Handbook of

North American Indians

Handbook of North American Indians

WILLIAM C. STURTEVANT
General Editor

VOLUME 5

Arctic

DAVID DAMAS

Volume Editor

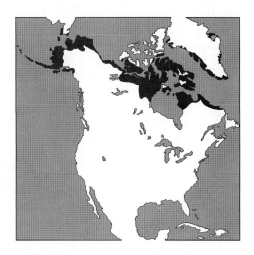

SMITHSONIAN INSTITUTION

WASHINGTON

1984

Copyright © 1984 by Smithsonian Insitution

For sale by the Superintendent of Documents,
U.S. Government Printing Office, Washington, D.C. 20402.

Library of Congress Cataloging in Publication Data

Handbook of North American Indians.

Bibliography.
Includes index.
CONTENTS:

v. 5 Arctic.

1. Indians of North America. 2. Eskimos.
I. Sturtevant, William C.

E77.H25   970′.004′97   77–17162

Arctic Volume Planning Committee

David Damas, Volume Editor

William C. Sturtevant, General Editor

Don E. Dumond, Coordinator for Prehistory chapters

James W. VanStone

Helge Kleivan

Bernard Saladin d'Anglure

Contents

This map is a diagrammatic guide to the coverage of this volume; it is not an authoritative depiction of territories for several reasons. Sharp boundaries have been drawn and no area is unassigned. The groups mapped are in some cases arbitrarily defined, subdivisions are not indicated, no joint or disputed occupations are shown, and different kinds of land use are not distinguished. Since the map depicts the situation at the earliest periods for which evidence is available, the ranges mapped for different groups often refer to different periods, and there may have been intervening movements, extinctions, and changes in range. Not shown are groups that came into separate existence later than the map period for their areas. In general, the simplified ranges shown are as of the mid-19th century; they are somewhat earlier for Kotzebue Sound, Northern Interior Alaska, and Labrador Coast Eskimo, and somewhat later for the Siberian, Pacific, and Greenland Eskimo. For more specific information see the maps and text in the appropriate chapters.

Key to Tribal Territories

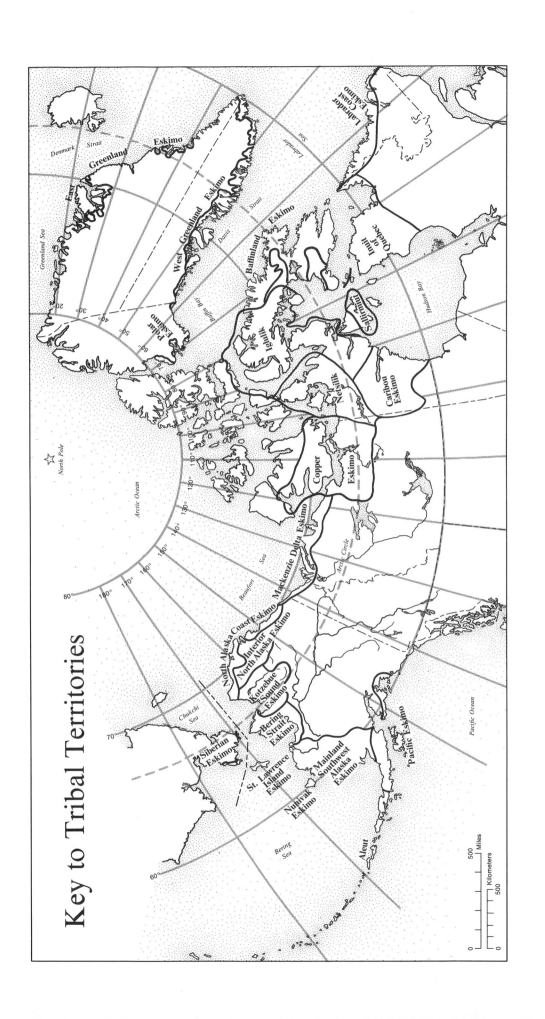

Technical Alphabet

Consonants

		bilabial	labiodental	dental	alveolar	alveopalatal	velar	back velar	glottal
stop	vl	p		t	t		k	q	ʔ
	vd	b		d	d		g	ġ	
affricate	vl				c	č			
	vd				3	ǯ			
fricative	vl	φ	f	θ	s	š	x	x̣	h
	vd	β	v	δ	z	ž	γ	γ̇	
nasal	vl	M			N		Ŋ		
	vd	m			n		ŋ	ṅ	
lateral	vl				ł				
	vd				l				
semivowel	vl	W				Y			
	vd	w				y			

vl = voiceless; vd = voiced

The standard symbol *r* (used in other volumes for a voiced medial flap, trill, or retroflex approximant) is replaced by *ř* in this volume, and *Ř* is used for its voiceless counterpart, in order to avoid confusion with the r of many Arctic Native language practical orthographies, which has the value [γ̇].

Modifications indicated for consonants are: glottalization (*t́*, *ḱ*, etc.), retroflexion (*ṭ*, *ç*, *ʒ̣*), palatalization (*tʸ*, *kʸ*, *nʸ*, *lʸ*), labialization (*kʷ*), aspiration (*tʰ*), length (*t·*). For vowels: length (*a·*), three-mora length (*a:*), nasalization (*ą*), voicelessness (*A*). The commonest prosodic markings are, for stress: *á* (primary) and *à* (secondary), and for pitch: *á* (high), *à* (low), *â* (falling), and *ă* (rising); however, the details of prosodic systems and the uses of accents differ widely from language to language.

Vowels

	front	central	back
high	i (ü)	ɨ	u (ɨ)
	I		U
mid	e (ö)	ə	o
	ε		ɔ
		Λ	
low	æ	a	a

Unparenthesized vowels are unrounded if front or central, and rounded if back; *ü* and *ö* are rounded; *ɨ* is unrounded. The special symbols for lax vowels (*I, U, ε, ɔ*) are generally used only where it is necessary to differentiate between tense and lax high or mid vowels. *ɨ* and *a* are used for both central and back vowels, as the two values seldom contrast in a given language.

Words in Arctic Native and Indian languages cited in italics in this volume are of two types. Those in Quebec and Greenlandic Eskimo are in the practical orthographies in use locally. Italicized words in other Arctic Native and Indian languages are written in phonemic transcription. That is, the letters and symbols are used in specific values defined for them by the structure of the sound system of the particular language. However, as far as possible, these phonemic transcriptions use letters and symbols in generally consistent values, as specified by the standard technical alphabet of the *Handbook*. Deviations from these standard values as well as specific details of the phonology of each language (or references to where they may be found) and information on practical orthographies are given in a footnote in each ethnographic chapter or an early chapter in each ethnographic section. Exceptionally, italics are used for Chinook Jargon words, which appear in the conventional English-based spellings of the sources (see vol. 6:x).

No italicized Native word is broken at a line end except when a hyphen would be present anyway as part of the word. Words in italicized phonemic transcription are never capitalized, but the practical orthographies use capitalization for names and sentence-initially. Pronunciations or phonetic values given in the standard technical alphabet without regard to phonemic analysis are put in square brackets rather than in italics. The glosses, or conventionalized translations, of native words are enclosed in single quotation marks.

Native words recorded by nonspecialists or before the phonemic systems of their languages had been analyzed are often not written accurately enough to allow respelling in phonemic transcription. Where phonemic retranscription has been possible the citation of source has been modified by the label "phonemicized" or "from." A few words that could not be phonemicized have been "normalized"—rewritten by mechanical substitution of the symbols of the standard technical alphabet. Others have been rationalized by eliminating redundant or potentially misleading diacritics and substituting nontechnical symbols. Words that do not use the standard technical alphabet occasionally contain some letters or diacritics used according to the values of other technical alphabets or traditional orthographies. All nonphonemic transcriptions give only incomplete, and sometimes imprecise, approximations of the correct pronunciation.

Nontechnical Equivalents

Correct pronunciation, as with any foreign language, requires extensive training and practice, but simplified (incorrect) pronunciations may be obtained by ignoring the diacritics and reading the vowels as in Italian or Spanish and the consonants as in English. For a closer approximation to the pronunciation or to rewrite into a nontechnical transcription the substitutions indicated in the following table may be made. The orthographic footnote for most languages contains a practical alphabet that may be used as an alternative by substituting the letters and letter groups for their correspondents in the list of technical symbols in the same footnote.

technical	nontechnical	technical	nontechnical	technical	nontechnical
æ	ae	M	mh	Y	yh
β	bh	N	nh	$ž$	zh
c	ts	ŋ	ng	ʒ	dz
č	ch	$N̦$	ngh	$ǯ$	j
δ	dh	ɔ	o	ʔ	'
ε	e	θ	th	$k̓, p̓, t̓$, etc.	k', p', t', etc.
γ	gh	φ	ph	$a·, e·, k·, s·$, etc.	aa, ee, kk, ss, etc.
ł	lh	š	sh	$ą, ę$, etc.	an, en, etc.
λ	dl	W	wh	k^y, t^y, etc.	ky, ty, etc.
ƛ	tlh	x	kh	k^w	kw

Transliteration of Russian Cyrillic

А	а	a		I	i [a]	ī		С	с	s		Ъ	ъ [b]	"
Б	б	b		Й	й	ĭ		Т	т	t		Ы	ы	y
В	в	v		К	к	k		У	у	u		Ь	ь	'
Г	г	g		Л	л	l		Ф	ф	f		Ѣ	ѣ [a]	ie
Д	д	d		М	м	m		Х	х	kh		Э	э	ė
Е	е	e		Н	н	n		Ц	ц	t͡s		Ю	ю	i͡u
Ё	ё	ë		О	о	o		Ч	ч	ch		Я	я	i͡a
Ж	ж	zh		П	п	p		Ш	ш	sh		Ѳ	ѳ [a]	ḟ
З	з	z		Р	р	r		Щ	щ	shch		Ѵ	ѵ [a]	ẏ
И	и	i												

[a] Not in the alphabet adopted in 1918.
[b] Disregarded in final position.

The transcription from Russian Cyrillic script is not entirely consistent. The Library of Congress transliteration displayed here has been used in the titles of items in the bibliography and in names and words that were available in Cyrillic, but the names of some authors appear in a simplified version. The names of historical personages and place-names are generally in the spellings used in the most available English sources or translations. The older alphabet has been followed when the sources use it.

English Pronunciations

The English pronunciations of the names of tribes and a few other words are indicated parenthetically in a dictionary-style orthography in which most letters have their usual English pronunciation. Special symbols are listed below, with sample words to be pronounced as in nonregional United States English. Approximate phonetic values are given in parentheses in the standard technical alphabet.

		ă:	bat (æ)				
ŋ:	thing (ŋ)	ä:	father (a)	ə:	about, gallop (ə)	ō:	boat (ow)
θ:	thin (θ)	ā:	bait (ey)	ĭ:	bit (I)	o͝o:	book (U)
ð:	this (ð)	e:	bet (ε)	ī:	bite (ay)	oo:	boot (uw)
zh:	vision (ž)	ē:	beat (iy)	ô:	bought (ɔ)	u:	but (ʌ)

'(primary stress), ‚(secondary stress): elevator (ˈelə‚vātər) (éləvèytər)

Conventions for Illustrations

Map Symbol

●   Native settlement

○   Abandoned settlement

■   Non-native or mixed settlement

□   Abandoned settlement

    Mountain range, peak

Marsh, swamp

River or stream

– – – – – –   National boundary

– – – – – –   Province or state boundary

– – – – – –   District or municipality boundary

Netsilik   Tribe

Aivilingmiut   Tribal subdivision

Ammassalik   Settlement, site

Colville R.   Geographical feature

Toned areas on tribal maps represent estimated territory.

Credits and Captions

Credit lines give the source of the illustrations or the collections where the artifacts shown are located. The numbers that follow are the catalog or inventory numbers of that repository. When the photographer mentioned in the caption is the source of the print reproduced, no credit line appears. "After" means that the *Handbook* illustrators have redrawn, rearranged, or abstracted the illustration from the one in the cited source. All maps and drawings not otherwise credited are by the *Handbook* illustrators. Measurements in captions are to the nearest millimeter if available; "about" indicates an estimate or a measurement converted from inches to centimeters. The following abbreviations are used in credit lines:

Amer.	American	Histl.	Historical
Anthr.	Anthropology, Anthropological	Ind.	Indian
		Inst.	Institute
Arch.	Archives	Instn.	Institution
Arch(a)eol	Arch(a)eology, Arch(a)ecological	Lib.	Library
		Mus.	Museum
Assoc.	Association	NAA	National Anthropological
Co.	County		Archives
Coll.	Collection(s)	Nat.	Natural
Dept.	Department	Natl.	National
Div.	Division	opp.	opposite
Ethnol.	Ethnology, Ethnological	pl(s).	plate(s)
fol.	folio	Prov.	Provincial
Ft.	Fort	Soc.	Society
Hist.	History	U.	University

Metric Equivalents

10 mm = 1 cm	10 cm = 3.937 in.	1 km = .62 mi.	1 in. = 2.54 cm	25 ft. = 7.62 m
100 cm = 1 m	1 m = 39.37 in.	5 km = 3.1 mi.	1 ft. = 30.48 cm	1 mi. = 1.60 km
1,000 m = 1 km	10 m = 32.81 ft.	10 km = 6.2 mi.	1 yd. = 91.44 cm	5 mi. = 8.02 km

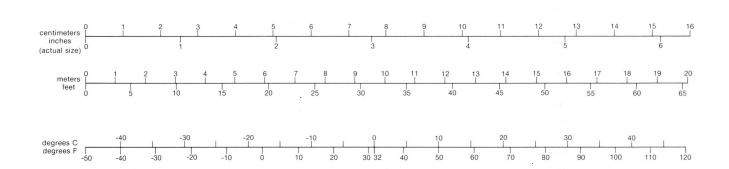

Preface

This is the sixth volume to be published of a 20-volume set planned to give an encyclopedic summary of what is known about the prehistory, history, and cultures of the aboriginal peoples of North America who lived north of the urban civilizations of central Mexico. Volumes 6–15 treat the other major culture areas of this region (see p. *i*).

Some topics relevant to the Arctic area are excluded from this volume because they are more appropriately discussed on a continent-wide basis. Readers should refer to volume 1, Introduction, for general descriptions of anthropological and historical methods and sources and for summaries for the whole continent of certain topics regarding social and political organization, religion, and the performing arts. Volume 2 contains detailed accounts of the different kinds of Indian and Eskimo communities in the twentieth century, especially during its third quarter, and describes their relations with one another and with the surrounding non-Indian societies and nations. Volume 3 gives the environmental and biological backgrounds within which Native American societies developed, summarizes the early and late human biology or physical anthropology of Indians, Eskimos, and Aleuts, and surveys the earliest prehistoric cultures. (Therefore detailed treatment of the evidence on the earliest migrations from Asia through the Arctic into the Americas is in volume 3 rather than in this volume.) Volume 4 contains details on the history of the relations between Whites and Native American societies. Volume 16 is a continent-wide survey of technology and the visual arts—of material cultures broadly defined. Volume 17 surveys the Native languages of North America, their characteristics and historical relationships. Volumes 18 and 19 are a biographical dictionary; included in the listing are many Eskimos and Aleuts. Volume 20 contains an index to the whole, which will serve to locate materials on Eskimos and Aleuts in other volumes as well as in this one; it also includes a list of errata found in all preceding volumes.

Preliminary discussions on the feasibility of the *Handbook* and alternatives for producing it began in 1965 in what was then the Smithsonian's Office of Anthropology. A history of the early development of the *Handbook* and a listing of the entire editorial staff will be found in volume 1. Detailed planning for the Arctic volume was undertaken at a meeting of the General Editor and the Volume Editor with a specially selected Planning Committee (listed on page *v*) held in Hamilton, Ontario, January 15–16, 1971. At that time a tentative table of contents was drawn up, and qualified specialists on each topic were listed as potential authors. The chapter headings in the final volume reproduce almost exactly the list decided upon at that meeting, and about two-thirds of the authors are those first invited. A few chapters were retitled, a couple were added, and some proposed authors had to be replaced as people were unable to accept invitations or later found that they could not meet their commitments to write.

At the time they were invited, the Volume Editor sent contributors instructions that gave brief article descriptions. This document outlined the volume's framework and was prepared jointly by the Volume Editor, Don E. Dumond, Bernard Saladin d'Anglure, and James W. VanStone. Authors were also sent a "Guide for Contributors" prepared by the General Editor describing the general aims and methods of the *Handbook* and the editorial conventions. One convention has been to avoid the present tense, where possible, in historical and cultural descriptions. Thus a statement in the past tense, with a recent date or approximate date, may also hold true for the time of writing. As they were received, the manuscripts were reviewed by the Volume Editor, the General Editor, and usually one or more referees—frequently including a member of the Planning Committee, and often authors of other chapters. James W. VanStone and Don E. Dumond were continually called upon to serve in this capacity. Suggestions for changes and additions often resulted. The published versions frequently reflect more editorial intervention than is customary for academic writings, since the encyclopedic aims and format of this publication made it necessary to attempt to eliminate duplication, avoid gaps in coverage, prevent contradictions, impose some standardization of organization and terminology, and keep within strict constraints on length. Where the evidence seemed so scanty or obscure as to allow different authorities to come to differing conclusions, authors have been permitted to elaborate whichever view they prefer, but the editors have endeavored to draw attention to alternative interpretations in other chapters.

The first draft manuscript submitted was received in the General Editor's office on January 30, 1972, and the last on March 10, 1983; the first acceptance of an author's manuscript was on November 23, 1972. In October 1981, all authors of manuscripts then on hand were requested to revise and bring them up to date. *xiii*

Most did so, and a few submitted substantially rewritten contributions. Edited manuscripts were sent from the Washington office to authors for their final approval between December 13, 1982, and July 15, 1983. These dates are given for each chapter in the list of Contributors.

The Editorial Assistant, Nikki L. Lanza, played an important role in organizing and supervising the complex flow of communications between authors and editors, especially during the final two years of editing.

Linguistic Editing

As far as possible, all cited words in Native languages were referred to consultants with expert knowledge of the respective languages and rewritten by them in the appropriate technical orthography. The consultants and the spelling systems are identified in the orthographic footnotes, drafted by the Linguistic Editor, Ives Goddard.

Statements about the genetic relationships of Eskimo and Aleut languages have also been checked with linguist consultants, to ensure conformity with recent findings and terminology in comparative linguistics and to avoid conflicting statements within the *Handbook*. In general, only the less remote genetic relationships are mentioned in the individual chapters. The chapter "Eskimo and Aleut Languages" discusses the relationships in the Eskimo-Aleut family as a whole and mentions proposed relationships to other families.

The Linguistic Editor served as coordinator and editor of these efforts by linguist consultants. A special debt is owed to these consultants, who provided advice and assistance without compensation and, in many cases, took time from their own research in order to check words with native speakers. The Linguistic Editor is especially grateful to Steven A. Jacobsen, Lawrence A. Kaplan, Michael E. Krauss, S.T. Mallon, and Anthony C. Woodbury.

In the case of words that could not be respelled in a technical orthography, an attempt has been made to rationalize the transcriptions used in earlier anthropological writings in order to eliminate phonetic symbols that are obsolete and diacritics that might convey a false impression of phonetic accuracy.

Synonymies

Toward the end of many chapters is a section called Synonymy. This describes the various names that have been applied to the groups and subgroups treated in that chapter (or set of chapters), giving the principal variant spellings used in English, and, frequently, in French and Russian, and often the names applied to the groups in neighboring Native languages.

Many synonymies have been expanded or reworked by the Linguistic Editor, who has added names and analyses from the literature, from other manuscripts submitted for the *Handbook* (from which they have then been deleted), and as provided by linguist consultants. Where a synonymy is wholly or substantially the work of the Linguistic Editor, a footnote specifying authorship is given.

These sections should assist in the identification of groups mentioned in the earlier historical and anthropological literature. They should also be examined for evidence on changes in the identifications and affiliations of groups, as seen by their own members as well as by neighbors and by outside observers.

Radiocarbon Dates

Authors were instructed to convert radiocarbon dates into dates in the Christian calendar. Such conversions normally have been made from the dates as originally published, without taking account of changes that may be required by developing research on revisions of the half-life of carbon 14, long-term changes in the amount of carbon 14 in the atmosphere, and other factors that may require modifications of absolute dates based on radiocarbon determinations.

Binomials

The scientific names of plant and animal genera and species, printed in italics, have been checked by the General Editor to ensure that they reflect modern usage by biological taxonomists. Scientific plant names have been brought into agreement with those accepted by Gray and Fernald (1950), Hultén (1968), and Böcher, Hulmen, and Jakobsen (1968), with assistance from Stanwyn G. Shetler in resolving inconsistencies among these three authorities. Zoological nomenclature has been revised in consultation with Smithsonian staff in the appropriate departments.

In most cases the English common names used for animals and plants have also been edited to avoid possible ambiguities. American as opposed to Old World usage has been followed in regard to the common names for *Rangifer tarandus*: all wild ones are caribou; only domesticates are reindeer. *Oncorhyncus tshawytscha* is usually referred to as king salmon, following Alaskan usage, rather than Chinook salmon (Hart's 1973 usage).

Bibliography

All references cited by contributors have been unified in a single list at the end of the volume. Citations within the text, by author, date, and often page, identify the works in this unified list. Wherever possible the *Handbook* Bibliographer, Lorraine H. Jacoby, has resolved conflicts between citations of different editions, corrected inaccuracies and omissions, and checked direct quotations against the originals. The bibliographic information has been verified by examination of the original work or from standard reliable library catalogs (especially the National Union Catalog and the published catalog of the Harvard Peabody Museum Library). The unified bibliography lists all and only the sources cited in the text of the volume, except personal communications. In the text "personal communications" to an author are distinguished from personal "communications to editors." The sections headed Sources at the ends of most chapters provide general guidance to the most important sources of information on the topics covered.

Place-Names

The standardization of place-names in the Arctic presented the editors with particularly complex challenges. Many places in the Soviet Union, Quebec, and Greenland have been known by an English name, a Russian, French, or Danish name, and one or more versions of an Eskimo name. Some may be uncomfortable with the variants of the names selected, but any consistent general principle of selection would have resulted in the use of unfamiliar names in some cases. In this volume the English names of geographical features in the USSR and Greenland are used when they are well established—for example, East Cape, Indian Point, Cape Farewell, and Wrangell Island (rather than the usual but incorrect Wrangel Island). Otherwise the Russian and Danish names are used, when they exist, but Siberian Yupik and Greenlandic names are generally used in referring to traditional settlements or when there is no other name. An attempt has been made to use the current Siberian Yupik roman orthography and the new Greenlandic orthography (introduced in 1972), but the editors acknowledge the likelihood of errors in the transcription of names for which full information was unavailable. (See also the footnote in "Paleo-Eskimo Cultures of Greenland," this vol.). For place-names in Quebec the usage of the *Canada Gazetteer Atlas* (1980) has been followed, which is said to reflect approved official local usage. Towns generally have their French name or an English or Eskimo name in French orthography, and the names of geographical features are in French or English form—for example the towns of Déception, Inoucdjouac, Cape-Hopes-Advance, but Deception Bay, Rivière Innuksuac, Cap Hopes Advance.

Illustrations

Authors were requested to submit suggestions for illustrations: photographs, maps, drawings, and lists and locations of objects that might be illustrated. To varying degrees they complied with this request. Yet considerations of space, balance, reproducibility, and availability required modifications in what was submitted. In addition much original material was provided by editorial staff members, from research they conducted in museums and other repositories, in the published literature, and from correspondence. Locating suitable photographs and earlier drawings and paintings was the responsibility of the Illustrations Researcher, Joanna Cohan Scherer. Artifacts in museum collections suitable for photographing or drawing were selected by the Artifact Researcher, Gayle Barsamian. All uncredited drawings are by the Scientific Illustrator, Jo Ann Moore.

All maps were drawn by the *Handbook* Cartographer, Judith Crawley Wojcik, who redrew some submitted by authors and compiled many new ones using information from the chapter manuscripts and from other sources. The base maps for all are authoritative standard ones, especially sheet maps produced by the U.S. Geological Survey and the Department of Energy, Mines and Resources, Surveys and Mapping Branch, Canada. When possible, the hydrography has been reconstructed for the date of each map.

Layout and design of the illustrations have been the responsibility of the Scientific Illustrator, Jo Ann Moore. Captions for illustrations were usually composed by Scherer, Barsamian, and Moore, and for maps by Wojcik. However, all illustrations, including maps and drawings, and all captions, have been approved by the General Editor, the Volume Editor, and the authors of the chapters in which they appear, and authors and editors frequently have participated actively in the selection process and in the improvement of captions.

We are indebted to individuals on the staffs of many museums for much time and effort spent in their collections locating photographs and artifacts and providing documentation on them. Many individuals, including professional photographers, have generously provided photographs free or at cost. Donnelley Cartographic Services devoted meticulous care to converting the map artwork into final film.

Acknowledgements

Beyond the members of the Planning Committee and those persons whose special contributions are identified in appropriate sections of the text, important aid was also received from Ernest S. Burch, Jr., Robert Petersen, J. Garth Taylor, Igor I. Krupnik, and Mikhail A. Chlenov. Special assistance in locating and documenting illustrations was received from Lydia T. Black (Aleut), Jean Blodgett (art), Bernadette Driscoll (clothing), William W. Fitzhugh (Alaska, Greenland), Hans-Christian Gulløv (Greenland), Susan A. Kaplan (Alaska, *xv*

Labrador), Molly Lee (baskets), James W. VanStone (Alaska), and David W. Zimmerly (kayaks). Throughout, Ives Goddard was of particular assistance on matters of historical and geographical accuracy as well as on decisions made by the General Editor regarding organization, consistency, and other editorial procedures. The help of many other individuals is acknowledged in footnotes, in credit lines, and as communications to editors.

During the first few years of this project, the *Handbook* editorial staff in Washington worked on materials for all volumes of the series. Since intensive preparation of this volume began in 1981, especially important contributions were provided by: the Editorial Assistant, Nikki L. Lanza; the Production Manager and Manuscript Editor, Diane Della-Loggia; the Bibliographer, Lorraine H. Jacoby; the Scientific Illustrator, Jo Ann Moore; the Cartographer, Judith Crawley Wojcik; the Graphic Arts Technicians, Tuleda Yvonne Poole and Barbara Frey; the Illustrations Researcher, Joanna Cohan Scherer; the Artifact Researcher, Gayle Barsamian; the Assistant Illustrations Researcher, Anne F. Morgan; the Management Services Assistant, Melvina Jackson; and the Secretaries, Valerie Smith and Nancy Schultz. Lottie Katz and Karen Keyes served as volunteer assistants for the Bibliographer and Artifact Researcher, respectively.

The Department of Anthropology, National Museum of Natural History, Smithsonian Institution, released the General Editor and the Linguistic Editor from part of their curatorial and research time.

The Department of Sociology and Anthropology, McMaster University, granted released time for the Volume Editor from January through April 1979.

Preparation and publication of this volume have been supported by federal appropriations made to the Smithsonian Institution, in part through its Bicentennial Programs.

Special thanks are extended to James W. VanStone, who assumed editorial duties when the Volume Editor was conducting field research.

July 29, 1983
William C. Sturtevant
David Damas

Introduction

DAVID DAMAS

The *Handbook of North American Indians* is organized according to geographical areas that in fact signify culture areas. The culture area concept has fallen into disrepute, doubtless because of early abuses that stemmed from theoretical propositions based on mechanistic conceptions of diffusion and on ecological associations that verged on environmental determinism. Later, scholars who dealt with surveys of native North American peoples used the concept merely as a classificatory device. These "areas provide a convenient framework for introducing some degree of order in the plethora of detail available about North American Indians" (Driver 1969:17). But in the case of the Arctic, there has existed a persistently strong series of associations among natural conditions, culture, language, and physical type that has made this area the darling of cultural arealists.

The commonest use of "arctic" is in reference to that part of the earth's surface above the Arctic Circle—the Land of the Midnight Sun. In "Physical Environment" (this vol.) the inadequacy of this definition is indicated; the tree line, the 10°C July isotherm, and the permafrost line reflect climatic criteria that set off a region to be described as "arctic" more accurately. The maps in this volume show that each of these lines moves north and south of the Arctic Circle at various points in North America due to local conditions. Other indicators can be found in the distributions of important fauna. Maps in "Arctic Ecosystems" (this vol.) illustrate close congruency of distributions of ringed seal, caribou, and Arctic char with the regions of Eskimo habitation. Among these associations the tree-line or taiga-tundra border coincides most closely with the boundary between Eskimo and Indian territory and has been applied to archeological (W.E. Taylor 1966) as well as to ethnological cultures.

While none of the lines conforms exactly to Eskimo habitation limits, together they form formidable evidence associating a people with a definite habitat zone.*

Among the early exponents of the culture-area concept was Mason (1896:646), who designated 18 "American Indian environments or culture areas" for the

Americas, and later 12 "ethnic environments" (Mason 1907:427) for America north of Mexico. Mason outlined the chief characteristics of the Arctic habitat including cold climate and great seasonal fluctuations in daylight, floral and faunal resources, and the occurrence of important raw materials for implement construction.

While Mason focused on the environmental background for Eskimo habitation and culture, we must ask what markers can be used to define the Eskimos as a population entity who occupy this Arctic zone. Surely language is the most reliable and yet uncontested criterion for this identification. The Eskimo-Aleut family of languages remains an undoubted basis for affinity and shows a high degree of distinctness from other languages either in the Old World or the New World. With regard to affinity of cultural traits and complexes Kroeber (1939:23) lists the following as common to all Eskimo peoples: "skin boats, harpoon, bladder or inflated skin, spear thrower, three- or four-pronged bird spear, two-winged salmon spear, lamp, stone pot, house platform, type of clothing, ivory carving, kashim or social house, shamanism, type of myth or tale." While this is an impressive list, not all items on it set off Eskimo culture sharply from that of neighboring peoples. Driver and Massey's (1957) maps reveal some of this overlapping. For example, the "rectanguloid earth-covered Alaskan house" is used by both Eskimos and Athapaskans, and hide boats are used in the interior of Alaska and the Quebec-Labrador peninsula as well as on the Arctic coast. Most Eskimo groups preserve meat by freezing or sun-drying but smoking is shared by the Mackenzie Eskimos with Subarctic peoples. However, clusters of features that relate to practices such as winter travel on the tundra and sea ice and various adaptive hunting and fishing techniques, as well as stylistic and content aspects of oral tradition, social usages, and tool type attest to a common cultural heritage and support the notion of an Eskimo culture area as separate from other culture areas.

One of the early critics of the culture-area concept was Sapir who in 1916 felt that it had been misused by application for descriptive rather than culture-historical purposes. He suggested that: "An historical analysis of North American culture would quite probably reduce the present culture areas to two or three fundamental ones, say a Mexican culture area, a Northwest Coast

*Another delimitation of the Arctic, which employs the geographical coordinates of longitude as well as latitude (Tremaine 1953–1975, 1:5–6), is an expansive designation that includes a great deal of the area covered in *Subarctic*, volume 6 of this series.

area, and a large Central area of which the Pueblo and the Eskimo areas are the most specialized developments: the former as conditioned by profound Mexican influences, the latter as conditioned by a very peculiar environment" (Mandelbaum 1951:427).

So even in the extreme reductionism employed by Sapir, the Eskimo area is accorded substantial distinctness. Wissler's (1917) six "food areas" provide another example of reductionism that lumps the Eskimo with Subarctic peoples in the "caribou area" and obscures the importance of Eskimo cultural distinctness as well as the importance of sea mammal hunting. His eventual plan of 10 culture areas does separate the Eskimo area from others in the continent. Kroeber (1939) utilizes a scheme of Grand culture areas, culture areas, and subareas; his roster of Grand areas includes the Arctic Coast, encompassing all Eskimo habitation regions. Other anthropologists who have sought to divide the continent into culture areas include Driver (1969), Spencer and Jennings (1965), and Oswalt (1966). These writers have all been influenced by Kroeber, use various versions of his plan, and favor separation of an Arctic area from others in North America.

This general acceptance of an Eskimo culture area that parallels linguistic distributions is sometimes supported by the notion of distinctness of physical type. For instance, Oschinsky (1962) has posited an Arctic Mongoloid racial type to be separated from New World and Old World Mongoloid types. By contrast Wissler (1917) was an early advocate of similarity between Eskimos and other native North Americans in physical type. Another view of this matter is expressed by Szathmary (1981) who sees the Reindeer Chukchi, all Eskimo populations (but not the Aleut, for whom comparable data are lacking), and Athapaskan speakers as forming a definite cluster in genetic traits as distinct from Algonquian speakers. Szathmary sees considerable continuity within Eskimo groups and maintains that Eskimos are genetically identifiable.

While most schemes of culture areas deal mainly with ethnographic horizons, a meaningful classification must take into account time perspective as well. In this regard Dumond ("Prehistory: Summary," this vol.) divides the prehistory of the Arctic into five stages but points out that during neither of the first two stages (before 2200 B.C.) can "the zone of later Eskimo occupation and the focus of this volume . . . be considered a culture area of itself." Later the carriers of the Arctic Small Tool tradition spread across the entire American Arctic to inhabit all areas that would ever be peopled. Since that stage there have been only minor fluctuations in the boundaries of Arctic habitation.

If, then, most archeological stages dealt with here are to be considered Arctic cultures, what can be said of the physical and linguistic affinities of the earlier Arctic peoples with the modern Eskimos? The problem of identifying racial type from Arctic archeology has two facets that currently hamper solution. First is the dearth of skeletal remains at all time periods throughout the area; secondly, the controversy over whether or not Eskimos are an identifiable racial type must also be resolved before anything but essentially speculative statements can be made.

As far as linguistic identification with archeological cultures is concerned, the populations that have inhabited the Aleutians seem firmly established as a branch of the major language family, while there has also been a strong tendency to identify Inuit-Inupiaq speakers with the Thule culture carriers (Dumond 1965). Association of language with other archeological cultures remains in doubt.

Any attempt to delimit the Arctic area must eventually come to grips with the possible effects of external contacts. Several scholars (J.G.E. Smith 1979) have addressed themselves to problems of Eskimo-Indian contacts. These papers reveal that while there were regional differences in the intensity of warfare between Indian and Eskimo elements, its effects can be exaggerated, and strong trade relationships existed side by side with fighting. While the effects of diffusion from outside the Eskimo area must be accorded importance in every study of Eskimo culture growth, it is likely that when the picture becomes more complete, the features and complexes characteristic of Eskimo culture will be seen to be overwhelmingly internal developments or products of contacts that occurred in the nascent stages of Eskimo culture history.

In considering the vast expanse of the Eskimo culture area, any detailed treatment such as is attempted in this volume must take into account subdivisions not only as valid cultural "subareas" but also in terms of practical considerations of manageability as well as reflecting interests and knowledge of the authors who participate.

The complexities involved in recognizing subareas begin to become apparent on the level of prehistory. The expansion of the carriers of the Arctic Small Tool tradition heralded a period of uniformity, but after about 1200 B.C. or 600 B.C. (depending on the region) diversity dominated. Later, during the Thule culture period, influences of a common culture were again felt, from Siberia to Greenland. While the relatively uniform Thule culture formed the basis for many ethnographic cultures, greater regional diversity once more characterized Eskimo cultures by the time of European contact. It is thus evident that both regional and temporal considerations must be observed in describing the archeology of the area. The decision to divide archeological chapters in the volume by region represents a compromise. The authors of individual chapters deal with relationships outside their region at various time periods and "Prehistory: Summary" draws together the various regional sequences using a temporal frame of organization.

Kroeber's (1939) scheme for dividing the Arctic area was designed to take into account both ethnographic and historical factors. His "Grand area" of the Arctic Coast is divided into two major areas—the Western, which includes the people of the Aleutians, Pacific Coast of Alaska, the Eskimos on both sides of the Bering Sea, north Alaska and the Mackenzie Eskimos; and a Central-Eastern area, which includes all other groups covered in this volume. He sees the Central-Eastern area as "pure Eskimo" and the Western area as "Eskimo plus a Northwest American and Northeast Asiatic addition" (Kroeber 1939:24). In this volume we have used major divisions of Western Arctic, Canadian Arctic, and Greenland, thus subdividing Kroeber's Central-Eastern area. Separation of Greenland from the Canadian Arctic seems justified on the basis of not only cultural differences but also the substantial geographical isolation of Eskimo populations in the ethnographic era as well as largely separate contact histories. The Polar Eskimo are intermediate between the cultures of Greenland and Arctic Canada, having experienced long periods of isolation from both major regions. They are classified here according to their geographical position as part of the subcontinent of Greenland. The Mackenzie Eskimo are grouped with the cultures of the Western Arctic because their cultural affinities with Alaska are greater than with central groups, comprising as they did the easternmost extension of the whaling complex in ethnographic times. Trade relations to the west were also more intense than to the east (see "Mackenzie Delta Eskimo," this vol.).

The most important segmentation of the volume follows general *Handbook* conventions in organizing ethnographic and culture-historical entries according to tribal or tribelike groupings. These correspond rather closely to the 25 "regional variants of Eskimo economic culture" recognized by Kroeber (1939: 23–24) as subdivisions of his two Eskimo areas. They also largely conform to Birket-Smith's (1936:225–227) 17 "tribal groups." Twenty-one chapters provide the basic ethnographic entries in this volume, while a shorter section (in "Central Eskimo: Introduction," this vol.) is devoted to the Sallirmiut of Southampton Island who were becoming extinct at the dawn of the ethnographic era. In some cases where sets of tribal entries represent close historical affinities and clusters of cultural complexes, separate introductory chapters are included (Southwest Alaska Eskimo, Asiatic Eskimo, North Alaska Eskimo, Central Eskimo, Greenland Eskimo).

The use of "tribe" and "tribal" to describe Eskimo groupings causes some special difficulties, although similar problems in identifying "tribes" face contributors and editors for *Handbook* volumes on other areas of North America. Certainly when societies are classified according to increasing levels of political integration as bands, tribes, or chiefdoms (Service 1962; cf. criticisms by Fried 1967), the tribal level is not appropriate for the American Arctic. Indeed, Birket-Smith (1936:225) early recognized that for Eskimos "the unit which may be regarded as a tribe is to a certain degree arbitrary, as a tribe has a purely geographical but never political character."

For the continent as a whole, some of the ways in which the term tribe has been used in North American ethnology are summarized by Spencer and Jennings (1965:6): "The names of Indian tribes have depended pretty much on convention; a designation has crept into the literature because a trader, a missionary, an Indian agent, or even an anthropologist found the term definitive and useful. Sometimes the name is that used by the group in referring to itself, sometimes it is the designation, not always complimentary, applied to a group by its neighbors."

Regarding the Eskimo, beginning with Boas's (1888) pioneering work there have been several attempts to make "tribal" identification on the basis of the native category of designations having the suffix-complex -*miut*, which is added to place-names to indicate inhabitants of locales. There are problems involved in this usage. For the Central Eskimos several authors (Stefánsson 1913; Jenness 1922; Mathiassen 1928) have pointed to the evanescent nature of groupings so designated, and Burch (1976a) detailed some of the problems of the usage as it applies to northern Alaska. Designations in -*miut* are applied to groups of several families and to populations of several hundreds or even thousands. The authors of individual entries have employed such designations, but they also indicate congruence or lack of congruence with the tribal identification in the particular cases.

Perhaps the best usage of the term tribe for societies at the level of hunting bands is the one suggested by Helm (1968:118) for the Northern Athapaskans: "the greatest extension of population throughout which there is sufficient intermarriage to maintain many-sided communications." This definition can be demonstrated as an ethnographic reality for groups such as the Netsilik, Copper, and Iglulik Eskimo, where genealogical research shows close approximations to discrete marriage universes or demes. Elsewhere evidence is lacking or ambiguous. Other compromises have had to be made in segmenting the Arctic area as we have; for instance, the very large regions and populations of West Greenland cannot be further divided because the long period of contact has obscured regional cultural differences (Birket-Smith 1924:234). On the other hand, there does not appear to be sufficient evidence for subdividing the units described in the individual ethnographic entries in this volume on the basis of significant cultural variations within them nor for applying the term "tribe" to any of their constitutent elements.

With regard to the format used in the entries, each

3

author follows a general outline, which allows reasonable freedom to deal with special problems of each of the regions and their populations. Uniformity is not met totally since data on all aspects of culture are not always available. To avoid repetitions of ethnographic details, in several cases after a topic is briefly introduced a cross-reference indicates where a fuller discussion occurs. This is especially the case in the Central Eskimo chapters.

Other chapters deal with acculturation or with special local situations. Most handle change on a large scale since in the twentieth century national boundaries and political associations have become significant realities.

With the identification of Eskimo populations as members of national states has come the self-image of being significant ethnic groups within these states, a consciousness of cultural and linguistic identity, and increased awareness of attitudes of other citizens. In this regard the terms Greenlander in English and *grønlænder* in Danish have long been accepted. Among Canadian Eskimos there has been a movement to adopt Inuit as the appropriate ethnic label in English and French. In this volume authors have usually been given the option to choose appropriate usage and, indeed, some of them use the terms Eskimo and Inuit interchangeably. Where designations of "tribes" such as Copper Eskimo and Caribou Eskimo are established in scholarly literature, they are used rather than neologisms such as Copper Inuit and Caribou Inuit. Since *inuit* means 'people' in many Inuit-Inupiaq dialects it could reasonably be applied to the peoples of Greenland and northern Alaska. However, even though there has been a tendency starting in the 1970s to revive the use of Inuit as a general term replacing Eskimo, this term has two main shortcomings as an all-encompassing appellation to be used throughout the volume. First, the uncertainty of language affiliations of most archeological cultures makes dubious its application for the prehistoric era. Second, the significant populations of Aleut and Yupik speakers do not use the term in self-reference in English nor does the word appear in their native vocabularies.

Eskimos were both the first native North American people to experience contact with Europeans, in the case of the Norsemen, and probably also the last to have direct contact, when Stefánsson met with elements of the Copper Eskimo in 1910.

The main era of important early contact came in the eighteenth century with the reestablishment of the Greenland colony and the coming of the missionaries to the coast of Labrador in the east, and the Russian intrusions in the extreme west. The central parts of the Eskimo area were explored chiefly during the nineteenth century in connection with the quest for the Northwest Passage, but whalers who reached the Mackenzie delta and all parts of Hudson Bay in the second

4

half of the century provided more significant influence on the Eskimos.

The fur trade, which had been established early by Scandinavians in Greenland and the Russians in Alaska and the Aleutians, became the chief factor in change in the Central Arctic in the third decade of the twentieth century. Due to a complex of factors the Eskimos of Canada abandoned their nomadic band settlement patterns first for dispersed hunting camps and then eventually concentrated into villages of mixed Eskimo-White composition. In Greenland several large port towns grew, but the bulk of the people remained in the isolated hunting and fishing villages. The Alaska Eskimos have long combined excursions to industrial centers with hunting and trapping, while the Siberian Eskimos are drawn tightly into the national state of the Soviet Union, being encouraged to become contributing producers to the greater Soviet economy.

Interest in the Eskimos has long concerned anthropologists. Franz Boas's visit to Baffin Island in 1882–1883 represents one of the very first field studies in professional ethnology. Ethnographic emphases dominated Eskimo anthropology of the late nineteenth century with the work of Hawkes (1916) in Labrador and Murdoch (1892) and Nelson (1899) in Alaska. The great ethnographic period in the Canadian Arctic was 1910 to 1924 and culminated in the renowned and highly productive Fifth Thule Expedition. Coincidental with the basically descriptive emphasis of this early period was the search for Eskimo origins that began with a strongly ethnographic orientation (Rink 1887–1891; Steensby 1917; Hatt 1916a; Birket-Smith 1929) but after about 1930 became largely the concern of archeologists, who still relate much of their research to this quest. The combined approaches of archeology and linguistics (Dumond 1965), and of these supplemented by physical anthropological inquiry (Dumond 1977a:151–154; Szathmary and Ossenberg 1978), have been enlisted in the search for origins.

Aside from several notable exceptions (Gabus 1944a; Lantis 1946) there was a virtual hiatus in ethnological inquiry among the Eskimos for about 30 years, though results of earlier research continued to be published. During the 1950s and 1960s a series of studies in the Western Arctic (Hughes 1960; VanStone 1962a; Oswalt 1963) broke the silence, and community studies sponsored by the Canadian government (VanStone and Oswalt 1959; Vallee 1962; Graburn 1964; Honigmann and Honigmann 1965, 1970) represented a new research emphasis. In Greenland, Scandinavian anthropologists (H. Kleivan 1969–1970; Kleivan 1969–1970; Jensen 1969–1970) studied change in the context of emerging Greenlander ethnic consciousness. Soviet anthropologists documented Siberian Eskimo participation in national economic and cultural programs (Hughes 1965).

Concern with the effects of environment on society

and culture has had a long history in the Arctic beginning with Boas (1888), continuing with Weyer's (1932) encyclopedic study, and later with the work of Freeman (1969–1970) and Damas (1969c).

Another interest that has flourished is concern with social organization and the approaches of social anthropology. Studies of kinship (Hughes 1958; Heinrich 1960; Damas 1963; Burch 1975a) and voluntary associations (Spencer 1958; Guemple 1972) were particularly prominent. These contributions and the comparative study of band organization (Damas 1969d; Guemple 1972a) brought Eskimo material to bear on general theoretical problems.

Other examples of current research include the multi-disciplinary work of members of the International Biological Program (Milan 1979), which brought teams to three Eskimo communities, one each in Alaska, Canada, and Greenland.

The Inuit Land Claims Report (Freeman 1976) represents another area of research that will continue to have importance. This is participation of anthropologists as data collectors and analysts representing native organizations.

Ethnohistory will be the most fruitful approach for those ethnologists who continue to be interested in the traditional Eskimo cultures. Many of the chapters in this volume reflect this approach. Workers such as Gad and I. Kleivan for Greenland; Hughes, Lantis, and VanStone for Alaska and Siberia; and Burch and J.G. Taylor for Canada have made important contributions in employing documentary sources.

Speculations on the future of the Eskimos are perilous at this juncture in history when change is accelerating due to a combination of factors, including mineral and oil exploitation, government programs, and increasing Eskimo political participation, but perhaps a few comments are appropriate. The danger of racial obliteration is not on the horizon. Nor does there appear to be the likelihood of Eskimos being outnumbered by outsiders in most locales. The situation contrasts to that in most of North America where native peoples have long competed for settlement space with immigrants. The question of the possible disappearance of Eskimo culture is another matter. Administrators have often assumed that native people will prefer to throw off all the trappings of a presumed impoverished background. Yet ready acceptance of the technical advantages of western innovations, which indeed dominate the scene in Arctic communities today, often disguises a simultaneous reluctance to abandon certain values and recognition of distinctiveness as a people.

Pan-Eskimo movements that would involve Alaskan, Canadian, and Greenlandic Eskimos, and perhaps the Eskimos of the Soviet Union, are developing ("The Pan-Eskimo Movement," this vol.) and may serve as media for information flow regarding common prob-lems, but the most effective action will probably derive from movements that operate within the context of each of the national states. There is ample evidence for a growing political sophistication of Eskimos, which is particularly effective where they represent numerically dominant ethnic groups. This influence is being expressed in legislative bodies and in dealings with industrial interests and has become a consideration for anthropologists who must take into account interests of the Eskimos themselves in organizing research projects.

Synonymy†

The name Eskimo is first attested in an English treatise of 1584 in the form Esquimawes, used for a people living at "graunde Bay" (Hakluyt 1935, 2:269; Benveniste 1953:244). The most common spelling in English in early usage was Esquimaux, used as a singular, plural, and attributive, the same as the common French plural of all periods. Thomas Gorst wrote Eskeimoes in 1671 (J.B. Tyrrell 1931:390). The French singular is Esquimau (rarely Esquimaud—Lemoine 1911), and the feminine Esquimau or, especially in Canada, Esquimaude. Eskimaux is also found in both languages, and English sources attest as well Esquimos, Eskemoes, Eskima, Eskimeaux, Esquimeaux, and others listed by Hodge (1907–1910, 1:436–437). The spelling Eskimo was used by Richardson (1851, 1:339, 2:38), though not appearing in the 1770 document he cites, and becomes more frequent after the mid-nineteenth century; it is unlikely to be from Danish *Eskimo*, as sometimes claimed, since this is a modern designation, applied to Canadian Eskimos but not Greenlanders.

The appearance of qu and -(e)aux in the earlier English forms might suggest a French source, but although these spellings reflect later influence from the French written forms no evidence has been found for this name in French in the sixteenth century. The earliest French form is the peculiar Excomminquois (and Latinized Excomminqui), reported by Pierre Biard from Acadia (Nova Scotia) in 1616 and 1611, respectively (JR 2:66, 3:68), which probably originated as a jocular deformation, to make a high-sounding word meaning 'excommunicated' (compare Benveniste 1953:243), of the word Hakluyt renders Esquimawes. The flavor of Excomminquois is the same as that of other early French ethnonyms, the mysterious Iroquois, the epithetical Huron (vol. 15:387), and the incongruously learned Souriquois 'Micmac', literally 'murine, pertaining to mice'. The French form Esquimaux seems to be first attested on a map of 1632 by Samuel Champlain (Martijn 1980:79, 89), who locates them on the lower North Shore at the western end of the Strait of Belle Isle. Later seventeenth-century references are generally to populations on the North

†This synonymy was written by Ives Goddard.   5

Shore of the Gulf of Saint Lawrence, beginning at least in 1640 (JR 18:226, 30:132).

An additional complication is that during the same early period the term Esquimaux was used by other French writers for the Micmac and for certain Montagnais groups on the central North Shore of the Gulf of Saint Lawrence. This multiple usage has been documented by Mailhot, Simard, and Vincent (1980) and Martijn (1980b), correcting the view that the early uses of the name all refer to the Montagnais or other non-Eskimos (J.G. Taylor 1978, 1980; vol.6:187). A distinction is made in the 1691 relation of Le Clercq (1910:417) between the Grands Eskimaux (the Labrador Eskimo) and the Petits Eskimaux (the Montagnais groups).

The French word and its uses appear to be closely linked to a Montagnais name *ayassime·w*, appearing in early French linguistic sources, with varying degrees of palatalization and cluster simplification, as aiachkime8- (phonemically *a·yaskʸime·w*), aiachtchime8- (*a·yasčime·w*), and aissimeu. In the twentieth-century upper (western) North Shore dialects this term refers to the Micmac, and in the central and lower North Shore dialects it designates the Eskimo. The early linguistic sources were based on the western dialects, and hence the early forms listed in them are always defined as 'Micmac'. The division of meaning between 'Eskimo' and 'Micmac' is clearly old and is directly reflected in the early French usage (Mailhot 1978; Mailhot, Simard, and Vincent 1980); the extension to some Montagnais groups is presumably a local innovation within French. This Algonquian word is also attested as Plains Cree *a·yaskime·w* 'Eskimo' (from Faries 1938:69, 248), and in unreduplicated form as Attikamek Cree *aškime·w* 'Eskimo' (Béland 1978:398) and Algonquin Eastern Ojibwa *aškime·winini* 'Micmac man', a loan from Montagnais (from Lemoine 1911). Names for the Eskimo in other Algonquian languages include upper North Shore Montagnais *ka·čiku·šu* and *ka·če·kwe·šu*, not analyzable but explained by speakers as meaning 'eater of raw meat', and earlier recorded as katchekakuashiueu and katshekuashueu (Mailhot 1978:63); and Ojibwa *e·škipot* 'one who eats raw', Algonquin Eastern Ojibwa *aškipo·k* 'raw eaters' (Baraga 1878–1880, 2:114; Cuoq 1886:13–14). In spite of the tenacity of the belief, both among Algonquian speakers and in the anthropological and general literature (Hodge 1907–1910, 1:434; Oxford English Dictionary, Supplement), that Eskimo means 'raw-meat eaters', this explanation fits only the cited Ojibwa forms (containing Proto-Algonquian *ašk-* 'raw' and *-po* 'eat') and cannot be correct for the presumed Montagnais source of the word Eskimo itself. The hypothesis that the Montagnais word contains an element *-m* 'speak' and a contraction of *a·nt-* (Cree-Montagnais *a·(h)t-* 'remove(d), different, foreign') and *-axky-* 'land'—hence 'speaker of (the language of) a foreign

land' (Mailhot 1978:65–66)—is also impossible, because there is no element *-m* in this meaning (only *-m* 'speak to' and *-mo* 'speak', which will not fit) and no parallel for the assumed contraction. The Montagnais word *ayassime·w* (in which *ay-* is a reduplication) and its unreduplicated Attikamek cognate exactly match Montagnais *assime·w*, Ojibwa *aškime·* 'she nets a snowshoe', and an origin from a form meaning 'snowshoe-netter' could be considered if the original Montagnais application (presumably before Montagnais contact with Eskimos) were to Algonquians.

The ultimate origin of the name Eskimo in Montagnais seems clearly indicated. The only other possible source known would be Micmac Esgemao 'Eskimo', pl. Esgemaĝ (Pacifique 1939:182), but this can hardly have been the source of the variety of Montagnais forms (and meanings). As for the Micmac form *esgimow* (A.D. DeBlois in Mailhot 1978), which has received some speculative discussion in the literature (Mailhot 1978:63; Mailhot, Simard, and Vincent 1980:74; Martijn 1980a:116, 124), this is pretty obviously just a recent anglicization of Pacifique's form or a reborrowing from English.

The exact path by which the Montagnais word diffused into English and French is uncertain, but it may be significant that a Spanish form of the name, esquimaos, is attested as early as 1625 in an account by a Basque historian, Lope de Isasti, and since this refers to the activities of Spanish Basque whalers in the Strait of Belle Isle in the second half of the sixteenth century it was presumably based on records from that period (Barkham 1980:54; Mailhot, Simard, and Vincent 1980:74; Martijn 1980a:109). The major landmark in the records of the Basque whalers was Gran Baya 'Grand Bay', the Strait of Belle Isle (Barkham 1980), and it must be significant that Hakluyt's first English reference to the "Esquimawes" locates them in "graunde Bay" and that Champlain's first French use of Esquimaux maps this name next to "La grande baye," at the western end of the Strait of Belle Isle (Martijn 1980:89). Although direct documentation may be lacking, not unexpectedly for this early period, the available evidence could easily support a conclusion that the early English and French uses of the name Eskimo were derived from Spanish-speaking Basque whalers who had picked up the word from the Montagnais who are known (Barkham 1980:54) to have traded with them and worked for them. Under this hypothesis the English spelling with -qu- would be equally as well accounted for as by a French intermediary, and in addition the otherwise puzzling initial E- would be explainable as a partial hispanicization of early Montagnais *a·yaskʸime·w* or the like (attested as aiachkime8-), influenced by the common Spanish word-initial pattern esc-(esqu-)/esp-/est-.

A second set of English terms for Eskimo, apparently reflecting an independent borrowing from a Cree form, is found in a 1749 account by a Hudson's Bay Company employee referring to those on the west coast of the Bay: Ehuskemay, Iskemay, Uskemau's, Uskemaw's (Isham 1949:118, 132, 153, 181); in the same set belong also Uskimay, 1744, and Eusquemays, 1754, in sources cited by Hodge (1907–1910, 1:436–437), and the Usquemows, 1751, of W. Coats (1852:15). The nineteenth-century name Huskemaw and especially its shortened form Husky (Huskey, Huskie, Hoskies) were apparently spread in English usage by Hudson's Bay Company employees and coastal whalers, in view of the attestation of the eighteenth-century forms and the statements of Dall (1877a:9) and Packard (1885:475) that Husky was used by these groups, but they seem to be best attested in Labrador and Newfoundland, where Husky survives as a localism in the twentieth century. (Otherwise English retains husky as the name of a breed of dog.)

The most widespread self-designations used by Eskimo speakers fall into two sets. Meaning simply 'person, people' are West Greenlandic and general Canadian *inuk* (pl. *inuit*) and Central Siberian Yupik *yu·k* (pl. *yuɣət*); meaning 'real, genuine person' are Mackenzie Delta *inuvialuk* (pl. *inuvialuit*); North Slope Inupiaq *inʸupiaq* (pl. *inʸupiat*) written Iñupiaq, Iñupiat in the standard orthography; general Central Alaskan Yupik *yúppik*, written Yup'ik; and Pacific Eskimo *súxpiaq* (written Sugpiaq), now archaic in this meaning and usage. Renderings of these terms have sometimes been used as English and French designations, the commonest being Inuit (for Canadian Eskimos), Inupiat (for those of North Alaska), Yupik (southwestern Alaska), and Yuit (Siberia and Saint Lawrence Island). There is some hesitation between the originally singular and plural forms in both languages with some writers favoring the invariant use of the forms given in the preceding sentence and others attempting to maintain the original number distinction, particularly in the case of Inuk and Inuit (though ignoring the Eskimo distinction between the plural *inuit*, used for three or more, and the dual *inu·k*, used for exactly two). In Alaska, Inupiat seems to predominate in local usage (and was used in vol. 6), but Inupiaq is favored by the Alaska Native Language Center, Fairbanks, and has been used in this volume.

In the 1970s in Canada the name Inuit all but replaced Eskimo in governmental and scientific publications and the mass media, largely in response to demands from Eskimo political associations. The erroneous belief that Eskimo was a pejorative term meaning 'eater of raw meat' had a major influence on this shift. The Inuit Circumpolar Conference meeting in Barrow, Alaska, in 1977 officially adopted Inuit as a designation for all Eskimos, regardless of their local usages (Mailhot 1978:59). This general use of Inuit was earlier promoted by Dall (1877a), who used the spelling Innuit, and this appears, for example, in the title of an early grammar of Yupik (Barnum 1901). An early use of Inuit as a singular is in Kipling (1895:145). The usual pronunciation in English is ('īnōō,īt), but hypercorrect ('īnyōō,it) and Eskimoized ('ēnōō,ēt) are also encountered.

Names for the Eskimo in Indian languages not already cited include the following. Several interior Alaska Athapaskan languages use names meaning 'coastal people': Ingalik *novoɣ́hə́tan*; Holikachuk *namaɣ́hə́tan* (both James M. Kari, communication to editors 1978); Koyukon *nobaɣ́ hŏtanə* (Eliza Jones, communication to editors 1978). These languages also have specific names for the Eskimos in certain specific areas. Tanaina has no general name for Eskimo but, in addition to local names, only the subgroup designations *dutna* '(southwestern Alaska) Yupik Eskimo' (vol. 6:557) and *ʔutčəna* 'Pacific Eskimo' (vol. 6:632). Some Tanaina dialects have a separate form for 'Yupik woman', Inland *dučay* and Lime Village *dužčay*. Ahtna has *nakeh* 'Eskimo' (Kari and Buck 1975:58), and Eyak uses *kudi·q̇*, apparently a loan from Tlingit *kuté·x̣ (qʷá·n)*, which means 'Eskimo' at Yakutat but 'Eyak' farther south (Krauss 1963–1970:280). Designations in other Alaskan languages are Haida *kudá·kws x̣a·tá·y* (Lawrence and Leer 1977:264), Tlingit *x̣atasa̓·q* (Naish and Story 1976:86), Western Kutchin *če·kʷai·* (Peter 1979:49), and Eastern Kutchin *ʔene·kai* (Ritter 1976:45). Other names in Canadian Athapaskan languages are Hare *ʔarakie*, literally 'enemies' (Keren D. Rice, communication to editors 1979) and Chipewyan *hotélʔená*, literally 'flat-place enemy' (Ronald Scollon, communication to editors 1979).

Old Norse *skrælingr* (pl. *skrælingar* and *skrælingjar*), a word applied to Greenlandic Eskimos and North American natives, appears to be the source of the Greenlandic self-designation *kalaaleq*, pl. *kalaallit* (Thalbitzer 1904:36).

History of Research Before 1945

HENRY B. COLLINS

The Eskimos have the greatest linear distribution of any people in the world, extending for over 6,000 miles from East Greenland and Labrador through northernmost Canada and Alaska to Bering Strait and the northeast coast of Siberia, then southward along the Alaska coast to Prince William Sound on the Pacific. In view of the enormous expanse of their territory, and of its remoteness, it is not entirely surprising but nevertheless a striking fact that Eskimos were both the first and the last native North Americans to be discovered by Europeans.

The voyages of Martin Frobisher, John Davis, Thomas Button, Robert Bylot, William Baffin, Jens Munk, and Luke Foxe in the sixteenth and seventeenth centuries provided some knowledge of the Eskimos and of their distribution in West Greenland and the eastern Canadian Arctic. Portraits of Eskimo men and women, showing their skin clothing, weapons, and boats, were made by European artists beginning in 1567 (Birket-Smith 1959a; Oswalt 1979) ("Baffinland Eskimo," figs. 2–3, "Historical Ethnography of the Labrador Coast," figs. 2–4, this vol.). Explorations in the eighteenth and nineteenth centuries brought fuller information on the Eskimos, not only those of the eastern Arctic but also those of Canada and Alaska. And yet it was not until the twentieth century that a major segment of the population, the Copper Eskimos of Coronation Gulf, were brought to the attention of the scientific world through the investigations of Vilhjálmur Stefánsson and Diamond Jenness.

Ethnology

Greenland

• WEST GREENLAND In 1721 the Lutheran missionary Hans Poulsen Egede, with three ships and 40 colonists, landed near the present town of Godhavn to begin the resettlement of Greenland. One of his primary aims was to bring Christianity back to the descendants of the medieval Norsemen thought still to be there, but finding only Eskimos he devoted himself to their conversion and education and to the guidance of the newly established colony. Egede's (1741, 1745) comprehensive description of Greenland as he knew it in 1729 is a basic historical work.

Poul Hansen Egede, who succeeded his father as director of the Greenland Mission, published the first Eskimo dictionary (P.H. Egede 1750) and the first Eskimo grammar (P.H. Egede 1760). David Cranz's (1767) work, like that of Hans Egede, covered all aspects of Greenland's history, geography, fauna, flora, climate, and native people. Egede and Cranz were the first to describe in any detail the customs, hunting methods, material culture, and religious beliefs of the Greenland Eskimo. Poul Egede's son-in-law Henric Glahn, missionary at Holsteinsborg, wrote several papers on Greenlandic ethnography in 1771 and 1784; his diaries (Ostermann 1921) also include ethnographic observations.

Otto Fabricius, who was stationed at the Frederikshåb mission from 1768 to 1773, made notable contributions to Greenlandic ethnography and linguistics. He improved and amplified Poul Egede's linguistic works (Fabricius 1801, 1804), and as a participant observer he produced the most accurate and detailed studies of Eskimo hunting practices made up to that time. Unlike his predecessors, Fabricius chose to live among the Greenlanders and participate in their activities. He lived in a stone and sod house and, clad in the waterproof garment of the Eskimo sealer, traveled and hunted in a kayak. He describes each animal species, its life habits, utilization by the Eskimos, method of capture (fig. 1), and, in the most minute detail, the hunting and fishing equipment used for the purpose. As many of Fabricius's ethnological observations were incorporated in his zoological papers and remained untranslated, they were seldom referred to except by Danish writers until the appearance of an English translation (Holtved 1962).

Samuel Kleinschmidt's (1851, 1871) basic works on the West Greenlandic language established the orthography and grammatical terminology followed by later scholars. Hinrich Rink's numerous writings on the West Greenland Eskimo included several papers on linguistics, most of which formed parts of his best-known work, *The Eskimo Tribes* (Rink 1887–1891). Rink directed his studies of Eskimo language and culture to a consideration of their migration to Greenland and of the origin and relationships of the Eskimo as a whole. He was the first and foremost champion of the theory that Eskimo culture had originated in America, among the riverine peoples of interior Alaska. Rink (1875, 1877) also de-

Kort- og Billedafdelingen, Kongelige Bibliotek, Copenhagen: Fabricius 1788:423.

Fig. 1. Trapping the Arctic fox, whose fur was an important item of trade in West Greenland in the late 18th century. The missionary, ethnographer, and naturalist Otto Fabricius (b. 1774, d. 1822) described 8 Greenlandic methods for capturing the fox, on the basis of his experiences at Iluilarssuk, south of Frederikshåb, in 1770–1773 (Holtved 1962:97–102). His illustration, an engraving published in 1788, depicts a kind of box trap made of stones.

scribed the history and geography of West Greenland and the economy and mode of life of its native people. William Thalbitzer (1904) dealt with the West Greenlandic dialect spoken at Disko Bay and Uummannaq Fjord. He also analyzed Eskimo grammar (Thalbitzer 1911). Both works give lexical and phonetic comparisons with Eskimo dialects in other parts of Greenland, Labrador, Canada, and Alaska. The former volume also contains sections on folk tales, songs and music, and a long list of Eskimo place-names in the Disko Bay–Uummannaq area and their meaning. Between 1900 and 1953 Thalbitzer published 302 titles. Further valuable contributions to West Greenlandic linguistics were Schultz-Lorentzen's dictionary (1927) and grammar (1945).

Gudmund Hatt's (1914) comparative analysis of skin clothing of the Arctic peoples of America and Eurasia includes precise descriptions of West Greenland clothing and footgear. Later substantial contributions were those of Morten Porsild (1915) on the material culture of the West Greenlanders and of Alfred Bertelsen (1929, 1935–1943) on health, living conditions, diseases, and sanitation. The first modern ethnography of the West Greenland Eskimo was by Birket-Smith (1924), who drew fully on all previous works and his own investigations in 1918. Birket-Smith (1928a) also published a useful summary of the distribution, history, physical characteristics, economy, and living conditions of the Greenland Eskimos as a whole.

• EAST GREENLAND Though only 500 miles from the Danish colonies in southern Greenland, the East Coast, because of its great masses of pack ice, remained unknown for many years. The Eskimos on the southern part of the East Coast had been seen by Peder Olsen Walløe in 1751 and by the naval officer Wilhelm Graah in 1829–1830, but it was not until 1884 that Gustav Holm, on a cartographic survey of the East Coast, dis-

covered the large unknown tribe of Eskimos living on Sermilik and Ammassalik fjords. Holm spent the winter of 1884–1885 among the Ammassalik Eskimos. The resulting report (Holm 1888) was to become one of the classics of American ethnology. It was one of the first scientific descriptions of an Eskimo tribe, a distinction shared with Franz Boas's (1888) work on the Central Eskimo. Holm's report, translated into English, formed a major part of the important monograph on the Ammassalik Eskimo (Thalbitzer 1914–1941), which included collected legends and tales, a study of the East Greenlandic dialect, and sections on physical anthropology, population distribution, and music. Important contributions in this work are by Thalbitzer, on ethnological collections from East Greenland, language and folklore, and social customs and mutual aid.

Under the leadership of Ejnar Mikkelsen Danish colonies, including Eskimo families from Ammassalik, were established on Scoresby Sound in 1924–1925. Mikkelsen (1934) and Mikkelsen and Sveistrup (1944) describe the colonization as well as population distribution and living conditions throughout East Greenland.

The Sixth and Seventh Thule Expeditions of 1931 and 1932–1933, under the direction of Knud Rasmussen, explored the East Coast up to Scoresby Sound and recorded observations on the Eskimos (Rasmussen 1932a, 1933), including notes on ethnology, mythology, and religion (Ostermann 1938, 1939).

• NORTH GREENLAND Just as the Ammassalik Eskimos had remained in isolation on the ice-bound coast of East Greenland, another tribe—the Polar Eskimos north of the glacier coast and ice-filled waters of Melville Bay—was unknown to their kinsmen in West Greenland. That the early Norsemen had penetrated their territory is known from Holtved's (1944, 1954) excavations, and there may have been limited contacts with the West Greenlanders after the Norse period. But there was no memory of such contacts, and when Sir John Ross discovered—or rediscovered—them in 1818 they believed themselves to be the only people in the world (Ross 1819). The Polar Eskimos, or as Ross called them, the Arctic Highlanders, had forgotten the use of skin boats, the bow and arrow, and the salmon spear; these were reintroduced to them by Iglulik Eskimos from Pond Inlet, northern Baffin Island, who immigrated to Smith Sound via Ellesmere Island in the 1860s.

Adm. Robert Peary made Smith Sound the base of his polar expeditions from 1891 to 1909, the success of which was due primarily to the Polar Eskimos who accompanied him on his sledge journeys. Without employing their mode of travel and hunting techniques, he could never have reached the Pole. Peary's and Mylius-Erichsen's close associations with the Polar Eskimos enabled them to describe in some detail the Eskimos' customs and way of life (Peary 1898; Mylius-Erichsen and Moltke 1906).

The first anthropological study of the Polar Eskimos was that of Kroeber (1900), based on comparative data from the explorers Ross, Émile Bessels, Isaac Israel Hayes, Elisha Kent Kane, and Peary, but essentially on information from six Eskimo informants brought to New York by Peary and on Peary's ethnological collection in the American Museum of Natural History, New York. This paper and his collection of tales of the Smith Sound Eskimo (Kroeber 1899) were Kroeber's first anthropological publications.

In 1910 Rasmussen established an Arctic Station and trading post at Thule. This was an event of far-reaching importance for it was mainly from the profits of his station that Rasmussen launched the succession of Thule Expeditions that contributed so greatly to scientific knowledge of northern Canada and Greenland. Rasmussen, part Eskimo himself, was born in Greenland and educated in Denmark. He had spoken Greenlandic Eskimo since childhood and had lived among the Polar Eskimos, as one of them, since 1903. His descriptions of the Polar Eskimos (e.g., 1908, 1921, 1921–1925, 1921b) display a depth of understanding, sensitivity, and insight that are unequaled in Arctic literature.

A comprehensive summary of Polar Eskimo ethnology and ecology was given by H.P. Steensby (1910), and further ecological studies were made by W.E. Ekblaw (1921, 1927–1928). Later substantial contributions

to Polar Eskimo ethnography, language, and folklore were those of Holtved (1951, 1967).

Canada

The earliest accounts giving explicit information on the Canadian Eskimo are those of the nineteenth-century British explorers searching for a Northwest Passage: notably Parry (1824, 1842), Lyon (1824), and Rae (1850, 1866) on the Iglulik; Lyon (1825) on the Sallirmiut (usually referred to by the older spelling Sadlermiut); and Back (1836) and Ross (1835) on the Netsilik. The most comprehensive descriptions of the Mackenzie Delta Eskimo are those of the missionary Émile Petitot (1876a, 1886, 1887).

The first scientific monograph on the Canadian Eskimos was Franz Boas's on the Central Eskimo (1888). This classic work, Boas's first major publication in anthropology, was based on field explorations in 1883–1884 in Cumberland Sound and the east coast of Baffin Island (fig. 2). As in the case of Holm, author of the first scientific monograph on the Greenland Eskimo, Boas's primary objective had been geographical exploration. His travels on foot, by boat, and by dog team covered some 2,400 miles and resulted in the first accurate charts of the shores of Cumberland Sound and eastern Baffin Island. Boas's work was far more than

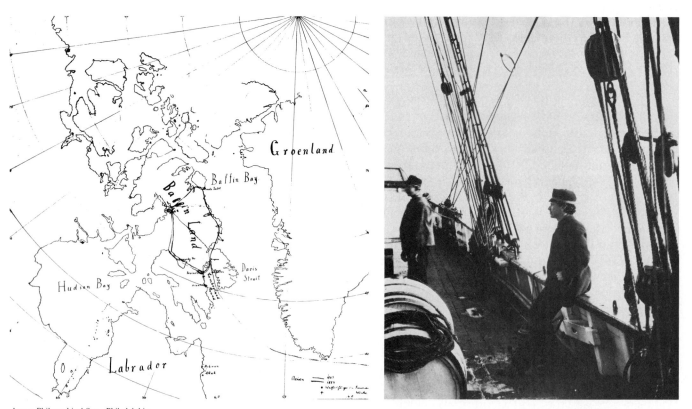

Amer. Philosophical Soc., Philadelphia.

Fig. 2. Franz Boas conducted geographical and ethnological research among the Baffinland Eskimo (Boas 1888). left, Watercolor map by Boas of his 1883–1884 trip. right, Boas on board the *Germania*, 1883.

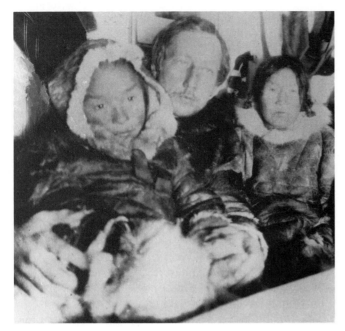

Fig. 3. Roald Amundsen, early visitor to the Netsilik, on his vessel the *Gjoa* with Kaiogolo (right), wife of his informant Teraiu, and their son Nutara. Photographed in Gjoa Haven, 1903–1905.

a description of the Eskimos—Oqomiut and Akudnirmiut and their several subtribes—with whom he had personal contact. Drawing on the works of Parry, Ross, Lyon, and others, he presented a rounded account of Eskimo culture in the eastern Canadian Arctic; and in

remarkable detail he described tribal distribution, intertribal relations, seasonal movements, and travel routes in Hudson Bay and Strait, Baffin Island, and areas to the west and north. Boas (1901–1907) presented data on the Eskimo of Baffin Island and Hudson Bay, based on collections and observations made for him by the whaling captains George Comer and James S. Mutch and the Rev. E.J. Peck.

The earliest description of the Labrador Eskimo was that of Cartwright (1792). The monographs by L.M. Turner (1894) and Hawkes (1916) provided the first full descriptions of these Eskimos. Other substantial works on Labrador and its people are those of Packard (1885), Low (1896), Gosling (1910), Hutton (1912, 1929), Grenfell et al. (1922), and Tanner (1947).

The western part of the Northwest Territories was the last section of the Canadian Arctic to be explored in modern times. On his first and second expeditions, 1908–1912 and 1913–1918, Stefánsson penetrated the country of the Copper Eskimos of Coronation Gulf and Victoria Island. This large and virtually unknown tribe consisted, he said, of 11 regional subgroups to whom Stefánsson gave the collective name Copper Eskimo. Through the studies of Stefánsson (1913, 1914, 1919, 1921) and of Jenness (1922, 1923, 1923a, 1924a, 1928a, 1946), a member of the second expedition, this last of the Eskimo tribes to be discovered in the Arctic became the most fully known (fig. 5). Jenness's (1922) classic monograph on the Copper Eskimos is generally regarded as the best description of a single Eskimo tribe.

The wide-ranging investigations of the Fifth Thule

Fig. 4. Drawing by an unknown Eskimo artist of Robert Flaherty directing and filming among the Eskimo of Hudson Bay. Pencil sketch, about 1913–1914. Flaherty later produced the film *Nanook of the North*.

11

Fig. 5. Ethnographers of the Copper Eskimo, members of the Canadian Arctic Expedition 1913–1918: Diamond Jenness (left) and Vilhjálmur Stefánsson. Photographs by George H. Wilkins, left, 1914–1916; right, 1916–1918.

Expedition, 1921–1924 under Rasmussen (fig. 6), marked a turning point in Arctic anthropology. In addition to basic reports on archeology, physical anthropology, physiography, geology, botany, and zoology, the ex-

pedition produced definitive monographs on the ethnology of the Caribou Eskimo (Birket-Smith 1929; Rasmussen 1930), Netsilik (Rasmussen 1931; Birket-Smith 1945), Iglulik (Mathiassen 1928; Rasmussen 1930), and Copper Eskimo (Rasmussen 1932; Birket-Smith 1945).

Birket-Smith's work (1929) was of particular significance because, in addition to its descriptive section and an analytical section tracing the distribution of Eskimo and Indian culture traits throughout northern America and Eurasia, it presented a far-reaching theory of the origin of Eskimo culture. Birket-Smith's theory was both an acceptance, in greatly elaborated form, of that of Steensby (1905, 1917) and an adjustment to Hatt's (1916, 1916a) theory opposing Steensby's.

Steensby had postulated a stratification of Eskimo culture, with an original Paleo-Eskimo form in the Central Arctic and a later Subarctic form, the Neo-Eskimo culture, in Alaska and Greenland. The Paleo-Eskimo culture had developed from a northern Indian base on the mainland around Coronation Gulf. Birket-Smith accepted this cultural stratification and terminology but added a still earlier, Proto-Eskimo, stage and a final, Eschato-Eskimo, stage. The Proto-Eskimo stage was represented by the modern Caribou Eskimos, most of whom lived in the interior and had no contact with the sea. This, Birket-Smith assumed, was an original condition; the Caribou Eskimo were, so to speak, the living ancestors of all the Eskimo. The few Caribou Eskimos now living on the west shore of Hudson Bay moved there only in recent centuries and represented the latest, or Eschato-Eskimo, stage of culture.

Hatt had proposed a reversal of Steensby's sequence. Steensby's Neo-Eskimo culture, in Hatt's view, was the older, representative of what he called the coast culture,

Fig. 6. Knud Rasmussen and some other members of the Fifth Thule Expedition, 1921–1924. left, Studio portrait (left to right): Leo Hansen, expedition photographer, Arnarulúnguaq, Qâvigarssuaq, and Rasmussen; photograph by the Lomen Brothers, probably 1924. The Natives were from Thule, Greenland. right, Heavily loaded sledge of the expedition preparing to leave Point Barrow. left to right, Arnarulúnguaq, Rasmussen, unidentified person, and Qâvigarssuaq. Photograph probably by Charles Brower, May 1924.

while the Paleo-Eskimo was a later intrusion of what he called the inland culture. Hatt's concept of two culture stages, "coast" and "inland," was based on his earlier analysis of skin clothing, footgear, and snowshoes in northern America and Eurasia, with the coastal complex, essentially Eskimo in character, representing an older stage and the inland complex a later one (Hatt 1914). Birket-Smith redefined Hatt's stages; the coast culture became the "ice-hunting" stage and the inland culture the "snowshoe" stage. Birket-Smith's theory was opposed by Mathiassen (1930), and its basic assumptions were questioned by Collins (1937a:379–380, 1940:542–544).

Ice-hunting and snowshoe, as classificatory terms, had only a limited impact on Arctic anthropology; but the simpler, basic concept of inland versus coastal, with inland inevitably the older, has had a pervasive, almost obsessive influence, as Arctic cultures, ancient and modern, were labeled and classified in line with the meaning if not the actual terminology of Steensby's original dichotomy. The lingering effects of this ethnologically based concept, applied to the interpretation of prehistoric cultures, have finally been dissipated by the factual findings of archeology.

Alaska

The North Pacific, Bering Sea, and Arctic coasts of Alaska were not discovered by Europeans until the eighteenth century, 200 years later than the opposite northeastern coasts of Canada and Greenland. Vitus Bering's second expedition, in 1741, was the first to encounter native Alaskans—Aleuts on the Shumagin Islands south of the Alaska Peninsula. Georg Wilhelm Steller, naturalist on Bering's expedition, was the first European to describe these people (Golder 1922–1925, 2:90–105). Steller noted the similarity of their skin-covered boats to those of the Greenland Eskimos; but from the physical appearance of the people themselves, their clothing, weapons, utensils, and food, he concluded that the Aleuts were related to the Kamchadals. Brief descriptions of the Aleuts by other early Russian explorers—Andreian Tolstykh in 1761, Ivan Korovin in 1763, Ivan Solovief 1764, Pëtr Krenitzin and Mikhail Levashev in 1768—were made available in English by Coxe (1803), Bancroft (1886), and Jochelson (1933). Somewhat fuller accounts of the Aleuts were given by the late eighteenth- and early nineteenth-century explorers and writers Capt. James Cook, Gavriil Sarychev, Martin Sauer, Iurii Lisīanskii, Georg Langsdorf, and Henrik Johan Holmberg. The ethnological information contained in these early accounts was assembled and presented in a useful topical arrangement by Hrdlička (1945). The most comprehensive description of the Aleuts was that by the Russian Orthodox missionary Ivan Ven-

iaminov (1840), later bishop Innocent and metropolitan of Moscow; although it has not been translated into English, lengthy sections of it have been published by Petroff (in U.S. Census Office 1884), Bancroft (1886), Jochelson (1933), and Hrdlička (1945).

The earliest work on Aleut linguistics was an 1820 manuscript by Rasmus Rask that suggested the relationship between the Aleut language and Greenlandic. Rask's manuscript was published by Thalbitzer (1922), who adduced additional evidence of the relationship of the two languages. Veniaminov's fuller study of Eastern Aleut (1846a) exists only in Russian, as does Jochelson's (1919) study based on Veniaminov's. However, Veniaminov's grammar was translated by Geoghegan (1944:17–83) and included in his study. A comparative grammar of Greenlandic, Mackenzie Delta Eskimo, and Aleut (Henry 1879) noted the structural similarity of the three languages despite word differences in Aleut. Studies by Swadesh (1951, 1952), Marsh and Swadesh (1951), and Hirsch (1954), employing the later controversial glottochronological technique for measuring elapsed time in the separation of related languages, concluded that Aleut and Eskimo had separated around 3,000 years ago.

Kodiak Island was discovered by the Russian fur hunter Stephan Glotov in 1763. The account of his eight-month stay on the island and his brief references to its Eskimo inhabitants, the Koniag, are related by Coxe (1803) and Sarychev. The most circumstantial contemporary accounts of the Koniags were those of Davydov and Shelikhov; these, and some of the historical accounts cited above for the Aleuts, are translated by Hrdlička (1944). Another valuable early source on the Koniags and other Alaska tribes is the journal of C.H. Merck, physician and naturalist on the Joseph Billings expedition (Jacobi 1937:116–136). The best account of Koniag material culture is that by Birket-Smith (1941), describing and illustrating clothing, ornaments, hunting implements, and utensils in the National Museum, Copenhagen, collected in 1851 by the Finnish naturalist Henrik Johan Holmberg. Lantis's (1938a) study of Koniag mythology includes results of her own fieldwork and everything available from the literature. Two other extensive works on Alaska ceremonialism (Lantis 1938, 1947) also include the Kodiak data on this subject.

The Chugach, southernmost of mainland Alaska Eskimos, were discovered by Captain Cook in 1778. Cook (Cook and King 1784) observed that the skin boats, clothing, weapons, and some of the words of the Chugach of Prince William Sound were like those of the eastern Eskimos, which confirmed his belief in the existence of a northwest passage between the east and west coasts of America. The narratives of later explorers contain very little on the Chugach, and they remained one of the least-known Eskimo tribes until publication of Birket-Smith's monograph (1953) based on

13

fieldwork in 1933. The Chugach are now one of the few Alaska tribes for which a full-scale ethnography exists.

The most valuable early source on the Bering Sea and interior Alaska Eskimos is Lt. L.A. Zagoskin. Not a professional in any field of science but a highly literate naval officer with broad interests, Zagoskin spent the years 1842–1844 exploring the interior of Alaska on foot and in a skin boat. His journal (Zagoskin 1967) is a mine of information on the geography and ethnography of the Norton Sound, Yukon, and Kuskokwim areas, particularly valuable for its detailed data on population, village location, and tribal identification in an area of ethnic complexity where Eskimo and Indian cultures meet. Dall (1870, 1877a) also discusses tribal identification in this area.

The principal source of information on the Bering Sea Eskimos is E.W. Nelson, who spent four years, 1877–1881, as an employee of the U.S. Army Signal Service at Saint Michael, with a secondary assignment to make ethnographic collections for the U.S. National Museum. Nelson made extensive sled journeys along the lower Yukon and Kuskokwim rivers and the Norton Sound coast from Saint Michael to Sledge Island. As naturalist on the U.S. revenue steamer *Corwin*, he also visited the Siberian and Alaskan coasts of Bering Strait and the Arctic coast as far north as Point Barrow. Nelson's (1899) report deals mainly with material culture, especially of the Norton Sound, Yukon, and Kuskokwim areas, with full descriptions and countless illustrations of houses, clothing, boats, sleds, implements, utensils, masks, and ornaments. He also records valuable information on mortuary customs, trade, warfare, games, dance festivals, religion, mythology, and other aspects of social life. More limited contributions to Eskimo ethnology of the area are those of Petroff (in U.S.

Census Office 1884), Gordon (1906, 1917), and Curtis (1907–1930, 20). Hawkes (1913, 1914) described dance festivals of the Bering Sea Eskimos, and Himmelheber (1938) discussed Eskimo art, especially masks. The first comprehensive studies of Alaska Eskimo ceremonialism were made by Lantis (1938, 1947), and her Nunivak monograph (1946) was the first full description of the social life of any Alaska Eskimo tribe.

Jenness's (1927, 1928, 1944) comparative linguistic studies of the Alaska, Mackenzie, and Coronation Gulf dialects included lexical and grammatical material for Bering Strait (Wales, King Island, and East Cape, Siberia), Inglestat (Norton Sound), and Nunivak Island. Jenness was the first to point out the sharp linguistic break between the Eskimo dialects south of Norton Sound and those of northern Alaska, which differed little from the dialects of the Canadian and Greenland Eskimos. Swadesh (1951, 1952), accepting Jenness's evidence of this linguistic alignment, adopted the name Yupik for the southern dialects and coined the since disfavored term Inupik for those from North Alaska to Greenland. He estimated that the two branches had separated around 1,000 years ago. Collins (1954a) believed that the evidence of archeology, ethnology, and physical anthropology, as well as the results of tree ring and radiocarbon dating, supported the linguistic evidence of a sharp break at Norton Sound and suggested that the movements of the Thule culture were the mechanisms responsible—an original eastward spread and later return movement to northern Alaska. Hirsch's (1954) more detailed linguistic analysis came to the same conclusion.

The earliest European explorers to contact the north Alaska Eskimos, Otto von Kotzebue in 1815–1818 and Frederick W. Beechey in 1825–1828, provided little

Fig. 7. T. Dale Stewart and an Eskimo from Nunivak Island in a one-hatch kayak. Stewart was collecting anthropometric data that was used by the physical anthropologist Aleš Hrdlička. Photograph by Henry B. Collins, summer 1927.

information on the people. The first substantive account of the Arctic coast Eskimos was that of Dr. John Simpson (1875), who was at Point Barrow in 1852–1853. The principal original source on the Point Barrow Eskimos is Murdoch (1892), which provides a full account of the material culture of the Point Barrow Eskimos of 1881–1883 but contains little on their social life and religion. Valuable information on the north Alaska Eskimos in the late nineteenth and early twentieth centuries is recorded by Cantwell (1887, 1889), Stoney (1900), Stefánsson (1914, 1919), and Jenness (1957).

Archeology

The first systematic excavations in the Arctic were made by Therkel Mathiassen (1927), archeologist of the Fifth Thule Expedition. The result was discovery of prehistoric sites west and north of Hudson Bay belonging to what Mathiassen called the Thule culture, more closely akin to that of Alaska and Greenland than to modern Central Eskimo. The Thule culture Eskimos were a maritime people who lived in permanent semi-subterranean houses of stones, whale bones, and turf, and in skin tents in summer; they hunted mainly whales, seals, walrus, caribou, and polar bears. The Thule culture, according to Mathiassen, had persisted in modified form in Baffin Island, Labrador, Southampton Island, and Smith Sound; but it was considered to be essentially a prehistoric culture of Alaskan origin that had disappeared from the central Canadian Arctic, to be replaced by that of the modern Central Eskimo. This view had been generally accepted, prior to VanStone's (1962) demonstration of a very close connection between Thule and modern Central Eskimo culture, with the latter in all probability a direct outgrowth of Thule. A number of other Thule sites were excavated in Greenland and Canada (Mathiassen 1931, 1931a, 1933, 1934; Mathiassen and Holtved 1936; Holtved 1944, 1954; Larsen 1934, 1938; Collins 1950, 1951a, 1952, 1955). According to the evidence of archeology, linguistics, and somatology the Thule culture was primarily responsible for the present distribution of an Eskimo population, culture, and language throughout the Arctic from Bering Strait to Greenland.

Excavations in Alaska revealed the earlier stages of culture preceding Thule: Okvik, Old Bering Sea, Birnirk (the stage directly ancestral to Thule), Punuk, and Western Thule (Jenness 1928c; Collins 1930, 1931, 1932, 1935, 1937; J.A. Mason 1930; Geist and Rainey 1936; Rainey 1941; Giddings 1952a; VanStone 1955; Ford 1959). Excavations at five sites at Gambell, Saint Lawrence Island, revealed an unbroken, 2,000-year sequence of Eskimo culture from Okvik–Old Bering Sea to the present time. The most characteristic features of these cultures were considered to be of Asiatic origin. Northeastern Siberia, between the Anadyr' and Kolyma

rivers, was postulated as the place of immediate origin, but the basic roots of the older cultures extended deeper into northern Eurasia (Collins 1937a). Later excavations in northeast Siberia produced abundant evidence of the prehistoric Saint Lawrence cultures (Rudenko 1961), and a pure site of Okvik culture was discovered by Otto W. Geist on Punuk Island (Rainey 1941). The series of related cultures beginning with Okvik–Old Bering Sea and leading to modern Eskimo, extending eastward from northeast Siberia to Greenland, represent a cultural continuum called the Northern Maritime tradition. Theoretical discussions of these cultures are to be found in Birket-Smith (1930, 1936, 1952), Mathiassen (1930, 1931b, 1935), Jenness (1928a, 1928c, 1933, 1940), Collins (1934, 1937a, 1940, 1951, 1954, 1954a, 1960), and De Laguna (1947, 1952).

De Laguna's (1947) report on excavations at Indian and Eskimo sites on the Yukon included a detailed trait analysis that traced the distribution and relative age of the particular culture elements wherever they occurred, among living or prehistoric peoples in America or the Old World, leading to a comprehensive reconstruction of culture growth and cultural configurations throughout northern North America.

Discovery of the Ipiutak culture at Point Hope on the Arctic coast of Alaska in 1939 (Larsen and Rainey 1948) introduced a new element in Arctic archeology, one that fell outside the culture sequence previously described. Closely related to Okvik–Old Bering Sea in art and implement typology, and only slightly younger, Ipiutak in other respects was divergent. It lacked typical western Eskimo features such as lamps, rubbed slate implements, sleds, harpoon floats and other evidence of whaling, bow drills, and pottery; some of its art motifs and animal carvings had close parallels in Scytho-Siberian art of northern Eurasia. However, chronological implications cannot be drawn from Ipiutak's divergence from other north Alaskan cultures, for an older, related stage of culture at Point Hope called Near Ipiutak (now known to be closely related to Norton) possessed rubbed slate implements, whaling harpoon heads, lamps, and pottery. Disregarding the original excessive claims for Ipiutak as an inland-oriented "Paleo-Eskimo" culture from which all other Eskimo cultures were derived, the true significance of Ipiutak, Near Ipiutak, and Norton is that they were the primary source of prehistoric and modern Eskimo culture in the Bering Sea region south of Norton Sound (Larsen and Rainey 1948; Larsen 1950; Collins 1955a). The Ipiutak flint industry was derived in large part from the Denbigh Flint complex (discovered by Louis Giddings after 1948), and it possessed side-bladed knives, arrows, and lances directly comparable to those of the Siberian Neolithic and European Mesolithic. These side-bladed implements held a central place in the hypothesis that the oldest roots of Eskimo culture were to be found in the early Siberian *15*

Neolithic and the Mesolithic of northern Europe (Collins 1943, 1951a). The problem of Ipiutak and its position in Eskimo culture has been discussed by Rainey (1941a, 1941b), De Laguna (1947, 1952), Larsen and Rainey (1948), Larsen (1952, 1953, 1954, 1961), Collins (1943, 1951, 1953, 1954, 1954b, 1961, 1963–1964, 1964, 1971; Collins 1973), Jenness (1952a), Giddings (1967), and Bandi (1969).

In 1925 Jenness, examining mixed collections of artifacts dug up by Eskimos at Cape Dorset and Coats Island, noticed that most of the bone and ivory objects were very small, deeply patinated, and typologically distinct from Thule and modern Eskimo artifacts; the accompanying stone implements were also entirely different. On the basis of this secondhand material Jenness (1925, 1928a, 1933) described a new Eskimo culture, the Cape Dorset, that had preceded the Thule culture in the Eastern Arctic. Jenness's reconstruction, not only of the relative age of the Dorset culture but also of the distribution, food economy, and way of life of the Dorset Eskimos, has been fully borne out by later investigations. The Dorset culture has been found from Newfoundland throughout the Central Canadian Arctic to Greenland (Wintemberg 1939–1940; Rowley 1940; Leechman 1943; Holtved 1944; Collins 1950, 1955, 1956, 1956a, 1957a, 1957; Harp 1951, 1953, 1958, 1964; Knuth 1952, 1954; O'Bryan 1953; Larsen and Meldgaard 1958; Mathiassen 1958; W.E. Taylor 1959, 1964, 1964a, 1965, 1968, 1972a; Meldgaard 1960, 1960a, 1962; Lowther 1962; Maxwell 1960, 1960a, 1962).

The Dorset culture had a time span of from around 1000 B.C. to A.D. 1300. After the arrival of the Thule Eskimos from Alaska about 1,000 years ago the two cultures coexisted for several centuries in the same areas. They should have influenced one another, and there are indications that several important features of Canadian Thule culture were borrowed from Dorset. The dominant form of modern harpoon head in the Central Arctic and Greenland is obviously derived from a Dorset prototype, and the same may be true of the snow knife (and therefore the snowhouse), soapstone pots, the side-bladed Sallirmiut lance, and the art of the Ammassalik Eskimos of East Greenland. The Manitounik culture on the Belcher Islands, off the east coast of Hudson Bay, seems to be a late Dorset, Thule-influenced culture (Quimby 1940; Jenness 1941), and future investigations will no doubt reveal further evidence of Dorset-Thule interchange. In this connection it has been suggested (De Laguna 1947; Collins 1953a) that the Sallirmiut of Southampton Island, whose peculiar culture included many Thule features, were actually a remnant Dorset group, with heavy Thule overlay. A test of this hypothesis would require discovery of Sallirmiut sites older than any now known, sites representing an earlier (tenth to fourteenth century ?) period when the Sallirmiut, like the Dorsets, had no dogs or bow drills.

Smithsonian, NAA:Hrdlička coll.

Fig. 8. Aleš Hrdlička and Mrs. Gordon Jones, wife of the superintendent of the Larsen's Bay Cannery at an excavation on Uyak Bay, Kodiak I., Alaska. Hats with nets and long gloves were worn to protect them from the mosquitoes. Photographed July 1931.

South Alaska was the most densely populated area of northern North America in the eighteenth century. The Aleutian Islands have been occupied by people with an Aleut form of culture for over 3,000 years, as shown by a radiocarbon-dated site, Chaluka, on Umnak Island (Laughlin and Marsh 1951). Following Jochelson's (1925) work on Unalaska, Umnak, Atka, and Attu in 1909–1910, Hrdlička (1945) excavated numerous prehistoric Aleut sites between Unalaska and Attu. In 1959 Laughlin and his coworkers inaugurated a long-range research program on Umnak Island, with investigations in archeology, somatology, zoology, and ecology (Laughlin 1952, 1952a, 1958, 1962, 1963, 1963a; Laughlin and Marsh 1951, 1954, 1956; Laughlin and Reeder 1966). In 1948–1952 the University of Michigan conducted archeological, ethnobotanical, and ecological studies on Unalaska, Umnak, Atka, Adak, Agattu, and other islands (Bank 1952b, 1953, 1953a, 1953b, 1953c; A.C. Spaulding 1953, 1962). The archeological materials excavated by Hrdlička (1944) on Kodiak Island (fig. 8) have been fully described and analyzed by Heizer (1956). At Port Moller on the north coast of the Alaska Peninsula, at the historic boundary between the Aleuts and Aglurmiut Eskimos, Weyer (1930) excavated a large midden containing materials culturally similar to Aleut and south Alaska Eskimo.

The basic works on the archeology of South Alaska are those of Frederica de Laguna. Her Cook Inlet (1934) and Prince William Sound (1956) monographs are the only full descriptions of the archeology of this part of Alaska. They not only present a detailed record of culture developments at the southern margin of Alaska Eskimo territory but also bring these into relationship with Eskimo culture generally.

History of Archeology After 1945

ELMER HARP, JR.

Immediately following World War II, archeological research resumed slowly in the North American Arctic, and by the end of the 1940s there were 15 separate field programs in progress. In the 1950s that number tripled, and during the 1960s and 1970s, when Arctic archeology truly came of age, there were well over 100 different field operations.

Western Arctic Problems

It is customary to identify a prehistoric Pacific-Aleut cultural tradition throughout southwestern Alaska and the Aleutian Islands, and Frederica de Laguna, an early pioneer in that area, returned to the field in 1949 to investigate protohistoric sites around Yakutat Bay (De Laguna et al. 1964). Later surveys by Wendell Oswalt (1955a) and Wilbur Davis (1960) further clarified recent aboriginal occupations in southern Alaska.

In the decades of the 1960s and 1970s Don Dumond worked intensively on the Alaska Peninsula, which he regards as the critical boundary between the Pacific-Aleut tradition and the Eskimo tradition of the Bering Sea area (Dumond 1969, 1977a). On the north side of the peninsula he excavated sites related to northern Eskimo sequences, while the Takli Alder phase on the south coast, dated about 4000 B.C., was suggested to be ancestral to Aleut culture. Research near Iliamna Lake by Sam-Joe and Joan Townsend, continued by Joan Townsend, has exposed a late Tanaina Indian community, some evidence of an earlier Norton-like Eskimo occupation, and clear indications of an occupation of the third millennium B.C., by people apparently related to contemporary inhabitants of Kodiak Island and the Pacific coast of the Alaska Peninsula (Townsend 1970; Townsend and Townsend 1961, 1964).

Aleutian Island prehistory is known largely from the research of William Laughlin, although Theodore Bank (1953a) also contributed substantially during four field seasons there. In the late 1940s and early 1950s Laughlin worked the Chaluka site on Umnak Island and delineated an occupation of Paleo-Aleuts that was established in the eastern Aleutians by 2000 B.C. and later moved westward throughout the island chain. Albert Spaulding's excavations on Agattu Island in 1949 confirmed that people, presumably Paleo-Aleuts, had reached the end of the archipelago by 500 B.C. (A.C. Spaulding 1962). Around A.D. 1000 this population contracted into the western portion of the chain and was replaced in the east by Neo-Aleuts (Laughlin and Marsh 1956). Meanwhile, Laughlin (1963a) continued his investigations on Anangula Island, there defining a distinctive Aleutian core and blade industry, dated to about 6000 B.C. Noting a similar blade technology in the lower levels of Chaluka, he suggested that Paleo-Aleut culture derived from this fundamental tradition.

Investigations by Donald Clark on Kodiak Island (Clark 1966), William Workman on Chirikoff Island, and Robert Ackerman in Glacier Bay National Monument also helped to detail this prehistoric Aleut-Pacific coastal spectrum, which Dumond summarized as follows. In the period 6000–5000 B.C. the northwest Pacific littoral was inhabited by a related group of Subarctic, coast-oriented cultures, characterized in part by a blade technology, of which variations have been found at Anangula Island (Aigner 1978a), Afognak Island (Clark 1979), Ground Hog Bay near Juneau (Ackerman 1973; Ackerman, Hamilton, and Stuckenrath 1979), Hidden Falls near Sitka (S.D. Davis 1980) in the Queen Charlotte Islands (Fladmark 1971), and on the coast of British Columbia (Carlson 1979). By 4000 B.C. Proto-Aleut had evolved from this base and occupied portions of the eastern Aleutians, the south coast of the Alaska Peninsula, and Kodiak Island. Aleut culture developed during the next two millennia, while the Pacific coast and Kodiak cultures differentiated further under influences from coastal groups as far south as British Columbia. After A.D. 1000 there was increasing cultural diffusion between the Bering Sea and Pacific coast across the Alaska Peninsula. This synthetic view has been questioned by some investigators (see "Prehistory: Summary," this vol.).

The classic Eskimo tradition developed in the arctic environments north of the Alaska Peninsula. Many scholars have done significant research in that area, but Louis Giddings deserves mention because of his prolific fieldwork. In 1948 he began a four-year campaign in Norton Bay, concentrating on two major sites, Nukleet and Iyatayet. Here he discovered the Denbigh Flint complex, a core and microblade industry with origins in the Old World Mesolithic. Originally estimated to be about 6,000 years old, but now dated about 2,000 years younger, the Denbigh complex has been widely accepted as a basic tradition in the composition of Eskimo culture. At Iyatayet, Giddings also discovered a later Norton horizon that dated around 500 B.C. This culture was based on sea mammal hunting and is recognized as one of the early, true Eskimo phases in the western Arctic (Giddings 1951, 1964).

Oswalt collected tree-ring dates in western Alaska in 1948 and 1952, and his 1950 excavations at Hooper Bay furnished material for an analysis of pottery there during the last two millennia (Oswalt 1949, 1955a). Helge Larsen and Erik Holtved explored the Bristol Bay–Kuskokwim area in 1948, and Larsen returned the following two years to excavate the Trail Creek caves. The stratified sequence there extended from historic times back to a lowermost horizon that Larsen thought antedated the Denbigh complex by perhaps 1,000 years (Larsen 1951, 1953, 1962, 1968). James VanStone (1957) investigated sites on Nunivak Island, most of them recent and containing evidence of late contact with the mainland; work by Nowak (1970) has established a Norton occupation of the island.

In 1956 Giddings explored a series of beach ridges on Choris Peninsula, finding on the oldest ridge a new variant of Eskimo culture that he named Choris. This dated in the first millennium B.C., between Denbigh and Norton (Giddings 1957, 1960). From 1958 to 1961 Giddings worked on the beach ridge chronology of Cape Krusenstern, and his excavations there furnished evidence of a 6,000-year panorama of Eskimo culture, ranging from western Thule, through Birnirk, Ipiutak, Choris–Trail Creek, Old Whaling, and Denbigh cultures. On the mainland behind the beachlines, Giddings discovered the still earlier Palisades phases, which he thought to resemble old flake industries in the Alaska interior.

Other research in this area in the 1960s included Frederick Hadleigh West's discovery of a Norton-like site on Seward Peninsula and a nearby cave that yielded Ipiutak culture and a suggestion of Denbigh technology. Farther south, Ackerman excavated sites near Platinum exhibiting a continuum from Norton to recent Eskimo, and his Security Cove collection, dated about 3000 B.C., resembled some of the Palisades material.

Some of these early mainland Eskimo cultures were ancestral to the classic Northern Maritime tradition originally identified through the pioneering research of Diamond Jenness, Henry B. Collins, Otto W. Geist, S.J. Rudenko, Louis Giddings, and Froelich Rainey. This includes the highly specialized maritime cultures called Okvik, Old Bering Sea, and Punuk, whose relationship is still obscured by chronological uncertainties. In response to this problem, Hans-Georg Bandi (1969) began investigations on Saint Lawrence Island in 1965. Ultimately, the Northern Maritime tradition, together with the Denbigh-Choris-Norton-Ipiutak sequence of the mainland, contributed to the formation of the Birnirk and Thule cultures during several centuries preceding A.D.1000; these cultures, in turn, evolved into the modern expression of Eskimo life.

In northern Alaska in the late 1940s and early 1950s, U.S. Geological Survey field parties discovered sites containing fluted points and polyhedral cores along various streams on the Arctic slope (R.M. Thompson 1948; Solecki 1950, 1950a, 1951a). Robert Hackman also found Denbigh materials at Natvakruak Lake (Solecki and Hackman 1951). In the early 1950s William Irving discovered evidence of the Denbigh compex in Anaktuvuk Pass, which stimulated his conceptual formulation of the Arctic Small Tool tradition. He suggested that this core and microblade technology had Old World Mesolithic origins and was a basic ingredient of the early coastal tundra cultures of the North American Arctic (Irving 1951, 1953, 1955, 1957). Dennis Stanford (1976) began explorations near Point Barrow in 1968, and his stratified Walakpa site yielded a full sequence from Denbigh to modern times.

In 1956–1959 John Campbell found a wide scattering of occupations in Anaktuvuk, including Kogruk, a crude flake assemblage, further evidence of Denbigh, a southern-influenced Plano component, a notched-point complex named Tuktu, and Ipiutak (Campbell 1959, 1961, 1962a, 1962b). Meanwhile, Irving (1962) excavated an Arctic Small Tool site at Itivlik Lake, Howard Pass. Herbert Alexander explored the Atigun valley in 1966, and again in 1967 with Robert Stuckenrath, finding sites related to Denbigh and Palisades. When the trans-Alaska oil pipeline was constructed in the late 1960s and early 1970s, John Cook directed all salvage archeology on the right-of-way. His field parties investigated a variety of early flake, Arctic Small Tool, and protohistoric sites in the Sagavanirktok and Atigun valleys.

The Central Arctic

In Canada, Richard MacNeish reconnoitered the arctic coast in 1954–1956, and his Engigstciak site on Firth River contained a noteworthy sequence (MacNeish 1956, 1959, 1962). The earliest level, British Mountain, was Mousterian-like and correlated with Kogruk; the succeeding Flint Creek phase related to the Northwest Microblade tradition of the interior; and New Mountain represented the Arctic Small Tool tradition of the coast. Six later phases tied in with the Alaska Eskimo sequence. However, solifluction had distorted the local stratification, creating uncertain mixed levels, so Gordon Lowther and Edwin Wilmsen reworked Engigstciak in 1961–1962. Wilmsen (1964) then proposed that British Mountain was one of several related Arctic flake industries that had diffused from Siberia and evolved into the Paleo-Indian tradition of the New World, but the only available radiocarbon evidence suggests a date for British Mountain later than 6000 B.C. (B.H.C. Gordon 1970).

Elmer Harp surveyed around Coronation Gulf in 1955, finding interior sites at Dismal Lake and Kamut Lake with assemblages of Arctic Small Tool materials. He interpreted these as a probable lead into the Dorset Eskimo continuum of the eastern Arctic (Harp 1958). Robert McGhee (1970) discovered a Pre-Dorset component at Bloody Falls on the Coppermine River in 1968, as well as evidence of an Archaic or Plano occupation. The following year he excavated an Arctic Small Tool site in the Mackenzie River delta.

In the Barren Grounds west of Hudson Bay in 1953, Giddings (1956a) found an assemblage of Denbigh-like materials on North Knife River, well within the eastern realm of the Dorset continuum. Guy Mary-Rousselière surveyed around Baker Lake, District of Keewatin, in 1955, and Elmer Harp explored the lower and middle Thelon River in 1958. His field data indicated a sequence of five occupations in the interior Barren Grounds, including a primary phase influenced by the southern Paleo-Indian tradition, a possible Pre-Dorset phase, Archaic Indian, Thule, and finally Caribou Eskimo. Harp (1959, 1961) believed that modern Caribou Eskimo culture had descended from Thule and therefore did not have southern origins.

Irving operated farther south in the Barren Grounds in the early 1960s and discovered Pre-Dorset at Twin Lakes near Churchill. In 1969, James Wright excavated the Aberdeen site, found by Harp on the Thelon, proving that the interior barrens had been inhabited by northern hunters for the previous 7,000 years, and further elaborating his concept of the Shield Archaic tradition (Wright 1972, 1972a). Bryan H.C. Gordon's (1975, 1976) excavations on the upper Thelon in the early 1970s stratigraphically confirmed and refined this Barren Grounds sequence.

Eastern Arctic Derivations

In the eastern Canadian Arctic and Greenland, most field research since 1945 has been involved with the origin and evolution of the Dorset Eskimo tradition. Eigil Knuth (1952) examined Thule sites in northeast Greenland and also found evidence of Paleo-Eskimo culture that he classified as Dorset. Subsequent investigations there led to his definition of the Independence I and II cultures, dating to 2000–1500 B.C. and 1000–500 B.C. respectively, which he thought were ancestral to Dorset (Knuth 1954, 1958). In 1948 Hans Mosegaard dug at Sarqaq, Disko Bay, West Greenland. His collections were analyzed and published by Jörgen Meldgaard (1952), who showed that Sarqaq was the pre-Thule "stone age" culture originally postulated by Solberg (1907). Meldgaard inferred Alaskan origins for

Sarqaq, and to check that hypothesis Helge Larsen and Meldgaard investigated the Sermermiut site in Disko Bay; Therkel Mathiassen (1958) also excavated there. The earliest occupation of Sermermiut was Sarqaq (Pre-Dorset), dated about 1500 B.C., the succeeding stratum Dorset around the beginning of the Christian era, and the final horizon classic Thule. Larsen and Meldgaard (1958) found no connections between Sarqaq and Dorset and therefore proposed a theory of separate migrations.

In the Canadian archipelago, Henry B. Collins (1950, 1955) excavated Crystal II on Frobisher Bay, Baffin Island, and at Resolute, Cornwallis Island. His sites produced sharp stratigraphic separation of Thule and underlying Dorset levels, and Collins's (1950) report included a typology of Dorset harpoon heads that expressed their value as horizon markers. Harp (1951, 1964) surveyed the Strait of Belle Isle area, discovering and testing several Dorset sites on the west coast of Newfoundland and Archaic sites in southern Labrador. Deric O'Bryan (1953) excavated a late Dorset site on Mill Island in Hudson Strait.

In 1954–1955 Collins's operations in the T-1 site on Southampton Island disclosed a new, early phase of Dorset culture (Collins 1956, 1956a, 1957, 1958). Concurrently, Meldgaard explored raised beachlines in the Igloolik area, finding an extensive seriation of Pre-Dorset, Dorset, and Thule settlements. Again, Meldgaard (1960, 1960a, 1962) emphasized the gap between Pre-Dorset and Dorset and suggested that Dorset origins must have occurred to the south in present-day boreal forest country.

The late 1950s and early 1960s brought a new surge of interest in the Eastern Arctic. Mary-Rousselière (1964, 1976, 1979) checked Pre-Dorset, Dorset, and Thule sites near Pelly Bay and spent two seasons at the Button Point Dorset site on Bylot Island. William Taylor worked three summers along the south shore of Hudson Strait and on several offshore islands. He discovered Eskimo skeletal material in association with presumed Dorset culture in the Imaha site (Laughlin and Taylor 1960) and found Pre-Dorset sites at Ivujivik and Arnapik. His evidence indicated that Pre-Dorset evolved directly into Dorset in the Eastern Arctic, without other significant influences (W.E. Taylor 1962, 1967, 1968).

Moreau Maxwell (1960) excavated around Lake Hazen on northern Ellesmere Island in 1958, finding mainly Thule and later occupations, but no evidence of prehistoric migrations through that area into Greenland. However, Knuth (1967), after continuing his research in Independence sites in northeast Greenland, proposed that Independence culture had followed the "Musk-Ox Way" out of Ellesmere Island. Maxwell (1962, 1973) mounted an extensive program on Juet Island and around Lake Harbour in southern Baffin Island, discovering a 3,000-year continuum of Pre-Dorset to Dorset evolution. His research there into the 1970s also established correlations between local climatic shifts and Dorset culture change (Maxwell 1967; Dekin 1969, 1970). Lowther (1962) found a Pre-Dorset site on Devon Island, and McGhee (1979) examined a full sequence of prehistoric Eskimo occupation on Grinnell Peninsula at the northwestern tip of Devon.

Harp returned to Newfoundland in 1961 and excavated for three seasons in the Port aux Choix–2 site on Cape Riche. There he traced a major Dorset occupation that persisted unacculturated and virtually unchanged through the first six centuries of the Christian era. His investigations in southern Labrador produced an Archaic occupation date of about 3500 B.C. (Harp 1964, 1964a, 1969–1970, 1976; Harp and Hughes 1968). William Fitzhugh (1972) discovered Pre-Dorset, Dorset, and Archaic sites around Hamilton Inlet in central Labrador, while in the 1960s Urve Linnamae (1975), Donald McLeod, and Helen Devereux concentrated on Newfoundland Dorset problems. Fitzhugh, McGhee, and James Tuck have pursued long-range research projects in Labrador, refining their concept of Maritime Archaic Indian culture and its spread into northern Labrador, as well as the southward diffusion of the Pre-Dorset and Dorset continuum into Newfoundland (see Cox 1978; Fitzhugh 1976a, 1976b, 1977; Jordan 1977; S. Kaplan 1980; McGhee 1976b; McGhee and Tuck 1975, 1976; Nagle 1978; Tuck 1975, 1976). Anne Stine Ingstad (1977) and Helge Ingstad excavated at L'Anse aux Meadows, Newfoundland, establishing the presence of an eleventh-century Norse settlement there.

In the early 1960s Taylor surveyed in the Central Arctic, discovering Thule sites on Bathurst and Somerset islands, and Pre-Dorset and Dorset sites on Victoria and Banks islands (W.E. Taylor 1964a, 1967, 1968). Hansjürgen Müller-Beck excavated for two seasons in a significant Pre-Dorset locale in the interior of Banks, while McGhee (1976b) found other Pre-Dorset sites on Victoria Island.

On the west coast of Hudson Bay, Ronald Nash investigated the previously known Twin Lakes and Thyazzi Pre-Dorset sites in 1965, and he later found Dorset components near Churchill (Nash 1969). The Thule occupation of northwestern Hudson Bay is well known from the pioneering research of Therkel Mathiassen on the Fifth Thule Expedition of 1921–1924, from the work of Charles Merbs (1968, 1968a), Urve Linnamae and Brenda Clark (1976; also B.L. Clark 1977), and especially from the extensive investigations of Allen McCartney (1977a, 1979). James VanStone (1962) analyzed archeological and osteological collections from Somerset Island and Boothia Peninsula, thus documenting the evolution of modern Netsilik culture from Thule forebears. Excavations in a site on Ellesmere Island produced Norse artifacts from a certain Thule context (Schledermann 1980).

In northern Ungava, Thomas Lee (1967) reexamined sites at Payne Lake, previously identified as Dorset by Taylor, and claimed for them a Norse origin; however, Patrick Plumet (1982) has reaffirmed the Dorset identity of these longhouse occupations. Bernard Saladin d'Anglure found Dorset sites with associated petroglyphs near Wakeham Bay, Ungava, in 1965–1966, while Plumet examined other Dorset sites in Diana Bay. Harp (1974–1975) explored the southeast coast of Hudson Bay, northward from Great Whale River, excavating a complex of late Dorset sites in the entrance to Richmond Gulf (fig. 1) and on the Nastapoka Islands. Plumet (1976) described a high Pre-Dorset site, dated about 1300 B.C., near the mouth of Great Whale River. Harp staged a reconnaissance of the Belcher Islands in 1974–1975, finding a Dorset occupation from about 1000 B.C. to A.D.1000. He found no evidence there of the Manitounik culture originally propounded by Quimby (1940) (see Benmouyal 1978; Harp 1976).

Archeological research in the Arctic has produced since 1945 an increasingly elaborate and specialized body of interpretive and operational theory. Earlier scholars had based themselves upon elementary distributional analysis and ethnographic comparison, derived without benefit of archeological wisdom. The first active archeologists, many of whom were Danes, followed suit. Noticeably influenced by the Kulturkreis school of continental Europe, the evolutionary stages they envisioned progressed from simple to more complex levels of economic and technological adaptation by means of diffusion and migration. Although in particular vogue before World War II, vestiges of this approach remained for sometime thereafter (for example, Collins 1951; De Laguna 1947; Larsen and Rainey 1948). Another va-

center right, Elmer Harp, Jr., Hanover, N.H.; bottom left, Henry B. Collins, Washington; bottom right, Guy Mary-Rousselière, Pond Inlet, N.W.T.
Fig. 1. Arctic archeologists in the field. top left and right, Gulf Hazard–1, a late Dorset site in the entrance to Richmond Gulf, Que., excavated Aug. 1967. top left, William Fitzhugh and Jack Rinker at the initial test. top right, Excavation of platform area in tent ring. center left, Tuurngasiti–2, an early Dorset site on Wiegand I., Belcher Is., N.W.T. Preparing for aerial photography over House–1, July 1975. Nylon airfoil is aloft in the sky as William Cavaney steadies the automatic motor-driven camera. When released the camera will be lifted to a predetermined point about 30 feet above the excavation, where it can be triggered by ground control. center right, Gulf Hazard–3 site, a late Thule site in the entrance to Richmond Gulf. Elmer Harp, Jr., excavating a small winter house with deep entrance passage, stone slab door jambs, cooking niche to left of entry, and subterranean floor. top left, top right, and center left, Photographs by Elmer Harp, Jr. center right, Photograph by Douglas Harp, Aug. 1967. bottom left, Henry B. Collins taking notes at Sallirmiut site, House 30, Native Point, Southampton I., 1955. bottom right, Guy Mary-Rousselière at the Arnakadlak site, both Dorset and Thule deposits, with Inuit helpers. Photograph by Jean-Louis de Gerlache, 1973.

HISTORY OF ARCHEOLOGY AFTER 1945

riety of early theoretical interpretation, with fewer proponents and in part a reaction to that just mentioned, exercised an unstructured functional analysis and emphasized in situ historical development with less regard for possibilities of migration, diffusion, or acculturation (for example, Birket-Smith 1959; cf. Giddings 1960).

As the horizons of archeological knowledge widened, students of Arctic prehistory have reduced their former stress on localized cultural diversity and have been more impressed by the high degree of cultural uniformity that has geographically pervaded the circumpolar homelands of the Eskimos. This awareness stimulated application of the "tradition" concept, a notion that implies the existence of a major ethnic and cultural entity extended through time (for example, Irving 1953; MacNeish 1959). Thus, regional culture sequences, viewed as specialized adaptations in response to fluctuating environments, can be subsumed within a theoretical framework of traditions, together with the broader patterns of circumpolar relationships and temporal continuity.

Methodologically, Arctic archeology has matured from basic levels of collection, description, and seriation to more sophisticated kinds of analysis that depend on the expert insights of numerous other scientific disciplines. The most obvious trend in this direction has been in the careful use of environmental information to generate interpretations of change with an explicitly defined ecological framework (for example, Fitzhugh 1977). At the same time, increased behavioral emphases are evident in ethnographic studies conducted for specifically archeological ends by archeologists (for example, Ackerman 1970; Binford 1978). Finally, changing legislative climates have dictated the development of programs by public agencies for the management and preservation of archeological remains as public resources, and these have entailed surveys and evaluations of scientific and historic merit on a scale undreamed of before the 1970s.

Settlement pattern analysis, demographic reconstruction, detailed biomass studies, computerized trait analysis, and other approaches may lead ultimately to better understanding of social structure and the intellectual concerns of northern peoples.

History of Ethnology After 1945

CHARLES C. HUGHES

By its nature, ethnological research has always been holistic in the conceptual approach taken toward the group being studied. Its ethos is integrative in character, for it strives to examine not simply the abstracted "parts" of a society, but also how such parts fit together to form an ongoing system of values and behavior and how that system itself functions in and adapts to a given habitat and social environment. Thus a typical ethnographic report on traditional groups in the Arctic (or anywhere) deals with the several institutional areas that comprise the pattern of sociocultural life—kinship, religion, politics, language, and so on, as well as techniques for subsisting from a given habitat. It might also have a chapter on changes and the impact of contact with the outside world, if that were significant.

Based on the pre-1945 literature, the Eskimos and Aleuts were usually depicted as a people with a primitive but ingenious technology and keen adaptive strategies oriented mainly to the hunting of maritime mammals; a common language from Greenland to southwestern Alaska; a highly animistic religious system in which sea mammal spirits figured prominently; modes of social control and political leadership that were implicit in the functioning of other institutions and not publicly designated as such; small population groups alternating between periods of separation and assembly at different points in the year, depending upon ecological opportunities; and a relatively simple kinship system much resembling that of the Euro-Canadian family in being nuclear or only slightly extended, bilateral in its reckoning of kinship, and characterized by having only a single term for 'cousin'.

It should be noted, of course, that there were major gaps in published knowledge of Eskimo societies—gaps known even then—and that, as would become much more evident later, the above characterization was overly simple and in many respects highly localized. For instance, in Alaska, many communities, especially in Yupik-speaking areas of the southwest, had never been studied; data from the Asiatic Eskimos were scanty and out of date; and Greenland had been an ethnographic isolate (at least to non-Danish readers) for many years. Yet even in the anthropological literature the cultural stereotype showed remarkable persistence.

Ethnological research in the Arctic since 1945 exemplifies both continuities and change compared to research prior to that time. Continuous is the abiding commitment to gathering comprehensive data on the ways of life of northern peoples. Representing change is not only the greater volume of literature produced but also the much greater scope of subject matters and problem areas considered relevant to that central ethnological purpose. There has also been greater variety in disciplines represented in the production of such ethnologic knowledge—not only anthropologists but also researchers in other fields, such as sociology, psychology, economics, geography, psychiatry, folklore, and ecology. Thus, while the goal of ethnological research has remained the same—understanding patterns of human life and adaptation—the conceptual framework for accomplishing such understanding has taken on a more variegated and cosmopolitan character.

At the same time, the environmental demands that challenge adaptation have shifted and become more complex. Beyond the conventional headings ethnography has begun to include problems such as the impact of social change upon personality and group, mental health and social deviance, local politics and law ways as they interact with non-Eskimo legal systems, the rise to consciousness and public examination of questions of group and self-identity, articulation of traditional subsistence economies with wage work and other sources of money income, native land claims and growth of political awareness, and possible (and demonstrated) environmental impacts of resource development.

Margaret Lantis (1957:126) succinctly and prophetically summarized trends that remained evident in the 1980s: "The substance of the situation is that *Eskimos are trying just as hard today to adapt as they did 500 or 900 years ago; the difficulty is that they are adapting not to the Arctic but to a Temperate Zone way of living.* The new people with their new standards have nearly overwhelmed the Eskimos, not in numbers but in wishes and wants."

The year 1945 is of course not an entirely arbitrary division point for ethnological research. It marked the end of a global conflict that had many portents for the life of the indigenous peoples of the Arctic. Historical events as well as accelerated technological developments quite beyond their control changed the nature of contact with the dominant national political powers, and in major ways the world of the Eskimos and Aleuts

23

became a different world. Some military installations were built in Greenland, Canada, and Alaska; some Eskimos served in the Alaska Territorial Guard; and most Aleuts were relocated to safe areas before the Japanese invasion of the Aleutian Islands.

But the war was a critical turning point for the people of the North not so much for its direct effects upon them during the conflict itself as for the era it presaged: the Cold War and heightened tensions between world powers, which had ramifications all across the Arctic. Military planners, by then schooled in a global strategy and provided with advanced electronic technology, could begin using the fact of the shorter polar air route to Europe and Asia for placement of numerous military installations. Thus came the construction by the United States of the large Thule Air Base in northern Greenland, forcing relocation of the Polar Eskimos, and the Distant Early Warning radar line stretching from Alaska to eastern Canada, which along with other installations to follow represented a massive invasion of many relatively untouched Eskimo areas (see Hughes 1965).

These incursions were soon followed by other types of interests: the beginnings of active exploration for oil and other natural resources, and the belated realization on the part of national governments that important needs of the native populations could not be ignored—health, education, social services, and political participation. (Recognition of such needs and actions to ameliorate perceived problems had occurred much earlier in Greenland and to some extent also in Siberia than was the case in Canada and Alaska.) There began also, especially in Canada and Alaska, stirrings of movements that would increasingly assume organized form and contemporary significance in the assertion of sociopolitical rights of the native peoples with respect to control of land, resources, and political destiny (for example, L.T. Rasmussen 1982, 1983).

Thus, relatively quickly, the post-1945 Eskimo world, before then manifested mainly as a number of scattered and small-scale ethnocentric societies, irrevocably became involved in multiple patterns of interdependence with and in many respects engulfment by the non-Eskimo world.

But more than just the character of the world the Eskimos confronted was changed. There was also an evolution in the conceptual frame of reference that guided and rationalized ethnological research in that changed environment. For a variety of reasons best illuminated by a sociology of knowledge perspective on the ways World War II affected the academic community, much research by anthropologists and other behavioral scientists began to take on a form that had implications for the problems of contemporary life. A great deal of the research not only was of interest to a new generation of anthropologists acquainted with interdisciplinary perspectives and with comprehensive studies of contemporary groups but also was designed explicitly to be of use to the administrator, the policy maker, and the economic developer.

Thus, ethnological studies done since 1945 that operationalize one aspect or another of a human ecological perspective have dealt with both conventional ethnographic concerns as well as those created by contemporary conditions of social and economic change. The historical dimension has always figured prominently in ethnological knowledge of any given people, and contemporary research has, by use of documents and recollections of informants, attempted to enhance our knowledge of traditional cultural patterns, as well as, through use of the cultural "experiments of nature" provided by Eskimo societies, to contribute further data toward examination of theoretical problems of importance to the field of anthropology generally. Some of these issues are: the structure and determinants of kinship systems and of local group formation, the use of voluntary relationships as a factor in societal stability, the dialectic between structure and flexibility in social relationships, and the basis and forms of political power in an acephalous society. Studies of the contemporary situation have addressed: interrelationships between sociocultural factors and personality dynamics; patterns of socialization and their consequences for personality structure; psychological, social, and economic impacts of cultural change; relationship between social change and community disintegration; optimal strategies for economic development; microeconomics of the transition from a subsistence to a cash- and job-based way of making a living; and bicultural problems posed by imposition of formal Western educational patterns.

It is impossible, of course, to discuss all the studies done. At best, they can be summarized here (except for linguistics, for which see "Eskimo and Aleut Languages," this vol.) in terms of the main theoretical problem areas or themes that they have addressed, together with a few illustrative or suggestive bibliographic citations that treat the topic either in part or in whole. Research themes of importance since 1945 have been:

• traditional material culture (for example, Freeman 1967; Oswalt 1972; VanStone 1972; Arima 1975; Nooter 1980; Van Gulik, Van der Straaten, and Van Wengen 1980; Fitzhugh and Kaplan 1982);

• ethnohistorical studies (for example, Giddings 1956, 1961; Spencer 1959; VanStone 1959, 1967, 1970; Oswalt 1960, 1963a; Dailey and Dailey 1961; Balikci 1970; Lantis 1970; Cooke 1973; Wells 1974; Ray 1975; Kennedy 1977; Burch 1978, 1979a; Laughlin 1980);

• art, mythology, music, film (for example, Steenhoven 1959a; Martijn 1964; Balikci and Brown 1966; Ray 1967, 1977, 1981; Oquilluk 1973; Hall 1975; Roch 1975; Silook 1976; Johnston 1976, 1977; Graburn 1976; Collins et al. 1973; Gulløv and Kapel 1979–1980; R.K. Nelson 1980; J.G.E. Smith 1980; Enel 1981);

24

• traditional empirical science such as ethnobotany, ethnomedicine, and ethno-anatomy (for example, Bank 1952b, 1953; Marsh and Laughlin 1956; Oswalt 1957; Lantis 1959; Laughlin 1963b; Young and Hall 1969; Lucier, VanStone, and Keats 1971; Milan 1974);

• kinship systems, interpersonal relationships, and primary social structures such as the local band; regional variations therein (for example, Lantis 1946; Hughes 1958, 1960; Heinrich 1960; Damas 1963, 1975; Befu 1964; Graburn 1964; Gamo 1964, 1980; Whitten 1964; Guemple 1965, 1972a; Burch 1975a; Lange 1977);

• alliances, partnerships, sharing patterns, dyadic associations and their role in exchange patterns and social stability (for example, Rubel 1961; Burch and Correll 1972; Damas 1972a; Guemple 1972, 1979; Jensen 1973; J.S. Matthiasson 1975);

• political dynamics, local leadership, and social factionalism (for example, Pospisil 1964; Hughes 1966, 1968; Freeman 1969–1972, 3; Lantis 1972; Nooter 1976);

• religion and ideational culture (for example, Balikci 1960, 1963a; Hughes 1960; Nelleman 1960; Burch 1971; J. Fisher 1973; Williamson 1973; Stephenson and Ahgook 1975; Robert-Lamblin 1981; Fitzhugh and Kaplan 1982);

• personality structure and dynamics, socialization, and life histories (for example, Lantis 1953, 1960; Glarborg 1962; S. Parker 1962; Lubart 1965; Nuligak 1966; Briggs 1970, 1975; Foulks 1972; Hippler 1974; Hughes 1975; C. Meyer 1977);

• demographics and control of population size, including suicide (for example, Leighton and Hughes 1955; Balikci 1967; Berg 1973; Robert-Lamblin 1971; Freeman 1971, 1971a, 1974–1975; Bloom 1972; Tussing and Arnold 1973; Riches 1974; Schrire and Steiger 1974; Kjellström 1974–1975; Milan 1974–1975; Damas 1975a; Gilberg 1976; Hobart 1976; Masnick and Katz 1976);

• ecological and economic studies of resource use (for example, Spencer 1959; J.D. Ferguson 1961; Nelleman 1961; Usher 1965, 1970–1971; Abrahamson 1963; Kleivan 1964; Freeman 1967; J.D. Abrahamson 1968; R.K. Nelson 1969; Worl 1980; Vesilind 1983);

• the replacement of traditional material culture with imported goods and tools, food, houses, furniture, weapons, sleds and boats, and clothing (for example, Cooper 1967; Thompson 1969; Honigmann 1972; L. Smith 1972; Usher 1972, 1976; Pelto and Müller-Wille 1972; Nowak 1977; Nooter 1980);

• ethnographically oriented studies of modern communities (for example, Berreman 1954; Malaurie 1956; VanStone and Oswalt 1959, 1960; Hughes 1960; Cohen 1962; VanStone 1962a; Oswalt 1963; Milan 1964; Balikci 1964a, 1970; Gubser 1965; Honigmann and Honigmann 1965, 1970; Vallee 1967; Gessain 1969; Hippler 1969, 1969a, 1970; Befu 1970; Gessain and Robert-Lamblin 1975; Jones 1976);

• changes in settlement patterns and consequences of

James VanStone, Chicago.
Fig. 1. James W. VanStone and John Long, a North Alaska Coast Eskimo of Point Hope where VanStone was conducting a community study (VanStone 1962a). Photographed in spring 1956.

such changes; the urbanization of the North through relocation and immigration and aggregating of people into larger population units, often of mixed ethnic characteristics (for example, W.D. Johnson 1962; Honigmann and Honigmann 1965, 1970; Vallee 1962; Stevenson 1968; Freeman 1969; Brody 1975; Honigmann 1975; Ben-Dor 1977; Petersen 1978);

• changes in family demographics and structure (for

Smithsonian, NAA: Honigmann Coll.
Fig. 2. Eetuk, a Baffinland Eskimo, and John J. Honigmann at Frobisher Bay, N.W.T., where Honigmann worked from March 1 to Aug. 27, 1963 (Honigmann and Honigmann 1965). Photograph probably by Irma Honigmann, 1963.

example, Wilmott 1961; Commission on Social Research in Greenland 1961, 2; Bentzon and Agersnap 1973; Damas 1971; Robert-Lamblin 1970, 1971; Burch 1975a);

• social change, stress, and personality disorder (for example, Chance 1960, 1965; Murphy and Hughes 1965; Lantis 1968; Vallee 1968; Lubart 1969; Olsen 1973; Bloom 1973; Berry 1976; Sampath 1976);

• socioeconomic change: emergence of a monetary standard of exchange and evaluation; incursion of wage work; search for new sources of monetary income—the job, welfare, sale of handicrafts; land claims reimbursement; and articulation of wage work with subsistence economics (for example, VanStone 1960a; Wilmott 1961; Brack 1962; Abrahamson 1963; Graburn 1963; Hughes 1965; Wolforth 1965; Riches 1966; Christensen 1968; Robert-Lamblin 1971; Nooter 1972–1973; Adam 1973; Borneman 1973; Boserup 1973; Lloyd 1973; Malaurie 1973a; Simpson and Bowles 1973; Tussing and Arnold 1973; Vdovin 1973; Weick et al. 1973; Brody 1978; Kupfer and Hobart 1978; Naylor and Gooding 1978; Hobfoll, Morgan, and Lehrman 1980; Kruse, Kleinfeld, and Travis 1981; Kruse 1982);

• acculturation and social disintegration (for example, Berreman 1955; Chance 1960a; Hughes 1960; Hippler 1970a; Bloom 1972a);

• alienation, development of socioeconomic classes, and castelike segmentation and institutionalized socioeconomic disadvantage (for example, Dunning 1959; Vallee 1962a, 1967; Berreman 1964; Jones 1973a; Malaurie 1973a; Rogers 1973; Brody 1975; Paine 1977);

• social deviance, alcoholism, personality disorder (for example, Berreman 1956; Borneman 1956; Balikci 1960; Commission on Social Research in Greenland 1961, 1; Nelleman 1962; Clairmont 1962, 1963; Lubart 1969a; Lynge 1976; Riches 1976; Thrasher 1976; Shinkwin and Pete 1982);

• crime, traditional law ways, and articulation with the Western legal system (for example, Steenhoven 1959; Commission on Social Research in Greenland 1961, 4; Goldschmidt 1955–1956; Hippler and Conn 1973, 1974; Jayewardene 1975; Hansen 1976);

• development of questions of identity, political consciousness, and organized sociopolitical "nativistic" movements (for example, S. Parker 1964; Graburn 1979; Townsend 1979; L.T. Rasmussen 1982, 1983; Vesilind 1983);

• new social forms of administration, political governance, and economic management (for example, Jenness 1962, 1964, 1965, 1967, 1968; Vallee 1964, 1966, 1967; Arbess 1966; Iglauer 1966; Lantis 1966; Broendsted 1973; Hoegh 1973; LeJeune 1973; Riches 1977; Brody 1978);

• pedagogical, psychological, and social consequences of new forms of education (for example, Ber-

thelsen 1960; Commission on Social Research in Greenland 1961, 3; Ray, Ryan, and Parker 1962; Hobart and Brant 1966; Chance 1972; Darnell 1972; Collier 1973; Pjettursson 1973; Brantenberg 1977);

• health problems and development of health services (for example, Parran 1954; Fortuine 1968, 1975; Ross 1971; Berg and Adler-Nissen 1976; Boesen 1976; Bloom and Richards 1976; Haraldson 1976; Reinhard 1976; Shephard and Itoh 1976; Tester 1976).

Arctic Bibliography, published periodically from 1953 to 1976, is an annotated bibliography of relevant materials in all subjects and all major languages (with abstracts in English). Periodicals that contain much material relating to the Eskimos and Aleuts are: *Arctic, Arctic Anthropology, The Anthropological Papers of the University of Alaska, Inuit Studies (Études Inuit), Folk, Inter/Nord (International Review of Arctic and Nordic Studies)*. Other useful bibliographies are those published periodically by the Centre d'Études Arctiques, École des Hautes Études at the Sorbonne (see also Gessain and Robert-Lamblin 1975; Perrot and Robert-Lamblin 1975); Hippler's (1970a) selected and annotated bibliography of Alaskan and other Eskimo acculturation studies; Murdock and O'Leary (1975, 1:1–34, 2:1–117); and Burch's (1979a) extensive discussion and bibliography structured around ethnographic data available on the Aleuts and designated Eskimo groups. Hughes (1965) extensively reviewed patterns and problems of culture change among the Eskimos (including Siberia) from the first half of the twentieth century through the 1950s. Jenness (1962, 1964, 1965, 1967, 1968), in dealing with the goals and structure of outside-imposed administration among the Eskimos (except for the Asiatic Eskimos), draws from numerous documents and other reports not normally consulted by the ethnologist. Periodic reports issued by the Institute of Social, Economic, and Government Research and the Alaska Native Language Center, both at the University of Alaska, represent useful sources; as does the extensive series of community, policy, demographic, economic, and ecological studies sponsored by the Canadian government's Department of Northern Affairs and Natural Resources beginning in the 1960s. Oswalt (1967) lists numerous specific sources for his review of Alaskan Eskimo cultures. Oswalt (1979) is exceptional in its synthesis and bibliographic scholarship for all sections of the Arctic. The U.S. Field Committee for Development Planning in Alaska (1968) provides a well-organized review of available ethnological and ecological data as background for planning, as Freeman (1976) does for Canada. The volume edited by Malaurie (1973a), consisting of papers from an international conference looking at effects of socioeconomic changes on the Eskimos, is a very helpful resource for the period up to the beginning of the 1970s.

Physical Environment

JOHN K. STAGER AND ROBERT J. MCSKIMMING

The Arctic regions in North America are commonly understood to be those portions of the mainland, islands, and neighboring seas that lie closest to the North Pole. They have a unique and distinguishable physical environment that is a consequence of an overriding characteristic, the relative absence of heat energy (Hare and Thomas 1974). It is the high latitude location that is paramount as a climatic control and enables the Arctic to be recognized as different from similar environments, like alpine regions, that are cold because of high elevation. With a climate of low heat energy there are corresponding biological and physical responses that have become incorporated in the definition of the boundaries of the Arctic.

Arctic Boundaries

The boundary to the Arctic, described first in the fifth century B.C., results from the fundamental relationship the earth has with the sun. The Arctic Circle at 66°30′ north latitude marks the northern limit of the year-round occurrence of daily alternating daylight and darkness. North of the Circle there are annual periods of continuous daylight and continuous darkness, which increase in length as one passes northward. For example, Cape Columbia (83°11′ north latitude), the most northerly point on the Canadian Arctic islands, has twilight appearing about February 6, then the sun first rises on February 20, when night and day is experienced until April 11, after which the sun stays above the horizon. On or about the first day of September the sun sets daily until October 2 when it disappears for the winter, although twilight persists until November 11 (see table 1).

Although latitude plays a role in the seasonal pattern of solar energy available in the north, the nature of the earth's surface, the distribution of land, sea, and ice-or snow-covered surfaces combine to produce a climate with an areal pattern that departs from strictly latitudinal zones. The best indication of this fact is the seasonal patterns of air temperature, which show in summer relatively high temperatures extending far north almost to the coast down the Mackenzie Valley (fig. 1a). Similarly, in Alaska on both sides of the Arctic Circle, inland from the sea over the intermontane plateaus, there is a region of high summer temperatures which are not matched elsewhere in the same latitude. As a contrast, on a latitudinal comparison, summer temperatures over Greenland are very low over the central ice cap and quite cool in coastal locations. In winter anomalously low temperatures are evident over the Brooks Range in Alaska, in a lobe of cold that dominates central Canada west of Hudson Bay, and over the Greenland ice cap (fig. 1b).

Several attempts to describe a climate boundary to the Arctic have failed to find agreement (Hamelin 1968). The most frequently recurring mappable limit is the mean 10°C isotherm in July (Sater 1969). In effect it marks the southern boundary of a zone that does not experience a warm summer and so is consistent with the concept of absence of heat energy. Another widely accepted boundary that delimits the Arctic is the tree line (Hare and Thomas 1974). It marks the limit of the extensive boreal forests north of which lies the treeless region or tundra that is usually thought of as the Arctic. The boundary is a visible one in vegetation zonation that represents the integration of climatic, soil, and topographic conditions on either side of which are distinct and different ecological zones. Even indigenous man has, for the most part, respected this natural division with the tundra as the home of the Eskimo and Subarctic forests as Indian lands.

With no warm summers and long, cold winters the ground remains frozen at depth except for most areas under large bodies of water (Price 1972). This climatically engendered physical condition is permafrost and in the mapping of its distribution, the southern limit of areas where permafrost continuously occurs is most important. This is another means of marking the southern limit of the Arctic itself. Although of only passing significance to indigenous man in the north, permafrost, especially continous permafrost, has been identified with the Arctic by industrial man and his works (see Price 1972).

Figure 1c plots the three boundaries—the 10° C July isotherm, the tree line, and the southern limit of continous permafrost. From Alaska east to Great Bear Lake these three lines are comparatively close together, seldom more than 200 miles apart. In the central Keewatin the permafrost boundary is more than 400 miles south of the 10° C July isotherm. East of Hudson Bay the permafrost line is well north of tree line. There

27

Table 1. Approximate Dates of Twilight and Daylight for Northern Latitudes

North Latitude	Civil Twilight Begins	Sun First Above the Horizon	Sun Continuously Above the Horizon	Sun First Below the Horizon	Sun Continuously Below the Horizon	Civil Twilight Ends
85°	February 19	March 5	April 1	September 12	October 8	October 22
80°	February 5	February 19	April 13	August 29	October 22	November 7
75°	January 17	February 5	April 28	August 16	November 5	November 28
70°	—	January 18	May 18	July 28	November 24	—
65°	—	—	—	—	—	—

SOURCE: Smithsonian Meteorological Tables 1963.

seems to be no satisfactory and widely acceptable means to devise a boundary that rationalizes these three climatic and biological limits. It is probably most meaningful to use the tree line as the southern boundary because it is related to the climate and adds a visual element. Rather than being a distinct line, the tree line is a zone in which trees become more sparse and more stunted northward before ceasing to exist. On a circumpolar scale, this zone is narrow, constituting in effect, a line. Greenland, then, would be considered entirely Arctic except for the most extreme southern tip (see Putnins 1970:4).

Climate Controls

The extent to which the Arctic climate differs from place to place around the pole results from factors such as the existence of mountain barriers, distance from open water bodies, surface cover of snow and ice, as well as the distinctive regime of daylight and darkness (Hare and Thomas 1974).

Insolation

The amount of solar energy received at the surface of the earth is a function of the sun's declination, the length of time the sun is above the horizon, and the cloudiness of the sky. In Arctic regions where the sun is very low on the horizon, and at times below it, the annual amount of insolation is small causing a negative radiation balance; that is, radiation loss from the earth's surface occurs all the year round but is offset during summer months by receipt of solar energy (Hare and Thomas 1974; Bird 1972).

The regional differences in insolation are quite marked, as the incoming solar radiation is affected by cloud type and amount, which vary from place to place. The area of the greatest cloud concentration seems to be over the Norwegian Sea, and as a result, minimum insolation is found there (Vowinckel and Orvig 1970:154). Eastern Siberia receives the maximum incoming solar radiation during the summer due to the relative absence of clouds,

which results from the extreme remoteness of the area from open water, and the dominance of anticyclonic circulation for the rest of the year. Northwestern Canada experiences a similar situation but not to the same extent (Hay 1969).

Long wave radiation, that is, terrestrial and counter-radiation, contributes most to the total radiation balance in the high latitudes. There is more long wave radiation into the atmosphere during the summer, and it is the only radiation heat source during the winter. The amount of incoming long radiation is dependent upon surface temperature and the moisture conditions of the atmosphere. Because the atmosphere will trap terrestrial radiation and either reradiate or reflect it back to earth there is an increased radiative heat source. This process is generally called the greenhouse effect of the atmosphere.

In total, the low net radiation totals of the Arctic give mean annual air temperatures well below freezing (fig. 1b–d). However, latitudinally the temperatures will not be constant because of other climate controls.

Atmospheric Circulation

In general, the Arctic circulation can be described as circumpolar with a large-scale cold core. The polar regions must import heat from the southerly latitudes to compensate for the net radiation loss to space from the surface and atmosphere. Thus the differential heating from equator to pole generates an upper air flow to redistribute heat energy northward, and with the earth's rotation, the flow pattern becomes circumpolar moving west to east—the so-called westerlies (Vowinckel and Orvig 1970:185–186). In winter when the thermal gradient from equator to pole is greatest, the circulation is most intense; in summer it is less strong. Near the pole itself, the flow is sluggish.

Within the westerly flow are standing long waves that depart from the west-east direction (Haurwitz 1975:175). They thread their way between the major pressure distributions. In the west, for example, is the Aleutian low pressure cell, a trough that lies in the Gulf of Alaska

28

and extends inland into Alaska and the Yukon in summer. Over the Atlantic near Greenland and Iceland is the Icelandic low pressure cell that in summer is farther to the west near Hudson Strait. In counter position to the lows are high pressure systems, which in the Arctic are shallow developments. During the winter the high is over the Mackenzie Valley, which retreats to a position over the Arctic Ocean in summer. In response to the pressure patterns there is an outflow of Arctic air dominating the Arctic Archipelago, the Keewatin, and Hudson Bay (Vowinckel and Orvig 1970:209–214).

Embedded in the general flow and moving at the surface are the cyclonic and anticyclonic cells that generate the changes in surface weather (Bird 1972). In winter the storms do not easily penetrate the high latitudes, although they may sweep northward into Baffin Bay and southern Greenland (Vowinckel and Orvig 1970:186). In summer, the track tends to lie farther north with variable weather the pattern across Alaska and southeast to Hudson Bay; the eastern Arctic can be stormy in almost any season.

Land-Sea Distribution

A major impact upon the distribution of certain climatic characteristics such as precipitation, air temperature, and wind direction is caused by the geographic distribution of the land mass with respect to water bodies. Large water bodies tend to reduce the annual temperature range in the surrounding region. Where water bodies freeze during the winter, they act like land masses in energy exchange processes (Hare and Thomas 1974:133). On the other hand, during the summer, open water tends to modify temperature extremes.

Mountain regions such as those along the Pacific and the mountainous region of Greenland interfere with the general zonal flow of the atmosphere (Putnins 1970:6). During winter, Pacific storms do not generally penetrate the mountain barriers into the Arctic regions. The Ural Mountains in the Soviet Union also act as barriers preventing storms from crossing into the Siberian region of that country. Greenland on the other hand disturbs the zonal flow not only because it is a topographic barrier but also because of a local high pressure cell due to cold subsiding over the icefields. Surface lows from the west are often diverted northward into the Arctic islands and polar sea. Also with the open water around Greenland surface low pressures may develop in the area and begin their zonal flow only to be blocked by Greenland and be diverted north (Putnins 1970:22, 25).

In the western part of the Arctic warm ocean currents through the Bering Strait have an impact on the climate. These currents tend to circulate through the Bering Strait into the Chukchi Sea, then mix with the general circulation of the Arctic waters themselves. The inclusion of much warmer water in this area and the associated air masses above it produces strong temperature gradients and strong zonal flow. However, this flow is usually deflected by the mountains south along the Pacific coast (Hare and Thomas 1974:36). On the other hand, over the continental interior, there is an absence of any considerable barrier to north-south movement of air masses (Vowinckel and Orvig 1970:185). In total then the resultant pattern of temperature has a north-west-southeast distribution pattern, rather than one that is latitudinal. For example, Nome in Alaska and Frobisher Bay on Baffin Island are on approximately the same latitudes, yet in January the average temperature for Nome is −16° C while at Frobisher Bay the temperature is −26° C.

The water body of Hudson Bay also influences surrounding air temperatures during the summer when it is ice-free (Hare and Thomas 1974:133; Bird 1972:10). As water tends to absorb radiation faster than land, and energy is mixed throughout the surface water, the air temperature will be generally cooler than over the surrounding land. Thus coastal locations tend to have lower temperatures than inland locations at the same latitude. Hence the summer isotherm bends farther south around Hudson Bay.

During July when there is no snow on the Arctic islands, their temperature is greater than the surrounding ice or water bodies. With increased minor breezes and unstable air there is a greater tendency for storm activity in the island area during the summer (Vowinckel and Orvig 1970:177).

Ocean Currents and Sea Ice

The general circulation of the Arctic Ocean tends to be counterclockwise. Throughout the year ocean currents transport heat from lower latitudes into the cooler Arctic regions. Warm water enters the Arctic basin in two areas, one near Spitsbergen into the Barents Sea and a second through the Bering Strait (Vowinckel and Orvig 1970:177). Figure 1e shows the general circulation of the ocean current in the North American portion of the Arctic Ocean. Currents move from the Spitsbergen area across the pole and divide with part of the circulation moving south along the east coast of Greenland, and part moving westward along the edge of the Canadian arctic archipelago, to form a clockwise gyral in the Bering Sea matched by a counterclockwise circulation in the Chukchi Sea (Bird 1972:20). Other currents move from the Arctic basin through the islands in northern Canada drifting eastward to form an outflow along the coast of Labrador. This general circulation results in less severe ice conditions in the Barents Sea and north of Bering Strait where warm water enters the Arctic Ocean. In the outflow area around Labrador pack ice may be extensive, and icebergs calved from the Greenland glaciers are common.

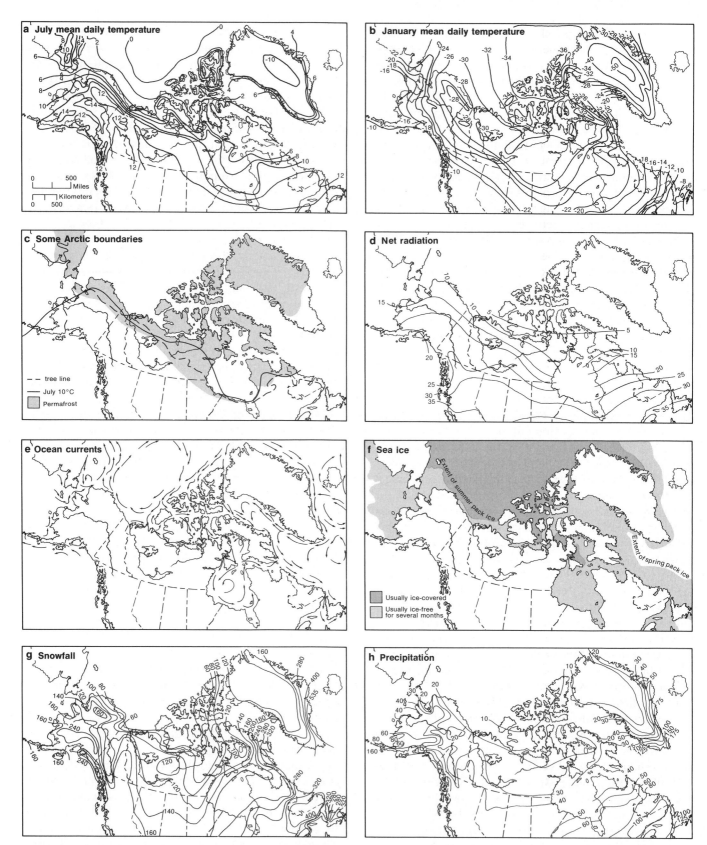

a **July mean daily temperature**

b **January mean daily temperature**

c **Some Arctic boundaries**

– – – tree line
——— July 10°C
▨ Permafrost

d **Net radiation**

e **Ocean currents**

f **Sea ice**

Extent of summer pack ice
Extent of spring pack ice

▨ Usually ice-covered
▨ Usually ice-free for several months

g **Snowfall**

h **Precipitation**

a–c, after Vowinckel and Orvig 1970, Hare and Thomas 1974; c, also after Pêwê 1983; d, g–h, after Hare and Hay 1974; e, after Vowinckel and Orvig 1970, Sater 1969, Weller and Bowling 1975; f, after Sater 1969.

Fig. 1. Climatic features of the Arctic: a, July mean air temperature (°C); b, Jan. mean air temperature (°C); c, limits of permafrost and trees, and 10°C July isotherm; d, annual net radiation (in kiloanglies); e, circulation of the ocean currents; f, sea ice; g, mean annual snowfall (in cm); h, total annual precipitation (in cm).

The extent of sea ice is shown in figure 1f. It is evident that the distribution of sea ice responds in part to the general circulation of the ocean currents. During summer the major portion of the polar ice pack is restricted mainly to the Arctic basin proper, although pack ice and landfast ice will usually remain between the High Arctic islands of Canada. This is due to the direction of ocean currents, prevailing wind, and restricted interisland passages. The pack itself is a slow-moving mass of ice pieces crushed together in rafted blocks and thick pressure ridges. Its margins change as wind is able to move ice so that it jams against the land in some places and exposes leads of open water in others.

In winter almost all sea surfaces are covered with ice. Between the islands of the Canadian Arctic the ice surfaces freeze "bank to bank" although wind and currents cause shifts, rafting, and periodic open leads. In Hudson Bay, a moving pack, developed after December and lasting into July, circulates slowly. Another pack moves around between Baffin Island and Greenland, and in this basin is to be found a zone in which open water is known to occur even in winter (Bird 1972:21). Sea ice persists in spring much longer than it takes for the land surface to become free of snow and for river and lake ice to disappear. Melting of sea ice begins off the mouths of major drainage channels, like the Mackenzie River, occurring later as one moves northward (see Mackay and Mackay 1972:87–89). Most ice disappears as a result of being moved and crushed by shifting winds, but in protected bays or in areas to the lee of prevailing wind, landfast ice lasts well into summer and sometimes all year in far northern locations.

Since the sea ice supports human existence, it is worth noting the character of its surface on the beach at the point of highest tide, where a narrow ice foot becomes frozen to the shore and moves only at times of high tide. Between this point and the lowest tide mark is a jumbled mass of broken ice that is constantly being lifted and dropped by the changes of the tide. Huge ice hummocks will gradually build over the boulders that lie on the botton of the tidal zone. In the western Arctic where the tide range is very small, a relatively smooth transition seaward is the case. Beyond the rough ice of the tide zone is smoother ice of the landfast floe. Floe ice will cover the surface of all marginal water bodies extending out to sea for as much as 10 miles. At the outer floe edge, huge sheets of ice break off under the press of wind and current to join the main mass of free-floating pack ice (Wilkinson 1970:26–27).

Wind

In general the mean annual wind speeds are greatest at exposed coastal stations. According to Sater, Ronhovde, and Van Allen (1971:127) there are certain regional characteristics in Arctic wind systems. For example, in eastern Siberia the wind systems are monsoon in character (see also Hare and Thomas 1974:131): thus, during the winter southerly winds prevail, and during the summer northerly winds prevail, bringing in a frequency of storms.

Areas of very flat or low elevation present no obstacle to the free interchange of air (Vowinckel and Orvig 1970:186). Also at several Arctic sites, the high surface winds associated with the strong pressure gradients are often enhanced by local effects. This is particularly true in the Keewatin region of northern Canada (Wilkinson 1970:19). Also many stations show locally influenced wind directions due to topography. Such local effects are best shown in Greenland where katabatic winds occur due to cold air from the Greenland ice cap channeling down fjord valleys toward the coast.

Fog

In most coastal locations fog is a feature of the environment in spring, summer, or fall. Fog is produced in moist air when surfaces of strong temperature contrast are close by one another. In spring after much of the land is free of snow and air temperatures over it rise, that air may come in contact with sea ice surfaces still in place to produce coastal fog (Vowinckel and Orvig 1970:207). Similarly, in summer cold sea water produces a fog bank that can be blown on shore. After freeze-up on the land in fall, moist air from open sea surfaces may cool to form fog over the land, although autumn fog is less common.

During winter, the sea ice may open to form leads exposing the sea water above which evaporation fog or "sea smoke" develops, but this phenomenon tends to be very local in its occurrence.

Rain, Snow, and Freshwater Ice

Snowfall is light in the Arctic, and stations in continental areas have maximum precipitation in late summer mostly in the form of rain (Hare and Thomas 1974:133). Most precipitation occurs from frontal storm activities; the annual amount decreases as one goes northward (Vowinckel and Orvig 1970:186–187). Figure 1g–h shows the mean annual snowfall distribution and total annual precipitation. Heavy snowfall occurs close to the location of low pressure cells in the north Atlantic and north Pacific. In the west the effect of the mountain barrier on the intrusion of frontal systems sees the concentration of precipitation on windward slopes (Hare and Thomas 1974:36).

Although the amount of precipitation is small in the Arctic, the ground may remain saturated for as long as it is not frozen (Pruitt 1978:20). Underground drainage is prevented by the permanently frozen subsoil (Cook 1967:262; Wilkinson 1970:56) or extensive areas of bedrock at or near the surface (Bird 1972:5). The very cool summer in much of the Arctic reduces the evaporation loss so that tundra surfaces do not always dry out (Wilkinson 1970:18). On the other hand, where good drainage exists drought conditions may prevail, especially in areas like the Queen Elizabeth Islands where the precipitation is as low as any desert regime in the world (Cook 1967:262).

The characteristics of the snow cover, such as thickness, density, and duration, have important effects on the heat and moisture exchange at the surface (Pruitt 1965). Sun and wind are perhaps the most important agents in determining snow properties.

Pruitt (1965) classified snow cover into two general categories, namely taiga and tundra. The former is snow that is not easily modified by external factors such as wind or incoming solar radiation as it lies protected beneath forest canopy. Tundra snow, on the other hand, is characterized by the fact that most of it has been moved by wind. Thus snow deposits are unevenly distributed and have highly varying density and hardness. The vigorous storms of autumn produce the first snowfalls with the amount greatest near major areas of still-open water (see also Hare and Thomas 1974:133). In winter, after complete freeze-up, little new snow is added but blowing snow is a constant feature especially in the windy belt of the Central Arctic (Hare 1970). Again fresh snow accumulates late in spring as moist air masses are able to penetrate the region.

Each year the areas of open water are frozen over into a continuous "land mass," which changes the thermal property of the surface (Bird 1972:10). Table 2 records the breakup and freeze-up of Arctic freshwater for various locations in Canada and Alaska. The surface water exposed to lower air temperatures and snowfall is cooled and ice forms along the shores, gradually extending over the entire surface. As the days grow colder the ice thickens. Lake ice freezes to a very flat, smooth surface if there is no wind (Wilkinson 1970:28). Freeze-up of lakes occurs before freeze-up of rivers with the result that the outflow of river water in some places runs over the top of lake ice, building up layers. Generally the turbulence of rivers delays ice formation by a week or two. Ice thicknesses may reach 2 to 2.5 meters over much of the Arctic so that shallow lakes freeze to the bottom and smaller streams have little or no flow.

During breakup snow melt water drains onto the ice of lakes and rivers. The combination of heat from melt water and radiation and rising air temperature begins to melt the ice. Small streams melt first, then larger rivers and ice around the river mouths, next the ice along the shores of lakes, and finally lake ice itself will melt (Wilkinson 1970:28). Wind is important in breaking up the lakes since it shifts and grinds the ice to hasten breakup (Bird 1972:21).

Table 2 indicates the mean date on which ice is first seen on lakes and rivers and when ice finally clears. Between the time that ice is first seen on the lakes until the time that rivers finally freeze over can be up to one month. Breakup, on the other hand, occurs very quickly on rivers and very slowly on lakes. Lakes often require a month longer than rivers to be free of ice.

Table 2. Times of Freeze-up and Breakup

	Fall/Winter				*Spring/Summer*			
	Ice First Seen		*Freeze-Over*		*Initial Breakup*		*Ice Cleared*	
	rivers	*lakes*	*rivers*	*lakes*	*rivers*	*lakes*	*rivers*	*lakes*
Canada								
Yellowknife	Oct. 15	Oct. 18	Nov. 9	Nov. 1	May 20	June 1	June 1	June 10
Inuvik	Oct. 5	Oct. 5	Oct. 15	Oct. 15	June 1	June 20	June 1	July 1
Churchill	Oct. 20	Oct. 19	Nov. 12	Oct. 27	June 10	June 20	June 10	July 1
Chesterfield	Oct. 9	Oct. 11	Nov. 1	Oct. 20	June 20	July 1	June 25	July 20
Port Harrison	Oct. 27	Oct. 18	Nov. 20	Oct. 27	June 10	June 15	June 20	July 1
Resolute[a]	Sep. 1	Sep. 20	Oct. 20	Sep. 25	July 1	July 10	July 10	Aug. 1
Frobisher Bay	Oct. 27	Oct. 15	Nov. 20	Nov. 10	June 10	June 15	June 20	July 10
Alaska								
Ft. Yukon			Oct. 28		May 14			
Kobuk			Oct. 21		May 19			
Unalakleet			Oct. 25		May 17			
Bethel			Oct. 29		May 15			
Susitna			Nov. 1		May 1			
Pt. Barrow (sea ice)			freeze-up Oct. 3				breakup July 22	

SOURCES: Johnson and Hartman 1969; Canada, Surveys and Mapping Branch 1971; Allen and Cudbird 1971.
[a] For lakes read bays (sea ice).

The Arctic Landscape

A number of physiographic provinces can be identified in the Arctic. There are high mountains, some covered by glacial ice, sedimentary plain, exposed bedrock, and lowlands (Bird 1972; Mackay 1964). Everywhere but in the mountainous region there is a curious sameness to the landscape. This was brought about by the scouring and deposition by massive continental glaciers that smoothed and rounded the surfaces of the land. The uniqueness of Arctic landforms is not due solely to geomorphic processes, for similar landforms are found in more temperate climates; rather the distinctiveness results more from features within the first 10 meters of the surface, where climate exerts its influence (Mackay 1964:60). Thus the sameness of landscape is made more complete by the absence of trees or other tall vegetation, as well as the winter-long blanket of snow and ice (Wilkinson 1970:18).

Frost

The action of frost in the soil is a primary environmental factor in the landscape morphology (Mackay 1964:60). The unique condition of frost in the soil is permafrost. Permafrost is perennially frozen ground—that is, earth materials such as soil and rock that have remained continuously below 0° C over at least one summer (Price 1972:7; Bird 1972:12–13; Mackay 1964:61). Permafrost describes the thermal condition of the ground; it does not imply the absence or presence of water in either the solid or liquid state. A negative heat balance in any year results in a layer being added to the permafrost (Pruitt 1978:18).

In Canada and in the Soviet Union, permafrost underlies about one-half of the land area; this is about 20 percent of the surface of the continents (Wilkinson 1970:54).

Throughout the area in which permafrost occurs the surface freezes and thaws annually with the passing of the seasons. The depth of this "active layer" varies with latitude, soil type, and vegetation cover, as well as aspect and angle of slope (Pruitt 1978:18). It is in the active layer that the freeze-thaw cycle can act as a geomorphic process.

Where there is water in permafrost soils, there may be a variety of ice formations (Price 1972:7). The largest quantities of ground ice in soil are normally found in silts (Bird 1972:14). They may act as a cementing agent in bonding together the soil grains or be segregated as distinct ice veins, lens ice, or massive tabular layers. In some places ice may make up much of the ground volume with soil in only small amounts.

Ice wedges, a type of ice lens, are common as irregular accumulations of ground ice. These structures are vertically oriented, wedge shaped masses of almost pure ice, ranging in diameter up to three meters near the surface and extending downward from three to four meters or more (Price 1972:11). They are caused by thermal contraction of the frozen tundra, which during the winter forms vertical cracks approximately one or two centimeters wide and a few meters deep. The cracks form a polygonal pattern, and in spring, melt water fills them and produces vertical veins of ice. These veins do not melt during the summer because they have formed in the permafrost, and in subsequent winters renewed thermal contraction can reopen the crack to receive in spring an increment of ice from melt water that enters and freezes. The many square miles of cracks forming a polygonal pattern are common in the Arctic and easily seen from the air or on air photographs.

Probably the most spectacular form of massive ground ice is in a pingo (Inuit-Inupiaq *piŋu* 'mound, hillock') (Mackay 1964:61). These ice-cored hills occur in large numbers in the Mackenzie delta region (Bird 1972:14). Pingos have also been found in eastern Greenland, usually occurring on slopes (Price 1972:16–17).

The Mackenzie pingos are formed from a "closed system" of unfrozen soil surrounded by an area of permafrost. A typical development follows this sequence (J. Ross Mackay, personal communication 1981; Mackay 1972): a large lake, beneath which there is no permafrost, fills with sediment or, more likely, is drained away; with the water gone, permafrost will form on the bottom and sides so as to trap a huge core of unfrozen, water-saturated soil above it; pressure from inward freezing forces the water upward toward the surface where it freezes forming an "ice blister" on the landscape.

The Greenland-type pingo is due to water seeping where artesian pressure develops in unfrozen soil beneath the permafrost (Price 1972:17). As the water under pressure approaches the surface and freezes, the continual supply of water allows the build-up of ice, which blisters the surface.

Massive ground ice is another feature of permafrost landscape (Mackay 1964:62; Bird 1972:14). It usually forms in areas of fine-grained material and takes the form of large horizontal ice sheets. The tops of these sheets frequently lie only a few meters below the ground surface; their thickness may range from one to 10 meters in depth, and then may underlie from tens to hundreds of square miles. They probably grow in place by the freezing of water being sucked up by capillary action and/or supplied by hydrostatic pressure from downward freezing permafrost (Mackay 1964:62).

Freezing and Thawing: Weathering and Mass Wasting

Frost heave is the predominantly vertical displacement of material, and as a process that affects land surfaces, it takes place in the active layer at the surface where freeze-thaw cycles occur (Price 1972:27). The pressure responsible for this heaving is due to the 9 percent volume change from water to ice and ice-crystal growth. Different heaving is unequal vertical displacement over a surface; it depends on the microenvironmental conditions (Pruitt 1978:20–21). For example, a poorly drained sediment with grass vegetation would be more susceptible to frost heaving than a well-drained, vegetation-free gravel area. In Arctic areas blocks may be heaved upward by the accumulation of water in cracks, with subsequent freezing forcing the block up. Upon thawing the block does not settle back to its original position due to debris falling in the void space (Price 1972:27). Needle ice, fine needlelike clusters of ice crystals occurring just below the ground surface, may be considered as a process of frost heave. In Arctic environments needle-ice development occurs mostly in oceanic areas where there is a more frequent diurnal freeze and thaw cycle (Price 1972:28) and are best developed in silty soils (Bird 1972:14). Needle ice is thought to have a major disruptive effect on vegetation (Pruitt 1978:21). In any case, frost heave of all kinds is important in the origin of patterned ground.

In areas underlain by permafrost, the surface of the ground is frequently broken up into geometric patterns of circles, ovals, polygons, and elongated ovals collectively called patterned ground (for example, Price 1972:29–34). Patterned grounds are classified not only on the basis of geometric form but also on whether there is sorting of materials such as stones, pebbles, or gravel.

Unsorted geometric forms may be delineated by a furrel, crack, or vegetation, but there is no order of large rocks or stones. In the geometric forms that are sorted, larger stones will border the figure and successively smaller material will be found in the center.

Circles vary in diameter from a few centimeters to over three meters and can extend to a depth of about one meter. They may occur singularly or in groups and are found on nearly horizontal surfaces. On sloping ground, circles become ovals or elongated ovals and even parallel stripes. Polygons, like circles, are best developed on horizontal ground. They may range in size from about five centimeters to approximately 30 meters. Polygons never occur singularly. All patterned grounds of the sorted variety have the size of their ordered stones increasing proportionately with the size of the landform.

Mass wasting is the downslope movement of soil and bedrock due to gravity. One process of mass wasting, slumping, is abundantly evident in areas of massive ground ice being undercut by thermal erosion. Probably the most widely recognized process of mass wasting is solifluction (Bird 1972:15). Solifluction occurs in the active layer of pemafrost, that is, the layer of soil which seasonally melts (see Bird 1972; Price 1972; Pruitt 1978). Solifluction is a mass of unconsolidated soil with high moisture content that moves downslope in the form of a flow. The material displaced downslope may take the form of discrete lobes or sheets. The action occurs on the most gentle slope and is best developed on slopes of less than 20° (Price 1972:37). In steeper areas, soil water is quickly lost, and the material is eroded away. The annual movement downslope varies depending on moisture availability, soil particle size, and degree of slope. Again, where best development occurs, annual displacement is commonly in the neighborhood of five centimeters (Bird 1972:15). Solifluction occurs widely: in Spitsbergen, Brooks Range in Alaska, in all parts of the Canadian Arctic except the flattest plains, and in many parts of the Soviet Union.

Boulder fields and rock glaciers are evidence of shattering due to the freeze-thaw cycle (Price 1972:38). Boulder fields are accumulations of angular blocks formed from weathering of the underlying bedrock. As the rocks are heaved to the surface the freeze-thaw cycle will cause them to fracture along planes of structural weaknesses or sedimentary bed cleavages. Boulder fields are usually found in fairly level areas; the blocks are large and small-grained material is lacking. Where boulder fields occur on slopes rock glaciers may form. These land forms are similar to true glaciers except that they are composed of coarse angular boulders produced from valley sides, valley headwalls, or underlying bedrock. Ice is usually present below the surface and plays a role along with gravity in rock glacier movement.

Freezing and Thawing: Erosion and Deposition

Much of the Arctic landscape was covered by massive continental glaciers that caused a variety of erosional and depositional surfaces (see Mackay 1964).

In many areas the evidence of glacial erosion takes the form of exposed, rounded bedrock from which the soil cover was stripped away. These surfaces were gouged by advancing ice, with alteration of pre-existing drainage patterns including the deepening of existing lake basins.

A great deal of the landscape in the Arctic region exhibits deposition from glaciers. The whole range of depositional forms is present, with thousands of square miles of till-covered plains sometimes fluted or drumlinized to show the directions of past glacial movement. There are sand plains, from the outwash of melt-waters, and coarse boulder fields of ablation moraine. Eskers, the sand and gravel ridges that are casts of subglacial streams, are very prominent features of the landscape. However, not all of the surface was glaciated, and much of eastern Siberia, Alaska, and perhaps a few of the High Arctic islands in Canada have no glacial erosion or deposition (Wilkinson 1970:47; Bird 1972:8). Instead the topography of these areas reflects their underlying structure as modified by postglacial erosional and depositional processes.

At the close of the glacial epoch, marine transgression

flooded most coastal lowlands as the ice withdrew (Bird 1972:8). As a result of crustal rebound, old beaches and shoreline features were elevated (Mackay 1964:60). This has been most extreme along the Hudson Bay shoreline, but raised shorelines are also common elsewhere in the Canadian Arctic. Along the coastal areas, many prominent gravelly beaches are found many miles inland and to heights of over 150 meters above present sea level.

The Arctic as a region of low temperature that sustains the phenomenon of permafrost may also show landforms that result from the disruption of the thermal regime. Unique landforms are found as a result of this thermal erosion (see Price 1972:18–23). It is most dramatic in the western Canadian Arctic and the north slopes of Alaska where ground ice is widely present (Bird 1972:15). Along exposed coasts wave attack frequently exposes ice to melting, and large areas of slumping and flowing mud are summer features, which taken over time have produced very rapid coastal retreat (Kerfoot and Mackay 1972:117). Even along riverbanks and on the shores of lakes the retreat process is evident. Thermokarst is the collective term applied to melting out of ground ice and subsequent alteration of landforms caused by it. Many lakes are thermokarst, basins from which ice has disappeared and the resulting depressions filled with water (Bird 1972:15).

Arctic Ecosystems

MILTON M.R. FREEMAN

This chapter discusses important characteristics of the arctic environment, especially the flora and fauna, that impinge directly on the human occupation of the region and describes the major cultural adjustments to this environment that the Eskimo population has made. The human population is, of course, an important and integral part of the Arctic ecosystem within which its varied and successive cultures have developed.

Ecologists increasingly turn to the ecosystem as the basic unit of study for two main reasons. First, the behavior of any species or population can only be fully defined and understood in the context of the total environment with which it interacts, and second, events in nature are seldom if ever due to, or explainable by, single or simple events. Thus, analysis of ecologic relationships requires consideration of a complex of interacting factors, a formidable and somewhat nebulous undertaking unless handled in strictly systematic fashion (see fig. 1).

Delimitation of ecosystems may be both subjective and arbitrary depending on the focus of investigation; nevertheless, there are three major and fairly distinct subsystems—the terrestrial, freshwater, and marine. Despite their obvious physical and biological differences, they will have certain shared characteristics, due to their common location in the arctic region. Perhaps the most important common characteristic is their youthfulness as ecological systems, resulting from the short period of time (8,000–10,000 years) that has elapsed since the retreat of the continental ice sheets that covered most of the region during the Pleistocene era (Dunbar 1968).

A number of other important features that follow from this relative recency of origin serve to distinguish ecosystems of the high latitudes from those in the temperate and tropical zones. For example, there are relatively few species that either have adapted to life in the arctic or have yet had time to migrate back since extinction or retreat of local populations occurred during earlier periods of climatic deterioration (not all ecologists subscribe to this view; cf. Pitelka 1969:338).

There is another possible explanation for the lack of biological diversity in the Arctic that advances ecologic, rather than historic, causes. In this view, the paucity and relative infertility of the arctic soil, together with the aridity (which results from the soil type and the generally low precipitation), the short growing seasons, and high wind velocity and frequency encourage the development of vegetation having a markedly low or prostrate characteristic life-form. This structural uniformity of the vegetation results in a lack of diversity among animal habitats, such that as one moves across the boundary from the tundra to the boreal forest, and on to lower latitudes, the number of species of animals increases dramatically.

An important ecologic consequence of this lack of diversity, following from the youthfulness and particular physical characteristics of the arctic, is the instability of the ecosystem, manifested by fluctuating population levels of certain dominant species. It should be noted that these fluctuations are most pronounced in the terrestrial ecosystems (and even there, probably only among certain species) and may be much less pronounced, or even absent, in freshwater and marine arctic ecosystems, where overall habitat diversity is much less a function of geographic location. There are quite basic differences surrounding the nature, functioning, and development of the three arctic subsystems.

Marine Subsystem

A major component of the arctic marine fauna is made up of marine mammals: whales, walrus, and seals especially, and the marine-adapted polar bear, whose obligate prey is the ringed seal (fig. 2). The two major species of seal occurring over most of the Eskimo range are ringed seal (*Phoca hispida*) and bearded seal (*Erignathus barbatus*), though in southwest Greenland hooded seal (*Cystophora cristata*) is an especially important quarry of hunters in some areas, and harp seal (*Phoca groenlandica*) are important at a few places in the eastern Arctic, especially in southern Greenland and at some Labrador locations where they pass inshore on their seasonal migrations. Harbor seal (*Phoca vitulina*) is a large seal, more usually associated with the subarctic marine environment, though locally important to some Labrador Eskimo groups and in some areas of the Frederikshåb district of southwest Greenland. Throughout the Arctic it has very localized occurrence, often found in freshwater and known for long journeys upstream into lakes (Mansfield 1967:4). One of the few

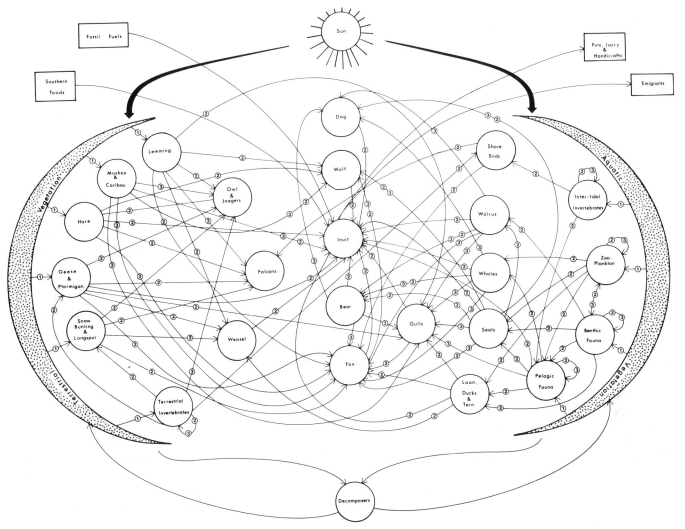

after Riewe 1977.

Fig. 1. Simplified representation of vertebrate predators in the High Arctic ecosystem. Arrows represent the direction of energy flow; numbers designate the type of nutrient transfer most often operating: 1, herbivorous; 2, carnivorous; 3, scavenging.

arctic areas where harbor seals are abundant is in northwest Alaska, where the North Alaska Coast Eskimos hunt them in open water, on ice pans, and close inshore near the river mouths (R.K. Nelson 1969:221).

Though the polar seas are commonly believed to be exceedingly productive, witness the presence of large baleen whales, large colonies of fur seals, walrus, and seabirds, these appearances belie the real situation. The areas of high productivity referred to tend to be either in the subpolar seas or situated close to areas of marine instability, where water masses originating from different parts of the oceans or polar basin flow together to cause local turbulence and upwelling of nutrients.

The appearance of high productivity in the northern seas can be accounted for in a variety of ways. First, a large standing crop may be observed at certain seasons. However, if these are huge baleen whales, or pods containing hundreds of smaller toothed whales, schools of harp seal, or thousands of sea ducks of many varieties,

it should be remembered that these are seasonal migrants into the region and that local production of food is required to sustain these visitors for only a few short months of the year.

Second, food chains in the northern seas are short; thus baleen whales feed on plankton, as do many of the seabirds. Individual arctic species also feed upon a wide range of food organisms, so that a large proportion of the available food species is taken by the few species feeding on them.

Third, growth and reproductive rates of many species are low. Thus a larger number of animals, growing and reproducing more slowly, can be supported by the same food production as would smaller numbers having higher metabolic demands for growth and reproduction. Whales and polar bear produce young once every three years when mature. Many seals produce young only once in two years and take many years to mature, and the same is true also of arctic char.

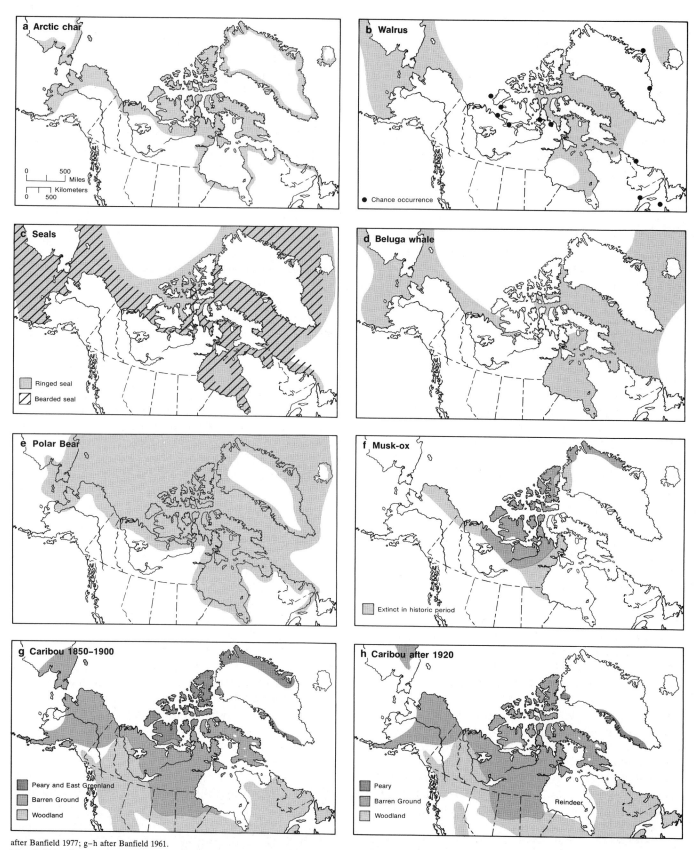

after Banfield 1977; g–h after Banfield 1961.

Fig. 2. Distribution of major fauna in the Arctic: a, Arctic char; b, walrus; c, ringed and bearded seals; d, beluga whale; e, polar bear; f, musk-ox; g, caribou 1850–1900; h, caribou after 1920.

Fourth, with less diversity in the fauna, individual species tend to be present in larger numbers. The general rule is for there to be fewer representatives of any class of animal the farther north one goes.

Last, whereas in the subarctic marine environment fishes are abundant and marine mammals relatively few, in the arctic proper the reverse is true so that the megafauna are far more visible to the human observer.

However, despite these reasons, which contribute to the appearance of high levels of production, northern seas do experience seasonal bursts of very high productivity and, in some particular locations, may even sustain high productivity for longer periods of time.

Overall, the arctic seas are from one-half to one-ninth as productive as the subarctic water masses to the south measured in terms of population size of zooplankton organisms. However, even within confined waters variation is noted, such that the standing crop of zooplankton is twice as large in the western part of Foxe Basin as it is in the eastern part (Grainger 1962:382). Incidentally, this greater local productivity is reflected in the megafauna too, for the Iglulik report that walrus are larger in northwest Foxe Basin than those in the eastern part of the area.

In addition to geographic variation in productivity, some year to year variation probably always occurs too at any locality, in response, for example, to the availability of nutrients, variation in ice cover, and variable mortality rates. Copper Eskimos have reported that seal pup production in Prince Albert Sound on western Victoria Island was almost nonexistent in 1974, an event they blamed on the very great movement of fox into the area from Banks Island, for arctic fox in that region ordinarily seek out and eat the newborn seals in their birth lairs on the fast ice.

Animal abundance is not always determined merely by food. A good example is provided by the ringed seal, which is probably the most important species in the economy of the majority of Eskimo groups exploiting coastal resources. Ringed seal are ubiquitous in the north, though they tend to be mostly inshore in distribution. The food of ringed seal consists of a wide variety of planktonic animals, and, when feeding inshore, fish also. As far as is known this seal is not particularly territorial, and indeed hunters sometimes take several seals at the same seal breathing hole in winter, or see several seals lying on the sea ice near a single breathing hole in spring. Thus, assuming that food is not limiting, one would believe that the population should grow at a rate that was dependent solely on the physiological fecundity of the female seals.

However, comparisons between different regions show this not to be the case: seals, in fact, are more productive in areas having coastlines characterized by features such as narrow and deep indentations and offshore, fringing islands. Such protected shorelines, having early

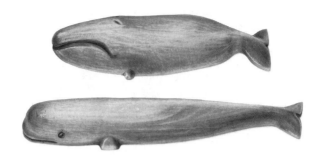

Smithsonian, Dept. of Anthr.: top, 45,131; bottom, 45,128.
Fig. 3. Eskimo ivory models of whales, representing genera recognizable from the anatomical accuracy of the carving. top, Bowhead with characteristic high-arched upper jaw; bottom, beluga. top, Length 4.8 cm; bottom same scale. Both collected by E.W. Nelson on Sledge I., Alaska, 1877–1881.

formation of sea ice in the fall and late breakup of sea ice in the spring, appear to provide optimal conditions for production of ringed seals. Furthermore, the individual seals appear, at any given age, to be larger than seals produced along less favorable coastlines. To be sure, food supply may be a factor, but the density of breeding seals appears to be positively correlated with extent and stability of coastal sea ice (MacLaren 1961:166).

Studies that compared seal production in the eastern and western Arctic have confirmed McLaren's earlier conclusions for the eastern regions. However, important differences in seal abundance and distribution are found in the west: lower seal population densities occur inshore but extend uniformly for many miles out from shore, in contrast to the east where ringed seal are mostly found inshore (T.G. Smith 1973a:124).

However, in the western Arctic, variation in seal production within a region is likewise related to ice conditions. Thus, Prince Albert Sound, on Victoria Island, has an uneven ice surface due to pressure-ridge formation with abundant snowdrift accumulations that are suitable locations for ringed seal birth lairs, whereas Minto Inlet immediately to the north has a smooth ice surface, formed without pressure ridges, thus allowing little snowdrift accumulation. The seal density in these adjacent inlets was 7.3 and 0.6 seals per square mile, respectively (T.G. Smith 1973:7).

Natl. Mus. of Canada, Ottawa: IV–B–787.
Fig. 4. Ivory model of a narwhal. Length about 11.4 cm; collected by A.P. Low, probably at Ramah, Labrador, Newf., 1899.

Fig. 5. Ivory carving of a polar bear. Length 10.0 cm; collected by
L.T. Burwash, Cape Dorset, Baffin I., probably 1925–1926.

Freshwater Subsystem

It is probably true to say that the freshwater subsystem
is of least (though not insignificant) importance to the
human occupants of the Arctic. Few Eskimo groups are
predominantly riverine or lacustrine in orientation, and
even among those dependent on fishes oftimes it is the
anadromous species, such as arctic char (*Salvelinus alpinus*) or Pacific salmon (*Oncorhynchus* spp.), which
move seasonally from sea to freshwater, that form the
economic basis of their particular aquatic orientation.

The greatest dependence on fish for subsistence is to
be found among various Alaska riverine and coastal
groups, especially the groups on the central and lower
Kobuk River, on the Noatak River, in Kotzebue Sound
as well as coastal groups in the Norton Sound, Kuskokwim, and Bristol Bay areas of the Bering Sea coast.
These people, together with Eskimos on Kodiak Island
and the Kenai Peninsula, had ready access to five species of salmon seasonally entering the rivers to spawn,
as well as several species of other freshwater fish (Oswalt 1967:22–23).

Compared to the subarctic or temperate zone, arctic
freshwater is low in productivity, a function of the characteristic thermal/density stratification of northern waters
and the low nutrient-quality of the surrounding drainage areas.

Annual production of char in arctic lakes averages
about one pound of fish per acre of lake surface per
year (Hunter 1971:104), which is about one-tenth the
level of fish production achieved in large lakes in the
temperate zone. However, char production is higher in
rivers than lakes and higher in shallow lakes than in
deep lakes.

Thus though daily (or seasonal) rates of biological
production have been found to be quite high in some
arctic aquatic environments, compared to temperate-
zone aquatic environments (Frey and Stahl 1958; J.W.
Moore 1974), the annual rates of production are very
low indeed.

The greatest individual component of secondary (animal) production is often that of aquatic larvae of insects, which though serving importantly as decomposers
in the ecological cycle and as food for fishes and shore
birds, contribute nothing directly to human subsistence.
The fishes, often heavily dependent on these aquatic
larvae, are in varying degrees important to many Eskimo groups; and it may be true that the contribution
made by fish to many Eskimo bands' survival is the
most consistently undervalued aspect of Eskimo subsistence. About 60 species of fish occur in arctic fresh-
waters (compared to about three times that number in
the Great Lakes drainage system) though only about
10 species are useful to man.

In the cold northern waters, despite low rates of biologic production by primary producers, most animal
species attain larger body size (and usually greater age)
than do representatives of the same species at lower
latitudes. Thus the energy return on hunting even individual fish can be favorable, and an effective array of
fishing gear is found throughout the Eskimo area both
prehistorically and historically.

Lake trout (*Salvelinus namaycush*) are the largest of
arctic freshwater fish, weighing up to 46 kilograms; other
species utilized include several species of whitefish or
cisco (*Coregonus* spp.), pike (*Esox lucius*), grayling
(*Thymallus arcticus*), and Pacific salmon (*Oncorhynchus* spp.). The arctic char is the most universally exploited species, especially because of its usual proximity
to and occurrence in coastal waters where the majority
of the Eskimo population is to be found. The importance of char may be reflected in the very exact nomenclature applied to this species; for example, Igluliks
of northern Baffin Island recognize three distinct forms
of char (iqaluppik), namely: tisuayuk, the anadromous
(sea-run) char; ivisaruk, a landlocked (lake) char with
pink flesh and a red belly, a thinner and deeper-bellied
form than tisuayuk; and nutidliayuk, a landlocked (lake)
char with white flesh and a yellow belly that occurs in
the same lakes as does ivisaruk.

In addition to these rather obvious distinctions, Eskimos normally can discriminate among local stocks of
char by reference to size, flavor, and degree of fatness
of particular local populations in the different drainage
systems present in their hunting and fishing territories.

Seasonal unavailability (through stability of the water
body) or low absolute values of nutrients are the principal cause of low production in arctic freshwater. The
higher production values of rivers are thereby understandable; and providing the silt content of arctic rivers
is not too great, rivers (and especially estuaries and
deltas) provide exceedingly rich areas during the brief
summer production season. Thus, the Mackenzie Delta
supports abundant populations of furbearers and wildfowl (Harding 1974), a condition that is repeated in the
deltas of other northern rivers, such as the Yukon and
Kuskokwim in Alaska. These abundant estuarine fish
resources attract various mammalian predators, in addition to man, to the rich feeding areas. However, much
of the faunal enrichment in the deltaic areas of the north

results from development of lush vegetation along active bank areas (Gill 1973) and is therefore more properly considered as part of the terrestrial subsystem.

Terrestrial Subsystem

As with the other two subsystems, low availability of nutrient supplies provides the major ultimate limitation to production of plant and animal material in the arctic terrestrial environment during the growing season. In part this is related to low temperature, for the undeveloped arctic soils are impoverished precisely because of the temperature-limited activity of soil-producing decomposers in the terrestrial ecosystem. However, in the far northern regions, conditions of extreme aridity combine with low nutrients to severely limit biological production, and it is obvious that seasonal variation in light intensity provides an absolute limit to the duration of biological production by plants.

Most arctic plants have well-developed root systems, which fact is important when considering secondary (animal) production in the arctic, for with five times more plant mass below ground than above (Johnson 1969:346), much plant material is unavailable to grazers who mainly crop the above-ground vegetative parts. However, arctic animals tend to have wide-ranging food preferences, which helps large animals such as musk-ox (*Ovibos moschatus*) to exist in far northern areas of the High Arctic archipelago, where vegetation is relatively scant.

Another feature that exerts important control over animal production in the Arctic is snow cover. Winter snowfall is an important source of moisture to plants during the spring growing season, so that hollows in the landscape, where snow accumulates, may reveal lush meadows when the snows melt away. Such meadow areas, even if small in extent, harbor an abundance of insects and small herbivores (lemmings and birds), which in turn attract predatory forms ensuring local nutrient enrichment as a result of the increased biological activity in the area. Snow provides an important protective cover for plants in the winter months, and it has been established that the more varied the snow cover, the more species of animals can use the area (Pruitt 1970:380).

However, unusually heavy snowfall can prevent animals such as caribou, musk-ox, and ptarmigan from reaching their food supply, and such periodic calamitous happenings will affect the smaller or weaker individuals in the population more severely than the older or stronger animals. In the High Arctic regions, where vegetation is patchy (due to the general aridity of the region) ptarmigan are often associated with musk-ox in the winter months and feed at the edge of the "craters" the large herbivores excavate in the hard-packed snow. On occasion the hardness of the snow completely cuts off the larger animals' access to their food supply, an event that may follow unseasonally mild weather in winter or late rains in the fall. Such happenings may cause massive mortality among the herds (Vibe 1967:187) and even extinction of a local population (Elton 1942:367).

The production of vegetation, upon which all other forms of life in the Arctic depend, varies greatly from place to place. Geology plays a part in causing this variation, for pure limestone and dolomite areas are unsuited to plant growth, as are all areas underlain with carbonate rocks. On the other hand, calcareous shale, argillaceous limestone, and shale and clay areas form soils suitable for plant growth, and the uneven distribution of musk-ox and caribou in some arctic areas has been related to the prevailing geologic formations in these regions (Thorsteinsson 1958; cf. Kelsall 1957, who disputes this influence on caribou distribution).

Despite considerable variation in plant production related to, for example, availability of moisture, nutrients, shelter, temperature, light intensity, and grazing, the annual rates of production are inevitably low compared to plant productivity in other global biomes. However, the daily rates of production during the short growing seasons are comparable to production rates for temperate-zone herbaceous communities, ranging from as low as 3 grams of dry plant matter per square meter in the Canadian High Arctic archipelago to 224 grams in wet meadows in northern Alaska (Bliss 1970:78). Within a small area, production values may halve between the wetter and drier parts of an arctic meadow (Bliss and Kerik 1973), and values of standing crop may vary 100 fold between hummocks and hollows one meter apart (Beschel 1970:86; Bliss et al. 1973 present a comprehensive review of tundra production).

The uniformity of the arctic vegetation over large areas results in a lack of diversity among the mammals inhabiting the northern regions. Over most of the Canadian mainland tundra, the so-called Barren Grounds, characteristic mammal species are the caribou (*Rangifer tarandus*), grizzly bear (*Ursus arctos*), wolf (*Canis lupus*), wolverine (*Gulo gulo*), arctic hare (*Lepus arcticus*), arctic fox (*Alopex lagopus*), least weasel (*Mustela*

Amer. Mus. of Nat. Hist., New York: 60/5686.
Fig. 6. Ivory carving representing a musk-ox, with horns a separate piece. Length about 7.5 cm; collected by George Comer, Hudson Bay, N.W.T., 1906.

41

erminea), ground squirrel (*Spermophilus parryii*), and a very few species of lemmings, mice, and shrew (MacPherson 1965 contains distribution maps for these tundra species). There are others, such as the musk-ox and tundra vole (*Microtus oeconomus*), that have local distribution on the tundra, and a great many others that occur more commonly in the taiga zone to the south but are sometimes encountered well within the tundra zone. These strays include red fox (*Vulpes vulpes*), moose (*Alces alces*), lynx (*Felis lynx*), mink (*Mustela vison*), marten (*Martes americana*), hoary marmot (*Marmota caligata*), and beaver (*Castor canadensis*). In the mountains west of the Mackenzie River and across northern Alaska, Dall sheep (*Ovis dalli*), porcupine (*Erethizon dorsatum*), black bear (*Ursus americanus*), and muskrat (*Ondatra zibethica*) are abundant in the area around the Mackenzie Delta. This fauna is greatly attenuated in the arctic archipelago (including Baffin Island and Greenland).

The arctic avifauna is quite varied, though only the raven (*Corvus corax*), ptarmigan (*Lagopus mutus*), and snowy owl (*Nyctea scandiaca*) remain during winter from among the 50 or more land and shore birds that mostly frequent the productive land-water interfaces during the short northern summer.

Human Exploitation of the Environment

It is commonplace to regard hunting as one of the most successful human adaptations. Justification for this conclusion stems from the long span of human history through which hunting has persisted, the wide geographical distribution of hunting peoples around the world, and the ability of hunters to occupy regions considered as environmentally demanding.

Arctic man the hunter is unique among hunting peoples, in that he has an obligate dependence on animal resources compared to hunting and gathering people elsewhere who derive a considerable proportion of their energy and nutritional requirements from vegetable sources. Hunting as a human activity has also been described as an efficient biobehavioral integrating system, wherein the physiological, behavioral, and social dimensions of an individual's life are given direction (Laughlin 1968:304), and others have stressed the complementarity of intrafamilial roles within particular phases of the hunting complex (Berreman 1954:105).

The ecologically integrative function of hunting can also be demonstrated by considering Eskimo hunting of walrus, as an example, wherein are integrated diverse elements of the marine, terrestrial and human subsystems, and various physical, biological, and cognitive interactions between the subsystems.

Walrus are a dominant element of the economy and culture of any Eskimo groups who are favored by the proximity of this resource. Certain environmental characteristics determine in large part the suitability of an area for walrus, for the animal is a specialized feeder on particular kinds of bottom-living invertebrates and also requires either areas of open water or unstable (and thus reforming and thin) ice in winter. Shallow sea areas, with suitable bottom sediments for shellfish, and at least periodic open water areas in winter occur in northern Hudson Bay and Foxe Basin in the eastern Canadian arctic, Inglefield Bay in northwest Greenland, and in the Bering Sea region. In each of these regions local Eskimo populations exploit the walrus herds. The Iglulik of Foxe Basin are generally regarded by neighboring groups as having the largest and best dog teams, a direct result of their having an abundance of the preferred dogfood. However, the presence of walrus is not an unmitigated benefit, for walrus tend to drive away ringed seal, which is a staple resource for most maritime Eskimo groups. Thus the seasonal presence of walrus in the customary seal-hunting areas will cause shortage of seal meat, seal oil, and sealskins unless these products are stored in anticipation of such shortages.

Seals are frightened of walrus for good reason: in some areas walrus hunt seals. The reason for this is known to the hunters and derives either from the scarcity or absence of the bottom-living clams (the preferred food for walrus) or from the separation of that walrus from its mother at the time of weaning so that it was never properly socialized as a bottom feeder and instead turned to the easy life of a seal predator. Thus carnivorous walrus can be encountered anywhere, but they are relatively more common in areas of deeper water, where bottom feeding is especially a problem (Fay 1960).

Unfortunately, carnivorous walrus are generally aggressive, and they present a decided danger to the hunter in a frail boat, so it becomes important to recognize such animals at a distance and to know how to kill them or avoid them. However, these walrus are readily identifiable: they have yellow tusks, with black surface etching clearly visible, and the tusks tend to be longer and more slender. Recognition is important not only because of the danger they pose whilst alive but also because their flesh can cause sickness in people and thus is customarily avoided.

The known aggressiveness of walrus has important survival value for the hunter, for he knows that no animal, not even the dreaded killer whale, will attack a walrus. Should a hunter be unfortunate enough to encounter a killer whale, or worse still, a pack of killer whales, his main hope of reaching safety lies in convincing the whales that walrus are in the vicinity. The various subterfuges include placing some white or gleaming object into the water (to simulate walrus tusks) or imitating the sound of a walrus roaring and transmitting this sound, perhaps via a paddle, into the water.

The walrus thus has an important role in several aspects of the hunters' exploitation of the marine subsystem: positively it represents a substantial yield of valued products—including the clams found in the stomach of the walrus—and it allows escape from a dangerous predator; negatively, its presence invariably precludes ringed seal, and it can contribute to sickness. However, knowledge of the various consequences of these interactions minimizes the attendant disadvantages; thus man's cultural system exerts certain control over inherent environmental limitations.

Eskimo Knowledge of the Environment

It is evident that successful hunting requires considerable knowledge of animal behavior, for not only are many arctic animals hard to locate and in somewhat limited supply, but also some are quite dangerous on account of their size or strength (polar bear, grizzly bear, bowhead whale, and narwhal) or ferocity, more especially when wounded (harbor seal and walrus). The comprehensive understanding of animal behavior has been discussed explicitly in respect to marine mammals (R.K. Nelson 1969) and certain land animals (Gubser 1965) in Alaska, and also for similar resources in Greenland (Anonymous 1964).

One of the important outcomes of this expert knowledge is that Eskimo groups have been able to exploit the highly productive ecotones that exist at the boundaries between the marine, freshwater, and terrestrial subsystems and between arctic and subarctic zones. In some instances Eskimo groups obtain a significant amount of their annual energy from animal populations that spend part of the year in the more productive temperate and subarctic zones south of the arctic environment itself.

Many resources upon which Eskimo groups depend in fact migrate out of the arctic; Barren Ground (mainland) caribou, whales, and wildfowl are major examples. Other species may migrate over large areas of the arctic, such as polar bears, or between different seasonal feeding locations, such as walrus, arctic char, some seals, and Peary caribou (in the arctic archipelago). Thus Eskimo settlement sites are normally to be found,

seasonally differentiated, at the best locations to intercept these migratory resources. An analysis of Eskimo hunting behavior at Point Hope in Alaska has statistically demonstrated what is perhaps the normal strategy of Eskimo hunters (who uniquely among hunting people depend on animal resources): that their food-getting behavior is oriented toward the intensive utilization of small and geographically scattered areas during short periods of time (Foote 1969–1970). Thus though Eskimo hunters appear to hunt over large areas, they make use of their detailed knowledge of animal behavior to concentrate hunting on small "core" areas where the likelihood of success is greatly enhanced. It is immediately apparent that in order to maximize energy returns and minimize energy expenditures, a hunter should be able to predict the best location for hunting. Insofar as animals do have certain seasonal habitat requirements, the experienced hunter can indeed maximize efficient food-getting practices.

In the winter, seal hunting takes place either in open water or at the seal breathing holes on the ice. It is important for the hunter to know whether the sea ice is stable or fissured at various, regular, pressure areas. If it is stable, seal breathing holes will be somewhat random, with a density that generally decreases beyond a certain distance offshore. Even on stable sea ice, areas with currents may retard sea-ice formation, thus providing preferred areas for breathing hole formation.

In areas of unstable ice, it is important to know where cracks form, as areas of refreezing, having thinner ice, are areas of abundant breathing holes, with relatively few holes occurring nearby on the thicker ice. Seals will be more abundant in the vicinity of these tide or pressure cracks and will maintain fewer individual breathing holes due to the large numbers of seals in the immediate vicinity. Thus hunters will have to wait for a shorter time for a seal to surface in such areas, compared to those hunting in areas of unbroken winter fast ice, who sometimes wait many hours for seals to surface at any particular breathing hole.

However, if only unbroken ice occurs in the seal-hunting territory, a group can shorten the time a hunter waits for a seal by collaborative hunting, where many hunters discover all the holes in the immediate area and

Smithsonian, Dept. of Anthr.: 37,571.
Fig. 7. Toggling harpoon head with copper point. The float line was attached with a line fastener to the short thong loop. The heads are stored on wooden mounts until they are fitted to the harpoon shaft for use. The multi-spurred base and the ivory incisions are characteristic of southern Alaska. The decoration is associated with hunting magic, sea mammals being displeased if hunted with ugly weapons (Fitzhugh and Kaplan 1982:242). Length 28.0 cm. Collected by E.W. Nelson at Anogok, Alaska, 1877–1881.

each guards one hole. This was the normal winter hunting practice of those Netsilik and Copper Eskimo in the Central Arctic who congregated in large winter camps on the sea ice (Damas 1969a:51); in the Eastern Arctic this collaborative practice is followed in the spring hunting, too (Freeman 1969:781).

There are many variations in hunting technique that utilize local conditions and detailed knowledge of seal behavior. The small band of Netsilik at Thom Bay has a different method of reducing the wait for seals in the winter, which is predicated on their knowledge that seals seek out breathing holes, even if open water is nearby. Thom Bay hunters construct an artificial breathing hole over a crack in the sea ice and harpoon the seals that are attracted to the breathing hole in preference to the open water (Rasmussen 1931:161), a technique that appears to have been used also by the Labrador Eskimo (J.G. Taylor 1974a:45).

In northern Hudson Bay, walrus follow a predictable seasonal migration pattern, such that their location and numbers can be forecast with some degree of reliability by the local hunters. The preferred season for hunting is the fall, and at that season the ratio of calves to adults or subadults in the hunting returns is lowest (1:3.0), whereas in the spring, when only a small amount of walrus hunting is practiced, the calf to adult or subadult ratio has risen to its highest level (1:1.75). The proportions of animals taken at the three walrus hunting seasons of the year at Southampton Island, namely spring, summer, and fall, are 1:2:9.5 respectively, indicating the adaptive manner in which hunting behavior maximizes return (carcass weight) for a given output of energy. In terms of yield, the Southampton Islander realized 0.167 walrus per day hunting in spring, compared to a high of 0.286 walrus per day in the fall (Freeman 1969–1970:159, table 3).

Similarly, the seasonal distribution of ringed seals in the winter months may account for preferences expressed in choice of hunting methods. In the early winter in many areas Eskimo hunters choose to hunt seals at the floe edge; however, as the winter advances, the distance to the floe edge increases and waiting at the seal breathing holes on the fast ice is increasingly preferred. In large part this change in technique results from the longer time needed to travel to the floe edge following the progressively extending fast-ice area. However, another variable contributing to the increasing return from breathing-hole hunting is that larger, adult seals during the winter months are found closer inshore beneath the fast ice, whereas seals taken at the floe edge in winter are smaller, immature animals.

Ice has an important effect on the abundance of polar bears at certain seasons. South Banks Island, one of the major denning areas for polar bear, will have no bears present when there is not pack ice in adjacent areas of the Beaufort Sea and Amundsen Gulf in the summer months (Usher 1970–1971, 2:74), and similar conditions greatly influence the availability of bears on the east coast of Southampton Island, the Simpson Peninsula, the Perry River area, and other Arctic coastlines (Harington 1968:11).

In the winter both male and female polar bears retire to dens on land for variable periods of time. The preferred locations for these dens in any area is known to local hunters; for example, on the east coast of Southampton Island dens are generally on elevated, south-facing slopes, often within 20 kilometers of the coast, and require a certain depth of snow of a suitable degree of softness (Harington 1968:12–13).

The physical conditions of the winter environment place similar restraints on caribou, the other great staple of the Eskimo hunting economy. It appears that though the majority of Barren Ground caribou leave the tundra areas for the forested taiga regions to the south, some animals always remain; and in certain years, and in some areas, these wintering animals are exceedingly numerous (Kelsall 1968:64).

However, caribou are restricted during winter to areas having snow conditions of particular characteristics. They avoid low-lying areas in which deep accumulations of snow occur (even though such areas might, in summer, provide the richest vegetation). In fact wintering caribou are mainly restricted to those places avoided as summer feeding areas, that is, the exposed ridges and slopes of hillsides where, due to abrasive wind action, no snow accumulates and little but lichen and woody growth is to be found.

It has been established that caribou have thresholds of sensitivity to not only the thickness but also the hardness and density of snow. Thus a snow depth of 60 centimeters will cause caribou to leave the area. Similarly, hardness of the snow equivalent to a bearing weight of 60 grams per square centimeter causes the animals to move away in search of snow having more suitable characteristics (Pruitt 1960:66). Though large areas of the summer and winter ranges of caribou are occupied by the animals for short periods of time, and often irregularly, the migration routes are often topographically distinguished (for instance, along drainage systems and eskers) and are quite regularly followed (Kelsall 1968:108ff.). Doubtless the degree of predictability of seasonal migrations, in contrast to the uncertainty of summer and winter feeding locations, allows success in caribou hunting among those inland bands having a major dependence on this particular species. The importance of these regular seasonal periods of caribou abundance and near predictability has allowed the construction of ambushing and coralling structures, and the development of collaborative hunting practices in the fall season in particular, to maximize returns during a very short period of hunting (Balikci 1964:11–16).

Biological Consideration

The important variables of a biological nature affecting hunting outcome include the numbers of a given species, their intrinsic rate of natural increase, the size and composition of individual carcasses, and the seasonal movements and groupings of the individuals.

Numbers are generally obtained by census methods, which include sample head counts as well as marking, release, and recapture of marked animals. Sample head counts have been used for dispersed populations such as caribou (discussed in Parker 1972) and ringed seal (MacLaren 1961; T.G. Smith 1973) and in the case of more gregarious species, such as walrus or musk-ox, may include a larger rather than smaller proportion of the total sample if the seasonal movements are already known. Recapture of marked individuals has been attempted with polar bear, walrus, arctic char, fox, whale, and ringed seals, but the main use of this technique is perhaps to gain more understanding of movements of individuals and the interrelationships of various local groupings.

The important components of recruitment are the natural rate of increase of the population (assuming stable, biologically determined birth and death rates) and the degree to which net migration of animals into and out of the area affects local numbers.

As a general rule annual rates of increase of arctic populations are not so high as in temperate zone populations, mainly due to the slower growth and maturation rates of individuals. As an example, female ringed seals generally become sexually mature in their fourth to seventh year, an important characteristic that varies individually and regionally (table 1). Taking into account natural mortality and the age and sex composition of the population, it has been calculated that the natural increase in ringed seal populations is about 8 percent a year (MacLaren 1962:175).

The importance of immigration of seals into the areas of intense exploitation is apparent, for human settlement areas are often strategically situated for maximizing a number of environmental benefits rather than achieving long-term equilibrium in respect to any one. Research has indicated that ringed seal harvests in the Cumberland Sound region of Baffin Island are above the sustainable yield levels for the area exploited but that immigration of seals into the area from underexploited areas immediately to the northeast allows the large annual harvests to continue being taken (T.G. Smith 1973b:49). This situation may be true for many regions of the Arctic, especially in Alaska and the western Canadian Arctic, where ringed seal appear to be markedly migratory in their habits and human settlements are individually larger and longer-lived than in the Eastern Arctic.

A distinction must be drawn between gross carcass

Table 1. Reproductive Rates for Female Ringed Seal

Age in Years	Percentage Reproductive Rate	
	East Baffin I.	Southwest Baffin I.
4	41	0
5	59	8
6	85	10
7	86	50
8	91	75
9	94	93
10–30	97	93

SOURCES: T.G. Smith 1973b (East Baffin); MacLaren 1958 (Southwest Baffin).

weight and weights of component parts utilizable by man, which includes those parts fed to dogs (an unvariable part of the human subsystem in the Arctic until about the 1960s). Table 2 indicates that about two-thirds of the total carcass weight of marine mammals harvested by the Southampton Island Eskimos was utilized by them and their dogs; in earlier times, when more seal oil was used (for lamps) than in the contemporary situation, this figure would likely have been even higher.

In terms of understanding ecosystems, the various component parts of different resources can be reduced to common units, more usually a measure of energy equivalence—the kilocalorie, which allows analysis of the dynamic between and within the various subsystems (Kemp 1971). Table 3 provides a balance sheet of energy origin and disposition within the High Arctic ecosystem. It can be seen that of the annual harvest by man, only about one-third of the total energy supply is used directly by him, with the remainder recycled by other animal components of the total ecosystem of which man is a part.

Carcass weight naturally varies, not just according to age of the animal, but also seasonally for any given individual. Generally the proportion of fat in the carcass is greatest in the early winter months, and at its lowest during the spring. This is an especially important variation for a number of important reasons.

The first such reason is dietetic. In the absence of carbohydrate in the diet, humans can utilize protein only in the presence of fat. Thus, whereas marine mammal hunters generally experience no critical shortages of fat, provided they can continue to hunt successfully, caribou hunting groups are very dependent on stored supplies obtained when the animals had maximal deposits of fat in their bodies. It is quite possible for inland groups to suffer severe nutritional stress in the late winter even if obtaining some caribou, hares, and fish at this season, for these animals will be lean and therefore provide physiologically nonutilizable foodstuffs.

The second important consequence of a seasonally varied fat cycle is related to the rate of retrieval of killed marine mammals. An important problem with marine

Table 2. Marine Mammal Hunting Production, Southampton Island, 1961

Species	Number	Average Weight in Kilograms	Total Biomass in Kilograms	Human Utilization Percentage	Human Utilization Weight in Kilograms	Dogfood Utilization Percentage	Dogfood Utilization Weight in Kilograms
Ringed seal	935	40	37,400	35	13,090	30	11,220
Bearded seal	165	270	44,550	10	4,455	55	24,503
White whale	30	450	13,500	14	1,890	60	8,100
Polar bear	60	365	21,900	10	2,190	35	7,665
Walrus							
Adult	108	512	55,296	5	2,765	65	35,942
Subadult	36	305	10,980	20	2,196	50	5,490
Calf	36	103	3,708	20	742	50	1,854
Total			187,334	14.5	27,328	50.5	94,774
Availability/per capita/per year (200 people; 400 dogs):				136.6 kilograms		236.9 kilograms	

SOURCE: Freeman 1969–1970.

mammal hunting is the loss through sinking, which occurs when seals, walrus, whales, and sometimes polar bear are killed in water (and wounded polar bears generally endeavor to reach water to effect their escape). The probability of sinking is a species characteristic, and it varies seasonally and according to individual circumstance. For example, white whales generally sink when killed, though younger individuals and pregnant females may float. Adult walrus generally sink when killed during the summer, though they generally float in the winter months; young walrus will generally float at any season when killed. For these reasons whale and walrus hunting in summer often takes place inshore where the animals can be retrieved from the bottom with hooks after several have been killed, or, in the case of walrus, killed outright as they sleep on ice pans (though in some areas they are never killed on traditional rock hauling-out places, *ullit*, for fear they will permanently desert that locality) (Freeman 1974–1975:149).

Losses through sinking are probably greatest among ringed seal, for a small carcass is harder to retrieve once having sunk than is a large carcass, especially in deeper water where ringed seal hunting usually occurs. Sinking rates are related to fat content of the carcass, the latitude (as loss of fat is related to the fasting and basking season, which is delayed the higher the latitude) and the density of seawater (which affects seal buoyancy). The relationships among these variables have been determined empirically (MacLaren 1961:171) and result in practice in 18 to 33 percent of seals being lost by sinking during open-water hunting (Foote 1969). Apart from using nets, there is no means of completely overcoming this sinking loss during seal hunting at certain seasons of the year. However, carefully conducted walrus hunts can result in negligible loss of carcasses through nonretrieval, despite the higher probability that individual animals will sink when killed. The interplay of

hunting methods, technology, and animal behavior contributing to this situation has been analyzed (Freeman 1969–1970).

Though the bowhead whale was probably widely hunted from Alaska to west Greenland until the early 1900s (though only rarely in the Central Arctic where ice-locked waters were inimical to its presence), it has become rare since the depredations of commercial whaling activity. Bowhead whale are still hunted in northwest Alaska on their annual migration, and the presence of this resource has occasioned unique social and technological response from the Eskimos of that region (Spencer 1959:332). It follows that the behavior and anatomy of whales must be well understood if man is to hunt them with any degree of success using hand weapons. To the south, Chugach Eskimo whaling was even more highly specialized, with few men allowed to participate and extreme secrecy surrounding the practice; among the Chugach, probably uniquely among Eskimo hunters, poison-tipped hunting lances were employed in whale hunting (Birket-Smith 1953:33). Small whales are also highly prized, for food, oil, and the excitement provided by their chase. Considerable skill is required to hunt whales, for in contrast to seals they are generally moving and therefore must be pursued or surprised.

The Human-Land Relationship

The harshness of much of the arctic environment has prompted ethnographers to see the Eskimo population in some sort of a Malthusian balance with the environment. Weyer (1932:50) wrote that "the Eskimo is a cultural success: he survives farther north than any other people on earth, in exceedingly wretched and difficult conditions—an exemplification of man's cultural adapt-

46

Table 3. Harvest and Distribution of Kilocalories by Grise Fiord Hunters, 1971–1972

Species	Number Harvested	Kilocalorie Equivalence	Percent of Total Kilocalorie	Kilocalories Consumed By people	By dogs	By scavengers and decomposers	Kilocalories exported as fur and skins
Arctic char	404	6.98×10^5	0.37	5.22×10^5	0	1.76×10^5	0
Snow geese	11	7.69×10^4	0.04	5.09×10^4	0	2.60×10^4	0
Ducks	60	1.37×10^5	0.01	8.30×10^4	0	5.44×10^4	0
Ptarmigan	117	1.72×10^5	0.09	1.06×10^5	0	6.55×10^4	0
Polar bear	27	2.27×10^7	11.90	1.03×10^6	5.92×10^6	1.36×10^7	2.16×10^6
Arctic fox	324	2.50×10^6	1.31	9.05×10^4	0	2.21×10^6	1.95×10^5
Walrus	12	1.75×10^7	9.14	1.28×10^6	1.09×10^6	1.51×10^7	0
Ringed seal	453	9.02×10^7	47.30	6.51×10^6	2.12×10^7	5.73×10^7	5.14×10^6
Harp seal	32	1.58×10^7	8.24	0	2.05×10^6	1.25×10^7	1.30×10^6
Bearded seal	28	2.49×10^7	13.00	6.60×10^6	3.40×10^6	1.49×10^7	0
Arctic hare	72	5.44×10^5	0.29	2.58×10^5	0	2.86×10^5	0
Peary caribou	26	2.15×10^6	1.13	9.35×10^5	0	1.21×10^6	0
Musk-ox	9	3.52×10^6	1.84	1.71×10^6	0	1.71×10^6	1.19×10^6
Narwhal	6	1.02×10^7	5.34	6.78×10^5	8.26×10^5	8.70×10^6	0
Total		1.91×10^8		2.00×10^7	3.45×10^7	1.28×10^8	9.99×10^6
Percent utilization of total harvest				10.5	18.1	67.0	5.2

SOURCE: Riewe 1977.

ability to nature in the raw." And Balikci (1968:82) provided this summary:

> Now within the vast Eskimo area there are great regional differences. . . . For instance, both northern Alaska and the Netsilik country may be considered to have harsh environments, yet the abundance of larger sea mammals in Alaska has allowed a much denser population to develop relatively sedentary patterns. Greater food availability seems to have reduced prolonged ecological pressure among the Alaskan Eskimos. . . . In the Netsilik area, on the other hand, prolonged pressure phases appear to have been much more frequent and severe. . . . The Caribou Eskimos dwelling inland illustrate another case of precarious ecological adaptation with frequent pressure phases.

Thus in many studies of traditional peoples—hunters, agriculturalists, and pastoralists alike—the tendency has been to explain their population processes (size, rate of growth, and movement) by considering an essentially biological concept, namely, the carrying capacity of their environment. This concept has been variously defined by ecologists but as used in studies of human ecology is often expressed as the maximum number of people that a given land area will maintain in perpetuity, under the prevailing system of resource exploitation, without causing any degradation of the land and wildlife resource base.

The usefulness of this concept has been questioned (Street 1969), especially on the grounds that constant innovation, in respect to improved technology and husbandry practices, causes progressive improvement in resource exploitation, thus requiring evaluation of an essentially moving target. In regard to Eskimo popu-lations in the north, the usefulness of the concept of carrying capacity is open to doubt for other reasons too; for example, for ringed seal hunting in Cumberland Sound, numbers taken by local hunters may be above the level of sustainable yield. However, degradation of the wildlife resource in this case appears unlikely to occur due to constant immigration of seals from underexploited stocks elsewhere. This situation of local overexploitation probably occurs in a number of Western Arctic localities as well, but it is sustained by immigration of young ringed seal from underexploited areas of high productivity in the Central Arctic (T.G. Smith 1973a:125).

Another factor that is ignored in the concept of carrying capacity is the complex and vital component of human behavior. Not only is there continual innovation in process, but also the dynamic introduced by human choice often overshadows any apparent environmental considerations that appear compelling determinants of human behavior (H. Kleivan 1964).

It appears that the notion of a population equilibrium (in human and nonhuman groups) being determined largely by available food supply is, in general terms, far too simplistic. One important staple resource for most Eskimo groups, namely the ringed seal, is not limited by food, and it is likely that the same holds true for several other species, who require (and oftimes compete for) resources other than food, such as mates, territory, breeding space, and so on.

Largely as a result of studies of social animals, the notion that population size is regulated by social means, rather than food supply, became advanced as an hypothesis having very general demographic applicability (Wynne-Edwards 1962). However, a number of ecologists have taken issue with some fundamental aspects of this hypothesis (see references in Wiens 1966; also Chitty 1967).

In regard to human populations, it seems that concerns about food are expressed more in respect to threatened, or imagined, shortages of preferred food, rather than in respect to the fear of outright starvation. Thus, human populations do regulate their fertility (to maintain particular sized populations), but more usually in response to limited access to social advantages rather than access to resources necessary for survival (Douglas 1966:272).

The concept of optimum population, rather than carrying capacity of the land, is preferred by some human ecologists, as it shifts the focus of concern from an implied prime importance (if not determinism) of the environment over human affairs, to the social and demographic spheres, whereby the population in question regulates its own demographic destiny by conscious choice. Optimum population is the term applied to a human group that maintains itself within the size range required for the suitable expression of a normative pattern of social organization and for the adequate reali-zation of certain internalized cultural goals. Such a population will normally stabilize itself below the biological carrying capacity of the environment (Freeman 1970:145).

This concept has value in explaining human settlement in the north insofar as it focuses attention on other than food as a factor in explaining human demographic processes. It especially allows explanation of the apparent ecological paradox of why large-sized winter settlements were found in areas of relative scarcity, such as the Central Arctic, whereas small-sized settlements occurred in areas of relative abundance, such as the Labrador coast. One explanation of this behavior suggests that the development of political structure and certain cultural systems of resource distribution are necessary prerequisites for the growth of such large seasonal groups (J.G. Taylor 1974a:95). Other studies of human demographic behavior in the Arctic similarly suggest that social factors may place greater restraint on the human population than do productivity characteristics of the environment (see Freeman 1971 and Riches 1974 for additional perspectives on the role of infanticide in Eskimo group behavior), suggesting once again that the ecosystem is an integrated system that necessarily includes inputs from the cultural subsystem created by man.

Eskimo and Aleut Languages

ANTHONY C. WOODBURY

The Eskimo-Aleut linguistic family consists of two distantly related branches, Eskimo and Aleut, each of which must have developed independently over a long period of time from a remote common ancestor, Proto–Eskimo-Aleut.* The Eskimo branch has two clearly differentiated subgroups, Yupik and Inuit-Inupiaq. Yupik, consisting of five languages, was spoken aboriginally on the coasts of the Chukchi Peninsula in Siberia and in Alaska from Norton Sound south to the Alaska Peninsula and then east along the Pacific to Prince William Sound. Inuit-Inupiaq, a continuum of closely related dialects, extended north from Norton Sound and east across Arctic Alaska and Canada to the coasts of Labrador and Greenland. The other great branch, Aleut, is represented by a single language, spoken aboriginally on the Aleutian Islands. The distribution of the languages in 1980 was largely unchanged from that at the time of first contact with Europeans (see fig. 1 for Alaska and Siberia), but such contact often severely affected the vigor of the languages in native communities (table 1).

Within each major grouping—Aleut, Yupik, and Inuit-Inupiaq—the relations among dialects (or languages) are the linguistic end products of very different sets of historical circumstances. In this chapter linguistic classification and prehistory are connected, where possible, with what is known about the prehistory of the speakers. Also discussed are the two most remote linguistic relationships in the family, Yupik–Inuit-Inupiaq, and Eskimo-Aleut, and their bearing on earlier Arctic prehistory.

Aleut

Although navigation, and hence communication, across the whole Aleut area is hampered by difficult waters,

*The transcriptions of Eskimo and Aleut words cited in this chapter generally follow the transcriptional systems described in the orthographic footnotes in the respective ethnographic chapters in this vol. However, to make the comparison of forms easier the transcription of Yupik words in this chapter follows the practical orthographies in not marking as long those vowels whose length is predictable from the rhythmic accent rules, and in not marking accent. The fourth vowel, traditionally written ï, is here transcribed ə, following the preference of some scholars; it is phonetically a high central [ɨ].

the Aleut language has just two main dialects, and their overall differences are less considerable than those found among the Inuit-Inupiaq dialects (Bergsland 1958:624).

Eastern Aleut, the first dialect to have been carefully studied (Veniaminov 1846a), was spoken by the three easternmost groups for which Bergsland (1959:11–14) gives tribal names, the Qagaan Tayaĝungin (Alaska Peninsula to Unimak Island), the Qigiiĝun (Krenitzin and adjacent islands between Unimak and Unalaska islands, as well as the eastern part of Unalaska Island), and the Qawalangin (Unalaska and Umnak islands to Amukta Island). Eastern Aleut has shown subdialectal differentiation in both the nineteenth and twentieth centuries (Veniaminov 1846a; Knut Bergsland, personal communication 1982). Speakers of Eastern Aleut were settled on the Pribilof Islands in the early nineteenth century, and the dialect was still spoken there in 1980.

Western Aleut included two known subdialects, Atkan and Attuan (Bergsland 1959), earlier called Central and Western Aleut, respectively (Bergsland 1951; Marsh and Swadesh 1951). Atkan was spoken by the Niiĝuĝis (Andreanof Islands from Seguam to Kanaga Island, including Atka), and Attuan by the Saskinan or Sasignan (Near Islands, including Attu). In the early nineteenth century, some Atkans and Attuans were taken by the Russians to the Commander Islands, but by 1980 there were very few speakers left of either dialect. Atkans and Attuans remaining in Alaska were resettled on Atka Island in 1945 after the upheavals of the Second World War. In 1980, Atkan survived there, but Attuan was extinct or nearly so.

Before the twentieth century a third Western-Aleut-speaking tribe, the Qax̂un, occupied the Rat Islands, between Atka and Attu. Their dialect is practically unknown (Bergsland 1959:13–14; Knut Bergsland, personal communication 1982).

Classification and Prehistory

Western Aleut may once have been a dialect continuum from Atka, to the Rat Islands, to Attu, with the loss of a Rat Islands dialect leading to the present Atkan-Attuan split (Knut Bergsland, personal communication 1982). Attuan differs from Atkan in having made a

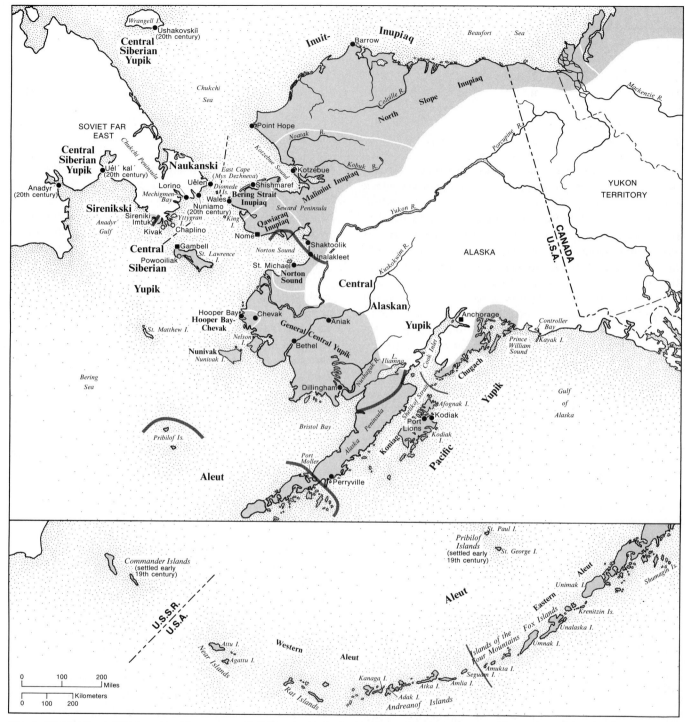

Fig. 1. Distribution of Eskimo-Aleut languages and dialects in the Soviet Far East and Alaska in 1980 (after Krauss 1975, 1982).

series of important phonological innovations (Bergsland 1951, 1956, 1958, 1967). Among these were: (1) the merger of Proto-Aleut *δ and *y into Attuan y; (2) the change of Proto-Aleut *w and *W to Attuan m and M, for example Atkan wan, Attuan man 'this one'; Atkan Waẋ, Attuan Maẋ 'smoke'; (3) the change of nasals to voiced fricatives before oral consonants (ex-

50 cept n before velar or uvular fricatives), for example,

Atkan qaŋlaaẋ, Attuan qaγlaaẋ 'raven'; Atkan aqmi-, and Attuan avqi- 'angry' (with vq from *mq after metathesis); Atkan kamγi-, Attuan kavi- 'head' (with v from *vγ by assimilation). It is interesting that (2) is a change that occurs independently in Sirenikski Yupik, and (3) a change that occurs independently in all Inuit-Inupiaq, proving that similar changes are not always connected historically. These changes are radical, and yet relatively recent and superficial, since underlying them, Attuan and Atkan share "morphological innovations and archaisms and a number of lexical items that distinguish them from Eastern Aleut" (Bergsland 1958:624). Therefore, it is reasonable to recognize an Eastern-Western historical division in Aleut, however much the earlier Eastern-Central-Western classification reflected the modern state of affairs.

In general, Western and Eastern Aleut innovated independently, in different ways. Of interest are a few cases where the same innovation has occurred at the two ends of the Aleut area but not in the middle. For example, Proto–Eskimo-Aleut final *t merges with *n in Attuan in the extreme west, and in all Eastern Aleut but that of nineteenth-century Umnak Island at the western end of the dialect area (Veniaminov 1846a:xii ff.); however, in late nineteenth-century Umnak and still in Atkan, final *t is realized as s and is distinct from final *n. It may be that this pattern is due to early contact, or it may be a case of independent innovation in the two areas. Whatever the explanation, such facts are a reminder that Aleut must be viewed as a complex of dialects where innovations and retentions overlap in different ways. Finally, all of Aleut innovated together during the historical period by accepting numerous loanwords first from Russian and then from American English.

It is to be expected that a single language would soon diversify when spoken over an area as large and as hostile to navigation and intercommunication as the Aleutians. If the linguistic ancestor of modern Aleut was there since Proto–Eskimo-Aleut times, it is almost certain that many Aleut-like or other unknown Eskimo-Aleut languages probably developed, diversified, and died there. The uniformity of the Aleut dialects surviving into the historical period suggests a relatively recent spread of Proto-Aleut from its place of origin over the entire island chain before the historical period, replacing all the dialects or languages spoken there. It may be that such a spread is connected in some way with the appearance of neo-Aleut artifacts around A.D. 1000 noted by archeologists (Laughlin 1958), although such an hypothesis cannot be confirmed by linguistic means.

Yupik

From Sirenikski in Siberia to Pacific Yupik in Alaska, the five Yupik languages form an intergrading chain where, in spite of considerable differences, neighbors share common innovations. Many of these innovations are old, so that while boundaries between languages may have moved from time to time, the relative geographical arrangement of the languages has probably remained constant for a great period.

Siberian Yupik

As recently as the seventeenth century it is likely that Yupik languages were spoken around the whole Chukchi Peninsula, and coastal toponyms around Anadyr´ Gulf to the southwest suggest an even broader distribution in earlier times (Dolgikh 1960; Rudenko 1961:20–22; Vdovin 1949:10). But by the beginning of the twentieth century, Yupik languages in Siberia for the most part occupied the much smaller, fragmented territory shown in figure 1, having lost ground to the advancing Chukchi. Three languages, known collectively as Siberian Yupik, Asiatic Eskimo, or Yuit (from yuγət 'people'), are clearly distinguished.

Sirenikski was confined to Sireniki village and nearby Imtuk at the beginning of the twentieth century, having once extended farther west, and by 1983 it had been replaced everywhere, except for two partial speakers, by Central Siberian Yupik, Chukchi, and Russian (Dolgikh 1972:23–24; Bogoras 1925:217, 219; Krauss 1980:10; Michael E. Krauss, personal communication 1982). It is remarkably divergent from the other Yupik languages of Siberia, with which it is mutually unintelligible (Menovshchikov 1964; Bergsland 1966).

Central Siberian Yupik, or Chaplinski in the Soviet literature, is the best-studied Siberian Yupik language (Menovshchikov 1962–1967; Rubtsova 1954, 1971; Krauss 1975a; Jacobson 1977, 1984). In the Soviet Union, where it is taken as the base for the standard form of literary Eskimo, it is spoken in villages around Chaplino and Sireniki at the southernmost corner of the Chukchi Peninsula, and since 1926 at Uel´kal´ on the Anadyr´ Gulf and on Wrangell Island in the Chukchi Sea.

Vocabularies recorded from inhabitants of Yttygran Island by J. Baer (1855) and J.M. Brooke (1855) of the John Rodgers North Pacific Exploring and Surveying Expedition show that the variety of Eskimo formerly spoken there was Chaplinski, and a former extension as far north as Mechigmen Bay, where Eskimos were still living in 1881 (Nelson 1899:27), may be indicated by the traditional connections between the Yttygran and Mechigmen groups (Krupnik and Chlenov 1979:23) and the statement of W.H. Hooper (1853:154) that the language of Lorino on Mechigmen Bay was "identical" to that of Chaplino and Kivak. Forty-two miles from Chaplino on Saint Lawrence Island, Alaska, a nearly identical dialect of Central Siberian Yupik is spoken. This similarity might be attributed to the repopulation of the island by mainlanders from the Chaplino region after a devastating famine or epidemic in 1878–1879 wiped out all but two island villages. Yet, the evidence of Saint Lawrence Island speech before the disaster—a wordlist from before 1822 (Khromchenko 1973:81–82)—reveals only a few minor differences from the modern language (Krauss 1975a:42–45). However, there is some scant dialect variation among mainlanders and among islanders that involves the same features. For example, *k and *q have become x and x̣ before voiceless continuants both at Ėstikhet (Avan) on the mainland and at Powooiliak on the island, possibly reflecting the recent migration (Krauss 1975a:44–45, 61).

Naukanski was spoken around East Cape (Mys Dezhneva) until 1958, when all speakers were relocated a short distance down the coast (Bogoras 1925:217–219; Menovshchikov 1975). In 1791 Karl Merck of the Joseph Billings expedition found Eskimos at Uélen and as far west as Cape Schmidt, but these people were assimilated by the Chukchi by the end of the nineteenth century, except for a remnant minority at Uélen (Dolgikh 1972:23). A vocabulary collected by Michael Rohbeck, on the same 1791 expedition, from Saint Lawrence Bay (Sarychev 1811:102–111), where there were still Eskimos in 1880 (Dall 1881:864), shows the former extent of Naukanski speech to the south (Michael E. Krauss, communication to editors 1983). Naukanski is at best partially mutually intelligible with Central Siberian Yupik. In an informal experiment in which Saint Lawrence Islanders and Central Alaskan Yupik speakers were played a tape-recorded Naukanski narrative, the Saint Lawrence Islanders had as much difficulty as the Central Alaskan Yupiks did in following what was said (Krauss 1980:9–10).

Alaskan Yupik

Two Yupik languages are found in Alaska, and both have well differentiated dialects.

Central Alaskan Yupik had four main dialects in 1980, and a fifth was attested in the nineteenth century. To a significant degree, the dialects do not coincide with social units recognized in standard sources (Zagoskin 1967; Nelson 1899; Oswalt 1967). Northernmost is the Norton Sound or Unaliq dialect (Swadesh 1951, 1952, 1952a, 1952b, 1952c; Jacobson 1980), which in historical times has been the only form of Yupik to share a border with Inuit-Inupiaq. It was spoken by the Unaliq, who as late as the nineteenth century were the sole inhabitants of the coast of Norton Sound from Saint Michael north to Golovnin Bay on Seward Peninsula or beyond (Ray 1975:137–138). By the mid-nineteenth century, southward movement of Qawiaraq and Malimiut Inupiaq speakers thinned the original Unaliq population north of Unalakleet, leaving small Yupik populations in the vicinity of Golovnin and Norton bays. West of Saint Michael (Kotlik and vicinity), the Norton Sound dialect is spoken in a slightly different form, called the Qiimiut dialect.

A second dialect is confined to the coastal villages of Hooper Bay and Chevak north of Nelson Island (Woodbury 1981; Jacobson 1983). No known tribal designation corresponds uniquely to this group, who have been assigned incorrectly to the General-Central-Yupik-speak-

Table 1. Speakers of Eskimo-Aleut Languages, 1980

	Population	Number of speakers
Aleut	2,000	700
Eskimo		
Yupik		
Sirenikski	—	2
Central Siberian	800 (USSR)	400
	1,050 (USA)	1,050
Naukanski	350	100
Central Alaskan	17,000	14,000
Pacific	3,000	1,000
Inuit-Inupiaq		
Alaska	12,000	5,000
Canada	24,000	20,000
Greenland	43,000[a]	43,000[a]
Total	103,200	85,252

SOURCES: Krauss 1979, 1980; Michael E. Krauss and L.J. Dorais, personal communications 1982.

[a] 2,000 in Denmark.

ing tribes to the northwest or south, the Maarmiut (Zagoskin 1967:210) or the Kayaligmiut (Nelson 1899:26, pl. II). It appears however that the significant social units were the two large and closely allied winter villages (Naparyaarmiut and Qissunamiut) that became modern Hooper Bay and Chevak (Woodbury 1978). Third and most divergent is the dialect of the Nunivak Island Eskimo (Khromchenko 1973:72–75; Hammerich 1953; Jacobson 1979, 1983). Nunivak Central Yupik is sometimes known as čux, from its cognate of yuk, the word for 'person' in most other Yupik (see table 2), but despite the phonological differences reflected there, it is mutually intelligible with the mainland dialects. The fourth modern dialect, General Central Yupik, has been by far the most widespread in the historical period and is described in greatest detail (Barnum 1901; Hinz 1944; Reed et al. 1977; sketch of Yupik in vol. 17). Within the General Central Yupik area tribal boundaries cut across the linguistic divisions, which can be described as an innovative "core" subdialect (Kuskokwim River below Aniak, and south along the coast from the Kuskokwim mouth to Bristol Bay), a conservative "peripheral" subdialect (Kuskokwim River above Aniak, Yukon River, Lake Iliamna), and mixed subdialects (Nelson Island, Nushagak River) (Jacobson 1983). Thus Kusquqvagmiut territory along the Kuskokwim is linguistically bisected, and in the complex Nushagak River area more linguistic research is needed even to associate subdialects and tribal affiliations.

A fifth dialect, attested only in the nineteenth century, is that of the Aglurmiut, called Aglëgmiut by the Russians. They inhabited the coastal Bristol Bay–Alaska Peninsula region in the 1820s but reportedly had earlier been forced there—and perhaps also to Nunivak Island—from the lower Kuskokwim–Nelson Island area by the Kusquqvagmiut (VanStone 1967:xxi, 118–121; Oswalt 1967:4–5). A few nineteenth-century Aglurmiut vocabularies were recorded (Voevodskiĭ 1858; Khromchenko 1973:54–56), and they indicate a Central Alaskan Yupik dialect with important similarities to that of Nunivak, but also some differences (Miyaoka 1974:78). Although many twentieth-century Bristol Bay residents identify themselves as Aglurmiut, the dialect preserved in the early vocabularies has disappeared (Steven A. Jacobson, personal communication 1982). A wordlist labeled as taken on the Gulf of Alaska near Mount Saint Elias (Voevodskiĭ 1858) has been found to represent a dialect with close affinities to nineteenth-century Aglurmiut (Miyaoka 1974). However, the Mount Saint Elias location is almost certainly erroneous, and the identification of this dialect with the Cilqarmiut of Controller Bay and Kayak Island (Miyaoka 1974), otherwise considered an abberant branch of the easternmost Chugach Pacific Yupik subtribe (Birket-Smith 1953:20), remains uncertain (Michael E. Krauss, personal communication 1982).

The broad patterns of Central Alaskan Yupik dialect geography suggest a rapid and relatively recent expansion of General Central Yupik that left the Nunivak and Hooper Bay–Chevak dialects in geographically isolated pockets. The distribution of General Central Yupik may reflect more recent connections between the lower Kuskokwim and Bristol Bay as the nineteenth-century Aglurmiut receded southward from there and their dialect disappeared. A grading of dialects from Norton Sound to General Central Yupik to Hooper Bay–Chevak to Nunivak is indicated by some complexes of phonological innovations, particularly those pertaining to rhythmic accent. Insofar as this reflects earlier geographical contiguities, it suggests that General Central Yupik may have spread from the region of the lower Yukon, between the Norton Sound and Hooper Bay–Chevak dialect areas. The position of nineteenth-century Aglurmiut is not clear from the scanty information available, and of course it is not possible to know from present linguistic evidence what was spoken to the immediate south and east of the dialects mentioned. However, nineteenth-century Aglurmiut shares some features with Nunivak and Pacific Yupik, and it has been suggested that it may have been a link in a dialect continuum extending from Hooper Bay–Chevak and Nunivak Central Alaskan Yupik, to Pacific Yupik (Michael E. Krauss, personal communication 1982).

Pacific Yupik, also called šuk/suk, Sugpiaq, Sugcestun, and, in Alaska, Alutiiq or Aleut, is clearly distinct from Central Alaskan Yupik. The Koniag dialect has two subdialects: Kodiak, spoken on Kodiak and Afognak islands (Leer 1978), and the Alaska Peninsula subdialect, spoken on the Alaska Peninsula as far west as Port Moller and Perryville, where it borders with Aleut (Leer 1977a). The varieties of the Koniag dialect spoken at Perryville (brought there from Katmai, opposite Kodiak Island) and Port Lions on Kodiak (originally from Afognak Island) share an apical fricative devoicing rule (ł for l and s for y, in some environments), in contrast to the rest of Koniag. This suggests that there may have been an earlier Shelikoff Strait subdialect of Koniag (Jeff Leer, personal communication 1982). It is not known whether the early nineteenth-century Alaska Peninsula Eskimos, who were replaced or absorbed by the 1850s by the Aglurmiut advance southward into their area (Oswalt 1967:4–5), were speakers of Pacific Yupik, Central Alaskan Yupik, or some intermediate form along an early coastal dialect continuum running from Central Alaskan to Pacific Yupik. Chugach, the other Pacific Yupik dialect, consists of a Prince William Sound subdialect spoken by the Chugach tribe proper, and a Kenai Peninsula subdialect, spoken by the Unegkurmiut (Leer 1978b, 1978a).

Classification and Prehistory

The Yupik languages of Siberia and Alaska were separated in 1800 by the Bering Strait, and by Inupiaq territory between the tip of Seward Peninsula and Golovnin Bay on its south coast. But in prehistoric times, Yupik languages almost certainly were spoken all the way across Seward Peninsula. Since the Bering Strait is known to have been crossed regularly by Eskimos from both sides, this must have amounted to a continuous Yupik-speaking region from Siberia to the southern parts of Alaska. The geographical configuration of Yupik and Inuit-Inupiaq has by itself long suggested to linguists that an Inuit-Inupiaq wedge entered the Yupik area and divided it (Hammerich 1960:87), and this view has been confirmed by emerging linguistic evidence that the Yupik languages form an intergrading chain in which neighbors—including those separated by the Inuit-Inupiaq wedge—share linguistic innovations. The chain follows the modern geographical arrangement of the languages: Sirenikski, Central Siberian Yupik, Naukanski, Central Alaskan Yupik, Pacific Yupik. A crude index of this chaining is the fact that each Yupik language is closest to being mutually intelligible with its nearest Yupik neighbors. Some of the better phonological evidence for the intergrading of the Yupik languages is reviewed here, especially that which may reflect early patterns of communication around the entire Yupik area.

A dramatic demonstration of Yupik intergrading is based on a complex of automatic accentual rules in Yupik phonology (Leer 1977). The simplest and perhaps most conservative accentual pattern is found in Central Siberian Yupik. Proceeding to Alaska, the accentual system becomes more and more complex from dialect to dialect, in this order: Norton Sound, General Central Yupik, Hooper Bay–Chevak, Nunivak, Kon-

Table 2. Comparative Yupik Vocabulary

	1	2	3 _indicative mood, first person sing._ subject[a]	4	5	6	7
	'blood'	'one'		'hear'	'drum'	'saliva'	'search'
Proto-Eskimo	*ařuk	*ataẏučiq	*-tu-ŋa	*naγa-t(ə)-	*čaγuyaq	*nuvak	*ivaẏ-
Sirenikski	acəx	ataẏəsix	-tə-ŋ	(tunəẏaẏ-)	saγəyax	yuvəx	?
Central Siberian Yupik	aakʷ	ataasiq	-tu-ŋa	naγa-tə-	saγuyaq	nuvak	ivaẏ-
Naukanski	aakʷ	ataasiq	-tu-a	nii-tə-	saγuyaq	nuvak	ivaẏ-
Norton Sound	auk	ataučiq	-tu-a	nii-tə-	čauyaq	nuak	yuaẏ-
General Central Yupik	auk	ataučiq	-tu-a	nii-tə-	čauyaq	nuak	yuaẏ-
Hooper Bay–Chevak	auk	ataučiq	-tu-a	nii-tə-	čauyaq	nuvak	ivaẏ-
Nunivak	aux	ataučix	-tu-a	nii-tə-	čauyax	nuvax	ivaẏ-
Koniag	auk	(atẋiluq, ał·iluq)	-tu-a	nii-tə-	čauya-t ('music')	naux-łuk	iwa-
Chugach	auk	(ał·iŋuq)	-tu-a	nii-tə-	čauya-t ('music')	naux-łuk	yuaẏ-aa-
Proto–Inuit-Inupiaq	*ařuk	*atausiq	*-tu-ŋa	*naa-lak-	*sauyaq	*nuvak	*ivaq-

[a] Only the post-consonantal allomorph is cited here.
[b] From an intermediate form *iuẏ-.
[c] Perhaps a loan from Central Siberian Yupik, since **qicə- would be expected.
[d] y occurs only when a vowel-initial suffix follows.
[e] Chevak only; Hooper Bay has yuk, probably a loan from General Central Yupik.

iag, Chugach. In each dialect beginning with Norton Sound, existing rules are modified or new rules are added, and the modifications and additions are shared, for the most part, by all the succeeding dialects in sequence. The following illustrates a part of this. In Central Siberian Yupik, a rule of rhythmic accent puts an accent (indicated here by ˆ) on every second syllable (syllables being here separated by dots): for example, nəẏ.yû.γa.qâ.tu 'and I want to eat it'. (In Yupik languages, accented syllables have rising pitch and, if they end in a vowel, increased duration.) All the Alaskan forms of Yupik complicate this simple pattern by adding a rule by which word-initial closed syllables (those ending in a consonant) are accented. Then, rhythmic accent is counted from that initial accent, thus Norton Sound nəẏ.yu.γâ.qa.łû. Next in line, General Central Yupik and the dialects beyond it modify rhythmic accent with accent retraction, a rule that eliminates sequences in which an unaccented closed syllable precedes an accented open syllable: compare Norton Sound ča.ŋâ.tən.ẏî.tu.kût 'we are all right', which has the sequence accent retraction is meant to avoid (tən.ẏî), with the same word in General Central Yupik, ča.ŋâ.tân.ẏi.tû.kut. Accent retraction converts tən.ẏî to tân.ẏi in General Central Yupik, and then rhythmic accent proceeds as usual to the end of the word. Innovations continue to accumulate in this way, and Pacific Yupik, at the end of the chain, attests an accentual system of phenomenal complexity. (Owing to the lack of adequate phonetic data, the status of Sirenikski and Naukanski accent is uncertain; however, preliminary investigations show Sirenikski to have recently superimposed the Central Siberian pattern on a more archaic and radically different system, and Naukanski to have a system basically like Central Siberian Yupik, but with some attraction of accent to initial and non-initial closed syllables counteracting rhythmic accent—Krauss 1982).

Because rhythmic accent—and perhaps other rules too—is shared across the Bering Strait, historical contact between Yupik groups on both sides can be inferred. That contact must have been early, since rhythmic accent is probably an old rule (because there are a number of phonological innovations, known to be old themselves, that clearly applied to the output of rhythmic accent). There is also a more unexpected way in which the Yupik accentual system indicates a continuous Yupik area across Bering Strait: it appears, in phonetically different form, in Bering Strait Inupiaq. In fact this dialect, spoken at the tip of the Seward Peninsula and on adjacent islands, reflects exactly the accentual pattern of Norton Sound Yupik (Leer 1977:11–13; Krauss 1979:825; Lawrence D. Kaplan, personal communication 1982), for example, Bering Strait (King Island) man.ni.ẏaq.tu.ut (reflecting underlying /mânni-qâq-tu-γût/) 'we have eggs', versus ma.ni.qa·.tu.γut (reflecting underlying /manî-qaq-tû-γut/) 'we have money'. In Bering Strait Inupiaq, the underlying accent is not heard as rising pitch and increased duration, as it is in Yupik. Instead, it is reflected by the lenition of consonants following _unaccented_ syllabic nuclei, as shown in the examples above. (Here the lenition is the weakening of q to ẏ, or to zero before a consonant, and of γ to zero.)

Table 2. Continued

8	9	10	11	12
'jell, stiffen'	'cry'	'wing'	'person'	'here'
*iɣřuɣ-, *iɣřuɣ-t(ə)-	*qiřa-	*iyaquq	*iŋuk ?	*uv-a-ni ?
?	qiyə-ᶜ	yaqəx	yux	ma-ni
iɣux-tə-	qiya-	yaquq	yuuk	xʷa-ni
iɣuɣ-	qiya-	yaquq	yuk	ɣʷa-ni
iɣuɣ-	qia-/qəya-	yaquq	yuk	ɣʷa-ni
əyuɣ-ᵇ	qia-/qəya-	yaquq	yuk	xʷa-ni
iɣuɣ-	qəya-	čaquq	čukᵉ	ɣʷa-ni
iɣuɣ-	qia-	čaqəx	čux	kʷa-ni
iɣux-tə-	qi(y)a-ᵈ	saquq	suk	ɣʷa-ni
yux-tə-	qi(y)a-ᵈ	saqəq	suk	xʷa-ni
*iɣřuq-	*qiřa-	*isaɣuq	*inuk	*uva-ni

This Inupiaq reflex of a Yupik pattern points to earlier communities in the region whose members were bilingual in Inupiaq and a form of Yupik resembling the Norton Sound dialect. It is not possible to determine whether the pattern arose as Yupik speakers became speakers of Inupiaq, or as bilingual Inupiaq speakers introduced a Yupik pattern into their own language.

The intergrading of Yupik languages is also revealed in the degree to which they have lost the Proto-Eskimo continuants *w, *ř, *γ, *ẏ, and *ŋ between vowels. In table 2 items 1–9 are cognate sets that illustrate some of the principal trends, with boxes enclosing those forms from which the Proto-Eskimo continuants have been lost in accordance with certain partially known rules (Bergsland 1967:208–214; Miyaoka 1976). Continuant loss escalates as one proceeds from west to east: Sirenikski is the most conservative (see items 1–2); next is Central Siberian Yupik (3–4); next Naukanski (5–9); and finally the Alaska Yupik languages. Thus Naukanski and to a lesser extent Central Siberian Yupik shared developments with their American neighbors across the Bering Strait. Within Alaskan Yupik, however, the pattern is different from that revealed by the distribution of accentual rules: innovations in General Central Yupik and usually Norton Sound Central Yupik did not reach Hooper Bay–Chevak and Nunivak (6–8). Meanwhile, what may well be an independent innovative trend is found in Pacific Yupik (6–8). Finally, certain individual lexical items follow more or less idiosyncratic patterns (9). In conclusion, intervocalic continuant loss reveals a more ancient layer of shared in-

novations among Alaskan Yupik, Naukanski, and, to a lesser degree, Central Siberian Yupik, and a set of more recent innovative trends in parts of Alaska that points to complicated patterns of intergroup contacts.

Table 2 also illustrates other, relatively local developments in Yupik languages. Phonological developments include: (i) the widespread reduction to ə of vowels in non-initial syllables in Sirenikski; (ii) the change of final *k and *q to x and χ in Sirenikski and Nunivak (see items 1, 2, 6, 10, 11); (iii) the change of *č to s in all Siberian Yupik (see 2, 5); (iv) the assimilation of vowel clusters in Central Siberian Yupik and Naukanski (see 1, 2); and (v) the different patterns of initial syllable loss in all forms of Yupik (see 10, 11, and 12). A few lexical developments are also illustrated in table 2, although a randomly chosen wordlist would probably show many more. In some instances a different word is used for a particular meaning (see item 2, Koniag and Chugach), and in some instances a partially similar word (see items 6, 7, Koniag and Chugach). Sometimes, a particular form is preserved in a daughter language, but its meaning changes (see item 5, Koniag and Chugach).

Siberian Yupik and Alaskan Yupik Subgroups

When Central Siberian Yupik was the only Asiatic Eskimo language for which extensive information was available, it appeared that a unified Proto-Yupik had early on divided into sharply distinct Siberian and Alaskan subgroups (Hammerich 1958). However, with Naukanski and especially Sirenikski better known a two-way division of this kind appears much less likely, because it is very difficult to find innovations common to all three Siberian languages and attributable to a time when they were distinct from Alaskan Yupik but not from each other. It seems, then, that the term Siberian Yupik does not correspond to a genetic subgroup, but it serves as a useful label for a group of languages sharing some of their recent history. Especially important is the incorporation into all three languages of a large body of loans from Chukchi, including very basic adverbial particles and connectives, for example, Central Siberian Yupik řəpał 'even, in fact, so much so that' (Chukchi ripet 'even'), and qənwat 'at last, finally' (Chukchi qinwer 'at last') (Steven A. Jacobson, personal communication 1983; Moll and Inénlikeĭ 1957). This suggests that the Chukchi-Yupik bilingualism found among Siberian Eskimos in the twentieth century is at least several centuries old. Finally, some common phonetic innovations are very recent. For example, recordings of Central Siberian Yupik as late as 1901 indicate that *č had not yet become s universally in that dialect (compare 'one' and 'drum', table 2) (Bogoras 1925:217–218; Krauss 1975a:45).

A somewhat better case might be made for the genetic unity of Alaskan Yupik. For example, initial-closed-syllable accent is characteristic of all forms and may be rather early. There are also lexical innovations and retentions characteristic of Alaskan Yupik. In historical times, the already distinct Alaskan Yupik languages and their dialects underwent many common developments, most notably the acquisition of many loans from Russian and then American English. (In contrast, the Siberian Yupik languages received English loans from American whalers and traders in the nineteenth century, and into the 1920s—Michael E. Krauss, personal communication 1982). Therefore, the grouping together of Central Alaskan and Pacific Yupik reflects the recent if not also the earliest history of those languages.

Inuit-Inupiaq

Inuit-Inupiaq, or Eastern Eskimo, is a continuum of dialects—more closely related to each other historically than are the Yupik languages—that stretches from the Seward Peninsula in Alaska across Arctic Canada down to the coasts of Quebec and Labrador, and up to the coasts of Greenland. While mutual intelligibility between contiguous dialects is generally high, speakers of widely separated dialects may have great difficulty understanding each other. From a speaker's viewpoint, the range of difference within Inuit-Inupiaq may even approach that within Yupik, and were the Inuit-Inupiaq continuum less smooth it would be possible to divide it into several mutually unintelligible languages. Important isoglosses demarcate four regions—Alaska, Western Canada, Eastern Canada, and Greenland—but these in no way constitute genetic units, since there are other equally significant isoglosses cutting across them. By far the greatest dialect diversity is found in Alaska and Greenland, while Canada is relatively uniform. Accordingly, the terms dialect and subdialect have different ranges in each area.

Inuit-Inupiaq has also been called Inupik (Swadesh 1951), but this term, coined from Inuit-Inupiaq inu(k)- 'person' and Yupik -pik 'genuine', is not correct in any variety of Eskimo and is not used by specialists.

Alaska

Collectively called Inupiaq, the four main Alaska dialects are paired into two groups: Bering Strait and Qawiaraq (Seward Peninsula group), and Malimiut and North Slope (North Alaska group) (see fig. 1). Bering Strait Inupiaq has three subdialects, one at Wales and Shishmaref on Seward Peninsula, one originally on the two Diomede islands straddling the USA-USSR frontier in the Bering Strait (now extinct in the USSR), and one on King Island to the southeast (abandoned for Nome in the 1960s) (Jenness 1927; Menovshchikov 1980a;

Kaplan 1981a, 1982, 1982a). Qawiaraq Inupiaq was transported by inhabitants of the Kuzitrin River to Shaktoolik and Unalakleet on Norton Sound beginning in the second half of the nineteenth century. Along with the early historical inhabitants of the Nome area, these groups spoke one of the two Qawiaraq subdialects. The other has been spoken in the Fish River region on Norton Sound at least since the mid-nineteenth century (Ray 1975:104; Burch 1980; Kaplan 1982a). Malimiut Inupiaq has a southern subdialect that was brought from the Buckland region near Kotzebue Sound to the eastern shore of Norton Sound. Along with those of the Qawiaraq, this group's movements are responsible for the thinning of Yupik populations between Golovnin Bay and Unalakleet. Farther north is the Kobuk River subdialect (including the Kotzebue and Selawik areas), and the Noatak River subdialect, which is transitional to North Slope Inupiaq (Ray 1975:130–139; Burch 1980; Kaplan 1981, 1982a). North Slope Inupiaq is quite uniform across a broad area but has divergent subdialects at Point Hope and among the inland Nunamiut. A North Slope form with Nunamiut affinities was brought to the Mackenzie Delta (around Aklavik and Inuvik) in the nineteenth and twentieth centuries (Kaplan 1981; Edna A. MacLean, personal communication 1982; Dorais and Lowe 1982).

Western Canada

Western Canada has four main dialects, and for the most part they correspond to the well-known social units. Westernmost is Mackenzie Coast (or Chiglit Inuvialuktun), centered around Tuktoyaktuk. It is in close contact with newly arrived North Slope Inupiaq, and the two have converged to a degree (Petitot 1876a; MacLean 1981; Edna A. McLean, personal communication 1982; Dorais and Lowe 1982). Next is Copper; texts show that there are subdialects (Rasmussen 1932; Métayer 1973), but no systematic dialectology has been done, and existing description is sketchy (Jenness 1928, 1944). Netsilik has at least two subdialects, one spoken by the Netsilingmiut proper, and the other by the Utkuhikhalingmiut. Between these two groups, close social ties existed (Rasmussen 1931; Webster and Zibell 1976; Damas 1969b:135; Thomas C. Correll, personal communication 1982). Caribou is divided into five subdialects corresponding to regional subgroups: Hauniqtuurmiut, Qairnirmiut, Harvaqtuurmiut, Ahiarmiut, and Paallirmiut (Webster and Zibell 1976).

Eastern Canada

Six main dialects have been recognized in Eastern Canada (Dorais 1977). Iglulik has two well-differentiated subdialects, Aivilingmiut and Iglulingmiut, spoken by subdivisions of the Iglulik. A third subdivision, the Tununirmiut of northeastern Baffin Island, also speak the Iglulingmiut subdialect (Mathiassen 1928:15–36; Dorais 1976, 1978a; K. Harper 1974, 1979). Two dialects are spoken in the southern part of Baffin Island: Southeast Baffin Eskimo (Southeast Baffin Inuktitut) from Cumberland Sound to Lake Harbour, and Kinngarmiut (Cape Dorset Inuktitut) in the southwest (K. Harper 1974, 1979; Dorais 1975, 1975a). The final three dialects, Itivimmiut (on Eastern Hudson Bay), Tarramiut (on Hudson Strait), and Labrador Eskimo (Labrador Inuttut), correspond to social and linguistic groups identified by L. Turner (1894); since then, Tarramiut has displaced Labrador Eskimo on the south and east coasts of Ungava Bay. Labrador Eskimo was first recorded in 1694 (Dorais 1980, 1980a), and has two subdialects, a uniquely conservative one in the south around Rigolet, as well as a remarkably innovative one to the north of it. In the northern area, elderly speakers who are members of the Moravian Church have preserved many features lost in the speech of others, perhaps under the influence of the Eskimo literary tradition fostered by the Moravians since the 1870s. Two-way subdialectal splits of lesser importance are found in the two Quebec dialects (Schneider 1966, 1970; Dorais 1975b, 1978, 1980; Bourquin 1891; L.R. Smith 1975).

Greenland

There are three main dialect areas on the coasts of Greenland. Polar Eskimo (North Greenlandic) is spoken in the extreme northwest above Melville Bay; it is geographically isolated and shows little internal dialectal variation (Holtved 1951, 1952). West Greenlandic is a complex of dialects with some significant differences and is by far the best-studied form of Eskimo-Aleut (Kleinschmidt 1851; Thalbitzer 1904; Bergsland 1955). The Central subdialect (Holsteinsborg to Fiskenæsset, including Godthåb) was the earliest to be documented in detail (Egede 1750, 1760; Fabricius 1804). Long taken as the spoken and written standard for all of Greenland,

it has made significant inroads into the other dialects. To the north are the Northern West Greenlandic (Disko Bay, Uummannaq) and Upernavik subdialects; the latter is sharply divergent from the rest and has East Greenlandic rather than North Greenlandic affinities. To the south are the Southern West Greenlandic subdialect (including the transitional Paamiut dialect at its northern edge) and Cape Farewell (Kap Farvel) subdialect (Thalbitzer 1904; Petersen 1969–1970, 1977; Rischel 1974, 1975, 1978; Fortescue 1981). When the Cape Farewell subdialect was recorded in 1914, the Cape Farewell area included recent East-Greenlandic–speaking immigrants from the east coast south of Ammassalik, which was completely abandoned by 1900 (Thalbitzer 1923:496–523; Petersen 1982). The dialect is in some ways transitional between West and East Greenlandic, being perhaps essentially a Southern West Greenlandic variety affected by the influx of East Greenlanders (Petersen 1982). In 1980 it was much closer lexically to the West Greenlandic dialects to the north of it than it was to East Greenlandic (Michael D. Fortescue, personal communication 1982). East Greenlandic was spoken in 1980 at Ammassalik, and at Scoresbysund to the north, which was settled in the twentieth century by natives of Ammassalik. According to native reports, dialect variation existed when greater portions of the coast were populated (Thalbitzer 1923:152–153), and a Southeast variety, spoken by those between Ammassalik and Cape Farewell, has been recognized (Petersen 1982). Since that time, some slight differences even at Ammassalik have been noted (Petersen 1977:2). Both phonologically and lexically, East Greenlandic is radically divergent from Central West Greenlandic (Thalbitzer 1923; Dorais 1981a; Gessain, Dorais, and Enel 1982).

Internal Linguistic Relations

It is assumed that the prehistoric bearers of Thule culture in north Alaska and then in the Central and Eastern

Smithsonian, Natl. Philatelic Coll.

Fig. 2. Greenlandic postage stamps. First issued in 1938 with the name of the country in Danish (left), beginning in 1969 issues had the name in Danish and Greenlandic (center), and in 1978 a change was made to the new Greenlandic orthography (right).

Table 3.   Inuit-Inupiaq Comparative Vocabulary

	1 'knife'	2 'cook, boil'	3 'people'	4 'enter'	5 'eye'
Proto-Eskimo	*čavik	*əγa-	*iŋuγ-(ə)t ?	*itəγ̇-	*ə̌řə
Bering Strait	sawik/čawik[a]	ia-/əa-[f]	inuit	itiq-/itaq-[f]	iři
North Alaska	savik/havik[b]	iγa-	inʸuič	isiq-/ihiq-[b]	iři
Mackenzie Coast	čavik	iγa-	inuit	itiq-	iyi
Copper	havik	iγa-	inuit	itiq-/ihiq-	iyi
Netsilik	(pilaut)[c]	iγa-	inuit	ihiq-	iři
Caribou	(pilaut)[c]/savik	iγa-	inuit	itiq-	iyi
Iglulik	savik	iγa-	inuit	itiq-/isiq-[i]	iyi
Southern Baffin	savik	iγa-	inuit	isiq-/itiq-[j]	iyi
Quebec	savik	iγa-	inuit	itiq-	iyi
Labrador	savik	iγa-	inuit	itiq-	iyi
Polar Eskimo	havik	iγa-	inuit	ihiq-	ihi
West Greenlandic	savik	iγa-/iŋa-[g]	inuit/inivit[h]	isiq-	iši/isi[k]
East Greenlandic	(pilagtaq)[d] /(pilaalaq)[e]	iŋa-	ii(vi)t	isiq-	(takungit)[d] /ili/(uitsat)[e]

[a] Second form: Fish River Qawiaraq.
[b] Second form: Nunamiut.
[c] Because of the lexical difference, this form does not show the reflex of *č, which is h in this subdialect.
[d] From Hanseeraq's 1884 wordlist, in West Greenlandic-based orthography (Rink 1914).
[e] Cited in Gessain, Dorais, and Enel 1982.
[f] Second form: Diomedes.
[g] Second form: Upernavik, Northern West Greenland, Cape Farewell.
[h] Second form: Upernavik, Southern West Greenland, Cape Farewell.
[i] Aivilingmiut/Iglulingmiut.
[j] Southeast Baffin/Cape Dorset.
[k] Conservative Central West Greenlandic/other West Greenlandic.
[l] Second form: Cape Farewell.

Arctic were speakers of earlier forms of Inuit-Inupiaq. Hypotheses of migration and intergroup communication during that millennium of spread must take into account the patterns of linguistic innovation and retention that such historical events have created in the modern Inuit-Inupiaq dialects. Typically, migrations are reflected linguistically by discontinuities, such as those brought about by the well-documented Qawiaraq and Malimiut movements into the Norton Sound area. However, when an isolated linguistic innovation is found in two separate regions, it is not sufficient evidence for migration, because it is very common for closely related languages or dialects to develop the same innovation independently. Table 3 presents 11 word sets illustrating nine important phonological innovations and one complex of lexical innovations. They are discussed below.

• LENITION   Under accentual conditions borrowed from Yupik, intervocalic p, s, k, and q in some Seward peninsula Inupiaq may become voiced fricatives (v, z, γ, and γ̇, respectively), for example, niγ̇i 'meat', other Inuit-Inupiaq niqi; v becomes w; and γ and γ̇ are deleted (as in table 3, items 1–2). This process is most productive in the Bering Strait dialect (Kaplan 1982a, Lawrence D. Kaplan, personal communication 1982).

• ELIMINATION OF THE FOURTH VOWEL *ə   Except in the Bering Strait Inupiaq of the Diomedes, where it is preserved under some conditions (Kaplan 1981a, 1982),

Proto-Eskimo *ə in Inuit-Inupiaq merges with *i under most conditions (otherwise it disappears or merges with one of the other vowels). This is shown by item 7 and, with unusual Diomede forms, 4 and 8. *ə is preserved in all Yupik.

• PROGRESSIVE ASSIBILATION   After *i (but not *ə), Proto-Eskimo *t assibilates to s (which becomes h in some areas) in North Alaska, Greenland, and sporadically in Canada: compare item 4, *itəq- 'enter', attested as isiq- or ihiq- in those dialects, with *ətəq 'anus', attested as itiq in all Inuit-Inupiaq. In the former but not the latter, *t follows *i (Rischel 1974:260–275; Kaplan 1981:76–115).

• PROGRESSIVE PALATALIZATION   In North Alaska, alveolar consonants—and in Kobuk Malimiut also velars—palatalize after Proto-Eskimo *i (but not *ə): see the reflexes of final *t in table 3, items 3 and 8, and of the nasal in *činə, which appears as nʸ in North Alaska (sinʸi), but as n elsewhere. (The controversial *ŋ in item 3 might have become *n or even *nʸ before the palatalization discussed here occurred; see Bergsland 1967; Miyaoka 1976.) Progressive palatalization has been found only in dialects that attest progressive assibilation and is likely to be a further extension of the same pattern. Thus Kobuk Malimiut, with progressive palatalization of velars, is most innovative, and Alaskan and Canadian dialects lacking even assibilation are most conservative

Table 3. Continued

6 'two'	7 'feather/hair (fur)'	8 'thou'	9 'eyebrow'	10 'bearded seal'	11 'blubber/oil'
*malẏuk	*məlquq	*əlpit	*qavluq	*uɣřuk	*uqřuq
malẏuk/maẏluuk^f	mitquq/mətquq^f	ilvin/ivlin^f	qavluq	uɣřuk	uqŘuq
malẏuk	mitquq	ilvič	qavluq	uɣřuk	uxŘuq
malẏuk	mitquq	ilvit	qavlu	uɣɣuk	uqčuq
malẏuk/malẏuuk	mitquq	ilvit	qavlu	uɣɣuk	uqhuq
mařẏuk/malẏuk	(huluit)	iřvit/ilvit	qavlu	uɣřuk	uqhuq
malẏuk/maẏẏuk	mitquq/miqquq	iɣvit/ilvit	qavlu	uɣɣuk	uqhuq/uqsuq
maẏẏuuk	miqquq	ivvit/iɣvit	qavlu/qallu^i	uɣɣuk	uqsuq
maẏẏuuk	miqquq	ivvit/iɣvit^j	qallu	uɣɣuk	uqsuq
maẏẏuuk	miqquq	ivvit	qallu	uyyuk	uqsuq
maẏẏuuk	miqquk	ivvit	qallu	uyyuk	utsuk
maẏluk	miqquq	ivlit	qavlu	uɣhuk	uɣhuq
ma^γlluk	miqquq	illit/ittit^l	qallu	uššuk/ussuk^k	u^γššuq/u^γssuq^k
ma^γttik	(qalequtit)^d /miqqiq	ittit	?	(angneq)^d	(mingugtoq)^d/u^γttuq /(amaqqaaq)^e

(Kaplan 1981:115). Progressive assibilation and palatalization are relatively early innovations, since they had to have preceded the merger of *i and *ə.

• REFLEXES OF PROTO-ESKIMO *y, *ř, AND *č Reflexes of these consonants are summarized in table 4 and illustrated in table 3. Phonologically, Canadian and Greenlandic dialects have innovated in divergent directions. In Canada, *ř merges with *č following *k or *q; in other environments, *ř merges with *y, except in some but not all forms of Netsilik (Rasmussen 1931; Michael D. Fortescue, personal communication 1982; Webster and Zibell 1976:276). In conservative Central West Greenlandic dialects, neither of these mergers takes place, but there and in all other Greenlandic, *kř falls together with *ɣř, and *qř falls together with *ẏř (compare items 10–11 in table 3). In all other Greenlandic too, all reflexes of *ř merge with those of *č. Because a complete merger cannot be reversed in cases like these, the conservative Central West Greenlandic system could not have developed from a Canadian-type system, nor could the opposite have taken place. However, it is logically possible for an innovative Greenlandic system to have developed from a Canadian system that lacks the merger of *ř and *y. Fortescue (1983) discusses some of these points.

Phonetically, *č has its original value as an affricate only in isolated locations in Western Canada and Alaska but becomes s or h elsewhere. It is likely that the h reflex resulted from a shift of *s to h that occurred late enough to have affected the reflexes of *ř (see item 11 in table 3) and of assibilated *t (see item 4) after they had merged with *č in Polar Eskimo and parts of the west.

• METATHESIS *lẏ and *lv (see table 3, items 6 and 8) are among the consonant clusters that undergo metathesis in Greenland as well as in the Diomedes. However, in Greenland *lv metathesis is sporadic; only metathesis involving *ẏ is regular there.

• CONSONANT CLUSTER ASSIMILATION In all Inuit-Inupiaq dialects there are classes of Proto-Eskimo consonant clusters that undergo partial or total assimilation. Proceeding eastward from Alaska, more and more are affected. Some idea of this complicated pattern is conveyed in table 3, items 6–11, where an enclosure is drawn around those reflexes attesting assimilation. These particular data do not happen to illustrate some other assimilations that begin as far west as Alaska, as in Malimiut itna 'thus' (contrast mannik 'egg'), but North Slope and points east inna (like mannik). However, in Canada, they show a stepwise increase in assimilation beginning with Copper and progressing east to North Baffin Island, south to East Hudson Bay via Cape Dorset, and east again to Labrador (Dorais 1977; Creider 1981). Though not identical, Polar Eskimo shows a

59

western Canadian stage of assimilation (Fortescue 1983a), and other Greenlandic shows a stage close to Quebec dialects. In Labrador and West Greenland, many unassimilated clusters are attested in the eighteenth and even nineteenth centuries (Bourquin 1891; L.R. Smith 1975; Dorais 1980; Egede 1750, 1760).

• HARMONIC UNROUNDING (*u>i) In Upernavik, South, and Cape Farewell West Greenlandic, as well as in East Greenlandic, some instances of *u in non-initial syllables become i or iv when not "protected" by nearby labials: see items 3, 6, 7 in table 3 (Petersen 1969–1970:331–332, 1977; Rischel 1975, 1978; Dorais 1981a).

• NASALIZATION OF INTERVOCALIC *γ In nearly the same set of West Greenlandic dialects and in East Greenlandic, intervocalic *γ becomes ŋ at least in some instances (item 2). This innovation has to an extent been undone in the twentieth century in some of northern West Greenlandic (Rischel 1974:167–173).

• LEXICAL INNOVATION IN EAST GREENLANDIC When visited in 1884–1885 and later, East Greenlanders avoided the names of deceased persons, and, since many personal names were taken from the ordinary lexicon, lexical turnover was greatly accelerated. In addition, other systems of lexical avoidance probably operated (Dorais 1981a:44–47). While the same observances are reported in many other Eskimo areas, the effect on the lexicon was greater in East Greenlandic, since there was less contact with other groups who would preserve the avoided word. Nevertheless, the geographical extent of East Greenlandic in the nineteenth century suggests transmission of lexical innovation beyond the community in which the avoidance was originally observed (Petersen 1982). The 1884 recordings of items 5 and 11 in table 3 are known to be avoidance terms and literally mean 'instrument for seeing' and 'that which greases', obvious circumlocutions for 'eye' and 'blubber'. Later, forms of the older words were recorded, perhaps due to new contact with West Greenlanders, as were yet further circumlocutions.

Discussion

At one level these few innovations illustrate something of the basis for dialect definition and classification: lenition (or deletion) of intervocalic consonants and retention of *ə distinguish Seward Peninsula Inupiaq and subparts, and suggest close contact with Yupik; progressive assibilation and palatalization distinguish North Alaskan Inupiaq; different mergers of *y, *ř, and *č distinguish modern Canada and modern Greenland from each other and from conservative Alaska; degrees of consonant cluster assimilation especially define Eastern Canada, but other regions too; and an unusual degree of lexical innovation is characteristic of East Greenlandic.

These innovations also show some geographical discontinuities, which then have to be interpreted historically. Assibilation and metathesis might suggest an Alaska-Greenland connection. The first of these is at least as old as the loss of *ə; yet, both are types of change that are common enough for independent innovations to have been suspected (Bergsland 1967:207–208 in the case of the first, and Fortescue 1983 in the case of the second). More strongly suggested by the linguistic evidence is the hypothesis that Polar Eskimo is a relatively recent arrival in Greenland from Canada (Holtved 1952; Rischel 1978), perhaps from as far west as the Copper area (Fortescue 1983): central-west Canada and Polar Eskimo both have h for primary and secondary *s; the Polar Eskimo system of *y-*ř-*č merger can be derived from a conservative Netsilik-type Canadian system; and Polar Eskimo has considerably less advanced consonant assimilation than other eastern dialects (however, the recency of much assimilation in West Greenlandic suggests that this may be less significant). Finally, harmonic unrounding and γ nasalization are found in north and south West Greenlandic and in East Greenlandic. Thalbitzer (1904:202–203, 1914:710–732) interpreted this as evidence for a connection via the prehistoric northeast Greenland group that is known to have existed (Bandi 1969:169), but whose language is unattested. Far more extensive information has led to the hypothesis that the West Greenlandic "fringe" dialects (Cape Farewell, Southern West Greenlandic, Upernavik) are the result of East Greenlandic–West Greenlandic contact, occurring in the case of Upernavik when survivors of the northernmost East Greenlandic settlements went west and south in response to climatic conditions in the middle of the second millennium A.D., and in Southern West Greenlandic by the more recent migrations westward around Cape Farewell (Rischel 1975, 1978; Fortescue 1981, 1983).

Earlier Eskimo-Aleut Prehistory

The linguistic divisions in the Eskimo-Aleut family that imply the greatest time-depth all fall in Western Alaska, and this fact has long been seen to point to an Alaska homeland for speakers of Proto–Eskimo-Aleut (Sapir 1916:82–83). Archeological evidence has also supported the hypothesis of an origin either in Alaska itself or nearby in the Bering Sea region ("Prehistory: Summary," this vol.). Linguistic facts alone are less useful in reconstructing the dates of major cleavages in a language family, since languages do not change at a constant rate (Bergsland and Vogt 1962). East Greenlandic is a famous case in this regard, since it has changed far more rapidly than its sister dialects. Speculations, based on statistical estimates of lexical turnover or subjective estimates of overall change, have usually placed the

Table 4. Reflexes of Proto-Eskimo Consonants in Inuit-Inupiaq Dialects

Inuit-Inupiaq Dialect	*y	*ř	*č	*ř following *k or *q
All Alaskan	y	ř	s	Ř
Netsilik	y	ř	h	h
Other Canadian	y	y	č/s/h	č/s/h
Polar Eskimo	y	h	h	h
Conservative Central West Greenlandic	y	š	s	š
Other West Greenlandic	y	s	s	s
East Greenlandic	y	l	s	sᵃ

ᵃ When geminate, East Greenlandic s is realized as a stop, tt.

Inuit-Inupiaq–Yupik split in the first millennium A.D. or slightly earlier, and the Eskimo-Aleut split at different points in the 4,000 years before that (the earlier dates seem more likely).

The Inuit-Inupiaq–Yupik Relationship

Both Yupik and Inuit-Inupiaq have characteristic innovations and retentions at all levels of grammar, and in their lexicons. In the case of Inuit-Inupiaq, there is good reason to consider at least some innovations common to all dialects as belonging to a period of independent Proto–Inuit-Inupiaq development. An example is an earlier round of consonant lenition affecting all Inuit-Inupiaq, in which among other things intervocalic *q and *k became $\dot{\gamma}$ and γ (see table 2, item 10), and some intervocalic continuants were lost after a and u (see table 2, item 4). Yet Proto–Inuit-Inupiaq is less clear-cut than it might be, because certain early innovations that occurred everywhere else in Inuit-Inupiaq bypassed Bering Strait Inupiaq (Bergsland 1967:216). For example, Proto-Eskimo nasals merge with oral consonants before oral consonants in Inuit-Inupiaq generally, but the distinction is preserved before q in Bering Strait Inupiaq. Thus Proto-Eskimo *nq and *lq are merged in other Inuit-Inupiaq as tq (and secondarily qq in the east), while in Bering Strait they are preserved as qq and tq, respectively: compare other Inuit-Inupiaq tatqiq 'moon' and mitquq 'feather' (eastern taqqiq, miqquq), with Bering Strait taqquq and mitquq, all reflecting Proto-Eskimo *tanqiq and *məlquq, preserved as such in Yupik. Because the distinction is preserved in Yupik, it may be that Yupik–Inuit-Inupiaq contact was significant enough at the time Inuit-Inupiaq was beginning to diversify to bring about the retention of the old pattern in Bering Strait Inupiaq. Then or later, all of Seward Peninsula Inupiaq acquired loans from Yupik neighbors (and in turn Naukanski and Norton Sound Central Alaskan Yupik took in Inupiaq loans) and developed underlying accentual patterns similar to those of Norton Sound Yupik.

Whether the Yupik languages have independent genetic unity is a more difficult question, and it has been suggested that they simply are the non–Inuit-Inupiaq forms of Eskimo (Bergsland 1967). In Bergsland's view, the innovations that all Yupik languages certainly share may well be due either to independent development, or to diffusion after isoglosses clearly distinguishing the daughter languages had already been established. Among the earliest and hence most controversial innovations (Miyaoka 1976) is the loss of the morphologically conditioned gemination that Inuit-Inupiaq preserves: compare Central Alaskan Yupik əɣan and North Slope Inupiaq iɣɣan 'cooking pot', which in both cases derived from *əɣa- 'cook' plus -(u)n 'device for . . .-ing'. Also early is initial syllable loss (table 2, items 10–12). Note in particular that *iy in item 10 and *iŋ (?) in 11 merge in all languages when at the beginning of a word and followed by a vowel. The question of whether these innovations stem from a Proto-Yupik period has not been fully resolved, and given the nature of dialect continua, it may not be resolvable. Sometimes, it is even unclear what is old and what is innovation, as in the case of the Proto–Inuit-Inupiaq ablative *-nən, which may either have occurred in Proto-Eskimo but been lost in all Yupik, or else have been innovated in Inuit-Inupiaq as a common-noun ablative to complement the existing demonstrative-noun ablative *-kən. Finally, the existence of a unified Proto-Yupik is called into question by cases where Inuit-Inupiaq shares possible innovations with part but not all of Yupik, as with Alaskan Yupik and all Inuit-Inupiaq relative second person singular *-pət versus Siberian Yupik *-pək, or most Alaskan Yupik and all Inuit-Inupiaq modalis case ending *-nək versus Hooper Bay–Chevak Alaskan Yupik and Siberian Yupik -nəŋ.

Several explanations have been offered for the sharp break between Yupik and Inuit-Inupiaq. One takes the Yupik-Inupiaq boundary in Western Alaska to be the southwestern terminus of an Inuit-Inupiaq back-migration that followed the original Thule migration eastward (Collins 1954a). In this view, Proto-Eskimo was homogeneous at the end of the first millennium A.D., and the Proto-Yupik speech community left behind by the Inuit-Inupiaq would have had to have occupied the entire Bering Strait region or conquered it linguistically shortly thereafter. It seems more reasonable to place the split earlier, at some point in the long period during which bearers of the Norton and then Old Bering Sea–Punuk and Birnirk cultures inhabited the coasts of the Bering Sea before Thule emergence, the middle of the first millennium B.C. to the end of the first millennium A.D. (Dumond 1977a:152). It must be realized that the attested Eskimo languages almost certainly represent tiny fragments of a far greater linguistic richness around the Bering Sea in that period, and that the Yupik–Inuit-Inupiaq break probably reflects the loss of many intermediate forms that did not survive (Krauss 1980:9–10). Furthermore, the archeological record in western Alaska shows a much greater cultural diversity in the early first millennium A.D. than in the historic period (William W. Fitzhugh, communication to editors 1982), and a corresponding linguistic diversity would be expected. Therefore, while evidence from modern Eskimo languages can suggest that diversity within Yupik may have developed at the same time as the Yupik–Inuit-Inupiaq split, it is not likely to reveal when and how the split took place during that long and complicated period around the Bering Sea.

The Eskimo-Aleut Relationship

The genetic relationship of Eskimo and Aleut, first presented in 1819 by Rasmus Rask (Thalbitzer 1916), has since been established on very firm ground (Bergsland 1951, 1958; Marsh and Swadesh 1951). Here the unity of each of the two branches is in no way in question. Among the many important innovations that characterize the attested forms of Aleut are the overall loss of a labial stop phoneme: Proto–Eskimo-Aleut *p* becomes *h* initially, as in Aleut *haqa-* 'come', *haqa-t-* 'come upon, find (out), bring about', versus Central Alaskan Yupik *paqətə-* 'go to see, inspect', North Slope Inupiaq *paqit-* 'to find'; and *p* becomes *M* medially, as in Aleut *aMa-t-* versus Central Alaskan Yupik *apətə-* 'ask'. Another change is the merger of Proto–Eskimo-Aleut *ə* with other vowels: Aleut *taγa-* 'test, try; understand, taste' versus Central Alaskan Yupik *naγə-* 'smell', and Aleut *tuMi-* 'fart' versus Central Alaskan Yupik *təpə-* 'odor' (Bergsland 1958:626, 630). Eskimo has innovated most strikingly by a morphosyntactic restructuring in which the Eskimo cognates of Aleut independent pronouns become fused into certain inflectional endings on Eskimo verbs, where they mark the agreement of the verb either with its subject or its direct object. This is part of the way in which Eskimo has developed large paradigms of inflectional endings (Bergsland 1964).

Firm linguistic evidence having a bearing on reasons for the enormous gap between Eskimo and Aleut is scarce. It was suggested that Aleut has a few Eyak, Tlingit, and Haida Indian loanwords (Bergsland 1958:625–626), although this has since been doubted (Michael E. Krauss, personal communication 1982). Further, it has been pointed out that the peculiar loss of labial stops in Aleut may reflect earlier proximity to Tlingit or Athapaskan, which both lack labial consonants almost entirely (Bergsland 1958:625–626). However, this does not necessarily mean that Indian groups were responsible for the original Eskimo-Aleut split by driving a wedge through a Proto–Eskimo-Aleut community located perhaps in the Bristol Bay–Cook Inlet region (Hirsch 1954; Hammerich 1960), and evidence in other languages that might support such a hypothesis

is missing: there are no Indian loans that can be reconstructed from all forms of modern Eskimo and attributed to the Proto-Eskimo period, there are no Aleut loans of any antiquity in Athapaskan, and Tlingit dialect distribution indicates a recent spread northward from far away in southernmost Alaska ("Northern Athapaskan Languages," vol. 6). Whether some unknown group once occupying territory between Eskimo-Aleut and Athapaskan-Eyak-Tlingit formed a wedge that separated Proto-Eskimo from Proto-Aleut is unknowable from linguistic evidence, because loans would be impossible to identify.

As in the case of Inuit-Inupiaq and Yupik, Proto-Eskimo and Proto-Aleut may each be a fragment of earlier linguistic diversity around the Bering Sea, and the Eskimo-Aleut "split" may reflect nothing more than the loss of intermediate forms along an ancient dialect continuum (Krauss 1980:9–10). It is likely, for example, that bearers of the Dorset culture, who occupied the Eastern Arctic at the beginning of the first millennium B.C., were speakers of some form or forms of Eskimo-Aleut (Jenness 1940). Perhaps these forms were distinct long before being taken eastward and were part of that ancient dialect continuum. However, no trace of Dorset language survived to be recorded, and, in spite of instances of Dorset-Thule contact after A.D. 1000, no evidence indicating a Dorset substratum of any kind has been found in any attested Inuit-Inupiaq dialect, although this is sometimes claimed for East Greenlandic (for example, Gessain 1969:16). A Dorset substratum in an Inuit-Inupiaq dialect would presumably have left Dorset loanwords or other features that would be recognizable as descendants of known Proto–Eskimo-Aleut forms, but would have undergone a history of regular sound changes different from that of the host dialect.

Remote Relationships

A number of hypotheses of distant relationships between Eskimo-Aleut and other language families have been advanced, including Indo-European (Hammerich 1951), Chukotko-Kamchatkan (Swadesh 1962; Hamp 1976:81–92), Uralic—with or without the proposed connections to Altaic and Yukagir—(Uhlenbeck 1905; Bergsland 1959a, Fortescue 1981), and many others. The hypothesis of a connection with Ural-Altaic is less controversial than the others, though none are necessarily mutually exclusive, but all are as yet unproved.

Sources

The most complete survey of the remarkably old and multinational scientific research in Eskimo-Aleut linguistics, with extensive bibliography, is Krauss (1973);

this has been updated, especially to account for the burgeoning practical and educational literature, in Krauss (1979). Purely bibliographical works include especially Pilling (1887) for earlier material. Bergsland (1968) provides a succinct introduction to the whole field of Eskimo-Aleut linguistics, while Hammerich (1976) treats key topics at more length. Miyaoka (1978), in Japanese, is the most detailed survey of the field for the general reader. Bergsland (1959) summarizes the history of Aleut linguistic studies, including the nineteenth-century work of Russian and Creole scholar-priests, except for the unpublished notes of John P. Harrington, which are available on microfilm (Mills 1981:1–8).

Even in 1980, Kleinschmidt's (1851) German grammar of West Greenlandic provided a brilliant introduction to Eskimo grammar for the serious student without extensive linguistic training, and it is acknowledged as the basis for the most accessible modern outline treatments in English, Schultz-Lorentzen (1945), which includes extensive paradigms, and Swadesh (1946), which stresses stem-formation and syntax. Bergsland's (1955) grammar of West Greenlandic, in 1980 by far the most complete and sophisticated technical account of any Eskimo language, treats syntax in very great detail. An introductory treatment of Central Alaskan Yupik is Reed et al. (1977).

Technical linguistic papers appear in the journals *Inuit Studies (Études Inuit),* the *International Journal of American Linguistics,* and others; significant collections are in Hamp (1976) and Dorais (1981).

Human Biology of the Arctic

EMŐKE J.E. SZATHMARY

Archeological evidence shows that Eskimos spread from the vicinity of the Bering Sea across the Arctic shore of North America. Linguistic evidence attests that their languages were derived from a single source. Biological evidence also characterizes these people, all of whom share to some degree the set of traits inherited from their common ancestors. The purpose of this chapter is to provide a survey of the anthropometric, physiologic, and genetic traits of Eskimo peoples that identify them as a single group and may distinguish them from eastern Siberians and adjacent Indians.

Anthropometric Characteristics

Body Build

One of the first summaries (as opposed to data lists) of Eskimo morphology made by a professional physical anthropologist was by Hrdlička (1930). His description of Alaskan Eskimos stated that compared to White Americans they were of medium to submedium stature rather than short. Large chests in combination with trunks that were long relative to the length of the legs gave an impression of stockiness. Hands and feet were small, but heads and faces were large, the face and mandible being particularly broad. Although Eskimos in the eastern Arctic were known to have narrow, elongated skulls, Eskimos of Alaska were more intermediate in skull form with a tendency to brachycephaly (roundheadedness) demonstrable from north to south and east to west in the region (Hrdlička 1930:239–249). Laughlin (1950:168) concurred in this description, adding that similar facial and body dimensions characterize Eskimos from Attu in the Aleutians to Greenland. He also noted that Eskimos are not fat, as is commonly believed, but are muscular people with heavy bones (Laughlin 1963:639).

Changes in body build as a consequence of increasing Westernization and through secular change (that is, the alteration of a morphological dimension over time in a population) have occurred in the Arctic since Hrdlička's study. Non-Eskimo genes from diverse sources and in differing amounts have entered Arctic populations, and these could also have had an impact on morphology. To date differences between "hybrids" and "nonhy-brids" have been published for north Alaskans only. These are important not only because they depict what changes have occurred in unadmixed Eskimos since Hrdlička's day but also because they quantify differences that are attributable to admixture. While the findings in north Alaska may not be rigorously applicable across the Arctic (because of variable amounts of gene flow), they may be indicative of the general effect of population mixture on the "typical" Eskimo form.

Most non-Eskimo genes entered north Alaskan Eskimo populations before 1925. Most were contributed by Western Europeans, but Africans, Asians, and Polynesians have also left descendants. In 1970 one-quarter to one-eighth of the genes on the average in north Alaskans were of non-Eskimo origin. Of the 30 craniofacial and body measurements taken on 272 nonhybrid and 70 hybrid Eskimos, nine were significantly different in men, and six, in women. Nevertheless Jamison (1978:52) found that when all measurements were used simultaneously in a statistical procedure (discriminant function) that classifies individuals into groups (such as hybrid or nonhybrid) 13.5% of the males and 17.2% of the females were identified incorrectly. These results suggest that admixture has had a small overall effect on morphology: hybrids are a little larger in body dimensions and a little smaller in head dimensions (Jamison 1978:51) than nonhybrids. The latter differ from Hrdlička's depiction by having neither very long trunks nor very short legs compared to those of American Whites; the size of their hands and feet relative to stature are also comparable to Whites, and they are round-headed (Jamison 1978:47).

Investigations carried out under the International Biological Program 1967–1974, in West Greenland, Northern Quebec, the Foxe Basin region of Canada, and north Alaska have described the anthropometric traits of modern Eskimos (Auger et al. 1980). Table 1 lists some of the metrics and relevant ratios for men, with comparative information on Chukchi, Asian Eskimos, and Subarctic Indians. These traits in Indians demonstrate relative consistency over time. A corresponding table for women is not provided because of a dearth of information on females from several (5 of 12) of the populations (Asiatic, Indian).

Eskimo populations vary in body size, with a general increase in dimensions (except stature) from east to

Table 1. Anthropometric Measures and Ratios of Adult Male Eskimos, Subarctic Indians, and Northeastern Siberians

Population	N[a]	Weight (kg)	Height (cm)	Sitting height (cm)	Biacromial breadth (cm)	Biliac breadth (cm)	Weight/ height squared	Sitting height/ height	Sources
Chukchi	88	63.2	164.5	—	38.3	28.7	23.4	.573[b]	Alekseev 1979a:77
Asian Eskimo	57	64.2	162.8	—	38.7	28.4	24.2	.563[b]	Alekseev 1979a:77
Alaska Eskimo	91	72.8	166.0	88.4	39.8	29.6	26.4	.533	Auger et al. 1980:244–245
Foxe Basin Eskimo	134	65.3	162.6	87.5	37.8	29.4	24.7	.538	Auger et al. 1980:244–245
Quebec Eskimo	92	66.8	165.6	—	—	—	—	—	Auger et al. 1980:244–245; Auger 1974:149
W. Greenland Eskimo	45	—	160.5	86.2	37.0	28.4	—	.537	Auger et al. 1980:244–245
Athapaskan Indians									
Chipewyan	44	—	166.4	89.4	—	—	—	.537	Grant 1930:30
Dogrib	60	66.6	165.4	—	—	—	24.3	—	Szathmary and Holt 1983
Algonquian Indians									
Ft. Severn Cree	15	67.0	173.5	90.1	—	—	22.5	.519	Hurlich and Steegmann 1979:264
Weagamow Lake Ojibwa	12	70.3	175.6	93.8	—	—	22.8	.534	Hurlich and Steegmann 1979:264
God's Lake Cree	17	—	172.0	90.0	—	—	—	.523	Grant 1929:20
Oxford House Cree	55	—	172.5	88.7	—	—	—	.514	Grant 1929:20
Island Lake Ojibwa	68	—	170.0	89.9	—	—	—	.528	Grant 1929:20

[a] Maximum number of cases. Sample sizes differ slightly for some measures.
[b] Trunk length/leg length: 50.4/88.0 = .573; 49.2/87.4 = .563.

west across the Arctic. Comparison with adjacent groups shows that marked differences in proportions occur with Subarctic Cree and Ojibwa Indians only. Crees and Ojibwas are absolutely taller, have less weight for height, and have longer legs than any of the others. The absence of transverse skeletal measures (biacromial and biliac breadths) for any of the Subarctic Indians prevents assessment of the general claim that Eskimos are "stockier," that is, also have greater breadth for unit height than Indians.

All evidence to date indicates that Eskimos in general cannot be considered "fat" if this is assessed by the same standards used in Canadian and other North American White populations (Schaefer 1977:1626). However, overweight has been increasing in Alaska since 1958 in both men and women (Colbert, Mann, and Hursh 1978:167), and obesity is becoming a problem among older women across the Arctic (Auger et al. 1980:254). More direct measures of body composition (deuterium oxide method) in lean Eskimos give greater percentages of body fat than predicted by skinfold readings. Shephard (1980:322) and Shephard and Rode (1976:96) suggest that the discrepancy is best explained by storage of fat in the deeper body tissues (omentum, mesentery, retroperitoneum) rather than under the skin. This suggestion, while intriguing, requires some additional confirmation.

The measurements obtained on children by the IBP studies, as well as the age breakdown of adult samples, show that Eskimos in the 1980s were taller than their parents. Adult stature is attained by the age of 20 years, with young men averaging heights of 166–168 centimeters and young women, 155–156 centimeters. Environmental differences, particularly nutritional differences, are implicated by variations between populations in stature, upper arm muscularity, and body fat measures, both as adults and children (Auger et al. 1980:242). Differences in protein consumption are unlikely, but reduced carbohydrate intake is evident, particularly in the Foxe Basin region in the decade before 1969 (Mayhall 1976:416).

Craniofacial Form

Hrdlička's (1930:263) observation that Eskimos have larger heads and broader faces than Caucasians is borne out by modern studies on Eskimos at Igloolik in the Foxe Basin (Colby and Cleall 1974:168) and at Wainwright, Alaska (Dahlberg 1980:176; Jamison 1978:47), the two study areas where X-rays were used to assess details of craniofacial growth and variation. These Eskimo groups have similar degrees of maxillary prognathism, flexion of the cranial base, and gonial angles; in both groups the mandibular body is very broad; and the lower part of the face is increasingly prominent until 30 years of age. Differences also exist, particularly in the more posterior positioning of the chin, and a much greater degree of maxillary and mandibular incisor protrusion in the Igloolik sample (Dahlberg et al. 1978:96–97; Colby and Cleall 1974:168–169). The Canadian study also showed that the greater size of the craniofacial complex of Eskimos is established by three years of age and is probably present at birth (Colby and Cleall

65

1974:169). Other measures, such as midfacial flatness in males and the size of the gonial angle, both considered important demarcations of Arctic Mongoloid face form, show age-related changes in adults (Dahlberg et al. 1978:95,97).

The IBP studies did not address the issue of similarity in facial appearance between Eskimos and Indians, once a matter of some concern (Hrdlička 1930; Shapiro 1931; Seltzer 1933), and relevant here because of the prevailing North American view that Eskimos are more Mongoloid in facial features than Indians (Laughlin 1962a:106–107, 1962:116). Soviet scientists are not so certain, for Debets's data show that "Eskimos resemble North American Indians despite some morphological differences" (Alekseev 1979a:67). To resolve this issue, assessment of the bony structure of the face is important, as is examination of the shape and distribution of soft tissue structures. Fair assessment requires comparison of Eskimos with Subarctic Indians, since it was among them that resemblances to Eskimos were seen (Hrdlička 1930:361; Shapiro 1931:378; Seltzer 1933:359–360; Collins 1951:445). This has not been done to anyone's satisfaction because skeletal remains of Subarctic Indians are largely unavailable. What data do exist indicate overlap between some Eskimos and some Indians, even in features such as facial flatness (Heathcote 1981:583).

In contrast to the dearth of skeletal data, anthropometric measures of Subarctic Indians are more plentiful from the period 1897 to 1936. Many Eskimo groups were also examined during that time, hence comparisons could be made for length and breadth dimensions of the head, face, and nose. Because morphologic shape is a better indicator of biological affinity than simple size, Penrose's (1954:338) "shape" distances (C_z^2) between populations were obtained from the craniofacial and nasal measurements. The "shape" distance measures the diversity among the differences between mean values of a character in two populations. It is, therefore, a variance statistic. For the Eskimo-Indian comparisons reported here the mean "shape" distance is 1.85 times the size of the average "size" distance. The results (Szathmary 1979) provide a vindication of Seltzer's (1933) findings: Cree Indians most resemble the Caribou Eskimos, Athapaskans most resemble Western Alaska and Saint Lawrence Island Eskimos. Figure 1 shows the pattern of craniofacial similarity among Eskimos and Indians, based on the "shape" distance statistics. It corroborates the subjective assessments others have made when looking at faces (Hrdlička 1930:99 on Kotzebue Eskimos in 1920; Collins 1951:445–446 on Eskimos of Pond Inlet and Frobisher Bay; Birket-Smith 1940:109 on Eskimos at Hudson Bay), or at photographs of faces (Collins 1951:442). However, it does not prove the similarity because the measurements were taken by several anthropometrists. Interobserver error in anthropometry can be considerable (Jamison and Zegura 1974:202–203), and confidence in a set of metrics varies inversely with the number of anthropometrists.

Morphological Adaptation

"Adaptation," in contrast to a term like "acclimatization," when used in biology refers to genetic adaptation: the existence of a genotype that was produced by the action of natural selection on an advantageous phenotype. In contrast, "acclimatization" refers to adjustments to the environment that occur during the lifetime of an individual but are not transmitted to offspring. Because Eskimos have lived for several thousand years in a land of climatic extremes, with long periods of cold occurring annually, much attention has focused on evidence for cold adaptation in body build, body weight, the shape of the head, face, and nose, and the size and shape of the frontal sinuses.

Warm-blooded animals exhibit temperature-associated variation in body shape, including the size of the appendages, as summarized by the zoological rules of Bergmann (1845–1847) and J.A. Allen (1877). Viewed globally, human populations occupying cold areas are heavier and have larger chests, relatively shorter extremities, and less body surface area per unit weight than inhabitants of the tropics (Steegmann 1975:162).

The Eskimo body build phenotype as described by IBP workers differs from that of Arctic-dwelling Lapps, and the difference has been attributed to genetic factors. Studies of Lapp and Eskimo children show that in spite of these differences, both Arctic populations differ in the same way from Icelandic children raised in the Subarctic portion of Iceland (Auger et al. 1980:218, 228, 237). Both groups have greater weight for height, and both show broader trunk dimensions relative to height than the Icelanders. Auger et al. (1980:254) concluded that both Eskimos and Lapps have some adaptation to climate in body build. To what degree, if any, the Eskimo body build is better adapted to cold than that of Subarctic Athapaskan Indians remains to be determined.

Dry cold stress, particularly frostbite stress, has been proposed as the selective force that led to the emergence of the Mongoloid face (Coon, Garn, and Birdsell 1950:67): a relatively round, flat structure, devoid of heavy brow ridges, but displaying prominent, fat-padded cheekbones, and eyes protected by fat-filled folds. Protruding, thin features were thought to be more in danger of freezing than the rounder features of Mongoloids. Steegmann (1972) tested this hypothesis in a laboratory using subjects of Asian and European descent. he found that the larger, prominent malar bones of Asians got colder than the cheekbones of Europeans when subjected to an air stream at 0°C for 70 minutes. The thicker fat layer of Asians could have insulated

66

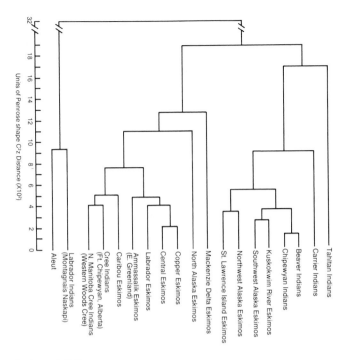

Szathmary 1979:33.
Fig. 1. Dendrogram showing craniofacial anthropometric similarities among Aleut, 11 Eskimo, and 7 Indian populations.

deeper structures of the face, but its effect at the surface was to lower skin temperatures. Nose shape and prominence, furthermore, were unrelated to nasal temperature, though the latter did increase with head size (Steegmann 1972:220–221). The Mongoloid face, then, could not have been produced by selection through frostbite stress (Steegmann 1975:160). Analysis of Siberian population data showed no association of temperature and the nasal index, facial flatness, or the height and width of the face (Bunak 1972 cited in Forsius 1980:194). Finally, the finding that facial flatness increases with age in Eskimos also argues against this distinctive feature being the product of cold adaptation (Dahlberg et al. 1978:96).

There is no evidence either that the Mongoloid eye serves to protect the eyeball from cold and glare (Laughlin 1966b:476). The palpebral fissure (opening between upper and lower eyelids), said to be narrower in Mongoloids, is not demonstrably narrower in Eskimos than in Lapps, Finns, and Icelanders. The fissure, moreover, decreases in width with age, as does the frequency of the epicanthic eyefold. The latter feature, it is worth noting, has a low frequency in Lapps (Forsius 1980:194–197) who have, nevertheless, occupied the Eurasian Arctic for several thousand years.

Other features of morphology that have been suggested as evidence for cold adaptation in the Eskimo face include the size of the frontal sinus (Koertvelyessy 1972:169), a narrow "nose" (the width of the bony aperture that supports the cartilaginous external nose—

Wolpoff 1968), and an expanded interior nasal chamber in conjunction with the narrow nose (Shea 1977:298–299). The mechanisms whereby adaptiveness is inferred for these structures differ, but each rests on the same basic observation. Each feature is associated with temperature, either inversely (frontal sinus volume) or directly (nose width, size of the nasal chamber). To confirm the claimed adaptiveness of these structures in Eskimos, more population data are necessary.

In contrast to the foregoing studies that sought evidence for cold adaptation in the Eskimo face, another body of investigations has focused on masticatory stress as *the* shaper of the Eskimo craniofacial complex. Although the hypothesis was first suggested by Hrdlička (1910), the most detailed analysis and exposition has been provided by Hylander (1977). In sum, he found that "the Eskimo skull is adapted to generate and dissipate large vertical biting forces" (Hylander 1977:161). Maximum chewing muscle efficiency, for example, occurs when the masseter and temporalis muscles are shifted anteriorly. The changes in the underlying bony framework that allow such muscular repositioning produce facial flatness. Other alterations involve buttressing the bony face to withstand high stress forces, and smoothing the forehead area to disperse these forces. Among the bony results are a narrowed nasal aperture, explained here as a consequence of the strengthening of the upper jaw; the reduction of brow ridge sizes, and the angulation (keeling) along the midline of the skull vault. Ethnographic evidence shows that Arctic Eskimos used the mouth frequently to hold objects when the hands were occupied in other tasks (during whaling, for example) or to shape and soften bone and skin objects. In Alaska a significant correlation exists between the occurrence of the "typical" Eskimo face and increased latitude, and the latitude is associated with increase in whaling activity (Wanner 1977:74–78). However, Mongoloid people elsewhere are also noted for facial flatness. These include interior Siberian peoples, some of whom are even more extreme in their nasiomalar and zygomaxillary angles (the measures of facial flatness) than Asiatic or North American Eskimos (Alekseev 1979:159; Heathcote 1981:583–584). Thus, while chewing power and chewing stress may have contributed to the formation of the Eskimo craniofacial complex, it is not likely to have been the only factor. The verdict, specifying the percentage contribution of masticatory stress and that of cold adaptation with a definition of its particular features, is still unavailable.

Physiology

Cold Adaptation

The central problem of Arctic survival is heat conservation and heat supply. Not only must the body core with its vital organs be protected from cold injury, but also the extremities must be kept warm without the danger of incurring too much core heat loss. The elaborate and ingenious aboriginal technology of Eskimos attest that this was the principal means through which life in the Arctic was made possible. Some biological cold adaptation has also taken place at least with respect to body form, and some degree of physiological adaptation is a possibility. Globally, the basal metabolic rate, or the minimum amount of heat produced by the resting body when it is not engaged in active digestion, mental activity, or subjected to emotional stress, is significantly and negatively associated with temperature (D.F. Roberts 1973:5). Eskimos, then, may be expected to manifest some physiologic adaptations to cold, and an elevated basal metabolic rate would seem to be obvious.

Indeed, 11 of the 14 studies on the Eskimo basal metabolic rate reported by Itoh (1980:286) have rates 13–33 percent above the Du Bois (normal) standard, with the highest values manifested by men still living traditional life-styles. Furthermore, no significant differences in basal metabolic rate were reported between Alaska Eskimos and central Alaska Athapaskan-speaking Indians (Milan, Hannon, and Evonuk 1963:380). Carefully controlled studies on Eskimos from Alaska and Canada show that the elevated basal metabolic rates found in these groups are mainly a product of diet, and to a lesser degree, test anxiety rather than any physiological adaptation (So 1980:69). Overactivity of the thyroid does not appear to be a factor in the elevated basal metabolic rates in either Eskimos or Indians (Itoh 1980:287).

The ability to withstand cold stress effectively can be evaluated by whole-body cooling and extremity cooling tests. The whole-body tests challenge individual capacity to maintain deep body temperature and surface temperatures on the trunk and extremities. Extremity cooling tests seek to establish surface temperatures of fingers, hands, or feet and to determine the physiological mechanisms whereby cold damage is avoided.

Three reviews of whole-body cooling tests on Eskimos conclude that there is no real physiological difference between the responses of Eskimos and Europeans (Steegmann 1975:158; Itoh 1980:288; So 1980:69), for both groups produce and release adequate amounts of body heat. The significant elevations of metabolic rate and skin temperature in Eskimos undergoing such tests are functions of their thermogenic diet, body build, and body composition (Steegmann 1975:158). That Eskimos can afford such a generous response to body cooling suggests that the real problem for them in the Arctic is not heat conservation or production, but heat dissipation (Rennie et al. 1962:331). The insulation provided by traditional clothing is such that even hunting activity does not put the individual at risk of either severe or chronic cold stress (Milan, Hannon, and Evonuk 1963:382). Thus, opinions differ not about the magnitude of heat lost by Eskimos, but how it is lost: less fat under the skin allowing heat escape (Rennie et al. 1962:331) or greater peripheral circulation allowing greater heat exchange (Milan, Hannon, and Evonuk 1963:381).

Heat loss is facilitated by sweating, and several investigators have noted excess sweat production by Eskimos at temperatures considered normal by Europeans (e.g., Rennie 1963:828; Shephard 1980:331). Although Eskimos have been reported to have a higher mean number of active sweat glands than Europeans (Kuno 1956), significantly greater numbers occur around the mouth and nose only, with significantly reduced numbers on the chest, abdomen, and upper and lower limbs (Schaefer et al. 1976:46–47). Relative to skin surface area, the fewest number of sweat glands are on the legs and feet, though the decrease elsewhere on the parts of the body that are normally clothed is striking. While reduced sweating in these areas is probably advantageous in an Arctic climate, the increased sweat output of the perioral region may not be sufficient for effective thermoregulation (Schaefer et al. 1976:49).

Every extremity cooling test that has compared responses of adult Eskimos and Indians with adult Europeans shows that Native Americans have superior responses to cold stress. The Native Americans tested have come from the North American Arctic and Subarctic as well as the Peruvian lowlands and highlands (Steegmann 1975:152). Warmer finger (and hand) temperatures, faster rewarming, and greater pain tolerance to cold have been reported for Eskimos (Eagan 1963:949–950) and Subarctic Indians (Eagan 1963:948; Meehan 1955:541). Some of these responses, particularly the reduction of cold-induced pain, are probably due to acclimatization; however, genetic factors must also be involved, for Eskimos who had spent nine months in the warmer state of Oregon still did better on extremity-cooling tests than Caucasian mountaineers acclimatized to Alaska (Eagan 1963:949).

Peripheral blood flow, cold-induced vasodilation (CIVD), and cold pressor response (elevation of blood pressure when the hand and forearm are immersed in ice water) have been examined as possible mechanisms that could account for cold adaptation of the extremities. Neither the rate of blood flow per minute when standardized by 100 milliliter hand volume nor the cold pressor responses are likely factors in Eskimos. The former does not differ significantly between Eskimos and Europeans (data of Krog and Wika in Itoh 1980:289); the latter is significantly lower in Eskimo adults and children than in control Whites (Igloolik data of Le Blanc in Itoh 1980:294). Earlier time of onset of CIVD appears to be the most consistent finding in circumpolar peoples, all of whom also show elevated CIVD re-

68

sponses (Itoh 1980:293). Itoh (1980:292) does not give CIVD onset times for Eskimos or Indians, but graphic data (Eagan 1963:948,949) suggest these occur within three to five minutes in Alaska Indians and within two to four minutes in Alaska Eskimos. These are lower than the absolute times reported for Lapps and other groups (Itoh 1980:292) and seem lower than the onset times of two groups of cold-acclimatized Cree and Ojibwa Indians (7.4 ± 5.6 minutes, 6.2 ± 7.6 minutes—Hurlich and Steegmann 1979:270).

Diet and Metabolism Adaptations

The aboriginal Arctic Eskimos were among the most heavily dependent on meat of any peoples in the world. High protein, high fat, and low carbohydrate intake occurred from Greenland (Draper 1980:259) to Alaska (Bell and Heller 1978:148). The central problem in such a diet is to produce sufficient glucose to fuel the nervous system and other body tissues. Diabetes mellitus in Eskimos was rare (Schaefer 1969:144) as was cardiovascular disease. The latter in temperate zone populations is associated with elevated levels of plasma lipids, triglycerides, and cholesterol, which are in turn influenced by the amount of dietary fat consumed. Adaptation to a high-fat, high-protein diet by Eskimos was a possibility, and such adaptation could explain the infrequency in Eskimos of the foregoing diseases (Schaefer, Crockford, and Romanowski 1972:738).

Environmental factors as well as genetic factors appear to be implicated in the low incidence of atherosclerotic heart disease. Eskimos consuming more traditional diets consistently have significantly lower amounts of total plasma lipids and lower levels of individual constituents (e.g., triglycerides, lipoproteins) of the total lipoprotein pattern than Eskimos consuming Western diets (Bang, Dyerberg, and Hjørne 1976:145; Feldman et al. 1978:181). A study on Greenlanders also showed that they differed from Danes by having altered proportions of their ester-bound fatty acids: some were significantly elevated and some were significantly lower (Bang, Dyerberg, and Hjørne 1976:145). The Greenlandic diet is the source of the polyunsaturated fatty acids (e.g., timnodinic acid) found elevated in Eskimos, which are thought to have a preventive function with respect to ischemic heart disease (Draper 1980:271).

The cholesterol content of the native Alaskan diet is modest (Draper 1976:125). Caribou, sea mammals, and fish have a high polyunsaturated fatty acid content, and this too may have contributed to the low serum cholesterol levels of unacculturated Eskimos. With increasing Westernization of the diet, increase in plasma cholesterol occurs and is documented within Alaska. Eskimos differ from American Whites in their very superior ability to absorb dietary cholesterol (absorption efficiency is 57%, Feldman et al. 1978:177) and in the elevation of the absolute amount of cholesterol absorbed. Furthermore, a cholesterol balance study showed that the total daily amount of cholesterol absorbed and cholesterol produced by the body was constant, with the maximal rate of inhibition of cholesterol synthesis (36%) being observed at the lowest level of dietary cholesterol intake. The net effect, if there is an increase in cholesterol consumption, is a faster turnover of absorbed cholesterol but also a proportional increase in plasma cholesterol level leading to hypercholesterolemia (Feldman et al. 1978:177–178). Thus, although more isolated villagers still have lower frequencies of hypertension and lower blood cholesterol levels than found in the general United States population, Eskimos in towns resemble non-Eskimos in these communities in the prevalence of cholesterol-associated disorders (Draper and Wo 1978:197).

Maturity-onset (Type II) diabetes is an uncommon condition among Eskimos and Alaska Indians, although the disorder is increasing both in Alaska (Mouratoff and Scott 1973:1346) and the Mackenzie delta (Schaefer, Crockford, and Romanowski 1972:736). Adaptation of the gut mucosa to a high protein diet was suggested as an explanation for Canadian Eskimos' poor insulin response to a load of oral carbohydrate, when this was consumed without a preceding protein meal (Schaefer, Crockford, and Romanowski 1972:737–738). Diet does appear to be a factor, for one- and two-hour plasma glucose levels were significantly lowered in Eskimo youths consuming a high carbohydrate diet compared to youths at home (Point Hope), with the former also having minor increases in insulin output. However, fasting plasma glucose levels as well as insulin levels at all hours were not significantly different. Subsequent tolbutamide tolerance tests on Point Hope residents showed normal sensitivity to plasma insulin and the existence of adequate insulin reserves despite low carbohydrate consumption before the test (Feldman et al. 1978:183). The precise role of dietary factors in Eskimo diabetes, then, is not known.

Lactose intolerance, common to populations without a history of dairying, and characterized by an increasing deficiency of the enzyme lactase during maturation, also occurs among Eskimos. Over 50 percent of Greenlanders, 80 percent of Alaska Eskimos and Indians (Duncan and Scott 1972:868), and 56–70 percent of Alaska Eskimo children are intolerant to the standard test dose (Draper 1980:279). Nevertheless, children and adults, with the exception of pregnant women, can consume nutritionally adequate amounts of lactose without difficulty (Draper 1980:280).

Sucrose intolerance, the result of the absence of the enzyme sucrase, is a genetically transmitted condition present in Greenland and north Alaska Eskimos. Prevalence data on this condition are as yet unavailable, but its absence in southwestern Alaska suggests it may be restricted in distribution to those regions of the Arctic where dietary sucrose, for example in berries, was absent (Draper 1980:281).

Population Genetics

Genetic Markers

Description of the genetic traits of Eskimos is often prefaced with the statement that they lack particular genes present in Indians. Foremost among these are Di^a (Diego blood groups), the serum proteins Tf^{DChi} (transferrins), Al^{Na} (albumins), and $Gm^{z,a,x;g}$ (immunoglobulin Gm). These genetic differences, when contrasted with genetic similarities of Eskimos to Asians (for example, B allele of the ABO blood group system) have been used to claim that Eskimos are more closely related to Asians than to Indians (Laughlin 1963:641; Laughlin and Wolfe 1979:5). To judge the merits of such claims information on the requisite genes in all relevant populations is necessary. The distribution of some genes is very well known, either globally or for specific hemispheres. In the former group falls Di^a; in the latter, Al^{Na}. It is not known, for example, whether any albumin variants occur in Siberia, although much is known about albumin variants in North and South America. Information on transferrins in northwestern North America is limited, and knowledge of the varieties of the immunoglobulins in both Siberia and North America is poor (Szathmary 1981:55–58). Although Di^a is absent in non-Asian Eskimos, it occurs in Chukchi and other Siberians. Tf^{DChi} has not been found in Reindeer Chukchi (Sukernik et al. 1981:126), nor has it been observed in Athapaskan-speaking Indians (Szathmary 1981:50); $Gm^{z,a,x;g}$ and Al^{Na} occur in the few Athapaskans tested for these systems, but no information on their presence or absence is available for Chukchi, Kamchadal, or Koryak of far eastern Siberia (Szathmary 1981:58). Clearly, to use single genetic markers as indices of population difference or affinity without adequate distributional information is foolhardy.

Eskimos do not seem to have any gene that is unique to them, with the exception of variants in the Gc (Group Specific α-Globulin) system. $Gc^{Igloolik}$ is present in Foxe Basin Eskimos with a frequency of 1 percent (Cox, Simpson, and Jantti 1978:345), while Gc^{Eskimo} occurs in Greenlanders (Persson and Tingsgard 1965). The two variants have been shown to be different by isoelectric focusing techniques (Cox, Simpson, and Jantti 1978:348). Detailed information is available on genetic characteristics of circumpolar peoples (Eriksson, Lehmann, and Simpson 1980), of Siberians north of the Arctic Circle (Rychkov and Sheremet´eva 1980), and of Siberian and northern North American peoples (Szathmary 1981).

Population Affinity

A debate is going on among physical anthropologists concerning the claimed biological distinctness of Eskimos from Indians (Laughlin 1966b:470–474; Ferrel et al. 1981; Szathmary and Ossenberg 1978; Szathmary 1981). Some see the Eskimo-Indian dichotomy as an artificial dichotomy, because it implies a morphological and genetic homogeneity of American Indians that is not the case (Stewart and Newman 1951; Spuhler 1979). Some Indians may indeed be phylogenetically closer to Eskimos than to other Indians—a notion that was favored by Hrdlička (1930:360–361).

Multivariate assessments of gene frequencies allow objective demonstrations of genetic similarities, which in many instances are also indicative of relationships. The restrictions on such analyses are that data must be available for the same system in all populations compared, and that accuracy is dependent on the total number of systems employed. The latter is hardly surprising,

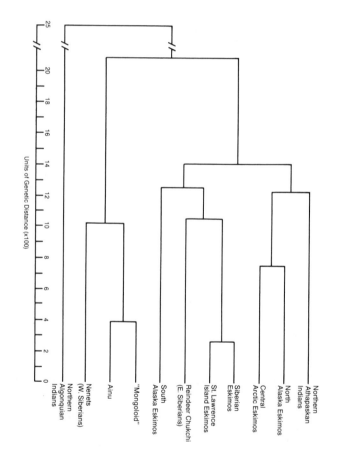

after Szathmary 1981:66.

Fig. 2. Dendrogram showing genetic affinities among 11 populations. Positions in the tree are based on Nei's standard distances obtained from information contained in 12 genetic systems.

since more than 100,000 structural gene loci are present in human chromosomes (Bodmer and Cavalli-Sforza 1976:132), while the ABO, Rh, and MNSs systems, by default the most commonly used in continent-wide analyses (for example, Spuhler 1979:144), add up to three. Fortunately, simulation studies show (Nei and Roychoudhury 1982) that information from 20 genetic systems is usually enough to allow stable patterns of genetic similarity to emerge in affinity studies. Figure 2 shows the dendrogram based on information from 12 loci, the largest array possible for the northern populations of interest here (Szathmary 1981:66). (Comparisons between figs. 1 and 2 are necessarily indirect because different populations were considered in each instance. Ideally, both morphological and genetic measurements should be obtained on the same people.)

Such a tree shows that northern Algonquians are more distant from a group of Eskimos—that is, more unlike them—than are a group of Asian populations. However, the Reindeer Chukchi and northern Athapaskans are shown as part of a cluster of Eskimo populations. Results such as this provoke the question: are Eskimos truly as distinct from Indians as has been believed? Indeed they are—from some—but not from all, and certainly not from the Athapaskan-speaking peoples of northwest North America (figs. 1–2).

Focusing attention on the position of Indians in a pattern of genetic similarity distracts from the obvious in figure 2: Eskimo groups cluster together. That the Chukchi, morphologicaly similar and geographically adjacent to the Siberian Eskimos—and according to some scholars distantly related linguistically—should be linked to them and the Saint Lawrence Islanders, is not unexpected. Spuhler (1979:155,162) established that Eskimos have the highest probability of any North American population of being correctly classified into their language family or culture area by the use of gene frequencies. This indicates, as other studies (Szathmary 1979), that Eskimos, regardless of geographic location, are genetically closely linked, and are indeed, genetically identifiable. Such identity is most commonly demonstrable in recently expanding populations who have not had significant genetic contact during this process with other human groups in the geographic area into which they have moved. An archeologist might say that this fits with what is known of the prehistoric eastward movement of Eskimos. Indeed, modern data confirm Hrdlička's (1930:361) assertion that although Eskimos and particularly the "latest branches" of the American Indian have a common origin in lower northern Asia, "the Eskimo are evidently a younger, smaller and still a more uniform member; which speaks strongly for their later origin, migration and internal differentiation" (Hrdlička 1930:365).

Prehistory: Summary

DON E. DUMOND

This chapter synthesizes the accounts that are provided in the individual chapters on regional archeology. It also discusses some models of the prehistory of the zone that have not been amenable to treatment within the individual chapters.

Archeological investigators in the extensive Arctic coastal and near-coastal zone have come from several nations and differing traditions of scholarship, so it is not surprising that the units of cultural taxonomy that have been used customarily in one corner of the Arctic may vary somewhat from those most in use in another. This variation has necessarily been preserved in the archeological chapters of this volume, as each author has sought to synthesize the sequence of prehistoric occupations and the archeological literature of his own area.

In order to keep faith with the regional authors, their own particular terminologies are used in figure 1. But to add for the purpose of this summary a cross-cutting means of integration, the whole has been divided into five historical-developmental stages. It should be noted that the beginning or ending dates of any one such roughly temporal unit are not necessarily identical in all local regions and that some of the stages do not logically apply at all within certain regions. The estimate of variance that is given for the beginning or end of most stages, for example, 2000 ± 300 B.C., is not a statement of uncertainty about the dates but rather indicates the variation that the beginning or ending of the stage appears to have in different locations. (In all cases these dates are derived without correction from radiocarbon determinations based on a half-life of 5,568 years.) Assemblages that appear idiosyncratic in the state of present knowledge are ignored.

Information not already included in the regional syntheses is added only for discussion of the first two stages, during neither of which the zone of later Eskimo occupation—and the focus of this volume—can be considered a culture area of itself, so that references to outside locations are particularly necessary. For ensuing stages the attention here is devoted specifically to matters that interrelate the various areas treated in the separate chapters. Thus considerable space is devoted to the first pan-Arctic cultural movement of Stage 3, and to the dynamic cultural changes occurring within Stage 4, whereas discussion of Stage 5 is limited to the last really dramatic pan-Arctic movement—the population shift that has been called the Thule migration—which took place in its opening years. For later prehistoric events the regional chapters could scarcely be improved upon.

Stage 1: 25,000 to 5000 B.C.

Through much of Stage 1 access from Alaska to more southerly portions of North America was presumably difficult because of glacial ice; the times during which it may have been possible at all have been the subject of disagreement (Bryan 1969; Reeves 1971). By the end of this period or very shortly afterward the entire region was virtually completely deglaciated and the seas had risen to substantially their present level, so that the conformation of the land mass was that of modern times. Nevertheless, there is no evidence that at the period's end there were people present in arctic Canada, in Greenland, or in the Kodiak region of Alaska.

The earliest putative evidence of human occupation is from an area now slightly outside the zone of Eskimo occupation, though geographically part of the unglaciated Alaska heartland of the Pleistocene. From the upper Porcupine River drainage, along the Old Crow River some 50 kilometers east of the United States–Canadian border, eroding sediments have yielded stream-deposited fossil animal bone of a number of species now extinct in the region, as well as some bones thought by some scholars to have been modified by man, which have been dated by radiocarbon and other means to about 25,000 B.C. and earlier (Bonnichsen 1979; Irving and Harington 1973; Morlan 1978, 1980). A similar, if smaller, assemblage of redeposited and apparently modified bone is also known from the vicinity of Chicken, Alaska, somewhat to the south of this locality (Porter 1979).

Excepting some few bone artifacts that can be placed only inferentially within a wider cultural context, debris that is of clearly attested antiquity and of absolutely indisputable human origin is almost totally confined to stone assemblages that are largely composed of products of the plentiful production of microblades and blades from cores of a certain variety in size and shape, but with some significant proportion of the blades pressed or struck from well-formed cores of carefully constructed wedge shape. Many of these assemblages also include generalized bifacial implements, some classes of burins, and few or no specialized projectile points. In this volume such collections are described both for northwestern and southwestern Alaska. Extremely similar collections also derive from various sites in the Alaska interior (in the Subarctic culture area), many of them from locations that were not heavily glaciated in the Pleistocene; among these collections are those used as a basis for the original definition of the Denali complex (West 1967). All these manifestations appear to date from 9000 to 6000 B.C. and can be presumed to be the products of hunters of terrestrial mammals, the remains of which, if they had been preserved, might include at least some species now extinct. However, with the exception of a very few occurrences of horse, bison, and elk, those fauna that in fact have been preserved in the sites appear to be essentially modern, with caribou especially well represented. It was artifactual assemblages such as these that were placed together in what was termed the American Paleo-Arctic tradition (Anderson 1968, 1970a).

In addition, there is at least one interior Alaska collection, the Chindadn unit from Healy Lake (J.P. Cook 1969), in which specialized projectile points are affiliated with an assemblage that may otherwise largely duplicate those just mentioned. It is also possible that a few similar collections may include fluted projectile points (Alexander 1974), although some uncertainties remain in regard to the derivation of most such artifacts.

Another variant includes collections in which, although the total blade-core technology is by no means completely divergent from those just mentioned, bifacial implements are lacking entirely. An example of this is the very thoroughly sampled Anangula blade assemblage, which derives from what is now an islet off the coast of Umnak Island in the eastern Aleutians, and which dates from about 6000 B.C. Given arguments that by 6000 B.C. Umnak Island had assumed an insular character that made necessary the use of boats in its original occupation and that the absence of rich strandflats at the time made true maritime, rather than simply littoral, food getting necessary (R.F. Black 1974, 1974a, 1975), it appears indeed possible that these people even at this early time were already well adapted to life on the ocean. Nonetheless, there is no particular specialization for ocean-edge life that is manifest in the stone remnants of the tool kits themselves. That the absence of bifaces at Anangula is not in itself such a manifestation seems indicated by the fact that the closest typological analog to the Anangula collection is the entirely unifacial and strikingly similar assemblage from the Gallagher Flint station of the eastern Brooks Range.

Despite this heterogeneity within the total series of blade-dominated collections, the assemblages of this period in Alaska are all alike in exhibiting formal similarities to material from interior Siberia of the same time or somewhat earlier; for that matter, in their heterogeneity they precisely duplicate the range of variation that appears between various Siberian "Paleolithic" and "Mesolithic" collections (as between the Diuktai and Sumnagin cultures). It is in part for this reason that some students have tended to lump together *all* the Alaska manifestations of this time into, for example, a single Early Boreal tradition (Borden 1975) or a single and all-inclusive Siberian-American Paleo-Arctic tradition (Dumond 1977a), or a similarly inclusive Beringian tradition (West 1981).

Within the New World, slightly later and derivative offshoots of this blade-dominated and properly Siberian material culture can be found only as far east as westernmost Northwest Territories in Canada, but as far south as southeastern Alaska and coastal and interior British Columbia—where they appear as early as 6000 B.C.—and even into south-central Washington (Borden 1975, 1979, with references), in what seems clearly to have been an early Holocene wave of influence that is marked particularly by the production of microblades.

Stage 2: 5000 to 2200 ± 300 B.C.

By about 4000 B.C. there is clearly evident a difference between assemblages of Pacific coastal dwellers and the contemporary tool kits of interior hunters. The coastal aspect has been the most explicitly set forth for Kodiak Island and the adjacent shore of the Alaska Peninsula, in what is termed the Ocean Bay I phase of culture. It also appears that an analog, possibly a close cultural relative, is represented on Anangula Island at the same time at the Village site (Laughlin 1975) although information is thus far incomplete. Even though the precise origin of the coastal peoples so represented is not clear, the presence of blademaking in the earliest of the Ocean Bay I sites seems to imply a beginning among the blademakers of Stage 1. Some excavators of Anangula argue for continuity between the Anangula Blade and Village sites (Laughlin 1975) although others are more cautious ("Prehistory of the Aleutian Region," this vol.).

At about the same time in Alaska north of the Alaska Peninsula, there appears both in the interior and near the coast what has been referred to (Anderson 1968) as the Northern Archaic tradition. This appearance is marked by collections such as are described in this volume for both northern and southwestern Alaska, which include some variety of notched, stemmed, and lanceolate projectile points, apparently the tool kits of terrestrial hunters and river fishermen. Once supposed to be almost entirely restricted to the boreal forest that was expanding within interior Alaska at this time,

Northern Archaic sites are now known to be distributed broadly through the tundra that lies north of the summit of the Brooks Range, as well as in the tundra strips that parallel so much of the coastline of the Bering and Chukchi seas (Anderson 1980).

Unlike the materials from Stage 1, outside of Alaska formal similarities to Northern Archaic assemblages are not notable in Asian collections but are more nearly restricted to those from North America. Similar assemblages are known from various locations in the Subarctic in Canada where, as in Alaska, these Stage 2 people have been presumed to stem ultimately from farther south in North America—where similar assemblages are known in the Archaic of eastern North America by at least 6000 B.C., and in the Great Basin of the western United States by at least as early—as a reflection of the northward movement of southern hunters following the final end of glaciation in response to the warming of the Thermal Maximum (Anderson 1968; Dumond 1969a).

This is not to say that collections within Alaska and northern Canada of this time are altogether homogeneous. Indeed, the variations around the central theme characterized above are substantial, both in the form of the implements and in the presence or absence of certain additional artifacts, especially microblades. The recovery of collections both with blades and without blades has been reported for northern and for southwestern Alaska, as well as from the Alaskan interior and closely adjacent Canada. The fluctuating presence of blades has been attributed variously to ecology, to changes through time (Dumond 1969a), and to blunders in excavation or analysis.

Nor is there agreement that the Northern Archaic tradition represents an occupation of Alaska by southerners. Indeed, the presence of blades in some Northern Archaic collections has been argued to be evidence of continuity from Stage 1 to Stage 2 (J.P. Cook 1969; Henn 1978), and in one case (J.P. Cook 1969) specifically as evidence that ancestral Athapaskans were present in interior Alaska by 9000 B.C.

Stage 3: 2200 ± 300 to 1200 ± 400 B.C.

During Stage 3 people first substantially completed the occupation of all of the American Arctic zone that was ever to be aboriginally occupied by man, and although the later evolution of culture was dramatic in some cases, in most significant aspects the essential character of all later prehistory was set.

By 2500 B.C. in the Kodiak region, people of the Takli culture had taken up the polishing of implements of slate, a characteristic that thereafter was to set the stone assemblages of the Kodiak zone dramatically apart from those of their neighbors of the Aleutian Islands, who were to persist in their emphasis upon chipped implements of hard rocks such as basalt virtually until the time when Europeans arrived. Although both in the prehistoric Aleutians and in the Pacific coastal regions of the Alaska Peninsula, on Kodiak Island, and around Prince William Sound, styles of implements—in both stone and bone—were to fluctuate with time and local area, these variations occurred within stable evolutionary pathways taken by people who were based solidly upon harvest of the products of the ocean, although peoples of both zones made use of whatever land-based fauna was available to them on the larger islands and on the mainland.

In the Aleutian Islands, indeed, developments were gradual enough, at least so far as present knowledge can be organized, that it is reasonable to speak of the establishment of an Aleutian tradition that was to persist until the arrival of Europeans, and to say that Stage 3 endured until about A.D. 1000 or even after, with Stage 4 as elsewhere known (fig. 1) not applicable to the region. In the Kodiak region, on the other hand, the typological differences recognized in the distinction of a Takli culture call for the separation of Stage 3 from a following Stage 4, despite the apparent traditional stability of the region from Stage 3 onward.

From the Alaska Peninsula north through Alaska and east through Canada to Greenland, the beginning of this stage (between about 2200 and 1900 B.C.) was marked by the appearance of peoples with a distinctive, miniaturized tool kit of delicately chipped end- and side-blades, of burins, microblades, and less frequent polished adz blades and burin-like grooving tools. These people, bearers of the Arctic Small Tool tradition (Irving 1962a, 1964), rapidly dispersed throughout virtually the entire portion of the maritime Arctic zone that was ever to be inhabited at all and within a few centuries would move into the Barren Grounds. It is this set of events that provides not only the beginning of the prehistory of most of the American Arctic but also one of its major integrating devices: the first indication of interest in and ability to colonize the High Arctic, that interest so basic to the popular conception of the nature of later Eskimos.

Ever since its initial discovery, the Arctic Small Tool tradition has been said to relate to microlithic assemblages of the Old World (Giddings 1951), and with the ensuing discovery of examples of what is here termed the Paleo-Arctic tradition of Stage 1, there has been a pronounced tendency either to align it with that tradition (Bandi 1969) or, as improved knowledge of chronology has developed, to derive it from that tradition (Anderson 1970b). Reasonably enough, because both these traditions are present within Alaska, it has often been presumed that any such descent also occurred there (Dumond 1965). But the increase in information regarding both the Paleo-Arctic and the Arctic Small Tool

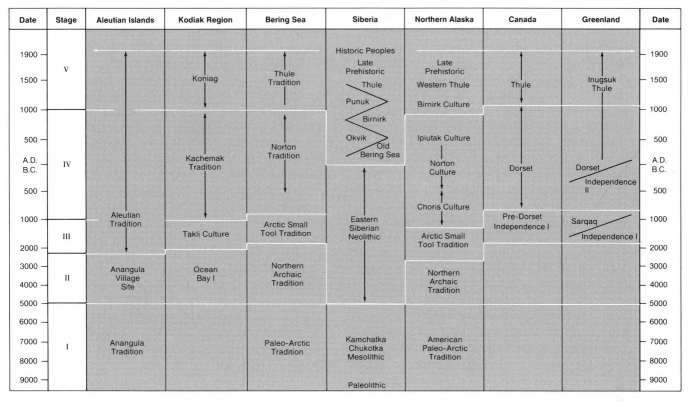

Fig. 1. Summary of the prehistoric occupations of the Arctic.

traditions within Alaska has brought no support of such a derivation of the one from the other on Alaskan soil, where, indeed, they seem to be definitively divided from one another by the Northern Archaic tradition of Stage 2.

One solution that has been suggested (Irving 1969–1970; Dumond 1969–1970, 1977a), which seems to violate none of the notions of relationship that have been held in the past, is that this descent occurred on Asian rather than American soil. The nature of the earlier Neolithic of eastern Siberia seems to reinforce this: Arctic Small Tool–like assemblages do occur there, and they can in turn and without too much problem be pictured as derived somewhere in that area from earlier terminal Paleolithic assemblages similar in cast to those of the American Paleo-Arctic tradition. It then becomes possible to suggest that the Arctic Small Tool tradition originated in the crystallization of a slightly new configuration of elements already present in Siberia and was then transported to the New World probably late in the third millennium B.C. Given the absence of evidence of people of the Arctic Small Tool tradition in the Aleutian zone and the evident continuity within that region since 2500 B.C., an implication of this model is that the linguistic separation of ancestral Eskimos and Aleuts may have occurred before the development of the Arctic Small Tool tradition, hence that speakers of Eskimo-Aleut languages entered the New World in two separate waves: one, perhaps as long ago as the flooding of the Bering Platform, bringing ancestors of Aleuts; the other, of the third millennium B.C., bringing ancestors of Eskimos.

Although the remains assigned to the Arctic Small Tool tradition within Alaska are remarkably uniform (excepting the variations in the proportions of certain artifacts in collections from the Alaska Peninsula, which can be used to set them slightly apart from the northern Denbigh Flint complex), they are much less uniform in the huge territory to the east. For that region, divergent views exist of the relationship between the so-called Independence I culture of northern Greenland and some High Arctic islands, and the Pre-Dorset culture in general (in which Greenland Sarqaq is provisionally included here). Nothing of a similar disagreement is in evidence for the Alaska zone, where the most drastic division among Small Tool materials is the separation of Proto-Denbigh, "Classic" Denbigh, and Late Denbigh.

Between collections from Alaska and most of those from the eastern Arctic, however, there are distinctions to be made. Although virtually all the Denbigh Flint complex artifacts can be duplicated somewhere in the eastern Arctic, the eastern assemblages as a whole stand apart from the Denbigh Flint complex: Independence I with its emphasis on stemmed projectiles, for instance; Pre-Dorset with its notched points and knives, not to mention its few polished points or knives and its few oil lamps. A number of radiocarbon determinations for eastern Small

Tool assemblages, if taken at face value, provide dates as early as 2500 B.C.—several centuries earlier than any acceptable determination relating to an Alaska Small Tool assemblage, despite the fact that there is unanimous agreement on the Alaska origin of the Small Tool people and most of their material culture.

It is unfortunate that organic materials are so often lacking in Small Tool collections, depriving students of the information they can provide not only in regard to the presence of useful items such as boats, sleds, and dogs, but also in the way of a direct indication of subsistence focus. Although in Alaska the only known examples of permanently constructed Small Tool habitations are located well away from the seacoast (specifically, toward the interior portion of the strip of tundra that parallels the sea edge) and it therefore seems that a major reliance was upon interior resources such as the caribou and (where available) river fish, it is also clear that seasonal visits were made to the coast for sealing. And it is even more evident that when these people moved into the eastern Arctic it was possible for them to subsist when necessary almost entirely upon sea-edge products, even though certain important techniques—such as those involved in hunting seals through the winter ice of the Arctic coasts—are nowhere in evidence. At the other extreme, when moving into the High Arctic of Greenland it was equally possible for the Independence I people to emphasize the hunting of land animals, here the musk-ox, almost to the exclusion of sea mammals. Thus, despite a shortage of organic food trash it seems clear that a broadly based economy, balanced among products of the land, the sea, and the rivers, was already established by 2000 B.C.—an economy that foreshadowed that of later Eskimos, who were over and over to exhibit their flexibility in wresting a living from often hostile environments, turning to the land or to the sea with equal success.

It is undoubtedly partly for this reason that so many students of Arctic prehistory have come to think of bearers of the Arctic Small Tool tradition as ancestral Eskimos.

Stage 4: 1200 ± 400 B.C. to A.D. 600 ± 500

The beginning of Stage 4 is marked by the disappearance of the Arctic Small Tool tradition; the end is marked by the appearance of a generalized Thule tradition. During its course certain previously established traditions continued their stable evolution; however, generally there was an increase in interest in use of products of the seacoast, the development of more nearly permanent coastal villages, and the use of properly maritime techniques in the taking of sea mammals.

In the Aleutian Islands the relative cultural and eco-

logical stability and the absence of any ready-made customary divisions into archeological units inhibit the separation of this stage from that which precedes it. For the Kodiak region, on the other hand, the recognition of a separate Kachemak tradition at this time does make possible the recognition of a separate Stage 4, despite the cultural and ecological continuity in evidence.

As with the Kodiak zone, in the eastern Arctic Stage 4 can be recognized with the presence of Dorset culture, which nevertheless in certain areas developed in unbroken succession from its parent Pre-Dorset—a succession of almost baffling ease and regularity, even though it occurred at about the time of colder weather, a retraction in geographic extent of occupation, and an apparent (if little understood) demographic crisis. The specific attributes of Dorset culture become evident between about 1000 and 800 B.C. and characterize most of the region east of the Mackenzie River, including Greenland.

In the zone between these eastern and southwestern regions of stable continuity, Alaska people of the coasts of the Bering and Chukchi seas were taking part in a development that, like the earlier rise of the Arctic Small Tool tradition, was shared with eastern Siberia, this time with a late Neolithic cultural aspect such as that of Belkachi and the burials of Ust'-Belaia. In northern Alaska this new development is manifest in cultural units termed Choris, Norton, near Ipiutak, and Ipiutak; south of Bering Strait the less heterogeneous manifestations have been called simply Norton.

The mechanism for this new evolutionary development is uncertain. Nearly all local chronologies appear disrupted at about this time, with an occupational hiatus common; however, the date of this often-unoccupied interval appears to vary: based on a single radiocarbon date calculated on the half-life of 5,730 years, the earliest post–Arctic Small Tool tradition development of the pottery-using Choris culture is sometimes said to date from the sixteenth century B.C. (or a century later using the 5,668 half-life). On the Alaska Peninsula, on the other hand, the Arctic Small Tool tradition persisted without substantial change until 1100 or even 1000 B.C. in (5,568 half-life) radiocarbon time, and the first pottery-bearing sites of the Norton cultural tradition can be dated no earlier than 500 B.C.

Furthermore, in the north the early Choris-affiliated assemblages appear in a number of places but are relatively heterogeneous, with variety in the forms of stone implements, some assemblages including pottery, and some without. The occurrence of the puzzling Old Whaling culture during the same interval simply adds to the sense of heterogeneity.

By the last centuries before the Christian era, however, a more broadly homogeneous culture of what may be termed the Norton tradition was spread along the coast from the Alaska Peninsula in southwestern Alaska to Firth River in extreme northwestern Canada. Although there was certainly some local diversity and variety in artifact styles, the range of variation was restricted, and the predominantly check-stamped ceramic ware was remarkably uniform. Direct evidence of maritime pursuits at this time is scanty (indeed, organic trash and implements of perishable materials are scarce for almost all Norton sites), being represented primarily by a pair of whaling harpoon heads that are attributed to Near Ipiutak occupation at Point Hope (Larsen and Rainey 1948:163). Indirect evidence exists in the relatively sudden appearance of substantial coastal sites from Wales on Bering Strait to the mouth of the Ugashik River on the Alaska Peninsula; in the initial occupation of islands such as Nunivak; and in the unmistakable coastal presence northward to Cape Krusenstern, Point Hope, Barrow, and beyond. Despite the existence of large coastal sites in some apparently suitable areas around Bristol Bay of the southern Bering Sea and of a continuing focus of settlement on some salmon streams away from the coast both in that region and farther north (Dumond 1979), it was an interest in coastal resources that apparently impelled some of these same people across the Alaska Peninsula from the Bering Sea to the sea mammal–rich Pacific coast. This coastward reorientation in Alaska was part of a systematic shift toward maritime resources that also involved contemporary peoples of the Asian coasts, particularly the shores of the Sea of Okhotsk (Dumond 1983).

In the zone north of Bering Strait, shortly after the beginning of the Christian era the Norton assemblages proper were replaced by those of the related, although strikingly distinct, Ipiutak culture, representing people who, although diverging artifactually from their Norton predecessors and particularly notable for their spectacular art so frequently found with burials, seem on the basis of present evidence to have shared a substantially similar culture (Lutz 1972). In the south, however, culture of a less drastically modified Norton tradition, with ceramics, oil lamps, and increasingly popular polished slate evolved steadily through all or most of the first millennium A.D.

Stage 5: A.D. 600 ± 500 to 1800 ± 100

Stage 5 begins with the appearance of what can be broadly defined as the Thule tradition and ends with the practical advent of the ethnographic present. As conceived here, the Thule tradition is substantially equivalent to "Neo-Eskimo" (Larsen and Rainey 1948:182) or to the "Northern Maritime tradition" (Collins 1964) and designates the maritime-oriented dwellers of northern coastlines, their close cultural relatives—who often did not show such extreme interest in purely maritime pursuits—and their descendants throughout the Arctic.

This Thule tradition is first manifest in the earliest cultures of the Bering Strait islands—cultures designated Old Bering Sea and Okvik, which are known primarily from Saint Lawrence and other islands, as well as from the Asiatic shore. Unfortunately, although there are various typological studies that can be cited, there has been no complete elucidation of the course of development of this particular culture or pair of cultures. Nonetheless, given the evident existence in eastern Siberia of Norton-like neolithic manifestations by 1000 B.C. and the irruption of peoples of a similar culture upon the Okhotsk Sea coast not long after, there can be little doubt that the maritime emphasis shown so quickly by people of Saint Lawrence Island and the western shore of Bering Strait was simply a precocious emphasis of the ocean-side interest that was general in both northeast Asia and Alaska.

This maritime interest and ability has been used to account for the striking expansion of people of this cultural stamp, first around the Chukchi Sea as Birnirk culture, and then in two divergent directions: to Bering Sea as Nukleet culture and related Thule people of Bristol Bay, who then moved on to the north Pacific in the Kodiak Island region, taking pottery and (according to one interpretation) a Yupik Eskimo language (Dumond 1965), and who even left traces in the eastern Aleutians; and to the east, where Thule people moved dramatically through northern Canada to Greenland over substantially the same path taken by their Arctic Small Tool predecessors, and along which they succeeded in submerging the still healthy Dorset culture of the zone. But it is also clear that this ability to deal with ocean hunting, which must certainly have been important to the continued success of Thule peoples throughout the Arctic, was not at the expense of comparable techniques applicable to subsistence up the rivers or in the tundra-covered interior. Rather, Thule economy, like that of its predecessors in both the eastern and western Arctic, was balanced, and Thule abilities ashore matched those afloat (W.E. Taylor 1966).

So it was that after the expansionist movements and related and explosive diffusion of the Thule period proper, from A.D. 900 to 1100, the cultural descendants of the broader Thule tradition were able not only to cope with challenges presented by the kayak- and umiak-hunting of sea mammals large and small, in a zone from the Pacific coast to southern Greenland, but also to expand up Alaska rivers into the edge of the boreal forest, to exploit the caribou herds of the Brooks Range and the Barren Grounds, and to take up again the migratory life of their Dorset predecessors in the Central Arctic as the deterioration of climate after A.D. 1400 rendered certain parts of the Thule culture no longer viable.

And thus they were found by the first European explorers.

77

Models of Eskimo-Aleut Prehistory

In the information and interpretations summarized here, there is material for more than one model of Eskimo-Aleut prehistory, and it should be clear from the areal summaries in this volume that no single model is acceptable to all the archeologist contributors. Indeed, the most fundamental area of disagreement may be that between prehistorians who are inclined to see the origins of Eskimos and Aleuts in the earliest cultural horizons that are fairly adequately known, and those prehistorians who are not. Some of these divergent views will be sketched briefly here (see also McGhee 1978).

The most far-reaching set of reconstructions of Eskimo-Aleut prehistory are those that derive both peoples from a common ancestor represented among assemblages of Stage 1 and that hypothesize that the Aleutian tradition, the Kachemak tradition, and the Arctic Small Tool tradition are all derived from it by divergent paths of cultural evolution. Whether other populations, such as ancestors of some American Indians, would also be represented among the possibly interrelated assemblages of Stage 1 is not necessarily relevant to a model of strictly Eskimo-Aleut prehistory, but there appears to be no compelling substantive reason that they should not be so represented. Beyond this question, and within this basic form, there is still room for a number of variations among the specific reconstructions of prehistory.

The first of these more specific models may be paraphrased thus: assemblages of Stage 1 include both ancestral Indians and ancestral Eskimo-Aleuts. Of these, the Anangula Blade site represents ancestral Eskimo-Aleuts, people who had long lived on the southern coastline of the Bering Platform and who, when the water of the Bering Sea had risen to flood the platform completely, had by 6000 B.C. or shortly thereafter found themselves upon an island (Umnak-Anangula), where they continued to practice their antique, effective, maritime way of life. As these seas continued to rise, however, some of them—or some of their very near relatives of the southern coast of the now-inundated platform—were forced northward toward the vicinity of the present mouth of the Kuskokwim River, and farther. As descendents of the remnant Anangula people become the modern Aleuts, those of these northward-migrating relatives became modern Eskimos (Aigner 1974; Laughlin 1967; cf. Dumond 1965).

Although parsimonious and cogent in many respects, a major problem with this version seems to lie in the argument that these ancestral peoples have been oriented toward the oceanside for at least 8,000 years, with the implication that such a clear maritime adaptation should be manifested by all ancestral Eskimos and in the further implication that some sort of developmental sequence from something like the Anangula blade complex to later Eskimo ancestors should be discoverable within Alaska. As has been suggested earlier, neither of these implications seems to be satisfied by what is understood of the subsistence orientation and material cultural affinities of the Arctic Small Tool tradition.

A second, although related, model eliminates some of this difficulty by conceiving of Eskimos and Aleuts as deriving from different populations of those peoples represented in Alaska during Stage 1, populations whose subsistence orientations were already divergent one from the other. In the south, people such as those at the Anangula Blade site were ancestral to modern Aleuts. In the north, more interior-oriented bearers of the American Paleo-Arctic tradition were ancestral to people of the Arctic Small Tool tradition and later Eskimos (Anderson 1970b). Clearly, this model also requires the eventual identification within Alaska of material cultures representing peoples ancestral to those of the Arctic Small Tool tradition and descended from those of the Paleo-Arctic tradition—an identification that is as yet extremely uncertain.

For some of the considerations indicated, a third and more complicated, although still related, model has appeared in which an all-embracing Paleo-Arctic tradition of Stage 1 is presumed to have been present both in Asia and America, with descendants of the common Eskimo-Aleut ancestors divided among themselves at least as early as the inundation of the Bering Platform at 11,000 to 10,000 B.C. From American descendants such as those at Anangula ultimately came modern Aleuts, and from some of their contemporary southern relatives—such as those represented by the Ugashik Narrows phase on the Alaska Peninsula—descended an Eskimo-Aleut group who provided a substantial part of the parentage of the modern Pacific Eskimos, who in their turn were to undergo a much later acculturation and language shift caused by the areally expanding Eskimos of the Thule tradition. Modern Eskimos of the Bering Sea and northward, on the other hand, are conceived of as descended from people represented by the Arctic Small Tool tradition, who in turn derived from the common Eskimo-Aleut ancestor not in America but in Siberia, and who entered the New World in a separate migratory movement between 3000 and 2000 B.C. (Dumond 1977a; cf. Irving 1969–1970). Aside from a lack of parsimony, this version suffers from the extreme view it takes of the degree of separation of Eskimos and Aleuts, as well as from its attribution of key events to a position offstage in the relative terra incognita of the eastern Siberian Neolithic.

Still a fourth reconstruction seeks to achieve greater economy by simply eliminating the Arctic Small Tool tradition from the model of Aleut relationship, making use of an organization in which Norton culture is derived from the earlier material culture of the Alaska Peninsula and the Pacific coastal regions. In one version

(Dumond 1972; McGhee 1976a) an ancestral connection between parental Norton people and early Alaska Peninsula people of either Pacific Eskimo or Aleut affinities is hypothesized for the time around 1000 B.C. after which the Norton progenitors expanded northward, acquiring Asian pottery, and then both Eskimos and Aleuts proceeded along developmental lines such as those assumed by the other models. A major difficulty here is the insufficient time-depth implied for the division between the Eskimo and Aleut branches of the Eskimo-Aleut language family, whose modern Aleut and Eskimo representatives have been compared in the degree of their divergence to English and Russian of the Germanic and Slavic branches of Indo-European (Swadesh 1968). The time-depth allowed by this model of prehistory would seem to correspond to the degree of divergence among the separate languages of the Eskimo branch of the family alone (Krauss 1973; Swadesh 1968) rather than to that between all Eskimo and all Aleut, however estimated.

This problem is avoided to a large extent by a second version of this same fourth model, which suggests hypothetically that the division between Eskimo and Aleut occurred at about the time of the earliest human occupation that is known in the eastern Aleutians and on the Alaska Peninsula—around 7000 to 6000 B.C. From these ancestral Eskimos ultimately developed people such as those represented on the lower Peninsula at Port Moller, who in turn gave rise to northward-moving early Norton people, who then spawned the later Eskimos (Clark 1979). There seems to be no particular violence done to well-established facts of Alaska prehistory by this organization, although some later features of movement or language shift seem necessary in order to account for the lack of intergrading speech communities between Eskimoan and Aleutian.

It is in the eastern Arctic, however, that the denial of Eskimo affiliation to people of the Arctic Small Tool tradition has its major impact. Given the steady progression from Pre-Dorset to Dorset that is now understood, this denial serves to set aside from the Eskimo stock the later people of Dorset culture as well. The rather general acceptance at this time of the Dorset people as some variety of Eskimos is no doubt in large measure intuitive, based upon the feelings about distribution and basic culture, for instance, as well as for the apparent ease with which Thule and Dorset seemed to accommodate as one absorbed the other. However, some supporting evidence does seem to exist in the Eskimo-like physical remains of the few Dorset skeletons that have been studied (Harp and Hughes 1968; Oschinsky 1964). That is, if the Dorset people were not "Eskimo," they appear to have been Arctic Mongoloids.

Indeed, most of the choice among the models hitherto described is based upon one's inclinations toward the Arctic Small Tool tradition. In the first place there is the question whether the people so represented were oriented toward a maritime life or not; in the second place there is the question whether their origin was within America; in the third place there is the question whether they were within the straight line of Eskimo development.

In contrast to all these models, some empirically oriented prehistorians are inclined to question the derivation of at least some of the later peoples of the northern littoral from *any* base in Stage 1 and to feel more comfortable with a model that takes up later, perhaps around 2500 B.C., and that does not presume to specify the archeological horizon upon which Eskimos and Aleuts are ultimately related, as their speech and physical characteristics indicate them to be. After the date given, any such model is substantially similar to those mentioned earlier. And indeed after that date the disagreement upon specific facts of Eskimo-Aleut prehistory grows relatively small—involving things such as the relative degree of Asian influence in the development of the maritime culture of Bering Strait in the early first millennium A.D., the precise nature of contacts between peoples of Canada and Greenland, the degree to which movements and adaptations can be termed environmental response, and so on.

Last of all, it must be noted that the models described above are those current among American prehistorians and some of their European colleagues. They are not, however, those subscribed to by many Russian prehistorians with an interest in their own northeast, who tend to see a significant portion of the total immigration to the New World Arctic as having occurred through the Commander and Aleutian islands, rather than across a more-or-less dry Bering Platform (for example, Arutiunov and Sergeev 1975; Black 1983 contains an English synthesis of Russian opinion). U.S. and Canadian investigators (for example, Hrdlička 1945; Laughlin and Marsh 1951) have tended to reject this same position on the basis of their reading of data from physical anthropology, archeology, and linguistics, although they have been able to draw on little comparative information from either the Russian mainland or the Commander Islands. Evidence from the latter is still unclear: Hrdlička (1945:397) concluded the islands to have been without prehistoric occupants at any time, and the study by Russians (Dikov 1977:111–112) is inconclusive. On the other hand, work is being done on the Pacific coast of the Kamchatka Peninsula, and the results are becoming available to American prehistorians (for example, Dikov 1977:112–117). It is conceivable that their position may eventually be modified.

Prehistory of North Alaska

DOUGLAS D. ANDERSON

The northwestern American Arctic from Nome, Alaska, to the Mackenzie River delta, Canada, includes the lands occupied in the twentieth century by western Inuit, and, along the Koyukuk River, by the Koyukuk River branch of the Koyukon Indians. The main geographical regions include: the Arctic coastal plain, comprising the flat lowlands north of the Arctic Slope; the Arctic Slope, which includes the northern foothills of the Brooks Range; the Brooks Range, which is a part of the Rocky Mountains; the Kotzebue-Kobuk lowland; the northern and western portions of Seward Peninsula; the Mackenzie River delta; and the upper part of the Koyukuk River.

The northwestern Arctic is noted archeologically for its important role in the development of early American Arctic cultures and, in more recent periods, in the development of Arctic Eskimo culture. It is also a region in which, along the southern boundary, Eskimos and Indians have interacted for millennia and in so doing have contributed a great deal to each other's culture.

A great many archeological sites have been recorded for this region (fig. 1). For this review the prehistory has been divided into five periods that reflect the more significant changes in culture and habitat: full-time tundra hunting, from earlier than 9000 B.C. to 6000 B.C.; adaptation to taiga-tundra hunting and fishing, from 6000 B.C. to 2200 B.C.; development of seasonal and year-round coastal hunting and fishing, from 2200 B.C. to A.D. 500; prehistoric Eskimo culture, from A.D. 500 to 1778; and historic Eskimo culture, from 1778 to the present.

Period 1: Full-time Tundra Hunting

Most archeologists believe that people have been in North America at least 20,000 years and perhaps as long as 60,000 years. The Old Crow Flats localities in northwestern Canada (in the Subarctic culture area) may document man's presence in northern North America prior to 25,000 years ago, and if so, sites at least as old are thus expectable in Arctic Alaska. However, as yet no one has been able to find conclusive evidence that people occupied the Alaskan Arctic prior to 11,000 years ago. Some excavated faunal remains are

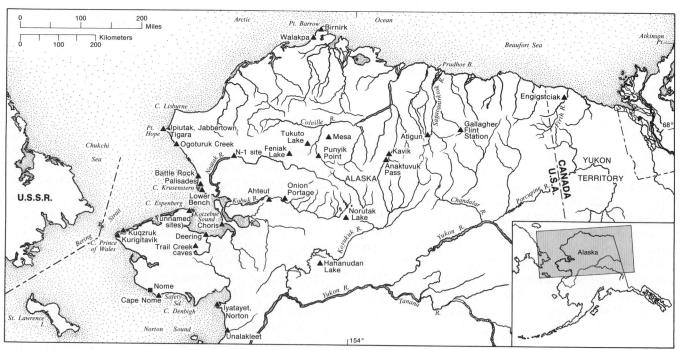

80   Fig. 1. Archeological sites of North Alaska.

older, but in each case there is some question whether they resulted from human activity. One of the likeliest of these questionable ancient sites in Arctic Alaska is Trail Creek cave number 9 on northern Seward Peninsula. A scapula of a horse (*Equus* sp.) and a calcaneus of a bison (*Bison* sp.), found in the lower level of the excavated floor outside cave 9, dated to 13,800 B.C. ± 350 (K1210) and 11,120 B.C. ± 280 (K1327), respectively (Larsen 1968:62–63). The calcaneus appears to have been broken by human beings for the purpose of extracting marrow. Unfortunately no artifacts were found associated with the bones; on the other hand, one crude bifaced point fragment came from a similarly low level just outside cave 2 at Trail Creek.

Other possibly early Arctic finds, thought to be younger than these, are fluted projectile points recovered from several parts of the Brooks Range (Humphrey 1966; Solecki 1951a; R.M. Thompson 1948; Kunz 1982; Bowers 1982; Dixon 1979) and the upper Koyukuk River drainage (Clark 1972). Although not well dated, they are thought by some experts to be historically related to Clovis and Folsom fluted points associated with extinct fauna in western North America. These archeologists believe that such points, whether found in Alaska or farther south, represent a big game hunting tradition that was widespread in North America between 12,000 and 8,000 years ago. Other experts see the points as but a variation on basally channeled points characteristic of several more recent Arctic cultures.

Among the earliest radiocarbon-dated archeological remains from the northwestern American Arctic are artifacts from the Gallagher Flint station, a multicomponent site on a glacial kame in the eastern Brooks Range. The site has yielded thousands of mudstone flakes and artifacts dated to before 8500 B.C. (Dixon 1975). The flakes were unpurposefully retouched and show signs of unidirectional use. Many are also elongate and ridged, resembling true blades. The latter flakes

were struck from blocky cores, and the cores often had multiple platforms for striking off the flakes. Such a flaking technique was perhaps a variant of the technique used in the polyhedral blade and core industry, in which cores were rotated, producing ever smaller blades, the smallest of which are called microblades.

American Paleo-Arctic Tradition

The earliest of the well-documented archeological traditions in the northwestern Arctic is the American Paleo-Arctic tradition (Anderson 1970a; Hall and Gal 1982; Davis et al. 1981). Originally identified from the Akmak and Kobuk assemblages at Onion Portage and an assemblage from the lower levels at Trail Creek caves, finds have subsequently been reported from the North Slope as well. Dates for the tradition are thus far available only from the original sites: Akmak has a date of 7907 B.C. ± 155 (K-1583), Kobuk has dates ranging from 6500 to 6100 B.C., and the early microblade layers at Trail Creek caves have a date of 7120 B.C. ± 150 (K-980).

Other sites in Alaska have also been assigned to the American Paleo-Arctic tradition (see "Prehistory of the Bering Sea Region," this vol.).

• AKMAK Vitreous chert (Inupiaq *akma·q*) was used for many tools in the Akmak complex. The assemblage is characterized by large cores on which steeply angled platforms were created for the purpose of striking off blade preforms. The preforms were reworked to make end scrapers, gouges, several kinds of knives, and shaft smoothers. Narrow grooved shaft straighteners of basalt suggest that bows and arrows were used. Microblades found in the complex were produced from narrow wedge-shaped cores of a type found at sites in Siberia, Mongolia, Japan, and central Alaska (there called Campus-type microblade cores); and the Akmak specimens undoubtedly owed their method of manufacture to tech-

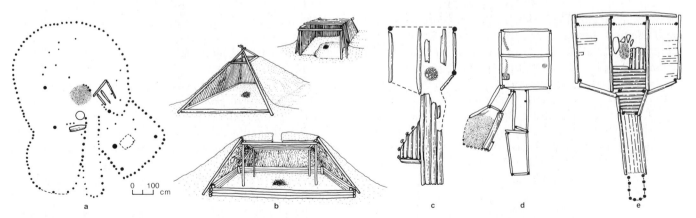

after Giddings and Anderson 1984.

Fig. 2. Alaska coast house-type plans: a, Old Whaling winter house 22, Cape Krusenstern, about 1300 B.C.; b, Ipiutak house types, Cape Krusenstern, A.D. 200–900; c, Birnirk period house 32, Cape Krusenstern, about A.D. 600; d, early western Thule period house, Cape Krusenstern, about A.D. 1200–1300; e, 15th-century house 5, Kotzebue Sound, of an interior type construction although built on the coast. a, c–e, Same scale; b, reconstructed houses not to scale.

Fig. 3. Period 1, Onion Portage, Alaska. Kobuk chert, 6000–6400 B.C.: a, blade; b, burin; c, narrow wedge-shaped microblade core. Akmak about 7800 B.C.: d, chert blade; e, blade from edge-faceted core; f, face-faceted blade core. Length of a, 7.5 cm; rest same scale.

niques developed earlier in Eurasia. In diverse areas of Eurasia and North America, microblades served different functions, but in northern Alaska they were tiny rectangular bladelets for insetting into the sides of arrow or spear heads. The Akmak assemblage bears close resemblance to finds from central and southwest Alaska (West 1981; Dumond 1981; Henn 1978) and from the Aldan region of eastern Siberia (Mochanov 1969, 1977). During the last centuries of the Bering land bridge and for several millennia afterward, Arctic groups throughout eastern Siberia and Alaska must have remained part of a broad interaction network.

• SETTLEMENTS Information about American Paleo-Arctic settlement patterns is scanty. Akmak was possibly a dwelling site, and the rest of the known sites appear to have been temporary campsites of caribou hunters. The possible Akmak dwelling site was on a well-drained, high bluff overlooking the Kobuk River at a place that afforded a broad view of the valley. The Akmak people who used the site carried out a wide range of activities including hide preparation, butchering, carving on soft and hard materials (perhaps on ivory), planing, chopping, and the manufacture of weapons. Stone tools apparently were finished and resharpened at the site but were blocked out or made elsewhere. The exotic cherts that gave Akmak its name were not local and may have been acquired from chert beds of the Noatak River or farther north.

Campsites of Kobuk complex hunters were found along the edges of the Kobuk River on moist overbank deposits sparsely covered with horsetails, sedges, and grasses. Though not so dry as higher, shrub-covered banks along the river, such sites afforded a ready supply of dead branches of poplar and willow scrub for fuel, an open place to spread out without having to clear brush, and a relatively mosquito-free campground. Twentieth-century Eskimos also select such spots as campsites. The ancient hunters made camp fires of willow branches and, in some cases, of caribou bones. Their fires were relatively small and frequently did not get hot enough to oxidize the moist sand upon which the fires were built. In some cases caribou bones were pulverized and boiled, probably to render fat, a practice that persisted until the twentieth century. Hunters sat close to their fires and worked at making or repairing their weapons. The remains of their manufactures lay scattered around the hearths to a distance of 4.5 feet.

The Trail Creek cave 2 site, the lower levels of which yielded American Paleo-Arctic artifacts, probably served as a shelter and a lookout for caribou hunters. The hunters may have built fires in the cave for cooking meat or for warmth, as people in later periods did, but the evidence for this is inconclusive. Other American Paleo-Arctic sites located in the Brooks Range and on the North Slope were short-term campsites, in which the artifacts were scattered over large areas (Anderson 1972; Davis et al. 1981). No trace of hearths is present in these sites, but even if hearths had been built in the rocky areas where most of the artifacts were located, their remains would not long have endured.

Period 2: Adaptation to Taiga-Tundra Hunting and Fishing

As a result of the post-Pleistocene warming trend and melting of glacial ice, by 6000 B.C. the sea level had risen to between 25 and 40 feet below its present height. In the northwestern Arctic the coast line was for the most part within a mile of the twentieth-century shore line. After this time sea level continued to rise slowly until it reached its present height between 2000 and 2500 B.C. During the period of maximum Holocene warming—known in other regions of North America as the Hypsithermal, when mean annual temperatures were warmer than now—most of the modern features of north Alaska vegetation were established. The shrubless tundra of the North Slope persisted in the lower, wetter coastal plain region, but in the higher southern elevations it was replaced by shrub tundra. Boreal woodland vegetation including spruce, alder, birch, and smaller woodland plants established itself in the Kobuk, Mackenzie, lower Noatak, and upper Selawik valleys (Schweger 1971; P.M. Anderson 1982).

The archeology of the period between 6000 and 4600 B.C. is, curiously, poorly known. Although numerous sites are present that may belong to that period, only one site, the Mesa site in the upper Colville River drainage system, dated to 5670 B.C. ± 95 (DIC-1589), is

82

demonstrably of that age (Kunz 1982). Lacking microblades characteristic of the American Paleo-Arctic tradition, the Mesa assemblage has, among other artifacts, a variety of bipointed and oblanceolate projectile points that appear unrelated to American Paleo-Arctic types. On the other hand, other sites attributed to this period do contain basically the same tool kit as the American Paleo-Arctic, except for some new varieties of microblade core types (Gal 1982; Gerlach 1982). Whether the differences between the Mesa assemblage and the assemblages of the microblade sites reflect the existence of two distinct cultural traditions or variations in activities conducted at the sites is a matter of debate.

Northern Archaic Tradition

After 4600 B.C. the cultures of the northwestern Arctic began to resemble those from the North American boreal woodlands. These cultural complexes, now identified as part of the Northern Archaic tradition (Anderson 1968), appeared in the north at about the same time that spruce began to grow along the southern edges of the Arctic, a coincidence that suggests some direct relationship between the two events. The oldest dated site affiliated with this new tradition is Tuktu, excavated in 1959 at Anaktuvuk Pass in the central Brooks Range (Campbell 1962b). Tuktu implements include side-notched projectile points, bifacial knives, end scrapers, notched pebble artifacts, and microblades made from broad cores. The artifacts were associated with a hearth that has been radiocarbon dated to 4560 B.C. ± 610 (SI-114) (Long 1965:250), about 700 years after the glaciers receded from the area.

In the southwestern part of the Brooks Range a somewhat later phase of the Northern Archaic tradition, known as Palisades, appeared around 4000 B.C. (Giddings 1960a). Palisades and its derivative Portage complex represent a long span of gradual cultural change that includes an evolution in chipped stone point forms from side-notched to corner-notched (or stemmed) and finally to lanceolate, the later form coincidentally like earlier Plano points of the North American Great Plains. Except that the Palisades and Portage complexes had no microblades, their tool forms were like those of Tuktu. The presence or absence of microblades in otherwise similar assemblages suggests that different activities were carried out at the different sites, but since caribou hunting and meat processing were the major endeavors at all the Palisades sites and at the Tuktu site, this suggestion does not seem to hold. It is interesting that both microblade and non-microblade notched point sites, also dating to between the fifth and third millennium B.C., have been found in central Alaska and the southwestern Yukon Territory of Canada as well (MacNeish 1964; Workman 1978; Cook 1977). Further analysis of these

sites should reveal whether microblades in the assemblages indicate special activities or geographical or temporal differences.

The association of Northern Archaic sites and the northern woodlands led archeologists initially to consider the tradition to represent the culture of people adapting to the spread of spruce habitats into earlier tundra-covered regions (Anderson 1968). However, subsequent archeological and palynological research has indicated that the relationships are much more complex. Northern Archaic sites have now been located in tundra areas far distant from the northern forest edge (Davis et al. 1981), so there is no longer a direct correlation between habitat and the archeological tradition. Palynological evidence indicates that although the tradition did appear along the southern flanks of the Brooks Range at the same time spruce appeared, the region did not begin to support a sizable spruce woodland until several millennia later (P.M. Anderson 1982). Obviously, a single spruce tree growing here or there in the tundra does not signal an effective change of habitat that would require a major change in culture. Thus, the replacement of the American Paleo-Arctic by the Northern Archaic tradition in the northwestern Arctic cannot presently be satisfactorily explained as adaptational change. On the other hand an alternative explanation, that the Northern Archaic tradition represents the cultural tradition of peoples moving northward into the Arctic, is equally unsatisfactory (Anderson 1979).

Although replaced in the northwestern Arctic by cultures of the Arctic Small Tool tradition about 2200 B.C., the Northern Archaic tradition continued in other parts of Alaska for several millennia. The tradition may also have had an influence on the development of the historic Athapaskan culture (Anderson 1978; Workman 1978; Dumond 1977a).

• SETTLEMENTS In the northwestern Arctic, settlements of the Northern Archaic tradition are known from semisubterranean house floors at Onion Portage, stone-lined tent rings in the Brooks Range and the North Slope, and unlined open campfire places throughout the region. The dwellings were probably skin-covered hemispherical tents made of flexible willow frames with unlined fireplaces located in the middle of the floors. Artifacts, scattered thickly over the entire floor, suggest that sleeping and working areas of the house were not spatially differentiated. At Onion Portage hearth areas outside the confines of the house floors contained thick lenses, often stratified, of burned caribou bones, oxidized sand, and charcoal. Artifacts were scattered around the hearths up to a radius of 7.5 feet, suggesting that tents had enclosed the space. The stone-lined tent rings of the Brooks Range, circular to oval in outline, measured 10–12 feet in diameter (Campbell 1961). In the Brooks Range other artifacts found in tight concentrations may also have once been associated with hearths, which lacking stone-lining subsequently were obliterated by the elements.

Period 3: Development of Seasonal and Year-Round Coastal Hunting and Fishing

Evidence is plentiful that the coasts of the northwestern Arctic have been inhabited by Arctic dwellers since the time sea level stabilized between 4,500 and 4,200 years ago. The sudden commencement of activity along the coast may be more apparent than real, however, because the waters rising prior to that time would have washed away traces of earlier coastal life.

Arctic Small Tool Tradition

The oldest coastal sites belonged to people of the Denbigh Flint complex, the first and most completely described of the Arctic Small Tool complexes. Discovered in 1948 at Cape Denbigh on Norton Sound (Giddings 1964), the complex was later found at Cape Espenberg, Cape Krusenstern, the Lower Bench site, Walakpa, Safety Sound, and Choris Peninsula. In all these sites the artifactual remains indicate only limited seasonal use, probably late spring or summer, of the coast. Denbigh sites, primarily winter and summer or fall sites, have also been located along tundra lakes (Hall 1974; Irving 1964; Solecki, Salwen, and Jacobson 1973), on lookout points in the Brooks Range and the North Slope, and in the woodlands of the Kobuk River. The earliest Denbigh phase, called proto-Denbigh, was found at Onion Portage along the Kobuk River, where it underlay classic Denbigh in stratigraphy (Anderson 1970b).

The proto-Denbigh assemblage was characterized by wide microblades used in a variety of ways, oval-platformed cuboid microblade cores, tiny bipointed end and side blades for inserting into antler arrow and spear heads, tanged end scrapers, large semilunar bifaced knives, flaked burins, unifaced flake knives, and notched stones presumably used as net sinkers. The burin spall artifacts may have been used as engraving tool points for incising designs on objects of organic material. Unfortunately organic artifacts are exceedingly rare in Denbigh sites, most such objects having decomposed long ago.

The classic Denbigh phase contained most of the above artifact types, but with alterations: chipping on the weapon insets was more regular and delicate, end scrapers had become triangular and untanged, microblade cores had become smaller and narrow, and microblades were narrower. Acute-angle-platformed microblade cores had become popular; and argiliceous slate, a material not used by proto-Denbigh people, was used by classic Denbigh toolmakers to make ground adz blades and burins.

84

Brown U., Haffenreffer Mus. of Anthr., Bristol, R.I.: a, 66–518; b, 66–572; c, 66–628; d, 474; e, 66–488; f, 65–4211; g, 64–3401; h, 66–1832; i, 66–1807; j, 66–1850; k, 66–1840.

Fig. 4. Period 3, Onion Portage, Alaska. Denbigh Flint complex, 2000–2100 B.C.: a, Denbigh-type burin, chert; b, arrowhead end blade inset, chert; c, arrowhead side blade inset, chert; d, flake knife, chert; e, microblade, obsidian. Portage complex, 2300–2600 B.C.: f–g, "Portage" points. Palisades complex, about 3800 B.C.: h–i, side-notched points; j, side scraper or flake knife; k, large semilunar knife biface. Length of a, 4.2 cm; rest same scale.

In the late-Denbigh phase the exquisite flaking technique of classic Denbigh declined and weaponhead insets began to resemble the earlier proto-Denbigh insets. The grinding of burins increased, and the burin blow was used to detach portions of the edges of bifacially flaked projectile points for a purpose still unknown.

One antler artifact from Trail Creek cave 9, possibly from Denbigh times, may provide a clue to Denbigh art styes. The object, perhaps an arrowhead, is covered with incised zigzag lines and dots (Larsen 1968:49). Other Denbigh antler weapon heads from Trail Creek have linear groove decorations, often as extensions of the sideblade slots. Another Denbigh antler arrowhead from Punyik Point is decorated with a single, narrow longitudinal groove with a rectangular cross-section (Irving 1962:77).

At interior Denbigh sites, caribou seem to have been the only large game animals sought by Denbigh hunters, but along the coast seals also were hunted. Coastal campsite refuse contains harpoon blade insets, but fewer in number than end or side blade insets used for land game. Stone lance heads were present, though rare, in both coastal and interior Denbigh sites. Fishing was indicated in proto-Denbigh sites by the one notched stone sinker from Onion Portage. In classic or late Denbigh times at Punyik Point, fishing was indicated by piles of fish scales in middens (Irving 1962:77) and by the locations of several of the sites along lakeshores.

• SETTLEMENTS Denbigh house styles at Onion Portage changed from squarish in floor and central hearth plan during the proto-Denbigh phase to round floor and hearth plans in classic and late Denbigh phases. Classic Denbigh houses, found only in the interior, probably resembled the hemispherical sod house (Inupiaq *ivrulik*) of historic interior Eskimos. They were slightly excavated into the ground, usually only to the bottom of the original sod line. Each house had a large, stone-lined central hearth in which willow—and at Onion Portage, also spruce and birch—were burned. The floors, between 12 and 16 feet across, were scattered with numerous artifacts, in a distribution suggesting that the houses had distinct activity areas for sleeping, cooking, and manufacturing. At Onion Portage, a Denbigh settlement consisted of only one or two houses. A possible Late Denbigh winter house at Punyik Point had an 11-foot-square floor with rounded corners, a hearth, possibly a wide wall alcove, and a deep 5-foot-long entrance passage leading to the floor (Irving 1964:82–86). The step-up from the tunnel to the floor anticipated the cold trap of more recent Arctic houses.

Denbigh dwellers on the coast left campsites of three to six hearths in a cluster. The hearth areas may have been enclosed by small tents, because artifacts were concentrated about the hearths out to a radius of 3 feet. Throughout the North Slope and Brooks Range, isolated stone rings 10 to 12 feet in diameter indicate that tundra Denbigh peoples camped in tents (Hall 1975a). Seal bones were burned in the coastal hearths, along with wood and seal fat. In contrast to the interior houses and camping areas, no differentiation in activity areas could be discerned from artifact distributions around the coastal hearths.

Denbigh artifact styles, particularly the small weapon insets, flake knives, and knife blades, are found along much of the Arctic and Subarctic coasts of North America. The Arctic Small Tool tradition was widespread in the second millennium B.C. (Irving 1964). Its predecessor may have been Asian, as tools very much like those of Denbigh have been located in the Aldan region of Siberia dating to the third millennium B.C. (Mochanov 1969; Irving 1969–1970, 3), but it may also have developed in Arctic America, where microblade cores

that are stylistically transitional between American Paleo-Arctic and Arctic Small Tool tradition are known (Anderson 1972:99–100).

Old Whaling Culture

Between 1400 and 1300 B.C., following the late Denbigh period, there appeared an unusual coastal culture at Cape Krusenstern called Old Whaling. It is known from the ruins of five very large, deeply dug winter houses arranged in a tight cluster adjacent to the ruins of five large, shallowly dug summer houses, also tightly clustered (Giddings 1961a:164–166). The large tools of Old Whaling point convincingly to a whaling economy: there were lance heads, weaponhead insets resembling in most respects the whaling harpoon head insets of recent times, and long-bladed butchering tools. Further evidence of whaling was a litter of whalebones on the beach ridge and a butchered whalehead in front of one of the houses. Old Whaling implements bear little stylistic relation to implements elsewhere in the Arctic. Old Whalers seem to have appeared suddenly at Cape Krusenstern, interrupting the long-standing occupation of the area by Arctic Small Tool peoples, but where the Old Whalers originated and why they disappeared suddenly are unanswered questions.

Choris Culture

The Denbigh Flint complex persisted in the northwestern Arctic with little material change from 2200 until about 1600 B.C. But during the sixteenth century B.C. it underwent a series of changes and emerged as a new complex called Choris, named after the seventh-

Brown U., Haffenreffer Mus. of Anthr., Bristol, R.I.: a, 61–579; b, 61–561; c, 61–3013; d, 61–872; e, 61–503; f, 61–598.

Fig. 5. Old Whaling culture, Cape Krusenstern, Alaska, about 1300 B.C. a, large knife biface, chalcedony; b, side-notched points, chert; c, biface (possible whaling harpoon blade inset), chert; d, side-notched point, chert; e, end scraper, chert; f, semilunar knife blade, chalcedony. Length of a, 21.6 cm; rest same scale.

century B.C. site on Choris peninsula (Giddings 1957:132). Choris complex, or culture, shows many continuities with Denbigh, particularly in its flaking techniques and inset forms, and clearly belongs to the Arctic Small Tool tradition. Denbigh-Choris transition and Choris assemblages have been found at Cape Krusenstern, at Onion Portage, at Walakpa (Stanford 1970), at Norutak Lake (Clark 1968:22–23), at Engigstciak on the Firth River in Canada (MacNeish 1959), at numerous sites in the Brooks Range and North Slope, and at Trail Creek caves (Larsen 1951), where the first points and knives of Choris culture were located.

A large cache of early Choris projectile points from Cape Krusenstern exhibits some of the controlled diagonal flaking characteristic of Denbigh, but on much larger artifacts. The points are surprisingly like much earlier Paleo-Indian points of the North American Great Plains: some are Scottsbluff-like, others Alberta-like, and others Angostura-like, but their similarities probably had nothing to do with historic relations. Burin spalls were produced by Choris as well as by Denbigh toolmakers, but the Choris spalls were struck from cores that were thick, irregular flakes or edges of bifaces. The absence of burins or other antler-grooving tools in the Choris culture suggests that Choris people employed a technique for grooving antler different from the technique used by Denbigh peoples.

As time progressed during the Arctic Small Tool Denbigh and Choris phases, microblades, Denbigh-style chipped and ground burins, Denbigh-style flake knives, and several other Denbigh tool types disappeared from the cultural inventory, while pottery (cord-wrap impressed, linear stamped, and linear incised with feather temper and thin walls), burin spalls from irregular flake cores, chipped adz blades, and new projectile point forms appeared.

Findings from numerous post-Denbigh sites in the northern half of the region suggest that the particular sequence of change differed considerably in each of the localities of the northwestern Arctic. In many areas, for example, Arctic Small Tool people ceased making microblades before they began making and using pottery, whereas in other areas they began to make pots before they ceased making microblades. Summarizing the culture history of this region, especially given that the bulk of the sites are single component surface sites incapable of precise dating by radiocarbon methods, is difficult.

Whereas Denbigh sites, regardless of location, had almost the same artifactual inventories, Choris tools and settlements varied regionally. Coastal, interior tundra, and woodland riverine sites each contained distinctive assemblages geared toward effectively obtaining and utilizing local resources. At Onion Portage, for example, present were some tool types like stone end scrapers for caribou hide processing and heavy notched

stones for fish netting that were lacking in other Choris sites where caribou hunting and fishing would not have been practicable. In later Choris, best known from the type site, delicately flaked butchering knives were rare, and instead ground slate knives, presumably for cutting through the skin and blubber of sea mammals, were common. Among the organic objects that have endured are fixed-shaft toggle points, and barbed darts with thick stone insets for sea mammal hunting and bifurcate tanged arrowheads for caribou hunting. Ivory, bone, and wood were made decorative by incising parallel grooved lines and by drilling deep dots. They were also carved into anthropomorphic faces. Tongue-shaped stone labrets also began to be worn.

The economy of Choris was also more varied than that of Denbigh. At Onion Portage, besides fishing, caribou hunting was obviously very important. In fact the only animal bones uncovered in the Choris layers there were of caribou. The number of Choris sites both north and south of the Brooks Range and their settings suggest that caribou may have been especially plentiful in late Choris times. At Choris Peninisula 80 percent of the bones uncovered were of two varieties of the genus *Rangifer*. One had large bones similar to the bones of modern caribou; the other had small bones like those of Siberian domesticated reindeer, an observation that led Giddings (1967:213–214) to suggest that reindeer herding might have found its way onto Alaskan soil at that early time. Fish, birds, seals, and white whales were also hunted at Choris Peninsula. Walrus and baleen whales, judging from the presence of ivory and large whale bones, were also a part of the Choris Peninsula economy, even though they were probably not hunted there.

At Cape Krusenstern, bearded and small seal bones accounted for the greatest percentage of faunal remains, pointing to a late spring or early summer use of the site.

• SETTLEMENTS The largest Choris settlement comes from the type site on Choris Peninsula. Here three houses with oval floors as large as 42 by 24 feet in area lay in a tight cluster that suggests concurrent occupation. One of the houses had a large central hearth, but the other two had no observable hearths. Thick clay and stone potsherds in the house floor middens indicated that food may also have been cooked over lamps.

The Choris settlement at Onion Portage was an arrangement of tents or hemispherical structures with large, central, stone-lined hearths adjacent to an excavated oval-floored structure with a short entrance passage and a large, square, central, stone-paved hearth. The floor areas of the smaller tentlike structures, out to a radius of about 5 feet, were scattered with implements for hide scraping and for butchering. In the larger structure, artifacts lay in clusters around the edges of the excavated floor: weapon insets, burin spalls, adz blades, and so on. They were mostly implements needed for manufacturing weapons and carving large objects of wood. The smaller structures were clearly family dwellings used for food preparation and hide-working (women's activities) and the larger structure was a workshop (men's activities)—a settlement pattern suggestive of some historic Eskimo groups.

At Cape Krusenstern, no Choris house ruins were located; as with Denbigh, the Choris remains were tightly clustered around hearths—usually two or three hearths in a group, but sometimes single ones in a pattern that suggests the use of tents. The beach ridge Choris hearths, which were round and paved with limestone cobbles, contained charred seal bones, seal fat, and charcoal. Potsherds were found in all the hearths, indicating the use of cooking pots.

While Choris people were developing a capability to live in permanent year-round settlements on the coast of northwestern Alaska, their relatives in the interior tundra region of north Alaska continued to lead a more transhumic existence centered on caribou hunting. Because of the temporary nature of these interior sites, the cultural identification and dating of the assemblages are difficult.

Choris-like assemblages with lanceolate knife blades and projectile points have been recovered from many surface sites in the Brooks Range, and although they have not been dated, few would argue against their belonging to the Arctic Small Tool cultural continuum and dating to a post-Denbigh period. But other finds, such as the Kayuk assemblages from Anaktuvuk Pass (Campbell 1962b), the middle Noatak River (Anderson 1972), and the upper Koyukuk River (Fetter and Shinkwin 1978), are similar to, yet also different from Choris, and there is a serious question whether these represent a regional variant of Choris phase or the remains of an unrecognized culture and time period.

One opinion is that the Kayuk lanceolate points and bifaces are northern stylistic variants of a late Paleo-Indian cultural tradition that stretched from the Plains to northern North America between approximately 6000 and 3000 B.C. (Irving 1962a:60–61). Another opinion, the one favored here, is that the lanceolate points in these interior Arctic assemblages are a product of functional needs for a weapon suited to the killing and butchering of open-country herd animals and that they had been made and used by Arctic peoples of several periods and cultural affiliations. The cultural affiliation of any undated lanceolate points in the northwest Arctic cannot be identified on the basis of stylistic attributes alone.

Norton Culture

Choris culture in north Alaska continued with little change until about 500 B.C., when again subsistence

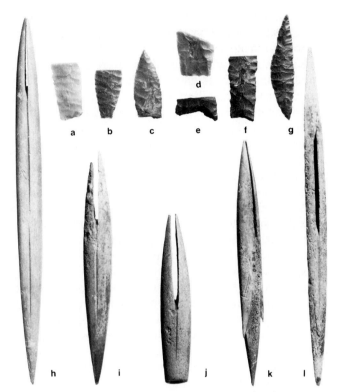

Brown U., Haffenreffer Mus. of Anthr., Bristol, R.I.: a, 61–3343; b, 61–3350; c, 61–3346; d, 61–3342; e, 61–3377; f, 61–3374; g, 61–3392; h, 61–3176; i, 61–3201; j, 61–3216; k, 61–3209; l, 61–3066.

Fig. 6. Battle Rock complex, Battle Rock, Alaska, about 500 B.C. a–f, bases of end blade insets of chert for insertion into the end-slotted weapon heads; g, side blade inset of chert for insertion into side-slotted weapon head; h–i, end-slotted weapon heads of antler; j, end-slotted weapon head, with socketed base, antler; k, barbed end-slotted weapon head, antler; l, side-slotted weapon head, antler. Length of h, 20.9 cm; rest same scale.

pursuits and settlement patterns began to take on a new form. Coastal settlements both north and south of Bering Strait became more numerous, and the subsistence pattern of coastal residents shifted toward a greater dependence on sea mammals and, in the south, fish (mainly salmon). Artifacts associated with these settlements belong to Norton culture, first isolated at Iyatayet, Cape Denbigh in Norton Sound (Giddings 1964:119–190). At Safety Sound, and southward, settlements became larger; northward they remained fairly small. Norton artifacts included end blade and side blade insets for arming seal-hunting and caribou-hunting weapons, notched pebbles for fish-net sinkers, bifaced knives for butchering, scrapers for hide working, ground burinlike implements for antler and ivory working, ground adz blades for ivory and wood working, linear and check-stamped pottery for cooking, and clay and stone lamps for light and heat. Net sinkers appeared in quantity at the Norton sites on Seward Peninsula, while at Safety Sound grooved, round line sinkers of a late Norton period indicated a different type of fishing (Bockstoce 1972:111–112).

Stylistically, much of Norton's chipped stone technology was derived from Denbigh, although because Norton toolmakers seldom used glassy silicates like chert, which Denbigh craftsmen used, the Norton tools appear cruder than the Denbigh tools. Check-stamped pottery decorations (a later Choris development) were adopted by Norton people, and the Norton clay and stone lamps for lighting and perhaps cooking are also indications of cultural continuity with Choris. Norton art is poorly represented in the archeological remains. One of the few artistic pieces is an ivory doll from the type site with a flat, uncarved face, crudely shaped legs, and no arms. Despite the absence of decorated organic artifacts from the type site, tiny pointed tools from there appear to have been used for incising. Norton artifacts from north of Bering Strait are, however, covered with bold incised decorations.

• SETTLEMENTS Norton house forms were quite varied, ranging from large, deep, square, winter houses with open central hearths and 7 to 11-foot-long tunnels at Safety Sound (or lacking tunnels as some at Safety Sound and at Unalakleet—Lutz 1972), to small houses with 10- to 12-foot-long tunnels at Iyatayet and Onion Portage. The house forms were unrelated to Choris forms. Norton settlements along the northern shores of Norton Sound were large, although because house ruins are found packed together so tightly at Safety Sound and Unalakleet it has been impossible to suggest the size of the settlement at any point in time.

The population north of Bering Strait during the Norton period does not seem to have increased as much as in the south, and it may have decreased. The residence pattern shifted from the large settlements of Choris to isolated winter houses. For example, at Point Hope only one house was found from this period (there called Near Ipiutak); at Cape Krusenstern, too, only one possible Norton–Near Ipiutak house was found, as also was the case on Kugzruk Island north of Cape Prince of Wales and at Onion Portage. At none of the northern coastal house sites was there evidence of net fishing. Perhaps net fishing had just been introduced to Norton residents at Iyatayet and other Bering Sea settlements and had not reached as far north as Point Hope and other Chukchi Sea settlements. More likely, though, net fishing north of Bering Strait was minimal because the water was too cold to support large schools of salmon.

Ipiutak Culture

At about the beginning of the Christian era a particularly striking phase of culture emerged in northwestern Alaska: the Ipiutak culture, notable at Point Hope especially for the elaborateness of its burial goods, and the earliest use of iron in Arctic Alaska. Burial objects included ivory carvings of linked chains, bizarre pretzellike objects, exquisite animal and anthropomorphic figures in a Scytho-Siberian art style, and pieces with delicately incised geometric designs (Larsen and Rainey 1948:145). Ipiutak art objects not associated with burials included tiny pebbles incised with designs resembling facial tattoos. Curiously enough, though Ipiutak people continued to manufacture many implements in the styles of their predecessors, other Near Ipiutak–Norton items such as pottery, ground slate, lamps, houses with tunnels, and whale hunting equipment—traits later found in coastal prehistoric Eskimo sites—were not adopted by the coastal Ipiutak people.

Ipiutak or Ipiutak-related sites were also found along the shores of Kotzebue Sound (Giddings and Anderson 1984; Anderson 1978a), at Anaktuvuk Pass, along lakeshores in the Arctic tundra (Hall 1974) and upper Koyukuk River drainage (Clark 1977), and along the Kobuk River at Onion Portage. The coastal Ipiutak site at Deering, dating to about A.D. 800, and the interior tundra lake site of Croxton, dating to A.D. 1100 or 1200 (Gal 1982) are the latest Ipiutak sites. Ipiutak people manufactured a wide variety of specialized tools and weapons, including delicate end and side bladed antler arrow and harpoon heads, the insets of which resemble Denbigh forms, Denbigh-like unifaced flake knives, Norton-related discoid scrapers, lunate knife bifaces, and ground stone burinlike implements.

Ipiutak is thought by some researchers to represent an early stage of Eskimo development, akin to Denbigh, in which people wintered in the interior and moved to the coast for spring and summer hunting and trading. Another interpretation of Ipiutak is that at least some Ipiutakers wintered on the coast at Point Hope and

Brown U., Haffenreffer Mus. of Anthr., Bristol, R.I.: a, 61–5245; b; c, 61–5243; d, 61–5434.

Fig. 7. Ground stone artifacts from the Ipiutak culture, Cape Krusenstern, Alaska, about A.D. 300. a, burinlike implement, silicified slate; b, hafted burinlike implement, wood and silicified slate; c, drill, silicified slate; d, planing adz, silicified slate. Length of a, 5.7 cm; rest same scale.

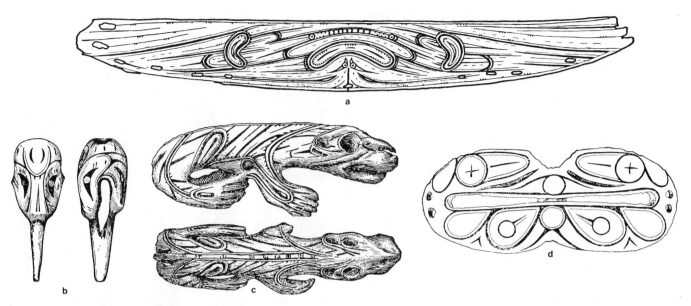

Larsen and Rainey 1948:74, 113, 125, 127, 136–137.

Fig. 8. Carved ivory objects of the Ipiutak culture, excavated from the village site at Ipiutak near Point Hope, Alaska. a, ornamented band, with pattern including a face with small round eyes and a downward curved mouth with teeth; b, socket piece carved to form an animal head with the tang extending from the base of the head. The socket piece is lashed to the harpoon shaft through the perforation. c, Figure of young walrus ornamented with a skeleton design and a boss on each hip. This design suggests that the carving represents a guardian spirit; judging from its location at excavation it was probably sewed to the shoulder of a shaman's garment. d, Snow goggles. Length of a 26.9 cm, rest same scale.

Cape Krusenstern and that their neglect of whale hunting indicates that whales were not then accessible because of unfavorable ice conditions. The absence of whales would have necessitated greater reliance on small sea mammals (obtained through advanced seal-hunting techniques) and caribou (requiring caribou to have wintered in the region) (Anderson 1962:127–131). The second interpretation of Ipiutak culture does not explain why Ipiutakers did not use slate or pottery or why their stone tools were so similar to Denbigh tools.

The Ipiutak-affiliated sites of the woodland region had essentially the same tool inventory as the coastal and tundra Ipiutak sites, but at Onion Portage there were some ground slate pieces and a few sherds of check-stamped pottery.

• SETTLEMENTS Coastal Ipiutak settlements were relatively large. At Point Hope more than 600 houses were uniformly spread along the beach ridges. Because house ruins were so close together, it was impossible to determine how many houses were occupied at one time; estimates range from nearly all to only a few. Ipiutak settlements at Cape Krusenstern, fortunately, were more dispersed. Seven settlements have been excavated, each composed of one large house (in one case, two large houses) surrounded by from 3 to 12 smaller houses. The Cape Krusenstern Ipiutak settlement at first suggested kinship both with Choris and with historic Eskimo settlements that included a large kashim; however, tools in the large Ipiutak structures were as much women's as men's. Thus, the large Ipiutak houses, instead of

being men's work houses as in the Choris or Eskimo cultures, seem to have been activity houses for the entire settlement (Anderson 1962:80). Although only one large Ipiutak house was excavated at Deering, it, too, suggested a kashim, primarily because of its size—six times the size of Point Hope dwellings—and its manufacturing evidence (Larsen 1951:83). However, it, too, contained numerous women's tools. An alternative interpretation is that the large dwellings in multidwelling settlements housed high-status families, but there is little in the archeology to support this view.

Ipiutak summer-spring campsites are also found along the northwest coast. The artifact surfaces of the campsites are large, dispersed areas that yield seal bones and an occasional hearth. They were probably tenting areas with either interior or exterior hearths.

Tundra Ipiutak settlements are smaller than at the coast. One square-floored winter house without raised benches was located at Itivlik Lake, and other camping areas were found at Anaktuvuk Pass. At Feniak Lake the floor plan appeared to be circular, with a short entrance passage (Hall 1974). The Ipiutak-affiliated remains at Onion Portage were mainly scattered around hearths, suggesting short-term camps. One house there had a short entrance passage and a square floor. At Hahanudan Lake one Ipiutak-affiliated settlement was comprised of three houses and another of two houses. Like the Onion Portage house these had short, floor-level entrances and at least some had square floors. Other house floors were nearly rectangular.

Despite regional differences, the Near Ipiutak, Norton, and Ipiutak complexes represent a generally similar culture that was spread throughout most of northwestern Alaska from about 500 B.C. to after A.D. 900.

Period 4: Prehistoric Eskimo Culture

At the end of the Ipiutak period, there came a dramatic change in the culture of residents of coastal northwestern Alaska. Some archeologists see the change as a result of new populations moving into the region from nearby coastal Asia or the islands around Bering Strait. Others see the change as a result of the introduction from Bering Strait of a new sea mammal hunting technology, and the rapid readaptation of the whole food-getting and processing material culture. This new culture, found at Safety Sound, Cape Prince of Wales, Cape Krusenstern, Point Hope, and Point Barrow, contains items closely related in style to implements of historic Inupiaq Eskimos, obviously the artifacts of their immediate forebears.

Birnirk Culture

Prehistoric Eskimos of the Birnirk culture used ground slate weapon heads and tools, chipped chert implements, multiple-spurred harpoon heads with single barbs and opposing chert side-blade insets, decorated and plain thick-walled clay lamps and cooking pots, and a variety of hunting and fishing tools in styles that continued almost unchanged until the nineteenth century. At Point Barrow, and perhaps elsewhere, Birnirk people hunted whales (Ford 1959:41), after a period of 500 years when no whale hunting had occurred in Arctic Alaska. Proof of their whaling came from a whaling harpoon head found on a house floor and the extensive use of baleen, whale bones, and whale effigies. At Point Barrow and along the rest of the northwestern Arctic coast Birnirk people's major economic pursuits were seal hunting over ice and open water (Stanford 1976); caribou hunting with bows and arrows and, probably, spears; bird hunting with arrows, spears, and bolas; and fishing with spears.

Birnirk culture ivory and other organic objects have not yet decayed, and there are many examples of Birnirk art. Decoration was achieved mostly by incising ivory objects with single or paired straight lines or paired arcs with ticked lines at right angles to the lines or arcs. The design elements were laid out in recurring patterns, often also paired. After the Birnirk phase, this style of decoration spread over a large region including northern Canada and Greenland. Birnirk pottery decoration consisted of intersecting curvilinear designs paddle-stamped into the pot surfaces. Figurines, probably dolls, with short arms and realistically shaped bodies were

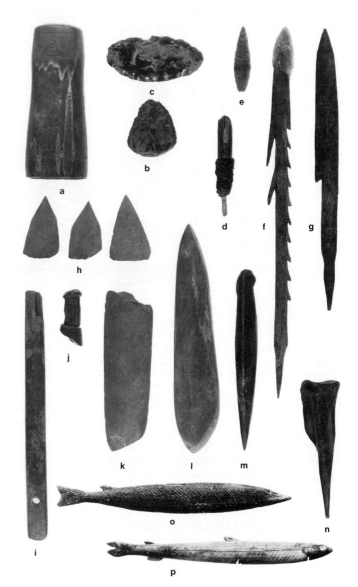

Brown U., Haffenreffer Mus. of Anthr., Bristol, R.I.: a, 65–a; b, 65–i; c, 65–h; d, 65–g; e, 65–b; f, 65–c; g, 65–d; h, 65–e; i, 65–1; j, 65–f; k, 65–0; l, 65–j; m, 65–n; n, 65–m; o, 65–q; p, 65–p.

Fig. 9. Early Inupiaq culture (Ahteut) coastal sea mammal hunting and interior hunting, fishing, and manufacturing equipment from Onion Portage, Alaska, about A.D. 1100. a, decorated harpoon socket piece, ivory; b, end scraper, chert; c, side scraper, chert; d, copper drill bit; e, arrowhead end blade inset, chert; f, arrowhead, antler and chert; g, arrowhead, antler; h, ground slate harpoon end blade insets; i, curved knife handle; j, inflation nozzle for a bladder dart float, ivory; k, knife blade, slate; l, whetstone, slate; m–n, awls of bone; o, fish lure in the shape of a pike, ivory; p, fish lure in the shape of a grayling (dorsal fin missing), ivory. Length of a, 9.2 cm; rest same scale.

carved of wood and bark, and small animal figures were carved of ivory. The Eskimo-style drum was also present.

• SETTLEMENTS   The Birnirk type site at Point Barrow (Ford 1959) was a series of 16 midden mounds from 2 to 10 feet high and from 50 to 120 feet across. The settlement pattern was not clear, but apparently several

90

small dwellings were built on each midden mound, often with timbers mined from earlier house ruins. The dwellings had single rooms 8 to 12 feet along a side, and long entrance tunnels, occasionally offset from the middle of the front wall. Sleeping platforms were usually at the back of the room opposite the entrance, although in one house the platform was along a side wall. Heat and light were furnished by means of lamps made from pottery and stone; no open hearths were built in the rooms. It is impossible to say how large a Birnirk village was at any one time, but probably it was quite small.

At Cape Krusenstern, two small Birnirk-related houses with entrance tunnels have been excavated (Giddings and Anderson 1984). Like one house at Birnirk, the Cape Krusenstern houses had a single sleeping platform along a side wall. One of the Cape Krusenstern houses had a small kitchen built off the front wall; to accommodate it, the entrance tunnel was placed off center, at an angle to the front wall. In the other house, charred bones and fat stains—indicating a hearth or lamp area—were on the main floor in front of the tunnel. At Cape Krusenstern both caribou and seal hunting were important Birnirk economic pursuits; whales were apparently not hunted at all. Birnirk people at Cape Krusenstern seem to have combined Ipiutak-style chert implements with Birnirk–Western Thule style slate, pottery, and antler objects.

Another Birnirk-related settlement, discovered at Safety Sound, was comprised of three house ruins (Bockstoce 1979). The two houses that were excavated were square in outline and had long entrance tunnels. One had an offset tunnel like the houses at Cape Krusenstern and at the Birnirk type site. Neither house had an attached kitchen, and both houses had an area in the center of the room for lamps or for burning seal fat. As at Cape Krusenstern in addition to the typically Birnirk smooth-ground slate artifacts, Ipiutak-style chipped stone artifacts were found. No pottery was located in either of the houses, a feature that distinguished the Safety Sound site from other Birnirk sites. Radiocarbon dates for the two houses ranged from A.D. 534 ± 92 to A.D. 699 ± 74.

One of the first Birnirk sites to be radiocarbon dated was the Kurigitavik midden at Cape Prince of Wales, where numerous well-preserved, Birnirk-style artifacts came from the lowest midden levels (Collins 1937b); they were dated to A.D. 597 ± 237 and A.D. 433 ± 237 (Rainey and Ralph 1959:368).

Birnirk-style weapons (harpoon heads, for instance), have been found over a large area—westward along parts of the northeastern Siberian coast as far as the mouth of the Kolyma River (Okladnikov and Beregovaīa 1971), and eastward as far as Atkinson Point, northwestern Canada. This indicates a far-reaching communication network, particularly westward, and calls to mind the extensive trade network of Eskimos around

Bering Strait during the nineteenth century (Thornton 1931:120).

The Birnirk phase of culture had little in common with earlier cultures on the mainland Alaska coast, except for Ipiutak-like bifacially flaked chert artifacts. Most of its traits were shared with Saint Lawrence Island's early Punuk culture. Early Punuk was a culture that developed from the Old Bering Sea and Okvik cultures on Saint Lawrence and neighboring islands and the adjacent northeast Asian coast. These three phases of Saint Lawrence Island culture evolved on the island during a period of 500 to 700 years, a fact that led some Arctic specialists to suggest that the Siberian coast and Saint Lawrence Island were the areas where Eskimo culture developed (Collins 1937; Ford 1959). On the other hand, certain Old Bering Sea traits, particularly the pottery style and slate grinding, seemed to relate to the still earlier Norton culture, and it may be that a pre–Old Bering Sea/Okvik coastal culture, distinct from Ipiutak in northwestern Alaska, developed over much of the southern half of the Alaska coast (Dumond 1965:1245).

While Birnirk people were flourishing along the coast, the population in the interior of northwestern Alaska seems to have diminished, perhaps the result of a decline in caribou. No Birnirk-related site has been found in the interior, but several of the interior Ipiutak sites date to Birnirk times and demonstrate that two cultural traditions, each representing Eskimo culture, coexisted in North Alaska for several centuries. Along the Kobuk River assemblages dating to about A.D. 500 represent the later stages of yet a third tradition, the Northern Archaic (Anderson 1970). From the Birnirk period onward, the cultural continuity of Arctic peoples into the twentieth century is clear. The continuity has been called by Birket-Smith (1959:194) the Neo-Eskimo tradition and by Collins (1964:91), who includes Saint Lawrence Island cultures, the Northern Maritime tradition.

Western Thule

Around A.D. 1000, or perhaps during the Birnirk period, a prehistoric Eskimo phase of culture called Thule spread from the northwest coast of Alaska eastward across northern Canada and Greenland (Ford 1959:243; W.E. Taylor 1963a:456; Stanford 1976). It was extensively investigated in the early twentieth century in eastern Canada, and when a western phase was discerned at Point Hope in 1939, it was given the name Western Thule for its obvious similarities to the Thule culture. Other Western Thule sites have been found at Cape Prince of Wales, Cape Krusenstern, Walakpa, and Point Barrow on the coast and Onion Portage and Ahteut in the woodland region. None has been located in the western tundra.

The Western Thule phase developed directly from Birnirk between A.D. 1000 or earlier and A.D. 1250 (Larsen and Rainey 1948:170–175), and its material goods were an elaboration of items developed in Birnirk times. Specialized tools were used increasingly, a trend that continued into the historic Eskimo period. At most sites the early Western Thule houses were single-room dwellings like the Birnirk houses; at Point Hope the houses were large, multi-room structures.

• SETTLEMENTS Western Thule sites reflect a broad economic base. Whaling was practiced in most of the coastal areas; caribou were obtained in large numbers, and sealing was an important occupation. Social groupings undoubtedly had to be restructured for the effective hunting of whales, and as a result they concentrated into larger settlements at locations like Point Barrow, Point Hope, and Cape Prince of Wales. At Cape Krusenstern the whaling settlements were made up of single-room dwellings flanking a multiple-room dwelling apparently occupied by the chief whaling family. After about A.D. 1400 at Cape Krusenstern, the large settlements gave way to sparsely populated settlements of small, single-room dwellings, a change apparently in response to the disappearance of whales and the declining food base that this triggered. The change in the resource potential of Kotzebue Sound put pressure on the people to seek a new reliable resource base, and this in turn gave rise to the focus on fishing that has influenced the subsistence and settlement patterns of the region ever since. At Point Hope and Barrow, whaling continued, and this was accompanied by a steady increase in the size and density of the settlements. However, the trend toward larger and more permanent settlements was not characteristic of the area between Barrow and the Mackenzie delta. Rather, winter settlements there usually contained only one to four small houses (MacNeish 1956a).

During the early Western Thule phase the Inuit also expanded into the interior Arctic woodlands. At Onion Portage at least one large eleventh century A.D. house contained artifacts like those of their coastal relatives. A century or so later Ahteut, a settlement of 60 or more houses along a quarter-mile stretch of the river below Onion Portage, shows that numerous Inuit were then wintering in the interior. As at Onion Portage the house floors were deep and the entrance tunnels long, features that were more attuned to coastal than to interior living (Giddings 1952a).

Between the fifteenth and the seventeenth centuries A.D. the small populations in the tundra regions of the Brooks Range and North Slope were supplemented by groups of Inuit from the Arctic coast and from the Kobuk and Noatak rivers (Hall 1975a).

The regional variations of the prehistoric Eskimo culture that followed the Western Thule phase were numerous, each variation known by its locally specific name. Along the coast, remains of cultures from the fifteenth century and later have been recovered from all the major coastal middens and beach ridge sites. All of them demonstrate an unbroken cultural continuity from the prehistoric period into the historic Eskimo period. As seen in the subtle changes in art and in technical styles that co-evolved throughout the region, there was undoubtedly a great deal of communication between settlements.

Along the coast after Western Thule times settlement patterns are not well known owing to the propensity of residents to live in tightly clustered settlements for long periods, a practice that has made it impossible to determine which houses were occupied when. In Kotzebue Sound, settlements were relocated from the prime sealing (and once prime whaling) sites to the major fishing sites. In the Mackenzie River delta from the fourteenth century on, large groups of Eskimos gathered in the summer to hunt white whales; whether they spent their winters in isolated small settlements around interior lakes or along the delta shores is not certain (McGhee 1971a).

In the Kobuk River valley, where late prehistoric excavations have been extensive, the sequence in house style has been from deeply excavated individual houses with long tunnels to shallowly excavated houses with short tunnels built in standardized forms. Gradually the settlements decreased in size until, by the beginning of the twentieth century, winter houses, at least in the upriver area, were built alone or in pairs. Fish netting increased in importance relative to hooking and spearing, and upriver people tended to remain year-round in the interior rather than to move in the early summer for sealing at the coast (Giddings 1952a:112–113; Hickey 1976). This change may relate to a decline in caribou or a rise in the importance of the fur trade, which in either case would have encouraged the dispersal of the populations during the winter.

Along the Noatak River, at least one settlement from the sixteenth century consisted of a single large house (Hall 1971a). How typical this was for the Noatak area is not known. Stylistically the artifacts were similar to implements of contemporaneous Kotzebue houses. An iron-bladed engraving tool and other evidences of the use of metal were recovered at the Noatak River site, so metal, presumably traded into the region, was in use along the Noatak before the period of direct European-American contact.

Interior Eskimo tundra sites increased in number dramatically beginning in the seventeenth century. Irving (1962:76–82) has located several that contained between 30 and 50 houses around lakes in the western Brooks Range. Hall (1971), too, has located numerous late Eskimo prehistoric settlements in the central Brooks Range.

In the central and eastern Brooks Range the late

prehistoric archeology is rather complex. Sites such as Kavik and Atigun contain artifacts attributed by some to Athapaskan Indian occupations of the region (Campbell 1968a; I.R. Wilson 1978), and if so they indicate a change in the regional distribution of Eskimos and Athapaskans in north Alaska during the late prehistoric period.

Period 5: Historic Eskimo Culture

The historic period for northern Alaska may be said to have begun in 1778, the year Capt. James Cook made the first recorded landfall by a European on the northern Alaska mainland. For nearly a century before that, Russians and Russian-sponsored expeditions had sailed into the Chukchi Sea, and although they undoubtedly carried on intercourse with the Eskimos of the region, there is little documentation of this. Russian trade items surely reached northern Alaska in the eighteenth century, and perhaps in the seventeenth probably through Eskimo traders at Cape Prince of Wales or Hotham Inlet; but trade items are rare in Eskimo sites until the middle of the nineteenth century, when New England whalers frequented the coast. Sites containing Eurasian trade items have been excavated at Cape Krusenstern (Giddings and Anderson 1984) and along the Kobuk River (Hickey 1969). Of the earliest trade items, only glass beads and metal have been found, and outside influences seem to have been insufficient to alter appreciably the aboriginal technology and settlement patterns. The greatest change from earlier periods was that bits of metal were used as blades for carving, whittling, and grooving knives; however, the style of the blades remained like the less frequently used stone blades.

When coastal exploration and whaling at the end of the nineteenth century brought in more people from the outside, trade intensified, particularly at a few key points (Foote 1965; Bockstoce 1977, 1977b). By 1890 western traders and prospectors were spending full years in northern Alaska, and although their presence certainly influenced the Eskimos, such indications barely show up archeologically. Also around 1890, missionaries and school teachers began to establish themselves in some of the permanent coastal settlements, and between 1895 and 1910 they induced some of the people scattered throughout the interior and the sparsely populated parts of the coast to come together to form permanent settlements.

A site on a bank of Ogotoruk Creek about 30 miles southeast of Point Hope is one of the few sites postdating the late nineteenth century to have been excavated. It was a small settlement from the mid-eighteenth century until 1922 (West 1966), and it well documented the transition from a culture using predominantly aboriginal goods, in the 1880s, to a culture using predominantly items of United States manufacture, in the 1920s.

Another excavated historic site, in the eastern Brooks Range, revealed a settlement of at least five winter houses, three tent rings, and one possible men's house of Nunamiut Eskimos occupied sometime between 1880 and 1890 (Corbin 1971). One rifle and numerous European and American goods were unearthed, but the prevailing items were of indigenous manufacture. For example, the rifle had not totally replaced the bow and arrow, and metal knives, though present, had not replaced stone-bladed knives. Likewise the large late nineteenth century settlement at Tukuto Lake in the central Brooks Range, excavated by Hall (1970), produced many more stone projectile points than rifle shells, even in the uppermost levels.

The history of the Nunamiut has been intensely investigated, and some archeologists believe the cultural boundary between the Nunamiut and Indians (Kutchin Athapaskans) shifted in the early historic period. According to Hall (1969:327–330), the Nunamiut may have moved into the eastern Brooks Range after 1800, displacing the region's Indian occupants. But excavations in the region have revealed early historic period tent rings containing Nunamiut-like artifacts, so the Nunamiut may have been in the eastern Brooks Range a long time (Bacon 1971:266–268). Other evidence suggests that the distribution of early historic Nunamiut may have coincided with the range of western Arctic caribou herds (Holmes 1971). There is good evidence, however, that western Nunamiut were somewhat culturally distinct from the eastern Nunamiut. This is most clearly seen in the use of pottery and semisubterranean houses by the western groups but not the eastern ones (Hall 1970:6–7).

A small coastal site at Prudhoe Bay occupied by two Eskimo families between 1921 and 1937 and by one family between 1940 and 1946 was excavated as part of the archeological survey sponsored by the Alyeska Company. After excavation, the former occupants of the settlement were interviewed, offering a unique opportunity to compare ethnographic and archeological data (Derry 1971).

Prehistory of the Bering Sea Region

DON E. DUMOND

This chapter deals with that portion of Alaska about the Bering Sea from a point on the Alaska Peninsula at 159° west longitude, northward to the vicinity of Nome on southern Seward Peninsula. Inland, the boundaries of the area accord with the interior boundary of Eskimos at the time of European contact (fig. 1).

Little attention was paid to the region by archeologists before World War II, even though some archeological remains were noted as early as the late 1870s (Nelson 1899:170). Between 1926 and 1931 the area was explored by Hrdlička, who, although chiefly in search of skeletal material, recorded the locations of a number of sites and settlements (Hrdlička 1930, 1943); a portion of the region was also visited by Stewart and Collins (Collins 1928; Hrdlička 1930:190). In 1935 De Laguna (1947) surveyed and excavated along the lower Yukon, but her area was upstream from Holy Cross and thus in the territory of modern Athapaskan Indians.

More intensive archeology began in 1948, when Larsen surveyed and tested around northern Bristol Bay—between modern Naknek and Platinum—and reported the discovery of "five hitherto unknown stages of Eskimo culture" (Larsen 1950:184). Giddings's (1949) work at Cape Denbigh in Norton Bay, an arm of Norton Sound, uncovered a stratified set of cultural remains that revealed a prehistoric sequence that appears to have prevailed throughout the entire area after about 2000 B.C.

The Paleo-Arctic Tradition

The first concrete suggestion of a terminal Pleistocene or early Recent occupation in this portion of southwestern Alaska was a blade-core site that in 1970 was discovered to have been almost completely destroyed at Igiugig, near the point where Iliamna Lake outlets to form the Kvichak River (Dixon and Johnson 1971). Although scant, the surviving materials are comparable to those that have been termed the Denali complex (West 1967) or that are here (after Anderson 1968, 1970a) assigned to the American Paleo-Arctic or, more simply, the Paleo-Arctic tradition.

A similar occupation was excavated at the mouth of the Kvichak River, yielding plentiful microblades, three cores, and a core tablet (a large core platform trimming

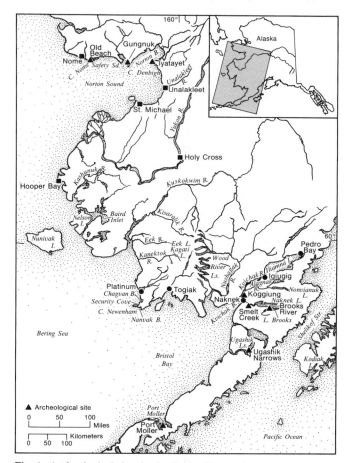

Fig. 1. Archeological sites in the Bering Sea region.

flake), which have been designated the Koggiung phase (fig. 2) (Dumond 1981).

Excavations between Upper and Lower Ugashik Lakes, 150 kilometers southwestward along the Alaska Peninsula from Koggiung, yielded material of what is designated the Ugashik Narrows phase (Dumond, Henn, and Stuckenrath 1976; Henn 1978) represented by 16 well-shaped microblade cores; more than 600 microblades and microblade fragments (fig. 3); larger blade cores of various forms; blades, core and flake bifaces, transverse burins, scrapers, knives; and one large and rather thick projectile point or knife with a thinned base. Although charcoal was present there were no clearly indicated campfire locations or pronounced living floors.

Surface reconnaissance in the inland region south and east of the mouth of the Kuskokwim River yielded evi-

U. of Oreg., Oreg. State Mus. of Anthr., Eugene: a, 1–0–3; b, 1–0–1; c, 16–0–5, B–1–3, 16–0–1, 16–1–1.

Fig. 2. Paleo-Arctic tradition, Koggiung phase artifacts, Koggiung (Graveyard Point) site (49 Nak 16), Alaska. a–b, top and front view of cores; c, blades. Length of b 5.3 cm; rest same scale.

dence of microblades and cores both at Kagati Lake, on the upper Kanektok River, and at one site in the middle portion of the Kisaralik River drainage (Ackerman 1979, 1980). These can be presumed to pertain to the Paleo-Arctic tradition.

Summarized in table 1, the available radiocarbon evidence suggests an uncorrected dating from about 7000 to 6000 B.C., with the Koggiung site slightly later than that at Ugashik Narrows. On the basis of core characteristics the date of the Iguigig site can be presumed to approximate that of Koggiung.

The Northern Archaic Tradition

The definition of this tradition follows Anderson (1968).

Security Cove and Lower Kuskokwim Region

A surface site discovered in 1962 on a terminal moraine facing Security Cove, immediately north and east of Cape Newenham, yielded a collection that consists of some 270 implements of chalcedony, quartzite, and argillite. One of the largest categories is that of chipped projectile blades, the most distinctive of which bear side

U. of Oreg., Oreg. State Mus. of Anthr., Eugene: a, W–7–3; b, V–7–4; c, K–11–34, K–11–24, K–11–349, J–11–1.

Fig. 3. Paleo-Arctic tradition artifacts, Ugashik River drainage, Ugashik Narrows site (49 Uga 1), Alaska. a–b, wedge-shaped microblade cores; c, microblades. Length of a 2.7 cm; rest same scale.

notches near their basal end and have a definitely indented base (Ackerman 1964:fig. 12). Also present are chipped lanceolate forms variously termed projectile blades, knives, and preforms; end and side scrapers, some of which appear to be equipped with a spur that has been used for graving; large, semilunar, heavy scrapers or choppers; and binotched stones of the sort commonly called net sinkers. No organic material of any kind was recovered that can be shown to be contemporary with the stone assemblage.

Materials similar in many respects to those from Security Cove are reported from Kagati Lake (Ackerman 1979; Glennan 1972). Lanceolate points apparently generally similar to those from both Security Cove and Kagati Lake are also reported from a surficial site in the middle course of the Kisalarik River drainage (Ackerman 1980).

Alaska Peninsula

At the narrows between Upper and Lower Ugashik Lakes, the Ugashik Knoll phase is represented at a single known site on a high ridge that provides clear visibility of the game crossing formed so conveniently by the constriction between the lakes (fig. 4a–c). Major implements are side-notched and stemmed projectile points, and plentiful scrapers and knives. Unlike Security Cove, there are also microblades, larger blades, and cores that lack the wedge-shaped style common to the Paleo-Arctic tradition that earlier appears in the

U. of Oreg., Oreg. State Mus. of Anthr., Eugene: a, 0–7–4, b, E–5–3; c, 0–7–3; d, BR 11–7, 10–3; e, BR 11–5, A–10–2; f, BR 20–2, 0–10–11; g, BR 10–7, 10–1; h, BR 10–7, 10–2.

Fig. 4. Northern Archaic tradition artifacts. a–c, Points, Ugashik Knoll phase, Ugashik River drainage, Ugashik Narrows site (49 Uga 6), Alaska. d–h, Brooks River Beachridge phase, upper Naknek drainage, Alaska: d, large biface; e–f, scrapers; g–h, leaf-shaped points. Length of a 4.7 cm, rest same scale.

same vicinity, consisting rather of small end-faceted pebbles, or roughly polyhedral or tabular forms derived from cobbles (Dumond, Henn, and Stuckenrath 1976; Henn 1978).

Notched projectile points similar to those of the Ugashik Knoll phase have been collected in some quantity by amateurs at the Koggiung site near the outlet of the Kvichak River at the base of the peninsula. None has thus far been directly collected by a professional in the region, despite the fact that professional archeologists have made surface collections of scrapers and less diagnostic artifacts, examined amateur collections, performed test excavations, and on the basis of all the artifacts examined have defined a largely hypothetical cultural unit designated the Graveyard phase; the phase is presumed to be dated by a single radiocarbon determination from a buried occupation zone (table 1) that unfortunately produced no truly diagnostic artifacts (Dumond 1981). The destroyed condition of the site made it impossible to determine whether microblades, present in the earlier Koggiung component of the same vicinity, were a part of the Graveyard phase.

A somewhat later period is represented by chipped lanceolate projectile or knife blades, heavy chopperlike semilunar scrapers, and small end scrapers in the Brooks River Beachridge phase (fig. 4d–h) of the upper Naknek drainage (Dumond 1981), in which hunting activity is evidenced by pulverized mammal bone in casual campsites. By reference to material from northwestern Alaska this complex can be considered to be a direct descendant of the notched-point-dominated collections just mentioned.

Radiocarbon evidence is given in table 1. Similarities of some of the artifacts from Security Cove, where the assemblage has not been dated by radiocarbon, with those from the Ugashik Knoll phase, as well as with those of the Palisades complex from Onion Portage, lead to the presumption that the side-notched point assemblages of southwestern Alaska can be dated around 3000 B.C., with those dominated by lanceolate forms, such as the Beachridge complex, dated as much as a millennium later. It is uncertain whether the presence of microblades in some collections is of specifically temporal significance.

A Tradition from the Pacific Coast

What were thought to be early historic or protohistoric Athapaskan houses were excavated at Pedro Bay on the northern shore of Iliamna Lake (Townsend and Townsend 1961), yielding glass beads, scraps of metal, implements of organic material, and a number of polished slate pieces, most of them large knife or lance blades. Later excavations have demonstrated that in fact the large slate implements pertained to a lower

Table 1. Radiocarbon Dates of Sites on the Alaska Peninsula

Ugashik Region	Naknek Region
Paleo-Arctic Tradition	
Ugashik Narrows phase	*Koggiung phase*
5725 B.C. ± 260 (SI-1998)	5815 B.C. ± 95 (SI-1955)
6475 B.C. ± 115 (SI-2641)	5945 B.C. ± 95 (SI-1956)
7045 B.C. ± 295 (SI-2492)	
Northern Archaic Tradition	
	Brooks River
	Beachridge phase
	1890 B.C. ± 130 (I-1630)
Ugashik Knoll phase	*Graveyard phase (probable)*
2860 B.C. ± 85 (SI-2640)	
2890 B.C. ± 80 (SI-2643)	3065 B.C. ± 70 (SI-1957)
3105 B.C. ± 70 (SI-2494)	

NOTE: Dates are unadjusted, calculated on half-life of 5,568 years; all are gas process dates.

deposit in the stratified site (Townsend 1970). The early Pedro Bay assemblage consists of a series of large polished slate projectile blades or knives, commonly with unthinned bases; numerous chipped projectile blades of basalt, some with stems and rounded shoulders, many of them of chalcedony. Implements of polished slate are confined to the large lance or knife blades.

A similar assemblage occurs at Brooks River, in the upper Naknek drainage, where it is termed the Brooks River Strand phase (Dumond 1981). That collection consists of large polished slate lance or knife blades both stemmed and unstemmed, with unthinned bases (fig. 5); large flaked lance or knife blades with stems, of shaly metamorphic rock; chipped side-notched knives and shallow D-shaped pecked stone lamps. Again, polished implements are confined to knife or lance blades.

One habitation, roughly teardrop in plan, had been lightly excavated into the contemporary surface; the floor was covered with crushed caribou bone and shale chips. Other areas of occupation were apparently more casual campsites, all of which included bits of caribou bone.

The radiocarbon evidence bearing upon the dating of the Pedro Bay assemblage and the Brooks River Strand phase is summarized in table 2. The date suggested, from about 2500 to 1900 B.C., is in complete accord with the evidently closely related manifestation of the Pacific coast of the Peninsula that is termed the Takli culture. On the basis both of stratigraphic evidence (in the upper Naknek River drainage) and of radiocarbon dates (tables 1–2) it seems clear that peoples of this Pacific coastal tradition and of the Northern Archaic tradition were substantially contemporaneous in southwestern Alaska.

U. of Oreg., Oreg. State Mus. of Anthr., Eugene: BR 20–T, 0–10–29; BR 11–5, C–8–1; BR 20–11, A–6–1.

Fig. 5. Polished slate lance blades, Brooks River Strand phase, upper Naknek drainage, Alaska. Length of bottom 28.0 cm, rest same scale.

The Arctic Small Tool Tradition

Two locations have yielded substantial and incontestable manifestations of the Arctic Small Tool tradition, which as defined by Irving (1962a:56) includes microblades, a particular form of burin and the spalls from it, small bifaces and sideblades of specialized form and fine workmanship, and a scarcity of ground or polished implements.

Cape Denbigh

The first manifestation to be reported was the Denbigh Flint complex (Giddings 1964). Located above Iyatayet Creek at Cape Denbigh on Norton Bay, the Iyatayet site yielded the materials from a stratified position beneath deposits both of Norton and Nukleet cultures.

The assemblage consisted chiefly of numerous microblades; of a class of small burins, most commonly made on a piece that was bifacially retouched before the burin blows were struck; of burin spalls, a number of which had apparently been used as engraving tools; of small bifacially chipped sideblades and endblades, both of which were commonly pointed on both ends, with the former asymmetrical and the latter frequently with basal edge grinding; of a series of well-fashioned endscrapers, as well as other unifacial implements termed "flake knives"; of a few triangular bifacial implements identified as harpoon endblades; and of occasional lance or larger double-edged knife blades. A few of the burins had traces of grinding on the flat faces of the body of

Table 2. Radiocarbon Dates for Early Alaska Peninsula Assemblages of Pacific Coastal Affiliation

Upper Naknek Drainage	Iliamna Lake
Brooks River Strand phase	*Pedro Bay*
1950 B.C. ± 120 (I-3144)	
2290 B.C. ± 250 (I-1634)	
2480 B.C. ± 110 (I-1946)	2370 B.C. ± 115 (I-3716)

NOTE: Dates are unadjusted, calculated on half-life of 5,568 years; all are gas process dates.

the piece, and some implements had a polished cutting edge; these latter are called "creasers" by Giddings (1964:238) and "polished burin-like implements" by others. At least one small adz blade, although later concluded to pertain to the overlying Norton culture deposit, was originally assigned to the Denbigh Flint complex (Giddings 1964:191).

The deposit contained no identifiable signs of aboriginal excavation for dwelling construction, and it was inferred that the cultural debris had been deposited directly upon a layer of sod (Giddings 1964:195). The positions of some fires were indicated by reddish discolorations accompanied by burned beach pebbles and a few charcoal flecks. The only identifiable bone was one or two charred fragments of seal.

Based upon the heavy preponderance of small sideblades and endblades over the triangular bifaces identified as harpoon blades, it was concluded that the remains were probably the result of camps established primarily for the hunting of caribou, rather than for sealing (Giddings 1964:242), although the presence of the seal bones is direct evidence of at least some sealing.

Naknek Drainage

The second location in which materials clearly attributable to the Arctic Small Tool tradition are known to occur is at Brooks River in the upper portion of the Naknek drainage system on the Alaska Peninsula, where the assemblage constitutes the Brooks River Gravels phase (fig. 6) (Dumond 1971a, 1981). Implements generally correspond to those from Cape Denbigh. The only significant class of implement from the Denbigh Flint complex that is absent entirely in the Gravels phase collections is the triangular endblade interpreted by Giddings (1964) as a harpoon blade. In drastically lower frequency at Brooks River are burins and microblades; in considerably higher frequency are the double-pointed endblades and, apparently, the well-fashioned scrapers. Adz blades with polished bits also occur, and inasmuch as these have appeared in Arctic Small Tool manifes-

97

U. of Oreg., Oreg. State Mus. of Anthr., Eugene: a, BR 16–2,5; b, BR15–9, 2–4; c, BR15–1, 65–16; BR 4–1, 21–11–1; e, BR5–1, K–7–1; f, BR 16–1, 64–14; g, BR 15–9, 2–9; h, BR–15–1,45; i, BR 10–3, C–6–9; j, BR 5–1, XT–7–10.
Fig. 6. Arctic Small Tool tradition, Brooks River Gravels phase artifacts from Brooks River site (49 MK 1), Alaska. a, burin; b–d, projectile points; e-f, scrapers; g, side blade or knife; h, polished adz blade; i–j, microblades. Length of a 2.7 cm; rest same scale.

Fig. 7. Arctic Small Tool tradition, Brooks River Gravels phase house (BR12–1) in the Brooks River site, Alaska. The measuring stick next to the hearth is 2.2 m in length. Photograph by Don E. Dumond, 1963.

tations at Onion Portage and elsewhere, it appears that Giddings's original attribution of the adz blade to the Denbigh Flint complex at Iyatayet was correct. Organic material is limited to a small amount of salmonid bone and teeth in trash of several house floors and to crushed mammal bone in a few fireplaces and campsites.

At Brooks River constructed, single-occupation habitations are common. In form these habitations were roughly square and about four meters on a side, excavated into the contemporary surface as much as 60 centimeters. A sloping entranceway led into the house, in which a central fireplace was usual (fig. 7). In only one case is there an apparent indication of four center posts. Roofs were not heavy but were covered with at least some sod. More informal campsites appear virtually all over the banks of the river, so that in addition to single occupation situations, Gravels phase material has been recovered from beneath Norton and Thule tradition remains, and from above remains of the Strand phase. The nature of the habitations suggests some winter occupation of the area, but the distribution of informal campsites suggests also that considerable occupation was focused upon the use of the river in summer, probably during salmon runs. Although some of the recovered salmonid bone is apparently that of trout, the teeth are probably those of anadromous salmon, which would support this suggestion.

Other Sites

Lutz and Anderson reported surface finds of apparent Arctic Small Tool material north of Unalakleet (Campbell 1970:240). Bockstoce (1979) reports at Cape Nome some evidence of similar material, presumably from a temporary campsite, underlying a habitation of Norton tradition, and Ackerman (1979) makes a comparable report with regard to a site at Eek Lake.

Small bifaces and a burin of clear Arctic Small Tool tradition cast were recovered from scattered deposits and from a portion of a square, semisubterranean house in the upper Ugashik River drainage (apparently similar to houses from Brooks River mentioned above), but as a part of an assemblage that includes a number of larger projectile points and sideblades clearly comparable to later Norton tradition forms and that seems to lack blades. On the basis of the relatively small sample available, this Ugashik Hillside phase, although variant, must be considered an Arctic Small Tool tradition affiliate, an assignment supported by the radiocarbon evidence that would place it (uncorrected) between about 1900 and 1500 B.C. (Dumond, Henn, and Stuckenrath 1976; Henn 1978).

When the final report on the Denbigh Flint complex was issued, the geologist David M. Hopkins, considering radiocarbon and other lines of evidence (Giddings

1964:250), concluded that the complex must date between 3000 and 2500 B.C. Remains at Brooks River, on the other hand, have been dated to the period between about 1900 and 1000 B.C. by means of 11 radiocarbon determinations, each on charcoal from a different hearth or house floor. This radiocarbon evidence is summarized in table 3.

Hopkins's conclusions rested heavily upon the date obtained from the lowermost peat overlying the Denbigh deposit at Iyatayet (2083 B.C. ± 280; P-105), which he tended to accept at the value of 2083 B.C. However, given the nature of radiocarbon, the true date of deposition of the peat may be as late as 1500 B.C., a date that would make generally acceptable any or all of the remaining Iyatayet radiocarbon determinations (table 3), would still provide time for the geologic processes taken into account by Hopkins, and would accord well with determinations from the Naknek drainage and elsewhere in Alaska. Considering the ambiguity present in some of the dates derived by measurements on solid carbon, it seems plausible to date the Iyatayet deposit at not earlier than about 2000 B.C.

The Norton Tradition

Since Giddings (1949) discovered the Norton culture deposits at Cape Denbigh and Larsen (1950) tested sites with related material at Platinum and at Nanvak and Chagvan bays, knowledge of the distribution of the Norton tradition has expanded almost yearly. Collections consist of chipped stone implements; of some rudimentary and rather scratchy ground slate; of pecked stone vessels, some of which were used as lamps; and of thin, hard pottery, usually decorated with check stamping, often fiber tempered. The chipped stone industry includes a variety of small projectile blades, both stemmed and unstemmed; asymmetrical sideblades in many forms; chipped drills; larger bifaces in a number of forms, some of them discoidal, which have been called "scrapers" by some investigators; small chipped adz blades, polished only at the bit; relatively small and very steeply retouched unifaces, sometimes termed "flake knives." Other implements include polished burinlike tools in hard stone, labrets, and the notched stones usually called net sinkers.

Cape Denbigh

The type collection is from Iyatayet (Giddings 1964), the site that produced the Denbigh Flint complex. In addition to items mentioned above, pottery here was also both plain and impressed with parallel grooves; the ceramic types have been designated Norton Check Stamped, Norton Linear Stamped, and Norton Plain (Griffin and Wilmeth 1964); the ware is predominantly fiber tempered. The majority of the small projectile blades are unstemmed, with a relatively square base; some have bases that contract to provide a somewhat diamond-shaped outline. Favored material was basalt.

Bone and antler material in frozen locations included parts of bird and fish spears; arrowheads for both endblades and sideblades; blunt arrowheads or "bunts"; toggling harpoon heads, both with and without line hole, of a form that has been called "primitive" (Giddings 1964:142); bilaterally barbed harpoon dart heads; other harpoon and dart pieces; and awls and implements thought to be stone flaking tools. The functions of most of these can be easily interpreted from similar implements in use by later Eskimos.

At Iyatayet and another nearby site (Gungnuk), Norton houses had been excavated into the ancient surface in a generally rectangular shape, with a relatively short entrance passage (Giddings 1964:136, 181). They were heated by interior fires.

Food debris included remains chiefly of small seal, with some bearded seal, white whale, walrus, and caribou also represented. From the numerous notched stones, Giddings (1964:168) inferred that fishing was important, and in the near absence of dog bones he concluded that the catch was used in human consumption. Small projectile blades were presumed to be used in caribou hunting, whereas the square-based points were thought harpoon points. Thus the overall conclusion was that the people were coastal dwellers with a strong interior subsistence interest.

Table 3. Radiocarbon Dates Applicable to the Arctic Small Tool Tradition

Cape Denbigh	Naknek Drainage
Peat overlying cultural deposit	
1043 B.C. ± 170 (P-104)	
(average of 3 runs)	
1123 B.C. + 210 (P-108)	*Brooks River Gravels phase*
(average of 2 runs)	1102 B.C. ± 250 (I-1159)
2083 B.C. ± 280 (P-105)	1138 B.C. ± 200 (I-1157)
	1150 B.C. ± 105 (SI-1857)
Denbigh Flint complex	1175 B.C. ± 200 (I-517)
1353 B.C. ± 200 (P-102)[a]	1300 B.C. ± 200 (I-518)
1523 B.C. ± 200 (P-103)[b]	1330 B.C. ± 60 (SI-1860)
(average of 2 runs)	1440 B.C. ± 110 (I-3115)
1557 B.C. ± 230 (C-792)[b]	1500 B.C. ± 110 (I-1947)
(average of 2 runs)	1520 B.C. ± 65 (SI-1859)
2019 B.C. ± 600 (W-298)[b]	1660 B.C. ± 85 (SI-1856)
2301 B.C. ± 290 (C-793)[a]	1950 B.C. ± 130 (I-1629)
3111 B.C. ± 340 (C-793)[a]	

NOTE: All Cape Denbigh dates are solid carbon dates except W-298, which is gas process; all Naknek drainage dates are gas process.

[a] P-102 and the two runs of C-793 were made on the same samples; the older C-793 date was obtained after washing in acid.

[b] P-103, C-792, and W-298 were obtained from samples from a single deposit; W-298 is the only CO_2 determination applicable to the Denbigh Flint complex at Iyatayet.

Naknek Drainage

In the Naknek drainage archeological remains of the Norton tradition are divided into three cultural phases (Dumond 1981). The first, the Smelt Creek phase, duplicates the stone and ceramic assemblage at Iyatayet fairly closely; minor exceptions occur in the far greater proportion of stemmed projectile blades and in the absence of linear stamped pottery (fig. 8a–e, j–o, s). The second, the Brooks River Weir phase, was apparently derived from the first, with changes in the styles of chipped stone endblades and sideblades (fig. 8f–g) and in the forms of some ululike knives of ground slate. Pottery changed shape, and ceramics became more often plain or carried check stamping of increased size (Dumond 1969b). The third phase, the Brooks River Falls phase, saw new styles in small stone points; chipped sideblades were almost completely replaced by ulus of ground slate, while large double-edged knife or lance blades of ground slate became fairly frequent. The pottery was almost always plain, and usually very thick, although still tempered predominantly with fiber. Organic material has not survived.

Habitations of the Smelt Creek and Brooks River Weir phases were roughly square and excavated slightly into the ancient surface, with a sloping entrance and internal fire—a form similar to that of the Arctic Small Tool tradition houses in the same locality—and at least some of them are presumed to have been for winter use. Although people of the Brooks River Falls phase are thought to have used similar habitations, the sites of this period have been so torn up by later aboriginal occupations that no satisfactory excavation has been possible.

Unlike the time of the earlier Arctic Small Tool tradition, for which remains are known thus far only from the upper portion of the Naknek drainage system (above Naknek Lake), during the time of the Norton tradition there was also a significant number of sites in the section of the river system that coincides with upper tidewater—below the lakes, but more than 25 kilometers from the present coast. Although there is suggestive evidence of a steadily increasing use of the upper portion of the drainage as the time of the Norton tradition wore on, there is no indication of any significant presence upon the coast itself (Dumond 1981:191–193).

Chagvan Bay

At the Chagvan Bay site Norton tradition remains have been divided into serial phases designated Chagvan Beach I, II, and III. The first of these is represented by only a few artifacts and no pottery and inasmuch as its departure from units assigned to the second phase is only in the absence of certain items, it seems simpler for present purposes to lump the first two phases.* Phase I-II, then, is similar in almost all respects to the Norton culture of Iyatayet, including the presence of both check- and linear-stamped ceramics. Chagvan Beach III compares more closely to the Brooks River Weir and Falls phases of the Naknek drainage (R.E. Ross 1971).

House of all phases were rounded, excavated to a shallow depth into the aboriginal ground surface, were entered by a sloping entrance passage, and contained an internal fire. The lack of food debris prevents any direct inference of subsistence practices.

Other Sites

Assemblages with clear affinity for the Norton culture of Iyatayet have been recovered from coastal locations near Cape Nome, where two phases of that culture have been distinguished (Bockstoce 1979) near Unalakleet, where "early" and "developed" aspects are noted (Lutz 1970, 1972, 1973); on Nunivak Island, where development within the Norton tradition for nearly a millennium seems indicated in the Duchikmiut phase (fig. 8 p–r) (Nowak 1970, 1974, 1982); the coastal lowlands between the mouths of the Kuskokwim and Yukon rivers (Shaw 1981); at Nanvak bay, where material similar to that at Chagvan Bay was recovered (Ackerman 1964; Larsen 1950); and at the mouth of the Ugashik River on the Alaska Peninsula, where a late (after A.D. 500) Norton manifestation appears (Henn 1978). At the first three of these, square houses, at least sometimes with sloping entrance passages, were present. At Unalakleet, the later "developed" aspect is represented by a large, rectangular structure that is thought to have been a ceremonial house or kashim (Lutz 1973).

To turn to more inland locations, it seems probable that some of the ceramics and chipped stone artifacts recovered from historic period house floors in the upper Nushagak drainage (VanStone 1968) pertain to the Norton tradition. A small amount of similar check-stamped pottery has been recovered in uncertain contexts at the site at Pedro Bay on Iliamna Lake, and stone implements almost certainly of a Norton assemblage were salvaged at the lower end of the same lake (Townsend and Townsend 1964). On Nonvianuk Lake in the Al-

---

*The radiocarbon dates derived from the Chagvan Bay excavations, especially those with the WSU (Washington State University) identification numbers, are internally inconsistent. Thus a substantial portion of the chronological ordering at that site was based upon a matrix analysis using the Robinson Index of Agreement. A characteristic of this statistic lies in its tendency to provide larger scores to comparisons in which paired units are both large, and smaller scores to comparisons in which one is large and the other is small. Thus the position of house 117, the only unit included in Chagvan Beach I, may well be an artifact of the technique. In content it departs from other units in Chagvan Beach II only in the absence of certain artifact types, a feature in keeping with its small size.

U. of Oreg., Oreg. State Mus. of Anthr., Eugene: a, N3, Z–3–4; b, N3, F–1–8; c, N3, B–5–16; d, N3, X–2–10; e, N3, W–5–3; f, Uga–2, M–2–28; g, BR 7, HP2–25; h, BR 20–1, B–6–2; i, Uga–1, M–2–50; j, BR11–6, F–6–19; k, SCI,695; l, SCI, 591; m, BR 20–C, A–3–1; n, BR11–6, E–6–1; o, BR 11–6, B–4–4; s; Colo. College, Colo. Springs: p, BC–4–186; q, MK2, HP1–13–215; r, MK 2, HP1B–10–265. Fig. 8. Norton tradition artifacts, Alaska. a–e, Smelt Creek phase sideblades from Smelt Creek site (49 Nak 3); f–g, Brooks River Weir phase endblades and sideblades from Brooks River site (49MK 1); h–i, Ugashik Lakes phase endblades from Ugashik Narrows site (49 Uga 2); j–n, Smelt Creek phase endblades from Brooks River site (j, m–n) and Smelt Creek site (k–l); o, Smelt Creek phase polished adz blade from Brooks River site; p–r, Duchikmiut phase harpoons from Nunivak Island (site MK 2); s, Smelt Creek phase check-stamped pot from Smelt Creek site. Length of r 8.5 cm, a–q same scale; height of s 24.0 cm.

agnak drainage a site has yielded pure Smelt Creek phase materials (Dumond 1960–1975; VanStone 1954: fig. 3). In the upper Ugashik River drainage, Norton tradition remains (designated the Ugashik Lakes phase,

fig. 8h–i) are especially plentiful, including substantial, square, semisubterranean houses, and appearing as early as 200 B.C.; only much later are similar remains known from the mouth of the same river (Henn 1978).

The radiocarbon evidence available for some material of the Norton tradition is summarized in table 4. Those collections that include linear-stamped pottery seem to be datable earlier than 200 B.C. although the distribution of linear-stamped ceramics, as opposed to the ubiquitous check-stamped, is erratic, including only Cape Denbigh, Chagvan Beach II, probably Nanvak Bay, a very uncertain context at Pedro Bay, and a similarly ambiguous context at Brooks River (Dumond 1969b). Assemblages most like the type collection in other respects appear to be those that are dated earlier than about A.D. 100. The end of the Norton tradition in the southern portion of the zone, as indicated by sudden changes in ceramics and stone implements, seems to have occurred very late in the first millennium A.D. (Dumond 1981).

The Thule Tradition

People of the Thule tradition are recognizable late prehistoric Eskimos of a material culture of the general sort described by Nelson (1899). Stone implements display a heavy reliance upon ground slate with polished ulus, projectile insert blades, and large barbed slate knives or lance blades characteristic of much of the region, although some chipped projectile blades continue to be represented in certain collections. Pottery consistently falls into a class of wares characterized by heavy gravel temper; that of earlier collections tends to be globular in form and may be decorated with impressed concentric-circle or spiral decorations; later, it is more flowerpotlike or bucketlike in form, and, except in the extreme south of the area, it is inscribed with lines and dots. Artifact collections commonly include high proportions of organic implements, in which hafted beaver-tooth knives are especially common; birchbark baskets, grass matting, and snowshoes also appear. Evidence of dog traction occurs only in the most recent collections. The house with the sunken entrance or cold trap was apparently universal. Although excavations have been made at sites of this tradition, only a few of them have been extensive enough to demonstrate changes through time within the tradition.

Cape Denbigh

The Nukleet assemblage from Cape Denbigh (Giddings 1964) appears to span considerable time. Harpoon heads were first decorated in a style known from the Early Punuk period of Saint Lawrence Island, later giving way to others apparently in a more localized style. Pottery underwent a parallel change from globular, concentric-

Table 4. Radiocarbon Dates Applicable to the Norton Tradition

Cape Nome[a]	Cape Denbigh	Unalakleet	Nunivak Island
			A.D. 995 ± 90 (I-5304)[d]
Late Norton phase	*Norton culture*	*Developed Norton*	*Duchikmiut phase*
A.D. 357 ± 89 (I-5380)	A.D. 492 ± 200 (C-506)[b]	A.D. 394 ± 48 (P-1530)[c]	A.D. 590 ± 95 (I-5303)
A.D. 288 ± 95 (I-5376)		A.D. 140 ± 40 (P-1772)[c]	
A.D. 231 ± 181 (I-5378)			
Early Norton phase		*Norton*	
23 B.C. ± 99 (I-5379)	16 B.C. ± 250 (C-562)[b]	26 B.C. ± 50 (P-1531)	A.D. 34 ± 95 (I-4486)[e]
97 B.C. ± 79 (I-5983)	255 B.C. ± 213 (P-13)	190 B.C. ± 47 (P-1532)	150 B.C. ± 105 (I-1948)[e]
266 B.C. ± 79 (I-6085)	403 B.C. ± 170 (P-13)[b]		
	770 B.C. ± 130 (M-1260)		

NOTE: Dates are unadjusted, calculated on the half-life of 5,568 years; all are gas process dates unless otherwise indicated.
[a] Cape Nome dates are converted to the half-life of 5,568 years from the citations of Bockstoce (1979).
[b] Solid carbon date.
[c] Dates P-1530 and P-1772 were derived from a single habitation.
[d] This date appears to apply to the latest appearance of check-stamped pottery.
[e] I-1948 and I-4486 were derived from the same habitation.
[f] WSU-119 and WSU-452 were derived from the same habitation.
[g] WSU-721 and I-4355 were derived from the same habitation.
[h] WSU-123 and I-4354 were derived from the same habitation.
[i] WSU-722 and I-4356 were derived from the same habitation.

circle marked ware to bucketlike vessels with line-and-dot decoration. Within the period, certain technological innovations appeared, including new ways of arrow hafting and the use of the sinew-backed bow. Subsistence was based upon sea hunting, land hunting, and fishing. Actual animal remains suggest that small seals were of first importance throughout the period of occupation. Caribou apparently declined in importance over time, as the taking of large sea mammals—walrus, white whale, and bearded seal—increased (Giddings 1964:91). Implements suggest a uniform importance of sealing by kayak and provide no evidence of either whaling or the winter hunting of seals through sea ice.

Naknek Drainage

In the Naknek drainage three phases appear in sequence. The first, the Brooks River Camp phase, is marked by the presence of numerous large barbed and stemmed lance and knife blades of polished slate projectile insert blades, and by thick pottery in globular shape (fig. 9). The second, the Brooks River Bluffs phase, is characterized by fewer large lance blades, a

change in the style of projectile insert blades and of adz blades, and the appearance of relatively thin pottery that may have appliquéd ridges on the exterior. The third, the Pavik phase, contains Russian and American trade goods, which shortly replaced most indigenous stone implements except for ground slate insert blades similar to those of the Bluffs phase. No line-dot markings occurred on the thin bucket- or flowerpot-shaped ceramic vessels. Organic implements still included harpoon dart heads, occasional relatively plain toggling harpoon heads, dart heads to take a stone or metal projectile insert tip, and other arrow and bird dart pieces (Dumond 1981).

In the interior portion of the area, food trash from all phases is primarily remains of salmon and caribou, although bird, beaver, bear, and some sea mammal bones also occur. On the coast, remains are chiefly of small seal, with walrus, caribou, and salmon also represented. For the first time settlements of significant size are known from the coast at the mouth of the Naknek River, but they do not appear at the expense of inland settlement, which also remains substantial. At the time of the historic Pavik phase there was a major

Table 4. Continued

Chagvan Bay	Naknek Region
Phase III	*Brooks River Falls phase*
A.D. 1720 ± 40 (WSU-119)[f]	
A.D. 1050 ± 370 (WSU-718)	A.D. 975 ± 120 (I-520)
A.D. 830 ± 180 (WSU-453)	A.D. 775 ± 125 (I-522)
	A.D. 750 ± 170 (I-519)
	A.D. 725 ± 130 (I-521)
	Brooks River Weir phase
A.D. 690 ± 270 (WSU-452)[f]	A.D. 720 ± 150 (I-526)
A.D. 610 ± 100 (I-4355)[g]	A.D. 515 ± 70 (SI-1858)
250 B.C. ± 400 (WSU-721)[g]	A.D. 505 ± 65 (SI-2074)
Phase II	A.D. 265 ± 70 (SI-1858)
A.D. 620 ± 60 (WSU-123)[h]	A.D. 260 ± 110 (I-3116)
	A.D. 160 ± 130 (I-1633)
	A.D. 160 ± 65 (SI-2073)
A.D. 100 ± 100 (I-4356)[i]	A.D. 100 ± 100 (I-200)
223 B.C. ± 382 (WSU-722)[i]	A.D. 55 ± 150 (I-1631)
400 B.C. ± 95 (I-4354)[h]	
Phase I	*Smelt Creek phase*
	A.D. 50 ± 150 (I-508)
	15 B.C. ± 75 (SI-1849)
	190 B.C. ± 105 (I-1948)
372 B.C. ± 380 (WSU-717)	305 B.C. ± 80 (SI-1850)

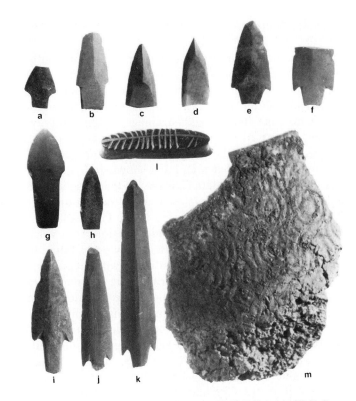

U. of Oreg., Oreg. State Mus. of Anthr., Eugene: a, BR 20-7, H-1-2; b, BR 20-C, D-3-2; c, S-630; d, BR 20-T, K-1-1; e, S-673; f, BR 20-C, D-4-10; g, BR 20-1, A-3-3; h, BR 20-A, E-6; i, BR 20-T, H-1-1; j, BR 20-1, D-2-5; k, S-663; l, BR 20-C, B-4-21; m, BR-1, 8.

Fig. 9. Thule tradition, Brooks River Camp phase artifacts from Brooks River site, Alaska (49 MK 1). a–h, polished slate projectile and knife insert tips; i–k, polished slate dart blades; l, coal labret; m, concentric-circle stamped potsherd. Length of c 4.9 cm; rest same scale.

permanent community (population about 200) located at the mouth of the Naknek River, and a second (with a population of about 150) in the upper reaches of the drainage system. The archeological evidence suggests year-round use of the upper drainage throughout all three phases. Accounts of modern informants suggest that the people of the upper drainage during historic times were accustomed to hunt sea mammals seasonally on the Pacific coast (W.A. Davis 1954; Dumond 1960–1975, 1981).

Other Sites

Materials pertaining to the Thule tradition have been excavated throughout the area—at Cape Nome (Bockstoce 1979), at Hooper Bay (Oswalt 1952, 1952a), on Nunivak Island in the Nash Harbor and Mekoryuk phases (Nowak 1970; VanStone 1954, 1957), in the Platinum vicinity (Ackerman 1964; Larsen 1950), at Togiak (Kowta 1963), and in the Ugashik drainage system (Henn 1978). In addition, on both the Kuskokwim and Nushagak river systems historic settlements with considerable ap-

plication to the late prehistoric period have been excavated (Oswalt and VanStone 1967; VanStone 1968, 1970a, 1971).

At the northern edge of the region, near Cape Nome, manifestations of Birnirk culture are reported (Bockstoce 1979) on the basis of house form and a small stone artifact assemblage, in which polished implements are much more numerous than in earlier Norton collections. The rectangular houses with sloping entrance passage and side bench contained no evidence of interior wood fires, but rather of fires of animal fat. No pottery was recovered. This is the southernmost reported occurrence of Birnirk culture, which according to criteria used here would be assigned to an early place within the Thule tradition.

Subsistence everywhere appears to have been extensively upon fish, particularly salmon, and upon caribou or seal or both, depending upon the location.

The radiocarbon evidence summarized in table 5 suggests that the tradition first appeared around A.D. 900 to 1000 throughout most of the area. The Birnirk or Birnirk-related materials are said to appear near Cape Nome at least as early as A.D. 600 (Bockstoce 1979).

Regional Distribution

Although the total area reported on here finds its southwestern boundary on the Alaska Peninsula at 159° west longitude, the cultural sequence described thus far seems to pertain to an area extending little farther southwestward than the Ugashik drainage system. Surveys in the vicinity of Chignik on the Pacific coast of the Peninsula and on the Bering Sea coast immediately northwestward of that area have shown rather clearly that the prehistoric material cultures of that zone around 159° west longitude are related to those found from Port Moller southwestward to the tip of the Peninsula (discussed in "Prehistory of the Aleutian Region," this vol.), a region that in the earliest period known was home to a people with a chipped-stone industry, without pottery. These early people persisted through the first millennia B.C. and A.D., at least, when they were intruded upon around A.D. 1000 by polished-slate-using people of evident Thule affiliation, who were to penetrate southwestward at least as far as Izembek Lagoon (Dumond, Henn, and Stuckenrath 1976). It is possible, although not certain, that this lower Peninsula cultural province of the turn of the Christian era may have extended as far northeastward as Cinder River, at about 158° west longitude (Dumond 1960–1975).

Conclusion

The archeology of the Bering Sea region has been summarized through the use of a number of traditions, the last three of which—Arctic Small Tool, Norton, and Thule—are presumed by many students to have been sequential developments in a single cultural and ethnic continuum leading to modern Eskimos. These traditions followed upon earlier periods when occupation was by peoples whose affiliations are considerably more ambiguous.

The first such people—of the time before about 6000 B.C.—are represented throughout much of both coastal and interior by a series of blade and core assemblages within which there is considerable heterogeneity, yet which are all clearly similar to contemporary or slightly earlier assemblages of eastern Siberia. The second people, of the period from about 4000 to 2000 B.C., deposited notched-point- and lanceolate-point-dominated and derivative assemblages throughout much of Alaska north of the Alaska Peninsula, largely in the interior yet not rarely on the coast, but unlike their predecessor, their assemblages relate with clarity not to Siberia but to Archaic assemblages of North America. Contemporary with these is an apparently more localized Pacific coastal culture in the Kodiak Island vicinity that also is represented sporadically at the southernmost edge of the Bering Sea drainage on the Alaska Peninsula.

Given the known distribution of the ensuing Arctic Small Tool tradition, and the apparent rapidity with which it displaced representatives of the Pacific coastal tradition and the Northern Archaic tradition within the Naknek drainage, its carriers must be presumed to have arrived in the Bering Sea region shortly after 2000 B.C. from the north—whatever its historical relationship elsewhere may have been to representatives of the widespread earlier traditions discussed here.

Of the two locations that have yielded substantial Arctic Small Tool remains in this area, Cape Denbigh

Table 5. Radiocarbon Dates Applicable to the Thule Tradition

Cape Nome[a]	Cape Denbigh	Nunivak Island	Naknek Region
Cape Nome phase A.D. 1656 ± 88 (I-5981)	Nukleet culture	Nash Harbor phase	Brooks River Bluffs phase A.D. 1720 ± 80 (I-209)
		A.D. 1600 ± 95 (I-3132)	A.D. 1595 ± 85 (SI-1853) A.D. 1500 ± 60 (Y-932) A.D. 1470 ± 90 (I-523)
		Mekoryuk River phase	Brooks River Camp phase A.D. 1650 ± 75 (I-524)
		A.D. 1280 ± 95 (I-4487) A.D. 1270 ± 95 (I-3131)	A.D. 1280 ± 105 (I-1632) A.D. 1270 ± 90 (I-525) A.D. 1255 ± 65 (SI-2072) A.D. 1105 ± 100 (I-1635)[c]
		A.D. 995 ± 90 (I-5304)[b]	A.D. 1070 ± 65 (SI-2075)[c]
	A.D. 900 ± 110 (M-1260)		
Birnirk culture A.D. 705 ± 74 (I-5982) A.D. 574 ± 92 (I-5377)			

NOTE: Dates are unadjusted, calculated on the half-life of 5,568 years; all are gas process dates.

[a] Cape Nome dates are converted to the half-life of 5,568 years from the citations of Bockstoce (1979).

[b] This apparently dates the transition from check-stamped to circle-stamped pottery.

[c] I-1635 and SI-2075 date ceramics that appear to retain some characteristics of the preceding Brooks River Falls phase, of Norton culture.

is coastal, whereas Brooks River is located about 80 kilometers from the coast. The Arctic Small Tool site in the Ugashik drainage is some 50 kilometers from the coast. In view of the fact that coastal regions have been generally explored much more fully than have the more interior zones, it appears likely that Small Tool remains, including habitations, will eventually be found to be more plentiful inland from the true coast and to occur especially along major streams. It seems likely that these people exploited caribou to a great extent, depended upon anadromous fish where available, and probably visited the coast only seasonally, where they engaged in some hunting of sea mammals.

The origin of the Norton tradition is obscure in that its manifestations seem everywhere to be preceded by a hiatus in the record. As Dumond (1971a, 1981) has pointed out there are a number of typological continuities that span the time between the end of the known persistence of the Arctic Small Tool tradition and the initiation of the Norton tradition. These include the house form, at least as houses occur in the Naknek drainage, as well as the form of certain small projectile blades and of the small chipped adz with polished bit. If the Arctic Small Tool tradition was indeed a Norton ancestor, however, to it as a base were added not only more elaborate forms of chipped stone artifacts but also pottery that must surely be Asian (Griffin 1969–1970), and shaped stone vessels and ground slate, a possible source for which was cultures of the Pacific coast south and east of the Alaska Peninsula.

If this is in fact the case, one would expect to find evidence somewhere in southwestern Alaska of an ancestral culture, intermediate between the Arctic Small Tool and Norton traditions, in which southern traits—stone vessels and ground slate—occurred, but to which pottery had not yet been added. Unambiguous pieces of this evidence are now lacking, although the Norton artifactual characteristics that occur in the Arctic Small

Tool–related Ugashik Hillside phase of the second millennium B.C. are certainly suggestive.

At any rate it seems evident that people of proper Norton tradition were spread throughout the region treated here by, or shortly after, the middle of the first millennium B.C.; that these people retained a substantial subsistence interest in the interior, while displaying a new interest in coastal subsistence resources as marked by the appearance of sizable settlements at some coastal locations; that as the centuries passed there was a tendency for local cultural divergences to evolve; and that in most of the area the tradition persisted through virtually all of the first millennium A.D. It has been suggested that this period was one of increasing population and sedentation (Dumond 1972a).

At most of the locations explored, a second hiatus appears between the Norton and the Thule materials, but there are also significant exceptions. On Nunivak Island a house floor dated A.D. 995 ± 90 (I-5304; Nowak 1974, personal communication 1973) yielded apparently transitional Norton-Thule pottery, with gravel-tempered, check-stamped sherds, and concentric-circle-impressed sherds appearing together. In the Naknek drainage, one deposit evidently as early as A.D. 1070 ± 65 (SI-2075) and another directly dated at 1105 ± 100 (I-1635) yielded pottery typologically transitional between that of the Brooks River Falls and Brooks River Camp phases (Dumond 1969b; Shields 1977). In both locations, although the transition was rapid it was not marked by discontinuity either in pottery or in other artifacts. This evidence, together with the apparent presence of a Birnirk-related occupation on southern Seward Peninsula several hundred years earlier, suggests that future work will reveal that the southwestern Alaska version of the Thule tradition was based firmly upon its long-established Norton predecessor and evolved under the stimulus of the early Christian era florescence of sea mammal hunting around Bering Strait.

Prehistory of the Asian Eskimo Zone

ROBERT E. ACKERMAN

Far from the mainstream of Asian cultural developments, the prehistoric Eskimo of Siberia lived along the shores of the East Siberian, Chukchi, and Bering seas (fig. 1). In the late twentieth century their settlements are restricted to a cluster of villages on the easternmost coast of the Chukchi Peninsula in the vicinity of the Bering Strait.

Compared to Alaska, interest in Siberian Eskimo prehistory was a comparatively late development. The pioneering work of Rudenko (1961) on the Chukchi Peninsula in 1945 represents the first scientific excavation of Eskimo prehistoric settlements. The material from these excavations was strikingly similar to that recovered by Jenness (1928) and Collins (1937b). Rudenko thus followed the phase sequence established by Collins (1937b) for Saint Lawrence Island but indicated that a local expression of the Okvik phase was present at the Uélen site (the Uélen-Okvik phase). He additionally disagreed with Collins's derivation of Eskimo culture from an Old World Mesolithic stage (Collins 1943, 1964; Rudenko 1961:177). Research of investigators in Eastern Siberia and the Soviet Far East since the 1960s has considerably altered the view of northern Asian prehistory.

Siberia and Eskimo Prehistory

The establishment of a culture history for the native peoples of Siberia has proceeded along several lines of inquiry, with the problem of each region being treated somewhat differently. Investigations along the Arctic coast between the Kolyma and Anadyr´ rivers and southward to Kamchatka and the Sea of Okhotsk, for example, focused on coastal settlements and emphasized sea-mammal hunting as a way of life (see fig. 1) (Beregovaia 1954, 1960; Rudenko 1947, 1961). The prehistoric cultural phases derived from the material recovered were essentially in agreement with the formulations of Danish, Canadian, and American archeologists covering a temporal span of some 2,000 years. In contrast, investigations in the interior of the continent revealed a more ancient cultural stratum that appeared to be derived from European and central Asiatic complexes. For continental Siberia, investigators constructed a sequence from the late Paleolithic through a transitional phase (Mesolithic?) into the Neolithic (chipped or ground stone tools with or without pottery, but nonagricultural), and then into the metal stages of Bronze and Iron, which carry on into the modern period (fig. 2) (Michael 1958; Okladnikov 1959, 1970).

Following World War II, Soviet archeologists conducted research studies in the Lake Baikal region, the Lena River valley from Lake Baikal to the Arctic coast, the interior Aldan River drainage system, the Upper to Lower Amur River region, the north shore of the Sea of Okhotsk, Kamchatka, Chukotka, the Maritime District, and Sakhalin Island, as well as expeditions into Mongolia. Through a consistent search for Eskimo origins, evidence from cultural antecedents prior to classic maritime adaptation has come to light (Arutiunov and Sergeev 1968, 1972, 1975; Bandi 1969, 1976; Chard 1955, 1961a, 1962, 1962a, 1962b, 1963a, 1973; Collins 1937a, 1939, 1940, 1943, 1951, 1962, 1963–1964, 1964, 1969–1970, 3; Dikov 1961b, 1965a, 1967, 1971a, 1974, 1977, 1979; Griffin 1960, 1962, 1969–1970, 3; Griffin and Wilmeth 1964; Levin 1958, 1958a; Okladnikov 1958, 1958a, 1960a, 1965; Rudenko 1961). This evidence will be reviewed with that from interior sites that may have a bearing on Eskimo prehistory.

Coastal Eskimo Cultural Phases

Paleo-Eskimo Stage

In 1975 Dikov (1977:210–212) discovered a nonceramic site (Chërtov Ovrag 'Devil's Gorge') on a southwestern promontory of Wrangell Island. Excavations by Tein (1979:54) extended the test area to 284 square meters. Around two camp fires and in a trash pit were found bones of walrus, seal, and ducks together with chipped stone tools and a toggling harpoon head (Dikov 1977:210–212, 1979:165–168; Tein 1979:53–63). The harpoon head had a single line hole, open socket, lashing groove for a binding to secure the foreshaft in the socket, asymmetric spur, and an open socket or bed for an endblade with a lashing groove on the opposite face (fig. 3k) (Dikov 1977, 1979). The harpoon head is illustrated with a stemmed, bifacial point as an endblade (Dikov 1979:156, fig. 66:1). The remainder of the assemblage consisted of stemmed, side notched, and ovate, bifa-

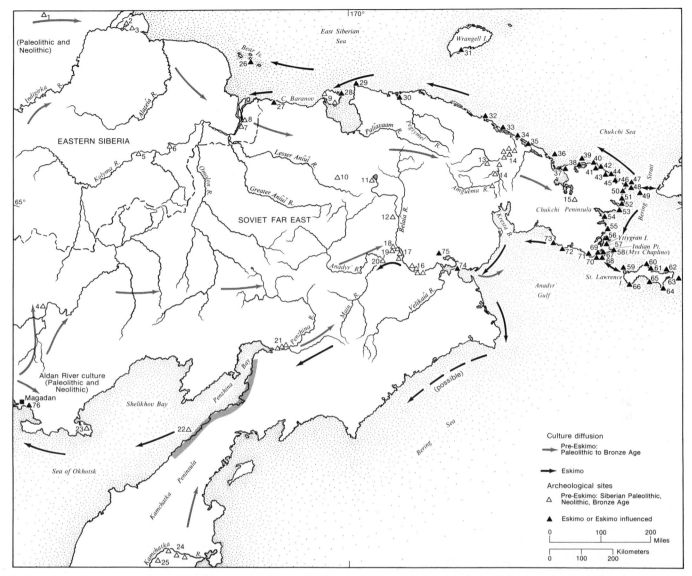

Fig. 1. Pre-Eskimo and Eskimo sites and site clusters in Eastern Siberia and the Soviet Far East. Pre-Eskimo: 1, Berelekh; 2, Lake Tat´īanino; 3, Ularovskaīa Channel; 4, Maiorych; 5, Lobuīa; 6, Pomazhina; 7, Kresta Kolymsk; 8, Petushki; 9, Aīon Island; 10, Lake Tytyl´; 11, Lake Ėl´gygytgyn; 12, Lake Chirovoe; 13, Ust´-Ėkityki; 14, Amguėma River sites; 15, Lake Ioni; 16, Chikaevo, Omrynskii; 17, Uvesnovaniīa, Utesiki, Vilka; 18, Ust´-Belaīa; 19, Snezhnoe; 20, Ust´-Main, Vakenaīa 1 and 2; 21, Penzhina River sites; 22, Penzhina Bay sites (Eskimo traits present); 23, P´īagina Peninsula sites (Eskimo traits present); 24, Kamchatka River sites; 25, Ushki. Eskimo: 26, Four Columns Island (Bear Islands); 27, Cape Baranov, Sarychev Bay, Second Bay; 28, Aīon Island; 29, Shalaurova Island; 30, Pegtymel´ River sites; 31, Chërtov Ovrag; 32, Cape Schmidt (Cape Ryrkaīpiīa); 33, Two Pilots Spit; 34, Nut Lagoon Spit; 35, Vankarem Spit, Cape Vankarem; 36, Kolīuchin Island; 37, Dzhenretlen; 38, Neshkana; 39, Ilitlen Island; 40, Ėnurmino; 41, Ikolivrunveem; 42, Seshan; 43, Chegitun; 44, Ėkichuverveem; 45, Uten; 46, Inchoun; 47, Uélen; 48, Naukan, Chenlun, East Cape; 49, Big Diomede, Little Diomede; 50, Ėkven; 51, Ėnmynytnyn, Chini; 52, Nunīamo; 53, Ĩandogaī; 54, Masik; 55, Nykhsirak; 56, Arakamchechen Island; 57, Siqluq; 58, Indian Point; 59, Gambell sites (Seklowaghyaget, Ievoghiyoq, Miyowagh, Hillside); 60, Kukulik; 61, S'keliyuk; 62, Camp Kolowiyi; 63, Punuk Islands; 64, Kialegak; 65, Siknik; 66, Southwest Cape sites; 67, Kivak; 68, Cape Chukotskii; 69, Plover Bay; 70, Avan, Hydrographic Lake; 71, Sireniki; 72, Nunligran; 73, Ėnmylen; 74, Anadyr´ Estuary; 75, Kanchalan; 76, Atargan (southeast of Magadan).

cially chipped projectile points; oblanceolate to weakly stemmed bifacial knives; stemmed side and end scrapers; adz blades with ground bits; flake knives and utilized flakes (fig. 3a–j) (Dikov 1977, 1979; Tein 1979). Neither ground slate tools nor ceramics were recovered from the site. Charcoal from the fire pits yielded a date of 1410 B.C. ± 155 (Dikov 1979:180). Dikov (1979:168) notes correspondences with the harpoon types of In-

dependence I in Greenland, but a closer analog appears to be the Old Whaling culture of Cape Krusenstern (Giddings 1961a:fig. 7), which dates to 1450–1250 B.C. (Anderson 1978:fig. 2-2).

Correspondences in the two assemblages are noteworthy: stemmed end scrapers, flake knife forms, the long, narrow bifacial knife form, adz blades, and the side-notched points.

107

Date	INTERIOR: STAGE	INTERIOR: PHASE	INTERIOR: SITE*	COAST AND ST. LAWRENCE ISLAND: STAGE	COAST AND ST. LAWRENCE ISLAND: PHASE	COAST AND ST. LAWRENCE ISLAND: SITE*
1500–A.D. 0 (1500, 1000, 500)	Relic-Neolithic; Ceramics- - - - - -Bronze - - - Iron	Kamchatka-Chukota localization of groups ancestral to Ainu, Koryak, Kamchadal, Yukagir, Chukchi, Eskimo.	16,20,21,24	Neo-Eskimo, Northern Maritime Tradition, Arctic Whaling Culture, or Relic-Neolithic	Late Prehistoric	26,28,33-35,42,49,50,54-57,59,60-66,69-73
					Thule	10,22,23,26,27,30,35,41,45,50,58,59,64,66,71-73,75
					Punuk	10,22,23,35,39,43,44,47,49,50,53,56,58-64,66,70-73,75,76
					Birnirk	26,27,35,38,40-42,45,47-49,52,59,60,66
					Okvik	47,48,51,59,60,63,68,71
A.D. 0 B.C.					Old Bering Sea	27,29,30,32,36,37,41,42,46-48,51,53,59,60,64,67-69,71,73,74
1000	Neolithic: Late	Kamchatka-Chukotka region cultural adaptations with hypothesized influences from the Aldan River region—Sumnagin, Syalakh, Bel-kachi, Ymyiakhtakh.	9-11,14,16,17,20,21,24,25,28,32	Paleo-Eskimo		31
2000	Neolithic: Middle		2,3,5-8,14,16-18,24,25	Coastal Beringian Cultulres?		
3000–4000	Neolithic: Early		13,14,18,25			
5000	Mesolithic		11,14,15,25,29			
10000–15000	Late Paleolithic	Diuktai Culture	1,4,25			

* see fig. 1 for location

after Arutiunov and Sergeev 1969; Collins 1964; Dikov 1965a, 1971, 1974, 1977, 1979; Giddings 1960; Mochanov 1969, 1969a, 1969b, 1969c, 1969d, 1970, 1977, 1980; Mochanov and Fedoseeva 1976; Okladnikov 1965; Rudenko 1961.

Fig. 2. Prehistoric cultures of the Asian Eskimo zone.

The Wrangell Island site is considerably older than other Eskimo sites along the north coast of Chukotka. Dikov (1979:168) has suggested that the Wrangell Island complex may have been derived from the Paleo-Eskimo cultures of Alaska or from some as yet unknown culture phase in northern Chukotka.

The intervening phases, Choris and Norton, have not been discovered by Soviet archeologists during their excavation of sites along the Chukotka coast. For this region the earliest occupation appears to be that of the Neo-Eskimo stage.

Neo-Eskimo Stage

• OLD BERING SEA–OKVIK PHASES The earliest evidence for an indisputable Eskimo occupation of the coastal region of northeastern Siberia is that found in the Bering Strait region. Here, as has been previously summarized by Chard (1955, 1958a) and Collins (1964), a fully developed maritime culture is represented by the Old Bering Sea and Okvik phases, which appeared during the last few centuries B.C. to the first few centuries of the Christian era (fig. 2). Considerable arguments have been advanced as to the temporal priority of one phase over the other (Anderson 1978; Bandi 1969; Collins 1943, 1953, 1964; Dumond 1977a; Giddings 1960; Rainey and Ralph 1959).

With the evidence available to them at the Ėkven and Uėlen sites Alekseev, Arutiunov, and Sergeev (1972:235) concluded that the two phases overlapped and remarked that differences in the artistic styles were a matter of regional emphasis. These investigators discovered, however, that the Old Bering Sea phase was earlier than the Okvik phase, which was contemporaneous with the developed and later aspects of the Old Bering Sea phase (Alekseev, Arutiunov, and Sergeev 1972:235; Arutiunov and Sergeev 1975:184). They also reported that the burial evidence at the Uėlen site indicated an association of Okvik and Birnirk harpoon head types (Arutiunov and Sergeev 1969:35). A dissenting view has been voiced by Dikov (1979:169–182), who saw in the artifacts of the Okvik phase archaic features that harkened back to earlier Neolithic cultures. Dikov (1979:182) noted, however, that the Okvik culture is still poorly known. It would be perhaps best at this point to consider the two phases as contemporaneous regional variants (cf. Dumond 1977a:119). Date ranges for the combined phases are: 72 B.C. ± 100 to A.D. 735 ± 30, or roughly A.D. 1–700 (Dikov 1977:243).

In terms of a cultural pattern, the technology of subsistence utilized by these two phases is virtually identical—hunting of sea mammals (walrus, seal, whale) with toggle harpoons along the sea ice edge; hunting of land mammals (caribou, bear) with bow and arrow; use of multi-pronged bird spear, sealing dart with throwing board, boats (kayak and umiak), hand-drawn small sled

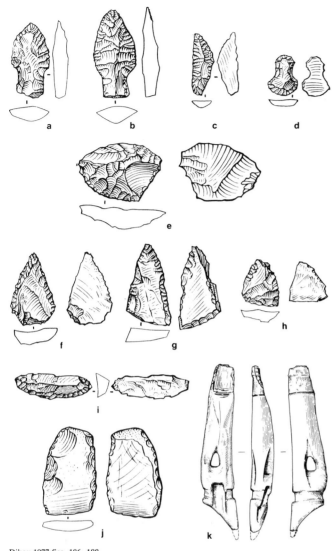

Dikov 1977:figs. 186–188.

Fig. 3. Paleo-Eskimo stone tool assemblage from Chërtov Ovrag (Devil's Gorge), Wrangell I. a–b, Stemmed endblades; c, side scraper; d, stemmed end scraper; e, large biface fragment; f, utilized flake (possibly sideblade); g, burin; h, scraping tool; i, keeled scraper; j, ground adz blade; k, open socket harpoon head with lashing slot for endblade. Length of a about 6.2 cm; rest same scale.

(no evidence of dog traction), snow goggles, fish leisters (spears with multiple serrated prongs), fishhooks; implements of chipped stone (knives, projectile points, side blades, drills, etc.) more numerous than tools made of ground stone (adzes, ulu blades, men's knife blades); a great number of bone, ivory, and antler tools (drills, skin scrapers, awls, needles, needle cases, mattocks, picks, harpoon parts—head, socket piece, foreshaft, ice pick; pottery with linear stamp or check stamp pattern (lamps and cooking pots); ivory carvings of animals and female figurines, and elaborate art styles found on harpoon heads; the enigmatic "winged figures" (bird or butterfly figures with outstretched wings), figurines, and drum handles (fig. 4).

Particular features of the art styles, harpoon head types, and constructional features of the semi-subterranean houses have been useful in distinguishing the Old Bering Sea and Okvik phases. The complexities of the art styles and the harpoon head typologies have been exhaustively detailed (Arutiunov and Sergeev 1969, 1972, 1975; Collins 1930, 1937, 1941; Dikov 1974, 1977, 1979; Geist and Rainey 1936; Rainey 1941; Rudenko 1947, 1961). In general, the elaborate art styles have been interpreted to indicate an early elaboration of hunting cults, inferring the interplay of magic and the forces of nature. On the more material side, the use of tailored clothing as a necessary adaptation to sea ice hunting is probable even if the evidence is not available. The discovery of gravers or burins with iron tips in the cemetery at Uélen indicates that there was trade with Iron Age societies to the west during the Old Bering Sea phase (Levin and Sergeev 1964).

The distribution of Old Bering Sea and Okvik settlements shows a localization in the Bering Strait region (figs. 1–2). The Okvik phase settlements are limited to Saint Lawrence Island and the eastern extremity of Chukchi Peninsula, while the cultural sphere of the Old Bering Sea phase extends from the Second Bay near Cape Baranov (Okladnikov and Beregovaiā 1971) to Ėnmylen (Rudenko 1961) on the south coast of the Chukchi Peninsula. The greater distribution of the Old Bering Sea phase to the west and south probably does not indicate a better environmental adjustment through technology but may simply reflect a greater need to extend the range of settlements once a maritime-oriented group is away from the rich resources of the Bering Strait area. Implicit also is the suggestion of a greater population, or perhaps a long duration of the Old Bering Sea phase, or both.

Much is still to be learned of these two early phases. They should be regarded as roughly contemporaneous localized cultures with the temporal priority of either phase still undecided. The major economic emphasis was on the hunting of walrus and seal with perhaps just the beginnings of a whale hunting complex. Settlements were small and rather widely separated. The finest artistic expressions of the two phases come from the cemeteries at Ekven (fig. 5) and Uélen (Arutiunov and Sergeev 1962, 1964, 1966, 1969, 1975; Arutiunov, Levin, and Sergeev 1964; Dikov 1967a; Levin 1959, 1964, 1964a; Levin and Sergeev 1970; Sergeev 1959), from the Chini cemetery (Dikov 1974), and from scattered finds on Saint Lawrence Island and the Punuk Islands (Collins 1937, Collins et al. 1973; Rainey 1941). This burial complex may be linked to a later elaboration at the Ipiutak site at Point Hope, Alaska (Larsen and Rainey 1948) and is undoubtedly reflected in the widespread cult of the dead found in eastern Siberia (Lopatin 1960).

• BIRNIRK—PUNUK PHASES Emerging as a development out of the Old Bering Sea and Okvik phases, the cultures represented by the Birnirk and Punuk phases were not simply amalgams of the antecedent technological traditions. In many ways these two cultural adaptations were different and yet were intertwined with shared cultural complexes. In figure 2 the Birnirk phase has been placed at an earlier time level and separate from that of Punuk (cf. Bandi 1969; Collins 1964; Giddings 1960; Rainey and Ralph 1959). This is a constraint imposed by a linear chart and does not accurately reflect the temporal relationships. Radiocarbon dates do give a temporal priority to Birnirk (Rainey and Ralph 1959), and Birnirk harpoon heads have been found in association with Old Bering Sea harpoon heads at the Uélen and Ėkven cemeteries, whereas Punuk harpoon heads have not (Arutiunov and Sergeev 1969). However, there is sufficient data to indicate that for the greater part of these two phases they were contemporaneous and in variable combination contributed to the following Thule phase. General date ranges are: Birnirk A.D. 300 or 400 to 800 or 900, Punuk A.D. 600 or 700 to 1000 or 1200 (Bandi 1969; Giddings 1960; Rainey and Ralph 1959).

In Siberia, sites containing artifacts belonging to the Birnirk phase are located on Saint Lawrence Island and along the coastline from Bering Strait to the Bear Islands off the mouth of the Kolyma in the west (fig. 6–7). As a cultural manifestation, the Birnirk phase is represented by a number of sites that have been briefly tested during archeological surveys (Beregovaĩa 1954, 1960; Chard 1955, 1959, 1961; Dikov 1958, 1961a, 1966, 1966a, 1971a, 1977, 1979; Rudenko 1961). The few sites of this phase to be systematically studied are those in the Cape Baranov area (Okladnikov 1947, 1970; Oklad-

nikov and Beregovaĩa 1971). Other Birnirk phase sites are found to the east, from Cape Prince of Wales (Collins 1937) to Point Barrow, Alaska (Ford 1959). The Eskimo of the Birnirk phase appear to have settled mainly along the Chukchi Sea coast and specialized in the hunting of seal at Uélen, Ėkven (Arutiunov and Sergeev 1969:36, 1972:307), and Cape Baranov (Okladnikov and Beregovaĩa 1971:19), while whale seems to have been hunted at Point Barrow (Ford 1959). The discovery of sealing harpoon heads of the Birnirk phase with Punuk whaling harpoon heads on Saint Lawrence Island may further indicate the lack of a whale hunting complex in Birnirk settlements (Ackerman 1961, 1962).

As a time segment of the Eskimo maritime adaptation, the cultural complex of the Birnirk phase reflected the continuity of the Old Bering Sea–Okvik cultural traditions. In brief, the cultural inventory included the accouterments of sea mammal hunting—toggle harpoon heads used with the heavy thrusting or light casting harpoon, seal dart with throwing board, sealskin floats, lances, boats (kayak and umiak); land mammal hunting—bow and arrow, spear, snares; fishing—nets, leisters, traps; and hunting of birds—snares, nets, bird spear. Within categories such as harpoon heads, change in form and surface decoration was evident and diagnostic for the phase. The small hand-drawn sled with bone or ivory runners was retained. Domestic tools were similar to those of the Old Bering Sea–Okvik phases, although ground stone largely replaced chipped stone in cutting, scraping, and chopping implements. Ornaments, carvings of wood, ivory, and bone, and toys continued. New elements added were bolas for snaring birds, elevated frame sled (perhaps used with dogs), baleen toboggan, wrist guard, reinforced bows, slat or hide armor, simplified art style based on the reduction of Old Bering Sea art motifs, curvilinear stamp pottery, house construction with whale bone supports, and new types of bone arrowheads.

Sites of the Punuk phase extend from Ėkichuverveem on the north (between Uélen and Koliuchin Bay) (Di-

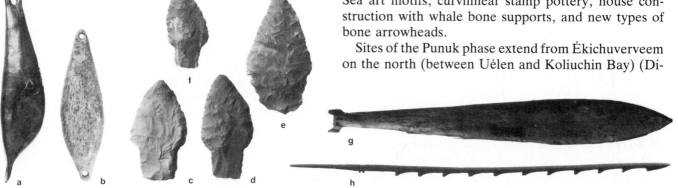

Smithsonian, Dept. of Anthr.: a, 370,735; b, 353,404; c, 352,675; d, 352,450; e, 352,447; f, 352,803; g, 371,052; h, 370,341.
Fig. 4. Old Bering Sea and Punuk cultures, St. Lawrence I., Alaska. a, Ivory fishline sinker; b, bone fishline sinker; c–d, chipped slate knife blades; e, chipped jasper knife blade; f, chipped chert knife blade or arrow point; g, toy paddle of baleen; h, ivory point for fish spear. a–b, g–h, Miyowagh site; rest Hillside site. Length of a about 10.4 cm; rest same scale.

Arutiunov and Sergeev 1975:figs. 48–49, 52.
Fig. 5. Old Bering Sea art from Ėkven site, Chukchi Peninsula, USSR: a, harpoon foreshaft; b–e, harpoon heads; f, kayak model; g, socket piece; h–j, harpoon heads; k, harpoon socketpiece; l, winged object; m–n, decorated ladles; o, bucket handle; p, bow drill; q, decorated masquette; r, chain of walrus ivory; s, bear's head; t, handle for a burin (cutting tool). Length of b about 19.0 cm; rest same scale.

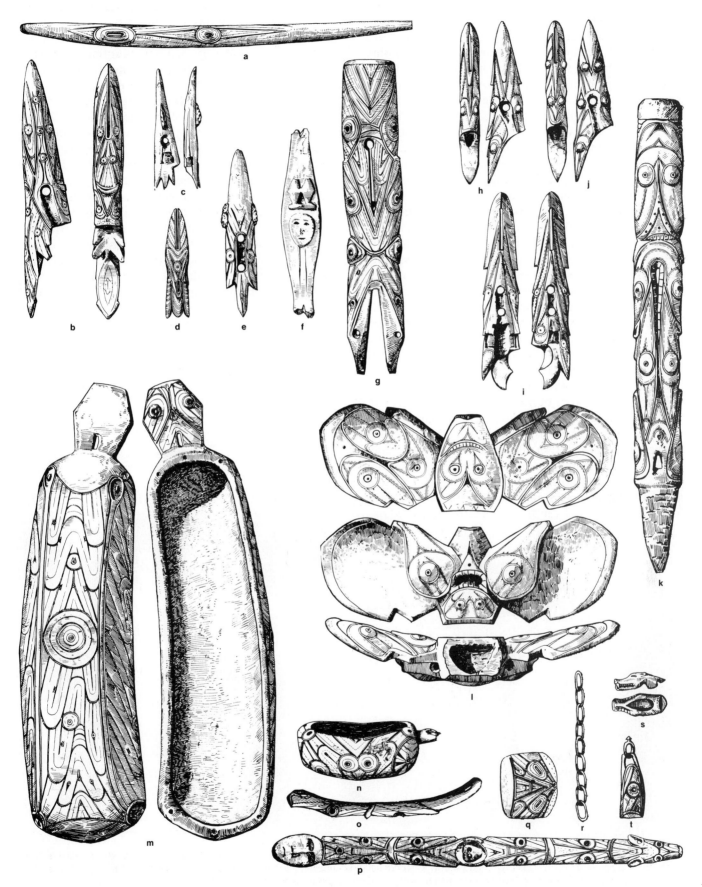

kov 1971a:34) to Ènmylen located on the south coast of the Chukchi Peninsula (Rudenko 1961:95–102). Elements of the artifact complexes of the Punuk phase are found in sites southwest of the Anadyr′ Gulf extending perhaps as far as Oliutor Bay and thence westward across the Kamchatka Peninsula to Shelikhov Bay and along the northern coast of the Sea of Okhotsk to the vicinity of Magadan (Chard 1957, 1959a, 1962; Dikov 1971a:34–35; Dikova 1965; Okladnikov 1958; Semenov 1965; Vasil′evskii 1964). Dikov (1971a:35) interprets the presence of these Punuk elements as evidence of cultural influences spreading from the Bering Sea area into the northern Sea of Okhotsk region. Transmission of cultural elements along the Anadyr′-Main and Penzhina river systems, linking Anadyr′ Gulf with Penzhina and Shelikhov bays is a possibility, but this is a lengthy interior route. Vasil′evskii acknowledges the possibility of a westward diffusion of Bering Sea culture traits but considers the impact of interior Neolithic traditions in combination with a maritime-oriented culture of the northern Sea of Okhotsk to be more significant in determining the specific character of the assemblages found in settlements along the northern coast of the Sea of Okhotsk (Vasil′evskii 1964, 1969, 1969a; see also Befu and Chard 1964; Collins 1969–1970, 3).

With the main area of occupation in the Bering Sea along the major migration routes of walrus and whales, the cultural complex of the Punuk phase is dominated by the subsistence pattern of large sea mammal hunting. Settlements are numerous, of large size, located at major coastal promontories, and marked by huge midden mounds. Whalebone is abundant at sites and was utilized often with rocks in the construction of dwellings (fig. 8), meat caches, drying racks, and boat racks. Direct pursuit and capture of whales is indicated by the presence of heavy harpoon equipment, floats, killing lances, and flensing tools. Other hunting and fishing implements are similar to those of the Birnirk phase.

Perhaps as an outgrowth of the expanding whaling economy, large population aggregates arose. With these concentrations, intergroup competition and conflict was undoubtedly unavoidable. These local encounters may have been, in part, responsible for the emergence of a warrior cult, for items such as slat armor, refinements in archery equipment (sinew-backed bow, bow braces, sinew twister, wrist guard, new arrow types), and long knives or daggers of ivory were found as part of the village midden debris. The emergence of a warrior class may also indicate an increasing contact with more advanced cultures to the south (Chard 1958, 1960, 1962; Collins 1937a, 1937; Okladnikov 1965; Rudenko 1961).

Art styles of engraving illustrate a continuance of late Old Bering Sea and Okvik patterns in what was to become a complex geometric style. Toward the end of the Punuk phase, the elaborate geometric pattern of engraving was reduced to a simple linear design (fig. 9) (Collins 1930, 1937; Collins et al. 1973). Periodization of the Punuk phase is based also on changes in harpoon head morphology. Early types closely resemble late Old

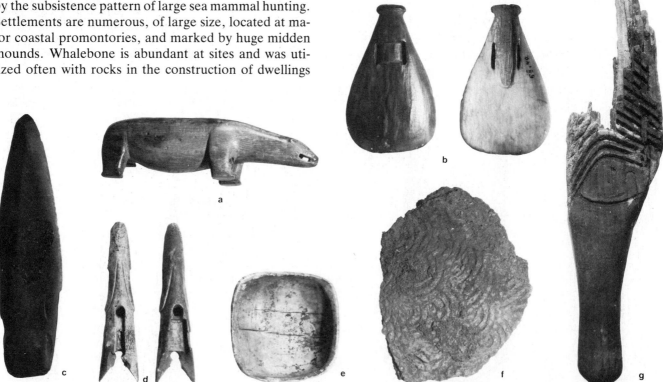

Institut Arkheologii, Leningrad (Ackerman photos).

Fig. 6. Old Bering Sea to Birnirk phase from Second Bay. a, Ivory bear; b, ivory spoon blade (obverse and reverse); c, ground slate blade; d, Old Bering Sea–type open socket harpoon head with double line hole and side blades; e, fat scraper; f, Birnirk-type pottery sherd stamped with curvilinear design; g, wood pottery paddle with herringbone design. Length of a about 23.7 cm; rest same scale.

ACKERMAN

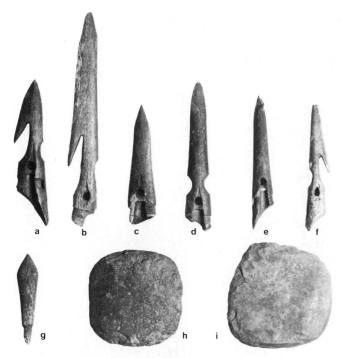

Institut Arkheologii, Leningrad (Ackerman photos).

Fig. 7. Birnirk phase. Cape Baranov: a–b, Open socket harpoon head with side barb and opposite side blade; c, harpoon head with opposing double side blades. Four Columns I.: d–f, open socket harpoon heads (Birnirk type), f with incompleted socket; g, blunt arrowhead; h–i, edge ground adz blades or hide scrapers. Length of a, about 18.0 cm; rest same scale.

Fig. 8. Birnirk-Punuk phase excavation showing use of whalebone and rock in probable dwelling construction site of S'keliyuk, St. Lawrence I. Photograph by Robert Ackerman, 1956.

Bering Sea forms, while later types are more comparable to late Okvik forms. Additionally, temporal shifts in the phase are marked by the evolution of the winged figures (harpoon shaft weights or crest figures surmounting a shaman's staff) from a realistic representation of a bird, human, or butterfly with outstretched wings to simplified "tridents," which are stylization of the earlier forms (fig. 9m) (Collins et al. 1973).

Rudenko (1961:172) has characterized the Punuk phase as being "marked by the further decay of primitive communal society." He has further suggested that the increased technological superiority of the Punuk phase was probably not only a function of advances in the material culture but also a reflection of the development of new social structures, that is, cooperative economic enterprises (hunting, trading, etc.) by local kindreds with an unequal distribution of goods (Rudenko 1961:163–168). Special status groups (shamans, warriors) may also have contributed to societal factionalism. In this phase is an imprint of the modern Eskimo culture that followed.

• THULE PHASE   The diversity of local cultures reflecting the major cultural traditions in the Chukchi and Bering seas continued from the Punuk or Thule phase into the modern era. On Saint Lawrence Island, Collins (1937) found that Eskimo culture underwent a gradual

transition from the Punuk phase to the late prehistoric-protohistoric phase. Thule phase harpoon heads have been recovered from what was a late Punuk context, indicating a contact between the people of the two cultural patterns, but insufficient for the establishment of the Thule phase on the island. In the vicinity of Bering Strait and in Siberia, implements of the Thule phase are found in the upper levels of Birnirk settlements from Bering Strait westward to the Bear Islands in the East Siberian Sea (Ackerman 1961; Bandi 1968, 1969; Beregovaĩa 1954; Chard 1955, 1958a, 1967, 1973; Collins 1930, 1937, 1964; Collins et al. 1973; Dikov 1958, 1966, 1966a, 1971, 1971a, 1972; Mathiassen 1930; Okladnikov 1947, 1970; Okladnikov and Beregovaia 1971; Rudenko 1961). Southward the Thule influences followed the path of the Punuk phase cultural expansion along the south coast of the Chukchi Peninsula to Anadyr´ Gulf and thence south and west to Shelikhov Bay on the north coast of the Sea of Okhotsk (Dikov 1971a; Rudenko 1961; Semenov 1965; Vasil´evskii 1964, 1969, 1969a). The date range for the Thule phase is roughly A.D. 800 or 900 to 1200 or 1500, a temporal ordering that parallels a considerable portion of the Punuk phase (Collins 1940; Giddings 1962; Rainey and Ralph 1959; W.E. Taylor 1963a).

From the pioneering work of Collins (1937) and Ford (1959) in Alaska, it is evident that the Thule phase was derived from some aspect of the Birnirk phase. Initially, the preliminary definition of the Thule phase was based upon the investigations by Mathiassen (1927) in the central Canadian Arctic. The basic economy of the Thule phase was categorized as maritime with an emphasis on   *113*

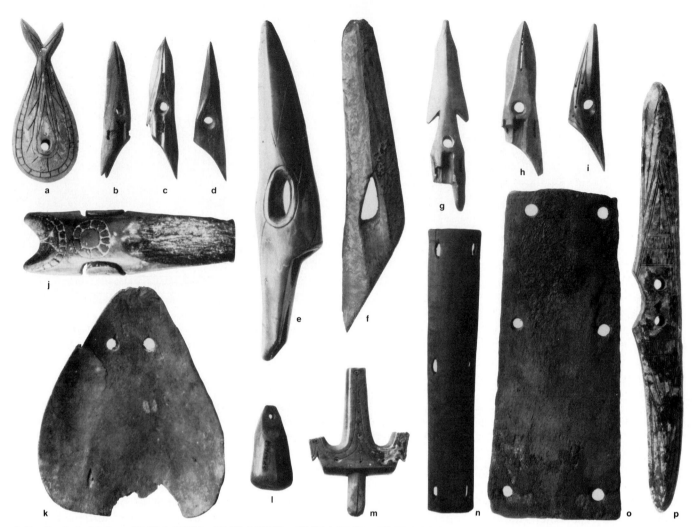

Smithsonian, Dept. of Anthr.: a, 372,036; b, 353,557; c, 371,868; d, 353,108; e, 371,846; f, 356,576; g, 355,252; h, 355, 596; i, 355,060; j, 371,903; k, 353,310; l, 371,255; m, 356,127; n, 355,982; o, 355,281; p, 355,775.

Fig. 9. Punuk culture, St. Lawrence I., Alaska. Miyowagh site: a, Decorated ivory object, an example of early Punuk art; b, bone harpoon head; c–d, ivory harpoon heads; e, ivory whaling harpoon head. Kukulik site; f, ivory whaling harpoon head. Ievoghiyoq site: g–i, ivory harpoon heads. Miyowagh site: j, ivory adz head; k, bone shovel. Ievoghiyoq site: l, ivory bola weight; m, ivory trident; n, piece of bone plate armor. Seklowaghyaget site: o, piece of bone plate armor. Ievoghiyoq site: p, decorated ivory object. Length of a about 9.0 cm; rest same scale.

whale hunting. Later research has shown that the subsistence pattern was variable, one local group adapting to a land-based resource, another to the sea, and a third to a combination of the two (W.E. Taylor 1966).

The Thule phase cultural complex, like that of previous phases, was undoubtedly not the result of a single progenitor. Cultural events propitious to the development of the Thule phase were occurring in North Alaska (Ford 1959), along the central Canadian Arctic coast (W.E. Taylor 1963a), Bering Strait (Collins 1937), and possibly along the Siberian Arctic coast, although most Soviet investigators concede an American origin for the Thule phase cultures (Dikov 1971a:34; Rudenko 1961:172). The specialization in whale hunting may have been a contribution of the Punuk phase as the one

whaling harpoon recovered from Ford's excavation at Point Barrow is a Punuk type rather than anything identifiable as Birnirk (Ford 1959:41, fig. 40:h).

Within the Chukchi and Bering Sea areas, there have been numerous excavations of the Thule phase components, but few of these discoveries have been adequately reported. In western Alaska and eastern Siberia, the Thule phase is carried forward as a cultural tradition into the modern era. The late prehistoric phase is not distinct as a new phase of Eskimo culture but rather reflects a period of increasing contact with other cultural groups.

The Eskimo of the Thule phase practiced sea mammal hunting (whale, walrus, seal), land mammal hunting (reindeer, bear, birds), and fishing; built large houses of stone, bone, turf and hide covering; developed dog driving, and used a raised frame sled—Ford (1959:156) has indicated the possibility of dog driving in the Birnirk phase, Rudenko (1961:152) for late Punuk; continued their use of kayak and umiak; made pottery lamps (with wick flanges) and cooking pots; manufactured hunting and domestic implements almost entirely of ground stone rather than chipped stone; maintained the well-developed tool kit of bone, ivory, antler and wood; played a game of dice with small ivory bird figures; utilized slat armor, the compound reinforced bow, unbarbed arrow heads, labrets, ornaments, toys, and with some modification, winged needlecases and combs.

The harpoon heads for seal and walrus are derived from Birnirk and Punuk forms. Whaling harpoon heads, where found, appear to represent innovations in form that may be unique to the phase. The drilling of lashing holes and rivet holes for the endblade on harpoon heads is another specific Thule phase technological innovation. Dog traction, if it originates in this phase, would be a major breakthrough in transportation and sea ice hunting. As some authors suggest, it may have been stimulated by contact with Siberian groups who drove reindeer (Ford 1959:156).

Late Prehistoric-Protohistoric Phase

The late prehistoric to protohistoric phase in the northern sector of the Soviet Far East was marked by extensive population movements, the expansion of the Chukchi, Koryak, and Yukagir and the retreat of the Eskimo to the farther reaches of the Chukchi Peninsula (Alekseev, Arutiunov, and Sergeev 1972; Menovshchikov 1963; Vdovin 1961). Alekseev has shown that the Chukchi and Eskimo are part of a genetically homogeneous population but that the Eskimo preceded the Chukchi by possibly two millennia in the Bering Sea region (Alekseev 1964; Alekseev, Arutiunov, and Sergeev 1972:241–242). The expansion of the Chukchi to the Anadyr´ lowlands is estimated to have occurred in the fourth to fifth centuries A.D., and there was armed confrontation with the Eskimo in the twelfth to sixteenth centuries A.D. In the sixteenth to seventeenth centuries A.D., the Chukchi adopted a maritime economy, and by the nineteenth century they had taken over a great number of Eskimo settlements, assimilating the local peoples (Alekseev, Arutiunov, and Sergeev 1972:242).

This pattern was repeated all along the Arctic coast from the mouth of the Kolyma to Bering Strait. The Shelagi, for example, who appear to have been an Eskimo group east of the Kolyma River in the vicinity of Cape Shelagskii, were displaced by Chukchi in the seventeenth to nineteenth centuries (Okladnikov and Beregovaĩa 1971:141–143; Dikov 1971:61–72, 1972). These descendant Thule groups were pressed eastward toward East Cape and the Bering Strait, where they settled for the last time. The ritual alignments of bowhead whale skulls and mandibles on Yttygran Island (north of Cape Chaplino, Chukchi Peninsula) may date to this time period (Arutiunov, Krupnik, and Chlenov 1982; Black 1982). In the late twentieth century the Eskimos of Siberia were a remnant group that is being gradually absorbed by the surrounding Chukchi.

Interior Chukchi Peninsula Prehistory

There are no interior cultural phases that have been directly identified with Eskimo populations. The investigation of the interior of Chukotka is still within the pioneering stage of research with most surveys along the lake and river systems. The site inventories are often small and are briefly noted in preliminary reports. Regional overviews are limited to those provided by Dikov and his research group (Dikov 1977, 1979).

The interior culture of hunter-fisher populations appears to have been derived from a late Paleolithic or Mesolithic base that was relatively unchanged throughout the Neolithic and into the later Bronze and Iron ages. This way of life was altered by the introduction of herding practices during the Christian era (Vasilevich 1969:80).

Sites near Lake Tytl´ (I-III) on the upper Lesser Aniui (tributary of the Kolyma River), by Lake Ioni (east of Kresta Bay), and on the lower Anadyr´ River (Krasnaia Kosa 'Red Point'; and Osinovaia Kosa 'Aspen Point') contained conical to prismatic blade cores, leaf-shaped projectile points, burins, wide scrapers, and end scrapers on blades (Dikov 1979:129–132; Kir´iak 1979). These assemblages are comparable to those recovered from the Sumnagin cultural phase in Yakutia (Dikov 1979:132; Kir´iak 1979:143) prompting Dikov to remark that in the fourth to third millennium B.C. there were ancient hunters in Chukotka who did not use pottery and whose method of working stone continued the Mesolithic core-and-blade tradition. Ceramics began to penetrate Chukotka in the third millennium B.C. with net-impressed and cordmarked pottery the earliest surface treatment. Check-stamp pottery has been dated at Chirovoe Lake at 850 B.C. ± 100 (Dikov 1979:133–134). Cordmarked pottery appears in Alaska during the Choris phase, and check-stamp in the following Norton phase (Anderson 1978, 1980; Griffin 1953, 1962, 1969–1970, 3; Griffin and Wilmeth 1964). While the Denbigh Flint complex has been broadly linked to Mesolithic or preceramic Neolithic traditions in Siberia (Dikov 1965a, 1971a; Mochanov 1973; Okladnikov 1960a, 1965), it is with the ceramic traditions, introduced perhaps from Yakutia, that there is a more positive relationship with Eskimo cultural phases.

Origins of Siberian Eskimo Culture

The search for the origins of Eskimo culture in Siberia involves two problems. The first is the development of the pattern of sea-mammal hunting while the second is broader, focusing upon the derivation of an Eskimo cultural precursor from an interior continental type of cultural adaptation. The data from Wrangell Island indicate that a maritime economy did exist in the Siberian area by at least 1410 B.C. ± 155 (Dikov 1979:168). This cultural complex, noted as analogous to the Old Whaling culture of Cape Krusenstern, Alaska, was preceded by the Arctic Small Tool tradition (Denbigh Flint complex), which dated to 2350–1650 B.C. (Anderson 1978).

In Siberia as in Alaska there is a series of interior cultural stages that are relevant to the problem of finding the precursors of Denbigh and the basis of the Eskimo culture. The search for cultural origins has lured archeologists not only into investigations of Neolithic cultural complexes but also into even the more remote complexes of the late Paleolithic (Dikov 1979:71–76; Mochanov 1969:142). Part of the problem involved in such a study is that much of the investigations involving the discovery, description, and definition of late Paleolithic cultural complexes in Eastern Siberia and the Soviet Far East is in its beginning stages.

In northeastern Asia, sites of late Paleolithic to early Mesolithic age have been located along the Kamchatka, Anadyr´, Kolyma, and Indigirka rivers (Chard 1958a, 1973; Dikov 1965a, 1968, 1969–1970, 3, 1971a, 1977, 1979; Mochanov 1970, 1972, 1976, 1977, 1980; Mochanov and Fedoseeva 1975, 1976; Powers 1973). Based upon data from the Aldan River region (north and east of Lake Baikal), Mochanov (1973, 1977, 1980) has hypothesized that eastern Siberia and the Soviet Far East were linked by the spread of people with a continental cultural tradition (Diuktai culture) based upon the hunting of mammoth, wooly rhinoceros, bison, horse, musk-ox, and reindeer. The associated lithic assemblage featured bifacial, leaf-shaped projectile points with a blade and core tradition of late Paleolithic to Mesolithic industries. The type site for this complex is Diuktai Cave on the Aldan River. The eastward spread of the Diuktai culture has been estimated to have occurred between 35,000 and 10,800 years ago (Mochanov 1969c, 1970, 1972, 1973, 1976, 1977, 1980).

Within the Aldan region, the late Paleolithic gave rise to the so-called Holocene Paleolithic, the Sumnagin culture, which is transitional between the late Paleolithic and Siberian Neolithic cultures (8850–4250 B.C.) (Mochanov 1977). For the Soviet Far East, this has been incorporated into the Kamchatka-Chukotka Mesolithic (Chard 1958a; Dikov 1971a, 1977, 1979). Neolithic cultural phases in the Aldan River drainage (Syalakh 4250–3050 B.C., Bel´kachi 3050–1950 B.C., and Ymyiakhtakh 1950–1150 B.C.) (Mochanov and Fedoseeva 1975, 1976)

do not have direct correlates in the Soviet Far East, for by the time of the Sumnagin culture, regionalization of peoples and cultures was taking place. The Neolithic cultural pattern, modified to some degree by the addition of metal tools obtained from metal age societies in the Amur River and Lake Baikal regions, was maintained until the period of historic contact. Dikov considered the northern groups in the Soviet Far East to be "relict" Neolithic societies, that is, continuing an earlier way of life while surrounded by more advanced cultures. It is during this period that the ethnic identity of the Chukchi, Eskimo, Koryak, Yukagir, and Ainu became evident (Dikov 1965a, 1971a, 1979).

Within the northern sector of the Soviet Far East, the chronology and phase differentiation is still not well established. The Neolithic has been broken up into early, middle, and late phases, with the early phase preceramic. The late phase is contemporary with metal-using societies to the west and south (Dikov 1965a, 1971a, 1979).

Two important areas of settlement in Chukotka, the northernmost sector of the Soviet Far East, during the Neolithic stage that may relate to the Eskimo problem are the Amguéma River valley and the lowland drained by the Anadyr´, Main, and Penzhina rivers. Little is known, unfortunately, about the Amguéma River settlements save for an occupation marked by scattered lithic debris that has been interpreted as indicating a Mesolithic to Neolithic type of culture (Chard 1955a, 1960, 1960a, 1961, 1973; Dikov 1958, 1960, 1961, 1965, 1967, 1971a, 1977, 1979; Krader 1952; Okladnikov 1953, 1960; Okladnikov and Nekrasov 1959; Saiapin and Dikov 1958). Dikov (1971a, 1979:134–140) has included these sites in a broad Neolithic cultural stage (Northern Chukotka Lake Neolithic culture) that extended from the lower Lena River area eastward to the Chukchi Peninsula. The Anadyr´-Main-Penzhina river valley lowlands have fortunately been more productive. From a series of sites on the Anadyr´ River and its tributaries, the Belaia and Main, there is evidence for a Neolithic upland hunting and riverine fishing economy (Ust´-Bel´skii culture) that may have contributed in part to the formation of an interior pattern of Eskimo culture (Chard 1955a, 1960b, 1973; Dikov 1958, 1958a, 1959, 1960, 1961a, 1961b, 1961c, 1963, 1965a, 1971a, 1977, 1979: 141–161; Okladnikov 1959a, 1960a; Okladnikov and Nekrasov 1962).

The Ust´-Bel´skii cultural complex is characterized by several sites (Ust´-Belaia, Omrynskii, Chikaevo, Utesiki, Vilka, and Uvesnovaniia) in the Anadyr´ River basin (Dikov 1979). The Ust´-Belaia settlement is the type site for this culture complex. The site consists of a village and cemetery located on the Belaia River at the spring and fall reindeer migration crossing point (Dikov 1979:141). The Ust´-Bel´skii complex has been divided into two components. The early component is from burial mounds 4, 11, 14, and 18 of the cemetery and estimated to date to 1650–50 B.C. The late component, characterized mainly by burial mounds 8 and 9 of the cemetery, has a date estimate of 2,000–1,000 years ago. A single radiocarbon date of 915 ± 95 B.C. has been assigned to the early component with the late component considered to be contemporary with Norton. The late component is distinguished by the presence of copper or bronze burins or incising tools. The two components are felt to belong to a single culture (Dikov 1979:147–148).

Dikov (1979:152–153) notes that the triangular arrowpoints, the carefully diagonally retouched points, the segmented side blades, and unifacial knives of the Ust´-Bel´skii complex are reminiscent of Denbigh forms; but the same tool forms plus rhombic, stemmed, and concave-based arrowpoints, small oval side blades, and side scrapers on flakes are more characteristic of Norton. The stemmed scrapers and side-notched points were seen as analogous to those of the Old Whaling culture. The linear-stamp pottery and an open socketed harpoon head with a line hole and without slots for end or side blades are also reminiscent of Norton (Dikov 1979:144). Griffin (1969–1970,3) has also noted correspondences between the Ust´-Bel´skii ceramics and those of Norton. Dikov adds a cautionary note, stating that although there are correspondences in artifact complexes, one must look at the overall site complex. Burial practices included dressing the head of the corpse with a cap covered with rows of mother-of-pearl beads and adding scatterings of bears' teeth and bone ornaments shaped like ravens' claws to the grave. Burials were in some instances partly or fully cremated (Dikov 1979:153). These burial elements are shared by taiga peoples such as the Even, Yukagir, and Chukchi, but not the Eskimo (Dikov 1979:154). The presence of microblades and cores as well as burins on flakes and bifaces in both components of the Ust´-Belaia site indicates that a cultural complex other than Norton, as it is known in Alaska, was represented (Dikov 1979:fig. 56).

Emergence of Maritime Adaptation

A recognizable maritime culture on Wrangell Island and a well-developed reindeer hunting economy in the Anadyr´ River basin are examples of both the coastal and interior Eskimo pattern by 1000 B.C. It is recognized that a genetically similar population of Chukchi and Eskimo peoples had their roots in the earlier Mesolithic and late Paleolithic cultural traditions. Okladnikov (1965:138) has labeled this aspect of Eskimo prehistory in Siberia the Northern Asiatic Continental phase. A comparable level of adaptation in Alaska would be the Arctic Small Tool tradition (Giddings 1964; Griffin 1960; Irving 1969–1970, 3; Okladnikov 1965).

The emergence of the maritime aspect of the Eskimo culture is then the departure point from this early interior continental orientation. Hypotheses advanced for this change in resource utilization range from ecological to cultural models. Dikov has noted that toward the end of the second millennium B.C. there was a climatic cooling with deforestation of the coastal zones. Interior hunters and fishers who had become familiar with sea mammals in the estuary of the Anadyr´ River would have been encouraged to adapt their technology to capture the resources of the open sea (Dikov 1965a:19, 1979:164). Though not discussed, the climatic model would have had to include a reduction in the productivity of land resources. A somewhat similar hypothesis was advanced by Larsen (1969–1970, 3:339).

An explanation for the origin of the northern maritime adaptation has also involved the use of a prior adaptive strategy developed in the warmer southern waters. Advances in open sea hunting in the Sea of Okhotsk region near the Amur River, Sakhalin Island, and the Japanese Islands were considered as prerequisite for the northern maritime hunting complexes (Okladnikov 1965:137–140). These coastal cultures typified by the Sidemi (shell mound) and Sea of Okhotsk cultures have been shown to be too recent to have served as the cultural models from which the sea-mammal hunting complexes of the Bering Sea were derived.

An origin for the Eskimo sea-mammal hunting complex on the now submerged intercontinental shelf between Chukotka and Alaska called Beringia has been suggested (Ackerman 1979a; Laughlin 1963). The coastal plains of Beringia constituted a dry land zone in what is now the Bering and Chukchi Sea basins. This land platform, stretching approximately 1,200 miles in a north-south axis, had coastal zones and a continental extension through the interior. Extensive river systems from Chukotka and Alaska threaded through this vast plain. Hunting patterns would have involved the use of tundra-, lake-, and river-based animals, basically an extension of the continental late Paleolithic to Mesolithic-Neolithic economy of Asia. Some local adjustments to utilize the resources at the mouths of the Anadyr´, Yukon, and Kuskokwim-Nushagak rivers may have been attempted at a rather early time. With the beginning of the rise in sea level about 16,000 to 14,000 years ago the river mouths would have been flooded, and a shallow sea would have extended over the lower elevations of the coastal plain. Present shorelines were reached by 7,000–6,000 years ago (Hopkins 1972, 1979). By that time a maritime economy may have been established at the Anangula Island site on the southern edge of the Bering Sea platform in what is now the eastern Aleutian Islands (Laughlin and Aigner 1975).

The proposed development of a coastal to maritime economy along the intercontinental shelf in the Bering Sea region is suggested by the ecological changes that

117

would have occurred in the river valleys and coastal plains as a result of the last marine transgression. As the land mass gave way to the encroaching sea, the riverine and shelf resources of plants and animals would have been replaced by those of the marine biome. Hunters and fishers, familiar with marine products from their earlier utilization of estuarine resources, would have been forced to shift from a partial to almost total reliance on a marine economy if they were to remain on the diminishing coastal shelf. For those who ultimately retreated to island areas this would have been their only recourse.

The intercontinental-shelf model for the development of a maritime economy provides a viable alternative to the hypothesized Sea of Okhotsk origin of sea-mammal hunting. It would additionally provide a greater time-depth for a maritime adaptation, which is then seen as developing as the sea encroached rather than after the flooding of the intercontinental shelf. The hypothesized development of a marine-oriented economy during the final stage of the marine transgression may explain the absence of the cultural precursors of Denbigh. Such sites would now be located well out to sea.

Summary

On a regional level, the study of the prehistoric cultures of northeastern Asia and Alaska reveals that this northern realm, often referred to as Beringia, was once a very large, continuous culture area. Late Paleolithic to Neolithic cultures were distributed over the region with a similar economic focus. By Neolithic times, however, local cultural patterns were discernible but were not significantly different as departures from the general adaptive pattern of resource exploitation. This continuity persisted in spite of the separation of Chukotka and Alaska by the sea level rise at the end of the Pleistocene. The inevitable forces of culture change were at work in Asia. To the south in China and Mongolia, pastoral and agricultural states were on the rise. Shock waves from that development were felt from the Ordos region to the Amur River, and to a lesser extent in Siberia beyond. The rise of the Old Bering Sea culture with its elaborate art style and burial complex is indicative of a cultural transfer of Amur River ceremonialism to the peoples of the Bering and Chukchi seas. In Alaska the Point Hope Ipiutak culture was the local equivalent. Later in Punuk and Thule times a more prosaic local development displaced the ceremonial art style of earlier centuries, giving the coastal regions once more a rather uniform cultural continuity. Within the interior of Chukotka, Tungusic-speaking peoples expanding northward from the Amur River region brought with them concepts of animal domestication that they applied to the wild reindeer. The relict Neolithic cultures soon fell under the influence of this new economy, moving as herdsmen toward the coasts in search of new pastures, eventually displacing or incorporating local enclaves of Eskimo peoples. These new economic patterns were not exported across the Bering Strait to Alaska. There, the Eskimo of the coast and interior continued their old way of life until interrupted by the appearance of European sailing ships off their shores.

Patterns of cultural adaptations to the land and its resources persist among the native peoples of Beringia. Their cultures, though complicated by the dictates of two different nation-states, can only be appreciated through an examination of their prehistoric past.

Prehistory of the Aleutian Region

ALLEN P. McCARTNEY

Prehistoric inhabitants of the Aleutian archipelago occupied a unique setting unlike that of other Arctic or Subarctic Eskimoid populations. Stretching for 1,050 miles into the northern Pacific, this chain of approximately 100 islands of one-half mile or greater size is isolated by the Pacific Ocean and Bering Sea. Natives entered the archipelago by way of the attenuated Alaska Peninsula, spreading to the chain's western end, and reaching a contact-period population of 12,000–15,000 (Lantis 1970). Despite the rugged island terrain and infamous weather, large human groups were capable of being sustained there in the past because of varied and productive coastal habitats (McCartney 1975; Yesner 1980).

The islands become smaller and farther apart from east to west. The dozen large and many smaller islands are clustered into five major groups beyond the tip of the Alaska Peninsula: the Fox Islands, the Islands of the Four Mountains, the Andreanof Islands (including the Delarof group), the Rat Islands, and the Near Islands (fig. 1). The following summaries of archeological research are organized according to these five groups plus the southwestern half of the Alaska Peninsula (west of 159° west longitude), because of their clear geographic separation from one another. This six-fold division presumes no cultural significance in the past, as there is little archeological evidence for where major or minor cultural divisions occurred. For example, it is not known whether the native cultural and linguistic regions of the early Russian period had much prehistoric time-depth (see Veniaminov 1840; Bergsland 1959; Black 1980).

The Aleut province is neatly bounded by water except at the Alaska Peninsula. The cultural demarcation between Aleuts and Peninsular Eskimos is not clearly known (Oswalt 1967). At the time of Russian contact, Aleuts lived in the archipelago proper and possibly in the Shumagin Islands and on the southwestern end of the Alaska Peninsula. Anthropologists have no direct evidence that Aleuts inhabited much of the peninsula in 1741 (Dumond 1974; Dumond, Conton, and Shields 1975). Early Russian explorers (e.g., Krenitsyn in Glushankov 1973) reported natives along the peninsula shores, but their cultural and linguistic affiliations were often not ascertained. By the second quarter of the nineteenth century, Lütke (1835–1836) noted three Aleut villages on the southern coast (Morzhovoi, Belkofski, and Pavlofski) and Veniaminov (in Hrdlička 1945:38, 41) cited their population totals. Ivan Petroff's Aleut–mainland Eskimo dividing line, from Port Heiden on the north to Pavlof Bay on the south at approximately 159° west longitude (U.S. Census Office 1884), suggests the easternmost occupation of mid-nineteenth-century Aleuts. But this boundary may be the result of the Russian-American Company's having moved Aleuts eastward from the island chain in order to exploit rich sea mammal hunting grounds. Russian colonists deliberately dispersed Aleut hunting groups into areas never previously occupied by those natives. Between 1741 and 1850, for instance, Aleuts were relocated in the Commander (Komandorskiye), Kuril (Kuril´skie), and Pribilof islands, possibly on Kamchatka Peninsula, and in southeastern Alaska and California (see Stejneger 1895; Jochelson 1925; Baba 1943; Hrdlička 1945; Bank 1962; McCartney 1969). Further confusing any ethnohistoric reconstruction of a precontact Aleut boundary is the fact that Russian period references often fail to discriminate among Aleuts, Peninsular Eskimos, and Koniags.

Although the possibility of a sharp boundary is supported by an Aleut-Eskimo linguistic separation somewhere on the Alaska Peninsula, archeological studies suggest that a cultural continuum existed during the late prehistoric period throughout the archipelago and the peninsula (McCartney 1974a; Dumond 1974). That continuum may have had great time-depth.

Models of Prehistory

A century of archeological investigation into past Aleutian culture reflects changing prehistoric models that parallel developments in anthropological thought. Outlined here are some theories of prehistoric change.

The first explicit prehistoric model set forth for the New World Arctic or Subarctic was Dall's (1877) evolutionary scheme of three periods or stages. The first, or Littoral Period (lowest strata), was characterized by a collecting subsistence (no fire, lamps, houses, clothing, ornaments, weapons, fishing or hunting equipment) and small communities. Next, the Fishing Period (middle strata) showed evidence of a fishing and collecting subsistence (chipped and ground stone imple-

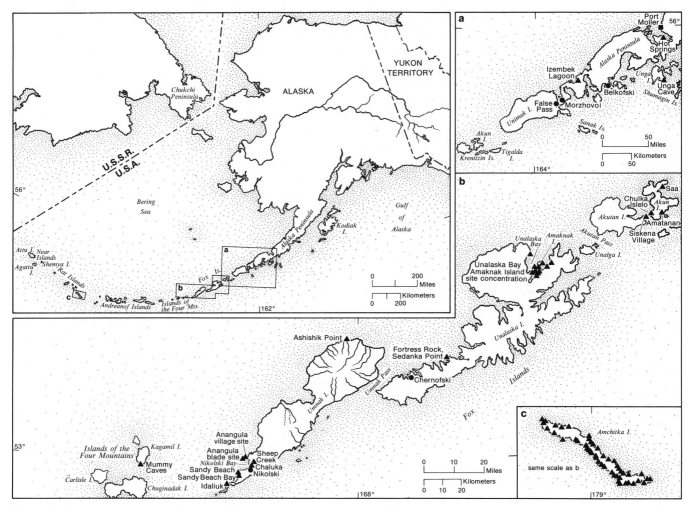

Fig. 1. Archeological site concentrations in the Aleutian region: a, Alaska Peninsula; b, Fox Islands; c, Amchitka Island (more than 70 sites).

ments, bone and ivory implements, skin boats, temporary huts, burials in wooden sarcophagi) and large communities. Finally, traits of the Hunting Period (upper strata) consisted of hunting, fishing, and collecting subsistence (harpoons, lamps, bow drills, labrets, anthropomorphic carvings), large whalebone houses with roof entries, and mummification.

Dall pointed out that despite these stage divisions, the midden succession indicated basic cultural continuity over time. This sequential, evolutionary scheme clearly derived from contemporary nineteenth-century stage or age models used for European prehistory and world ethnology. Dall claimed that multiple migrations from the east peopled the chain, with early occupants appearing culturally more similar to Eskimos than did historic Aleuts.

Another three-stage model (Quimby 1945, 1948), based on artistic decoration of bone projectile heads and other incised objects, is flawed by a mixed artifact sample and by using decoration that is not independent of artifact types (McCartney 1967).

Jochelson (1925) refuted the three-stage scheme of Dall and replaced it with one stressing greater cultural uniformity. The earliest Aleuts had a "relatively high primitive culture," and cultural changes were slight over their long occupation. In part, these gradual changes were due to the Aleuts adapting to their unique archipelago environment. Continuity was supported by the similarity between ancient midden site implements and those of the early historic period. Jochelson found no confirmation for isolated development of the Aleut but rather theorized that the archipelago was populated by migrants from the mainland. No temporal subdivisions based on human skeletal or cultural remains were postulated for the Aleutian area.

Hrdlička (1945) provided temporal and skeletal subdivisions for Jochelson's uniformity model. He suggested that the chain was occupied by two major populations with their attendant cultural peculiarities. Paralleling his earlier Kodiak sequence of pre-Koniag and Koniag (Hrdlička 1944), longheaded pre-Aleuts made up the early population and were followed by later Aleuts who had broad heads. Neither population was regarded as biologically close to mainland Eskimos. Whereas the pre-Aleuts entered the chain in "the earlier part of the Christian era," the Aleuts appeared within the last "few hundred years" and gradually spread westward (Hrdlička 1945:586). While hypothesizing skeletal differences, Hrdlička noted that there existed no clear cultural separation between these prehistoric natives. Each group possessed "the same classes of objects, though differing in form and other details" between them (Hrdlička 1945:474). However, cultural separation between the two populations was unlikely to be detected since Hrdlička divided skeletons from midden sites on the basis of morphology rather than stratigraphy (Laughlin and Marsh 1951).

A slightly altered version of this two-stage model was proposed after World War II. The term pre-Aleut became Paleo-Aleut and Aleut became Neo-Aleut (Laughlin and Marsh 1951; Laughlin 1952, 1963a). This model emphasizes that Aleuts are basically Eskimoid in physical type, language, and culture. Further, Neo-Aleuts only replaced Paleo-Aleuts in the eastern islands, while longheaded natives derived from earlier Paleo-Aleuts survived until Russian contact in the western islands. Whereas there is no exact fit among race, language, and culture, strong artifactual continuity is found throughout the midden sites, and there is no meaningful cultural break corresponding to Paleo- and Neo-Aleut populations.

A significant addition to the Aleutian cultural sequence was added with the excavation of the Anangula core and blade site (Laughlin 1951a, 1963; Laughlin and Marsh 1954; Black and Laughlin 1964; McCartney and Turner 1966a; Aigner 1974). It has been argued that technologic continuity exists between this 8,000-year-old site and later ones, in much the same way that midden sites of the past 4,500 years exhibit an unbroken sequence up to the Russian period. This technologic continuity is based on the occurrence of Anangula's unifacially flaked stone tools that are similar to those from the lower strata of Chaluka midden nearby. Other artifacts from 1960s Anangula excavations, such as stone vessels, pumice abraders, and ocher grinders, are seen as further evidence of continuity (Laughlin 1967).

Since the 1970s, Aleutian prehistory has increasingly been viewed within ecological and systemic frameworks (McCartney 1975, 1977; Laughlin and Aigner 1975; Yesner 1980; Yesner and Aigner 1976). Food and raw material procurement, predator-prey impacts, and biomass estimates have become the focus for archeological research. Pan-Aleutian animal censuses conducted by the U.S. Fish and Wildlife Service (for example, Sekora 1973) and in-depth ecological studies of marine and terrestrial animals and plants (for example, Merritt and Fuller 1977; Love 1976) have provided a quantitative background for the interpretation of archeological materials.

Overview

Aleutian culture history can be summarized as follows. The midden period (2000 B.C.-historic period) is marked by cultural continuity but a racial dichotomy (Turner

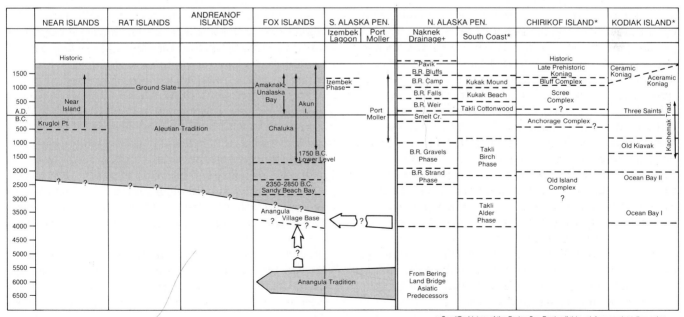

+ See "Prehistory of the Bering Sea Region," this vol. for complete discussion.
* See "Prehistory of the Pacific Eskimo Region," this vol. for complete discussion.
B.R. = Brooks River

Fig. 2. Prehistoric cultures of the Aleutian Islands and adjacent areas.

1974). In spite of Hrdlička's (1945) questionable field procedures used in dividing early longheaded peoples from later broadheaded ones, physical anthropologists still support this two-population model. In fact, Hrdlička's contention that Aleuts were late prehistoric or early historic people is supported by study of midden stratigraphy during the 1960s and 1970s (Turner, Aigner, and Richards 1974).

The 4,000 years of Aleutian midden occupation are marked by strong cultural ties over time and space. Whereas little attention has been given to interisland artifact comparisons, almost all Aleutian investigators have been impressed with the lack of marked artifact changes in midden stratigraphy (Dall 1877; Jochelson 1925; Laughlin and Marsh 1951; Laughlin 1963, 1967; Bank 1953a; McCartney 1967; Aigner 1976a). But assemblage comparisons between islands and island groups also reveal strong horizontal relationships. Reasons for cultural homogeneity within the archipelago include a common insular environment, common marine-oriented procurement systems used to acquire the same species found throughout island groups if not the entire chain, movement of styles through exchange and the movement of people for social, economic, political, and warfare purposes, and geographic isolation of the chain from external cultural influences except along the eastern extremity.

This unbroken cultural sequence may, in part, reflect the nature of the midden matrix in which artifacts are found. Mixed, even reversed, stratigraphy results from natives living on these refuse mounds for long periods and digging graves, house foundations, and other excavations into the ever-rising surfaces. Only major vertical divisions are possible to detect across a midden site, and three or four meters of accumulation may correspond to several thousands of years. Very few single-component, short-term features are known, such as late prehistoric and historic sarcophagi, which permit a precise statement about contemporaneous cultural materials.

Aleutian artifacts, while basically Eskimoid, are often of particular styles found only in southwestern Alaska and sometimes only in the archipelago proper. Artifact functions and their use contexts cannot always be identified, but the major deficiency is the lack of even cursory typological studies prerequisite to establishing major time-space divisions for the chain. Within the middens, slow changes in artifact styles occurred, but few horizon markers are known save the introduction of ground slate grinding during the first millennium A.D. or the spread of artifact styles such as long, unilaterally barbed bone points and long, rodlike socket pieces during the second millennium A.D.

No archeological phases have been defined for the area considered here, except for the Izembek phase at the tip of the Alaska Peninsula (McCartney 1974a). This phase has been compared to a sequence of archeological phases at the base of the peninsula (Dumond 1971a).

Anangula: Earliest Evidence of Occupation

Ananiuliak or Anangula is a small island at the northern edge of Nikolski Bay, Umnak Island (Laughlin and Marsh 1954; Turner 1963; McCartney and Turner 1966a). A large site found there in 1938 reveals a unique core and blade assemblage with cultural affinities to a few early Alaska mainland sites (fig. 2). A thin artifact stratum is sealed beneath multiple ash layers from regional vulcanism; only a few burned bone fragments and no typical midden debris of shells and urchin spines have been found. The deeply buried and protected cultural stratum and the large size (approximately 90 by 250 meters) make the site one of the most important places to study early Alaskans.

The Anangula core and blade assemblage is the oldest known evidence of human occupation in the Aleutian chain. About three dozen radiocarbon dates cluster around 6000 B.C. for the thin cultural layer, making this site the most abundantly dated Aleutian site (Laughlin 1974–1975, 1975; R.F. Black 1976; Aigner 1976). The cultural layer measures only about 20 centimeters thick and suggests a relatively short occupation span of perhaps a century or less.

Excavations at the Anangula site exposed part of a depression in the original living surface that McCartney and Turner (1966a) called an "occupation pit" rather than a house because the possible feature had not been fully excavated. Six depressions were discovered during 1970 amid scattered lithic artifacts and debris, and these have been referred to as "houses" (Laughlin 1974–1975; Aigner 1974). Structural particulars have not been published for comparison, and therefore these depressions cannot be evaluated in relation to stone-walled houses dating from 2000 B.C. to the historic period (Turner, Aigner, and Richards 1974; Aigner 1978).

The Anangula assemblage is dominated by small to large blades struck from polyhedral cores of wedge and other shapes, and flakes and platform tablets from this manufacturing technique. Transverse burins/scrapers and spalls and obsidian end and side scrapers are also typically found (fig. 3). Although some artifact classes such as stone vessels, grinding slabs, rubbing stones, hammerstones, and scoria abraders are similar to those from later Aleut midden sites, no other site less than 4,500 years old is known to share in the core and blade technology, the burinated scrapers, and the exclusive use of unifacial retouch flaking of blades and flakes (McCartney and Turner 1966; Laughlin and Aigner 1966; Aigner 1970). No bifacially flaked projectile points or knives have been found among thousands of artifacts retrieved. Also, the general artifact classes mentioned

U. of Conn., Dept. of Anthr., Storrs: uncatalogued.

Fig. 3. Stone artifacts, Anangula (Fox Islands), Alaska, about 6,000 B.C.: a–d, small to large blades showing secondary edge retouching; e–f, polyhedral cores with blade scars seen at the right edges; g, double-ended transverse burin, ventral view; h, single-ended transverse burin made from a blade, ventral view; i, single-ended transverse burin made from a blade, showing a typical burin spall above, ventral view; j–k, unifacially flaked end and side scrapers of obsidian; l, scoria abrader; m, carved bowl fragments that fit together. Length of a, 11.7 cm; rest same scale.

above are common to most southwestern Alaska sites and do not distinguish Aleutian from non-Aleutian sites. These artifact classes are highly related to the availability of particular raw materials such as pumice for abraders, welded tuff for bowls, and obsidian for end scrapers.

Whether Anangula and nearby Umnak were islands when first occupied, requiring the presence of watercraft, or were attached to the other eastern islands to form an expanded Alaska Peninsula depends on the interpretation given to sea level fluctuations. A previous interpretation held that the ancient sea level was approximately 8–20 meters below that of the mid-twentieth century. The Fox Islands would have consisted of fewer but longer islands with only narrow passes between them, if not a solid peninusla (Black and Laughlin 1964; R.F. Black 1966; McCartney and Turner 1966a). Natives could have reached Anangula from the north-

east by following the then-exposed Beringian coast ultimately from the Kamchatka–Sea of Okhostk (Okhotskoe More) region (Chard 1963; Laughlin 1967). Deglaciation of this region occurred at about 11,000–9,000 B.C. (R.F. Black 1976). Mainland terrestrial mammals such as caribou could also have expanded along this peninsula or the closely spaced islands to form a distribution similar to that of the historic period on the Alaska Peninsula and Unimak (McCartney and Turner 1966a).

However, R.F. Black (1974, 1976) has reinterpreted the sea level of 8,000 years ago as having been essentially what it is in the mid-twentieth century A.D. Hence, early natives would require boats to reach Anangula. The location on the Bering Sea coast, of course, suggests that Anangula people were marine-oriented, but there is no direct evidence that they possessed boats or the degree of maritime expertise expressed by later Aleuts. Unlike the previous interpretation, which limited terrestrially oriented early man to Anangula and the peninsula formed to the east, the possibility of boat travel opens up all parts of the archipelago to these early colonists. However, no other Anangula-type site has been found anywhere in the chain.

The Anangula site was likely abandoned as a result of being buried by a thick blanket of volcanic ash (Black and Laughlin 1964; McCartney and Turner 1966a).

Dual Tradition Model

A century of archeological scholarship has shown the basic relatedness of Aleut midden site cultures, but the relationship of Anangula to the midden cultures is far from resolved. There are three broad explanations that might apply to the connection between early and late period sites. First, Anangula peoples were the first occupants of the chain and their culture developed in isolation into that of recent Aleuts, thus yielding an 8,000-year cultural, racial, and linguistic continuum. Second, recent Aleut culture is a blend of later Eskimoid influences from the Alaska Peninsula and the older Anangula substratum; thus both external and in situ influences joined together. Or, third, Anangula peoples died out after their initial occupation of the chain; recent Aleuts derive from a second or later major occupation of the chain beginning at least 4,500 years ago.

The first and second alternatives conform closely to the previously stated model of cultural continuity. The third alternative, that of minimal congruence between Anangula and the later midden cultures, has been referred to (Laughlin 1951a; Turner 1963; Dumond 1971; McCartney 1971, 1974) but has not been fully explained. In the briefest form, this dual tradition model states that the basic stone technology differs from Anangula to later industries and that different technologies reflect distinctive cultural traditions not closely related. Race and language of these culture bearers may have been equally unrelated, especially because of the apparent 3,500-year gap separating the two traditions. The lack of bone implements or human skeletal remains and all but a few scraps of charred faunal elements from Anangula preclude direct comparisons of these materials with more recent sites.

The two distinguishable traditions are the Anangula tradition and the Aleutian tradition. The Anangula tradition, dated about 6000 B.C., is known only from the Anangula site in the Fox Islands. It is a core and blade tradition consisting of small to large prismatic cores, blades, core rejuvenation tablets (struck horizontally rather than vertically as blades), preparatory flakes, and blade-derived tools such as transverse burins, edge-retouched knives, steep end scrapers, and side scrapers. Unifacial edge retouch predominates; no bifacially flaked projectile points are known. No bone industry has been found. Influence of core and blade technology out of northeastern Asia is strong.

In contrast, the Aleutian tradition dates to about 2500 B.C.–A.D. 1800 and is known from throughout the archipelago. This is an irregular core and flake tradition that includes bifacially trimmed implements made from flakes such as projectile points, tanged and untanged knives and scrapers, and drills. Chipped and ground adz and ulu blades are found, as is an elaborate bone industry. Alaska mainland Eskimo influences are strong.

It is the general lack of core and blade evidence in the older midden sites such as Chaluka that supports a model of cultural discontinuity. The tool manufacturing complex of prismatic cores, unretouched blades, transverse burins, burin spalls, and core tablets have never been found to date as recently as 2500 B.C. Excavations during 1974 at a midden site located almost adjacent to the older Anangula core and blade site (referred to as the Anangula village site) produced an assemblage that may be a mixture of the two sites' artifacts. Only a brief description of this village site collection has been published (Laughlin 1975, 1980). Included in this collection are two bifacially flaked projectile points with contracting bases that appear typologically to date after the core and blade period. These points are very similar to projectile points from Port Moller or to those of the Takli Alder and Birch phases of the Shelikof Strait area (G.H. Clark 1977). This collection's position in Aleutian culture history awaits a detailed analysis.

Whereas unifacial versus bifacial tool percentages have been compared between these traditions (Laughlin and Marsh 1954, 1956; Denniston 1966; Aigner 1970), confusion of stone technologies has often resulted. Anangula *and* some midden tools (knives and scrapers) are unifacially flaked. Yet the former are made from blades of polyhedral cores whereas the latter are extensively retouched irregular flakes from non-polyhedral cores. By edge retouch, nonparallel-sided flakes may be shaped into parallel-sided scrapers and knives. Therefore, while the resulting Aleutian tradition implements are sometimes similar in shape to those from the Anangula tradition, they represent a different series of manufacturing steps. Lack of bifacially flaked tools at Anangula and lack of core and blade derived tools at midden period sites suggest a significant cultural separation.

Whenever people occupied the Aleutians, a full maritime subsistence adaptation was required. The same general environmental limitations existed for both Anangula and later natives (R.F. Black 1974, 1976). Both early and late natives likely utilized comparable implement classes in similar procurement and preparation systems, but the styles or types were distinctive if the evidence of stone tool technology and resulting tools are an adequate measure.

Although the Anangula tradition appears to have been brief when compared with the Aleutian tradition, it is actually the isolated remnant of a much older, Asiatic tradition with few expressions in the New World Arctic and Subarctic (McCartney and Turner 1966; Laughlin 1967, 1975). This tradition derived from the great Upper Paleolithic traditions of late Pleistocene age that swept into Siberia about 15,000–20,000 years ago (Müller-Beck 1967; Chard 1974). While the parental tradition in the Old World is called the Siberian Paleolithic, some Alaska core and blade finds are grouped as the Paleo-Arctic tradition (Anderson 1970a; cf. Dumond 1977a). However, there is no uniform application of this latter term by Alaska archeologists, so the more specific label Anangula tradition is preferred for the Aleutian Island core and blade culture. Just as the Aleutian tradition is distinctive among later Alaska culture groupings, so too the Anangula tradition appears, on current evidence, to be distinctive among early core and blade finds.

When the Anangula assemblage is compared with other Alaska core and blade site assemblages of 8500–5000 B.C., broad similarities may be noted as well as peculiarities (see Anderson 1970a; Dixon 1975; Henn 1978; Dumond 1980). The most important differences between Anangula and other assemblages (for example Akmak, Gallagher Flint Station, Ugashik Narrows, and Koggiung) center on the absence of bifaces at Anangula, the absence of transverse burins at some other sites, and the presence at Anangula of a wider size range of blades produced from polyhedral cores.

It is true that Anangula peoples are the oldest known occupants in the archipelago and hence are "Paleo-Aleuts" or perhaps even "pre-Aleuts." However, terms such as pre-Aleut, Paleo-Aleut, Aleut, and Neo-Aleut have established connotations. Therefore, Anangula and Aleutian are better rubrics to differentiate these major traditions.

Areal Summaries

Alaska Peninsula

The southwestern half of the Alaska Peninsula, an attenuation of the mainland, is distinctive in having a mixture of continental terrestrial fauna and rich marine fauna. Caribou, brown bear, porcupine, wolf, wolverine, and other small mammals extend to the end of the peninsula and, in some cases, onto Unimak Island (O.J. Murie 1959). Walruses frequent the winter drift ice along the peninsular shore, and salmon streams are more numerous than in the adjacent islands. This half of the Alaska Peninsula shows a vegetational gradient in which alder, willow, and dwarf birch thickets decrease in size and frequency from northeast to southwest, expressing the transition from continental to marine climate.

The only sites excavated in this area are at Port Moller and Izembek Lagoon, the only two embayments on this low Bering Sea coast (fig. 1). No archeological testing has occurred on the mountainous Pacific shore west of Chignik.

• PORT MOLLER The Hot Springs village site covers a headland that faces a shallow bay some 20 miles inland from the Bering Sea coast (Weyer 1930; Oka, Sugihara, and Watanabe 1961; Workman 1966). One of the largest southwestern Alaska sites, it has over 200 possible dwelling depressions pockmarked over the surface. These oval, semisubterranean dwellings have internal hearths and clay-lined and stone-lined storage pits. Most lack entrance passages, and they may have had whalebone or wooden supports for a roof (Okada and Okada 1974; Okada et al. 1976).

A suite of radiocarbon dates suggests that the site was occupied over three periods: 1500–1000 B.C., A.D. 500–600, and A.D. 1300–1500 (Okada 1980). Faunal remains from the thick midden strata represent over 50 species of sea and land mammals, fish, birds, and invertebrates. Caribou and fox bones are the most common evidence of land mammals found throughout the site (Kotani 1980). The twentieth-century caribou range extends westward only to Unimak Island, the first Aleutian Island. Large numbers of notched and grooved sinkers, fishhooks, and leister barbs suggest that summer fishing was an important subsistence activity.

A rich bone and stone industry reflects an intermediate cultural position between the Aleutians on the west and the mainland on the east (figs. 4–5) (Workman 1966; McCartney 1969; Dumond, Conton, and Shields 1975). Harpoon heads, arrowheads, adz heads and blades, labrets, projectile points, knives, and scrapers are some of the important artifact classes. Thick gravel-tempered pottery is known at Izembek Lagoon, just to the west of Port Moller, at about A.D. 1000 (Yarborough 1974), and similar pottery is contemporaneously known at the base of the Alaska Peninsula in the Brooks River Camp and Kukak Mound phases

at about A.D. 1000–1400 (Dumond 1971a). Why no pottery has yet been discovered at the Hot Springs site remains an enigma.

Some of the Port Moller flaked stone knives and projectile points (fig. 4) are similar to those of the Takli Birch phase on Shelikof Strait, near Kodiak Island (G.H. Clark 1977). The Takli Birch phase dates to 2100–800 B.C. and is therefore contemporaneous with the early Hot Springs site.

Red ocher is associated with half of the burials found at the site, and human remains have been identified as expressing either Aleut (Laughlin 1966a) or Eskimo physical characteristics (Okada and Yamaguchi 1975).

• IZEMBEK LAGOON Several prehistoric village sites, similar to the Hot Springs site, dot the shores of this coastal indentation near the peninsula tip. Over 100 dwelling depressions are known that appear to have served as spots for light shelters or tents. These villages were probably occupied during the summer when salmon ran and during the autumn when large flocks of migratory waterfowl congregated on this shallow lagoon. The only known permanent house structure, constructed of whalebones and boulders, is located on a low knoll at the inner lagoon shore (McCartney 1974a). It measures eight by nine meters and has a collapsed superstructure of at least 32 large whale mandibles. A low wall of boulders outlines the structure; no entrance was located. A large hearth and small stone-encircled storage pits were found dug into the house floor.

Anchorage Histl. and Fine Arts Mus., Alaska: uncatalogued.

Fig. 4. Stone artifacts, Port Moller, Alaska Peninsula, 1000 B.C.–early first millennium A.D.?: a–d, flaked projectile points; e–g, flaked knife blades with tangs; h, flaked knife or scraper blade with tang; i, flaked knife blade lacking a tang; j, pecked stone weight with lashing grooves; k, flaked knife blade; l, knife blade made from a large flake; m, beach cobble weight with double-drilled line hole. Length of a, 9.1 cm; rest same scale.

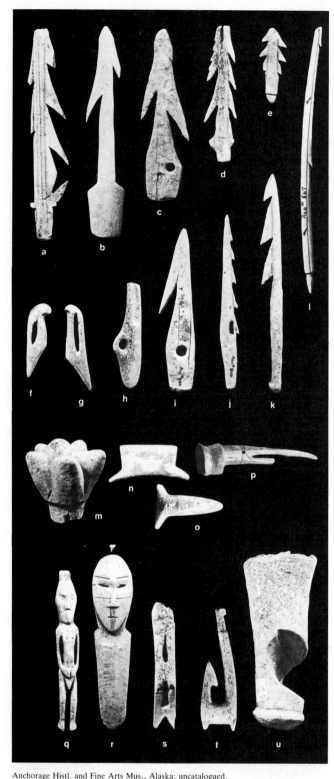

Fig. 5. Bone artifacts, Port Moller, Alaska Peninsula, 1000 B.C.–
early first millennium A.D.?: a–e, bilaterally barbed harpoon
points; f–g, fish spear barbs; h–k, unilaterally barbed harpoon
points (h is missing the barbed tip); l, unilaterally barbed
arrowpoint (warped); m, star-shaped dart bunt; n–p, ivory labrets;
q, carved human figurine; r, carved human head and attached
thorax, with cheek and chin lines indicating tattooing; s, toggle
harpoon head; t, simple fishhook; u, side-notched adz head.
Length of a 12.8 cm; rest same scale.

Dates from the whalebone house and two nearby sites
cluster at about A.D. 1000. Because the sites found thus
far along Izembek Lagoon have similar surface features,
they probably all date to the early second millennium
A.D. However, just as the Hot Springs site reflects several periods of occupation, the Izembek sites may be
shown to have older lower strata as well.

Bone artifacts are infrequent and poorly preserved
due to lack of thick, buffering midden layers. The poor
bone implement sample precludes meaningful comparisons with either Aleutian or Port Moller and other
Alaska Peninsula bone assemblages. Unlike the Hot
Springs site, the Izembek Lagoon sites sampled thus far
reveal gravel-tempered pottery and abundant ground
slate projectile points and knives (fig. 6). Pottery and
ground slate spread, perhaps separately, down the
peninsula from the Naknek-Kodiak region just before

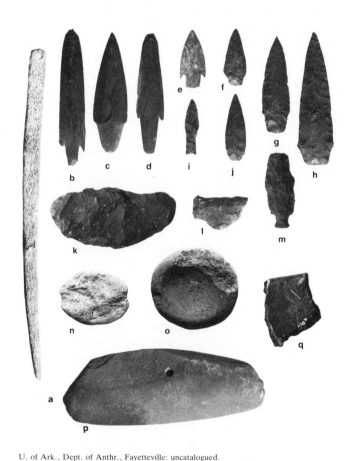

Fig. 6. Artifacts from Izembek Lagoon, Alaska Peninsula, about
A.D. 1050: a, large bone "needle" with drilled eye; b, ground slate
projectile point with diamond-shaped cross-section; c–d, ground
slate projectile points with lenticular cross-sections; e, ground
stone projectile point; f–h, flaked projectile points; i, flaked
"fishtail" projectile point; j, flaked projectile point lacking a
shouldered tang; k, large flaked knife blade; l, flaked asymmetrical
knife blade with tang; m, flaked knife blade with tang; n, beach
pebble weight with notches for lashing; o, small carved stone lamp;
p, ground slate ulu blade with double-drilled lashing hole; q,
gravel-tempered pottery rim sherd. Length of a, 26.2 cm; rest same
scale.

McCARTNEY

A.D. 1000 (see Dumond 1971a). Conversely, most of the flaked stone industry shows strong similarity to Aleutian assemblages. Notched stone sinkers are very numerous at both Izembek Lagoon and Port Moller, and they suggest the primacy of seasonal fishing at both locales. Other major artifact classes include flaked projectile points, knives, and scrapers, ground adz blades and slate ulu blades, scoria abraders, and small to large stone lamps. Pottery has not been located in the Aleutian chain, and the Izembek Lagoon pottery stands as the westernmost on the Alaska Peninsula (McCartney 1970; Yarborough 1974).

The intermingling of western and eastern influences in the Izembek phase suggests its intermediate position between dominant Aleutian and mainland cultural spheres. No sharp cultural division appears between the Aleut and the Alaska Peninsula Eskimo in the late prehistoric period, based on limited materials for study. This model of cultural intergradation parallels Laughlin's (1951:113, 1952:73, 1958:525) view of racial intergradation in the same region where "what data do exist indicate that no line can be drawn separating Aleuts from western Eskimos."

• SHUMAGIN ISLANDS Investigations into the prehistory of this island group lying south of the Alaska Peninsula are few. Pinart (1875), Lot-Falck (1957), and Dall (1875, 1880:28–31) collected and described late prehistoric or early historic period mummies and wooden artifacts from a site on Delarof Harbor, Unga Island. These burials were assumed to have been of Aleut origin but this cultural association remains conjectural. Besides providing the first archeological evidence of mummification and cave or rockshelter burials referred to in Russian period literature (for example, Veniaminov 1840), the painted masks (fig. 7) and other artifacts of wood show a facet of material culture not preserved in middens. Only in caves and rockshelters such as those on Unga or Kagamil are wooden artifacts, baskets (fig. 8), and mats well preserved. The excellent state of preservation is clear evidence of their late prehistoric or early Russian period age.

No other organized excavations have occurred in the entire Shumagin group. A boat survey around most of the islands in 1973 located a few sites (McCartney 1974b). No large middens comparable in size to those commonly found in the Aleutian archipelago were found. A detailed surveying and site testing program will be required to establish the cultural sequence in this island group and its relationship to those of Kodiak, the Alaska Peninsula, and the eastern Aleutians.

Fox Islands

The easternmost group of islands contains three of the largest islands in the chain, Unimak, Unalaska, and

Smithsonian, Dept. of Anthr.: 7,604.
Fig. 7. Wooden mask with light traces of coloring remaining; one ear is missing as are the teeth, which were single pegs. Height about 32.0 cm. Collected from a cave at Delarof Harbor, Unga I., Alaska, 1868.

Umnak. The following overview is arranged geographically by major islands from east to west.

• TIGALDA-AKUN Archeological investigations of the Tigalda site on Tigalda Island showed that this midden site includes a precontact occupation from the first millennium A.D. up to Russian contact, which is evidenced by manufactured trade goods (Grayson 1969). Several flaked-stone artifact types are similar to the Izembek assemblage, and the Tigalda specimens are very similar to those from Akun (Turner and Turner 1974).

The Chulka site on Akun is dated to A.D. 780–1870, with both Russian and American trade goods found; this site was ancestral to the modern village of Akutan on Akutan Island (Turner 1972; Turner and Turner 1974). The prehistoric assemblage is typical for the Fox Islands but has a large proportion of ground slate ulu blades from throughout the dated sequence. Other common artifacts include flake scrapers, whetstones, abraders, projectile points, adz blades, bird bone awls, needles, bone wedges, and harpoon heads. Fragments of bottles, china, plate glass, and iron implements are abundant among the historical artifacts (Turner 1975). With the exception of pottery and long, ground slate points, the Chulka-Izembek comparisons are very close.

Iselelo is a site made up of a thin horizon of charcoal and artifacts covering a small promontory. The cultural horizon dates to 1155 B.C. Testing at Siskena village on nearby Akutan reveals both aboriginal and trade items (Turner and Turner 1974). Of nine additional Akun sites, two, Saa and Amatanan, are large middens (Turner 1973). These midden sites along with Chulka are interpreted by Turner to be the three main village localities of the late prehistoric period. The Saa site is par-

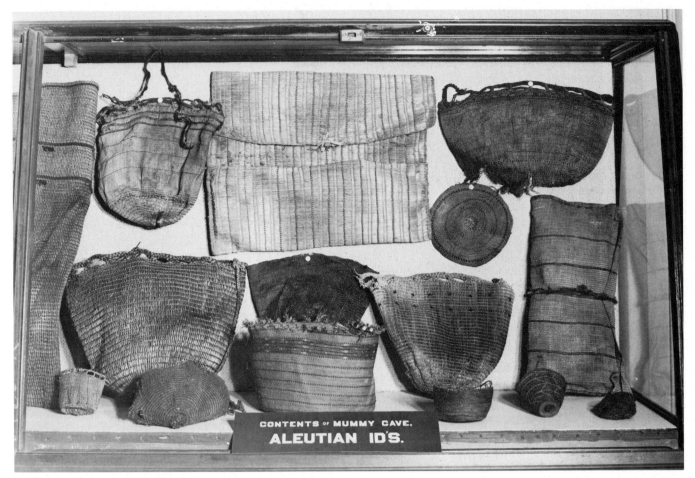

Smithsonian, NAA: 32680–V.

Fig. 8. Prehistoric twined basketry on display in former Smithsonian exhibit. (For modern examples see "Aleut," fig. 4, this vol.). All collected by Aleš Hrdlička from Kagamil caves, Islands of the Four Mountains, Alaska, 1937.

ticularly noteworthy because it contains water-saturated strata in which very well-preserved wooden artifacts are found. It is Turner's belief that the degree of artifactual variation displayed among different Akun sites is greater than that usually attributed to the entire archipelago. But few other islands have been sufficiently tested to make possible comparisons of intra-island variation.

• UNALASKA Unalaska, especially the Unalaska Bay region, is an area where archeological research was first undertaken. Further, the extensive site surveying and collecting by Lt. Comdr. Alvin Cahn during World War II makes this region one of the best studied in the chain. Historically, Dutch Harbor and Iliuliuk (Unalaska village) formed the most important Russian period community in the archipelago. Nineteen sites were located around Unalaska Bay and on Amaknak Island during the 1940s. Artifacts salvaged from military constructions came mainly from five sites. These collections are housed at the Field Museum of Natural History, Chicago, and the American Museum of Natural History, New York (Quimby 1946, 1948; McCartney 1967). They compose the largest collections for all the islands east

of Umnak and date from A.D. 1–1500. Although most of the pieces lack provenience details within sites, the wide range of artifact styles represented is valuable for typological and distributional studies.

Bone implements and decorative pieces fashioned from a wide spectrum of animals such as whales, sea lions, foxes, and birds were collected during 1941–1945 (fig. 9). Flaked stone projectile points, knives, and scrapers were commonly made of basalt (fig. 10). Labrets or lip plugs were made of jet, bone, and ivory. An analysis of the Amaknak bone industry revealed no marked discontinuities in Site D, one of the largest and deepest on that small island (McCartney 1967). In addition, some Amaknak bone artifacts were shown to be rather similar to those of Kodiak Island (Three Saints and Koniag phases; Clark 1966). Comparison to western island assemblages demonstrated that bone implement styles were not uniform throughout the eastern, central, and western island groups.

Bank (1953a) suggested, in contrast to Hrdlička's two-migration theory, that different human populations and cultural periods may be explained by isolation along the

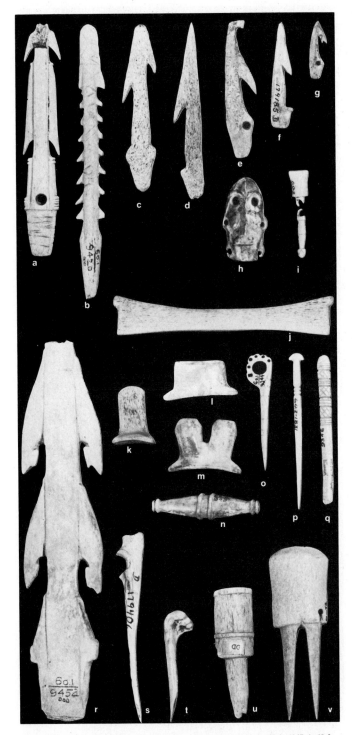

Amer. Mus. of Nat. Hist., New York: a, 60.2–470; b, 60.1–9420; h, 60.2–4867; i, 60.2–442/1513; k, 60.1–9144; n, 60.2–942; o, 60.1–9144; p, 60.2–1831; q, 60.1–9346; r, 60.1–9452; v, 60.2–2198; Field Mus., Chicago: c, 179,363; d, 179,252; e, 179,624; f, 179,185; g, 179,181; j, 178,941; l, 256,035; m, 179,406; s, 179,406; t, 256,035; u, 179,276.

Fig. 9. Bone artifacts, Amaknak (Fox Is.), about A.D. 1–1500: a–c, bilaterally barbed harpoon points; d–g, unilaterally barbed harpoon points; h, carved ivory face, use uncertain; i, broken 2-piece pendant; j, "gauge" with end pips, use uncertain; k–m, bone and ivory labrets; n, decorated cylinder of uncertain use; o–q, decorated ivory bodkins(?) or awls, q missing the pointed end; r, bilaterally barbed harpoon head blank, partially finished; s, fox ulna awl; t, puffin humerus awl; u, half of a 2-piece harpoon socket piece; v, harpoon socket piece. Length of a, 13.8 cm; rest same scale.

Field Mus., Chicago: a, 179,680; b, 178,934; c, 178,421; d, 256,008; e, 178,481; f, 178,618; g, 178,528; h, 178,419; i, 256,008; j, 178,425; k, 178,521; l, 178,468; m, 178,534; n, 178,531; o, 178,769; p, 178,481; q, 178,751–1; r, 178,403.

Fig. 10. Stone artifacts, Amaknak (Fox Is.) about A.D. 1–1500. a, jet (coal) nose(?) ornament; b, jet labret; c, flaked projectile point; d–f, flaked knife blades with tangs, f missing the tip; g, flaked bipointed projectile point or knife blade; h, flaked projectile point with erratically serrated edges; i, small flaked asymmetrical knife blade; j, tip section of a flaked knife blade; k, flaked side scraper with tang; l–m, flaked knife blades with side-notched tangs; n, basal section of an ovoid flaked knife blade; o, flaked knife or scraper blade with tang; p, flaked triangular knife blade; q, basal section of a flaked asymmetrical knife blade with tang; r, partially ground adz blade. Length of d 12.9 cm; rest same scale.

linear archipelago, which would allow development of regional variations. Such variations from one post-Anangula stock could thus form a kind of racial, linguistic, and technologic gradation from east to west.

The excavation of an Aleutian mummy site on a small islet at Sedanka Point is especially important in revealing late prehistoric artifacts (fig. 11) (Weyer 1931;

McCracken 1930). The wooden mummy sarcophagus and associated wood, bone, and stone artifacts probably date to A.D. 1550–1700 (fig. 12). Mummies are typically tightly flexed bodies with mat wrappings (Hrdlička 1945). Wooden sarcophagi or shelters are referred to in ethnohistoric literature, and burials with wooden covers have been excavated on Umnak (Jochelson 1925) and Amchitka (Desautels et al. 1970) as well. Late prehistoric or early Russian-period mummies placed in rock crevasses were also found at Sedanka Point. Similar burials in crevasses, rockshelters, and caves are common to the Unalaska area.

• UMNAK   The modern village of Nikolski has been the focal point for prehistoric research at the southwestern end of Umnak Island. Part of this village rests on the prehistoric site called Chaluka, a midden site measuring approximately 100 by 240 meters by 10 meters deep that has been extensively excavated since 1909 (Jochelson 1925; Hrdlička 1945; Laughlin and Marsh 1951). Other Nikolski area sites such as Sheep Creek, Sandy Beach, Oglodax, and a midden site on Anangula Island nearby have also been studied.

Chaluka midden has been the source of the greatest number of artifacts, burials, faunal refuse, and dated radiocarbon samples of any site in the Aleutians. The site has been more or less continually occupied, with few significant breaks, from about 2000 B.C. until the present (Denniston 1966; Turner, Aigner, and Richards 1974). The midden rests on a small isthmus separating Nikolski Bay from a freshwater lake. A volcanic ash layer referred to as Ash IV is intermixed with the lower midden strata (R.F. Black 1976). This thick and often unweathered ash layer was the uppermost of four primary ash strata found in the Anangula core and blade site stratigraphy. The core and blade artifacts are sealed beneath Ash III (McCartney and Turner 1966a). The time interval represented between Ash III and Ash IV is approximately 3,500–4,000 years.

At the base of Chaluka midden are found coursed stone walls of houses that probably had whalebone roof supports. Stone-lined storage holes are associated with these lower houses (Turner, Aigner, and Richards 1974; Aigner 1978). Chaluka artifact and faunal descriptions are supplied by Aigner (1966), Denniston (1966), and Lippold (1966).

An even older site on southwestern Umnak is one at Sandy Beach (Aigner et al. 1976). Excavation there uncovered eight house floors. Five radiocarbon dates indicate that the site may have been occupied 500 years earlier than Chaluka, or by 2500 B.C. The site's cultural horizon falls just beneath Ash IV of the Anangula-Chaluka ash sequence (R.F. Black 1976). The stone industry of this old site conforms to those of other Aleutian tradition sites in having lamps, bowls, adz blades, basalt knife blades, scrapers, bifacially flaked knives, and ocher grinders. The excavators conclude that this

130

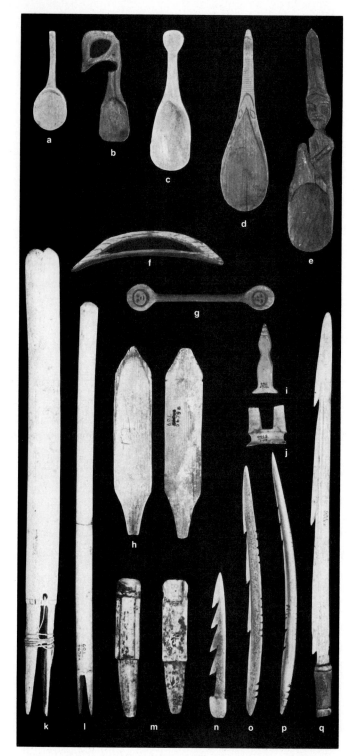

Amer. Mus. of Nat. Hist., New York: a, 60.1–5690; b, 60.1–5753; c, 60.1–5755; d, 60.1–5754; e, 60.1–5752; f, 60.1–5719–1; j, 60.1–5700; k, 60.1–5673; l, 60.1–5676–a; m, 60.1–5681; n–p, 60.1–5719; q, 60.1–5674.

Fig. 11. Artifacts from Sedanka Point (Fox Is.), Alaska, about A.D. 1500–1740: a–e, wooden spoons; f, wooden handle of uncertain use; g, wooden "barbell" piece with opposing faces, uncertain use; h, 2-piece wooden case of uncertain use, obverse and reverse shown; i–j, fine-grained limestone labrets; k–l, harpoon socket pieces; m, 2-piece ivory harpoon socket, obverse and reverse shown; n, unilaterally barbed harpoon point; o–p, fish or bird spear prongs; q, unilaterally barbed lance point set into a wooden shaft fragment. Length of a 9.0 cm; rest same scale.

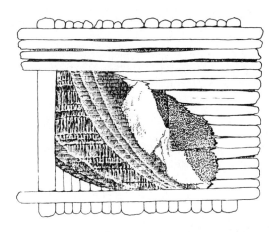

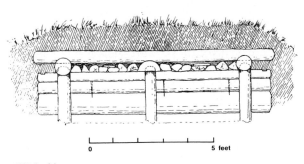

Weyer 1931:fig. 2 b–c.

Fig. 12. Driftwood sarcophagus. top, Top view showing layer of matting between the 2 wooden lids; bottom, side view in situ, Unalaska I., Alaska.

early Sandy Beach site is technologically more similar to Chaluka midden than it is to the much older Anangula core and blade site.

A second site on Sandy Beach has a cultural horizon just above Ash IV, dating to about 1000 B.C. Still another site, located at Idaliuk west of Sandy Beach, has a date of about 2200 B.C. (R.F. Black 1976).

Chaluka midden has provided one of the largest human skeletal series of any site in the chain (Jochelson 1925; Hrdlička 1945; Laughlin 1951). Burials dug into the midden strata are known only by skeletal remains, usually in flexed position, and surrounding ocher powder and durable artifacts. No wooden covers, mat wrappings, or skin clothing are preserved, as is typical of mummies from rockshelters and caves. A second type of subsurface burial has been discovered in pits dug between inverted V-shaped drainage trenches. The points of these trenches are directed uphill on slopes in order to divert ground water. These features are known from Umnak and other central islands in the chain including Kagamil and Atka (Aigner and Veltre 1976; Veltre 1979). These V-shaped features are likely the remnants of cache pits that were secondarily used as burial pits. Whalebone fragments have been found associated with these burials as well as mummy cave burials, suggesting some symbolic connection between whales and those interred (see Aigner and Veltre 1976; May 1951; Hrdlička 1945).

The only site excavated at the northeastern end of Umnak is that at Ashishik Point. It dates from as early as A.D. 200 and continues until the late prehistoric period with some occupational gaps. Although the artifact collection is small in comparison with other Umnak and Unalaska collections, Denniston's (1972, 1974) analysis of Aleut economic patterns is a pioneering demonstration for this area. She analyzed the faunal debris as a means of understanding food resources, subsistence seasonality, and nutritional adequacy of the diet. Major food classes are quantified as to edible weight, and the results form an estimate for relative food importance. The ratio determined was 1.0 part marine invertebrates, 1.8 parts birds, 35.9 parts fish, and 51.7 parts sea mammals. Marine and terrestrial vegetation, although not identified in the midden debris, provided only an insignificant quantity of food in the Aleut diet. Yesner (1981) estimates prehistoric Aleutian biomass and harvesting strategies based on archeological site fauna.

Islands of the Four Mountains

No midden sites have been excavated by archeologists in the Islands of the Four Mountains, a seven-island group, although they occur there as on surrounding islands. These islands are best known for the Aleutian mummies that come from one of them, Kagamil (Dall 1875, 1880; Hrdlička 1945:237–246, 417–420). Similar burial caves were investigated at Shiprock (between Unalaska and Umnak), Chernofski (Unalaska), and Ilak (Delarof group; Hrdlička 1945:312–337, 412–417). The Kagamil mummy series (63+ skeletons, 30 separate skulls, and other loose bones) is the largest for one island. Both sexes of all ages were carefully placed in such caves and crevasses with weapons, clothing, and other equipment. Besides the biologic data and evidence of mummification techniques gained from the Kagamil burials, the best Aleutian collection of organic materials was found with them. Artifacts of wood include dishes, combs, shields, slat armor, and kayak frames. Clothing and containers of gut, feathers, and skin were found. All manner of vegetable fiber mats, nets, baskets, and cordage are included in the burial inventory. Other materials include seaweed, sinew, and baleen (Dall 1880; Hrdlička 1945:238–242, 478–479, 589–610).

The excellent artifact preservation and folklore accounts of burials on Kagamil attributed to historic-period Aleuts suggest that these mummies, as others in the chain, date to the late prehistoric period.

Andreanof Islands

Knowledge of Aleut prehistory is more limited for the Andreanof Islands than for any other major island group. Excavations during the past century on Amlia, Atka,

Adak, Kanaga, and Tanaga have been poorly published, and the resulting museum collections have not yet been thoroughly studied (Dall 1877; Jochelson 1925; Hrdlička 1945; Bank 1952, 1952a). Contents of a minor burial cave are reported from Kanaga (Nelson and Barnett 1955).

Extensive excavations during the 1970s on Atka reveal a long sequence of prehistoric and historic age on northeastern Atka (Veltre 1979). This is the site known from the Russian period as Korovinski, a major Russian-American Company post in the Andreanof group. A prehistoric midden dating between A.D. 1 and 1400 underlies the early nineteenth-century historic occupation by Aleuts and Russians. the Korovinski excavation provides a rare glimpse of Russian trade items such as beads, window glass, iron nails, and bricks. Turner's (1973) Akun excavation and the excavation on Tigalda referred to above are the only other sites to reveal historic trade goods in quantity. The prehistoric artifacts from Korovinski and other sites in the Andreanof group appear, on the whole, similar in style and material to those from the eastern Aleutians. Such similar types include basalt knives, scrapers, and projectile points; stone lamps, abraders, whetstones, and weights; bone harpoon heads, socket pieces, fishhooks, awls, and wedges.

Rat Islands

Amchitka is the only island of the group that has been studied in any archeological detail, although sites were tested during the nineteenth century on Kiska and Little Kiska as well (Dall 1877; Hrdlička 1945). This long, flat island is relatively accessible and received special attention as an atomic testing ground during the late 1960s and early 1970s (Merritt and Fuller 1977). Working from a World War II period map of 40 sites (Guggenheim 1945), the Atomic Energy Commission sponsored archeological surveys that increased the known site total to 73 (Turner 1970; McCartney 1977). Testing and excavations at about 20 midden sites provide almost 11,000 artifacts and several radiocarbon dates that confirm a prehistoric occupation as early as 600 B.C. (Desautels et al. 1970). While some artifact styles appear to be unique to this island group and to the Near Islands to the west, others show cultural connection with the central and eastern islands. Of particular interest are a dozen iron knife (?) fragments found in the upper strata of five sites (Desautels et al. 1970:243ff.; Cook, Dixon, and Holmes 1972). Some of these are likely of early historic age but some may date to the late prehistoric period. Whatever their age, these iron pieces came from an exchange network based in Asia, as no native iron occurs in the chain or southwestern Alaska.

A permanent house with wooden superstructure, also found on Amchitka, is the only fully excavated prehis-

toric house west of the Fox Islands that includes architectural details (Cook, Dixon, and Holmes 1972:91–101). Dating to about A.D. 1500, this house measures six by seven and one-half meters. Apparently very little whalebone was used in building it, making it quite different from the whalebone house at Izembek Lagoon. However, the Amchitka and Izembek Lagoon houses are similar in size, and they stand in contrast to the much larger communal houses known from the early Russian period in the eastern Aleutians.

Near Islands

The westernmost island group, that designated "nearest" the Asiatic mainland by early Russian seamen, is the smallest group of the five. L.M. Turner (1886) tested Attu sites in 1880–1881 but his collections, now in the Smithsonian Institution, were never published. Dall (1877), Jochelson (1925), and Hrdlička (1945) all excavated on Attu or Agattu and published some illustrations of artifacts from these major islands. Many small artifact collections were made by servicemen during World War II. However, only a few of these have been deposited in museums or published (Hurt 1950; McCartney 1971).

Following the war, a small crew dug at Krugloi Point on Agattu at a site dating to the middle of the first millennium B.C. (A.C. Spaulding 1962). Spaulding concluded, on the basis of a poor bone artifact sample, that isolation caused the archaic and simple inventory found. However, it has been demonstrated, on the basis of other collections from nearby Shemya and Attu, that cultural impoverishment does not characterize the Near Islands (McCartney 1971). The same classes of artifacts found farther to the east in the chain occur in this island group as well (figs. 13–14). It is true that this island cluster is the most isolated in all the chain because of its placement at the end and because it is separated from the neighboring Rat Islands by the widest interisland pass. This isolation is seen technologically in several styles of stone and bone artifacts that are found only in this group or are shared with the Rat Islands just to the east.

Aleut Cultural Patterns

Marine Adaptations

Aleut interaction with the sea was almost exclusive and unquestionably rewarding. The mixing Pacific and Bering Sea currents are highly productive and the resulting food web was sampled at several levels, from kelp to puffins and seals. The convoluted shores around the islands and embayments increase the exploitable area over a straighter coast. Skin boats permitted hunting in

Fig. 13. Bone artifacts, Shemya and Attu Is., Alaska, late first millennium B.C.–A.D. 1500: a, trimming tablet showing multiple cutting scars; b, ivory ferrule or blunt projectile point with broken socket at the upper end; c, incised bird bone awl section; d, step-scarfed object of uncertain use; e, pierced pendant with notched edges; f–g, pendants with carved knobs; h, harpoon socket piece with broken basal tang; i, composite fishhook points or barbs (secured to shanks when used); j, lure or decorative fish figurine; k, drilled bone piece of uncertain use; l–m, bilaterally barbed harpoon points; n–o, unilaterally barbed harpoon points; p, toggle harpoon head; q, toggle harpoon head; r, carved labret. Length of a 7.5 cm; rest same scale.

Fig. 14. Stone artifacts, Shemya and Attu Is., Alaska, late first millennium B.C.–A.D. 1500: a–f, flaked projectile points; g–i, pointed basal sections of flaked projectile points; j–k, unifacially flaked side scrapers; l–m, partially ground adz blades; n–o, narrow flaked knife blades; p–r, narrow flaked projectile point; s, narrow flaked scraper with ground ventral surface (dorsal side shown). Length of a 4.5 cm; rest same scale.

open water beyond the shore. Another geographic advantage of the chain and peninsula was ready access to migrating sea mammals and birds passing through this archipelago filter, augmenting the resident marine life and avifauna.

The following shore habitats were those principally exploited by prehistoric Aleuts: beaches as hauling spots for pinnepeds and sites for washed-up whales, intertidal reefs or flats where crustaceans, mollusks, echinoderms, and various seaweeds occur, stream mouths where salmon run annually, and precipitous cliffs where birds and their eggs are found. The Aleuts favored three water habitats: onshore shallow areas for netting fish or fishing with lines from shore, deeper offshore areas for line fishing from boats and sea mammal hunting, and marine or lake waters for hunting waterfowl (see McCartney 1975, 1977 for a discussion of Aleut procurement patterns).

Faunal analyses of midden samples throughout the chain show general consistency from site to site of those animals serving as primary sources of food, skins, bones for artifacts, and other products (Jochelson 1925; Eyerdam 1936; Hrdlička 1945; Lippold 1966; Denniston 1972; Desautels et al. 1970; Turner and Turner 1974). Minor intersite variation in animal species and proportions occurs, but there are too few careful faunal studies to reveal frequency patterns of prehistoric animal use. The principal, but by no means the only, animals utilized include: sea otters, harbor seals, northern fur seals, northern sea lions, large and small whales, porpoises, foxes, cormorants, ducks, gulls, cod, halibut, rock greenling, Irish lord, salmon, sea urchins, limpets, mussels, clams, periwinkles, chitons, and scallops. Whereas the Aleuts west of Unimak depended almost totally on these sea animals for food, inhabitants of Unimak and the end of the Alaska Peninsula added walruses and a terrestrial mammalian fauna (Kotani 1980). But with the exception of caribou, the added land animals contributed little as dietary staples.

Distribution of animal species along the chain is dictated by geographic factors such as shore shape, availability of strand flats, and shallow waters around islands. Each island differs in kinds and extent of coastal habitats, and therefore islands differ as to species abundance (see Sekora 1973). Volcanic eruptions from some of the 45 known Aleutian volcanoes, with their related earthquakes, tsunamis, lava flows, or ash falls, are common throughout the chain (Coats 1950). These cataclysmic events caused one or more islands' vegetation and littoral sea life to be adversely affected, sometimes for months at a time (Wilcox 1959; Workman 1979; Black 1979). Dependence on marine resources was, thus, periodically interrupted on or near active volcanic islands. Volcanic eruptions probably caused Aleuts to shift their residence temporarily to unaffected areas on nearby islands.

Settlement Patterns

Little is known about varieties of prehistoric communities and their seasonal occupation, although general habitation patterns appear to be shared throughout the chain. No complete site survey has been conducted for all the Aleutian Islands, but village or camp sites are found on essentially all islands with circumferences greater than two or three miles. Large, deep midden sites of accumulated shell and bone debris and soil horizons mark the most permanent settlements, probably occupied for most of the year (Bank 1953b). These coastal sites are commonly found on embayments and sometimes on headlands. They are almost always found on low coasts with easy access to the sea (see McCartney 1974b, 1977 for locational factors). Coastal spits usually have prehistoric sites on them. It has been estimated that only 5 to 10 percent of the total Aleutian coastline is low enough for sites (McCartney 1974b). The majority of coast consists of high or steep cliffs and shores undergoing mass wasting.

Sites tend to be reused for periods of up to thousands of years. The supporting food base permitted demographic stability and the conservative continuity of these communities makes for few cultural hiatuses over time. No inland sites of lasting duration are known; all sites are situated on island shores or the shores of the Alaska Peninsula. Few activities other than bird, plant, stone, and mineral collecting took Aleuts away from the coastal zone. Camps of more temporary occupation were probably established during the summer near salmon streams and possibly bird rookeries. These sites have much less midden accumulation and often show surface depressions from temporary shelter foundations.

Permanent houses are little understood. At Russian contact, large semisubterranean barabaras or pit houses of up to 50 meters long and housing many families were used. But houses as early as 2000 B.C. were small, probably single-family dwellings made of boulders and whale bones or driftwood. The Izembek and Amchitka houses described above are more similar to the early style, although they were built after A.D. 1000. Just when the transition occurred from small to large houses is unknown, but it probably dates to the past 500 years.

Technology

Nineteenth-century ethnographic collections exhibit limited varieties of stone and bone tools and implements, while archeological research reveals a much fuller picture of these native technologies. Conversely, organic materials such as wooden implements, matting, basketry and cordage fragments, and skin clothing are rare in collections older than the late prehistoric period (see Hrdlička 1945:589–610). The great majority of harpoon shafts, boat fragments, bowls, and woven pieces are from the historic period. Wooden objects were abundantly fashioned from drift logs, but these are not well preserved in most middens. Trees are not native to the Aleutian archipelago.

Hunting implements include harpoons, lances, darts and throwing-boards, bows and arrows, and clubs. Harpoons and dart heads are both of the toggling and nontoggling types, but nontoggling heads are more frequent. Lines with hooks (simple or compound) and weights, and nets with floats and weights are some of the fishing implements used. Bone picks, mattocks, and shovels were used as collecting and digging tools. Wood- and boneworking tools include wedges, adzes, drills,

134

knives with flaked stone blades, scrapers, and scoria and pumice abraders or smoothers. Skin preparation was done with ulu knives with ground slate blades, various knives and scrapers, bone awls and punches, needles, and trimming tablets. Also found are miscellaneous household items such as whale vertebra bowls, bone and wooden spoons and scoops, hammerstones, stone lamps, grinding slabs and rubbing stones for preparing ocher powder and other materials, and tabular stone griddles. Decorative items include bone, ivory, and jet labrets, spools, pins and pendants, carved bone chains, animal effigies, and other finely made decorative pieces of uncertain function.

The Aleutian artifact collections form a continuum from east to west. By inspecting major collections from one island group to the next, one gets a distinct impression that each group has artifact styles not found elsewhere but also styles shared with adjacent groups. Although stylistic variation occurs between island groups, artifacts such as those listed above occur throughout the chain. The common equipment is directly related to common marine adaptations in similar coastal habitats. Unfortunately, such a horizontal cultural continuum has never been studied in detail or quantified.

Raw materials for tools, clothing, boats, and other objects made by Aleuts were spread, albeit unevenly, throughout the archipelago. Bones, skins, driftwood, and basalt are available on most larger islands, requiring no long-distance trade for these basic materials. For example, it has been shown that all the rocks used for lithic implements on Umnak (such as silicified argillite, basalt, andesite, obsidian, scoria/pumice, and welded tuff) are found on that island (see R.F. Black 1976). Obsidian is an example of a relatively rare rock used for projectile points and scrapers that was traded from eastern Aleutian sources (McCartney 1977:108–109). It is only infrequently found in Rat and Near Island collections, suggesting that implement materials were, in most cases, of local origin.

Old World Contacts

Attu is the western terminus of the Aleutian culture area. Two hundred and twenty-five miles to the west lie the Commander Islands, made up of Bering and Copper Islands and small islets. There is no good evidence to date that these islands were occupied by Aleuts or other natives prior to Vitus Bering's discovery of the Aleutians in 1741 (Hrdlička 1945). Bering expedition survivors who camped on the islands on their return from the New World did not relate sightings of human occupants or their settlements. Despite the intermediate position of the Commander Islands between Kamchatka Peninsula and the Aleutians, there is no archeological basis for believing that native populations ever entered the Aleutians by this water route. Sailing vessels of Asian origin may have occasionally wrecked on Aleutian shores prior to 1741, but there is no incontrovertible evidence that intentional trade contacts existed between Asia and the Aleutian chain before the Russian period.

However, convergent cultural development based on maritime-dependent adaptations is seen between Aleutian and marine hunting and gathering cultures of the Old World Pacific rim such as the Okhotsk and prehistoric Kurile cultures (e.g., Befu and Chard 1964; Vasil´evskii 1969–1970; Ohyi 1975; McCartney 1974). Such convergence stems largely from different peoples occupying similar cold ocean islands or coasts and subsisting on the same or similar sea mammals, birds, fish, and invertebrate species. Cold ocean convergence can also be demonstrated between the Aleut and Fuegian areas at opposite ends of the New World (for example, Dall 1877:53–54; McCartney 1975).

Prehistory of the Pacific Eskimo Region

DONALD W. CLARK

The Pacific Eskimo area—from the middle Alaska Peninsula west of Kodiak Island to the Copper River—is the homeland of a distinctive series of prehistoric maritime cultures. Although it has not formed a single historic block at all times, local distinctions found principally among Prince William Sound, Kachemak Bay, Kodiak Island, the Pacific side of the upper Alaska Peninsula, and Chirikof Island together with the middle Alaska Peninsula can be interpreted within a co-tradition framework.

History of Research

Concerted archeological research in the Pacific area began in the 1930s with projects by Frederica de Laguna and Aleš Hrdlička. During four field seasons De Laguna excavated part of the thick midden or refuse deposits at several sites on Yukon Island and Cottonwood Creek in Kachemak Bay, outer Cook Inlet, and at Palugvik in Prince William Sound (De Laguna 1934, 1956). In addition, she examined numerous other occupation sites, rock-art localities, and burial caves or rockshelters. Hrdlička's several seasons on Kodiak, from 1931 to 1936, were directed toward excavation of the Uyak or "Our Point" site, located on the Shelikof Strait side of the island (Hrdlička 1944; Heizer 1956). Hrdlička recovered evidence for a succession of cultures, Pre-Koniag and Koniag. The Pre-Koniag culture is essentially the same as De Laguna's Kachemak series. Hrdlička's conclusion that the Koniag succession was a swift population replacement has been questioned, and thus his work has set one of the major problems for continued research in the Pacific area.

Excavations on the Pacific side of the Alaska Peninsula at Kukak in 1953 by W.A. Davis (1960) and the next year at Kaflia Bay by Wendell Oswalt (1955) added to the scant knowledge of the upper Peninsula region; but the 7,000-year sequence for that subarea was not developed until after 1964 when D.E. Dumond shifted the focus of his investigations in the Naknek drainage on the Alaska Peninsula, where the archeology shows predominantly northern relationships, to include Takli Island and Kukak on the Pacific coast opposite Kodiak (Dumond 1971a, 1972; G.H. Clark 1977). Also, from 1961 through 1964 archeologists under the direction of W.S. Laughlin tested several sites located on the eastern side of the Kodiak group. They defined a late prehistoric pottery-using facies of Koniag Eskimo, previously suggested by Heizer (1949), at Rolling Bay and Kiavak (Clark 1966a, 1974a); further explicated the Kachemak tradition or Uyak lower (Pre-Koniag) culture at Three Saints, Crag Point, and Old Kiavak (Clark 1966, 1970); surveyed Chirikof Island (Workman 1969a); and discovered at Ocean Bay two previously unrecognized earlier cultures (Clark 1979). Additional work done on Kodiak includes minor excavations (Clark 1974; Milan in Clark 1974), further investigation of the Ocean Bay culture in 1971 and in 1977–1978 at two Afognak sites (Clark 1979) and on Uganik Island (Nowak 1978), respectively, and agency surveys (Nowak 1978; Righter and Jordan 1980).

Kachemak Bay again became the focus of a sustained program of fieldwork in 1974 (Lobdell 1980; Workman, Lobdell, and Workman 1980; Workman and Lobdell 1981; Workman 1977; K.W. Workman 1977). Investigation of the peripherally related middle and upper Cook Inlet region has had an unspectacular history, beginning with De Laguna's survey and continuing to the 1980s, although the results and complex are significant (R.G. Dixon 1980; Dumond and Mace 1968; Hibben 1943; De Laguna 1934; Reger 1977; Thorson, Plasket, and Dixon 1980; Townsend and Townsend 1961; Townsend 1970a). Sites are mapped in figure 1.

Culture History: The Earlier Traditions

Comparison of progressions in the regional sequences (fig. 2) reveals gaps in knowledge about each subarea. The sequence is controlled primarily by radiocarbon dating (table 1) and secondarily by stratigraphy and typological considerations.

By 7,000 years ago maritime hunters were living on Kodiak Island, the adjacent Alaska Peninsula, and probably throughout the Pacific area.* These people

* Approximately 6,000 years ago according to unadjusted radiocarbon dates. Except for the initial date given here all dates, ranges, and estimates in this article are based on unadjusted radiocarbon dates provided in table 1. Radiocarbon dates cited in the text by laboratory number have been rounded to the nearest 50 years. Adjustment of radiocarbon dates to derive "true" age is discussed in the note to table 1.

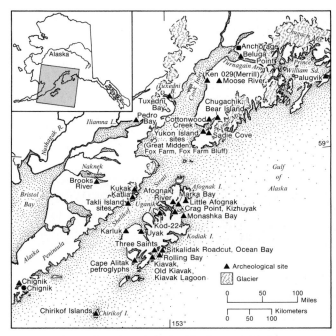

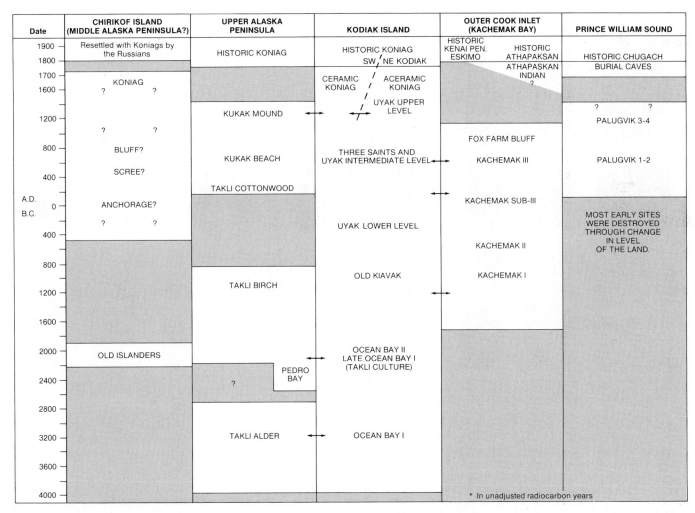

Fig. 1. Archeological sites of the Pacific Coast of Alaska.

left the chipped tools and other remains of the Ocean Bay I culture on Kodiak (fig. 3a–d, i–k, u) (Clark 1966, 1975, 1979; Nowak 1978) and the closely related Takli Alder phase of the mainland opposite (G.H. Clark 1977). Their forebears probably lived in the same area, and certainly older occupations of the Pacific area can be expected judging from the earlier prehistory of adjacent coastal areas and the Bering Sea drainage of the Alaska Peninsula (Dumond, Henn, and Stuckenrath 1976). Eventually, any projection will come to the time, about 10,000 years ago, when late Pleistocene glaciers covered most of the area excluding any human occupation and when people in the North Pacific region might not as yet have developed the specialized maritime hunting economy required for living on Kodiak Island.

During the summer, Ocean Bay people camped at the mouths of streams in order to exploit the salmon runs, probably through the use of spears and traps. They continued then in their principal pursuit, the sea mammal chase. In addition to seals and sea lions, they took sea otter, porpoise, probably larger whales, fowl, and the occasional land mammal. Shellfish were gathered when available or when required. Presumably cod, scul-

Fig. 2. Prehistoric cultures of the Pacific Eskimo region.

pin, and halibut were taken offshore, and bird rookeries were raided. This type of economy also is characteristic of later Pacific area cultures (Clark 1979; Dumond 1977).

Ocean Bay I people rarely ground slate although they were aware of the technique (fig. 3i). Eventually, about 2500 B.C., increased interest was shown in the production of slate implements, particularly points, lances, and large stemmed knives, using a distinctive technology in which sheets of slate were sawed into long strips and then scraped to shape before they were finished by grinding (fig. 3g–h) (Clark 1975, 1979, 1980). Within a couple of centuries some groups on Kodiak almost gave up stone flaking in favor of slate working, thus giving rise to Ocean Bay II; however, on the mainland and among other Kodiak communities, the new slate technology and implements simply were added to the earlier base of flaked chert and basalt. This is the late Ocean Bay I phase of Kodiak (Clark 1979), in part the

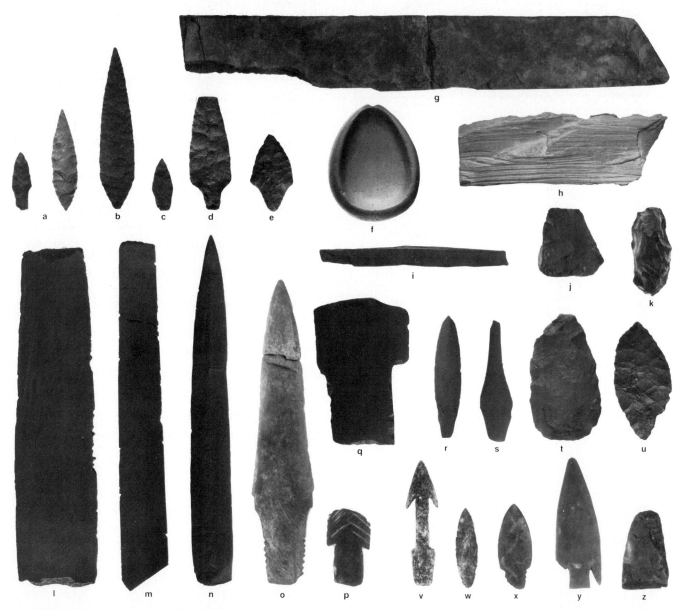

U. of Alaska, Anchorage: a, b, e–n, t, u; U. of Wis., Madison: c, d, o–s, v–z.

Fig. 3. Ocean Bay (OB) phase. Chipped stone projectile points from Afognak I., Alaska: a, OB I; b–d, OB I or succeeding transition; e, late OB I or succeeding transition. From Afognak I.: f, miniature but functional stone lamp, OB II, also found in other periods; g, sawn slate strip (blank) and h, scraped slate, both representing distinctive fabrication processes of OB II; i, slate beach shingle rod slightly modified by grinding, early OB I; j, *pièce esquillée* (wedge), OB I; k, microblade core, base view, OB I; l, ground slate blade fragment, OB II; m, slate bayonet-shaped blade with ornamental barbs, incomplete, OB II; n, slate bayonet-shaped blade, incomplete proximal end, OB II. Ground slate objects from Sitkalidak Roadcut site: o, projectile point or knife blade, OB II; p, projectile point stem fragment, OB I or II; q, broad double-edged blade stem fragment, OB II; r, point, OB II; s, double-edged knife, blade reduced by sharpening, OB II. Chipped stone from Afognak I.: t, flaked adz blade, with trace of grinding on the ventral surface, OB I or II; u, biface blade, OB I. Old Kiavak phase, Kiavak Lagoon site 419: v, harpoon head; w, flaked point; x, knife or blade; y, blade; z, adz bit. Length of g, 29.1 cm; rest same scale.

CLARK

Takli Birch of the peninsula opposite (G.H. Clark 1977; Dumond 1971a), and peripherally the older Pedro Bay component of Lake Iliamna (Townsend 1970); here it will be called the Takli culture though it is regarded as part of the Ocean Bay tradition. On the northern part of Kodiak, Takli and Ocean Bay II people seemingly coexisted and interacted until at least 1800 B.C., when the present record of investigations becomes inadequate. On the Shelikof Strait side of the island Takli is superceded by the Kachemak tradition after 1200 B.C. (Nowak 1979), while across the strait on the Alaska Peninsula Takli Birch continues into a much later period, though evidently under the influence of the Kachemak tradition. This reconstruction is based on the sequences at the Sitkalidak Roadcut site at Ocean Bay, two Afognak River sites on Afognak Island off northern Kodiak, Kod-224 on the Shelikof Strait side of the island, and two Takli Island and one Kukak site on the Alaska Peninsula, as dated in table 1.

Further cultural diversity at this time is illustrated by the Old Islander culture of tiny Chirikof Island, equally remote from Kodiak and the Alaska Peninsula (Workman 1966a, 1969a). The Old Islanders of 2100 B.C. (P-1050) also employed the dual technology (flaking stone and grinding slate) but they produced implement styles different from the Takli and Ocean Bay II culture and did not scrape or saw slate. They probably formed a regional phase of the central and western Alaska Peninsula and offshore islands although presently only the one site is known. Townsend (1970) has described another contemporary variation, the 4,500-year-old (I-3176, I-4161) Pedro Bay assemblage of Lake Iliamna at the base of the Alaska Peninsula, which is geographically marginal to the Pacific area. The Pedro Bay ground slate industry is almost identical to Ocean Bay II, but some flaked implements differ. Another assemblage from the Bering Sea slope of the upper Alaska Peninsula that is relatable to Ocean Bay II on the basis of its ground slate industry and age is the Brooks River Strand phase (Dumond 1981).

On the Alaska Peninsula the persisting Takli Birch underwent little cultural elaboration or development, although some of the earlier point styles lapse; and single-edged slate knives (ulus), the rare stone drill, and labrets come into use (G.H. Clark 1977). The developments seen in later Takli Birch have close counterparts on Kodiak and in outer Cook Inlet and may be indicative of communication throughout the region.

Elsewhere during the second millennium B.C. a new culture appeared in the Pacific area. This was the Kachemak tradition, a culture that through two and one-half millennia became progressively more elaborated and then was amalgamated with Neo-Eskimo to form the Pacific Eskimo (Clark 1975). Continuity from Ocean Bay II or Takli to the Kachemak tradition remains to be documented, although it is plausible if viewed along certain lines of evidence. The earliest Kachemak people had an unelaborated material kit as found in the rudimentary Kachemak I sample (De Laguna 1934). They flaked and ground stone (although not in the Ocean Bay II and Takli styles and techniques), wore labrets, and lighted their dwellings with oil lamps. Among their distinctive implements are a stone weight, grooved plummet-style about one end (fig. 4a), and an archaic-appearing toggle harpoon head. Their economy was characteristically North Pacific maritime and not basically different from that indicated for Ocean Bay culture.

Through time—essentially the first millennium B.C. in Kachemak II including the Old Kiavak phase of Kodiak (De Laguna 1934; Clark 1966; Workman, Lobdell, and Workman 1980)—material culture became more complex, but still there was little elaboration of implements and artwork (fig. 3v–z). Kachemak II people began to practice a range of burial customs that were to characterize their descendants. They were active fishermen and to this end produced for weights large numbers of notched pebbles and several varieties of grooved stones. Many implements were flaked from flinty material, but on Kodiak ground-slate tools were common. Affiliations with or influence from Norton culture of the Bering Sea region is evident in a number of implement styles (K.W. Workman 1977; Workman 1981). This stage or range of the Kachemak tradition is not well dated, but there are first and second century B.C. dates for the succeeding sub-III and III periods, one of nearly 400 B.C. for late Kachemak II at Chugachik Island (S-1062), a less certain dating to 800 B.C. (UGa-2343) (Workman, Lobdell, and Workman 1980:table 1), and an earlier date from Kodiak (P-1039) that might apply to an antecedent stage.

Kachemak culture continued to develop through periods sub-III and III at Kachemak Bay (De Laguna 1934; Workman 1980), in the Three Saints phase and Uyak site intermediate and lower levels of Kodiak (Clark 1970a; Heizer 1956), and it also is recognized in the middle Cook Inlet region (Reger 1977, 1981; R.G. Dixon 1980) and in Prince William Sound (De Laguna 1956).

In the original periodization of the Kachemak Bay sequence sub-III was seen as developmental leading from II into the height of cultural elaboration found in period III. An age of 400 B.C. to 1 B.C. has been suggested, especially on the basis of later work on Chugachik Island, which spans late Kachemak II through early Kachemak III (K.W. Workman 1977; Workman 1980). However, it is uncertain if specific details of this periodization can be applied elsewhere or even throughout Kachemak Bay considering local variation or "anomalies" (Workman 1980:77).

Kachemak III, or Late Kachemak in more general terms, essentially spans the first millennium of the Christian era. It was the zenith of the Kachemak tra-   *139*

U. of Wis., Madison: a, 215:2; b, 209:8; c, 139; d, 241:29.1; e, 241:82.4; f, 241:72.11; g, 244:105.2; h, 241:111:27; i, 241:63.3; j, 241:61.4; k, 241:139.3.

Fig. 4. Kachemak tradition, Alaska. a, Early Kachemak plummet-type grooved stone, a diagnostic horizon style, Woody I.; b, modified boulder spall characteristic of the tradition, Kodiak I.; c, small flat adz bit characteristic of the tradition, Three Saints, Kodiak I., d–h, Crag Point, Kodiak I.: d, slate point or knife fragment with serrated stem distinctive of Kachemak and Ocean Bay II; e, stone saw; f–g, bone adz hafts (notched form is a horizon marker); h, bone wedge; i–j, bone harpoon heads; k, unidentified object, distinctive of the Kachemak tradition. Length of b, 18.0 cm; rest same scale.

dition. The distinctiveness of late Kachemak culture on Kodiak is seen best when it is contrasted with the succeeding Koniag culture (Clark 1974a). Although there is considerable similarity in the types of implements used, late Kachemak produced better-finished implements and hunting equipment (fig. 4b–k, fig. 5b cf. fig. 12e, fig. 6b cf. fig. 12b).

Late Kachemak people were appreciative of personal adornment and art and produced a large variety of beads, pendants, figurines, labrets, and ornamental pins in bone, ivory, jet, shell, and soft red stone (figs. 5o, 6a–d, 7). Designs often were incised on carefully barbed slate points (fig. 8). Their most noteworthy achievement was the production of massive pecked-stone lamps weighing up to 95 pounds with human figures, animals, and fe-

male breasts carved in the bowl in high relief or on the exterior in lower relief (fig. 9) (Marsh 1956; J.A. Mason 1928; Hrdlička 1944:App. A). Occupation sites and refuse deposits are replete with evidence for varied practices with the dead including cut and drilled human bones, trophy heads, dismembered and secondary burials, artificial eyes, and probably cannibalism (Hrdlička 1941, 1941a; De Laguna 1934; Workman, Lobdell, and Workman 1980:392–393).

The inhabitants of Prince William Sound, who make their first appearance in the record at this time (probably because earlier sites have been destroyed through lowering of the relative land level), are characterized by a less sharply defined phase of Kachemak culture related to Kachemak III (De Laguna 1956). Some of the most basic and simple late Kachemak implements, like the ubiquitous boulder flakes (fig. 4b) and notched pebbles, are rare or absent at Palugvik, the principal excavated site. Although much of the Palugvik assemblage has a very generalized appearance, highly specific cross-ties between Palugvik and late Kachemak are seen in styles of slate points, fishhooks, labrets, and stone lamps.

During certain periods Eskimoid cultures also are found in the middle and upper Cook Inlet region, an area that has been occupied by Tanaina Indians from some time before historic contact. Assemblages are not so rich as those from the outer inlet, and much of this material thus has a more generalized Kachemak tradition or Pacific Eskimo cast (dates from Merrill, Moose River, and Beluga Point sites, table 1) (R.G. Dixon 1980; Dumond and Mace 1968; J.A. Mason 1928; Reger 1977, 1981).

On the Alaska Peninsula there is a long hiatus in the sampled sequence of occupation, which reappears in the small Takli Cottonwood phase assemblage of A.D. 200 (I-1942) to possibly 500 (Dumond 1971a; G. H. Clark 1977). Apparently Takli Birch descendants had continued to live in the area and, with occasional changes and development through the centuries, became the authors of the Takli Cottonwood artifacts. Slate frequently was worked, but the majority of Cottonwood tools and points are flaked. Contact with the Kachemak tradition across the 25 miles of water separating the peninsula from Kodiak evidently continued, and some Cottonwood implements, such as the breasted lamp (Dumond 1971a: fig. 5a), are of distinctive late Kachemak styles. The unity with diversity seen throughout the Pacific area at this time is well expressed in the co-tradition concept (Workman 1980:50–54).

Influence from the Bering Sea region also is discernable in the Cottonwood phase. Diagnostic elements of Norton flaked stone technology appeared on the Pacific coast late in the first millennium B.C. in the Cook Inlet and Kachemak Bay areas. Ceramics appear in the Cottonwood phase. These elements became more conspic-

U. of Wis., Madison: a, 241:54.2; b, Kod 439: x.39; c, 241:102.10; d, 241:46.1; e, 241:200.7; f, 241:x.520; g, 241:64.20; r, 241:x.37; U. of Alaska, Anchorage: h–q.

Fig. 5. Late Kachemak tradition. a, flaked slate blade, Crag Point, Kodiak I., Alaska; b, ulu blade from Kodiak I. area (precise semilunar form is a horizon marker); c, spear side-prong, Crag Point; d, sawn bone tube, Crag Point; e, bipointed bone gorge(?), Crag Point; f, fishhook (shank portion), Crag Point; g, fishhook (barbed portion), Crag Point. Kachemak III from Chugachik I.: h–i, flaked stone points; j, bone arrowhead with blade slits; k, barbed dart; e, toggle harpoon head; m, bone seal(?) image. n, notched ulu from Cottonwood Creek site. Fox Farm Bluff site, Yukon I.: o, jet labret; p, flaked stone drill; q, chert wedge. r, Terminal Kachemak tradition U-notched beach shingle scraper(?), Crag Point. Length of b, about 14.0 cm; rest same scale.

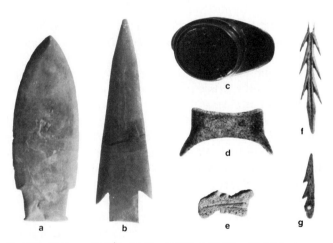

U. of Wis., Madison a, 401:68; b, 401:10; c, 401:134; d, 401:101; e, 401:132; f, no number; g, 401:118.

Fig. 6. Three Saints phase of Kachemak tradition from Kodiak I., Alaska: a, ground slate knife with "lugged" indented haft (diagnostic style); b, ground slate projectile point (preparation of the base is a diagnostic attribute); c, labret of jet (coal) formerly inlayed with red ocher; d, labret, a diagnostic horizon style; e, pumice abrader; f, bone barbed arrow point, slotted for endblade; g, bone harpoon head, the small size indicative of either a harpoon arrow or a nonfunctional miniature. Length of a about 11.2 cm; rest same scale.

uous after A.D. 500 in the first post-III phase at Kachemak Bay, in the Kukak Beach phase of A.D. 500 to 1000 that succeeds Cottonwood, and on Chirikof Island.

Kukak Beach stone technology is a blend of the southern Bering Sea and the Pacific; perhaps its people also are a blend or mixture (Dumond 1969, 1971a, 1972; G.H. Clark 1977). Kukak Beach used characteristic Pacific (late Kachemak tradition) forms of ground- and pecked-stone implements and harpoon heads. But pottery of northern affinity, as well as flaked artifacts, also are present. By this time typical Pacific slate implements appear in the southern Bering Sea province, possibly indicating people and influence flowing in both directions. But the salient feature of Kukak Beach is a strong reemphasis on stone flaking, which is completely unlike events on Kodiak and in Prince William Sound but is not unlike those at Kachemak Bay and in the west, as on Chirikof Island.

After the Old Islanders, Chirikof Island was only sporadically occupied until late in the first millennium B.C. when a group apparently moved there from the Alaska Peninsula (Workman 1969, 1969a). Although an occasional implement was ground from slate, most

141

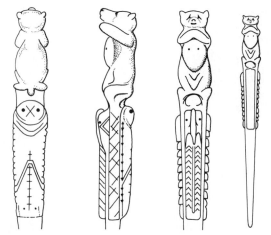

after Clark 1970:fig. 4.

Fig. 7. Ornamental pin, Late Kachemak tradition, Three Saints, Kodiak I., Alaska. At the top is a bear clasping a human head to its chest. On one side a sea otter or otter lies on its back below the bear, and on the other side is an abstract form, probably zoomorphic. Length of pin about 5.1 cm.

of the undated Anchorage-complex artifacts, including characteristic stemmed and notched knives, were flaked from basalt. This technology continues into the Scree complex, which also has a strong emphasis on ground slate, particularly the highly distinctive first millennium late Kachemak forms of Kodiak. Continuity with change is seen from Scree to the Bluff complex, the last phase of the Chirikof middle period. Slate is used less frequently than before and is not so distinctive of the Kachemak tradition. Bluff, though undated, appears to be related to late first-millennium cultures on both the Pacific and Bering Sea sides of the Alaska Peninsula.

Chirikof Island, at this period, can be interpreted as an outlier of a culture subarea located along the largely unexplored south-central part of the Alaska Peninsula (but see Dumond, Henn, and Stuckenrath 1976 for Chignik locality). The technology combines Aleutian, Norton, and Alaska Peninsula flaked forms with Kodiak-style ground-slate and pecked-stone implements. The slightly more recent (A.D. 1050) Izembek phase in

Clark 1970:fig. 3.

Fig. 8. Late Kachemak tradition incised ground slate points. First 2 at left, Crag Point site, all others, Three Saints site, Kodiak I., Alaska. Length of far left 5.6 cm; rest same scale.

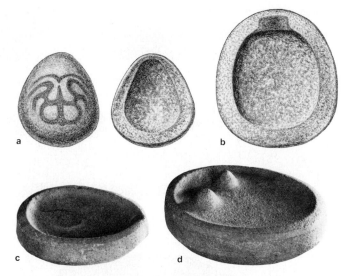

Smithsonian, Dept. of Anthr.: a, 375,505; b, 375,504; c, 375,270; d, 377,861.

Fig. 9. Stone lamps of diorite from Uyak site, Kodiak Is., Alaska. a, Koniag style Type I.B.1 from the upper level, the convex bottom of the lamp showing a pecked design representing a human face; b, late Pacific-Eskimo style Type I.A.1 from the upper level, with a wide, flat upper rim, a wide wick channel, and a shallow bowl; c, Type I.B.2 subtype a from the lower level, with a simple prow and a raised ovoid shape in the bowl cavity; d, late Kachemak tradition style Type I.B.2 subtype e from the lower level, with protrusions representing female breasts in the bowl cavity. (See Heizer 1956:32–37). Length of c 22.9 cm, rest same scale.

historic Aleut territory on the outer Alaska Peninsula also partakes of features of this regional or co-tradition branch (McCartney 1974a). Whether this involves a linguistic and ethnic group different from the Kachemak tradition and upper Alaska Peninsula or represents continuous variation across the later Aleut-Eskimo boundary remains an issue (McCartney 1974a:69; Dumond 1974a).

Following or partially contemporary with Kachemak III in the outer Cook Inlet sequence is the Yukon Fox Farm Bluff site ceramic component, which is dated at about A.D. 800–900 or, considering the total range of dates and their reliability, from A.D. 500 to 1000 (table 1) (Workman 1980; Workman and Lobdell 1979; Workman, Lobdell, and Workman 1980). This material, discovered in 1978, considerably alters De Laguna's (1934) original tentative definition of a Kachemak IV stage. Collections for this period from the multi-component Yukon Fox Farm Bluff site feature a resurgence of stone flaking, especially in specific styles of late Norton culture, coupled with a continuity of late Kachemak implements in bone and other material. Lithic preferences change to exotic material, and native copper is utilized for the first time at Kachemak Bay. Pottery is significantly present, though it probably was introduced later than the Norton flaked artifact types. The thick, gravel-tempered ware with impressed curvilinear surface treatment is characteristic of the Birnirk (late first millen-

Table 1. Selected Chronology of Radiocarbon Dates, Pacific Area

Laboratory Number	Age and Date		Applies to	Sources
Chirikof Island, Site No. 9				Stuckenrath, Coe, and Ralph 1966
P-1050	4029 ± 63	2079 B.C.	Old Islander	
Ocean Bay (Sitkalidak Roadcut site), Site No. 438 (Kod 119) (Kodiak Islands)				Stuckenrath, Coe, and Ralph 1966
P-1036	3929 ± 65	1979 B.C.	Ocean Bay II	
P-1034	5503 ± 78	3553 B.C.	Ocean Bay I base of site	
Afognak River, Site Afo-106 (AFG 008) (Kodiak Islands)				Clark 1979
GaK-3802	4150 ± 200	2200 B.C.	Late Ocean Bay I or Takli Birchlike–transition	
GaK-3801	5750 ± 240	3800 B.C.	Ocean Bay I base of site	
Afognak River, Site Afo-109 (AFG 011) (Kodiak Islands)				
S-1418	4480 ± 160	2530 B.C.	Ocean Bay II, base of site	Rutherford, Wittenberg, and Wilmeth 1981
GaK-3804	4200 ± 140	2250 B.C.	Ocean Bay II, basal zone	Clark 1979
S-1419	4480 ± 130	2525 B.C.	Ocean Bay II, lower levels	Rutherford, Wittenberg, and Wilmeth 1981
GaK-3803	3890 ± 110	1940 B.C.	Ocean Bay II, high upper	Clark 1979
Uganik Island, Site Kod-224 (Kodiak Islands)				Nowak 1978, 1979
UGa-2820	3130 ± 85	1180 B.C.	Late Takli (like Birch)	
UGa-2822	3365 ± 70	1415 B.C.	Late Takli	
UGa-1931	5065 ± 135	3115 B.C.	Late Ocean Bay I	
DIC-1236	6220 ± 70	4270 B.C.	Earliest Ocean Bay I	
Takli Island Takli site, AK1 (MK-12) (Alaska Peninsula)				Buckley and Willis 1970
I-1639	4110 ± 160	2160 B.C.	Takli Birch phase, base	
I-1941	2910 ± 105	960 B.C.	Takli Birch phase, Upper	
I-3733	2810 ± 100	860 B.C.	Takli Birch phase, Upper	
I-1940	5650 ± 115	3700 B.C.	Takli Alder phase, Lower (Ocean Bay I)	
Takli Island, Hook Point site AK3 (MK-14) (Alaska Peninsula)				Buckley and Willis 1970
I-1943	3470 ± 110	1520 B.C.	Takli Birch	
I-1942	1680 ± 100	A.D. 270	Takli Cottonwood	
Kukak Isolated Housepit Site KK1a (MK-6a) (Alaska Peninsula)				
I-1945	5830 ± 120	3880 B.C.	Takli Alder phase (Ocean Bay I)	Buckley and Willis 1970
Pedro Bay (Lake Iliamna) (Alaska Peninsula)				
I-3176	4320 ± 115	2370 B.C.	Older component	Buckley and Willis 1969
I-4161	4530 ± 110	2580 B.C.	Older component related to Ocean Bay culture	Buckley and Willis 1970
Old Kiavak Site No. 419 (Kodiak Islands)				Stuckenrath, Coe, and Ralph 1966
P-1039	3263 ± 61	1313 B.C.	Old Kiavak	
P-1041	937 ± 49	A.D. 1013	Ceramic, early Koniag (charred oil)	
Chugachik (Indian) Island site (SEL 033) (Kachemak Bay)				Workman 1980; Workman, Lobdell, and Workman 1980
UGa-2343	2740 ± 75	790 B.C.	Base of site	
S-1062	2310 ± 70	360 B.C.	Base of site, Kachemak II or sub-III	Rutherford, Wittenberg, and Wilmeth 1981
UGa-2342	1940 ± 90	A.D. 10		Workman 1980; Workman, Lobdell, and Workman 1980
S-1063	1705 ± 70	A.D. 245	Upper zone of site	Rutherford, Wittenberg, and Wilmeth 1981
UGa-2344	1475 ± 70	A.D. 475	Upper zone of site, Kachemak II or sub-III	Workman 1980; Workman, Lobdell, and Workman 1980

Table 1. Selected Chronology of Radiocarbon Dates, Pacific Area (Continued)

Laboratory Number	Age and Date		Applies to	Sources
Cottonwood Creek site (SEL 030) (Kachemak Bay)				Rutherford, Wittenberg, and Wilmeth 1981
S-1042	1750 ± 70	A.D. 200	Lower Kachemak III	
S-1043	1750 ± 130	A.D. 200	Lower Kachemak III	
S-1054	1560 ± 80	A.D. 390	Top of Kachemak III	
Yukon Island Site (SEL 001) (Kachemak Bay)				Ralph and Ackerman 1961
P-139	2706 ± 118	748 B.C.	Kachemak I	
P-138	1369 ± 102 (from 1954)	A.D. 589	Kachemak III	
Three Saints, Site No. 401 (Kodiak Islands)				Stuckenrath, Coe, and Ralph 1966
P-1042	2028 ± 55	78 B.C.	Three Saints phase (Kachemak III-related)	
P-1043	1119 ± 49	A.D. 831	Three Saints phase, upper levels	
Crag Point, Site No. 241 Anton Larsen Bay (Kodiak Island)				
P-1057	2033 ± 52	83 B.C.	Three Saints-Kachemak III	Stuckenrath, Coe, and Ralph 1966
B-835	1110 ± 100	A.D. 850	Transition to Koniag phase? (charred oil)	Oeschger, Riesen, and Lerman 1970
Yukon Fox Farm Bluff site (SEL 041) (Kachemak Bay)				Workman 1980; Workman, Lobdell, and Workman 1980
UGa-2341	1315 ± 250	A.D. 625	Kachemak III derivative	
UGa-2339	1090 ± 195	A.D. 860	Kachemak III derivative, ceramics	
UGa-2340	1130 ± 120	A.D. 820	Kachemak III derivative, ceramics	
Palugvik (Prince William Sound)				Ralph and Ackerman 1961
P-174	1753 ± 105	A.D. 205	Palugvik I	
P-192	1727 ± 105 (from 1954)	A.D. 231(+83)	Palugvik I	
Kukak Site KK1 (Alaska Peninsula)				
I-1637	1450 ± 130	A.D. 500	Kukak Beach	Buckley and Willis 1970
I-1638	1075 ± 100	A.D. 875	Kukak Beach	Buckley and Willis 1970
I-1944	1460 ± 95	A.D. 490	Kukak Beach	Buckley and Willis 1970
I-505	775 ± 95	A.D. 1175	Kukak Mound	Trautman 1964
I-1636	775 ± 110	A.D. 1175	Kukak Mound	Buckley and Willis 1970
Brooks River Camp component (Naknek Drainage) (Alaska Peninsula)				
I-524	300 ± 75	A.D. 1650	Camp phase, upper	Trautman 1964
I-525	680 ± 90	A.D. 1270	Camp phase, basal	Trautman 1964
I-1635	845 ± 100	A.D. 1105	Camp phase	Buckley and Willis 1970
Kiavak, Site 418 (Kodiak Islands)				Stuckenrath, Coe, and Ralph 1966
P-1044	280 ± 44	A.D. 1670	Ceramic Koniag	
P-1045	391 ± 48	A.D. 1559	Ceramic Koniag	
Rolling Bay, Site 420 (Kodiak Islands)				Stuckenrath, Coe, and Ralph 1966
P-1047	393 ± 40	A.D. 1557	Ceramic Koniag	
P-1048	353 ± 44	A.D. 1597	Ceramic Koniag	
Monashka Bay (Kodiak Islands)				Stuckenrath, Coe, and Ralph 1966
P-1049	298 ± 44	A.D. 1652	Aceramic Koniag, middle	
Kizhuyak, site No. 240 Anton Larsen Bay (Kodiak Islands)				Oeschger, Riesen, and Lerman 1970
144 B-835	600 ± 100	A.D. 1350	Aceramic Koniag, base	

Table 1. Selected Chronology of Radiocarbon Dates, Pacific Area (Continued)

Laboratory Number	Age and Date		Applies to	Sources
Merrill site (Ken 029) Kenai River (Cook Inlet)				Rutherford, Wittenberg, and Wilmeth 1981
S-1040	2560 ± 300	610 B.C.	Uppermost layer	
S-1041	2250 ± 120	300 B.C.	Lowest layer, Kachemak II/ Norton culture affinities	
Moose River site (Ken 043) Kenai River area (Cook Inlet)				R.G. Dixon 1980; cf. Reger 1981
GX-5039	1515 ± 125	A.D. 435	Eskimoid culture, generalized Kachemak III, House 1	
WSU-1888	1495 ± 70	A.D. 455	Eskimoid culture, generalized Kachemak III, House 1	
Beluga Point North (ANC 054) Turnagain Arm (Cook Inlet)				Reger 1981
GX-4409	790 ± 120	A.D. 1160	Component III, Generalized Pacific Eskimo	
WSU-1887	650 ± 70	A.D. 1300	Component III, Generalized Pacific Eskimo	

NOTE: Two corrections may be applied. Dates on charred oil residues (P-1041, B-835) generally are found to be older than dates obtained on wood charcoal, but there is no agreement on the correction to be applied.

Ralph, Michael, and Han (1973) provide a schedule for converting radiocarbon dates to "true" age, which is necessitated by the fact that the availability of the carbon 14 isotope has not been constant through time. The following approximate corrections may be applied to arrive at apparently true ages: Ocean Bay I, older range, add 800 years (900 years in the case of D1C-1236); Ocean Bay I, younger range, add 700 years; Ocean Bay II, oldest Takli Birch, add 600 years; Takli Birch (1520 B.C.), add 400 years; Old Kiavak, add 300 years; Kachemak II or sub-III (790 B.C.), add 150–200 years; Merrill site, Kenai River, add 100 years; Kachemak III, Three Saints, Takli Cottonwood, Cottonwood Creek, Kukak Beach phase, Yukon Fox Farm Bluff, Kukak Mound phase, early Koniag phase, generally 100 B.C. to A.D. 1350, proposed adjustment less than 50 years, generally to a younger age; Middle and late Koniag phase (A.D. 1500–1700), adjustment variable and in some cases inconclusive, generally add 50–140 years.

nium) and succeeding second millennium coastal cultures of northwestern Alaska.

Whether this amount of change with its influx of Bering Sea ideas, and presumably people, can be accommodated within the Kachemak tradition, or whether it is the beginning of a pronounced change in language, ethnic identity, and material culture remains to be determined. Events of the next 800 years preceding historic contact, during which the Kenai Peninsula branch of Pacific Eskimo attained their historic configuration and the greater part of Cook Inlet was occupied by Tanaina Indians, are poorly documented by a number of small undated collections that are subject to various interpretations.

Events Leading to the Modern Pacific Eskimo

The last centuries of the first millenium A.D. were ones of fusion of Bering Sea and Pacific ideas, undoubtedly coupled with ongoing development. In most areas cultural continuity is evident though some immigration is probable. This period is significant to the ethnogenesis of the historically known Pacific Eskimo, although additional events taking place over the next several centuries lead more directly into the later prehistory of the region.

Heretofore, northerly influences on the Pacific coast have been seen as arising from Norton culture, which

was thriving only a few miles away inland on the Alaska Peninsula (Dumond 1971a; Henn 1978), but any later follow-through cannot be identified with Norton, perhaps because Norton itself ceases to exist as a distinct congeries of tool types and technology around A.D. 1000. But soon so too does the Kachemak tradition. The former case, and perhaps both, involve one of the broader trends in Arctic prehistory commonly designated as the spread of Thule culture although the term Neo-Eskimo also is appropriate (see "Prehistory: Summary," this vol.). A better understanding of the specific mechanisms that account for the spread of these trends may be seen from the analysis of local events.

In Prince William Sound, unlike other parts of the Pacific area, there appears to have been continuity with change across the A.D. 1000 temporal boundary. There was little or no influence from the Bering Sea region and none that is expressed in the stone artifacts, which include items such as heavy grooved splitting adzes accompanying native copper points. However, data from that area are poorly suited to answer these questions inasmuch as occupation of Palugvik, the principal excavated site, ended at some unestablished date possibly well before contact, and the ethnic attribution of this site cannot be certain.

The outer Cook Inlet sequence after A.D. 1000 also is poorly known, but judging from the sparsity of ceramics and Norton-type implements in various undated

a–b, after Clark 1970a:figs. 2–3; c, after Heizer 1947.
Fig. 10. Rock art probably of the Koniag phase. a, Group of petroglyphs near Afognak village, Kodiak area, Alaska; b, individual petroglyphs found at Marka Bay, Afognak I.; c, individual petroglyphs from Cape Alitak, Kodiak I. a, Width about 91.0 cm; b same scale; c not to scale.

collections of late appearance it is doubtful if the Yukon Fox Farm Bluff culture persisted. It is thus pertinent to note that the introduction of pottery into another late Kachemak tradition settlement, Crag Point, on the northern part of Kodiak Island also failed to persist. As was the case at Kachemak Bay (Fox Farm Bluff) there appears to have been an assimilation and eventual partial rejection of northern influence. The appearance of distinctive Pacific styles of ground slate implements and of gravel-tempered pottery in the A.D. 1050 Iz-embek phase of the outer Alaska Peninsula presents yet another example of the outward dissemination of ideas, followed by the rejection of certain elements, ceramics in particular. On the southern part of Kodiak,

however, the introduction of ceramics, probably at a later date, was an outstanding success.

These developments underscore a period of change underlying the formation of the historic Pacific Eskimo whose ancestors may have been present on the Alaska Peninsula in the Kukak Mound phase, commencing about A.D. 1100, and on Kodiak in the Koniag phase. In most respects the Kukak Mound phase and the Koniag phase are identical, and both are closely related to the Brooks River Camp phase in the Naknek drainage on the other side of the peninsula, which also begins about A.D. 1100 (Dumond 1964, 1971a), and the Ugashik River phase of the same region (Henn 1978). The Kukak Mound and tentatively the Brooks River Camp and River phases are interpreted as local facies of the Koniag phase, with a moderate degree of precedence that provides time slope to any northwest-southeast diffusion model. Specific similarities are seen in ground slate points and knives, labret styles, planing adzes, nontoggling harpoon dart heads, and gravel-tempered ceramics. Tying these phases together places Kodiak, the Pacific side of the Alaska Peninsula, and the Bering sea drainage in a single historical context that bridges two major components of the Eskimo community.

The inception of these phases perhaps culminates in the unsettling events of the centuries immediately preceding though technologically they represent new directions or reversals. Change in the Naknek drainage between the Brooks River Camp phase and its antecedent there was rapid "representing something of a technological revolution" (Dumond 1971a:19), though not completely abrupt and without transition. This entailed both replacement of flaked implements with ones of ground slate and a change to thick gravel-tempered pottery. Ceramics changed similarly in the Kukak Beach phase on Shelikof Strait as also did lithic tools. These changes are explained primarily through Thule culture influence from the north. Recognition of Thule influence is complicated by the fact that whereas Thule stone technology is distinct from Norton, it differed little from the ground slate industry already extant in the Pacific area.

A long series of events and the ongoing operation of cultural processes tending to obliterate cultural differences is involved in the formation of the Pacific Eskimo and their neighbors. The Norton influences and possible migrations of the late first millennium of the Christian era, the subsequent Thule-influenced transformation on the Alaska Peninsula at the beginning of the second millennium, or ongoing local development cannot explain fully the later prehistoric and ethnographic cultures of the region. Ethnographically and archeologically, there also is an impressive body of material and nonmaterial culture with a distinctive North Pacific cast variously shared by the Pacific Eskimo, Aleut, and Eyak and other Northwest Coast peoples. This includes mum-

after DeLaguna 1934:pls. 64–66, 68, 1956:figs. 22–23.

Fig. 11. Rock paintings in hematite pigment (perhaps mixed with fat). a–f, Tuxedni Bay, Cook Inlet, Alaska; a group in a single line: a, swan; b, killer whale; c, man in kayak; d, man; e, umiak; f, man. g–k, Bear Island, Cook Inlet, unrelated figures: g, woman; h, kid or faun; i, seal and young seal; j, wounded sea mammal; k, sea mammal wounded with bladder dart. l, Sadie Cove, Cook Inlet, group of blackfish whales and conventionalized animals. m–o, Hawkins I., Prince William Sound, Alaska, unrelated figures on a cliff: m, headless man; n, cross; o, face. p–q, Hawkins I., unrelated figures from wall of burial cave: p, whale; q, conventionalized figure. Entire length of l, about 20.5 cm; rest same scale.

mification, petroglyphs (fig. 10), rock painting (fig. 11), certain types of cradles, types of mauls, grooved splitting adzes and other woodworking tools, an incised slate figurine ritual, lance or dart whaling ostensibly with aconite poison, deep saltwater fishing equipment, and a fondness for the vapor sweatbath in which water was dashed over rocks. To illustrate late prehistoric events more fully, the Koniag phase, as found on Kodiak, is liberally interpreted below.

Kodiak had active lines of communication to the southern Bering Sea area as well as northeast to Cook Inlet and Prince William Sound. Contact consisted of trading partnerships, exchange festivals, intermarriage, and raids. Strong influences and settlers, at Crag Point, from the Bering Sea via the mainland near A.D. 1000 were assimilated on northern Kodiak without permanently altering the late Kachemak technology and culture there. But Kodiak continued to be subject to pressure through several channels of communication. People, probably from Cook Inlet and areas farther east, were moving in on their host villages, family by family, first to Afognak, then to Kodiak proper. It is difficult to say who assimilated whom, but the unelaborated material culture of the newcomers, who brought new kinds of activities, prevailed by A.D. 1100–1200. The vapor sweatbath became very popular, wood was split with heavy grooved splitting adzes (Clark 1974), and for one

of their rituals people made and discarded numerous incised slate figurines (fig. 12) (Clark 1974; Heizer 1952a).

Clark 1964:figs. 2, 4.

Fig. 12. Early Koniag phase incised tablets, Monashka Bay site, Kodiak I., Alaska. left, Length about 15 cm; rest same scale.

U. of Wis., Madison: a, Kod 418:no number; b, Kod 418:c9 – ½.1, c9-½.2; c, Kod 403:3SB-3/TP 1.1.1; d, Kod 403:3SB-C/c-1; e, Kod 403:3SB-3/c-2; f, 122.3.

Fig. 13. Koniag phase from Kodiak I., Alaska. a, labret, probably simulating a tooth; b, late Koniag phase ground slate projectile points (found in association). Protohistoric or historic Koniag: c, abrasive stone, also characteristic of other phases; d, (human?) ribs inserted through vertebrae, a phenomenon widespread in sites of Thule and Thule-related or influenced cultures; e, ulu blade, large elongate form characteristic of phase; f, splitting adz from Little Afognak. g–h, Ceramic pots from Rolling Bay: g, Koniag phase ceramic variant; h, in situ with stone slab cover. Length of a, 3.2 cm; length of c, 7.8 cm, b, d–f same scale.

Hunters pecked figures of whales, human faces, and various other designs into rock exposures (Heizer 1947; Clark 1970a); and elsewhere they painted pictographs (De Laguna 1934:149–154, 1956).

Similarly, but perhaps somewhat later, on southwestern Kodiak families were moving in from the Alaska Peninsula. Some stayed on the Pacific side of the peninsula where they had kinspeople, but others went on to Kodiak in such numbers that they were able to introduce new practices like pottery making (fig. 13g–h), which in the north had been introduced a few centuries earlier but was given up. They amalgamated with the recently modified local base to form the ceramic facies of Koniag culture about A.D. 1200–1500 (poorly dated). In doing so they only partially accepted or later lost interest in some practices recently introduced from the northeast, like the incised figurine ritual. Conversely, the northern half of Kodiak (and the Chugach too) remained aceramic. Through succeeding centuries many additional developments appeared in Koniag culture, but the hybrid development on antecedent base may be reflected in subdialect level differences in speech existing at the time of European contact in 1761 (Davydov 1977:147). Continuing interaction, respectively, with differing parts of the Pacific area and mobility across the Alaska Peninsula probably also has helped to maintain diversity.

To recapitulate, the Koniag phase, and in general the Pacific Eskimo, is neither an in situ development nor a direct result of a population and cultural replacement; rather it is an amalgamation of old and new elements and replacement or loss of numerous former traits during the course of several centuries, accompanied by population mobility. As seen from the Pacific, a salient feature of this period is the introduction or updating of some elements of Bering Sea Eskimo culture, including the Pacific dialects of Yupik Eskimo speech (see Dumond 1965), but these form only one component of Pacific Eskimo culture.

Exploration and Contact History of Western Alaska

JAMES W. VANSTONE

Early Exploration and Trade

Before the end of the sixteenth century, Russian fur traders had crossed the Urals and during the next 40 years gradually extended their operations eastward across northern Asia. In 1648 a party of Cossacks, traders, and hunters under the leadership of Semën Dezhnev sailed from the Kolyma River, which flows into the Arctic Ocean, to the mouth of the Anadyr´ River on the Pacific coast thus becoming the first Europeans to sail through the strait separating northeastern Asia from northwestern America (fig. 1) (Fisher 1981).

In Saint Petersburg Tsar Peter the Great realized the potential importance of establishing trade relations with the inhabitants of northwestern America. He ordered the organization of an expedition that was directed to extend the explorations of the Cossack navigators and to go from Kamchatka to America to reconnoiter the coast (Fisher 1977:152). The command of this expedition was given to Vitus Bering, a Dane and fleet captain in the Russian navy. In July 1728, after constructing a vessel at Nizhne-Kamchatsk on the Kamchatka River, he sailed northward in two small vessels along the coast of Siberia as far as Cape Dezhnev. Having passed through the strait that now bears his name, he returned to Okhotsk without having sighted the American continent (Golder 1922–1925, 1:6–20; Fisher 1977:80–107).

In spite of its modest achievements, the interest aroused by Bering's first voyage led to the organization of a second expedition, the purpose of which was to establish Russian sovereignty in northwestern America so that fur and mineral resources could be exploited (Fisher 1977:152). In June 1741 this expedition sailed from Kamchatka in two vessels commanded by Bering and Aleksei Chirikov. The ships soon separated and on July 18 (Old Style) Bering sighted the American coast. A few days later a landing was made on Kayak Island. Human habitations were observed, but no natives were encountered. The ship was eventually wrecked on Bering Island and many members of the crew, including Bering, died during the winter. The survivors built a

small vessel from the wreckage and returned to Kamchatka the following summer.

Chirikov, meanwhile, sighted the American continent near Cross Sound on July 15 (Old Style). An attempt to land resulted in the loss of two boats and the death of nearly one-third of his crew, apparently at the hands of the Tlingit Indians. The navigator hastily returned to Kamchatka, sighting a few of the Aleutian Islands during his voyage (Golder 1922–1925, 1; Fisher 1977:147–150).

Although Bering's explorations failed to establish Russian sovereignty, fur hunters began to exploit those areas of the north Pacific where fabulous riches in furs had been reported. These hardy Siberians, known as promyshlenniki, reached the Commander Islands within two years after the return of Bering's party. Subsequently they succeeded in pushing their way eastward along the Aleutian chain to the mainland of Alaska (Masterson and Brower 1948).

Some of these fur hunters reached Kodiak Island as early as 1762, by which time it was already apparent that foxes, sea otters, and other furbearers were becoming scarce in the Aleutians. Because the hunting and trading voyages were growing less profitable, it was necessary to look toward the northeast for new areas to exploit. Up to this time, fur gathering had been in the hands of individual entrepreneurs or a few small companies. Then in 1781 a well-organized company of eastern Siberian merchants was formed to exploit the American fur trade. The leader of this new organization was Grigorii Shelikhov, an Irkutsk merchant who, in 1784, supervised the establishment of a small colony at Three Saints Bay near the southwestern end of Kodiak Island. From there the Shelikhov Company extended its trading operations to the neighboring islands and mainland.

In 1792 Aleksandr Baranov was appointed chief director of the company's American interests, a post that he held for 25 years. Virtually alone, he developed the company to the point where it was able to overcome its rivals for control of the fur trade and become established, under the name of the Russian-American Com-

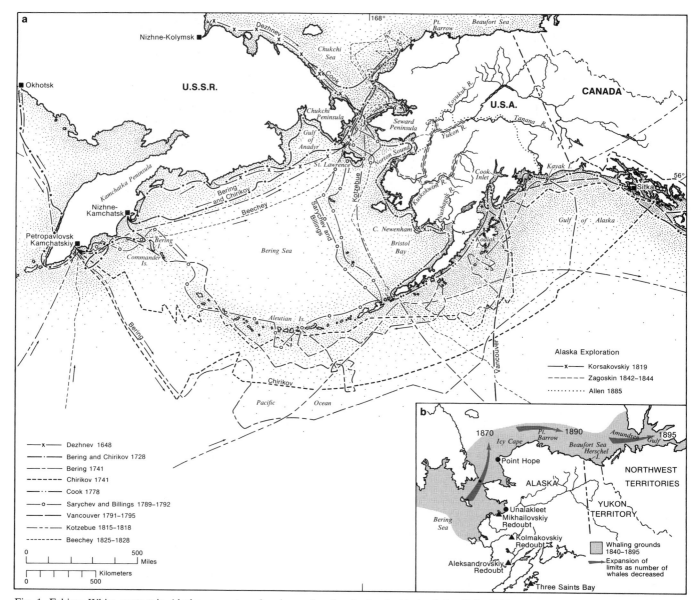

Fig. 1. Eskimo-White contact in Alaska: a, routes of major exploration in Arctic Alaska (after Friis 1967; Zagoskin 1967; Federova 1973; Brooks 1953; Beechey 1832); b, whaling activity (after John R. Bockstoce, communication to editors 1983) and major fur trade posts.

pany, as a state monopoly by imperial decree in 1799 (Tikhmenev 1978:41–61).

Exploration of Southwestern Alaska

By the time Baranov was relieved of his duties in 1818, Russia's North American domain extended from the Aleutian Islands down the coast of southeastern Alaska to Sitka. He moved his headquarters from Kodiak Island to Sitka in 1800 and this small settlement became the capital of Russian Alaska. Although the Russians were familiar with the coastal areas in this region, virtually nothing was known of the coast or interior to the north. Early in the nineteenth century, as the number of fur-bearing animals continued to decline in the traditionally exploited areas, the Russian-American Com-

pany was forced to turn its attention to the vast area of southwestern Alaska north of the Alaska Peninsula. This was an unknown region in which it was hoped that new profits could be reaped through trade with the Eskimo inhabitants for beaver pelts.

In 1818 and 1819 expeditions under the direction of Pëtr Korsakovskiy were dispatched to explore the region to the north of Bristol Bay. The primary aim of these expeditions was to establish a redoubt at the mouth of the Nushagak River, the major river flowing into Bristol Bay, that would serve as a departure point for explorations into the interior of southwestern Alaska. An exploration of the Kuskokwim River was also planned, but it was abandoned. In 1819 Korsakovskiy established the small post, called Aleksandrovskiy Redoubt, which was left in the charge of Fëdor Kolmakov, an energetic creole trader who quickly established trade relations with Eskimos living in the vicinity (Berkh 1823:46–49; Fedorova 1973:68–69). As a result of this expedition and the efforts of Kolmakov, the Russian-American Company learned that beaver were plentiful in the area, the native inhabitants friendly, and most important of all, the region was drained by a number of rivers that would make penetration of the interior relatively easy. At the same time, Eskimos of the interior had easy access to coastal trading posts. Aleksandrovskiy Redoubt seemed ideally situated to attract Eskimos with furs and to serve as a point of departure for explorations and trading parties into the interior.

Although the Korsakovskiy expedition reached the mouth of the Kuskokwim River in 1819, coastal explorations of southwestern Alaska did not really begin until the following year. Then both the imperial government and the Russian-American Company sponsored expeditions to survey the coast between Bristol Bay and Norton Sound. Indeed, the government expedition, under the command of Capt. Lt. Mikhail N. Vasiliev and Gleb Shishmaref, was directed to survey the northern coasts and at the same time to look for the fabled Northwest Passage. The company expedition, under the command of Vasilii Khromchenko and Adolph K. Etolin, did not begin until 1821. In that year and the following, extensive surveys were made along the coast between Cape Newenham and Norton Bay (Berkh 1823a:45–58). Vasiliev's expedition (Berkh 1823a:1–21) added little to data obtained by Capt. James Cook 40 years earlier, but Khromchenko and Etolin made contacts with Eskimos all along the coast (Khromchenko 1824; Van-Stone 1973). These contacts provided a foundation for trade relations that later proved extremely profitable to the company.

In fact, it is no exaggeration to state that the explorations of the Korsakovskiy expeditions and the two voyages of Khromchenko and Etolin laid the groundwork for the opening up of all southwestern Alaska to the fur trade. They were followed by the interior explorations of Ivan Ya. Vasil´ev and Fëdor Kolmakov between 1829 and 1832, which brought the Eskimos of the Nushagak and Kuskokwim rivers within the sphere of influence of Aleksandrovskiy Redoubt. In 1832 Kolmakov established the redoubt on the middle Kuskokwim that was later to bear his name. In 1833 Mikhailovskiy Redoubt was constructed opposite Stuart Island and the way was open for Russian penetration of the Yukon the following year (Russian-American Company Records 1818–1865, 6(244):folios 478, 482, 7(257):folio 269; Tikhmenev 1978:180–181; Zagoskin 1967:79–81, 252).

These activities led to the finest achievement of exploration by Russians in Alaska: that of Lt. Lavrentii Zagoskin in 1842–1844. Zagoskin was commissioned by the Russian-American Company to ascertain how

British Mus.: 1929–12–18–1.

Fig. 2. Carved wooden mask painted red and black. Length 23.0 cm. Collected (probably at Unalaska, Black 1982a:34) by Otto von Kotzebue, leader of a Russian voyage seeking an entrance to a Northwest Passage, 1816–1817.

the trade of the middle Yukon could be channeled to the company rather than to Seward Peninsula and, through Eskimo middlemen, across Bering Strait to the Chukchi. In carrying out this task, he explored the Yukon almost to the mouth of the Tanana, as well as much

Peabody Mus., Salem, Mass.: E 3662.

Fig. 3. Seal gut garments. Material acquired by sea captains on the Alaska coast was often traded far and wide. This finely decorated cape, parka, and pants are probably Aleut, but they were presented to Capt. Thomas Meek in 1817 by King Kamehameha I of the Hawaiian Is., to whom they were undoubtedly given by another captain involved in the triangular trade among Alaska, Hawaii, and China. Length of cape 144.0 cm.

151

of the Kuskokwim and Koyukuk rivers. His excellent report contains much valuable information on the Indians and Eskimos with whom he came in contact and on the fur trade in general (Zagoskin 1967).

East of the areas visited by Zagoskin, the American explorer Lt. Henry T. Allen made an equally impressive reconnaissance in the spring and summer of 1885. Ascending the Copper River and crossing the divide to the valley of the upper Tanana, Allen descended that river to its junction with the Yukon and then proceeded downstream, reaching Saint Michael (Mikhailovskiy Redoubt) in late August (Allen 1887). This journey was the first to pass from the Prince William Sound country directly to the Yukon. Although Allen's explorations were almost entirely in areas occupied by Indians rather than Eskimos, like Zagoskin's journey, his also demonstrated the extensive interaction of native peoples in interior Alaska.

Exploration of Northern Alaska

The exploration of southwestern Alaska was, for the most part, directly related to the expansion of the fur trade. It is undoubtedly also true, however, that in response to the political pressures created as a result of explorations in the north Pacific conducted by other nations, the Russians felt compelled to extend their influence into regions with which they had not been traditionally associated.

The most extensive of these non-Russian explorations of Alaska during the Russian period was, of course, that of Capt. James Cook, who in 1776–1780 explored the coast between Bristol Bay and Icy Cape on the third and last of his great voyages. The map of Alaska as we know it today first began to take shape as a result of Cook's thorough exploration of the coastline (Cook and King 1784). Almost equally skillful from the standpoint of navigation was the careful examination of the coast of southeastern Alaska north to Cook Inlet by Capt. George Vancouver in 1790–1795 (Vancouver 1798). It is little wonder that with professional seamanship of this order exhibited within their area of influence, the Russians were concerned with emphasizing their claim to all Alaska. Thus, Capt. Otto von Kotzebue explored the sound that bears his name in 1815 (Kotzebue 1821), M.N. Vasiliev and Shishmaref, on their voyage (undertaken, significantly, for the imperial government rather than the Russian-American Company) reached almost to Icy Cape in 1820 (Berkh 1823a:1–21), while Khromchenko and Etolin surveyed Golovnin Bay and parts of Norton Sound in 1822 (Khromchenko 1824; VanStone 1973).

In 1823 Capt. Frederick W. Beechey of the British Royal Navy attempted to work his way east along the arctic coast but was frustrated by ice not far beyond the farthest north reached by Captain Cook. However,

members of his crew did reach Point Barrow in the ship's boat, the first Europeans to do so, in 1826 (Beechey 1832). Not long afterward the Russians also made an attempt to explore the northern coast when a party led by Aleksandr Kashevarov, traveling in Eskimo skin boats, reached a point 30 miles east of Point Barrow in 1838 (Kashevarov 1879; VanStone 1977).

Penetration of the interior of northwest Alaska, contrary to the situation in the southwestern region, hardly occurred at all during the Russian period. Much of interior Seward Peninsula was explored in connection with the various gold discoveries in the late nineteenth and early twentieth centuries, while the United States Navy and Department of the Treasury Revenue Marine were responsible for explorations of the rivers flowing into Kotzebue Sound in the 1880s (Healy 1887, 1889; Hooper 1881; Stoney 1900; Sherwood 1965:119–132). The extensive northern interior received some attention as a by-product of coastal whaling activity at the turn of the

Fig. 4. Drawing of early dress styles. On the left is depicted an Aleut wearing a hooded waterproof hunting shirt and wooden hat. Around his neck is an embroidered gutskin bag for small implements. The man on the right is a Koniag Eskimo wearing a ceremonial hat and a parka of cormorant skins trimmed with fur strips. Detail of watercolor (in private collection), probably by Alexander Postels, artist with the Theodor Lütke (F.P. Litke) Expedition, 1826–1829.

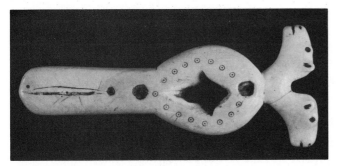

British Mus.: 1376.

Fig. 5. Implement used to straighten the wooden shafts of hunter's arrows. Caribou are often depicted on such tools; here there are 2 caribou heads, plus decoration of beads and incised circle and dot motif. Length 14.0 cm; collected by F.W. Beechey in northern Alaska, 1826–1827.

Gonzaga U., Crosby Lib., Spokane, Wash.: Oreg. Prov. Arch. Coll.

Fig. 6. Children in the Roman Catholic mission at Akulurak in the Yukon-Kuskokwim delta at the time of their first communion. Photograph possibly by Jules Jetté, about 1900–1915.

century, but it remained for the U.S. Geological Survey to carry out thorough investigations after 1900 (Schrader 1904; Smith and Mertie 1930; Sherwood 1965:169–186).

In summary, by the middle of the nineteenth century, much of southwestern Alaska had at least been roughly mapped and the inhabitants brought within the orbit of various coastal and interior trading posts. In northwestern Alaska, although the basic coastal explorations took place somewhat earlier, the interior regions remained virtually unexplored until the end of the century. At the same time, the rationale for exploration along the northern coasts was quite different from that which motivated those Russians who penetrated the interior river systems between Bristol Bay and the Yukon River. Cook and Kotzebue were concerned primarily with increasing geographical knowledge or, particularly in the case of Kotzebue, geopolitical maneuvering. Beechey's accomplishments were associated with Sir John Franklin's explorations of the Mackenzie River. These prominent navigators, along with the later English and American explorers involved in the search for Franklin's third expedition, affected the Eskimo population only slightly. In fact they appear to have had little or no interest in the local inhabitants aside from the possibility that they could supply information, food, and water.

Missionary Activities

With reference to missionary activity throughout Eskimo Alaska, it is possible to note a significant discrepancy between southwestern and northwestern Alaska, as to both time and intensity of contact. In most of southwestern Alaska, Russian Orthodox missionaries followed closely on the heels of the trade-oriented explorers, and by the middle of the century all the Eskimos, with the possible exception of those in some Yukon Delta communities, had at least a superficial acquaintance with the Orthodox brand of Christianity.

In northwest Alaska, on the other hand, even those Eskimos in the relatively accessible coastal villages were almost completely unacquainted with Christianity until Congregational, Episcopal, and Presbyterian missionaries contacted them at the end of the nineteenth century. It is likely, however, that in this area missionaries had a greater initial impact because they frequently opened schools and offered medical services along with their missionary activities (VanStone 1964). Because the villages of northern Alaska were less scattered than those along the river systems and coast of the southwestern area, missionaries could reach a greater proportion of the population more regularly and thus more effectively. The northern missionary did not have to travel extensively; in fact, one factor in the depopulation of the northern interior was the existence of well-established mission stations in the coastal communities. The Orthodox missionaries, and later the Moravians and churchmen of other denominations in southwestern Alaska, usually lived in the coastal trading centers and had to travel frequently and far if they wished to see all their scattered and highly mobile parishioners. Even under the best of circumstances, they were seldom able to visit individual villages more than twice a year (DRHA 2:144). Therefore, they could not possibly achieve the same intensity of exposure as missionaries living permanently in the large, sedentary coastal villages of the north.

In both areas at least the superficial aspects of Christian ritual and belief were rapidly accepted, perhaps because the time was propitious for all kinds of changes as the Eskimos were increasingly drawn into a trapping-trading economy (Oswalt 1963a:153–154; VanStone 1964; Ray 1975:250–251). It is probably true, then, that although missionary activity began somewhat earlier in the southwest and the missionaries played a vital and lasting role as agents of change during most of the nine-

Glenbow-Alberta Inst., Calgary, Alta.: ND–1–1337A.

Fig. 7. Lavinia Wallace Young Mission for Eskimos at Nome, known as the "Eskimo Church," established in 1911–1912 by the Methodists and active at least into the 1940s. Photograph by the Lomen Brothers, probably Easter Sunday, 1917.

teenth century, the end result in the two regions is roughly comparable because of the more intensive relations between Eskimos and their spiritual advisors in the north. An interesting fact is that in both areas, denominations making the original conversions have continued to receive major support from the people in spite of attempts by later church groups to dislodge them. This situation is particularly remarkable in southwestern Alaska where the Russian Orthodox Church enjoys wide support despite rudimentary organization and scarcity of trained clergy.

Economic Activities

Fur Trade

The Russian-American Company was established in southwestern Alaska by the second decade of the nineteenth century, and within 30 years most of the region had been opened to the fur trade. The relatively small number of individuals who carried out this expansion appear to have established their role among the people with caution. Company traders had no force to back up their position and thus could not afford to oppress the people as they had been able to do in the Aleutians and throughout southeastern Alaska.

From unpublished records of the Russian-American Company it is possible to extract some information concerning the methods by which the company post managers throughout southwestern Alaska dealt with the

Eskimos for furs. When new contacts were established with remote villages, an attempt was made to identify the community leaders, who were then appointed toions by the Russians (Russian *toĭon*) (vol. 6:631). Those individuals were given silver medals; the post managers were supposed to keep a close account of the medals distributed and even to try to retrieve them from the families of toions who died so that they might be awarded once again. The toions were supposed to be individuals held in respect by the people and whose friendly relations with the Russians would be of definite benefit to the company. They encouraged their fellow villagers to hunt and to bring their furs to the redoubt, or they collected furs for delivery to a representative of the company when he visited the settlement to trade (Russian-American Company Records 1818–1865, 8(322):folio 247, 9(460):folio 350, 16(467):folios 178–179, 17(387):folios 370–371).

It is doubtful whether the toions ever actually had as much power and authority in their communities as company officials may have believed. Nevertheless, in one way or another, a faithful toion could encourage the hunters in his village to expend more energy in the company's behalf than they might otherwise have been inclined to do.

Although specific documentation is lacking it can be assumed that the Eskimos of southwestern Alaska, as elsewhere throughout the history of the North American fur trade, were encouraged to become indebted to the Russian-American Company since the more closely trappers were bound to the company, the more they relied on the trader for supplies and items of European manufacture, and the less likely they were to pursue vigorously traditional subsistence activities. The company thus assumed a paternal role not only by controlling the goods that the Eskimos could obtain, but also by carefully regulating how much they were to receive. The purchase of Alaska by the United States in 1867 probably did not alter the basic relationship between Eskimos and traders, although the number and variety of trade goods entering the region were greatly increased.

In northwest Alaska, the Eskimos had access to trade goods at a much earlier date than in the southwestern region. By the middle of the seventeenth century, the Russians had penetrated northeastern Siberia, and European goods began to flow into Alaska from the Chukchi and the Siberian Eskimo by way of inhabitants of the Diomede Islands and settlements on Seward Peninsula. As early as the beginning of the eighteenth century the people of Sledge Island, the Diomedes, and Cape Prince of Wales became the middlemen of this intercontinental trade. Trading centers, such as the one at Hotham Inlet near the present village of Kotzebue, became important distribution centers not only for all of northwestern Alaska but also for Eskimos in the

Yukon and Kuskokwim regions (Ray 1964:86, 1975:97–102). In fact, it was this trade that Zagoskin was sent to investigate in 1842–1844 (Zagoskin 1967:82). The Russians were concerned about the extent to which furs were being diverted from company posts to the middlemen of the Siberian trade.

Whaling and Fishing

After 1850, commercial whaling ships began to frequent the Arctic Ocean in large numbers every summer and from them the northern Eskimos first received trade goods in large quantities. The whalers, who were interested in obtaining baleen, traded for it with the Eskimos and also took large quantities with their own ships. Some Eskimos worked on these whaling vessels and also at shore-based whaling stations. Inhabitants in all the villages from Port Clarence to Point Barrow were eager to obtain trade goods and looked forward to the arrival of the whaling ships every spring. The people were paid in items such as flour, crackers, tobacco, matches, lead, firearms, ammunition, and molasses (VanStone 1958; Ray 1975:198–201).

Toward the end of the nineteenth century, when the demand for baleen began to fall off, some whaling vessels found it profitable to combine trading with whaling, and the first regularly established trade contacts with the settlements of northwest Alaska came about in this way. Thus traders were fixtures in some villages by the time whaling ended in the second decade of the twentieth century (VanStone 1960a:176).

It would be difficult to consider the history of contact and culture change throughout Eskimo Alaska without reference to the commercial salmon fishing industry that grew up in the Bristol Bay region after 1880 and almost immediately began to influence the Eskimo inhabitants of the area. Although Eskimos apparently

found little employment during the early years of the industry, the presence of the canneries and the large number of outsiders they attracted had a profound effect on the native inhabitants of Bristol Bay and eventually on those of all southwestern Alaska. As the canneries became established, flourished, declined, and were abandoned, they were directly responsible for population shifts and changes in subsistence patterns among the coastal and interior Eskimos of the bay area. To a lesser extent they effected similar changes among inhabitants of the Kuskokwim and Yukon river regions (VanStone 1967:63–82).

top, U. of Alaska Arch., Fairbanks: Bunnell Coll. 58-1026-2291; bottom, Muzeĭ Antropologii i Étnografii, Akademiĭa Nauk SSSR, Leningrad.
Fig. 8. Mikhailovskiy Redoubt, the trading post on Norton Sound east of the mouth of the Yukon River established by the Russian-American Company in 1833. From this post Russian fur traders explored the Yukon River and penetrated most of western and southwestern Alaska. top, Abandoned blockhouse of Mikhailovskiy Redoubt at St. Michael, photographed about 1900. bottom, Drawing by I.G. Voznesenskiĭ, 1843.

Smithsonian, Dept. of Anthr.: top, 48,519; bottom, 176,172.
Fig. 9. Engraved depictions on bow drill bows, showing whaling ships. European men are recognizable by their brimmed hats. top, Length of detail 10.7 cm, bottom same scale. Both collected by E.W. Nelson, top, Kotzebue Sound, Alaska; bottom, Golovnin Bay, Alaska, 1877–1881.

In some ways the fishing industry parallels the development of commercial whaling in the north. Both were seasonal activities and agents of intensive change; however, the differences are more significant. Commercial fishing represented an earlier introduction to true wage employment than any commercial development in the north, and no period of adjustment was required paralleling the one that was necessary in northwest Alaska after the decline in baleen prices brought an end to the whaling industry. The whalers were drawn to the Eskimo villages, and although a certain coalescence of population took place during the summer months as a result of the presence of whaling ships, no lasting changes in settlement pattern occurred. The population groupings in the 1970s along the northwest coast of Alaska were much the same as they were at the beginning of the contact period.

In a sense, therefore, whaling and commercial fishing represent attempts by the Eskimos of both areas to obtain trade goods through the barter of environmental products. Only in southwestern Alaska has this particular type of economic endeavor endured, and the economic history of the area has continued to be conditioned to a large degree by attempts on the part of both Eskimos and other residents to achieve a greater and more profitable role in the harvest of this renewable resource.

Mining

Beginning in the last decade of the nineteenth century, miners must be considered as significant agents of change in some areas of Alaska, even though most of their activities took place in regions occupied by Athapaskan Indians. In southwestern Alaska the number of known individuals who searched for minerals throughout much of the area was small, and they probably offered the Eskimos comparatively little in the way of trade goods. This statement does not apply to the Yukon River region, since that river was a major route to the gold fields of the Yukon Territory and there were a number of stampedes along its tributaries. The Eskimos of the lower Yukon experienced their first extensive contact with Euro-Americans as a result of heavy traffic through the area after 1885.

In northwest Alaska the influence of miners was also important although it is unlikely that they played a role comparable in any way to that of other agents of change. Persons hoping to reach the gold fields, particularly at Nome, went north on the whaling ships and then deserted in Eskimo villages (Ray 1975:245). Although some individuals spent a year or more in different communities, there is no indication that the knowledge of Euro-American material and social culture obtained by the Eskimos from these people in any way rivaled the influx of ideas and objects that were coming into villages from other sources, particularly the whaling ships. After 1940, however, many north Alaskan Eskimos obtained summer employment with mining companies involved in dredging operations near Fairbanks and Nome (VanStone 1962a:61).

Reindeer Herding

The Eskimos of southwestern Alaska participated only marginally in the reindeer-herding program instituted by the Bureau of Education in 1892 for the benefit of northern Eskimos who were suffering from the decline in sea mammals caused by unrestricted killing of whales, walrus, and seals. Largely through the efforts of Moravian missionaries, the Kuskokwim Eskimos became involved in the reindeer program as early as 1901, but they served mainly as hired herders. Although large herds were involved in the beginning, it is doubtful whether the effects of the herding program were either extensive or long lasting. The basic skills of close herding were never learned well by the Eskimos of the region, and the industry perished leaving very little visible effect on Eskimo life ("North Alaska Eskimo: Introduction," fig. 1, this vol.) (Jackson 1897:131–132; Oswalt 1963a:46–47).

Mus. of the Am. Ind., Heye Foundation, New York: 21/4677.
Fig. 10. Ivory model of a sailing ship made by Eskimos, probably for trade to whalers as were ivory pipes. Length 30.5 cm; collected at Point Barrow, Alaska, before 1949.

156

Fig. 11. Eskimos trading native goods for Euro-American material. top, Encounter with St. Lawrence I. Eskimos during the Frederick William Beechey Expedition, July 1826. In offering to trade nets, walrus ivory, skin shirts, harpoons, bows and arrows, small birds and skins, the Eskimos displayed a knowledge of trading practices. James Wolfe, Admiralty Mate, recorded that "The ship's side was lined with officers and men holding out tobacco, beads, buttons or whatever was thought likely to be acceptable exhibiting a variety of passions and feelings in their anxiety to procure the trinkets of these people, exceeding perhaps their eagerness for our wares" (Bockstoce 1977:104). center left, Natives from Provideniia Bay wearing rain parkas of seal intestines, trading with sailors on board the American ship *Bear* at Uélen. Photograph by Alfred M. Bailey, July 1921. center right, Bering Strait Eskimos trading with passengers on the steamer *Roanoke* bringing gold miners to Alaska. The kayak design indicates the Norton Sound region, possibly near St. Michael. Sleds tied to the kayak sterns are for pulling the vessels over the ice or along the beach. Photograph by Eric A. Hegg, probably 1897–1898. bottom, North Alaska Coast Eskimos in the store at Wainwright. The customer is receiving tobacco in exchange for a walrus tusk. Photograph by Alfred M. Bailey, 1921–1922.

EXPLORATION AND CONTACT HISTORY OF WESTERN ALASKA

In northwest Alaska the story was somewhat different, even though the program eventually failed there too. At Point Hope, for example, the reindeer herd served as the Eskimos' introduction to Euro-American economic methods. Deer were first introduced in 1908, and after 1926 all animals owned by individual villagers were counted into a single herd owned by a joint stock company. A board of directors elected from among the shareholders ran the herd and a store as well. In the late 1920s the store separated from the reindeer herd, probably because the store was much more successful. The tradition of a village-owned store persisted, however, and eventually it became affiliated with the Alaska Native Industries Cooperative Association and later still, a completely independent, village-owned store (VanStone 1962a:139–140). Unquestionably, the knowledge and skills gained through the operation of the reindeer company helped to prepare the Eskimos of Point Hope and other northern villages for a more sophisticated involvement in a new type of economic existence. This legacy has made the long-defunct reindeer-herding program a more significant agent of change in the north than in the south.

Educational Services

Although some educational facilities were available in southwestern Alaska earlier than in most other areas, relatively few individuals were in a position to take advantage of them. The Russian Orthodox Church provided some education for residents of the Russian-American Company's posts. A school was started at the company's redoubt on the Nushagak River as early as 1842, and the Moravians instructed Eskimo children as part of their mission work in the Nushagak region beginning in 1888 (Barsukov 1886–1888, 1:222, VanStone

1967:90–91). These endeavors had little effect on the Eskimos of the interior regions. Along the Kuskokwim and Yukon rivers inland penetration of educational facilities, particularly those associated with missions, took place somewhat earlier than along the Nushagak; but in all three regions it has been only since the 1930s that formal education played an important part in the life of young people. In northwest Alaska, on the other hand, education was firmly established in most villages by the first missionaries near the close of the nineteenth century, and government schools followed rapidly in the easily accessible coastal villages (VanStone 1962a:24–25). Because of this solid foundation and the continuity of educational services, education has been a vital acculturative factor and young people from northern villages are being drawn increasingly into the mainstream of American life by means of their involvement in formal education (Ray 1975:244–245). By 1960, virtually all graduates of the eight grades taught in the various village schools continued their education in regional high schools, schools in the larger Alaskan cities, or the government school at Mount Edgecumbe. By 1975 a growing number had enrolled in specialized training centers outside Alaska and were attending colleges and universities. Although this trend is also developing in the southern regions, it has tended to lag well behind similar developments in the north.

Medical Services

The extent to which medical services have been provided to the Eskimos of Alaska has varied considerably. In the north, some of the first missionaries were men who also had medical training, and they seem first to have gained the confidence of the people through their ability to cure illnesses and to free the Eskimos from

left, Gonzaga U., Crosby Lib., Spokane, Wash.: Oreg. Prov. Arch. Coll.; right, U. of Pa., U. Mus., Philadelphia.

Fig. 12. Schools. left, Girls learning beadwork in the Roman Catholic mission school at Akulurak in the Yukon-Kuskokwim delta. Photograph possibly by Jules Jetté, about 1900–1915. right, Bering Strait Eskimo children at the government school on Little Diomede I. At the left is Mena Delook, interpreter and assistant teacher. Photograph possibly by E.W. Hawkes about 1910.

their fear of shamans (VanStone 1962a:155). In the southwestern area, medical missionaries also played an important role (Schwalbe 1951:61–62). Although in both areas formal medical services sponsored by the government may have been introduced relatively late, they were able to build on the solid foundations laid by the earlier practitioners.

Since Alaskan Eskimos were continually exposed to virulent epidemics throughout the period of historic contact, evidence in all areas suggests that the long experience that the people have had with introduced European diseases has conditioned them to accept unusual forms of treatment for unusual diseases from outsiders, particularly in comparison to many other areas of the world. Disease causation and the basic tenets of preventative medicine may be understood no better in Alaska than they are in other marginal areas, but people are usually willing to accept professional help to at least the partial exclusion of local traditional remedies (VanStone 1962a:129–133, 1967:99–105; Ray 1975:178–179, 243–244).

Conclusion

Perhaps the most important single point to emerge from this comparative overview of the activities of agents of change throughout Eskimo Alaska is the significance of the early penetration of the interior by these agents in the southwestern region. At the time the whalers were establishing the first intensive contacts with Eskimos in northwest Alaska, the area between the mouth of the Yukon River and Bristol Bay was already open to the fur trade and to the influence of the Russian Orthodox Church. Because transportation between the coast and the interior was relatively easy in this region and game and furbearing animals continued to be plentiful, the interior was never depopulated and the communities there did not experience a marked decline as the coastal trading centers grew in importance. Of course the activities of the various agents of change had a profound effect on the subsistence pattern, and consequently on the settlement pattern throughout the region, but interior communities tended to coalesce or move within the interior setting. This pattern contrasts markedly with the situation in northwest Alaska where the entire arctic slope region was rapidly abandoned as a result of the intensive contacts established by agents of change in the coastal communities (Gubser 1965:23).

Yet in spite of the many differences affecting the pattern and rates of change through Eskimo Alaska north of the Alaska Peninsula, the end result does not reflect so many of these differences as might be expected. The acculturation level throughout the areas under discussion is remarkably uniform.

At the same time, it seems worthwhile to stress the difference with reference to one basic fact of life in the 1960s and 1970s: the extent to which Eskimos throughout Alaska were drawn into a wage economy and the effect this had on their traditional subsistence activities. Throughout their long history, the coastal villages of northwest Alaska have enjoyed the benefits of their location in one of the best sea mammal hunting areas in the world. Because of this almost complete dependence on sea mammals, subsistence activities in the coastal settlements closely reflect the movements of the sea ice and take on their characteristic cyclical pattern. A notable feature of this cycle has been the fact that the summer months, when the sea ice is absent from the vicinity of the villages, have always been a time of relative inactivity. Since employment opportunities in Alaska are, to a marked degree, confined to summer months, the people of the northern villages have been able to fit wage employment into the seasonal cycle at a time when the most jobs are available and when few traditional subsistence activities are possible. As a result, they have achieved considerable success in a combination of traditional subsistence activities and wage economies, which allows them to retain their aboriginal methods of obtaining food and at the same time satisfy material wants created by contact with the outside world (VanStone 1960a:190).

In southwestern Alaska the continuity between past and present is more noticeable. The Eskimos of this area, although affected to some extent by wage employment opportunities that have become available in the period since World War II, have remained closely connected to the trapping-trading economy and the seasonal commercial fishery. Commercial fishing also takes place during a time of the year that does not interfere with traditional subsistence activities, since subsistence fishing can be carried on at the same time as the commercial variety. Some areas of southwestern Alaska have adjusted successfully to the new conditions because their involvement in the commercial fishery has been marginal. In other areas, particularly in the Bristol Bay region, there has been more disruption. Changes in the settlement pattern near the close of the nineteenth century, together with a later depletion of the fur and game resources, have almost eliminated the aboriginal subsistence pattern. Increasing involvement of the people of this area in the commercial fishery has caused them to depend on their cash income earned during the summer, and a certain amount of subsistence fishing, to support themselves for the entire year. Thus both diversified hunting and trapping have suffered a marked decline (VanStone 1967:165–166).

The postcontact history of both northwest and southwest Alaska shows clearly for how long and to what extent the Eskimos have been heavily dependent on economic conditions that show little indication of long range stability. The northern Eskimos would seem to be in a slightly better position because of their continued strong commitment to traditional subsistence activities. In southwestern Alaska the Eskimos' increasing dependency on income earned through participation in the commercial fishery could in time lead to the same sort of economic insecurity that has been associated with a trapping-trading economy throughout the North American Arctic and Subarctic.

Aleut

MARGARET LANTIS

Language

The Aleut (ˈălē,ōōt) language is one of the two major branches of Eskimo-Aleut and is assumed to have been distinct from Eskimo by 1000 B.C. (Dumond 1965; Krauss 1980:7). There are Eastern and Western branches of Aleut. Of the two Western dialects of Aleut, Atkan was still being spoken by children on Atka in 1980, but Attuan was nearly extinct.* Other Western dialects were formerly spoken on the Andreanof and Rat islands. The Unalaska or Eastern dialect is spoken in the Fox Islands (fig. 1), on the Alaska Peninsula, and in the Shumagin, Sanak, and Pribilof island groups. School books have been published in the Eastern and Western dialects (Krauss 1980:42–43).

Territory and Environment

From the westernmost section of the Alaska Peninsula and the Shumagin Islands south of it, along the curving Aleutian chain to Attu, the last island east of the international date line, Aleut territory covers nearly 29 degrees of longitude. The international date line has been bent westward to accommodate the national and geographic integrity of the Aleutian chain. The geographically similar Bering and Copper islands, closer to Asia, that have remained in Russian possession, are considered "eastern," not "western" even though peopled partly by Aleuts brought there by the Russians. Modern Aleuts listening to their household radios can receive broadcasts from more Japanese and Russian stations than from North American ones, yet they are, as they always have been, soundly Alaskan.

Environmental conditions in Aleut territory are remarkably uniform. Absent are permafrost, ocean ice except in Izembek Lagoon and Cold Bay on the Alaska Peninsula, and trees, although there is strong growth of grasses and flowers. A broken coastline is protected by reefs and islets except where cliffs dip straight into the sea. Earthquakes and hot springs show evidence of an unstable crustal zone. Temperatures remain moderate, but sudden fierce storms, fog, and rain are common. There is abundant marine life. Although the mountains at the east end of Aleut territory are higher than those in the west, for example, the difference between 4,000 or 6,000 and 8,000 feet has not mattered for people whose lives are spent at sea level. Depth of the sea does matter, however. Because the cold waters and winds of the relatively shallow Bering Sea meet the warm water and air of the Japan Current as it crosses the north Pacific above the extremely deep Aleutian Trench, either air turbulence or fog is brewed at all seasons, and the tide waters moving through narrow straits between some of the islands become mountainous riptides. Life in such a situation, dependent on only local resources, required special adaptation, producing from a general Eskimo base the Aleut culture.

There is uncertainty regarding the eastern boundary of Aleut culture in prehistoric and historic times. From the archeological evidence, McCartney (1969) thinks that along the north side of the Alaska Peninsula there was a zone of mixed Aleut-Eskimo culture and speculates that the people probably were bilingual. Most students think that the boundary at European contact was, as later, across the Peninsula where it narrows between Port Moller on the north side and Stepovak Bay on the south side (cf. Dumond 1974:1, 7).

East of the Peninsula, many Pacific Eskimos have accepted for perhaps three generations the Aleut designation extended to them by the Russians. This is true

*The phonemes of Atkan Aleut are: (voiceless stops and affricate) t, č, k, q; (voiced fricatives) δ, z (between [z] and [ž]), γ, γ̇; (voiceless fricatives) s (between [s] and [š]), x, x̣; (voiced nasals) m, n, ŋ; (voiceless preaspirated nasals) M, N, N̦; (voiced liquid) l; (voiceless preaspirated liquid) ł; (voiced glides) w, y; (voiceless aspirate or preaspirated glides) W, Y, h; (short vowels) i, a, u; (long vowels) i·, a·, u·. In addition, loanwords have p, b, d, g, v, f, ř (a retroflex trill or English-type r), and the vowels e, e·, o, and o·.

The Attuan variety of Western Aleut differs from Atkan in having an additional affricate č̣ and a native v, and in lacking z and W. Eastern Aleut differs from Atkan in lacking z and the voiceless glides (W, Y, h), and in lacking all the voiceless preaspirates except in the oldest speakers (Michael E. Krauss, communication to editors 1982).

In the practical orthography used by the Alaska Native Language Center and others (based on the earlier Aleut Cyrillic alphabet, in which there was widespread literacy) the native Atkan Aleut phonemes are written: t, ch, k, q; d, z, ĝ; s, x, x̂; m, n, ng; hm, hn, hng; l; hl; w, y; hw, hy, h; i, a, u; ii, aa, uu. The phonemes appearing in loans are written: p, b, d, g, v, f, r; e, ee, o, oo.

Information on Aleut phonology and the phonemic transcription of Aleut words were obtained from Bergsland (1956, 1959) and Bergsland and Dirks (1978, 1978a). Unlabeled forms are the same in both Atkan and Eastern Aleut. The plural ending -n is found in most of Eastern Aleut and in Attuan, the ending -s in Atkan.

161

at Port Graham and other small settlements in the Seldovia area of the Kenai Peninsula as well as on Kodiak Island and the neighboring mainland and along Bristol Bay (Anderson and Eells 1935:9; Krauss 1980:7). This broadened use of the name Aleut has caused confusion or, among nonanthropologists, a misunderstanding of the real size of the Aleut population. The Pacific Eskimos who prefer to be called Aleuts, and who may have had a few Aleut ancestors, inflate the census reports of the Aleut population.

The boundary of the 1970 Aleutian Census Division (No. 1) is, like the preceding one (No. 14), farther east than the above-mentioned boundary: it crosses the Alaska Peninsula from Port Heiden on the north to Kujulik Bay on the south, thus including the Eskimo communities of Chignik and Perryville (Lin 1971:maps 1 and

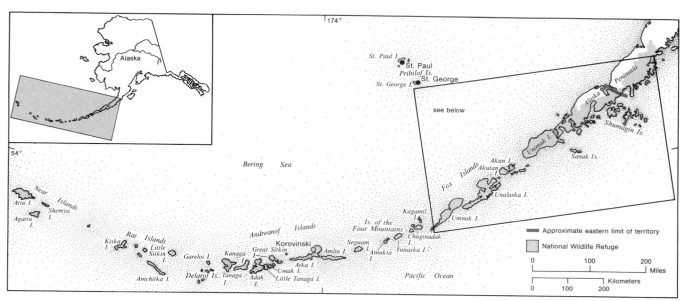

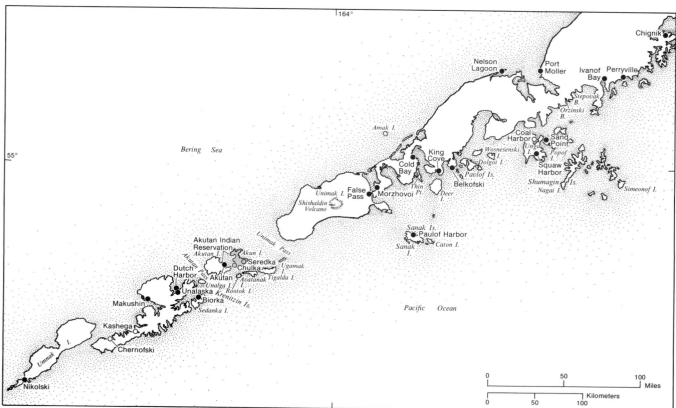

162   Fig. 1. Tribal territory.

2). In recognition of the Pribilof Islands (Seal Islands) Aleut, they are included in Census Division 1.

Because the islands are naturally grouped into clusters, with greater distances between the clusters than the width of straits within them, both Aleuts and Russians noted cultural, including linguistic, affinities within the groups and differences among them.

Within the Eastern division, the linguistic and social ("tribal") subdivisions as classified by Atkans are: Alaska Peninsula, Deer Island and other small islands near the coast, Shumagin Islands, Unimak, Sanak Islands; Krenitzin Islands, the principal community of which has been, in modern times, Akutan; Unalaska, Umnak, Islands of the Four Mountains; Pribilof Islands, peopled largely by Aleuts from Unalaska and Umnak. The Western division comprises Seguam, Amlia, Atka, Great Sitkin, Adak, Kanaga, and smaller islands near all of them; Tanaga (sometimes classed with Kanaga), Gareloi and smaller islands in the Delarof group; Amchitka, Kiska, and smaller islands in the Rat Islands; Agattu, Attu, and smaller islands in the Near Islands (Bergsland 1959:11–14).

The "capital" of the Aleutians in both Russian and American periods was Unalaska village, *ilu·lux̣* in Aleut (Bergsland 1959:12).

Demography

Population

Without examining the evidence, writers for many years have been repeating that the aboriginal Aleut population was 16,000 to 20,000. Lantis (1970,2:172–175) after reviewing the early sources, has agreed with the estimate made by the most knowledgeable and careful of the early observers, Ivan Veniaminov, that the population was 12,000 to 15,000. An accurate count cannot be given because early fur hunters and explorers often recorded only household heads or adult males (hunters) or tribute payers or number of villages with estimate of their size. Also, they sometimes did not distinguish between summer and winter villages. By the time that actual head counts were made, the population had declined drastically—80 percent according to the estimate of Lantis, and as high as 90 percent according to some others. In the first two generations of Russian domination, that is, approximately from 1750 to 1800 when the Russian-American Company gained control, people died from introduced diseases, punishment for resistance, malnutrition, suicide, and exposure in the forced sea mammal hunting that transported hunters away from their home territory, leaving dependents without adequate provision (Turner, Richards, and Turner 1976; Milan 1974:19–21). Although the decline continued when Aleut hunters were taken farther and farther away, the

more vicious practices were gradually ended in the first quarter of the nineteenth century, and there were some counterbalancing factors: the end of inter-island warfare, the care of children and youths who worked for the Russians, protection by priests, and the special attention to Creoles (persons of Russian-Native descent), many of whom remained in the Islands. See table 1 for figures on the most populous district.

In the 1830s smallpox ravaged much of Alaska. It reached the Aleuts in 1838–1839, killing 85 on Unalaska Island and an unknown number elsewhere. Because of vaccination instituted during the epidemic, the loss was not so great as in southeast Alaska (Bancroft 1886:561–562). In 1845 the population of Kodiak district was 69 Russians, 472 Creoles, and 3,440 Natives, over half of whom were listed as Aleuts. In Unalaska district were counted 27 Russians, 124 Creoles, and 1,259 Aleuts. Of the Russian-occupied communities in Alaska, Sitka, then containing the governor's headquarters, was the largest with 1,278 people. Less than 500 were Russian, 671 were Creoles, and the rest were Native people (Hulley 1970:171). The total population of Aleuts was 4,287, by Russian count, probably too large a figure as some Eskimos in the Kodiak-Alaska Peninsula area already were being counted as Aleuts. Nevertheless, there had been some recovery from the early devastation.

The problems of comparing Russian and American census tables are shown in the figures given by Hrdlička, who compiled 15 population reports covering the period 1781–1871, several of which were secondhand reports and a third of which gave only generalized round-figure totals. They do show some consistency, the totals ranging between about 1,800 and 2,500, supposedly including the Peninsula throughout the 90 years. There was neither steady increase nor decrease, but instead a fluctuation that may have been due to differences in quality of enumeration as much as to real changes in population. Six of the eight censuses that give numbers by sex report more females than males, an indication of the attrition among the hunters (Hrdlička 1945:33).

The size of villages about the time of the purchase by the United States is indicated by Pinart (1871), who traveled by kayak from Unalaska to Kodiak. Of eight settlements he visited, only one, Belkofski, on the Alaska Peninsula, had as many as 40 houses and a population of about 250 (see also U.S. Census Office 1893:87). Next in size was Unga with about 20 Native houses and nearly 200 people. The remaining settlements ranged from 1 to 12 households.

By 1890 available data were more accurate (table 2). What happened between the 1890 and 1910 censuses is not known, but only 1,491 Aleuts were recorded in 1910. These are possible explanations of the decrease: change in the designation of Aleut, a real decline due to increase of disease such as tuberculosis, out-migra-

Table 1.   Unalaska District, 1834

| Place | Population | | | Houses[a] | Kayaks[b] |
	Male	Female	Total		
Unalaska	214	256	470	65	58
Umnak	49	60	109	16	18
Akun	42	43	85	14	21
Biorka	17	27	44	6	7
Unalga	10	13	23	3	4
Avatanak	24	25	49	5	9
Akutan	6	7	13	2	1
Tigalda	38	59	97	6	14
Unimak	38	53	91	2	4
Peninsula	93	113	206	25	31
Unga	52	64	116	13	15
Pribilofs	88	94	182		
Outside Aleutians	10	18	28		
Total	681	832	1,513		

SOURCE: Veniaminov 1840, 2:202–204.

[a] Exclusive of houses belonging to the Russian-American Company.

[b] "Only such boats counted in this are those not belonging to the Company, and capable of being used for hunting sea-otter, which is not more than about one-half of the total" (Hrdlička 1945:41).

tion and mixing with other populations, incomplete enumeration. In contrast, the 1920 figure seems appropriate—2,942.

Although there were some big local fluctuations through the next 40 years (see D.C. Jones 1970:table 1), total Aleut population more than doubled, to 6,581, some of the increase being accountable to better reporting, some to the continuing tendency of the mixed Aleut-Eskimo-White population, especially in the Kodiak Census Division, to identify itself as Aleut. In 1980, only 1,815 were recorded in the Aleutian Islands Census Area, the remaining 6,275 Aleuts in Alaska (self-identified in the U.S. Census) located outside it (table 3). Even though nearly as many lived in Anchorage as in the islands, more than two-thirds of the total Aleut population still lived in villages and smaller towns, but outside the original area.

Table 3 shows the Aleut population relative to that of other ethnic populations in the Aleutian Census Area. Much of the Asian population, attracted by the large seafood industry, is seasonal and fluctuating.

The greater percent of females than of males separated, widowed, or divorced in 1980 might be explained by a more sedentary life of women than of no longer married males, so that they were accessible for enumeration, or possibly by the women's greater tendency to marry non-Natives and by the instability of these marriages. In 1980 there was an average of 3.44 persons per Aleut household. This compares to 3.32 persons for Alaska Indian households and 4.31 for Alaska Eskimos.

Table 2.   Unalaska District, 1890

Place	Population	Houses	Families
Akutan	80	20	20
Atka	132	25	36
Attu	101	22	24
Belkofski	185	48	56
Biorka	57	9	15
Chernofski	78	20	20
Coal Harbor	15	5	5
Kashigin (Kashega)	46	13	13
Korovinski	41	4	10
Makushin	51	11	14
Morzhovoi	68	22	23
Ozernoi (Orzinski Bay)	45	3	3
Popof Island	146	15	15
Saint George	93	20	23
Saint Paul	244	61	67
Sanak	132	29	30
Semenovsky (Simeonof)	3	3	3
Thin Point	231	5	5
Umnak	94	30	31
Unalaska	317	65	79
Unga	159	35	40
Voznesensky (Wosnesenski)	43	11	12
Total	2,361[a]	476	544[a]

SOURCE: U.S. Census Office 1893:163.

[a] Above totals yield an average of 4.34 persons per family, but when 440 White and 137 Chinese males without families are deducted from total population, the average family size is 3.28. A slight excess of married Aleut or mixed-Aleut females over married Aleut males indicates marriage to White men.

Communities were founded, abandoned, and moved from one locality to another, making difficult a comparison of district counts in the nineteenth and early twentieth centuries. While some groups merely moved from one part of their island to another, or outlying settlements were consolidated into one village on an island, there were also long-distance movements. Through most of the Russian period, Aleut hunters were transported to newly acquired hunting territory as the Russians moved north but principally east and then south. After discovery of the Pribilof Islands in 1786, Russians took hunters there, in 1823–1826 establishing settlements (Black 1981:125). Some Attuans were taken east to Unalaska and others west to Copper Island, where after the purchase of Alaska they were cut off from their relatives. Atkans also were taken to Bering and Copper islands in the still Russian-held Commander group (Bergsland 1959:14–15). By 1790 the Delarof Islands were entirely depopulated and Tanaga nearly so (Bergsland 1959:14). In contrast, when Baron Ferdinand von Wrangell visited Fort Ross in northern California in 1833, he reported a population of 199 (128 males and 71 females), including 41 Russians, 42 Aleuts, the remainder Creole or Indian (Okun' 1951:141). The movement of men was large, even allowing for exaggeration in early accounts. When the famous Russian-American Company governor, Aleksandr Baranov, sailed from Kodiak to establish a station at Sitka, he was accompanied by nearly 350 "canoes," at least some and probably all of which were two-man kayaks. Thirty were lost in a storm and 13 in a Tlingit Indian attack. This must have meant a loss of 75 or more men (Bancroft 1886:386–387). The party undoubtedly contained both Aleuts and Pacific Eskimos. According to Hulley (1970:124–125), in 1800 nearly 200 Aleuts (probably including some Kodiak Islanders) died from eating mussels in Peril Strait, southeast Alaska. In 1802 when the Tlingits attacked Sitka, some Aleut men were killed along with the Russians, although most escaped because they were out hunting, fishing, and on other missions.

Most of the early community moves are now unknown. The following are important recorded ones. In 1826 Amlia Island people were moved to Atka; then in 1838 when foxes were introduced, a community was reestablished at Amlia and flourished. Dall reported 150 on Amlia Island in 1867. Some time after 1870, the Amlia community was again consolidated with that on Atka Island and has never been permanently settled (Bergsland 1959:13–14). On the south side of the Alaska Peninsula, Belkofski was peopled from Sanak in 1823; King Cove was established in 1911 by a mixed Aleut-White population from various islands. Perryville was formed by Eskimos moving southwestward into Aleut

Table 3. Aleut Population in Alaska, 1980

Rural (places under 2,500)	5,624
Urban	2,466
Total	8,090
Anchorage	1,512
Cordova	231
Dillingham	422
Kodiak (city)	573
Unalaska	182
Bristol Bay Borough	305
Kenai Peninsula Borough	589
Kodiak Island Borough	1,810
Dillingham Census Area	1,225
Racial Composition of Aleutian Islands Census Area	
White	4,775
Aleut	1,815
Filipino	354
Black	329
American Indian	92
Vietnamese	85
Other Asian and Pacific	141
Other	150
Total Native Alaskan 1,934	
Total non-Native 5,834	
Age: 16 years and over	5,383
Under 16 years	2,707
Median age 22.5	

Marital status of those 15 years and over

	Male	Female
Single	1,287	820
Married	1,248	1,379
Separated	47	63
Widowed	79	210
Divorced	188	261
Total	2,849	2,733
Percent separated, widowed, divorced	11	19.5

SOURCE: U.S. Bureau of the Census 1980.

territory following the great Katmai eruption in 1912. During and after World War II, people congregated at Cold Bay chiefly because its airport has made it a transportation center. Jones (1973) gives a good account of these moves.

Changes in the Krenitzin Islands are better known than most others (table 4). Not shown in the table is the rise and fall of the village of Chulka on Akun Island. Because of its harbor, the Russians induced people to move there from Avatanak, Tigalda, and Rootok islands. After an American trading company settled at the present site of Akutan village about 1879 people began to move there, and Chulka and other settlements were abandoned. A codfish packing station was established at Akutan in 1904 and a whaling station in 1912. A reasonable and responsible trader settled there about the same time, and a dam to provide water and a schoolhouse were built in 1921. The economic and service base of Akutan thus was made firm, and all other islands in the group were abandoned. D.C. Jones's (1970:table 1) comparison of four Aleut villages shows that Akutan grew most consistently in the twentieth century, although like the other three it suffered a population loss in the 1960s.

In 1942 came the biggest move of all. After the Japanese had invaded Kiska and Attu Islands and had bombed and strafed villages and installations elsewhere, all Aleuts west of Unimak Island were removed to southeast Alaska, except the Attuans. The small Attu group and one of its teachers (the other one was killed) were captured and kept at Otaru, Hokkaido, for three years; in 1945 those who had survived were taken to Atka for resettlement (Bergsland 1959:127). On the American side 41 people from Akutan, 72 from Nikolski on Umnak Island and 47 Unalaskans from Biorka, Kashega, and Makushin were removed to Ward Lake near Ketchikan; 143 people from Unalaska village to Burnett Inlet near Wrangell; 477 Pribilof people to Funter Bay west of Juneau; 83 Atkans to Killisnoo, near Angoon.

Data for the village of Atka obtained by Bergsland and by Lantis show that between at least 1890 and 1950, there was intermarriage among villages. Of 37 adults 20 years old or older in 1950, living in Atka, 13 had come from another island, 9 of these from the Unalaska district (Bergsland 1959:15). Thus the postwar settlement of Attuans on Atka does not account for all the migration and intermarriage.

D.C. Jones's (1970) study of changes in Aleutian Island population structure demonstrates a movement that, for somewhat different reasons, has been occurring periodically since the beginning of Aleut recorded history: movement of young adults out of the islands. Even though more females than males are emigrating, the remaining females are rearing as many children as the former total, due to better protection of child health and apparently to a positive value on large families. "The higher female emigration rate may reflect the greater opportunity for females to marry white out-

siders" (D.C. Jones 1970:6). With 4,653 males and only 1,239 females 18 years old or older recorded in the Aleutian Islands Division in 1970, most of the "extra" men being Whites in military or civilian government service or commercial fishermen, it is not surprising that women have had an opportunity to marry and move away. This is an old situation, indicated by the number of Creoles in Alaska in the Russian period.

Settlement Pattern

Since the late eighteenth century most Peninsula settlements have been on its south coast, and this may have been true in precontact time, due to winter ice on the north coast. In the eastern islands and on Atka, settlements generally were on north shores until after the coming of the Russians, perhaps because the Pacific ocean swell made landing more difficult or because hunting and fishing were better on the Bering Sea. On the Rat Islands archeological sites have been found on both north and south shores (McCartney 1977:64). A typical village was located near a stream emptying into a bay and near a headland providing a handy lookout. Since it was not everywhere possible to go on foot from village to village, beaches and kayaks were essential for peaceful or martial travel as well as for hunting.

Structures

Because a house was large, containing stall-like living spaces strung along the sides for the several nuclear families, with a long common space in the center under the large roof hole for entrance and light, there evidently was no need for a ceremonial structure larger than the residential buildings. At least the eastern Aleuts must have known about their Eskimo neighbors' kashims (ceremonial houses), but there is no evidence that Aleuts built them in precontact times. There is also no evidence that they had either the dry-heat sweatbath of southwest Alaska Eskimos or the steam bath, but the latter was speedily acquired from the Russians and their Siberian helpers. The traditional esteemed form of bathing was, as with the Indians in south Alaska, in the sea or other cold water. It was enjoined on youths and hunters at least to wade in cold water, and young children might be put in it to stop their crying.

A house (called locally a barabara [bə'räbər,u]; Aleut *ulax*) was built in an oblong to rectangular shape with a frame of drift logs and, where necessary, of whale bones. It was semisubterranean, the walls sunk three to four feet into the ground (fig. 2). According to Veniaminov a row of posts was set along the wall, their tops even with the surface of the ground, about a fathom apart. Two rows of posts, twice as tall, were set to form an inner rectangle. "Over these posts round logs were

Table 4. Population of the Krenitzin Islands, 1830–1953

Island and Village	About 1830	1880	1953
Akun		85	54	0
Artelnov	32		
Recheshnoe	37		
Seredka	16		
Avatanak		49	19	0
Akutan		13	631	92
Tigalda		97	Unreported	9
Total	244	136	92

SOURCE: Spaulding 1955:13–14.

Fig. 2. Drawings of Aleut settlement and houses. left, Settlement on Unga Island. Old-style semisubterranean windowless dwellings of logs and sod were inhabited by the Aleuts. The 4-walled structures with windows and doors were occupied by Russian-American Company employees. Drying racks, gardens, the Russian-American Company flag on hilltop in center, and a sailing ship in harbor are also depicted. Pencil drawing by Ilĭa Gavrilovich Voznesenskiĭ, 1843. right, Interior of a semisubterranean house with roof of driftwood timbers overlain with dry grass and then sod. In the roof were 2 openings, one for light and one to admit the inhabitants via a notched log ladder. Occupants slept in mat-covered trenches along the walls. After the Russian occupation such communal structures might be up to 240 feet long, 40 feet wide, and occupied by 10–40 families or 150 individuals (Collins, Clark, and Walker 1945:23). Drawing copied by John Webber, 1781–1784 (Joppien 1978), from his original sketches made on James Cook's Third Expedition, 1778.

laid. Then other pieces of wood were laid across these logs at small intervals," forming the rafters. Over these were laid skins or, more often mentioned by others, dry grass, then sods (Veniaminov 1840, 2:204–205). Fine mats covered the ground where people sat and slept and were hung as curtains around the personal spaces. These cubicles later were separated by plank walls.

The houses were soon modified by the Russians. Although they continued to be built partly underground and to be sod covered, a door through the wall was added (as booted Europeans undoubtedly could not negotiate the notched-log ladder from the roof en-

trance), benches were substituted for the troughlike side compartments, and even plank flooring came into use. Then much later a window, stove, and metal chimney pipe might be added. Finally, in the American period, houses with siding of imported lumber and with shingle roofs were constructed. Lantis (1970, 2:187–189) gives more information on housing.

Culture

The Aleuts show what a people with a basically Eskimo culture living in a rich hunting and fishing area could

Fig. 3. Settlements and dwellings. left, Log and sod houses on Barbara I., in the Andreanof Is., Alaska. Photograph by Asahel Curtis, about 1914. right, Aerial view of the village of Attu. Buildings include a church, schoolhouse, and residences of the approximately 38 Natives. Photograph by Bureau of Aeronautics, U.S. Navy, 1934.

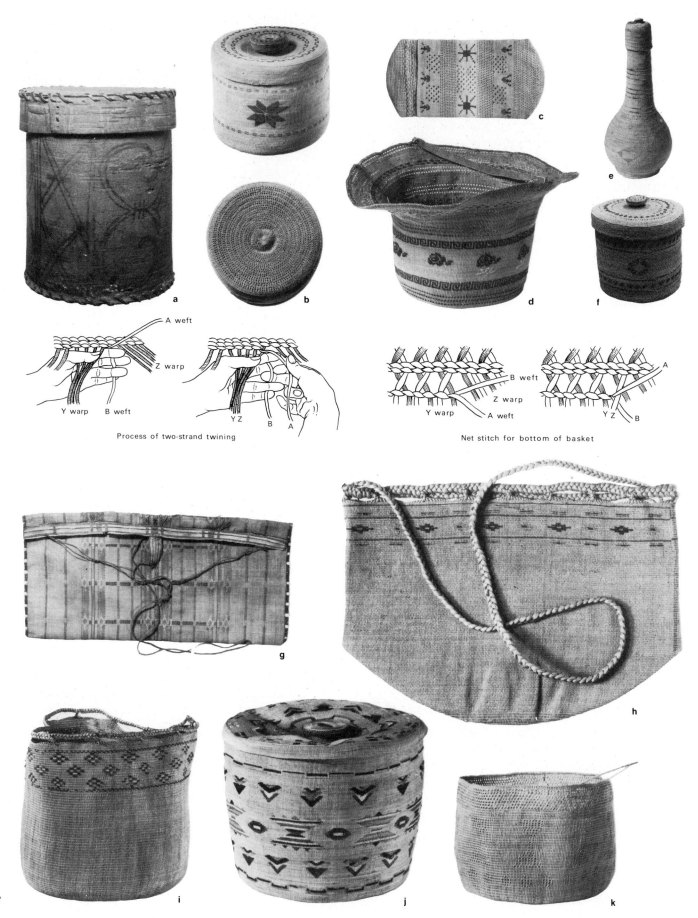

a

b

c

d

e

f

A weft

Z warp

Y warp   B weft

Process of two-strand twining

B weft

Z warp

Y warp   A weft

A

Y Z   B

Net stitch for bottom of basket

g

h

i

j

k

achieve in wealth and social differentiation. Their mountainous terrain and other environmental factors made some complexes like dog traction and ceramics unnecessary, maladaptive, or impossible. Some complexes were different from the Eskimo, notably the technology of whaling (possibly because the umiak was not used) and treatment of the dead. Others were quite similar to the Asiatic Eskimo, for example bride service, distinction between older and younger siblings, positive value of suicide, and many details of technology.

Technology

When traveling or at home, Aleuts used small stone lamps, round or more often oval or flatiron shaped. They would stand or squat over these lamps to warm themselves. An open fire seldom was made in the house, much of the food being eaten raw. An early fur buyer, Andrei Tolstykh, wrote that men made fire by striking flintstones, igniting sulphur and bird down placed on one stone, then from that igniting dry grass, which was placed as a wick in a lamp of sea mammal oil (Jochelson 1933:11). There also were wooden fire drills, but whether in bow drill or hand drill form is not clear.

Household utensils comprised wooden buckets and bowls, some carved to shape, others with carved bottom and bentwood vertical side (bent around and pegged or stitched); large spoons; the woman's stone knife in ulu shape, hafted at the back; the man's stone knife, hafted at the end. In the eastern district, the Aleuts had a few iron knives before the Russian conquest. See Jochelson (1925:63–65, pl. 16) for illustrations of tools and utensils. For materials see McCartney (1977:86, table 7). Cook's (1799) journal notes that in 1778 people might broil or boil their food, cooking techniques probably learned from the Russians. By this time, at least on Unalaska Island, people had small brass kettles. There was a flat stone paint grinder, and Jochelson (1925:pl. 21) identified a large flat stone as a "frying pan," that

is, meat was cooked on the heated stone over a fire pit.

Aleuts did not make pottery (McCartney 1977:105) but would build up clay sides on a flat stone bottom. The unbaked clay turned white when soup was boiled in it over a fire pit. Their volcanic islands were not likely to have good pottery clay, and they had substitutes. There is no mention of stone-boiling, but there is a reference to pit cooking of a whole carcass. This may have been aboriginal. Noticeable to Europeans in the house was the typically Eskimo wooden "trough" receptacle for urine in which skins were soaked. There were at least two good reasons for the paucity of rigid containers: the use of flexible and lightweight skins and mammal organs and of fine basketry for containers. Stomach, bladder, intestine casing, esophagus as well as whole skin of a sea mammal might be used, as were bird skins. The large kelp also might be used as a tube to carry water.

The finest craft product was and remains basketry (fig. 4) (Ray 1981:46, figs. 17, 23). Although using the two-strand twining technique almost exclusively, the weaving was not simple because of the variation in handling the warps. Aleut women produced not only baskets for storing and carrying, mats for the houses, and a mat for the kayak paddler to sit on, but also finely woven and decorated mats in which to wrap the remains of illustrious people, the famous mummy bundles (see Dall 1880:12–16, 24, pls. 4–5). A baby's cradle consisted of closely woven, pouch-shaped matting attached to an oval wood frame (Hrdlička 1945:fig. 17). The fiber most often used was dune grass (*Elymus arenarius*, subspecies *mollis*) in Alaska called wild rye or wild barley, which was split into fine strands (Jochelson 1933:61–62). To prevent its breaking, the dried grass had to be kept moist while being woven but baskets have not been woven under water, despite White people's beliefs about the famous "Attu baskets." To maintain perpendicular sides of the trinket baskets, they were woven upside down (fig. 5). In the prehistoric matting used as burial

a, Yale U., Peabody Mus.: 3660/9945; Smithsonian, Dept. of Anthr.: b. 417,767; h, 14,976; k, 65,174; U. of Pa., U. Mus., Philadelphia: c, NA 3284; i, NA 1238; j, NA 3280; Alaska State Mus., Juneau: d, II-F-285; e, II-F-132; f, Anchorage Histl. and Fine Arts Mus., Alaska: 80.59; g, British Mus.: NWC 14.

Fig. 4. Basketry. a, Birchbark container, from the late 18th–early 19th century, decorated with burnished curvilinear motifs, which probably once had a cord handle. Although birchbark, imported from the mainland, is found among women's grave goods, only a few baskets survive (Black 1982a:1511–52). Height 18.0 cm. Collected before 1925. Aleut grass work (b-k), especially baskets from Attu and Atka, became well known and highly prized items of trade. The quality and production were probably at their peak from the mid-19th to the early 20th century. Women made baskets in variations of 2-strand twining. b, Basket with embroidered designs and rattling seeds in the lid knob. The bottom was worked in a type of net stitch that produces a pattern and quickly increases circumference. The bottom was suspended from a string or put over a form to hold it upside down, and weaving proceeded from left to right (see drawings, center, after Shapsnikoff and Hudson 1974). Made in 1935 on Attu. c, Cigar case, a popular form made specifically for trade, has 2 pieces that fit into each other. The false embroidery is red and lavender worsted. Collected on Attu before 1915. d, Flared basket, showing Euro-American influence in the shape and in the key borders and rose motif. Collected before 1976. e, Bottle covered with basketry, a type made for sale; design in pink and blue silk thread, 40 stitches per inch horizontally and 51 per inch vertically. Collected before 1957. f, Miniature basket made for sale in 1980. a-f to same scale. Traditional basketry items (g-k) include grass hats, socks, mittens, and mats (for walls, furnishings, clothing, and burial shrouds), as well as storage containers. g, Housewife made from a piece of matting folded twice, decorated with false embroidery and edged with decorated rawhide. Width 39.0 cm; probably collected by Capt. James Cook, 1778. h, Decorated carrying bag with braided trim and handle, collected by W.H. Dall, 1874. i, Decorated fish basket with braided trim and handle, collected by G.B. Gordon, 1905. j, Covered cylindrical basket from Attu, distinct from those from Atka and Unalaska in its lid knob, shape, fineness, and style of corners (Shapsnikoff and Hudson 1974:56); collected before 1915. k, Open twining worked into pattern; collected by Lucien Turner on Atka, 1879. g-k to same scale.

Fig. 5. Aleut basket being constructed upside down and suspended. Shredded grass is woven in a 2-strand twining technique. Photograph possibly by C. Gadsen Porcher, 1904.

bottles, and other objects made for trade in the peak period of this craft, early in the twentieth century. For materials, weaves, and designs, see Shapsnikoff and Hudson (1974).

Clothing and Adornment

The parkas, whether made of fur, birdskins, or intestine casing (fig. 7), were as praiseworthy as the basketry, it appears, although the stitchery never has received a modern analysis. The Aleut garment differed from the Eskimo one in having a standing collar instead of a hood except on the rain parka or kamleika (Russian *kamleĭā, kamleĭka*). Lacking a hood, the woman's parka also lacked a pouchlike enlargement in which to carry a baby on the upper back. The baby was carried instead in a cradle. The parka for both sexes reached to the ankles and was straight around the bottom, unlike Eskimo parkas (Ray 1981:figs. 7, 18–21).

The Aleut people, incredibly, were said to have no foot covering except on and near the Alaska Peninsula, where they had boots (fig. 8) and trousers. Steller, the first European to describe Aleuts, reported these on Shumagin Islanders (Golder 1922–1925, 2:97). Dall's (1880) good account of clothing and wrappings in mummy bundles and of women's sewing kits containing mate-

wrappings, colored patterns were formed with feathers and other materials. To satisfy the American newcomers' demand, women substituted embroidery silk thread to produce overlay patterns on the cigar cases, covered

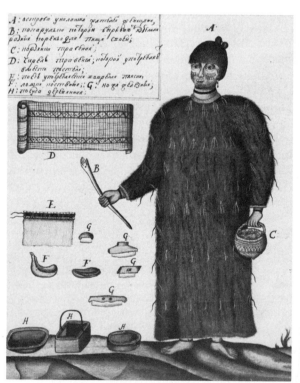

Fig. 6. Early drawings of Aleut. left: A, Woman with facial tattooing wearing a fur garment probably sealskin; B, tool for digging roots; C, grass basket; D, grass sleeping mat; E, belt used in dances; F, bone spoons; G, iron knives including an ulu; H, wooden bowls. center, Woman of Unalaska in a long coat with embroidered cuffs and lower edge. Her face is tattooed and her hair tied in a knot. right, Man from Unalaska holding a wooden visor decorated with sea lion whiskers. left, Drawing by Mikhail Dmitrievich Levashov, 1768–1769. center and right, Watercolors by John Webber, on James Cook's Third Expedition, Oct. 1778.

LANTIS

Suomen Kansallismuseo, Helsinki:VK275.

Fig. 7. Gut shirt. Horizontal strips of walrus intestine are decoratively sewn together and bordered with gut and skin strips, colored yarn, cormorant feathers, and eagle down. Women processed the gut and sewed these waterproof garments; both men and women wore them. The style of this example and of gutskin capes was probably influenced by Russian clothing. See Black (1982a:157–163) for a full discussion of the sewing technique. Length 125.0 cm. Collected by A.K. Etolin on the Pribilof Islands, Alaska, before 1847.

Smithsonian, Dept. of Anthr.: 48,102.

Fig. 8. Boots. The sole and foot portions are separate pieces of dark leather and the uppers are light leather. The leg portion has a vertical seam decorated with tufts of red wool and hair and an upper border of fur. Height 47.0 cm. Collected by E.W. Nelson on Unalaska, Alaska, 1877–1881.

rials for ornament should be consulted for an understanding of the material elaboration in this culture.

Most often described and pictured were the wooden hats and eye shades (fig. 9), worn by hunters in their kayaks, which were like a deep inverted scoop. The thin wood was bent around to shape and stitched up the back. The best were painted with concentric stripes and animal figures; at or near the peak were ivory figurines of animals. Simpler than these hats with their magical appurtenances were smaller, decorated yet plainer ones without a crown, that is, cut off across the top. Every man would have one of these whereas only the wealthy upper-class men would own the full-size and fully decorated hats, which cost one to three slaves (Ray 1981:32–34, figs. 5, 10; Veniaminov 1840, 2:218).

Art

Like Eskimos in the Bering Sea region, Aleuts would bleach white the sea mammal esophagus, bladder, and other body parts by hanging them outside in freezing weather, then would use them to make decorative borders, small bags, and other niceties. Not having so much ivory as the coastal Eskimos or so much wood as the river people, Aleuts were limited in art media; and the motifs most often were simple cross-hatch, zigzag, circle, and other geometric forms and unelaborated hu-

man and animal forms. Bird figures and some sea otters (fig. 10) show more detail, and most masks representing human faces were naturalistic (Ray 1981:fig. 39). The wooden bowls were plain, but the stone lamps might be sculptured. Spear throwers (fig. 11), paddles, and hunting-implement shafts were painted black and red. For materials used, see Ray (1981:19).

Implements

There was great variety in the heads of hunting implements and possibly also those used in warfare. The long implement heads showed many combinations of large and small barbs, evenly or unevenly spaced or combinations of both. These might have circle-and-dot and line decoration incised on the walrus ivory or bone. Besides harpoons and lances for sea mammals, there were multipronged bird darts and fish spears, arrows, and composite fishhooks although the Northwest Coast halibut hook probably was not obtained until the European period. For examples of implements, see Jochelson (1925:pls. 22–27, figs. 45–83). For implement distributions, see McCartney (1969:table 1), and for techniques and implements used in eight food procurement systems, McCartney (1977:81–82, table 5).

The bow is not useful in a kayak as it requires two hands. Bow and arrow were used almost solely in warfare and by Aleuts on the Alaska Peninsula in hunting caribou and other large land animals. The bow was small. Whether the composite sinew-backed bow, as well as the simple bow, was made is not definitely known (Jochelson 1925:121).

171

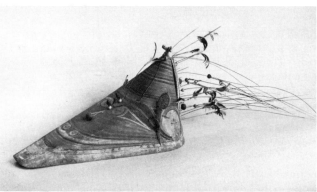

top, British Mus.: NWC 3; center, Suomen Kansallismuseo, Helsinki: VK 207; bottom, Peabody Mus. of Salem, Mass.: E 3486.

Fig. 9. Wooden headgear. Although wooden hats and visors were worn by men when hunting sea mammals throughout western Alaska, the Aleutian examples are distinctive for their long fronts, polychrome painting, and elaborate decoration. top, Wooden visor, perhaps a type of headgear that preceded the conical hat (Ray 1981:33), made of 3 pieces of wood bent and joined. It has an abstract design painted in blue, black, and red on a ground probably once painted white, and originally (as sketched by John Webber) had an ivory ornament attached at each side; an ivory figure remains as do sea lion whiskers with blue glass beads (King 1981:48–49). center, Painted conical bentwood hat with carved ivory decoration, beads, sea lion whiskers, and feathers. bottom, Conical bentwood hat painted with red, green, yellow, black, and blue designs. Other decorative elements include metal side pieces, carved ivory birds, beads, circular shell inlay, and sea lion whiskers. The long front apparently shielded the eyes from sun and glare but was removed in strong winds to avoid the risk of capsizing. Length 45.7 cm; rest to same scale. top, Collected by Capt. James Cook on Unalaska, Alaska, 1778; center, by A.K. Etolin before 1847; bottom, by William Osgood on Unalaska, 1829.

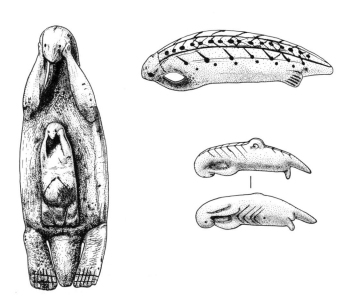

left, Muzeĭ Antropologii i Étnografii, Akademiĭa Nauk SSSR, Leningrad: 2938-6; Smithsonian, Dept. of Anthr.: top right, 35,905; bottom right, 35,893.

Fig. 10. Sea otter carvings of ivory, used as decorations on wooden hats, as amulets, and possibly as fasteners on kayaks. left, Length, 16.8 cm, collected in the early 19th century. top right, Length 4.5 cm; bottom right, same scale; both collected by Lucien Turner, 1879.

Transportation

Compared with the kayaks of Bering Sea Eskimos, Aleut kayaks (in the historical literature called baidarkas) were of shallow draft and long in proportion to beam, appearing light and fragile (fig. 13). The unique two-hatch kayak may have been pre-Russian, but the three-hole boat definitely was designed to carry conqueror hunters and officials, with the passenger in the middle hatch. The larger boats called in the historical sources baidaras might have been open skin-covered boats like the Es-

kimo umiak, but in modern times (at least on Umnak Island) this term designates the two-hatch kayak. Veniaminov (1840) did not mention an open skinboat, even for carrying freight. Although Jochelson (1933:56, 58) published photographs of an Aleut umiak on one of the Pribilof Islands (which he must have seen in 1909–1910), this might well have been copied from Eskimo boats (fig. 14).

Besides hunting implements, spear thrower, double-bladed paddles, a wooden tube to serve as bail, stones for ballast, a flat wood seat, and domestic possessions

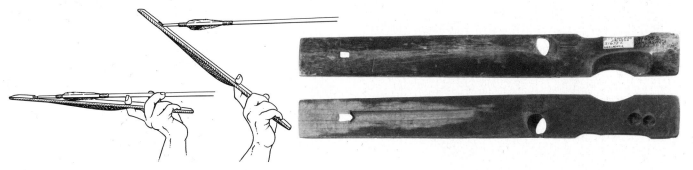

Smithsonian, Dept. of Anthr.: 316,752.

Fig. 11. Throwing-board. This thin straight-sided wooden board is used to project darts and harpoons, increasing the power and speed of the throw. The length is determined by the distance between the user's elbow and the end of his forefinger. The weapon is laid in the groove against the ivory hook and propelled as shown. Although the method of use is the same, the shape and ornament of the board varies by region (compare "Bering Strait Eskimo," fig. 3, this vol.). The back side is painted red, the top black, with red in depressions and the carved design by the index-finger hole. Length 45.0 cm. Collected by Sheldon Jackson on Unalaska, Alaska, before 1910.

for heating and eating, the kayakman always carried a float of sea mammal stomach that he could use to support himself while righting an overturned boat, to help keep afloat a boat that was taking water, or even to repair a torn cover. A disabled kayak might be tied between two others or laid across them. In rough weather, kayakmen would lash their boats together, and each would fasten himself to the cockpit rim, so that the boat could not take water. Each man built his kayak to his own body measurements (Robert-Lamblin 1980). In a good one-hatch kayak he could travel as fast as seven miles an hour and could travel even against a current. The only situation in which he might be helpless was in one of the whirling riptides passing through the straits between islands.

The presence of dogs is questionable except for archeological evidence of a small terrierlike dog from

Smithsonian, Dept. of Anthr.: 389,861.

Fig. 12. Wooden shield, made of 2 boards lashed together, used as protection against darts and arrows during combat. A geometric design is painted in red on the front; the back has 2 knobs for attaching a handle. The lashing is a museum reconstruction, and the design has been retraced; there were originally crossbars on the back. Length 69.0 cm; collected by Aleš Hrdlička from a burial cave on Kagamil I., Alaska, 1937.

Akun Island at the east end of the chain (Turner 1976). On rugged terrain that precluded much overland travel and along broken hazardous shores, the use of dogs for sledging, packing, or towing boats was inappropriate, and artifacts connected with such use have not been found.

Knowledge

In the foggy Aleutian climate, men had to navigate by the currents, which they learned by instruction and experience, at any given time and place taking account also of wind direction and tide. In an emergency they could travel at night, seeing almost nothing but feeling the direction of the water beneath them and the wind above them.

The Aleuts' knowledge of anatomy has drawn special attention (Marsh and Laughlin 1956). This derived from and conversely facilitated two complexes: mummification and bloodletting and other medical practices. Veniaminov (1840,2:259) was told that before warfare was stopped, Aleut doctors dissected dead enemies and slaves, who usually were captives. If the various accounts are correct, for preservation of a body the viscera were removed through the pelvic girdle or a hole in the chest. The body was laid in a clear running stream until thoroughly cleansed, then dried and stuffed with dry grass or sphagnum moss, possibly oiled, dressed in a birdskin parka or wrapped in fur skins, then further wrapped in layers of fine matting or hides and lashed (Dall 1880). The mummy bundle was placed in a dry cave, often suspended in a kind of cradle. Only the bodies of important people and cherished children were so treated.

In medical treatment, the bloodletting, at least as practiced in the twentieth century, might have been learned from the Russians. It was done for a number of ailments whenever it was thought that bad blood was the cause. For example, in the 1930s, for rheumatism *173*

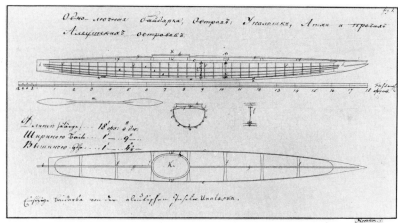

left, Muzeĭ Antropologii i Ėtnografii, Akademiĭa Nauk SSSR, Leningrad; right, Bancroft Lib., U. of Calif., Berkeley.

Fig. 13. Single-seated kayaks. left, Man in kayak wearing waterproof parka and protector that keeps the opening watertight. The long-visored open crown hat has decorative sea lion whiskers protruding. Drawing by M.D. Levashev, 1818. right, Plan and elevation of kayak of "Unalaska, Atka, and others of the Aleutian Islands." Drawn by Ivan Petrovich Korukin, shipbuilding expert on N.P. Rezanov's Expedition, 1803–1807.

in the knee an incision was made in the flesh of the leg, avoiding a blood vessel, with a small two-edged knife. (A century earlier, a stone lancet was used.) The incision was not sewed or clamped but was bound. Or, the skin might be pinched up and the lancet thrust through it, with very little blood lost.

Intentional bleeding appears at first to be opposite to the practice of Bering Sea Eskimos, who tried to stop any bleeding as they feared that the soul essence could flow out in the blood. However, Veniaminov (1840, 2:262) explained the treatment for an expectorating tuberculosis patient as the withdrawal of bad blood and the "bad odor or soul." Since Aleuts may not have had tuberculosis before the Russian conquest, one wonders whether the disease and the treatment were acquired together and syncretized with an old belief. For early health conditions see Milan (1974:17–18).

An alternative has been the Eskimo type of tattooing: on Atka Island a moistened thread covered with gunpowder (probably soot in former times) would be sewed through the pinched-up skin near an aching joint or across the back over the region of a pain, leaving black lines.

As a last resort for a very ill person, Aleut doctors used "piercing," evidently a form of acupuncture (Veniaminov 1840, 2:263).

As Bank (1953) has written, old women would rub and manipulate the abdomen to get the organs into their proper place, and midwives also tried to move a fetus by manipulation. An elderly Atka male doctor was observed by Lantis (1933–1934) to rub almost constantly the chest and sides of a young child who evidently had pneumonia, in an effort to move the pain away from the heart, which he saw in this case was a fruitless effort.

Much of the Aleut medical knowledge and use of plants in doctoring has been assembled by Bank (1953:428), who also has presented former uses of local products, plant and mineral, for evil magic and for protective magic.

Like the Koniag, Aleuts probably made a poison from the root of monkshood (*Aconitum maximum*), which they put on the slate spear points used in whaling. Modern hunters have had vague traditions of use of some plant as a poison but usually have not attributed this to monkshood. Several Umnak people told Bank (1953:429) that it is not poisonous. If it was used, it was mixed with or used in conjunction with a magic poison: some part of a human body, apparently the body of a great whaler. Very little is known about this restricted practice. An elderly Atkan told Lantis (1933–1934) that every whale hunter hid his poison, which he made himself. No one should know another's poison. This could have referred to the theft and use of human remains or other magic "poisons" as well as to plants. Like the knowledge of anatomy, the pharmacognosy was extensive (see B.S. Smith 1973).

The seasons were named for natural changes in weather, fauna, and flora or for periods of human plenty and scarcity. Measures were based on distances between human body parts, hence were relative. Cardinal points were really cardinal areas from which the winds blew (Jochelson 1933:85–86). Astronomical knowledge evidently was meager and was of little use in the Aleutian fog and cloud overcast. In an area in which the weather was usually bad, there were of course many weather signs from the behavior of birds and mammals.

Subsistence

Most food came from the sea: all local whale species except the sperm whale (Veniaminov 1840, 2:229–230) and killer whale (McCartney 1975:294), sea lions, fur

top, © Natl. Geographic Soc., Washington; bottom, Natl. Arch., Washington: RG22-WB-61899.

Fig. 14. Umiaks, probably introduced to the Pribilof Is. by Eskimo workers or Aleuts in contact with Eskimos. top, Villagers of St. Paul Island rowing out to meet an incoming supply vessel. Photograph by Victor B. Scheffer, May 1950. bottom, Collecting murre eggs in a canvas-covered umiak. Photograph by W.W. Collins, 1936.

seals, sea otters, and occasionally walrus. The fish were salmon, halibut, codfish, flounder, herring, sculpin; of invertebrates, chiefly sea urchins but clams, limpets, and mussels also might be eaten. The shrimp and king crab, of high value in the modern fishing industry, were not mentioned in early accounts although Veniaminov did mention "lobster." It is likely that the enjoyment of octopus meat is not only recent. Birds eaten were ducks and geese, occasionally cormorants and others. More often the eggs of other species were taken.

The foxes found on the eastern islands at contact (McCartney 1975:292) evidently were not eaten. Both Russians and Americans brought foxes to the islands.

Other than foxes, indigenous land animals could be found only on the Alaska Peninsula except that caribou, bears, and wolves had migrated also to Unimak Island. In the period of American domination, whaling disappeared except commercial whaling at Akutan. When the sea otter had become nearly extinct and the fur seal herd on the Pribilof Islands had dwindled, the hunting of both was forbidden by the United States government except when done by government agencies (Hulley 1970:184–186, 276–278). In the twentieth century, do-

mesticated reindeer, originally imported from Siberia, were introduced to Umnak, Atka, and the Pribilof islands but never became economically important. On Umnak, sheep ranching supplemented subsistence activities.

Veniaminov observed regarding the hunting of baleen whales in the 1820s that in the Unalaska area, "though the hunters there spear from 30 to 60 every year, they only secure 33 of them on the average, and sometimes no more than 10" (1840, 2:231). He did not say whether whales were being hunted in the old way, that is, speared with a poisoned point, then left to drift ashore in some accessible, not too distant place. Unlike Arctic Eskimo whalers, they did not harpoon the animals and try to hang onto them. It is understandable that with this technique a small proportion was obtained, and magic was relied on more than skill.

A hunt at which Aleuts were expert was an important reason for their conquest by the Russians: the hunting of sea otters (Black 1981:127–128). In the Russian period and presumably in aboriginal times, several kayakmen would proceed in an arc until sea otters were sighted. At a signal, some would move to close a circle around the animals; then all would throw their harpoons. The animals having to surface to breathe and the females impeded by the young, which they carried in their forepaws, could be killed with greater certainty than in some types of hunting. This success eventually led to near extinction of the species.

Sea birds and their eggs were taken from their rookeries by the lowering of a man down a cliff by several others or by men climbing up a cliff, both methods dangerous. Choris, on the Otto von Kotzebue expedition in 1816–1817, wrote, "They gather among the crags a great quantity of eggs, with which the ships that arrive supply themselves; we took several barrels of them. They preserve very well in oil" (Van Stone 1960:157).

From the diary of the merchant Tolstykh, one of the earliest visitors to the islands, Jochelson (1933:11) translated the method of fishing for halibut and cod: "by hooks tied to lines about 150 fathoms long, made of sea-weeds, which are as thick as an ordinary iron wire and twice more enduring than a hemp cord." The fish might be cooked or, more often, eaten raw. Tolstykh said Aleuts also used small baglike dragnets made of whale sinew, to catch fish in the small rivers. When hunting was unsuccessful, especially when the sea was too rough, people dug edible roots. In winter when this was difficult, they collected seaweed and shellfish on the beach.

Veniaminov (1840, 2) noted the same attitude that was common to all Bering Sea Eskimos: without seal oil, no matter how many fresh or dried fish they had, they thought they might starve or become ill. With it, they could eat dried roots, shellfish, or other foods less nutritious or less palatable than meat; and it was regarded as an essential condiment for even favored foods.

Jochelson (1933:51) described the technique of fishing for each species in the period 1910–1912. Because so many changes had been made by Russians in the eighteenth century it is uncertain whether weirs or seines (the latter especially important by 1910) were used before the Aleuts were forced to adopt efficient techniques of collecting large quantities of food to feed their conquerors as well as themselves. Spaulding (1955) has attempted to show for the Krenitzin Islands the shift in food gathering in a period of 50 to 100 years.

Aleuts know and have used the edible plants, for example cow parsnip (*Heracleum lanatum*), cranberry (*Vaccinium vitis-idaea*), and crowberry (*Empetrum nigrum*). They also ate a lily bulb (*Fritillaria camschatcensis*, Kamtchatka fritillary), cowslip (*Caltha palustris*), and anemone (*Anemone narcissiflora*) greens, and the roots of anemone and lupine (*Lupinus nootkatensis*) (Collins, Clark, and Walker 1945:69). The wild parsnip (*Angelica lucida*) known locally as wild celery or puchki, kelp, a considerable variety of berries, and the several greens that could be collected along beach edges nearly all year had greater importance than most writers have credited (for a list of available food plants and animals, see McCartney 1975:305–310, table 1). Because of abundant food resources in aboriginal times and the damp weather, poor for drying, not much food was stored except for the festivals. When population was decimated and life habits disturbed, there seems to have been even less food storage. Under American influence in the twentieth century, trade staples such as potatoes, rice, and dried fruits have supplemented local fresh foods, obviating much storage.

Sociopolitical Organization

Before the Russians consolidated the population, it was scattered in many small settlements. The typical house was large, containing several nuclear families, most of them related through males—for example, a man, his wife (wives) and children, eldest son and family, younger brother and family, and a sister's son whom he was training, the avunculate being a strong relationship. "In fact, a whole village might be composed basically of kindred" (Lantis 1970, 2:292).

Since both polyandry and polygyny were permitted, it is not surprising to find also that both simultaneous and successive levirate and sororate were acceptable marriages and that the kin terms reflected these relationships. A man could take his wife's younger sisters, apparently with or without formal marriage, and younger brothers had access to an elder brother's wife, in the early twentieth century, "only when the younger brother is not married" (Jochelson 1933:72). An elder brother could not cohabit with a younger brother's wife because he was a substitute father for his brother, but his wife obviously was not seen as a substitute mother. A parallel set of obligations and taboos evidently governed relations between elder and younger sisters and their spouses. Age seniority was an important principle; there were kin terms for elder and younger brothers and elder and younger sisters, and rights and duties were designated on this basis.

The approved way of getting a wife was by bride service for one to two years, during which the betrothed couple might have intercourse. It appears that the youth's service frequently was combined with the avunculate. He was already living with and working for his mother's brother; when he then married the uncle's daughter, he was of course marrying his cross-cousin, a preferred marriage partnership. Parallel cousins were as siblings, in terminology and in behavior, while cross-cousins were potential spouses.

There appears to have been no rigidly enforced rule of residence although the most common was matripatrilocal. The young couple would likely remain with the woman's parents until after the birth of the first child and then would move to the man's family home. If, however, the wife's father needed help and the husband's father had other sons to help him, the young man might remain with his uncle–father-in-law. Although it cannot be proved, there is some evidence that the rule of descent was matrilineal.

Yet the special rights and powers of whale hunting were said to pass from father to son, as did chieftainship. It may have been that kin membership was separate from inheritance of office or privileged position. Whaling was confined to a few families and brought high status. Before the Russian period, a "chief" was the head of a deme, that is, village composed of kin, or of the strongest extended family in a settlement if there were more than one. "There was a tendency to inheritance of chieftainship although the higher chief for a group of villages or a whole island was chosen from among the lesser chiefs. Beyond one island there was no authority" (Lantis 1970, 2:295). The chief (*tukux̣*, called in Russian *toĭon*) was expected to be a leader by force of personal qualities and by the number of friends and relatives, both consanguineal and affinal. He had to protect his kindred's hunting grounds, control his people's behavior so that it did not arouse the hostility of other groups, and command if war became necessary. He received a share, but no larger share than others, of every subordinate's catch and therefore usually became wealthy. He could not decide punishment or decide on war without the consent of the "honorables" (Lantis 1970, 2:250–253). A system of first, second, and even third chiefs for each community was established by the Russians, who also defined the chiefs' authority; and these offices tended to become hereditary, especially that of first chief.

In the Krenitzin Islands anciently the house and all that it contained, exclusive of men's hunting and fishing gear, kayak, and tools, belonged to the wife. The house was inherited in the female line, that is, by the eldest daughter, whereas a man's possessions were inherited in the male line (Spaulding 1955:97–98). This suggests that the eldest daughter continued to live with her parents following marriage. If she had married her cross-cousin, her husband would simply continue to live where he had worked for her parents in his youth. As a member of the Russian Orthodox church, "a man is expected to leave his belongings to a nephew, a son, or a god-child" (Spaulding 1955:98). Aleuts, like Eskimos, have been quite flexible in modifying rules to fit circumstances.

Before European contact, there were feuds between kindreds and between islands, the result of insults, raids, and murders being avenged. Because many men might be out hunting, leaving their families without defense, some of the settlements were reported to have been fortified or built on places with natural protection. Passageways and side compartments of the houses also were built for hideaway and escape. In warfare, Aleuts and Pacific Eskimos resembled their Indian neighbors more than their Eskimo cousins, especially in the size and organization of war parties and in their taking high-status prisoners to serve as hostages or slaves; nevertheless, there were resemblances to Asiatic Eskimo warfare. Their motives for attack were more likely revenge than territorial disputes. Preferred methods of attack involved deceit and surprising sleeping people in the early dawn. Mistreatment of prisoners and defiling of bodies were common. Warfare and the taking of slaves probably were the most important means of culture diffusion.

Aleuts resembled the Tlingit Indians in regard to status or class differences, with their high-status wealthy people, common people, and slaves, who most often were captives. The son of a chief might be captured, but customarily the enemy warriors would be killed while women were taken as slave concubines. Offspring of these unions were (or could be?) free, but children not fathered by a local man, that is, one of the conquerors, remained in slavery. Wealth was important, not only the usual Eskimo wealth of furs and food but also dentalium shells, amber, and slaves. Because the sociopolitical structure was changed so drastically and so quickly, the indigenous Aleut and the Aleut-Creole-Russian societies have been confused in the accounts of the early nineteenth century. Also, Aleuts may have described their old system so that it resembled that of the Tlingits with whom they were brought in contact by their Russian masters.

If the customary behavior that Spaulding observed or that was reported to him on Akutan at mid-twentieth century can be accepted as indicating the old ways, which is possible because Akutan people have been sufficiently strong and self-assured to maintain some of their traditional culture, the successful hunter or fisherman would give food to others on three principles: obligation to relatives or partners, payment for the loan of a motor or supplies, and generosity to less fortunate families. People would gather when a man returned with his catch. If he had enough, he would give them part of it on a first come, first served basis. Eggs collected on the cliff rookeries were pooled for the whole village, then divided; but a man bringing a few game birds could give them only to those to whom he was obligated (Spaulding 1955:77–80). A traveler in others' territory was expected never to take game or other food but would be generously fed if he came to a camp or village.

Participants in a hunting party, directed by the head of an extended family, probably were members of one household, living in one of the large multifamily houses. "Rivalry and competition did exist, but the expression was not disintegrative . . . to the community" (Spaulding 1955:114–115). This probably states the general traditional Aleut situation. Besides rivalry in hunting, there was competition in singing, dancing, and feats of strength. Choris wrote that if two Aleuts had animosity toward each other, they would enter a verbal duel (apparently in principle resembling the song duels of Greenland but spoken rather than sung), each man required to listen to his antagonist without showing anger (VanStone 1960:154). Other than control by chiefs and honorables, control seems to have been exerted principally by shaming and for women and children by the men's intimidation of them in the guise of spirits.

Religion

According to Marsh (1954:21), Eskimo-Aleut religion acknowledges five categories of interacting powers: "1) charms, amulets, talismans and magic formulas; 2) the immortal and perpetually reincarnated souls of men and animals; 3) the 'persons' of creatures [and places and things]; 4) the demonic spirits of the earth and air; and 5) the 'persons' or spirit-powers directing the universe and forces of nature." By exploiting the system of interaction of these powers, "humans may exert control over the operation of the universe." Throughout Alaska, there were personal guardian spirits and large public ceremonials—beliefs and rituals lacking in the Central and Eastern Eskimo regions. In all the Eskimo-Aleut area, the Aleut religion is the least known. Although Marsh has not cited sources, his summary survey can be substantiated and should be consulted for explanation of the beliefs.

Christian influence was small until the nineteenth century. On Unalaska in 1824 and on Atka Island in 1825 permanent Russian Orthodox missions were founded (Veniaminov 1840, 2:156–164). In 1828 the first Creole priest, trained at Irkutsk Seminary, arrived at the Atka mission (B.S. Smith 1980:121). Thereafter, in religion Aleuts were thoroughly Russianized, and in the twentieth century the Russian Orthodox Church was well established (fig. 15). The biggest annual community event was a traditional celebration of the Julian New Year. On the character of the Russian Orthodoxy introduced, see B.S. Smith (1980:3–17) and Black (1981:134–137).

Knowledge of the aboriginal religion is fragmentary. Marsh (1954:29) found the primary deity to be agudar or *aγu·ɣuχ* 'creator', a name later used for the Christian God. Apparently related to the sun, this deity was the source of "hunting luck, protection from harm, and the reincarnation of souls." This great spirit seems to have been the counterpart of the Eskimo deity of weather, atmosphere, or world above (Pacific Eskimo *ł̣am sua;* Inuit *silap inua)*. Veniaminov wrote that the creator named Agoughhoukh was not connected with the management of the world and was not worshipped. Instead, the people "came to worship everything that seemed more powerful than they. As rulers of everything in their surroundings thay have acknowledged . . . . two kinds of spirits, who likewise regulated the fate of man in every respect. The first they called Khougakh and the second Aglikhaiakh" (Veniaminov 1840, 2:119). Marsh (1954) reported that a demonic spirit was called *quɣaχ*, obviously Veniaminov's Khougakh. The second kind must have been the helpful spirits.

Near every village there was a sacred place such as a high rock or cliff and a cave under it strictly forbidden to females and young men. At these places, adult males made offerings, "akhakhilik, that is, 'All his to him he gave'," which were of two kinds: any objects, princi-

Fig. 15. Julian Golley, an Aleut lay preacher of the Russian Orthodox church at Atka, Andreanof Is. Photographed about 1940.

pally animal skins, brought with prayers for help in war or chase; and the feathers of some species of birds, smeared with paint and then thrown into the wind, the votary uttering his request, to be borne to the spirits by the feathers (Veniaminov 1840, 2:121–122). The localities tabooed to the uninitiated may have been also the places where the whalers performed their preparatory rites or the places where the men, who formed a "secret society" of all adult males, prepared for their dramas representing spirits by which they intimidated women and children. For beliefs and practices relating to whalers, sea-otters, and other animals, see Black (1981:116, 126–130).

Aleuts believed that there were three worlds, each with its beings and doings: the highest one, called Akadan Kougoudakh, with no night, where there was a "multitude of people"; the earthly world; and the subterranean one, called Sitkoughikh Kouyudakh, where there were also many people in the afterlife (Veniaminov 1840, 2:121). In the division into three levels, this perception resembles the belief of Eskimos farther north. Souls of the dead, conceived as shadows, "remained invisible among their people, accompanying them on land and sea, especially those whom they had loved" and could do good as well as evil. At what stages souls resided in the heavenly world and in the earthly world was not recorded. Aleut pre-Christian religion has never been fully explained.

Although details are lacking, the general form and function of shamanism were recorded. Practice consisted of singing, dancing, drumming, and "contortions." Here as elsewhere, shamans were mediators between the visible and invisible worlds. Shamanic powers were invoked to foretell the future and for good hunting, health, and weather, rescue from danger at sea, and for help in cases of difficult birth. They did not initially seek the spirits, but from about 15 years of age they were troubled by "apparitions in the shape of animals or marvelous beings until they were bewildered and willing to submit to their inevitable masters" (Veniaminov 1840, 2:122, 125–126).

Of the many amulets and other means of protection, two were highly valued: an inherited girdle "plaited of sinews and grasses under invocations, with secret knots," worn under the clothing as protection from death; and a specific bicolored hollow pebble, rarely found on the beach, kept hidden by the hunter-owner to draw sea otters to him (Veniaminov 1840, 2:131–132). Figurines on the large wood hats of hunters and on the kayaks probably were amulets (Ray 1981:fig. 33).

Early explorers and Russian traders reported seeing public ceremonies and festivals, with both men and women singing and the women dancing, beginning with gentle movements and at last becoming violent. Almost invariably the women were said to wave "blown bladders" (sometimes containing stones or teeth to form

Fig. 16. Calendar. A peg was moved around the circular wooden board; each represents a day of the year. Tradition has it that Father Veniaminov invented the calendars so that natives in areas with no Russian Orthodox priests could keep track of feast days, but it may be that they developed from the Aleuts' own lunar calendar (Black 1982a:124). Diameter about 11.1 cm. Collected on Unalaska I., Alaska, 1889.

Fig. 17. Dance described as a Bladder dance, probably at Atka, about 1756–1762. Men at left wear wooden hats or visors, labrets, and long shirtlike garments; 2 in foreground beat tambourine drums, and dancer in center holds bladder. Women have facial tattooing and hair knots, possibly also hats, while one holds dancer's inflated seal bladder. In background is diagram of Aleut semisubterranean structure with 2 entrance ladders. Drawing on manuscript map by Pëtr Bashmakov or Andrei Tolstykh (Black 1982a:[x]).

rattles), which could have been inflated bladders, stomachs, or lengths of intestine of the sea mammals (fig. 17). The "games," held through the winter until the beginning of whaling and again after a whale was caught, were staged to please the spirits who would, in return, send more whales. The performers wore masks representing the spirits that had appeared to the shamans. (Aleut masks in museums show that both animal and human beings were represented.) The festivals included competitive and amusing feats of agility. Men's and women's dances, as described in 1791, must have been almost identical to those of east Bering Sea Eskimos: the men presenting scenes of hunting and mimetic dances of ridicule, the women dancing in unison in more formal, less individualistic fashion (Lantis 1947:76–78).

Sometimes one village would entertain others, each village trying to outdo the other in the invention and skill of their performance and wealth of their feast. The biggest occasion was the memorial feast and distribution of goods at the end of a mourning period of 40 days, but there were other occasions. The big winter festivals featured lavish entertainment. The chief and honorables dressed in their best clothes and displayed trophies of war and hunting to prove the greatness of their ancestors. Dall said that images made of wood or stuffed skins, which could become possessed by spirits, were carried from island to island in these festivals, then were destroyed at the end of the season. Parts of a nearly life-size wood figure of a human being were found,

along with masks and other cultural remains as well as human remains, in a cave on Unga Island (Lantis 1947:77–79).

Life Cycle

Observations marking the stages of life naturally had a large religious element, but there were also social considerations. The common concept of the special state and the power to harm of a person undergoing a transformation (whether called unclean or sacred) was illustrated by taboos on women at every menstrual period and following childbirth. A girl at puberty or a parturient woman was isolated, while a woman otherwise was not completely isolated but could not touch her husband's hunting amulets and gear or go near river or sea. She bathed at the end of the period of uncleanness. Details on requirements to protect family and community can be found in Lantis (1970, 2:197–205).

A girl evidently could marry at 13 years, even before puberty if she was proficient in woman's work or if the parents had arranged the marriage, perhaps long before, and wanted it to occur. The bridegroom was expected to be a hunter, that is, 18 years old or older. There was an exchange of gifts, but there is no mention of ritual before acceptance of Christianity. A man seems to have had greater freedom in returning a woman to her kin than a woman had in leaving her husband, and a man could lend a wife or concubine to an honored guest. As on Kodiak Island, male transvestites who did women's work were openly accepted (Lantis 1970, 2:205–214).

Behavior connected with a death has been noted more often than other life crises. The Aleuts' lack of fear of the dead made it possible for them to place a body in a side compartment of the house and then wall it up, to keep the bundled body of a beloved infant in the family quarters, to handle the bodies of important people in the mummification process. The mourning period, especially for a widow, was 40 days, the same as for a woman following childbirth. This statement, like most of Veniaminov's ethnography, pertained almost exclusively to the eastern Aleutians. In the central Aleutian district a father maintained the mourning fast for an infant 10 days, the mother 20; man or woman mourned the death of a spouse 60 days except when a man had perished at sea, and then only 30 days. In any mourning period, people lamented, often at the place of burial, did not eat meat or oily food, and kept themselves physically and sexually "clean." Some might commit suicide or give away large quantities of possessions (Veniaminov 1840, 3:12).

History

The hunting of sea otters continued after the American purchase of Alaska, principally in the Peninsula-Shumagin-Sanak region, the animals having become rare farther west. By a 1911 treaty among Japan, Russia, Great Britain (covering Canada), and the United States, hunting of the valuable animal, then nearly extinct, was totally forbidden, and the taking of fur seals was limited to the United States government, with net income of sale of the fur to be divided among treaty signers. Actually the killing of fur seals was limited to the breeding grounds on the Pribilof Islands, where nearly all employees were Aleuts, as has been the case under private company lessees.

In 1913 the Aleutian chain, with five islands in the eastern region excepted (Akun, Akutan, Tigalda, Unalaska, Umnak), was reserved as a national wildlife refuge. Later, the Izembek Wildlife Range was established on the western end of the Alaska Peninsula. With the above treaty exceptions, Aleuts could take any wildlife for subsistence and could catch foxes for sale of the fur. Reindeer brought to Atka, Umnak, and Saint Paul islands by the federal government in the period of World War I have been minor in the economy.

Small reserves of land for schools and a hospital were created by presidential executive order, beginning with Unalaska in 1897, but there as elsewhere in Alaska the whole system of Indian reservations, with their superintendents, was not introduced. Only the Akutan reservation on Akun and Akutan islands was set aside (in 1943) for the exclusive use of its people. This seems not to have affected the people's lives.

Since World War II, defense installations have been maintained on Adak (the largest), Shemya, and Attu islands. On Adak, a civilian community with school and other services developed for the families of military and civilian personnel, chiefly White but with a few Native employees. Aleut men have worked for the Atomic Energy Commission and the U.S. Department of the Interior Fish and Wildlife Service in preliminary and follow-up studies connected with an atomic underground explosion on Amchitka Island (Operation Longshot) and for the state in its program of counting and relocating sea otters. Such work providing good experience and pay has been available for only a few people.

Until the formation of the Alaska Federation of Natives in 1967, only eight Aleut communities had petitioned for hearings to determine possessory rights under the Indian Reorganization Act, extended to Alaska in 1936. Even fewer had elected councils under this act. Because the aboriginal and Russian system of chiefs had survived, the councils, under schoolteachers' impetus and tutelage rather than indigenous leadership, were generally ineffective. The exception was the Saint Paul council in the Pribilofs. Whereas the Russians had dominated the selection of chiefs, the tendency under American rule was inheritance of office or tacit acceptance of a leader by the community. There might be an amalgam of old and new. At Nikolski, for example, men of the Orthodox Church Brotherhood selected the chief who was, at least in the late 1940s, a son of the former chief. The council president was another person, supposedly elected by the entire adult community, whose choice actually was strongly influenced by an elderly leader. The president's function was to deal with White authority (Shade 1949). By 1970 the chief and council president roles had been combined.

A regional association formed in December 1967, the Aleut League, joined other regional associations in the Alaska Federation of Natives. There still was locally little formal organization. By 1970 only three communities were incorporated under Alaska law as cities: King Cove, Sand Point, and Unalaska (see table 5).

Due to the distances between island groups, poor travel conditions, differences in non-Natives' influence and in economic opportunity, culture history in the twentieth century has been different in the several Aleut districts. There were, however, a few universal influences. Besides the Russian Orthodox Church, the schools had an acculturative influence earlier than in many parts of Alaska. The Aleut religious schools taught written Aleut and Russian until the last one, at Unalaska, was forcibly closed in 1912 by education officials who opposed the use of Native languages (Krauss 1980:24; Hulley 1970:180, 239). Methodist coeducational schools had been established at Unga in 1886 and at Unalaska in 1890, but in 1911 only Unalaska and Atka had them.

By 1930, several Aleut villages had federal schools, King Cove and Unalaska had territorial schools, supplanting the mission ones, and the Pribilof Islands had a school provided by the U.S. Department of Commerce Bureau of Fisheries, which was the successor of the schools established by a private company (Anderson and Eells 1935:349). In 1940, 76 percent of children 5–14 years inclusive were enrolled, a higher proportion than among Indians or Eskimos. After World War II, Aleut students were transported to the Bureau of Indian Affairs boarding high school at Sitka, but later some began attending Anchorage high schools.

Aleutian village schools, formerly provided by the Bureau of Indian Affairs and later in the Alaska state-operated school system, in the 1970s began to receive bilingual, bicultural training. In 1973 four Aleuts received training at Atka for teaching in Aleut as well as English, a reversal of the long-time policy of both federal and state schools.

Medical care and health instruction were less available than formal education. Unless a person west of Unalaska could manage to go to the Indian Bureau hospital there (built in the early 1930s and destroyed in 1942), the only professional service came when the ship's surgeon of a Coast Guard cutter visited briefly in the summer. Because Unalaska–Dutch Harbor was the summer home port for Coast Guard and Navy, it had had more attention for years. Also, in the early decades of the twentieth century a physician headed the Methodist children's home. There were occasionally other privately supported doctors, as at the gold mine on Unga Island in the 1890s. Otherwise, people relied on teachers' first aid and provision of common medicines, and on folk medicine and midwifery, unequal to the pervasive tuberculosis in the 1920s to 1940s. The death rate was high, especially among infants, with many infant deaths unrecorded (Milan 1974:24–26, 35).

After 1945 and notably after 1955, public health care improved, but weather always has interfered. In 1972, Atka still had only monthly boat service, and sometimes weather prevented that. Because of the Pribilofs' isolation and poor transportation, the U.S. Public Health Service maintained a physician and small hospital on Saint Paul Island (Milan 1974:26–29, 35–36).

In the late 1960s and early 1970s, Office of Economic Opportunity and other federal programs reached the Aleuts. In 1973 the regional director of the Aleutian Planning Commission was an Aleut. In 1974 the Aleut League, headquartered in Anchorage, was one of the prime sponsors of a variety of "Indian" manpower programs, for which it received nearly $99,000 under the Comprehensive Employment and Training Act. Because Aleuts had been literate in English for two generations or more and had worked with Whites a long time, they could take such positions and responsibilities when available. Unfortunately, not many technical, clerical, and administrative jobs had been available.

By autumn 1974, under provisions of the Alaska Native Claims Settlement Act of 1971, of about 76,500 people enrolled in Alaska's first enrollment (of the 12

Table 5. Aleut Community Inventory, 1970–1971

| Place | 1970 Population | | | Form of Government | Housing Units | School | | Transport Facilities | |
	Native	Other	Total			Enrollment	Grades	By Water (Dock)	By Air
Atka	86	2	88	IRA[a]	22	27	K–8	Boat	None
Akutan	90	11	101	Traditional	22	17	1–8	Boat	Seaplane
Belkofski	53	6	59	Traditional	22	17	1–8	No data	Seaplane
Cold Bay	32	224	256	Not Aleut community	75	23	1–8	Ship	Airplane
False Pass	58	4	62	No data	16	20	1–8	Ship	Airplane
Ivanof Bay	46	2	48	Traditional	11	16	1–8	Ship	Seaplane
King Cove	252	31	283	2d-class city	61	69	1–8	Ship	Airplane, seaplane
Nelson Lagoon	39	4	43	Traditional	16	13	1–8	Via Port Moller	Via Port Moller
Nikolski	52	5	57	IRA[a]	27	11	1–8	No data	Airplane
Paulof Harbor	38	1	39	No data	14	No data		No data	Seaplane
Saint George I.	156	7	163	Traditional	32	54	K–8	No data	Airplane
Saint Paul I.	428	22	450	IRA[a]	97	117	K–8	None	Airplane
Sand Point	265	95	360	4th-class city	94	93	1–8	Ship	Airplane
Squaw Harbor	52	13	65	No data	15			Ship	Seaplane
Unalaska	121	57	178	1st-class city	72	108	K–12	Ship	Airplane

SOURCE: U.S. Federal Field Committee for Development Planning in Alaska 1971.
[a] Organized under Indian Reorganization Act.

regional corporations), 3,353 were in the Aleut Corporation, each a shareholder. At this time, the corporations were to receive, each in proportion to its number of enrollees, the third payment, bringing the total paid under the act to $209,000,000, with more to come in succeeding years, from Congressional appropriation and an overriding two percent of mineral royalties and leases in Alaska. Ten percent would be distributed to the stockholders living in villages, with an additional amount to nonvillage stockholders, and 90 percent kept by the regional corporations for resource development and other investment. For subsequent developments, see "The Land Claims Era in Alaska," this volume.

Aleuts, more fully than most Alaska Eskimos, have operated in a money economy. Chiefly because of a good harbor and proximity to Akutan and Unimak Passes through the Aleutian chain, Unalaska early became a commercial center. In 1890 when whaling in the Arctic still was strong, "the number of arrivals and departures of vessels during the season reaches into the hundreds. . . . Trading and hunting schooners and steamers, freight carriers under sail and steam, colliers, revenue marine and naval vessels, and a numerous whaling fleet under steam and canvas make this port a regular place of call," to coal, water, refit, and handle mail, although there was not yet government mail service (U.S. Census Office 1893:89). This must have provided some employment for local people even when hunters were away in the sea otter hunt. When commerical whaling neared its end, the Nome gold rush developed at the turn of the century. Dutch Harbor was the busy port of entry, with a customhouse, for Bering Sea and the Arctic Ocean.

A San Francisco company was already well established at its Alaska headquarters in Unalaska. In 1890 it owned two-thirds of the buildings including some of the Native housing, the wharf, and the water supply (U.S. Census Office 1893:88). As supply of the vessels declined, its economic base became increasingly the fur trade. In the 1920s and early 1930s, when fox fur prices were high, the three communities west of Unalaska as well as individuals and companies had leases on specific "fox islands" (without permanent human habitation) for commercial trapping. Atka could trap on its own island but depended principally on Amchitka and Amlia (11 smaller islands were "owned" by Atka individuals), while Nikolski trappers got red fox on their own island, Umnak, and blue fox on Tanaga. Attu trappers worked on Agattu as well as Attu. A community usually made a contract with a trading company for supplies (coal, lumber, food, traps), promising to sell its furs to the company. Any funds remaining after payment of trappers and debt payment were divided per capita, including children. Hence people liked to adopt children. Additionally, a man might trap his own leased island with relatives or hire trappers from other villages. Men from eastern Aleutian communities that did not "own"

fox islands hired out to companies or individuals. Thus, a party of trappers on an island like Kiska might comprise a White man and one or two each from Unalaska, Akutan, or another community. One effect of the system was that the communities and some of the individuals were almost continuously and heavily in debt to their suppliers. Another effect was acquisition of more varied goods, particularly household goods.

After the Depression of the 1930s and the loss of fashion interest in long fur, the next and greatest blow was the wartime evacuation to southeast Alaska, where all suffered from anxiety and change in natural environment and where the Atkans had an especially difficult time because of inadequate housing. However, they and Nikolski people were said to be better able to construct housing and boats than the Pribilof people, who had depended a long time on the federal government for such things. When Aleuts were returned home, they found at Atka, Nikolski, and Unalaska a general destruction, by Japanese strafing, U.S. military burning at Atka to prevent Japanese use, "Aleutian weather and three years of neglect," and by "GI moonlight requisitioners and souvenir hunters," as the Army weekly, *Yank*, reported in 1945. The dories, necessary for hunting and fishing, were gone, even locked houses were rifled, and community facilities were in ruins. Pribilovians had killed their cattle and chickens before leaving. The communities were given rabbits—presumably to provide a steady food supply—a few of which survived as pets on Umnak Island, but all of which soon succumbed to rat and human predation on Atka. With heavy government assistance, villages were rebuilt, but Umnak and Atka never developed an economic base, especially not one largely in their own control, to succeed the fox trade. A White-owned and operated sheep-raising business has existed on Umnak Island since 1934, offering some employment. Atka men must go east to work in the commercial fishery to obtain an adequate cash income.

Codfish salteries and salmon-packing plants were built by Whites in the 1880s in the Alaska Peninsula–Shumagin Island region. The seafood industry was later extended westward to Akutan and Unalaska. At Unalaska in the 1930s there was a herring packing business that employed both women and men, then, after World War II, a lean period until the king crab boom. By 1966 there were three crab processing plants and more came later, greatly increasing the non-Native population.

In the Shumagin Islands the codfish salting and salmon packing businesses, gold mines, and stamping mills brought prosperity from about 1885 to 1915. Some hunting of sea otter and fur seal and trapping of locally stocked blue fox continued. After World War I, the only production that continued and gradually increased was salmon canning. Although the large companies brought East Asian workers for the canneries and there were Scandinavian and American fishermen, in later decades local women in the canneries and local men on the fishing boats supplanted them.

On Akutan Island in the Krenitzin group there was a commercial whaling station from 1912 to 1942, modern successor to the nineteenth century whaling in that area. Aleuts received wages for the processing work and meat for home consumption. About 1879 a fur trading post had attracted people to Akutan from neighboring Akun Island. In 1915 a man different from most entrepreneurs entering the islands started a codfish packing business that employed local people. With his help, the community acquired modern facilities, getting materials from a sulphur mine that had closed, and became stronger and more independent.

Most Aleut communities have gone through cycles of rapid economic development and severe decline, usually because of outside decisions from various sources. The villages that have remained under one controlling agency, since 1970 called the Department of Commerce National Marine Fisheries Service, for most of the twentieth century have been Saint Paul and Saint George, on the Pribilof Islands. Although services were provided, this federal agency, managing the fur seal kill and market, controlled Aleuts' lives by weekly inspections of homes, by paying in scrip redeemable only locally, and trying to prevent political participation. As part of the Native organization and civil rights and land rights demands of the 1960s and 1970s, the Pribilovians have gradually acquired self direction although management decisions regarding the seal herd must be made by the agency (Milan 1974:35–36).

All groups have continued to depend on the marine fauna, principally salmon. Sea lions, ducks, geese, and octopus continued as subsistence items; fish and crustaceans as both subsistence and commercial products. The gun had supplanted the harpoon in the late nineteenth and early twentieth centuries, and by 1940 the dory had supplanted the kayak even in the isolated areas, although there were not yet many outboard motors. Outboard and even inboard fishing boats became common after World War II. Any kind of fishing gear that Aleuts had seen elsewhere when hunting for the Russians or working as crew on American boats was used if adaptable to their streams and coasts.

Income from craft work has been meager. Since World War II, a half-dozen or fewer women could or would make the fine "Aleut" or "Attu" baskets. Women's crafts became knitting and crocheting. Occasionally a man would make a small model kayak. By the 1980s old-style items were sold at high prices, but the production was too small to be remunerative.

The U.S. Federal Field Committee for Development Planning in Alaska (1968) found that "the Aleuts look mainly to wage employment for their livelihood. Jobs are found in a broad range of activities, with few of a permanent nature and with no large-scale employers." The principal permanent jobs were those of government employees in several agencies, as janitors and maintenance personnel, postmasters, and health and welfare aides. (The "welfare" system was abolished in Alaska about 1969.) There were seasonal jobs in the seafood industry, the government sealing operation, and on special projects. Subsistence resources are utilized to supplement store-bought goods or are depended upon when income and credit are depleted by extended unemployment.

Due to the distances among island groups, poor travel conditions, differences in non-Natives' influence and in economic opportunity, recent culture history has been quite different in the several Aleut districts (Jones 1976). The 1971 Congressional settlement of the Alaska Native claims probably will tend to equalize the communities, not only because of the provided funds but also because of the required corporate organization.

Except where otherwise cited, material for this section has been drawn from Anderson and Eells (1935), Berreman (1955, 1964), Foote, Fischer, and Rogers (1968), Jones (1969, 1973, 1976), Lantis (1933–1934), Morgan (1974), and Spaulding (1955).

Synonymy

Aleut is not a word of Aleut origin. It is thought to have come from the Koryak language or Chukchi language and to have been given by the early Russian visitors and the east Siberians who accompanied them to the Aleutian Islands. It is probable that within a decade of the discovery of the Aleutian Islands, that is, by 1750, the Russian name *Aleut* (pl. *Aleuty*) was applied to their inhabitants. In Coxe's (1787) translation of a 1768–1769 journal of Russian naval officers, it was stated that people in the Fox Islands were already calling themselves Aleyut. In a translation of a 1776 work, Aleütian was used (Coxe 1787:75, 125, 219). The origin of the name is uncertain, but it was suggested as early as 1774 (Bancroft 1886:106; Bergsland 1959:11) that the Russians probably extended eastward the name of the village of Alut (Russian adjective *Oliútorskoe*) on the coast of Kamchatka, whose inhabitants, though closely related to the Koryak, were, like the Aleuts, whale hunters. The most commonly cited of other suggested sources is Chukchi aliat 'island'. Menovshchikov's (1980) derivation from Aleut *alitxux̣* 'war, troop of warriors' involves complex assumptions.

In the Aleut language, the self-designation is *unaŋax̣* (pl. Atkan *unaŋas*, Attuan and Unalaskan *unaŋan*), apparently based on a stem *un(a)-* 'extended below there (e.g. at the coast)' that occurs in several names of islands (Bergsland 1959:11). In Atkan, the eastern groups are called *qayakuris* 'easterners', and *na·Mirus* 'westerners' may have been applied to all west of the Four Mountains group of islands (as Veniaminov claimed for the Unalaskan cognate) or just to the people on Tanaga and the Delarof islands, as claimed by one of Bergsland's (1959:13–14) principal Atka informants.

The Aleuts have also borrowed the name Aleut for themselves, attested Atkan plurals being *aliɣutas* and *aliu·tas* (Bergsland 1959:11).

Sources

There are extensive gaps in the published and archival ethnographic records of the Aleutians. The period 1790 to 1835 is covered by the reports of early explorers (summarized in Berkh 1823a), but of much greater significance is Veniaminov's (1840) pioneer study of Aleut language and culture. Activities of the Russian-American Company and the Russian Orthodox church during this period may be found in the Records of the Russian-American Company, National Archives, Washington; and the Archives of the Russian Orthodox church in Alaska, Library of Congress, Washington. Between 1870 and 1915 the works of Dall (1870), Pinart (1871), federal censuses (U.S. Census Office 1884, 1893), and Jochelson (1925, 1933) are important.

Early archeological excavations in the Aleutians were carried out by Dall (1873, 1877, 1880) and Hrdlička (1945). In the late 1940s sustained archeological and ecological programs were begun under the direction of Laughlin (1963, 1966, 1975), his colleagues, and his students (McCartney 1969, 1970, 1975).

Except for the special case of the Pribilof Islands (Foote, Fischer, and Rogers 1968), a government monopoly since the U.S. purchase of Alaska, little has been published on modern Aleut. The principal student of the Aleut socioeconomic and political situation in the 1960s and 1970s has been a sociologist, Jones (1969, 1972, 1973, 1976).

Archeological collections from the Aleutians are widely dispersed in American museums, the largest located in the American Museum of Natural History, New York; Field Museum of Natural History, Chicago; and the Smithsonian Institution Museum of Natural History, Washington, which also has an extensive collection of skeletal material. Aleut ethnographic collections can be found in the R.H. Lowie Museum, University of California, Berkeley; Smithsonian Museum of Natural History; Muzeĭ Antropologii i Ėtnografii, Akademiia Nauk SSSR, Leningrad; Muzeĭ Antropologii Moskovskogo Gosudarstvennogo Universiteta im. M.V. Lomonosova, Moscow.

Pacific Eskimo: Historical Ethnography

DONALD W. CLARK

Language, Territory, and Environment

When the Russian promyshlenniks (fur hunters or trappers) reached the mainland coasts of Alaska after 1760 they found the series of Eskimo groups now collectively termed Pacific Eskimo. The populous Koniag ('kōnē͵ăg) possessed Kodiak Island. With them are grouped the Eskimo of the Alaska Peninsula, from Kupreanof Point eastward to Cook Inlet (cf. Dall 1877a:map; Dumond 1972:30–31; Oswalt 1967:map 2). The Chugach ('chōōgăch) occupied Prince William Sound east nearly to Cordova and had hunting camps beyond on the offshore islands of Kayak, Wingham, and Middleton (fig. 1). The Eskimo of the lower Kenai Peninsula may have been a separate group, but there is little early information extant for them. At one time they occupied a more extensive portion of Cook Inlet (Dumond and Mace 1968; De Laguna 1934:13–15, 1956:34–36). It is possible that there were others among the Pacific Eskimo (Miyaoka 1974).

Historic accounts indicate that, as is the case in the twentieth century, the same language was spoken on Kodiak and at Prince William Sound (Shelekhov 1981:55), although there were subdialects within and between these and other parts of the Pacific area (Davydov 1977:147; Veniaminov 1846). This language is called by linguists Pacific Eskimo or Pacific Yupik* ("Eskimo and Aleut Languages," this vol.), but a number of names based on native words have also been used including šuk/suk (Hammerich 1958), Sugpiaq (Krauss 1975), and Alutiiq (Leer 1978:1–2,4). Pacific Eskimo is one of the five Yupik languages (also referred to as Western Eskimo), which are distributed from southern Alaska to Siberia. With the nearest of these, Central Alaskan

Yupik of the mainland north of the Alaska Peninsula, it shows a low level of mutual intelligibility (Krauss 1973:819–820, 827).

The Pacific Eskimo are essentially a discrete cultural, linguistic, and historic entity, although, in these terms, there is no absolute boundary with the Bering Sea region, a fact that also has been inferred from their seemingly intrusive position between the Aleuts and Indians. Yet, in another sense, depending upon the set of data emphasized, their culture, like that of their non-Eskimo neighbors, is characteristically North Pacific. A single or common origin in antiquity has yet to be demonstrated, although archeologists have traced Pacific Eskimo roots well into the prehistoric past.

Evidence for a common identity above the level of the major self-named groups, mainly the Koniag and Chugach, is lacking. Neither was a tribe in the sense of an organized body, but informally structured organization may have permeated society both above and below the level of the local village cluster. Eight local groups have been delineated for the Chugach (Birket-Smith 1953:20–21; De Laguna 1956:11). Detailed traditional information is lacking for the Koniags but Davydov's (1977:190) statement that some of the chiefs rule over many settlements suggests that on Kodiak there also were local groups, and later there was a degree of village territoriality (Moser 1902:247).

Settlement was limited to the fringes of the coast, although occasionally a salmon-fishing camp was on a stream a few miles inland. The economy was primarily littoral and maritime following the zones of greatest economic opportunity. Except for inlets that receive and trap fresh water, the Pacific area is free of winter ice, and thus ice-hunting techniques were little utilized. Nevertheless, the damp, raw climate with temperatures

---

*The phonemes of Pacific Yupik are: (plain voiceless stops) p, t, č, k, kʷ, q; (voiceless continuants) f, ł, s ([s], [š]), x, xʷ, x̣; (voiced continuants) l, y, γ, γʷ ([γʷ-w]), γ̇; (voiced nasals) m, n, ŋ; (voiceless nasals) M, N, Ŋ: (retroflex resonant) ř; (short vowels) i, a, u, ə; (long vowels) i·, a·, u·.

In the practical orthography used by the Alaska Native Language Center the Pacific Yupik phonemes are written: p, t, c, k, kw, q; f, ll, s, gg, ggw, rr; l, y, g, w (syllable-initially) - uĝ (syllable-finally), r; m, n, ng; hm, hn, hng; ř; i, a, u, e; ii, aa, uu. In certain positions where voicelessness is predictable the voiceless velar and back velar continuants are written with single rather than double letters and the voiceless nasals are written without the h. Certain long vowels that

are predictable by rhythmic accentual rules are written with single vowel letters, and short stressed vowels are written double in accordance with other rhythmic patterns. An apostrophe is used as a diacritic after consonants to indicate gemination that is not predictable from the regular accentual rules, between vowel letters to show that the rules treat them as heterosyllabic vowels, and between consonant letters that have their separate rather than combined values. An acute accent (v́) indicates irregular stress and length.

Information on Pacific Eskimo phonology and orthography and the spelling of the words cited in italics was obtained from Leer (1978) and Jeff Leer (communications to editors 1974, 1982).

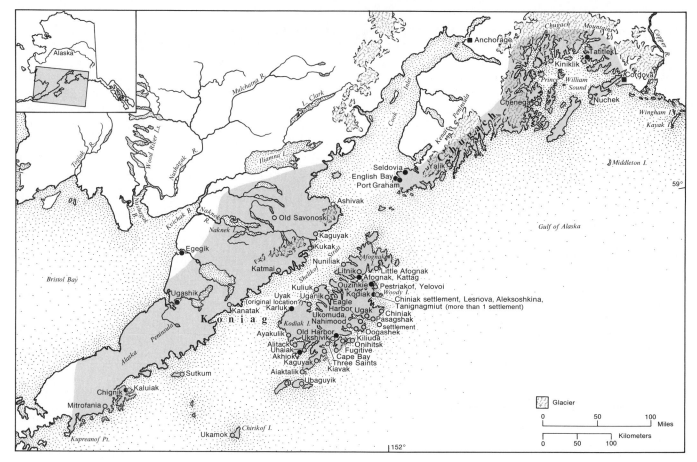

Fig. 1. Pacific Eskimo territory in about 1900 with 19th-century villages.

occasionally dropping below 0°F and the stormy seas (De Laguna 1956:8) probably did not make the life of the southern maritime hunter any more pleasant than that of his northern counterpart. The primary pursuit was the sea-mammal chase, supplemented by saltwater fishing and augmented with gathering. The salient summer activity was salmon fishing at the innumerable but generally small salmon streams and rivers. Few species of larger land animals other than brown bear, foxes, and river otter are available on Kodiak and the islands of Prince William Sound; and although a wider assemblage including caribou is found on the Alaska Peninsula, and more yet on the rest of the mainland (Manville and Young 1965:distribution maps), land fauna was of lesser economic significance (Clark 1975; De Laguna 1956:49 ff.). Essentially only a single type of environment, punctuated by the absence of spruce forests in the western third (Griggs 1934), was occupied and exploited.

External Relations

Traditions tell of internecine raiding between Koniags and Aleuts (Davydov 1977) and other neighboring tribes (Gedeon in Valaam Monastery 1978) and between the Chugach and their purportedly bitter enemies, the northern Tlingit. Likewise, traditions of contact between the Tanaina and their Eskimo neighbors deal predominantly with conflict (Osgood 1937; Shelekhov 1981:89). Raids and feuds that resulted in capturing slaves (Merck 1980:109) took place between Koniags and Chugach (Gedeon in Valaam Monastery 1978:128) and even between related villages (Birket-Smith 1953 after Zaikov). Peace could be established by exchanging hostages (Gedeon in Valaam Monastery 1978).

Tales of raid may be a biased attribute of the genre; presumably the extent of technology and custom common to the Aleut, Koniag, Chugach, Tanaina, Eyak, and Tlingit indicates some amicable interaction. Trade within and beyond area boundaries is seen in the example of Aleutian dentalia (Hrdlička 1945), which ultimately derived from the Northwest Coast. The Russians, at an early date, deterred intergroup conflicts and at the same time diverted native trade into their own hands; thus, the historic accounts poorly relate the functional context of intertribal relationships.

History

The first contact between the Pacific Eskimo and Europeans was a silent encounter. Vitus Bering's second expedition, which is credited with the discovery of Alaska,

186

saw dwellings on and near Kayak Island east of the Copper River in 1741, but the inhabitants, probably Chugach, had fled. Gifts were left for them (Steller's account in Stejneger 1936:269–270; Waxell 1952:105–106, interpreted by Birket-Smith 1953). In 1761 Dimitrii Pan'kov (Shelekhov 1981:41) or in 1763 Stephen Glotov and crew (Coxe 1803; Berkh 1974:35–36) spent the winter on Kodiak although their presence was vigorously resisted by the Koniags. In 1776 Dimitrii Bragin (Dimitrii Polutov according to Berkh 1974:50), who had arrived to trade, was forced to leave the island (Berkh 1974; Hrdlička 1944:11), as was another ship-based trader, Ivan Ocheredin who overwintered there in 1779–1780 (Berkh 1974:57–58). A large party of fur hunters in three ships under Potap Zaikov reached Prince William Sound (Chugatsk Bay) in 1783 where they overwintered although they were constrained from hunting by the hostile Chugach (Shelekhov 1981; Berkh 1974:62–63). By this time other European powers, particularly the English (since James Cook in 1778) and the Spaniards also had been probing into Prince William Sound and Cook Inlet (Birket-Smith 1953:8–11; Gormly 1977; De Laguna 1956:10). The primary stage of European discovery of the Pacific area had been accomplished. From among the Europeans the Russians settled in the area.

Grigorii Shelekhov forcibly overcame Koniag resistance, established a post at Three Saints Bay on Kodiak in 1784, and ordered exploration and the establishment of small posts elsewhere in the region (Coxe 1803; Shelekhov 1981:46–48). In 1785 Shelekhov sent an exploration party to Prince William Sound and outer Cook Inlet (Shelekhov 1981:46). Later, a small post was established in Cook Inlet. Again, in 1788, a party led by Gerasim Ismailov and Dimitrii Bocharov left Three Saints Harbor for Prince William Sound and the mainland coasts eastward as far as Lituya Bay. At Prince William Sound they only missed by days meeting vessels from other countries (Shelekhov 1981:84). In 1792 Aleksandr Baranov, the recently arrived manager at Kodiak, took hostages in Prince William Sound and engaged in a night battle apparently with a roving company of Tlingit Indians. The following year a different Russian trading company placed a post near Nuchek (Bancroft 1886:324–328). Rival companies, to be consolidated by the end of the century, by then also had established stations on Cook Inlet, especially among the Tanaina Indians living adjacent to the Kenai Peninsula Eskimo (Bancroft 1886:334 ff.; Berkh 1974:65).

Hostages were demanded and these, usually children of traditional chiefs, were kept at Kodiak (Coxe 1803:351 after Sauer 1802; Shelekhov 1981:15). The natives were organized into a work force under appointed chiefs and Russian overseers (Davydov 1977; Gedeon in Valaam Monastery 1978:136; Gideon in Black 1977). All men and women were required to work for the company for a certain period and meet a quota. This included service in a sea-otter hunting brigade, bird hunting, or at fox trapping and work artels (small settlements with primarily native work crews, the actual personnel by some definitions being the artel) to secure a diverse array of foodstuffs including dried salmon, whale meat, and edible roots. There appears to have been more than one category of persons required to serve the company or to fulfill a quota, though some accounts do not make a consistent distinction between them. Provisions, though sometimes scant, and reimbursement were provided by the company, particularly when one's take of furs exceeded the quota (Davydov 1977; Gedeon in Valaam Monastery 1978). Men and hunting parties were freely dispersed over coastal Alaska and even to California and the Asiatic side of the North Pacific Ocean. These demands and dispersals severely disrupted the native lifeway and resulted in a rapid population decline although attempts at directed culture change appear to have been minimal. From an estimated population of more than 9,000 at the time of first sustained contact in 1784, the Pacific Eskimo decreased to less than 6,000 by 1800, soon to 5,000, following a smallpox epidemic to 3,000 by the middle of the nineteenth century, and possibly minus a few hundred more persons by the time of the first U.S. census there in 1880. With the inclusion of 600 to 800 persons of mixed descent, there were then 278 Chugach (a group that may never have been numerous), 205 Kenai Eskimo, and 2,458 Koniags, who earlier numbered about 8,000 inclusive of the adjacent Alaska Peninsula (calculations based on U.S. Census Office 1884).

Culture

Exploration accounts and traditional information provide ample information for certain aspects of Pacific Eskimo culture at the time of contact, which is the time base for the following description.

Subsistence

The sea is calm, a mobile gray mass emerges from the depths, breaks water—a sharp prick! The wounded whale dives, the rear paddler in the two-hatch kayak backs off to avoid danger, and the hunters of the whalers' caste are gone too, back to the shore to wait quietly three to six or more days for the dead whale to float. It is not known whether the efficacy of the dart—a slate-tipped feathered shaft five feet long—was due to the aconitine poison smeared on the tip during secret whaling rites or to inflammation produced by salt water and the 12-inch-long ground slate tip (Heizer 1943; Lantis 1938; Lisīanskiī 1814). Unlike harpoon whaling, no physical tie was maintained with the whale, but the deeply embayed coast is preeminently suited for re-

Fig. 2. Early depictions of Pacific Eskimo. top left, *toion Nankok of Kodiak, baptized Nikita*. He wears a headdress of red feathers, with black and white beads, has red tattooed or painted lines on his face, and holds a rattle made of wooden rings with puffin beaks tied in clusters (Birket-Smith 1941:157–159). Watercolor by Mikhail Tikhanov, 1818. top right, *A Man of Prince William's Sound* wearing a waterproof gutskin parka, basketry hat with red and black painted decoration, and nose ornament with a bead on either end. His lower lip is perforated to hold labrets. bottom left, *A Woman of Prince William's Sound*, with fur cape, face paint, labrets, and ear and nose ornaments. bottom right, *A native of Prince William Sound* wearing fur garment with small mammal tails or fur strips as decoration, face paint, necklace, beadlike labrets, and ornament inserted through pierced nasal septum. top right and bottom, Watercolors by John Webber, who accompanied James Cook, 1778 (for other versions of these by Webber, see Beaglehole 1967:pls. 44b, 45 ab; Bushnell 1928:pl. 6).

covering dead whales. Whales were desired for their blubber (fat), meat, and especially oil derived from the blubber.

Another drama takes place when a party of hunters in their kayaks surrounds a sea otter: "The prey [is] so sure, that scarcely one animal out of a hundred can save itself from its pursuers" (Lisīanskiĭ 1814:203). The surround method of hunting with harpoon arrows and darts (Fassett 1960) is widely distributed in the northern North Pacific, probably due to postcontact introduction by fur traders though it may have been indigenous among the Pacific Eskimo. Firearms did not successfully replace native implements, which were especially well adapted for recovering prey in the water. Sea otters also were clubbed when forced ashore during storms.

The Pacific Eskimo, together with the Aleuts, are noted for their development of the two-hatch kayak, used especially in the sea otter hunt. Under Russian instigation this craft was enlarged to a three-hatch form (fig. 3). Both are historically known by the Russian designation *baĭdarka*. Dugouts also are reported for Prince William Sound (Merck 1980:122). Probably the only known illustration of the other craft commonly used by Eskimos, the umiak (Pacific Yupik *áŋyaq*), in its original Chugach Eskimo form prior to modification by the Russians, is reproduced in figure 5.

Seal hunting ranked high in economic value along with the salmon fishery, saltwater fishery, and whaling. Harbor seals were harpooned from kayaks, harpooned from the shore after being attracted within range through a decoy consisting of a helmet (fig. 6) or inflated sealskin, clubbed at hauling grounds, or trapped and entangled with large nets (Lisīanskiĭ 1814). Two other important marine sources of food and raw material—porpoises and sea lions—were harpooned.

Sea birds were taken by a variety of projectiles and in nets, but the bolas was not employed.

It is evident from the natural distribution of fauna and the recovery of faunal refuse in archeological sites (Clark 1974; De Laguna 1956) that land mammals were of considerably lesser economic importance than marine mammals, although nearly all available species were trapped, snared, or hunted. Where locally available, ground squirrels were intensively snared for their fur, which was used in parkas (Davydov 1977; Holmberg 1856:364). Although not obtained in large numbers,

caribou were sought on the Alaska Peninsula and mountain goat and marmot around Prince William Sound. Their products—horns, antler, fur, and hides—were traded to other parts of the Pacific area (Holmberg 1856:366; Merck 1980:205); however, most hunting, trapping, and fishing were for subsistence.

Too little is known about fisheries considering their value, according to some observers, as the main source of food. Denizens of the sea, particularly cod, halibut, and sculpin were hooked from deep water. Historically, halibut hooks were similar to those used by the Tlingit on the Northwest Coast (Birket-Smith 1941:fig. 22),

top, Natl. Arch.: RG22-FA-5269; bottom, © Natl. Geographic Soc., Washington.
Fig. 3. Kayaks with upturned bow characteristic of Pacific Eskimo. top, One with 2 hatches at Old Harbor, Kodiak I. Photograph by N.B. Miller, 1888–1889. bottom, Type with extra hatch said to have been introduced to transport Russian passengers. Photograph by George C. Martin at Iliamna Bay, 1912.

Fig. 4. Quiver. Two vertical pieces of wood are bound with sinew to form a cylinder, which is decorated with incising and black and red paint. It was placed on top of a kayak between 2 hunters to hold arrows for both; skin quivers were used when hunting on land (Birket-Smith 1953:28,37). Length 94.0 cm. Collected on Kodiak I., Alaska, 1868–1898.

while the apparatus for taking cod (described by Homberg 1856:385) evidently was more distinctive of the area (for these and most other material objects see illustrations in Birket-Smith 1941, 1953; Heizer 1952). Salmon fishing was concentrated at spawning streams where, at weirs, salmon were speared, gaffed, or harpooned. Among the Chugach herring were taken with a fish rake. Reports of fish nets are not to be accepted without questioning their precontact indigenous application. Shellfish (sea urchins, periwinkles, clams, blue mussels, chitons, etc.) were consumed in large quantities judging from shell midden deposits at late prehistoric and early historic settlement sites. Shellfish exploitation often is interpreted as primarily an activity of the late winter season of scarcity (Lisīanskiĭ 1814:173), but circumstantial evidence consisting of clamshells at inland summer salmon fishing sites suggests that there also was an epicurian interest in shellfish.

Economic activities followed a natural annual cycle that probably formed a calendar for other aspects of Pacific Eskimo life. Only one brief account of the annual cycle, from three related sources, is available for the early contact period (Merck 1980:105, 205). Even

by 1790 the activities reported for Kodiak may have been altered to suit the fur trade. Fur seals were hunted from February until April, according to the Julian calendar. After then until June hunters departed to the outlying islands for sea otter. Harbor seals, porpoise, and sea lions were hunted from April through October, sea lions particularly during June and July when whales also were killed. Salmon were available from May through September, and halibut were readily caught early in the season before the salmon runs of five species reached their peak. Dried salmon was prepared during July.

The Chugach took whales, sea otter, and halibut throughout the year; fur seal in May; salmon, herring, halibut, cod, and eulachon during the summer; sea lion mainly during the fall but also throughout the year; mountain goat during the fall and winter; and bear and harbor seal during the winter (Birket-Smith 1953).

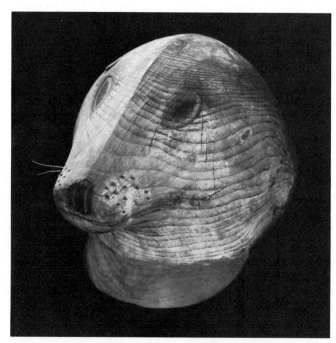

Fig. 5. Europeans coming ashore at Chugach Bay. The natives on left wear traditional clothing and one is pulling a kayak onto the beach. Three large umiaks are beached and one provides shelter for 2 women. Engraving based on sketch made about July 25, 1790.

Fig. 6. Wooden decoy helmet carved to represent a seal and painted white, red, and black. Attaching it with the rawhide chin strap, the hunter lay among rocks until seals approached close enough to be killed. Length 25.4 cm. Collected by Edward G. Fast on Kodiak I., Alaska, 1867–1868.

Smithsonian, Dept. of Anthr.: 68,623.

Fig. 8. Wooden bowl used as a food dish, carved to represent a bird and decorated with grooves, inlaid white seed beads, and red coloring on the interior. The right wing is partly missing and repaired with a metal staple. Length 37.5 cm. Collected by William J. Fisher at Prince William Sound, Alaska, 1893.

Smithsonian, Dept. of Anthr.: 90,429; 90,428; 72,528.

Fig. 7. Spoons of mountain goat horn, decorated with incising and inlaid white seed beads. The handles are carved in a style resembling that of Northwest Coast Indians. Simpler spoons and ladles were carved in bone and wood. bottom, Width of ladle 6.5 cm, rest same scale. Collected by William J. Fisher on Kodiak I., Alaska, 1882–1883.

In the autumn, prior to the winter festivities, the families returned to their main settlements. Too, in the late summer the women picked berries and dug certain edible roots, among them cranberry (*Vaccinium vitis-idaea*) and the bulbs of the Kamchatka fritillary (*Fritillaria camschatcensis*), to be mixed or eaten with oil rendered from sea mammal fat.

Structures

Winter villages were located behind a headland, in the lee of a small island, or in a small embayment. Fishing camps or summer villages were located around the mouth of a salmon stream, especially where there were heavy runs of several species. Defensive positions on relatively inaccessible rocks were occupied when the need was felt to be impending or all the able men had departed the village on an expedition (Davydov 1977:173; Gedeon in Valaam Monastery 1978:124).

Dwellings were not numerous, but several families, up to 20 persons, lived in each house; thus a settlement easily aggregated 100 to 200 persons (Holmberg 1856:376). Each morning, the day permitting, one could find the male residents sitting quietly upon the turf- and straw-covered roof of their semisubterranean home contemplating the sunrise at sea (Davydov 1977:173; Lisīanskiĭ 1814). Inside, the main or common room, with its central hearth and unkept floor, served as the kitchen while families and even their dogs slept and found privacy in the several appended better-kept, floored side-chambers. The common room also could be used as a workshop where, when not similarly occupied outside, men fashioned pieces for kayak and umiak frames, spear throwers, slat armor, bows, quivers and a large array of arrows, harpoons, and darts; and women wove baskets (fig. 9) and hats and sewed bags and clothing. Here too they held gatherings, ceremonies, and dances in villages that did not have a hall. The private side rooms were heated with hot rocks and were employed also for sweatbaths (vapor or steambath) (Holmberg 1856:377; Merck 1980:100), which were taken by both sexes for ritual purification as well as for enjoyment. There should be no question that the vapor sweatbath antedates the arrival of the Russians. Although the Koniag house is described by nearly every historical ethnographer, some structural details would be open to interpretation were it not for the fact that photographs are available for similar houses that continued to be built to the beginning of the twentieth century on the Alaska Peninsula (Martin 1913). The Chugach had, at least during historic time, wooden plank houses, but the organization into a common room and private compartments still applied (Birket-Smith 1953).

Fig. 9. Spruce root baskets. Two-strand or plain twined basketry decorated with false embroidery of grass and maidenhair fern made by Pacific Eskimos can be distinguished from similar work by Tlingit Indians on the basis of its concentric rings of 3-strand twining on the base, the weft of unpolished grade of spruce root, the lower stitch count, a primary and secondary design field, and differences in design elements (M. Lee 1981). left, Height 14.0 cm, collected on the Vancouver Expedition, 1794; right, same scale, collected by A.K. Etolin before 1847.

Social Organization

The structure of a domicile group has not been recorded, but inasmuch as a young man, upon marriage, customarily went to live with his wife's parents (Merck 1980:108), usually temporarily, a household probably contained several sisters and their families, any unmarried siblings, an older couple, and an assortment of peripheral persons such as poor relatives and orphans. The status of those peripheral persons was little higher than that of the occasional slave obtained through trade or war.

Life Cycle

Marriage was initiated either through consultation between mutually inclined principals and their own parents or between the prospective in-laws, and the exchange of valuable gifts (statements regarding these points vary among the several early sources of which Gedeon in Valaam Monastery 1978 is the most detailed). It was consummated when the man effected the gift exchange, if there was any, and took residence with his wife. Gifts notwithstanding, wives were not purchased (Merck 1980:108). Women had relatively high status, although they did not participate directly in public affairs or councils (Davydov 1977:165). A woman might have two husbands, the second one with status little above that of a servant (Gedeon in Valaam Monastery 1978:128), and spouses could separate and remarry.

Birth took place near the house in a small temporary hut (Davydov 1977:171) where the mother remained 5 or 10 days (Gedeon in Valaam Monastery 1978:127) or longer (multiples of the ritual number 5). Women and girls also had to retire to these huts or to a sleeping compartment for 10 days at the first menstruation and for the period of all subsequent ones. Similar seclusion occured when a child died (Lisīanskiĭ 1814:200). After birth seclusion, the mother and child were taken into the sweatbath, and at this time on Kodiak perforations were started for labrets and nose pins. Cradling resulted in very broad, occipitally flattened heads, but the use of cradles is not fully described (Davydov 1977:154, 164), and occipital flattening may have been unintentional, Pinart's (1873) description notwithstanding.

Children were nursed until about the age of three, or longer among the Chugach (Birket-Smith 1953). They were raised permissively and not let cry, but at the same time they were taught stoicism, for instance by immersion in cold water. Children were disciplined by admonition and, if necessary, through scorn and ridicule (Gedeon in Valaam Monastery 1978:127). Six-year-old girls started to perform productive tasks like mat weaving, while the play of boys, throwing toy spears for instance, and later their assistance at fish camps, led into adult activities. From the age of about 12 years boys were under adult tutelage, particularly an uncle, and by the age of 16 they were accompanying hunting parties in their own kayaks. It may be inferred that some nephews (potential sons-in-law?) of the adult men stayed with the family temporarily although the avunculate was not a formally developed institution. Tattooing of the chin signaled that a girl had reached puberty (Merck 1980:103). Sometimes the parents had wanted a child of the opposite sex; thus, a girl might be given a masculine name and be raised and trained as a son (Gedeon in Valaam Monastery 1978:121). More often the reverse occurred, and the male transvestite (with chin tattoos) continued in that esteemed role through life.

Departure by death was not a total breakoff of interpersonal relationships as the dead were kept at hand in a side chamber of a house, nearby within the settlement area (Merck 1980:108) (Chugach excepted?), or, in the case of rich persons and special categories, were taken to secluded places and preserved in a form of mummification, sometimes for participation in secret whaling rituals (Lisīanskiĭ 1814:174). Following the initial mourning and interment, at which a slave sometimes accompanied a person of high rank (Lisīanskiĭ 1814:200), close relatives of the deceased cropped or singed their hair, blackened their faces, and went into seclusion. Songs might be sung at the grave or food and water taken there at twilight for 40 days or longer, possibly until the deceased had been honored at the winter celebrations.

192

Ceremonies

Feasts, public gatherings and restricted ceremonies and business meetings were held in the men's hall or kashim (Pacific Yupik *qásxiq,* rendered khasu by Merck 1980:100; Russian *kazhim*). The kashim does not appear to have been the men's dormitory and club house that it was in the southern Bering Sea region, although the Russians did designate native barracks by this term. Not every village had a hall, and it may have been completely lacking among the Chugach: a large residence served for this purpose. A kashim was built by a rich leader (*aŋá·yuqaq*) and could be rented out for individually sponsored fetes, such as a wedding party, but it was used primarily for winter ceremonies.

A considerable battery of ceremonies, dances, masked performances, rituals and feasts followed in rapid succession in the early winter for as long as the food reserves permitted or was held at other times for certain purposes (Davydov 1977:183; Gedeon in Valaam Monastery 1978:122–126; Merck 1980:100). Although purpose cannot always be ascertained from the early descriptions, these evidently included the memorial feast for the dead, an animal increase ceremony, invitational potlatches (which included trading), ceremonies on the occasion of securing a whale (Chugach only?), planning a war party, the succession of chiefs, the announcement of an invitational potlatch, and various first events in a life cycle.

Smithsonian, Dept. of Anthr.: 90,453.
Fig. 11. Headdress, probably worn by women on festive occasions. Varied sizes of opaque, faceted, and clear glass beads in red, white, blues, black, gold, and green are strung on sinew between horizontal leather separator strips. There is a circle of leather at the crown and dangling fringe over the forehead and ears as well as the tail at the back. Necklaces and earrings were also made from these trade beads. Total length from crown 51.0 cm; collected by William J. Fisher at Ugashik, Alaska, 1883.

Political Organization

References are found in the historical literature to the owner of a kashim, to a rich man (criteria given by Gedeon in Valaam Monastery 1978:121), and to a leader, referred to by various renderings of Pacific Yupik *aŋá·yuqaq*: anaiugak (Gedeon in Valaam Monastery 1978:121), ngayokak (Merck 1980), or anayugak. These may be essentially one and the same and Gedeon defines the last as 'village chief'. Although a position of leadership was inherited, or at least filled by one of noble class (Holmberg 1856:358), it had to be maintained on a personal basis through advice, gifts, and respect. Gedeon (in Valaam Monastery 1978:121) states that an aging chief would decide whom among his varied categories of relatives would become his successor and inherit his kashim. In personal undertakings, but not communal proceedings decided in a gathering, a man followed his own will, unless he were a slave. Holmberg (1856:358) suggests that slavery was not highly developed as an economic institution. Classes may have been less rigid than the use of European terms (noble, com-

Smithsonian, Dept. of Anthr.: 90,438.
Fig. 10. Rattle. Puffin beaks are tied with sinew to the framework of twigs bent into concentric circles and attached to the central wood cross-pieces. Probably shaken by dancers. Diameter 24.0 cm; collected by William J. Fisher on Uganik I., Alaska, 1883.

moner, slave) implies. Each settlement had its chief (fig. 12), but some chiefs exercised influence over a number of villages (Davydov 1977:190).

Although exploration accounts dwell on personal adornment, tattooing, and face painting (cf. Merck 1980:103) no indication is given that the designs signal any aspect of lineage or social organization.

Shamanism and Religion

Among other roles or part-time practitioners were the shaman or medicine man (*kałá·aləq,* rendered kaha-hulik in Merck 1980), the "wise-man," and the curer. Shamanism was commonly resorted to when one wanted to forecast the success or the proper timing of an undertaking, to forecast or control the weather, to cure, or to ascertain events—like the well-being of a relative—at a different place (Merck 1980:107). Although contact with the supernatural was attained through a trance, it also was found or implemented through masks (fig. 13) and dolls. Usually, there was no special costume, but the face was painted and feathers adorned the head, and sometimes a shaman performed naked (Gedeon in Valaam Monastery 1978:135). A garment might be reversed or its sex changed in the case of the relatively common male transvestite medicine man. Women also could be shamans.

Much curing was done not by shamans but by healers, usually women, whose bloodletting practices, involving incision of various parts of the body, suggest an affinity to acupuncture. They also knew several herbal cures and employed extraction methods, such as sucking out the cause of illness.

© Natl. Geographic Soc., Washington.
Fig. 12. Alexi, chief of the village at Chignik, in front of sod-covered structure. Photograph by Bernard R. Hubbard, summer 1930.

194

Smithsonian, Dept. of Anthr.: 20,269.
Fig. 13. Carved wooden dance mask painted red around the mouth, on one eye, designs on the forehead, and in a dot on the back; the nose and several forehead strips are green. The nostril holes serve as peepholes, and there is a bar across the back. Originally there were probably also feather decorations. Length 45.0 cm, collected at Prince William Sound, Alaska, before 1875.

On Kodiak the organization and conduct of religious ceremonies, including the perpetuation of all requisite knowledge, and according to one source the composition of poetry, was in the hands of wise-men (*kássaq* sg., rendered kaseks, kachaks, and kasiats), who later were terminologically equated to priests (Lisīanskiĭ 1814:208). The deity *łam sua* 'spirit of the sky' was described as the high diety among the Koniag (hlam-choua in Pinart 1873), but as but one of the three major "owners" of the universe among the Chugach (Birket-Smith 1953:120–121). Several classes of spirits and beings, from giants to benign dwarfs to evil shamans' helpers with pointed heads, also inhabited the Pacific Eskimo's world. At the individual level there was considerable use of amulets and songs and adherence to behavioral proscriptions to secure luck and other desired results.

Clothing

Traditional clothing for both sexes of the Pacific Eskimo differed from that of their high arctic congeners, though in many aspects it was like that of the Aleuts. The principal garments were very long, usually hoodless, fur and bird-skin parkas and hooded rain parkas (known by the Siberian Russian term *kamleǐka*) sewn from strips of intestine (Davydov 1977:102, 155; Holmberg 1856:364; Merck 1980:111). Trousers were not worn and gloves are not reported. Boots and other footwear were poorly developed and were not worn during the warm season.

To work while wearing a parka, people inserted their arms through slits at the side rather than through the virtually nonfunctional sleeves. At sea hunters wore decorated scalene (slanted) conical bent-wood hats, characteristic also of the Aleutian Islands and southern Bering Sea region, and two forms of woven spruce root hats (fig. 14) characteristic of and evidently traded and copied from the Indian tribes of the Northwest Coast. Some later caps show Russian influence. For indoor wear early in the nineteenth century imported fabric clothing replaced the garments, described above, which could be shed if not needed, but traditional clothing continued to be worn outside. Evidently, suitable alternatives were not available among imported clothing.

Synonymy†

In the early sources the Koniag and the Chugach are always named separately.

Early variants of the name Koniag include Kanagist, 1763 (Glotov in Coxe 1803), Koniagi and Kanjagi, 1791 (Jacobi 1937:116, 127), Kanīag-, 1802 (Sarychev in Bergsland 1959:11), Koniaga, 1810 (Davydov 1977:148), and Konjagen (Holmberg 1856:355). These are ultimately derived from the Aleut name for the Eskimo of the Alaska Peninsula and Kodiak Island, Atkan pl. *kana·ɣis* (Bergsland 1959:11). Early writers show some confusion about the origin of the name; some take it as a self-designation (Glotov, Davydov) though Bolotov (in Black 1977:84) says it is not known why they are called Kanyag, especially since the name, unlike that of many other peoples, is not derived from the locality this group occupies. The statement that Kaniagi was applied to the Aleut (Merck 1980:109) appears to be a mistranslation (cf. Jacobi 1937:127). Later Russian writers used the name *Kad'íakfsy* (adjective *Kad'íakskiï*), derived from the Russian name of Kodiak Island, *Kad'íak* (Wrangell 1839), itself of unknown origin. The hybrid name Kaniagmiut (Hodge 1907–1910, 1:652) is an incorrect coinage of W.H. Dall.

Both the Koniag and the Chugach use the Pacific Yupik name *qikəxtaɣmiut* 'island people' for the Koniag; this appears as Kychtagmytt (Merck 1937:127), Kykhtagmiut (Merck 1980:109), Kikhtagmute (Petroff in U.S. Census Office 1884:136), and Qiqtarmiut (Birket-Smith 1953:99).

The name Chugach first appears in the historical literature as Schugatschi or Shugarski in Zaikov's account (in Pallas 1781–1793; see also Masterson and Brower 1948), apparently recorded in 1775–1778 from outside the region prior to Zaikov's recorded visit to Prince William Sound in 1783. A few years later the Russian forms Chiugachi (assumed from Shelekhov 1981:46) and Chugachi, 1792 (assumed from Merck 1980:111), are found, and Wrangell (1839:67) has Chugachik´; Jacobi

†This synonymy was written by Donald Clark and Ives Goddard.

PACIFIC ESKIMO: HISTORICAL ETHNOGRAPHY

British Mus.: NWC 4.

Fig. 14. Conical basketry hat of twined spruce root with painted designs in red, mauve, and green, red and white beads, and leather chin straps. Both the shape and the design style resemble Northwest Coast Indian hats. Diameter 47.0 cm; probably collected at Prince William Sound, Alaska, 1780.

(1937:116) has German Tschuwatschi. It is possible that the source of this name is Pacific Yupik *suá·ciq* (pl. *suá·cit*), recorded by Birket-Smith (1953:19) as a self-designation, but Jeff Leer (communication to editors 1982) has pointed out difficulties with this derivation. The phonetics do not match very precisely (even with *s* in its Chugach pronunciation [š]), and although there is an Alaska Peninsula dialect form *suɣá·ciq* that is closer, the Russians had little contact with that area. Furthermore, contemporary Pacific Yupik speakers regard *suá·cit* as a pejorative term used for people of different background; although on Kodiak it is applied to the Chugach, on the Kenai Peninsula it is given to people of Athapaskan ancestry. A recent borrowing from Chinook Jargon *siwash* 'Indian' is possible. Leer suggests that a more likely source of Chugach is the Pacific Yupik place-name *cú·ŋá·ciq* 'Cook Inlet'; in this case Dall's Chūgăch´ig-mūt, the basis of the Chugachigmiut of Hodge (1907–1910, 1:294), could be a genuine form rather than one of his coinages (as Birket-Smith thought).

The Russians extended the name Aleut (see the syn- *195*

onymy in "Aleut," this vol.) to all the Pacific Eskimo as well. This usage is attested at least as early as 1805, when Langsdorff (1813–1814) referred to the Kodiak Islanders by this name, and is preferred by many Pacific Eskimo. In the 1970s the desire among natives and scholars to differentiate the distinct Alaska groups called Aleut led to the proposal of a series of alternative names, including Sugpiaq (representing *súxpiaq*, an archaic expression for 'a real person') and, for their language, Sugcestun (*súxčəstun* [súxtstun] 'like people'). By 1982 the name Alutiiq (*alú·tíq* 'a Pacific Eskimo person', the native borrowing of Aleut in the current practical orthography) was being widely adopted as the English name for both the people (with plural Alutiiqs) and the language (Krauss 1979:815; Leer 1978:1–2, 4, 35). Names including the term Eskimo tended to be disfavored because of a strongly felt cultural and ethnic distinctness from the Eskimos to the north. The Tanaina call the Pacific Eskimo *ʔułčəna* (Kari 1977:94).

Sources

Several historical ethnographies give particular attention to the Koniags. There are far fewer accounts of the Chugach and almost none of the Kenai Peninsula Eskimo.

For the first contacts on Kodiak there are accounts of Pan'kov's or Glotov's visit in 1761 or 1763 (in Coxe 1803:185–196), Bragin's attempt to trade in 1776 (in Masterson and Brower 1948:71–73), and Shelekhov's establishment of Three Saints in 1784 (Shelekhov 1981). From the scientific expedition led by Capt. Joseph Billings and Capt. Gavril Sarychev, which visited Three Saints in 1790 when Russian control was well established, there are four accounts (Sarychev 1802; Sauer 1802; Merck 1980; Billings in Merck 1980).

The most valuable works are Merck (1980) and the trio dating to 1803–1806 of Davydov (1977), Lisīanskiĭ (1814), and Gedeon (in Valaam Monastery 1978; Gideon in Black 1977), supplemented by Bolotov's brief account (in Black 1977). Langsdorff (1813–1814), like others, discusses Russian life and treatment of natives. By the first decade of the nineteenth century it had become necessary to refer to former as well as contemporary conditions.

Holmberg's (1856) account of the middle of the nineteenth century is a blend of original observations and those of others, while subsequent Koniag ethnographies are largely derivatives or specialized synthetic studies (Bancroft 1886a, 1:96ff.; Birket-Smith 1941; Heizer 1943; Hewes 1947; Lantis 1938, 1938a, 1947; Hrdlička 1944; U.S. Census Office 1884:136–145; Oswalt 1967). There are in addition Pinart's (1873) enigmatic account of world view and his notes in the Bancroft Library, University of California, Berkeley, and collections of folklore (Golder 1903, 1907, 1909).

Ethnographic collections are described by Birket-Smith (1941) for items in Nationalmuseet, Copenhagen, Denmark, collected by H.J. Holmberg, by Heizer (1952) for the Alaska Commercial Company collection in the Robert H. Lowie Museum of Anthropology, University of California, Berkeley, and by Lipshits (1950, 1955) for some items in the Muzeĭ Antropologii i Ėtnografii, Leningrad. Additional specimens in the Leningrad museum are illustrated by Ivanov (1930), Ray (1981), and Zolotarevskaja, Blomkvist, and Zibert (1958). Lot-Falck (1957) describes masks in the Musée des Beaux-Arts et d'Archéologie, Boulogne-sur-Mer, France, collected by Pinart (1872). Important material from Kodiak is located in the Suomen Kansallimuseo, the national museum of Finland, Helsinki, which has items collected by Arvid A. Etholen.

This massive body of historical ethnography suffers from the defects common to its genre: it provides a great deal of particular facts but very little to give an integrated overview of lifeways including social and territorial organization and the annual cycle.

Ethnographic work among the Koniag since the 1950s has focused primarily on contemporary situations (Befu 1970; Davis 1970, 1971; Hammerich 1954; K.L. Kemp 1981; Lundsgaarde 1962; Oswalt 1955; Rathburn 1981; Taylor 1966).

Soon after their penetration of the Kodiak area, the Russians were visiting Prince William Sound from the west while numerous ships of other European powers reached Chugach Eskimo territory principally by sailing up the Pacific Coast (Bancroft 1886:255–281; Birket-Smith 1953:8–11), but accounts of ethnographic value arising from these early explorations, undertaken largely during 1785–1800, are brief (cf. Cook and King 1785, 2; Ellis 1782; Beresford 1789; Meares 1790; Merck 1980; Portlock 1789). Gormly (1977) provides a thorough guide to ethnographic source material, which exists primarily in manuscripts, from several Spanish voyages of this period. Information from the Russian explorations is extremely brief, as is noted by Birket-Smith (1953) and De Laguna (1956). Bushnell (1928) and Gunther (1972) draw on the graphics from Cook's and other voyages. Except for collecting activities, subsequent contributions to Chugach ethnography were scant until 1933 when Birket-Smith, with De Laguna, undertook fieldwork for an ethnography integrating exploration accounts, museum collections, and original fieldwork.

Dall (1880), Jacobsen (1884), and Meany (1906) made collections and have left some information on Chugach burial caves and mummies (summarized in De Laguna 1956:66–101). Chugach artifacts in the Museum für Völkerkunde, Berlin, collected by Jacobsen are described by Birket-Smith (1953) together with a few specimens in the Danish national museum acquired in 1933. A few weapons are located in the Historisches Museum, Bern, Switzerland (Bandi 1958). Two collections of masks are described by Dall (1884, illustrated in Birket-Smith 1953:fig. 41) and Lot-Falck (1957). Other Chugach masks are located in the Smithsonian Institution, in the Sheldon Jackson Museum, Sitka, Alaska (Collins et al. 1973: Nos.142–143, 145; Ray 1981:fig. 47), in Madrid (Ray 1981:fig 48), and in the Burke Memorial Washington State Museum, Seattle (Ray 1967:pl. 40). Finally, it should be noted that the material culture of the Pacific Eskimo during the eighteenth century at and immediately preceding contact is represented in certain late archeological collections (see "Prehistory of the Pacific Eskimo Region," this vol.).

Contemporary Pacific Eskimo

NANCY YAW DAVIS

The three historically distinct groups of the Pacific Eskimo (or Pacific Gulf Eskimo) are the Koniag, the Chugach, and the Unegkurmiut on the lower Kenai Peninsula. The local and often preferred use of the name Aleut for these groups is discussed in the synonymy in "Pacific Eskimo: Historical Ethnography" (this vol.).

In 1980 descendants of these traditional groups of Pacific Eskimo lived in 15 villages and five towns, as well as in the larger cities of Alaska and elsewhere (fig. 1). This chapter deals primarily with events since 1960 and description of the contemporary villages, but recognition should be given to important, continuous ties that extend to nearby towns and beyond. After considering some common characteristics shared by these southernmost village Eskimo, the distinctiveness of the villages will be reviewed by area.

All the villages are located on the seacoast and all are small. The largest community is Old Harbor on Kodiak Island, with 340 people, and the smallest is Ivanof Bay with 40 residents in 1980 (census). The villages maintain distinct identities as semi–self-sufficient units of people who live in relative isolation. The means of physical communication are limited to air and sea; no roads connect the villages with any other community. Radio contact is maintained between the villages and the nearest major town, but travel to town is usually limited to periodic pleasure or medical visits.

Although most villagers in the 1980s shared a common fluency in English, they originally all shared a linguistic affiliation with the Pacific Eskimo branch of Yupik.* By 1970 only an estimated 1,000 out of 4,000 Pacific Eskimo spoke this language, and only at English Bay were the school children able to speak it. The Alaska Native Language Center in Fairbanks began working with the people of English Bay in 1973 to develop materials to help keep the language alive (Krauss 1973a:19), and it has since produced practical introductory dictionaries for three dialects (Leer 1978:2–3) and other educational material (Sawden and Pulu 1979).

The villages have experienced a similar sequence of historical contacts with the western world. From the

late eighteenth century until 1867, they came under Russian influence that resulted in the establishment of a strong commitment to the Russian Orthodox Church. Then, starting in the 1880s in the American period, the village economies were profoundly affected by the establishment of salmon canneries and commercial fishing. In the twentieth century, other new institutions were introduced: schools, missions from different faiths, and government agencies such as the Public Health Service and the Bureau of Indian Affairs. During the 1960s, federal programs like community action agencies, Vista and Headstart, and state programs including health, welfare, and other social service aid, and the Alaska State troopers, have further increased, though unevenly, the internal differentiation of each community. In the details of response to these forces of change, the villages vary but the fact of increasing government involvement is constant. With each new agency has come a wider web of ties with the world beyond the village and beyond the nearest cannery (Davis 1969). Modernization processes accelerated in the 1970s by the introduction of new or improved facilities under both federal and state auspices included new houses, water and sewer systems, community-wide electrical services, telephones, and television. Airstrips, bridges, and local roads were built or expanded in many of the communities; a few boat harbors were added.

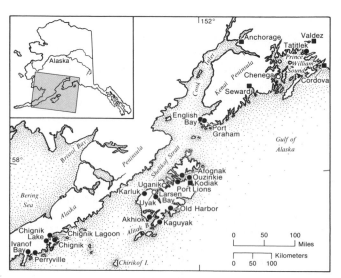

Fig. 1. Pacific Eskimo villages.

---

*For the orthography of Pacific Eskimo words, see the footnote in "Pacific Eskimo: Historical Ethnography" (this vol.). Jeff Leer (communication to editors 1982) provided the name of the Kenai Peninsula people.

Two events have had profound effects on the villages of the area. The first of these was the great Alaska earthquake of 1964 with its accompanying tsunamis (seismic sea waves), which brought about displacement of people for varying periods and, ultimately, resettlement and the reorganization of several of the villages. The second was the passing of the Alaska Native Claims Settlement Act of 1971, which forced the villagers to share common problems of urgent decision making, complex land selections, enrollment procedures, increased stratification, and new demands for leadership. Each village formed a local corporation and also became part of a larger regional corporation (see "The Land Claims Era in Alaska," this vol.). Traditional alignments have been redirected through the groupings of the Chugach and the Unegkurmiut to form Chugach Natives, Inc., and the affiliation of some Pacific villages with their northern neighbors in Bristol Bay Native Corporation though they have closer ties with Kodiak. Only the Koniag of Kodiak have retained their traditionally separate ethnic affiliation through their enrollment to Koniag, Incorporated.

Villages

The Pacific Yupik villages are located in four distinct geographic areas: the Alaska Peninsula, the Kenai Peninsula, Prince William Sound, and Kodiak Island (fig. 1).

The historical ethnic ties of the cluster of five villages on the Pacific side of the Alaska Peninsula have not been clearly established, but linguistically they are known to be Koniag (Leer 1978:6). Social and economic ties continue with the Kodiak area (Davis 1979) and social ties with Port Heiden, Ugashik, and Pilot Point (Petterson, Palinkas, and Harris 1982). Of the original 12 villages of the nineteenth century (see "Pacific Eskimo: Historical Ethnography," fig. 1, this vol.), only Chignik survives with its original name and location. All the villages between 57° and 59° west longitude were abandoned. Perryville is located near the site of the nineteenth-century village of Mitrofania. Two new villages were recorded in the 1960 census: Chignik Lagoon and Chignik Lake; by 1970 another new village appeared: Ivanof Bay. The main occupation in these villages was commercial fishing.

No ethnographic study has been made of these villages on the Alaska Peninsula. Neither is there a study of the Kenai Peninsula Eskimo, who share only a slightly less obscure ethnic identity. The Chugach called the Kenai Peninsula Eskimo *unáxkúýmiut* 'people out that way' (i.e., toward the open sea), rendered Unikhkurmiut (Birket-Smith 1953:99) and Unegkurmiut (practical orthography). Oswalt (1967:9) refers to them as Unixkugmiut but adds that "hardly anything more than

the name is known." Three of the former five villages were occupied in 1980. English Bay is the most traditional; the Alutiiq language and subsistence activities are integral parts of contemporary life (Stratton 1981). Port Graham, a cannery-based village, shares with English Bay a concern about possible disruption of subsistence activities from oil and gas development in Cook Inlet and from increasing numbers of nonresidents who come to hunt and fish.

An ethnography based on Birket-Smith's 1933 expedition to Prince William Sound is available for the Chugach (1953). Even at that time the scarce population of the area was noted but not explained. By 1970 only one village, Tatitlek, was still occupied. Three nearby towns, Cordova, Valdez, and Seward, have some native residents, but the exact composition and origin of these people is not known. Cordova in 1980 had a population of 1,879, including 286 Natives, most of whom probably were Chugach Eskimo. Valdez, population 3,079, had 175 Natives in 1980. The town of Valdez became an actively growing community in 1974; the trans-Alaska oil pipeline route terminates there.

Both Tatitlek and Chenega were located very near the epicenter of the great Alaska earthquake of 1964. Tatitlek was spared damage from the ensuing seismic waves, but Chenega was inundated by water shortly after the earthquake. Twenty-three persons, one third of the village, were drowned. All homes and the Russian Orthodox Church were destroyed. The survivors were evacuated to Cordova and relocated in Tatitlek; later they moved to Cordova or Anchorage.

Under the Alaska Native Claims Settlement Act nearly all the original Chenegans chose to enroll back to their original village. In 1974 court hearings confirmed eligibility for land, and plans to establish a new village began. By 1982 a new site was chosen on Evans Island and funds obtained to rebuild.

The Koniag of Kodiak Island live in six villages and the city of Kodiak. Only five of the more than 39 villages of the nineteenth century were permanently occupied in 1970. The sixth, Larsen Bay in Uyak Bay, may be near the former village of Ooiatsk. A few isolated households were located in the otherwise abandoned areas, such as Uganik and Uyak.

In the northern part of the Kodiak cluster of islands are two villages, Ouzinkie and Port Lions. The people of Port Lions include former residents of the village of Afognak. In 1880 two villages were listed for Afognak; Hrdlička (1930:184) in 1926 reported a nearby summer village. By 1939 the villages had been consolidated. A locally owned sawmill provided some income, but fishing here, as elsewhere on the coast, was the mainstay.

The tsunami following the earthquake of 1964 flooded the village, contaminated the wells, and destroyed or damaged about half the buildings. The International Lions Club "adopted" the village and assisted in relocating the community at a new site, called Port Lions. The villagers moved in December 1964.

Many of the original Afognak residents chose to enroll to their original village. The villagers won their case in village eligibility hearings and began making plans to return to Afognak Island. In the meantime, Wakefield Company built a modern cannery in Port Lions that provided the community with a steady source of income until 1975 when the cannery burned. In 1978 Afognak merged its village corporation with Port Lions.

On Spruce Island, north of the city of Kodiak, is Ouzinkie, a community of 173 residents in 1980. Until 1964 Ouzinkie had a cannery and a store in the center of the village, but the tidal wave following the earthquake destroyed the cannery, store, and two homes. Two local men drowned. Following the disaster the store was rebuilt, but the cannery was not. In the 1960s some families moved to Kodiak and village numbers declined. However, the village incorporated as a city and made positive plans for the future.

Before the earthquake of 1964, three villages continued to be occupied on the southern coast of Kodiak: Akhiok, Kaguyak, and Old Harbor.

Akhiok is the farthest south, located on a rocky, treeless bluff above the surf. Nearby, at Alitak Bay, the cannery expanded in 1959 to a year-round operation processing crab. Although most of the labor is imported from outside the state, residents of Akhiok do have access to employment, when they choose, and to the cannery store. As in most Alaska villages, the school complex comprises the largest and most modern building.

A smaller village of Kaguyak was located nearby on a low, narrow spit of land between Kaguyak Bay and a freshwater lake. In the nineteenth century it boasted several stores and many people. However, after whaling declined, the village dwindled in size and numbered only 36 persons in 1964. After the earthquake, the fourth tsunami destroyed the village with the loss of two lives. Survivors were evacuated first to Kodiak, then to Anchorage, before being relocated at Akhiok. However, the combining of two villages led to some initial difficulties including duplicating roles and authority.

Following the Alaska Native Claims Settlement Act the Kaguyakans enrolled to their original village. In 1974 plans were being made to return and rebuild the village, but by 1978 they had merged their corporation with Akhiok, and resettlement plans were discontinued.

The village that experienced the greatest increase in population in the twentieth century was Old Harbor. This community is located on a very narrow strip of land just above sea level at the base of a mountain near Three Saints Bay, the site of the first Russian community in North America. After whaling declined in the 1920s, people converged at Old Harbor from surrounding small communities. From 1926 until 1964 their economic base was the Kodiak Fisheries Company at Shearwater, 22 miles away. Old Harbor grew from 84 residents in 1929 to 340 in 1980.

Like Kaguyak, Old Harbor was destroyed by the massive tsunami in 1964, but after six weeks in Anchorage, the villagers were returned to resettle at the former sea-level site, where new housing was built (fig. 2).

Baseline ethnographic data is available for Old Harbor through an ethnographic sketch published by Befu (1970), who spent three weeks in Old Harbor in the

Nancy Yaw Davis, Anchorage, Alaska.
Fig. 2. High tide at Old Harbor, Kodiak I. The village was rebuilt following the 1964 earthquake and tsunami. Photograph by Paul Duncan, 1970.

summer of 1960. In addition to a general history of the community, Befu provides a community demography and an analysis of kinship and marriage. Perhaps most important is his perceptive account of the village's economic relationships both within the community and with the nearby cannery.

Befu's analysis of the degree of indebtedness of villagers to the cannery helps to explain the predicament experienced at Karluk on the other side of the island. Taylor (1966) in his demographic study based on fieldwork in 1962, 1963, and 1964, reports the cannery withdrew its credit system and instigated a system of paying the balance of a worker's wages in cash at the end of the short, intensive summer fishing season. The villagers experienced difficulty making that small amount of cash last through the winter.

Once the site of the greatest salmon fisheries of the Pacific, Karluk experienced great decline in numbers, from 192 residents in 1929 to 96 in 1980. Apparently more women than men left the village. Taylor found Karluk to have an unusual sex ratio of 155:100. He also found that many ancestors of present residents were originally from other places on the island. Marriage patterns, church relationships, and pregnancy records are included in Taylor's study.

Davis's research in the 1960s showed examples of the continuity of traditional patterns in family relationships, adoption patterns, and the suggestion of matrilocal residence and matrilineal-like ties between brothers and sisters, mothers and daughters (Davis 1971). Also, the Pacific Yupik people remain distinctive in the selective manner in which they have combined Russian and American influences.

In summary, no traditional ethnography is available for the Koniag, the Kenai Peninsula Unegkurmiut, or the people of the Alaska Peninsula. Only limited research since the 1960s is available for a few villages in the whole north Pacific area.

Major Historical Influences

Two institutions continue to figure importantly in village life, the church and the cannery, and two major events have profoundly affected village life, the 1964 Alaska earthquake and the 1971 land claims act. A more detailed consideration of these four topics can provide a greater understanding of the chief forces that have shaped the lives of contemporary village peoples of the north Pacific rim.

The Church

The most lasting influence of the Russian period was the establishment of the Russian Orthodox Church and local lay leadership. Most villages have at least one lay

reader who conducts regular church services; an annual visit from a priest supports this local leadership. In each established village a prominent landmark is the church building (fig. 3). Services are held regularly Saturday night and Sunday morning, and occasionally on Sunday afternoon. In addition, every village has its own saint's day, a holiday when special services are conducted. Major ceremonies occur at Christmas and Easter.

The integration of the Orthodox Church into community life can be seen in at least four dimensions beyond the religious one: language, economics, social activities, and kinship. Until the late 1960s the Russian language was used in all church services, and resistance was marked to a change to English, which was recommended by a regional priest. Further, some Russian words have been incorporated into the local dialect of English. Economically, the church is the only institution sustained by local funds. Other institutions, such as schools, other churches, and federal and state programs, are supported by sources outside the community. But in the villages, donations to the church after fishing season are expected.

Social activities also have a church reference. The major social events of the year coincide with church holidays, particularly Christmas and Easter. With the exception of a traditional town visit and, for some, an associated drinking bout after fishing season, accepted times for parties occur in reference to the church calendar. The church also regulates times for not drinking: Saturday, Sunday, and during Lent. Most village-wide social activities are church-related ones.

Finally, kinship and marriage are influenced by the

© Natl. Geographic Soc., Washington.

Fig. 3. Native church at Kodiak, built 1874, destroyed 1943. The first Russian Orthodox Church in Alaska, Holy Resurrection of Our Lord, was built on this site 1795–1796 (B.S. Smith 1980). The third church built there was dedicated in 1947. Associated with this continuing center of Orthodoxy, St. Herman's Pastoral School was accredited as a seminary in 1977, training Native priests, readers, teachers, and song leaders. By 1983, 8 Native priests had completed the 4-year course and were ordained. Photograph by John E. Thwaites, before June 1912.

church. Kin relationships are extended and reinforced by the godparent tradition (Taylor 1966). People related to each other through this system were excluded as potential spouses.

The prominence of the church was further highlighted during and after the 1964 earthquake when it influenced people's willingness to be relocated, their interpretations of the reasons for the disaster, and their choice of leaders (Davis 1970). Finally, subsequent revitalization of the church is symbolized in the canonization of Father Herman (b. 1757, d. 1837) in Kodiak in 1970, and the establishment in 1972 of a seminary for the training of priests and lay readers (Rathburn 1981).

Other denominations also have been influential, but to a lesser extent. In the Kodiak area, the Baptists have been active since about 1896. The Ouzinkie Baptist Mission cared for 124 children in 1906. It listed 34 converts in 1907 and 56 converts in 1913 (Baptist Newsletter 1906–1920). The Baptist laity and clergy continue to work primarily in Kodiak. Arctic Mission efforts in Perryville in the 1960s led several families to move and found a new village, Ivanof Bay, which is the only Native community on the North Pacific that is not predominantly Russian Orthodox.

The Canneries

In the late nineteenth century one of the richest salmon fisheries in the Pacific was located on the west coast of Kodiak near the present villages of Karluk and Larsen Bay. Exploitation of this resource resulted in the establishment of canneries, the first of which was built in 1882. At the height of production, six canneries were operating, and a total of 3.5 million fish were processed in 1891 (Moser 1899). Soon the fragile renewable resource was drastically reduced by overfishing. By 1907 only one cannery was operating on the west coast of Kodiak, and the population of the area declined.

A study of the impact of canneries on native settlements is available for the Bristol Bay area (VanStone 1967:63–82). Possibly some of the same kinds of changes occurred on the north Pacific rim, though precedence for dependence on an outside economic institution had previously been introduced, and probably well established, during the Russian fur trade period. Some data suggest that a consolidation of villages may have occurred twice, once in the early nineteenth century under Russian rule, and then again in the late nineteenth century around the commercial fishing enterprise. Okun' (1951:202) reports that 67 villages had been brought together by 1842 to form seven larger communities. Although Clark ("Pacific Eskimo: Historical Ethnography," this vol.) has identified over 40 villages that existed in the nineteenth century, only 14 villages on Kodiak appear on the 1880 census. Of those only seven, including the present city of Kodiak, are listed in the

Fig. 4. Don and Nick Kompkoff with kayak in Chenega, Prince William Sound. Photograph by John Poling, 1945.

1980 census. Each of the six villages is affiliated with one cannery, and in the case of the city, many fish processing factories. The changing settlement patterns of the Pacific Eskimo, as reflected in the census, include the abandonment of many villages, the growth of others, and the development of several new villages. These changes may well prove to be in direct response to the rise and fall of canneries in key locations.

Certainly during the first half of the twentieth century, the villagers came to depend almost wholly on commercial fishing for cash and credit. The canneries were large summer factories that controlled resources and labor. They dealt in a specific cash crop: salmon or (later) crab. The canneries controlled the means of catching the resource by renting boats and fishing gear. People in these cannery-based villages are wage-earning, store-buying people. Money has long been a pervasive mode of exchange within the village, but the year-round ties with the company were on a credit system. Finally, commitment and loyalty to only one cannery company was expected. Further discussion of the canneries may be found in Befu (1970) and Taylor (1966).

In the 1950s the crab industry was introduced and some Pacific Eskimo bought larger boats and crab gear, thus extending their season and income far beyond the salmon run. However, many villagers could not obtain or risk the capital investment required for this new industry. When Alaska began regulating salmon-fishing permits in the 1970s, some Natives lost their livelihood and others did very well, especially in the Chignik area.

Natural Disasters

All the villages on the north Pacific rim are located in one of the most active tectonic regions of the world. Much of the formation of land masses along the whole crescent is the result of tectonic activity (R.F. Black 1966:7), and earthquakes continue to occur frequently.

Lisīānskiĭ (1814:185) reported an earthquake in 1788 that led to flooding of the new Russian colony of Three Saints Bay. Davydov (1810–1812:156) referred to another major earthquake in 1792. In later historic times 22 major earthquakes, including two tsunami in the twentieth century, have been reported in the area. Another natural calamity was the Katmai Eruption of 1912, which destroyed the Koniag village of Katmai, located on the Alaska Peninsula (fig. 5), and led to the relocation of the villagers at Perryville.

The great Alaska earthquake of March 27, 1964, may be the most significant single event in the twentieth century for the five villages that suffered major destruction by the resulting tsunami. Two other villages, Tatitlek and Akhiok, were permanently changed as well, when survivors of two of the destroyed villages were relocated to them. More significant than the natural disaster were the irreversible social consequences of subsequent extensive government involvement in the affected communities (Davis 1971). Narratives of what happened in six villages have been written by Norton and Haas (1970:357–399); and a detailed description and analysis of events before, during, and after the

© Natl. Geographic Soc., Washington.
Fig. 5. Ash covered villages after the eruptions of the Mt. Katmai volcano in early June 1912. top, Katmai village looking north toward the volcano, which is hidden by the clouds, Aug. 13, 1912. This village was deserted at the time of the eruptions, the inhabitants being at their summer fishing camps. bottom, A semi-subterranean dwelling at Kaguyak village, Kodiak I., July 14, 1912. Photographs by George C. Martin.

earthquake through the first year of resettlement of Old Harbor and Kaguyak can be found in Davis (1971).

Alaska Native Claims Settlement Act of 1971

All Alaska villages found eligible for benefits under the Alaska Native Claims Settlement Act of 1971 were first organized as land-owning business corporations. Complex enrollment procedures, detailed land selections, village and regional corporation meetings, board elections, proxy solicitations, distribution of funds, and resulting legal entanglements have greatly increased Native political tempo and involvement. The Chugach Natives, Inc., encountered boundary difficulties with the Tlingits of Sealaska Corporation and extensive U.S. Forest Service involvement with conveyance of lands from the Chugach National Forest. Studies of historical and cemetery sites beginning in 1975 led to considerable new information documenting traditional locations and subsistence uses in the Prince William Sound area. Koniag, Incorporated, has had an involved legal history relating to enrollments to nine villages that were appealed, transfer of lands selected on the Alaska Peninsula in exchange for additional acres on the well-forested Afognak Island, and an accumulation of litigation concerning management, conveyance, proxy material, and mergers. The five Koniag villages enrolled to Bristol Bay Native Corporation have had a marginal role in the activities centering in Dillingham; their economic success as fishermen combined with isolation has moderated their interest and participation in corporation affairs.

The following figures are the approximate numbers available in 1982 concerning the original enrollments, expected land conveyance, and the final cash distributions for the three regions involving Pacific Eskimo. Koniag, Incorporated, had 3,267 enrollees, about 1,800 residing in the region. The region received 41 million dollars over a 10-year period and anticipated a total of 1.4 million acres of land. The Chugach Natives, Incorporated, enrolled 1,908 persons, received 24 million dollars, and expected eventual conveyance of about one million acres of land. The five villages on the Pacific coast of the Alaska Peninsula belong to the Bristol Bay Native Corporation, a region of 5,400 original enrollees. A total of 67 million dollars was received from the Alaska Native Fund, and 2.7 million acres is their land entitlement. The exact distribution of funds and lands to individuals, to village corporations, and to regional corporations is based on a complex formula determined by the act (Arnold 1976) and amendments, including the Alaska National Interest Lands Conservation Act of 1980.

The 1964 Alaska earthquake and the 1971 settlement act have profoundly affected the north Pacific rim. The first was the more localized and immediate; the second   *203* was more general and long-ranged. They served both to separate the villages in new ways and to articulate them with state and national economies and politics in ways not possible before.

Sources

Compared to other groups addressed in this volume, little information is available about the contemporary Pacific Eskimo. The main ethnographic work is by Birket-Smith (1953) and by Clark ("Pacific Eskimo: Historical Ethnography," this vol.). Shorter and village-specific studies were made by Befu (1970),Taylor (1966), and Davis (1970, 1971).

Federal and state laws have led to studies of current and future conditions; while not traditional ethnographies, they provide additional descriptive data about the communities. Concern about subsistence use (Stratton 1981) and the proximity of these activities to federal parklands also received some attention (Tuten 1977). The need to prepare environmental impact statements prior to outercontinental shelf oil and gas lease sales resulted in the preparation of community descriptions and forecasts of cultural changes assuming petroleum development (Bennett 1979; Davis 1979; Braund and Behnke 1979; Petterson, Palinkas, and Harris 1982).

Regional corporation newsletters and annual reports to shareholders provide information about land claims matters and corporation activities. In addition, the non-profit Native corporations and the State of Alaska have generated some regional studies, planning documents, and village profiles (North Pacific Rim 1977, 1981; Kodiak Area Native Association 1978, 1979; Dowl Engineering 1981). Research on the location of historical and cemetery sites, required by the 1971 claims act, has been undertaken by the National Park Service. Some of the social implications of the act were identified by Davis (1979a).

Linguistic work (Leer 1978); preparation of school material in Alutiiq (Sawden and Pulu 1979); and the publication of history, biographies, and local customs written by high school students (Kenai Peninsula Borough School District 1980–1981, 1981–1982; Anonymous 1978) add important contributions to the knowledge of the coastal villages of the North Pacific.

Southwest Alaska Eskimo: Introduction

JAMES W. VANSTONE

Environment

In the two chapters dealing with the Eskimos of southwest Alaska, detailed consideration is given to the geographic, physiographic, and climatic conditions characteristic of the region. Here it is sufficient to note that the natural area is an extremely varied one combining a coastal tundra setting of grasses, lichens, and mosses with interior forests at low elevations, portions of major river systems, and a large island of volcanic origin.

Geographically, southwest Alaska is dominated by four river systems; from north to south they are the Yukon, Kuskokwim, Togiak, and Nushagak. This extensive network of waterways gives easy access to the vast intermontane interior and has been of the utmost importance to the Eskimo inhabitants, furnishing them with fish for food and easy routes of travel. The topography of the mainland area varies considerably. In addition to delta lowlands and river valleys, there are mountains that approach the coast in the vicinity of Bristol Bay and reach the sea near the mouth of the Togiak River and north of the mouth of the Yukon. Nunivak Island, lying off the coast just north of Kuskokwim Bay, has a low coastline that gradually rises to form rolling hills near the center and along its western shore.

Between the mouths of the Yukon and Kuskokwim rivers the relief is low with poor drainage and large numbers of sloughs and lakes. Coastal waters north of Bristol Bay are extremely shallow due to deposition from the rivers, a circumstance that discouraged extensive exploration in the late eighteenth and early nineteenth centuries. As a result, the coastal and delta Eskimos experienced intensive contact with Europeans later than those living along interior riverbanks.

Throughout southwest Alaska the climate is cold and damp in winter and ranges from cool to cold in summer; precipitation is moderate. At the village of Naknek on Bristol Bay the mean annual temperature is 35°F with 24.1 inches of precipitation during 92 days in an average year. Farther to the north at Hooper Bay Village on the Bering Sea coast in the Yukon delta the mean annual temperature is 30°F and the precipitation 17.1 inches over 144 days of the year. Inland along the rivers temperatures are higher in summer and lower in winter, but precipitation is approximately the same as in coastal areas (Oswalt 1967:17).

Determining the boundaries of the southwest Alaska cultural zone is relatively easy. To the east they are delimited by the boundary between Eskimo and Athapaskan Indian speakers, and to the west by the Bering Sea. For the purposes of this volume, the northern boundary is the mouth of the Yukon River, although many students of Eskimo culture would draw it farther north on southern Seward Peninsula in the area where the Yupik and Inupiaq languages adjoin. The southern extent of the cultural zone is more difficult to determine since considerable uncertainty exists about what kind of Eskimos aboriginally inhabited the upper Alaska Peninsula. It is not necessary to go into detail here concerning these uncertainties (see Oswalt 1967:8; Dumond 1973). It can be stated that Yupik-speaking Eskimos, at contact, inhabited all the upper Peninsula to some point southwest of Ugashik.*

It is apparent, therefore, that both linguistic boundaries and geographical features are of significance in defining the cultural zone called southwest Alaska, with neither being of paramount importance. As in northwest Alaska, however, the geographic and cultural positions of the inhabitants have combined to bring about rather specialized adaptations and pronounced varia-

*The phonemes of Central Alaska Yupik are: (plain voiceless stops and affricate) *p, t, č, k, q*; (voiced fricatives) *v, l, z, γ, γ̇, γʷ, γ̇ʷ*; (voiceless fricatives) *f, ł, s, x, x̣, xʷ, x̣ʷ*; (voiced nasals) *m, n, ŋ*; (voiceless nasals) *M, N, Ŋ*; (semivowels) *w, y*; (short vowels) *i, a, u, ə* ([ɨ]); (long vowels) *i·, a·, u·*. The distribution and details of pronunciation of these vary slightly among the dialects. There is a largely predictable stress accent (v́).

In the standard orthography used by the Alaska Native Language Center and others the Yupik phonemes are written: p, t, c, k, q; v, l, s, g, r, u͡g, u͡r; vv, ll, ss, gg, rr, w, u͡rr; m, n, ng; ḿ, ń, ńg; v, y; i, a, u, e; ii, aa, uu. In certain positions where voicelessness is predictable the voiceless continuants are written with single rather than double letters, and the accent is omitted from the voiceless nasals. Certain long vowels that are predictable by rhythmic accentual rules are written with single vowel letters. An apostrophe is used as a diacritic between consonants to indicate that they are pronounced separately rather than interpreted as a combination, after consonants to indicate gemination that is not predictable from the rhythmic accentual rules, and in certain other such cases.

Information on Yupik phonology was obtained from Reed et al. (1977:1–17) and the sketch of the Yupik language in vol. 17.

tions in basic Eskimo cultural patterns (see "North Alaska Eskimo: Introduction," this vol."). Thus the zones of southwest Alaska Eskimo culture are defined by the particular cultural adaptations and economic emphasis of the people in combination with their geographic position within the total cultural zone.

Although considerable physiographic variability has been noted for southwest Alaska, human habitation is confined for the most part to the lowland tundra areas of the Yukon-Kuskokwim delta, and along the banks of these and other rivers in the region. In both areas there were, at the time of first European contact, large, permanent villages as well as small hunting, trapping, and fishing camps. Nunivak Island, although isolated to some extent both geographically and linguistically from the mainland, exhibited a similar configuration with settlements at the mouths and on the banks of rivers as well as in other lowland locations.

As in all Eskimo cultures, the basic subsistence pattern of the people of the southwest Alaska culture zone was dependence on hunting. The area has a rich land and sea fauna, more so even than the north Alaska culture zone. Seals, beluga, and, in some areas, walrus are abundant along the coast, while all species of Pacific salmon ascend the rivers annually in great numbers. In addition to these important fish, the numerous lakes and streams on the tundra contain whitefish, trout, pike, and a variety of other fish. The consequent emphasis on fishing gives a stability to life on the tundra and along the river banks that is equal to that of the sea mammal hunting communities on the coast. Local variations in hunting and fishing patterns are closely related to the inland-coastal settlement distribution and led to the development of culture patterns similar to those in

north Alaska, notwithstanding the coastal emphasis in north Alaska.

In summary, the natural area was not simply a suitable location for human population, but one so abundant in natural resources that it permitted the heaviest concentration of Eskimos in the largest communities to be found anywhere in the arctic regions, except on Kodiak Island. Periods of want and scarcity, although occasionally occurring, were probably less prevalent in southwest Alaska than in regions to the north and east.

Subsistence

In southwest Alaska, as in north Alaska, there are two basic ecological focuses—maritime and inland.

The maritime focus is practiced by the coastal communities of Bristol Bay, the Yukon delta, and Nunivak Island. For the inhabitants of villages in these areas the hunting of sea mammals was of primary significance with the seal being the most important game animal. On the adjacent tundra there was some emphasis on the hunting of caribou, and fishing for salmon was significant at the mouths of rivers and in certain favored bays, particularly Bristol Bay. Hunting mobility enabled the Eskimos to take full advantage of the varied subsistence possibilities characteristic of their rich environment. Coastal peoples ventured inland to hunt caribou and fish in inland lakes, and Eskimos whose permanent villages were inland on the tundra, while subsisting primarily on lake fish supplemented with caribou hunting, also occasionally visited the coast to hunt sea mammals. Seals and belugas sometimes ventured a short way up the sloughs and major rivers. Actually,

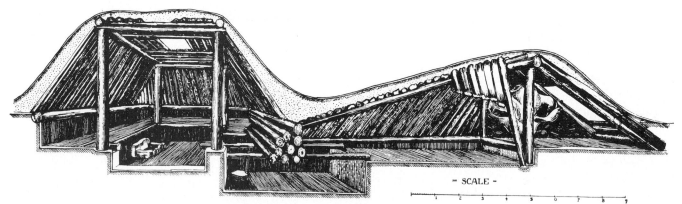

Fig. 25.—Cross-section of an Eskimo house on Nunivak Island.

Collins 1937:258–260.

Fig. 1. Cross-section of a house on Nunivak Island, Alaska. This house, made of driftwood logs, is typical of the style found in southwest Alaska. The entrance opens into a very small anteroom, the walls of which are formed by 2 upright whale skulls spanned by short timbers. From there an inner connecting room, the floor of which is 16 inches lower than the entrance, leads to the inner living room through a sunken passage that is 2.5 feet below the entrance floor. Where the passage is spanned by the lower wall beams it is less than 3 feet high making it necessary to enter the living room on hands and knees. The 10-foot square living area has a 3- or 4-foot-wide bench or platform on 3 sides. The stone lined fireplace is located on the earthen floor against the bench opposite the entrance. This bench is used for storage. The benches on the two sides parallel to the entrance are used for sleeping.

the tundra offered little in the way of food to sustain a sedentary population. It was the presence of predictable supplies of fish that made possible large and stable concentrations of population.

The inland focus was practiced by the riverine communities on the lower Yukon, lower and central Kuskokwim, Togiak, and Nushagak rivers. The Yupik speakers' penetration of the four major river systems in southwest Alaska was made possible by the abundance of salmon and familiarity with fishing technology enabling the people to exploit the rivers effectively. Salmon fishing is a more reliable subsistence activity than coastal sea mammal hunting. Although the size of salmon runs may vary, the supply has never been known to fail completely. In Bristol Bay these annual runs were probably much larger in late prehistoric times than they were in the 1980s after more than 80 years of commercial fishing.

Interior and tundra hunting of land animals such as caribou and moose was also possible for the inland-dwelling riverine Eskimos who tended to concentrate in sizable villages along riverbanks during the summer months when the salmon runs occur, and then to disperse in smaller groups for hunting at other times of the year. Unlike all the other inland Eskimos, with the possible exception of those on the upper Kobuk River in north Alaska, the culture of the riverine Eskimos of southwest Alaska was specifically adapted to a riverine setting and to northern forests. In this respect their way of life closely resembled that of the Athapaskan Indians who were their neighbors throughout much of the area.

It would be misleading, however, to overemphasize these ecological differences and the distinction between the maritime and inland focuses. Cultural differences between the inhabitants of the two focuses in southwest Alaska are of less significance than related distinctions in north Alaska. There was considerable mobility of individuals and groups across ecological boundaries. On the Kuskokwim, Eskimos exploited both the tundra and forested zones, while in the Bristol Bay area coastal dwellers traveled up the rivers to fish in the lakes of the interior. The Nushagak River region is perhaps the only area in Alaska where one Eskimo dialect group occupied the mouth of a river and another inhabited the riverbanks in the nineteenth century; however, the dialect differences were apparently minimal and did not impede movements of peoples from the coast to the interior and vice versa. (The distinct coastal dialect, Aglurmiut, which the Russians called Aglëgmiut, is extinct.) Each focus had its own special products and, as in north Alaska, the products of one were in demand by the inhabitants of the other. However, ritualized trade between inhabitants of the two focuses was perhaps less significant in southwest Alaska because of this mobility, which was motivated by ceremonial as well as subsistence requirements.

The inhabitants of Nunivak Island, a tundra people, were a partial exception to this wholesale crossing of ecological boundaries. Nevertheless, they too were highly mobile, drawn into the mainstream of southwest Alaska culture through their frequent contacts with the Eskimos of Nelson Island and elsewhere on the Yukon delta and Kuskokwim Bay. The island was plentifully supplied with caribou in the late prehistoric and early historic periods, so the inhabitants, as much as those of any coastal communities on the adjacent mainland, exploited a rich environment that included fish of many species (including salmon), seals, sea lions, and caribou.

It is important to emphasize that the pattern of reciprocities created by the desire of maritime and inland people for each other's products, although less ritualized, was as important in southwest as in north Alaska. This configuration is probably of considerable antiquity, but knowledge of the prehistory of the region is limited. Most students have maintained that the maritime adjustment is the older and that at some time in the not too distant past, maritime peoples penetrated the major rivers and their tributaries. Their mobility and consequent familiarity with fishing and land hunting subsistence techniques made it easy for them to adapt to the inland areas. It is possible, however, that a much older inland population related to the Arctic Small Tool tradition farther north may have preceded this penetration and may even have been at least partly ancestral to its people (Dumond 1969:1114, 1979:15, 1981:194–195).

The Cultural Position of Southwest Alaska

The two following chapters indicate the serious gaps that exist in knowledge of the Eskimos of southwest Alaska. With the exception of an early study by Nelson (1899), devoted for the most part to material culture, there are no ethnographies for the mainland areas of the region. The Yukon delta in particular is largely unknown. An important monograph by Lantis (1946) on Nunivak Island provides valuable information concerning aboriginal social culture, but very little concerning material culture and subsistence. For the Kuskokwim River, the studies of Oswalt (1963, 1963a, 1980; Oswalt and VanStone 1967) are devoted in part to the reconstruction of traditional culture, but primarily to the history of culture change and the nature of contemporary Eskimo life. VanStone's (1967, 1971) research in the Nushagak River region has been almost exclusively ethnohistorical. Accounts by early explorers, traders, and missionaries are useful for an understanding of the process of culture change and their writings will be referred to in the chapters that follow. However, since the Eskimos were exposed to the fur trade and Christianity at a relatively early date, these studies provide only limited information concerning precontact culture. The most useful ethnohistorical account is that of Zagoskin (1967).

Although relevant literature is limited, it is nevertheless clear that southwest Alaska represents a basic configuration of Eskimo culture with types and degrees of specialization that distinguish it from other areas. Spencer ("North Alaska Eskimo: Introduction," this vol.) has defined north Alaska as culturally and geographically isolated, although by virtue of its central role in the dispersal of the prehistoric Thule culture, he questions the area's cultural marginality. It is certainly true that southwest Alaska, parts of which are as isolated as any region of Alaska, is geographically marginal. However, as far as the elaboration of culture is concerned, the southwest is far from marginal, with more complex forms of social and ceremonial life than are found in any other region occupied by Eskimos.

It has frequently been suggested that the vigorous cultures of the Northwest Coast culture area influenced cultural development in southwest Alaska and were in part responsible for the elaborate social and ceremonial life to be found there. Certainly the importance of the men's house (kashim) and the elaborate seasonal cycle of ceremonies held therein indicate that southwest Alaska was the key Eskimo area with reference to the dissemination of cultural elaborations to the north and east. Abundant natural resources, a large and stable population, together with geographical proximity to cultures with highly developed social and ceremonial systems all emphasize the importance of southwest Alaska within the total configuration of Eskimo culture.

Nunivak Eskimo

MARGARET LANTIS

Territory and Environment

The Nunivak ('nōōnĭ,văk) Eskimo inhabit an island in the Bering Sea, on 60° north latitude about 25 miles from the mainland, between the mouths of the Yukon and Kuskokwim rivers. Nunivak Island is more than 50 miles long on its east-west (longest) axis. It is characterized by tundra and low relief, with the highest point, Mount Robert, about 490 meters high. Nunivak lies well within Beringia, the prehistoric exposed continental shelf. Shallow depth of the sea, especially around the northeast coast, makes very dangerous the approach close to shore by any vessel of more than two fathoms draft. The winter ice of Etolin Strait between Nunivak and Nelson islands may be thick but often is too broken and liable to movement or at times too slushy for small vessel or sled travel.

Compared with the climate of the mainland interior, the summer climate is foggy and chill, thus resembling islands at the north edge of the Bering Sea; yet the Nunivak climate is more equable than in either of these other regions. Temperature ranges from a summer high of 21°C to winter low of −31°C. In most years, the sea is open from June to the end of October, ponds and small rivers from May to early October. Precipitation in summer and winter is greater than on the Alaska coast north of Bering Strait, so that grasses and most other vegetation grow better; but there are no trees other than the several species of *Salix* (willow), none of which, even in protected places, grows more than about one meter tall.

Most villages have had geographic advantages for comfortable living that mainland villages like Hooper Bay and Kwigillingok lacked: for example, raised well-drained land and sand beaches instead of mud.

Several factors fostered the islanders' isolation from European contact. Large whales and commercial whalers remained in deeper water to the west, only the smaller white whale (beluga) routinely entering the shallow bays along the mainland coast. For life on an aboriginal basis, Nunivak was well located: six months' annual isolation from raids and epidemics, adequate supply of driftwood, variety and abundance of food, a climate that was not extreme, and freedom from predatory animals, except occasional wolves, in precontact time.

Although the sea provided well, the insular position limited land mammal species: no wolverine, lynx or bear, but also no muskrat, marmot, otter, squirrel, or beaver. White and red foxes, mink, ermine (rare), and a few caribou, the last killed off in the second half of the nineteenth century, comprised the wild mammalian fauna. In number of species (89) and in population, the avifauna was abundant (for example, six or more species of ducks), with occasional large birds like the cranes but mostly with sea birds such as cormorant, puffin, and murre. The fish most exploited were salmon, char (Dolly Varden), cod, halibut, flounder, needlefish (stickleback), and, especially in winter, tomcod. There were some herring. The mainstay among game animals was the small hair seal (harbor seal) although there always were also spotted seal, bearded seal, and walrus. Other species were rarities.

The sociocultural boundary included more territory than the geographic one. Nunivakers regarded the people of Nelson Island, whose principal settlement was Tununak, and others along the coast from Tununak northward to Hooper Bay as distant relatives and similar to themselves. Those to the north and to the south, in the Yukon and Kuskokwim areas respectively, were regarded as strangers and at times enemies. The culture of the mainland coastal communities, while incorporating some elements of upriver culture, still formed with Nunivak a subarea of the great river-delta Yupik region.

Language

The Nunivak Eskimo speak a dialect of Central Alaskan Yupik, the most divergent of the four dialects of this language spoken in the twentieth century but mutually intelligible with the others.* Although some of its divergent features are shown by nineteenth-century vocabularies to be recent (Michael Krauss, communication to editors 1982), others point to an affinity with the Hooper Bay–Chevak dialect enclave on the nearby mainland and with the extinct nineteenth-century dialect of the Aglëgmiut of the Bristol Bay area ("Eskimo and Aleut Languages," this vol.). These affinities could

---

*For the orthography of Yupik, see the footnote in "Southwest Alaska Eskimo: Introduction," this vol.

indicate that these similar dialects are remnant pockets of a formerly more widespread type or that some of their speakers dispersed into their historical locations by recent migration, as indicated by Wrangell's 1839 (1970:17) account. Hammerich (1958) refers to Nunivak as the *čux* dialect on the basis of its word for 'man' (Chevak *čuk,* General Central Yupik *yuk*).

Prehistory

The prehistoric cultures identified on the island thus far begin with one that resembles Norton culture on the mainland from Norton Sound to Bristol Bay or farther: the Duchikmiut phase with radiocarbon dates from 150 B.C. to A.D. 590. Fish, walrus, seal, and probably birds were major food sources. Because the number of potsherds excavated was five times the total number of stone and bone tools in this period and nine times the number of tools in the next known period, Mekoryuk River, A.D. 900–1400, they can best characterize the prehistoric cultures. Regarding Duchikmiut lithic and organic artifacts, see Nowak (1982).

In the early period of the Norton-like culture (Duchikmiut), before A.D. 250, pottery was hair tempered, thin walled, and quite well made, of bucket or barrel form, check stamped (most common), plain, or linear stamped. Later in this phase, a check stamp made differently became more frequent, with plain and linear stamped sherds declining somewhat. The late Duchikmiut ware was thicker and sand tempered. This last characteristic related Nunivak to the Bristol Bay region more than to northern regions.

In the Mekoryuk River phase (considered by Nowak 1974 as early western Thule), although 96 percent of the potsherds were plain, there was greater variety in the remainder: concentric circle or check or linear stamped, ridged, banded, incised or raised line. The ware is relatively thick, with feather and gravel temper, and only gravel used in the common plain ware late in the phase. The characteristic form is globular.

The greatest change in stone tools from early to middle phase was the large increase in ground slate (97% of Mekoryuk River artifacts) used instead of flaked igneous or metamorphic rock (97% in Duchikmiut). From the few specimens excavated, it appears that the closed-socket toggling harpoon supplanted the open-socket, lashed toggling harpoon in late Duchikmiut and early Mekoryuk River phases.

In the Nash Harbor phase (A.D. 1500 to 1700 or probably 1800), potsherds were five times more numerous than excavated stone, bone, and wood implements. Plain pots continued dominant, with a few edged, incised line, or dot decorated specimens. In this phase, all stone tools except a few abraders were of ground slate. None of the lithic tool forms was new. Of bone artifacts, only in this phase have sealing clubs, large fishhooks, and arrowheads been excavated although they might have been used earlier. For Nunivak prehistory see Nowak (1974).

History

In the summer of 1821, Mikhail N. Vasiliev in one expedition and A.K. Etolin in another independently discovered Nunivak. Vasiliev named it Discovery Island, applying the name of his ship (Ray 1975:70), but others evidently did not know or did not accept the name. "Presumably from Etolin's report, Tikhmenev . . . [stated]: '. . . These islanders lead a sedentary life, coming to the mainland in the summer to barter seal skins, blubber, and a few foxes for tobacco from the local natives. They are very little acquainted with the use of dry goods and do not use it for clothes' " (VanStone 1957:97).

There are stories of two or more whaling ships being wrecked on a Nunivak coast, and an occasional vessel may have sought shelter in its lee, but the next recorded purposeful visit was that by William H. Dall in 1874. He commented that Nunivak people "seemed to have few trade goods compared to other peoples of Alaska with whom he was familiar" (see VanStone 1957:98). In 1880 and 1891, the U.S. Revenue Steamer *Corwin* stopped at Nunivak, on the second occasion for the 1890 census. This was the first time that any outsider had gone most of the distance or possibly all around the island, describing settlements and geographic features. From 1900–1910 inclusive, there were four more shipwrecks, undoubtedly providing hardware to the Eskimos.

The first trader (of Russian-Eskimo ancestry) who brought his family and settled on the island came in 1920, bringing 10 reindeer owned by a Nome trading and reindeer-breeding family. With good forage and without wild predators, the reindeer flourished, as did the trader.

In 1924 a White teacher and his wife were established at Nash Harbor by the U.S. Bureau of Education, to be followed a few years later by Eskimo teachers. In 1936–1937 an Eskimo missionary established an Evangelical Covenant Church at Mekoryuk, and in 1939 a new school was built there by the Bureau of Indian Affairs, which had succeeded the Bureau of Education. All assets of the private trading company were purchased by the federal government, and in 1940 the store was transferred to the community while the reindeer were managed by the BIA. Island residents were organized under the Indian Reorganization Act, and a council representing both Nash Harbor and Mekoryuk was elected.

In 1934 the U.S. Biological Survey (Department of

Agriculture) brought 34 musk-oxen from Greenland in an effort to reestablish musk-oxen in Alaska. Alaska Territorial biologists introduced 10 caribou to improve the local reindeer. Scientists and people interested in game management came at rare intervals. Until after World War II the only regular visitors and only in the summer were the BIA supply ship and a Coast Guard cutter that gave brief medical service by the ship's surgeon. Nunivak Island had no regular mail service and remained remarkably isolated; however, there still was enough contact to bring epidemics. About 1900, many died of an unidentified disease. The great influenza epidemic of 1918–1919, pertussis (whooping cough), tuberculosis and other respiratory diseases, and in 1942 a measles epidemic killed people of all ages.

From 1940 onward, Nunivak Island received increasing federal attention. During World War II, two Signal Corps men were stationed there. In 1943 a reindeer abattoir was built at Nash Harbor, later moved to Mekoryuk and expanded. This initiated the greatest change, which accelerated phenomenally in the 1950s and 1960s. A National Guard unit was formed and men were taken to Fort Richardson for training. Although mail service by air began in 1946, it was not until 1957 that the state of Alaska built an airstrip and a road from it to the village of Mekoryuk, by then the only village. In the 1960s came the Headstart program for preschool children, VISTA workers to aid community development, and other federal programs. A new village school was built in 1965. In the 1970s Mekoryuk received more dependable electric power under the Department of Agriculture Rural Electrification Administration, a water and sewer project, a new reindeer slaughter-house, and a home construction project.

After school, storekeeper, and reindeer came to the island, everyone would be employed for a day or two in the annual bringing ashore of supplies; a few men would be hired to round up deer for slaughter, and a man or woman would work occasionally on some construction or sewing. Since the workers were usually paid in goods instead of cash, real cash value was scarcely understood. Another income source before 1940 had also been craft work. Baskets, carved walrus tusks (fig. 1), and even implements like wooden dishes as well as masks (fig. 2) were sold to storekeepers, ship's crews, and visiting officials; Nunivak became known as a place where traditional items could be obtained. In the 1970s the sale of masks was a lucrative business (Ray 1981:69–70).

After 1940, as regular jobs became available, especially at the reindeer project after 1944 and in the National Guard to which all able-bodied men belonged, Nunivakers learned about time clocks, wage rates, and Social Security. In learning to use a whole new technology, they underwent rapid change.

Many of the changes that had occurred by 1960–1961 have been documented (Lantis 1972). By that time, the teachers already were set apart from the community, which met to decide community policy without the presence of any outsider. Community institutions were stronger and more independent than those in many mainland villages in the lower Kuskokwim region. The reindeer project supervisors knew more of the new technology, became more involved in community interests, and became increasingly the culture models in contrast with teachers and missionaries. Yet, when the project was transferred to Mekoryuk in 1970 for management by the community, it had a difficult time. After 25 years

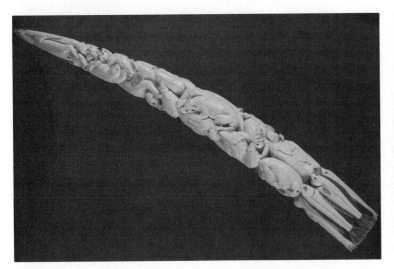

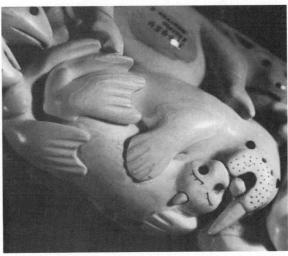

Smithsonian, Dept. of Anthr.: 394,454.

Fig. 1. Walrus tusk, ivory with intertwined representations of fish and mammals carved in high relief; at the tip is a sea mammal tail and at the base a group of fish and one seal. This type of object, a "Nunivak tusk," was introduced in 1920 when the Lomen Company provided ivory and bought the products for the souvenir trade; by the 1970s such carvings were no longer made (Ray 1981:65–66). Length about 76.2 cm; collected on Nunivak I., Alaska, 1926–1940.

NUNIVAK ESKIMO

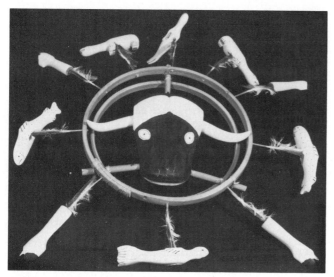

Natl. Mus. of Canada, Ottawa: IV-E-1095.

Fig. 2. Carved wood musk-ox head mask with ivory horns. The carved wooden appendages represent musk-ox feet, bears, seals, and fish. The mask is painted reddish orange, cream, black, and red and has feathers added. Made by Andrew Noatak, for whom musk-oxen were a favorite subject after the animals were introduced to the island in 1936 (Ray 1981:70). Concentric rings with attached appendages were common elements of dance masks. In the 1980s masks were made by men, only for sale. Diameter of outer hoop 28.5 cm; made at Mekoryuk, Nunivak I., Alaska, 1978.

of presumably efficient experience, there still were for the local managers uncertainties and mistakes in decisions on herd management and selection of workers.

The reindeer never were a large source of food or skins. When they were owned privately, Nunivak people had to purchase deer even though more than 10,000 grazed free on their land. Under federal management, people could buy meat from the abattoir or could get whole deer by hunting them under regulations set by the council and reindeer superintendent; yet by the 1960s few of the younger hunters were interested in hunting reindeer. Under local management, as of 1973 each family was allotted four animals, mostly hunted in conjunction with roundups for slaughter in August.

An old bull musk-ox was for local people a fearsome animal and in fact all musk-oxen were avoided until 1964, when a man from Vermont brought helpers to catch young animals to be reared at the University of Alaska experimental farm at Fairbanks. Despite difficulties then and again in 1976 some calves were taken and successfully bred and raised. For these little expeditions, for archeologists, and for government officials, Nunivak men were employed to provide guide service and boat transportation. Because outside hunters were not allowed, there was no other employment for guides until fall 1975 and spring 1976 when the Alaska Fish and Game Department permitted 10 hunters of musk-oxen in the fall and 40 in the spring.

By 1973, 15 people worked part-time in a native in-

dustries program, and 20 women were also working part-time in knitting qiviut, the very fine and soft wool from the undercoat of the musk-ox (fig. 3); in 1981 a few were thus employed.

Besides paid work, "over two-thirds of the adult males still engage in some form of aboriginal subsistence activity, many of them in multiple forms at different times of the year." An even higher proportion of the women engaged in gathering shellfish, berries, and greens in summer, and in fishing through the ice in winter (Novak 1974:1). It was estimated in 1973 that between one-fourth and one-half of the total food intake consisted of store-bought foods; by 1981 three-fourths was commercial. If both husband and wife were employed, there was a good cash income. Poor people who could not support themselves were given federal financial aid. For an account of Nunivak economy in the mid-1970s see Nowak (1975, 1977).

Demography

Etolin reported that there were 400 people (in 16 villages) living on the island in 1821. Although one wonders how he obtained this figure, it may have been approximately correct. The 1890 census (U.S. Census

U.S. Dept. of the Interior, Indian Arts and Crafts Board, Washington: W-71.26.1.

Fig. 3. Scarf handknit of qiviut, the under wool of the domesticated musk-ox. Such work has been done only since 1969 under a program initiated by the Institute of Northern Agricultural Research, which established a musk-ox breeding station in Alaska (Griffiths 1971). Yarn is provided to knitters in scattered villages and marketed through the Musk Ox Producers' Cooperative in Anchorage, Alaska. Length 117.0 cm; made by Elizabeth Speed, Nunivak I., Alaska, 1970.

Office 1893, 6:158) figure of 702 is suspect. The first reliable population total, in 1940, was 218, excluding Eskimos from the mainland. The obvious population decline was due not to out-migration but to inadequate medical services. The number of children under 20 years old who were recorded in the 1970 census (table 1) probably indicates chiefly the increased number of children kept alive between 1955 and 1970 due to improved health care. It cannot be argued that emigration of only those over 20 years explains the smaller number of young adults. In the 1960s and 1970s families with many children as well as single adults moved off the island, and there was no comparable movement onto it. The population had increased more than table 1 indicates. By 1980, the island population was 153 (96 male, 57 female), of whom 105 were age 16 or older (U.S. Bureau of the Census 1982:table 55).

The number of settlements had been declining for 80 years or more, due to loss of population, concentration in places where traders, government services, and employment were available, and also, less often, due to change in natural food resources. In 1940, there were seven winter villages, five of which each had fewer than 20 persons. In 1970, there was one village. There still were satellite seasonally occupied village sites for fishing or sealing, but very few compared with the 90 or more named sites of old villages, permanent and seasonal. The movement had been generally from south coast to north coast.

When transportation was by ship, Nunivak was oriented principally north to Saint Michael and Nome, areas from which modern economic and religious influences came. On leaving the island, people moved in that direction. When the airplane became the vehicle for movement of people to the mainland for medical care and jobs, they went east to Bethel on the Kuskokwim River and beyond it to Anchorage. Probably a total of 75 Nunivak people were settled in those communities by 1982.

Legal Status

Nunivak Island is a National Wildlife Refuge, comprising more than one million acres, a status that does

Table 1. Nunivak Population Distribution by Age, 1970

Age	Number	Age	Number
Under 5	30	45–49	2
5– 9	35	50–54	6
10–14	39	55–59	8
15–19	31	60–64	4
20–24	20	65–69	6
25–29	26	70–74	2
30–34	14	75–79	2
35–39	8	80 +	3
40–44	13	Total	249

SOURCE: University of Alaska. Institute of Social, Economic and Government Research 1973:37.

not prevent hunting, trapping, and fishing by local residents (except for the protected musk-ox) but that does control such activity by others. Mekoryuk is incorporated as a fourth-class city. Its residents are stockholder-members of the Calista Corporation (headquartered at Bethel), one of the 12 regional corporations formed under the Alaska Native Claims Settlement Act of 1971. The community also is incorporated under that act.

Traditional Culture

Subsistence

In the aboriginal economy, except for an occasional seal taken in summer, all seals were caught in the spring by men hunting from kayaks on the open sea and among ice floes or in the autumn by two men cooperating in setting a net under the shore ice before it became too thick. Most men said that Nunivak people never hunted at seal breathing holes, but one man said that this was done on the south side of the Island before the period of White settlement. An annual catch of about 600, including all species, was considered normal. Of these, 20–30 would be the large bearded seals. Walrus similarly were hunted from kayaks, yielding an annual island total of about 35. Only a few beluga were caught: with harpoon or by the animal blundering into a net. The beluga was prized not only for food but also for its long sinews for thread and cord. Seals were the ob-

Smithsonian, Dept. of Anthr.: 16,251.
Fig. 4. Breast yoke used to help carry loads on the back. A cord permanently fixed to one end of the yoke is passed over the load with the loop at the other end of the cord slipped over the ridged end of the yoke. The carved wood yoke has inset caribou teeth; the image of the tattooed woman at the center served as a charm to protect the wearer (Fitzhugh and Kaplan 1982:99) Width 51.0 cm. Collected by William H. Dall, Cape Etolin, Nunivak I., Alaska, 1874.

213

NUNIVAK ESKIMO

vious staple, providing food, oil for light (not usually for heating, as the houses had stone hearths), boat covers, and materials for clothing. Walrus additionally provided ivory for many implements and most ornaments.

Although fish might be caught in the bays and open sea by hook and line, the principal techniques were these: in a small river, a stone weir with a long cone-shaped trap, made of thin slats, set in its opening; spearing most fish with multipronged spear (fig. 5) or harpooning a large salmon; in winter, spearing fish through a hole in the ice on river or bay. The modern fish wheel was not used. Fish were eaten boiled, frozen, or sun-dried, not smoked. Mussels, the principal shellfish, were eaten raw. An effort was made to store large quantities of dried or frozen seal meat and oil, the oil in "pokes" made of whole sealskins, as well as fish for winter consumption. Although some fish was placed in pits, to be frozen for winter use, this probably was not done so much as in mainland villages. Considerable quantities of wild greens were stored in clay-lined pits. Berries apparently were kept in large wooden containers.

Birds were sought not solely for food, as the skins of some species, especially cormorant, eider, and murre, made warm parkas; and beaks, feathers, and feet could be used for ornaments, decoration of ceremonial objects, and of course arrows. They were caught by nets on the cliff rookeries, by multipronged bird spears on open water.

In most hunting, the spear-thrower, used with spear or harpoon, was preferable to bow and arrow because the former requires only one free hand when hunting from kayaks. The long barbed bone arrowheads were used against caribou or people. When warfare ended and mainlanders ventured to go to Nunivak to hunt, its few caribou were exterminated. The exact date is unknown, but it appears that from about 1880 to 1920 Eskimos of the immediate Nunivak area did not have access to wild or domestic reindeer.

One man who, in the late nineteenth century, several times found a dead whale on the southwest side of the Island, became wealthy. A family that lost its principal hunter, killed or crippled in one of the frequent accidents, would have a difficult time.

There was not general sharing of food except in a case like that of finding a whale and except on life cycle and festival occasions. Food and other products of the

Fig. 5. Fishing and fish preparation. top, Woman using a 3-prong fish spear to spear tomcods through the ice on a river. To the left is an open mesh grass bag for carrying the fish and to the right a wooden scoop to remove slush ice from the hole. The woman is wearing old-style waist-length sealskin boots. Photograph by Margaret Lantis, 1939–1940. center, Husband and wife, wearing waterproof seal gutskin parkas, seining for chum salmon in the mouth of a river, probably the Mekoryuk. bottom, Woman using an ulu to prepare chum salmon for drying on a rack. center and bottom, Photographs by Jerry Hout, 1966.

214

hunt might be given to a kinsman or a partner as a favor or an obligation in an unspoken exchange of goods and services. Prosperous hunters who were kin-group or community leaders were expected to feed orphans and elderly people who needed help, but they did not always perform according to the code. Evidently no one starved while others had food; nevertheless, wide differences between family conditions persisted.

Trade

In 1891 the census enumerator observed trading in the vicinity of present Mekoryuk when an umiak came from the mainland bringing leaf tobacco, flour, calico print, gunpowder and lead, matches, and the usual small items like knives and needles. In exchange, Nunivak people gave bearded-seal skins, a few fox skins, seal oil in pokes, "and several thousand fathoms of seal and walrus line." On the Nunivak side of the exchange, a local trader served as middleman for his compatriots (U.S. Census Office 1893:114–115). In this period, according to later report, Nunivakers not only went to trade with their friends on the neighboring mainland coast, who in turn traded inland as had been done for a long time, but also went up the Yukon and Kuskokwim Rivers themselves.

Later, Nunivak men took pokes of oil and sealskins (whole or cut and prepared for bootsoles and other uses) up the Kuskokwim River, receiving squirrel, wolverine, and other furs from the interior region. Still later, for example, in the 1950s, they sold the much-desired oil for a high price in cash. Before the storekeeper began business in 1920 and for a while afterward, the trading expeditions were made chiefly for an exchange of coastal and inland products, not for exchange of local native and introduced commercial goods. The commercial goods were obtained, probably in exchange for arctic fox skins, from occasional small White-owned trading vessels that called at the island or from some enterprising local trader who went to Saint Michael for goods. The important characteristic of this trade was that it remained largely under local control and was not a fully developed fox fur trade until after 1920.

Technology

To 1940, Nunivak differed from the better-known Inupiaq technology of northwest Alaska and, in some of its ways, differed from its Yupik relatives for three reasons: it shared traits of material culture with other Yupik of its region that differed from Inupiaq traits functionally identical but different in form; it had a few distinctive, chiefly stylistic characteristics; it was conservative, preserving old forms and ways that had disappeared elsewhere.

Although its technology has not been fully studied,

some examples can be given. Nunivak differed from the Inupiaq and was like the Yupik of the Yukon-Kuskokwim Delta in making and using saucer-shaped pottery lamps (fig. 6) instead of stone lamps, in having benches along two sides and the back wall of the house (the rear bench used more for storage) rather than one wide bench across the back, and in having stylistic differences in implement handles and needlecases (fig. 7).

Cases of lag were the sled-dog complex and type of storehouse. The Nunivak small sled that people pushed, sometimes helped by dogs tied to the sides of the sled by a primitive grass-rope harness, clearly antedated the tandem-hitched team.

The traditional Nunivak storehouse was a small semisubterranean sod-covered structure, not the Alaskan log structure at ground level or on posts that has been publicized in modern times. By the 1920s there were some log storehouses at ground level, with sod roof. Probably the ancient cache was a small room opening from the underground passage that connected two or three houses and a men's house or kashim (*qayγi* in the Nunivak dialect). Another conservative segment of culture was clothing. As late as 1940, some women still wore parkas curved up at the sides instead of straight around the bottom, worn with boot-trousers, each boot leg a whole sealskin. Some boys and men still wore bonnet-type fur caps with the parka hood thrown back (Lantis 1946:231, 232).

The great use of grass, for kayak mats, matting on house benches and walls, coarse mats over drying fish to keep off flies, carrying and storage baskets (fig. 8), trinket baskets, socks and boot insoles, rope, and ceremonial ornamentation, was a characteristic shared with other Yupik, especially those on the Pacific coast, and with Aleuts. Although the workmanship was good, the result was not nearly so fine as the Aleut products. Wood also was a commonly used material, for dishes, trays, cups, buckets, and boxes (fig. 9), the dishes varying in size from the child's personal dish (every person

Smithsonian, Dept. of Anthr.: 16,383.
Fig. 6. Pottery lamp, saucer-shaped, fired with concentric incised rings on the interior surface. Diameter 20.0 cm; collected by William H. Dall, Nunivak I., Alaska, 1874.

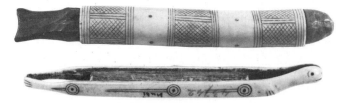

top, U. of Pa., U. Mus., Philadelphia: NA540; bottom, Smithsonian, Dep. of Anthr.: 43,742.

Fig. 7. Sewing implements. Women kept their tools, including a separate container for their ivory or metal needles, in a special housewife bag. top, Needlecase of hollowed bone with incised decoration has wooden ends carved to represent the tail and head of a fish. Cases with stoppered ends are characteristic of southern Alaska. bottom, Reel or spool of carved ivory representing a seal, used to hold sinew thread. Length 12.5 cm; collected by E.W. Nelson on Nunivak I., Alaska, 1877–1881. top, same scale, collected by G.B. Gordon on Nunivak I., Alaska, 1905.

Smithsonian, Dept. of Anthr.: top, 16,095; bottom, 16,147.

Fig. 9. Tobacco implements. Tobacco was ground and sifted to produce snuff, used by both men and women, which was kept in boxes made in a variety of shapes and designs. top, Round bentwood container, with ivory piece at side join, is painted red with black designs. The separate lid has a carved face with inlaid ivory labrets. bottom, Snuff tube made from a hollow waterfowl wing bone has 2 incised lines at one end. The user put one end in the box, the other in a nostril, and inhaled. Tubes were sometimes attached to the boxes but were also carried separately. top, Height 5.5 cm; bottom, same scale. Both collected by William H. Dall, Cape Etolin, Nunivak I., Alaska, 1874.

had his own) to very large storage and feast dishes, for dolls, for wooden hats, eyeshades, and snow-goggles, and for elaborate masks (see Lantis 1946:175–176, 190–192, 215). These were added to the usual Eskimo requirement for wood shafts and handles, net floats, boat frames and house frames, and other uses. With a greater quantity of driftwood than the northern coastal Inupiaq had, and with more ivory than the inland Yupik and Pacific Eskimo had, these materials were used in place of stone, bone, and hides or "bladders" for a variety

of containers and implements; however, Nunivak people did have the usual men's and women's stone knives, chisels, and scrapers of their region, and some containers made from animal organs.

Several aspects of culture were distinctive to Nunivak people, among them the large heavy kayak. After contact, there was the carving of whole walrus tusks in high relief, the subjects being sinuously intertwined animals (Ray 1981:figs. 123–131). In addition, possibly details of women's work that have not been adequately studied were unique to Nunivak.

It should be understood that other parts of the technology not specifically mentioned here were basically like those of the lower Yukon-Kuskokwim area: semi-subterranean houses, umiak and kayak, a great variety of hunting implements, and many niceties of small tools and ornaments—labrets, ear pendants, and nose pendants (figs. 10–11) (Ray 1981:fig. 62). There were also fur parkas, birdskin parkas, and rain parkas made of sea-mammal intestine casing, fishskin boot tops, fur boots and mittens, but of course no caribou or moose-skin socks and other items of clothing.

Social Organization

In traditional organization the institutionalized relationships were the family, usually extended beyond the nuclear family; the household; the patrilineal lineage, defined here as an extended unilateral family having no essential territorial association or restriction; the men's house (kashim), a unit in a factional division of the

Fig. 8. Woman making a twined carrying and storage basket of dunegrass (*Elymus arenarius*). Photograph by Leonard Lee Rue III, at Mekoryuk, Nunivak I., 1969.

216

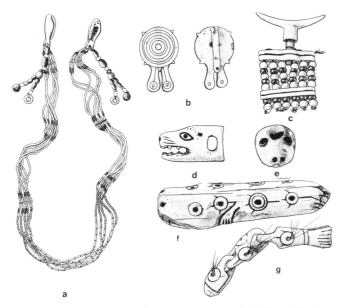

Smithsonian, Dept, of Anthr.: a, 340,331; b, 48,306; c, 16,204; d, 43,722; e, 43,879; f, 43,736; g, 16,184.

Fig. 10. Personal adornment. a, Man's ear ornaments with ivory pieces connected by strands of beads that hang under the chin. Total length 63.5 cm. b, Woman's ear ornaments, not connected by beads; these have a characteristic shape and incised concentric circles. c, Man's ivory labret fastened with a wood stem to an ivory crosspiece with red and white beads attached. Women's labrets were usually sickle-shaped ivory. Other types of ornaments include: d, belt fastener in shape of an otter head; e, belt button in shape of seal head; f, belt ornament representing an otter, and g, ivory pendant of 3 linked pieces incised and decorated with seal hair. b, Length 3.2 cm; c-g same scale. All collected on Nunivak I., Alaska. a, by Henry Collins and T. Dale Stewart, 1927; b, d, e, f by E.W. Nelson 1877–1881; c, g, by W.H. Dall, 1874.

community if there were two or more kashims, and a unit in the sex-linked division of society; the winter village, with seasonal settlements that did not belong solely to one village although peopled mostly from one; partnerships; and a separation between shamans and laymen, not that shamans formed a fraternity, but a shaman, his family, and his apprentice helper formed a unit apart from others.

The nuclear family contracted when a child was given to others, usually relatives, for adoption, which was a common occurrence. It expanded when a prosperous man added a second wife. Nuclear and extended families, therefore their households, varied in many ways. With the customary bride service by young suitor or husband, he and the first child born to the couple would be added to help support the family although he lived in the men's house. A household of kin might comprise, for example, two brothers and their families, or an older couple with grandchildren or niece and nephew, or a couple and their children with the children of either parent (or both parents) from a previous marriage (Lantis 1946:162–168, 235–244).

The house actually was inhabited only by women and children until the twentieth century when the men's house ceased to function as an institution for more than social sweatbathing. A man's possessions were kept in the family's house or storehouse. He would visit his wife more or less secretly during the night and might spend some time at home during the day. Women controlled the family's supplies of food and those materials that they had provided or made: the many fathoms of sinew cord, great bundles of dry grass, and skins prepared for clothing. Men kept their hunting implements and ritual paraphernalia out of reach of women and children.

When the men and older boys still lived and worked in the kashim, with the women bringing their meals to them, there was a strong sex division in the society, ritualized in the Bladder Festival (Lantis 1946:186). A person might have four or more marriages in a lifetime, but there were a few strong enduring marital attachments. A boy, sent to live with the men sometimes as early as five years old, would progressively identify with them, listening and watching the men, thus learning their crafts and lore. Acquiring knowledge of local geography, of game animals and their habits, was essential for a people almost completely self-dependent. Similarly, a girl had to associate with women to learn essentials such as skinning seals and making waterproof boots.

If the village was small and there was only one men's house, its members were close affinal and consanguineal relatives of its leader (usually referred to later as "boss" or "chief"). If the village was large and there were two or more kashims, their members were likely to form factions and their leaders were competitors. Within the men's house or within the community there were well-defined status differences. The great hunter was more prosperous because hunting was the source of wealth. The organizer of action such as building a new men's house, leading a group of families to another settlement when there was conflict, and organizing a trading or feuding expedition to the mainland, was powerful; he was admired, followed, and sometimes feared. Status was formalized within the kashim. The "boss" and respected elders had their places at the rear opposite the entrance. Ordinary hunter–family heads had places along the sides, with boys of their families on benches above them, while poor dependants sat beside the drafty entrance.

Throughout social relations, an age principle operated. Older children cared for and controlled younger ones; older women made the younger women work hard; young men were expected to listen to their elders. Age differences and the skills appropriate to different ages were recognized ritually.

Villages varied greatly in size: one might have only two houses, three or four storehouses, and a kashim, while another had a dozen or more houses (some occupied by two nuclear families), two kashims, and store-

217

left, Natl. Arch.: B-31082; center, Glenbow-Alberta Inst., Calgary, Alta.: NC-1-888; right, Natl. Arch.: RG22-WA-370.

Fig. 11 Female head decorations including beaded nose rings. left, Woman and child shipboard visitors. She wears nasal ornament and labrets and ear ornaments with beaded pendants. Photograph by W.B. Miller, June 1925. center, Child wearing cap with button decoration and beaded pendants, used for dancing. Photograph (cropped) by Loman Brothers, 1908–1915. right, Woman wearing simple walrus ivory labrets. Photograph (cropped) by Homer Jewell, Aug. 1936.

houses in proportion to number of families. In a large village, there would be two or three shamans. The statuses of "wealthy man" and "poor man" were clearly recognized.

Food was shared within the household; but only when honoring someone in his family would a man give food to the other men and only at feast time would all the productive families feed the entire village and guests from another community. Older people who could no longer produce much were fed, although not always well. This depended on family relationships and community attitudes. Elders were, however, not abandoned. A shaman regarded as evil would be avoided to the extent that families would move away or the shaman would be so ostracized that he and his family would move from the community or even to the mainland, or reportedly there would be an attempt to kill the offender. Otherwise, punishment or hostility toward a rival was a problem for personal and family action.

According to legend, raids were made by mainlanders, especially from the Yukon Delta, and Nunivakers raided in retaliation. Because the intent was to surprise people in the houses and kill everyone, only a very few women and children might be taken captive. They were not regarded as slaves. The amount of this warfare is unknown (Lantis 1946:168–169).

Perhaps because Euro-Americans have been so accustomed to hierarchical social systems, most of them have not seen the important horizontal relationships in Alaska Eskimo communities. Partnerships were universal and vital, that is, every person, not only adult males, had several partners, forming a network of cooperative work, personal defense, behavior control, and friendly giving. Partnerships were of three types: pat-

rilineally inherited mutual aid; inherited joking; and personally arranged trading and assistance partnerships, which were infrequent, for off-island protection.

The lineage was patrilineal, without inheritance of titles or formal prerogatives but with a likelihood of sons having the status and powers of the father, particularly in the families of successful hunters and of shamans. The secret knowledge that was thought essential for success passed from father to son by instruction and by inheritance of objects and songs having special powers and of symbolic designs representing a power source, for example a species of bird. With growth of the family, in time collateral as well as lineal relatives would have the same *ínɣu* 'power'. The sense of identity of lineage males is indicated by the set of property marks, on hunting implements for example, owned by the lineage, marks that did not appear to be amuletic.

A woman was expected to become a member of her husband's family, and after the birth of children, she even would learn her husband's hunting songs and secrets of his lineage. Although daughters knew the traditions and rules, their behavior was controlled by them only insofar as a woman's work was involved. A man, for example, could not hunt, eat, sell, or give away his animal helper except possibly to use its head as a forehead mask or its claws or other parts as amulets. There was no stated rule of exogamy, but because marriage between parallel cousins (the same as siblings) was prohibited, it was unlikely that people with the same talismanic animal would marry. Further, there apparently was no concept of a kin-group larger than the lineage.

Regarding marriage rules, the only forbidden marriages besides that between parent and child and two siblings (including parallel cousins) was marriage of any people in uncle-niece or aunt-nephew relationship. Levirate and sororate, although permitted, were not common. In polygyny and polyandry, which also occurred infrequently, there was a tendency to marry two sisters or two brothers. Other types of marriages also occurred infrequently. For example, a man might marry a woman and her daughter or marry his stepmother after his father's death. In the genealogies, there was no case of a man marrying his maternal uncle's widow (Lantis 1960). Marriage with a cross-cousin or with an inherited partner, serious or joking, was acceptable. Because the original partners seem to have been offspring of one mother but different fathers, they and their descendants would belong to different lineages.

In small communities with a dearth of people of appropriate age, it was realistic for a man and woman of greatly different ages to marry. The preferred first marriage was, however, between a youth about 20 years old and a girl about 13.

In family relationships, there was required of both men and women the most distant and respectful behavior toward both parents-in-law. Maintenance of the cross-sex formality and distance was facilitated by the separate living quarters for men and women. In same-sex dealings, a man, for example, would not look at his father-in-law when talking with him or would ask his wife to speak for him.

The age principle was formalized in and maintained by the kinship terminology that distinguished between older and younger brother, older and younger sister, with parallel cousins identified with siblings and sibling terms of reference applied to them. The Nunivak system was not the "Eskimo system" but the "Iroquois" or "Western Eskimo." There was, however, only one term for cross-cousins regardless of age and sex, except the special term for a man's female cross-cousin who was his joking partner. There were four terms for parents' siblings and four nepotic terms. (For other characteristics of the kinship system, see Lantis 1946:235–236.)

Because of taboos on use of what Nunivakers regarded as "the real name," there was a variety of devices to avoid its use. It was problematic whether or not the name contained a soul, but it at least named or represented the essential intrinsic being or a vital essence of the person. Use of the real name was avoided by three means: teknonymy; descriptive nicknames referring to a personal trait, accident, or accomplishment of the person and given by others; and pet names elaborated from kin terms and given by family members. These last were used in direct address. Teknonymy and the use of many nicknames would so completely supplant the real name that a young child would not know the names of its parents and the other adults. In adulthood, gradually the names of elders would be learned but could not be used in direct address by younger to older person. Among the names acquired at puberty were those like "Little older sister," "Mother's young brother," "Real daughter-in-law." Hearing such a name, a child would use it even though the addressee did not stand in sister, uncle, or daughter-in-law relation to the speaker (Lantis 1946:237–239).

Because Nunivak people have been reluctant to discuss kin relationships and practices, the full rationale of the system has not been recorded, especially the origin of inherited partnerships. As in the Barrow region (North Alaska Coast Eskimo), they may have arisen through spouse exchange. The complex family composition, difficult to describe, is best seen in the genealogies (Lantis 1960:189–213).

Life Cycle

In the Nunivak scheme of things there were three kinds of crises in an individual's life, not consciously categorized; but behavior at different life crises was consistently different. One life crisis behavior pattern was connected with physiological change: childbirth, girl's puberty, and death. These changes represented unnatural conditions and were potentially dangerous; therefore, the mother at childbirth, the pubescent girl, and the relatives of recently deceased had to take precautions. Taboos were put on fresh foods, sexual intercourse, wearing of ornaments, joking and playing, certain important economic activities, and important food-getting implements, like kayaks and harpoons. Other associated taboos also applied with regard to looking around and dress while out of doors. Punishments for breaking taboos at these times were thought to be illness or other misfortune to the individual or to members of his or her family, but the community as a whole would suffer only secondarily from infractions.

A related crisis that did not have a physiological basis was the occasion of a young man's killing his first bearded seal. While the boy would usually be beyond puberty at this stage, the situation called for almost point by point adherence to the girls' puberty observances. "At the same time where was a social element in his father's presenting gifts to the people at the Bladder Feast" (Lantis 1946:230). This public factor was an important ingredient in a second main type of life crisis that related to a change in one's status with regard to obtaining food resources. Berry picking, gathering of grass by girls, first killing of bird or hair seal by boys—all these events required recognition by the whole community since these activities involved its food supply and celebrated the addition of another producer to the community. The child's parents were proud to call the occasion to the attention of the whole community by distributing gifts.

Gift giving by parents to the community also marked events such as first appearance of an infant in the kashim, a boy's first drum, or first dancing in the kashim by either boy or girl.

The third kind of crisis was a change in social status, which to a Nunivaker was no crisis at all. Under this heading were marriage, divorce, and adoption. These did not involve either food supply or ritual. There were no taboos and no official participation by the community. A suitor would give the girl's mother the furs from which to make a parka for her. If the marriage was acceptable, the girl would take to the young man in the kashim a dish of her best food. Each one thus symbolized the sex-appropriate ability to provide.

Two other changes of social status were recognized by the community, for different reasons. When a novice shaman was ready to demonstrate his powers, he was urged to do so before the assembled residents. If successful, he was acclaimed. When a wealthy man organized and served as host for the great infrequent Messenger Feast, he too would be acclaimed and would be called henceforth by a term often translated as "chief." He was not a political leader or officeholder but an economic leader, who, even though he might be tyrannical in the village, obviously was acting correctly in the natural-supernatural universe (Lantis 1946:223–233).

Religion

• BELIEF Spirit powers, objects containing those powers, and songs derived from and invoking the powers form the core of the religion. Nothing important could be accomplished without the help of an *ín*ɣ̇*u*. The shaman possessed a greater variety of and stronger powers than the layman, yet it is doubtful whether he was as essential to the individual as was the person's own amulets and songs, most of which were inherited from ancestors, and a few of which derived from personal experience. The shaman's real strenth, apart from the impressive but unessential tricks, was based on the same compulsive influences over the supernatural that every man and woman possessed to some degree.

Ghosts—even though to be feared—were not prominent in the belief system or in personal experience. Most important were the souls of sea mammals which, if treated properly, would be reincarnated. Each species had its own villages under the sea, to which the shaman might journey to request its elder to send some of the younger animals to the hunters. There was no mother of the animals: masters of the animals were male.

Any animal could take human form. Actually not only mammals but also birds and fish could appear and speak as human beings. The nonhuman, nonanimal species were dwarfs, of two or more kinds and very common; giants, more rare; half-people, being only one side of a person, and half-birds; creatures that were half-human and half-animal or on whom one side of the face was normal, the other side distorted; wanderers, who formerly were human; a spirit with large mouth on the chest; a string-figure spirit; the northern lights, which

Smithsonian, Dibner Lib.: 83-3665.
Fig. 12. Man wearing a forehead mask of a predatory bird carrying a fish in his mouth. Carved wings were mounted on 3-inch feathers stuck into the hoop. "A miniature spear, feather-mounted, was stuck in the top of the bird's head" (Curtis 1907–1930, 20:39). Photograph by Edward S. Curtis, 1927.

were walrus spirits playing ball with a human skull; water monsters in the lakes; a large man-worm with human face on the head; a caribou with antlers branching like a willow; Big Eagle; and Raven.

The great Universe Being or Spirit of the World (*łam čua*) occasionally was heard but never seen. Nunivakers had difficulty in formulating his powers and functions. He probably was the great regulator of the world. A male moon spirit would come to the earth to get a wife or to help a mistreated person, and the shaman might journey to the moon to get help.

The underworld was a dark unpleasant place; the sky-world was pleasant and, as among other Eskimos, a person who died a violent death was rewarded by his or her soul going up to the heaven-world. Like Pacific Eskimos, Nunivak people thought that there was a series of sky-worlds, one above the other.

• RITUAL Much of Nunivak ritual was personal and individual. Although most of the Bladder Festival (the Feast for Seals' Souls) was communal, "the most important part of the ceremony was given by lineages, . . . the dispatching of the seals back to the sea and the singing of sacred hunting songs" (Lantis 1946:195–196).

Fig. 13. Clapper-drum. Bentwood frame with gut head secured with sinew is attached to a wooden handle shaped like a bird's head at the drum end. A thin strip of baleen is attached to the handle with willow root. It was beaten or clapped against the rim, the single head providing resonance. These small drums were used in addition to large tambourine drums during the Bladder festival (Lantis 1946:182–187). Length 42.0 cm; collected by Margaret Lantis at Mekoryuk, Nunivak I., Alaska, 1940.

The ritual opening of the spring hunting season, fundamental in Nunivak life, was performed entirely by families and whenever each family was ready. Regarding family taboos relating to seals see Ray (1981:56) and Lantis (1947:39).

Along with each hunter's bundle of sea-mammal bladders hung up in the kashim for the festival (the animal's soul was in the bladder), the first little birds killed by any boys during the year also were hung up to be honored. As the community's relations with the natural-supernatural world were set right and confirmed by the Bladder Festival's many parts, so its social relations were confirmed by the Messenger Feast, at which one village entertained one or more others. Whereas the Bladder Festival had to be given annually, the Messenger Feast could not be, because it required too much wealth and effort. Also, even though it contained some religious elements, it was not essentially a religious ceremony, therefore not on the calendar of rituals.

• SHAMANISM When a shaman saw one or more of the spirits, he often received a song. He would carve an amulet or might compose a song or carve a mask to represent the spirit and its power. He customarily would receive a specific power: to drive away bad weather, prevent illness or witchcraft, to bring herring, and so on. The shaman could give amulets having curative power to a patient as part of his doctoring. For public welfare, most shaman songs were sung in public. Only the means of the power displays, such as being burned and returning whole or freeing oneself of knotted bindings, appear to have been secret. A shaman sometimes would be thought to practice witchcraft.

There were female shamans, whose principal activity was curing. A woman shaman had a drum and used it herself, the only woman who could do this. Usually, however, in a doctoring session others would sing and drum for her while she worked over the patient.

For either sex, there were stories of only a few instances of genuine trance, hysteria, or any other unsimulated abnormal condition. Although trance did occur, there is not clear evidence that it was routinely sought. When a shaman demonstrated his powers, "both he and the audience undoubtedly experienced great excitement and suspense, for different reasons. Shamans did feel that they had power. This seems clear" (Lantis 1946:200).

The common method of curing was extraction: the shaman's sucking or pulling out the pain, usually a prolonged activity accompanied by drumming and singing and anciently the wearing of a mask. Curing by recovery of a lost soul was less common. This was accomplished by a shaman's spirit-flight to recover a soul stolen by the spirits. "Sometimes in case of sickness or other misfortune, the shaman would call upon a person to confess his sins in the kazigi [kashim]" (Lantis 1946:202–203).

For other elements of religion, ceremonial, and curing, see Lantis (1946:182–205).

Art

Because Nunivak art was still produced and sold in the 1980s while little traditional art was available from most other Yupik, it has become well known to Alaska collectors and to anthropologists elsewhere. Most of the wooden Nunivak dishes made in the 1980s were, however, inferior to those being made and used in the 1930s. There was, in the 1970s, also some carving and etching of ivory, both traditional and innovative (Ray 1981; Lantis 1946:190).

The X-ray or anatomical style of painted animals on wood has been spare, formalized, yet curvilinear, showing excellent control of the brush. Incised ("etched") figures on ivory hunting-implement socket-pieces have been similarly well controlled but more rectilinear, somewhat more reminiscent of Punuk style. The workmanship, although characterized by meticulous care, has shown a willingness to vary, to experiment.

There were also the following. A totemic figure was painted along the side of the boat cover. Drumheads had painted figures and drum handles were carved. Wooden dolls without appendages were rather crudely carved as were toy boats. Other toys were usually made by the youthful players. Wooden eyeshades were carved and painted. Wooden hunting hats were not only painted

left, U. of Pa., U. Mus., Philadelphia: NA 762; Natl. Mus. of Canada, Ottawa: center IV-E-970; right, IV-E-975.

Fig. 14. Coiled baskets. Traditional basketry (mats, baskets, socks, and mittens) were twined. It is not clear when coiled baskets were first made, but their production increased in 1920 when a manager for the Lomen Company provided a steady market for them and encouraged the women to make finer baskets and to vary size, shape, and decoration. left, Covered basket; center, covered basket with blue, brown, and yellow dyed pattern; right, covered basket with openwork zigzag bands. left, Height 17.5 cm; collected by G.B. Gordon on Nunivak I., Alaska, 1905. center and right, Same scale; collected by Diamond Jenness on Nunivak I., Alaska, 1926.

but also held carved ivory pieces representing inherited spirit-powers. The most abundant carved ivory objects were the amulets, which might be worn on a thong or be attached to net or implement. An artifact like the toggle used to fasten together two parts of a harpoon line would be carved in the form of an animal-spirit or other spirit-helper. The handle of the woman's knife (ulu) was most likely to have a geometric design, as were the ear pendants and other ornaments.

The women's art was limited to simple, although carefully and pleasingly made, decoration on the borders of clothing, twined basketry, and pottery vessels, principally lamps. Such decoration was likely to be long or short parallel lines and dots. It is uncertain when the women began to make coiled baskets for sale, decorated with either geometric designs (fig. 14) or figures from nature such as insects, birds, and dogs—perhaps in the 1920s as the trader claimed (Ray 1981:figs. 75, 83; Lantis 1950).

Mythology

Myths and tales showed a combination of familiar motifs from the Pacific coast (Tlingit Indian and Pacific Eskimo) and from Bering and Arctic coast Eskimos. Dog Husband, Raven, Son-in-law Tests, Younger Brother ridding the world of monsters, and the Haughty Girl all appeared. Besides origin myths, there were war legends and short amusing animal tales. In agreement with kinship terminology and kinship taboos, Sun Sister and Moon Brother here is Sun Aunt and Moon Nephew.

As songs accompanied many of the string-figures, so also songs were part of many stories. If a character was said to sing, the storyteller thereupon sang the song (Himmelheber 1951). Sonne (1980) analyzed Nunivak mythology for social content, and Lantis (1953) for psychological implications.

Synonymy†

The Nunivak Eskimo take their name from their island, called in General Central Yupik *nuní·va·q* (practical orthography Nunivaaq) and in the Nunivak dialect *nuṇí·wáx̣* (Nunivaar). This appears to be a derivative of *nuna* 'land', but the precise meaning is unknown. In General Central Yupik the people of Nunivak are called *nuní·vá·γ̇miut,* in the Nunivak dialect *nuṇí·wáγ̇miut* (both Nunivaarmiut).

The name of the village Mekoryuk is in the Nunivak dialect *mikúγ̇yax̣* (Mikuryar), meaning 'gathering', considered locally to refer to a swarm of mosquitoes.

Sources

The 1890 census (U.S. Census Office 1893) is an important early source for Nunivak. Curtis (1907–1930, 20) visited the island in 1927. Henry B. Collins and T. Dale Stewart of the Smithsonian Institution stopped

†This synonymy was written by Margaret Lantis and Ives Goddard incorporating linguistic forms furnished by Steven A. Jacobson and Anthony C. Woodbury (communications to editors 1982).

222

Fig. 15. New and old structures in Mekoryuk. Photograph by Jerry Hout, March 1967.

there in 1927; their collection of Nunivak artifacts is in the National Museum of Natural History, Smithsonian Institution, Washington. Himmelheber (1938, 1951) was on the island in 1936–1937 studying its graphic arts and mythology. Lantis's fieldwork resulted in studies in social culture (1946, 1953, 1960, 1972).

Archeological reconnaissance was done by VanStone (1957) and Nowak (1974, 1982), who also studied diet (1975, 1977). Hammerich (1958) did linguistic research on Nunivak in 1950 and 1953, and the extensive work by Steven A. Jacobson in the 1970s was in 1982 being included in the Central Alaskan Yupik dictionary being produced by the Alaska Native Language Center.

There are small collections of artifacts in the Burke Memorial Washington State Museum, University of Washington, Seattle; Lowie Museum of Anthropology, University of California, Berkeley; Museum of Anthropology, University of Kentucky, Lexington; and the Buffalo Museum of Science, New York.

Mainland Southwest Alaska Eskimo

JAMES W. VANSTONE

Language and Territory

Although it is convenient to think of southwestern Alaska, excluding Nunivak Island, as a geographical and cultural unit, the region has actually been occupied in historic times by seven groups of Central-Alaskan-Yupik–speaking Eskimos* (fig. 1). The problem of accurately identifying the subcultural affiliations of these Eskimos is complicated by vague and conflicting statements in the early historic sources, and by movements of people throughout the region, movements that were influenced to a marked degree by historical factors.

In the Yukon delta region, subcultural boundaries cannot be determined with certainty, but there is general agreement that three groups were involved. To the north, along the banks of the lower Yukon River lived the Kuigpagmiut, Eskimos who came in contact with the Ingalik Indians near the present settlement of Holy Cross. The Eskimos between the south bank of the Yukon and north bank of the Kuskokwim are generally separated into two tribal groupings, the Maarmiut and Kayaligmiut, although the basis for such a separation is weak. In the language of the local Eskimos, all the people of the delta area are called *akúlmiut* 'dwellers in between' or 'tundra people'. The Kayaligmiut lived in the vicinity of Hazen Bay and on Nelson Island, while the Maarmiut were an inland people living near the settlement of Mountain Village. In 1880 the Kuigpagmiut, Maarmiut, and Kayaligmiut had a combined population of approximately 3,100 (Nelson 1899:26; Oswalt 1967:5–7, map 2; Petroff 1884:11–12, 126; Zagoskin 1967:210).

The Kusquqvagmiut, with an estimated population of 3,100 in 1880, inhabited the banks of the Kuskokwim River as far inland as the present village of Aniak. Beyond that point on the central Kuskokwim as far as the mouth of the Holitna River was an area of joint occupancy with the Georgetown subgroup of the Ingalik. To the south, the Kusquqvagmiut occupied the village of Tikchik on the lake of that name, which is in the Nushagak drainage. They may also have controlled the lakes to the north toward the Kuskokwim, but it is doubtful if they utilized this vast area very extensively

(Bailey 1880:26–27; Oswalt 1962:1–4, 1967:7; Russian-American Company 1818–1865, vol. 6, no. 244:folio 478).

South of the territory of the Kusquqvagmiut are the Tuyuryarmiut, who occupied the banks of the Togiak River, its tributaries, and the adjacent coast. Population estimates for this group are untrustworthy, but there may have been as many as 1,000 in 1880 (Bailey 1880:27; Oswalt 1967:8–9; Petroff 1884:17, 134–135).

In the Nushagak River region there was a basic distinction between the coastal Eskimos in the Nushagak Bay area and those who lived along the river and its tributaries. Nushagak Bay was inhabited by the Aglurmiut, whose territory has generally been thought to have included most of the Alaska Peninsula to the southwest as far as Port Moller, and to the northeast up to and including the western two-thirds of Iliamna Lake (VanStone 1967:xxi). However, later research (Dumond, Conton, and Shields 1975:fig. 1) suggests that the Aglurmiut may not have extended to the south as far as Ugashik, nor much beyond the Naknek River to the north.

The Nushagak River Eskimos have the ethnic name of Kiatagmiut (the correct Yupik form is uncertain). This subgroup of central-Alaskan-Yupik–speakers occupied the entire Nushagak River, the lower Mulchatna River, and the area to the north possibly including the Wood River Lakes. The more northerly Tikchik Lakes were within the territory of the Kusquqvagmiut. To the east, the Kiatagmiut occupied the upper Kvichak River and probably the lower end of Iliamna Lake (Dumond, Conton, and Shields 1975:fig. 1). A reliable population estimate of 900 for the combined Aglurmiut-Kiatagmiut exists as early as 1829 (Russian-American Company 1818–1865, vol. 6, no. 460:folio 349; VanStone 1967:xxi–xxii, 110–112).

Considering the diversity of ethnic boundaries within the relatively restricted area of southwestern Alaska, it is not surprising that the distinction between the various subgroups just described has become blurred as a result of European contact. Epidemics of introduced European diseases, the establishment of schools and missions, and particularly the emergence of the fur trade and an important commercial salmon-fishing industry in Bristol Bay resulted in considerable movement of Eskimos throughout the region, the coalescence of some

---

*For the orthography used to spell Yupik words, see the footnote in "Southwest Alaska Eskimo: Introduction."

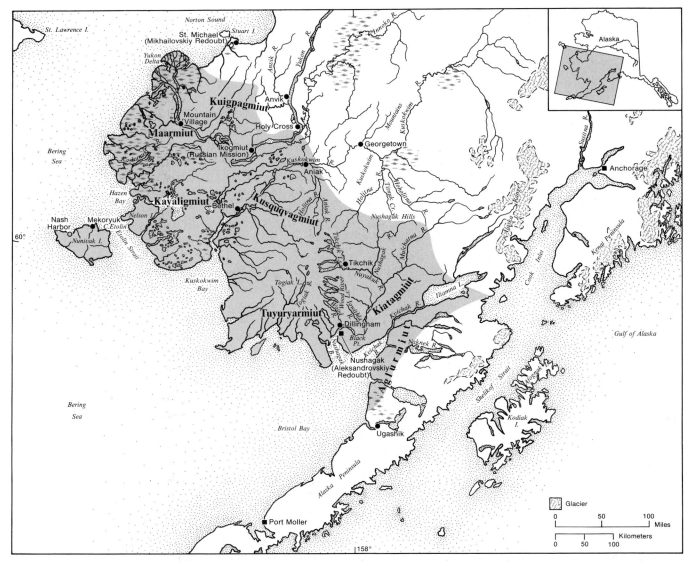

Fig. 1. Approximate locations of Southwest Alaska Eskimo groups in the 19th century.

populations and the dispersal of others. These population movements have been going on since the very beginning of the historical period and the subgroups discussed here are based on a consensus of the historic sources, early census reports and, in some cases, informants' statements. It is significant that many Eskimos resident in the Nushagak River region in the mid-twentieth century recognized the distinction between the Aglurmiut and the Kiatagmiut as having both a linguistic and a cultural basis, even though a slight one (VanStone 1967:120).

Environment

The broad lowland including the deltas of both the Yukon and Kuskokwim rivers has a breadth of more than 200 miles. In the north it begins near 63° north latitude where the Yukon divides into a number of channels, the most important of which is Aphrewn Pass. These channels head in the direction of the sea in a generally northern and northwesterly direction. The area is characterized by an intricate maze of waterways, some of which flow into Bering Sea while some connect with other channels. Many are simply sloughs that lead nowhere and make travel in the area extremely difficult. The land between and around the sloughs and streams, no more than 10 feet above low tide, is swampy and dotted with many small lakes. The delta of the Kuskokwim is similar to that of the Yukon, except for the deep channel that winds through it, and the fact that the land surface is broken to a greater degree by occasional low, isolated hills. Shoreline at the mouth of the Kuskokwim is characterized by a large number of inlets, islands, and tidal lagoons. The coastal plain throughout the entire lowland area extends a long distance seaward in the form of mud flats, which are visible at low tide.

225

The upper reaches of the lower Yukon are heavily forested, but as the river approaches the sea trees become scattered. Finally, a few miles down the delta the trees disappear entirely and there is nothing to interrupt the flat moss and grass-covered tundra.

The valley of the Kuskokwim River within the area occupied by Eskimos is broad, and on the south the river is bordered in most places by wide lowlands. About 100 miles above the delta, spruce vegetation begins to thin out and the country becomes flat with the waters of the river meandering sluggishly toward the sea. Uplands are represented only by occasional rounded hills and low ridges (Brooks 1953:22–25).

The areas drained by the Togiak and Nushagak rivers are a region of greater relief and general topographical variety. The main topographic feature is, of course, the Nushagak River, which rises in the Nushagak Hills and flows in a southwesterly direction to the head of Nushagak Bay. A tributary of the Nushagak, the Nuyakuk River, drains the six northern Tikchik Lakes to the west. The four lakes immediately to the south of these are drained by the Wood River, which flows into Nushagak Bay. These are called the Wood River Lakes. Also included in the area occupied by Eskimos are the lower reaches of the Mulchatna River, the only significant eastern tributary of the Nushagak.

A geologist who traveled extensively in the Nushagak River region in the 1930s divided the area into three geographic units: the lowland region of the river and bay, the Nushagak Hills, and the Tikchik Mountains (Mertie 1938:9). The lowland region can, in turn, be divided into two sections: the flat, almost treeless region around Nushagak and Kvichak bays, and the alluvial

flats of the river. The country bordering on the bay is, for the most part, a swampy lowland, virtually treeless and characterized by a tundra type of vegetation. In the vicinity of the community of Dillingham, stands of spruce begin to appear and continue northward as isolated patches to the Wood River Lakes.

The vast valley lowland of the Nushagak River spreads about 90 miles to the north and is approximately 60 miles wide from the eastern extremities of the Tikchik Mountains to the Kvichak River. The river estuary, which spreads from Black Point to the mouth of the Wood River, is bordered on both sides by gray mud flats. Above Black Point the Nushagak is a moderately swift, shallow stream that is frequently braided with sloughs and channels. From a point about 10 miles east of Black Point and continuing upstream for about 10 miles the river is divided into two channels of approximately equal size.

The west bank of the Nushagak from the Iowithla River upstream to a point approximately 10 miles above the mouth of the Mulchatna River is bordered by a steep bluff that ranges from 40 to 200 feet above the level of the river. This bluff is the eastern edge of a gravel, sand, and clay plain that forms the topography of the vast stretch of country between the Nushagak River and the Tikchik Mountains. This plain is primarily covered with moss, grass, and brush; but along the river, beginning just above Black Point, stands a strip of timber that continues upstream into the Nushagak Hills. This timber consists mainly of spruce and poplar with some birch in the better-drained areas along the west bank.

The east bank of the Nushagak from Portage Creek

Fig. 2. View of Hooper Bay, a coastal village in the Yukon-Kuskokwim Delta. At the far right is an elevated storage cache and a kayak elevated on a rack so that dogs cannot chew the skin cover. The houses at Hooper Bay are on top of an extensive midden deposit, the upper levels of which date to approximately A.D. 1600 (Oswalt 1952a). Photograph by Lomen Brothers, 1908–1915.

northward to the Nuyakuk is much lower than the west bank. The Mulchatna is also timbered along its course and the vast, low plain of this important tributary is an undrained lowland covered with hundreds of small lakes. The Mulchatna has its headwaters in the southern foothills of the Alaska Range that border Iliamna Lake.

The Tikchik Mountains constitute the eastern part of an extensive range known as the Kuskokwim Mountains (Wood River Mountains on U.S. Geological Survey quadrangle maps), the southern limit of which is about 20 miles north of the head of Nushagak Bay. The Togiak River drains these rugged mountains, but to the east in the interlake region the peaks are less abrupt and their tops are either flat or rounded. At many places these rounded hills occur as isolated buttes, or groups of several buttes, separated from one another by broad, low, alluviated valleys. The easternmost spurs of these hills project outward into the lowland of the Nushagak River (Mertie 1938:9–24).

Prehistory

The cultural center of the Central-Alaskan-Yupik–speaking peoples was not forested river valleys like those just described, but the central Bering Sea coast. In this area, from the earliest times people were oriented toward a maritime economy in which the seal was the most important animal hunted. On the adjacent tundra there was some caribou hunting, and fishing for salmon was significant at the mouths of rivers and in certain bays.

The prehistoric archeology of the entire region under consideration is poorly known, but it is possible that extensive archeological excavations carried out in the Naknek River region on the Alaska Peninsula may throw some light on prehistoric developments to the north. In the Naknek region Dumond (1969:1114, 1981:189–190) has postulated that by 2500 B.C. the interior portion of the Alaska Peninsula northwest of the Aleutian Range was inhabited by an inland-oriented people who were probably Indians. Around 1900 B.C. these people were displaced by a movement of ancestral Eskimos from the north bearing the so-called Arctic Small Tool tradition who by 1000 B.C. had moved out to the coast. By 300 B.C. the upper portion of the Naknek drainage had been reinhabited by descendants of the Arctic Small Tool people and from that time, continuity of population down to historic times can be demonstrated.

It is, of course, risky to assume that prehistoric movements of people throughout southwestern Alaska paralleled exactly those in the Naknek drainage; nevertheless, the possibility exists that such a pattern might

top, U. of Alaska Arch., Fairbanks: White Coll., 76-2-115; bottom, Smithsonian, NAA: S.I. 6371.

Fig. 3. Kuigpagmiut villages. top, Summer house at Ikogmiut (Russian Mission) on the lower Yukon River. Upright planks form the front and rear walls, while the lateral walls are of horizontal logs. Over the gabled roof of hewn poles are boards and a layer of bark. Light enters through small holes cut in the wall planks. Dwellings like this sheltered up to 3 families. Photograph probably by J.T. White, 1899–1901. bottom, Winter village of Razboinski on the lower Yukon River. The log houses are summer structures that face a creek. In front are semi-subterranean winter houses, which appear as raised snow-covered mounds. Photograph by E.W. Nelson, 1877–1881.

Fig. 5. Grave monuments in a cemetery on the lower Kuskokwim River. Over the grave on the left, possessions of the deceased (kayak paddle, rifle, bucket, bow, harpoon line holder) are displayed on poles and intended for the use of his spirit after death. Over the grave on the right is a wooden effigy and backboard, probably erected as a memorial or to please the spirit of the deceased. Photograph by George B. Gordon, 1907.

apply to a wider area and the question naturally arises why the remains of those who repopulated the interior have not been found. The fact is that much of southwestern Alaska is an extremely unrewarding area in which to conduct archeological investigations. The rivers are heavily forested, and the Kuskokwim and Yukon have unstable banks. Thus, human habitation sites are likely either to have been cut away or to be obscured by dense growth of trees and brush. Regardless of when the inland movements of population took place, it was certainly their already acquired salmon-fishing technology that enabled the Eskimos to exploit effectively an inland environment like that along the Nushagak, Togiak, Kuskokwim, and lower Yukon rivers.

Culture

Subsistence

It is well to keep in mind that although the tundra and taiga environments of southwestern Alaska imposed rather strict limitations on the ways in which people could make their living, Eskimos of this area did not experience the extreme environmental pressures felt by inhabitants of the High Arctic. Hunting, fishing, and collecting were all practiced in the area, but fishing was by far the most important. Hunting supplemented the food supply and provided the skins necessary for clothing (fig. 6), but the collection of wild plants was minimal. An understanding of subsistence pursuits is important not only in itself, but also to make clear much of Eskimo life that is not directly related to subsistence.

Fig. 4. Log structures. top, Semisubterranean houses at Hooper Bay. Storm sheds made from drift logs protect the tunnel and main entrance from cold winds and afford storage space for hunting equipment and household items. Photograph by Lomen Brothers, 1908–1915. center, House at the coastal village of Quinhagak on Kuskokwim Bay. This type of above-ground log dwelling with a storm shed replaced traditional semisubterranean structures in Alaska Eskimo villages. Blocks of sod placed against the walls and on the roof keep out the wind. Photograph by George B. Gordon, 1907. bottom, Elevated cache at the village of Nushagak. Dried salmon for dog food, and sleds, harnesses, and other equipment were stored in caches like this one, constructed of split logs with sod on the roof. A net and drying fish are hanging from the structure. The Eskimos are dressed in the combination of traditional and European clothing that was characteristic of this area at the beginning of the 20th century. Photograph by N.B. Miller, 1890.

Smithsonian, NAA: S.I. 6914.

Fig. 6. A couple from a settlement on the Kuskokwim River wearing typical winter clothing. The man's coat appears to be made of ground-squirrel skins and the woman's of beaver or muskrat. Both are decorated with strips of skin. Clothing in the Yupik-speaking area was more varied than among the Inupiaq, the garments often fitting loosely and lacking the tailor-made appearance characteristic of more northern peoples. Photograph by E.W. Nelson, 1877–1881.

It should be stated at the outset that it is no longer possible to reconstruct with certainty the aboriginal life of any part of southwestern Alaska. The Eskimos were drawn into the fur trade before their precontact way of life could be recorded, and by the time the most reliable historic sources begin to describe the people and their lifeways, considerable change had already taken place. This is particularly true for the area of subsistence activities where involvement in the fur trade brought about

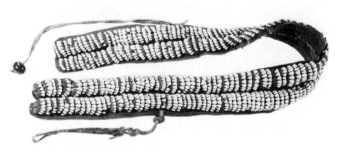

Smithsonian, Dept. of Anthr.: 76,703.

Fig. 7. Caribou-tooth belt. Women wore belts made by men from trimmed lower mandibles of caribou sewn onto leather strips. A double row of incisors is the product of an accomplished hunter. Leather ties and a large blue bead serve as fastener. Belts used by many generations of women acquired curing powers (Fitzhugh and Kaplan 1982:146). Length 87.0 cm; collected by J.W. Johnson at Nushagak, Alaska, 1885.

immediate, radical changes. Much of the information that is available and presented here applies to the period between 1880 and 1910, although reliable informants such as Zagoskin (1967) give significant glimpses of life several decades earlier.

Because subsistence activities were rather uniform throughout the lower and central Kuskokwim, in the Nushagak region, and, to some extent, in the Yukon delta, it is possible to consider the entire area as a subsistence unit even though localized variations did, of course, exist. Probably the greatest variations were characteristic of the Yukon delta region where little detailed ethnographic research has been undertaken. Known variations will be included in the discussion whenever they seem to be pertinent. Most of the following account of the seasonal round has been adapted from Oswalt (1963a:116–132, 1978:101–143) and VanStone (1967:122–130).

Throughout the region, the subsistence year can be said to have ended with the coming of spring. By late March or early April winter food supplies began to be severely depleted. Although starvation sometimes threatened, it rarely occurred. At this time of the year, Eskimo inhabitants of the Kuskokwim and Nushagak rivers prepared to abandon their winter villages. Sledges were refurbished, open skin boats were repaired, and other equipment was gathered and packed for the trip to spring camps. Residents of the lower Kuskokwim generally had their camps in the open tundra country. Middle River Eskimos ascended the various tributaries of the Kuskokwim. Nushagak River families moved to camps along the streams in the mountainous country of the interior. Boats and all household equipment were moved by dog sledge even though some families did not leave their villages until April.

Dwellings in the tundra camps of the Kuskokwim Eskimos were simple structures about 10 feet square, with walls of cut sod approximately six feet in height. The split log ceiling was supported by four vertical posts set in the corners. Additional sod was placed on the ceiling to make the dwelling relatively waterproof. Some tundra houses were more elaborate and resembled those built in the villages. Occasionally the tundra camp contained a kashim (Yupik *qázγiq*) or ceremonial house. In fact, the tundra camps can hardly be called temporary since they frequently were occupied over several generations.

The main spring occupation in both the Kuskokwim and Nushagak areas in the early historic period was the taking of fur-bearing animals. On the tundra, the Kuskokwim people trapped muskrat, mink, otter, ground squirrel, and marmots. In the middle Kuskokwim and Nushagak areas, beaver, otter, red fox, arctic fox, marten, lynx, mink, and muskrat were the most valuable pelts. Traps included fixed and spring-pole snares, traditional trapping devices being preferred even after 229

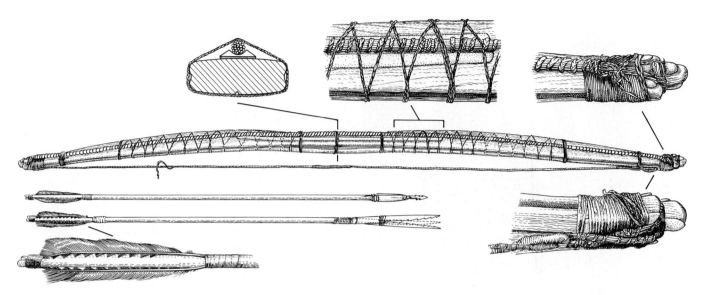

Smithsonian, Dept. of Anthr.: top, 43,914; center, 36,149; bottom, 36,169.

Fig. 8. Bow and arrows. top, Bow of the southern Alaska type (Murdoch 1884), broad and flat, tapering to the nocks (which are ivory reinforced) and narrowed at the handle. The edges are grooved, and a piece of ivory stiffens the back. The sinew backing is parallel strands spirally lashed into a single cable. The bowstring is twisted sinew with root reinforcing wound at the center for better grip. Northern bows are usually shorter and have a more elaborate backing, greater reinforcement being needed because of weaker and less plentiful wood. center and bottom, Arrows used for killing fish (different varieties were used for birds and mammals). top, Length 140.0 cm, rest same scale. All collected by E.W. Nelson in Alaska; top, on the Yukon River; center, Kashunuk; bottom, Big Lake; 1877–1881.

commercial steel traps became available. Migrating game birds were taken in large numbers in the riverine areas and Yukon delta, with fine-meshed nets, snares, or spears. A characteristic form of bird spear had a cluster of three barbed points at the end and was thrown with the aid of a throwing board (figs. 10–11). Caribou hunting was also an important spring activity in some locations and, at least in the tundra camps, whitefish were abundant in the lakes and streams and could be taken easily with gill nets.

While the river Eskimos were in the interior trapping and hunting caribou, residents of Nushagak Bay and the Yukon delta hunted seals at favored locations along the coast (in addition to interior trapping). Barbed harpoon darts, sometimes feathered at the base of the shaft, were more commonly used than toggle-headed harpoons for taking seals. These darts (fig. 12) were thrown from a kayak with the aid of a throwing board (Mason 1902:294). Dip netting for smelt was also an important late spring activity for these people.

By no later than the middle of June and sometimes earlier, the spring camps were abandoned and families returned by boat to their permanent villages along the riverbanks to prepare for salmon fishing. Smelt ascended the Kuskokwim at this time of year and were taken in large numbers with dip nets. Both belugas and seals also ascended the Kuskokwim in late spring in pursuit of the smelt and were hunted extensively.

The village dwellings usually consisted of a small anteroom connected to a main living area by a short, ground-level passage or a semisubterranean tunnel. This tunnel or passage prevented cold air from entering the living room, the entrance to which was covered by a woven grass mat or skin curtain. The main living area, usually about 15 feet square, was built into an excavation approximately three feet deep. Either vertical or horizontal logs formed the side walls, and the roof was supported by four posts, either set against the front and rear walls, or standing free in the room. Short, split logs covered the roof with an opening in the center fitted with sewed fish skins to serve as a window. The entire structure was covered with sheets of birchbark or bundles of grass, and then a layer of sod was added. Thus the house appeared as a dome-shaped mound of earth

Smithsonian, Dept. of Anthr.: top, 127,497; bottom, 127,636.

Fig. 9. Skin scrapers. Long-handled tools are used by women for working hide from the lower Kuskokwim to northern Norton Sound (see "Kotzebue Sound Eskimo," fig. 9, this vol. for northern style). top, Curved wooden handle, groove running in center of each side and a stone blade lashed on with root. bottom, Wooden handle with separate wooden crosspiece at one end and stone blade bound with root. Length 32.5 cm; collected by J.W. Johnson at Nushagak, Alaska, 1886. top, Same scale; collected by S. Applegate, Togiak River, Alaska, 1886.

Fig. 10. Bird hunters from Quinhagak in kayaks at the mouth of the Kuskokwim River. The large bow holes in these vessels are characteristic of kayaks from Nunivak I. and the adjacent mainland. In front of the hunter in the nearest vessel is a bird spear and throwing-board. Photograph by G.B. Gordon, 1907.

from the outside. A fireplace was usually located near the center of the floor, and sleeping benches paralleled the side walls and sometimes the rear wall as well.

In addition to artifacts associated with subsistence activities, a village house would contain numerous clay

Fig. 11. Eskimo boy holding a bird spear, throwing-board, and Canada geese he has killed on Kashunuk Slough in the Yukon-Kuskokwim Delta near the Kuigpagmiut village of Marshall. Photograph by O.J. Murie, July 1924.

cooking pots, birchbark baskets, and skillfully made grass baskets woven by twining or coiling (fig. 13). There would also be expertly constructed wooden boxes, trays, buckets, and dishes of diverse shapes to be used for a variety of purposes (fig. 14). Light in the house was provided by shallow, saucer-shaped clay lamps, which frequently were raised on wooden stands (Nelson 1899:63–72, 201–204; Oswalt and VanStone 1967:90–91).

An important early spring activity in the village was the repairing of nets and traps in preparation for the first salmon runs. By mid-June, the huge king salmon (*Oncorhynchus tshawytscha*) were making their appearance, to be followed by other varieties. Along the Nushagak these fish were taken primarily with gill nets, although there were certain locations where funnel-shaped basket traps as well as spears with barbed harpoon dart heads could be used effectively. Nets were made of sinew and held vertical in the water by means of wooden floats and stone sinkers; mesh sizes were measured with gauges.

On the Kuskokwim drift netting was practiced extensively for all the varieties of salmon. A single fisherman, utilizing a straight stretch of river, floated in his kayak or canoe while paying out his gill net and removing the fish from it as they were caught. When the drift had been completed, the fisherman would paddle upstream and begin again. A drift of about two miles is said to have been average.

Along the lower reaches of the rivers of southwestern Alaska each man owned a sealskin-covered kayak, the frame of which had a projecting stern piece and a large hole at the bow. Farther up the river, small birchbark canoes were used in addition to kayaks.

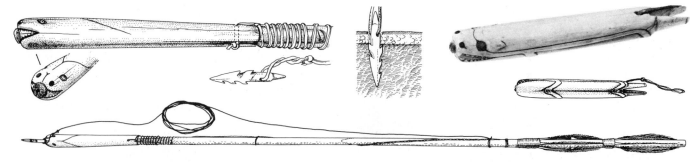

Smithsonian, Dept. of Anthr.: left, 37,350; right, 176,248.

Fig. 12. Seal dart. Seals were hunted in the summer from kayaks using a dart made of a wooden shaft (sometimes fletched as here), with an ivory socketpiece. At the end of the socketpiece is a wooden plug into which is inserted a barbed harpoon point. Unlike a toggling harpoon point, the barbed point (the drawing shows penetration) is used only on small mammals as it would pull out if used on larger animals. The point is attached by a line to the shaft. The weapon was projected with a throwing-board. Although missing from this example, an inflated bladder on a line to the shaft kept the dart and seal afloat. The decorated socketpieces (right) often represent animal predators, probably to aid the hunter's luck. left, Length 139.0 cm, right, 20.0 cm; both collected by E.W. Nelson at Cape Vancouver, Alaska, 1877–1881.

Some villages on both the lower Kuskokwim and Nushagak rivers had summer fish camps where the villagers went during the salmon fishing season. On the Kuskokwim, these frequently were located not only near good drifting grounds, but also with easy access to a tundra stream where traps could be set all summer for whitefish. Nushagak fish camps were located in good areas for gill netting. Fish caught were split and then hung across a pole frame drying rack in order to dry in the air and sun (fig. 16).

The fall run of coho salmon (*Oncorhynchus kisutch*) ended the fishing season, although on the upper Nushagak and its tributaries these fish could be taken until freeze-up. By early September Eskimos throughout the region prepared once again to leave their summer fish camps and villages. In the tundra lakes adjacent to the lower Kuskokwim, gill nets were set for whitefish, blackfish, and pike. These fish were staple food items for early winter. Along the central Kuskokwim, the men traveled to the headwaters of the river's tributaries to hunt caribou and take fur-bearing animals. After hunting for a month or more, the men assembled their catch near a stream and constructed a boat for their trip to the main river. The canoes with which they had ascended the tributaries were cached to be picked up during the winter.

As early as mid-August, the men of Nushagak River villages began to ascend the tributaries of that river to hunt and trap, leaving the women, children, and elderly in the villages to watch over the full fish caches. Caribou hunting was particularly good at this time of the year, and many skins were secured for winter clothing. The animals were caught in snares or killed with bows and arrows after being lured past concealed hunters or driven into narrow valleys. By mid-September the fur of the beaver was in prime condition and these animals were taken in wooden deadfalls or their dams were broken and the water allowed to run out, thus exposing the beaver. This hunting and trapping continued until the first snowfall in October when the men returned once again to their winter villages.

Prior to European contact, caribou skins and various furs were used extensively for clothing, but Russian and American traders discouraged this practice as being detrimental to the fur trade and encouraged the Eskimos to wear far less suitable European clothing. In the aboriginal period men wore long, hooded parkas reaching to the knees or below. Beneath the parka, belted knee-length trousers were worn by both sexes. The parkas of women tended to be shorter than those of men and were cut up the sides to form front and rear flaps. Eskimos of the Yukon-Kuskokwim region used a greater variety of animal skins as parka materials than did more northern people. Both sexes wore skin boots, sometimes with woven grass socks (fig. 17). Fishskin trousers

Diocese of Fairbanks, Chancery Office, Alaska.

Fig. 13. Eskimo women in the Yukon-Kuskokwim Delta region making coiled baskets of dried rye-grass. The woman at left is wearing a parka made of ground-squirrel skins. Photograph by Bernard R. Hubbard, about 1925.

and parkas were frequently worn in summer (Nelson 1899:30–38; Oswalt 1963a:26–27).

In winter the people of the lower Kuskokwim did not fish a great deal; they relied heavily on their accumulated surplus of dried salmon for food. Most central river Eskimos continued to fish during the early part of the winter, taking a species of cod in traps and spearing whitefish and pike with leisters through holes in the river ice. Along the Nushagak, some early fall trapping seems to have been done near the villages, and in November, traps for whitefish were placed under the ice and grayling were taken with hooks through holes in the ice. It is likely too that caribou were hunted near the villages and perhaps for some distance up the river and its tributaries.

For people along the lower Kuskokwim, winter was an extended period of enforced leisure, while along the middle river this leisure was broken by occasional hunting and trapping trips. On the Nushagak, most fall activities in both river and coastal communities ended early in December, when severe weather settled in.

The major winter activity throughout all of southwestern Alaska was the dance festivals that began in late December or early January and lasted until February. Some of these ceremonies were purely secular, while others had supernatural implications and seem to have centered around the propitiation of the dead and possibly the magical revival of game animals. The center of these winter festivities was the kashim, at least one of which was to be found in all the larger settlements. Residents of other settlements would be invited for many of the festivals, and the singing and dancing in the kashim frequently continued for 10 days or more at a time. Ceremonial equipment used at these festivals included elaborate face masks (fig. 18), usually made by shamans, and the characteristic Eskimo tambourine drum.

The annual cycle that has been described for the Nushagak and Kuskokwim rivers was roughly the same for those people living in the coastal settlements. Only in the spring did major differences occur, as this was when the coastal people did most of their sea mammal hunting. It has been suggested that the distinction between the coastal and interior way of life may have been greater in the aboriginal period before both groups of people were drawn into the fur trade. In any event, it is important to emphasize that the Aglurmiut of Bristol Bay, and very likely other coastal groups throughout the region, were never primarily sea mammal hunters but concentrated on fishing and were always more inland-oriented than many coastal Eskimos to the north.

Social Organization

Throughout the area under discussion, nuclear families lived together in the same house, forming an extended family household, only at tundra or hunting camps and in summer fish camps. When the permanent villages were occupied, the men and older boys lived in the kashim, while only the women and children occupied other dwellings. Among the Kusquqvagmiut and, as nearly as can be determined, the Nushagak area Eskimos too, residence tended to be duolocal (matrilocal for females), so that a woman not only raised her daughters in the house while her sons eventually went to live in the kashim, but the daughters in turn would raise the next generation of children in the same house.

Village life centered around the kashim since it was there that decisions concerning the whole village were made and ceremonial events took place. A kashim was somewhat similar in construction to a house except that it was about twice as large and had a cribbed roof. The tunnel was usually semisubterranean with entry to the main room through a hole in the floor. There was an open area which served as a fire pit when the kashim was used as a bathhouse. This opening was closed when not in use.

Women brought meals to the men in the kashim and collected firewood for use there. The structure was also a bathhouse for males, the firebath being characteristic until the steam bath involving heated stones was introduced by the Russians. In the kashim young men learned the lore of their people, frequently listening to elders recounting tales explaining the formation of the natural world, origin of the sun, moon, and other natural features, as well as the basis of environmental relationships. These mythological tales, often quite elaborate, provided a partial background for religious behavior. The kashim also served as a workshop for teaching subsistence techniques and as a guest house for male visitors from other villages.

As might be expected, division of labor was very marked among the Eskimos of southwestern Alaska. Women prepared and processed food, cared for children, made and repaired clothing (fig. 21), and performed various gathering activities. Men provided fish and land mammals for food and clothing. The only specialists were shamans and dance leaders, but even these individuals did some hunting and fishing like other men.

Along with duolocal residence, it is also likely that village endogamy was preferred, but since many settlements were quite small, some men, of necessity, had to leave the community in order to find wives. Polygamy probably did not occur often, but when it did, it tended to be sororal. Kinship was reckoned bilaterally and descent or descent groups are unreported. Cousins were designated according to the Iroquois type, so that brother and sister terms were extended to include parallel cousins, while cross-cousins were given separate terms.

Although there is little definite information concerning leadership and authority among the Eskimos of southwestern Alaska, it seems likely that there were

233

a

b

c

d

e

f

g

rim

groove

bottom

h

i

234

few occasions when it was necessary for decisions to be made that affected the entire community. This situation probably resulted from the fact that subsistence activities were largely a matter of individual rather than community concern. It is probable that older men exercised a certain amount of authority and helped to settle disputes. The most powerful member of any community was the shaman, most of whose performances were designed to diagnose and cure illness. Shamans were feared because of their affiliation with supernatural beings (Oswalt 1978:112–119).

History

Explorations of Bristol Bay and the Nushagak River by the Russian-American Company in the early nineteenth century opened the interior regions to the fur trade. A series of trading stations was built at various points along the middle Kuskokwim and supplied from Aleksandrovskiy Redoubt at the mouth of the Nushagak (established 1818). The route up the Nushagak to its headwaters, across the divide, and down the Holitna or Hoholitna to the Kuskokwim became a heavily traveled route with supplies going upriver into the Kuskokwim region and furs proceeding in the opposite direction (VanStone 1967:10–11).

In 1833 Mikhailovskiy Redoubt was established approximately 60 miles north of the mouth of the Yukon, and the Russian-American Company expanded its interior explorations to the north in the hope of bringing more Eskimos into the fur trade. European discovery of the Yukon took place during the winter of 1834 when Andrey Glazunov reached this great waterway by an overland route down the Anvik River (VanStone 1959). It is significant that this discovery came about as a result of interior exploration rather than an inland penetration from the coast, a fact that emphasizes the barren, inhospitable nature of the coast in this area with the complex Yukon mouth and its bewildering number of sloughs.

In 1836 the first trading post on the Yukon was established at Ikogmiut by Glazunov. Two years later Pëtr Malakhov traveled from Mikhailovskiy along the Unalakleet River and then overland to the Yukon in the vicinity of Nulato. He then traveled upstream as far as

Smithsonian, Dept. of Anthr.: 37,871.

Fig. 15. Fishskin container for clothing. With a circular bottom piece, drawstring top, and ornamental bands of dyed red skin, applique, and embroidery. Height 38.0 cm; collected by E.W. Nelson at Askinuk (Hooper Bay), Alaska, 1877–1881.

the mouth of the Koyukuk River and, in the spring of 1839, descended the Yukon to Mikhailovskiy. He was thus the first European to descend the Yukon by boat to the coast. Malakhov opened the middle Yukon, occupied by Athapaskan Indians, to the fur trade; a post was established at Nulato in 1839. Meanwhile, the previous year, the Ikogmiut post was destroyed by natives from either the Kuskokwim or the lower Yukon who held the Russians responsible, as indeed they were, for the smallpox epidemic of 1838–1839. Ikogmiut had been a successful post during its brief period of operation, so it was reestablished in 1840 (Zagoskin 1967:10, 81–82, 201, 248, 275, 342).

By the time of L.A. Zagoskin's explorations in 1842–1844, the Yukon was well known to the Russians, particularly the area between Mikhailovskiy Redoubt and Ikogmiut, which virtually encompasses that part of the river inhabited by Eskimos. The delta of the Yukon, however, remained almost completely unknown and unvisited by outsiders until well into the American period; even today it is one of the most isolated areas of Alaska. When Edward W. Nelson, an American naturalist and collector of ethnographic materials for the

Smithsonian, Dept. of Anthr.: a, 38,066; b, 38,508; c, 38,508; d, 127,655; e, 260,312; f, 260,310; g, 38,678; h, 56,033; i, 38,844.

Fig. 14. Wooden utensils. Well-made implements of wood are used for food preparation and serving. They are often decorated with painted designs (fixed with blood so they do not rub off) representing animals and mythological creatures that may serve as amulets and have other symbolic associations (Fitzhugh and Kaplan 1982:123). a–c, Ladles carved from single pieces of wood and painted with black and red patterns. d, Wooden dish of one piece of wood, with bands of red and black with a decapitated caribou painted in black on the interior. e, Wooden dish with rim painted red and designs in black on interior. f, Tray with bottom piece and separate wooden rim decorated with inlaid pieces of bone (round on the side and lozenge shaped on the top of the rim) (see drawing bottom left for construction details). g, Wood oil bowl with a carved head serving as a handle. h, Berry container, of bent wood overlapped and laced together; the bottom is a separate piece as is the bone handle. The exterior is painted with black and red. i, Pestle, with a groove around the rim of the handle, used with a dish to crush berries. f, 34.5 cm long, rest same scale. a–c, g, i collected in Alaska by E.W. Nelson, 1877–1881: a, Anogok; b–c, Kuskokwim River; g, Kongiganak; i, Big Lake. d, collected by J.W. Johnson at Nushagak, Alaska, 1886; e–f, Lower Yukon, 1910. h, collected by C.L. McKay, Bristol Bay, Alaska, 1881–1882.

236

top, Smithsonian, NAA: SI 6913; center left, Alaska Histl. Lib., Juneau: Andrews Coll.; bottom left, *Tundra Times*, Anchorage, Alaska.

Fig. 16. Fishing and the preservation of fish. top, Setting a fish trap for ling, whitefish, and pike through the ice of the Yukon River near Ikogmiut. Photograph by E.W. Nelson, 1877–1881. center left, Fish trap of willow branches in Hamilton, near the mouth of the Yukon River. The opening to the right is large to admit fish such as king salmon but narrows abruptly so that once the fish are inside they cannot find their way out. Photograph by Clarence L. Andrews, about 1920. center right, Racks of drying herring braided together with grass at Umkumiut, a fish camp on Nelson Island. When it rains, the fish are covered with canvas or sealskins as shown here. Photograph by James H. Barker, 1976. bottom left, Dip netting for whitefish, probably on the lower Yukon River near Emmonak. The row of stakes forms a fence that directs the fish toward the fisherman or the trap. Photographer unknown, 1970s. bottom right, Commercial fishermen bringing their catch of Kuskokwim River king salmon (*Oncorhyncus tshawytscha*) to a weighing scale near Bethel where the fish will be sold. In the 1980s commercial fishing was the most important source of cash income for the Eskimo of western and southwestern Alaska. Photograph by James H. Barker, 1975.

Smithsonian Institution, visited Hooper Bay in December of 1878 he noted that the people appeared to have seen few, if any, White men (Nelson 1899:249–250).

Compared to the interior, the delta area is rich in neither furs nor mineral resources and, as various explorers in both the Russian and American periods quickly learned, the coastal waters are shallow and treacherous. This combination of inaccessibility with little in the way of attractive resources was sufficient to keep White trappers, traders, prospectors, and even missionaries out of the delta country until nearly the end of the nineteenth century. And yet in terms of subsistence resources, the area is a rich one where heavy and predictable annual runs of salmon enabled people to live in larger settlements than anywhere else throughout the vast regions occupied by Eskimos.

Culture Change

Between 1818 and 1867 the most important external influences on the Eskimos of the Nushagak and Kuskokwim rivers were the result of activities involving interaction with representatives of the Russian-American Company and the Russian Orthodox Church. Company influence was the most immediate, but the Orthodox Church has remained significant through the area. Contact between the Russians and the Eskimos of the Yukon delta did not begin until after the establishment of Mikhailovskiy Redoubt in 1833, but from that time they too were heavily involved with the Russian-American Company and the Church.

Of the various changes introduced by the Russians, the most obvious were related to the subsistence cycle. Throughout much of their period of influence, they were chiefly interested in obtaining beaver pelts. Trade was on an exchange basis, the pelts being exchanged for various trade items including glass beads, copper bracelets, iron axes and other metal tools, items of clothing, and, later, food. Because of a desire for these and other goods, the Eskimos were obliged to make a major shift in their subsistence activities with more emphasis placed on fur trapping. This meant that more time was spent in the pursuit of game that had little or no food value, with the result that the Eskimos became increasingly dependent on the trading posts for the necessities of life. This process was a slow one and the Eskimos did not become totally dependent on such trade until well into the American period.

Smithsonian, Dept. of Anthr.: left, 90461; center, 90462; right, U. of Pa., U. Mus., Philadelphia: NA1546.

Fig. 17. Mittens and socks. left, Mittens made of several pieces of fishskin, with the bottom edge turned up to form a drawstring casing. center, Twined grass mittens worn as liners inside the fishskin ones. right, Socks made in the same technique as grass mittens; both provided insulation and absorbed moisture that came through the outer layer. left, Length 31.3 cm; rest, same scale. left and center, Collected by William Fisher at Egegik, Alaska, 1883; right, collected by G.B. Gordon, Kuskokwim River, Alaska, 1907.

237

MAINLAND SOUTHWEST ALASKA ESKIMO

top, Newark Mus., N.J.: 38,345; bottom, Smithsonian, Dept. of Anthr.: 36,234.

Fig. 18. Masks. top, Wooden dance mask with a body representing a combined fish and bird with flippers attached with bird quills. The center of the back is a face that opens to reveal another face, perhaps the animal's spirit. Masks were highly individualized and rich in symbolic content. bottom, Fingermasks, worn by women of the Bering Sea area during ceremonies, one on each hand, their arms and hands moving slowly to the drumbeat (Riggs 1980). Wooden disc with fingergrips with a face carved on one side and a symbolic circle and crescent form painted in red on the reverse. A strip of caribou hair is tied around the outer edge. Height excluding fringe 12.0 cm; collected by E.W. Nelson at Chalit, Alaska, 1877–1881. top, Same scale; collected by W.R. Olsen, Kuskokwim River, Alaska, before 1938.

It is important to note that it was the people of the Nushagak and middle Kuskokwim who were most heavily involved in the beaver trade. The lower Kuskokwim and Yukon delta Eskimos had relatively few fur-bearing animals in their areas that were of interest to the Russians. It was not until the price of mink began to rise around 1900 that these people became involved in intensive fur trapping (Oswalt 1963a:129–130).

In 1841 the first Russian Orthodox church north of the Alaska Peninsula was established at Aleksandrovskiy Redoubt, and missionaries began to penetrate the Nushagak and Kuskokwim areas. Little is known concerning the exact nature of missionary contact with Eskimos of the interior regions, but apparently it was extremely effective. By the end of the Russian era, it is probable that most of the Eskimos throughout southwestern Alaska considered themselves to be Christians. The early Orthodox missionaries were successful in conveying to the Eskimos the basic belief system of Christianity and, even more important, the role of the church as an established institution and part of their lives (VanStone 1964:21–22; Oswalt 1978:124).

Tangible manifestations of Russian contact throughout southwestern Alaska were the trading and mission centers. In addition to redoubts in the interior and along the Bering Sea coast, there was an Orthodox Church center at Russian Mission (Ikogmiut) on the lower Yukon. These settlements, which might be termed contact communities, were located either in small Eskimo communities or on previously unoccupied sites near aboriginal settlements. The outposts were supplied under conditions that necessitated hazardous sea voyages or long trips with portages along inland rivers and streams. Trading center inventories appear always to have been limited in variety and abundance. Each post was manned by a few individuals representing the Russian-American Company, the Orthodox Church, or both, and resident Eskimos aided in maintaining the establishments. The traders and mission officials were often of a mixed racial and cultural heritage, educated by the Russians, and thus reasonably familiar with both Russian and Eskimo ways. From these centers, particularly the redoubts, trade goods and food products flowed to the adjacent settlements, primarily in exchange for furs. The spheres of influence of these isolated posts represented zones of intense contact between the Russians and Eskimos (VanStone 1970:62–63).

With the sale of Alaska to the United States, this overall pattern did not change a great deal. An American firm, the Alaska Commercial Company, acquired the holdings of the Russian-American Company and continued to maintain the same trading centers. There are indications, however, that the inventory of goods traded to the Eskimos of southwestern Alaska increased considerably. In fact, from an economic standpoint it is probable that not until the advent of commercial salmon fishing in Bristol Bay in the 1880s did the inhabitants of any part of southwestern Alaska begin to experience contact situations radically different from those they had been accustomed to during the Russian period.

The Russian Orthodox Church began to experience competition from other churches in the early American period. The Moravians established missions near Bethel on the lower Kuskokwim in 1885 and near the community of Nushagak in 1887. The Nushagak mission lasted only 20 years, but the Moravians have remained active on the Kuskokwim. On the Yukon River, the Episcopalians established a mission station at Anvik in 1887 and the Roman Catholics at Holy Cross the following year. Since that time, various evangelical Protestant denominations have gained a foothold throughout the region, but their activities are confined almost exclusively to the larger trading centers of the region.

Although Christianity and the fur trade emerge as factors of major acculturational importance in southwestern Alaska during the Russian period, the commercial salmon-fishing industry that began to develop in Bristol Bay during the 1880s was eventually to have far greater significance. During the early years of the

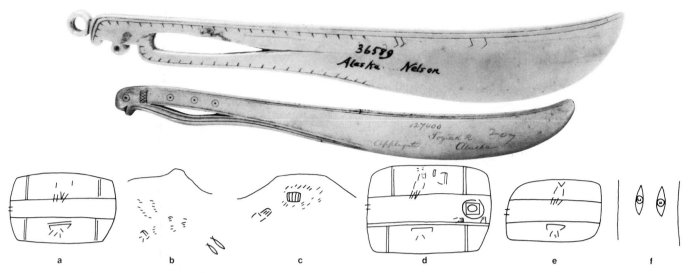

Smithsonian, Dept. of Anthr.: top, 36,589; center, 127,403; bottom, after Oswalt 1964:318.

Fig: 19. Storyknives. Sharp pointed objects are used by girls, about 5 to 16 years old, to draw pictures in the mud or snow to illustrate stories they tell each other. The storyknife complex is found only in southwest Alaska (Ager 1974). In the 1960s kitchen knives were used, but the traditional knives (top, center) made by a girl's father were carved ivory of varied style incised on both sides and along the flattened top. top, Curved blade. center, Knife with handle end probably representing a bird's head. Length 28.3 cm, collected by S. Applegate, Togiak River, Alaska, 1886. top, Same scale; collected by E.W. Nelson at Big Lake, Alaska, 1877–1881. bottom, Stories often concern a girl and her grandmother and use standardized symbols and themes. The drawing (a) representing a traditional style house is the first drawing for a story that begins "Once there were an old woman and her granddaughter. The old woman always said, 'Don't go over to that hill over there.' " The story continues with the girl going to the hill to cut grass (b) and discovering a door (c) into a house (d). Inside she finds a girl who she eventually kills with an arrow. Returning to her grandmother (e) she said "I killed that girl, the one you are always afraid of. The grandmother said 'Let's move from here' " and they take their kayaks (f) to the water (Oswalt 1964:318).

fishery, most of the actual fishing was done by Euro-Americans while a cannery work force was provided by imported Chinese and later other laborers. Large numbers of Eskimos were attracted to Nushagak Bay during the fishing seasons, and gradually some were able to obtain employment in the canneries in spite of considerable prejudice against them and their abilities as workers. Nevertheless, it was not until after World War II that Eskimos participated fully in the industry.

As might be expected, the Nushagak region itself was affected the most by the developing commercial fishery, but eventually Eskimos from even the most remote villages throughout southwestern Alaska were attracted to Bristol Bay during the summer months where they came into direct and instructive contact with many different races and nationalities (VanStone 1967:63–82).

Other historical economic developments, including mining and the reindeer-herding program, had only regional significance for the Eskimos of southwestern Alaska. At the end of the nineteenth century, Mikhailovskiy, or Saint Michael as it was known in the American period, became a busy trading center and port of entry to and departure from Alaska for thousands of miners headed for the Klondike to seek their fortunes. Since dramatic discoveries of gold-bearing deposits were never made in the Kuskokwim and Nushagak regions, the Eskimos living there had relatively little contact with miners. However, an important item of material culture introduced by the miners was the fish wheel. This device is a log raft on which is mounted a horizontal axle hung with basket-shaped paddles. The current propels the paddles and fish are entrapped in them, from which they slide into a live box at the side of the raft. Such a device, effective only in muddy water, has been and still is used extensively along the Kuskokwim and Yukon rivers, where it has replaced most other methods of taking fish (Oswalt 1978:126).

The 1970s

Eskimos throughout the region pursued traditional subsistence activities, but only to a limited extent. In the Nushagak River region the importance of such pursuits has declined steadily, particularly since World War II, and had reached the point where the inhabitants are as much removed from traditional subsistence patterns as any group of Eskimos in Alaska outside of urban areas. Even trapping, not a traditional subsistence activity but nevertheless an important aspect of the economy as far back as information on the people can be obtained, no longer played a truly major part in the yearly economic cycle.

The salmon canneries were primarily responsible for the decline of subsistence activities. Relatively high incomes could be earned during the summer months, making it possible for many families to subsist through *239*

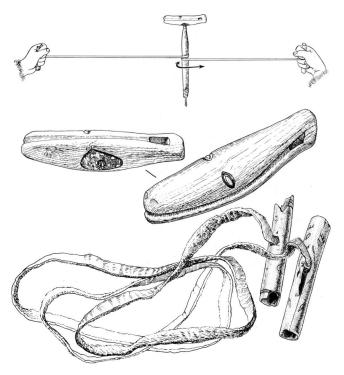

Smithsonian, Dept. of Anthr.: 36,318.

Fig. 20. Strap drill. Used in southwest Alaska, rather than the bow drill, to make holes and fire. The wooden drill cap with an inset stone socket is carved as an animal head. The hole at one end is to hold the strap when not in use. The strap, which is wound around the drill (a wooden piece with metal bit), has decorated bone handles. To use, a stick would probably be lashed to the cap (some caps have a projection), which would then be held in the mouth; the drill is rotated by pulling on the strap or one man presses on the cap while another works the strap. Length of cap 15.0 cm; collected by E.W. Nelson at Chalit, Alaska, 1877–1881.

Smithsonian, Dept. of Anthr.: 127,353.

Fig. 21. Housewife used by women in the Bering Sea region to carry their sewing equipment. When not in use it is rolled up, the leather thong at the top wrapped around it with the decorated ivory crosspiece (bag fastener) slipped under to secure the thong. The fastener is usually incised in one of a variety of styles and the bag itself is decorated. Here the outside is fur and the interior surface has skin painted red and bordered at the sides with embroidery, applique, tufts of red yarn, and fur. The U-shaped top flap is a characteristic woman's motif and echoes the lower cut of the woman's fur top (Fitzhugh and Kaplan 1982:132). Length 28.0 cm, excluding thong; collected by S. Applegate, Togiak River, Alaska, 1886.

the winter with only marginal involvement in hunting and trapping. This was particularly true following the Second World War when Eskimo participation in the fishing industry increased until in the 1960s all adult males from river communities were normally involved.

Limited entry fishing, a state law that restricts Bristol Bay fishing to those with a permit, was inaugurated in 1975. Local residents and outsiders received permits based on their participation in the fishery in past years, but many Eskimos were excluded because, for one reason or another, they failed to fish during specified qualifying years. Fishing permits, limited in number, can be bought and sold and bring extremely high prices. The permit system, the effects of which have been extensively debated, at least put a stop to fishermen entering the Bristol Bay region in increasing numbers.

Multiple factors are responsible for the decline in trapping. Generally low fur prices have affected all Alaska Eskimos as they have trappers throughout northern North America. As a result, many Nushagak Eskimos have found that with income derived from summer fishing, credit against next season's earnings, a certain amount

of hunting and fishing, and unearned income from various sources, they can subsist during the year. Thus it is not surprising to find that most people are interested in subsistence activities and trapping only to the extent that these are necessary in order to live from one fishing season to the next (VanStone 1967:142–143).

It is worth noting that subsistence fishing throughout southwestern Alaska, once considered the most stable form of resource utilization, has declined rapidly since about 1968, when mechanized snow vehicles were introduced in the area. They quite suddenly replaced dog teams as the major form of transportation, and large amounts of dried fish are no longer required for dog food.

Although Eskimos from other parts of southwestern Alaska do not participate in the Bristol Bay commercial fishery to the same extent as those in the Nushagak region, the economic trends noted above nevertheless exist. Wage labor of some kind during the summer months has been a factor in the lives of all Alaska Eskimos since the Second World War and the effects upon traditional subsistence activities have been similar. Un-

240

earned income from various federal agencies is equally important throughout the region.

A charcteristic of most of Eskimo Alaska has been the emergence of cosmopolitan trading centers in various regions. On the Kuskokwim, Bethel has emerged as the most important urban area, while Dillingham is the largest and most important town in the Nushagak region. Saint Michael fills a similar role for the lower Yukon and is the only former Russian post in southwestern Alaska to grow in importance during the American period. Many Eskimo families have found it desirable to establish residence at these centers, where the best educational, health, and community services are available. This has happened to a lesser extent on the Kuskokwim where small villages continue to flourish within a relatively short distance of Bethel.

All Alaska Eskimos are increasingly dependent upon economic conditions that are unlikely to have long range stability. At the same time, they are increasingly unwilling and unable to live by traditional subsistence activities alone. Within southwestern Alaska, there is some variability in adaptation to the facts of acculturation. The Nushagak Eskimos would appear to be in the least satisfactory circumstances, since they are most closely tied to the unpredictable commercial fishing industry. Their traditional settlement and subsistence patterns have been severely disrupted, and they appear to be ill-equipped to cope with an uncertain future. Those Eskimos of the Kuskokwim and Yukon delta, on the other hand, are for the most part living in villages that have been established for a long time and have relatively stable populations that feel close ties with the area where

Fig. 22. Eskimos from Hooper Bay performing at a dance festival in Bethel. The man, wearing a mask, is telling the story from a kneeling position while the women mimic his moves. Movements of the dancers are in time to a beat provided by drummers. The dance paraphernaiia are newly made, but the movements of the dancers to the accompaniment of tambourine drums is traditional. Photograph by Jerry L. Hout, 1973.

they live. This association has helped to develop a sense of community cohesiveness, which has been and will continue to be an excellent protection against the uncertainties of the contact situation.

Passage of the Alaska Native Claims Settlement Act in 1971 resulted in the creation of two regional corporations representing the Eskimos of southwestern Alaska: the Bristol Bay Native Corporation for the Nushagak River region and the Calista Corporation for the Yukon Delta and lower Yukon and Kuskokwim rivers. A primary purpose of these corporations is to convey money and land to villages and individuals as required by the act. Funds are also retained by the corporations for investment. Although both Calista and the Bristol Bay corporations invested in a variety of business ventures, as of 1981 relatively little money or land had been distributed at the village level in southwestern Alaska (see Oswalt 1978:139–140).

Synonymy†

The names of the seven groups of Central-Alaskan-Yupik-speaking Eskimos treated in this chapter are discussed here in alphabetical order. Except for that of the Kiatagmiut, which was not available from modern speakers, the names used here as the standard English names are the Yupik names in the Yupik practical orthography. Most earlier variants are attempts to spell the same forms.

The Aglurmiut (Yupik *áɣlúẏmiut* 'people of the ridgepole') are referred to in early Russian sources as Aglegmiut (Khromchenko 1824:34–41; Zagoskin 1967:210; VanStone 1967:109–110), probably intended for Aglëgmiut (ë indicating the value [yó]). Other variants are Glakhmiut (Berkh 1823:47), Agolegmĩuty (Wrangell 1839:70), Agolegmüten (Wrangell 1839a:121), Agolegmyut (Wrangell 1970:14), and the Aglemiut of Hodge (1907–1910, 1:24), who gives others (but incorrectly follows William H. Dall in including as synonyms renditions of *akúlmiut*, a general name for the Yukon delta people). Wrangell (1970:17) reported a tradition that the Aglurmiut took their name from a former village Agolegma on the Kuskokwim. In the twentieth century the Yupik name *áɣlúẏmiut* is applied to the Yupik of the Bristol Bay area (Steven A. Jacobson, communication to editors 1982), who do not (or no longer) speak the distinctive dialect recorded in the area in the early nineteenth century ("Eskimo and Aleut Languages," this vol.). The Inland Tanaina name for the Eskimos in this area is *aɣəluxtan* (Kari 1977:94).

The Kayaligmiut (Yupik *kayá·líɣmiut*) have their name from the former village Kayalik or Kayalivik just north

†This synonymy was written by James W. VanStone and Ives Goddard.

241

of Nelson Island, whose inhabitants abandoned it for the modern village of Newtok nearby (Anthony C. Woodbury, communication to editors 1982). Variant forms include Kaialigamiut (Oswalt 1967:6), Kaialigmiut (Hodge 1907–1910, 1:641), and Kaialigumute (Petroff 1884:126). This group may be that referred to by Zagoskin, 1844 (1956:80, 1967:103, 210) as the Kvikhlīūagmĭuty (Russian), that is Kvikhlyuagmyut (English), whose speech was "very different" from neighboring types of Yupik.

The name Kiatagmiut is used here in the spelling adopted as standard by Hodge (1907–1910, 1:682), who gives early variants; the correct Yupik form is not known. Early Russian names are Kĭīataĭgmĭuty and (with Russian suffix) Kĭīatentsy (Wrangell 1839:70), anglicized as Kiyataygmyut and Kiyatentsy (Wrangell 1970:14; Zagoskin 1967:210–211). This group has been equated with the Nushagagmiut 'people of the Nushagak River' (VanStone 1967:109–111).

Kuigpagmiut (Yupik kúixpáɣmiut 'people of the Yukon River') also appears as Kwikpagmiut (Hodge 1907–1910, 1:748; Oswalt 1967:5) and Kvikhpagmyut (Zagoskin 1967:209). Another name is Ikogmiut (Oswalt 1967:5), also applied to Russian Mission, with variants Ikogmute (Petroff 1884:126), Ikogmut (Nelson 1899:26), and others given by Hodge (1907–1910, 1:597), representing Yupik iqúɣmiut (Iugmiut).

For Kusquqvagmiut (Yupik kúsquqfáɣmiut 'people of the Kuskokwim') variants are Kuskokvigmĭuty and Kuskokvigmyut (Zagoskin 1956:80, 1967:103), Kushkukkhvak´´mĭuty and in Russian Kuskokvimtsy (Wrangell 1839:75), and the more divergent Kuskwogmiut (Hodge 1907–1910, 1:738) and Kuskowagamiut (Oswalt 1967:7, 1962:1–4), as well as others listed by Hodge.

The name of the Maarmiut can be established as Yupik má·ɣmiut 'people of the marshy or muddy lowlands' on the basis of Zagoskin's (1956:80, 1967:103, 210) 1844 recordings of Magmiut and Magagmiut; these show optional dropping of intervocalic ɣ in the element maɣaɣ-, a sporadic rule in this sequence that is obligatory in this word in modern Yupik (Anthony C. Woodbury, communication to editors 1982). Other variants are Magemiut (Hodge 1907–1910, 1:783; Oswalt 1967:7) and those listed by Hodge. Wrangell (1839:69, 70, 71, 1970:14, 15) appears to distinguish one or two Athapaskan groups called Magachmĭuty and Magimĭuty from the Eskimo group Magmĭuty, but there may be some confusion with these names.

The name Tuyuryarmiut (Yupik tuyúɣyáɣmiut 'people of the Togiak River') also appears as Togiagamiut (Hodge 1907–1910, 2:770; Oswalt 1967:8) and Togiagamute (Petroff 1884:134).

Sources

A characteristic feature of source material on the Eskimos of southwestern Alaska is unevenness. Considerable research has been carried out among Eskimos of the Nushagak and Kuskokwim rivers, but the Yukon delta region and the Togiak River are virtually unknown anthropologically. An essential published historical reference for the entire area is Zagoskin's (1967) account of his travels on the Kuskokwim and Yukon in 1842–1844, which provides the only ethnographic data available for the period immediately following historic contact. A valuable archival source for the history of the fur trade throughout the region is Russian-American Company (1818–1865) in the National Archives. It is available on microfilm.

Considerable ethnographic, historical, and recent archeological research has been undertaken along the Kuskokwim River by Wendell H. Oswalt. Of particular importance is a historical reconstruction of Kuskokwim Eskimo life with emphasis on the period from 1884 to 1925 (Oswalt 1963a). In addition, a study made in 1955–1956 of a Kuskokwim Eskimo community provides most of the available information on contemporary riverine Eskimo life in southwestern Alaska (Oswalt 1978). A useful archeological study containing some ethnographic data is Oswalt and VanStone (1967), which details the excavation of a site along the Kuskokwim occupied by Eskimos between approximately 1830 and 1912 and documents some of the material changes that took place during this period. Oswalt (1980) describes materials excavated at Kolmakovskiy Redoubt and reconstructs the history of contact for the period during which the post was occupied.

VanStone (1967) deals with the history of contact among Eskimos, Russians, and Euro-Americans and with changing socioeconomic life in the Nushagak River region. VanStone (1971) has also excavated a number of historic archeological sites along the river and its tributaries and undertaken an extensive settlement pattern study of the area in historic times.

Eskimo material culture in southwestern Alaska has been exhaustively described in Nelson (1899), which is based on extensive collections in the Smithsonian Institution, Washington. Fitzhugh and Kaplan (1982) also describe and illustrate Nelson's collection.

Asiatic Eskimo: Introduction

CHARLES C. HUGHES

The term Asiatic Eskimos designates the 2,000 or so Eskimos who lived in the 1980s in several widely scattered villages on the Chukchi Peninsula, the northeastern tip of Siberia in the Soviet Union, and on Saint Lawrence Island, part of the State of Alaska, including a few that have moved from these areas in the twentieth century. Saint Lawrence Island lies about 40 miles to the southeast of the Siberian mainland but about 125 miles from that of Alaska. For most of their history this proximity of the island to the Siberian mainland as well as its distance from the North American continent were important features in structuring the cultural relations that existed between the two populations. Since 1948 the international boundary between the Soviet Union and the United States has effectively separated these two groups of people, but for centuries before that there was extensive contact in the form of migration of peoples, voyages for trade and visiting of relatives, and raiding and warfare. Based both upon archeological evidence from the cultural past as well as upon known historic contacts that nourished cultural similarities, it is clear that the people of Saint Lawrence Island and the Eskimos of the Siberian shore are basically to be classed together as of the same cultural population.

The Asiatic Eskimos are a distinctive subgroup of the larger Eskimo population, with internal differences among them the result largely of local ecological and climatological constraints and the greater immediate population pressure (on the Siberian shore) from Paleo-Siberian groups. Aside from such internal differences, when the level of contrast is with other Eskimo groups, the Asiatic Eskimos can be sharply differentiated, particularly on the basis of language and certain aspects of social organization and kinship terminology.

The present-day Asiatic Eskimos are the cultural heirs to, if not in all cases the lineal descendants of, peoples who several thousand years ago established an ancient and highly successful cultural adaptation oriented primarily to a maritime and coastal habitat. The specifics of interpretation of the artifactual record are always subject to revision, but the main outlines indicate that by as early as 2,000 years ago an economy based upon hunting of maritime mammals (walrus, seal, and to some extent whales) had evolved along the Siberian shore and on Saint Lawrence Island, an economy and culture known as Old Bering Sea. Closely allied in time and

cultural type in the same region was the Okvik culture. This period (or periods), dated from about the beginning of the Christian era to approximately A.D. 500, evolved into the Punuk culture, in which whaling became much more predominant in the hunting complex than had been the case with the Old Bering Sea and Okvik cultures. Another phase, occurring about the same time, or possibly a little earlier, was the Birnirk culture. The Punuk and Birnirk cultures extended through the end of the first millennium A.D. Finally, certain elements of the Thule culture are found on Saint Lawrence Island and in Siberia, dated from about A.D. 800–900 to 1200–1500. Evidence of Thule culture on Saint Lawrence Island suggests that this culture was intrusive from other locations in the Bering Sea area.

Thus, the Asiatic Eskimos now live in the region that has offered some of the most critical and definitive artifactual remains for the reconstruction of generic Eskimo culture history. The search for the ultimate origins of Eskimo culture is being pushed, especially by Soviet scholars, in other directions (such as farther south along the Pacific coast, or inland along river systems). Whatever the outcome of such research, it is clear that the archeological cultures of Old Bering Sea, Okvik, Bir-

Fig. 1. Bering Strait Eskimos of Little Diomede Island meeting with Siberian Eskimos on the ice at the international date line and trying out each other's rifles. The snowmobile belongs to the Bering Strait Eskimos. Photograph by Fred Bruemmer, April 1975.

nirk, and Punuk—all originally conceptualized on the basis of finds in the territory of the contemporary Asiatic Eskimos—represent some of the most crucial data in the theoretical formulation of the distinctive kinds of cultural adaptations termed Eskimo.

It is clear also that in the past the territory occupied by Eskimos was much more extensive than it is now. What appears to have happened is that the current Eskimo populations in Siberia, living as they do surrounded by and in modern times intermixed with Maritime Chukchi peoples, are a remnant population, having apparently been subject to considerable population pressure and crowding toward the east by the expanding Chukchi and other Siberian groups over the past several hundred years.

The Asiatic Eskimo speak three sharply divergent dialects or distinct languages of the Yupik branch of the Eskimo family: Sirenikski, Central Siberian Yupik, and Naukanski. All of these are spoken in Siberia, with Central Siberian Yupik also spoken, in virtually identical form, on Saint Lawrence Island.* These three varieties of Asiatic Eskimo have generally been considered to constitute a separate Siberian Yupik division (Oswalt 1967; Krauss 1973, 1975a, 1979:814), but there is some evidence that the Siberian and mainland Alaskan varieties of Yupik form an intergrading chain, with a less sharp break between the types of Yupik in the two areas than earlier assumed (Krauss 1980:9–10; "Eskimo and Aleut Languages," this vol.). The Siberian Yupik languages show considerable lexical influence from Chukchi, even in expressions for concepts central to Eskimo culture; for example, the Central Siberian Yupik suffix -řamka, commonly used both on Saint Lawrence Island and in Siberia in referring to the localized clan or lineage, is of Chukchi origin.

The Asiatic Eskimos differ from many Eskimo groups, especially in Alaska, in lacking a traditional kashim or communal men's house. While functional equivalents may have existed in the form of the large, semi-subterranean dwellings that could house numerous people, and in small villages that could well include most

of the population (in fact, Sergeev and Arutiunov 1975 claim this was the case), the formal institution of the kashim, with its many attendant functions (social, religious, and political) was absent.

The Asiatic Eskimos also differ sharply from the other Eskimo groups in having clans or lineages based upon patrilineal affiliation. Members of such a group tend to trace ancestry to a common progenitor, even though the names of intervening relatives and the number of generations may be unclear. Whether these groups are called clans (as here) or lineages depends on which technical anthropological definitions are followed. While possibly foreshadowed to a certain extent in some of the Bering Sea Alaska villages (see Giddings 1952), the full and unequivocal development of clans—a trait presumably antithetical to the "Eskimo type" of social organization (cf. Hughes 1958)—was a characteristic feature of the social organization (even in the 1980s, at least on Saint Lawrence Island).

The origin of such clans may have lain in simply the naming of local territorial groupings, reinforced by perceptions and pressures from other such groups (cf. Hughes 1958); or, as suggested by Soviet authors, it may have represented an inexorable feature of the social evolution of all Eskimo societies, with the lack of such clans elsewhere being explained by disruptions in expected cultural development caused by the intrusion of Europeans (cf. Fainberg 1955). Whatever the theory of choice, the fact is that such clans were the pivotal social units in community structure. Membership in a clan influenced marriage patterns (traditionally clan exogamous), hunting patterns (boat crews were composed traditionally only of clansmen), settlement patterns (various sections of the village "belonged" to particular clans), burial patterns (at least in Siberia, where clansmen were all buried together in particular sites), religious activities (in both Siberia and on Saint Lawrence Island there were unique hunting and other rituals distinctive of particular clans), folklore (unique tales of origin, intergroup relations, and cosmology, both in Siberia and Saint Lawrence), and even subdialectical differences.

Along with the existence of clans, kinship terminology also differed rather markedly from other Eskimo groups. Strongly reflecting a patrilineal emphasis in other aspects of the social organization, it grouped cross-cousins together under a single term, while differentiating patrilineal parallel cousins from matrilineal parallel cousins, each with a distinctive term (Hughes 1958, 1960). A comparison of the Saint Lawrence Island terms with the only known listing for the Siberian groups is contained in "Saint Lawrence Island Eskimo," this volume. The overall identity of the two lists is quite evident.

In religion, the Asiatic Eskimos again show a familial similarity to other Eskimo groups but at the same time have developed particular emphases. Highly animistic

---

*The phonemes of Central Siberian Yupik are: (voiceless stops) p, t, k, k^w, q, q^w; (voiced fricatives) v, z, γ, w ([w], [γ^w]), $\dot{\gamma}$, $\dot{\gamma}^w$; (voiceless fricatives) f, s, x, x^w, χ, χ^w; (voiced nasals) m, n, η, η^w; (voiceless nasals) M, N, $\mathcal{N}$, $\mathcal{N}^w$; (voiced retroflex and lateral) $\check{r}$, l; (voiceless retroflex and lateral) $\check{R}$, $ł$; (glides) y, h; (short vowels) i, a, u, ∂; (long vowels) $i\cdot$, $a\cdot$, $u\cdot$; (extralong vowels) $i\colon$, $a\colon$, $u\colon$; stress ($\acute{v}$).

In the practical orthography developed in 1971 for Saint Lawrence Island these phonemes are written: p, t, k, kw, q, qw; v, z, g, w, gh, ghw; f, s, gg, wh, ghh, ghhw; m, n, ng, ngw; mm, nn, ngng, ngngw; r, l; rr, ll; y, h; i, a, u, e; ii, aa, uu. The stress, some long vowels, and all extralong vowels are accounted for by prosodic rules. An apostrophe is used to separate consonants that have separate values.

Information on Central Siberian Yupik phonology and orthography is from Krauss (1975a), who also discusses the Soviet systems. The phonemicizations of the words cited in italics were provided by Steven A. Jacobsen and Michael E. Krauss (communication to editors 1982).

244

in character, their religious practices were oriented to placation of the marine animals they must kill in order to survive: whales, seals, walruses, and polar bears. Ceremonies in anticipation of the hunt, ceremonies in thankfulness for a successful hunt, individual private

behavioral injunctions for both men and women in regard to life crises as well as normal events, ceremonies marking the first killing of various species of animals and birds—all these were found in both places. Rituals of thanksgiving and remembrance of ancestors illustrate the widespread belief in ghosts and other spirits, both of people and other animals as well as disembodied spirits, which could bring both good fortune as well as tragedies in life, such as illness and unanticipated death or poor hunting. Belief in witches and their malevolent powers was prevalent, and the strong development of a shamanic cult provided not only a sense of supernatural control over untoward events but also healing resources for illness of all types, psychosomatic and organic. The shamans as well as some lay people had a pharmacopeia composed of plants and animal products.

Subsistence patterns were organized to take advantage of the abundant supply of marine mammals that inhabit the northern Bering Sea. Beginning with the Punuk culture of about A.D. 500, whaling became, and has remained through the late twentieth century, the most dramatic if not most provident form of the maritime hunt, providing the focus for acquisition of great prestige and renown for the successful boat captain. Walruses and seals provided the bulk of the animal food, although especially on the Siberian shore reindeer

Field Mus., Chicago: a, 34,150; b, 34,151; c, 34,152 and 34,153; Muzeĭ Antropologii i Étnografii; Akademiiā Nauk SSSR, Leningrad: 593–54.

Fig. 2. Armor. Warfare was common among the Asiatic Eskimo and men protected themselves with skin armor. bottom, Suit of armor consisting of a, wooden shield covered with sealskin; b, hoop body plates, the first made of a sealskin-covered baleen strip, the rest double pieces of sealskin; and c, shin guards of mammoth ivory, length 27.0 cm, rest to same scale. All collected at East Cape, USSR, before 1905. top, Museum mannikin, wearing armor collected on St. Lawrence Island, Alaska, by I.G. Voznesenski, 1843, demonstrates the cumbersome position of the heavy shield, attached to the middle of the back and the left arm. After shooting, the warrior turned, using the shield as a barrier; it also protected his neck.

245

were also an important food resource. In addition, fishing, bird-hunting, and collecting and gathering of plants were important in the total food economy.

Contact with Europeans began earlier on the Siberian shore than on Saint Lawrence Island. During the seventeenth century parties of Cossack adventurers in search of furs explored the area, during the eighteenth century a few European explorers such as Vitus Bering and James Cook visited the region, and in the nineteenth century Europeans and Americans began making commercial incursions into the Bering Strait area for whales and other maritime products, which greatly increased opportunities for the Eskimos to obtain new technology (as well as new diseases). Acquisition of the rifle changed some basic aspects of walrus and seal hunting, and the purchase of whaling equipment (such as harpoon guns) from the commercial ships also added new power to the hunt for the bowhead, finback, and gray whales. Hunting technology was further improved by the gasoline-powered outboard motor for the hunting boats. On Saint Lawrence Island widespread adoption occurred in the 1920s, and the motors became common on the Siberian shore after 1945.

Both the Soviet and American populations of Asiatic Eskimos have been subjected to a wide range of acculturation pressures, pressures that deeply affect every institution of their societies: subsistence, economic, kinship, educational, religious, political, and linguistic. At the same time, they remain loyal to the ecological imperatives established so many hundreds of years ago, in that they still go forth onto the sea in their search for food.

Siberian Eskimo

CHARLES C. HUGHES

The reason for including Eskimos living in Siberia in the *Handbook of North American Indians*, is, of course, that whatever their ultimate cultural origin, they represent the westernmost members of a cultural group that extends more than 3,000 miles to the east across the North American continent, to the eastern shore of Greenland. In the early 1960s there were approximately 1,200 Asiatic Eskimos living in the Soviet Far East. Heirs to a long cultural tradition in this region, in historic times and during the period of exploration of the north Bering Sea they were found in small villages scattered along the eastern coastline of the Chukchi Peninsula (*Chukotskiǐ Poluostrov*), a coastline that they shared with the Maritime Chukchis (fig. 1). That tradition of close contact with the Chukchi—shown in many items of material, social, and religious culture, intermarriage and intermingling of the populations (sometimes even sharing of the same village), bilingualism, and (in the past) warfare—has continued into the late twentieth century.

The Siberian Eskimos and those of Saint Lawrence Island (part of Alaska, offshore some 40 miles from Siberia) are the two populations that comprise the Asiatic Eskimo subgroup of the Eskimo population. Traditionally there were close material, social, and ideational cultural ties between the two groups. Their* treatment in two separate chapters in the *Handbook* does not reflect cultural distinctness but rather follows from their location in different nations and the consequent divergence in twentieth-century cultural and political history and separate bodies of scientific literature. In fact, the Saint Lawrence Islanders speak a variety of Eskimo that is nearly identical to one of the three varieties spoken in Siberia, that of the former settlement of Chaplino and others nearby, and these two groups maintained occasional contacts until 1948, when with the onset of the Cold War an earlier agreement to permit these contacts was revoked.

The use of the name Siberia for the part of the Soviet Union where the Eskimos are found follows traditional American English and earlier Russian usage. In archeological and ethnological writings the Eskimo have generally been included among the peoples of Siberia in this sense. However, in official Soviet geographical terminology Siberia extends to the east only far enough to include the Kolyma River system (excluding its easternmost portions), beyond which lies the Soviet Far East. In this sense the specific region in which the Siberian Eskimo are located is Chukotka, not Siberia.

Language

The Siberian Eskimo are linguistically divided into three sharply different dialects or separate languages, called in the Soviet literature Sirenikski, Chaplinski, and Naukanski. These have been the subject of separate grammatical treatments by Menovshchikov (1962–1967, 1964, 1975). Of these, Chaplinski is the language shared with Saint Lawrence Island, these two very similar varieties being classed together as Central Siberian Yupik,† and it is also the one officially recognized as standard Eskimo and the one referred to when the name Asiatic Eskimo is used as an unqualified linguistic term.

Chaplinski was spoken in the village of Chaplino on Indian Point (*Mys Chaplino*) until this was closed and the population resettled in 1958. It had previously been spoken, with minor dialectal variation, in several villages between Yttygran Island and Sireniki, variously listed by Bogoras (1904–1909, 1:29), Menovshchikov (1962–1967, 1:3), and Krupnik and Chlenov (1979:21–24). With the dislocation of population occasioned by Soviet developmental policies, these Eskimos have ended up in New Chaplino (*Novoe Chaplino*), Sireniki, the transplanted communities of Uél'kal' and Wrangell Island (where small groups were relocated in 1924), the predominantly Chukchi town of Lorino, the predominantly Russian towns of Provideniia and, far to the west, Anadyr', and other scattered places. The approximately 500 at New Chaplino and 300 at Sireniki were the only

---

*The rest of this paragraph, the one following, and the section on language were written by Ives Goddard.

†For the transcriptional system used to write Central Siberian Yupik words (labeled CSY), see the footnote in "Asiatic Eskimo: Introduction" (this vol.). The phonemicizations were supplied by Steven A. Jacobsen (communication to editors 1982). Complete phonemic analyses of Sirenikski and Naukanski are not available. Eskimo words available only in Cyrillic have been given in roman with the transcription of the special digraphs into phonetic symbols. Chukchi and Koryak words from Bogoras (1904–1909) have been transliterated into the *Handbook* technical alphabet.

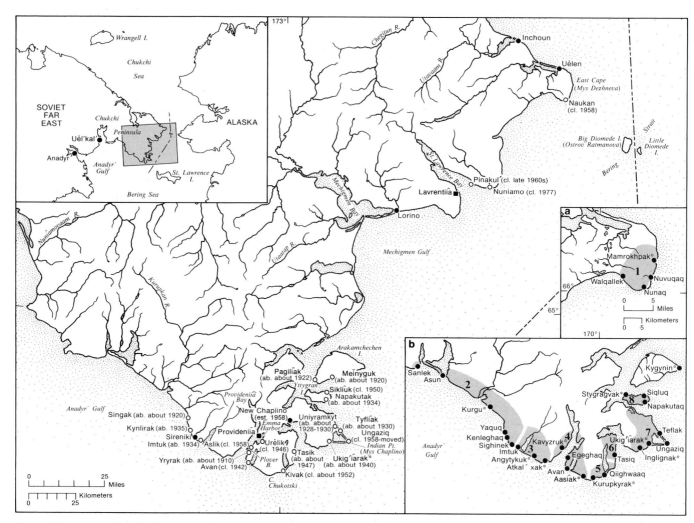

Fig. 1. 20th-century Siberian Eskimo settlements (cl-closed; ab-abandoned; est-established). Insets show late 19th-century settlements and group territories (according to Krupnik and Chlenov 1979; Igor I. Krupnik, Mikhail A. Chlenov, and Ernest S. Burch, communications to editors 1983). a, East Cape: 1. Nuvuqaghhmiit; b, southern Chukchi Peninsula: 2, Sirinegmiit; 3, Imtugmiit (2 groups before the 1880s); 4, Avatmiit; 5, Qiighwaaghmiit; 6, Tasighmiit; 7, Ungazighmiit; 8, Napakutaghmiit. The group names and 19th-century settlement names have been checked for conformity with the Central Siberian Yupik roman orthography by Michael E. Krauss (communication to editors 1983); the 19th-century settlement names marked by asterisks and all the 20th-century settlement names are transliterated from Cyrillic. The settlements and groups shown on each map were not contemporaneous in a few instances.

large communities in 1980, and only in New Chaplino were any of the Siberian Eskimos a local majority.

Naukanski was spoken in the single relatively large village of Naukan on East Cape (*Mys Dezhneva*) until Naukan, like Chaplino, was closed in 1958. There is evidence of other associated communities formerly in the area (Krupnik and Chlenov 1979:21). In 1958 the population was moved to the villages of Pinakul' and Nuniamo on Saint Lawrence Bay, and many went to the Russian administrative center of Lavrentiia. Pinakul' was closed in the late 1960s and Nuniamo in 1977; about 70 Naukanski speakers went back to East Cape to the large Chukchi town of Uėlen, while the rest dispersed to other settlements, everywhere as a small minority.

Sirenikski was the old language of Sireniki village but in 1980 was remembered by only two elderly women,

the rest of the population being predominantly Chukchi or of Chaplinski origin. It is in some ways the most divergent variety of Eskimo known, with both unique innovations and archaic features.

A fourth Eskimo language formerly spoken in the Soviet Union is that of Big Diomede Island (Russian *Ostrov Ratmanova*; Inupiaq *imaqłiq*), a variety of Inupiaq nearly identical to that spoken on Little Diomede (*Ostrov Kruzenshterna*), across the international boundary in Alaska (Menovshchikov 1980a). This population generally went to Little Diomede or was absorbed by the people of Naukan, with whom they had traditional trading contacts, and the last residents of the island were removed by the authorities in 1948. Because of their linguistic affiliation the Big Diomede people (Inupiaq *imaqłit*) are generally not classed with the Asiatic Eskimo, and because of their location they are omitted

Smithsonian, Dept. of Anthr.: 56,531.

Fig. 2. Ivory carvings. Small carvings representing a fox and ducks or geese, from a set of 25. They were probably used in a children's game and are similar to those made in other parts of the Arctic (see "Saint Lawrence Island Eskimo," fig. **9**, this vol.). Length of fox 7.0 cm; collected by P.H. Ray, Plover Bay, USSR, 1881.

from treatments of Alaska Eskimos. They are not separately discussed in the *Handbook*, but for Little Diomede see "Bering Strait Eskimo" and "North Alaska Coast Eskimo" (this vol.).

Culture

The Asiatic Eskimo are marked off from those of North America not only by the putative distinctness of their languages ("Asiatic Eskimo: Introduction," this vol.), but also by other cultural traits: on the Siberian shore, much greater cultural influences from Paleo-Siberian tribes (especially the Chukchi), and, on Saint Lawrence Island, by a cultural orientation (and cultural past) dependent upon the Siberian shore, since direct contacts with Alaska (125 miles away) were impossible in premodern times. Consequently, a cultural axis existed between Saint Lawrence Island and Chukotka that included not only many elements of material culture but also certain forms of social organization and kinship terminology, as well as religious concepts and forms of ritualism that separated these people from all other Eskimo groups.

Only since the 1950s has the region of the north Bering Sea occupied by the Asiatic Eskimos been the focus for the extensive archeological research ultimately necessary to complete the picture of the evolution of Eskimo societies on the Siberian mainland ("Prehistory of the Asian Eskimo Zone," this vol.). This chapter describes their cultural life from late Punuk or early modern times (the early 1880s). Most of the primary sources employed in this effort are writings of Soviet ethnographers, most of whose works have not been translated from Russian. While the most significant of these works have been consulted, unavailability of some potential sources has prevented a complete examination of possibly relevant literature.

Subsistence

The following discussion of subsistence activities and material culture is adapted largely from Menovshchikov and Shnakenburg (1956). In its traditional form, the subsistence patterns of the Siberian Eskimos closely resembled those of many other circum–Bering Sea Eskimo groups. That is to say, they depended primarily upon whales, seals, and especially walruses, with some more limited use being made of reindeer; in addition, there was some fishing (fig. 3), gathering, and hunting of birds and fur-bearing animals such as wild reindeer and mountain sheep.

Returns from sea mammal hunting satisfied all the vital needs of the indigenous Eskimo economy and way of life. Meat and fat were food for both people and dogs; from skins, clothing and footwear were sewn; the skins also were used as material in the construction of houses and the manufacture of hunting weapons and tools; and the blubber was used in heating and lighting the houses.

Smithsonian, Dept. of Anthr.: top, 46,248; bottom, 46,249.

Fig. 3. Needles of bone with hole at one end, used for stringing fish on a line as soon as they are caught. Length of top 27.0 cm; bottom, same scale. Both collected at Plover Bay, USSR, 1880.

Until the middle of the nineteenth century (when trade goods became available from whaling and other ships), the principal weapons for hunting sea mammals were lances, harpoons, and thong nets; bows and stone- or bone-tipped arrows were used for land mammals. To illustrate the variety of hunting methods employed with these weapons, the taking of the single most important species, the walrus, may be cited. The methods and strategy chosen depended upon the seasonal conditions. In the early spring, when the walruses were found resting on drifting icebergs, they were hunted from open, walrus hide–covered boats. A harpoon attached to an inflated sealskin float was thrown into an animal to prevent its sinking, and it was then dispatched with a lance. Another method of hunting walrus was the "drive." Hunters in boats encircled a group of walrus near the shore and used a special whalebone flapper that made a sound like that of the killer whale, a rapacious enemy of the walrus. The noise of this flapper so frightened the walruses that they beached themselves on the land, where they could be easily killed by lances and harpoons.

When firearms became available from whalers and trading vessels, harpoons began to play a subsidiary role in hunting, and the use of guns greatly increased the animal kill. Then the hunters would shoot a walrus first and then throw a harpoon with float in order to drag the carcass onto the ice or shore for butchering. The pattern for seal hunting changed also. Whereas the earlier pattern had been that of a hunter throwing a spear or harpoon from a kayak or from the shore, creeping up on the sleeping animals lying on the ice while the hunter was covered with a sealskin, or lying in wait at a seal's breathing hole with a harpoon ready, now, with guns, hunters could sit at the edge of the winter shore ice, rest their rifles on supports, and wait for an animal's head to break the surface. The carcass was then snared with a barbed wooden float.

With the extensive commercial exploitation of whales during the late nineteenth century, hunting of that animal by the Eskimos declined because of fewer animals

Smithsonian, Dept. of Anthr.: 46,257.
Fig. 4. Drinking cup of mountain sheep horn with handle carved from the same piece, bent and inserted into a hole near the cup rim. Bogoras (1904–1909:188) reports that these were highly valued objects. Length 21.0 cm; collected by E.P. Herendeen at Plover Bay, USSR, 1880.

Amer. Mus. of Nat. Hist., New York: 60/3613.
Fig. 5. Woman's knife, with metal blade set into an engraved ivory handle. Length about 20.0 cm; collected by W. Bogoras at Indian Point, USSR, 1900–1901.

available, although it was still an important subsistence and ritual animal in Eskimo life. A single animal's body could provide blubber and meat for an entire village for several months, as well as valuable trade items, such as whalebone and oil. It required the cooperative activities of several boats, each equipped with harpoons and lances—and later, harpoon guns—to kill the animal.

As was common with other indigenous northern people, the trapping of the arctic white fox for trade became very important to the Eskimos toward the end of the nineteenth century, and it remained important in the 1980s.

It was the hunt that provided practically all the food for the Eskimos (although the products of gathering activities, such as plants and seaweeds, were also much valued as relish for the meats). Meat was eaten in a dried, frozen, or boiled form, and the black, elastic, and rubbery skin of the whale with a bit of the blubber attached was considered a delicacy and eaten in a raw form. Reindeer meat was also valued highly.

The Eskimos used several kinds of boats for hunting and other subsistence activities. Before the advent of trade with the outside, the principal crafts were the well-known kayak, a single seat skin-covered canoe with a cockpit where the hunter sat dressed in waterproof clothing made from walrus intestine; and the umiak, an open, flat-bottomed skin canoe built of walrus hide stretched and sewed over a wooden lattice frame (CSY aŋyáꞏpik, earlier aŋyaq, which is now just 'boat'; Russian baĭdara). Some of these boats had a carrying ca-

Amer. Mus. of Nat. Hist., New York: 60/3653.
Fig. 6. Wrist guard of ivory, tied to the arm to protect the skin from the snap of the bow string. Wrist guards were sometimes decoratively incised. Length 14.3 cm; collected by W. Bogoras at Chaplino, Indian Point, USSR, 1900–1901.

Fig. 7. Ice creepers, rectangular piece of ivory with points carved out on one side. Leather ties were used to strap them to the bottom of boots. They provided traction, allowing easier movement over ice or snow crust. Length 8.5 cm., collected by W.M. Noyes, at Plover Bay, USSR, 1880.

pacity of up to four tons. The umiak was propelled by oars and sails, and it was a craft ideally suited to hunting in the ice floes, for, because of its lightness, it could quickly be pulled up out of the water and its tough skin sides were not easily punctured by the sharp edges of the ice. After contact with the whaling ships, wooden whaleboats were also used.

Land transportation was provided by several kinds of sleds. Up to the middle of the nineteenth century the primary form of dog-teaming sled was an arch-stanchioned sled with a fan-shaped harness; that style was superseded by the more customary form found among other northeastern Siberian peoples (such as the Chukchis, Koryaks, and Kamchadals), where the dogs are hitched in pairs to a central trace. The other type of sled used, the *qáꞏnřak*, dated from Old Bering Sea culture times. This was a small, short sled, without stanchions, made of walrus tusks and wood. The sleds were pulled by the hunters themselves in carrying meat and in transporting the umiaks to and from the water.

Other articles of the hunt included snowshoes and special ice cleats (fig. 7).

Structures

Up to the middle of the nineteenth century the winter house was the ancient large, communal, semi-subterranean house (*nəŋlu*) in which several families lived. Sergeev (1962) states that legends assert all the members of a given clan–from 250 to 400 people—lived in such a dwelling, but this seems impossible based on structural possibilities for such a building. In any case, such houses were used not only as living quarters but also for religious ceremonies, dances, and other large-scale communal gatherings.

By about the middle of the nineteenth century the *nəŋlu* was replaced by another type of house modeled closely after the Chukchi winter tent. This house, the *maŋtɔ́ɣaq*, was constructed of plank siding and a wooden lattice roof covered with walrus hides. Often turf and stone were also piled up around the outside to provide additional support and insulation.

The typical summer house was also basically a walrus-hide (or later, tarpaulin) tent stretched over a wooden framework, rectangular in shape with the roof sloping to the rear. Inside the house there was a small bed platform often simply suspended on thongs.

Fig. 8. Dwellings at Plover Bay. left, Village of summer tents, some of canvas and some of skins; right, Winter house made of whalebone framework, sod walls, and walrus-hide roof. Photographs by Edward S. Curtis, July 1899.

SIBERIAN ESKIMO

Fig. 9. Frame of a winter lodge. The roof supports and crossbeams are of wood while the wall supports are usually of whalebone.

In the late nineteenth century the more prosperous Eskimos began to build wooden frame houses with gable roofs and windows, the design and materials originally being acquired from American traders; however, often such houses were used only during the summer months, with the *maŋtə́ɣaq* remaining the predominant form of the winter house until the twentieth century. By the 1950s it had disappeared completely.

Clothing

In most respects the clothing of the Siberian Eskimos was very similar to that of other Eskimo groups. All of it was constructed from skins and other animal materials. Men's clothing consisted of tight sealskin underpants, a hoodless shirt of reindeer fur similar to that of the Chukchi, fur trousers, and boots. The summer shirt was sewn from one piece of hide with the fur turned in, and the winter shirt, of two pieces of hide, with fur both inside and outside. A belt of sealskin embroidered with white reindeer hair cinched in at the hips. Fur stockings and sealskin boots of varying heights completed the costume. For added warmth during the winter a hooded parka of reindeer fur extending to the knees was worn. One of the unusual features of the Siberian Eskimo clothing style was that the parka was

Fig. 10. Bone implement. Described as a "louse whacker" by the collector, this carved and incised tool was used to beat fur clothing that had become infested; badly infested clothing was cut up and burnt. It was probably also used for brushing snow from clothing. A stouter version was used to beat frost out of skins, in winter inside the dwelling. Length 62.5 cm; collected by W.H. Dall at Plover Bay, USSR, 1880.

252

hoodless; it is asserted, in fact, that "men and women wore fur caps and mittens only in travel. The rest of the time, even in the strongest cold and wind, they went with the head uncovered" (Menovshchikov and Shnakenburg 1956). While the literal truth of the statement may be questioned on the basis of sheer climatic conditions, it is clear that the usual costume was hoodless.

Women's clothing consisted of fur underpants over which was worn fur overalls. The women's boots (fig. 13) were similar to the men's but covered the entire calf; in the wintertime they were often of reindeer fur.

Another traditional form of winter garment was birdskin parkas, worn up to the end of the nineteenth century and supplanted by reindeer fur when the reindeer became more abundant with the development of trade with the Reindeer Chukchi. Sleeping mats and beds were also made from birdskins.

Women wore their hair parted in the middle and braided on the sides. Facial tattooing was very common. Although men sometimes cut their hair so that a long lock was left on top, the usual form was that of shaving it off at the top and leaving a fringe of hair around the head.

Fig. 11. Man from Lütke Harbor, St. Lawrence Bay, wearing a waterproof parka made of walrus intestine. The visor is worn by a boat captain as a mark of status. He sits in front of a sod house with a walrus-hide roof held down by rocks. Photograph by Henry Collins, 1929.

top, Amer. Mus. of Nat. Hist., New York: 60/3564; bottom, U. of Pa., U. Mus., Philadelphia: NA 226.

Fig. 12. Mittens and boots. top, Mittens of tanned sealskin with bands of embroidery on the thumb and bottom border, used in summer. bottom, Man's reindeer-skin boots with bands of embroidery. Although reported by the collectors as acquired from Eskimo, the style of these pieces is typically Chukchi. The same patterns and materials were utilized by both groups. top, Length 25.0 cm; collected by W. Bogoras, at Chaplino, USSR, 1900–1901. bottom, Same scale, collected by G.B. Gordon, East Cape, USSR, 1905.

Social Organization

Extensive published data concerning the traditional social organization of the Siberian Eskimos are hard to come by. The chief primary sources for social structural material used here are the articles by Sergeev (1962) and Menovshchikov (1962). Rubtsova's book (1954) dealing with folklore and mythology provides the only detailed listing of kinship terms. Subsidiary materials relating to social organization are found in Menovshchikov and Shnakenburg (1956) and Sergeev and Arutiunov (1975).

Citing Hughes (1958) on clans among the Saint Lawrence Island Eskimo, both Sergeev and Menovshchikov

U. of Iowa, Mus. of Nat. Hist., Iowa City: 10,910.

Fig. 13. Woman's boots. The sole is sealskin, with toe and heel crimping, sewed to a piece of red tanned sealskin; the leg is made of 4 pieces of reindeer skin alternating brown and mottled white. The top bands are marten, clipped caribou skin, and sealskin with blue and red wool stripes. A drawstring runs through the top, and there are ties around the ankles. These boots were worn in the winter over deerskin stockings. Length about 76.2 cm; collected by Frank Russell at East Cape, USSR, 1892–1894.

provide data that clearly establish the existence of a patrilineal clan system also among the Siberian Eskimo in traditional times, with clan names and the constituent families having been preserved, in Menovshchikov's (1962:31) phrase, "since time immemorial." Sergeev (1962) discusses a number of features of the traditional kinship system and social structure, as well as asserting the linear evolution of the patrilineal clan out of an earlier matriarchal form—an interpretation universal in writings of Soviet authors, which leads them, for example, to emphasize the role of females in religious ceremonies and in the mythology as "survivals" of the matriarchal stage. For instance, Fainberg (1955) asserts that there were matrilineal clans among all Eskimo groups, but their (theoretically expected) transition into patrilineal forms was prevented by extensive and disruptive contact with the outside world, a deviation that did not occur among the Siberian Eskimos. Sergeev gives an overall picture of the distribution of the various clans in the villages of Sireniki, Chaplino, and Naukan. He gathered his data in the periods 1953–1956 and 1958–1961. Chichlo (1981) also comments on the clan system in Naukan.

Sergeev (1962:36) discovered the existence of groups that are "impossible to call anything other than patrilineal clans." He notes that in Chukotka as a whole there are 30 such clans, each with a distinctive name, and he provides a list of those clans according to the settlements with which they are principally associated. For the village of Chaplino (the village closest to Saint Lawrence Island), both he and Menovshchikov list several clans, members of which are found in the village of Gambell on the island. However, there is some discrepancy between the two accounts. Sergeev (1962:36) lists eight clans in Chaplino, and Menovshchikov

Glenbow-Alberta Inst., Calgary, Alta.: left NC-1-357, right ND-1-166.

Fig. 14. East Cape women's clothing and facial tattoos. left, Mother wearing skin parka and child, wearing hood decorated with beads. right, Hootna wearing gutskin waterproof garment. She has tattooed lines on her chin and nose. Photographs by Lomen Brothers, 1908–1915.

(1962:30) lists 10. Of the clans found in Gambell on Saint Lawrence Island, Sergeev lists the *aymá·řamkət* (one of the most powerful on the island), the *lá·kaɣmi·t*, and the *uɣá·li·t*; Menovshchikov lists those three and the Pakagmit and also lists the names of the individual family heads for most of the groups.

Other indicators of the prevalence and strength of an overall patrilineal organization are also found. For instance, the rule of descent was patrilineal, kinship reckoning was more detailed on the patrilineal side, inheritance was patrilineally structured, and each clan had its own defined residential area in the village, as well as plots for its meat-drying racks and racks for tying down the hunting boats. Sergeev mentions also that in the village of Naukan the best locations for these racks were occupied by those clans considered to be aboriginal to the place, which consisted of six out of the nine clans in the village. It should be noted that the division of territory according to ownership by clan did not extend to hunting areas (for example, the shore) that were held in common by all villagers.

Even up to the beginning of the twentieth century, each clan was headed by an elderly male, called the *nuná·ləxtaq*. The duties of such a person included the direction and regulation of the social and subsistence activities of the clan. For example, he opened and closed the hunting season, determined when to undertake trips

to the reindeer herders (Chukchi) to trade for skins, and directed the carrying out of the religious ceremonies of the clan. In conjunction with elders of the other clans, he settled quarrels and altercations. According to Sergeev (1962) the position of clan head was hereditary, always in the patrilineal line and usually from father to son. Frequently, Sergeev notes, the clan head from one

Harvard U., Peabody Mus.: 10-24-60/76076.

Fig. 15. Ball used primarily by children to play kickball. Pieces of dark and light sealskin are sewn together, appliquéd with X's, and decorated with tufts of hair. It is probably stuffed with hair or moss. Diameter 10.0 cm; collected at East Cape, USSR, before 1910.

254

of the most powerful and respected clans exercised the function of leader for the entire village.

Apparently until the 1950s, there were distinctive burial grounds for each clan. In this, as in areas designated for residence, the most convenient locations were allocated to clans aboriginal to the given village, and they were usually located on slopes of hills nearest the village. Furthermore, each clan had its own special rituals, traditions, and legends pertaining to its origins, its relations (often of warfare) with other clans and groups (including Saint Lawrence Island; for example, Rubtsova 1954:225 ff.), and the rationale for religious ceremonies. A common theme in such legends had to do with the facile transmutability between humans and animals, and the parallelism between the character of human motivation and that of the maritime mammals.

In addition, clans held distinctive rites in honor of clan ancestors. Menovshchikov (1962:33), in fact, witnessed such a ceremony held in the ruins of an ancient nəŋlu in 1954, a ceremony that consisted of pounding on the skin drum, talking with the spirits of the dead ancestors (who, it was believed, still dwelled in the ruins), offering sacrificial foods, and eating a communal meal.

From about the middle of the nineteenth century, the character and distribution patterns of the collective hunting activities changed with the advent of commodity values. Gradually, the boat captains became the owners of the whaleboats, and unequal division of the products ensued, with the captain receiving a larger share. Prior to that time distribution of products of the hunt, such as meat, skins, and blubber, had been equal among all clan members, including children of deceased members (Sergeev 1962). Despite the disintegrative effects that boat ownership by a single person had upon some aspects of the clan system, the basis for crew membership remained, as in the past, that of close clanship ties and widespread if not equal sharing among clan members.

Thus, up until the middle of the 1930s the fundamental production unit (the hunting crew) was based primarily upon the clan unit. Until the collectivization of the hunting activities and the reorganization of hunters into work units, or "brigades," each clan had up to three or more hunting crews. In Naukan at the beginning of the twentieth century there were 11 such crews, each containing from 10 to 12 men. Aside from the hunting crew and the special boats used for that purpose, each clan had its own larger vessel, used for longer voyages, such as those for trade or warfare. The primarily clan-based composition of the hunting crew is demonstrated by Sergeev (1962:38) with data pertinent to the village of Naukan in 1934.

The rule of exogamy, commonly a key indicator of a clan-organized society, retained its cultural force until at least the 1960s. Data from a survey conducted in 1960 by Sergeev (1962:40) in the villages of Sireniki, Chaplino, and Naukan concerned with marital relations both between clans and within clans showed that in the majority of marriages even as late as this date the partners belonged to different clans. In former times marriage with someone from the same clan was strictly forbidden. The dire consequences of doing so are reported in some of the legends, in which one youth was killed by his father for marrying the father's brother's daughter. In a sample table given by Sergeev (1962:41) on clan origin of 12 married couples from Naukan the existence of clan exogamy is clear. He adduces further support for the principle of clan exogamy by noting that the Central Siberian Yupik kinship term for father's brother (atá:ta) is sharply differentiated from that for mother's brother (aŋak).

Sometimes engagement of small children was concluded between adult members of the two different families involved, and occasionally even at their birth, a practice also found on Saint Lawrence Island. Sergeev (1962:40) implies that there existed into the 1930s the custom of formalized wife exchange with "trading partners" and also polygyny, practiced most commonly by the wealthy and powerful, such as shamans. However, the existence of plural wives was a comparatively rare occurrence and depended upon the material wealth of the family.

In the case of the death of an older brother, invariably the surviving wife became the wife of the younger brother, even if the brother was already married. The care of the children of the deceased devolved entirely upon the younger brother and the entire clan. Sergeev's table (1962:41) included one instance of the levirate.

Menovshchikov (1962) cites other indicators of a patrilineal clan organization in former times: patrilateral parallel cousins were differentiated from matrilateral parallel cousins, with the former calling each other 'brother' and 'sister' and the children in each case considering their paternal uncle, his wife and children, the same as their own nuclear family relatives; and each clan group worked collectively during the taking down

Amer. Mus. of Nat. Hist., New York: 60/3724.
Fig. 16. Tobacco pipe of one piece, with pewter bowl, stem and inlay in wood center section; the shape is derived from the Chinese opium pipe. All the pewter was cast together in 2 end molds connected by a paper tube over the carved wood section. The pipe was finished with knife and file (Bogoras 1904–1909:202). Although such pipes became integrated into Eskimo life it is not clear whether Eskimos manufactured them themselves. Length 26.0 cm; collected by W. Bogoras at Indian Point, USSR, 1900–1901.

255

and putting up of the winter and summer dwelling units of each family. He also corroborates Sergeev's observations concerning the clan composition of the hunting crews. Menovshchikov's statement about cousin terms appears to be contradicted by the set in Rubtsova (1954:502–503), which includes a separate term for patrilateral parallel cousin (*atálɣun*), but both usages are found on Saint Lawrence Island as alternates ("Saint Lawrence Island Eskimo," fig. 10, this vol.), and probably this is the case in Chaplinski as well.

Religion

Religious ideas of the Siberian Eskimos had much in common with those of the Chukchi (Menovshchikov and Shnakenburg 1956; Bogoras 1904–1909). Both groups believed in the existence of benevolent as well as harmful spirits. Aside from belief in a distant supreme being or creator, there was also conceived to be a goddess of the sea, Məɣətaɣna, in the familiar Eskimo manner (Sergeev and Arutiunov 1975). The malevolent spirits were called *tuɣnəɣaˑt*, and they were considered extremely dangerous for people, believed to cause all kinds of sickness, accidents, and other mishaps. For protection from these spirits people relied upon amulets and marked their faces with stripes of red ocher or graphite as a symbol of anointment. Such marking was especially done during illness. It is also indicated by Menovshchikov and Shnakenburg that sometimes a sick person's face was tattooed with schematic figures of people, but the reason is not given; the rationale may be similar to that found for the custom on Saint Lawrence Island, in which a sick person would sometimes wear clothes different from what he usually wore in order to confuse the spirits into thinking it was a different person and thereby induced them to turn their malevolent energies elsewhere.

Among the Siberian Eskimos there was widespread worship of several animals and birds, the killing of which was forbidden. Wolves, ravens, and swallows were so regarded. The swallow cult had great significance, the Eskimos believing that the swallow protected the hunter on the sea, and that in the wintertime the swallow turned into a wolf and punished miserly reindeer herders by eating their reindeer if they did not give meat and reindeer hides to the coastal dwellers. Wooden figures of the swallow were worn on the belts as amulets, and a depiction of the bird was drawn upon the hunting boats and whaleboats.

Eskimo ritualism was accompanied by dramatic presentations and dancing, and the ceremonies, as well as an extensive series of taboos, were principally concerned with the cult of sea animals. The ceremonies had two purposes—to beseech the spirits of the animals for a rich hunt in the forthcoming season, and to pay gratitude to those spirits in thanks for a successful hunt.

The rites ranged from simple acts, such as showing respect and thanks to the soul of a slain walrus, seal, or whale, through offering a drink of water and some "food" to the dead animal, to complex ceremonies that required much preparation and the participation of many people.

Sergeev and Arutiunov (1975) describe a ritual of propitiation to the walrus conducted until the beginning of the twentieth century that has not been discussed elsewhere. In order to ensure continued abundance of the walruses during future hunts, the head of the first walrus killed on a given hauling-up area was taken back to the village, where it was consulted as to the appropriate strategy for the ensuing hunt and for choosing which of the hunters should lead the killing. After the slaughter was over, the head of the first walrus killed during the actual hunt, with its tusks intact, was placed upon a cliff overlooking the hauling ground, or else nearby. Every year this was repeated. The heads of walruses with their tusks facing the sea were placed in even rows, sometimes forming two or three tiers, and the number of such heads was thus a marker of the number of years in which a walrus kill had occurred at a given area.

Another example of a propitiatory rite, this time relating to the whale (Sergeev and Arutiunov 1975), is similar to a ceremony found on Saint Lawrence Island. When a whale (bowhead or right whale) was being towed to the shore, the hunters called out "Okh, Okh," which notified the villagers to come to the shore for ritual propitiation of the animal. The wife or mother of the hunter who had killed the whale offered a trencher or basin of sacrificial foods (such as reindeer meat, mukluk seal, and special leaves of plants). A vessel containing fresh water was also brought. The whale was "fed" and "watered," some of the food was sacrificed to the sea, and the rest was eaten by the participants. Old men bent down to the whale's head and whispered words of conciliation, words that were passed down from generation to generation. Part of the head, eyes, flippers, lips, and tongue, and the heart were placed in a pit and saved until the beginning of another ceremony that was to take place during the fall in preparation for subsequent whale hunting, the rite attigak, practiced at least until the 1930s (see also Voblov 1952).

Each settlement had its own most powerful shaman, who was important in curing sickness and in divination, services for which he was paid in valuable goods. Usually shamans were men, but at times there were also powerful female shamans. Among the Eskimos there was no special costume for the shaman, but pendants, tassels, and a tobacco pouch worn on his usual clothing indicated to other people that the person was a shaman.

Generally speaking, women played an important part in the religious ceremonies, especially in invocations and magical activities and the preparation of the ritual food. The oldest women in the family did the tattooing, marked the sign of anointment in sickness, and figured importantly in the social drama of the rituals as well.

The religious beliefs were reflected in the Eskimos' art and mythology, for example, in carved wooden representations of the spirit protectors (amulets), and in decoration of ritual clothing with special ornaments. Collections of Siberian Eskimo mythology have been published by Bogoras (1913), Rubfsova (1954), and Menovshchikov (1958, 1974). Krauss (1973, 1979) discusses published materials relating to linguistics and folklore.

History

Although direct changes in the Siberian Eskimo way of life as a result of contact with the technologically more advanced world had begun during the middle of the nineteenth century (indeed, even in the seventeenth century, when Cossack explorers visited them), it was not until the late 1920s that the most significant and far-reaching effects of such contact began (Sergeev and Arutiunov 1975). With the advent of the Soviet government following the revolution of 1917–1918, policy formulations and administrative developments got underway that were to result in major changes in the social, economic, political, educational, and cultural life of all minority peoples of the North, including the Eskimos.

At first it was proposed that the instrument of such development be self-governing units or councils (soviets) based upon local tribal units and having a wide scope of authority. Practically all areas of community life were implicated in the proposed changes: regulations for hunting and preservation of resources, organization of mutual aid societies (which transcended the traditional form of mutual aid society, the clan and extended family), health and educational development, establishment of community reserves, and sharing of ammunition, reindeer, and other food supplies. For example, public meat storage pits were established. In addition, a vast complex of measures for land tenure was instituted. During this time, as a temporary measure until the achievement of given general cultural and economic goals, the Siberian Eskimos (and all other minority peoples of the North) were freed from taxation, military service, and other civic responsibilities.

But there were problems with the soviets' accomplishing all these goals, problems that arose in part, at least, because of antecedent sociocultural conditions. For example, great difficulties were encountered in drawing young people and women into the activities of the councils, and a great deal of work had to be done to make the new cultural and economic goals understandable, and acceptable, to all parts of the population (especially, one would guess, to those segments of the population whose traditional activities and privileges were threatened by the new schemes). But beyond this, structural factors were found to be critical impediments to change. For example, Sergeev and Arutiunov (1975) assert that "the pressure of a tradition of subordination to the voice of the elders in these small communities would sometimes result in the chairman of a tribal council identifying the council with himself and thereby acting without the consent of others." Armstrong (1966:68) enlarges on this point:

> It was first decided, in 1926, that the clan should be the basic unit, and that the local equivalent of the village soviets of the rest of the country should be clan-based "native soviets." This was put into practice, but it was discovered to be, from the regime's point of view, a mistake. The elders of the clan simply became the officials of the soviet, and the chance of such a body carrying through novel and probably unpopular measures was obviously small. There was a change-over, therefore, for purely ideological reasons, to territorial soviets. This was made during the period 1929–32 by creating "national districts," with the main object of helping to fashion a national culture for the peoples.

The organization of the populations into national regions or "okrugs" of mixed ethnic groups had the purpose of heightening political activities and reorganizing economic and cultural development at the regional as well as at the local level. Both in places where an already settled population was found as well as in those places where nomadism was the way of life (as with nomadic hunters or reindeer herders), local governing councils were formed. Circuit and regional courts, village and nomadic public courts were created in a similar fashion.

The Siberian Eskimos live in the Chukchi National Area (*Chukotskiĭ Nafsional'nyĭ Okrug*), Magadan Province. The Chukchi National Area (shared primarily between the Eskimos and the Chukchis, so far as aborig-

Denver Mus. of Nat. Hist., Dept. of Anthr., Colo.: BA21-401C.
Fig. 17. Natives of Provideniia Bay speaking to Soviet official (left in uniform) aboard the U.S. ship *Bear*; John Burnham, U.S. Biological Survey, in center. Photograph by Alfred M. Bailey, Emma Harbor, 1921.

inal groups are concerned) was officially constituted in 1930, as were most of the other national areas populated by minority nationalities of the North. According to the 1959 census, in the Chukchi National Area the general population was composed of 46,700 people, of whom 11,700 were Chukchis; 1,200 were Eskimos, who originally had settled virtually isolated places of this region; 2,000 Even (Lamut); and smaller numbers of other kinds of indigenous nationalities of the North. The number of Eskimos in the region changed only slightly by the time of the 1970 census (1,308, 785 of whom were Eskimo speakers) but did increase significantly in the 1979 census (to 1,500) (Brown et al. 1982:71). The precision of these ethnic population estimates may be questioned on the basis of the extensive intermarriage between Eskimos and other ethnic groups (especially Chukchis) and the encouragement of the authorities to take on a national rather than an ethnic identity (Krauss 1973; Gurvich and Fainberg 1964:59).

Along with the new administrative format for the population beginning in the 1930s, there came also attempts to settle the population, which affected the reindeer herders, of course, more than the Eskimo populations, and to collectivize production. A large number of small settlements were changed into numerous larger settlements and organized sociopolitical and socioeconomic units. Krauss (1973) and Chichlo (1981) note the removal of the Eskimos of Naukan to Nuniamo, in 1958, where they became a minority group living among the Chukchis. Later the inhabitants of Nuniamo itself were dispersed into larger settlements. Large kolkhoz (collective farm or hunting and fishing cooperative) and sovkhoz villages (collectives owned outright by the state) grew either in areas where small settlements used to be or else in entirely new areas. After these changes there were numbers of Eskimos in Uél'kal', Uélen, New Chaplino, Sireniki, Nuniamo, and other places, where they live alongside or intermixed with the Chukchi.

According to Sergeev and Arutiunov (1975), the Eskimo population of Chukotka is organized for production purposes into several large kolkhozes and sovkhozes, forms of the social and economic organization of production that represent the long and comprehensive process of sociocultural change that began in the 1930s. The goal of this effort is to organize and coordinate indigenous subsistence activities toward the end of greater efficiency and productivity for the group as a whole. In addition, all these activities were to be translated into an explicitly monetary framework, both for assessing the value of the productive efforts of the group as a whole as well as for rewarding the efforts of a given worker (that is, in the form of payment for work in the collective).

The problems involved obviously were many: the usual psychological resistance from those who were well-favored by the existing system (such as boat captains), the threat of changes in social affiliation and political relationships implied by the proposed new schemes, the conceptual complexities inherent in a monetary system of reckoning, as well as the sheer technological and empirical problems involved in trying to make the ecological necessities of, for example, nomadic reindeer herding fit with the sociopolitical imperatives of a development plan calling for sedentarization.

But the effort continued, with mixed successes, during the 1930s and 1940s, with the one major change from the original format being the institution of collectives based not upon a single subsistence pursuit (such as hunting), but upon the mixing of varied activities organized under a single administrative unit. In the end, what was accomplished could perhaps best be described, in the case of the Eskimos, as the superimposition of a comprehensive socialist sociopolitical order over a system that had theretofore been organized on the basis of many values that stressed communalism, at least at the level of family and clan relationships. The effort required many years to accomplish, and in the Chukchi National Area it is asserted that "1950 was the year of virtual completion of collectivization" (Vasil'ev, Simchenko, and Sokolova 1966:11). An illustration, in some considerable detail, of how the process of collectivization was functioning in the Chukchi National Area during the 1950s is presented in Hughes's (1965) translation of a section of Smoliak's (1957) monograph.

What is apparent in the accounts of collectivization among the Siberian Eskimos is the mixture of continuity and change in their subsistence pursuits and forms of social organization for exploiting the natural environment. Thus, the major productive efforts are still oriented toward utilization of walruses, seals, whales, and reindeer, and the use of products from those animals for satisfying life's needs; the types of animals hunted and many of the strategies employed are still dictated by the presence or absence of ice, and ice of different kinds, all dependent upon the shifting ecological possibilities that structure the migration routes of the animals; there still is a marked tendency toward division of labor between males and females; the production units are still small groups of hunters (or herders); there is still some individual hunting activity and retention by the individual of at least some of the products of that hunt, while at the same time sharing with others the meat and other products from other types of hunting.

But changes are also obvious. Quite beyond the much greater use of new weapons and technological hardware, there is also an overarching set of regulations and norms that dictate the patterns of coordination, establishment of new social networks for accomplishing that task, and of distribution of the products. And all this is explicitly set within the context of a monetary system, of specified production goals to be reached, and of man-

258

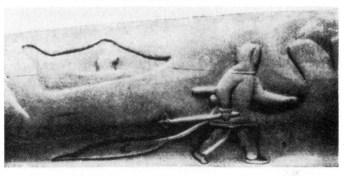

top, Mitlĩãnskaĩã 1976:fig. 49; Muzeĩ Antropologii i Étnografii, Akademiĩã Nauk SSSR, Leningrad: bottom left, 6010-19; bottom right, 6010-47.

Fig. 18. Contemporary ivory carving by Eskimos from Naukan. top, *Hunter and a Sea Lion* by Khukhutan, 1956, with a scene of walrus butchering engraved at the base. Khukhutan (b. 1904, d. 1969) began carving in 1928 after losing a leg in a hunting accident and became a master carver, working in Naukan, Nuniamo, and Uélen. bottom left, Portion of engraved tusk depicting the shooting of polar bears with rifles. The sea is painted deep blue, and the people, bears, and boats in brown and yellow. Length of tusk 54.0 cm; carved by Ul'gun (b. 1927, d. 1975), who worked in Naukan and Uélen. bottom right, Portion of tusk carved in relief with scene of hunter dragging seal. Length of tusk 63.0 cm; carved by Zhirintan (b. 1908, d. 1968).

datory concern for conservation of the various species. Another aspect of the new situation is that of mixed populations and mixed cultural backgrounds of the units organized for production purposes; no longer, apparently, is it appropriate to think of an "Eskimo" brigade going out from some of these villages, but rather, of a unit that may include Soviet citizens from any of the several population groups represented—Eskimo, Chukchi, or even Russian.

One would like to have further data to make the above statement more specific, but they are not to be found in the accessible literature. Another interesting and related research question would be, specifically, whether the hunting crews, the brigades based in Eskimo villages, are still composed mostly of patrilineally related males, or has that ancient principle of the social organization of hunting been fundamentally changed by the sociopolitical goals developed since 1950?

Synonymy‡

The name Asiatic Eskimo has been used by Bogoras

‡This synonymy was written by Charles C. Hughes and Ives Goddard.

(1904–1909, 1:11) and others as the equivalent of Siberian Eskimo. In the *Handbook* these expressions are differentiated, with Asiatic Eskimo including the Saint Lawrence Islanders, and Siberian Eskimo excluding them.

The Siberian Eskimo use as self-designations forms and derivatives of the same widespread Eskimo word that is also the basis of the names Inuit, Inupiaq, and Yupik: CSY *yu·k* 'person' (*yuɣət* pl.) and *yupik* 'authentic person' (*yupí·ɣət* pl.). The English name Yuit (Hodge 1907–1910, 2:1007) and such transcriptions of Cyrillic as juit and ĩuit are renderings of *yuɣət*. The use of these terms has been consistently reported (Bogoras 1904–1909, 1:11, 20; Menovshchikov and Shnakenburg 1956; Sergeev and Arutiunov 1975), but Orlova (1941) has disputed the existence of a collective term, claiming that only specific, locality-based designations were found.

The Siberian Eskimo were usually not differentiated from the culturally similar Maritime Chukchi in the accounts of early explorers such as Vitus Bering and Otto von Kotzebue. In fact, the Maritime Chukchi make the same generalization in calling themselves and other maritime peoples collectively aŋqa´lɪt 'sea people' or rama´ɣlat 'seacoast dwellers' (Bogoras 1904–1909, 1:11). The singular of the first of these terms, aŋqa´lɪn, is *259* evidently the source of the name Onkilon, applied by Ferdinand von Wrangell to the Siberian Eskimo, and similarly the name Namollo, used by Theodor Lütke (Fëdor Litke), also in Russian form as Namolly, appears to be from the general Koryak word nıʹmıḷu 'maritime settlers', corresponding to Chukchi nıʹmılıt 'inhabitants'. A similar notion is reflected in the expression sedentary Chukchi, used in the literature of the Billings-Sarychev expedition of 1787–1792 for the Siberian Eskimo (Bogoras 1904–1909, 1:21; Menovshchikov and Shnakenburg 1956:934; M.B. Chernenko in Zagoskin 1967:331, 332). The phrase sedentary Chukchi-Namolly has the same reference (Zagoskin 1967:105).

Kotzebue (1967:196) reported that the Saint Lawrence Islanders called the Siberian Eskimo Wemen; the origin of this term is unknown.

Subgroups

Sirenikski. The Sirenikski-speaking Eskimos are called in Russian sireniktsy or sirenikovtsy (adjective sirenikskii or sirenikovskii), forms based on the name of their principal village Sireniki (also Sirenik; Serenek in Voblov 1952:334), in CSY siɣíʹnǝk (practical orthography Sighinek; in Russian sources usually Siɣǝnǝk, perhaps the Sirenikski form). The Sireniki people are in CSY siɣíʹnǝɣmiʹt. The Chukchi call the village wuteʹen or wuʹturen, and the people from it and other former settlements of the same language wuteʹelit.

The names of other former villages are given by Bogoras (1904–1909, 1:29), Menovshchikov (1964:7–8), and Krupnik and Chlenov (1979:22).

Chaplinski. The Chaplinski-speaking Eskimos are called in Russian chaplintsy (adjective chaplinskii), forms derived from the Russian name of Indian Point, Mys Chaplino (earlier also Mys Chaplin). The Eskimo name of their principal traditional village of Old Chaplino is CSY uŋáʹziq (practical orthography Ungaziq), the people from there being uŋáʹziɣmiʹt. The Chukchi name for Old Chaplino is uŋiʹin (in Russian sources unyyn), but the general name for the people of all the Chaplinski-speaking villages is aiwaʹnat (sg. aiʹwan). The term aiʹwan was also applied to any Maritime Chukchi who owned no reindeer, and both the Maritime Chukchi and Siberian Eskimo also used the name aiwaʹnat for the Saint Lawrence Islanders (Bogoras 1904–1909, 1:19–20; Menovshchikov 1964:6).

The names of other former Chaplinski-speaking villages are given by Bogoras (1904–1909, 1–29), Menovshchikov (1962–1967, 1:3), and Krupnik and Chlenov (1979:21–24).

Naukanski. The Naukanski-speaking Eskimos are called in Russian naukantsy (adjective naukanskii), after Naukan, the Russian name of their principal traditional village on East Cape (from Chukchi noʹǫkan). The Eskimo name for Naukan is CSY nǝvúʹqaq (practical or-

thography Nevuqaq), and the people from there are nǝvúʹqaɣmiʹt (in Chukchi noʹǫkalıt; or derisively peʹekit, from peʹek 'East Cape').

The names of this and other former Naukanski-speaking villages are given by Bogoras (1904–1909, 1:20, 30), Menovshchikov (1975:9), Krupnik and Chlenov (1979:21), and Chichlo (1981:32).

Sources

The most detailed bibliographic sources for the cultural study of Siberian Eskimos are found in the Russian literature, especially for fieldwork done during the modern period. Of general importance within this category is the journal Sovetskaĭa Ėtnografiĭa [Soviet Ethnography], in which appeared, for example, the two primary articles used here giving data on the clan system and other aspects of the traditional social structure (Sergeev 1962; Menovshchikov 1962). A less detailed source for an ethnographic sketch of the people is found in a chapter by Menovshchikov and Shnakenburg in the USSR Academy of Sciences publication Narody Sibiri [Peoples of Siberia] (Levin and Potapov 1956). Other publications of relevance, especially for studies of the changing economic and political life and the process of collectivization, are the considerable publications of the Institute of Ethnography of the USSR Academy of Sciences, such as Smoliak (1957), Sergeev (1955), or Vasil'ev, Simchenko, and Sokolova (1966). Publications in English dealing with the socioeconomic transformations in the Soviet North are those by Dunn and Dunn (1963), Dunn (1968), and a brief overview by Hughes (1965). Chichlo (1981) writes of the social and cultural impact of resettlement of the Eskimos of Naukan based on fieldwork in 1976. Chlenov (1973) discusses social organization, and Krupnik and Chlenov (1979) give a detailed discussion of settlements, clans, and their history.

Voblov's (1952) description of the ritualism and ceremonialism is highly useful in giving details of the aboriginal religious rites as described (and, to a limited extent, functioning) during the 1930s. Another work based on data collected in the 1930s (Orlova 1941) has discussions mainly of material culture.

Rubtsova's (1954) collection of folklore, which exists only in Russian and Eskimo, provides a rich resource for the student of comparative Eskimo mythology and folklore. It also contains valuable appendices on aspects of linguistics, kinship terms, and a number of drawings having to do with aboriginal life. Other collections of folklore have been published by Menovshchikov (1958, 1974). An early collection of folktales was made by Bogoras (1913). Krauss (1973) provides linguistic and folklore materials dealing with Siberian Yupik.

For bibliographic sources published earlier, the reader

should of course consult the two classics that have some material on the cultural situation of the Siberian Eskimos toward the end of the nineteenth century: Nelson (1899) and Bogoras (1904–1909). The Nelson volume contains scattered references to the Eskimos living on the Siberian shore, which deal mostly with material culture, and is deficient in regard to religion and social organization. The same may be said of Bogoras's volume, which is, of course, indispensable for data on the Chukchi. Consequently, although one can inferentially obtain considerable information about the Eskimos from the discussion of the Maritime Chukchi (Bogoras says that in material culture they were identical), the other scattered references to social culture and especially matters of social organization do not provide the kind of ethnographic detail desired. Nonetheless, the volume remains a valuable ancillary source.

Finally, for the most comprehensive and easily accessible bibliographic guide to all the literature available on the Siberian Eskimos up to 1975, consult the 16 volumes of the *Arctic Bibliography,* which provides English summaries of all the sources it cites.

Saint Lawrence Island Eskimo

CHARLES C. HUGHES

Territory and Environment

Saint Lawrence Island was given its European name by Vitus Bering in 1728, while on his first voyage of discovery into the North Pacific. Obviously it had been "discovered" many centuries earlier by ancestors of people now called Eskimos, for it is the largest island in the Bering Sea, about 100 miles long and averaging from 20 to 30 miles wide. Less than 200 miles south of Bering Strait and about 125 miles southwest of Nome, Alaska, its northwestern tip is only 40 miles from Siberia, which can be seen on a clear day (fig. 1).

Although technically located in the Subarctic rather than the Arctic (lying between 168°45′ and 171°50′ west longitude and between 63°00′ and 63°38′ north latitude), in a functional sense Saint Lawrence Island is fully an Arctic environment. It is a largely flat, treeless, tundra island, punctuated by several mountainous features of volcanic, igneous, and sedimentary origin. Surrounded by the ice pack for much of the year, it is beset by winds of high velocity alternating with heavy fog and cloud cover. There is no great accumulation of snowfall, but what does come down is piled into high drifts by the winds. The lowest recorded temperature is −30°F, but with the high winds, the wind chill factor seems considerably lower—especially to hunters out on the ocean ice. The ground cover is termed subarctic, containing the types of lichens, grasses, mosses, and flowering plants found elsewhere in such an inclement environment.

The island is one of the few remaining nonsubmerged parts of what had been a wide land bridge intermittently connecting the New World with the Old during the Pleistocene period and serving as a wide portal of entry for migrants from Asia, who were to become the indigenous peoples of North America, the first wave beginning possibly as long ago as 25,000 B.C. (Hopkins 1967; Müller-Beck 1967; Laughlin 1967). The key structural position of Saint Lawrence Island in such an episodic land bridge can be illustrated best by noting that a decline in present sea level of only 46 meters would create a land passage between Siberia and Alaska by way of Saint Lawrence, and sea level fell that much, and more, several times from about 30,000 years ago to possibly 10,000 years ago (Hopkins 1967:460, 464–465). Also, during the several periods of submergence

of the rest of the bridge over that time, the mountainous land mass that was eventually to be named Saint Lawrence Island might well have served as a refuge for populations that did not move elsewhere to escape the encroaching waters. This could be particularly likely for a human group that had developed subsistence techniques based upon exploitation of maritime and shoreline resources—groups such as the ancestors of present-day Eskimos and Aleuts (Laughlin 1963, 1967).

Prehistory

In any case, an impressive artifactual record of sea-mammal hunters was left on the island, which began to be uncovered by archeological investigations in the 1920s. The island has provided highly significant sites in the development of Bering Sea prehistory (Collins 1964). It was on the basis of work in the 1930s (Collins 1937; Geist and Rainey 1936) that the major outlines of the archeologically known cultures on the island—Old Bering Sea, Okvik, Punuk, Birnirk, and Thule—were laid out, although, as will no doubt continue with additional finds and reformulations, there are alternative views

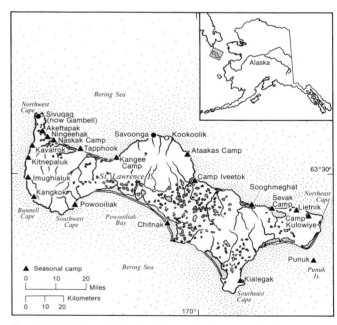

Fig. 1. St. Lawrence Island settlements and seasonal camps occupied before the famine of 1879–1880; some were used as summer camps in the 1980s.

among scholars on certain questions, such as how Okvik relates to Old Bering Sea or whether Birnirk was indigenous or intrusive (Ackerman 1962; Bandi 1969; Arutiunov and Sergeev 1968). However, there does appear to be concurrence on a dating of about 2,000 years ago for the appearance of Okvik and Old Bering Sea on Saint Lawrence Island, with Punuk appearing several hundred years later, followed by intrusive Thule influences (Giddings 1960; Ackerman 1976). In all cases the artifactual evidence points to a people who were very efficient at hunting and extensively utilizing sea mammals: walruses, seals of various types, and several kinds of whales provided flesh for food, light, and heat; bones and tusks for tools; and skins for implements, clothing, boots, and house and boat covers. They had done so for centuries before Euro-American contact, when first the rifle and then the pressure lamp, canned foods, heating oil, mail-order clothing, imported lumber for houses, gasoline-run vehicles, and electricity greatly changed the subsistence patterns by which the Saint Lawrence Islanders adapt to their Arctic environment.

History

After the sighting and naming of Saint Lawrence Island by Bering in 1728, the island was seen by several other Russian and European explorers over the next century, including Otto von Kotzebue, Gleb Shishmaref, and Capt. James Cook in 1778. Toward the middle of the nineteenth century the island became caught up in activities connected with the appearance of American and other commercial whaling ships in the North Pacific Ocean, and the Bering, Chukchi, and Beaufort seas. It became the regular pattern for such ships to stop at Eskimo villages to replenish water casks, to carouse, and to trade for ivory, baleen, and warm skin clothing. In return the Eskimos acquired firearms, whaling equipment (such as bomb guns, hemp rope, steel cutting-tools, and wooden whaleboats), liquor, disease, and sometimes long-term guests, for in a few places on the Alaskan shore stations were established for some members of the ships' crews to stay over the winter to hunt whales with the help of local Eskimos until the return of the ship the following spring. It is uncertain whether such stations were established on Saint Lawrence Island, but it is not unlikely, and at any rate it is quite apparent that people of the island had considerable commerce with visiting vessels. One account explicitly comments on the Saint Lawrence Islanders' being taken on as crew members of whaling ships (Foote 1964).

It may have been an encounter of this kind that led to wholesale tragedy for the Saint Lawrence Island Eskimos (Hughes 1960). Contradictory versions of exactly what happened exist, but one account has it that in the

fall of 1878 some of the whaling vessels moving south with the oncoming winter freeze-up traded large amounts of liquor just at the time when normally intensive hunting of the walrus herds would have occurred. In the debauch that followed, little hunting was done and consequently meat supplies for the coming months—until the usual walrus harvest in the spring—were very low. Such bad weather followed that it was impossible to hunt the few animals that did remain in the area over the winter. Starvation, then sickness, then slow death for much of the island's population ensued (Collins 1937). Whatever the cause—alcoholic debauch or simply the periodic year of stormy weather and bad hunting (Burgess 1974)—it is estimated that about 1,000 of the island's population of 1,500 or so had died by the next summer, a loss never recovered. The population in the late 1950s was still only about 600; in 1970 it was about 700 (U.S. Bureau of Indian Affairs 1977, 1977a); the 1980 census gives 936 for Gambell and Savoonga (which includes non-Natives). So devastated was the island that when the U.S. revenue cutter *Corwin* investigated reports of mass starvation in the summer of 1880, one of its passengers, the noted naturalist John Muir, described entire settlements containing nothing but bleached bones, with bodies lying in houses, about the village, or on the path to the burial ground (Muir 1917).

The first recorded long-term residence by a White man began in 1894, when the Presbyterian missionary Vene C. Gambell arrived with his wife and established a station in the major village of the island, then known as Sivuqaq (*sivú·qaq*; Sivokakh in Gambell 1898). Located on the northwestern tip of the island, it had been a place of habitation for several thousand years, with signs of earliest settlement found on the slopes of the mountain that stands as a bold landmark for many miles out to sea. Gambell and his family died in 1898 when the ship on which they were returning after a leave was lost at sea. The village was renamed in his honor (in English usage), and others came to take up his post as missionary, teacher, and representative of the United States government. One of the most effective was Dr. E.O. Campbell, a medical missionary, who remained for over 10 years after the turn of the century and kept a detailed diary of many of the important events occurring during his stay. In it he recounts his battles with shamans for the conversion of the Eskimos to Presbyterianism, with Siberians over trading whiskey to local Eskimos, with domineering Eskimo boat captains who wanted no part of his interference with traditional hunting rites, and with his own isolation and disappointments at lack of success. One of the legacies he left was the building of the reindeer herd on the island. As part of a general scheme by the U.S. government to restore stability to the native economy, in 1900 42 reindeer and several Lapp herders were placed on the island to help the Eskimos develop and manage a food resource. The

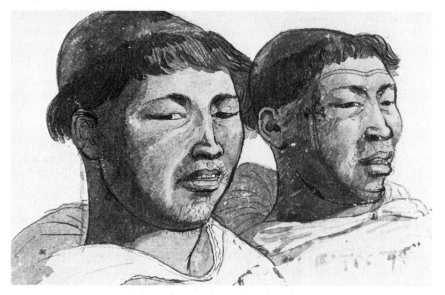

top left and right, Yale U., The Beinecke Rare Book and Manuscript Lib.; bottom left, U. of Alaska Arch., Fairbanks: Geist Coll., 64-98-264; bottom right, Smithsonian, NAA: 30951-B.
Fig. 2. Clothing and hairstyles. top left, Hoodless parka and tonsured haircut, which remained common into the 20th century. Men's facial tattooing was rare by 1912 (Moore 1923:345). top right, Man with facial tattooing, probably of ritual significance. The shaving of the entire head is unusual. Earrings were worn by both men and women (Doty 1900). The beads attached to the headband suggest a shaman's ritual adornment. Watercolors by Louis Choris, St. Lawrence Island, 1816–1817. bottom left, Florence Nupok. Photograph by Otto Geist, 1927. bottom right, Children whose clothing and hairstyles are the same as those of adults. Men shaved the tops of their heads, women wore the hair long and loose or braided. The boys wear reindeer skin parkas with the hair turned inward, and the boy in center wears his knife on a belt in adult fashion. Photograph by an officer of ship *Bear*, about 1888.

herd was successful with respect to that aim for about 30 years or more (reaching a size of at least several thousand animals), but by the mid-1950s it had practically disappeared, most likely through range devegetation. In the early 1970s the herd had increased to 800–1,000 (U.S. Bureau of Indian Affairs 1977a).

Other missionaries and government-appointed teachers followed Dr. Campbell. The notes of one of these record the first use of an outboard motor on the hunting boats in 1917 (Hughes 1960), and those of another,

some 10 years later, the formation of the first village council on an elective basis.

The 1920s were good years for the Saint Lawrence Islanders, based upon a mixed economy of indigenous pursuits and trapping the Arctic fox (*Alopex lagopus*), whose pelts brought up to $60 each (Hughes 1960; Ackerman 1976). Indeed, some of the most successful trappers could earn several thousand dollars a year during those years from trapping alone. Such income even surpassed what had been possible some 30 and more years

264

U. of Alaska Mus., Fairbanks: UA 66-23-2.
Fig. 3. Doll dressed in an infant's combination garment of traditional style. The suit of reindeer fawnskin has the sleeves and feet sewn closed as protection from the cold. The crotch is cut out and a diaper (which was padded with moss and hair) is sewn on at the back and tied around the front, making for easy changing. Charms are attached to the hands and belt. Babies were carried on the mother's shoulders rather than inside the parka. Children began to wear adult-style clothes at about 6 to 8 but the diaper (without filler) was retained longer. Height about 27.8 cm, made by Miriam Kilowiyi at Savoonga, Saint Lawrence I., Alaska, 1966.

earlier, when the Eskimos had had a highly profitable trade in whale baleen with commercial vessels, a market that had begun to decline after the turn of the century, leaving the Eskimos with only the sale of Arctic fox furs as an important source of cash income, supplemented by the sale of carved ivory objects (fig. 7). But the Arctic fox market also began to fade in the late 1930s. With the onset of World War II it became highly uncertain and remained so after the war.

The Saint Lawrence Islanders were affected in other ways also by the war. Some of their young men served in the Alaska Territorial Guard, a few even seeing combat in the Alaskan theater of operations, and at one point the Islanders felt threatened with invasion by Japanese forces. Following the war what had been mostly year-round isolation from close contact with the outside world came to an end, when there was established near the village a small U.S. military installation and a weather station. The effects of both of these firsthand illustrations of mainland life upon the evolving cultural system of the Saint Lawrence Islanders were profound (Hughes 1960). By the middle 1950s the pattern had been set: the teacher, missionary, and public health nurse were still the "traditional" representatives of the mainland world, but increasingly the island has become more interdependent with the Alaskan mainland. By the mid-

dle 1970s, the following changes had begun to influence the island: statehood and its implications for local government; implementation of the Alaska Native Claims Settlement Act (under which the island is owned by the Native people and managed by the native corporations in Gambell and Savoonga); stricter controls on the hunting of maritime animals and sale of their products (under provisions of the 1972 Marine Mammals Protection Act); tourism as an industry, dependence on monetary income from jobs; enhanced communication capabilities (exemplified in satellite-beamed television reception); exploration for mineral resources; and emigration to the Alaskan mainland (U.S. Bureau of Indian Affairs 1977, 1977a; Ellana 1980). Above all, Natives needed to deal with three separate but overlapping local governmental structures in each village—the council established by the Indian Reorganization Act, the city council, established under Alaska state authority, and the village corporation, established under the Alaska claims act. While the cultural pattern presented here derives from data gathered in the mid-1950s, its principal outlines, especially social structure, remained valid into the 1980s (Burgess 1974; Ackerman 1976; Hughes 1977; Jørgen B. Jørgenson, personal communication 1982; Ronald L. Little, personal communication 1982).

Culture

The Saint Lawrence Islanders belong culturally to the Asiatic Eskimo population, rather than to that of North America. This relationship is shown by a number of major cultural features but especially by their language, which is nearly identical to the variety of Eskimo spoken on the Siberian mainland called Chaplinski in the Soviet Union; the two together constitute the Central Siberian Yupik language* (Krauss 1973, 1975a; "Eskimo and Aleut Languages," this vol.).

Besides the speakers of Central Siberian Yupik, who bridge the international boundary, the other Asiatic Eskimos are found in Siberia. In addition to language, the features that differentiate the Asiatic from the North American Eskimos are the existence of patrilineal descent groups; the absence of the formal men's house found in Alaska villages; house, clothing, and cosmetic styles; and major features of the ceremonial system (which shows strong similarities to that of the Maritime Chukchis on the Siberian shore).

*For the orthographic systems used to spell Saint Lawrence Island Eskimo words in the *Handbook,* see the footnote in "Asiatic Eskimo: Introduction," this vol.

Eskimo place-names and band or lineage names are normalized to the standard spelling of the Saint Lawrence Island practical orthography, with a phonemic transcription added in italics at the first occurrence. The words spelled atrruk and chkwaek were not available to the editors in phonemic transcription.

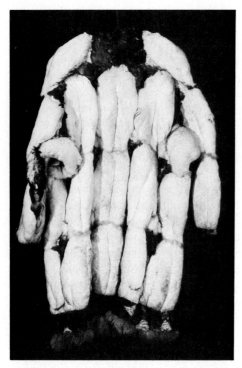 

Fig. 4. Men's clothing. Tops, with or without hoods, are made of fur or bird skins. left, Parka, of guillemot breast skins which hung to about knee level. Length from top of hood 116.0 cm; collected by E. Tappen Adney on St. Lawrence I., Alaska, 1899. right, Gutskin parka, worn over the skin garment for protection. Made of pieces of gut (seal or walrus) that have been soaked, scraped, inflated, and dried. The opaque, rather than translucent, quality of the gut is obtained by putting it in the sun to bleach. The pieces are sewn together with the seams on the outside and are decorated with skin strips, crested auklet feathers, and fur. The hood has a drawstring closing. Worn with the tops were pants with drawstring waists and bottoms and boots. The number of layers of clothing (and whether the fur faced in or out) depended on the weather. Width 80.5 cm; collected by Riley D. Moore, on St. Lawrence I., Alaska, 1912.

Social Organization

In most respects, any treatment of the Saint Lawrence Island Eskimos should be viewed as a partial discussion of the larger cultural grouping, the Siberian or Asiatic Eskimos; this is particularly true of any discussion of

Fig. 5. Traditional male dance costume, worn inside the warm winter house. Note the distinctive Asiatic Eskimo and Chukchi tonsure. Drawing by Florence Nupok, a St. Lawrence I. Eskimo woman, Sept. 1928.

social organization. For several hundred years at least (and probably a few millennia), there has been considerable interchange between the Saint Lawrence Islanders and Eskimos and Chukchis living on the Siberian shore, only 40 or so miles to the northwest. Such interactions involved extensive trade relations, intermarriage, warfare, and migration; in fact, at least one of the existing clan groups on Saint Lawrence Island is known historically to have originated in the village of Old Chaplino (Ungaziq, *uŋá·ziq*) on Indian Point (*Mys Chaplino*) on the Siberian shore, and one of the clans living there in 1962 bore the same name, Aymaramket (*aymářamkət*) (Menovshchikov 1962:30).

One of the principal features of traditional Siberian Eskimo social structure is the existence of patrilineal clans or lineages (Hughes 1958, 1960; Fainberg 1955; Sergeev 1962; Menovshchikov 1962; Chichlo 1981). Soviet scholars broaden this issue, asserting that a clan structure was found everywhere in Eskimo societies, and that an evolutionary process had occurred whereby such groups had changed from a primitive communal form of social structure to a matrilineal organization and finally would reach a patrilineal mode of organization. One aspect of this argument is that vestiges of the presumed former matrilineal stage of development are everywhere to be seen as "survivals" in cultural

266

left, Smithsonian, NAA:left, 76-705, right, 3106-D-27. right, Mus. of the Amer. Ind., Heye Foundation, New York: 13/3520.

Fig. 6. Wrestling on St. Lawrence I. for fun, prestige, and resolution of arguments. left, Fourth of July celebration at Gambell with festivities and athletic contests such as traditional wrestling matches. In the background is the Presbyterian church, which was also used as a school. Photograph by Riley D. Moore, July 1912. right, Ivory sculpture representing a wrestling match. Those who excel at such activities are known as "strong men" (Moore 1923:364). Height 6.4 cm, collected by A.E. Thompson at Kookoolik, Saint Lawrence I., Alaska, before 1925.

features such as the presence of female deities in the religion, the participation of females in rituals, and the like.

The general issue of clans among the Eskimos notwithstanding, there is no question of the existence—and viability—of patrilineal descent groups among the Saint Lawrence Islanders in historic times. These groups may be called clans (Hughes 1958) in conformance with criteria discussed by Murdock (1949).

The development and stabilization of these patrilineal clans may be conjectured as an outcome of particular historical, social, and ecological circumstances. In brief, the Saint Lawrence Islanders formerly were dispersed into a number of settlements scattered around the island, each settlement a patrilineally dominated extended family group similar to the social organizational and settlement pattern found in traditional North American Eskimo bands. In general the bands were

designated, by themselves and others, by the place-name; they were, for example, the Meregtemiit (məřáxtəmi·t) 'the people of Meregta (məřáxta)'. In a sense such groups may be thought of as "tribes," or at least incipient tribes (early reports called them this—for example, Moore 1923); for each had an overall group identification that was meaningful to members of the group itself and also served to differentiate each group from all others. In addition, it is said that there were slight dialectal differences apparent among the bands, as well as some distinctive religious practices and social lore.

Smithsonian, Dept. of Anthr.: 45,721.

Fig. 8. Wooden mask representing a human face, with wrinkles carved into the brow. A quill is added through the nose, wooden pegs are set in as teeth, and added pieces of wood represent labrets (one labret is missing here). The mask, held in place with the leather thongs tied through a hole in each side, is stained red, with black painted eyebrows and beard and white paint on teeth and around the eyes. Length 25.0 cm; collected by C.L. Hooper on Saint Lawrence I., Alaska, 1877-1881.

Smithsonian, Dept. of Anthr.: 332,298 and 332,299.

Fig. 7. Napkin rings, one of a variety of types of ivory carving made for sale. These napkin rings have a pattern of openwork and seals carved in relief. left, Height 3.6 cm; right, same scale. Both collected by A. Hrdlička on Saint Lawrence I., Alaska, 1926.

Smithsonian, Dept. of Anthr.: top, 63,452; bottom, 63,480.
Fig. 9. Carved ornaments. Ivory birds such as these are a common and ancient Eskimo artifact type, found all across the Arctic. bottom, Set of birds with flat bottoms that may have been used as a game; they were strung together through tail holes. top, Larger carving with dots over its body, perhaps used as an amulet. Length 6.9 cm; bottom, length about 4.0 cm each. Both collected by E.W. Nelson on Saint Lawrence I., Alaska, 1877-1881.

For reasons having to do with hunting opportunities as well as the catastrophic famine and decimation of the population in the winter of 1878–1879, all of these small outlying settlements were completely destroyed. The only survivors were about 30 at Powooiliak (Pugughileq, *puɣú·ɣiləq*) on Southwest Cape, about 300 at what became the principal village on the island, Gambell, and one at Kialegak (Kiyalighaq, *kiyá·liɣaq*) on Southeast Cape, who went to Powooiliak (Krauss 1973:820, 1975a:43–44). This catastrophe no doubt simply accelerated and consolidated a process of seasonal settlement from a central base that had already been going on, given the excellence of Gambell as a hunting site (Burgess 1974). The population of Powooiliak was absorbed by Gambell in the twentieth century. The other year-round settlement, Savoonga (Sivunga, *sivú·ŋa*), was started as a reindeer camp in 1914 as an offshoot of Gambell village; its social organizational format is similar to that of Gambell (Ackerman 1976), which it surpassed in population in the 1970s.

In the context of that new social environment, Gambell village, the band or extended-family designations by which people were known became more pronounced. Whereas in the outlying settlements, the issue of what group a person belonged to was seldom raised in that local context (it being taken for granted), in Gambell village, with its heterogeneous population, such

a group affiliation became a more important dimension of ongoing interpersonal relations, thus reinforcing a person's sense of kinship with a patriline. In addition, these groups continued to function in such a manner as to underscore the sense of identification and mutual need, for example, hunting together, conducting their own indigenous religious services, and serving as a person's reserve line of defense in quarrels with other villagers (Hughes 1966, 1968). In Gambell village since about the 1940s three such clans were dominant, the Meregtemiit, Aymaramket, and Pugughileghmiit (*puɣú·ɣiləɣmi·t*), with several others having fewer members and, largely because of that, being relatively powerless in intravillage politics.

It should also be noted that there are subclans within these larger descent groupings and that the specific terms by which the group and subgroup are known might well depend on the situation and the level of specificity required. For example, the broad group to which a person belongs might be the Meregtemiit when the issue is one of differentiating him from the Aymaramket; but if the focus is on the internal structure of the Meregtemiit, his "real" affiliation might be with the Nangupagaghmiit (*nanú·paɣáɣmi·t*) (Hughes 1960:252).

• KINSHIP Using Murdock's (1949) criteria, one may label the social organization of the Saint Lawrence Islanders as a variant of Iroquoian (Hughes 1960:227ff.), that is, there are distinctive cousin terms for father's brother's children (*atálɣun,* sg.) and mother's sister's children (*aɣnálɣun,* sg.), with one term covering cousins linked to ego through father's sister and mother's brother (fig. 10). This single cross-cousin term, *ilú·ɣaq,* designates what is primarily a joking relationship, with none of the more serious and helpful interpersonal dimensions found with the other two types of cousin bonds. The two parallel cousin relationships are not the same, for the bond between a male (especially) and his father's brother's children is one of the strongest and most enduring of all relationships in the entire social organization. It is the base on which the boat crew is built and is the cornerstone of the patrilineal descent group. There is, in fact, social recognition of the importance—and closeness—of this relationship, expressed in a collective term for a group of patrilineal parallel cousins (*kəmə́kR̆akúlɣi·t*), which is translated 'those that have the same flesh'. So close behaviorally are individuals who stand in this relation that commonly, in fact, terms for one's own siblings rather than cousin terms are used in reference and in direct discourse.

The rest of the kinship terminology may be described as bifurcate collateral, with relatively more development of the patrilineal principle as expressed in number of terms and importance of social function accorded to persons standing in that relationship. Thus the patriline is firmly ensconced both in extended family and lineage activities, while matrilineal relatives function only pe-

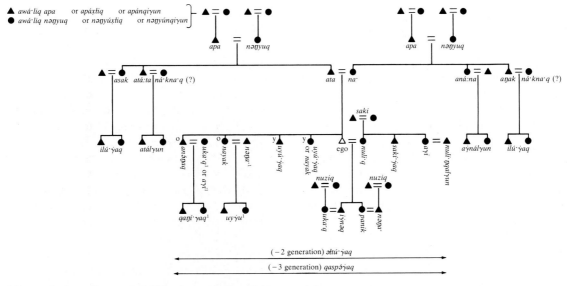

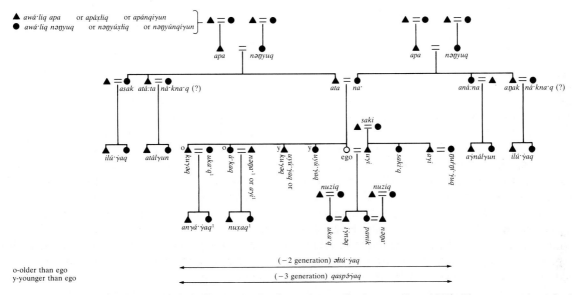

[1] These are also the terms for spouses and children of younger brothers and sisters, respectively.

o-older than ego
y-younger than ego

Fig. 10. Central Siberian Yupik kinship terminology (Steven A. Jacobson, communication to editors 1982). These terms, from St. Lawrence Island, are identical to those collected on the Siberian mainland (Rubtsova 1954:502-503), allowing for variant transcriptions and the use of equivalent descriptive terms in some of the less central categories. top, Male ego; bottom, female ego.

riodically and irregularly in activities relating to ego's life-cycle events and small-scale domestic needs (for example, sharing of food or borrowing of tools).

Thus, for a given individual, there are concentric circles of social groupings, varying according to their bases and the scope of activities for which they are relevant to ego. The inmost grouping is the domestic family, which may be either nuclear or extended. Beyond the nuclear family the extended form may include either a grandparental generation, or else married or unmarried siblings at the parental level. The next kind of social grouping—and this is especially important for a male—is that of the patrilateral parallel cousin grouping. Then there is the kindred, ego's close relatives on both fa-

ther's and mother's sides. Finally comes the most influential and dominant of the social bonds, this one expressed in a definite social group that has time and generational depth, the patrilineal clans (ilá·kʷá·qulɣi·t).

• MARRIAGE Even though there was a clear lineage principle as the organizing structure of the social system, at least in historic times this was apparently not coupled with any consistent rule so far as exogamy was concerned, although clan exogamy was perhaps the dominant mode. The Siberian Eskimos are varyingly reported to have been exogamous between clans. In this respect Saint Lawrence Island cultural practice appears to resemble that of North American Eskimo groups, the only restriction upon marriage partner being that against marrying a "close" relative (in kindred terms). Thus on Saint Lawrence Island a person could and did marry someone belonging to the same descent group, and in the past, when the population lived in the small settlements before the gathering of the clans into the two dominant villages, this probably occurred frequently.

Traditionally, arrangements for marriage were made by the parents and elders of the young people concerned (see Hughes 1960:276ff.; Shinen 1963). Sometimes, in fact, there was infant betrothal. In any case, at some point in adolescence deemed appropriate, the sequence of events that comprised the "marriage" began. The first step was that of the young man's moving into the home of the young woman's parents to render "groom-work" for a period of time, usually about a year in duration. The move was preceded by gifts of tools, weapons, and other economic goods from the boy's family to that of the girl. His duties were practically boundless: he was to hunt with his future father-in-law (and in his boat) and to do all other things appropriate to a male in the household (fig. 11). It is said that some men took advantage of this arrangement, exacting great labors from the prospective son-in-law, only then to refuse to carry through the rest of the bargain by giving the daughter up.

At the end of the work period, during which time the young people usually began sexual relations, the next formal step in social recognition occurred, and this one was the most decisive. The young couple moved back into the house of the boy's parents. The traditional rule of residence was thus matri-patrilocal or, more accurately, uxori-virilocal. The actual move was accompanied by a group of the girl's kinsmen (or close relatives if the marriage was lineage-endogamous) pulling a sled loaded with gifts of useful goods, such as walrus-hide rope, walrus skins, hunting tools, stores of food (meat, preserved plant food), ivory or baleen. With the receipt of the girl and the sledload of gifts, the marriage contract was sealed. No other formal ritualization occurred to mark the event.

The ensuing adjustment of the young bride to a new home environment was not always easy. Frictions either with the in-laws or with the new husband not uncommonly led to divorce. When it did occur, divorce, like the marriage itself, was not highly formalized. In fact, all that was required was for the woman either to leave or to be told to leave, returning to her original home and kinsmen. Although both marriage and divorce have changed with respect to Alaska state law, most features of the traditional pattern remained in the 1950s (see Shinen 1963).

• PARTNERSHIP One other type of institutionalized social bond—the trading and singing partner—is very important in Eskimo groups. On Saint Lawrence Island this fictive kin relation was known as *naŋsá·γaq*. The

Fig. 11. Roger Slwooko taking meat out of an underground storage cellar as part of his "groom work" under the direction of his future father-in-law, Moses Soongarook. Photograph by Charles C. Hughes, 1955.

principal form such a relationship took was that of an alliance between two nonclan mates, whereby they functioned as "brothers" in support of each other—sharing goods, giving support and hospitality, providing staged occasions of entertainment and singing matches, as well as sexual access to each other's wives. In the past, such "brother" relations were most often found between two men living on different parts of the island or with someone in Siberia; because of the distance, the other partner's residence would serve as a "home away from home." Once a relationship of this type had been agreed upon by two men, they would formalize it in a ritual that included participation by their wives, exchange of gifts, and the public sanction provided by many guests participating in the affair.

Subsistence

For as long as there is any evidence, the Saint Lawrence Islanders have relied chiefly upon the sea for food and for many of their tools to wrest a living from their severe environment (see Hughes 1960:101–226). The island lies astraddle migration routes for the Pacific walrus (*Odobenus divergens*) and several species of whales, the bowhead (*Balaena mysticetus*), finback (*Balaenoptera physalus*), and the gray or summer whale (*Eschrichtius robustus*). In addition, the spotted seal (*Phoca vitulina*), ringed seal (*P. hispida*), and the bearded seal or ugrug (*makłak*) (*Erignathus barbatus*) are found in considerable numbers at different times of the year, either along coasts or out among the ice floes. It has been the flesh of these animals, with occasional addition of polar bear, that has provided the great bulk of food.

270

Fig. 12. Woman splitting a female walrus hide. They were split longitudinally in a very exacting and laborious process and then sewn together for umiak covers or in earlier times for house roofs. Photograph by Otto Geist, 1928.

Fig. 13. Container. Since wood was not plentiful, food bowls were often made of strips of baleen, as here, softened, bent, and sewed together with thinner strips of baleen. The bottom is a fitted piece of wood. Height 18.5 cm; collected by E.W. Nelson on Saint Lawrence I., Alaska, 1877-1881.

Particularly important was the walrus. In the 1950s, for example, in a good year hunters of Gambell village would often kill up to 300 of these large animals, the males each weighing about a ton; in 1982, 1,000 were killed (Ronald L. Little, personal communication 1982). And it was not simply the flesh and internal organs that were used (practically everything except the spleen was eaten—flesh, heart, lung, kidney, stomach, intestines), but also the hide of the females (fig. 12), the ivory tusks, and the flippers (of baby walruses). If not eaten, the intestines were used to make waterproof parkas. Until the 1970s, when snowmobiles replaced dog teams for transportation, walrus meat was also important for dog food.

Other clothing was made of sealskins—parkas, boots, pants, mittens—and reindeer furs, obtained in trade from Siberia before the Saint Lawrence Islanders had their own herd. Tough ropes for whaling were made from baby walrus hide; before the coming of the whaling vessels the harpoon heads were of walrus ivory tipped with stone; and the floats used on both the whaling line and the harpoon line for walrus or seals were made of inflated sealskins. Finally, seal and walrus blubber gave heat and light, and walrus hides were used as covers for the hunting boats and one of the types of houses built by the Saint Lawrence Islanders. That house was the maŋtəɣaq, a structure of driftwood roofed with skin (fig. 14). It was adopted from Siberia during the nineteenth century as an alternative winter house to the traditional semisubterranean, sod-covered nəŋlu, which phased out of use in the late 1800s. Traditionally summer houses were skin tents. With the importation of

Fig. 14. Houses. left, Large house of the style adopted during the early to middle 19th century from the Siberian shore. The roof is made of walrus hides lashed down over driftwood logs and lumber sides. A drying rack keeps the furs and foodstuffs well out of the way of the dogs. Photograph by Samuel Call, 1898. right, Inside Soonogarook's summer house. Photograph by Riley D. Moore, 1912.

271

SAINT LAWRENCE ISLAND ESKIMO

lumber during the affluent 1920s, there began a shift to a single lumber structure used year round. By the 1950s this change was complete.

Although maritime mammals were the basis of life, the diet was supplemented by fishing in streams, through the winter ice, or from boats; by netting birds; and by the picking and preserving of many types of plants. The most commonly used plant was the *nuní·vak* (*Sedum rosea*, roseroot), the leaves of which were tightly packed and stored in a water-filled sealskin to preserve for the winter, when it was used as a succulent for ordinary meals and, in small portions, ceremonial offerings on ritual occasions.

Patterns of hunting took two basic forms. In one, an individual hunter would stalk seals and walruses at the ice edge where currents opened up breathing spaces in the ocean ice, or else would stand—sometimes for hours—at breathing holes on the stable ice. This type of hunting occurred only during the heart of the winter, when the ocean was so covered with ice that it was unfeasible to use boats. There were other times of the year also when boats were not used, such as early fall, when seals would come close to shore for feeding and could be netted or, after the introduction of the rifle, shot and their carcasses snared with a thrown hook.

But the chief mode of hunting, and the most productive, took the form of hunting walruses, seals, and especially whales with use of a boat. The most intensive hunting, in fact, occurred during the spring breakup of the ocean ice, at a time when walruses were beginning to work their way back north in huge herds, and whales were sporting about in the opening ocean. For the Saint Lawrence Islanders this was from March through May. After May, the walruses had mostly passed, the whales were rarely seen, and the seals could easily avoid being shot in the open sea.

The boats used were principally umiaks (*aŋyaq* 'boat', or *aŋyá·pik* 'authentic boat'), constructed of driftwood and covered with split female walrus hides. In recent historic times, at least, this was the boat mostly used by the Saint Lawrence Islanders. Data are unclear on how much the kayak (*qayaq*) was used. Certain archeological artifacts from the Old Bering Sea and Punuk cultures are interpreted as belonging to kayak frames (Collins 1937; Bandi 1969); and a drawing in a late nineteenth-century U.S. government publication depicts the Islanders using kayaks for harpooning walruses (Maynard 1898:pl. XXIII). But the data base for that drawing is not discussed and it is highly relevant that kayaks are not mentioned in other contemporary accounts of the Islanders (for example, Maynard 1898:305; Elliott 1898:163–164). Otto von Kotzebue, who visited in 1816, also does not mention them (quoted in Collins 1937:19–22), and Nelson (1899:218), in fact, denies their presence: "A smaller boat or canoe, called [kayak], is also used along the American coast and the adjacent islands; but I have never seen one among the people of the Siberian coast nor among the St. Lawrence Islanders." Corroborating Nelson is the lack of reference to kayaks among the twentieth-century Eskimos on the Siberian coast by Rubtsova (1954). Fieldwork in the 1950s also did not discover either their use or remembered use on Saint Lawrence Island (Hughes and Hughes

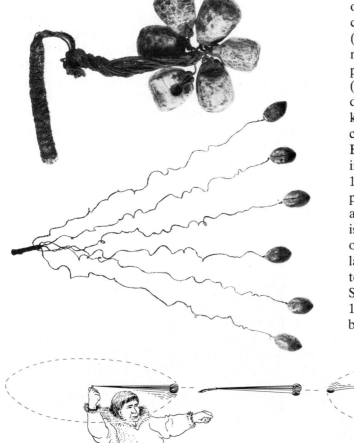

Smithsonian, Dept. of Anthr.: top, 63,263; bottom 63, 261.

Fig. 15. Bolas, used on land and sea to hunt birds in flight. These examples were probably used on land since their ivory weights would not float; those used over water had driftwood weights. The weights are tied to braided sinew lines that are bound together at the handle—a bundle of bird quills from which the feathers are now missing. When not in use the lines were looped up, but could be quickly straightened out; the weapon was whirled around the head and thrown at a passing flock (see drawing). The lines wrap around a bird and force it down. top, Length of handle 9.0 cm; bottom, 6.5 cm. Both collected by E.W. Nelson on Saint Lawrence I., Alaska, 1887-1881.

272

1954–1955). On the other hand, Doty (1900:203) noted that "kayaks are used in the summer and early fall by a few natives on lagoons."

In any case, the open umiak, powered by paddles—and for whaling, by sail—was the most efficient and productive hunting device for centuries (fig. 17), made even more effective when outboard gasoline motors were placed in it and high-powered rifles added to its weaponry after contact with the American mainland.

The makeup of the crew for each boat also served as a key example of the functioning of the principal structure in the social organization, the patrilineal clans, for crews were composed of some six to eight members drawn from the sons of a man (acting as captain), sometimes his brothers, and his brother's sons. This group was highly solidary, working together as a hunting unit and tied together with overriding bonds of kinship and clanship. Indeed, the core of the boat crew, companions on whom a person could rely through the many dangers of ice floe, freezing weather, and animal vengeance, was the group of patrilateral parallel cousins.

Religion

Saint Lawrence Island traditional religion was a variant of the beliefs and practices oriented to the supernatural world found elsewhere in Eskimo groups, although it showed strong similarities to that of the Chukchi on the Siberian shore (Bogoras 1904–1909, 2). It was, as elsewhere, directed primarily at the mollification and beseechment of animals to ensure continued good hunting, and at the warding off or cure of sickness. Its social forms were individual and personal (such as taboos and prescriptions placed upon the hunter) as well as collective and public (as in rituals of thanksgiving upon the killing of a whale). Finally, into a number of these religious contexts, both private and public, there came the person of the shaman (*aŋátkuq*) (Ackerman 1976), the vital link between man and the encompassing spiritual world (see Hughes 1960:261–265).

The spiritual world is best described as highly animistic. Most features of observable nature were thought to have indwelling spiritual essences, in some cases capable of taking diverse forms. Rocks, mountains, and other features of landscape were included under such a spiritual umbrella. But more important in the affairs of men were the souls of animals—seals, walruses, whales, polar bears—that were the quarry in the life-and-death encounters out on the sea. The souls of these animals

Fig. 16. Hunting mammals. top, Abraham Kaningok and Joe Slwooko shooting walruses on an ice floe. center, Jerry Tungyan, John Apongalook, and Leonard Apongalook cutting in a bowhead whale around the baleen. Empty heating oil drums were used as floats. bottom, Samuel Irrigoo with seal he has just killed along the shore ice. His gun case is strapped to his back. Photographs by Charles C. Hughes, 1955.

Smithsonian, NAA: 43458-D.

Fig. 17. Hunting umiak. The sail may be of several walrus skins sewed together. Photograph by an officer of the U.S. ship *Bear*, about 1888.

were conceived to be very much like those of human beings, subject to the same range of emotions and thoughts, of resentments and desires. Hence it was important to treat them with respect and dignity, such as offering a prayer to the soul of a seal before killing or lifting a cup of water to the animal's lips before the carcass was taken inside the house. Legend has it that such souls, if properly treated, would willingly release the body for use of man and harbor no grudge; indeed, they would return to villages at the bottom of the sea where they were thought to live, there to tell their fellows of the respectful manner in which they had been treated by men. A great many of the individual, private ritual prescriptions placed upon the hunter and upon his wife had to do with this goal of showing the animal that it was a valued cobeing with man in the scheme of things.

At times, such respect took the form of public ceremonies. Strangely (given its importance in the diet) there were no mass ceremonies in honor of the walrus, nor any to honor the seal comparable in magnitude and importance to those of the Alaskan mainland. The most dramatic ceremonies of this nature were performed for the polar bear and, especially, for the whale; they involved the ritual sacrifice of foodstuffs, singing and dancing in honor of the soul of the slain animal, and activities that functioned to unify the boat crew and the clan the crew belonged to (see Hughes 1960; Keim 1969).

• WHALE CEREMONIALISM Whaling was a focal concern, one that acted in the social realm as the principal arbiter of prestige and value, for the hunters considered to be the greatest and most powerful boat captains were those who had killed at least one whale. The supernatural ritualization of the whale's importance extended over several months, being marked by discrete events, either those of preparation for whaling or thankfulness

after a successful hunt. The main ritual event of the winter occurred from February through April, when each of the hunting boats conducted a ceremony in preparation for whaling. This was called the atrruk or chkwaek (meaning 'the sacrifice'), and its details were traditional for each clan with its one or several hunting boats. The ceremony was held only at the time of the full moon, and it was customary that no two boats could conduct the ritual on the same day.

Preparations for the ceremony were begun long in advance. Throughout the previous spring and summer, greens from the mountain had been collected and sorted in a special place; reindeer fat (gotten from Siberia in the days before the Saint Lawrence herd) was similarly set aside; tobacco traded from the Russians made up part of the sacrificial foods; and a final item usually was fish of some kind. All these foods were considered extremely holy and were placed in sealskin pokes on a meat rack, out of the reach of children and dogs.

When later in the winter the day for the ceremony finally arrived, the boat captain, his wife, his harpooner, and sometimes the rest of the crew took all the foods down from the meat rack and, working on several wooden platters, molded them into long low mounds. These were placed in the center of the room in the boat captain's house and covered with a walrus skin. Over the foods were hung the captain's hunting gear—such as his special visor, worn only on the hunt and symbolic of his status as well as presumably possessing an inherent power. The captain's bag of special hunting charms was also hung over the foods, which was a small sealskin container in which were placed various bits of flesh or organs of animals the captain had killed—whale, polar bear, walrus, or sometimes even a sea gull if there had been something unusual about its killing. The captain and the rest of the group then sat around the foods singing and praying through the night.

Long before sunrise all the participants went down to the shore, carrying the trays of food with them. There they lowered the boat into the water, all the crew got into the craft, and they paddled out a short distance from shore, where once more they uttered prayers. Then they returned to the shore to await the coming of sunrise. At dawn, the sacrifice of food began. The captain took a small portion from each platter, broke this into small bits, and threw these into the air, into the sea, and onto the land. As he did so, he recited prayers asking for a successful hunt during the coming season. Following the sacrificing of ritual foods, the crew ate what was left on the platters, and anything remaining after that was distributed to other people in the village.

If a boat was successful in killing a whale, a different sort of ceremony occurred. First, out on the water before the animal was towed back to land, the captain, raising his special paddle (another mark of status and, like the visor, embodying supernatural power), shouted

274

"Ho-ho-ho-ho." Then his boat circled the whale, stopping at the front and at the back once again while the captain shouted in the same way. The purpose of such shouting was to inform *kiyáγnəq*, the all-powerful, Supreme God (also known as *apa* 'grandfather'), that the whale had been captured and to thank him. Before towing the animal to the shore, the captain cut four small pieces of flesh from the tips of the tail and flukes and threw them back into the sea. This was again a mark of sacrifice to *kiyáγnəq* and to the animal spirits. During the towing to shore the captain twice shouted in his distinctive way.

With the animal finally tied up to the shore, the cutting began. While this was occurring, women of the captain's clan gathered to sing in front of his house, with the captain's wife wearing a special costume for the occasion, part of which was a band of white reindeer hair decorating her head.

From the cutting in of the whale, several pieces had been saved: bits of the flukes, eyes, and nose. Immediately after the cutting in was completed, the boat crew (along with the entire clan of the boat that had killed the whale) went to the captain's house, in front of which all these various parts of the animal were spread out on the ground in a diagrammatic form suggestive of the whale's body. A fire was built in front of the animal's nose, and then the captain's wife brought a pail of water containing small pieces of whale meat and *nuní·vak*. She offered a part of the water and *nuní·vak* to the whale, symbolically putting some into its mouth. Next she threw portions of the whale meat into the fire (in an act of feeding the ancestors). After this all the family walked around the parts of the whale and then on top of them.

Finally, all the pieces were taken into the captain's house and hung up over the fire for five days, while songs were chanted and stories told. No hunting was possible during this time, similar to the prohibition on hunting after the killing of a polar bear. At the end of the period, most of the parts of the animal were distributed among clan relatives and eaten. Parts not eaten were the mid-section of the tail, which was saved for a ceremony during the coming summer, and the eyeball of the whale, from which was made a black substance used for painting special ritual designs on the captain's paddle and on the bow of the boat.

• SPIRITS While it was the souls of animals that, in their incarnate form, sustained the Saint Lawrence Islanders in the empirical world, other spirits made them fearful and apprehensive. Aside from the spirits of observable natural phenomena (rocks, hills) and beyond the souls of animals, there were thought to be at least two other types of spirits. One of these types was sometimes beneficial to man, responding to an appeal for aid or special power (as in regard to the shaman's alliance with a spiritual helper). These were the *taγnśγa·t*

(*taγnśγaq* sg.), and they, like the second kind, could assume many forms, visible and invisible. The second aid or special power (as in regard to the shaman's always evil and maleficent toward man. They caused accidents, sickness, poor weather, loss of soul or of valuable objects, and all other manner of ill fortune. In the translation of the early missionaries these were known as 'devils', and however ethnocentric the term may be, in orientation it connotes the essential character of these spirits, who were said to be everywhere, but especially around the village, looking for the chance to create trouble and worry.

• SHAMANS When sickness or some other perplexing problem arose that did not respond to home solutions, the Saint Lawrence Islanders turned to a shaman for help. Shamans, most of whom were men, acquired their presumed powers and their special alliance with the spiritual world through a quest out on the tundra or in some other lonely, isolated place. After striking a bargain with one or more spirits—by which the shaman was given power in return for what could be called a token or symbolic part of the valuable goods he would receive from clients—the shaman set himself up in the business of divination, prophecy, diagnosis, and therapy. His approach included dreams, ventriloquism, sleight-of-hand artistry, and, no doubt, acute observational and inference skills (Hughes 1960).

In the case of sickness of the Saint Lawrence Islanders, three causes were believed paramount—loss of soul, intrusion of some malignant object or spirit, and breach of taboo. The shaman's task was to discover which cause or causes were operating, and then to bring about the conditions for health. If loss of soul was indicated, the shaman would conduct a seance—with darkened lights in the room crowded with relatives, beating of the walrus-stomach drum, singing in an archaic language—in which his own soul would depart his body to wander in search of the soul of the patient. If it was theft of soul, then through his power he would overcome the evil spirit that had done the deed. The shaman's soul would "return" from wandering the spiritual world, reenter his own body, and tell those in the room and the patient what he had done and what the patient should now do to get better. Usually this would include some directives for the patient's behavior—to abstain from certain food, or to wear a particular amulet, and the like—and sometimes, too, restrictions of similar nature were placed on the patient's family.

In his curative procedures the shaman also was adept at use of empirical medicine—giving emetics, applying poultices, staunching wounds—but he was no doubt careful never to let such common-sense techniques overshadow the definition of the situation he had created in the minds of the viewers, namely, that this was a religious, and hence dangerous, procedure, one in which he was the expert and not they.

275

For such expert aid he was, of course, paid, and paid well. The patient's family gave him walrus-hide rope, food, reindeer fat, and many other kinds of valuable goods. After the patient-oriented ceremony was over, the shaman then had to satisfy his own spiritual obligation to those agents that had helped him, by throwing into a fire small bits cut from each of the items he had been paid, uttering as he did so prayers of thanksgiving to his spirit-familiars, and prayers also to the supreme being *kiyáɣnəq*, thought to have ultimate control (however loose it was at times) over all affairs of men.

• CULTURAL PERSISTENCE The preceding descriptions of ritual and belief belong to a past time in the culture history of the Saint Lawrence Islanders. Yet a number of the dominant beliefs that structured the Saint Lawrence Islanders' view of the supernatural world still operate to some degree in the current scene: in attitudes toward animals; in vague, inchoate fears of spirits or retributive events of nature; and in an apperception of an unseen power that influences man's fate, his health, and his well-being. It is probable that only to some extent have these beliefs been eradicated by Christianity, which began to influence their lives when Presbyterian missionaries arrived in 1894, followed during the 1940s by another Christian denomination, the Seventh-Day Adventists. Both groups had been so successful that by the late 1950s there was only one person still avowedly and openly practicing the indigenous religion. For the rest, the social influences of American culture on the Alaska mainland were as profound in the area of religious practice as they were in most other spheres of life—esthetic, recreational, material-cultural, and ideological. The one area where the press of a dominant environment retains its impact upon social, psychological, and economic reality is hunting, representing perhaps the most dramatic continuity of Saint

Fig. 18. The Savoonga comedy dancers performing at the 1981 Alaska Federation of Natives convention in Anchorage.
Photograph by Bill Hess, Dec. 1981.

Lawrence Island Eskimo present with its past (see Hughes 1960, 1977; Burgess 1974).

Synonymy†

In the 1970s the Saint Lawrence Islanders applied the name Sivuqaq (*sivú·qaq*) to both the entire island and the town of Gambell, and the derived form *sivú·qaxMi·t* could mean either 'Saint Lawrence Islanders' or 'Gambellites' (Krauss 1975a:43, 68; Michael E. Krauss, communication to editors 1982).

The meaning of this name and its original application are uncertain, and the historical sources and islanders interviewed in 1955 appear to vary on the scope of the terms. From a man who had lived on the island before 1820 Khromchenko recorded its name as Chuakak. Kotzebue learned Tschibocki as the name of the island from the people he met in the southwest and found that those in the northwest likewise called themselves Tschibocko, but he later understood from people on the east that they applied the name Tschibocka to the western part and Kealegack (the same as the settlement name *kiyá·liɣaq*) to the east (Collins 1937:20–22). These and other early spellings, like Chibukak and Chebukak, render *sivú·qaq* and reflect the nineteenth-century pronunciation [čiβó·qaq], before the shift of [č] (recorded as late as 1901) to s (Krauss 1975a:45). Moore (1923) claims that in 1922 the group name (Sivokakhmeit) was used for the inhabitants of Gambell, but in 1955, although one informant used Sivuqaq for the entire island, others did not commonly use the group name to refer even to all the people just in Gambell, but rather only to some of them. This can be understood as reflecting the importance of clan groupings and clan identification in the traditional social structure.

Part of the difficulty in fixing a single term for the Saint Lawrence Islanders may be the assumption by outsiders that geographic space must be identical with social psychological reality. In view of Saint Lawrence Island cultural history, this clearly is not so. Shifting frames of social affiliation and identification have overlain the dispersion and consolidation of groups, such that at only one point in recent history might it have been possible to characterize the population of the island by the one term—when (as Moore noted in 1912) all the population was, in fact, centered in Gambell village as the basic point of residence.

The Chukchi name of Saint Lawrence Island has been recorded as Eiwugi-nu, 1792 (Merck 1980:194), also Eivugen, E-oo-vogen, Eivoogiena (Orth 1967:826–827), and eiwhue´n, and the Chukchi name for the people has been given as eiwhue´ lɪt; in the form Eiwhuelit this has been used as the English name for the islanders in

†This synonymy was written by Charles C. Hughes and Ives Goddard.

some sources (Hodge 1907–1910, 1:419; U.S. Federal Field Committee for Development Planning in Alaska 1968:107). There is evidence that this term traditionally designated only one of the groups living in Gambell, the (now small) *uɣá·li·t* clan whose ancestors founded and therefore "own" the village (Collins 1937:18; Moore 1923; Hughes 1960).

The claim that the Saint Lawrence Islanders and the Chaplinski-speaking Siberian Eskimos called themselves Massinga 'good men' (Doty 1900) appears to be based on a misunderstanding of a polite term of address derived from Chukchi (Michael E. Krauss, communication to editors 1982).

Hodge (1907–1910, 1:419) gives a few other names.

Sources

An excellent review of the relevant literature up to the mid-1930s is in Collins (1937), which includes excerpts from early explorers such as Semën Dezhnev and Otto von Kotzebue. An extensive review, with illustrations, of the material culture of the nineteenth century is given by Nelson (1899), which is skimpy on social organization. Other observations from the late nineteenth century are those of Hooper (1881) and Muir (1917); and in the renowned study of the Chukchis by Bogoras (1904–1909), there are numerous comments about the Islanders. Materials also exist in government reports (for instance, Maynard 1898; Elliott 1898). An excellent source of information (sometimes erroneous, sometimes quite accurate) is the annual reports on the introduction of domestic reindeer into Alaska (U.S. Bureau of Education 1896–1905). Of particular interest in that source are statements by Gambell (1898) and a lengthy "ethnographic" report by his successor, Doty (1900). Several photographs of interest are also found in these volumes.

The earliest formal "ethnological" account of the Saint Lawrence Islanders is that of Moore (1923), based on data gathered in 1912. Basic archeological monographs contain much valuable information on contemporary cultural patterns as well (Collins 1937; Geist and Rainey 1936). Hughes (1960) provides a comprehensive ethnography and study of sociocultural change through the middle 1950s; and J. M. Hughes (1960) analyzes mental health data from the same field study. Corroborative material on marriage is found in Shinen (1963). A brief overview of the archeology and contemporary culture of the island, focusing especially on Savoonga, is provided by Ackerman (1976), which speaks of economic and sociopolitical developments up to the middle 1970s. A collection of myths has been published by Silook (1976). Ethnobotany is described by Young and Hall (1969). Finally, a novelistic account of several nine-

teenth-century historical events in the life of the Saint Lawrence Islanders based upon the field notes of Otto Geist is found in Murie (1977).

Burgess (1974) provides a report on resource utilization of the Islanders, including a detailed compilation of documentary and archival sources relating to the nineteenth century history of the island. Two other dissertations dealing with the people of the Island—both in biological anthropology—have been completed (Byard 1980; Heathcote 1982). A brief grammar of the language has been produced by Jacobson (1977).

Various reports since the 1960s relate to aspects of planning for the political, social, and economic changes that would be affecting Eskimo populations. The comprehensive review of the situation of Alaska natives (U.S. Federal Field Committee for Development Planning in Alaska 1968) is one such example. Others are that by Ellana (1980), a background document relating to the sociocultural impacts of petroleum exploration in the Bering Sea–Norton Sound area, and the two reports produced by the U.S. Bureau of Indian Affairs (1977, 1977a) intended as resource documents for the people of Gambell and Savoonga as they plan their economic futures. See Little and Robbins (1982).

Unpublished data exist in the diaries, letters, and reports written by missionaries and school teachers, for example, those of Dr. E.O. Campbell, missionary from 1901 to 1911. Reputedly the original diary—as well as other such diaries and reports—were sent to the Bureau of Indian Affairs office in Juneau; undoubtedly there also exist in that office many other types of primary data in the form of reports and memoranda. The papers of Sheldon Jackson are available in the Presbyterian Historical Society, Philadelphia.

A.H. Leighton and D.C. Leighton conducted research on Saint Lawrence in 1940. Their field notes on life histories are deposited in the archives of the University of Alaska, Fairbanks.

Popular or semipopular accounts date from Gambell's posthumously published article (Stephens 1900) and include articles appearing in *Alaskan Sportsman* through the years, occasionally in magazines such as *Life,* and in Alaska newspapers. In the 1960s documentary films were made that show aspects of Saint Lawrence Island life and people (*At The Time of Whaling* and *On the Spring Ice,* available from Documentary Educational Resources, Inc., Somerville, Massachusetts). A biography of one of the pioneers in Saint Lawrence Island archeological and cultural research, Otto Wilhelm Geist, contains some useful and previously unpublished cultural data, especially on ceremonies that were not being performed in the 1950s (Keim 1969). It also has excellent photographs showing people, housing and clothing styles, graves, hunting scenes, and other views from the 1920s and 1930s.

North Alaska Eskimo: Introduction

ROBERT F. SPENCER

Environment and Territory

Each of the sections treating the various peoples of north Alaska describes in some detail the physiographic, climatic, and related natural features characteristic of the regions they inhabit. This zone of Eskimo culture falls in the main north of the Arctic Circle and reflects generally an arctic tundra and maritime configuration both in land form and native culture. North Alaska is marginal both geographically and culturally.

The area is definable geographically because of the presence of the Brooks Range, which lies south of the tundra. These glaciated mountains, forested on the southside approaches to the Yukon valley, bare and denuded across their northern divide, form a natural barrier to north-south movement. They run east and west virtually from the sea at the Alaska-Canada border, reaching peaks of 8,000 feet, and gradually taper downward in elevation in the west. On the western side, the Brooks Range bifurcates to form the DeLong and Baird mountains, giving rise to spurs, such as the Waring Range east of Kotzebue Sound and the Bendeleben Mountains in the Seward Peninsula. The higher segments of the mountains to the east have some natural passes, such as the Chandalar and Anaktuvuk, while in the west the river systems of the Noatak, Kobuk, and Selawik provide some avenues of access to the interior (Kachadoorian 1966).

Still, in general, north Alaska is a natural cul-de-sac. Mountain ranges define the southern limits of the area, the sea to the west and north. On the maritime side, the north Alaskan focus begins with the Bering Strait with its Diomede Islands, proceeds along the north coast of the Seward Peninsula, and ultimately edges the Alaskan coasts from Kotzebue Sound to Point Hope and beyond to the northernmost limit at Point Barrow. Delineation of the eastern boundary of North Alaska Eskimo must be arbitrary, since Mackenzie Delta Eskimo probably also hunted and certainly traveled for trade along the same coast.

A result of the geographic position of the area was the creation of a cultural isolate, not necessarily a wholly distinctive brand of Eskimo culture, but one suggesting variations of degree as southern Alaska is considered or when compared with the Eskimo groups farther to the east. Geographic and cultural positions combine in the area to produce a series of subphrasings of basic Eskimo patterns.

Admittedly, a basic problem exists in respect to the definition of the southern limits of the north Alaskan Eskimo cultural zone. Here were people who might cover extensive areas in their pursuit of economic goals. The Brooks Range, it is true, provided a southern boundary for most Alaska Eskimo, but hunting of mountain sheep and caribou drew hunting groups through the passes. Similarly, in the general Kotzebue Sound area and on the Seward Peninsula, the same drift toward the south might apply. The southern boundaries of ethnic distribution are thus clouded. However, at the same time, the networks of relationship and economic activity, coupled with familiarity of terrain, served to locate the northern peoples with some exactness. The zones of north Alaska culture can thus be defined not by any exact territorial boundaries but rather by the cultural preoccupations and economic focuses of the peoples participating in it (Larsen 1952, 1973).

A tundra configuration marks the interior regions to the north of the ranges. The east-west mountains shade off into a foothill province, one inhabited by various Eskimo groups in precontact times. This in turn gives way to the coastal plain, a section ranging from 30 to 90 miles in width in the far north of Alaska. The Noatak system provides the western drainage, while the Colville and its tributaries becomes the major river pattern of the tundra interior. The tundra itself is characterized by an extremely flat surface with summer bogs, but frozen 9 to 10 months of the year, in short, an area marked by tundra landform and vegetation, as well as by permafrost (Allen and Weedfall 1966). Although the tundra area of the arctic slope was important for hunting, for temporary camps such as at fishing stations, it was not primarily a focus of human habitation. On the northern side, these camps were found chiefly at the foothill edge, occasionally along the rivers, and on the coasts. Toward the west, in the Noatak and Kobuk drainages, human groups at times moved into the mountains for hunting and occasional summer gathering (Giddings 1952a:3–4, 64).

Like Eskimo cultures elsewhere, the basic subsistence level of north Alaska was dependent on hunting. Vegetal resources were virtually ignored (Johnson et al. 1966). An exceedingly rich array of fauna characterizes the area. There was, to be sure, local variation in hunting pattern—seasonal differences in activity—but the basic hunting focus remained primary. Land as against sea faunal distributions played an important role in the development of areal culture patterns. Caribou, fur-bearing predators, brown bears, an occasional mountain sheep, ptarmigan, various rodents, and freshwater fishes may be contrasted with the sea mammal inventory of whales (both bowhead and beluga), walrus, polar bear, and the many species and varieties of seals, as well as of wildfowl (Spencer 1959:23–38).

In summary, the natural area, despite long, cold winters and short summers, intense winds, basic tundra landscape and permafrost, proved wholly adequate for human adaptation and habitation. For all groups in the area there were occasional periods of want and sometimes of starvation; however, these were an exception to the prevailing adequacy of the environment for human adjustment.

Subsistence

Faunal range, land form, and access to the sea or foothill province played significant parts in the human balance in north Alaska. Specialized adaptations to the circumstances of hunting and selection of game created some sharply defined differences in basic mode of life among the groups in the area. Perhaps the most dramatic of the Eskimo cultures in Alaska were those developed by the peoples from the Bering Strait up to Point Barrow, where whaling became an economic mainstay and was involved in turn with social and ceremonial institutions. Yet whaling appeared only at certain sites favorable to such hunting along the northern coasts. Elsewhere the adaptation differed, since there were coastal communities not immediately involved in the whaling complex. Inland, the focus centered on the caribou, with associated communal drives at campsites determined by the spring and fall caribou movements (Lent 1966).

The human ecological pattern for the north Alaskan culture area thus falls into a twofold arrangement: a maritime focus and an inland focus.

The maritime focus primarily means whaling communities, such as those at Point Barrow, Point Hope, Cape Prince of Wales, and the Diomede Islands. A secondary configuration of maritime life appears in areas south of Point Barrow, with communities such as Wainwright, Utukok, and Point Lay, including various groups and communities in Kotzebue Sound and the north edge of the Seward Peninsula. For these groups, while sea mammal hunting figured prominently, there was no adjacent whaling. Yet hunting mobility in the area was

not unknown; men from the maritime groups where whaling appeared might join whalers at coastal centers for the spring hunt (Spencer 1972).

As for the inland focus, what the whale was to the northwestern Alaskan coasts, the caribou was to the peoples of the interior. Clearly, a very different kind of adjustment was necessary for the inland peoples. A community centered on whaling as the keystone of annual activities of subsistence tended toward a degree of permanence; because of the migratory nature of the caribou, the interior peoples tended toward much more annual and seasonal movement (Larsen and Rainey 1948).

The result was a sharp contrast in human ecological and subsistence mode. So far as language and basic cultural orientations were concerned, there seem to have been no significant differences. All groups in the area spoke Inupiaq.* Localisms and some dialectal difference appeared, but there was mutual intelligibility across the area. Similarly, the basic patterns of kinship organization, associations, leadership, religion and world view ran fairly consistently across the entire area. It can be seen that if the whale was a center of ritual and ceremonial activity among the maritime villages that practiced whaling, the interior peoples might accord the same ritual patterns to their economic mainstay, the caribou (Spencer 1959:331–357).

These ecological differences have been conceptualized by the native peoples themselves. This is the distinction between the Taġiuġmiut (*taɣiuɣmiut*)—tareumiut in Spencer (1959); tareormiut in Larsen (1973)—and the Nunamiut (*nunamiut*) (Gubser 1965). The former refers to the peoples resident on the coasts, groups adapted to whaling and other sea mammal hunting. The latter term, 'people of the land', is reserved for the caribou-hunting inhabitants of the interior regions north of the mountain ranges. The way in which these two terms have been employed in ethnographic description

---

*The phonemes of Inupiaq Eskimo are: (plain voiceless stops and affricate) p, t, č, k, q, ʔ; (voiceless fricatives) s, x, x̣, h; (voiced or unmarked fricatives) v, γ, ɣ̇; (nasals) m, n, nʸ, ŋ; (voiced laterals) l, lʸ; (voiceless laterals) ł, łʸ; (voiced retroflex) ř ([z] or [ɹ]); (voiceless retroflex) Ř ([ṣ] or [ṛ]); (semivowel) y; (short vowels) i, a, u; (long vowels) iˑ, aˑ, uˑ. In a cluster with a voiceless consonant v is devoiced to [f] or [ɸ], in the latter case perhaps to be taken as a continuant allophone of p. The rules of consonant assimilation, which affect fricativization, devoicing, and nasalization, differ somewhat from dialect to dialect. Some dialects lack some of the phonemes listed.

In the practical orthography used by the Alaska Native Language Center and others the Inupiaq phonemes are written as follows: p, t, ch/ṭ, k, q, '; s, kh/k, qh/q/h, h; v, g, ġ; m, n, ñ, ŋ; l, ḷ; ł, ḷ̣; r, sr; y; i, a, u; ii, aa, uu.

Information on Inupiaq phonology has been taken from Webster and Zibell (1970:ix–xii), MacLean (1980:xvii–xx), and Kaplan (1981:19–34). The transcriptions of Inupiaq words used in the *Handbook* were obtained from these sources and from James Nageak (communication to the editors 1973) and Lawrence A. Kaplan (communication to the editors 1982).

280

top left, U. of Alaska Arch., Fairbanks: Call Coll., A66-10-328; top right, Field Mus., Chicago: 17013; Glenbow-Alberta Inst., Calgary, Alta.: center left, NC-1-597, center right, NC-1-547; bottom, Denver Mus. of Nat. Hist., Colo.: Bailey Coll., BA 21-080A; THIS PAGE, Anchorage Histl. and Fine Arts Mus., Alaska: 72.115.3.

Fig. 1. Chukchi herdsmen from Siberia were brought to Alaska with the reindeer herds in 1891–1892 at the suggestion of Sheldon Jackson, a Presbyterian missionary, and with the help of Capt. Michael A. Healy of the U.S. Revenue Marine Service. Herds were introduced on the Aleutians in 1891, at Teller on the Seward Peninsula in 1892, at Kotzebue in 1901, and at Kivalina and Deering in 1905. In addition to their proposed use as food, to replace depleted native subsistence sources, Jackson hoped they would replace dogs for local sled transportation. The Chukchi herdsmen were also probably helpful in introducing items of material culture (reindeer collars, Siberian-style sleds and whips) associated with the reindeer transport they knew in Siberia. Herds were, at first, frequently owned by non-Eskimos, especially individuals at the missions. The Lapps who were brought in to teach herding practices (after the Chukchi proved unsatisfactory) also became important herd owners. By 1918, however, ownership was about 69% Eskimo and 23% Lapp. Then, after 1918, the reindeer industry gradually became dominated by companies, such as the Lomen Brothers, who owned trading posts and transport as well as stock. Their monopoly continued until the Reindeer Act of 1937, which restricted the holdings of domesticated reindeer to Natives. The industry by that time had declined in importance. In 1976, the NANA Regional Corp. took up reindeering again as a hedge against the decline of other subsistence sources. top left, Siberian herdsman with rope and whip. Photograph by Samuel J. Call, 1891–1892. top right, Alaska Eskimo herdsmen at Port Clarence, Seward Peninsula, Alaska. The man on far right may be Miner W. Bruce, superintendent of the Teller Reindeer Station, 1892–1893. Photographed about 1892–1893. center left, Alaska Eskimo with reindeer harnessed as sled transport. The sled is an Alaska built-up type. center right, Harnessed reindeer with decorated harness blanket. The Eskimo holds a whip. center right and left, Photographed by Lomen Brothers, 1908–1915. bottom, North Alaska Coast Eskimos at reindeer round-up using ice slab corrals. This was done in late autumn when the herdsmen counted and earmarked the herd (A.M. Bailey 1971:107). Photograph by Alfred M. Bailey, Wainwright, 1921. THIS PAGE, Annual fall corralling of reindeer by Bering Strait Eskimos of Shishmaref, Seward Peninsula. India ink on bleached hide by George Ahgupuk of Shishmaref, about 1942.

has been criticized by Burch (1976a,1980), quite justifiably, since the implication is one of two highly contrasting modes of life.

There is, it is true, some fairly sharp contrast especially in economic aspects and in material culture. But the distinction is one of shading rather than one of a precise boundary of difference (Burch 1976a, 1980; Spencer 1959:124–146). Local groups, bands, demes, or communities were fairly well fixed so far as geographic location, but mobility of persons and groups between settled areas and across an ecological boundary could and did occur. From the interior, people at times made their way to the sea and were drawn into maritime hunting. The reverse was equally true. Not that there was any wholesale mobility at any time; individuals and families tended to remain in the areas most familiar to them, as well as in the kind of activity reflecting specialization. However, groups did expand and contract depending on the availability of resources and the presence of demonstrable social ties. Even if strangers were suspect and feuds not uncommon, networks of social relations could cross ecological boundaries. This is why it is difficult to delineate with exactness the names and locations of groups. In Eskimo usage, these applied to place; the personnel associated with a place could change and often did (cf. Burch 1976a). The shading from one mode of subsistence to another can be demonstrated not only in the Kotzebue Sound region but also at any point where rivers provided access to the sea or offered an avenue inland. Nunamiut came to the sea via the

281

Kuk, Utukok, and Noatak-Kobuk-Selawik rivers. The result is a blurring and it is only the whaling communities that stand out with precision.

But if the whaling focus is set against the caribou concentration, the two ecological systems appear to have some validity in fact. The mutual interdependence of the two systems deserves comment when it is considered that trade played so significant a part in the aboriginal cultures (Spencer 1959:198–209). Each focus had its own special products, much in demand by the other. Pokes of sea mammal oil were traded for caribou skins, meaning that food and fuel from the coasts were brought inland while caribou skins for clothing and bedding were required on the coastal side. The result was a set of balanced and regularized reciprocities in which the two ecological systems stand side by side and in which patterns of social interaction could develop (Burch 1970a).

Precontact north Alaska, having created such a balance, had clearly depended on it for a considerable period of time (cf. Larsen and Rainey 1948; Larsen 1952). A question is sometimes raised as to the temporal priority of one system as against the other (cf. Larsen 1973). If archeological evidence is considered for the general range of Eskimo cultures, the stress appears to lie on a maritime adjustment, not necessarily of whaling, but rather of adaptations to seal hunting by netting and harpooning. The suggestion is of a stress on individualized rather than on elaborately organized group activity. Group patterns, it is true, rise from this base; this is particularly true in north Alaska where the whaling crew of the Taġiuġmiut can be contrasted with the caribou drive of the interior peoples. Given a basic pattern of sea mammal hunting without whales, it may be suggested that the whaling focus on the one hand represents a specialization of an initial coastal and maritime focus. Intensive inland caribou hunting, by the same reasoning, appears to represent yet another specialized development.

That these were well founded in north Alaska there can be no doubt even if the Nunamiut, with the exception of a few small bands that remain in the 1980s, are gone. In the precontact period there seems adequate evidence that the inland people outnumbered those settled on the coasts (Spencer 1959:19). The sea hunters, at least those concentrating on the whale and living in settlements in which whales could be taken, represent, if anything, a minority of population. The social relations, however, become somewhat clouded at this point. Aside from the whaling "captain," the organizer and leader of a hunting expedition was a specialist; so also was the skilled harpooner he was required to enlist. Other men were variously recuited, and they could derive from both inland and maritime locations. Specializations and skills did tend to keep individuals within their respective provinces. Those who whaled, for example, tended to laugh at "landlubbers" and their fear of the open sea. A high degree of skill was also required for a successful caribou drive where wholesale slaughtering was the rule and vast quantities of meat were taken. Yet there was overlapping and the presence of groups that, like some of the Eskimo farther east, moved back and forth from sea to land (Spencer 1972).

The ecology of north Alaska, in summary, suggests variability rather than firm lines of distinction. This is why it is difficult to define "tribes" as such (but see Burch 1980). It is more reasonable, considering the circumstances of life, to define the human components in terms of their particularized adaptations.

The Cultural Position of North Alaska

The area under consideration appears to represent a basic configuration of Eskimo culture with degrees of economic specialization. The area is marginal both culturally and geographically. Geographic marginality is

top, U. of Calif., Lowie Mus., Berkeley: 2–149; bottom, Smithsonian, Dept. of Anthr: 260,110.
Fig. 2. Reindeer herders. The non-Eskimo herders brought to Alaska in connection with the reindeer project were one subject of the ivory carver. top, Engraved tusk with scene depicting Chukchi men (one in sled and the other standing) with herd of reindeer. bottom, Tool with engraving showing Lapp herders, recognizable by their 4-cornered hats. Length 26.5 cm, collected at Norton Sound, Alaska, before 1910. bottom, length 49.8 cm, collected by Charles L. Hall, probably at or near Port Clarence, Alaska, before 1894.

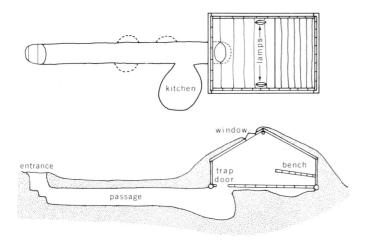
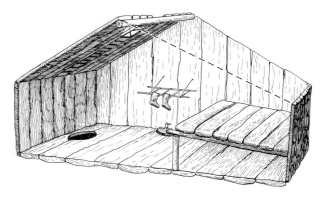

after Murdoch 1892:72-74 with alterations based on the *Utgiagvik Archaeology Project, North Slope Borough* published at the State University of New York at Binghamton.

Fig. 3. Cross section and plan of a winter house at Point Barrow, Alaska. The entrance is a vertical shaft about 6 feet deep with wood steps leading to a dark, icy passage about 25 feet long and about 4 feet wide and high with roof and walls supported by whalebone. Various storage recesses and the kitchen, with its wooden roof containing a central smoke hole, open off the passageway. The passage ends in a circular trapdoor in the floor of the living room. The living area is generally 12–14 feet long and 8–10 feet wide and is constructed of thick planks of driftwood that have been dressed smooth and fitted together. The window is covered by a translucent membrane of sewed seal gut, and there is a ventilation hole between the window and the ridgepole. A sloping platform about 5 feet wide and 30 inches high runs across the length of the room opposite the entrance and serves as a sleeping and lounging place. Oil lamps and suspended racks for drying clothing are located at the 2 end walls. Usually 2 families occupy a house, with each wife occupying an end of the room with a lamp.

clear by virtue of the isolation of the region. Considering, however, that the Thule movement of Eskimos fanned out across the Arctic from a north Alaskan center, and that there are the specializations of inland and maritime hunting, it may be questioned whether the area does represent an attenuated phrasing (cf. Collins 1951).

It does when compared to the Alaskan groups farther to the south. As Lantis (1947:114–115) points out, outside the Bering Sea, ceremonials, life cycle rites, rituals, public festivals, art forms, and many other features tend to be less elaborate. Wales, it is clear, was more elaborate in its attention to public ceremony than was either Point Hope or Barrow, and at that, Point Hope was more complex in such forms than were the Barrow villages. To put the matter another way, north Alaska, coastal and inland, looks more like the Thule configuration despite its specializations.

Resemblances to other Eskimo come out in aspects of both material and social culture. Like Eskimo generally, north Alaska shares in a host of "circumpolar" traits, elements of culture that reflect affinities not only to the American arctic but also to the Eurasiatic land mass. Harpoon types, the lamp, dog traction, tanning methods and clothing manufacture, clothing styles, world view and religious concepts, including shamanism, are elements in a vast array of circumpolar traits (Bogoras 1929). The phrasing of such historically derived elements gives north Alaska some distinctness, it is true, since local modifications occur. The house types, for example, however much they conform, as on the coasts, to a semisubterranean trans-Bering complex, possess certain distinctive attributes. The domed snow lodge does not appear in north Alaska. Within the area, there were housing variations as between the inland and coastal groups (Spencer 1959:43–61; Giddings 1952a:11–34).

On the social side, north Alaska is suggestive of Eskimo to the east rather than those to the south and west. The stress on kinship is strong and the structure is one of bilateral extensions with a variation on the theme of an "Eskimo" kinship terminology, that is, merging lineal relationships, distinguishing siblings from cousins (Lantis 1947; Burch 1976a). This pattern contrasts both in structure and in terminology with the unilineal patterns found in the south of Alaska, the Bering Sea, and possibly the Aleutians. It is a southern focus of Alaska Eskimo culture that appears to have been making an imprint farther north at the time of contact. The virile cultures of the Northwest Coast, in southeast Alaska and British Columbia, unquestionably made their mark on the development of southern Alaska and Bering Sea cultures. A marginal reflection of such influence is seen in the growing stress on wealth that the precontact north Alaskan groups exhibit. Many of the public ceremonies are gone by the time one reaches the north. The one that appears to have rooted itself with considerable success, in both coastal and inland groups, was the Messenger Feast, an institution strongly reminiscent of the potlatch of southeastern Alaska (Spencer 1959:210–228). At the time of contact, the *283* native cultures were in a state of change. Left alone, they may have received further stimuli from southern sources.

Yet another element that shows southern influences and is not characteristic of groups to the east is the men's house, the focus of hunting groups and the limited public ceremonials of the area. Along with the Messenger Feast and the wealth emphasis, this institution was growing at the time of contact. Owned by men of skill and substance, the kashim (*qařγi*) appears to take on the aspect of a leader's or chief's house (Oswalt 1967:87). Political organization as such was not a char-

acteristic of Eskimo culture; both legal and political controls were informal and kin-centered. But in north Alaska, as a result of an incipient system of prestige wealth, chieftainship as a political factor may have been in process of development (Spencer 1972).

The summation of north Alaska cultures thus points to a Thule-like configuration in which the economic specializations of whaling as against caribou concentration arose, with the retention of a basic sea mammal and caribou hunting focus, and the superimposition of extraneous elements such as wealth and incipient chieftainship.

Bering Strait Eskimo

DOROTHY JEAN RAY

Territory and Environment

Tribes included in the Bering Strait area occupied the eastern shores of Norton Sound as far south as Pastolik, all the islands offshore and in the strait, and all of Seward Peninsula with the exception of its northeast corner.

Compare these boundaries with those in "North Alaska Eskimo: Introduction" and "Southwest Alaska Eskimo: Introduction," this volume. In terms of economic emphases and because of other cultural factors resulting from special historical circumstances, the groups described in this chapter actually are quite distinct from groups to the north or south. They are grouped in this volume with neighbors to the north because most of the Bering Strait Eskimo were Inupiaq speakers. With a few exceptions, the ethnographic data herein refer to the early and mid-nineteenth century.

The Bering Strait tribes occupied almost 26,000 square miles, 49 square miles of which lie north of the Arctic Circle (fig. 1). The natural environment has changed little since the nineteenth century: it is a mostly rolling and flat, treeless tundra, but there are several mountain ranges and extensive pond and lagoon areas. Large stands of spruce and birch forests extend from Golovin to Unalakleet. The islands are treeless and rocky.

Nome has an average yearly precipitation of 17.88 inches and an average July temperature of 54.6°F. It has a January maximum average of 11.5°F and a minimum average of −2.7°F. Wales is colder and windier throughout the year, and Unalakleet, warmer. Temperatures in the interior of Seward Peninsula repeatedly reach 80°F with correspondingly cold winters. Severe storms are common along all the coast in October and November.

The pack ice arrives in October and leaves in June, but little intercontinental travel was undertaken on foot or by dogsled because the ice in the strait was constantly churning and shifting. Consequently, the umiak, or skin boat, was the traditional means of communication across the strait.

Culture

Social and Political Organization

• THE TRIBE, OR LOCAL GROUP During the nineteenth century there were 22 autonomous groups that may be called tribes,* each associated with a major village and exclusively occupied territory. English names are used here because in the 1970s most tribes continued to occupy traditional areas, using at the same time English names instead of Eskimo.

Maps of this area have customarily shown four "tribal" divisions, which were originally presented by Ivan Petroff (in U.S. Census Office 1884:125–126) as the Kingigumute, Kaviagmute, Mahlemute, and Oonaligmute. The first two were names for specific tribes, the people of Wales (Inupiaq *kiŋiɣin*) and of Kauwerak (*qaviař̆aq*, east of Teller), who occupied much less territory than ascribed to them by Petroff, but the last two were general terms, Inupiaq *malimiut* (see the synonymy in "Kotzebue Sound Eskimo," this vol.; Zagoskin 1967:103, 124, 291) and *unalliɣmiut* or *unaliq* (Yupik *uná·liq*), applied to the original Yupik-speaking inhabitants of Norton Sound.

Both Inupiaq and Yupik varieties of Eskimo were found in the Bering Strait area.† The Unaliq (or Unaluk) subdialect of Central Alaskan Yupik was spoken on Norton Sound between Pastolik and Solomon, with a separate Qiimiut subvariety in the Pastolik area itself. The Malimiut, who spoke an Inupiaq dialect, lived on the south shore of Kotzebue Sound between the eastern boundary of the Goodhope tribe and the eastern boundary of Buckland, and included the Deering and Buckland tribes (Kangiġmiut and Pitaġmiut in "Kotzebue Sound Eskimo," this vol.) and, after a southward migration, on eastern Norton Sound. The remaining tribes spoke related Inupiaq dialects that differed considerably from Malimiut.

A tribe consisted of people with a common language and culture living within well-defined boundaries recognized by themselves and contiguous tribes. A tribal territory usually included a large river and all the land

---

*The usage of "tribe" in this chapter appears to follow that employed by Nelson (1899) and differs from that found in other parts of the volume. For instance, it refers to much smaller populations than those of the Copper, Netsilik, and Iglulik Eskimo tribes (see "Central Eskimo: Introduction," this vol.).—Volume Editor.

†For the orthographies used to write Inupiaq and Yupik words, see the footnotes in "North Alaska Eskimo: Introduction" and "Southwest Alaska Eskimo: Introduction" (this vol.). The phonemic spelling of Eskimo words was furnished by Lawrence D. Kaplan, Steven Jacobson, and Edna MacLean, and Steven Jacobson supplied the information on the Qiimiut subdialect (communications to editors 1982).

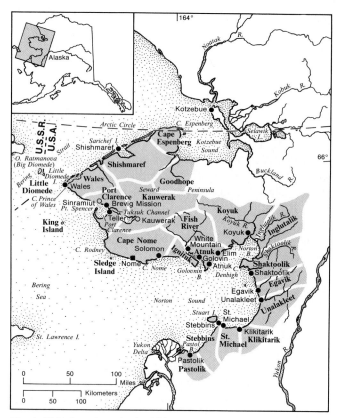

Fig. 1. Tribal territory in the 19th century.

drained by its tributaries, but several islands and coastal areas like Wales were autonomous units. The principal settlement was a winter village whose site name with the addition of *-miut* 'people of' lent its name to the tribe. Several smaller winter villages and numerous summer fishing campsites were also included.

• SETTLEMENT AND HOUSEHOLD PATTERNS With the exception of Kauwerak and Fish River Village, the principal settlement of a tribal group was located on the ocean, if possible on or near a high point of land for scouting sea mammals. The size of winter villages ranged from one to more than 60 houses, as in Wales (Trollope 1854; Jackson 1895:97). In summer, the residents dispersed in family groups to their accustomed fishing sites along the ocean or on the river, usually one family to a site.

The basic social unit was the household that occupied a separate dwelling. The household might consist of the wife and husband and one or two children or possibly a number of other relatives. A one-dwelling settlement sometimes had as many as 27 persons under one roof (Jacobsen 1884:240–241). In the larger villages, related households often lived in the same area of the village on patrilineally inherited plots near a structure called the kashim (Yupik *qazɣiq*; Inupiaq *qařɣi*).

• LEADERSHIP, THE KASHIM, AND LAW Each village had one or more chiefs (umialiks) for each kashim or local group. These men were members of politically

effective factions, and on King Island, were synonymous with a strong umiak captain and his crew. The focal point of the community was the kashim that served as political and social center, men's workroom, and guest house (fig. 2). A boy's education centered in the kashim, but a girl's in the home. Wales had four kashims and King Island, three, but all other villages had only one. Little Diomede had several kashim organizations that met in homes. Family areas in the kashim were inherited, and its continuance and upkeep were the chief's responsibility (Ray 1967a:377–379, 1972a). On King Island, the membership of each kashim came from all factions but was dominated by the captain of only one (Bogojavlensky 1969:175). Although the original meaning of Inupiaq *umialik* is 'umiak captain', not every boat owner was an umialik, and away from the sea umialiks had no umiaks.

The chief and the council arbitrated in intratribal and intertribal affairs, including division of labor in cooperative ventures, duties to be performed during ceremonials, disposition of food during a famine, strategy during impending invasion, and the like. However, a strong chief made the final decision alone.

Punishment and theft ranged from restitution to temporary ostracism; adultery was often punished by beating; and murder was dealt with by banishment or execution by a member of the family wronged. The murder sanction often resulted in a long-standing feud between families.

• MARRIAGE AND KINSHIP Chiefs and good hunters often had two and sometimes more wives. In the Nome area the first wife did all the sewing, and the second—a younger woman—all the household chores. Among the Unaliq, and possibly the northern groups, girls were betrothed as young as 10 years of age to an older man (Khromchenko 1824:311; Ray 1961–1968). Marriage was entered into without a formal ceremony, but the man usually gave the girl a parka or other apparel to show his intent. There were two forms of marriage, primary residential marriage and supplementary marriage, which included both spouse exchange and the social bonds that continued between a man and a woman after a primary marriage had broken up (Heinrich 1972). Sexual relations before marriage were not condemned, but infidelity afterward could dissolve a marriage or lead to harsh treatment, especially for a wife at the hands of her husband. Unions were sought outside the local group not only to establish intertribal ties but also to observe incest taboos or rules of kin exogamy. Kinship was reckoned bilaterally, and residence on the village level was either matrilocal or patrilocal, or rarely neolocal.

The kinship terminology was of the Iroquois type. Cross-cousins, matrilateral parallel cousins, and patrilateral parallel cousins were differentiated; sibling terms could be applied to all cousins; siblings were differen-

286

tiated according to sex and age; spouses of cousins and of siblings were terminologically equated; patrilateral and matrilateral aunts and uncles were differentiated; wives of uncles had a special term but could be called a regular aunt term; husbands of aunts were given a term homophonous with para-father or classed as affinal. Parallel and cross nepotics had different terms, and their spouses were known as sons- and daughters-in-law and their children were called grandchildren (Heinrich 1963a:58–59).

The wide range of kin produced through primary marriage, supplementary marriage, adoption, and continuing ties after divorce produced a complex interrelatedness of local groups.

• INTERTRIBAL RELATIONS The Bering Strait Eskimos were traditional enemies of the Siberians across the strait to the west, of the Athapaskan Indians on their eastern boundaries, and of nonallied Eskimo tribes. Alliances were usually made between coastal villages and inland villages or between island and mainland tribes. Despite the reciprocal usage of other lands for subsistence activities through trading partners and marriage, it was a political agreement on tribal lands with the tacit consent of the tribe as a whole. Trading partnerships formed between two men of different villages, though entailing a symbolic exchange of wives, were also entirely political, though given a place in the kinship terminology.

Nonallied tribes were theoretically enemies, and individual members could be killed if found in foreign territory. Indians were often blamed for the mysterious disappearance of a hunter in inland territory. A popular folk theme of entire villages being wiped out by another tribe or by Indians is not substantiated, at least after Capt. James Cook's time of 1778 (Ray 1967a:384–388).

Tales of Siberian-Alaskan Eskimo conflicts abound in Bering Strait folklore and early Russian writings. Because of this animosity, intercontinental communication was doubtless very limited before the late eighteenth century, when a trade in Russian goods increased across the strait. Consequently the Kotzebue market, which drew both Siberian and Alaskan traders, was probably a local, small affair until trade in European merchandise made travel safe and profitable. A trade fair at Point Spencer antedated the Kotzebue market, drawing Eskimos from Saint Michael to Kotzebue Sound for a preponderantly native trade. These markets provided not only considerable tribal interaction on a peaceful basis, but also a marriage market (Ray 1961–1968, 1972a).

Trade was responsible for the migration of Kobuk River and Kotzebue Sound people—later to be called Malimiut—to Norton Sound at the beginning of the nineteenth century. At first, individual traders traveled south with European goods obtained from Siberian markets like the Anyui Fair on the Kolyma River. Later,

entire families followed, especially during the 1860s when Buckland people accompanied a large caribou migration to the Koyuk and Inglutalik area (Ray 1972a).

Subsistence

The large area involved and the diversity of subsistence patterns necessitate a summary treatment of resources and yearly activities. Food and a large proportion of raw materials for clothing, boats, and tents were obtained from sea mammals and caribou; but all tribes gathered large quantities of greens, berries, roots, and eggs and hunted migratory birds, ptarmigan, Arctic hares, and ground squirrels (fig. 3).

All tribes depended upon fish and seals for a large part of their diet. Some tribes also depended heavily on walrus and whales; others, on caribou. Wales, Little Diomede, and King Island peoples were the principal walrus, whale, and polar bear hunters, but Sledge Islanders were said to have hunted walrus and whales during the eighteenth century. The Kauwerak people were the main caribou hunters; they accumulated tons of meat by the end of a good season. The Fish River, Koyuk, Egavik, and Inglutalik people also depended more or less on caribou. The rest of the coastal tribes pursued a sealing-fishing round of activities with limited caribou hunting in their upland territories (Ray 1964, 1972a).

The black whale and walrus migrated north through the strait from April to June, and caribou traveled customary routes in the interior of the peninsula during winter, often going to the coast in small groups in summer. Seals were hunted everywhere, and even the Kauwerak and Fish River peoples traveled to coastal bays for seal hunting. Bearded seals (Inupiaq *uɣřuk,* Yupik *maklak*) and beluga (white whales) were found in special areas: bearded seals mainly around Sledge and King islands, along the *tapqaq* ('sandy strand') north of Wales (especially off Sarichef Island), at the mouth of the Solomon River, and in Port Clarence; the beluga, in the shallow offshore waters around Nome, Koyuk, Inglutalik, Golovnin Bay, and Pastolik (Ray 1964, 1972a).

• ANNUAL ROUND Generally the sequence of seasonal activities was the same throughout the area. By October, almost all families had returned to their winter homes from summer fishing and trading. Seal hunting began when the water became cold enough to keep the thong nets from rotting. Nets were hauled out at freeze-up but were replaced in holes in the ice, usually in December. The quantity of seals obtained was tremendous. Even Wales, with its walruses and whales, annually harvested 4,000 to 5,000 seals for a population of about 500 during the 1890s.

The end of December and the beginning of January was the most idle and leisurely time of the year, when preparations were made for local or intertribal cere-

a

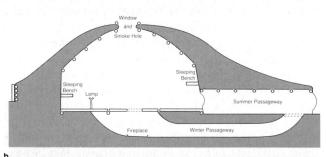

b

Window and Smoke Hole

Sleeping Bench

Sleeping Bench

Lamp

Fireplace

Summer Passageway

Winter Passageway

c

d

e

f

monies like the Messenger Feast. From December until the ice left the strait in June, the most daring men hunted polar bears, mainly as a thrilling sport. In fall and winter, flounders were speared through the sea ice, especially north of Wales and near Teller, and whitefish were caught through the river ice. The principal caribou hunting was carried on during the February and March migration, usually by driving the animals between posts, men, or rock piles.

From January to March, crabs were caught in favorable spots a mile or more from shore near Wales, Nome, Unalakleet, and around the islands. During the winter months of a poor migration, the caribou-hunting tribes eked out their rations with hares and ptarmigan caught in snares or nets and with fish snagged through the river ice. April was often a "hungry" month for tribes not hunting walrus and whales, and families might move away from the winter village to a dependable fishing place like Atnuk or Tuksuk Channel. Yet even in that area of abundance, unfavorable weather could limit the food supply.

Extensive ceremonies accompanied all phases of whale hunting in April and May. In the spring and again in the fall, beluga were chased ashore in kayaks and speared. During April and May many ducks and geese were caught with bolas. Swans, cranes, puffins, murres, auklets, and arctic owls were also captured and eaten. In the spring, the people of Norton Sound caught large quantities of herring. During May and June, some tribes like Wales and Unalakleet hunted caribou, the Wales people going to the interior of their territory and those of Unalakleet, inland and to Pastolik. Ground squirrels were snared at birthing time during a two-week period in April or May and again in September.

Coho, chum, and some king salmon were caught in knotted sinew nets beginning in June in the Unalakleet area and in July farther north. Families left the main village for their accustomed campsites where they split, scored, and dried salmon on driftwood racks for both men and dogs. Every year at this time, some families from Wales, King Island, and Little Diomede went to the Kotzebue market, combining trading and salmon fishing. Sledge Island traders went to Saint Michael and Pastol Bay to trade after the end of fishing there.

During late spring and summer, women gathered many vegetal foods, such as willow leaves, wild celery, and sourdock; and in late July and August they picked salmonberries, cranberries, and blueberries. Later on, they gathered roots, especially cotton grass root (*pikniq*) and licorice root (*mazut*) from underground caches stored by mice. In September, beluga hunting was best at Pastol and Norton bays. The fishing and trading families tried to arrive home before the annual storms of September and October to repair their dwellings, to open the community house for the winter, and to begin preparations for seal hunting and festivities of the season (Ray 1964, 1972a).

Clothing

Sealskin and summer caribou skins were used for trousers and hooded coats (Inupiaq *atiɣi*), called parkas by the Russians (figs. 10–11). Ground-squirrel skins were made into dress-up parkas, but hare fur was rarely used because of its fragility.

Winter caribou skins and sometimes polar-bear skins served as bedding. Sealskin and summer and winter caribou leg fur were used for land boots that varied from ankle to hip height. Waterproof boots were made of bleached dehaired sealskin. Hard soles of dehaired, split bearded sealskin were attached to the uppers of both kinds of boots with a waterproof seam of sinew.

The Eskimo seamstress sewed together sea-mammal intestines into coats to be worn over fur parkas, waterproof jackets for wearing in kayaks, and neck-high suits to wear while setting salmon nets in deep water. She made mittens and gloves, but no hats. She made bags out of whole sealskins for food and clothing storage. The absorbent ptarmigan feathers were carefully kept for cleansing purposes and for diapers (Ray 1961–1968).

Transportation

All tribes used the one-holed kayak and the umiak made of split walrus or bearded seal hides over driftwood frames. Kayaks were used mainly for salmon netting in the ocean and rivers, for seal hunting, and for caribou hunting in lakes, but the King Islanders also hunted walrus in them. The largest umiaks (some were 40 feet long) were made by the people who hunted walrus and whales (fig. 12). The Norton Sound inhabitants had

top, Smithsonian, NAA: SI 6908; a, Fitzhugh and Kaplan 1982: fig. 196; Smithsonian, Dept. of Anthr.: b, 176,172; c, T1847; d, 38,850; e, Smithsonian, Arch.: 80-1377.

Fig. 2. The kashim. Sweatbaths, dances, festivals and games were held in the kashim, which is similar in construction to family dwellings but much larger. top, Kashim at St. Michael, Alaska. Photograph by E. W. Nelson, 1877–1881. a, Diagram showing the interior. Entry in summer is through the ground-level passageway; in winter the outside door is closed off to seal out cold air and entry is through the underground passageway. b, Scene on a bow drill, showing cross-section of a kashim with drummers and dancers inside. To the left are 2 men wrestling, a competition held during gatherings. Length of detail 7.0 cm; collected by E. W. Nelson at Golovnin Bay, Alaska, 1877–1881. c, Bow drill scene showing bladders hanging from kashim roof. Length of detail 6.3 cm. d, Respirators of grass or wood shavings used to protect a man's lungs in the heat of the sweatbath in the kashim. Shavings are bound together with cord, with a mouthpiece stick across the back. Width 14.0 cm; collected by E. W. Nelson at Shaktoolik, Alaska, 1877–1881. e, Man with a respirator over his mouth. The birdskin cap shown is appropriate for a sweatbath, but no other clothing was worn. Sketch by William H. Dall at Klikitarik, east of St. Michael, Alaska, Oct. 1866.

Smithsonian, Dept. of Anthr.: a, 46,078; b, 24,336; c, and e, 43,360; d, 24,553; g, 44,788; h, 63,686; i, 33,438; j, 44,285; k, 43,401; 1, 63,633; m, 176,273; n, 45,364; f,o,p,q, Royal Ont. Mus., Toronto: 917.11.

Fig. 3. Subsistence technology. a, Set of lance tips, with metal points, kept in a leather pouch filled with straw. South of the Yukon individual wooden sheaths were used to protect points. A personal mark has been carved into the wooden shaft. b, Throwing-board with ivory finger pegs. c, Portion of a bow drill handle with an engraving of walrus-hunting from a umiak. d, Detail from bow drill depicting caribou hunt on land with bow and arrows. e, Bow drill pictograph showing caribou hunting from kayaks and hauling a dead seal over ice. Birds were hunted in a variety of ways including f, from kayak using a spear; o, on land with nets; p, on land or water with snares. These engravings along with q, marmots being snared, are scenes on a tusk attributed to Happy Jack (see VanStone 1963). g-j, Harpoons and darts used in hunting sea mammals, with floats, their inflation nozzles and plugs made of ivory as small sculptures or engraved with geometric designs. k-n, Fishhooks, elaborately decorated and intended for specific fish—m, sculpin hook and sinker; k and n, tomcod hook and sinker. a, Length of sheath 12.0 cm, b same scale. a collected by W. H. Dall at Port Clarence, Alaska, 1880. b and d collected by Lucien Turner at St. Michael, Alaska, 1876. c and e collected by E. W. Nelson, Cape Prince of Wales, Alaska, 1877–1881. g-n collected by E. W. Nelson in Alaska; g, Length 7.5 cm (g-n same scale), Sledge I.; h and l Diomede Is.; i, St. Michael; j, Cape Darby; k, Cape Prince of Wales; m and n, Cape Nome; 1877–1881. f,o,p,q from Happy Jack tusk; acquired in 1917.

fewer and smaller ones. Kayaks were propelled by paddles, and umiaks, by paddles and by sails (the sails were probably not aboriginal). The earliest allusion to umiaks in the literature is the statement of a report of 1711 that Eskimos "can row across [the strait] with oars" (Müller 1758). Umiaks were often towed with a rope when a hard offshore wind was blowing. Motors were used first in the 1910s.

Sleds were usually drawn by three dogs, but a rich man might have five.

Structures

Winter homes on the mainland were turf and wood semisubterranean dwellings, which looked like mounds, and on the islands, rock, turf, and driftwood. The dwellings had either an entrance room (entered with a ladder) as at Cape Nome, or a long, underground entranceway, as at Shishmaref and Wales, and from one to three other rooms averaging 10 feet square or more (fig. 13). They were lined with smoothly finished driftlogs (Kotzebue 1821, 1:200–201; Nelson 1899:241–256).

Summer dwellings in many permanent campsites, especially in the Yupik-speaking area, were wooden structures built above ground. Captain Cook described such a building in 1778 at Cape Denbigh: "a sloping roof,

without any side-walls, composed of logs, and covered with grass and earth" (Cook and King 1784, 2:484). When on the move, the Eskimos generally used a hemispherical tent of caribou or seal skin, but the Wales and Nome people also used conical tents of seal or split walrus, sometimes with a gutskin window, as observed in 1791 at Cape Rodney (Jacobi 1937:135). The King Islanders erected a square box of translucent walrus hide, on stilts, for summer use adjacent to the winter home (fig. 14) (Nelson 1899:256).

Technology

The earliest explorers observed Eskimos using round clay pots for cooking. They also used baskets (fig. 16) and mats made of beach grass, and bowls, buckets, and spoons of wood. They produced sparks for a fire with a two-man drill and made holes and split wood with a bow drill. The woman's most important implement was the half-moon–shaped ulu, a knife indispensable for cutting fish and skins.

At Cape Rodney in 1791, the Joseph Billings expedition saw armor of wood and bone, sinew-backed bows, arrows, wrist-guards, and spears with ivory and iron points. They also saw jade adzes, apparently traded from the Kobuk River.

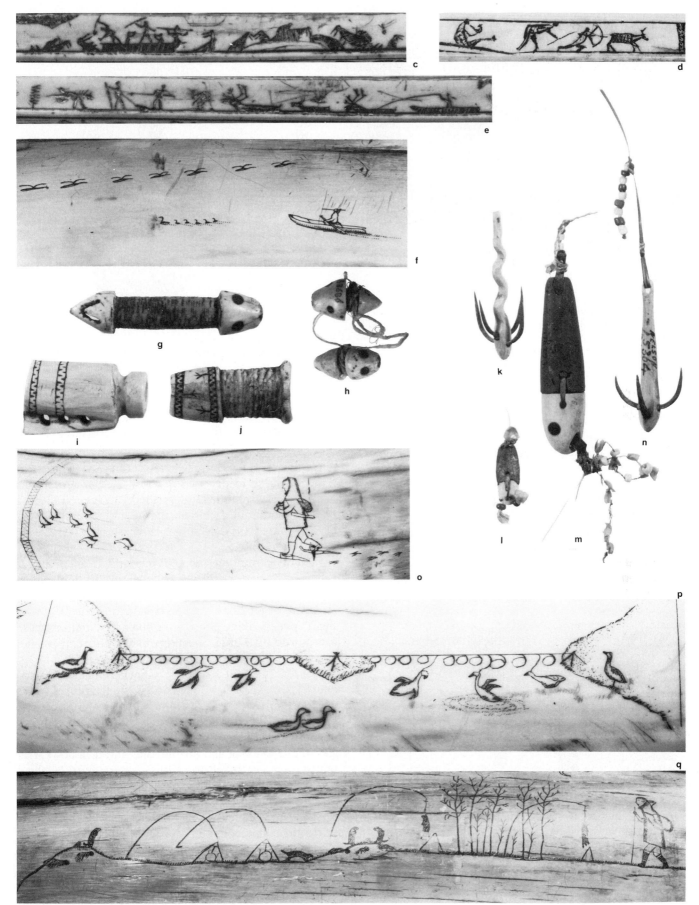

BERING STRAIT ESKIMO

Fig. 4. Putting meat or blubber into sealskin pokes. Blubber placed into the poke liquified into oil after some time had elapsed. Photographed on Cape Prince of Wales, about 1920–1925.

Photographs and descriptions of typical nineteenth-century implements can be found in H.M.W. Edmonds's report (Ray 1966) and Nelson (1899).

Art and Ceremonials

In traditional times all mainland groups had a feast on the first anniversary of a relative's burial, sometimes with a considerable amount of goods given away as presents. The Messenger Feast, a trading festival called nilga at Bering Strait, was celebrated at year's end by all mainland tribes, usually between a coastal and an inland village for an exchange of land and sea products. Nilga was organized at the request of one or more chiefs, who with their relatives' help accumulated large amounts of food and gifts to be dispensed to the invited village, which reciprocated as host another year.

The Messenger Feast was probably a fairly late development after dog traction made possible long-dis-

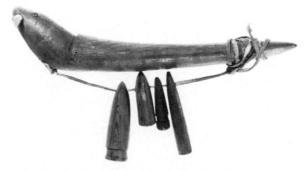

Fig. 5. Seal plugs. A seal killed in spring is thin and likely to sink, so the hunter blew air into holes cut in the skin to inflate it. The plugs were put in these holes, keeping the air in, and making the seal easier to tow behind the kayak (VanStone 1976:12). The wedge-shaped wooden pieces are fastened by a line to a larger plug, which has the head of a seal carved at one end with bead eyes and seal hair whiskers. Length 33.3 cm, collected by Minor Bruce at Port Clarence, Alaska, 1894.

Fig. 6. Mask used at the Inviting-In Feast held in January to appeal to the spirits for successful hunting in the coming year. This is a comic one, worn on the first of 3 days, meant to caricature an Indian. Carved of wood, with an exaggerated nose, the features are painted red and black. The central feather is loon with a ptarmigan tuft; the others are duck (Hawkes 1913). Width 12.0 cm; collected by E. W. Hawkes at St. Michael, Alaska, 1912.

tance travel. The Bering Strait ceremony, which differed in many respects from those farther north, has never been systematically described, but several sources provide numerous details (Kakaruk and Oquilluk 1964; D.S. Neuman 1914; Neuman 1914; Rasmussen 1932b; Ray 1961–1968).

Lengthy ceremonies and considerable ritual behavior occurred during whaling, caribou hunting, and polar-bear hunting. The Bladder Festival for propitiation of seals and other game animals was held in the fall by all the Yupik-speaking peoples. A boy's first animals were recognized by a little ceremony in the entire area, and a present of food was usually given to visitors.

A great deal of artwork, especially masks, marionettes, and various wooden and ivory sculptures, were made to be used in the ceremonies. Bering Strait Eskimos enjoyed considerable fame as "Eskimo artists," beginning in the mid-nineteenth century when they began to engrave bag and box handles and drill bows with realistic scenes to sell to sailors. Later, Saint Michael and Nome became centers of souvenir art. However, traditional sculptures and masks were made almost exclusively for religious and magical purposes, for honoring spirits in ceremonials, or as amulets (fig. 19) (Ray 1961, 1967, 1969).

Wooden sculptures other than masks ceased to exist as popular art forms after ivory engraving and carving were demanded by nonnatives. Carved of spruce drift-

top left, Glenbow-Alberta Inst., Calgary, Alta.: NC-1-438a; top right, Denver Mus. of Nat. Hist.: Bailey Coll. BA21- 395G; center left, Smithsonian, NAA: SI 3846; center right, Glenbow-Alberta Inst., Calgary, Alta.: NC-1-916b. bottom, Glenbow-Alberta Inst., Calgary, Alta.: left, ND-1-714, right, NC–1–21.

Fig. 7. Subsistence and transportation. top left, Hunters searching for seal among the ice floes of the Bering Sea, in kayaks of the King Island type, with sleds attached. Kayaks were often carried by sled to the sealing area (R. K. Nelson 1969: 287–290). top right, Dragging a bearded seal from the water's edge. Photograph by Alfred M. Bailey, Wales, May 1922. center left, Kayaks of the Norton Sound type (Nelson 1899:pl. 79(3) and 220). Photograph by E.W. Nelson, 1877–1881. center right, Waterproof gutskin clothing secured around the opening of a King Island kayak. top right and center, Photographs by Lomen Brothers, 1908–1915. bottom left, Tomcod fishing in winter on the frozen Nome River. bottom right, Summer fish camp at Nome with small fish drying. Photographs by Lomen Brothers, 1908–1915.

Fig. 8. Charms and amulets. top, Ceremonial headband of leather decorated with large blue and white beads, probably worn by the captain of a whaling umiak. bottom, Charms used by men—pieces of leather sewed together and stuffed, with tufts of fur as trim. Diameter 6.5 cm; collected by G. B. Gordon at Cape Prince of Wales, Alaska, 1905. top, Same scale; collected by Gordon on King I., Alaska, 1905.

wood, they were made to be used as house protectors, grave images, and sometimes personal amulets. Early explorers were usually unsuccessful in acquiring such objects.

Small ivory animal and human figurines have been found in archeological sites of almost all periods. Dur-

Fig. 9. Carved wooden containers for storing lance or harpoon points. top, Box carved to represent a seal, with eyes of white beads. The box lid represents another seal, with red bead eyes. There is red stain at the head and flippers, green on the body, and one white bead inset on the bottom. bottom, Whale with inset blue bead eye. The lid fitted into the bottom is missing. Length 29.0 cm; collected by W. Van Valin on Sledge I., Alaska, 1916. top, Same scale; collected by Lucien Turner, Norton Sound area, Alaska, 1879.

Fig. 10. Clothing and adornment. top, Men from Shishmaref Inlet with tonsured hair, labrets, bead earrings, and headbands. Watercolor by Louis Choris, 1816. bottom, Family from St. Michael or Yukon River area, in dress-up parkas. The woman's belt is made of caribou teeth. The man has labrets and the woman's chin is tattooed. Watercolor by Guy Kakarook, an Eskimo from St. Michael, Alaska, about 1895.

ing historical times they were also used as amulets to be hung on boats, in houses, and fastened to fishing gear, buckets, boxes, and many other objects. The Eskimo carver also strove to make the simplest of his utensils and implements in a shape pleasing to himself as well as to the spirits for whom much of his artwork was intended.

Demography

The population of the Bering Strait area (excluding the north shore of Seward Peninsula, but including Pastolik on the south) was probably between 2,100 and 2,400 during the last half of the nineteenth century. The pub-

Smithsonian, NAA: right, 3904-A.

Fig. 11. Woman from Port Clarence. Unger-ke-kuk in a parka of caribou fawn skin. The white triangular inserts are probably domesticated reindeer skin. She has tattooed lines on her chin. Photograph by William Dinwiddie in Washington, 1894.

Table 1. Bering Strait Estimated Population about 1850

Tribes, north to south	Eskimo name of principal village in the local dialect, Inupiaq (I.) or Yupik (Y.).	Population
Goodhope	I. *pitaq*	25
Cape Espenberg		30
Kauwerak	I. *kaviařaq*	80
Shishmaref	I. *qiẏiqtaq*	125
Wales	I. *kiŋiɣin*	600[a]
Little Diomede	I. *iŋaliq*	120
Port Clarence	I. *sinẏa(ẏ)miut*	200
King Island	I. *uɣiuvak*	140
Sledge Island	I. *aya·q*	60
Cape Nome	I. *aya·saẏiaq*	60
Fish River	I. *iẏałuit*	50
Ignituk	I. *iɣniqtaq*	50
Atnuk	I. *atniq*, Y. *átnəq*	60
Koyuk	I. *ku·yuk*	25
Inglutalik	I. *iɣlutalik*, Y. *əŋlutá·lək*	25
Shaktoolik	Y. *čáxtulək*	50
Egavik	I. *iɣavik*	20
Unalakleet	I. *uŋallaqłi·t*, Y. *uŋá·laqłi·t*	100
Klikitarik	I. *qikiqtaẏřuk*	50
St. Michael	Y. *tačíq*	25
Stebbins	Y. *áttəẏvik*	100
Pastolik	Y. *pástuliq*	180[b]
Total		2,175

[a] Including Agianamiut, Kiata(na)miut, and Tin City.
[b] Including Pikmitalik (Y. *pətMixtá·lək*).

lished figures seem a little low, and in the early 1800s the population may have exceeded the upper figure by 100 or 200 (see table 1).

The following early population estimates of northwest Alaska show that this area did not traditionally support the huge populations often attributed to it: 2,500 persons from the Seward Peninsula to the Arctic coast in 1826–1827 (Beechey 1831, 2:568); 3,750 including Saint Michael in 1870 (Dall 1870:537); 3,000 in 1881 by C.L. Hooper, skipper of the *Corwin* (1884:101); and 3,177 Eskimos between Pastolik and Point Barrow in the 1890 census. Of this figure, 2,022 lived between Saint Michael and the north coast of Seward Peninsula (U.S. Census Office 1893:7, 8, 162, 165).

The Eskimo population increased greatly after the late nineteenth century because of reduced infant mortality and greater longevity. During the 1890s when false assertions were made about an "Eskimo decimation," teachers, who usually obtained the most accurate figures, said that births always exceeded deaths, and that the population was growing.

Major population shifts of the nineteenth and twentieth centuries were the Malimiut immigration to the Norton Sound area; the gold rush of 1899–1900 and migration of Eskimos to Nome from surrounding areas; the measles epidemic of 1900 and depopulation of several small villages; the migration of Hooper Bay people to Stebbins in the 1910s; the 1918 influenza epidemic and subsequent high Eskimo mortality and abandonment of small villages; the influx of many Eskimos into

Nome and Unalakleet after World War II; and in 1969, the permanent move of King Islanders to Nome, which had been their summer home since the gold rush (Ray 1961–1968).

In 1838 a smallpox epidemic, which reduced the population of Unalakleet to 13 (Zagoskin 1967:95), apparently did not reach north of Koyuk.

In 1900 the measles epidemic extended from the lower Yukon to Point Hope and into Siberia. It was estimated that the population of some villages was reduced by one-third or one-half.

In 1918 an influenza epidemic extended as far north as Wales, but barricades prevented its entry into Shishmaref. Hundreds died in this epidemic. Sledge Island and Ayasayuk on Cape Nome were severely reduced, and the survivors moved to Nome (Ray 1961–1968).

Smaller "epidemics" and illnesses seemed constantly to beset the various tribes. For example, in 1866 members of the Western Union Telegraph Expedition said that about 15 years before, a sickness of some kind had reduced the populations of Atnuk and Koyuk (Harrington 1867:37; Taggart 1954:154). Between 1890 and 1900, school teachers reported many outbreaks of pneumonia and bronchitis, such as an "epidemic of pneu-

top left, U. of Santa Clara Arch., Calif.: Hubbard Coll.; top right, © Natl. Geographic Soc., Washington; Glenbow-Alberta Inst., Calgary, Alta.: bottom left ND-1-440024, bottom right NC-1-1135.

Fig. 12. Umiaks. top left, Lashing the wooden frame together. Photograph by Bernard R. Hubbard, King I., 1938. top right, Three umiaks covered with walrus skin, towing a whale. Photograph by Henry Collins, Cape Prince of Wales, 1936. bottom left, A hunter waiting at the ice edge in the Bering Sea. Sealskin floats protrude from the boat and he holds a spear. bottom right, Umiak under sail on the Bering Sea. Photograph by Lomen Brothers, 1908–1915.

monia" following very bad weather in the fall of 1890 at Wales where 26 died (Lopp and Thornton 1891:360–361).

Botulism from fish and meat was known to have killed whole families, and all early explorers reported universally infected eyes and respiratory diseases from poorly ventilated and smoke-filled houses. Stomach ailments, scrofula, and boils were common. Lice were everywhere.

History

The earliest information about any part of Alaska was obtained in Siberia by Russian Cossacks from the Chukchi and Eskimos who were acquainted with people on the American side of the Bering Strait. Long before Vitus Bering "discovered" Alaska in 1741, considerable information about inhabitants of the Alaskan Bering Strait had already been gathered into reports of 1711 and 1718 (Müller 1758, 1761:xxiv–xxvii). The reports said that the land was rich in furs, food animals, and vegetable products. The people lived in earthen dwellings; the men wore ivory labrets in their chins and fox tails on the back of their belts; some went barefoot and had "feet like ravens." They fought among themselves, and were often at war with the Siberians. Their population was estimated to be two to three times that of the Chukchi.

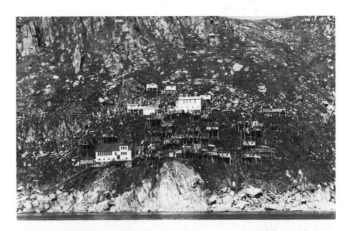

Fig. 13. Cape Prince of Wales winter house. top, Upper entrance with sled on rack (background) and fishing equipment protruding from the snow. center, Underground approach to dwelling area, lined and floored with planks. Snowshoes, clothes, dried fish, furs, and inflated sealskin floats are stored here. bottom, House interior, where residents partially disrobe because of the warmth. An oil lamp is behind the man. The wall contains beaded ornaments, 2 adzes, bells, metal spoons, and other household goods. Photographs by Lomen Brothers, 1908–1915.

Fig. 14. King Island houses built on the cliffs. top, View in 1938. Large building near top of settlement is the Roman Catholic Church. The lower large building is the school. Photograph by Bernard R. Hubbard. center, Skins on stretcher frames against the houses and household goods hung about the houses. Photograph by Lomen Brothers, 1908–1915. bottom, Woman working on a ramp outside her house. Photograph by Bernard R. Hubbard, 1938.

Fig. 15. Norton Sound man, woman with child in parka, and house to left. A kayak lies on the beach to the right. Watercolor by John Webber, 1778.

Explorations before 1848

Alaska, therefore, was far from unknown when Mikhail Gvozdev and Ivan Fedorov made the first actual discovery of Alaska in 1732 in the *Gabriel* near Cape Prince of Wales. They landed on Big Diomede Island (which Vitus Bering had discovered in 1728 during his voyage along the Siberian coast) after being shot at with arrows. They discovered Little Diomede, but "meeting with an unfriendly reception," did not land. They discovered

Fig. 16. Coiled baskets made of marsh grass. Bands of zigzag openwork resemble those on coiled baskets made by the Inuit of Labrador (see "Historical Ethnography of the Labrador Coast," fig. 13, this vol.). The similarity may be due to the Moravian missionaries who worked in both areas. bottom, Oblong basket with a leather handle on lid. bottom, Height 27.0 cm; top, same scale. Both collected by G.B. Gordon at St. Michael, Alaska, 1905.

Fig. 17. Dance costumes. left, Kauwerak Eskimos dressed for a Wolf Dance, including wolf head masks and mittens decorated with puffin beaks. Men always wore gloves when dancing; masks, special pants, and fur armlets were also worn during ceremonies. In the rear is a rectangular box drum (Ray 1964a: 10). Photograph by Lomen Brothers, 1918. right, Sealskin dance mittens with puffin beaks that rattle as the dancer moves. The border is pierced skin and fur with several feathers attached. Length 55.0 cm; collected by E.W. Nelson, on Sledge I., Alaska, 1877–1881.

Smithsonian, Dept. of Anthr.: left, 64,226; center, 316,705; right, U. of Pa., U. Mus., Philadelphia: NA4574.

Fig. 18. King Island masks. Although stylistically simpler than those made in southwest Alaska, masks were much used north of Norton Sound. left, Carved wood mask with teeth of inset wooden pegs, painted white with black hair and red mouth. center, Wooden mask painted white with black hair. right, Wooden mask with separate movable tongue piece, stained red, with painted black hair. It may represent a bear. Length 20.0 cm, rest same scale. Collected by W. Van Valin in 1916. left, Collected by E. W. Nelson, 1877–1881; center collected by Sheldon Jackson in 1890.

King Island and talked to a man who came to their ship in a kayak. The *Gabriel* anchored two and one-half miles from Wales but was forced out to sea by wind. On returning home, Gvozdev made a map with a remarkably accurate outline of the Wales coastline and islands in the strait (Efimov 1948:160–175, 236–243; Golder 1914:160–162; Grekov 1960:49–54; Anonymous 1850:389–402; Gvozdev 1851:78–107; Ray 1972a).

In 1765 the first specific information about Seward Peninsula—a drawing of a village on a "Kheuveren River"—was placed on a map made in Siberia by a Chukchi Cossack, Nikolai Daurkin. According to Daurkin, this village (which can be no other than Kauwerak) was established in 1761 by a ruler named Inalun. In 1779 the Russian Cossack, Ivan Kobelev, interpreted it to be a Russian fort inhabited by descendants of sailors who supposedly had been shipwrecked in 1648. The fort was entirely fictional, but many Russian writers continue to believe in its existence (Belov 1956; Grekov 1960; Efimov 1950; Chernenko 1957; Fedorova 1964, 1971a, 1971:62–64; Masterson and Brower 1948:94; Pallas 1781–1793, 4:108; Ray 1964a, 1972a).

Until mid-nineteenth century, European contacts with the Bering Strait tribes were short and haphazard. In 1778 Captain Cook landed on Sledge Island but did not see its inhabitants. He saw people in the Shaktoolik and Elim area for the first time. In 1779 Kobelev was the first European to go ashore on Little Diomede Island. From information obtained there he made a map of Seward Peninsula villages. (This extraordinary map is reproduced or discussed in Fedorova 1971; Masterson and Brower 1948:facing 92; Pallas 1781–1793, 4; Ray 1964a, 1971:4–6). In 1791 the Billings expedition stayed several days in the vicinity of Cape Rodney, and Kobelev, an employee of the expedition, again visited both Diomedes and attempted to reach Kauwerak by skin boat but was turned back by ice. He was the first European to land on King Island. By 1791 the Bering Strait Eskimos were using bells, bracelets, harpoon and lance points made of metal, and glass beads, but little tobacco and apparently no iron pots (Chernenko 1957; Fedorova 1971a; Jacobi 1937; Sarychev 1806–1807, 1; Sauer 1802).

The Eskimos of Shishmaref, Cape Espenberg, and Goodhope River were seen for the first time when Otto von Kotzebue visited them in 1816 (Kotzebue 1821, 1). In 1821 Mikhail N. Vasiliev met the Stebbins people at their Stuart Island camps, and V.S. Khromchenko discovered Golovnin Bay, where Sledge Islanders were met for the first time. In 1826 and 1827, Beechey (1831, 1:255–291) wrote the first description of Wales people who were fishing and trading at Kotzebue Sound.

In 1833 Saint Michael was founded by the Russian-American Company on Norton Sound at a site considered to be favorable for the fur trade of both the Yukon River and the Bering Strait. In 1840 or 1841, Unalakleet became a subdepot. Few native traders were employed by the company because most of the trading was done by an annual company vessel, which went from Sitka as far north as Kotzebue Sound. Lt. L.A. Zagoskin arrived in Saint Michael in 1842 for a two-year visit to evaluate the fur trade and to establish a post on Kotzebue Sound to intercept the Bering Strait fur trade. He did not accomplish the latter objective (Zagoskin 1967). *299*

Whaling and Commercial Enterprises

The year 1848 marks the beginning of intensive whaling and trading, and of the six-year search for Sir John Franklin in the Bering Strait area. Commercial whaling activities were of consequence only to the people of the islands after the 1860s when ships stopped to buy fur clothing and to hire seamstresses and hunters, and to the Port Clarence people after 1884 when a coal stockpile was established for the new steam whaling fleet based in San Francisco. Commercial whalers made less of an impact on Eskimo life in this area by decreasing the number of whalers, which was really inconsiderable, than by trading liquor and guns and mixing genes with the native population.

In 1854 the Franklin searchers were the first Europeans to visit and describe the villages of Kauwerak, Sinramiut, and Wales. Vessels remained over the winter three times in Port Clarence between 1849 and 1854 (Collinson 1889; Great Britain. Parliament. House of Commons. Sessional Papers 1852–1853, 60:82, 1854–1855, 35:1898; Seemann 1853).

In 1866 members of the Western Union Telegraph Expedition built the first non-Native settlement—five small wooden buildings—north of Saint Michael at Port Clarence. The buildings were given to an Eskimo chief when the project was abandoned in 1867. Between 1865 and 1867, members of the expedition employed many Eskimos as interpreters, packers, post-hole diggers, and cooks at Port Clarence, Koyuk, Unalakleet, and Saint Michael (Dall 1870; James 1942; Taggart 1954, 1956; Whymper 1869).

The first and only "Indian agent" in the Bering Strait area, Frederick S. Hall, lived in Saint Michael between June 1873 and the end of summer 1874 to enforce the prohibition against selling liquor to Natives. After his agency was abolished he recommended that a revenue marine patrol or a military post be established (McCoy 1956). Liquor had become a serious problem all along the coast, and in 1877 about 20 Wales Eskimos—apparently intoxicated—were killed in an altercation on the brig *William H. Allen* (Aldrich 1889:143–146; Ray 1961–1968).

In 1880 an annual revenue marine service patrol was inaugurated for Bering Strait and northward (Bailey 1880; Healy 1887, 1889; Hooper 1881, 1884). The revenue steamers gave unlimited assistance to scientists, and partly because of his trip on the *Corwin* in 1881, E.W. Nelson was able to make a large collection of artifacts north of Saint Michael for the Smithsonian Institution (W.J. Hoffman 1897; Nelson 1899; Fitzhugh and Kaplan 1982). Thereafter, many other collectors and explorers came to Saint Michael and vicinity, including J.A. Jacobsen in 1882 and H.M.W. Edmonds in 1889–1890 and 1898. Both wrote extensive ethnographic notes (Jacobsen 1884; Ray 1966).

In 1880, apparently by accident, galena ore was discovered in the vicinity of Golovin, and the Omilak Silver Mine inaugurated the first mining venture in the area. The miners exploited the Eskimos as laborers during the following two decades and killed two of them (Ray 1972a).

Missions, Schools, and Reindeer

The establishment of missions, schools, and reindeer herding brought permanence of non-Eskimo culture to the Bering Strait area as no other activities had before. The Russians had provided a chapel in Saint Michael but no school. American schools were begun at Unalakleet and Golovin in 1887 and 1889 under the Mission Covenant of Sweden and at Wales in 1890 under the joint auspices of the Congregational Church and the Bureau of Education (a "contract school"). Schools, missions, and the reindeer industry were interrelated under the guidance of Sheldon Jackson, first agent for education in Alaska, until his removal from office in 1907. Schools were established in several other villages under the Bureau of Education until 1907, and thereafter under the Bureau of Indian Affairs. Several public schools—Teller, Dime Creek, and Nome—were established for White and mixed-blood children. Many Native children went to Indian boarding schools outside Alaska. A Bureau of Indian Affairs school was established in Nome; it was closed in 1950. In the 1970s, Bureau of Indian Affairs schools (usually only through the eighth grade) were in operation at Brevig Mission, Elim, Golovin, Koyuk, Little Diomede, Saint Michael, Shaktoolik, Shishmaref, Stebbins, Unalakleet, Wales, and White Mountain. Nome and Teller had state-operated schools, and Nome also had a regional boarding high school (Ray 1961–1968).

Between 1892 and 1902, Jackson had enlisted the aid of the revenue cutter *Bear* to transport about 1,280 domesticated reindeer from Siberia to the reindeer station at Port Clarence for Eskimo benefit. This venture did not become the success that he had envisioned, either culturally or financially. In 1971 only 12 Eskimo-owned herds with a total of 19,389 animals were located on Seward Peninsula (Ray 1964; U.S. Bureau of Indian Affairs 1971:4).

The Gold Rush and the Twentieth Century

Gold was discovered on Anvil Creek near the present town of Nome in 1898; and during 1899 and 1900 more than 40,000 prospectors covered almost every mile of the Seward Peninsula, many of them going overland from Saint Michael, which had been the port for the water route to the Canadian Klondike in 1896–1897. The miners disturbed camping sites and diverted the water of some streams, but the greatest changes in settlement patterns were due to Eskimos' moving from small villages and campsites to Nome. At first they came only in summertime to sell game and handicrafts (fig. 19), but later they remained to work at longshoring and odd jobs and to attend school. Gradually over the years, the Eskimos of Nome and Unalakleet depended less on their old seasonal round of pursuits and more on a wage subsistence, although Unalakleet remained a subsistence village to a large extent. After the 1950s the Eskimos obtained increasing work as store clerks, secretaries, bank clerks, teachers, and administrators (Ray 1961–1968).

Unemployment, welfare, and aid to dependent children checks became a common source of income after World War II. The Native population of Nome increased, and the smaller villages decreased in size (with the exception of Unalakleet, of whose population of 610, 500 were Natives in 1969). In 1880 the population of a 100-square-mile area around Nome, including Sledge Island, was only about 140. In 1906 in Nome alone there were about 150 permanent Native residents, with 1,000 transients in summer. In 1925 the Native population had grown to 455 of a total of 1,429; in 1942, 500 of 1,250; in 1967, 1,534 of 2,450; and in 1969, 1,950 of a total of 2,800 (U.S. Census Office 1884:11; U.S. Federal Field Committee for Development and Planning in Alaska 1967, 1969; Ray 1961–1968).

Despite many interracial marriages, bigotry was widespread, especially in Nome. Until 1945 when the Alaska Territorial Legislature passed the Equal Rights Bill, Eskimos were not permitted to eat in restaurants, to rent rooms in hotels, or to sit wherever they chose in the theater.

In 1939 the Nome Eskimo Community was organized pursuant to the Indian Reorganization Act of 1934, but there was little cooperation among the various tribes living in Nome. In the 1940s, an attempt by the Alaska Native Brotherhood of southeast Alaska to organize a northwest chapter met with initial failure (Ray 1961–1968). In 1966, with the prospect of settling their aboriginal land claims through congressional action, the Eskimos of this area united for the first time under the name Seward Peninsula Native Association and joined the state-wide Alaska Federation of Natives in bringing a money and land settlement to a successful close in the Alaska Native Claims Settlement Act of 1971. By June 1972 each of 12 Native corporations—including the Bering Straits Native Corporation—formed under terms of the act received $500,000 as initial settlement. This corporation narrowly escaped bankruptcy in the late 1970s.

By 1982 a large proportion of the work force in all of the towns and villages of the Bering Strait area was Eskimo. Many young people had completed technical and professional courses in high school and college, including the Northwest Community College, established in Nome in 1975.

Synonymy

The principal variations of the names of several tribes are as follows (see table 1 for Eskimo names and Ray 1964 and 1971 for a more extensive treatment of village names and their meanings).

Cape Nome: Azichigiag, Ayacheruk, and Aiacheruk (Hodge 1907–1910, 1:31).

Kauwerak: Cuv-vi-e-rook, Kaiyóruk, Kaviak, Kaviarazakhmute, Kow-ee-ruk, Qaveŕak, and Kaviagmiut (Hodge 1907–1910, 1:666).

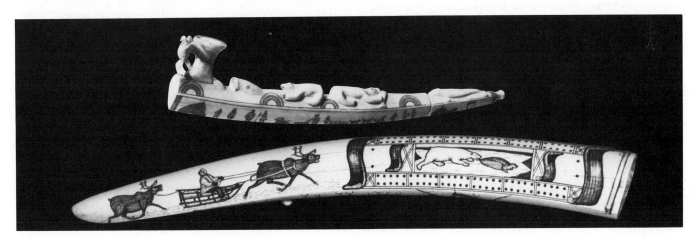

top, Smithsonian, Dept. of Anthr.: 260, 095; bottom, U. of Alaska Mus., Fairbanks: UA 717-116.

Fig. 19. Ivory carving. Men probably began making non-traditional ivory carvings at the request of early traders. top, Pipe not made to be smoked. The sides are engraved with scenes and geometric motifs, and animals are carved in relief on the top. bottom, Cribbage board, which has a map of the Seward Peninsula on the reverse side, attributed to Komanaciak (Komonaseak) of Wales, Alaska. Happy Jack (Angokwazhuk), recognized as the founder of contemporary Alaskan ivory carving (see Ray 1980), made and sold in Nome some of the first cribbage boards carved in walrus tusk. These scrimshaw-inspired engravings are more realistic than traditional designs. Nome became a center for ivory carvers with the gold rush. Length 55.9 cm, made about 1905. top, Same scale, collected before 1910.

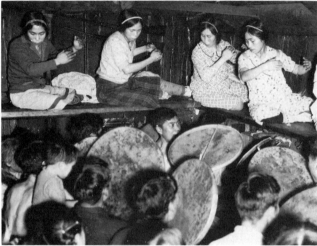

top, Glenbow-Alberta Inst., Calgary, Alta: ND-1-3; bottom, U. of Santa Clara Arch., Calif.: Hubbard Coll.

Fig. 20. Dancers accompanied by drummers. top, Man dancing on a piece of skin spread before an umiak, turned on its side for a shelter. Photograph by Lomen Brothers, 1908–1915. bottom, Women performing the bench dance in the kashim on King I. Photograph by Bernard Hubbard, winter 1937–1938.

King Island: Okibyan, Ukipen, Ookivok, Oo-ghe-a-boak, and Ukivogmiut (Hodge 1907–1910, 2:864).

Little Diomede: Igailin, Ignalitke, Inalit, Ig nee´shook, Ig-narlook, and Inguklimiut (Hodge 1907–1910, 1:609).

Sledge Island: Aiak, Aiakamut, Aziak, and Ahyak (Hodge 1907–1910, 1:122).

Wales, the combined villages of Kiatanamiut, the north village, and Agianamiut, the south village: Kiñugumut, Kigygmin, King-a-ghee, Kingigamute, and Kinugumiut (Hodge 1907–1910, 1:690, 698). The name Kigin Elyat on Ivan Lvov's map of 1710 probably refers to Wales (Efimov 1964:pl. 55). If so, it is the first record of any

Alaska place-name. Variations of the names of the two Wales villages are Agivaemeet and Agenamete; Kiatomeet and Gaytarnamete.

When Zagoskin (1956:80) in 1842 asked some Norton Sound Yupik speakers what they called themselves collectively they told him Chnagmiut 'coastal people' (čэNáγmiut), but this is not the name of an Eskimo tribe; the English translation (Zagoskin 1967:103) omits the word vse 'all' that indicates that this is a general term referring to several local groups.

Sources

Many of the sources cited for the history also contain limited ethnographic data. For the Bering Strait in general, see Nelson (1899), Ray (1961, 1964, 1966, 1967, 1967a, 1969, 1972, 1975), and Burch (1980). Additional major sources for specific villages include: for Golovin, Khromchenko (1824); for Ignituk, Harrington (1867) and Jacobsen (1884); for Kauwerak, Great Britain. Parliament. House of Commons. Sessional Papers (1854–1855), Jacobsen (1884), and Ray (1961–1968, 1964a, 1972a); for King Island, Renner (1979), Bogojavlensky (1969), Curtis (1907–1930, 20), and LaFortune (1929–1942); for Koyuk, Meyers (1957). For data on Little Diomede Island, see Curtis (1907–1930, 20), Heinrich (1963, 1963a, 1972), and Weyer (1932). The Nome area is covered in Ray (1964a, 1967a, 1972a). Other village sources are: for Port Clarence, Bruce (1894), Great Britain. Parliament. House of Commons. Sessional Papers (1852–1853, 1854–1855), Harrington (1867), and Brevig (1944); for Saint Michael, Dall (1870), Ray (1966), and Zagoskin (1967); for Shishmaref, Keithahn (1963); for Unalakleet, Zagoskin (1967); for Wales, Bernardi (1912), Curtis (1907–1930, 20), The Eskimo Bulletin 1893–1902, Great Britain. Parliament. House of Commons. Sessional Papers (1854–1855), Lopp and Thornton (1891), and Thornton (1931).

Major references for ceremonials and art are W.J. Hoffman (1897), Nelson (1899), and Ray (1961, 1967, 1969, 1972). Major sources for the reindeer industry are the annual reindeer reports (1891–1908), Lantis (1950a), Olson (1969), and Ray (1964). For kinship and social organization, see Bogojavlensky (1969) and Heinrich (1960, 1963, 1963a, 1972).

Sources for a detailed history of the land claims legislation are in U.S. Federal Field Committee for Development Planning in Alaska (1968) and in articles in the *Tundra Times* since 1962.

Kotzebue Sound Eskimo

ERNEST S. BURCH, JR.

Territory and Environment

The Kotzebue region comprises the coastal zone of northwest Alaska bordering Kotzebue Sound between Cape Thompson, on the north, and Cape Espenberg, on the south, and the inland districts drained by rivers reaching the coast between those points. It encompasses approximately 36,000 square miles and is drained by three major river systems—Noatak, Kobuk, and Selawik—in its central portion, and a number of minor ones toward its northern and southern peripheries.

The region has a varied topography that includes broad level plains, rolling hills, and, particularly between the upper Noatak and upper Kobuk rivers, high rugged mountains. Tundra vegetation (lichens, mosses, grasses, sedges) predominates in all districts, although high willow and alder growth occurs along the rivers and most streams even at relatively high elevations. The lower Noatak, Kobuk, Selawik, and some of the smaller rivers in the southern portion of the region have spruce growing along their banks and along the sides of the valley floors. The region has an Arctic climate, with long cold winters, short cool summers, and little annual precipitation (8–9 inches). Temperatures are more extreme inland—with a maximum of 96°F, and a minimum of −72°F on the upper Kobuk (Tony Bernhardt, personal communication 1970)—than they are along the coast, with a maximum of 85°F and minimum of −52°F at Kotzebue.

The Kotzebue region was inhabited in the early nineteenth century by the members of 10 "tribes" (Ray 1967a, 1975:87ff., 103ff.) or "societies" (fig. 1) (Burch 1975a:235ff., 1980): (1) Kivaliñiġmiut, of the Kivalina and Wilik river drainages and adjacent coastline; (2) Napaaqtuġmiut, of the lower Noatak River basin, and Chukchi Sea coast directly to the west; (3) Nuataaġmiut, of the upper Noatak River basin; (4) Qikiqtaġrungmiut, of the extreme lower Noatak River, Baldwin Peninsula, and the northern shore of the inner reaches of Kotzebue Sound; (5) Kuungmiut, of the Kobuk River delta; (6) Akuniġmiut, of the middle Kobuk River basin; (7) Kuuvaum Kangianiġmiut, of the upper Kobuk River drainage; (8) Siiḷvingmiut, of the Selawik River basin; (9) Kangiġmiut, of the Buckland River drainage and adjacent coastline; and (10) Pitaġmiut, of the Goodhope River and the coastline adjacent to its mouth.[*]

With the possible exception of the Kivaliñiġmiut, who may have spoken the Northern dialect, all the inhabitants of the region spoke the Malimiut dialect of the Inupiaq Eskimo language (Krauss 1980:49).[†] For a generation or two early in the nineteenth century the extreme upper Noatak valley was occupied by the Dihai Kutchin (vol. 6:516) (Burch 1979a:124ff., 1981:7ff.; Gubser 1965:44ff.; West 1959) and, after about 1870, by the Nunamiut Eskimos (Burch 1976a, 1980:280–281; cf. Campbell 1968; Gubser 1965:28ff.; Stoney 1900:569ff., 812ff.).

Immediate neighbors to the north were the Tikiġaġmiut and Utuqqaġmiut Eskimos of the Point Hope and Utukok River districts, respectively (Burch 1980:291, 294, 1981a:11ff.). Several groups of Koyukon Indians (Clark 1974) inhabited the adjacent territory to the east and southeast. The Tapqaamiut (Shishmaref) and Qaviaṙaġmiut (Kuzitrin River) Inupiaq-speaking Eskimos resided immediately to the west and southwest, while the Yupik-speaking people of the Fish River and Koyuk River districts lived to the south (Ray 1967a:372, 1975:103ff.).

Culture

Social Organization

Each of the 10 traditional societies in the Kotzebue region was comprised of a set of relatively autonomous,

*This chapter and "Bering Strait Eskimo" offer significantly different interpretations of the Pitaġmiut and Tapqaamiut districts. In part this reflects a genuine difference of opinion, but mostly it is a consequence of the paucity of information on this particular region for the early nineteenth century; the few data admit of a wide range of reasonable interpretations.

†The Inupiaq words written in italics in this chapter are in the phonemic system described in the orthographic footnote in "North Alaska Eskimo: Introduction" (this vol.). The names of the societies (or tribes) used as English designations, and hence not in italics, are the Inupiaq names in their respective local dialectal forms transcribed in the practical orthography also described in that footnote (but with ng substituted for ŋ, and ř for r). The major differences between these spelling systems that are exemplified in these names are as follows: practical g = phonemic γ; ġ = γ̇; ñ = nʸ; ng = ŋ; ḷ = ɬ; ii = iˑ, aa = aˑ; uu = uˑ.

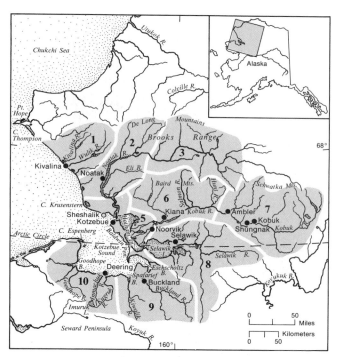

Fig. 1. Societal territories, about 1800 to 1825: 1, Kivaliñiġmiut; 2, Napaaqtuġmiut; 3, Nuataaġmiut; 4, Qikiqtaġřungmiut; 5, Kuungmiut; 6, Akuniġmiut; 7, Kuuvaum Kangianiġmiut; 8, Siilvingmiut; 9, Kangiġmiut; 10, Pitaġmiut.

self-sufficient social segments. Of the type commonly referred to in the anthropological literature on hunting-gathering societies as "villages," "local groups," or "bands," these units actually were what students of any other type of society would call "families" (Burch 1975a:235ff.). Some were small, geographically isolated conjugal families involving perhaps six people. Others were extremely large, bilaterally extended "local" families that sometimes involved as many as 100 or more people but that ordinarily were in the 20 to 30 member range. Each local family of any size was subdivided into two or more "domestic family" units (Burch 1975a; Foote 1965:213ff.) whose members lived in separate dwellings.

Local families were relatively self-sufficient in the sense that the members of each were capable of surviving for considerable periods without contact with the members of any others. Production and consumption took place primarily in terms of local families, and power and responsibility were allocated primarily at that level. Each local family was under the leadership of a "chief" or umialik (V.L. Smith 1966:24–25; Spencer 1959:152–155). Many included one or more shamans (sg. aŋatkuq). Families made up of more than three or four households, or domestic families, normally had a community hall, or kashim (Correll 1972; Spencer 1959:182–192). For all the people most of the time, the local family formed *the* social context in which daily activities were carried out.

304   The domestic families, or households, that comprised

a local family unit involved an average of about seven persons (Foote 1965:233ff.), although the range extended from around four to as many as 20 or more. Most households consisted of some type of extended family, while a few were comprised of polygamous (usually polygynous, rarely polyandrous) conjugal families Residence was bilocal.

The several relatively autonomous local families that comprised each society were found together by a variety of connections of which five were particularly important. The first was intermarriage, which was frequent among the local families within a society but uncommon between local families in different societies. Each society, therefore, constituted a deme (Burch and Correll 1972). Most of them were probably of the type Adams and Kasakoff (1976) have referred to as an "80 percent group," meaning that the endogamy rate averaged around that level. A second unifying factor was identification with a particular territory, which its members owned to the exclusion of all other people. Third, each society was characterized by a distinctive annual cycle of movement. A fourth unifying factor was that, although relatively self-sufficient most of the time, the members of the different local families within a given society were dependent upon one another for support in time of crisis (famine, war), and they also had to join together occasionally to conduct properly the feasts, dances, ceremonies, and games that were an important feature of Native life in this area. Finally, the members of each society spoke a subdialect of the Inupiaq language. The several subdialects were mutually intelligible, but distinctive enough to serve to identify an individual belonging to a particular society (Burch and Correll 1972; Correll 1972; Stefánsson 1933:314) to the members of any of the others.

The five factors listed above, along with regional differences in clothing, traditions, taboos, rituals, subsistence base, and various other factors combined to impart a sense of unity to the members of each society and of separateness from people belonging to the other societies. Intersociety prejudice was very strong in traditional times (Burch 1979a:126, 1980:277ff.; V.L. Smith 1966:25ff.).

Regional Integration

Despite the fact that the 10 societies in the Kotzebue region were completely separate social systems at the beginning of the historic period, there was a more abstract general unity underlying the Kotzebue region as a whole. This unity reflected not only the geographic integrity of the region but also a common cultural heritage derived from several centuries during which the historic populations developed out of a prehistoric Thule culture base.

The geographic unity of the Kotzebue region was

created by the combination of the deep eastward penetration of Kotzebue Sound into the Alaskan land mass and the focus of several river systems on it. At all times of year, but particularly in summer, it was physically easier for the members of most of the different societies in the region to converge on the inner portion of the Sound by traveling downriver than it was for them to communicate overland even between adjacent territories. The convergence of the different populations is precisely what happened every summer at the Sheshalik (*sisualik*) fair (fig. 2).

The fair regularly involved the entire populations of Napaaqtuġmiut, Nuataaġmiut, Qikiqtaġřungmiut, Kuungmiut, and Kangiġmiut, an average of perhaps 10 percent of the inhabitants of the Kotzebue region, as well as people located outside the region, such as the Tikiġaġmiut, Tapqaamiut, and Kingikmiut (Wales). Often a boatload or two of people from the Bering Strait islands, and occasionally even from the Asiatic mainland, would attend. The resulting gathering of some 2,000 or more people was the largest regular concentration of people in the entire Eskimo world.

The fair (*katŋut*) lasted for two or three weeks. Although increasingly oriented to intersocietal trade as commerce in furs, firearms (fig. 3), and whiskey expanded during the nineteenth century, the fair was al-

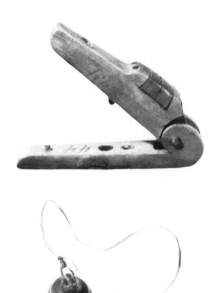

Fig. 3. Ammunition paraphernalia. Muzzle-loading firearms were acquired from the early Russian traders, and native materials were adapted to the new technology. top, Reloading tool of hinged pieces of ivory has a round hole in one side for the cartridge case and a tamper on the opposite piece. bottom, Wood container with plug top used to hold percussion caps. Height 5.0 cm; collected at Cape Espenberg, Alaska, 1881. top, Same scale, collected at Kotzebue Sound, Alaska, before 1910.

ways a multi-faceted event. In addition to private contacts between partners (Burch 1970a, 1979a:129; Burch and Correll 1972:25–26; Spencer 1959:167ff.), there were intersocietal feasts, dancing, and athletic competitions, and exhibitions of shamanistic prowess. A truly comprehensive social occasion, it was made possible both by the confluence of the Noatak, Kobuk, and Selawik rivers near Sheshalik and by the relatively large (and temporary) concentration of natural resources there (particularly beluga and salmon) just prior to and during the fair.

There are many sources on the Sheshalik fair (Brower 1945:160–161; Burch 1975a:249, 251–252; Burch and Correll 1972:30–31; Cantwell 1889:71–73; Curtis 1907–1930, 20:161–162; Hickey 1979; Hooper 1881:26–27, 1884:39; Nelson 1899:261; Oquilluk 1973:101ff.; J. Simpson 1875:236; V.L. Smith 1966:21–23; VanStone 1962b; Wells and Kelly 1890:25).

Miniature versions of the fair took place from time to time in winter, usually during the holiday season of late November to early January. These were the Messenger Feasts, which ordinarily involved the members of two local families in different societies whose heads were partners. One family would invite the other to visit for a week or two during which a whole series of feasts, rituals, games, dances, and other special events would take place. Whereas the Sheshalik fair occurred

Fig. 2. Kotzebue Sound people, probably Nuataaġmiut, at the Sheshalik fair. The tents are covered with caribou skins over which a layer of drilling has been placed as waterproofing. The 4 men in the center are wearing caribou-skin parkas with the hair side in. The woman (extreme right) and the boy (extreme left) are wearing calico parkas. The unusually large labrets on one man probably denote his status as umialik. Photograph by E.W. Nelson, July 15, 1881.

every year, Messenger Feasts were held only in times of abundance. Also like the fair, Messenger Feasts were not restricted to societies in the Kotzebue region, although they apparently did involve two societies from within it a high percentage of the time.

The Sheshalik fair and Messenger Feasts, while they indeed fostered social integration at the regional, as opposed to the societal, level, by no means eliminated intersocietal hostility. Mutual suspicion and prejudice were pervasive tendencies in early historic northwest Alaska. From time to time these hostile attitudes erupted into outright war (Burch 1974, 1979a:129, 1980:272–273; Burch and Correll 1972:34). Indeed, some of the same people who participated peacefully in the Sheshalik fair in July could be trying to annihilate one another the following November. However, during the nineteenth century, intersocietal warfare seems to have been directed more toward societies outside the Kotzebue region—particularly toward Point Hope—than it was to societies within it.

Subsistence

The traditional populations of the Kotzebue region had hunting-gathering economies based on resources that were relatively rich and varied for an area this far north. Caribou, mountain sheep, bears (grizzly, black, polar), several species of sea mammal (bearded seal, ringed seal, spotted seal, beluga, walrus, bowhead whale), fish (char, several species of salmon and whitefish, sheefish, grayling, burbot, Arctic cod), small game (ground squirrels, hare), furbearers (white fox, colored fox, hoary marmot, wolverine, lynx, wolf, otter, mink, muskrat, ermine), and birds (ptarmigan, snowy owls, sandhill cranes, whistling swans, several varieties of ducks and geese, seacliff nesting birds) comprised the harvestable fauna. The harvestable flora included several varieties of berry, greens, roots, shrubs (with edible or otherwise

top, VanStone 1980: 51; bottom, U. of Alaska Mus.; Fairbanks: UA 70-50-57.
Fig. 4. Birchbark containers. top, Traditional birchbark storage basket, basically a single piece of bark, heated, folded, then held in place with a rim stitched (sometimes decoratively) with willow root, and reinforced with a strip of willow around the center (Ray 1965). bottom, Basket with sides of reversed and interlaced strips of birchbark sewn with spruce root to willow rods at rim and base; a type made for sale. Height about 11.4 cm; made at Ambler, Alaska in 1970.

useful leaves or bark), mosses, and trees (especially spruce, birch, cottonwood); driftwood was abundant along the coast. Useful mineral resources included chert, slate, jade, and clay.

The relative abundance of the different resources varied from one societal territory to another, as did the precise timing of animal and fish movements. The environmental differences created the basis for societally distinctive economies and annual cycles of movement and for the comprehensive system of intersocietal trade. If the members of a given society did not have direct access to a particular resource in their own territory,

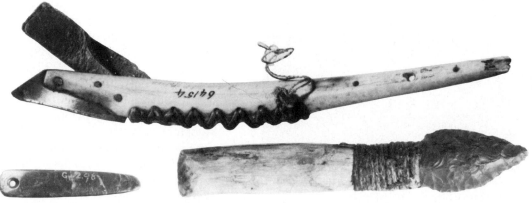

Smithsonian, Dept. of Anthr.: top, 64,154; bottom left, 63,762; bottom right, 63,722.
Fig. 5. Men's tools. top, Curved knife with metal blade fixed to a bone handle with metal rivets; leather sheath is attached to cover the blade edge. bottom left, Sharpening tool of jadite, a prized stone, used for both metal and stone blades. The hole at the end held a thong to tie the stone to a man's belt or hang around his neck. bottom right, Fish-skinning knife with chipped stone blade set into a wooden handle and bound with braided sinew. Length 19.0 cm, rest same scale. All collected by E.W. Nelson at Hotham Inlet, Alaska, 1877–1881.

Fig. 6. Bow drill. The northern drill type consisted of a mouthpiece and drill bit as in the south but instead of a pull strap to rotate the drill it had a bow with a leather strap. This is more efficient as it frees one hand. The bows were usually of ivory and often elaborately engraved. Ray (1982:258) suggests that the engraved bows collected in the Kotzebue Sound area may have originated elsewhere and been traded at the fairs held there. Length 34.5 cm, collected by E.W. Nelson at Hotham Inlet, Alaska, 1877–1881.

either at all or at the desired level, they could acquire what they needed either by moving to where the resource was, or by trade, or by some combination of the two. For example, both the Nuataaġmiut and the Kuuvaum Kangianiġmiut, living a considerable distance inland, had no access to sea mammals, hence to oil, in their respective homelands. The Nuataaġmiut dealt with the problem by traveling en masse to the coast each summer to participate in both the major beluga hunt and the fair that took place at Sheshalik. The Kuuvaum Kangianiġmiut, on the other hand, sent a few families of specialist traders to the fair to obtain sea mammal products, while the rest of the women stayed home and fished, and the rest of the men walked north into (temporarily) abandoned Nuataaġmiut country to hunt for caribou, marmots, and mountain sheep.

Interdistrict travel in summer for subsistence purposes was extensive, and it was a key element in the institutionalized pattern of intersocietal relations. Almost the entire population of Nuataaġmiut passed right through the heart of Napaaqtuġmiut country while the latter were elsewhere hunting seals, spent several weeks in Qikiqtaġrungmiut country harvesting beluga, a major local resource, and returned home again each year with little or no conflict. In winter, small groups could traverse one another's territory en route to or from a Mesenger Feast. But any movement across societal boundaries at any other time of year, or for any other purpose was considered an act of war and was treated as such. The overall pattern of interdistrict movement and trade, which must have evolved gradually over many centuries, enabled the people of the Kotzebue region to exploit the general resource base more effectively, and thus to have a higher material standard of living, than would have been possible otherwise.

Brief summaries of the subsistence base and annual cycle of each of the traditional northwest Alaska societies are contained in Burch (1980:285–295).

Structures

Several forms of dwelling were used by the Eskimos of the Kotzebue region, the specific type varying with the season and, to some extent, with the society. Most groups spent the summer living either in tepeelike tents (Nelson 1899:261; Seeman 1853:59) or in dome-shaped tents (Nelson 1899:260). Along the Kobuk River the willow pole dome framework was often covered with bark (Curtis 1907–1930, 20:209); in the Selawik district, by moss and grass (Anderson and Anderson 1977:50).

The most widespread type of winter dwelling was a semisubterranean "four-post center" building (Giddings 1952a:11–33; J. Simpson 1875:256), usually with a long entrance tunnel. Such a house consisted of a square or rectangular room having a hearth located on the floor below a skylight, and a gently sloping roof supported by a post at each corner. One, frequently two, and occasionally three sleeping areas would be built as separate alcoves off the sides of this central

Fig. 7. Kotzebue woman processing beluga muktuk. The muktuk is cut into linked rectangular sections and hung to dry for 2–3 days, then boiled in salt water, drained (on the wire mesh), and stored in seal or beluga oil. Photograph by W. Robert Moore, before Aug. 1955.

KOTZEBUE SOUND ESKIMO

area. The wooden framework would be covered by saplings, logs, sod, grass and/or moss, the precise combination depending on the local availability of building materials.

The four-post center house with sleeping alcoves was distinctive of the Kotzebue region. It contrasted with the more widespread north Alaska house in which a single sleeping platform was located at the back of the central living area, of which it was an integral part.

Dome-shaped structures were also used as temporary winter dwellings in all the societies in the Kotzebue region; in some, their use was quite common. Depending on the society, the degree of dwelling permanence, and the availability of materials, the dome-shaped sapling framework would be covered with caribou skins (Stoney 1900:813) or bark (Grinnell 1901:49–50). The typical Kivaliñiġmiut winter house, however, was a particularly large dome covered with layers of thin saplings, grass, moss, and snow (Brower 1945:158, 1950:32). Some of the Napaaqtuġmiut built rectangular log cabins as winter houses (Brower 1950:33–34). Small rectangular snowhouses were built as temporary shelters in all districts. The Kuungmiut, Qikiqtaġrungmiut, Napaaqtuġmiut, Kivaliñiġmiut, and occasionally the Pitaġmiut also built snowhouses when they lived on the sea ice for a few weeks early each spring (J. Simpson 1875:259).

Houses in all regions were lit by locally made pottery, or, rarely, by imported soapstone seal-oil lamps. Heat was also provided by these lamps, although in most districts an open fire (built on the floor in the center of the house) was used to heat rocks for the one cooked meal that the people ate each day. The internal arrangements and furnishings of houses have been described by Cantwell (1889:87–88), Giddings (1952a),

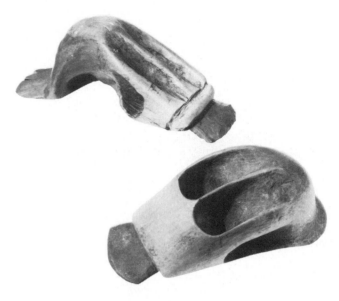

Fig. 9. Skin scrapers. Made to fit the contours of a woman's hand, these handles are of wood; ivory and bone handles were also made. The inset blades are stone. top, Length 14.2 cm; collected by G. Stoney at Hotham Inlet, Alaska, 1883–1886. bottom, Same scale, red stain on handle; collected by E.W. Nelson at Hotham Inlet, Alaska, 1877–1881.

and J. Simpson (1875:257). For the many different kinds of implements, utensils, and tools used in the house see Anderson and Anderson (1977:86ff., 150ff., 289ff.), Giddings (1952a:64–80, 93–104), Murdoch (1892:86ff., 150ff., 289ff.), Nelson (1899:63ff., 90ff.), and V.L. Smith (1966:19).

Clothing

Clothing was made from untanned skins shaped and sewed together (with caribou sinew) into six basic types of garment: an inner pullover parka with the hair inside, an outer pullover parka with the hair outside, inner pants (hair inside), outer pants (hair outside), socks, and boots. Both the inner (*il*ʸ*upa·q*) and outer (*qusuŋŋaq*) men's parkas had rounded hoods; they extended down to about hip level, and were cut off evenly all around. The comparable garment for women had a pointed hood and greater fullness in both the hood and in the body (for packing infants and small children). It extended to well below the knees in rounded flaps in both front and back. Men's inner (*ařvaukkaq*) and outer (*qaẏlik*) pants went from waist to ankle and were held up with a drawstring. Skin socks (*atula·piaq*), boots (*kamik*), and an outer belt (*pamiuqtaq*) (with a wolverine or ermine tail in the middle of the back) that went around the outer parka completed the basic wardrobe. For females the outside pants (*sivuẏalik*) were similar to those of the men, but the inside pants and socks were sewn together into a single garment (*mamẏuk*).

The basic wardrobe could be varied in a number of

Fig. 8. Kivalina houses. The sod house, owned by Austin and Mabel Thomas and built on the Shishmaref model, was traditional in appearance except for the split oil barrels used to cover the stormshed. The pole, which traditionally would have had household amulets suspended from it, was used to support a radio antenna. The frame house on the right was owned by Mabel's son Russell Adams and his wife Gladys. By 1982 both dwellings, as well as all others in the village, had been replaced by frame houses 3–4 times larger. Photograph by E.S. Burch, Jr., Sept. 1965.

Field Mus., Chicago: 20,756.

Fig. 11. Woman's summer parka made of ground-squirrel skins with wolf fur trim around the hood and decorative borders of clipped caribou fur, white reindeer skin, red yarn, and wolf fur. The deep side slits and elongated U-shaped bottom are characteristic of the region north of Norton Sound and contrast with the short slit and straighter hemline seen on women's parkas farther south. Collected by Minor Bruce at Kotzebue Sound, Alaska, 1894.

Fig. 10. Women from Selawik, including Esther Outwater on top right and bottom center, in elaborately decorated parkas. Photographs by Douglas D. Anderson, Nov. 1971.

ways according to season, regional differences in style, and the personal taste and expertise of the seamstress. The resulting diversity was considerable. An idea of what the possibilities were is indicated by the fact that the Nuataaġmiut alone made at least 15 distinctly different types of boot, each with a different name, using only seal and caribou skins as raw materials. Additional information on clothing and related accouterments can be found in the following sources: Beechey (1832, 1:340–341, 360, 396–397, 402), Giddings (1952a:87–89, 1961:139–140), Nelson (1899:30ff.), Seeman (1853:52–53), and J. Simpson (1875:238–245).

Technology

Hunting equipment consisted of the bow and a variety of special-purpose arrows, various types of thrusting

Smithsonian, Dept. of Anthr.: 44,146B.

Fig. 12. Gloves. Made of leather with the fur inside, each of the fingers is a separate piece sewed to the hand portion. The border is decorated with wolverine fur and clipped fur sewed in bands. The leather strip connecting them was passed around the neck, keeping the gloves readily available when removed. Length 19.0 cm; collected by E.W. Nelson at Selawik Lake, Alaska, 1877–1881.

309

Smithsonian, Dept. of Anthr.: top, 49,164; bottom, 48,546.

Fig. 13. Boots. top, Boots with hard sealskin soles crimped at the toe and heel; the upper is pieced reindeer skin with a horizontal band of wolverine fur and red yarn. The top of the boots is held up by a drawstring and the leather thongs are bound around the ankle. Height 46.0 cm. bottom, Boot sole creaser of incised ivory with separate animal carving linked to one end; used to crimp the soles during manufacture and also to reshape them when they became wet. Length 11.7 cm. Both collected by E.W. Nelson at Kotzebue Sound, Alaska, 1877–1881.

and throwing spears, and several kinds of harpoons. Bolas were used to kill waterfowl, deadfalls were employed to catch fur-bearing animals, and snares were used to take both small game (such as rabbits and ptarmigan) and large (such as caribou, grizzly bears, mountain sheep). Other sources give detailed information on hunting equipment and techniques (Anderson et al. 1977; Cantwell 1889:86–87; Giddings 1952a:42–52, 1956, 1961:130–133; Murdoch 1892:191ff.; Nelson 1899:118ff.; Seeman 1853:53; Stoney 1900:837–840).

Fish were caught with several types of net (gill net, dip net, seine) made from sealskin, caribou sinew (fig. 14), baleen, or willow bark, and with leisters, weirs, and hook and line. Sources include Cantwell (1887:42), Giddings (1952a:34–41, 1956, 1961:129–130, 133–135), Murdoch (1892:279ff.), Nelson (1899:173ff.), and Stoney (1900:840–842).

Transportation

Transportation in summer was either on foot (with or without pack dogs) or by boat. For the movement of bulk goods and large numbers of people the primary means of conveyance was the umiak (Inupiaq *umiaq*).

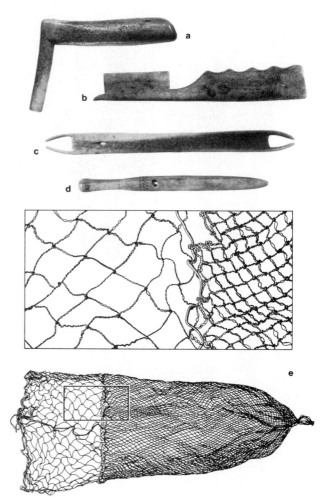

Field Mus., Chicago: a, 20,720; b, 20,211; d, 20,522; Smithsonian, Dept. of Anthr.: c, 48,538; e, 127,945.

Fig. 14. Netmaking. Nets are used in hunting and fishing; the size of the tools varies with the size of the net. a and b, Mesh gauges used to keep the size of the net openings uniform. c, Bone shuttle to keep sinew or baleen for netting. Like the gauges, shuttles may also be of ivory or wood. d, Needle for repairing nets. A spike (not shown) was used for tying and slipping the meshes (see Nelson 1899:193). e, Small sinew net gathered and tied at one end to form a funnel. c, Length 16.5 cm, rest same scale. a–c, Collected by Minor Bruce at Kotzebue Sound, Alaska, 1894; d, by E.W. Nelson at Kotzebue Sound, Alaska, 1877–1881; e, by G. Stoney, Kobuk River, Alaska, 1883–1886.

In the Kotzebue region these boats ranged between 25 and nearly 50 feet in length and consisted of a wooden frame covered by 6 to 16 bearded seal skins. An eight-skin (approximately 30-foot) boat was capable of carrying a payload of over a ton, plus a crew of 10. The boats were powered by square-rigged sails, or else by dogs and people, who tracked them along the seacoast or river bank. See Beechey (1832, 1:346, 389–390, 404–405), Giddings (1961:145–148), Nelson (1899:23, 216ff.), and Stoney (1900:836–837) for more detailed data.

Boat hunting by individuals in most areas was done by men in kayaks (Inupiaq *qayaq,* sg.). In the Siilvingmiut and the three Kobuk River districts, however, the

310

most common type was a relatively small, wooden, canoelike craft (Cantwell 1887:50, 1889:84–85; Foote 1966:23–25).

The primary means of transportation in winter was the basket sled, which was pulled by dogs, people, or, most often, both. Flat sleds were also used, particularly for hauling boats and unusually large or heavy loads. People in many districts, but particularly in the Kobuk River region, employed snowshoes to get about in deep snow. Sources on winter transportation include Burch (1975, 1976), Giddings (1952a:58–63, 1956, 1961:144–145), Nelson (1899:205ff.), and Stoney (1900:846–847).

Personal Appearance

The traditional Eskimos of the Kotzebue region were described by the early explorers as being strong, vigorous, robust, and healthy in appearance despite the fact that they were also characterized as being extremely dirty. Beechey (1832, 1:360) reported that the tallest man he encountered was five feet, nine inches and the tallest woman was five feet, four inches. Inlanders, particularly the people living in the upper Noatak district, averaged some two or three inches taller and were generally huskier than the coastal people seen by Beechey (McLenegan 1887:75; Nelson 1899:27–28; Wells and Kelly 1890:15; Woolfe 1893:15).

Excellent eyewitness descriptions of people in the Kotzebue region from the first half of the nineteenth century were published by Beechey (1832, 1:339ff., 360, 456), Kotzebue (1821:46–47, 60–61), Seeman (1853:51), and J. Simpson (1875:238–241, 244–245). According to their accounts, men cut their hair in an even line across the forehead and had it cropped very short on the crown. The balance, a strip about two inches wide, was permitted to grow long, increasingly so toward the back of the head. Personal adornment for men consisted of strings of beads in the hair and on the clothing, pendants and amulets worn about the neck and on the clothing, and labrets (of blue glass, ivory, jade, steatite, or other stones) worn in the sides of the lower lip (fig. 19).

Women let their hair grow long, with a part down the middle; they usually had two braids, which were occasionally wound around the head. Virtually every woman had three lines tattooed from the lower lip to

Fig. 16. Umiak of traditional style modified for use with outboard motor, belonging to Lawrence Sage of Kivalina. It is 30 feet long, and made of a wooden frame over which a cover made from bearded seal skins has been stretched. It is slightly narrower than the traditional model, hence has a faster hull speed. It retains the traditional features of light weight (2 men could lift it), buoyancy (3-inch draft when empty), and large capacity (about 3,000 pounds). Used for fall fishing and spring seal hunting in 1982, this frame was by then covered with plywood and fiberglass. Photograph by E.S. Burch, Jr., Sept. 1964.

the underpart of the chin. Many women had pierced ears from which strings of small beads were suspended; a few had pierced noses from which a bead was hung; and the occasional woman had bracelets of iron or copper, apparently obtained through trade with Chukchi.

Personality

Eskimos in northwest Alaska generally have been described as "friendly, open, genial, warm, and outgoing"

Smithsonian, Dept. of Anthr.: 127,907.
Fig. 17. Goggles, wooden eyepieces connected by strands of red and white seed beads with a leather spreader. Sinew and leather thongs tied the goggles around the head. Such shades protected against snow blindness. There is a wide range of goggle styles but those made north of Norton Sound, like these, are usually not so sculptural as those made in the south (Fitzhugh and Kaplan 1982:100). Width 14.0 cm without ties; collected by G. Stoney, Kobuk River, Alaska, 1883–1886.

Smithsonian, Dept. of Anthr.: 127,882.
Fig. 15. Antler comb with tines carved at each end, used to divide and clean sinew to create the strands for sewing. Length 10.0 cm; collected by G. Stoney, Kobuk River, Alaska, 1883–1886.

to strangers (Chance 1966:77). Such statements in fact describe a facade that the Eskimos presented only to people who were clearly more powerful than they. Burch's (1960–1961) informants described their own ancestors as having been "open, genial, warm, and outgoing" in only a limited number of social contexts, most commonly those involving close relatives and trading partners.

The informant accounts are supported by the experiences of the earliest explorers in the region. For example, Beechey (1832, 1:362, 2:277ff., 283–284); and Kashevarov (VanStone 1977:59ff.) both found the Natives insolent and threatening unless they were specifically seeking trade or unless they were in very small parties (cf. J. Simpson 1875:246ff.). It was only after their numbers had been profoundly reduced by disease and famine that this aggressive demeanor toward strangers moderated. Even as late as the winter of 1886 Stoney (1900:572) had to contend with an aggressive chief on the upper Kobuk River.

A more accurate view of traditional Eskimo personality in the Kotzebue region is symbolized by the "spartan ethic" (Burch 1974:2). According to this standard an individual was supposed to develop and display the qualities of competence, toughness, and discipline, both mental and physical, in virtually all spheres of activity. These characteristics were presented to others through quality performance, a dignified bearing, and emotional restraint. Informants invariably described their parents and grandparents as stoics who rarely manifested any emotion except within the confines of their own house, and in the kashim on certain occasions when the emotional display of pleasure or sorrow (but not pain) was considered appropriate.

The traditional Eskimos of the Kotzebue region were highly competitive (Burch 1975a:206; Charles Lucier, personal communication 1970), another characteristic that contrasts with the stereotyped view. Both individuals and groups competed with one another in practically every activity in which strength, endurance, skill, and knowledge were judged to be important factors. Such activities included sewing, carving, carpentry, hunting, story telling, dancing, trading, a wide variety of contests of physical strength and agility, and the game of football (similar to soccer and rugby combined). The list did not include certain other games, such as "stickball" (similar to American baseball), which in the Eskimo view did not require important personal qualities, and which, therefore, were engaged in simply for pleasure. The ethic of dignity and restraint required that individuals should keep feelings of pride or disappointment to themselves, and competition was often very subtle. Despite the covert nature of much of this rivalry, the desire to be better than one's fellows (or the shame of being bettered) was an important element in traditional Eskimo personality in this region.

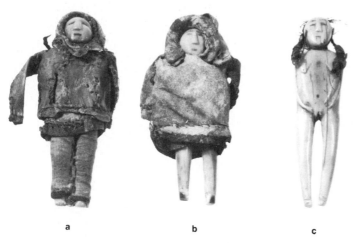

a   b   c

d

left, Smithsonian, Dept. of Anthr.: a, 64,210; b, 64,211; c, 64,206; d, 64,208; right, Alaska State Mus., Juneau: II-A-5250.

Fig. 18. Dolls. left, Traditionally carved ivory figures made by fathers as toys for their daughters. Clothes were sometimes removable and changeable; arms carved close to or as part of the torso are typical. a, Male with leather parka and cloth pants; b, female with leather parka; c, female with added hair; d, male with blue beads inset as labrets. a, Height 8.5 cm, rest same scale. All collected by E.W. Nelson at Hotham Inlet, Alaska, 1877–1881. right, Doll made for sale by Ethel Washington of Kotzebue, Alaska, who made dolls portraying individuals she knew. The woman holds a minature wooden spoon in one hand and a birchbark basket in the other. Height about 25.5 cm. Probably made in the 1930s.

312

Fig. 19. Sketches of Pitaġmiut men and women observed along the coast of Kotzebue Sound between Cape Espenberg and the Goodhope River. top left, Faces with tattooing on the chin are those of women, as is the arm, which shows copper and iron bracelets. The man in the upper right, probably a chief, wears labrets made from walrus ivory and inlaid beads and a headband of blue and white glass beads. The beads were obtained in trade from Asiatic Eskimos or Chukchi. The figure in the center wears a complete summer outfit. top right, The man at left wears a winter parka and a headband of blue and white trade beads. bottom left, These sketches illustrate the head and facial hairstyles favored by men of Kotzebue Sound at the beginning of the historic period. The paddle blades at left are painted with designs that probably indicated ownership; they may also have had ritual significance. A small ulu is below the paddles. At lower right is the stern (above) and bow (below) of an umiak. bottom right, Boy and tent frame. The explorers on Otto von Kotzebue's Russian expedition, of whom the artist was one, were amazed that the Eskimos found it warm enough to be without boots; many were wearing only breeches in the 50°F weather. Watercolors by Louis Choris, 1816.

History

Early Exploration and Contact

The era of early exploration and contact lasted from 1816, when Otto von Kotzebue "discovered" the region, to 1849–1850, when the *Plover,* of the John Franklin search expeditions, became the first European ship to overwinter there. Although contacted by Kotzebue, the Frederick W. Beechey expedition in 1826 and 1827, and by A.F. Kashevarov in 1838, the natives continued to act in a basically traditional manner throughout the period. The Pitaġmiut apparently were decimated early in or just prior to the period by a disaster, the nature

313

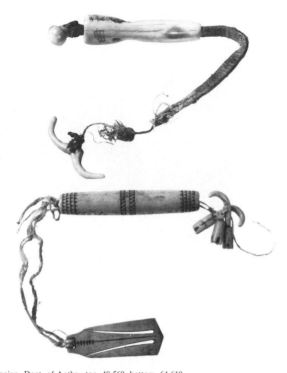

Smithsonian, Dept. of Anthr.: top, 48,569; bottom, 64,610.

Fig. 20. Needlecases. Unlike stoppered cases made south of Norton Sound, needlecases in north Alaska are carved ivory tubes with a strap running through. Needles are kept in the strap, which is exposed by pulling it up, and returned to the tube by pulling down on the end of the strap (which often has ivory ornaments attached). Also tied on are thimble guards, varying from cresent shaped to ornamented slotted ivory pieces, used to hold sealskin thimbles. top, Ivory case in form of a whale; bottom, ivory tube with sinew rather than sealskin strap. Length of case 8.9 cm, top same scale. Both collected by E.W. Nelson at Kotzebue Sound, Alaska, 1877–1881.

of which remains unknown, but that was probably unrelated to contact with Europeans.

Sources on the era of early exploration and contact include Anderson et al. (1981:64–80), Beechey (1832), Bockstoce (1977), Burch (1975a), Foote (1965), Foote and Williamson (1966), Gough (1973), Kotzebue (1821), T.E.L. Moore (1851), Ray (1975, 1975a), Seeman (1853), J. Simpson (1975), and VanStone (1977).

Period of Destruction

The period of destruction lasted from 1850 to 1897. The years from about 1850 to 1880 were marked by increasing contact with American trading vessels, particularly just before and during the Sheshalik fair, which resulted in the gradual spread of European diseases, and in the acquisition of firearms and alcohol by the Natives. Regular patrols by the U.S. Department of the Treasury Revenue Marine to halt the firearm and whiskey trade were inaugurated in 1880, and the first explorations of the interior—made by detachments from those patrols—were conducted by John C. Cantwell, S.B. McLenegan, and George M. Stoney.

Most of the Kangiġmiut emigrated south to Norton Sound during this period, leaving their homeland very sparsely settled. The Great Famine of 1881–1883 decimated the Kivaliñiġmiut, Napaaqtuġmiut, Qikiqtaġřungmiut, and Kuungmiut populations, and many of the survivors emigrated to the north. Faced with rapidly declining numbers of caribou, the Nuataaġmiut abandoned their homeland in 1886; most of them moved to the Arctic coast. The Siiḷvingmiut, Akuniġmiut, and Kuuvaum Kangianiġmiut continued to occupy their traditional territories, although their populations steadily declined because of disease and emigration.

Sources on the period of destruction include Anderson (1974–1975), W.W. Anderson (1974–1975), Anderson and Anderson (1977), Bertholf (1899a:18–19, 1899:111–114), Burch (1972, 1975a:26, 202, 253, 1979a), Cantwell (1887, 1889), Foote (1959–1962), Giddings (1952a, 1956, 1961), Grinnell (1901), Healy (1887, 1889), Hooper (1881, 1884), Jacobsen (1884, 1977), Jarvis (1899:61–62, 67), Larsen (1958), Mendenhall (1902), McLenegan (1887, 1889), Nelson (1899), Ostermann and Ostermann (1952), U.S. Census Office (1884), Ray (1975), Rosse (1883), Sherwood (1965), V.L. Smith (1966), Stoney (1900), C.H. Townsend (1887), VanStone (1962b), Wells and Kelly (1890), and Woolfe (1893).

Period of Consolidation

The period of consolidation began in 1897, when a Society of Friends mission was established at the site of the modern town of Kotzebue. This was followed in 1898–1899 by a gold rush to the Noatak and especially to the Kobuk River, and to the Seward Peninsula a year later. Between 1905 and 1915 several other missions, as well as schools, were built in various locations throughout the region, and domesticated reindeer herds were established to replace the entirely depleted caribou population.

The mission-school clusters rapidly became focuses for the Natives. However, people continued to reside for most of the year in dispersed settlements and to live a seminomadic way of life, since fur hunting and reindeer herding required that many people remain "on the land" throughout much of the year. When the reindeer population crashed and fur hunting ceased to be profitable during the Depression of the 1930s, the Eskimos became sedentarized in the mission-school villages. At that point, the map of the Kotzebue region aquired essentially its present form.

The caribou began to return during the late 1940s and increased considerably in numbers during the 1950s. Moose moved into the region in growing numbers as well. These developments, combined with the general maintenance of fish and sea mammal stocks, enabled the Natives to continue to harvest local faunal resources for much of their nutrition and for some of their clothing. The Native population grew rapidly during the 1940s and 1950s despite an appalling mortality rate. During the 1950s the U.S. Public Health Service successfully waged war against contagious diseases, and the Native population began to grow even faster subsequently. Many Whites moved into the region, especially to Kotzebue, after World War II.

By 1960 the population was distributed among 10 permanent villages of which Kotzebue was by far the largest; an eleventh, Ambler, was founded in the 1960s in a traditional settlement locality. Each village had a school (through grade eight), one or more stores and churches, a National Guard Armory (which in many cases served also as a community hall), and an all-weather airstrip. The people on the coast lived in wooden frame houses heated by a combination of seal blubber, driftwood, and willows; inland they used timber. Light was provided by gasoline lantern or kerosene lamp. Houses were occupied for the most part by single conjugal family units, albeit very large ones due to the presence of many children. Local government was by elected village councils. The people made their living through a combination of hunting and fishing, welfare, and wage employment, this last being largely seasonal, and primarily outside the Kotzebue region. English began to vie with Inupiaq as the first language of the Native population.

Sources on the period of consolidation include Gagnon (1959), Anderson et al. (1977), Anderson and Eells (1935), Andrews (1939), A.M. Bailey (1971), Burch (1975a:30ff., 222ff., 269ff., 1979a), U.S. Federal Field Committee for Development Planning in Alaska (1968), Foote (1959, 1959–1962, 1966), Foote and Cooke (1960), Foote and Williamson (1966), Green (1959), Grinnell (1901), Hadley (1969), Hawkins (1956), Hippler (1970), Hrdlička (1930), Jackson (1904), Jenness (1962), Olson (1969), Ostermann and Ostermann (1952), S. Parker (1964), Saario and Kessel (1966), P.S. Smith (1913), Smith and Mertie (1930), V.L. Smith (1966), Stern (1977), and Stern et al. (1980).

Land Claims Period

The "land claims period" began around 1960, with the first stirrings of political unrest among the Native population of northwestern Alaska, and culminated with the passage of the Alaska Native Claims Settlement Act in 1971.

The decade of the 1960s witnessed the formation of Native political organizations throughout the state. In the Kotzebue region specifically this trend began primarily as a protest against the Project Chariot scheme of the United States Atomic Energy Commission to blast a harbor out of the coastline near Cape Thompson, at the northern boundary of the region. It led eventually to the formation of the Northwest Alaska Native Association, in 1966. This organization represented the Natives of the Kotzebue region in the statewide push for recognition of Native rights in general, and of land rights in particular. The passage of the claims act concluded this phase of political activity.

Under the terms of the act, Alaska Natives were to receive $962.5 million and 44 million acres of land over a period of years, both to be granted to and administered by 13 regional corporations and more than 200 village corporations. One of the 13 regional corporations was NANA Regional Corporation, Inc., whose domain coincides almost exactly with that of the Kotzebue region as defined here. The inhabitants of Point Hope, who had been affiliated with the earlier Northwest Alaska Native Association, joined the Arctic Slope Regional Corporation.

Ten of the 11 village corporations initially established in the Kotzebue region—one for each village—were judged too small to operate profitably on their own. Accordingly, in 1976, they merged with NANA Regional Corporation. The eleventh, the Kikiktagruk Inupiat Corporation, of Kotzebue, was considered large enough to continue operating as an independent entity. During the 1970s both Kikiktagruk Inupiat Corporation and NANA Regional Corporation opened or joined in a number of business ventures in several different parts of the state. NANA was one of the most successful of the 13 regional corporations during this period. A nonprofit corporation, the Maniilaq Association, was created to provide a variety of social services to the inhabitants of the region.

Creation of extensive conservation areas was another outgrowth of the land claims act. After nearly a decade of intense debate between or among conservation groups, pro-development groups, and Native groups, the Alaska National Interest Land Conservation Act became law in December 1980. This legislation created within the Kotzebue region all or part of one national park, one national monument, two national preserves, and two national wildlife refuges, totaling more than 12 million acres. In addition, the Kobuk, Salmon, Noatak, and Selawik rivers were added to the National Wild and Scenic Rivers system.

During the land claims period several other developments took place that were not directly related to the act. One was the gradual surrender of the responsibility for Native education in the region by the Bureau of Indian Affairs to the state-operated school system. In 1976 the state system was dissolved, being replaced by regional and local school districts. One school district serves the village of Selawik. The Northwest Arctic School District has responsibility for schools in all the other villages in the Kotzebue region. By 1980 most villages had schools with a curriculum from kindergarten to twelfth grade, and with impressive physical plants, including modern classrooms and full-size gymnasiums. Among other innovations, the curriculum included a focus on local and regional Native culture, including courses in Native music and dance, oral history, language, hunting and fishing techniques, and crafts.

With the partial exception of the village of Kivalina, where subsistence whaling was resumed in 1966 after a hiatus that began with the Great Famine of 1881–1883, the people of the Kotzebue region remained essentially outside the controversies surrounding Native whaling (Bockstoce 1977a, 1980). However, they were very actively involved in other subsistence issues. These included debates over limits on caribou hunting, which were imposed following an extremely rapid (but temporary) decline of the Western Brooks caribou herd in the mid-1970s, and about who, if anyone, should be permitted to hunt on National Interest Lands.

In 1980 the people of the Kotzebue region were distributed among 11 permanent villages. For the most part, they lived in multi-roomed frame houses constructed by the state or federal government or by NANA Regional Corporation. All the villages had electricity and television and telephone service. Dwellings were heated by a combination of stove oil, firewood, and propane gas. All the villages except Noatak and Selawik technically were second-class cities, a status acquired during the 1960s in order to qualify for government grants to cities. They were governed by locally elected mayors and city councils. People still made their living through a combination of hunting and fishing (figs. 21–

22), welfare, and wage employment. In contrast to the situation in 1960, much of the employment could be obtained either within the region, particularly in Kotzebue, or in other parts of the state under the auspices of NANA Regional Corporation (or its subsidiaries) and Kikiktagruk Inupiat Corporation. English had become the first language of the majority of the Native population, although most adults were bilingual in English and Inupiaq.

Sources on the land claims period in the Kotzebue region include Anderson et al. (1981), Alaska State Housing Authority (1971), Arctic Environmental Information and Data Center (1976), Grabowski (1973, 1974), Hale (1979, 1979a), and Uhl and Uhl (1977, 1979). For a more general treatment of this period, and for additional references, see "The Land Claims Era in Alaska," this volume.

Population

Population estimates are presented in table 1. The figures refer to the total population of each district, which, from 1900 on, included non-Natives. The figures for 1800, 1850, and 1880 represent the populations of the traditional societies in their respective districts.

No reliable contemporary population estimates exist for any period prior to 1910. The U.S. Census Bureau began its work in the Kotzebue region in 1880, but the

Table 1. Population Estimates

District (Traditional Society)	1800	1850	1880	1900	1920	1940	1960	1980
Buckland (Kangiġmiut)	300	200	50	25	150	275	190	180
Goodhope Bay (Pitaġmiut)	300	75	50	25	75	230	95	135
Kivalina (Kivaliñiġmiut)	300	300	275	50	80	100	140	265
Kobuk Delta (Kuungmiut)	250	250	200	25	25	0	0	0
Kotzebue (Qikiqtaġruŋmiut)	375	400	225	100	225	375	1,290	2,525
Lower Noatak (Napaaqtuġmiut)	225	225	200	125	150	325	275	260
Middle Kobuk (Akuniġmiut)	375	375	325	100	380	375	640	870
Selawik (Siiḷvingmiut)	775	775	725	300	275	250	350	505
Upper Kobuk (Kuuvaum Kangianiġmiut)	500	500	450	300	100	225	260	475
Noatak (Nuataaġmiut)	550	575	600	0	0	0	0	0
Totals	3,950	3,675	3,100	1,050	1,460	2,155	3,240	5,215

SOURCES: 1800–1900, Burch's estimates based on personal observation and indirect evidence; 1920–1980, based on U.S. Census data, rounded off.

Natl. Park Service, Alaska Regional Office, Anchorage: 229531.
Fig. 21. Minnie Gray dressing out a caribou in Ambler, on the Kobuk River. She is dressed in conventional mid-20th-century style, with a calico-covered parka, slacks, and traditional mukluks. The caribou had been killed just as it approached the Kobuk River near Onion Portage and was brought to the village by boat. Photograph by Robert Belous, Sept. 1978.

Natl. Park Service, Alaska Regional Office, Anchorage: B100023.
Fig. 22. Minnie Gray (left) and a relative removing whitefish from a gill net near Ambler, in a temperature of −35° F. To set the net a series of holes was chopped at appropriate intervals in the ice, and a line was stretched from one to the next with the pole. After the line had been extended between the 2 most distant holes, the net was attached to it and stretched between them under the ice. The women return periodically, chop free the lines at each end, and retrieve their catch. Photograph by Robert Belous, late Nov., about 1974.

results for that year are very incomplete, as well as questionable on other grounds. The figures are totally unreliable for 1890 and 1900 and are only slightly better for 1910. However, from 1920 on the government figures are reasonably accurate.

Several disasters are represented in table 1. The earliest is an unknown event (or events) that all but terminated the Pitaġmiut of Goodhope Bay. The second was an accident in which large numbers of Qikiqtaġřungmiut drowned, presumably, but by no means definitely, between 1838 and 1850. A third is a famine that struck the Kuulugřuaġmiut, of Meade River, on the Arctic coastal plain, also apparently sometime between 1838 and 1850. Many of the survivors of that disaster fled as refugees to the Nuataaġmiut district, which accounts in part for the growth in the upper Noatak River population around mid-century. A fourth tragedy was the Great Famine of 1881–1883, which decimated the Kivaliñiġmiut, Napaaqtuġmiut, Qikiqtaġřungmiut, and Kuungmiut.

Extensive migration is also apparent in the numbers. The most extreme cases were the movement of the original Kangiġmiut south to Norton Sound after 1840, and particularly after 1850; and of the Nuataaġmiut, primarily to the Arctic coast, partly to Qikiqtaġřungmiut territory, in the 1880s. The declining figures for most districts after 1850 reflect both the impact of European diseases and the slow but persistent movement of families out of all sectors of the Kotzebue region toward the north and northeast in response to the de-

clining caribou population. Some of these migrants lived for a time in Nuataaġmiut territory before moving east in the Endicott Mountains or north to the Arctic coast. The nadir for the region as a whole was reached about 1900. Subsequently the population began to recover. In part this was due to the influx of non-Natives, including missionaries, teachers, traders, and especially miners to certain districts, especially to the former Kangiġmiut and Pitaġmiut districts. More important, however, was the general stabilization of the food supply, and the decline of emigration. The rapid overall growth after 1940 was a consequence of very high birth rates and steadily declining death rates. Much of the subsequent loss of population in some districts, such as Goodhope Bay, Buckland, and the lower Noatak River was associated with migration to the town of Kotzebue. The growth of Kotzebue after the end of World War II reflects a combination of internal growth and emigration from practically all sectors of northwest Alaska, as well as from other parts of the state and beyond.

Synonymy

The assignment of names to populations n the Kotzebue Region historically has been characterized by considerable confusion. What follows is a list of the most important "group names."

Akuniġmiut (*akuniẏmiut*), the people of the middle Kobuk River, first identified as a society and first named by Burch (1980:291). The term does not refer to any living population.

Kangiġmiut (*kaŋiẏmiut*), the Buckland River people, first identified in 1843 by Zagoskin (1967:216) and reported under the name Kanykgmiut. The 1880 census (U.S. Census 1884:4) renders it Kongigamiut. Traditionally, the term referred to both a settlement and a society. It is applied in 1982 to the inhabitants of Buckland village.

Kivaliñiġmiut (*kivalinʸiẏmiut*), the people of the Kivalina district. This population was first named Kivalinagmiut and correctly identified as a "tribe" by Kashevarov (VanStone 1977:59) in 1838. Zagoskin (1967:126) copied him, rendering it Kivualinagmyut. Kelly's seemingly fantastic account of the "Kevalinyes" (Wells and Kelly 1890:13) actually represents with some accuracy the chaos and population dispersal that followed the Great Famine of 1881–1883. The term is now used to designate the inhabitants of Kivalina village.

Kuungmiut (*ku·ŋmiut* 'river people'), first identified by Burch and Correll (1972:22–23) as Kobuk Delta Society. The ethnonym first appeared in Burch (1980:289). It is not applied to any currently existing population.

Kuuvangmiut (*ku·vaŋmiut* 'big river (Kobuk) people'), the inhabitants of the Kobuk River. This term first appeared in its correct subdialect form in Anderson et al. (1977), but "Kubok" was identified—very inadequately—as a population center by Zagoskin (1967:126) as early as 1843. The term, in its many literary variants, refers to all the inhabitants of the Kobuk River drainage. Traditionally it included the Kuungmiut, Akuniġmiut, and Kuuvaum Kangianiġmiut under a single geographic (but not social) heading. The special 1910 census report (U.S. Bureau of the Census 1915:113) illustrates some of the confusion formerly surrounding the term. The term now designates collectively the inhabitants of the several Kobuk River villages: Noorvik, Kiana, Ambler, Shungnak, and Kobuk.

Kuuvaum Kangianiġmiut (*ku·vaum kaŋianiẏmiut* 'people of the head of the big river (Kobuk)'), first identified as a society by Burch (1980:293–294), who also published the name for the first time. These people should not be confused with the Kangianiġmiut who inhabited the upper Colville River in the late nineteenth

century. The term is not applied to any living population.

Malimiut also appears as Malemut, Malemiut, Mahlemute, and Maleygmyut (Zagoskin 1967:103). This term is used by residents of the Norton Sound region to refer generally to the inhabitants of the Kotzebue region and to local people of Kotzebue origin and their distinctive dialect (Krauss 1980:49). In the early historical literature Malimiut was often employed to refer to emigrants from Kotzebue Sound, particularly from the Buckland River district (Kangiġmiut), who moved to Norton Sound after about 1840. The term was reported, almost always at least partly incorrectly, by observers who gained their perspective and most of their information on the Norton sound side of the Seward Peninsula (Zagoskin 1967:124; Dall 1877a:map; Nelson 1899:pl. II; Jacobsen 1977:123ff.; U.S. Bureau of the Census 1915:113). Early observers such as John Kelly, whose knowledge of Eskimo life was orginally acquired to the north of Seward Peninsula, never used the term and possibly never even heard it (see Wells and Kelly 1890). Ray (1975:133ff.) presents a useful discussion of the term and some of its referents.

Napaaqtuġmiut (*napaˑqtuẏmiut* 'spruce tree people'), of the lower Noatak basin, were first referred to in print by Kelly, under the label Napakato Mutes, but he had them confused with the Nuataaġmiut (Wells and Kelly 1890:14). Napartoo also appeared as referring to nine persons "enumerated in the vicinity of Point Barrow" (U.S. Bureau of the Census 1915:114). The census takers no doubt had found refugees from the lower Noatak River region who had fled northward after the Great Famine of 1881–1883. Stefánsson (1913:282) used the word more accurately, but the first really correct identification of the "Naupaktomiut" was in Foote and Williamson (1966:1045). The term is not applied to any living population.

Nuataaġmiut (*nuataˑẏmiut*) were the inhabitants of the upper Noatak basin. The earliest use of Nooatoks was by Kelly, who confused them with the Napaaqtuġmiut (Wells and Kelly 1890:14). His confusion is understandable, since the few Nuataaġmiut still residing on the Noatak River after about 1886 were becoming intermingled with survivors of the Napaaqtuġmiut. The term was employed more accurately by Stefánsson (1913:282), but Foote and Williamson (1966:1046) were the first to fully identify its correct referent. The term usually appears as Noatagmiut in the literature. The former Nuataaġmiut population was usually lumped together with the Napaaqtuġmiut and sometimes even with the three Kobuk River populations under the heading of Nunataaġmiut. Nuataaġmiut now refers exclusively to the inhabitants of Noatak village, which happens to be located in former Napaaqtuġmiut territory.

Nunataaġmiut (*nunataˑẏmiut*) has usually designated the inhabitants of the entire Noatak River drainage, encompassing both the Napaaqtuġmiut and Nuataaġmiut populations (see Dall 1877a:map). Beyond that, the referent has varied. Petroff (U.S. Census Office 1884:125), for example, said that it applied to the inhabitants of the Kobuk as well as the Noatak River. Nelson (1899) broadened its scope by including the Selawik district and much of the western Arctic Slope as well. Stefánsson (1913:282), on the other hand, claimed that the term applied only to a tiny group residing somewhere between the upper Noatak and the upper Colville rivers. The special census of 1910 (U.S. Bureau of the Census 1915:114) simply admits to confusion. However, the Inupiaq-speaking people of the Kobuk River used this word (in its subdialect form, Nunataaġmiut) to refer specifically to the inhabitants of the upper Noatak River. Apparently, many of the groups on the Arctic Slope also did this. The Nunataaġmiut who appeared on the Arctic coast east of the Colville River after 1886 initially were emigrant Nuataaġmiut, although the term rapidly became generalized to refer to all former inland-dwelling people in the area regardless of their specific point of origin.

Pitaġmiut (*pitaẏmiut*), of the Goodhope River (pitaq) district. The earliest mention of Pitukmiut was in the special census of 1910 (U.S. Bureau of the Census 1915:114), but virtually nothing was known about the people enumerated under that heading. See Ray (1964:83–84, 1975:153) and Burch (1980:288) for further discussion.

Qikiqtaġřungmiut (*qikiqtaẏřuŋmiut* 'big island people'), of the Kotzebue district, were first noted and correctly identified as a tribe in 1838 by Kashevarov, who reported them as Kyktagagmiut (VanStone 1977:62). Other variations included Zagoskin's (1967:126) Kikikhtagyuk and Petroff's Kikiktagamute (U.S. Census Office 1884:4). The term is used in the 1980s to refer to the inhabitants of Kotzebue, and homonymous designations apply to Herschel Island in the Arctic Ocean and Klikitarik on Norton Sound.

Siilvingmiut (*si·lʸviŋmiut* 'shee-fish place (Selawik River) people'), of the Selawik River drainage. Zagoskin, 1843, was apparently the first European to learn of Chilivik (1967:126), although he may have heard about them from Kashevarov's interpreter of 1838. He described it, incorrectly, as a settlement. So did Petroff (U.S. Census Office 1884:4), under the heading of Selawigamute. The Selawigmiut were listed as a tribe in the special census of 1910 (U.S. Bureau of the Census 1915:114). The term in the 1980s designates the inhabitants of Selawik village.

Sources

An ethnographic description of the Kotzebue region as a whole has never been published. Truly comprehensive accounts even at the district level are limited to the upper and middle Kobuk River districts. The Kuungmiut have scarcely even been mentioned in the literature. The situation is only slightly better for the Kivaliñiġmiut and Qikiqtaġřungmiut. Information on the Siilvingmiut, Kangiġmiut, Nuataaġmiut, and Napaaqtuġmiut falls somewhere between the two extremes. Even the existence of a separate society of Pitaġmiut remains in doubt.

The literature on the Eskimos of the Kotzebue region includes a number of strictly anthropological studies, but also a number of important explorers' accounts. A considerable quantity of useful information for the post-1880 period is contained in documents produced by historians, and particularly by representatives of various government agencies. During the 1970s NANA Regional Corporation sponsored research in conjunction with the NANA Cultural Heritage Project, although the information thus obtained has not been made available in published form.

This chapter was based primarily on Burch's (1981) study of the oral history of the region, significantly supplemented by the cited published reports.

Descriptions of many individual aspects of the traditional culture of the Kotzebue Sound region have been published. These include art (Ray 1977, 1981a), athletic contests and games (Hooper 1881:26–27; Nelson 1899:330ff.; Stoney 1900:835–836), dancing (Beechey 1832, 1:395–396; Jacobsen 1884, 1977; Johnston 1974, 1975), ceremonies (Lantis 1947; Ostermann and Ostermann 1952:77–82; Wells and Kelly 1890:24), feasts (Giddings 1956:37–38, 43–46; 1961:22–30, 53–60, 151–153; Hawkes 1913; Ostermann and Ostermann 1952:103–112; V.L. Smith 1966:29–31; Spencer 1959:210ff.), kinship and marriage (Burch 1970, 1975a; Heinrich 1955, 1955a, 1960, 1963; V.L. Smith 1966:31ff.), medicine (Lucier, VanStone, and Keats 1971), music (Johnston 1974, 1976, 1976a, 1976b, 1978), myths and legends (Curtis 1907–1930, 20; Lucier 1954, 1958; Giddings 1961:65–122; Hall 1975), place-names (Anderson and Anderson 1977; Anderson et al. 1977; Ray 1964, 1971), partnerships (Burch 1970a), stories and story telling (Curtis 1907–1930, 20; Giddings 1961:65–121; Hall 1975; Ostermann and Ostermann 1952), technology (Bockstoce 1977a; Giddings 1952a, 1956; D.W. Larsen 1972; Matthiassen 1930a; Nelson 1899; J. Simpson 1875, VanStone 1976), trading (Burch 1970a; V.L. Smith 1966:21ff.; Foote 1965; Spencer 1959:192–209), travel (Burch 1975, 1976), warfare (Burch 1974; V.L. Smith 1966:25–29), world view (Burch 1971), and life cycle (Spencer 1959:229–254; Gubser 1965:107–122; Giddings 1961:49–50; Nelson 1899:289–292).

North Alaska Coast Eskimo

ROBERT F. SPENCER

Although not all the settlements of Eskimos in the coastal zones of northern and northwestern Alaska were adapted to whaling, it was this activity that lent the area its specialized character. Some population enclaves were located away from the seasonal migration routes taken by the bowhead whales and so developed other economic pursuits. Where whaling occurred, it was an activity added to a variety of other hunting patterns. But even if a group or community did not engage in whaling, there were men from such locations who might have membership in a spring whaling crew and who sometimes traveled long distances in order to participate. Moreover, even in a settlement where whaling did occur, there were persons who took no active part, preferring to concentrate on other kinds of hunting. Thus, even though selective as a pursuit, the rewards of successful whaling were so great that all to some degree benefited. The result is that whaling became a virtual hallmark of the coastal cultures (Spencer 1959:25–38) (figs. 1–3).

It is clear that whales were of considerable economic importance; their flesh and oil as well as other by-products were extensively traded through the area. Forms of social solidarity arose through whaling, since membership in a hunting group or formally constituted crew was a social and economic asset. There was a ritual complex associated with whaling. All these factors combined to effect patterns of social solidarity in the area and to establish a degree of interdependence between whaler and nonwhaler (Spencer 1959:25–27; Worl 1980: 306–308).

The whaling centers of the precontact past, into the early twentieth century, were located in northern Alaska on a northeast-southwest axis from Point Barrow to Point Hope and so across to the tip of the Seward Peninsula to include Cape Prince of Wales and the Diomede Islands in the Bering Strait (fig. 4). In their northward movement the herds of whales tended to avoid the shallow waters of Kotzebue Sound and the shelf along much of the arctic slope. Other sea mammals could be taken in such waters, while there was also access to the inland caribou, but in the general area of the arctic slope none of the nonwhaling settlements had the permanence and longevity of those located on whaling grounds.

Environment

Northern Alaska, including for purposes of this treatment an extension of the whaling focus to the tip of the Seward Peninsula, is made up of 76,000 square miles of the arctic slope. The region is in general set off by the Brooks Range, the topographic barrier between the Yukon valley and the foothill-tundra domain to the north. These mountains come close to the border of Canada and the sea on the eastern side, reaching elevations of over 9,000 feet. As the range proceeds westward, elevations are reduced and the mountains fork into several lesser ranges and drainage systems. Although the foothill province to the north and west of the Brooks Range has significance for some of the native cultures, the coastal peoples were relegated to the tundra. This coastal plain, 20 to 90 miles in width, its greatest expanse being south of Point Barrow, is undrained except where a river system such as the Colville makes its meandering way from the Noatak divide in the De Long branch of the Brooks Range to its delta well east of Point Barrow. A few smaller riverine patterns also appear; however, none is so important as the Colville.

The tundra in general is marked by permafrost and lack of summer drainage creating the characteristic polygonal pattern of the area. At places the coastal plain simply shades off into the shallow sea. Winter ice action may also create bluffs and benches, rarely more than 25 feet in height but suitable for the location of human habitation. The climate of the area is high arctic, with long cold winters and relatively short cool summers. In contrast to zones of continental climate temperatures reach no great extreme in either summer or winter with yearly averages of 8°–12° F. The summer tundra is marked by a profusion of vegetation. Plants are very small and of virtually no economic importance to the native peoples. Forested areas apppear south of the Brooks Range. To the north stands of willows form the principal larger plants, although these too fade away in the tundra proper. Temperature averages rise slightly and the vegetal cover increases the farther south one moves along the coasts. The same is true of rainfall. Highly limited in the extreme north (5–7 inches yearly), precipitation and fogs

increase in the Bering Strait (Wilimovsky and Wolfe 1966).

Two features that relate to climate and landscape stand out. The solsticial light-darkness occurrence is marked, with, for example, 72 days of full light at Point Barrow between June and August with a corresponding absence of sun and light from December through February. Suggestions as to the effects of such changes on human physiology have been made (Simpson, Lobban, and Halberg 1970). A second element of importance to the area is the ice pattern. Although the freezing and opening of ocean waters is rarely predictable, ice has formed on the sea by mid-October, going through various phases of freeze, and the ocean may be ice-free again in June or July. Storms break the ice pack at times, pushing large floes against the beaches. Similarly, the ice pack may form open leads in the spring (R.K. Nelson 1969). It is through these that the whales swim.

Human adaptation centers around the fauna of the area. The native peoples made a conceptual differentiation between animals of the land and those of the sea. Throughout the tundra caribou (*Rangifer tarandus granti*) appeared in spring and were hunted until fall. Trapping of foxes, wolves, and wolverines, as well as of various rodents was important. To the south brown bears and mountain sheep were taken. Fish were trapped and netted on the tundra streams in summer, and much attention was given to the hunting of various waterfowl, especially along the coasts. Saltwater fishes were of little economic significance except for the occasional runs of eulachon. But in the main, the coastal peoples concentrated on sea mammal hunting.

top, U. of Alaska Arch., Fairbanks: Call Coll.; bottom, *Tundra Times,* Anchorage, Alaska.
Fig. 1. Whale hunting. top, Umiaks with flags at Point Barrow, celebrating the return from a whale hunt. Photograph probably by Samuel J. Call, about 1898. bottom, A beached whale possibly at Point Barrow. Photographed 1976.

The baleen whale, variously known as the bowhead, Greenland, or polar whale (*Balaena mysticetus*) makes its way, beginning in early spring as the ice leads open, through the Bering Strait. In herds of varying numbers, although rarely more than 50, the whales pass Cape Prince of Wales, Point Hope, and move in a northeasterly direction toward Point Barrow. Summering under the polar ice pack, the whales return southward as the winter freeze begins. While random whales might be hunted on the ice-free sea in the fall, it was the whale hunt in the spring, with its attendant preparation and ceremony, that marked the beginning of the yearly round of activity for the coastal peoples. The spring whaling was followed by the advent of the Pacific walrus, herds being encountered on floes at sea beginning in late June,

321

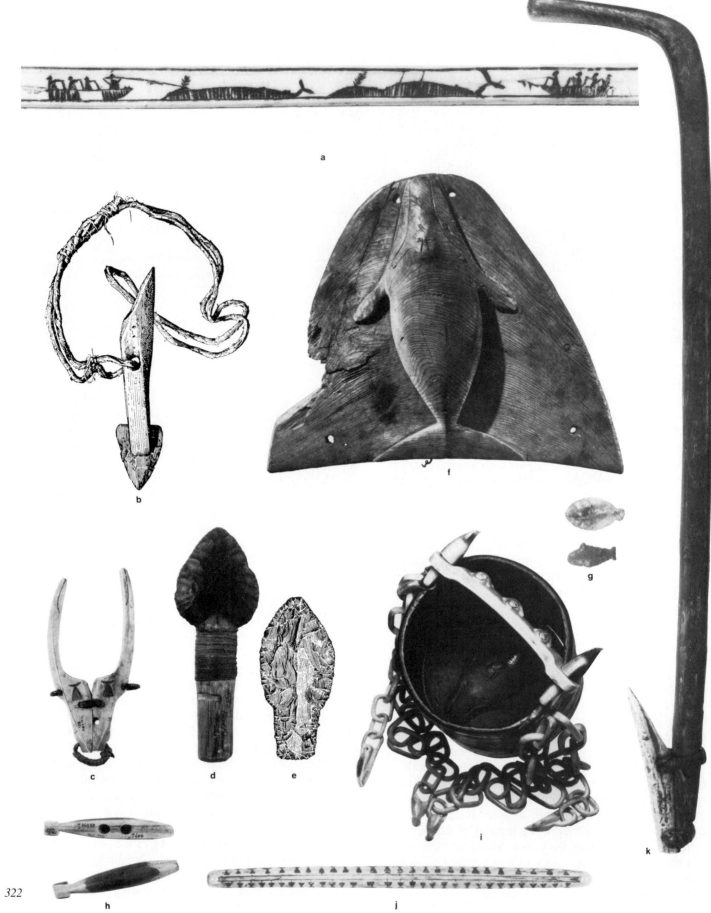

a

b

c

d

e

f

g

h

i

j

k

a movement lasting into August. Some belugas, narwhal, and polar bear, as well as the many seals of the area, including the ugrug (*Erignathus barbatus*, bearded seal), were taken as encountered. Individual hunting of seals occupied the dark months (fig. 5). Given the food resources of the area, the native inhabitants were able to adapt wholly successfully to the environment in which they lived and to make capital of both sea and land hunting (Spencer 1959:9–38).

The Traditional Peoples

The groups resident in the area, those of Point Barrow, Point Hope, and of Cape Prince of Wales and its environs, as they are seen at the time of contact, can only with difficulty be designated as tribes. While the concept "tribe" need have no political significance, referring rather to a sense of in-group identity (Oswalt 1967), the settlements that did exist were made up of kinship segments. These far transcended any consciousness of local group identity per se. While it was true that continuing community endogamy effected a continuing replenishment of kinship ties, the primary focus of relationship clearly went beyond the boundaries of the single settlement. There was in general a uniform language (Inupiaq, northern Alaska Eskimo) with some slight dialectal variation, but this again was not so distinct as to create boundaries between settled groups* (Correll 1972).

It is probably true that the presence of whaling created some distinctiveness among the north Alaska coastal dwellers. The hunt itself was attractive and so fascinating as to draw individuals into its sphere from various groups and communities. It was not unusual to find men from Wales at the Barrow villages, or to see inland people making an adaptation to the coast. It is for this reason that the population of coastal north Alaska seems to be rather diverse and suggests at times social and

---

*For the transcription and sources of Inupiaq words, see the footnote in "North Alaska Eskimo: Introduction" (this vol.). The names used here as the English designations of Eskimo groups and places are the Inupiaq names in the standard Inupiaq practical orthography. The names in italics are phonemic transcriptions.

cultural discontinuities. A reflection of this is seen in the changing composition of the coastal communities. There is a gradient of activities rather than a precise and single focus.

As Burch (1976a, 1980) has suggested, the ecological distinction of Nunamiut 'people of the land' and Taġiuġmiut 'people of the sea' may be somewhat overdone and not wholly faithful to social reality in the area. At its extremes, considering the Nunamiut of the general Anaktuvuk Pass region (cf. Larsen 1973; Gubser 1965; Ingstad 1954), as against the tried whalers of Point Hope or Point Barrow, the distinction is striking. When, however, the intermediate foothill-tundra-coastal zones are considered, the distinction is less apparent. The presence of a network of social relationships across the coastal and adjacent inland settlements blurs any sense of tribal distinction. The suffix *-miut* 'people of' is regularly employed in Inupiaq to refer to the residents of any definable place. This can be a large inclusive unit, such as 'those of the sea coast' or merely the inhabitants of a minute locality named for a natural feature. Since people could and did change their localities, it follows that they might be variously and differently identified. To put the matter another way, there was some sense of community, some notion of locality and local origins, but clearly, no sense of broader political or necessarily of territorial affiliation. There was, to be sure, familiarity with a section of terrain, involving detailed knowledge of what to the outsider appears as an undifferentiated mass of tundra. Similarly, people know the conditions of tide, ice, wind, and sea action on a stretch of familiar coast. Clearly, this kind of knowledge tended to make for some stability of population. But since the potential for mobility also existed, difficulties arise in respect to the designations of the groups encountered. It is eminently clear that given the firm bases of kinship and voluntary association the native peoples were wholly conversant with the implications of both group membership and mobility. These must be seen from their eyes rather than from taxa arbitrarily imposed by ethnology (Spencer 1959:126–146; see also Burch 1975a, 1980).

Membership in a group initially rested on kinship.

Smithsonian, Dept. of Anthr.: a, 63,802; b, 89,744; d, 89,596; e, 56,667; g, 89,613 and 89,577; h, 56,598; j, 89,424; k, 89,836; c, U. of Pa., U. Mus., Philadelphia: 42,101; f, Field Mus., Chicago: 53,424; i, Calif. Academy of Sciences, San Francisco: Liebes Coll. 5–428.

Fig. 2. Whaling complex. a, Pictographic scene of whaling with umiaks, on a bow drill handle. Length of detail 17.0 cm; collected by E.W. Nelson at Point Hope, Alaska, 1877–1881. b, Whale harpoon head with part of line attached. c, Harpoon rest, 2 pieces of ivory, incised with whale tails, to be lashed between the gunwales where they meet at the bow; used only when whaling, to support the heavy harpoon while approaching a whale. d–e, Lance heads of chipped stone used to kill the whale after it is harpooned; d, shows the manner of attachment to the wooden shaft. f, Carved wooden image of a whale with blue bead eyes, to serve as a umiak charm, probably attached to the bow between the gunwales. g, Chipped-stone charms carried by hunters. h, Pair of carved ivory whales used on a line probably to toggle the dead whale's flippers together while it was towed to ice. i, Wooden water bucket with a whale carved on the inside bottom and others on the elaborately carved ivory handle, used by the captain's wife to offer the dead whale a ceremonial drink of water. j, Bag handle with whale flukes engraved on it, probably a hunting tally. k, Blubber hook with wooden handle and ivory hook used to engage pieces of blubber or flesh; it may have been used as a boat hook as well. Length 88.6 cm, b-i same scale. b,d,e,g,h,j,k, collected by P.H. Ray at Point Barrow, Alaska, 1881–1883; c, by E.A. McIllhenny at Point Barrow, Alaska, 1898; f, by Minor Bruce at Point Hope, Alaska, 1897; i, by Arnold Liebes at Point Barrow, Alaska, before 1960.

Beyond this were the associations arising in membership in a hunting group and in the quasi-kinship extensions of partnership and friendship (Spencer 1959:193–209; Burch 1970a).

There is a fairly general agreement as to band, deme, or group names for the area. However, this chapter, recognizing that "tribe" per se has little or no validity, but rather that group names depend on local provenience within territorial definitions conceived by the native cultures themselves, is obliged to come to grips with varying designations for the component peoples. Thus, recognizing that Nuvuk was a settlement at the tip of Point Barrow, the residents there being designated Nuvugmiut, there is still the problem of shifting population. Persons could be designated by the place in which they tended to continue to live, even if their origins might be elsewhere. This has created a problem of general designation and creates some problems in providing precise delineations of local groupings both in ethnographic and ethnohistorical literature.

Stefánsson, for example, in his mapping of the area locates the Kigirktarugmiut (*qikiqtaẏřuẏmiut*) on the coast off Herschel Island (1914:facing p. 10). This, noted elsewhere as the Kikiktarmiut, cannot be regarded as a permanent group. Its members were variable, depending on family segments that moved in summer to the Colville area for trade. The same is true of Stefánsson's Kittegaryumiut east of the Mackenzie Delta. In the river systems inland from Wainwright inlet, Stefánsson locates the Oturkagmiut (*utuqqaẏmiut*). Along the western Colville, he locates the Kangianirmiut (*kaṇianiẏmiut*), Noatagmiut (*nuata·ẏmiut*), Nunatagmiut (*nunata·ẏmiut*), Kuvugmiut (*ku·vaṇmiut*), Killirmiut (*killiẏmiut*), and Kagmallirmiut (*qaṇmaliẏmiut*).

The Nuvungmiut (*nuvuṇmiut*), Utkiavigmiut (*utqiaẏviẏmiut*), and Kugmiut (*ku·ẏmiut*) are located between Point Barrow proper and Wainwright. P.H. Ray's (1885) account lists place-names, such as Nuwuk at Point Barrow, Uglaamie, Cape Smythe, the modern town of Barrow, Kuñmeum (*ku·ṇmiut*, a southern form of *ku·ẏmiut*) (Wainwright), and Sidáru (southwest of Point Belcher). Nelson (1899:22–23) places the Kaviagmut (Qaviaragmiut) back of Cape Nome and the Kiñugumiut (Kingikmiut) in the Wales area, both on the Seward Peninsula, and the Malemut (Malimiut) from Shishmaref Inlet to Point Hope.

While all such terms have validity and convey meaning to the inhabitants of the general area, they have no precise value as anything beyond local designation. Indeed, the societal organization and the ecological focus, together with some dialectal variation, especially as re-

top, U. of Alaska Arch., Fairbanks: Yasuda Coll.; bottom left, *Tundra Times,* Anchorage, Alaska; bottom right, Alaska Northwest Publishing Company, Edmonds, Wash.

Fig. 3. Ceremonial whale feast. top, Blanket toss in a sealskin blanket, at the celebration of a successful whale hunt. Photograph by Hannah Yasuda, 1935. bottom left, Whaling crew slicing up flukes into muktuk. Photograph by Frank Whaley, 1970s. bottom right, Point Hope 3-day springtime whale feast. Participants sitting in the shelter of their umiaks, waiting for the ceremonial division of the whale. Photograph by Lael Morgan, probably 1975.

324

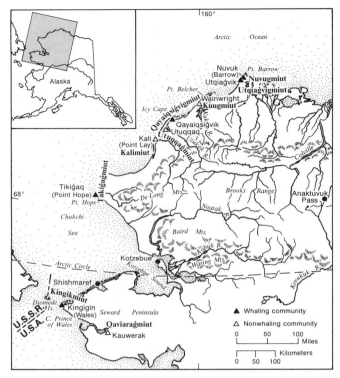

Fig. 4. Eskimo groups of the north Alaska coast in the 19th century.

lates to the Seward Peninsula as against the north slope, are more reflective of group reality.

The groups practicing whaling were found in three areas. In the north there were at Point Barrow (Nuvuk) the Nuvugmiut; at Cape Smyth (Utqiaġvik) the Utqiaġvigmiut; and, at Icy Cape (Qayaiqsiġvik) the Qayaiqsiġvigmiut. In the west were the Tikiġaġmiut, at Point Hope (Tikiġaq). In the southwest were the Kingikmiut, at Cape Prince of Wales (Kingigin), and those on the Diomede Islands.

The groups not primarily adapted to whaling were found in three areas. In the north there were on the Kuk River near Wainwright the Kuugmiut; at the Utukok River mouth (Utuqqaq) the Utuqqaġmiut; and, at Point Lay (Kali) the Kalimiut. Groups inhabiting Kotzebue Sound and environs are discussed in "Kotzebue Sound Eskimo," this volume. In the Seward Peninsula at Kauwerak there were the Qaviaraġmiut. For the Seward Peninsula groups see also "Bering Strait Eskimo," this volume.

Demography

The area to the east of Point Barrow was used for a camping, hunting, and fishing territory both by the people of the Barrow region and by the groups resident

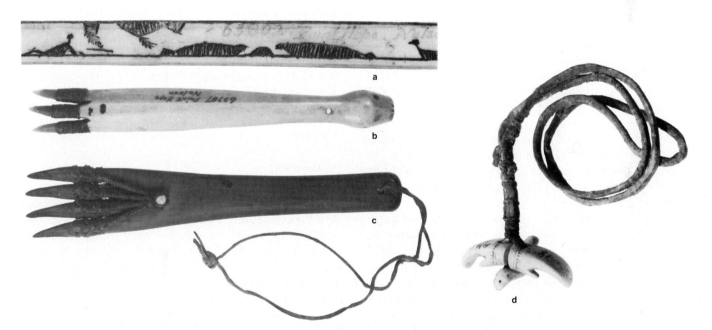

Smithsonian, Dept. of Anthr.: a, 63,802; b, 63,787; c, 56,557; d, 56,625.

Fig. 5. Sealing. a, When seals lay sleeping in the sun on the ice in late winter and spring the hunter, as shown in this bow drill pictograph, stalked them by crawling forward on the ice. Although he wears large polar bear skin mittens and knee pads the movement wakens his quarry. To reassure the animal the hunter scratches on the ice with a special implement, imitating the sound of a seal. b, Ivory scratcher with a seal head carved on one end and 3 seal claws lashed with sinew to the other. c, Wooden scratcher with an ivory stud to hold the claw lashings and a strap through a hole in the handle end. For the kill the hunter used a spear or braining stone. d, Seal drag used to take the kill home. The line is looped through an incision in the seal's lower jaw and the handle is attached to a longer line or a dog's harness. The seal is dragged on its back. This example has a handle made of 3 pieces of ivory carved to represent mittens with a seal between them. Width of handle 7.5 cm, rest to same scale. a and b, Collected by E.W. Nelson at Point Hope, Alaska, 1877–1881; c and d, collected by P.H. Ray at Point Barrow, Alaska, 1881–1883.

along the Colville tributaries. At Nigalik, on the delta of the Colville, was a well-known trading site, but it was not continuously inhabited. Although there were sometimes a few people at Barter Island and also at Herschel Island, the next major grouping to the east lay at the mouth of the Mackenzie. Omitting the groups living virtually exclusively in the interior, the coastal settlements vary as to population depending on food supply and shortage, mobility, and epidemic disease.

At Nuvuk, J. Simpson (1875) listed 54 houses in 1852–1853 and 309 people, 166 male. P.H. Ray (1885) listed 150. The settlement was reduced thereafter and abandoned in 1936.

At Utqiaġvik in 1852–1853 J. Simpson (1875) showed a count of 250 people in 40 houses. An immediate decline took place, the result of an influenza epidemic. P.H. Ray (1885) counted 23 families with a population of 130 in 1882. The coming of the Euro-American whalers from the 1880 to 1900 both reduced the population and increased it by in-migration. The town of Barrow grew up at the expense of other communities both on the coast and inland, gradually reaching, as a result of its location as a service center, a population of more than 2,000 in 1925.

Although these two "villages" were primary, they were not the only settlements. A localized dwelling, a single family house, might be found at any point on the coast from Nuvuk on southward. For example, there were houses at Bernirk (piẏniq, the place from which the well-known archeological site of Birnirk takes its name) and any number of sites containing one to three houses spread along the coasts. Such settlements were abandoned as commercial whaling, trapping, and the fur market developed and as service towns such as Barrow and Kotzebue arose.

A group of perhaps 50 people in eight families were resident at Point Belcher in 1882 (P.H. Ray 1885). At Icy Cape some whaling was undertaken by an estimated 60 people until about 1900 when the site was abandoned. That this community, that of the Qayaiqsiġvigmiut, was of some whaling importance is shown by the presence of a single men's house and participation in the Messenger Feast. At other points along the northwest coast, shallow water and a coastal indentation precluded whaling. Since sections of the areas were favorable for caribou hunting, some inland groups pushed to the sea. The town of Wainwright on the Kuk had 80 people in 1882 (P.H. Ray 1885), while a parallel situation arose at the mouth of the Utukok. Point Lay was founded by a group of inland people but was "colonized" in the twentieth century by a group from Point Hope (Rainey 1947). With the exception of Wainwright, all such communities have been abandoned.

At Tigara ((Tikiġaq), 276 people are listed at Point Hope in the 1880 census (VanStone 1962a). The presence of outlying settlements increased this number at times to as much as 400–500. As with the other communities, there has been considerable expansion and contraction of population. Burch (1981) discusses the Point Hope population in the nineteenth century.

The Wales group includes Cape Prince of Wales and the Diomede Islands. The town of Wales itself consists of a northern and a southern "village." This, with its segments, may have run as high as 900, although 500–600 seems to offer an average between 1854 and 1895 (Ray 1964). To this figure may be added another 200–300 for the Diomede Islands, as well as some 200 along the north coast of the Seward Peninsula toward Shishmaref and Cape Espenberg.

The figures stated above, drawn from many differing sources, are faced with the difficulty that population movement at any given time, the advent of epidemics, the onset of commercial ventures such as fur trapping in the twentieth century and whaling in the late nineteenth, blur the picture. For the Taġiuġmiut of the period 1850–1890, using the term to refer specifically to the whale hunters, a figure of 1,850 seems fairly reasonable. It may be recalled that this does not take into account the various Nunamiut, even those resident at coastal sites such as the mouth of the Utukok. If the peoples in the interior in the same period are considered, their number is probably double, perhaps 3,000–4,000. Although prehistoric sites reveal a long dependence on whaling at sites where it could occur, populations were probably never much greater. The question of what happened to the Nunamiut of the interior can be answered in terms of population decimation through introduced diseases and of migration to the coasts (cf. Kroeber 1939:20–27; Burch 1976a).

Culture

Settlements

Even if Nuvuk, Utqiaġvik, Tigara (Tikiġaq), Wales, and the communities on the Diomede Islands offer what seem to be towns or villages, they lacked corporate reality as such. Ties of kinship were primary, meaning that a settlement consisted of a series of separate, bilateral extended families. Nor were these limited to a single community, since a network of kinship relationships could apply. There was some sense of local endogamy, largely a matter of expediency, but this did not prevent movement and marriage into or out of the settlement. The separate bilateral families could and did intermarry, with the result that a child brought his maternal and paternal kindred groupings together. In the north Alaska coast societies, extended genealogical reckoning did not play an important role; definitions of relationship were pragmatically conceived and in large measure tied up with residence arrangements. Rela-

top left and right, Alaska Histl. Lib., Juneau; bottom left, Denver Mus. of Nat. Hist., Colo.: Bailey Coll. BA21–289.

Fig. 6. Structures. top left, Winter houses and storage racks at Point Hope. Whale bones outline the sod house at right. Photographed in 1880s. right, Wooden house with partial sod covering. Photograph by Clarence L. Andrews, 1920s. bottom left, Woman tending an oil lamp inside a house. Photograph by Alfred M. Bailey, Wainwright, Aug. 1921.

tionships were reckoned through those living or in recent memory, thus rarely beyond kindred in the great-grandparental generation. This meant that a settlement was made up of a series of more or less permanently inhabited houses (Spencer 1959:75–92).

Since primary loyalties were directed to the household group, thence to the kindred group, and only incidentally to affinal kin, it follows that these extended familial units existed side by side rather than together. Feud or an uneasy truce might exist between unrelated groups. There was no definable political organization, except perhaps an incipient one in the presence of hunt leaders. The problem that the native cultures faced was the creation of a situation where benign and cooperative relations could exist between persons and groups possessing no other tie than propinquity. How this was achieved explains much of the organization of the society of the area.

The community thus begins with the house. On the

coasts, houses were well constructed of blocks of sod over an excavation (fig. 6). The house was entered through a passage starting at ground level and inclining gradually downward. Storage rooms or areas were located on the sides of the passage, which ended in a cooking place, a meat cellar in the permafrost, and a well leading upward into the main room. This was an area often lined and floored with beached driftwood and sometimes whalebone. The sod forming the walls and roof was domed and banked. A skylight of gut was placed in the roof. At one end, that away from the entrance well, was a bench. The inhabitants slept there or on the floor. Furnishing included furs and skins for bedding, racks for drying of boots and clothing, and the ubiquitous Eskimo lamp. Such houses, ranging in size from 10 to 12 or more feet in diameter, could accommodate 8 to 12 persons. As noted, these were close relatives, siblings, their wives (or husbands) and various dependents. Two or three able-bodied men could supply the economic needs of the household, while women prepared food and dress. There was, in short, the balanced sexual division of labor that so characterizes Eskimo society generally (Spencer 1959:44–61).

Related people might occupy adjacent houses or build a common passageway. Relatives in nearby houses could stand together in cases of emergency, such as feud, abduction, or murder. No precise rules of residence existed. Living arrangements depended on practical necessity. Yet it was in the household and the extended family involvements related to it that the community may be said to begin to function (Spencer 1959:182–192).

In each community were several whaling crews, the number varying from time to time as personnel could be recruited. It was on this level that kinship could be set aside, men joining the banner of a whaling captain, an umialik, who functioned to organize the spring hunt. It is because of the presence of men on whaling crews from different localities and residence situations that it is difficult to delineate the composition of the community or "tribe" as such. An element in the community beyond the household was the kashim or men's house

(Inupiaq *qařɣi*). This was a social center, a dance house, a place to which men went for leisure time activity, and a work center. Not wholly the domain of men, since women could enter, often bringing men their food when they stayed there, and participating in festivals, the kashim was usually associated with one or more whaling crews, the building erected by the hunt leaders. Rivalry between whaling captains, crews, and the various kashims themselves was at times a divisive factor in the settlement. A community came to have reality not because of the houses within it but rather because of the existence of the kashim. It did not have to be a special structure, since a normal dwelling would serve; however, a captain of substance tried to erect one, usually a large rectangular building with a shorter passageway than would be characteristic of the usual house (Spencer 1972).

Subsistence and Technology

Hunting was carried out either individually or as a group effort. There was the development of the hunting group or crew and the emergence of the hunt leader (Spencer 1979). The work ideal of the culture demanded activity; it did not require joining a group. Individual hunting could involve sealing, fishing (usually a women's task), trapping, fowling, or any other task of which a person was capable. Group hunting related to the capture of large mammals, the whale primarily, but also walrus (fig. 7), ugrug, sometimes polar bear, and the communal activity of a caribou drive. Most individuals were associated with a crew and also hunted alone as often as possible.

It is in respect to hunting that the significant material array of Eskimo life is encountered. A full discussion

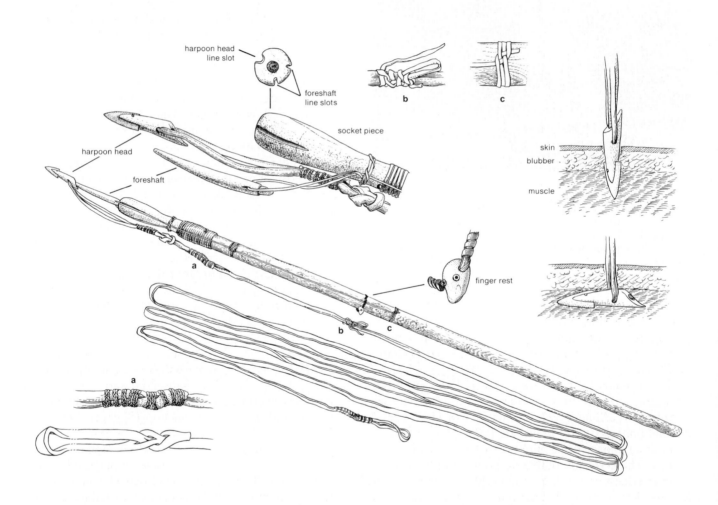

Fig. 7. Walrus harpoon. Walrus were usually hunted from the umiak, but not in so organized a manner as whales. The harpoon varied in size depending on the size of the owner, and when in use had floats attached. The captured walrus was towed to the nearest ice for butchering. This complete harpoon has a wooden shaft, heavy ivory socket piece, ivory foreshaft, toggle harpoon head with metal point (see drawing for penetration), and a finger rest carved in the shape of a seal. Length, excluding point, 183.0 cm; collected by P.H. Ray at Point Barrow, Alaska, 1881–1883.

of the elements of material culture is to be found in Murdoch (1892). North Alaska, it is true, is somewhat less well endowed materially than groups to the south and generally reflects, in terms of archeological remains, a late Thule configuration. Weapon assemblage, including the complex harpoon with detachable shaft, the spear thrower, and the bola, suggests the range of possibility. The sod house, clothing (figs. 8–10), and footgear, sleds and sledges, as well as a variety of containers not excluding a simple pottery, reflect the native inventive adaptations. Water transport, which was vital, was mainly by umiak, the open whaling boat. Made by men, the boat, still widely employed in the 1970s, was 15 to 20 feet in length. A frame was made of whatever materials were conveniently at hand, such as wood obtained from driftwood and bone. If sufficient wood was available, a deck of boards was laid over the keel in the three-feet-deep craft. The frame was covered with ugrug skins, six such being required for an average boat.

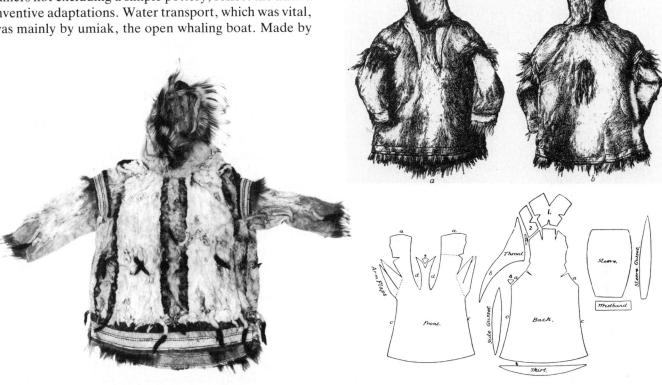

left, Smithsonian, Dept. of Anthr.: 56,757; right, Murdoch 1892:figs. 57, 59.

Fig. 8. Men's parkas. left, Typical slightly rounded bottom reaching just below the hips (unlike the longer style of southern Alaska), but the hood is not fitted to the sides as is usual. The material—brown and white ermine skins for the body—marks it for special occasions. The hood is reindeer and mountain sheep skin bordered with wolfskin. Decorative bands of clipped hair, red beads, and red dyed skin border the bottom and shoulders. right, Nearly white mountain sheep skin with decorative shoulder and bottom borders probably also for special wear. Its hood is closer fitting; pattern is below. left, Length from top of hood 97.0 cm. Both collected by P.H. Ray at Point Barrow, Alaska, 1881–1883.

Smithsonian, Dept. of Anthr.: 89,544.

Fig. 9. Ptarmigan quill belt. Men and women wore belts outside their parkas to prevent updrafts of cold air. This man's belt is particularly elaborate, having black tail quills and white wing quills woven in a checkerboard pattern (see Murdoch 1892:136–137 for description of technique). The edges are bound with deerskin and a point hangs from the back as an amulet. The end tab is sealskin and the tie braided sinew. Length 87.0 cm, excluding tie. Collected by P.H. Ray at Point Barrow, Alaska, 1881–1883.

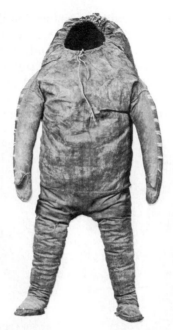

Fig. 10. One-piece waterproof skin garment decorated with tufts of hair along the outer seam of each arm. The large hood, which allowed it to be stepped into, has a drawstring closure. Length 153.8 cm; probably from the Point Barrow region, Alaska.

The skins were stitched carefully by women, allowing watertightness, and lashed over the gunwales to the keel. The craft was paddled with single-bladed paddles, each man in a crew kneeling on the deck and paddling on one side. The umiak could accommodate 6 to 12 persons (Spencer 1959:201–203).

With the opening of the ice leads, lookouts for whales were posted. With the onset of late winter light, a whaling crew went aside to prepare the gear. The whaling season marked a world renewal—new lines, new clothing, and a new cover for the umiak or whaleboat frame. Whaling magic, sexual continence, and solemnity marked the preparation. The umialik had a virtual priestly role, both in the preparation and in the greeting of the captured whale. He had also enlisted the services of a skilled harpooner. A camp was set up on the ice in March or as the whales were sighted. The crew, 7–10 men, ran the umiak into the ice lead when a whale was sighted. The whale was harpooned as many times as possible, so arranged as to allow the shaft to come free, and was tied with lines and inflated sealskin floats. After the

Fig. 11. Snowknife of ivory, with sinew lacing on grip. It was used to knock snow off boots and garments and to cut blocks of snow for temporary snow structures or to be melted for water. Length 38.5 cm. Collected by P.H. Ray at Point Barrow, Alaska, 1881–1883.

dangerous task of subduing the whale, it was lanced in a vital spot by the harpooner. Crews might cooperate both in hunting and in towing the whale back to the ice edge, dividing the meat according to respective efforts in the kill. The whale was greeted by the wife of an umialik, dressed in new finery and acting as a priestess. This woman offered fresh water to the whale, addressing it with words of greeting. The butchering followed, each crew member and members of assisting crews obtaining shares (figs. 2–4). Generosity patterns demanded that the boat owner give freely of the meat to all in the community and beyond it. The meat was stored in ice cellars in the permafrost. The cellar had to be emptied before the next season (Spencer 1959:26–27).

Crew activity was next directed to the walrus. The meat of this animal was less prized but used for the dogs. Ivory and meat were shared by crew members. The same division applied to all animals taken by joint endeavor. In summer crew activity might extend to caribou, meaning a trip inland. But after the whaling, crews tended to break up, men and their families traveling widely on various activities. Thus a family head might leave his dependents at a fishing station, going upstream in the interior with an umiak and summer gear. He would then engage in caribou hunting, return for the walrus, or go on trading expeditions. The umiak was pulled by dogs; when the freeze began, a sled was taken from the umiak, the boat mounted on it, and the dogs pulled the load back on the ice (Spencer 1959:27–32, 33–34).

Late summer saw the formal preparations for the trading expeditions of the area. Indeed, some of the period had to be spent getting goods ready for trading, mainly pokes of sea mammal oil. At the mouth of the Colville, on the Utukok, on the Noatak, at Shishmaref on the Seward Peninsula, and at several other sites were the trading centers. People with formally constituted partners met with them and engaged in a structured trade. Here is where the Nunamiut-Tagiuġmiut distinction becomes clearest. The people from the coast traded oil to the land hunters of the interior for caribou skins for clothing. In the area arose a mutual interdependence on this basis, one marked by formality of trade and mechanisms of association in the form of trading partnerships stretching across ecological boundaries (Spencer 1959:193–209; Burch 1970a).

The onset of the winter freeze saw the traders returned, often picking up their families on the way, and the settling down to the winter months. Crew activity now ceased and men went out alone for seal netting (fig. 12) and spearing. The winter months, while much given to social activities centered in the men's houses, were also a period of work, relating to various crafts and manufactures of weapons, lines, clothing, nets, tanning, and so through an array of the material products of the culture.

Social Organization

The primary focus of societal integration in the area lay in the bilateral extended family. The major theme of family membership was cooperation, mutual aid, and defense. Kindred were bound to each other by the principle of collective responsibility. There was no recognized family authority, each individual being free to make his own decisions as to activity. At the same time, the strength of the society lay in the conceptual ordering of kinship relationships, as far as these were reckoned by the kindred grouping. The emphasis was always on consanguineal relatives. Collective responsibility being primary, affinal relationships were less important. In other words, support for a brother, cousin, or anyone else defined by a consanguineal kinship term took precedence over any spouse's relative. In cases of feud, a person related to groups in conflict faced a tragic dilemma (Spencer 1959:62–96, 99–118, 1979; Burch 1975a:43–74).

While there was no abhorrence of incest, marriage or sexual relationships with anyone designated by a kinship term were seen as inappropriate. This is because the basic principle in the sociocultural system was to extend to nonkindred the rights and privileges of kinship. There was, in short, the development of a quasi-kinship, unrelated people brought together in a cooperative relationship not unlike that of consanguinity. This principle applied initially at marriage, or indeed, in any circumstance in which sexual relations had taken place. Implicit was a concept of mutual aid and support.

U. of Pa., U. Mus., Philadelphia: top, NA 10,070; bottom, NA 2749.
Fig. 12. Carved wooden figures with ivory rattles strung on hoop of ivory (top) and metal (bottom). They may have been used as floats for seal nets or were attached to a string and shaken on the ice to attract seals to the net (Murdoch 1892:254). Height of top 13.5 cm; bottom, same scale. Collected by W. Van Valin 1917–1919: top at Point Hope, Alaska; bottom, Point Barrow, Alaska.

It follows that if one had a wife, one was bound through her to a circle of affinal kin. By the same reasoning, one avoided the wife's sisters sexually, the argument being that one was already involved with them in a system of mutual aid. Polyandry and polygyny might exist, but they were never fraternal or sororal (Spencer 1959:75–82).

Because there is thus a continuum of sexual relationship from the casual affair or rape, moving on to a more permanent union, and ultimately coming to marriage itself, the various shadings of marriage and sex are difficult to define. Chastity was not prized. Girls after puberty could cohabit with a number of men. These men stood in a special relationship to each other by virtue of having had sexual relations with the same woman. This might result in benign relations between them. In any case, it was here that the institution of partnership, of nonkinship relationships, and of quasi-kinship had its beginnings.

In marriage, a couple simply settled down in joint residence. There were no rules regarding this, since practical circumstances dictated where a couple might live. They could set up a new household, live with parents or siblings on either side, or move to a new community. A man ran the risk of having his wife abducted by a stronger person with a backing of kin. In this case, he married again, usually in the same community. If endogamy in the community tends to be the practice, it is not reflective of any rule, but simply of familiarity with persons in a known area. After children were born, after the marital relationship was generally recognized, when there was allocation of ownership of property such as game, the hunter owning it until he brought it into the household when it belonged to his wife—then could a marriage be said really to exist (Spencer 1959:75–82).

The sexual principle continued to operate after marriage. A wife could be lent to another man for temporary sexual relationships. This was a means by which ties between unrelated persons could be cemented. Thus in attracting and holding members of a hunting crew, an umialik could lend his wife to a crew member and take his in turn. These men thereafter entered into a partnership relationship, one virtually as strong as kinship. The children of such men, in fact, retained a recognized relationship to each other by virtue of the wife exchange of their parents (Spencer 1959:83–84; Burch 1975a:106–111).

Associations and Alliances

Aside from the extended family, the crew relationship was primary. The umialik, a man of skill, strength, and wealth, could take over a crew from an older relative, or, given the backing of his kindred, could organize one. He sought, both by judicious gift-giving and support and by wife exchange on a temporary basis, to

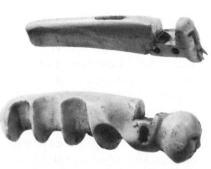

Fig. 13. Dancing and drumming. top left, Drawing of a family sitting outside their sod-covered house just south of Point Hope, Alaska. The man with labrets is drumming, while the woman appears to be dancing. A sled is elevated on one of the whalebone racks and an inflated sealskin rests on the other one. At the far right is another sled. Watercolor by Richard B. Beechey, 1826. bottom left, Performance at Wainwright, 1921. Men traditionally wore mittens when they danced possibly in imitation of seal flippers. Photograph by Alfred M. Bailey. bottom right, Drummers from Wainwright at the Eskimo Olympics, 1974. On the right is Weir Negavana. Photograph by Steve Preston. top right, Handles for tambourine drums, the only musical instrument used; they have a wooden frame over which a membrane is stretched. The player holds the drum in his left hand, gripping it by the handle, which is a separate piece tied onto the rim. These examples are ivory; both have faces carved at the distal ends. upper, The upturned face has inset ivory tusks, perhaps representing a walrus man; the grip is plain. lower, This human face is carved with an open mouth, suggesting singing. The handle has separate grooves for the thumb and fingers. upper 12.0 cm, lower same scale; both collected by P.H. Ray, at Point Barrow, Alaska, 1881–1883.

enlist and retain his crew. Men could leave a crew if dissatisfied or if the leader was unsuccessful. The umialik vied with others to keep crew members, resulting in no little competitive rivalry. An umialik required a good deal of surplus food and property to keep his crew; here lay the importance of the backing of his own kindred. He had further to acquire the songs, charms, and magic necessary to the successful hunt. As noted, the whaling communities lacked political organization outside of the familial lines. In the umialik, as a man of wealth and status, there may be said to be the beginnings of a political organization (Spencer 1959:177–182; Van-Stone 1962a:38–58; Worl 1980).

Within the community and indeed, beyond it, were relationships between persons, mainly between men, but also between women, that can best be seen as institutionalized friendships. These partnerships, usually so termed in the literature (Spencer 1959:177–182, 1972; Burch 1970a), were of several different kinds. They might be for purposes of sociability and economic aid if they occurred between individuals of the same general age-grade and the same area. The crew relationship was often a variation on this theme, although such patterned friendships might take place between crew members as well as with the umialik. Wife lending might serve to effect a permanent partnership. There were also joking partnerships, a reflection of the highly developed humor of the region. These involved competitive horseplay and were often no more than an extension of formalized friendship. In other words, one might have a series of partners, friends, with some of whom a joking license was allowed.

Trading partnerships were of a somewhat different order, most frequently between persons with differing economic pursuits. The most common was between a man from the coast and several inland caribou hunters. At the yearly fairs, the great trading conclaves held in the early fall at various sites, men sought out those with whom they had established a relationship and effected an extensive trade of goods, although primarily pokes of oil for caribou skins. In general, such trading partnerships did not involve a sexual exchange.

When partners had effected wife exchange, especially if they lived in different communities, those traveling were urged to seek out their relatives' partners, especially those of the parents. Not quite so dependable as kindred, a relative's partner could vouch for one in an alien community. The attitude toward the stranger, one who could establish no ties at all in another group, was marked by hostility. A stranger could be killed at sight, his goods and wife or wives taken. The rationale for such suspicion lay in recollections of killings and feuds.

While the feud was always a kindred matter, people could call on partners for assistance. The partnership alliance, coupled with family membership and responsibility, allowed for a situation as close to war as these groups came. The noninvolved preferred to stand aside. Despite armor, ambush, and other techniques of war, the fighting personnel were generally drawn from a single kinship grouping. Others were drawn in only incidentally.

The Messenger Feast

The peoples to the south along the Alaska coasts, generally speaking, south of Wales (cf. Nelson 1899), had a series of socioceremonial festivals. To the north, although religious ritual surrounding the food quest was important, social festivals were restricted to the Messenger Feast. This reflected a relationship between men of substance, umialik, who, sending messengers to their counterparts in other communities, invited them, feasted them, gave lavishly of gifts, and expected to be invited in return. The Messenger Feast (fig. 15) appears to be a variation on the theme of the Northwest Coast potlatch. There was the same idea of rivalry, of over-

right, Smithsonian, Dept. of Anthr.: 89,800.

Fig. 14. Games. left, Joshua Okpik of Barrow establishing a world record in the ear weight competition at the 1982 World Eskimo Indian Olympics at Fairbanks. Photograph by Bill Hess, Aug. 1982. right, Bull-roarer, a children's toy that makes a loud whining noise when swung. The handle is a wooden rod with a notch at one end to which is tied a line of braided sinew also attached to the oval board with notched sides. Both pieces are painted with black and red designs. Length of rod 34.5 cm; collected by P.H. Ray at Point Barrow, Alaska, 1881–1883.

Denver Mus. of Nat. Hist., Colo.: Bailey Coll. BA21–460.

Fig. 15. Kunuyuq, a native of Wainwright, wearing a yellow-billed loon headdress of the Messenger Feast. His lip is punctured for a labret. Photograph by Alfred M. Bailey, 1921.

whelming a guest with food and largesse, and of social status tied up with the distribution of surplus goods. Divisive elements in a whaling community there may have been; clearly, however, the Messenger Feast, held in the fall or winter, had an effect of allowing all residents in a given area, far beyond the confines of a single community, to achieve a share in distributed goods. Generally, one umialik, aided by his crew, feasted another along with his men. The messages sent by runner were often humorous and insulting, suggesting a joking-partner arrangement (Spencer 1959:227–229).

Religion and Ritual

The basic world view of the area, paralleling that of Eskimos in other regions and other northern hunters, was linked intimately with the realm of animals. An elaboration of folklore and myth demonstrates that animals were morally and intellectually superior to men, that the game hunted allowed itself to be taken or could be coerced by ritual and magic. The religious elements thus fall into two major groupings, hunting ritual and shamanism, the shamanism involving the theory of illness and its cure.

The whaling peoples of north Alaska made the most of the cult of the whale. The hunt itself could be seen as a world renewal rite, marking the beginning of the yearly cycle. Preparations required avoiding at all cost giving offense to the whale, or indeed, to any animal, which would, if offended, withhold itself and resist the compelling magic. The refurbishing of the gear, the solemn approach to the hunt, and during the hunt greeting the whale and the offering to it of fresh water—all combined to create solidarity among crew members, involved their wives and families, and so by extension, an entire community. Songs, charms (fig. 16), and amulets were a vital part of the whaling process. These were owned usually by the umialik and the harpooner, but also by any crew member. Such magic was sold and inherited. Whoever owned one of these or indeed, any charm, song, or name, had a certain food taboo tied up with the ownership, as for example, being forbidden the back fat of a female caribou or the hind flippers of the ribbon seal. In whaling and other hunting, ritual duties were incumbent both on a hunter and on his wife, a factor in creating marital stability (Spencer 1959:267–277).

All sea mammals, on being taken, were offered cold fresh water as a welcoming libation. Land animals, when trapped, were given gifts, needle cases or knives. Animals had to be treated with care, the throat cut or the brain pan opened when taken so as to free the soul. Any breach in these areas gave offense and prevented future success. Caribou likewise had to be treated with care, there being among the peoples of the interior a parallel to the coastal whaling cult. A vast lore existed

in the native cultures about the animal realm. Beyond animal spirits, there were no divine or other spiritual beings of significance. Monsters, trolls, and dwarfs figure in the folklore and belief but play no part in any cosmogonic system. Nor was there a defined sense of afterlife. Names of the dead were given to the newly born, suggesting a vague sense of reincarnation, but unlike the animal beliefs, these patterns lacked any systematization (Burch 1971).

Because the shaman participated in other economic activities, as a hunter or a crew member, he could not actually be said to belong to a class apart. There were usually several persons, more often men, who possessed the shamanistic call and acted as curers and incidentally as magicians. Shamanism in the area was mainly of the ecstatic type; spirit possession, while not unknown, does not seem to reach the same level as among the Siberian Eskimo. The shaman had a special kind of power that enabled him to perceive the cause of disease (offense to the animal world), to control weather, and to find lost items. As commonly described for other areas, the shaman was likely to be an hysteric, schizoid and schizophrenic, highly compulsive. A novice was usually apprenticed to another shaman. Once he mastered the patterns of his art, he might be sought to cure. He was paid for his services in manufactured goods, food, or sexual rights. His knowledge consisted of ability to perform legerdemain as well of possession of magic songs. He performed as a curer and as a magician in the winter months, singing his songs accompanied by the usual Eskimo tambourine.

Illness arose from the breaking of prohibitions. This might involve offense to an animal spirit or the eating of food that ownership of a name, charm, or song had

U. of Pa., U. Mus., Philadelphia: NA 335.
Fig. 16. Bracelets of leather with fur trim and inset blue beads, worn by men to secure the cuffs of their waterproof parkas and probably also serving as charms. Diameter 9.0 cm. Collected by G.B. Gordon at Point Hope, Alaska, 1905.

tabooed. This infraction caused the soul to wander. It was the shaman's task to entice the errant soul or personality back into the body. Illness could also be caused by an intruded object shot into the patient's body by an enemy. The shaman removed this from the body by singing and sucking. Given anxiety as a not infrequent cause of illness, it follows that the ministrations of the shaman were frequently successful (Spencer 1959:299–330).

Summary

The picture that emerges of the whaling cultures of the north Alaska coasts is one of remarkable success, a society integrated in family and founded in exploitation of the resources of the terrain. Within the boundaries of the whaling cultures lay an essentially common societal organization, a generally common language, with, to be sure, some dialectic diversity, and a common set of cultural premises. Local variation in economy existed, and similarly, there was movement of persons and groups within the defined area. The social units cannot be defined with precision when it is considered that one activity shades off into another, when whaling gives way to sea mammal hunting, and this in turn fades into an inland caribou hunting adjustment.

If differences there were, they lay more in intensity than in sharp lines of differentiation. It seems evident that the kashim of the Wales area was extremely elaborate. This aspect was retained at Point Hope, where festivals held in the kashim involved dramatic performances, masked figures, and carvings of men and animals with moveable joints. Although vastly different in style, there is some suggestion of the parallel drama of the Northwest Coast. At Barrow, there was considerably less by way of such ritual and recreational paraphernalia. In other words, in this feature and in a good many others, such as the Messenger Feast, the focus becomes most intense in the Wales–Point Hope region, and is attenuated farther north.

Prehistory

Since the whaling area is striking as a distinctive phrasing of Eskimo culture, any culture-historical treatment of north Alaska begins with this adaptation. The cultures of the area reflect the detailed sequences of both pre-Eskimo and prehistoric Eskimo cultures. The beginnings of a whaling crew are traced archeologically in Okvik, Old Bering Sea, Birnirk, and Thule sequences, even if Ipiutak, the striking prehistoric culture at Point Hope, lacked whaling. Elements from all coalesce to produce the cultures of the ethnographic present. Yet the whaling cultures of the north coasts, lacking the full array of technical and artistic elements of the

remoter past, may not reflect a direct continuity. The problem of the inland as against the maritime specializations raises some points not yet fully resolved. Any culture-historical analysis should take such questions into account. In part, they may be answered by archeology, in part by an analysis through comparative ethnology of the distributions of the component traits. By the early nineteenth century, the north Alaska whaling cultures had reached the patterns as described. With contact with outsiders a rapid series of changes began.

History

The historic and ethnohistoric backgrounds of the Alaska coasts are described in detail by Gubser (1965). With the exception of the peoples around the Bering Strait, contacted in the late eighteenth century by the Russians, the coasts were left in relative isolation, contacted only sporadically by various expeditions (Beechey 1832; Simpson 1843; J. Simpson 1875; P.H. Ray 1885; Murdoch 1892) of British and American origin. An interest in trade goods on the part of the Eskimo was marked. Iron tools and especially tobacco were avidly sought after. There was little beyond various items effecting material change until the beginning of intensive whaling by outsiders in the 1880s. The coming of commercial whalers from New England and elsewhere had a marked impact on the native population. In both maritime and inland people it proved to be the main avenue of culture change.

On the heels of the whalers came other agencies of change. The reindeer industry affected the area, fur trapping and sale of pelts developed, and there were the beginnings of intensive missionization. Negative ef-

Hydrographer of the Navy, Taunton, England.
Fig. 17. Woman and child from Icy Cape. Pencil sketch by Capt. Frederick William Beechey, during the voyage of H.M.S. *Blossom*, 1826–1827.

fects on the native populations arose following contact with the appearance of epidemic diseases—influenza, measles, and tuberculosis—all of which took a fearful toll of the Eskimo. Decimation and relocation of populations continued from the late nineteenth century until well into the twentieth. Such changes related also to the economy of the area; they were furthered not only by missionaries but also by the development of administrative units such as the U.S. Bureau of Indian Affairs with welfare and educational programs. Alaska statehood has effected marked changes again. The north Alaska Eskimo, in a money economy, have begun to take a more positive role in the direction of their own destiny. A final element of change in the area lay in the development by the U.S. Navy of the Petroleum Reserve No. 4. The explorations for oil, natural gas, and similar resources (Tussing, Rogers, and Fisher 1971) presaged the development of the trans-Alaska pipeline.

It was the commercial whalers who first enlisted the services of Eskimos as crew members. The prize was baleen, used in the corset stays of the late Victorian period. Between 1880 and 1905, baleen ranged from $2.00 to $5.00 per pound. Despite governmental attempts at paternalistic protection, the whalers introduced alcohol and diseases and contributed to a marked period of disorganization. Interior peoples drifted down to the coasts for the goods available there, disrupting the human ecological balance of the entire area.

By the 1880s steam-driven ships were introduced into the arctic, permitting overwintering by the alien whalers. The effect was to disrupt the integrity of the native crew system and to introduce goods in payment for services. By enlisting the natives in whaling, older skills were laid aside, no attention being paid as to whether a native hired on a ship came from an inland or maritime group. One effect of this was to destroy the balanced relations between population enclaves whose previous subsistence patterns had been well defined. Native modes of whaling were changed by the introduction of the darting gun and the whale bomb, items still used in the 1970s (VanStone 1958, 1962a).

By 1905, baleen was no longer marketable (fig. 18). Furs were bought by the storekeepers and fur companies that had begun to set up posts at various locations on the coasts. By the 1920s payment in goods gave way to payment in cash. Furs remained a profitable source of native income until the Depression of 1930. At the same time, beginning as early as 1892, attempts were made to introduce the Eskimo to reindeer herding. Herds were imported from Siberia and Scandinavia along with herdsmen to teach the new skill. By 1914 there was moderate success, although not too many individuals were interested in leaving their settlements for the lonely tundra vigils that herding demanded. There were still some herds in 1948, but the peak, reached in the 1920s, tapered off as the herds were lost through overgrazing, mixing with caribou, and disease.

The development of the Petroleum Reserve during World War II caused the town of Barrow to grow at the expense of other settlements on the coasts. Employment opportunities rose as the area was investigated for its oil and gas deposits (Rogers 1970), and the emergence of a full money economy took place. Whaling continued, as it does in the 1980s, but as a reflection of the patterns imposed by the alien whalers rather than in aboriginal terms. Many lived in the area who were not involved in hunting at all but who depended for food, apart from what was imported, on the knowledge and skills of a dwindling few. Air travel, increased communication with the outside, and native

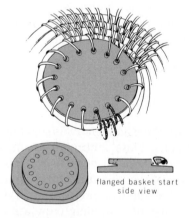

flanged basket start
side view

left, U. of Alaska Mus., Fairbanks: UA-67-98-108 A&B; right, Smithsonian Dept. of Anthr.: 418,393.

Fig. 18. Baleen baskets. This craft developed after 1905 at the suggestion of Point Barrow trader Charles Brower, to utilize stockpiled baleen for which there was a declining world market. The baleen is soaked in water, cut into strips, dried, then scraped, shaped, and polished for use in a single-rod coiling technique. The start of the bottom and lid is a simple or flanged piece of ivory. The lid piece is often carved to represent an animal. These baskets, which are made for sale, are usually made by men, perhaps because of their traditional skills in net making and ivory carving (M. Lee 1981:21). left, Dark baleen (the color can vary from black to gray to white) decorated with quills and a polar bear finial. Height about 9.5 cm, made by Robert James of Wainwright, Alaska, about 1960. right, Carved ivory finial representing a walrus. Height 8.0 cm, made by Toorak of Wainwright, Alaska, probably late 1940s.

336

organizations and claims payments have begun to create an arctic urbanism, at least in the Barrow and Kotzebue areas. Schools, hospitals, churches, welfare assistance, and employment opportunity suggest the intensive modification of the culture. Finally, the effects of the trans-Alaska pipeline, whether supported by the state, the federal authority, or industry, introduced further changes in the situation of the Eskimo of north Alaska.

Something does remain of the aboriginal past. The dogs are now rivaled by the snowmobile. But even if partnerships as they were, wife exchange, shamanism, the importance of the kashim, and the older world view are gone, the bonds of kinship remain. Much has been made in this discussion of the import of the bilateral extended family. It was important; it continues to be.

Synonymy

There is no established Eskimo or English name applied specifically to the Eskimo grouping treated in this chapter. Individual group names recognized in this study and in the past are given in the body of the text. Other lists are in Zagoskin, 1842 (1956:108–11, 1967:125–127), and Burch (1980).

Sources

The initial phase of ethnographic description of the north Alaska coastal regions begins in the 1830s and relates to voyages of discovery and exploration undertaken mainly by British naval vessels. Russian interest in the far north was minimal. Of interest are the narratives of Capt. F.W. Beechey (1832) and of Thomas Simpson (1843), both of whom provide some sense of a minimally changed aboriginal Eskimo culture. After 1848, the intensive search for the lost expedition of Sir John Franklin brought new outside contacts to the region, giving rise to the various Admiralty Reports of the British government and to the sensitive observations of Dr. John Simpson (1875).

Systematic ethnography followed the acquisition of Alaska by the United States. This is reflected in the work at Point Barrow of the International Polar Expedition of 1881 and in the ethnographic descriptions of Lt. P.H. Ray (1885). The work of the expedition involved the sketching of the natural as well as the human resources, resulting in the classic ethnographic monograph for the general area by Murdoch (1892). The works of Ray and Murdoch lay heavy stress on the material culture, a not unexpected development considering the problems of linguistic communication and the concerns of the day with primitive technology. From Ray and Murdoch can be obtained a fairly precise sense of the distribution of peoples in the area. Another study of the general period, one focusing on the groups to the south along the Seward Peninsula and so to the Bering Strait, is that by Nelson (1899). This provides more ethnographic detail and a fuller delineation of group distributions (see Foote 1965).

Modern ethnography may be said to begin after 1900 when the area, opened by whaling ships, became more readily accessible. It is not until Stefánsson's (1914, 1919) accounts that a more complete picture of the ethnographic character of the region begins to emerge. Rasmussen (1952) had visited the area on his trek across the north in 1924, and it had been visited by Jenness (1957) in 1913–1914. But it is not until after World War II that reconstruction of the precontact cultures was begun. Archeology received more attention in the intervening period, with the delineation of the Ipiutak, Birnirk, and Thule cultures.

Ethnographic analyses after 1950 treat the culture and society of the north Alaska Eskimo as they were just prior to contact, relying on the data supplied by native respondents. There are also fairly extensive accounts of culture change. Burch (1970a, 1971), Burch and Correll (1972), Campbell (1968), Heinrich (1960), Rainey (1947), Ray (1964, 1967a), Spencer (1959, 1972), and VanStone (1962a) deal in the main with the coastal peoples, their cultural background, ecological adaptations, and societal organization, as these institutions appeared in the nineteenth and early twentieth centuries. The special north Alaska question of the relations between the maritime Eskimo and those situated inland—the problem of the Nunamiut—is considered by Burch (1976a), Giddings (1952a), Gubser (1965), Ingstad (1954), Larsen (1973), Larsen and Rainey (1948), and Spencer (1959).

Questions of social and cultural change may go beyond the specifically ethnographic literature. While some of the sources listed above treat contemporary problems of change, the works by Chance (1966), R.K. Nelson (1969), Rogers (1970), Spencer (1959), Tussing, Rogers, and Fisher (1971), and VanStone (1962a) relate to the ways in which the Eskimo of north Alaska have been obliged to adapt to changes from without.

Interior North Alaska Eskimo

EDWIN S. HALL, JR.

Language and Territory

The Interior Eskimos of northern Alaska included the Mountain Eskimos, Colville River Eskimos, Utukok River Eskimos, and Meade and Ikpikpuk River Eskimos (fig. 1). Each group spoke a dialect of the Inupiaq language of the Eskimo family.*

The Interior Eskimos of northern Alaska were those groups who spent the better part of each year, particularly the fall and winter months, living along the willow-cloaked reaches of the major river valleys between the Brooks Range divide and the arctic coast (specifically the Colville River and its northward-flowing tributaries and the Kukpowruk, Kokolik, Utukok, Meade, Ikpikpuk, Kuparuk, and Sagavanirktok rivers). This entire area lies north of the tree line. Three physiographic provinces are represented: the Brooks Range proper, a rugged belt of east-west trending mountains ranging in height from 4,000 to 10,000 feet; the arctic foothills to the north, consisting mostly of rolling hills and long steep dry-topped ridges; and, stretching to the northern coast, the arctic coastal plain with low relief, sluggish, meandering streams, and myriad lakes (Solecki 1951:476).

*For the transcription of Inupiaq words and their sources, see the footnote in "North Alaska Eskimo: Introduction" (this vol.). The names Nunamiut, Taġiuġmiut, and Utqiaġvigmiut, used here as the English designations of these groups, are the Inupiaq names in the standard Inupiaq practical orthography.

Knowledge of the Interior Eskimos is derived primarily from archeological and ethnographical investigations, though historical sources and physical anthropology provide some data. Unfortunately, most archeological researchers in the area have concentrated on sites of earlier time levels and tested late prehistoric and historic Eskimo sites in only a limited number of locations. Also, virtually all the ethnographic data on the Interior Eskimos is derived from informants now living at Anaktuvuk Pass, in the central Brooks Range, and apparently these data apply mainly to Mountain Eskimos who lived east of the Killik River in the late 1800s (Oswalt 1967:234; Hall 1970; Burch 1979a, 1980). Differences in population density, house type, and the presence or absence of pottery and of substantially built, permanent, men's houses distinguish the peoples living to the east of the Killik River from those to the west in the Brooks Range and upper Colville River basin, suggesting major variation in other aspects of culture as well. Only Burch (cf. 1976a; Burch and Correll 1972) has interviewed the few knowledgeable informants from the western Brooks Range and Colville basin who now live in coastal villages or along the Kobuk River. Hence, the following ethnographic description must refer, unless otherwise noted, primarily to the late nineteenth-century eastern Brooks Range peoples, for whom the information is soundest. However, the basic description undoubtedly applies to the western groups as well. Information on the peoples of the rivers flowing directly

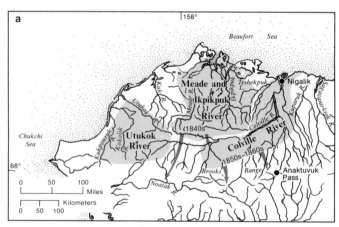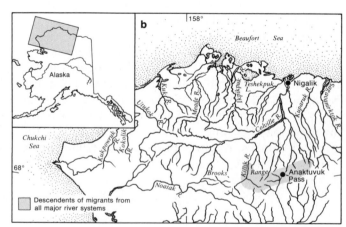

after Burch 1979a, 1980.

Fig. 1. Northern interior Alaska societies: a, 1816–1842 with movements in the mid-19th century; b, 1900, except for the Mountain Eskimo, shown as in 1880.

into the Arctic Ocean is even more scanty. The Meade River region, for example, was depopulated in the early 1800s (Gubser 1965:9). Descriptions of the Meade and Ikpikpuk river group (and to a lesser extent the Utukok River Eskimos) depend on extension of ethnographic data from Anaktuvuk Pass, supplemented with occasional fragments of direct evidence.

Prehistory

Though interior northern Alaska was occupied in earlier times, the people who became known historically as the Interior Eskimos moved into the unoccupied Brooks Range and Colville basin from the Noatak/Kobuk river region sometime after A.D. 1400 (Hall 1976). Apparently the initial occupation was by a few scattered families utilizing relatively impermanent, slightly semisubterranean oval tents. The increasing utilization of dog traction after A.D. 1600 by Eskimos of northern Alaska accelerated the occupation and exploitation of the Brooks Range and Colville basin (Hall 1978). By the end of the sixteenth century the western part of the interior was relatively heavily populated as evidenced by a number of lakeside villages of well-built, deep semisubterranean, rectangular houses with long entrance passages (Hall 1976). The mountains east of the Killik River were not inhabited by Eskimo peoples until after the arrival in northern Alaska of European trade goods, probably shortly after 1800.

Culture

Social Organization

Though considerable fluidity in terms of social units and territorial utilization has pertained throughout the period the interior has been occupied, by 1850 several distinct demes or societies had formed, characterized by high levels of endogamy, identification with a particular territory that was occupied by the members as least during the fall (and usually the winter) of every year, a distinctive yearly cycle, and a distinctive dialect (Burch 1976a, 1979a, 1980). The most important of these societies were the Mountain Eskimos of the Brooks Range proper, the Eskimos of the Colville basin, those living along the Utukok River, and the group that inhabited the valleys of the Meade and Ikpikpuk rivers. Estimates of the population of each group and of the Interior Eskimos in total prior to 1920 vary greatly (table 1). The figures for 1842, which are based on data from informants and a critical reviews of the early literature, may be the most accurate.

The Mountain Eskimo society was divided into several bands, the exact number depending upon the population density and the food resources available at a given time. Six to 12 extended families formed a band, under the leadership of an umialik or rich man, to take full advantage of hunting large caribou herds during the spring and fall migrations. The constituent families of a band tended to be related but the band was essentially an economic, political, and social group that almost always included several extended families not related to the others of the band.

The nuclear family was the basic structural unit of Mountain Eskimo society, but the household was the primary social group. The nuclear family was concerned with procreation, socialization of young children, and education of the older ones in terms of major economic skills. Though occasional nuclear families lived alone, most often such families were incorporated into the more inclusive extended family of one of the spouse's parents, preferably on the wife's side. Most households consisted of extended families forming the basic unit of economic production and consumption (Pospisil 1964; cf. Gubser 1965; Burch 1975a).

Every Mountain Eskimo individual was the center of another social group, the kindred or bilateral kin group. An individual's kindred included those paternal and maternal consanguineal (and adopted) relatives who extended as far as the third ascending and descending generations. Outsiders, even though they might be genealogically related to an individual, were considered strangers. The exogamous kindred was an exceedingly important social unit in that a Mountain Eskimo held in common with members of his kindred both responsibility for his and their offenses against outsiders and the mutual duty of blood revenge. Members of one's kindred also provided economic support on a daily basis as well as in times of crisis (Pospisil 1964; Gubser 1965:134ff.; Burch 1975a).

Two other sets of relationships were important to an individual: trading partnerships and friendships. Trading partnerships were relationships voluntarily established between two individuals, who were not related on a kinship basis, primarily for the exchange of goods and services (Burch 1970a:50). Most of an Eskimo's needs were met through his kindred or affinal relatives, but some material goods were procurable only through a trading partnership. For example, a Mountain Eskimo might exchange caribou skins with a coastal Eskimo for seal oil and skins. Trading partnerships provided protection for an individual in a context where relatives, who normally had this obligation, were not present. Trading partners also were supposed to be good friends and help each other under any circumstances in time of need. Often partners met at a Messenger Feast, a gathering that brought together members of different societies (coastal Eskimo, interior Eskimo, and Athapaskan Indian) in the winter months for a week or more of trading, feasting, story telling, and athletic competition. Friendships beyond the trading partnerships were

Table 1. Population Estimates, 1400–1979

Number	Date	Area	Sources
0	before A.D. 1400	Interior Eskimos as defined here	Hall 1976
few	A.D. 1400–1600	Interior Eskimos as defined here	Hall 1976
fewer than 1,500	A.D. 1600–1800	Interior Eskimos as defined here	Hall 1976
1,050	1842	Utukok River (250), Colville River (500), Arctic coastal plain (300)	Burch 1980
1,400	1870	Upper Noatak, Brooks Range, Colville River (300–400), Anaktuvuk Pass (100), Chandler Lake (150), Killik River (100–150)	Campbell 1962:387–394, 1968:1
300	1875	Upper Noatak River, Colville River	Collins 1954:123–124
1,000 +	1880	Brooks Range, Colville River basin, Sagavanirktok River	Gubser 1965:52
42	1890	Upper Noatak River, Colville River	Collins 1954:123–124
500	early 1900s[a]	Colville River basin	Rasmussen 1927:317
300	1900	Brooks Range, Colville River basin	Gubser 1965:20
800	1900	Noatak River to Mackenzie delta	Ingstad 1954:29–30
3,000	1895–1905	Kobuk River, Selawik River, Brooks Range, Colville basin, rivers flowing into Arctic Ocean	Larsen and Rainey 1948:31; Spencer 1959:21
150–200	1905	Brooks Range, Colville basin, Sagavanirktok River	Gubser 1965:55
few families	1913–1914	Colville Basin, Sagavanirktok River (one family)	Leffingwell 1919:67
20 +	1920	Brooks Range, Colville basin, Sagavanirktok River	Gubser 1965:55
0	shortly after 1920	Brooks Range, Colville basin, Sagavanirktok River	Gubser 1965:55
3 families	1938	Brooks Range, Colville basin, Sagavanirktok River	Gubser 1965:55
less than 50	1939–1941	Brooks Range, Colville basin, Sagavanirktok River	Gubser 1965:55
65	1949	Vicinity of Anaktuvuk Pass	Ingstad 1954:26; Larsen 1958:574
71	1951	Vicinity of Anaktuvuk Pass	Rausch 1951:154
48	prior to 1954	Vicinity of Anaktuvuk Pass	Collins 1954:123–124
78	1955	Vicinity of Anaktuvuk Pass	Laughlin 1957:7
85	1957	Vicinity of Anaktuvuk Pass	Pospisil and Laughlin 1963:180
96	1960	Vicinity of Anaktuvuk Pass	Gubser 1965:96
133	1969	Vicinity of Anaktuvuk Pass	Hanson 1969
180	1979	Anaktuvuk Pass	Spearman 1979

[a] Based on number at Colville mouth in spring; probably not 1924 as suggested by Larsen and Rainey 1948:31.

not based on exchange of economic goods through trade but they also involved mutual aid and support.

The presence of the kindred, the trading partnership, and friendships structured a Mountain Eskimo's relations with those around him. Relationships between larger social units, the Mountain Eskimos and other Eskimo societies for example, were complex and fluid in nature, involving both alliance and conflict. The nineteenth century in northern Alaska appears to have been a time of evolution, with numerous small societies coalescing into a smaller number of larger ones (Burch 1979a, 1980). Mountain Eskimos' relations with outside groups were structured around relationships between specific individuals or families in each society or else through meetings, friendly in the case of feasts and trading fairs, hostile in the case of conflict, involving a number of individuals from more than one society. Societies were cemented together in alliances by marriage or trading partnership bonds between two individuals in different societies. Military alliances between two or more societies also were possible, built around partnerships or marriages. Finally, at various times during the nineteenth century, economic conditions forced families to migrate from one region to another, bringing members of different societies together (Burch and Correll 1972).

Conflict did occur. Feuds took place between members of two different extended family units (Spencer

340

Fig. 2. Mountain Eskimo leading his pack dogs on a summer caribou hunt. Packs were made of untanned caribou hide and could carry a load of 25–30 pounds. Dogs were trained to walk behind but frequently darted off after hares and the pack often got wet. The tent in the background was John Campbell's field headquarters during his work on the Kogruk archeological site. Photograph by Edwin S. Hall, Jr., near the village of Anaktuvuk Pass, 1959.

Fig. 3. Fleshing a caribou hide for eventual use for clothing. Photograph by Lael Morgan at Anaktuvuk Pass, 1972.

1959:71ff.). Interregional warfare, involving as many as several dozen men in ambush with bows and arrows, also was common during the nineteenth century, existing side by side with peaceful bonds of marriage and partnership binding the warring societies. Members of two regional groups typically engaged in both during a single annual cycle. But the presence of alliances between different societies prevented the spread of longterm armed conflict (Burch 1974; Burch and Correll 1972).

Relations between the Mountain Eskimos and Athapaskan-speaking Indians to the south have been typified as friendly in the case of the Koyukon (Gubser 1965:49–50; Clark and Clark 1976) and generally hostile in the case of the Kutchin (Gubser 1965:44–49; Hall 1969). Most anthropologists have drawn a sharp boundary, linguistically and culturally, between the Eskimos and Indians of northern Alaska; but some authors, utilizing basically archeological data, have cast doubt on the existence of this boundary (Anderson 1970; A.M. Clark 1970; Hall 1969; Giddings 1965; Burch 1979a). Marriages and trading partnerships existed between Eskimos and Athapaskans, and the same pattern of alliance and conflict prevailed as between various Eskimo societies (Burch and Correll 1972; Clark and Clark 1976).

Political Organization

On the band level, leadership in the Mountain Eskimo society revolved around the umialik, an individual who possessed material wealth (beads, dogs, animal pelts, and a skin boat), usually accrued by hard work and

from his kindred. This individual was a skillful hunter, with the characteristics of generosity, assertiveness, and general wisdom. Usually only one umialik was dominant in each band. An umialik held a position of power in a very subtle, almost imperceptible way and exerted his influence in organizing and informally controlling activities such as the large caribou drives, trading expeditions, and extraband relationships. The position was not a secure one, as it depended on the acquiescence and support of the rest of the band (Gubser 1965:180ff.).

Subsistence

For the Mountain Eskimos, the caribou was the axis upon which life turned. During the period of the year the people were inland, caribou constituted more than 90 percent of their diet and provided skins for clothing and shelter, sinew for sewing, and bone and antler for manufacture. Twice a year, spring and fall, caribou migrated through Mountain Eskimo territory in great numbers. Under the direction of the umialik, each band planned large-scale caribou drives, using long converging rows of rock or sod fences to funnel the animals into a lake or corral where they could be easily speared or shot. At other times during the year small bands of feeding caribou were stalked by men with bows and arrows or caught in snares set along well-traveled paths. Mountain sheep, bear, moose, ground squirrels, ptarmigan and other birds, and fish provided variety in the diet or were sought when caribou were scarce.

The annual cycle of the Mountain Eskimo involved semiannual coalescence and dissolution of the band.

Fig. 4. Sod house (top) and caribou meat drying rack (bottom) at Anaktuvuk Pass. Sod houses were extended-family dwellings used only in winter since they leaked and were too warm in summer. Made with logs hauled 40 miles from the timberline, sod houses were still in occasional use in the 1970s by young men interested in privacy. Photographs by Gil Mull, July 1963.

During the winter the Eskimos lived in small extended family groups, scattered across the northern Brooks Range, constantly on the move in search of caribou and other game. Occasionally some families briefly moved south of the divide into the spruce forest along tributaries of the Koyukon River. The typical winter shelter was a ground level, willow-frame, skin-covered oval or round tent. Another, less common, house type had a willow frame covered with moss or sod and sometimes a short entrance passage (Corbin 1976; Campbell 1962). In April, the various families making up a band gathered at a traditional corralling location for the spring hunt. Here a kashim (ceremonial or men's house; Inupiaq *qařɣi*) would be built, on the same pattern as a skin tent but much larger. This structure served as a central location for community activity, including eating, working, and dancing as well as planning and ceremonially preparing for the coming caribou drive. Women were not excluded from the kashim; they and the children joined the men there for the main meal of the day.

Fig. 5. Domed dwellings, an overturned umiak, and a fish-drying rack at a summer camp on the Kupik River (lower Colville River). Photograph by Frank C. Schrader, 1901.

After the caribou drive, when the meat and skins were processed, dried, and cached, most Mountain Eskimos traveled north by dog team to locations along the Colville River where their large skin boats had been left the previous fall. When the ice in the Colville went out, the people journeyed downstream to Nigalik, where the Colville meets the sea. Nigalik was the location of one of the two great trading fairs in northern Alaska (Sheśhalik, on Kotzebue Sound, was the other) where Eskimos from many different regions came to trade each year (Burch 1970a; Burch and Correll 1972). At Nigalik the Mountain Eskimos lived in conical, tepee-like skin tents, while waiting for the Utqiaġvigmiut Eskimos, with whom they traded caribou skins and sinew, other animal skins, and snowshoes, for seal oil and skins, ivory, and other marine products. After trading, in the early fall, the Mountain Eskimos ascended the

Fig. 6. Simon Paneak at Tuluak Lake camp. His clothing is trimmed with wolf fur; such trim was almost exclusively wolf or wolverine from traditional into modern times. Wolf skins hang on the rack, along with snowshoes used mainly in the forest area south of Tuluak Lake. The sleds are shod with metal. In the 1950s wolves were hunted for the $50 bounty and the skins. Photograph by Laurence Irving, Feb.-March 1952.

342

Colville to where their skin boats were to be cached and, after the first snow, dog-teamed back to the mountain valleys to spend the winter. Bands formed again for the fall caribou drive, and trading took place between the people who had visited the coast and those who spent the summer inland.

Life Cycle

Family life within the Mountain Eskimo society was close and rewarding. Children were greatly desired and were treated with considerable permissiveness. Childhood was a long period, lasting from the age of one and one-half years to 14 years or later. Children spent much of their time playing, but also gradually began to learn the skills necessary for survival by carrying out small tasks in imitation of their elders. Young girls sought firewood, gathered roots and berries, learned how to scrape and sew skins. Boys used dog teams to bring meat back to camp, chopped firewood, and went on short hunting trips. Gradually adolescence was assumed, a stage that lasted from puberty to marriage. Young men and women were a definite economic asset to their families, as they took almost a full role in the various daily activities.

Individuals usually married when between 16 and 25 years of age. Initially the relationship between man and woman was one of sexual cohabitation, common residence, and economic cooperation (Gubser 1965:115). Though often there was some initial affection between the two young persons, usually this bond greatly strengthened after several children were born and the new household became an integral part of the community. Divorce was uncommon, particularly after the arrival of children.

A Mountain Eskimo thought of old age as that time when the hair turned gray and the body became less agile, usually after 60 years of age. Older people frequently lived in the household of a married child. They continued to pursue economic activities when possible and contributed to the well-being of the household.

Yale U., Peabody Mus.: 202767.

Fig. 8. Pump drill made of spruce wood and caribou thong with platform; used for starting fire. Length of drill about 30.5 cm; collected by Leopold Pospisil, Brooks Range, Alaska, 1957.

Abandonment, as well as infanticide, seem to have been rare. After death, the body was dressed in finery by the deceased's relatives, wrapped in caribou hides, and, accompanied by a few tools, left on high, dry ground. A brief period of mourning followed.

Religion

The Mountain Eskimo did not have an especially complex or integrated cosmology, and speculation regarding the universe and natural phenomena was not an important feature in the culture. Mountain Eskimo attitudes toward the universe are found largely in folktales, telling of which was an art. Additionally, a number of nonempirical creatures, including ghosts, dragons, and giant fish and birds, inhabited the environment (Burch 1971).

It was toward control of the supernatural that most religious behavior was directed. Both the individual and the specially endowed and trained shaman (aŋatkuq) used songs, formulas, and rituals in an attempt to control the weather and other natural phenomena and, especially, the animal world. Animals had the ability to reason and talk much as did humans and if not treated with proper respect would withhold themselves from man, with the ultimate result of human starvation. Thus much effort was expended on propitiating the various animal species so necessary for survival.

Though every individual owned magic songs and other

Yale U., Peabody Mus.: 202765.

Fig. 7. Hammer of gray polished stone with spruce wood handle. Used for crushing long bones for marrow. Length about 22.9 cm; collected by Leopold Pospisil, Brooks Range, Alaska, 1957.

Fig. 9. Gun case made of caribou hide. Length about 100.2 cm; collected by Leopold Pospisil, Brooks Range, Alaska, 1957.

powers, the shaman had a much greater degree of power and familiarity with the supernatural world. Shamanism involved curing (usually illnesses caused by breaking a taboo), finding lost articles, foretelling the future, speaking to the dead, and performing shamanistic seances where the shaman served as intermediary between the people and the supernatural world. Shamans were not full-time religious practitioners; an ordinary man or woman became a shaman when a spirit, usually from a particular species of animal, directed the individual into the calling. Since shamans were feared as much as venerated because of their power, the role involved a certain amount of tension (Spencer 1959:255ff.).

Other Interior Eskimos

Groups of Mountain Eskimos living west of the Killik River and the people of the Colville, Utukok, and Meade-Ikpikpuk rivers lived in larger, more permanent villages of deep semisubterranean rectangular houses built of spruce logs or heavy willows, and sod. They followed a slightly different annual cycle from that described for the Mountain Eskimos, though most families spent the fall and winter inland and the summer at the coast. Trade, especially during the late 1800s, became very important in the western interior, as the Eskimos there served as middlemen for goods passing between Siberia and the Canadian Arctic (cf. Stefánsson 1914).

History

The years following 1850 marked the decline of the Interior Eskimos. Depopulation because of disease, starvation because of a decline in the caribou herds, and the attraction of the coast, where whaling and, later, fox trapping were lucrative economic activities, resulted in the abandonment of the interior shortly after 1920. Many interior families became assimilated into coastal villages, but in 1938 a few families returned to the interior. They lived much as their ancestors had, until the early 1950s when they settled more or less permanently in Anaktuvuk Pass (Amsden 1977).

The village there has grown steadily and has become

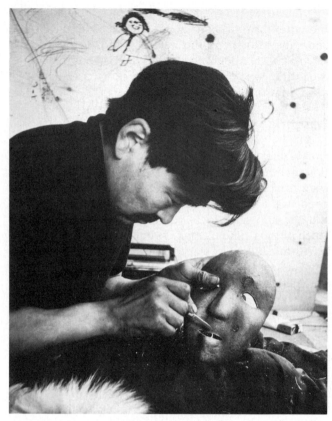

Fig. 10. Man from Anaktuvuk Pass trimming caribou hide mask. Photograph by George Motley, Nov. 1968.

well known through the visits of scientists, tourists, and other outsiders. An all-season airfield was constructed in 1960.

An eight-million-dollar school, featuring classrooms, offices, a large shop, a full-sized gymnasium, and a swimming pool, was completed in 1979 (Spearman 1979). The Alaska Native Claims Settlement Act of 1971 has brought about the establishment of Eskimo-dominated political units, such as the Arctic Slope Regional Corporation and the North Slope Borough, resulting in new jobs and increased extra-village responsibilities for many of the Anaktuvuk Pass people. The additional monies flowing into the village help to offset the strict limits placed on the hunting of caribou after the severe decline of that all-important species in the mid-1970s; imported foodstuffs necessarily play an increasing role in subsistence. Health problems have been alleviated through better and more regular medical care.

The use of all-terrain vehicles and the construction of a winter tote road through the pass to the North Slope oil fields have disrupted the environment. The future of Anaktuvuk Pass as a viable village in the face of these conflicting forces remains in doubt. Many of the younger people see their future in the more heterogeneous centers of Alaska. However, for the foreseeable future, the Anaktuvuk Pass people are likely

344

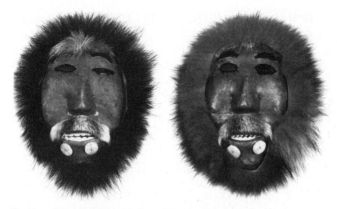

Nat. Mus. of Canada, Ottawa: left, IV-E-1053; right, IV-E-1054.

Fig. 11. Skin masks, not a traditional artifact type. Caribou skin masks were first sewed for a Christmas festival in 1951, and not until 1956 were they made for sale as curios (Atamian 1966). To speed production wet caribou skin is stretched over a wooden form until it dries, to create the molded face; both these masks may have been made on the same form. Fur around the face suggests a parka ruff, and eyelashes, eyebrows, and moustache of fur are also added. These examples have carved ivory teeth and labrets. Men and women both are involved in this craft, which was an important source of income at Anaktuvuk Pass through the 1960s. Both, face length about 21.6 cm, made by Elijah Kakinya, Anaktuvuk Pass, Alaska, about 1963.

to remain in the Brooks Range, the last remnants of a once numerous people, held by the strong ties of their past and their land as well as the difficulties of finding security and happiness in a White-oriented world.

Synonymy

The interior people originally were referred to as the Nunatarmiut (specifically 'people of the Nunatak or Noatak' River, but generalized to include all interior groups) as early as 1875 by John Simpson (1875) who spent the years between 1849 and 1853 in northern Alaska. The same term was used by other anthropologists working in northern Alaska prior to 1950 (H.P. Ray 1885; Murdoch 1885; Stefánsson 1919; Jenness 1957). After this date the term Nunamiut gained currency, being utilized by anthropologists and others studying the Anaktuvuk Pass people (cf. Gubser 1965). Nunamiut is Inupiaq *nunamiut*, formed from *nuna* 'land' and *miut* 'people of ', and is contrasted with Taġiuġmiut (Tareumiut, Tariumiut), or 'people of the sea', the term for coastal dwellers.

Some authors have been more specific, concentrating on the names of local groups. Thus we have Killikmiut (*killiẏmiut*) 'people of the Killik River', Tulugakmiut (*tuluɣaẏmiut*) 'people of Tulugak Lake', Utukokmiut (*utuqqaẏmiut*) 'people of the Utukok River', and so on (Gubser 1965:338–339).

In any case, the meaning conveyed by combining a place-name with the suffix -*miut* is ambiguous in both anthropological and Eskimo usage. Burch (1976a) has

pointed out that the term Nunamiut is not utilized by Eskimos (except, perhaps, when the Anaktuvuk Pass people talk to anthropologists), has taken on many meanings in the professional literature, and has generally been the source of considerable ambiguity. Burch's (1976a) alternate suggestion, followed here, is to speak of a number of regional units. For the north Alaskan interior, then, there are the Mountain Eskimos, the Colville basin Eskimos, the Utukok River Eskimos, and the Meade–Ikpikpuk River Eskimos.

The general term Interior Eskimos, used here, should be unambiguous in context, though most anthropologists would extend the term to include inland groups living along the Noatak, Kobuk, and Selawik rivers and in the Seward Peninsula interior.

Sources

Few exploration parties visited interior Northern Alaska prior to abandonment of the area; hence few historical accounts of the Interior Eskimos are available. Howard (in Stoney 1900) does briefly describe the Eskimos he met in the upper Colville basin and along the Ikpikpuk River in 1886.

The three primary ethnographic accounts dealing with the Mountain Eskimos are by Spencer (1959), Gubser (1965), and Ingstad (1954). Spencer's detailed work, an ethnographic reconstruction, confuses the inland and coastal Eskimos in some respects and too sharply distinguishes between them in others (cf. Oswalt 1967:234); however, this study did serve to initiate further work in the area. Gubser's well-written and insightful study deals mostly with the Eskimos who settled in Anaktuvuk Pass and is also a reconstruction. Ingstad's book is a popularized description of the Anaktuvuk Pass people. By combining these three accounts and the following shorter papers dealing with specific aspects of Mountain Eskimo culture, a relatively well-rounded picture of this group is available: on knowledge of the animal world (Rausch 1951; L. Irving 1953, 1958, 1960; Irving and Paneak 1954); on demography (Hanson 1969; Binford 1972; Binford and Chasko 1976); on settlement patterns (Campbell 1968; Amsden 1977); on kinship (Pospisil and Laughlin 1963; Heinrich 1960); on law and social structure (Pospisil 1964); on trade (Stefánsson 1914); on radioactive body count (Hanson 1965, 1965a, 1967; Hanson, Watson, and Perkins 1967); on physical anthropology (Laughlin 1957); education (Cline 1975); and ethnoarcheology (Binford 1978). Mountain Eskimo life in general is treated by Larsen (1958, 1973) and Solecki (1950).

Sources dealing with interior societies other than that of the Mountain Eskimos include Spencer (1959), Jenness (1952, 1957), Ostermann (1952), Stefánsson (1919), Larsen and Rainey (1948) and, particularly, the excellent papers of Burch (1970, 1970a, 1971, 1974, 1975, 1975a, 1976, 1976a, 1979a, 1980; Burch and Correll 1972). Ethnographic research on the Interior Eskimos has been summarized by Burch (1979b).

Archeological reports with data on the Interior Eskimos include those of Alexander (1969) and Corbin (1976) on the Galbraith Lake region, Campbell (1962, 1968) on Anaktuvuk Pass, Irving (1962, 1964) on the Itivluk Lake region, and Hall (1970, 1976, 1978) on the upper Colville River basin.

Archeological and ethnological specimens from interior northern Alaska are found primarily at the Peabody Museum of Yale University, the University of Alaska Museum at College, the Smithsonian Institution, and the Maxwell Museum of Anthropology of the University of New Mexico, at Albuquerque.

Mackenzie Delta Eskimo

DEREK G. SMITH

Language, Territory, and Environment

In the twentieth century there were two distinct dialects of Inuit-Inupiaq Eskimo spoken in the Mackenzie Delta region. One of these, centered around the town of Tuktoyaktuk, is the dialect of the Mackenzie Delta Eskimo described in this chapter.* It is called the Coast dialect locally and has been referred to in earlier literature as the Mackenzie River Delta dialect or Mackenzie (Jenness 1924, 1928, 1944; Swadesh 1951, 1952) and as Chiglit or Tchiglit (Petitot 1876b); it is called the Mackenzie Coast dialect in "Eskimo and Aleut Languages" (this vol.). Its closest affinities are with the Copper Eskimo dialect to the east. The other dialect in the region, spoken around Aklavik and Inuvik, is a variety of inland North Slope Inupiaq that displaced the earlier dialect of the delta itself as a result of the population changes of the late nineteenth and early twentieth centuries described at the end of this chapter. This is the dialect that is locally called the Delta dialect in the twentieth century.

Cape Bathurst and the Baillie Islands marked the eastern limits of Mackenzie Eskimo occupation in the late precontact times (Collinson 1889). Stefánsson (1914:12, 1919:25) indicates that the 300-mile unoccupied area between the Mackenzie Eskimo of the Baillie Islands and the Copper Eskimo at Cape Bexley was occupied in earlier times, probably by Mackenzie Eskimos. Considerable disagreement exists regarding the group's western limits. Petitot (1876:831, 1876b:1, 1886:3, 1887:279) places these limits variously at the Colville River, Point Barrow, and Herschel Island; Stefánsson (1914:6), at the western edge of the Mackenzie Delta; yet others suggest Demarcation Point or Barter Island. Whether or not Mackenzie Eskimos permanently occupied any portion of the Alaska north coast, this was clearly an important area for seasonal trade and contact between them and their western neighbors (Stefánsson 1914). Except seasonally, Mackenzie Eskimo occupation was largely confined to the Arctic coast, especially at the mouths of streams and rivers. Inland penetration was most extensive in the tundra east of the Mackenzie Delta. This occupation overlapped that of Indian groups to the extent that Eskimos used it in summer, Indians in winter.

There were five named Mackenzie Eskimo subgroups (fig. 1), the largest of which occupied the islands at the mouth of the Mackenzie Delta and was centered at the large permanent village of Kittigazuit (Kittegaryuit, Kitikârjuit). Relations among these five groups were extensive and friendly so that they "almost formed one community" (Stefánsson 1914:6).

The Mackenzie River Delta, some 4,700 square miles in area, was the dominating feature of Mackenzie Eskimo territory. Both the Peel and Mackenzie rivers drain through this delta in a complex series of channels. Some 40 percent of the delta is covered by shallow lakes and ponds, which in summer, with day-round sunlight for several weeks, are ideal breeding grounds for mosquitoes. Several hundred feet of permafrost underlie the whole area. There is an "active layer" or surface thaw zone of approximately three feet in the summer months. The southern two-thirds of the land area is wooded with stunted spruce, alder, and poplar, and much arctic willow. These species and ample driftwood provided material for fuel, housing, and manufactures. The northern edge of the delta consists of low alluvial islands with a vegetation of low sedges, grasses, and horsetails. Here the land is tussocky and damp, with many shallow ponds. Channels of the delta and connected lakes contain an abundance of fish, which were an important supply of food for humans and draft dogs.

To the west of the delta the Richardson Mountains, a northern extension of the American Cordillera, rise steeply to elevations of over 5,000 feet. They are covered with typical tundra vegetation and drain into the delta by complex braided streams, some of which have steep canyons in their middle reaches. While difficult to traverse, especially in summer, they provided several species of land mammals economically important to the Mackenzie Eskimo. Woodland caribou passed through this area in spring and early autumn on their seasonal migration to and from the Arctic coast. Their migration paths were diverse and variable. Mountain sheep, grizzly and brown bears, marten, and wolverine were also sig-

---

*The phonemes of the Tuktoyaktuk dialect are: (voiceless stops and affricate) *p, t, č, k, q*; (voiced fricatives) *v, y* ([y], [ž], [ȝ]), γ, γ̇; (voiceless fricatives) *s, h*; (nasals) *m, n, ŋ*; (lateral) *l*; (short vowels) *i, a, u*; (long vowels) *i·, a·, u·*.

Information on Mackenzie phonology is from Webster and Zibell (1976:275).

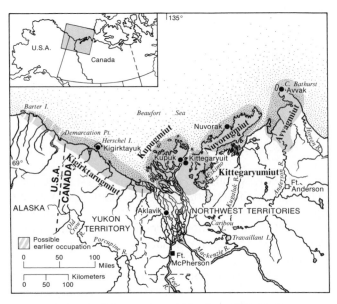

Fig. 1. Mackenzie Eskimo subgroups in about 1850 (Stefánsson 1919; McGhee 1974).

nificant resources. Several valued species of berries were found both here and in the delta.

East of the delta, the land rises quickly through the scarp of the so-called Caribou mountains to open, rolling tundra. Barren Ground caribou penetrated this area.

A low, narrow coastal plain extends from both sides of the delta. Beluga were abundant off the mouth of the delta and its western margin in late summer. Seals were more abundant along the coast east of the delta and in the Eskimo Lakes. Walrus were not present.

External Relations

Culturally, the Mackenzie Eskimo had close affinities with North Alaska Coast Eskimo groups. They were the most easterly group of what might be known as the Alaska whaling complex. There were basic similarities in subsistence patterns and associated technology, in house types and village structure, in details of dress and ornamentation (labrets, tattoos), in family organization, and in the whale cult (cf. Lantis 1938; Mickey 1955). Close linguistic connection is indicated by Jenness (1928), while Swadesh (1951, 1952) also finds a close affinity with Copper Eskimo. Mackenzie Eskimos recognized and had names for most western Eskimo groups extending as far as Bering Strait (Petitot 1876a:xi), and it is with these groups that they had most extensive trading relations (Petitot 1876a:xvi, xxvi, 1887:197; Stefánsson 1914:9–13).

Petitot (1876a:xi, xxiv, 1886:5, 1887:122, 131, 141, 161–166, 194), Stefánsson (1919:24), and Slobodin (1962) refer to a deep-seated antipathy and distrust that periodically resulted in violence and murder between the Mackenzie Eskimo and their Indian neighbors. Never-

theless, Stefánsson (1919:15) indicates that voluntary marriages and adoptions sometimes occurred between these groups. Trading relations were maintained with Indian groups, especially the Hare to the south of the delta, since about 1825. This relationship, an important early source of European trade goods, operated both through silent barter and, in later times, through a local trade jargon of which no details survive (Petitot 1876a:i).

Population Distribution

Estimates of population size and distribution are fragmentary and conflicting. There are no formal census data. Table 1 indicates the best estimates available for selected dates. Stefánsson's (1913a) estimate of 4,000 persons in aboriginal times seems to be far too high, although before decimation the Mackenzie Delta Eskimo were one of the largest Eskimo populations in the Canadian Arctic (McGhee 1974:xi). Series of infectious disease epidemics, beginning with scarlet fever and measles in 1865 and culminating in a severe epidemic of measles and influenza in 1900–1902, were major factors in population decline. Tuberculosis was widespread after about 1880. Several sources (for example, Jenness 1964:14) cite liquor and firearms as additional factors. Dispersal of the Mackenzie Eskimo along the North Alaska coast, with cultural and genetic absorption of those remaining in the Mackenzie Delta area by immigrant Alaska Eskimos during the traumatic and short-lived whaling era, 1889 to 1908, has perhaps been considerably underestimated as a factor in population decline. Stefánsson (1913:60–79, 1913a:451) refers to Mackenzie Eskimos permanently resident at Point Barrow after decimation of the aboriginal population there. Both he and Jenness repeatedly refer to a profound cultural and linguistic "Alaskanization" of remaining Mackenzie Eskimos.

From various sources Usher (1971a:169–171) has reconstructed population sizes for Mackenzie Eskimo subgroups as they were in 1850, but he does not identify the groups by name. His estimates, shown in table 2 with group names as given by Stefánsson (1919), may be a little too high. Each subgroup centered in one or two villages in each area during winter and dispersed into small groups for fishing and hunting and into groups of intermediate size in July and August for whaling. The permanent village of Kittigazuit was very large by Eskimo standards, being occupied by about 1,000 people in early contact times according to several accounts. Stefánsson (1913a:452) identifies eight more large villages (fig. 1), two of which contained 200–300 people.

The most easterly subgroup of Mackenzie Eskimo, centered around Cape Bathurst, differs in certain features of material culture and seasonal economic cycle from the other subgroups (Collinson 1889; Höhn 1963;

Table 1. Mackenzie Eskimo Population Estimates, 1826–1930

Year	Population	Source
1826	2,000	Franklin 1828:86–228
1850	2,500	Usher 1971a:169–171
1865	2,000	Petitot 1876a:x
1905	250	RCMP 1906:129
1910	130	RCMP 1911:151
1930	10	Jenness 1964:14

Table 2. Mackenzie Eskimo Subgroup Population Estimates, about 1850

Subgroup (Stefánsson 1919: opp. 10, opp. 32)	Estimate (Usher 1971a:169–171)
Kigirktarugmiut	250
Kittegaryumiut	1,000
Kupugmiut	250
Nuvorugmiut	500
Avvagmiut	500
Total	2,500

Damas 1969:136–137). These differences, which relate the Cape Bathurst group more closely to Copper Eskimo practices, reflect ecological features of the Cape Bathurst area, which demanded a more marine- than riverine-oriented way of life, and are especially associated with an emphasis on breathing-hole sealing. It is also likely that there had been cultural contact between the Cape Bathurst subgroup and the Copper Eskimo (McGhee 1974:7–18).

Culture

The following discussion describes the nineteenth century, as observed and as reconstructed from later informants.

Technology

Mackenzie Eskimo material culture reflects a strong orientation to land and marine mammal hunting and, especially in contact times after the introduction of gill nets, to riverine fishing. The umiak, a large wood-framed boat covered with beluga skin and propelled by single-bladed paddles, was extensively used for transportation and whaling. The wood-framed skin kayak with double-bladed paddles was in extensive use for sea mammal hunting (fig. 2). Sleds with iced bone or antler runners drawn by small dog teams (five or six dogs) were used for sealing at the floe edge and for tundra land mammal hunting. Several types of toggling harpoons (some with inflated skin floats and drogues), fixed barbed point

spears, lances, hunting arrows with stone or barbed bone or antler points, bird bunts, and fishing leisters and tridents (for use at fish weirs) are described and illustrated by Petitot (1876b, 1970; Russell 1898). The Mackenzie Eskimo were the most easterly group to use bird bolas (Murdoch 1888a:334). Throwing boards for projecting harpoons were in common use. Composite bone fishhooks without barbs were common (fig. 4). Simple arc and double recurved sinew-backed bows were used with a wide variety of simple and composite arrows. Wood, bone, antler, and ivory were the most common working materials. Some copper was in use before contact; it was of Russian and European origin, traded in fron Alaska and the southern Mackenzie. Cold-beaten native copper was also used. Chipped-stone projectile points (triangular forms, usually tanged) and points of polished stone were manufactured. Polished stone adzes were present. Labrets, beads and ornaments, and in later times, tobacco pipes were made of polished steatite. Steatite cooking pots and a small number of characteristic Eskimo stove oil lamps were traded in from eastern groups. Lamps were in less common use here, for there was an abundance of wood to fuel open fires. Bow drills were used for making fires.

Bone- and antler-backed polished stone and metal women's knives (ulus) were extensively used. Examples from the Smithsonian Institution collection are shown by Mason (1891:pl. LVI). Men's knives, double-edged daggers, were of bone, ivory, and metal. Large bone snow knives were present but less common than among Central and Eastern Eskimos since snowhouses were less commonly constructed.

Small boxes, needle cases, beads, hair combs, snow visors, harness toggles, and buckles were made of bone, antler, ivory, and wood. There were shallow wooden food-serving trays and serving ladles of wood and horn.

Structures

Although small snowhouses built on the sea ice were used for winter habitation, particularly in the eastern ranges of the territory, the characteristic winter house was a large, wood-framed and planked semi-subterranean structure covered with sod and glazed with ice similar to North Alaska forms. Access was gained by a tunnel up to 20 feet in length, sometimes curved, which opened into the house at floor level through a small door closed with a skin flap. A skylight of oiled membrane admitted some light. There was an open central floor area with normally three chambers with sloping roofs opening off it. These chambers were occupied by raised sleeping platforms covered with skins. Each platform was used by a single nuclear family that was usually but not necessarily closely related to other families occupying the house. Each nuclear family had a separate cooking lamp with a rack over it for drying

clothing placed by its sleeping platform. Tools and other possessions were stored along the inner sides of these platforms or suspended from the ceiling. Pokes of oil and food stuffs were stored in the cool entrance tunnel or in small niches in its walls. Most cooking was done here over an open wood fire (Petitot 1876a:xxi).

Snowhouses were rather small, domed structures, usually occupied by a single nuclear family. There was a small door at floor level, and an unroofed windbreak of snow blocks rather than an entrance tunnel. Snowhouses were used extensively when traveling. Summer habitations were small skin tents erected over willow frames. Near any dwelling occupied for any length of time, each nuclear family erected platform stages reached by a sloping log for a ladder for storage of food beyond the reach of dogs and predators.

Winter houses were occupied from October through May while the weather was sufficiently cool to keep roofs from dripping. In these winter months, life was relatively sedentary, with hunting and trapping excursions from fixed base camps and villages. By mid-June, after breakup of the river ice and the recession of water levels, the population dispersed to fishing camps until mid-July. Some caribou were hunted at this time, but most caribou hunts took place in September and October. In late July and August, some people of the eastern subgroups hunted in the Eskimo Lakes region, but many people returned to whaling camps at or near their winter villages (Petitot 1876a; Stefánsson 1919). Damas (1969:136–137) notes certain cultural features of the Cape Bathurst subgroup reminiscent of Copper Eskimo practices. These features are associated with a greater emphasis on breathing-hole sealing in the Cape Bathurst area rather than on floe-edge sealing as in the other four Mackenzie Eskimo sugroups.

While Stefánsson (1919:36) reports the presence of men's clubhouses or kashims (Delta *qařɣi,* Coast *qayɣi(q),* sg.) at the winter villages, it is likely that these were a late intrusion from Alaska. Both Lantis (1938) and Spencer (1959:44) state that in early times these structures were not found east of Point Barrow. Petitot (1876a:xxx) makes passing reference to the presence of men's clubhouses but specifically says that their use was derived from Alaska groups. They were large timbered structures, covered with sod, but with an open roof. An open fire burned in the center of the floor. They were used only in autumn before the weather became severe and winter houses were reoccupied. Adult men took

Smithsonian, Dept. of Anthr.: 7,442.

Fig. 3. Wolf killer. A strip of baleen sharpened at the ends was softened, bent, and bound into shape. After it dried the cord was removed and it was covered with oil, wrapped in blubber, fishskin, or meat, and placed where wolves or foxes were likely to find it and gulp it down. The digestive juices and warmth of the stomach cause it to straighten out again, piercing the animal and killing it or weakening it so that the pursuing hunter can easily make the kill. Wolf skins were used for clothing and in trade. Length 7.0 cm; collected by R. MacFarlane, Ft. Anderson, N.W.T., 1869.

their meals there, although women and children were occasionally admitted. Shamanistic performances often took place there (see also Damas 1969:136).

Subsistence

Fish caught in spring and summer were preserved for winter use by several techniques. Most were split and scored, then air-dried with light smoking over a willow smudge fire (Petitot 1876a:xx). Some were allowed to dry and decay slightly in open racks, without being dressed, for subsequent storage in permafrost pits. Some fish were placed directly in these pits, and some were preserved in pokes of oil suspended in the trees beyond reach of predators. The meat of mammals and birds was usually stored directly in permafrost pits, but small amounts were dried or allowed to decay slightly before use. Sea mammals were prized mostly for their oils and fats. A favored festival food was made by preserving three-inch squares of beluga meat in pokes of rendered blubber. Muktuk, or beluga skin and blubber, was less in favor than among Alaska groups. It was usually eaten fresh after boiling, but some was used in the fermented state. There was a widespread taboo aversion to birds' eggs. Muskrat and beaver meat was dried in a manner similar to fish (Stefánsson 1919).

Vegetable foods were in limited use. Most important were berries, used fresh or frozen. Edible roots included young willow; the starchy, slightly astringent, nutlike roots of knotweed; and sainfoin. These were boiled or preserved in oil, as were the somewhat acidic leaves of

top, Prov. Arch. of Alta., Edmonton: E. Brown Coll. B9963; center, Natl. Mus. of Canada, Ottawa: 37136; bottom left, Hudson's Bay Company Lib., Winnipeg, Man.; bottom right, Nationalmuseet, Copenhagen: 2037.

Fig. 2. Settlement life. top, Eskimo youths in kayaks on the Mackenzie River. The kayak in the background has a spear in the straps on the bow, and the youth with labrets is using a double-bladed paddle. The kayak in the foreground has a double-bladed paddle strapped to the stern while the youth uses a single-bladed paddle. Photograph by Charles W. Mathers, 1895–1901. center, Winter log and sod house, tents, and drying racks at Shingle Point, Mackenzie Delta. Photograph by Diamond Jenness, 1914. bottom left, Koklik and his wife at their summer camp at Ft. McPherson in Kutchin Indian territory. A metal trade pot is suspended on a tripod over a fire directly behind the couple. Photograph by Elizabeth Taylor, 1892. bottom right, Anguisinaoq from Baillie Island. Photograph by Leo Hansen, 1923.

351

mountain sorrel ("Eskimo rhubarb") and the pith of flowering rushes (Stefánsson 1919; Petitot 1887:194, 239). Table 3 indicates the principal species economically significant to the Mackenzie Eskimo.

By preference, fish were eaten raw and frozen. Unlike Alaska groups, Mackenzie Eskimos preferred meats boiled or roasted. Most foods were served with animal oils and fats. Fatty marrow and brains were highly valued. The common beverage was water or stock from boiled foods. There was usually only one large meal per day, prepared in late afternoon or evening. Remains of this meal were kept for smaller meals or snacks at other times (Stefánsson 1919).

Clothing and Adornment

Men's clothing consisted of an undershirt, underpants, and stockings of muskrat pelts covered with a hip-length hooded parka, calf-length pantaloons of soft caribou skin, knee-length boots of caribou leg-skins with crimped beluga skin soles, and caribou skin mittens. Mitten liners were made of soft seal skin. Women's clothing was distinguished by a parka of knee length with a flap before and behind. The hood of a woman's parka was much larger than a man's in order to accommodate her hairstyle, consisting of a double-bun chignon with two long side braids. The woman's characteristic lower garment was a one-piece culotte instead of the man's pantaloons and boots. Clothing for young children consisted of a one-piece head-to-foot garment of caribou fawn skin with the animal's ears preserved in the hood for ornamentation. Underclothing was worn with the hair side turned in, outer clothing (with the exception of mittens) with the hair side turned out. Fish skin and seal skin rain clothing and kayak coats were known but were not common. Summer clothing consisted of the previous winter's underclothes worn with the hair side turned out (Stefánsson 1919; Petitot 1876a:xiv–xvi, xxviii, 1879:541–542, 1887:4, 43, 55–57, 79–80).

Paired cheek labrets were worn by men after puberty. These were usually made of polished stone or ivory, and in late times were ornamented with blue glass bead insets. Pendants were worn in pierced earlobes and nasal septa by both sexes, but especially by men (fig. 9). Men's tattoos consisted of two or three transverse blue lines on the cheeks worn by homicides and of small blue crosses on the shoulder worn by whalers. Women's tat-

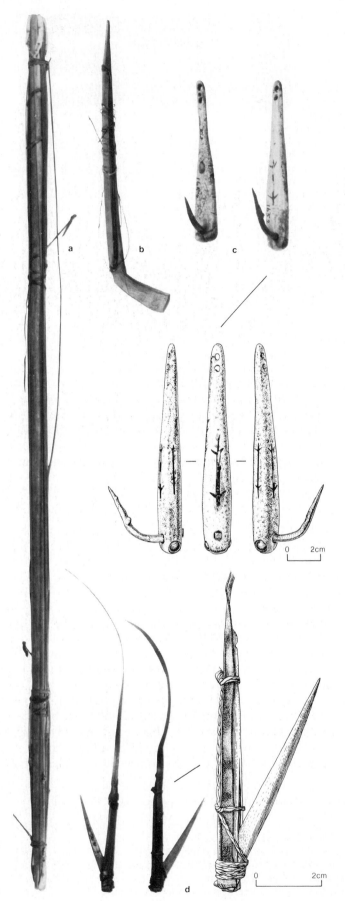

Smithsonian, Dept. of Anthr.: a, 7,475; b, 2,193; c, 1,652; d, 2,197.

Fig. 4. Fishing equipment. Although net fishing was probably more frequent, hooks and line were also used. a, Wooden reel with notched ends with pieces of ivory as guides for the baleen line; b, Wooden reel with wooden pegs through its shaft as line guides; c, metal hooks placed in ivory shafts that are decorated with blue beads and incised designs; d, bone hooks attached with sinew to wooden shaft. The line at the end is baleen. a, Length 66.0 cm, rest same scale. All collected by R. MacFarlane, N.W.T., a, 1869; b–d, 1866.

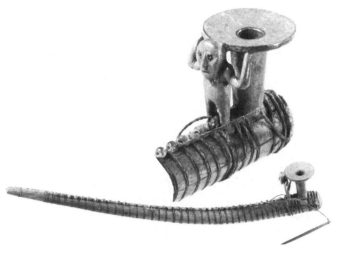

Smithsonian, Dept. of Anthr.: 2,159.

Fig. 5. Pipe. Tobacco was introduced to Alaska from Asia, and the shape of Eskimo pipes reflects those used in China and Japan (Nelson 1899:280). The stem of this example is made of 2 pieces of carved wood decoratively bound together with sinew strung with blue beads. The lead bowl has a standing figure with blue beads inset as eyes. A carved bone tamper is attached. Length 30.3 cm; collected by R. MacFarlane, Anderson River, N.W.T., 1866.

Smithsonian, Dept. of Anthr.: a, 1,663; b, 7,726; c, Glenbow-Alberta Inst., Calgary, Alta.: AB 783.

Fig. 6. Containers. a–b, Decorated wolverine skin bags used to carry tobacco, pipe, flint, steel, and tinder. a, Decorated with blue and red seed beads sewed to bands of clipped hair; leather thong with large blue bead and fur at the end. b, Bands of clipped hair decorate top portion of the bag; the thong has 2 blue beads and a piece of fur at the end. a, Length 22.0 cm excluding fringe, rest same scale. Both collected by R. MacFarlane, Anderson River, N.W.T.: a, 1866; b, 1869. c, Coiled spruce root basket used as a tinder container. Collected by S.T. Wood, Mackenzie River, N.W.T., 1919–1924.

toos consisted of small blue crosses at the corners of the mouth and of several vertical blue lines on the chin (Petitot 1876a:xxviii, xxxiv–xxxv).

Social Organization

Data on kinship organization and terminology and on group structure and dynamics are very fragmentary and scanty. Both Petitot (1876a:140, 237) and Stefánsson (1919) record the occurrence of polygamy (certainly polygyny and possibly also polyandry), although polygamous marriages constituted no more than 5 percent of all marriages. Wife-lending between friends is well attested.

Production units varied seasonally in size from single nuclear families or small groups of them in fishing and hunting seasons to large groups of 75 to 200 or 300 or more persons in whaling camps. The principal collaborative economic activities were whaling, weir fishing, caribou drives, and floe-edge sealing. Produce was shared according to need among families participating in these groups. The basic consumption unit was the nuclear family. In winter residence each nuclear family maintained its own cooking lamp or fire and food stores and prepared its meals separately, although complementary food sharing between families in a house was institutionalized with a precise etiquette (Stefánsson 1919:135).

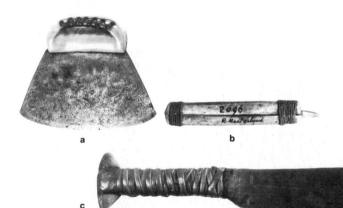

Smithsonian, Dept. of Anthr.: a, 1,630; b, 2,096; c, 1,307.

Fig. 7. Knives. a, Ulu with a metal blade set into a slit in the ivory handle. There is a depression on each side of the handle for the fingers and decorative lacing of baleen strips. Length 12.0 cm. b, Tool made of 2 pieces of bone bound together with sinew, with a short metal blade set in the tip. It was probably used for engraving ivory. Length 13.0 cm. a–b, Collected by R. MacFarlane, Anderson River, N.W.T., 1866. c, Large metal blade set into a wooden shaft with a bone end-piece, used for cutting blubber. Length 52.3 cm. Collected by C.P. Gaudet, Anderson River, N.W.T., 1866.

Smithsonian, Dept. of Anthr.: 2,208.
Fig. 8. Toolboard. Wooden board, probably used to grind and mix paint, with tools tied together at one end with sinew cord: an ivory needle, 2 pieces of leather wrapping pigment, and a small knife with a metal blade. Length of board 16.5 cm. Collected by R. Kennicott, Anderson River, N.W.T., 1866.

There was no formal chieftainship. Men admired for their skills and personal attributes (such as generosity and modesty) constituted "situational leaders" in various activities. Some of these leaders may also have been shamans (Petitot 1890:24–25). While Stefánsson (1919:168, 170, 172) notes that each village had a chief or headman especially concerned with whaling-boat crew organization (reminiscent of the umialik tradition of Alaska groups) and that these headmen succeeded to their positions patrilineally (reminiscent of the Eastern and Central Eskimo isumataq tradition, cf. Damas 1969:137), it is quite possible, even most likely, that these features were acquired in late prehistoric and early historic contacts with Alaska and Central Eskimo groups.

Close "partnerships" between pairs of men were a significant feature of social organization. These were often contracted between potential enemies, and a specialized variant, the trading partnership, was often established with Eskimos of other groups and with Indians. Partners referred to each other as their "double." In partnerships there was pervasive mutual sharing of resources and a guarantee of mutual support and protection. They were unbreakable once established (Petitot 1876a; Stefánsson 1919).

Formal social control was institutionalized as a right of direct reprisal or "self-help." Murder, wife stealing, and theft were the principal offenses treated in this manner. Men were publicly executed by stabbing with a dagger, while women were strangled. This feature of Mackenzie Eskimo social organization is probably often erroneously called blood feud, but Petitot (1876a:xxxiv–xxxv) does state that it could engender longstanding hate and distrust between families that could develop into recurrent violence.

Children were treated very affectionately and warmly. They were seldom or never harshly disciplined. Apparently infanticide was not practiced or was sporadic and minimal. Many children were named after deceased

354

Table 3. Animal and Plant Species Utilized by the Mackenzie Eskimo

Common Name	Species
Land Mammals	
Woodland caribou	*Rangifer tarandus caribou*
Barren Ground caribou	*Rangifer tarandus groenlandicus*
Moose	*Alces alces*
Grizzly bear	*Ursus horribilis*
Brown bear	*Ursus arctos*
Wolverine	*Gulo gulo*
Marten	*Martes americana*
Muskrat	*Ondatra zibethicus*
Beaver	*Castor canadensis*
Lynx	*Felis lynx*
Mink	*Mustela vison*
Arctic fox	*Alopex lagopus*
Red fox	*Vulpes vulpes*
Arctic hare	*Lepus arcticus*
Snowshoe hare	*Lepus americanus*
Dall's sheep	*Ovis dalli*
Sea Mammals	
Beluga	*Delphinapterus leucas*
Ringed seal	*Phoca hispida*
Bearded seal	*Erignathus barbatus*
Fish	
Lumpback whitefish	*Coregonus clupeaformis*
Broad whitefish	*Coregonus nasus*
Inconnu	*Stenodus leucichthys*
Burbot (loche)	*Lota lota*
Northern pike	*Esox lucius*
Herring	*Clupea harengus*
Arctic char	*Salvelinus alpinus*
Birds	
Snow goose	*Chen caerulescens*
Canada goose	*Branta canadensis*
Brant	*Branta bernicla*
Willow ptarmigan	*Lagopus lagopus*
Rock ptarmigan	*Lagopus mutus*
Tundra swan	*Cygnus colombianus*
Old-squaw	*Clangula hyemalis*
Mallard	*Anas platyrhynchos*
Pintail	*Anas acuta*
American widgeon	*Anas americana*
Canvasback	*Aythya valisineria*
Green-winged teal	*Anas carolinensis*
Common eider	*Somateria mollissima*
Red-breasted merganser	*Mergus serrator*
White-winged scooter	*Melanitta fusca*
Greater scaup	*Aythya marila*
Plants	
Cranberry	*Vaccinium vitis-idaea*
Bog blueberry	*Vaccinium uliginosum*
Crowberry	*Empetrum nigrum*
Cloudberry	*Rubus chamaemorus*
Viviparous knotweed	*Polygonum viviparum*
Wild sweet pea, sainfoin	*Hedysarum mackenzii*
Mountain sorrel	*Oxyria digyna*

SOURCES: Petitot 1876, 1876a, 1876b, 1886, 1887; Stefánsson 1913, 1913a, 1919, 1921; Russell 1898.

left, Smithsonian, NAA: 77-7115; Smithsonian, Dept. of Anthr.: top center, 5,817; bottom center, 2251; right, Anglican Church of Canada, General Synod Arch., Toronto, Ont.: Stringer Coll. P7517-163.

Fig. 9. Clothing and ornaments. left, Man of the Anderson River region with decorated fur parka, leggings, and boots, holding a pipe and knife. Around his waist is a belt with a whole skin of a small mammal attached, perhaps as an amulet. He wears labrets; the tattooed lines across his face indicate that he had committed homicide (Petitot 1887:100). Pen and ink drawing by Émile Petitot, 1862–1883. top center, Labret made of an ivory mouth piece with 2 blue beads attached with wooden dowels. Width 2.8 cm; collected by R. MacFarlane, Anderson River, N.W.T., 1868. bottom center, Pendants of ivory joined with blue beads strung on sinew, worn in the ear or through the nasal septum. Length 5.5 cm; collected by R. Kennicott, Anderson River, N.W.T., 1866. right, Avumnuk and his wife from Herschel Island. She wears a bead necklace and a pouch suspended from her neck. Photograph by Issac O. Stringer, 1892–1905.

grandparents and were treated with the respect previously accorded their namesakes. Most names could be used by both sexes. People who had the same name could not marry each other. Each person had several names, but only one might be in common use. Names were ceremoniously bestowed by shamans (Petitot 1887:145).

Petitot (1887:279, 1893:352) refers to three puberty rites of passage: filing of lower incisors to gum level, perforation of the earlobes, perforation of the cheeks for labrets. These were ceremoniously performed on boys at the age of 12 or 13. In addition, a boy's first kill of a large game animal was an event for celebration, and after it he joined exclusively in men's activities.

Burial of the dead was effected by placing the corpse on the ground, usually on the top of a low hill near water, and covering it with driftwood. Personal possessions of the deceased, including kayaks, umiaks, and sleds, were placed in or on top of the grave. There was a general fear of the dead and of objects with which the dead had been in contact. Corpses were removed from dwellings by a hole made in a wall rather than by the doorway.

Beliefs

Hostile sorcery, consisting of chants and ritual gestures, was practiced against people who had caused offense in cases where direct reprisal was impossible or would not be publicly condoned. One of the instruments used was a thin, supple wand with a small talisman attached to the end by a lanyard. As the dance and gestures became more excited, the lanyard wound and unwound around the wand, which it seems was pointed in the general direction of the victim (Petitot 1876a:90–92).

Curative magic consisted of chants and spells. A frequent feature was bloodletting and the making of incisions over affected parts (Petitot 1876a:195).

Taboos, mostly restrictions on eating certain foods or parts of animals, were prevalent. The wearing of talismans against evil was commonly practiced. Recorded objects of this kind include the skins, tails, or feathers of ravens, owls, eagles, ermine, wolves, foxes, falcons, and wolverine and small objects of metal or ivory. There was a general belief in evil spirits (tunɣaˑq).

Several cosmogonic myths state that the beaver created two brothers: one was the ancestor of the Mackenzie Eskimo, the other of all other western Eskimos. There are several myths—of a primeval deluge, of disappointed lovers (a brother and a sister) who became the man in the moon and the woman in the sun, and of the bringing of daylight—that are very similar to North Alaska versions.

Dances were accompanied by songs and large tambourine-type drums struck on the wooden rim rather than on the skin covering (fig. 12). There was a wealth

U. of Iowa, Mus. of Nat. Hist., Iowa City: left, 10,905; center, 10,903; right, Smithsonian Dept. of Anthr.: 128,407.

Fig. 10. Clothing. left, Woman's caribou fur parka with decorative borders of sheepskin with red and blue wool in the seams, and wolverine fur. center, Women's trousers with stockings attached worn with the caribou fur inside; boots were worn over this garment. right, Man's dance coat of brown and white fur with decorative borders of seed beads, clipped hair, and fur. There are tufts of hair sewed all over the garment. The hood ends in a cone shape. This parka is similar to dance costumes farther east (see "Copper Eskimo," fig. 16, this vol.). left, Back length about 96.5 cm; center, same scale. Both collected by Frank Russell on Herschel I., Yukon Terr., 1892–1894. right, Width, 60 cm; collected by E.P. Herenden on Herschel I., Yukon Terr., 1881–1883.

of string figures and accompanying stories (see Jenness 1924a).

Intriguingly, Petitot (1883:698, 1887:141) refers to a woman's version of the language, which employed distinctive vocabulary, expressions, and suffixes. These, he says, were never used by men. Unfortunately there are no details of this interesting feature, and the reliability of the observation cannot be confirmed.

The Twentieth Century

The presence of American whaling ships along the coast of the Mackenzie Delta after 1889 greatly disrupted the traditional culture of the Mackenzie Eskimos. The whaling era, here as elsewhere, was accompanied by swift population decline due to the effects of alcohol and introduced European diseases. In addition, many

North Alaska Eskimos, both coastal and inland peoples, having moved to Herschel Island to profit from interaction with the crews of whaling ships, moved east and repopulated the Delta once bowhead whaling declined. The remaining indigenous Delta population was dispersed, and a large-scale reorganization of the aboriginal economic and social system occurred. The Mackenzie Eskimos were in effect extinct by the 1920s (McGhee 1974:5–6).

Around 1906 a large number of inland Alaska Eskimos, many of them from the Colville River region, moved to the Delta to trap furs. Subsequently other people, both Indians and Eskimos, came into the area from the Central Arctic, the upper Mackenzie Valley, and the Yukon Territory. From southern Canada came White trappers, traders, missionaries, policemen, and government administrators. This heavy migration of Native and non-Native peoples had profound effects on

Smithsonian, Dept. of Anthr.: 7,733.

Fig. 11. Eyeshade. A strip of sealskin with slits cut for the eyes, and blue and red beads strung through the nose hole, secured around the head with ties at the back. It was probably used in the same way as wooden goggles to protect the wearer's eyes from snow blindness. Width 26.0 cm; collected by R. MacFarlane at Ft. Anderson, N.W.T., 1869.

the area, not the least of which was the establishment in 1959 of Inuvik, essentially a government town dedicated to the ideal of "modernizing" the north. The results of this experiment in "planned development" have been described in detail by Honigmann and Honigmann (1970:13–63). At Inuvik and other Delta settlements they had defined a distinctive frontier culture adapted to settled life in towns and an economy based primarily on wage labor and dependence on government social services. This way of life has virtually no relationship to the traditional culture of the Mackenzie Eskimos.

Hudson's Bay Company Lib., Winnipeg, Man.:E–120.

Fig. 12. Dance at Ft. McPherson, N.W.T. Koklik is in the background playing a drum and singing. Photograph by Elizabeth Taylor, 1892.

Public Arch. of Canada, Ottawa: PA 114833.

Fig. 13. Drum dance held in the federal day school at Aklavik, N.W.T., in honor of Gov.-Gen. Vincent Massey's visit, March 1956. The woman wears a calico dress. In Alaska and the western Canadian Arctic calico became a popular material to use as a cover over imported woolen duffle. The hood ruff of the woman's parka was known as a "sunburst," a reference to the long-haired fur of the wolf, which radiates from the face. This dress retains the hood to carry a child but is less capacious and comfortable than that of the traditional design. (Caption by Bernadette Driscoll, 1982). Photograph by Gar Lunney.

Synonymy

Mackenzie Eskimo is the most frequent designation in English for this group. However, it has frequently been used in a culturally loose sense simply to designate any Eskimo resident in the traditional Mackenzie Eskimo territory, and by the early twentieth century this included only a very small number of aboriginal inhabitants. The less well-known but more precise designation Chiglit or Tchiglit (*siɣlit*) should really be preferred but has enjoyed only limited use (Petitot 1876a). The name refers to the paired labrets worn in perforations in the cheeks near the mouth by adult Mackenzie Eskimo males. The name Kopagmiut was used by Hodge (1907–1910, 1:725–726), who lists variants.

Sources

Alexander Mackenzie, the first to explore the Mackenzie River (named after him) to the Arctic coast, in the summer of 1789, made no direct contact with Eskimos. He mentions only some recently abandoned camps (Mackenzie 1801). John Franklin (1828) records contact with Mackenzie Eskimos by exploring parties under his own and Dr. John Richardson's direction at the eastern and western edges of the Mackenzie Delta in 1826. He provides some ethnographic data, mostly on material culture; he illustrates houses and camp arrangements.

Contact in both cases, at first friendly, became hostile and ended in pillaging and harassment of the explorers' parties. Two or three traders and missionaries who attempted to enter the Mackenzie Delta in the late 1840s were slain by Eskimos. Richardson (1851) gives further ethnographic notes from a subsequent expedition of 1848 in search of the missing Franklin expedition.

In 1857 Roderick Ross MacFarlane, Hudson's Bay Company employee, explored the Anderson River and in 1861 established Fort Anderson, the first built specifically for the Eskimo trade. It was closed in 1866 (Höhn 1963). MacFarlane (1891, 1905) made substantial ethnographic and biological collections, most of which were deposited in the Smithsonian Institution.

Historical data on pre-European life in the Mackenzie Delta has been summarized by McGhee (1974:7–24). By far the most comprehensive and best-quality published ethnographic observations were made by Petitot (1876, 1876a, 1876b, 1886, 1887). While partly indebted to MacFarlane's previous works, especially for map data, he collected a large amount of linguistic material, including an extensive dictionary, and made systematic observations on most phases of Mackenzie Es-

kimo cultural and social life. While the data are best and most complete on material culture and weakest on social groups and structures, they must unquestionably be considered to represent the ethnographic baseline for the Mackenzie Eskimo. Petitot (1970) is a valuable précis and systematization of Petitot's work, along with an extensive bibliography. Later ethnographic descriptions, with the exception of Jenness (1924, 1924a, 1928, 1944) and Stefánsson (1908, 1913a, 1914, 1919), must be considered as less valuable. Not only do other works describe highly acculturated and culturally mixed conditions, but also they often fail to distinguish Mackenzie Eskimo practices from those of immigrant Eskimos. Ostermann's (1942) observations on the Mackenzie Eskimo, based on Knud Rasmussen's notes, are a good example of this; in his volume, "Mackenzie Eskimo" refers simply to Eskimos resident in the Mackenzie Delta area at the time of Rasmussen's visit. Many of the practices described are of Alaskan origin.

Details of cultural differences among the Cape Bathurst subgroup and the four other Mackenzie Eskimo subgroups are evidenced in Collinson (1889), Höhn (1963), and Damas (1969:136–137).

Pre-Dorset and Dorset Prehistory of Canada

MOREAU S. MAXWELL

Around the mid-point of the third millennium B.C. pioneering bands of hunters, presumably preadapted to a frozen coast economy and techniques of marine mammal hunting, entered the Eastern Arctic as the first human inhabitants of that region. Their point of origin is still unknown. Since their material culture has no known prototypes in the east but does have suggestions of origin in the Western Arctic and on into Siberia, they probably came from the west. Although Western Arctic evidence does not suggest either population pressures or food scarcity at this point, the eastward move seems to have involved more than just a few scattered bands. They appear to have traveled rapidly through the Central and Eastern Arctic to ecological limits in northeastern Greenland and northern Labrador. Geomorphological evidence suggests that this apparently rapid and possibly large-scale movement took place some 4,000 years after the retreat of Pleistocene ice had opened Hudson Bay and Hudson Strait to Atlantic waters (Blake 1966). At this time the climate was warmer than at present, and at least part of the immigration must have been by boat (Maxwell 1960a). Lacking other evidence, scholars can only assume that a combination of optimal conditions led to an exploitable biomass of such proportions that it lured hunters eastward.

Distinctive lithic artifacts of this eastward-moving complex, referred to as the Arctic Small Tool tradition, include: spalled burins and burin spalls, microblades and microcores, small side and end scrapers in a variety of forms; end-hafted bifaces of straight-stemmed, contracting-stemmed, and triangular stemless forms; ovate and half-moon-shaped side blades, drills (rare); polished adzes, retouched flakes including some retouched to tiny tips, like those of Paleo-Indians, used for graving.

Nonlithic artifacts are less well known because of the differential preservation in early sites, but the high frequency of stone tools for processing hard organic materials suggests an originally rich inventory of bone, antler, and ivory foreshafts; lance and arrow tips; and harpoon heads.

Interpreting this pioneering immigration depends in large part on chronological evidence, which at this point is questionable. Materials submitted for carbon-14 analysis include disparate substances such as charred marine mammal fat, thought to give too old a date, and caribou antler, thought to give one too young. McGhee and Tuck (1976) suggest either that all but indigenous floral dates be ignored or that dates based on marine substances be reduced by 400 years. Arundale (1981) takes fractionation corrections into consideration. The choice of alternative chronologies obviously leads to opposing interpretations of the region's prehistory. An approximate time frame would be as follows: Independence I of the High Arctic, 2000–1600 B.C.; Pre-Dorset of the Low Arctic, either 2200 B.C. or 1800 B.C.–800 B.C. depending on controversial interpretations; a transitional phase including Independence II and Groswater Dorset, 800–500 B.C.; and Dorset 500 B.C.–A.D. 1450.

Independence I

The oldest wood (indigenous willow) dates available from the Eastern Arctic come from the cultural complex that Knuth (1967) has called Independence I. Sites that he considers belong to this culture extend across northern Greenland from the northeastern corner and through northern Ellesmere to Eureka Sound on the west coast. On the basis of 11 carbon dates on willow charcoal, dates range from 1810 B.C. (K-1262) to 2000 B.C. (K-938). Although the lithic assemblages of these sites can be described in terms of the general tool categories of the Eastern Arctic Small Tool tradition, there are discrete characteristics that tend to set off the Independence I complex from others of the eastern Paleo-Eskimo.

Until 1972 many archeologists considered that Independence I was simply a regional variant of the more widespread Pre-Dorset culture. In summer 1972 McGhee (1976, 1979), excavating on the south coast of the Grinnel Peninsula, Devon Island, found convincing proof of the separation of an early Pre-Dorset complex from an Independence I complex. At Port Refuge, along a limited expanse of beach he found two distinct sets of settlements, with different house patterns, different artifact complexes, and at different sea-level elevations. The upper, and presumably older (because of sea-level decline and isostasy), had linear strings of houses with internal stone boxes, a lithic complex resembling Independence I, and unusual nontoggling harpoon heads.

359

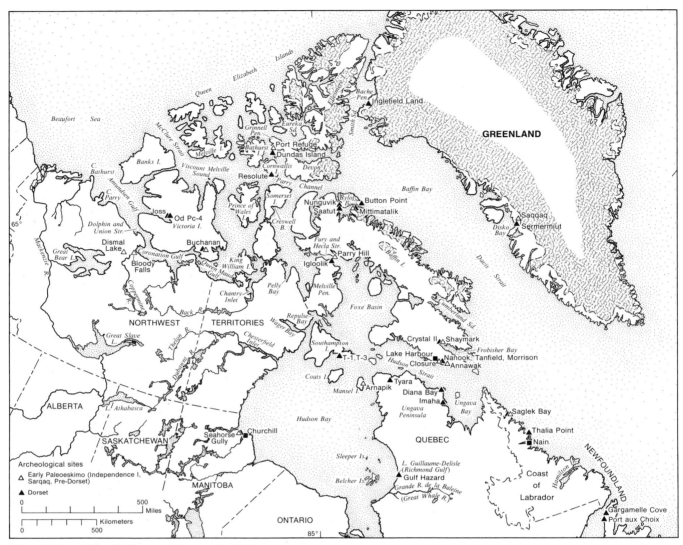

Fig. 1. Primary Paleo-Eskimo and Dorset sites in Canada.

Houses in the lower settlement tended to cluster; lacked internal stone features; and contained artifacts, including toggling harpoon heads, common to more southerly Pre-Dorset sites.

McGhee (1976) interprets this evidence as indicating a temporal and cultural gap between the two, with the earliest migration to the Eastern Arctic consisting of "sequential occupations by two distinct populations with quite different traditions." He suggests that the Independence I occupation taking place around 2000 B.C. may have preceded the Pre-Dorset one by approximately 300 years. Tuck's (1976) earliest Paleo-Eskimo material from Saglek Bay, northern Labrador, provisionally dated 1880 B.C. with charcoal, tends to support this position. Here the lithic complex (no nonlithic tools have been recovered) differs significantly from a Pre-Dorset one, in the direction of Independence I artifacts.

Pre-Dorset Culture

If "unadjusted" carbon dates on marine materials such as charred seal fat, sea mammal bones, and ivory (Wil-

meth 1978) are accepted, then Pre-Dorset (figs. 2–3) must be seen as the earliest culture in the Eastern Arctic. The Closure site on the south coast of Baffin Island; the Mittimatalik site at Pond Inlet on the northeastern coast of Baffin Island; the Parry Hill site (Kaleruserk) near Igloolik, northwestern Foxe Basin; and the Shaymark site at Frobisher Bay, southeastern Baffin Island—all date, on marine materials, between 2500 B.C. and 2000 B.C.

The distribution of Pre-Dorset sites, as distinct from other Paleo-Eskimo complexes such as Independence I and Dorset, appears to extend from central Labrador north along the coast and eastern Baffin Island to the northwestern corner of Devon Island. They are located along both shores of the Hudson Strait, out to Mansel Island, south on the east coast of Hudson Bay to Great Whale River, and on the west coast to Churchill. There are sites in northwestern Foxe Basin, Pelly Bay on the central mainland littoral, southern Victoria Island, and Banks Island. But the region has been poorly explored, and there is no current evidence to indicate whether

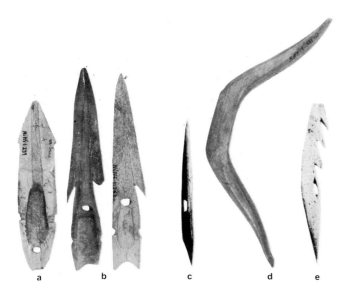

Natl. Mus. Canada, Ottawa

Fig. 2. Pre-Dorset culture artifacts: a, open socket ivory lance head stepped for endblade, Igloolik region, early Pre-Dorset; b, open socket antler harpoon heads, Igloolik region, early Pre-Dorset; c, open socket ivory harpoon head; Bucharan site, Victoria I., N.W.T., late Pre-Dorset; d, antler bow brace, Igloolik region; e, antler bird or fish spear side barb, Buchanan site. Length of a, 9.0 cm, rest same scale.

these are isolated settlements, or whether the population was relatively continuous along these vast distances. In the west there is penetration of Pre-Dorset into the interior at Bloody Falls on the Coppermine (McGhee 1970) and south to Dismal Lake (Harp 1958). Noble (1971) sees its influence continuing well into the taiga and south of Great Bear Lake (see "Prehistory of the Great Slave Lake and Great Bear Lake Region," vol. 6).

Like the beginning date for Pre-Dorset, its termination is also confused by carbon dates based on a number of disparate substances (Arundale 1981). A terminal date for Pre-Dorset between 800 B.C. and 500 B.C. would be generally acceptable to most archeologists. Those distinctive cultural characteristics that mark the end of this period and the beginning of Dorset would be much less widely accepted.

• SEA MAMMAL HUNTING The seacoast locations of settlements and, where preserved, the presence of harpoon heads and numerous other artifacts of seal and walrus bone and ivory attest the importance of seal and walrus in the economy. Evidence for beluga and narwhal hunting is less conclusive but sufficient to suggest at least occasional hunting.

The harpoon heads for sea mammal hunting appear to follow a stylistic progression through Pre-Dorset time with closely similar forms being apparently coeval in far-distant sites. The earliest version, known from Igloolik, Mittimatalik, and Port Refuge, has a single line

hole, is self-bladed, with single or bilateral barbs, and an open socket. Through time the Pre-Dorset harpoon heads lose the side barbs and become smaller but retain their open sockets. While most of those recovered have been self-bladed, there is adequate evidence that many were tipped with triangular chert points.

• TERRESTRIAL HUNTING Bones of musk-ox, caribou, polar bear, and birds appear in the middens. Hunters seem to have been well equipped for taking this game with bows, arrows, and lances of both throwing and thrusting types. Antler bow braces and handle segments (Meldgaard 1962) indicate that bows were small, sharply recurved, composite bows like those documented for the Central Eskimo. Arrows (W.E. Taylor 1964) had long, slender bone or antler foreshafts, which ended either in blunt tips for birds or small game or in a gouged-out bed for a stone tip. Chert end blades for these arrows are thin, slender, and double-tapered or else triangular. These tips often have minutely serrated edges and polished facets on dorsal and ventral faces.

The characteristic lance heads, of antler, were long, open-socketed, and usually perforated near the base with a small line groove that produces a "cloven hoof" effect. Many had end blades and half-moon-shaped side blades set in slots just above the socket or low lateral ridges in lieu of side blades (W.E. Taylor 1963). Throughout the span of Pre-Dorset and into Dorset there is very little variation in the shape of these lances. Help in hunting land animals may have come from large Greenlandic-type dogs. Their remains, although always rare, occur throughout the Pre-Dorset duration at Igloolik (Meldgaard 1962).

• TECHNOLOGY Analysis indicates that many categories of stone tools were used in fabricating ivory, bone, and antler. This would include a variety of burins, small spoke-shave side scrapers, and tiny end scrapers of chert and quartz crystal. A suite of stemmed and side-notched knives, both symmetric and asymmetric, was more appropriate for cutting wood or meat. Ground slate knives, apparently restricted to only a few regions, would have served well in separating seal blubber from the carcass or perhaps in working soft wood; they are too fragile for other functions. Chert drills, or reamers, appear in several complexes in contrast to Dorset assemblages.

Microblades, pressed from chisel-shaped quartz crystals and from random-shaped chert cores; retouched burin spall awls, cup-shaped skin scrapers of bear or seal skull; bone awls, and ivory needles, round in cross-section with small round eyes and blunt butt ends—all suggest tailored clothing of seal and caribou skin.

Soapstone lamps—small oval or round bowls for burning seal fat—are part of the Pre-Dorset inventory but are so rare that their use may have been restricted to special situations, such as heating snowhouses. More common practices were to burn chunks of fat on small,

Fig. 3. Pre-Dorset culture artifacts: a, burins, unifacially and bifacially flaked, polished and unpolished, Shaymark site, Baffin I., N.W.T.; b, bifacially flaked knife, Shaymark site; c, end scrapers, Annawak site, Lake Harbour region, N.W.T.; d, side scrapers, Shaymark site; e, burin spalls, several modified for use as tools, Shaymark site; f, sideblades for lances, Shaymark site; g, end scraper, Shaymark site; h, angular-tipped burinlike tool, Annawak site; i, microblades, Shaymark site; j, limestone adz, Shaymark site; k, stemmed endblades for knives or lances, one on the right shattered by impact on distal end, Shaymark site; l, endblades for harpoons and arrows, some delicately serrated and polished on both faces prior to retouching, Shaymark site. Length of b, 4.4 cm, rest same scale.

flat stones, or to burn wood and fatty bones in open hearths.

• ART According to J. Meldgaard (personal communication 1972), Pre-Dorset artistic activities at Igloolik include geometric designs on tubular needle cases and on a caribou scapula. There are a few naturalistic animal carvings and, in later Pre-Dorset, small ivory human maskettes similar to those from Dorset complexes.

• STRUCTURES There are apparently seasonal differences in Pre-Dorset dwellings. Summer tent rings, small ovals seldom more than two meters long and a meter and one-half wide, may be marked at the periphery by a ring of boulders, but more commonly there is simply a small oval area within which there is a greater concentration of artifacts and small rocks (Dekin 1976). Throughout the area there are structures thought to be Pre-Dorset winter houses. These are small oval areas with mid-passages (probably actually meat preparation centers) and fire boxes defined by stone slabs set in vertical rows. However, if McGhee (1976) is correct, this trait is confined, in the early period, to Independence I and is not characteristic of earliest Pre-Dorset.

Regional Variants

There is sufficient similarity between specific artifacts and artifact complexes of Devon Island, northern Baffin Island, the Fury and Hecla Strait region, Pelly Bay, Mansel Island, northern Ungava, and the southeast coast of Baffin Island to suggest close contact among the Pre-Dorset peoples of these regions. The more southerly sites lack preserved nonlithic artifacts but show little variation in their lithic traits.

The western sites of Victoria and Banks islands (W.E. Taylor 1964, 1967, 1972a; C.D. Arnold 1980) have a majority of traits in common with this core area in addition to certain distinctive artifacts that have yet to appear in other Pre-Dorset sites. Some of these traits appear to have affinities with Alaska. On the other hand, the Bloody Falls assemblage (McGhee 1970), which appears to be coeval, has closer resemblance to the eastern sites. This may be, in part, because no nonlithic materials were preserved at Bloody Falls.

The appearance of the site assemblages, the relatively late carbon dates, and the absence of distinctively early sites has led McGhee (1976) and Maxwell (1973) to suggest that the early eastward migration passed rapidly through the west and that at a later date, prior to 1500 B.C., Pre-Dorset people moved back westward to occupy Banks and Victoria islands, possibly to develop in relative isolation from the eastern centers. Taylor (W.E. 1964) disagrees and sees the situation as one in which there has been insufficient site survey to locate earlier western sites.

The Seahorse Gully Pre-Dorset component near Churchill, at the south-central periphery of the Pre-Dorset sphere, also appears to be a regional variant of the basic complex (Nash 1969, 1972, 1976). Here, along with standard late Pre-Dorset lithic traits, there is a peculiar group of large chert mattocks, picks, and gouges that has no parallel in other Pre-Dorset or Dorset sites.

Fitzhugh (1972, 1976a) feels that the Pre-Dorset of Thalia Point, north of Nain, Labrador, also varies from the Hudson Strait–Foxe Basin complex in the direction of more Greenlandic manifestations of Paleo-Eskimo, although the evidence is not so clear-cut as that at Saglek Bay.

Dorset Culture

There is general agreement among archeologists working in the area that Dorset culture (figs. 4–6) emerges from Pre-Dorset without the introduction of distinctive cultural features from outside the Eastern Arctic or the immigration of a new population. There is much less agreement, or understanding, of the nature of the transition or its causes, a situation compounded by a lack of reliable dates. Available evidence suggests some change from a Pre-Dorset configuration to a Dorset configuration between 800 B.C. and 500 B.C.; however, since the majority of cultural traits persist from Pre-Dorset into Dorset with only slight stylistic variation, it is difficult to define the differences between late sites of the one and early sites of the other. J. Meldgaard (personal communication 1972) sees the transitional period as one of marked increase in the rate of stylistic change, particularly in nonlithic artifacts. McGhee (1976) and Knuth (1967) see Independence II as a transitional phase in the High Arctic, as Fitzhugh (1976) sees Groswater Dorset in Labrador. However, at Lake Harbour, where there is no preserved organic material from sites prior to 500 B.C., there are changes in artifact frequen-

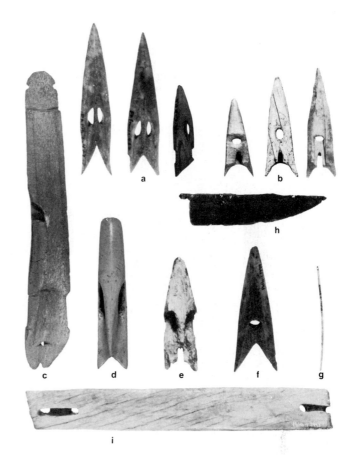

Natl. Mus. of Canada, Ottawa.

Fig. 4. Dorset culture artifacts: a, 2 closed socket, double line hole harpoon heads, Button Point, Bylot I., N.W.T., and one open socket fishing harpoon head, Coats I., northern Hudson Bay, late Dorset; b, "sliced" harpoon heads, 2 on the left slotted for endblades, Tanfield site, Lake Harbour region, Baffin I., N.W.T., early Dorset; c, open socket antler lance head slotted on the edge for a sideblade and stepped for an endblade, Igloolik region; d, walrus hunting harpoon head of ivory, Maxwell Bay, Devon I., N.W.T., late Dorset; e, walrus hunting harpoon head of ivory, Tanfield site, early Dorset; f, closed socket harpoon head, Saatut site, Navy Board Inlet, northern Baffin I., N.W.T., middle Dorset; g, ivory needle with blunt proximal end, Saatut site, middle Dorset; h, wooden toy sled, Tanfield site; i, narwhal ivory sled shoe, Nunguvik site, Navy Board Inlet, early Dorset. Length of c, 16.0 cm, rest same scale.

cies but little change in artifact type or style. A number of lithic traits considered "guide fossils" for beginning Dorset make their first appearance in several sites. The fact that many of these were present at Lake Harbour for several preceding centuries implies that at least the lithic traits characteristic of developing Dorset over a broad area may have their genesis on the north shore of Hudson Strait and spread outward at this time.

Through this transition, harpoon heads, known mainly from Igloolik sites, pass rapidly from an open socket form to a closed one through intermediate steps. With the beginning of Dorset, bone sled shoes (presumably for small hand-drawn sleds), snow knives for snowhouse

Fig. 5. Dorset culture artifacts: a, chert harpoon endblades, Tanfield site, Lake Harbour region, Baffin I., N.W.T., early Dorset; b, chert harpoon endblades with serrated edges, Crystal II site, Baffin I., N.W.T., late Dorset; c, chert end scrapers, Crystal II site; d, chert side scrapers, Crystal II site; e, angular-tipped burinlike tools of nephrite, Tanfield site; f, square-ended burinlike tools of chert and chalcedony, Tanfield site; g, chert side-notched knives with angled edges, Crystal II site, late Dorset. Length of a (far left) 2.1 cm, rest same scale.

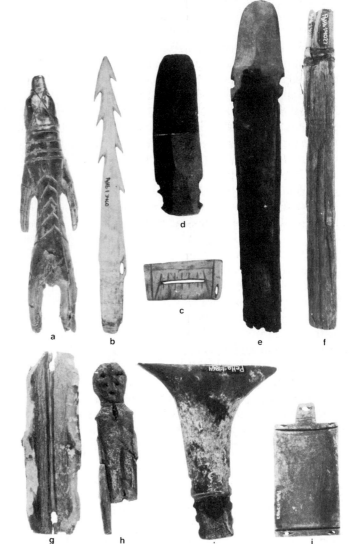

Fig. 6. Dorset culture artifacts: a, ivory bear with engraved skeletal motif, Nanook site, Lake Harbour region, Baffin I., N.W.T.; b, ivory fish spear, Nunguvik site, Navy Board Inlet, northern Baffin I., N.W.T.; c, ivory "shaman's teeth," Coats I., northern Hudson Bay; d, slate knife blade, Tanfield site, Lake Harbour region, Baffin I., N.W.T.; e, slate knife in original wooden handle, Tanfield site; f, side-hafted microblade in original composite wooden handle, Nunguvik site; g, antler ice creeper for strapping on boot (one of a pair), Morrisson site, Lake Harbour region, Baffin I., N.W.T.; h, wooden female figurine with removable arms and legs and neck region pierced and filled with red ocher, Button Point, Bylot I., N.W.T.; i, antler adz socket, Saatut site, Navy Board Inlet, Baffin I., N.W.T.; j, antler amulet box, Nunguvik site. Length of a, 13.6 cm, rest same scale.

building, and ice creepers of antler or ivory make their appearance. Dogs, bows and arrows, and drills apparently drop from the cultural inventory, although there is sporadic evidence for them later in Dorset.

The appearance of these winter hunting traits and a proportional increase in stone lamps may imply a shift in emphasis toward the greater importance of sea-ice hunting. Possibly there is a concomitant reduction in the winter stalking of caribou with dogs and bow and arrow as well as an increase in hunting caribou in warmer months when they could be driven into lakes and speared. Dekin (1975) finds this to be a climatic period marked in the Eastern Arctic by colder and more unstable conditions with increased precipitation in winter and declines in land fauna dependent on foraging for winter survival.

Fitzhugh (1976) also suggests evidence for caribou decline in the Ungava as a related factor in the development of Dorset. As one of a number of alternative suggestions he proposes that increased ice conditions and the decrease of open-water hunting areas in Hudson Bay at this time may have led to a population with-

drawal back to Hudson Strait where demographic compressions could have been a causative factor in Dorset development.

Adequate faunal reports are few, but even with scanty data the following propositions are apparent: Dorset hunters were highly skilled and efficient, they were selective in harvesting faunal resources, and their hunting equipment was less complicated and functionally specific than that of Thule and modern Eskimo.

• SEA MAMMAL HUNTING Most, although not all, Dorset sites have in the food refuse a predominance of seal bones of several species. Walrus bones appear in middens in relationship to access to the better hunting sites, although, except for some peripheral locations such as Newfoundland, walrus hunting appears to have been an important activity throughout. Narwhal and beluga hunting was less common, although since beluga was probably butchered at the coast, there should be few bones in the midden. Sheets of baleen, large chunks of whale bone, and whale-bone sled shoes, which occasionally appear in Dorset sites, have usually been interpreted as the residue of stranded whales. However, Mary-Rousselière (1976) suggests that hunting the baleen whale is less dangerous than walrus hunting and that this may have been a Dorset activity, although not organized to the extent that it was in Thule culture.

There is no evidence for the throwing board or other projecting equipment or for floats or drags for fastening to the harpoon line. Preserved wooden harpoon shaft fragments from the Lake Harbour sites (Maxwell 1974–1975) indicate that the shaft ended in a scarfed surface rather than a socket and that a caribou bone foreshaft, bound to the slanting surface, slid along it on impact, releasing the toggling head. Harpoon heads, of ivory and antler, both self-bladed and slotted for stone tips, appear to follow a regular stylistic progression throughout the Dorset sphere and provide reasonably reliable time markers.

• TERRESTRIAL HUNTING The common weapon for taking land animals was the lance with bone foreshaft and open-socketed head, little changed in discrete attributes from Pre-Dorset times. With the lance, quantities of caribou and musk-ox, where available, were killed. The high concentration of caribou bones in lakeshore sites suggests that animals were driven into the water and speared there perhaps with harpoon as well as lance (W.E. Taylor 1967:223).

It is hard to imagine that as useful a weapon as the bow and arrow, present in the Pre-Dorset inventory, should have dropped from use. However, in sites such as those from Lake Harbour and Button Point, where wooden fragments are well preserved, there are no traces of arrow shafts or bow parts. The only arrow parts reported in the literature are two from Victoria Island sites excavated by McGhee (1971:pl. II, 1). Here, at the Joss site and site OdPc-4, he recovered two slotted foreshafts prepared for side blades, which must be arrowheads. They differ significantly from Western Arctic ones, but their source cannot easily have been eastern Dorset.

Hunting dogs disappear in Dorset, according to the evidence from Igloolik and other sites, although an identified dog skull (and possibly fragments of a second dog) appears in the Nanook midden of about 200 B.C. (Maxwell 1973). Hunting polar bears without dogs and with only hand-held lances would have been extremely dangerous and suggests cooperative efforts. The mystical importance of the bear is reflected in Dorset art and in what appears to be a ceremonial treatment of bear skulls and forearm bones in a late Dorset site at Dundas Island (McGhee 1976).

Dorset sites are often in good fishing locations and near old stone fish weirs; however, the fishing equipment shows little sophistication or variety. There are no known hooks or gorges for line fishing and only occasionally artifacts interpreted as line weights or fish lures. Artifacts that may be Dorset leisters, so useful in taking Arctic char from streams and weirs, are reported only from Dundas Island (McGhee 1976) and Newfoundland. A trident, similar in effectiveness to the leister, comes in very late and may be the result of Thule influence. The ubiquitous artifact interpreted as a Dorset fish-spear tip is a very small, fragile point with bilateral barbs, a line hole usually asymmetrically placed, and either an open socket or a pointed proximal end.

• DOMESTIC ACTIVITIES Dorset fire making remains enigmatic. Meldgaard (1960) at Igloolik and Maxwell (1973) at Lake Harbour recovered a few chunks of iron pyrites, but they are rare. Mary-Rousselière (1976) found parts of what appears to be a fire plough, but no other mechanical means of making fire have been reported. There are many indications that some cooking was carried on inside the dwelling over driftwood fires, but soapstone lamps and vessels attest to cooking over wick and seal oil heat. Most of the lamps, rectangular in early Dorset and oval in late, are so small that they would hardly give more heat than three or four candles. Many of the bowls, grooved at the narrow ends for suspension, are so small that they would hardly hold more than a cup of soup.

Fragments of cut and stitched skins, numerous ivory and bone needles with oval eyes and sharpened butt ends, and skins cut with microblades all attest to tailored clothing. However, there is little indication of costume. On the basis of several carvings, high collars extending above the ears may have supplanted parka hoods. A sealskin boot fragment from the Nanook site was identical to the modern kamik, with bearded seal skin sole, harp seal instep, and ring seal upper.

• TRANSPORTATION Shoes presumably for hand-drawn sleds appear early in Dorset and last until the end, the early ones being flat sections of whale bones, the later ones narrower, of ivory, with binding perforations running from one lateral margin to the other. Wooden sled models (eight were recovered from the Tanfield site), if they were proportional, indicate that full-sized ones would have been about eight inches high and six to eight feet long, with solid driftwood runners and four or five cross slats. Kayak parts and model kayaks recovered from Button Point (Mary-Rousellière 1979) do not differ from Thule ones. Similar fragments recovered from the Nanook site (Maxwell 1973; Arundale 1976) also suggest small kayaks.

• STRUCTURES Snow block houses have been inferred for Dorset on the basis of recovered snow knives. In addition there appears to be a variety of dwelling types. Variants are presumably based on seasonal needs. The rich and extensive Tanfield site midden contained so few rocks that dwellings there can only be of sod chunks with a skin roof, but there is no suggestion of size or shape. Summer tent rings may be small circles of extremely large boulders, ovals of small rocks, or large rectangular areas with internal compartments defined with rocks. At the Seahorse Gully site, Nash (1972) has excavated five houses or tents. These are oval or rectangular, with outer boundaries either poorly defined or marked with stone slabs. A central platform about three feet wide, marked with stone slabs set vertically and running lengthwise through the middle, divides the shelter into two equal parts. Lengths of these houses range from about 14 to 24 feet, and widths from about 8 to 22 feet. McGhee (1976) reports several similar structures from Devon Island. A late Dorset dwelling in Richmond Gulf incorporates many of the internal features, such as fire boxes defined by vertical stone slabs that are a recurrent theme in Dorset winter (?) dwellings. These fire boxes; the stone-slab-defined mid-passages, or food preparation centers; and side sleeping benches are particularly well defined in the relatively large semisubterranean houses of the Port aux Choix community, Newfoundland (Harp 1976).

At approximately A.D. 500 a different type of structure is added to the suite. These are large structures from 14 meters to more than 40 meters long (Meldgaard 1960; Laughlin and Taylor 1960; W.E. Taylor 1967; Plumet 1969; Lee 1969; McGhee 1971; Schledermann 1981). They appear sporadically in sites from Ungava to Victoria Island, and Ellesmere Island. Some may have been multi-family dwellings, but many contain so few artifacts and so little refuse that they can hardly have been residences.

• BURIALS In spite of the relatively large numbers of known Dorset sites, mortuary information is very scanty. This implies that the majority of Dorset dead were exposed either on the tundra or on sea ice, leaving no trace for archeologists. It also raises the question of why the few burials that are known, with their reflections of ideational behavior, were singled out for special treatment. A burial at the Imaha site, Payne Bay (Laughlin and Taylor 1960), accompanied by a few generalized stone tools, is that of an Eskimo physical type and probably Dorset. A mandible from the Tyara site, unquestionably Dorset, is surely Eskimo in type, as is a mandible from a late Dorset site on Mansel Island (Oschinsky 1960).

Harp and Hughes (1968) report an infant burial in House 12 of the Port aux Choix 2 site, Newfoundland. The 20-month-old infant had been buried in a tightly contracted upright position in a pit two feet deep and two feet in diameter in the central hearth trench. Grave goods, an interesting combination of technological and ideational artifacts, were scattered around the infant; the grave was filled; and then it was capped with a limestone slab. In the same fireplace trench was an adult mandible and charcoal carbon dated A.D. 363. Nearby, in a cave at Gargamelle Cove, amateurs located a grave or graves containing remains of four infants and four or five adults with associated artifacts, both utilitarian and ideational, clearly Dorset of the Newfoundland type. Anderson and Tuck (1974) report three additional cave burials from Newfoundland. Associated remains are like those from the Gargamelle Cove site and unquestionably Dorset. Cranial morphology shows major features typical of Eskimo.

• ART The artistic expression of carvers and engravers is the most interesting and exotic Dorset activity. One of the best statements on Dorset art is in Taylor and Swinton (1967). In general, artistic pieces of ivory, antler, bone, wood, and stone are small but carved to scale. Few artifacts that are functional in the technical sense have been decorated, since "most if not all Dorset art [was] concerned with supernatural matters—with shamanism, burial practices, sympathetic magic" (Taylor and Swinton 1967:44). Three-dimensional carvings may be naturalistic, with accurate anatomical detail, or highly stylized, or abstract in the sense of one anatomical feature standing for the whole animal (fig. 7). Line engraving is almost exclusively in unembellished straight lines that cross, form X's, are parallel, or chevroned and often represent a "skeletal" effect.

While bears, sea mammals, caribou, and birds are all depicted, the greatest variety is seen in the representation of humans. The Button Point site (W.E. Taylor 1972a) has produced two life-sized wooden masks, which showed facial tattooing and, originally, had moustache and hair pegged into place. Maskettes of ivory, antler, wood, and steatite have been recovered from a number of sites dating from earliest Dorset to latest. Small wooden dolls with removable arms and legs have been found in sites widely separated in space and time, as have antler segments covered with clusters of faces. Some figures of both bears and humans have small slits in throat or back, filled with red ocher, and then closed with wooden slivers, suggesting a form of sympathetic magic. The very close similarity of some of the art pieces and the fact that they are often found in close association in situ suggests that this was a highly specialized activity, perhaps restricted to the shaman. As Swinton (Taylor and Swinton 1967:41) has explained, "magical symbols would not be applied to anything by anybody other than one who is familiar with magic and its powerful effects. Magic is not something with which to fool around."

Culture Change and Style Shift

Statements about development within Dorset suffer from a dearth of monographic reports and quantified information as well as from questionable carbon dates. Present published sources allow little more than statements about an early phase and a late phase. Relying on available carbon dates, the early phase would extend from about 500 B.C. to A.D. 300, and the late phase from then to about A.D. 1400.

Within an area bounded by sites on both sides of Hudson Strait, the islands at the north end of Hudson Bay, the Fury and Hecla Strait, and probably the north end of Baffin Island, there is a high level of homogeneity of traits, comparable continuities of style shifts, and apparent synchronous changes in artifact form. This all suggests a long-continued and intense interaction within an apparent "core area." Published information on early developments within this core area is fairly complete with site reports from T-1, Southampton Island (Collins 1956, 1957); Tyara, Sugluk Island (W.E. Taylor 1968); Nunguvik, Navy Board Inlet (Mary-Rousselière 1976); and Tanfield, south Baffin Island (Maxwell 1976). These sites are all dated on sea mammal material (undoubtedly some centuries too early) within a 60-year period beginning in 720 B.C. Additionally, Meldgaard (1960, 1960a, 1962) has published summaries of this early Dorset material from the Fury and Hecla Strait. A less securely dated sequence of sites follows this group (Maxwell 1976), and then another cluster—T-3 (Collins 1957), the top level at Tyara (W.E. Taylor 1968), and the Nanook on the south shore of Baffin Island (Maxwell 1973)—with a central tendency around 250 B.C. From this time on there is a scattering of published site reports, many of the sites not yet dated, which demonstrate regular and concomitant style shifts throughout the core area. In the late phase the core area appears to extend northward at least as far as Devon Island (Lethbridge 1939) where materials from the Dundas Island site (McGhee 1976) and Resolute, Cornwallis Island (Collins 1955), seem closely linked to the more southerly sites. This northerly expansion of the core area, or at least of the traits that distinguish it, continues to Ellesmere Island (Bentham and Jenness 1941; Schledermann 1981), and onto Inglefield Land, Greenland (Holtved 1944).

Within the core area, changes in the material culture inventory from early to late seem to be only minor stylistic shifts, many of them not easily recognized as being more functional or adaptive. Except for periods in which there appear to be geographic extensions of Dorset influence, there is no evidence of major dimensions of cultural change. The picture of Dorset development in regions peripheral to the core area differs somewhat, with apparent periods in which there is relatively close contact with the core, periods of isolation, and apparent gaps in continuity marked either by the extinction of regional groups or by population withdrawal into more advantageous ecological situations. The peripheral region of the Labrador coast and Newfoundland appears to reflect more regional variation and the effects of isolation. The evidence from Saglek Bay (Tuck 1976) and from the Groswater Dorset phase of Hamilton Inlet (Fitzhugh 1972, 1976a) suggests a very early Dorset migration along the Labrador coast, at least as early as 740 B.C., and local development, possibly isolated from the Hudson Strait–Foxe Basin area but perhaps not from the High Arctic–Greenland area until at least 300 B.C.

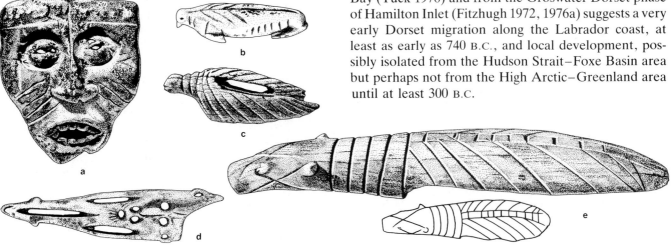

a and c, after Société des Amis du Musée de l'Homme 1969:4,15; b, d, and e, after Canadian Arts Council 1971:11,4,10.

Fig. 7. Dorset art. These objects, associated with shamanism, probably served as amulets and carvings of spirit-helpers. They are characterized by their small scale, incised designs (including crosses and skeletal motif), and fine carving. a, Miniature mask made from a fragment of a soapstone lamp, one of the few examples of Dorset art in soapstone; incised lines on the face may represent tattoo marks on a woman's face; Igloolik region. Ivory carvings: b, Walrus with incised skeletal marks, Igloolik region; c, falcon, incised with deeply excised underside, Angekok site, Mansel I., N.W.T. d, Stylized bear that inverted becomes a human face (the combination of different species on a single piece is common in Dorset art), Button Point site, Bylot I., N.W.T. e, Stylized bear with skeletal motif, larger than many Dorset pieces. The grooves and perforations on the underside show traces of red ocher, Sleeper Is., N.W.T. Length of b, 3.5 cm, rest same scale.

In the first century A.D. there appears to have been an additional outward expansion of Dorset affecting western Greenland, Labrador, and Newfoundland. At this time there is a movement, characterized by artifacts virtually identical to those of the core area, into Disko Bay (Larsen and Meldgaard 1958; Mathiassen 1958). It also seems to mark the appearance of Dorset in Newfoundland at the Port aux Choix site (Harp 1964, 1969–1970, 1976; Harp and Hughes 1968). Although the Sermermiut Disko Bay settlement may have been short-lived, the Newfoundland settlers remained from A.D. 162 to A.D. 589, living in relatively large, semi-subterranean, rectangular houses with central fire boxes or "mid-passages."

The east coast of Hudson Bay, still largely an archeological terra incognita, appears to have been peripheral in the sense of being a refuge for a terminal Dorset population. Harp's (1976) excavations in Richmond Gulf and Gulf Hazard point to a very late Dorset occupation. However, on the west coast of Hudson Bay, Nash (1972, 1976) sees the early Dorset occupation at Seahorse Gully to be linked typologically with the core area and, unlike the earlier Pre-Dorset in the region, to demonstrate no specific regional diversity. Farther north, at Chesterfield Inlet, McCartney (1972) reports material also comparable to the core area.

Disagreement over interpreting the Dorset sites on Victoria Island can be resolved only by future survey and excavation. W.E. Taylor (1964, 1967, 1972a) feels that future work will demonstrate a continuity of settlement and that there is no essential difference between Dorset on Victoria and that of the core area. McGhee (1976), on the other hand, sees essentially two periods of occupation, the first between 500 B.C. and A.D. 100, and the second no earlier than A.D. 500, with a gap in continuity between. In either case, these western sites show some regional diversity through traits not yet reported from elsewhere, such as ice chisels, barbed dart heads, hooked implements possibly for spear slings, and stone-tipped arrowheads equipped for side blades.

Terminal Dorset

The question of what happened to Dorset people and culture remains one of the most intriguing problems in Arctic archeology. The most recent carbon dates for Dorset are around A.D. 1400 at Gulf Hazard (Harp 1976) and northern Ungava (Plumet 1979). These, like a date of A.D. 1350 from Igloolik, overlap the entry of Thule people into the Eastern Arctic (see "Thule Prehistory of Canada," this vol.). Dorset culture as such virtually disappears, although there are no indications of widespread hostility between the two groups. Logically, Thule economy with its whale hunting, dog traction, and umiak simply provided more efficient ways of deriving energy from the environment. Dorset people may have dwindled in numbers as the better caribou crossings and fish weirs were taken over by bow and arrow–equipped Thule people, able to operate in larger social groups by virtue of the quantities of whale meat that supported their communities. Dorset people and culture may have been pushed to peripheral, less desirable regions, or the majority of Dorset people may simply have substituted Thule culture for their own. In all probability a complex combination of these events took place. Jordan (1979) finds several discrete traits of eastern Thule that may have derived their stimulus from Dorset culture. As Collins (1950) pointed out, the Thule transverse-line-hole harpoon tip was undoubtedly derived from Dorset. So, probably, was the snow knife and knowledge of snowhouse building, whalebone sled shoes, and the substitution of soapstone for pottery in the making of lamps and vessels. On the other hand, Meldgaard (1962) and Plumet (1979) see Thule-derived changes in the late Dorset houses at Igloolik and on Diana Bay with cold-trap entrances, side rooms for storage, and rear sleeping platforms.

Both the Sallirmiut Eskimo of Southampton Island (Collins 1957; W.E. Taylor 1960) and the modern Ammassalik of East Greenland (Meldgaard 1960b), who have stood out as ethnographically distinct from other eastern Eskimos, have been seen as modern vestiges of Dorset people strongly modified by Thule culture. Ammassalik art is particularly reminiscent of Dorset, and chert artifacts of the Sallirmiut have close parallels in Dorset assemblages, as do some of the attributes of their harpoon heads.

Whatever the fate of Dorset, the entry of Thule people after the beginning of the second millennium A.D. seems to have triggered the process that finally disrupted a continuity that had lasted for 3,000 years. This long-lasting continuity and the relative conservatism reflected in material culture from earliest Pre-Dorset to latest Dorset times appears unique in North American prehistory.

Thule Prehistory of Canada

ROBERT McGHEE

The Central Eskimo tribes of the Canadian Arctic, between Mackenzie River and Labrador, have since the nineteenth century posed a number of historical problems to ethnographers and culture historians These groups, inhabiting some of the most desolate regions of the Arctic, lacked many of the more sophisticated and productive elements of technology and economic adaptation found among the maritime-oriented Eskimos of Alaska and Greenland. However, biologically and linguistically they appeared to be closely related to the Alaska and Greenland Eskimos and to form part of a remarkably uniform Eskimo population inhabiting most Arctic areas between Bering Strait and the Atlantic Ocean.

Early ethnologists such as Rink (1887–1891), Steensby (1917), and Birket-Smith (1929) attempted to provide a historical explanation for this situation, basing their hypotheses on studies of the distribution of myths, elements of material culture, dialect, and biological traits among the various Eskimo populations. These studies generally placed the origin of Eskimo culture in the interior regions of the Central Arctic, from whence hypothetical Indianlike ancestors of the Eskimos had at some time in the past moved northward and adapted to an Arctic coastal way of life. The Central Eskimos of Arctic Canada, whose manner of life involving interior caribou hunting and fishing as well as winter ice-hunting somewhat resembled that of northern Indians, were considered to be the most recent immigrants from the south.

The first coordinated program of archeological research in the North American Arctic was directed to the investigation of the problem of Central Eskimo origins and to the testing of the hypotheses based on distribution studies. This program, undertaken by Therkel Mathiassen of the Fifth Thule Expedition, 1921–1924, resulted in the definition of Thule culture, the questioning of the earlier hypotheses on the origin of the Central Eskimos, and the first successful archeological attempt to explain a major part of Eskimo prehistory (Mathiassen 1927, 2).

The remains left by the Thule people are the most obvious archeological ruins in Arctic Canada. Settlements of one to several dozen semisubterranean houses occur along most of the mainland and Arctic island coasts as well as in Greenland, where a site near the settlement of Thule gave its name to the culture. Excavation of these houses yields abundant and well-preserved artifacts and food refuse that reflect a typically Eskimo cultural pattern, but one that was technologically more specialized, uniform, and economically more productive than that of the various Central Eskimo tribes of the historic period.

Origin of the Thule Culture

Present archeological knowledge confirms Mathiassen's original hypothesis that Thule culture originated in North Alaska, from whence it spread eastward across Arctic Canada as far as Greenland (fig. 1). The distinctive Thule technology and cultural pattern can be traced from the Birnirk culture, a Norton-derived development centered in the North Alaska coast between roughly A.D. 500 and 900. The Birnirk people, particularly those revealed by Ford's (1959) and Stanford's (1976) excavations at Point Barrow, were coastal sea-mammal hunters, who did not hunt the large bowhead whales (*Balaena mysticetus*) as did their Thule descendants. Although W.E. Taylor (1963a) has suggested that Birnirk development may have occurred as far east as Amundsen Gulf, Birnirk sites have not yet been found east of the North Alaska coast.

During this period, prior to about A.D. 1000, the central and eastern Canadian Arctic was occupied by Eskimos of the Dorset culture. Dorset sites are known as far west as Dolphin and Union Strait, but no evidence of Dorset occupation has been found in the area between Amundsen Gulf and North Alaska. The Dorset people, developing in an apparent 3,000-year isolation from the Norton and Birnirk populations of Alaska, must have spoken a different dialect, followed different social customs, and certainly had a different technology and economic adaptation from that of their Alaska relatives. Yet at some time around A.D. 1000 their isolation was broken, and within one or two centuries the Dorset cultural pattern was supplanted by the Alaska-derived Thule pattern. The apparently rapid shift in adaptive emphasis at this time, combined with the massive, abrupt, and almost total technological change from the Dorset to the Thule pattern, suggest that population replacement accompanied culture change. The first phase of Canadian Thule development was apparently one of rapid migration or population expansion, which carried these people and their culture across the Canadian Arctic to Greenland. Although there is isolated evidence of small-scale cultural diffusion between Dorset and Thule populations, this is not sufficient to warrant the hypothesis that the Dorset population adopted Thule culture through a process of diffusion from Alaska, as suggested by Giddings (1967:100).

The most likely explanation for the rapid eastward expansion of Thule people at this time, after several centuries of relative geographical stability, involves environmental change and the expansion of an environmental zone to which the Birnirk/early Thule people were adjusted. McGhee (1969–1970) and McCartney (1977a:23) have argued that a warming climatic trend, which affected much of the northern hemisphere after approximately A.D. 900, caused a reduction in the seasonal and regional extent of summer pack ice throughout the Arctic seas. This in turn permitted a greater number of bowhead whales to spend the summer in the productive feeding grounds of the Beaufort Sea and adjacent waters in the western Canadian Arctic. In these

areas, whales could be spotted and chased throughout the summer, while in North Alaska they were available only during the spring and fall migrations. This situation may have attracted Birnirk/early Thule whalers eastward along the coast of Beaufort Sea and Amundsen Gulf and been the impulse that stimulated the Thule migration across the Canadian Arctic.

Canadian Thule Expansion: Phase 1

The route followed by the early Thule migrants can be traced by plotting the archeological occurrence of certain artifact types distinctive of the early Thule period. The most useful artifact type for this purpose is the Sicco sealing harpoon head with marked central constriction, an early form of the Thule 3 type. Sicco-like harpoon heads are found in the Birnirk and Nunagiak phases at Point Barrow (Ford 1959:83); at four sites around the Amundsen Gulf coast in the western Canadian Arctic (W.E. Taylor 1963a:458; McGhee 1969–1970:179); at Resolute on Cornwallis Island (Collins 1952:51) and Maxwell Bay on Devon Island (W.E. Taylor 1963a:458), both on the north coast of Parry Channel in the Canadian High Arctic; at Turnstone Beach (Lethbridge 1939:fig. 9, no. 4) and Bache Peninsula (Schle-

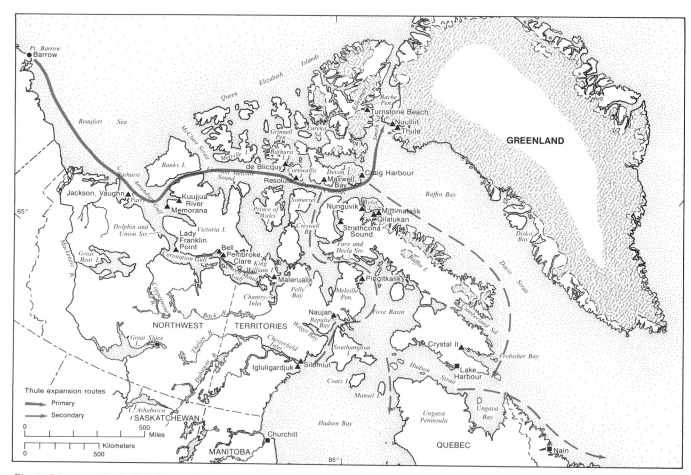

370   Fig. 1. Primary archeological sites and probable routes of Thule expansion across Arctic Canada.

McGHEE

dermann and McCullough 1980) in eastern Ellesmere Island; and at Thule and Nuulliit on the adjacent coast of northwestern Greenland (Holtved 1944:pl. 3, no. 14, 1954:pl. 1, nos. 1–3).

The distribution of Sicco-like harpoon heads at sites along the coasts of Amundsen Gulf, Parry Channel, and Smith Sound suggests that the migration followed a route through the Canadian High Arctic. This distribution and the presence of Thule sites containing large numbers of whale bones on Bathurst, Cornwallis, Devon, and Somerset islands suggest that during the Thule expansion period the western Arctic bowhead whale population may have been continuous with the eastern Arctic Greenland whale population (also *Balaena mysticetus*) across Parry Channel. In the mid-twentieth century bowhead whales are excluded from Parry Channel by extensive pack ice in Melville Sound. If this were so, the Thule migrants could move from Alaska to Greenland while hunting the same quarry by the same techniques, without major changes in their adaptive pattern. Such a situation appears to be reflected in the uniformity of artifacts found across the entire range of the early Thule expansion.

Thule Adaptations to Arctic Canada

Having reached the area east of Mackenzie River, these migrants were forced to make several changes in their way of life. The results of these changes can be discerned from the winter villages in which they sheltered and serve to define Canadian Thule culture as distinct from its Birnirk antecedents. Thule winter villages are generally smaller than the large villages of the North Alaska coast. Most Thule sites consist of from one to four winter houses; and at the larger sites, which may have several dozen houses, there is little evidence to suggest that more than a few houses were occupied simultaneously. The small size of the winter social unit probably reflects the hunting pattern followed by the Thule people, involving whaling in the open sea rather than in shore leads as is done in North Alaska. The Alaska technique is more consistently productive but can be carried out in only a few favored localities between Bering Strait and Point Barrow. At these locations, where migrating whales were channeled close to shore by narrow leads in the spring pack ice, large villages were supported in the historic period by several trained whaling crews operating from umiaks launched from the shore ice (Spencer 1959). The conditions for this kind of hunting are not present in most areas of the Canadian Arctic.

The technique that must have been used by most Thule people and the one that was followed by their historic period descendants in the eastern Arctic involved stalking and chasing whales in the open sea using an umiak and a small fleet of kayaks. It seems unlikely that this technique would often capture more than one whale at any one locality during the summer season, so that the Thule social group during the winter was probably limited to the few related families who comprised the summer whaling unit. This small group, typically of perhaps 10 to 50 people, would have been highly mobile, traveling by umiak and kayak in the extensive open-water seasons of the period and building winter houses wherever a sufficient store of food and fuel could be accumulated by the killing of a whale, sealing, fishing, or hunting land mammals.

The food refuse bones and hunting weapons found at Thule sites indicate the wide range of hunting techniques used by these people in coping with their new environment (fig. 2). Most impressive are the bones of bowhead whales and the large whaling harpoon heads used in conjunction with skin floats, represented archeologically by ivory or wood plugs and toggles. A Thule umiak frame found in northern Greenland (Knuth 1952) indicates the type of large open skin boat used in whaling and traveling. Kayak parts are found, and a few toys and engraved representations suggest that the Thule kayak was a sea-going craft with upturned bow and stern. The throwing-board was used, probably in kayak hunting, to throw multiple-pronged bird-darts and barbed bladder-darts for seals, walrus, and small whales. Sealing is represented by a range of distinctive harpoon heads, used with a loose foreshaft that was attached to the harpoon shaft by means of a heavy socket. Ice picks, scoops, and three-legged stools are associated with winter hunting of ringed seals (*Phoca hispida*) at their breathing holes. All sea mammals found in Arctic waters are represented by bones in the food refuse of Thule villages.

The sinew-backed composite bow was the main weapon used in land hunting. Bow equipment and antler arrowheads are common on most Thule sites, and the results of the chase can be seen in bones of caribou, musk-ox, bear, and smaller mammals that may have been trapped or snared. Bola weights of antler or bone indicate the use of this bird-hunting weapon. Fishing was probably important in most areas, undertaken with fish spears of both the trident and leister types, composite fishhooks, and gorges. Although baleen whales were the largest and most impressive quarry hunted, the Thule people did not neglect food obtainable from other sources (W.E. Taylor 1966) and in many areas depended entirely on such sources.

Adaptations in winter shelter and heating technology were also made by the Thule migrants. In North Alaska, Birnirk houses were built as semisubterranean rectangular cribs of driftwood logs, with log floors, rear sleeping platforms, and cold-trap entrance tunnels (Ford 1959:33–53). Similar houses are found at the Thule period Jackson and Vaughn sites at Cape Parry on the

Amundsen Gulf coast (W.E. Taylor 1972a), but the scarcity of driftwood on most Canadian Arctic coasts resulted in the development of a house built of different materials and necessarily of a somewhat different style. The typical Canadian Thule house was round to oval in shape, with the floor and rear sleeping platform paved with gravel or stone slabs, the walls of the entrance tunnel and room built of boulders, stone slabs, or whale bones, and the roof framed with whale ribs and covered with sod. For the same reason, boulder-covered cist

graves were used by the Thule people as a substitute for the driftwood-covered graves used by their Birnirk ancestors (Ford 1959:32).

Winter heat and light were supplied by soapstone lamps, crescentic in shape with a row of knobs dividing the shallow well into two longitudinal sections. Pottery lamps of a shallow saucer shape had been used by the Birnirk people (Ford 1959:202), and it seems that the early Thule migrants gave these up in favor of more durable lamps made from soapstone found in the central Arctic. The previous Dorset inhabitants of Arctic Canada had used soapstone lamps for some 2,000 years (Meldgaard 1962:pl. 5), and the Thule people may have learned the use of this material from their Dorset antecedents; it should be noted, though, that the large crescentic Thule lamps bear scant resemblance to the shallow oval lamps used by the Dorset people. Soapstone cooking pots, oval to rectangular in shape, were also used by the early Thule people and may also have originated from a Dorset source.

Another important technological complex that was adopted by the early Thule migrants may have been derived from their Dorset predecessors. This was the domed snowhouse, evidenced archeologically by large bone snow knives and snow probes found on early Thule sites. These artifacts do not occur in the Birnirk/early Thule sequence in Alaska, while ivory snow knives are found at Dorset sites in the Central Arctic (Meldgaard 1962:92). The use of the domed snowhouse allowed extensive periods of hunting and travel on the sea ice without the necessity of remaining close to permanent coastal winter houses.

Aside from these few pieces of technology that first appeared in Arctic Canada, the great bulk of Thule material culture reflects its Alaska heritage: most of the hunting and fishing gear mentioned above; men's tools such as whalebone mattocks, adzes with ground stone blades, and the bow drill, which was the basic tool used

Natl. Mus. of Canada, Ottawa: a, IX-C:614; b, IX-C:4227; c, IX-C:7305; d, IX-C:1480; e, IX-C:3835b; f, NdPd-1:11; g, OdPq-1:90; h, IX-C:764; i, IX-C:5355; j, IX-C:3462; k, IX-C:3651; l, IX-C:3429d; m, OdPq-1:207; n, IX-C:4316c, IX-C4315; o, IX-C:4636; p, IX-C:4633; q, IX-C:1345; r, IX-C:4304; s, IX-C:749; t, IX-C:2758; u, IX-C:1909.

Fig. 2. Characteristic Thule culture artifacts: a, Thule 2 harpoon head, north side of Strathcona Sound, Baffin I., N.W.T.; b, Thule 3 harpoon head, Pingitkalik, Melville Peninsula; c, Sicco open socket harpoon head, near mouth of Kuujjua River, N.W.T.; d, "flat" harpoon head, Pond Inlet, Baffin I., N.W.T.; e, fish spear barb, Foxe Basin, N.W.T.; f, arrowhead, Lady Franklin Point site, Victoria I., N.W.T.; g, bird dart side prong, Memorana site, Victoria I.; h, wound pin, north side of Strathcona Sound, Baffin I., N.W.T.; i, ulu handle, Mill Island, Hudson Strait; j, ulu blade, Belcher Is., N.W.T.; k, dog harness trace buckle, Craig Harbour, Ellesmere I.; l, harpoon blade, Belcher Is.; m, whale effigy, Memorana site; n, human/bird figures, Igloolik, N.W.T.; o, decorated plaque, Belcher Is.; p, decorated handle, Belcher Is.; q, pendant, Pond Inlet, Baffin I., N.W.T.; r, toy comb, Igloolik, N.W.T.; s, doll, north side Strathcona Sound; t, lamp trimmer, Admiralty Inlet; u, needle case, Pond Inlet. Length of c, 8.3 cm, rest same scale.

in working bone and ivory; men's knives of various forms with large ground-slate blades; women's ulus with ground-slate blades; scrapers of several types; wing-shaped needle cases and anchor-shaped thimble holders; combs; snow goggles; beads and pendants; engraving motifs; and many other items of material culture that are preserved archeologically in the frozen earth of collapsed winter houses. There can be little doubt that the language and much of the mythology and social customs of the Thule people were also derived from Alaska.

Canadian Thule Expansion: Phase 2

The second phase of Canadian Thule development was one of expansion into areas that were more ecologically diverse than that along which they had made their initial

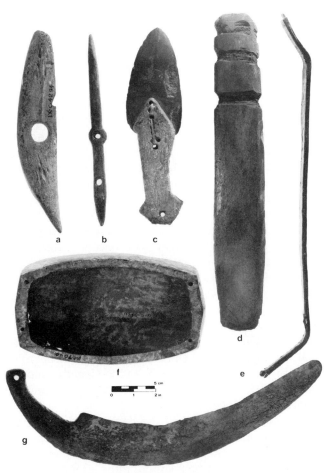

Natl. Mus. of Canada, Ottawa: a, IX-C:4294; b, IX-C:586; c, IX-C:688 d, PeJq-1:Q33; e, QjLe-1 D-186; f, IX-C:7040; g, IX-C:1671.
Fig. 3. Characteristic Thule culture artifacts: a, whaling harpoon head, Igloolik, N.W.T.; b, harpoon foreshaft, north side of Strathcona Sound, Baffin I., N.W.T.; c, flensing knife, north side of Strathcona Sound; d, mattock blade, Quadak site, north shore of Creswell Bay, Somerset I., N.W.T.; e, toy baleen bow, de Blicquy site, Bathurst I., N.W.T.; f, soapstone pot, location unknown; g, snow knife, Pond Inlet, Baffin I., N.W.T. Length of g 24.0 cm, rest same scale.

rapid migration. This movement probably began shortly after the original spread, but the few radiocarbon dates available give only a vague picture of the timing of this phase. The earliest acceptable dates on Canadian Thule sites occur during the eleventh and early twelfth centuries A.D. and are obtained on sites along the shores of Amundsen Gulf, Parry Channel, and in Ellesmere Island, on the early migration route. Twelfth and thirteenth century dates have been obtained on sites in Coronation Gulf, on the west coast of Hudson Bay, and in northern Ungava (Wilmeth 1978; Plumet 1979). At these sites the early Sicco-like harpoon heads have been replaced by the Thule 3 type without central constriction, and with decoration minimal or absent.

By A.D. 1200–1300 the second phase of Thule expansion had populated most of the southern Arctic Archipelago, the coasts of Hudson Bay, and the coastal mainland to the west. Expansion down the coast of Labrador as far as Hamilton Inlet probably took place at a later date, since Bird (1945), Fitzhugh (1972), Schledermann (1971), and Jordan (1978) have failed to find Thule occupations of Labrador earlier than the fifteenth or sixteenth centuries. Mathiassen's "classic" Thule sites of Naujan, Qilalukan, Mittimatalik, and Malerualik belong in this second phase of Thule expansion and probably date from the twelfth and thirteenth centuries. The characteristic Thule artifact types listed by Mathiassen (1927, 2:4, fig. 1) refer specifically to this phase in the development of Thule technology.

During this period there was increased regional diversification of Thule material culture, probably resulting from regional isolation and the development of local types of economic adaptation. McGhee (1969–1970:180) has suggested that this diversification may reflect, on the social level, the formation of regional "tribes" isolated from one another to about the same extent as the various Canadian Eskimo "tribes" of the historic period. For example, Thule people living around the Amundsen Gulf coast at Cape Parry (W.E. Taylor 1972a), Cape Kellett on Banks Island (Manning 1956), Memorana on Victoria Island, Bloody Falls on the Coppermine River (McGhee 1972), and in western Coronation Gulf (Morrison 1981) differed from Mathiassen's "typical" Foxe Basin Thule. They resembled their North Alaska neighbors to the west in using plain and crudely made pottery lamps and cooking pots, building winter houses of driftwood, and showing a preference for barbed harpoon heads of the Thule 2 type. Thule people living on the Baffin Bay coasts of Greenland and Baffin Island resembled more closely the "typical" Foxe Basin Thule but differed in a more extensive use of "flat" harpoon heads with multiple drilled lashing holes, dolls with top-knot hair arrangements, paddle tips of bone, and a few other items (Holtved 1944; Mathiassen 1927, 1; Collins 1950; Schledermann 1975).

These regional populations were not completely isolated from one another, and there is evidence of widespread trade. Iron, rather surprisingly, may have been an important trade commodity, for small pieces of iron are found in many Thule collections. Iron of meteoric and European smelted origin found on Thule sites in the central and eastern Arctic probably originated from Greenland, where many items of Norse manufacture are found on Thule sites (Holtved 1944). Other objects of European manufacture are found in several Thule sites across the High Arctic, indicating at least indirect contact over a period of several centuries with the Norse Greenland colonies (Schledermann 1981; McGhee 1982). Iron found at western Arctic sites such as Memorana (McGhee 1972) may have come from Siberia by way of Alaska. Lamps and pots carved from the soapstone deposits of the central Canadian Arctic are found in Thule sites around Foxe Basin, and at some time after about A.D. 1200 they began to be traded westward to the North Alaska coast (Ford 1959:200). The appearance of several traits of Canadian Thule material culture in North Alaska during the few centuries before European contact has been interpreted as evidence for a return migration of Thule people to the west (Collins 1937:366; Ford 1959:241); however, the evidence of long-standing trade between the central and western Arctic and the existence of an Amundsen Gulf Thule population, which seems to have been culturally intermediate between Canadian Thule and Western Thule, suggest that Canadian Thule traits may have reached North Alaska by trade and diffusion rather than by population movement. Perhaps the increased number of Thule traits appearing in North Alaska during the century prior to European contact may be linked to an acceleration in trading brought about by increased availability of Russian iron and other trade objects in Alaska at this time.

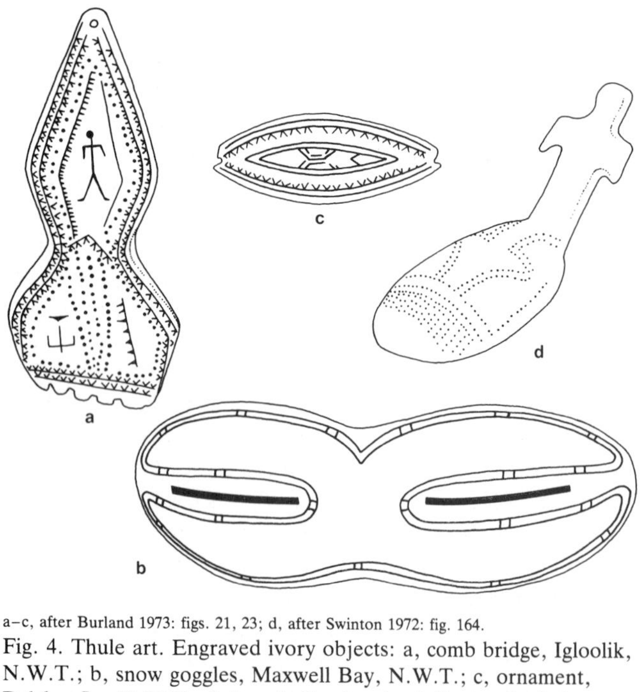

During the second phase of Thule expansion, whaling was still an important activity in areas where whales were available, but villages were now located along channels of the central Arctic Archipelago that were outside the bowhead whale feeding range. Malerualik on King William Island (Mathiassen 1927, 1); the Pembroke, Clare, Bell, and Lady Franklin Point sites on southern Victoria Island (W.E. Taylor 1966); and sites in western Coronation Gulf (Morrison 1981) show Thule subsistence patterns based on caribou, fish, and ringed seals. The absence of whalebone house ruins in these Central Arctic regions strongly suggests that whaling was never an important activity to populations occupying the area.

Transition from Thule to Historic Eskimo Cultures

The diversification of economy that took place during the twelfth and thirteenth centuries set the stage for the third phase of Canadian Thule development, a broad and poorly defined process of cultural change that may have begun as early as the thirteenth century and that continued to the historic period. The most obvious archeological symptoms of this change are the progressive restriction of whaling activities throughout much of the Canadian Arctic and the abandonment of the Parry Channel region, which had been occupied during the original eastward migration. Birket-Smith (1929, 2:233) suggested that isostatic uplift caused shoaling of the channels in the Arctic Archipelago, restricting the movement of whales and causing a decline in the Thule whaling economy in much of the Central Arctic. Andrews, McGhee, and McKenzie-Pollock (1971) indicate that isostatic rebound since Thule times has been less than 10 meters in all parts of Arctic Canada, and this small change could not have effected major changes in whale movements.

A more likely cause for the decline of whaling and the abandonment of the central High Arctic can be seen in deteriorating climatic conditions, which began to be felt in the northern hemisphere after about A.D. 1200 and which culminated in the "Little Ice Age" between approximately 1650 and 1850. W.E. Taylor (1965:11), McGhee (1969–1970:190), and McCartney (1977a:27) have argued that increased sea-ice accumulation and slower melting of summer pack ice impeded the movement of bowhead whales into certain Arctic areas and brought about a widespread decline in Thule whaling activities. Populations of other sea mammals such as

a–c, after Burland 1973: figs. 21, 23; d, after Swinton 1972: fig. 164.

Fig. 4. Thule art. Engraved ivory objects: a, comb bridge, Igloolik, N.W.T.; b, snow goggles, Maxwell Bay, N.W.T.; c, ornament, Belcher Is., N.W.T.; d, female figurine (such "swimming" figures of woman and birds are frequent), Igloolik area. Length of a, 10.4 cm, rest same scale.

walrus, narwhal, and beluga may have been restricted for the same reasons, while ringed seal populations may have increased and expanded geographically with an increase in the stable winter ice under which these animals live and reproduce. The changed conditions probably had less effect on the availability of land mammals. Although the types of adaptation in such a cooling period would vary in different parts of the Arctic, they would generally tend toward a reduction in the importance of maritime hunting and a related increase in the importance of summer inland hunting of land mammals and winter ice-hunting of ringed seals. In general, these are the major trends that were followed by the Thule populations during this period of climatic deterioration.

Along Parry Channel and the High Arctic islands to the north, adaptation seems to have been impossible and the area was abandoned at an unknown date. Maxwell's (1960:88) work in northern Ellesmere Island indicates that this area was inhabited until about A.D. 1450. Knuth (1967:63) reports a radiocarbon date of A.D. 1380 ± 100 (K-1259) on Thule ruins from Ellesmere Island, a date of A.D. 1490 ± 100 (K-566) on a Thule umiak from northeastern Greenland, and a date of A.D. 1540 ± 100 (K-567) on a Thule ruin in the same region. There is no evidence that northern Greenland (outside the Thule region), the Queen Elizabeth Islands, and the coasts of Parry Channel were occupied after the sixteenth century.

In the southern Arctic islands and along the mainland coast, adaptation to environmental change was possible, and these areas continued to be occupied. Regional diversification increased as adaptation to changing local conditions accelerated. This adaptation was the most important process in the transformation of regional Thule cultural variants to the various Eskimo tribes of the historic period. Work in several areas of Arctic Canada has indicated local continuities between Thule and historic Eskimo groups and has traced the changes that took place during the centuries preceding European contact in the eighteenth and nineteenth centuries. These changes are more marked in the Central Arctic than in either the east or the west.

In Labrador, where environmental change appears to have been minimized by the Subarctic location and proximity to the Atlantic Ocean, very little change can be detected between the earliest known Thule occupation of the fifteenth or sixteenth centuries and the historic Labrador Eskimo of the contact period (Schledermann 1971). There were a few stylistic changes in material culture and a shift from single-family winter houses to multifamily dwellings during the seventeenth or eighteenth centuries, which may have coincided with a decline in whaling, or perhaps with involvement in a trading economy with European whalers (Jordan 1978), but no great change in the basic way of life.

In northern Baffin Island Mathiassen (1927, 2:191) first described the transition from Thule culture to historic Baffin Island Eskimo. Again there were a number of stylistic changes in tools and weapons, but the major change was the abandonment of the semisubterranean winter houses used during the Thule period. The historic Eskimos of this area spent part of the winter in a type of house known as the *qarmaq*, which Mathiassen (1927, 2:134) considered to be a degenerate form of the Thule house in which a skin roof had replaced the thick sod roof of the earlier period. The remainder of the winter was spent in snowhouses, which were probably used more extensively than during the Thule period. As in Labrador, the umiak and whaling harpoons were still used by the historic Baffin Island Eskimo.

Very little is known of developments along Hudson Strait and the east coast of Hudson Bay. The work of Quimby (1940) and Jenness (1941) has revealed a rather strange Thule variant on the Belcher Islands, but these collections are not dated, and their relation to the historic occupants of the islands and the adjacent areas of the eastern Hudson Bay coast is unknown. Mathiassen's (1927, 1) work on Southampton Island suggested a Thule ancestry for the historic Sallirmiut who inhabited the island until their extinction in 1902. On the adjacent west coast of Hudson Bay, McCartney's (1977a) work indicates cultural continuity between the Thule and historic periods, but a major change in subsistence pattern occurring shortly after A.D. 1200. After this period, semisubterranean winter houses were no longer built, implying that winter was spent in snowhouses on the sea ice, and that whaling was no longer an important economic activity that could supply winter food and fuel for sedentary coastal occupants.

In the Barren Ground area west of Hudson Bay, Harp (1961) found traces of Thule occupations that were probably left by people who made short forays into the interior to hunt caribou or obtain wood. No permanent Thule occupation was found, and no continuous occupation of the area between the Thule and historic periods. This leaves unsolved the problem of the origin and development of Caribou Eskimo culture; these historic inhabitants of the Barren Ground were considered by Birket-Smith (1929) to be the descendants of a primitive interior Eskimo group that had inhabited the Barren Ground for several millennia. Neither the work of Harp (1961) nor that of Irving (1968) has revealed traces of Caribou Eskimo occupations prior to the nineteenth century, and it now seems likely that this anomalous interior adaptation was begun during the early historic period after the late eighteenth-century abandonment of the area by Chipewyan Indians (B.L. Clark 1977). It is not known yet whether the ancestors of the Caribou Eskimo moved to the interior from the Hudson Bay coast as suggested by Harp (1961) and B.L. Clark (1977) or southward from the Arctic coast as postulated by W.E. Taylor (1966) and Burch (1979), but each of these

375

workers agrees with Mathiassen's (1930) hypothesis that the Caribou Eskimo are recently derived from a coastal Thule ancestry. For another account of possible Caribou origins, which differs somewhat from this one, see "Caribou Eskimo," this volume.

The work of VanStone (1962) and McGhee (1972) on the recent prehistory of the Netsilik and the Copper Eskimo, respectively, has suggested that these historic tribes of the Central Arctic coast developed from local variants of Thule culture. The Thule whaling economy was never established in this area, and Thule subsistence was based from the beginning on caribou, fish, and seals (W.E. Taylor 1966). Developments during the five or six centuries preceding European contact paralleled those in other areas of Arctic Canada, but here were carried further. Permanent winter houses were abandoned completely in favor of the snowhouse, umiaks went out of use, and kayaks were used only for hunting caribou in inland rivers and lakes. Stone-covered graves were not built, and corpses were merely exposed on the surface. As in other areas, there was a marked simplification in technology, a decrease in ornamentation applied to artifacts, and the general impression of a poorer and less secure way of life as resources diminished with a deteriorating climate.

In summary then, archeology has provided fairly certain evidence that all Canadian Eskimo tribes of the historic period are descended biologically and culturally from the Thule people who first swept across the area from Alaska after the tenth century. Thule culture is the historical factor that explains the biological, linguistic, and cultural similarities of all Eskimo between Bering Strait and Greenland. Cultural adaptation to regional environmental variations and to deteriorating environmental conditions after the thirteenth century is the basic process that brought about the diversification and technological simplification of the Canadian Eskimo tribes of the historic period. This process was accentuated by indirect and direct contacts with Europeans and with European technology prior to the period during which the Canadian Eskimos were described by ethnographers.

Exploration and History of the Canadian Arctic

L.H. NEATBY

The first contact between Europeans and the natives of the American Arctic occurred about A.D. 1000 when Norsemen from Greenland made a temporary settlement on American soil, probably at L'Anse aux Meadows on the northern tip of Newfoundland (Ingstad 1966:7). Relations between the newcomers and the native Skraelings, presumably Eskimos, were marked by mutual mistrust and open hostility. The Norsemen were strong enough to repel the attacks of the natives, but the manifest impossibility of maintaining a tiny settlement separated by a wide stretch of ocean from the founding state caused the early abandonment of the colony (Oswalt 1979:5–24). It was 500 years before Europeans arrived again.

Exploration

A few decades after Christopher Columbus rediscovered America, Europeans established contact with the Eskimos in Labrador (fig. 1) (see "Historical Ethnography of the Labrador Coast," this vol.). In 1576 the Englishman Martin Frobisher appeared on the east shore of lower Baffin Island (fig. 2). At that date the seafaring nations of Europe were competing for the wealth to be obtained in the New World and the Spice Islands of the Far East. As the Spaniards were dominant in America, and the Portuguese claimed a monopoly of the trade by way of the Cape of Good Hope, Frobisher sought a channel for English commerce with China by way of the Arctic sea. He made his landfall on Baffin Island and sailed 150 miles up Frobisher Bay, finding no end to it, and persuaded himself that he had found the strait that divided America from Asia. His two subsequent voyages were gold hunts, and consequently he did not discover his error. The Eskimos whom he encountered rejected his friendly gestures and kidnapped five of his men (fig. 3). Since Eskimos were seldom guilty of unprovoked hostility on their first encounter with Europeans, it may be conjectured that these people had already suffered ill usage at the hands of European fishermen, who mistrusted them and had not the explorer's motive for cultivating their good will. It may also be noted that Frobisher himself kidnapped three Eskimos (Hakluyt 1907–1910,5:131–171; Stefánsson 1938; Morison 1971:497–550).

In three summer voyages, 1585–1587, John Davis discovered Davis Strait leading into Baffin Bay, and on its west side explored the great gulf of Cumberland Sound. He roughly delineated the Atlantic face of North America from the Strait of Belle Isle to well up the Baffin Island east shore (Markham 1880; Oswalt 1979:37–41; Morison 1971:583–605).

Both Frobisher and Davis had been aware of a tide-vexed gulf between Baffin Island and Cape Chidley, the northernmost point of Labrador. In 1610 Henry Hudson, employed by English merchants to trace the elusive Northwest Passage, proved this to be a strait leading into the great inland sea of Hudson Bay. There Hudson with some loyal crewmen was marooned and left to starve by mutineers. On their way out some of these men landed at the west end of Hudson Strait and were set upon by Eskimos, losing four of their number. The killing was evidently unprovoked as the Europeans had held a friendly conference with the natives the previous day and had come ashore unarmed (Powys 1927; Oswalt 1979:52–54).

Other explorers followed in Hudson's track: Thomas Button in 1612 (Rundall 1849), the Dane Jens Munk in 1619–1620 (Gosch 1897), Luke Foxe in 1631, and Thomas James in 1631–1632 (Christy 1894). Their explorations disclosed harbors at the mouths of the Nelson and Churchill rivers. The Hudson's Bay Company, founded in 1670, utilized these ports of entry for opening a trade in furs with the Indians of the western forests. Though this traffic was long restricted to Subarctic areas and was concerned chiefly with Indians, it led indirectly to penetration of the true Arctic and to renewed Eskimo contacts.

In 1719 James Knight, undertaking a fresh search for the Northwest Passage, disappeared with his ships *Albany* and *Discovery* in northern Hudson Bay. The traders at Churchill accepted without question the hypothesis that "every man was killed by the Eskimos." Later they opened up a trade with the natives to the north of Churchill, and by voyages in 1767 and 1769 established that Knight's crews had perished in a winter camp on Marble Island and that their neglected ships had sunk offshore. The Eskimos reported that they had died, as John Franklin's crews were to die, of famine and scurvy (Morton 1939:142–146; Neatby 1968:99). The com-

377

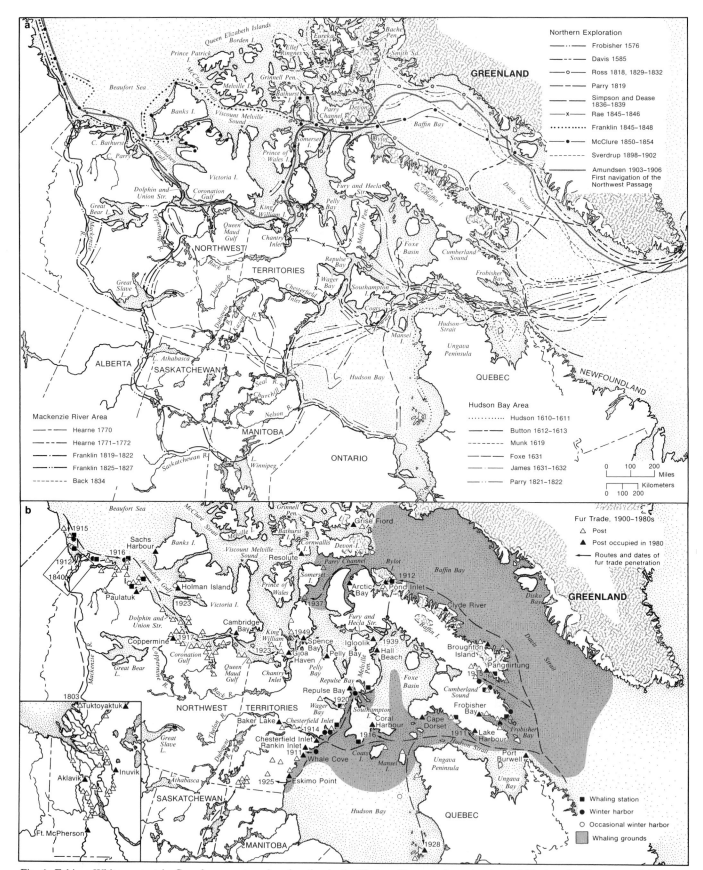

Fig. 1. Eskimo-White contact in Canada: a, routes of exploration in the Hudson Bay, northern Arctic, and Mackenzie River areas (after Burpee 1927; Chalmers, Eccles, and Fullard 1966); b, whaling activity in Davis Strait 1719–1911, Hudson Bay 1860–1915, and Beaufort Sea 1889–1908 (after Ross 1978, 1979) and fur trade posts with routes and dates of penetration in the Canadian Arctic (after Usher 1971).

NEATBY

Fig. 2. Frobisher excavations. top, A mine or possibly a reservoir used by Martin Frobisher and his men. Charles Francis Hall, the first White to visit since the Frobisher crew departed in 1578, located and described this feature when he discovered the site in 1861–1862. bottom, Remains of a stone cache. Both photographs by William Fitzhugh, Kodlunarn I., Countess of Warwick Sound, Frobisher Bay, 1981.

ment made by Moses Norton, governor of Fort Churchill, illustrates the traders' policy of dealing with the natives without mistrust: "I don't doubt but what some of the said vessels' crews might be destroyed by the Esquemays, as they was at that time not in the least Civilized, but I have the vanity to think that if any accident was to happen to an English vessel now, as did to Knight and Borlow [George Berley?] (which God forbid) I have reason to believe that the Natives as far north as Marble Island would rather assist a man in distress than to do otherwise by him" (Morton 1939:146).

The penetration of the American North by Europeans and Euro-Americans was a peaceful process, seldom disfigured by the suspicion, hatred, and reciprocal murder that marked the advance of the European in other parts of the New World. For this there were a number of reasons: the nomadic hunters of the Far North were too few and too widely dispersed to excite the fears of the traders; their soil was unproductive and worthless to Europeans; and as it contained no readily accessible precious metals, there was no incentive to rob, dispossess, and enslave them. Their services were required as guides and trappers, but this demanded not compulsion but the cultivation of mutual good will.

The directors of the Hudson's Bay Company spared themselves the cost of armaments by building posts on the shore of the bay only and inviting the Indians there to traffic. Though this diminished the flow of furs it kept the unruly servants of the company under the immediate eye of the local governor. It was not for trade but to disprove the existence of a practicable Northwest Passage that Governor Norton sent the sailor, Samuel Hearne, overland from Fort Churchill northwest to the Arctic shore. After two unsuccessful attempts Hearne made this long and hazardous journey in 1770–1772. With an escort of Indians he passed north of Great Slave Lake and descended the Coppermine River to the ice-choked ocean at its mouth. He was the first White man to reach the Arctic littoral of North America. The hostility of Indian for Eskimo often mentioned in early accounts was demonstrated by the massacre by Hearne's Indian companions of a band of Eskimos tenting at the riverside not far from the sea (Hearne 1958).

In the late eighteenth century the Hudson's Bay Company was forced to adopt a more active trade policy. The Saint Lawrence settlements of New France were now a British possession: Montreal traders, among them the New Englander Peter Pond, and the Scottish adventurers as shrewd and resolute as he (Morton 1939:328ff.) had opened up a trade route by river and lake across the continent to the fur forests of the extreme northwest around Lake Athabasca and Great Slave Lake; and the traders on the bay were obliged to move inland or see their trade cut off at its source. A channel of trade was opened up by way of the Hayes River to Lake Winnipeg, on up the Saskatchewan and Churchill rivers, and over the height of land to the basin of Great Slave Lake. The remotest posts were on the north side of that body of water. Though in 1789 Alexander Mackenzie explored the river highway of the Mackenzie to the Arctic Ocean, neither of the rival companies was operating beyond the treeline in the true Arctic or trafficking with its Eskimo inhabitants. But they had set up a system of annual transport by river boat that gave explorer and scientist ready access to that field of research. In 1819 Capt. John Franklin of the Royal Navy with three other officers arrived at Great Slave Lake to recruit boatmen from the fur brigades and with them to explore the polar shore.

379

Commercial aims had little to do with this renewed quest for the mythical Passage. The British government had set it on foot with two motives: to confirm its territorial claims against Russia, whose activities in Alaska, as elsewhere, were regarded by the statesmen of western Europe with chronic distrust, and to promote geography and the other natural sciences.

At the time of Franklin's first overland journey the Arctic seaboard of America was unknown except for the mouths of the Coppermine and Mackenzie rivers, where Hearne and Mackenzie respectively had barely reached tidewater. Of the vast archipelago beyond only a few disconnected stretches of the shores of Baffin, Devon, and Ellesmere islands had been sighted.

Franklin's orders were to go down the Coppermine River and map the Arctic shore eastward as far as Hudson Bay by canoe. The traders warned him that he and his party would be murdered on the way—a plausible supposition, for the enmity of their Indian foes would dispose the Eskimos to regard any strangers from the south as hostile and dangerous. Actually Franklin found them harmless but too frightened to be easily approached. Denied their help he cruised eastward, explored Coronation Gulf, and laid down 550 miles of coastline before terminating his mission. He lost half his party by cold and hunger on the overland trek back to his base near the source of the Coppermine (Franklin 1823). But now he understood the conditions with which the Arctic traveler had to cope. He came back with a well-organized expedition and objectives that were attainable and clearly defined. In 1826 he went down the Mackenzie to the head of the delta and sent Dr. John Richardson with two boats to map the coast east to the Coppermine, while he with two others was to strike west along the Alaskan shore. While groping amid shoals for a western outlet from the delta Franklin's detachment came upon a large Eskimo encampment and narrowly escaped wholesale plunder. Both Eskimos and Indians were more prone to aggression when numbers gave them confidence. In this instance Franklin attributed their violence to the instigation of a few firebrands, whom the authority of the well-disposed leaders was insufficient to restrain. The courage and tact of Augustus, an Eskimo interpreter from Hudson Bay (fig. 4), whose dialect was intelligible to the local inhabitants, brought about a truce, permitting the explorers to make their escape on the rising tide. Franklin traced over 300 miles of Canadian and Alaskan shorelines, gave the name of Prudhoe Bay to a shallow indentation near his journey's end, and obtained a distant sight of Point Beechey to the west. On the way back his crews were shown much kindness by a small group of Eskimos camping near the shore. Richardson, too, came back with his mission fully accomplished. In his two expeditions Franklin had laid bare half the Arctic seaboard of America (Franklin 1971).

In 1834 Commander George Back, a former officer of Franklin's, ran a skewer through the unknown northeastern angle of the continent by boating down the Great Fish (Back) River in an unsuccessful search for the missing crew of John Ross's *Victory*. Eskimos encamped on the river bank above Chantrey Inlet had learned by the native grapevine of Edward Parry's friendly dealings with their compatriots in upper Foxe Basin and gave Back a hospitable reception (Back 1836:328–388). In 1836–1839 the fur traders Thomas Simpson and Peter Warren Dease extended Franklin's Alaska discoveries and then extended the coastal chart eastward to the west side of Boothia Isthmus (Simpson 1843; A. Simpson 1845). In 1845–1846 Dr. John Rae (1850) also of the Hudson's Bay Company, filled in the map from Repulse Bay around Melville Peninsula to the east side of Boothia Isthmus, a stubborn obstacle, which made the geographical Northwest Passage still incomplete.

In the meantime seagoing cruisers had been groping for a Passage at a more northerly latitude. There are three breaches in the barrier rock that guards the eastern seaboard of Canada: the Gulf of Saint Lawrence, Hudson Strait, and, far to the north, Lancaster Sound. In 1616 the explorers Robert Bylot and William Baffin had marked the last-named feature as a bay. On his 1818 voyage Capt. John Ross had endorsed this opinion. In 1819 Lt. Edward Parry was sent with the ships *Hecla* and *Griper* to test this conclusion. After much intricate maneuvering in the ice, including a 100-mile lunge down Prince Regent Inlet, Parry found a channel to the west and took his ships, powered of course by sail only, 500 miles west, through Lancaster Sound, Barrow Strait, and Viscount Melville Sound (which combined form Parry Channel) to a winter anchorage on Melville Island. There he observed traces of petroleum deposits and carved the names of his ships on his famous Monument at Winter Harbour. Further progress west was barred by the dense ice pack of McClure Strait (Parry 1821).

In 1821 Captain Parry in the *Fury* accompanied by Commander George F. Lyon in the *Hecla* came in by way of Hudson Strait to seek a western outlet at the tip of Hudson Bay. They spent two winters in Foxe Basin, the first at Winter Island, the second at Igloolik, off the east end of Fury and Hecla Strait. Both captains had lively contact with Eskimos encamped on shore. Parry found them to be excellent geographers: they traced for him what Rae later found to be an accurate outline of the west side of Melville Peninsula. Lyon visited the natives in their homes, was admitted to witness the Eskimo women's version of the "Follies," and in return invited the shaman Toolemak on board the *Hecla* to cure the sickness of one of its officers. The skipper's portrayal of himself and the medicine man

Fig. 3. Exploration and the Canadian Eskimo. top left, Baffinland Eskimos of the Upper Savage Is. (near Big I.), Hudson Strait, in their kayaks and umiaks, trading with the Hudson's Bay Company ships *Prince of Wales* and *Eddystone*. Watercolor by Robert Hood, member of John Franklin Expedition, Aug. 1819. top right, Hostilities between the Baffinland Eskimos and members of the Martin Frobisher Expedition. Pen and watercolor by John White, 1577. center right, Baffinland Eskimos on board the *Neptune*, near Ashe Inlet, Big I. Photograph by Robert Bell, Aug. 1884. center left, Iglulik woman drying skins by pegging them to a wall of snow, which is the hull of the ice-bound ship *Era*. A cannon protrudes from the snow-laden deck. Photograph by George Comer, Cape Fullerton, March 1901. bottom, Ice-bound *Neptune,* in winter quarters at Cape Fullerton (snowhouses, possibly of Iglulik, to left). Photograph by Albert Peter Low, 1903–1904.

EXPLORATION AND HISTORY OF THE CANADIAN ARCTIC

left, Hudson's Bay Company Lib., Winnipeg, Man.: 69–24; right, Scott Polar Research Inst., U. of Cambridge, England.

Fig. 4. Eskimos portrayed by early explorers. left, Captioned on the original "Tattannaaeuk, Esquimaux Interpreter, named, by the English in Hudson's Bay, Augustus, the faithful follower of Captains Sr. John Franklin, & Sr. Geo. Back, & Dr. Richardson, in their Arctic land Expeditions in N. America." He was from the west shore of Hudson Bay, probably a Caribou Eskimo. He holds 2 tridents for fishing and a bow and arrow for hunting. A kayak with paddle is behind him. Watercolor by John Halkett, after a sketch made at York Factory in 1832. right, "Konyaroklik (or Bald-head)," a Netsilik visitor of John Ross. Ross says this man "came at the same time with Neweetioke, and had one son, called Ulla, of whom he was very proud; he was still more so of his *bald head,* which was unique here, being the only instance we saw of it. He was five feet six inches high, about fifty years of age, and rather good-looking. He brought us some skins, for which he was liberally paid, and was delighted when he saw his portrait, which I made of him. His costume was a dark deer-skin jacket and bear-skin trousers" (Ross 1835:48). Watercolor by John Ross, 1830–1833.

hobnobbing in the captain's cabin would be amusing did it not foreshadow the excesses that Eskimos were later tempted into by less responsible hosts (Parry 1824; Lyon 1824; Neatby 1970; Oswalt 1979:169–176, 178–181).

Capt. John Ross, the first to experiment with steam propulsion in the Arctic, brought in the paddle-wheeler *Victory* in 1829 and was permanently ice-bound in Lord Mayor's Bay at the bottom of Prince Regent Inlet. After three years the crew made their escape by boat to the whalers' fishing grounds, but in the meantime all might well have perished without the aid of the natives of Boothia (fig. 5). These people fraternized with the Europeans, hunted with them, supplied them with fresh meat, and initiated the captain's nephew, James Clark Ross (later the discoverer of Ross Island and McMurdo Sound in Antarctica) into the techniques of travel by sledge (Ross 1835). Hitherto the British had explored in the Arctic by ship or boat exclusively. The skills first taught Ross by the Eskimos of Boothia made possible the long journeys and extensive discoveries of the Franklin search.

In 1846 Franklin with the ships *Erebus* and *Terror* attempted to navigate the Northwest Passage by sailing south from Lancaster Sound through Peel Sound and Franklin Strait. His vessels were caught in a perennial icejam northwest of King William Island. After 18 months the crews deserted the ships to make for the continent but perished to the last man from scurvy and famine (Cyriax 1939). Eskimos refashioned materials of the abandoned ship and its equipment for their own use (figs. 6–7).

Franklin must have been much favored by wind and ice conditions during his descent through Peel Sound, for rescue parties found that strait so persistently ice-choked that they ignored it and directed their search elsewhere. For seven seasons (1848–1854) British and American expeditions groped through the Canadian archipelago, mapping most of its islands, but never attaining the object of their search (Neatby 1970; Mirsky 1970:322–324). In 1854 Rae, journeying from Repulse Bay to Boothia for an entirely different purpose, learned in a casual encounter with Eskimos that some years before a party of Europeans had been seen sledging down the west shore of King William Island and that later 40 bodies had been found on the continental shore near the mouth of the Back River (Rae 1963:274–277). When Rae's report became known in England the belief that the castaways had been massacred by the Eskimos found wide acceptance. Rae steadfastly rejected this

382

Fig. 5. Ikmallik and his wife Apellagliu, Netsiliks, being shown a map of the land between Repulse Bay and Prince Regent Inlet and westward during an interview with Capt. John Ross, Jan. 12, 1830, on board the *Victory*. Ikmallik recognized the land and added information to the map. Ross (1835:259–260, App.:53) found him to be very accurate in his cartography. Watercolor by John Ross, 1830–1833.

version (Neatby 1970:246), apparently with good reason. For in 1859 when Capt. Leopold McClintock of the *Fox* visited King William Island to gather what information he could of the Franklin catastrophe, he placed himself and his lone sledge crew completely in the power of the supposed assassins. "The men were stout, hearty fellows, and the women were arrant thieves, but all were good-humoured and friendly." "There was not a trace of fear, every countenance was lighted up with joy; even the children were not shy, nor backward either, in crowding about us, and poking in everywhere" (M'Clintock 1859:212, 236).

One of the voyages of the often misdirected Franklin search was the 1850–1854 cruise of Commander Robert McClure in H.M.S. *Investigator*. It was McClure who

Fig. 6. Relics of John Franklin's third Arctic expedition, a search for the Northwest Passage. left, Cooking vessel made of copper obtained from the ships; right, powder horn, length 27.0 cm, left, same scale. Both collected by George Comer from Netsilik Eskimos, 1902.

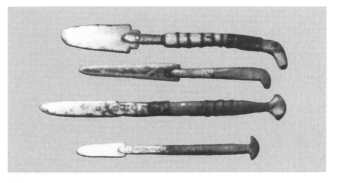

Fig. 7. Snow knives. The metal blades and rivets of these knives are of materials salvaged by natives from the abandoned Franklin ships and reworked by them in traditional forms. In addition to the Franklin ships the many search parties also were a source of new materials. Collected by F.L. McClintock, 1857–1859.

discovered Prince of Wales Strait, the key to the only Northwest Passage navigable by ships of any considerable size (Armstrong 1857). Another interesting circumstance of the *Investigator*'s famous cruise is the presence on board of Johann August Miertsching, who belonged to the Labrador Mission of the Moravian Church, and had been enlisted to serve as interpreter among the natives of the western Arctic. He affords some lively glimpses of the Eskimos of the north shore of Alaska and Canada to whom Europeans had been until then unknown, and of himself as the type of the missionary whose role it was to combat the possible adverse effects of Western culture thrust suddenly upon them. McClure (who came in by way of Bering Strait) missed no opportunity taking a boat ashore at various places to question the natives about the missing ships. When the Eskimos menaced them with weapons and hostile gestures Miertsching would advance in Eskimo garb and, speaking their dialect, never failed to calm their fears, though, "to these simple folk our ship seemed some sort of great monster; they called it a swimming island, etc. At every movement of the ship, although it was half an hour's pull distant, they showed fresh alarm and an electric shock, as it were, went through them all" (Miertsching 1967:45). At one encampment after asking the routine questions relating to Franklin, Miertsching told his new friends something of his own religion and listened courteously to their leader's exposition of the native creed and cosmogony. The man asked him to remain with his people as their teacher but Miertsching begged off, telling him something of McClure's mission. At an isolated settlement on Victoria Island McClure's party found a people who practiced barter but seemed not to have the Europeans' conception of a gift. When McClure wrapped a scarf about the neck of a young Eskimo woman "she was much startled at this and said that she had nothing to give in return; then she drew her little child from her hood and, in great distress and still covering it with *383* kisses, offered it to the captain as payment for the shawl, which she had not ventured to touch; only after I had declared to her clearly and emphatically that it was a gift, she looked at the captain in a very friendly manner and laughed, delighted that she could keep her child" (Miertsching 1967:118).

McClure found that these people were, like the Eskimos of Igloolik, excellent mapmakers with accurate knowledge of the shores and islands for some distance roundabout (Miertsching 1967:116–117). Miertsching (1967:46) confesses candidly and not without humor that some of his new friends were thievish: "Mr. Ford, our carpenter, detected in the skin-boat a small ice-anchor and the iron crank belonging to the windlass; on the latter sat a woman in order to hide it. I scolded her and called her 'thief'; she retorted that *she* was no thief—her husband, not she, had taken it into the boat."

McClure's traveling parties found no Eskimo settlements on Banks Island, though they came upon several traces of former habitation both there and on the north shore of Victoria Island (Miertsching 1967:120–121).

The impetus of the search for Franklin carried the frontier of geographical knowledge far beyond the immediate range of trader or scientist. Exploration was renewed at the turn of the century. In 1898–1902 the Norwegian Otto Sverdrup passed up Jones Sound to discover Axel Heiberg, Amund Ringnes, Ellef Ringnes, and King Christian islands. Sverdrup (1904) and others gave shape to the large Ellesmere Island. In 1908–1918 Vilhjalmur Stefánsson and R.M. Anderson made a study of the Copper Eskimos, whose hunting grounds lay between Cape Wise and the Coppermine River and who were the only remaining Eskimos who had not yet come into direct contact with Europeans.

In 1913–1918 Stefánsson, under the auspices of the Canadian government, added Brock, Borden, Mackenzie King, and Meighen islands to the map, completing

U. i Oslo, Etnografisk Mus.: 15,728.
Fig. 9. Wooden snow goggles made especially for Capt. Roald Amundsen, leader of the Gjøa Expedition on its successful trip through the Northwest Passage. The face carved between the eye slits may be a caricature of Amundsen (J.G. Taylor 1974: 53). Most explorers and researchers in the Arctic have found it beneficial to adopt native dress. Length 16.2 cm; collected by Amundsen on King William I., N.W.T., 1903–1905.

the raw chart of the vast archipelago unknown a century before (Stefánsson 1943). McClure had found traces of Eskimo settlement on the north side of Banks Island, and Greely (1886) and Sverdrup on Ellesmere Island, which are areas beyond the range of contact period habitation.

Eskimo History

Geographical discovery has revealed four ways of approach by water to the country of the Eskimo: by way of Davis Strait, Baffin Bay, and Lancaster Sound; through Hudson Strait and Bay; down the navigable Mackenzie River; and by way of Bering Strait. Air transport now provides a ready means of access to all northern regions.

Permanent relations with the Eskimos were established by whaling ships in and around Cumberland Sound and at Pond Inlet about 1840, and at a somewhat later date, along the northwest shore of Hudson Bay. The Scots and New Englanders who plied this trade were more sparing of their liquor than the San Francisco-based skippers who entered the western Arctic in the 1880s; nonetheless, their coming affected the native culture and economy. Charles Francis Hall, who spent the seasons 1860–1862 on or near Cumberland Sound, and was indebted to the whalers for transportation and shelter, is naturally reticent on this question; the German ornithologist Bernhard Hantzsch, who passed the winter of 1909–1910 on Blacklead Island in Cumberland Sound and quotes in part Eskimo tradition, states that the whaling crews who wintered over "treated the natives in shameless fashion, betraying the men with a little tobacco and the women with *Branntwein* . . . . The poor Eskimos . . . . yielded themselves to degrading influences . . . . not from badness of character, but from frivolity, good-humoured compliance and heathenish ignorance" (Hantzsch 1977:98–99). This passionate indictment must substantially be founded on fact, as Hantzsch's elderly Eskimo informant could not have forged it. The natives were employed to aid in hunting with the whale boat, especially in spring when the open

Natl. Mus. of Canada, Ottawa: 50705.
Fig. 8. George H. Wilkins showing motion pictures to Copper Eskimos. The women all have chin tattooing. Photographed on Canadian Arctic Expedition, 1914–1916, led by Vilhalmur Stefánsson.

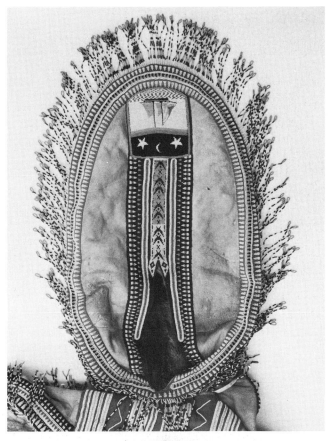

sea was navigable, but the ships were still locked in the ice of a sheltered anchorage. They gave up to some degree their seminomadic life and clustered around whaling base and trading post. Thus diverted from full-time subsistence hunting by the demands of the whale and fur trades, the Eskimos in Hantzsch's time had become dependent on the trading post on Kekerten Island for firearms, ammunition, and to some extent, food supplies. The wreck of the annual Cumberland Sound supply ship in 1909 brought near starvation to the Eskimos gathered around the mission station on Blacklead Island and the trading post at Kekerten; and Hantzsch was obliged to turn over some of his ammunition and food stores to avert a crisis (Hantzsch 1977; Fleming 1932). Conditions were similar in Hudson Bay. "On the whole, the whalers may be taken as beneficial to the Eskimos, and now that the latter have long been dependent upon the whalers for guns, ammunition and other articles of civilization, there is no doubt that many would perish should the whaling stations be closed without other provisions being made for the accustomed supplies" (Low 1906:10).

The impact of the whaler on the natives of the Western Arctic was more damaging. In 1888 whaling vessels, having fished out the Bering and Chukchi seas, moved into Canadian waters and set up base on Herschel Island between the Alaska boundary and the Mackenzie Delta. The number of ships availing themselves of this winter anchorage was great: Amundsen (1908, 2:146) found five there in the winter of 1905–1906 when the trade was declining (Jenness 1964:14), and the disruption of native ways was great in proportion. Drunkenness and syphilis wrought fearful havoc, and by Jenness's computation the native population of Herschel Island and the Mackenzie Delta in 1930 was only one-tenth of what it had been in the time of Franklin, and of the 200 who remained only a dozen were of local descent, the rest being immigrants who had moved from Alaska into Canadian territory (Jenness 1964:14, 19, 24).

The central-dwelling Copper Eskimos, who frequented the region of Coronation Gulf, remained longer in isolation and were spared the catastrophe that overtook their compatriots in the west. Dealings with the transient explorers of the Franklin era had been slight; the 1908–1912 expedition of Stefánsson and Anderson was purely scientific in purpose, and its members carefully avoided wounding Eskimo susceptibilities. But by Stefánsson's time traders were finding their way in by the Mackenzie River and its eastern tributary of Great

U. of Pa., U. Mus., Philadelphia: NA 2844.
Fig. 10. Iglulik woman's parka. The availability of trade goods had its influence on traditional clothing. This caribou skin inner parka is elaborately decorated with seed beads and cloth. A beaded scene on the hood portrays a whaling ship and the floral motifs on the front are probably European derived. Width at shoulders 72.0 cm; collected by George Comer, Repulse Bay, N.W.T., 1913.

Natl. Mus. of Canada, Ottawa: left, IV-C-2690; right, IV-B-1151.
Fig. 11. Ivory carvings. Small scale carvings, for example, bears, birds, and other animals, have a long tradition in the Arctic. As new tools and products were introduced from outside and integrated into native life they too became the subjects for carving. Outsiders also provided a market for native carvings from the early 1800s to the present (Blodgett 1979a). left, Model of a rifle, length 14.5 cm, collected by J.D. Soper, Cape Dorset, Baffin I., N.W.T., 1924–1925. right, Model of a saw, same scale, collected at Hebron, Labrador, Newf., 1912.

Bear River and Lake. The murder of the Roman Catholic fathers Jean-Baptiste Rouvière and Guillaume LeRoux (Whalley 1960) at Bloody Falls by Copper Eskimo brought in the police (fig. 12).

By 1916 more missionaries came and with them the Hudson's Bay company trader. The natives were equipped with firearms and encouraged to trap furs. This deemphasized the winter seal hunt on which they earlier largely depended for food; with high-powered rifles they so ravaged the caribou herds that according to one estimate in the decade 1910–1920 the number annually migrating across Coronation Gulf was cut down nine-tenths (Jenness 1921:548). This made the Copper Eskimo partly dependent on the trader for food and clothing as well as for firearms. The ultimate consequence of the economic revolution, manifest in the 1950s, has been for the Eskimo to give up the old roving life in pursuit of seal and caribou and to congregate in coastal settlements sited not for convenience in hunting but for harbor facilities and nearness to trader and missionary. The Hudson's Bay trader came late to the true Arctic but arrived in time to avert the catastrophe that Low (1906) apprehended from the decay of the whaling trade and to ensure the supply of goods and equipment that had become necessities. Between 1921 and 1931 the company established at least 15 new trading posts, while Anglican and Catholic missions and the police expanded their activities (Jenness 1964; Usher 1971).

During the 1920s the fur trade prospered, especially in the Mackenzie Delta, where the muskrat, unknown elsewhere in the Arctic, was plentiful. Often after bartering part of his catch for necessary goods the successful hunter was left with a cash surplus that he spent on watches, cameras, safety razors, and other articles of little utility (Kitto 1930:68). Family unity, the core of Eskimo life, was impaired by the father's long absences on the trap line.

The collapse of fur prices in the 1930s put an end to this period of affluence, though in the delta and on Banks Island fish and game were a plentiful means of subsistence. Farther east, in the King William Island and Boothia region, the slump brought much distress to the Eskimo and would have caused widespread starvation but for aid furnished by the Canadian government and the Hudson's Bay Company (Jenness 1964:50–51; Usher 1970–1971, 1).

In 1934 a number of families, 40 persons in all, were transferred from the hunted-out areas of Cape Dorset and Pond Inlet to the south shore of Devon Island in the High Arctic. The experiment broke down. A few of the migrants found fruitful hunting farther south on the Boothia Peninsula; the rest went back to their old haunts (Jenness 1964:59–61). After a temporary success the experiment of bringing reindeer into the Mackenzie Valley failed owing to economic conditions and the inaptitude of the Eskimo (partly due to lack of adequate training) for the task of herdsman (Canada. Department of Mines and Resources 1944:70; for another attempt at Eskimo relocation see "The Grise Fiord Project," this vol.).

Christian Missions

Missionaries of the Anglican and Roman Catholic Churches have done much to lessen the shock of the revolution in Eskimo life that whaler and trader brought

Glenbow-Alberta Inst., Calgary, Alta.: NA–2939–2.
Fig. 12. Copper Eskimos from the Coronation Gulf area, Sinnisiak and Uluksak, brought to Edmonton for trial in 1917 for the homicide of the Oblate priests Rouvière and LeRoux. After the jury at Edmonton reached no verdict, a second trial at Calgary found them guilty but commuted their death sentences to a few years in prison. back row, left to right, Charles C. McCaul, Crown counsel, Inspector C.O. "Denny" LaNauze, James E. Wallbridge (defense counsel), and Corp. James E. Wight. Front row, left to right, Ilavinik (interpreter), Koeha (witness for the prosecution), Sinnisiak, Uluksak, Patsy Klenkenberg (part Eskimo). Photograph by McDermid Studios, Edmonton, Aug. 1917.

NEATBY

about (fig. 13). "The wise and devoted missionary . . . could strengthen and restore their spiritual equilibrium, which had been profoundly shaken . . . and left them [the Eskimos] drifting, bewildered and without guidance, in an unfamiliar and swiftly changing universe. . . . The understanding missionary, who knew something both of the old life and the new, . . . could counsel them in their troubles and interpret for them the perplexing unknowns" (Jenness 1964:15). This idealized appreciation has a very substantial basis in fact. In 1868 the Oblate Father Emile Petitot visited the Mackenzie Delta and compiled a dictionary of the local dialect (Jenness 1964:15). In 1876 an Anglican minister, E.J. Peck, began the work of translating parts of the New Testament and some hymns into the Eskimo tongue. He set up a number of schools, with the result that a brief quasi-literacy spread in the Hudson Bay and Baffin Island areas to an impressive degree (D.B. Marsh 1967; Low 1906:139–140). In 1894 Peck established a mission station on Blacklead Island in Cumberland Sound. Through his insistence two candidates for the mission field were given basic medical training to provide the health services that were otherwise unavailable. A shack on Blacklead Island "can be considered the first hospital in the Arctic" (D.B. Marsh 1967:9). The Anglican Church inaugurated the first regular dental service in the western Arctic in 1930 (D.B. Marsh 1967:9). Edgar Greenshield, the missionary on Blacklead Island, ministered to the health of his congregation, taught music, and trained his converts to conduct the church service admitting the gifted speakers among them to his pulpit (Hantzsch 1977:37–38). Until 1945 it was the churches that were the major force in health and education in the Canadian Arctic, and though they have been largely supplanted in these fields by public institutions, the good they did before the state awoke to its responsibilities is incalculable.

The Hudson's Bay Company

The traders, principally the agents of the Hudson's Bay Company, moved in with their trade goods as the whaler moved out. Unlike the transient seafarers who preceded them, the traders often had a sense of responsibility and a permanent interest in the welfare of their native clientele (Rasmussen 1927:299). Generally they seem to have dealt fairly with their customers in the prosperous 1920s and in the hungry 1930s gave them credit "to the limit that sound business warranted and often beyond" (Jenness 1964:41). The Révillon Frères made advances of bacon, flour, and beans "to enable the natives to ride over the evil days" (Sexé 1923). The Hudson's Bay Company obtained a virtual monopoly of trade on the understanding that no native would be permitted to starve within reach of any one of its posts.

In the hard winter of 1934 a local manager wrote that he had sent out a sledge to rescue nine starving persons, and that 16 others in his area had died of want (Jenness 1964:51, 54). At the same time the post managers, along with the police, served as distributors of public relief, as, later on, they looked after the distribution of family allowances and social security benefits. With the expansion of government activities since the 1940s the trader has become a shopkeeper and the religious teacher has also been relegated to his normal functions.

Government Activities

The Canadian federal government was slow in exercising the Arctic sovereignty ceded to it by Great Britain in 1880. In 1903 a detachment of the North West Mounted Police (now the Royal Canadian Mounted Police) was sent to enforce the law among whalers and Eskimos on Herschel Island. Other stations were set up in the Arctic, chiefly to assert Canadian sovereignty, threatened, for instance, by the 1898–1902 explorations of Otto Sverdrup within the so-called Canadian Arctic sector. Church missions were granted a pittance to support hospitals and schools. In periods of want relief was distributed through the agency of trader or police officer. After World War II the government began to assume full responsibility for the health, education, and welfare of the Eskimo, who, like other Canadian citizens, became entitled to all types of state assistance. Settlements in the eastern Arctic, which had been served irregularly by a Hudson's Bay Company ship, were made more accessible by the introduction of the icebreaker; the precarious navigation of Barrow Strait was thus made relatively secure for the burdened freighter. A station was set up at Resolute Bay on the south shore of Cornwallis Island with airstrip and harbor facilities. There freighters call annually to unload supplies, which are delivered in spring and autumn airlifts to the Canada–United States weather stations on the far northern islands.

In the 1980s the Eskimo was provided with efficient health services by airplane and icebreaker. Tuberculosis hospitals operated for some time in Hamilton, Ontario, and Edmonton, Alberta, for patients from the North, and the incidence of the disease there was much reduced, though still well above the national average. Every year a team of doctors, dentists, nurses, and X-ray technicians visits the eastern settlements by icebreaker. A similar group operates from the Mackenzie River to Cambridge Bay. Twelve nursing stations were scattered over the North, the nurse in charge being able at all times to contact a physician by radio. At the same time efforts were being made to remove the menace to Eskimo health represented by poor housing, poor clothing, and malnutrition. Not all change has been progress. Venereal disease was prevalent. Liquor, from which the

387

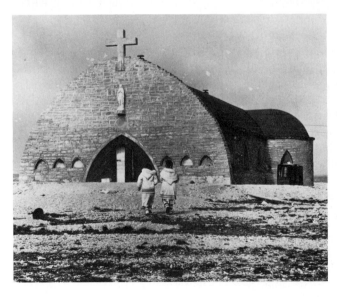

Fig. 13. Christian influence. top left, Baffinland Eskimo church choir in the Anglican mission at Cape Dorset. Photograph by Tessa Macintosh, 1974. top right, Exterior of the Anglican Mission at Cape Dorset. Photograph by B. Korda, Aug. 1961. center left, Interior of the Catholic Church of the Caribou Eskimo at Padlei, N.W.T. Photograph by Richard Harrington, 1949–1950. center right, Labrador Eskimo choir at the Moravian Mission at Nain. Photograph by Hermann Jannasch, 1880s. bottom left, The Roman Catholic Church at Igloolik. Photograph by Villy Svarre, Aug. 1961. bottom right, The first Eskimo nun, Sister Naya Pelagie, takes her vows on entering the Order of the Grey Nuns at a ceremony in the Roman Catholic Church, Chesterfield Inlet, N.W.T., a Caribou Eskimo community. Photograph by Douglas Wilkinson, March 1951.

Eskimo can no longer be protected, produced the familiar contemporary phenomenon of adolescent disorders in large centers such as Inuvik and Frobisher (Jenness 1964:160, 174; Gzowski 1975:33–36).

Nonetheless, much has been achieved; the Eskimo population numbering 8,646 in 1951 was 10,751 in 1960. In 1975 there were 15,800 Canadian Eskimos, of whom 4,395 lived in Quebec or Labrador (Canada. Statistics Canada 1976).

Education

The tendency of the once-scattered Eskimo population to cluster around mission station or trading post had created centers of some importance, such as Frobisher, Cambridge Bay, Coppermine, and Aklavik-Inuvik. Despite its drawbacks this development has facilitated the administration of public services, including education. The first government school was opened at Tuktoyaktuk in 1947. By 1982 more than 30 had been set up in the Arctic. There was a federal school at Inuvik, capable of accommodating 625 pupils and flanked by two hostels, one Roman Catholic, one Anglican. A smaller institution of the same type was operated at Chesterfield on Hudson Bay. The government operated

a student hostel at Frobisher. Of necessity instruction was given in English by teachers, few of whom speak Eskimo. In consequence it was not easy for the pupil to attain the academic level that fit him for the urgently needed technical training. Mission schools were restricted to the giving of religious instruction. Civic consciousness was being promoted: natives sat on the Northwest Territories Council at Yellowknife and on local district councils. The drawback, that they contributed little to discussion when Europeans participated, is one that time will remedy (Jenness 1964:120–138).

Sources

A comprehensive chronological listing of explorations in the Canadian Arctic with extensive bibliographies is provided by Cooke and Holland (1978). Important narrative summaries are those of Morison (1971), Morton (1939), Neatby (1968), and Quinn (1977:347–384, 417–428). The primary source for early exploration is Hakluyt (1907–1910), and late Jacobean discoveries are dealt with in Christy's (1894) introduction to the voyages of Foxe and James; most of the primary documents are

Fig. 14. Hudson's Bay Company influence. left, Quebec Eskimo woman with chin tattooing and small child in her parka hood, carrying Hudson's Bay Company supplies at Fort Wolstenholme, Ungava Peninsula. Photograph by Harvey Bassett, 1934. right, Baffinland Eskimos at Pangnirtung unloading supplies. Photograph by W. Doucette, July 1951.

printed, with useful introductions, by Quinn (1979). Other useful summaries of discovery are by Barrow (1818,1846). Later exploration is dealt with by Sverdrup (1904) and Stefánsson (1943).

Interaction between Eskimos and explorers throughout the Arctic has been summarized by Oswalt (1979). Useful primary accounts are found in the writings of nineteenth-century explorers who were concerned with all branches of science and thus needed advice and guidance from the Eskimos with whom they came in contact. Lyon (1824) made himself familiar with the domestic ways of the Eskimos, while Parry (1821, 1824) concerned himself specifically with their languages and music. John Ross (1835) learned much about hunting and travel techniques from the natives of Boothia Peninsula. Franklin's own writings contain relatively little information about native peoples, but closer relations and more intimate details emerge from the search for the lost ships of his last expedition, for there was an urgent need to seek out and question the indigenous population (see Armstrong 1857; Rae 1850; M'Clintock 1859; Miertsching 1967; Neatby 1970).

The history of postexploration Eskimo contacts in Canada to 1950 is covered in considerable detail by Jenness (1964). For later history, see other chapters in this volume.

Central Eskimo: Introduction

DAVID DAMAS

The five chapters that follow contain ethnographic accounts of the Copper, Netsilik, Iglulik, Caribou, and Baffinland Eskimo, the groups here considered to be the Central Eskimo (fig. 1). This designation has been used in other ways; each sense has combined geographical with cultural criteria. Boas's (1888:420) Central Eskimo included the people from King William Island, the interior of the District of Keewatin, the Boothia and Melville peninsulas, Baffin Island, and the Smith Sound region of northwestern Greenland. His omission of the Copper Eskimo is notable and probably resulted from the dearth at that time of ethnography for the Coronation Gulf–Victoria Island regions. In their survey of mythology and religion, Nungak and Arima (1969) name the Copper Eskimo along with the groups mentioned by Boas as Central Eskimo. They argue for the inclusion of the Polar Eskimo of Smith Sound, although they qualify this by pointing out that their chief source for Polar Eskimo mythology, Holtved (1951), used as chief informant a native whose mother had come from Baffinland in the 1860s (Nungak and Arima 1969:112). Mathiassen (1927:1) excludes the Polar Eskimo and considers Baffinlanders as well as the Labrador Eskimo to be peripheral to the "Central Eskimo proper." The *Handbook* classification agrees most closely with that of Birket-Smith, who speaks of five Central Eskimo dialect groups "which may be termed the Cumberland Sound, the Iglulik, the Netsilik, the Coronation Gulf, and the Barren Grounds groups" (Birket-Smith 1928:23).

While separation of the Eskimos of the Mackenzie delta region from this scheme is justified by their much closer similarities to the Western Eskimo groups, it is more difficult to define boundaries on cultural and linguistic grounds with neighbors to the southeast and northeast. The chief reason for excluding the Polar Eskimo and those of the Quebec-Labrador peninsula is their considerable geographical separation. The conditions of recent cultural contact also provide administrative-political grounds for excluding the Quebec and Labrador groups.

The people here designated Central Eskimo occupy the area fittingly called the Central Arctic, which lies about both the east-west and the north-south centers of Eskimo country, as opposed to those other groups that are marginal to those regions.

Ecological Zones

Basic contrasts in habitat as related to native technology and techniques of exploitation allow the differentiation of three main ecological zones in the Central Arctic (Damas 1969a). One of these comprised the regions of the Copper and Netsilik Eskimo, from Coronation Gulf eastward through Queen Maud Gulf, Rasmussen Basin, Boothia Peninsula, and Pelly Bay. This area was characterized by unbroken expanses of landfast ice that joined the islands and peninsulas of the region in winter but disappeared during the summer months. Open water with fringing floe edges occurred only on the margins of the area and did not figure prominently in the winter economy of the aboriginal Copper and Netsilik Eskimo. This was the region where the winter economy was almost entirely restricted to breathing-hole sealing, large sea mammals being virtually absent and surface sealing poorly developed. The summer orientation was entirely an inland one with caribou hunting and fishing the predominant modes of exploitation. The kayak was used in inland lakes and streams but not for hunting in the

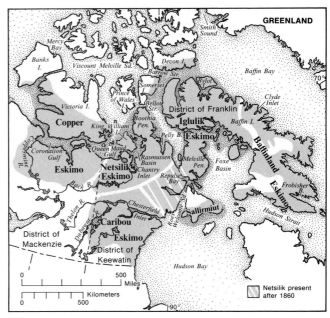

Fig. 1. Distribution of central Eskimo tribes about 1900. The boundary for Netsilik Eskimo represents the pre-1860 range, before emigration of parts of this tribe to the Hudson Bay.

sea. The Inuit of this zone hunted polar bear and musk-oxen whenever encountered, but only locally and only irregularly did these animals comprise important food sources.

By contrast, the habitat of the Iglulik Eskimo (Melville Peninsula and northern Baffin Island) offered large sea mammals such as the bearded seal, walrus, beluga, narwhal, and occasionally the Greenland whale. In the winter, floe edge hunting of these animals was common as a supplement to breathing-hole sealing. In summer, groups often split, some hunting caribou inland and some using kayaks to pursue coastal sea mammals. The same pattern was apparently followed by the Baffinland Eskimo. Thus, this second ecological zone included eastern and southern Baffin Island as well as the Iglulik territory.

A third zone was the interior of the District of Keewatin, which became the habitat of the Caribou Eskimo and the people of the upper Back River. This tundra area supported seasonally large herds of caribou as the first line of subsistence, with supplementary food sources being fish and the smaller numbers of caribou that remained in winter.*

To some degree these three exploitative zones also represented different levels of subsistence success, though variations within each zone were sometimes significant as well. The most dramatic gauge of differences in levels of subsistence are population statistics and other evidence for the presence or absence of selective female infanticide as a forced response to subsistence pressures. For the Copper Eskimo (Rasmussen 1932:70; Jenness 1922:42, 166) and the Netsilik (Rasmussen 1931:84, 139–142) statements regarding the existence of female infanticide and the associated imbalance of males over females indicate a very marginal subsistence situation, indeed. For both the Iglulik Eskimo (Mathiassen 1928:20) and the Baffinlanders (Boas 1888:426) there was a slight preponderance of females, probably attesting to the absence of female infanticide and to the more hazardous occupations of males, in particular kayak drownings in the sea and loss of life during the dan-

gerous thin ice hunting at the floe edge. The material from the Caribou Eskimo (Birket-Smith 1929:66–68, 98), however, is somewhat ambiguous with regard to the practice of female infanticide.†

The number of dogs that could be supported by a hunter has also been used as a measure of subsistence level (Damas 1963:203, 1975a). It was only in the Iglulik Eskimo regions that real teams of any size could be said to have been common, with one to three dogs per hunter being more common throughout the remainder of the regions considered here.

The length of time during the year's cycle when Inuit subsisted from stores might be enlisted as another such gauge of subsistence level. For instance, the Copper Eskimo squeezed through a period of two to four weeks in the fall, sometimes on short rations, before commencing the winter sealing (Jenness 1922:110), while the summer and autumn stores of the Repulse Bay Aivilingmiut sometimes lasted them until March or April (Boas 1888:446–447). On the other hand, the situation of the Caribou Eskimo was one of forced rather than preferential reliance on stored food since the largest kill of caribou had to be made before the winter period of relative sparseness of their chief game animal, and famines often occurred before the end of the winter.

Aboriginal Distributions

One might expect these differences in exploitation to have been expressed in the material culture. Indeed, Mathiassen (1928:239) relates the presence of special kayak implements and the walrus hunting harpoon among the Iglulik and Baffinland Eskimo to the use of the kayak in the sea. Certainly the design of kayak types such as those of the Copper and Netsilik Eskimo attested to their use only in inland waters. Birket-Smith's (1929:102–132) inventory of Caribou Eskimo hunting implements clearly shows the dearth of seal hunting tools as a reflection of the predominantly inland economic life of that tribe. Different materials, depending

---

*There are some exceptions to this scheme of ecological zones. Thus Balikci (1964:19) reports surface sealing to have been an important spring activity for the Pelly Bay Netsilik, and Boas (1888:452–453) inferred from John Ross's account that the same people may have spent most of some winters living inland on autumn stores and winter-killed musk-oxen. Floe-edge sealing was not practiced by the Clyde Inlet Baffinlanders because of the great distance of the edge from land. Stefánsson (1919:30) thought that some Copper Eskimo who visited Banks Island during winter months subsisted mainly on polar bear at that season. The Utkuhikhalingmiut of the lower Back River and Chantry Inlet have been represented by Rasmussen (1931:481–489) as having an inland orientation like the Caribou Eskimo, but differing in relying more heavily on fish. Damas (1968) indicates that they shared subsistence activities with the Netsilik proper, sealing on the ice of Chantry Inlet in winter at the time of Rasmussen's visit in 1923.

†The imbalance of sexes in Birket-Smith's census of 1922–1923 is only slight with 221 males to 211 females being recorded (though the Ahiarmiut figure of 35 is not broken down by sex). Birket-Smith (1929:661) noted that there was a predominance of males in the children counted but the opposite proportion was noted among adults. Arima ("Caribou Eskimo," this vol.) considers that these figures indicate the practice of female infanticide and also the relative hazardousness of the male occupations in adult years. However, it is not clear what criteria have been used for adulthood. For instance, in the case of censuses in this and neighboring regions taken by Capt. George Comer, adult females are those with children. Considering the early age of marriage, it is possible that many teenaged males are counted as children and teenaged females as adults, thus exaggerating the age-linked associations in his and possibly Birket-Smith's censuses (Damas 1975a:412, 417), and casting some doubt on the widespread occurrence of selective female infanticide among the Caribou Eskimo.

on their availability, were used for the same important tools and implements from region to region. Clothing styles also varied to some extent within the Central Eskimo area. However, Birket-Smith (1945:218) indicates that when the same artifact types occur among the Netsilik, Caribou, and Iglulik, they are practically indistinguishable in detail, whereas those of the Copper Eskimo seem rather distinct. Birket-Smith (1928) posited separate dialects for each of the tribal groups named here, but as yet dialect geography has been insufficiently studied; it is not known whether recognizable dialectal boundaries coincided with those of the tribal ranges outlined in the following ethnographic chapters.

McGhee (1972) has used the Fifth Thule Expedition data on material culture along with that of Jenness (1946) in a quantitative study and has arrived at virtually the same conclusion as Birket-Smith. McGhee (1972:126) suggested that the distinctiveness of Copper Eskimo material culture resulted from indirect influences of European trade.‡ He also expanded his comparison to physical anthropology (blood-group gene frequencies and cranial data) and to linguistics (lexicostatistics), using material from Copper, Netsilik, Iglulik, and Caribou as well as North Alaskan and Greenland groups. He found a high degree of correspondence among the Central groups considered, with Copper Eskimo again showing greater divergence in cranial and blood group traits. This divergence he attributes either to genetic drift or to possible Athapaskan contacts. However, the general degree of correspondence in all of his indices leads him to believe in a common Thule origin for all Central Eskimo, with little evidence of Dorset influences. (McGhee 1972:20).

Some aspects of Central Eskimo social organization show significant variation. Damas (1975) and material in the following chapters indicate that each of the tribes had a distinctive system of cousin terminology. Regional differences occurred in other terminological categories as well. The family organization of the Copper Eskimo is alone in conforming to the stereotype (Murdock 1949) of the isolated Eskimo nuclear family; some form of the extended family occurred elsewhere. Variations in marriage practices can also be noted in the area (Damas 1975a). Analysis of band organization shows that the Copper, Netsilik, and Iglulik groupings were

‡J.G. Taylor (1974:166–169) disagrees with both Birket-Smith and McGhee regarding the distributions of material culture items along the Northwest Passage, finding close affinities between Netsilik and Copper Eskimo and a greater separation between Netsilik and Iglulik materials than they perceived. He attributes the apparent discrepancy to the variation between the Fifth Thule collections used by Birket-Smith and McGhee in their analyses and the Amundsen collection used by Taylor himself, suggesting increased contacts between Iglulik and Netsilik Eskimo after the time of Amundsen's visit (1903–1905) to account for much of the similarity previously reported in the material culture of the latter groups.

very similar, all having a pronounced male-oriented slant to the primary kin ties involved in the largest aggregations, while the structure of smaller hunting groups varied among the tribes (Damas 1969b).

In social organization, the Copper Eskimo were relatively distinct in family organization and hunting group composition, and each major group of the region had a distinct terminology for cousins. Otherwise variation in social organization does not coincide with the present classification into major groups (Damas 1969a). Neither do these variations always coincide with the ecological zones indicated above; certain uniformities cross ecological boundaries, and variations (particularly in family organization) occur within the Netsilik-Copper zone. On the other hand, Damas (1969a, 1975a) argues for a chain of associations regarding exploitative zones, demography, marriage practices, and to some extent cousin terminologies.

Several historical processes account for the distribution of trait complexes in material culture, physical anthropology, linguistics, and social organization. Common heritage from a Thule base and continued contact and diffusion among the Central Eskimo groups are, of course, evident. On the other hand, the distinctiveness of each of the kinship terminological systems, especially in the cousin terms, together with the separateness of the Copper Eskimo in several of the comparative categories, indicate the probable operation of forces working for diversity that were based on conditions of relative isolation.

On the basis of the above comparative studies it is indeed difficult to justify classifying the Central Eskimo into major named groups, with the possible exception of the Copper Eskimo. The rationale of the members of the Fifth Thule Expedition (Mathiassen 1928:1; Birket-Smith 1945:15) for designating each of them as a distinct "tribe" would not seem to be strongly supported.

However, there are other criteria that do support the separation into these named tribes (if the political sense of the term tribe is discounted). One of these is geographical or territorial. Each of the tribes is separated from the neighboring ones by an expanse of usually uninhabited country, or at least each was until late nineteenth and twentieth-century contact with Westerners altered ranges of habitation. Contacts among the groups named here were generally sporadic and occurred in the context of intertribal trade or raids. This is not to say that the concept of defended territories existed, but rather that customary tribal hunting grounds seldom overlapped.

A strong case can be made for the separation of the Central Eskimo into tribes on genealogical grounds. Work by Damas (1969b) on Copper, Netsilik, and Iglulik material and by Arima ("Caribou Eskimo," this vol.) on the Caribou Eskimo genealogies based on the

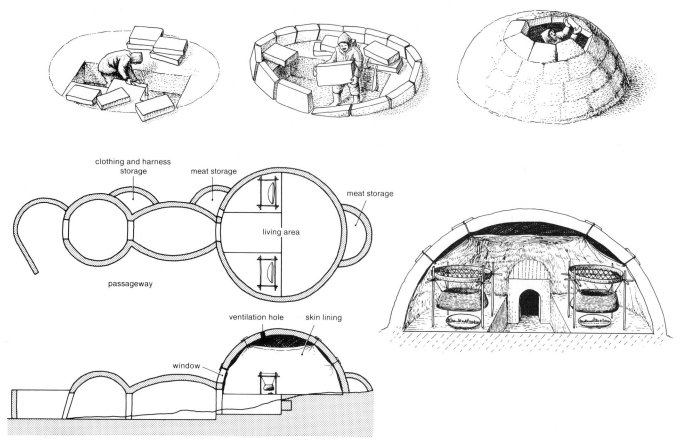

after Boas 1888:539–546; J.A. Maxwell 1978:360.

Fig. 2. Snowhouses were constructed for two purposes. A small snowhouse about five feet high and seven feet in diameter was built as a temporary dwelling while on winter hunts or journeys. A larger snowhouse with vaults 10–12 feet high and 12–15 feet in diameter was built to house families through the winter season until warming spring temperatures necessitated abandonment to tents. The principles of construction were the same for both types. The building blocks had to be cut from a snowbank formed by a single storm so they would hold together when cut and measure about 3–4 feet long, 2 feet high, and 6–8 inches thick. The first row of blocks is put up in a circle. Then the top of the first block is cut down to the ground and the slanting line of the cut continued around the circle to form the base of a spiral. As new blocks cut into a trapezoid shape are added to the spiral they are inclined increasingly inward and their edges cut at a more slanted angle, forming a self-supported vault. When the vault is finished, the joints between the blocks are filled with snow and scraps of blocks. Two or sometimes 3 smaller vaults are attached to the main building to form a passageway connected by low doors. Additional vaults can be added for storerooms. In the main dome a window is cut above the door and is either covered with a translucent membrane of sewn seal gut or a block of freshwater ice. The bank of snow at the rear is the sleeping area. The two benches on either side of the entrance trench are work areas each with an oil lamp and frame supporting a drying rack and a suspended kettle. Usually, two families occupy a house with each wife having a bench and a lamp. Near the top of the dome a small hole is cut through the wall for ventilation. Cold air enters through the passage, is warmed by the lamps as it slowly rises from the trench and escapes through the ventilation hole. Some of the Central Eskimo groups, particularly those along Davis Strait, lined the living area of the snowhouse with skins suspended from the roof by small ropes held by toggles on the outside of the wall. The lining, by trapping a layer of colder air against the walls, allows the temperature of the room to be warmer without melting the snow blocks. Unlined houses frequently drip and the temperature averages around 2–3° C, while in lined houses it can be from 10–20° C.

censuses of the Fifth Thule Expedition of 1921–1924 shows that in fact these groups can be regarded as being virtual demes. There is some doubt as to possible internal division of the tribes into "sub-demes," particularly in the cases of the Copper, Caribou, and Baffinland Eskimo, but in general the degree of contact and marriage within tribes was much higher than contact or marriage between segments of different tribal groups as designated here.

Culture History

The preceding three chapters describe the archeological and early historical background of the Canadian Eskimo, including the Central Eskimo. The culture of the Central Eskimo was little influenced by contact with European and American explorers of the sixteenth through the nineteenth centuries, whose goals were the expansion of geographical knowledge rather than a search for commercial opportunities. Inadvertently, however, the abandonment of Robert McClure's *Investigator* at Mercy Bay in 1853 (Stefánsson 1919:38–39) and John Ross's *Victory* near Thom Bay in 1832 (Rasmussen 1931:27) brought wood and metal into the areas of the Copper Eskimo and the Netsilik and stimulated intertribal contact. The ships of explorers entered the Central Arctic either via the Bering Sea and Alaska or from the Atlantic; barriers of ice delayed first the discovery and subsequently the navigation of the Northwest Passage. A few overland explorers like John Franklin and George Back operated from continental bases.

Whaling influences from the east brought about more profound situations of contact. Both Scottish and New England whalers early affected the lives of the Baffinland Eskimo. At the time of Boas's fieldwork, 1883–1884, considerable depopulation had occurred, and a number of European artifacts had been introduced. After 1860 whalers penetrated into the northwestern Hudson Bay area, where Aivilingmiut (Iglulik Eskimo) men were hired as hunters and members of whaling parties, and women as seamstresses (Robinson 1973). Some of the Caribou Eskimo and Netsilik Eskimo were also drawn to the Roes Welcome Sound area to participate in whaling activity or the associated trade (C.F. Hall 1879:274–275, 278; Robinson 1973).

In the west, while whaling operations via Bering Strait profoundly influenced the population structure and culture of the Mackenzie Eskimo, their effect was not apparent in the Central Eskimo region, though the Copper Eskimo did receive goods from the west in the early nineteenth century and later via the overland trade routes (Stefánsson 1914).

The fur trade was a force that affected all the Central Eskimo tribes. The people of the west coast of Hudson Bay were the first to have direct contact with the fur trade, out of Churchill beginning in the eighteenth century. Direct contact with traders was delayed for the remaining groups until after 1900. In the west Christian Klengenberg's over-wintering in 1905–1906 and William Mogg's in 1907–1908 (Jenness 1922:31) began effective direct trade contact for the Copper Eskimo, though when Stefánsson visited them in 1910 and 1911 they still offered the closest approach to an aboriginal state that an ethnographer could observe among the Central Eskimo tribes. The Fifth Thule Expedition arrived at the brink of the transition throughout the Central Arctic between either aboriginal or whaling periods on the one hand and the advent of trading posts on the other. For the Iglulik, Baffinland, Caribou, and Netsilik Eskimo the fur trade was for the most part represented by the expansion of the Hudson's Bay Company into their regions. For the Copper Eskimo, however, for more than 20 years after 1920 competition between smaller companies and the Company itself dominated the scene, with the eventual emergence of the Company

during the period of lowered fur prices in World War II (Usher 1971:101–102).

The Hudson's Bay Company tried to span the east-west barriers with a post at Fort Ross on Bellot Strait (Jenness 1964:61), but conditions of navigation continued to make the two spheres distinct until the advent of the airplane.

The following chapters contain references to the era of the fur trader, the missionary, and the police. This was a stabilized period during which the traditional seasonal cycle was modified, considerable quantities of European goods were introduced, nominal religious conversion took place, and the Inuit were brought under the influence of the Canadian legal system. This phase resembled closely the situation that had crystallized earlier in the Canadian Subarctic (Helm and Damas 1963).

Although the airplane eased many of the supply and transportation problems in the Central Arctic, the great change came with the increased interest of the Canadian government beginning in the late 1950s. The rapid concentration of the population into a few centers resulted in the merging of elements of the various tribal groups, as well as some divisions among them. Trapping and hunting were often replaced by wage labor, handicrafts, and social welfare as chief sources of income and support. The problems of adjustment to this changed situation are discussed to some measure in the ethnographic chapters but more specifically in "Contemporary Canadian Inuit," this volume.

Sallirmiut

The Sallirmiut should be included among Central Eskimo groups even though their demise before they could be visited by an ethnologist limits our information severely ("Iglulik," fig. 1, this vol.).

Boas (1888) noted Parry's finding traces of Eskimo at Duke of York Bay on Southampton Island in 1821 and the first meeting with the Sallirmiut by Lyon on Coats Island in 1824. Boas (1888:51) also mentions discovery of other people at Manico Point by an American whaler in 1865. According to Mathiassen (1927), their country in the years just preceding their extinction in 1902–1903 included only the southern parts of Southampton Island. Mathiassen combined information from published material, especially the accounts of Comer (1910) and Munn (1919), with interpretations of his own archeological finds, and accounts of Aivilingmiut who had lived on Southampton Island, to produce the only ethnographic sketch of the Sallirmiut.

Mathiassen (1927:285) saw the Sallirmiut as clearly derived from Thule with minor Dorset influences (a view shared by Collins 1953a, 1957), with singular features of culture developing under conditions of extreme isolation. Maritime emphasis dominated the economy with walrus and polar bear especially important. Sallirmiut practiced the usual Eskimo methods of breathing hole and surface sealing and hunted both seals and walrus from the floe edge. Caribou, fish, and fowl comprised secondary sources of food during summer months. The strong maritime emphasis was expressed in the wardrobe, which made extensive use of bearskin, and in the permanent winter dwellings built near favorite locales for sea mammal hunting. A number of these dwellings had the unique feature of supporting pillars of limestone slabs, and the wide use of limestone for lamps and cooking pots (Mathiassen 1927:228, 231) attests to the absence of soapstone and lack of contact with groups trading that material.

The high development of flint chipping and the absence of rubbed slate and (for later cultures) iron distinguished the material culture of the Sallirmiut from that of Thule and modern Central Eskimo (Collins 1953:33).

Considerable quantities of whale bone are found in some houses, and sled runners were also made from that material (Mathiassen 1927:275, 277); these practices likely indicate a shortage of driftwood as does perhaps the absence of the umiak, whose construction is favored by good timber. Whales and other sea mammals were hunted from kayaks, but that craft was not used in hunting caribou.

Mathiassen's (1927:268–283) Aivilingmiut informants recalled pan-Eskimo customs such as shamanism, child betrothal, spouse exchange, and a body of taboos concerning menstruating and pregnant women, but there seemed to be a lack of concern with separating the products of land and sea. Two origin myths are reported, one citing the Wager Bay area as the point of emigration to Southampton Island, and the other, Baffin Island.

The notion that the Sallirmiut died off because of the failure of the caribou herds (Low 1906) was rejected by Mathiassen. His own view that they perished as a result of an epidemic (perhaps typhus) is supported by the testimony of an Aivilingmiut who claimed to be a survivor of that calamity (Mathiassen 1927:284). The Sallirmiut were probably never numerous and Mathiassen estimated their number as 58 just before the epidemic.

Copper Eskimo

DAVID DAMAS

Territory

The Copper Eskimo are the westernmost of the groups that are regarded as being the Central Eskimo. The normal western boundary of Copper Eskimo country on the mainland of Canada seems to have been at Wise Point (Stefánsson 1913:167). In the northwest the south coast of Banks Island was visited in the region from DeSalis Bay to Nelson Head. In the south the Copper Eskimo knew of Great Bear Lake (Stefánsson 1919:260) and also visited Beechey Lake on the Back River (Rasmussen 1932:119) and Contwoyto Lake (Damas 1962–1963). In the east, Perry River is regarded as having been the boundary between Copper Eskimo and Netsilik countries (Damas 1968). Much of Victoria Island was hunted over but usually the area south of a line drawn from Walker Bay to Denmark Bay is considered to be their region of travel and occupation (fig. 1).

Stefánsson (1914) has presented a survey of trade routes across the Canadian north that were active during the nineteenth century and that involved the Copper Eskimo in contacts with neighboring groups. One of these connected with the Mackenzie Delta Eskimo along the south shore of Amundsen Gulf and another across that gulf from Banks Island. Contact by these routes is believed to have ceased by about 1830.

Encounters with Athapaskan Indians to the south appear to have been rare in the period between Samuel Hearne's visit to Bloody Falls in 1771 and Vilhjálmur Stefánsson's joining of elements of Copper Eskimo and Slavey in the summer of 1910 (Jenness 1922:47).

Both Stefánsson (1914) and Jenness (1922:48) refer to trading expeditions to Akiliniq on the Thelon River where the Caribou Eskimo were encountered. Trading contacts with the Netsilik usually occurred on the ice of Victoria Strait and also near Hat Island in eastern Queen Maud Gulf (Jenness 1922; Rasmussen 1931, 1932).

Intermarriage appears to have been infrequent between Copper Eskimos and other groups, and accordingly they represented a close approach to a discrete marriage universe or deme (Damas 1969b). Comparison of vocabularies from the eastern and western part of the Copper Eskimo area (Rasmussen 1932:333–345) indicates a very close correspondence in language, and in a 1968 survey Webster and Zibell (1976:275) found the same set of phonemes used by Coppermine and Cambridge Bay speakers. It is probably accurate then, to refer to a Copper Eskimo dialect, which is in the Inuit-Inupiaq (Eastern Eskimo) division.[*]

Viewed in archeological perspective all three major phases of prehistoric Canadian Eskimo culture are represented—the Pre-Dorset, Dorset (W.E. Taylor 1965), and Thule (McGhee 1968)—though Mathiassen (1927, 2) noted a gap in the distribution of classic Thule traits such as whalebone and earth houses in an area that includes the country of the Copper Eskimo. Other important Thule characteristics do appear in the archeology, and there is a clear transition to modern Copper Eskimo culture in the sites of the area (McGhee 1968).

Environment

The land of the Copper Eskimo is largely tundra and reaches wooded areas only on the southwestern margins and along the Coppermine River, though willow is found in considerable quantities in a number of places. Physiographically the region is divided into Pre-Cambrian Lowland and scarpland of the coast of the mainland and part of northwestern Victoria Island, and other areas that are comprised of sedimentary strata from later geological ages.

The area is Arctic in climate with February mean temperatures from $-20°$ to $-28°F$ and July means ranging in the high 40°s for most localities. Most of the light precipitation falls in the form of snow in spring and fall, while the blizzards of winter serve mainly to shift the accumulation of snow according to wind direction.

The straits and gulfs of the Copper Eskimo regions are covered by a continuous sheet of ice from October or November until sometime in July, and many of the lakes have ice cover for an even longer period. The

---

[*]The phonemes of Copper Eskimo are: (voiceless stops) *p, t, k, q*; (voiced fricatives) *v, y* ([ž]~[ʒ] intervocalically; [y]), *ɣ, ɣ́*; (voiceless fricatives) *s, h*; (nasals) *m, n, ŋ*; (lateral) *l*; (short vowels) *i, a, u*; (long vowels) *i·, a·, u·*. If *s* is found only in *ts* clusters it is not distinct from *h* phonemically. Before nasals *ɣ́* is [ŋ]. *ll* is [dl].

In the practical orthography generally in use the Copper Eskimo phonemes are written: p, t, k, q; v, j, g, r; s, h; m, n, ng; l; i, a, u; ii, aa, uu. Before nasals *ɣ́* [ŋ] may be written r or rng.

Information on Copper Eskimo phonology and the transcription of words is from David Damas, Webster and Zibell (1976:274–276), and Anthony C. Woodbury (communication to editors 1982).

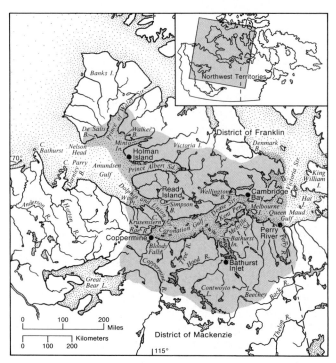

Fig. 1. Copper Eskimo territory, about 1900.

seasonality of climate is paralleled by the cycle of the sun, which disappears in most of the region for two or more months and circles the horizon again for an equal period in summer. Taken together such yearly changes can be seen to have had marked effects upon the annual economic cycle.

Culture

Subsistence

During the second half of May the aboriginal Copper Eskimo abandoned the snowhouse villages on the sea ice and moved to land. Despite the presence of migrating herds of caribou on the ice of Dolphin and Union Strait in the west and Dease Strait in the east, little attempt was made to hunt the animals in the spring (Jenness 1922:123). It is also significant that seldom were seals hunted as they slept on the surface of the sea ice (Stefánsson 1913:205). Neither was sealing practiced in the open water of summer. The chief sources of food from late May until November were caribou, fish, fowl, and small game.

Chief emphasis on either caribou or fish varied according to season as well as locale. Generally, fishing through ice in lakes was more important in spring and the early part of summer while caribou hunting tended to dominate from about the beginning of August, when the animals were fatter and the skins most suitable for clothing. This phase was interrupted briefly by a period of fishing from weirs in streams when the arctic char returned inland after their period in the sea. In some

localities like southeastern Victoria Island, fishing tended to be more important while on the mainland around Bathurst Inlet and east to Perry River, large herds of caribou made hunting that animal more profitable (Jenness 1922:122 ff.; Rasmussen 1932:76–77).

Caribou were generally hunted in drives between rows of stones set in converging lines to resemble men, while women and children chased the animals toward waiting hunters who used bows and lances from their firing pits. Another method was hunting with lances from kayaks at crossing places in lakes (Jenness 1922:148–149). Techniques for hunting caribou were essentially the same as for other Central Eskimo groups (see "Caribou Eskimo," this vol.).

Men, women, and children all participated in fishing whether jigging through the ice for trout or char in the spring or in spearing the char in weirs in late summer (fig. 2).

Wildfowl, including the ptarmigan and several species of geese and ducks, were secured during the summer with bow and arrow and also with snares (Jenness 1922:152).

Beginning some time in November for a period of two weeks or a month the Copper Eskimo were relatively idle, with subsistence coming mainly from cached food such as sun-dried caribou meat and fish and frozen meat and fish. Some jigging for fish at nearby lakes took place, but sewing of the winter garments by the women was the most important activity at this period.

From December until May breathing-hole sealing was the chief activity in most of the Copper Eskimo area. This method was carried out with a number of hunters and their specially trained dogs who located the breathing holes. Each hunter stationed himself at a hole to wait quietly for the rise of a seal to breathe. The common ringed seal was usually caught, but occasionally the bearded or squareflipper seal weighing 600 to 800 pounds was taken as well (Stefánsson 1913:268). The method of hunting seals at the breathing hole was identical with that of the Netsilik Eskimo.

Polar bears were an important part of the winter larder of those Copper Eskimos who wintered off the southeast coast of Banks Island (Stefánsson 1919:30). They were also often met with in Victoria Strait but less frequently in other parts of the area. Bears were usually held at bay by dogs and dispatched with harpoons or lances made from knives lashed to poles.

Musk-oxen were another occasional summer quarry of the Copper Eskimo. They were most numerous around Bathurst Inlet but could be encountered in small herds almost anywhere.

Settlement Pattern

Just as the economic cycle was strongly influenced by seasonal fluctuations in the availability of the various

Natl. Mus. of Canada, Ottawa: top, 51187; bottom left, A-12; bottom right, 50927.
Fig. 2. Fishing. top, Stone weirs at Nulahugyuk Creek near Bernard Harbour. Sometimes 4 dams were built at 25-yard intervals. The lower 3 had a path into the next dam, the upper one blocked the passage altogether (Jenness 1922:155). The man in the distance at the mouth of the creek tries to prevent the salmon from escaping. Men and women are spearing the fish, with tridents and leisters. Photograph by Diamond Jenness, 1914. bottom left, Setting a gill net across the mouth of a stream at Bathurst Inlet. Photograph by David Damas, summer 1963. bottom right, Kilavdluak (wearing snow goggles) jigging for fish in an ice-crack near Bernard Harbour, with wooden fishing rod and line probably made from plaited caribou leg sinew or baleen. A fish spear lies in foreground. Photograph by George H. Wilkins, 1914–1916.

species and by hunting conditions that changed over the seasons, so was the patterning of local aggregations to a large extent shaped by the conditions of the year's economic round. During the period from May to November Copper Eskimo groups were quite variable in size and composition. At times the nuclear family comprised the local groupings for a few days at a time when foraging was especially difficult and subsistence reduced

to fishing in lakes and hunting small game. More often groups of a dozen or more people would stay together for longer periods, especially when caribou hunting was favorable or when the best fishing places were inhabited. The largest summer period aggregations were probably about 50 at sites of the summer char runs (Damas 1969b).

A more regular sort of aggregation occurred for a

period of two to four weeks in the late autumn in conjunction with the sewing period. Summer groups that hunted in a large general area gathered at traditionally used points of land at that time. Jenness's (1922:fig. 2) map indicates 11 of these gathering places while omitting several known for the eastern part of the region (Damas 1962–1963) and also for the Prince Albert Sound–Minto Inlet people. It seems likely that there were 16 to 18 of these 'finishing places' (*innakhaγvi·t*). If Rasmussen's census of 816 is a typical Copper Eskimo population figure it means that the sewing groups averaged 45 to 50 persons. Other Copper Eskimo population estimates for the aboriginal or early contact period are Stefánsson's (1919:25–40) 1,100 and Jenness's 700 or 800 (1922:42). Neither of these ethnologists had contact with or accurate information for the eastern groups of Copper Eskimo. Rasmussen's census appears to be the most complete for the whole area.

The third type of aggregation occurred in conjunction with the winter sealing village. While there was probably an advantage for splitting into small groups during the summer period, and while the sewing group size was probably not related to subsistence activity (since stores were used at that period), there appears to be a close association between economic advantage and the large groups of the winter period. Stefánsson (1913:170) notes that each seal probably has a number of breathing holes and given this condition there is an obvious advantage to covering as many holes in a given area as is possible. Jenness's map indicates eight of these sealing sites, though he lacked information for some parts of the area. Accordingly, each winter the total population of Copper Eskimos merged into seven to nine of these aggregations for much of the sealing period. Using Rasmussen's figures again, the mean sizes then ranged from about 91 to 117. The largest number seems to be represented by Stefánsson's group of about 150 at Prince Albert Sound and the Bathurst Inlet group of 166. The minimum size seems to have been about 50 persons (Damas 1969b).

It is thus possible to distinguish three types of settlement for the aboriginal period Copper Eskimo, as follows: the winter sealing encampment or maximal bands, the sewing-place gathering or minimal band, and the evanescent summer hunting group (Damas 1972b).

As is often the case, it is difficult to identify these designations with native categories. Group names ending in *-miut* 'people of' cannot be made to correspond with exactitude to the above classification. The closest correspondent in the ethnographical material is those who exploit a wide general summer hunting region (table 1). Damas's (1962–1963) research raises the number above Rasmussen's for the eastern part of the area to give a total of about 16 *-miut* groups for the entire Copper Eskimo country. This number nearly coincides with the sewing-place group or minimal band, which is

identified with those who gather after having exploited the same general region in summer. In actual fact there would seem to be more *-miut* groups (16 to 18) because in one or two cases, two of these units comprised the sewing-period group.

The maximal band was also often designated by a name in *-miut* by outsiders, with the group name being taken from the name of one of the constituent minimal bands (Damas 1962–1963).

Social Organization

The fluctuations in group size that in large part harmonized with the year's economic cycle were accompanied by changes in characteristics of group composition. Jenness (1922:125–142) has given an account of the activities and changing composition and size of a hunting group that he accompanied during the spring, summer, and autumn of 1915. Analysis of his material indicates that the group fluctuated in size from 3 to 19 members and that bilateral kinship ties were evident though there was one break in the continuity of primary ties within the maximum aggregation (Damas 1960).

Informants from the eastern part of the Copper Eskimo area gave a picture of no set pattern of relationships for the summer hunting groups. At times father-son ties were evident, at times brother-brother bonds, at times more distant connections were apparent, and sometimes kinship connections were denied (Damas 1969b).

The sewing-place aggregations were occasions for the renewal of kinship ties and bonds of friendship that were split during the May to November period. It is apparent that there generally were breaks in the chain of primary kin ties in these groups.

During the winter sealing period when the largest aggregations occurred, the continuity of primary kinship ties reached virtual completeness with only a few nuclear families being detached from the main body with regard to primary ties. In most cases these families were newcomers or travelers. One could expect that about two-thirds of the members of one winter aggregation would return the following year. Analysis of kinship composition of these winter aggregations or maximal bands reveals a pronounced slant toward male-male as opposed to female-female connections (Damas 1969b).

If one uses criteria of kinship, coresidence, economic criteria, and criteria of mutual aid for identifying the extended family, only a weak case can be made for its existence among the Copper Eskimo. Therefore, the isolated nuclear family that has been associated with the Eskimo in general is exemplified by the Copper Eskimo.

The kinship system of the Copper Eskimo has been presented as being an example of the "Eskimo type"

Table 1. Group Designations of Copper Eskimo by Summer Hunting Regions

Stefánsson (1919:26–32)	Jenness (1922:33–41)	Rasmussen (1932:7, 69–70, 76–77)
1. Akuliakattagmiut Interior south of Dolphin and Union Strait	1. Akulliakattangmiut Akulliakattak Lake	1. Ahungahungârmiut, earlier Piuvlermiut Both sides of Dolphin and Union Strait
2. Noahonirmiut Interior north of Rae River	2. Haneragmiut North of Dolphin and Union Strait, extinct 1915	2. Nuvungmiut Behind Cape Krusenstern
3. Kañianermiut, also Uallirgmiut Headwaters of Rae River	3. Noahognirmiut Next east of group 1	3. Qor(d)lortôrmiut Bloody Falls
4. Pallirmiut West end of Coronation Gulf	4. Puivlirmiut Colville Hills to Simpson Bay	4. Nägjugtôrmiut Victoria Island southeast of group 1
5. Kogluktogmiut Bloody Falls	5. Uwalliarmiut Richardson River	5. Agiarmiut Tree River region
6. Kugaryuagmiut Just west of Coppermine River	6. Nagyuktogmiut Southwest Victoria Island	6. Kiluhigtormiut Bathurst Inlet
7. Pingangnaktogmiut West of Tree River	7. Kogluktomiut Bloody Falls	7. Umingmaktôrmiut, also Malerisiorfingmiut Bathurst Inlet
8. Kogluktualugmiut, also Utkusiksaligmiut Tree River	8. Asiagmiut East of Coppermine River	8. Kêgdlingujârmiut Kent Peninsula
9. Kogluktuaryumiut East of Tree River	9. Pingangnaktomiut South and east of Tree River	9. Kûngmiut Victoria Island, west of Cambridge Bay
10. Umingmûktogmiut Kent Peninsula	10. Nennitagmiut Behind Cape Barrow	10. Eqalugtôrmiut Cambridge Bay
11. Ahiagmiut Ogden Bay	11. Kilusiktomiut Bathurst Inlet	11. Nuvungmiut Victoria Island opposite Melbourne Island
12. Ugyuligmiut Banks Island, extinct 1910	12. Umingmaktomiut South of Melville Sound	12. Ahiarmiut Mainland, between Kent Peninsula and Ogden Bay
13. Haneragmiut Colville Hills	13. Asiagmiut West of Kent Peninsula	13. Kangerjuarmiut Prince Albert Sound
14. Puiplirmiut North of Simpson Bay	14. Ekaluktomiut North of Wellington Bay	14. Kangarjuätjiarmiut Minto Inlet
15. Nagyuktogmiut, also Killinermiut South shore Victoria Island	15. Kiglinirmiut East of group 14	
16. Kilusiktogmiut Just east of group 15	16. Kanghiryuarmiut Around Prince Albert Sound	
17. Ekalluktogmiut East end of Victoria Island	17. Kanghiryuatjagmiut Minto Inlet region	
18. Kanhiryuarmiut Prince Albert Sound region		
19. Kanhiryuatjiagmiut Minto Inlet region		

(Murdock 1949:227) with a common term for cousins distinct from siblings and linear aunt–niece terms. However, this characterization seems to have stemmed from an erroneous presentation by Jenness (1922:83–84). Figure 3 applies to the eastern part of the Copper Eskimo area, and cousin and aunt–niece terms have been checked with informants from the western part of the area. Significant terminological features include two terms for cousins, bifurcate collateral terms for uncles, aunts, nieces, and nephews, and the inclusion of affines in the first ascending generation. This last characteristic appears to be related to the frequent marriages among relatives as does the separation of sisters from female cousins (Damas 1975).

Marriage was arranged during infancy or at birth, and in most documented cases, betrothal was arranged between some sort of cousins. Marriage was acknowledged when both of the betrothed, or more frequently, when the girl reached puberty. This often followed a period of bride service but afterward a separate household was established.

Adoption was widely practiced, and there was a kinship obligation involved for supplying parents and older siblings with children if they desired them. Adoption of nonrelatives was usually accompanied by a payment.

Another area in which kinship played an important role was that of the vendetta. Rasmussen (1932:17) remarked that all the adult males of a village that he

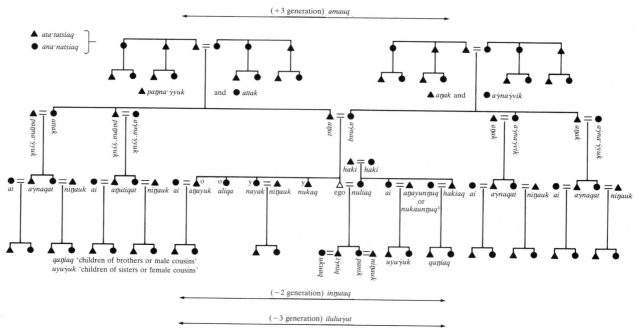

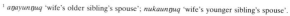

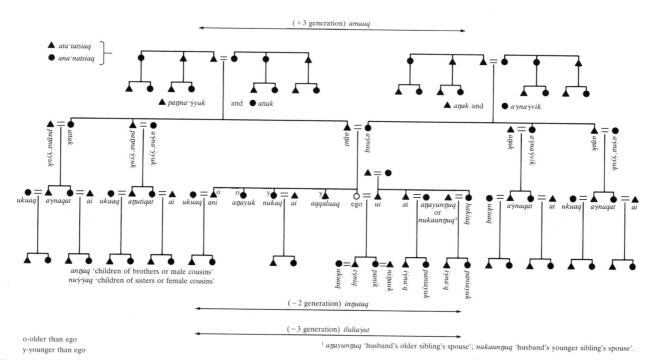

Fig. 3. Kinship terminology. top, Male ego; bottom, female ego.

visited had been involved in feuds, and during the following years the Royal Canadian Mounted Police investigated a number of murders, several of which were attributed to revenge killings.

While the blood feud, betrothal, and adoption all had important kinship ingredients the realms of economics and of household residence were more closely associated with factors of locality and voluntary relationships (Damas 1972).

During the summer months food and skins were cached separately for each nuclear family, but current consumption was in the form of communal eating within whatever local group that occurred. During the sewing period when subsistence came largely from cached food, communal eating and gift-giving of meat were both important. The meat giving was purely voluntary and did not involve kinship obligations or formalized partnerships (Damas 1972a).

Fig. 4. Sewing. Eskimo women had the major responsibility for making and repairing the family clothing. Some seasons required more sewing than others, with the autumn being the hardest in the urgent necessity to prepare for winter (Jenness 1946:87). left, Higilak making clothing, possibly for the Canadian Arctic Expedition (Jenness 1922:142). She wears a thimble and sews with sinew. On her parka front she wears amulets or charms, evidently mandibles of a small mammal. Photograph by George H. Wilkins, near Bernard Harbour, autumn 1915. right, Rosie Kongyona and Patrick Ekalun in a tent. He is carving and she is making duffel socks using a portable sewing machine. Photograph by Fred Bruemmer, May 1969.

During the breathing-hole sealing season the main food sharing procedure was the *piqatiɣi·t* system of partitioning the seal (Rasmussen 1932:106–107; Damas 1972a). Each hunter had a partner for sharing a particular part of the animal with which he would reciprocate when he was successful in the hunt. Partners were appointed at the time of a youth's first kill, and kinship factors were irrelevant since both kindred and non-kindred made up an individual's inventory of partners. (Compare the similar description of seal sharing partnerships in "Netsilik Eskimo," this vol.).

Other important sorts of partnerships involved spouse exchange and association in dancing, relationships that excluded kindred; and joking relationships, which encompassed both kindred and persons apparently unrelated. Avoidance and respect relationships existed among certain classes of kin, and the namesake partnerships pertained between persons named for the same deceased person. All these sorts of dyads appear to have operated exclusively in an affective sphere and did not involve economic obligations (Damas 1972).

In summary, the Copper Eskimo appear at first glance to have approached the widespread characterization of the loosely organized, even anarchical society, attributed to the Eskimo in general. The lack of family organization above the nuclear level, the absence of formalized leadership above that level, the amorphous character of summer groupings, the absence of descent

Fig. 5. Food utensils. Meat and blubber were served in wooden dishes. top, Oblong dish of single piece of wood repaired with copper rivets. center, Dish with bentwood side strip held together with copper nails and separate bottom piece. bottom, Meat forks used for removing meat from the cooking pot but not for eating. This decorated bone fork is particularly elaborate. Length 25.3 cm. Small spatula-shaped tools were used for extracting marrow from bones. top, Length 30.8 cm, center same scale. top, center collected by Diamond Jenness, Bernard Harbour, N.W.T., 1914–1916; bottom, by J. Bernard, Coronation Gulf, N.W.T., before 1921.

Fig. 6. Use of the ulu, the woman's knife. left, Kukilugak splitting arctic char. The fish when split and cleaned will be dried for winter consumption. A sealskin water bucket is next to her (Jenness 1946:74). She is tattooed on the forehead, cheeks, chin, hands, and arms. Photograph by James Harold Webster, Coppermine, Aug. 1945. right, Lucy Anagaik eating meat from a caribou leg. Her cheeks, hands, and wrists are tattooed. Photograph by Richard Harrington at Iksik's camp between Bathurst Inlet and Perry River, N.W.T., Feb. 1949.

groups, the apparently subordinate role of kinship—all tend to contribute to that picture. However, with the substantial elaboration of voluntary relationships, especially as expressed in the complex system of dyadic terminologies, definite structure can be perceived.

Technology

The inventories of hunting implements varied according to the quarry and, indirectly, with the season of the hunt. Sealing implements, used in winter, included a harpoon consisting of several sections of bone and wood with a blade of bone, copper, or trade iron, a butt of antler, a lanyard of sealskin or plaited sinew; a bone indicator; a scoop for clearing the hole; skewers for

closing wounds; a toggle for the dog to drag the seal home (fig. 7); and a fur tool bag, which also served as a foot pad (Birket-Smith 1945:172–178; Jenness 1946:115–142).

The spring and early summer economy centered on fishing through ice in lakes. Sometimes a large copper or iron hook was attached to the line, which wound around a curved rod. At other times the hook was substituted for by a lure of bear's tooth, and a leister was used to dispatch the fish. Later, during the summer run of char, fish were caught in weirs with a trident, and under conditions of plentiful supplies of fish a rake with curved copper prongs was brought into play (fig. 8) (Birket-Smith 1945:178–183; Jenness 1946:105–115).

Caribou were hunted chiefly with bow and arrow. The bows of spruce, antler, or musk-oxen horn were most often composite with the sections scarfed together with sinew. Invariably the bows were backed with a strip of sealskin and braided sinew (fig. 9). Arrows were

Fig. 7. Dog toggle. Used by the hunter in winter seal hunting when dogs are used to find breathing holes. The large loop hangs over the man's wrist and the small toggle goes into a loop at the end of the dog trace. Total length 30.0 cm, collected by Diamond Jenness, Bernard Harbour, N.W.T., 1914–1916.

Fig. 8. Fish rake used to catch arctic char. Two copper hooks inserted into a piece of antler lashed to a wooden handle. Put under water and pulled up with a jerk, the rake usually caught several fish on the spikes at each pass. Length 63.0 cm; collected by Diamond Jenness, Bernard Harbour, N.W.T., 1914–1916.

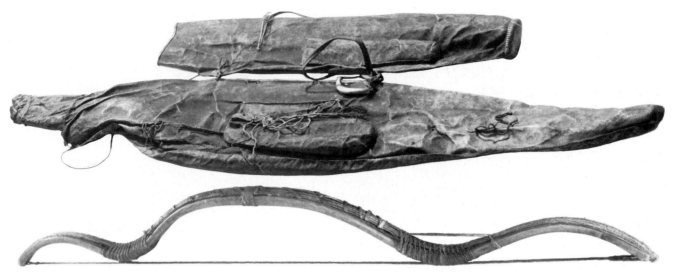

U. of Pa., U. Mus., Philadelphia: NA 4030.

Fig. 9. Bow and sealskin bowcase with attached quiver and snow knife sheath. Toggles and needles were also attached to the case. This bow is made of wood and is sinew-backed for strengthening; bows were sometimes made of several pieces of wood and also of musk-ox horn. The bowstring is twisted sinew. Length of bow 135.0 cm; collected by J. Bernard, Victoria I., N.W.T., 1915.

tipped with copper, iron, bone, or antler, and were feathered. The hunter carried his bow in a special sealskin case together with the quiver and a pouch or bag that contained a number of tools. When caribou were hunted at crossing places in kayaks a special lance was used, usually having a bone head and copper blade. If bears were encountered, the sealing harpoon or a lance improvised from a knife fastened to a pole were the usual weapons (Birket-Smith 1945:161–172; Jenness 1946:122–135).

Transport

Although dogs can be considered to have been chiefly hunting animals and few Copper Eskimos had more than two (Stefánsson 1919:238), they were, of course, used in transportation as well. During the summer they carried sizable loads on their backs, and in winter they pulled the heavily loaded sleds with the help of the men and women (fig. 10). The standard Copper Eskimo sled was comprised of wooden runners and a platform of cross slats. Jenness (1946:136) reports that the usual length was 14 to 15 feet. Runners were sometimes shoed with the rarely available whalebone, but more often mud or peat, which served as a base for the all-important icing, was placed on the wood (Birket-Smith 1945:183; Jenness 1946:5, 136–137).

Kayaks are to be considered more hunting implements than transportation devices in this area, though at times they would be used for ferrying across streams. The craft was rather longer but also lighter than most of the sea-going kayaks used in the western and eastern Arctic and was propelled with the familiar double-bladed paddle (Birket-Smith 1945:187–189; Jenness 1946:139–140).

Structures

Each season had its special form of shelter. The domed snowhouse was used from sometime in October until May. Composite forms of the snowhouse were relatively common, and Jenness (1922:65–76) shows a number of methods of enlarging or joining houses. Distinguishing the Copper Eskimo house from those used farther east was the use of straight-sided and flat-topped entranceways as opposed to a series of domes that formed the porches of the more eastern Central Eskimo houses. The platforms were covered with the skins of caribou, polar bear, and musk-oxen, with sleeping bags for two persons being the common cover (Jenness 1946:79). A variety of household utensils—soapstone lamps and cooking pots, bone skewers, the semilunar woman's knife, needles of copper, bone skin scrapers, baskets of willow twigs, skin clothing bags (fig. 11) and chamber pots—made up the furnishings (Birket-Smith 1945:189–192; Jenness 1946:55–79).

After a period of transition in May when the melting roofs of snowhouses were covered with skin, a heavy tent of caribou skin was used with a wall and entranceway of snow blocks. In summer lighter tents of caribou or sealskin were employed (fig. 13), some having a ridged construction and others being conical, much like a tepee (Jenness 1922:77–82; Birket-Smith 1945:191–192).

Clothing

Caribou skin had its most important use in clothing. The basic wardrobe was the double suit of summer-killed skins, the inner with fur inward and the outer with the fur on the outside. The inner suit was usually

Natl. Mus. of Canada, Ottawa: center, 38571; bottom, 43343.

Fig. 10. Land transportation. In the early period when only a few dogs were affordable, husband and wife helped pull the sled. Later, when more dogs could be fed and kept (because rifles increased productivity) teams of dogs came into use. top left, Peter Agliogoitok icing mud-coated sled runners. The sled dogs, at rest, are hitched in a Nome or Alaska-style hitch and may be wearing shoes to protect their paws from the sharp ice. top right, Rosie Kongyona and Patrick Ekalun loading their sled to move to their spring camp in June. top, Photographs by Fred Bruemmer, 1969. center, Sleds of Tree River natives heavily laden with equipment and game. The women help the dogs pull. Photograph by J.J. O'Neill, Oct. 1915. bottom, Summer packing of Coppermine River Eskimos on their way to Great Bear Lake. Shoulder strap and tumpline are used to carry their pack of skin and gear. The dogs are also heavily loaded, each carrying about 30–40 pounds of equipment (Jenness 1946:139). Photograph by Kenneth G. Chipman, Coronation Gulf, June 1916.

Fig. 11. Bag for clothing storage made of caribou leg fur strips sewed together with a round bottom. The top is closed with a leather drawstring. Men used smaller skin bags to hold their tools. Diameter 75.0 cm; collected by V. Stefánsson at Coronation Gulf, N.W.T., 1908–1912.

worn alone during the warmer months (fig. 14). Each man had, in addition, a very long coat for sealing and a lighter, elaborately trimmed swallowtail coat for ceremonial occasions (figs. 15–16). Slippers of sealskin were worn over two sets of fur stockings in winter (Birket-Smith 1945:141–151; Jenness 1946:11–34).

The woman's costume had exaggerated shoulders and hoods, and one-piece combination leggings and boots, features that set off the costume markedly from that of men (Birket-Smith 1945:152–157).

The material culture of the Copper Eskimo had a more fortunate base in raw materials than that of groups such as the Caribou Eskimo and the Netsiliks, given the accessibility of wooded areas, the good sources of soapstone, and the presence of copper.

Beliefs

The seasonal changes also had some indirect effect upon the belief system of the Copper Eskimo in that certain observances were related to the separation of land and sea animals, which was linked to seasonal exploitation. The Sedna myth was known in the area, the sea goddess being called Arnapkapfaaluk 'the big, bad woman.'

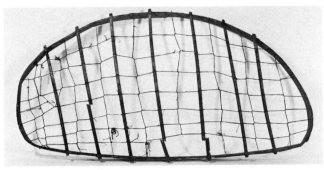

Fig. 12. Drying rack. Oval wooden frame with wood crosspieces and rawhide lacing, placed horizontally on wood supports above the lamp. Wet clothes were put on the frame to dry. Length about 116.8 cm; collected by Diamond Jenness, Bernard Harbour, N.W.T., 1914–1916.

However, the associated body of restrictions and observances was less complete than was the case farther east.

The seasonal aspect of the land-sea split was expressed in prohibition against sewing caribou skin clothing during the early winter at the beginning of the sealing season, but the association is most clearly with the period of darkness, for after the return of the sun in January it was again permissible to sew garments (Stefánsson 1913:266, 1919:48; Jenness 1922:182–184, 188; Rasmussen 1932:36).

Other regulations that bear more directly on the separation of land and sea mammal products include the following: products of the land and the sea must never be cooked in the same pot at the same time, seal blood cannot be used for splicing arrows intended for caribou hunting, and fresh seal meat cannot be placed on the side platform of the snowhouse alongside caribou meat (Rasmussen 1932:36–40).

Taboos related to women, which are fairly widespread in other Eskimo regions, are not so highly developed among the Copper Eskimo, especially with regard to menstruation, except that there is a rather elaborate set of observances surrounding childbirth (Rasmussen 1932:40–44). Another important life crisis event that is accompanied by ritual observances is the event of the boy's first kill of a seal, at which time the body of the seal is dragged over the boy's body by a relative (Damas 1962–1963).

Death was also accompanied by a series of observances with regard to handling the body. Burial was usually in the form of abandoning the body in a snowhouse in winter or wrapping it in skins and laying it on the surface in summer (Jenness 1922:171–172; Rasmussen 1932:44–47).

The shaman served as an intermediary between the people and the spirit world and was believed to receive his power from the *hilap inui* 'the spirits of the air'. Both men and women could be shamans though usually they were expected to have had some kind of visionary experience. Special tricks, including ventriloquism, had to be performed at intervals in order for the shaman to demonstrate his powers so that he would be trusted to have efficacy in performing his main functions of curing the sick, controlling the weather, improving hunting, and warding off evil spirits (Jenness 1922:9, 217; Rasmussen 1932:27–33).

The mythology of the Copper Eskimo contains, in addition to the Sedna myth, a number of epiclike tales and the pan-Eskimo hero, Kiviuq. The widespread myth of the mating of a dog with an Eskimo woman to produce White people and Indians is also known. The songs and stories of the Copper Eskimo have a number of motifs including hunger, man's impotence in the universe, hunting, vengeance, and death. Rasmussen (1932:5, 16) felt that the Copper Eskimo, especially the

Fig. 13. Summer tents made of deerskin, sealskin, or a combination and later of canvas. left, Tent on Banks Peninsula with bundles of black birch and willow fuel. Photograph by R.M. Anderson, May 1916. right, Woman cooking seal meat in front of her canvas tent. Photograph by Don Blair, Cambridge Bay, 1954.

Umingmaktuurmiut of the eastern part of the area, were very gifted poetically. The ethnography (Jenness 1924a; Roberts and Jenness 1925; Rasmussen 1932) contains an impressive collection of myths and songs, indicating that this phase of culture was significantly represented among the Copper Eskimo.

History

The period from first effective contact in 1910 until about 1925 was one of transition from a stabilized tra-

ditional economy, society, and culture to an altered but perhaps equally stable "contact-traditional" situation (Helm and Damas 1963).

The exploratory journey of Stefánsson in 1910–1911 and the presence of the Canadian Arctic Expedition in 1914–1917 were important factors, but the influx of goods brought by trading ships from the west and the establishment of a number of trading posts in the Coronation Gulf area during the early 1920s (Usher 1971:101–105) were the chief determinants of changes in material culture, economy, and social organization.

Fig. 14. Clothing. left, Dressing-up for the dance of welcome. A family from Prince Albert Sound had arrived to visit and trade at a camp on Tahiryuak Lake, Victoria I. They danced the first evening they were together (Jenness 1922:52). The clothing shows the beginning of a transition from all skin to part cloth, the checked garments being made from trade cloth. Photograph by Diamond Jenness, 1915. right, Manigurin and her baby, Itayuk, in coat hood. She wears undecorated inner garments. Photograph by J.R. Cox, May 1916.

408

Missionization moved slowly after the first Roman Catholic priests were killed near Bloody Falls in 1913 and the Rev. H. Girling of the Church of England entered the area in 1915. The RCMP became involved in the investigation of the frequent homicides in the area at about the same time and established a post at Tree River in the early 1920s (Jenness 1922:10, 31; Rasmussen 1932:61–65).

Already during Jenness's stay, 1914–1916, the use of rifles had begun to alter the seasonal economic cycle in the western part of the area with the sealing grounds being abandoned about a month earlier for caribou hunts on both sides of Dolphin and Union Strait. By 1923–1924 numbers of Copper Eskimos were spending a substantial part of the winter inland (Ostermann 1942:36–42), while the basic breathing-hole sealing economy persisted both in the eastern part of Copper Eskimo country and in the Dolphin and Union Strait region and would do so for a number of years to come (Rasmussen 1932; Hoare 1927; Damas 1972b). The steel trap, fish net, and the rifle together made life away from the sea feasible, and by some time in the 1930s the bulk of the population south of Coronation Gulf and Queen Maud Sound camped throughout the winter on lakes in the interior. Caribou were taken at all seasons when they were present. In direct reversal of the aboriginal economic cycle a descent to the sea was usually made for part of the summer and seals were taken from small wooden boats (Damas 1972b).

Greater mobility on trap lines and for caribou hunting and for travel in general was made possible by the increased number of dogs that could be supported, each Eskimo hunter having a team of five, six, or more dogs as compared to one to three for the aboriginal period. Trade goods become an important part of the material culture. Rifles, nets, traps, steel knives, canvas tents, and cloth clothing (for summer wear) were all superior to their counterpart equipment in the native inventory. Consumable goods were restricted largely to tobacco, tea, flour, and ammunition with diet continuing to be based on various game foods.

Changes in settlement pattern have been noted in the inland emphasis and the gradual abandonment of the sea ice encampment. Settlement size and composition most closely resembled the summer hunting groups, among the aboriginal group types, both with regard to average size of 10 to 20 and in the irregular sorts of kinship bonds operating together with fortuitous factors in group composition (Damas 1972b).

The *piqatiγiˑt* network faded as emphasis on breathing-hole sealing declined, but communal eating continued to be important for distributing food as well as presenting opportunities for social interaction. A number of voluntary alliances persisted, and child betrothal and adoption continued in force into the 1960s as did spouse exchange. Female infanticide appears to have

been practiced until about 1940 (Damas 1972b). The lack of leadership that characterized the aboriginal period was somewhat supplanted by the influence of the traders, the RCMP, and the missionaries, as the Copper Eskimo began to be peripherally involved in the economic, legal, and religious systems of Canadian society (Damas 1972b).

Another influence in the area that began during the exploratory period of the early part of the twentieth century was the influx of western Eskimos. They introduced changes in clothing styles, the use of the Nome or paired-dog hitch, and instruction in the use of trap lines. Intermarriage also occurred, largely between Copper Eskimo women and western Eskimo men.

Beginning about 1955 a new phase of Copper Eskimo history began with the increasing concentration of population in a small number of focal communities. In the east, Cambridge Bay became the chief settlement, though the all-native camp survived in southeast Victoria Island, around Bathurst Inlet and Perry Island, for another 10 years. In the west, Coppermine developed into a sprawling community of several hundred Copper Eskimos in addition to an increasing number of Whites. Holman Island and Read Island (abandoned in 1962) were smaller centralized communities in the west (Abrahamson et al. 1964; Usher 1965).

Motives for centralization were varied. One important force was the wage labor offered by the construction of the military Distant Early Warning line. The growth of the community at Cambridge Bay, which was a main radar site, was especially affected by this factor. The decline in numbers of caribou was certainly a prominent factor that began to make camp life in the interior precarious by the 1950s. In some areas, as around Bathurst Inlet, the shortage of caribou effected a reorientation to the sea, and settlement shifted more and more to coastal sites. Elsewhere, as around Cambridge Bay, and in the west around Coppermine, centralization followed in the wake of the caribou depopulation. The uncertainty of the market and supply of the white fox also became acute in the same period and resulted in the decline of the fur trade. The services offered in the new communities, such as health care, welfare, and education, together with the socializing and entertainment possibilities, all acted as attractions. In the beginning housing was comprised mainly of shacks constructed from scrap lumber from dumps of DEW-line sites, but by 1965 nearly all the Copper Eskimo who were living in the centralized communities had been supplied with insulated, oil-heated, frame houses by the government (Damas 1972b).

Centralization in the three main communities of Holman Island, Coppermine, and Cambridge Bay proceeded rapidly with the abandonment of Hudson's Bay Company posts at Read Island in 1962 and in the Bathurst Inlet area in 1970. The last of the Perry River

Natl. Mus. of Canada, Ottawa: 36914.

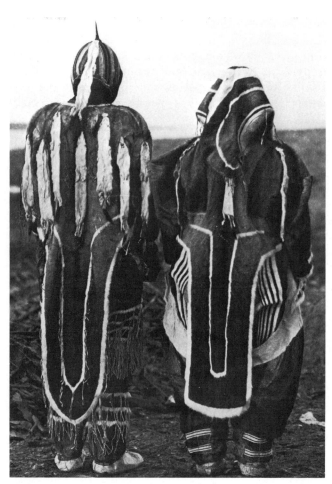

Fig. 15. Back view of traditional dance costumes worn by Ikpakhuak and his wife Higilak, Tahiryuak Lake (for front view see Jenness 1922: frontispiece). For a description of a dance in which Ikpakhuak and Higilak participated see Jenness (1922:224–225). The man's coat is hoodless, with ermine pelts down the back. His striped peaked cap has a loon's bill rising from the top and an ermine pelt hanging from the base (Birket-Smith 1945:142, 150). Photograph by George H. Wilkins, 1915.

people left that region in 1968, and by 1971 people from all the southeastern Victoria Island camps had moved to Cambridge Bay, with only a few families remaining on the land in the Bathurst area through the 1970s (Farquharson 1976; Momatiuk and Eastcott 1977). Trapping and hunting excursions continued to be important from the main centers of settlement with the snowmobile largely replacing the dog sled. Use of this vehicle obviated the need for amassing large quantities of meat for dog food, but it also brought on some tight budgetary demands, considering the high initial expenditure and the rising fuel costs (T.G. Smith 1973a, 1979–1980). Carving and handicrafts accounted for some cash income, and a momentary boom in the sealskin market during the 1960s and 1970s brought on resurgences in seal hunting that faded rapidly as prices fell again (Damas 1972b; T.G. Smith 1973).

Younger children attended primary schools in the communities within the area, but residential high schools were in Inuvik and Yellowknife. Experiences at these places brought on problems of adjustment for youths, with considerable disorientation a result when they returned to their homes (Hobart 1970). Other problems of Arctic community living included those of inadequate water and sewage facilities, and by the late 1970s, further housing needs (Kay 1979).

By the early 1960s there was little left of the externals of Copper Eskimo culture, and that condition has continued to prevail. Fur clothing was seldom evident, with European costumes often reflecting style as much as adaptive utility. Outboard motors and plywood canoes have long replaced the kayak, and the number of sled dogs declined steadily. Motion pictures, canned foods, alcoholic beverages, and radios were all important parts of the visible culture in the 1980s. Religion became more immediate as people centralized near the missions, with evangelical missionaries competing with the efforts of the Church of England and the Catholic workers.

The temporary population decline in the period 1924–1941 was followed by recovery after 1941 according to census figures: 1941, 793; 1951, 919; 1956, 900; 1961, 939; 1963, 1,115 (Abrahamson et al. 1964:19). These figures do not accurately reflect natural increase, since a number of Western Eskimos and a few Netsiliks moved into the area. The 1963 figure probably includes 900 to 950 who can actually be considered Copper Eskimo.

Precise census figures for the 1970s are difficult to

Natl. Mus. of Canada, Ottawa: a, IV-D-963; f, IV-D-1644; U. of Pa., U. Mus., Philadelphia: b, NA 4232; c, NA 4234; d, NA 4243; e, NA 4233. top right, Nationalmuseet, Copenhagen: 2274.

Fig. 16. Clothing and dancing. The finest clothes are worn for dances. a, Woman's caribou fur outer parka with narrow bands of red dyed skin edged and dotted with running stitches of white skin down the front. Men's and women's parkas are similar except the woman's has broader shoulders and a hood that is almost a bag. b, Woman's caribou skin boots with decorative fur bands and fringe. The straps at the top supported them from the belt. c, Sealskin shoes with decorative crimping at the toe and heal. (Plain shoes were also made.) A casing around the top edge has a drawstring. d, Woman's trousers with vertical striping on the front, plain in the rear. e, Loonskin dance cap. A luxury item owned by a few, they were lent freely during the evening entertainment, being worn by men and women. The cap is caribou fur with bands of red, white, and black dyed skin; this example has 2 loon beaks and feathers with an ermine skin at the rear that the dancer tries to rotate, synchronizing its swing to the rhythm of the drum. f, Drum, the only musical instrument used, with short and heavy wooden drumstick. top right, Dance of natives of Dolphin and Union Strait given at a farewell celebration for members of the Fifth Thule Expedition. The dancer, accompanied by a drum, sings songs he composed and owns. Others in the group may join in the refrain. Photograph by Leo Hansen, 1924. a, Collected by Diamond Jenness, Bernard Harbour, N.W.T., 1914–1916. b–e, Collected by J. Bernard, Coppermine River, N.W.T., 1915. f, Collected by Bernard at Coronation Gulf, N.W.T., before 1921. a, Width at shoulders 75.0 cm, b–d and f same scale. e, Height 36.0 cm.

a

b

c

d

e

f

411

Fig. 17. Scissors with sinew-wrapped ivory handles and metal shears attached with rivets. The prototypes were acquired probably as early as the mid-19th century from Hudson Bay natives who got them through the Hudson's Bay Company and whalers (Jenness 1946:96). Scissors were probably used for cutting hair and sewing. Length 13.0 cm; collected by J. Bernard from a grave at Cape Hamilton, N.W.T., 1915.

Fig. 18. Playing at building a snowhouse, a teenage boy and girl at Colville hills, Victoria I., making houses of pebbles. Photograph by Diamond Jenness, 1913–1918.

Fig. 19. Parka with fur mosaic work. This nontraditional woman's top is for wearing over a cloth dress. Length 116.0 cm; made in Coppermine, N.W.T., 1948.

abstract, but table 2 gives population data for settlements in the traditional Copper Eskimo territory.

Applying the 1978 percentages to the 1979 numbers yields a population of about 1,750 Inuit in the area. Again, this number can only approximate a Copper Eskimo population since not only has there been intermarriage with, and immigration of, people from other tribes, but also there may be people of Copper Eskimo ancestry living outside the area. However, it is clear from even these rough figures that the population explosion continued through the 1970s. A continued high birth rate and infant survival is also indicated in that about 40 percent of the population was below the age of 15 in the 1978 figures (Devine and Wood 1981).

Conclusion

The traditional Copper Eskimo represented a close approach to popular stereotypes of a generalized Eskimo. It is true that many features of common Eskimo heritage did obtain: the language, general inventories of tools,

methods of hunting, a large part of the kinship terminology, a great part of the oral culture and religious beliefs, the importance of betrothal and adoption, all bear the unmistakable stamp of pan-Eskimo culture. Other features were not so widely shared in the Eskimo area but were held in common with Central Eskimo groups: the use of the snowhouse as the only winter dwelling, the general outlines of the year's economic cycle with its special emphases on caribou hunting and breathing-hole sealing, the nearly exclusive use of caribou skin in clothing, and the nomadic settlement pattern. Still other features show distinctness among the Copper Eskimo. Among these are the wide use of copper in implements (fig. 20), distinctive tailoring of clothing, and the complex of the nuclear family household, fragmentation of summer hunting groups, and the nar-

Table 2. Population of Copper Eskimo Settlements, 1971–1979

Settlement	1971	1979	Percent Inuit in 1978
Holman Island	241	336	88.4
Coppermine	637	766	91.7
Cambridge Bay	743	864	76.8
Bathurst Inlet	82	96	100.0

SOURCE: Devine and Wood 1981.

Natl. Mus. of Canada, Ottawa: a, IV-D-427; b, IV-D-1476; c, IV-D-439; d, IV-D-432; e, IV-D-1635. Glenbow-Alberta Inst., Calgary, Alta.: f, AB788; g, AB787; h, AB761.

Fig. 20. Copper tools. Copper, considered a type of stone by the natives, was worked into shape by cold hammering. It was used in place of stone, bone, or ivory in many implements: a, Woman's knife with antler handle; iron replaced copper when it became available. b, Adz with antler handle and sealskin lashings. c, Skin scraper. d, Knife, imitating a European example, used for cutting snow. e, Lance; f, ice pick; g, knife; h, knife with sharpener attached. Length of h 24.5 cm, rest same scale. a–d, collected by Diamond Jenness, Bernard Harbour, N.W.T., 1914–1916; e, by J. Bernard before 1921; f–h, by S.T. Wood, 1919–1924.

row scope of kinship-directed behavioral norms (Damas 1969b).

The influence of seasonality in climate and resources is especially important as a determinant of Copper Eskimo culture and society. Broad ecological factors made their contribution, but historical processes that had little to do with ecology were also influential (Damas 1969a). Only a careful comparative study can attempt to isolate these various determinants.

Although aboriginal trade routes linked the Copper Eskimo with both eastern and western contact influences through other tribes, during the period of most intensive contact in the twentieth century they fell solidly within the western scope of influence both through the trading operations of Whites entering the area from the Pacific side and also through the Western Eskimos who contributed substantially to the contact-traditional Copper Eskimo culture.

The problems that faced the Copper Eskimo during the 1960s and 1970s were little different from those that were encountered by most other Eskimos of Canada in the same period.

Synonymy

Although Stefánsson (1919:33) has usually been given credit for naming the Copper Eskimo (because of the extensive use of float copper in their implements), there is an earlier use of the term as a synonym by Schwatka (1884:543): "Still farther west are the Kidnelik (copper Eskimo)." This designation has dominated ethnological writings, but terms used by other Eskimo groups are also worthy of note. The Netsilik and other groups to the east refer to them as Killinirmiut, translated by Rasmussen (1932:12) as 'the people of the boundary (Victoria Island)'. Schwatka's Kidnelik is presumably a garbled form of the place-name Killiniq, the basis of this group name. Stefánsson (1913:162, 1919:24) indicates that the Mackenzie Delta Eskimo called the Copper Eskimo Nagyuktogmiut (*naɣyuktu·ɣmiut* 'the people of the caribou antler'), a term that he later found to apply more accurately to a small subgroup of Copper Eskimo.

Sources

Several exploratory parties passed through the area during the nineteenth century. The expeditions of John Franklin, John Richardson, Thomas Simpson, Robert McClure, and Richard Collinson helped explore the coastlines of the country, but only Collinson's had more than fleeting contact with people, and none of the early accounts contributes significantly to the ethnography of the Copper Eskimo.

Hanbury's (1904) account of his journey through the area in 1903 gives only slight information about the Copper Eskimo. Stefánsson's visit to the western part of the area in 1910–1911 produced the first important ethnography, which is represented in both popular (Stefánsson 1913) and professional (Stefánsson 1919) publications. The most important source for the Copper Eskimo is Jenness (1922, 1923, 1923b, 1924, 1924a, 1928, 1944, 1946; Roberts and Jenness 1925), whose nine volumes probably represent the most complete ethnography of any Eskimo group. Rasmussen's (1932) account from the eastern part of Copper Eskimo country is also important since it covers regions not visited by the above-mentioned anthropologists.

After Rasmussen's visit in 1923–1924 the only information for a long period came from popular sources (Finnie 1940; R. Harrington 1952; de Coccola and King 1956), and government reports (Hoare 1927; Reports of the RCMP 1917–1918, 1919–1962).

Damas spent a year with the Copper Eskimo in 1962–1963 and paid two brief visits to that group in 1965. This chapter and Damas (1972b) are the main sources based on this fieldwork. Abrahamson et al. (1964) and Usher (1965) provide important historical information and depict the situation of the 1960s for the area. Condon (1982) describes the effects of seasonal variations on interpersonal conflict at Holman Island as well as reveals some more general aspects of Copper Eskimo social adjustments.

Netsilik

ASEN BALIKCI

Environment and Territory

The habitat of the Netsilik (ˌnet'sīlĭk) covers an immense area from Committee Bay in the east to Victoria Strait to the west, and from Bellot Strait in the north to Garry Lake to the south (fig. 1). This part of the Arctic contains large land masses: the generally flat King William Island, Adelaide and Simpson peninsulas, and Boothia Peninsula covered by rocky Precambrian hills. The coast is cut by ocean inlets and lined by islands. Lakes and rivers abound. The area lies entirely in the arctic tundra biogeographical zone. Lichens, mosses, and various grasslike plants cover the tundra and hills. The climate is rigorous, winters are cold, and in midwinter the sea ice is six to seven feet thick. Summers are short, cool, and misty. Precipitation is low.

The Netsilik speak a variety of Inuit-Inupiaq Eskimo quite similar to that of their neighbors on both sides.*

The Netsilik comprised several nomadic bands, each identified with a particular hunting area. Since movement of people among bands is frequent, as was temporary or permanent emigration outside the Netsilik area, the composition of local bands is variable and their social boundaries elastic. There are no precise territorial boundaries either; a band's geographic area is best defined by a number of strategic hunting-camping sites. The band nomenclature given below follows Rasmussen's (1931:8) survey of 1923, with references to band movements for earlier times.

*The phonemes of Netsilik Eskimo are: (voiceless stops) *p, t, k, q, ʔ*; (voiced fricatives) *v, y, ž, γ, γ̇* ([ŋ] before nasals); (voiceless fricatives) *h* ([s] after stops); (nasals) *m, n, ŋ;* (lateral) *l*; (short vowels) *i, a, u;* (long vowels) *iˑ, aˑ, uˑ*.

In the practical orthography generally in use the Netsilik phonemes are written: p, t, k, q, '; v, j, z̧, g, r; s, h; m, n, ng; l; i, a, u; ii, aa, uu.

Information on Netsilik Eskimo phonology and the transcription of words is from Anthony C. Woodbury and Webster and Zibell (1976:276). Rasmussen's (1931) orthography was influenced by Greenlandic, and there may be some errors in the *Handbook* transcriptions based on them. The name Nârssuk was available only in its Greenlandic spelling.

Group names used as English designations are in the practical orthography, but with y instead of j. For groups associated with the Netsilik spellings with h are used rather than the corresponding s of some other dialects; hence Hinimiut rather than Sinimiut, Hanningayurmiut rather than Saningajormiut.

The easternmost Netsilik group is the Arviligyuarmiut in Pelly Bay, Simpson Peninsula, and the area immediately south. There is some evidence that traditionally this southern region was inhabited by a distinct group called Hinimiut, which disappeared in 1902–1903 following an epidemic (Boas 1888; Birket-Smith 1945:16). Beginning in the 1870s many eastern Netsilik moved eastward to Repulse Bay, attracted by the whalers and, later, by the establishment of a trading post.

The hunting grounds of the Netsilik proper (or Natsilingmiut) were located around Boothia Isthmus and Willersted Lake. This group moved westward during the second half of the nineteenth century, evidently motivated by a search for driftwood, which was lacking on Boothia Peninsula. In their wandering they displaced the Ugyulingmiut (called Ogluli Eskimos by Amundsen 1908), who at one time occupied Adelaide Peninsula and King William Island. At the time of the Thule Expedition, in 1923, these two areas were inhabited, respectively, by the Ilivilirmiut and the Qiqiqtarmiut. The Kuungmiut lived along Murchison River and around Shepherd Bay, while the group located northwest of Boothia Isthmus was called Killirmiut. Still farther north, around Bellot Strait, resided the Arviqtuurmiut, an unstable group reported to consist mostly of murderers and wife-stealers (Rasmussen 1931:88). The people at Back River, as inland dwellers, have certain distinct cultural characteristics, yet they can be considered as part of the Netsilik group. At the time of the Fifth Thule Expedition the Utkuhikhalingmiut lived near the mouth of the river, the Hanningayurmiut farther up the course of Back River, and the Uvaliarlit resided mostly around Garry Lake.

There is little agreement on the band movements of the Back River people during the nineteenth century. According to local tradition the ancestors of the Utkuhikhalingmiut and probably also of the other two groups lived on Adelaide Peninsula and around Queen Maud Gulf. According to Rasmussen (1931:473) a famine at an unspecified time determined the survivors to seek refuge at the rich fishing sites of Back River, where they were joined by the Ugyulingmiut, who were fleeing for the same reason. Earlier explorers (Gilder 1881:77) emphasize the hostility toward neighboring Netsilik. Briggs (1970:13ff.) considers the movement south to have been gradual and motivated primarily by economic 415 reasons, namely the desire to obtain guns from the trading post at Baker Lake.

External Relations

Rae (1850:121) mentions that the Aivilingmiut (Iglulik) around Repulse Bay were fearful of Netsilik hostility, but by the 1920s peaceful visiting prevailed (Rasmussen 1931:11). Relations between the Netsilik and the Killinirmiut (Copper Eskimos) from Victoria Island to the west were usually hostile with mutual accusations of ferocity and treachery (Jenness 1922:49; Rasmussen 1931:50, 73, 76). However, there is evidence of barter activities between the two groups near Melbourne Island, the Netsilik acquiring driftwood and native copper in exchange for iron knives and harpoon heads locally made from the abundant supply of iron left by the ship of John Ross (Jenness 1922:49, 150; Rasmussen 1931:27, 481). Further, the Pelly Bay and Back River people were in the habit of undertaking long sledge journeys south to Akiliniq near the Thelon River, where they met with Caribou Eskimos from whom they obtained wood (Rasmussen 1931:26, 489).

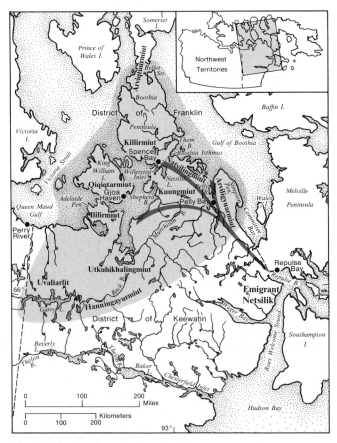

Fig. 1. Tribal territory in the early 20th century with subgroups at different historical periods. Arrows show Netsilik movement between 1860 and 1920.

Culture

Technology

The Netsilik bands shared basically the same material, social, and intellectual culture. The following will describe this common pattern with only occasional references to regional differences easily explicable by the uneven distribution of resources and wide separation of bands.

In reference to the raw materials employed, the material culture of the Netsilik can be divided into four major technological complexes: snow and ice, skin, bone, and stone (Balikci 1970). The snow and ice complex mostly found application in architecture: igloos, their porches and entrances, beds and kitchen tables, high meat stands outside, and shelters for the sealskin sleds were all made of snow. Ice slabs were used as window panels, and the runners of the sleds were covered with ice. Often in the fall rectangular icehouses were built and covered with skin roofs. The tools associated with the snow complex were the snow knife made of caribou antler, the snow shovel with an antler frame (fig. 2), the bone pointed ice chisel, and the ice scoop.

The skin complex implied several techniques for processing caribou fur and sealskin: these techniques included stretching, drying, scraping, softening, occasionally shaving and sewing (Rasmussen 1931:179). Depending on the utilization of the skin, different curing methods were employed. Tailored clothing for all seasons (both inner and outer coats) (fig. 3) was made of caribou fur, except for summer boots and kayakers' jackets of sealskin (Birket-Smith 1945:22ff.). Further utilization of sealskin was in summer tents (fig. 4), kayak covers, sledge building, mattresses, various containers for water and oil, and, most important, thongs mainly for packing and dog harnessing. Caribou sinew was used for threading material. The main tools for skin work were the woman's semilunar knife, a variety of iron-tipped or bone scrapers, and the bone and caribou sinew needle.

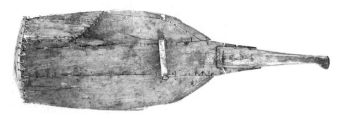

U. i Oslo, Etnografisk Mus.: 15,894.

Fig. 2. Snow shovel made of thin pieces of wood joined with sinew; the edges, blade, and a cross grip are of antler. It is used in the last phase of snowhouse construction to shovel loose snow around the base of the wall and for building platforms and in midwinter to cover the whole house with snow for insulation. Length 90.5 cm; collected by Roald Amundsen on King William I., N.W.T., 1903–1905.

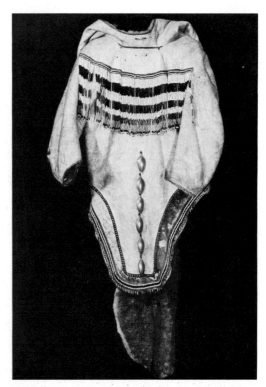

left and center, Scott Polar Research Inst., U. of Cambridge, England; right, Amer. Mus. of Nat. Hist., New York: 60/4663.

Fig. 3. Clothing. left, Man, wearing skin parka with long flap down the back, trousers with fur side out, holding a fishing leister. center, Kakikagiu (Kakikakiu) a native of Akullee, about 25 years old, wearing fur parka with long flap in back and shorter flap in front, both fringed. She has chin and forehead tattooed and has her hair made up in hairsticks. Ross (1835, App.:39) reported that she had 2 husbands. Watercolors by John Ross, 1829–1833. right, Woman's parka with fur on inside, decorated with trade items—spoons, fringed border of beads, and pieces of metal. There is no baby pouch. Back length, hood to bottom, 166.0 cm; collected by George Comer, 1902.

The bone complex comprised the manufacture of tools, weapons, and transportation devices made of bone (mostly antler), some driftwood, and later iron (Birket-Smith 1945:102ff.). Every man owned a tool kit including a bow drill, adz, saw, and whittling and splitting knives. Considering the extreme scarcity of driftwood, the Netsilik relied greatly on bone antler and musk-ox bone as the essential materials to make sealing harpoons and harpoon points, tool handles, the composite bow, arrow points, leisters and fishing harpoons, spear and ice chisel points, ice scoops, the many specialized instruments associated with breathing-hole seal hunting (VandeVelde 1958), and cross bars for sledges (fig. 6). Sections of driftwood were pieced together to make spear shafts, kayak frames, and tent poles.

The stone complex included the rectangular cooking pot and semilunar oil lamp carved in soapstone (fig. 7) (Birket-Smith 1945:89) and the utilization of stones for tent rings, cairns, graves, and various stands.

A precise division of labor following sex lines was associated with the handling of the technological complexes. Practically all work on snow was done by men, although women used the snow shovel to heap loose snow over the igloos and to repair leaking rooftops. Similarly, work on bone, wood, iron, and stone was a male task. Almost the whole of the skin complex fell in the women's domain with the exception of scraping and softening caribou fur skins, which was performed by men. Ownership rights did not affect closely this sexual division of labor. Household furnishings including pots and lamps, the tools associated with the processing of skins, and summer tents belonged to women; men owned their tools and weapons, sledges, and kayaks (Balikci 1964:39).

With these four technological complexes, the Netsilik were able to exploit the resources of the area, protect themselves from and adapt to the rigorous climate and environment.

Subsistence

In aboriginal times the Netsilik lived almost entirely by hunting and fishing. The year was divided into a sea mammal hunting season in winter and spring and a fishing and land animal hunting phase in summer and fall. This dual adaptation had profound effects on the social organization, band structure, and intellectual culture of the Netsilik (Rasmussen 1931:142–182).

In midwinter, around December or January, after the completion of their new winter clothes, the Netsilik left their fall fishing sites and set up large snowhouse settlements in the bays and inlets where seal hunting was

417

Natl. Film Board of Canada Phototheque, Ottawa: top, 64-2370; center, 64-2371; bottom, 64-2380.

Fig. 4. Breaking summer camp in the Pelly Bay area after fishing at the weir has been exhausted. The skin tent is made of seal skins. A ring of heavy boulders marks the floor of the tent and the sealskin thongs are fastened to the ring stones to secure the tent from the gale winds. top, Packing skins on a staff to be carried on the back. A metal pot and skin container (water pail?) are to the right. center, Collapsed tent. bottom, Strapping a load on the dog's back. Frequent stops will be made to adjust the packs of dogs and people as they move over the marshy tundra (Balikci 1970:26–31). Photographs by Douglas Wilkinson, Aug. 1963.

U. i Oslo, Etnografisk Mus.: top, 16,183; bottom 16,184.

Fig. 5. Hair sticks, tapered wooden rods with skin caps at base used by women to create a distinctive hairstyle, stiffening and lengthening their own hair. Worn in pairs, half of the hair is wound around each and is then wrapped with a strip of caribou fur, as here, or of decorated fur and cloth. Length about 37.0 cm; collected by Roald Amundsen on King William I., N.W.T., 1903–1905.

to be conducted under the new sea ice. Sealing at the breathing holes was a highly developed art among the Netsilik and necessitated the collaboration of numerous hunters (Rasmussen 1931:159). This aggregation was needed because of certain biogeographic characteristics of the seal. This air-breathing mammal keeps open a number of breathing holes through the thick ice and may use any one of them. Thus, the larger the number of hunters attending each particular breathing hole in a restricted area, the better the chances for a speedy catch. Each hunter carried his special seal-hunting implements: the thrusting harpoon, made entirely of antler reinforced with sealskin thongs and provided at one end with an ice-pick used to enlarge the breathing hole after the seal had been caught; the harpoon point, generally made of antler or bear bone; the down or the

Natl. Film Board of Canada Phototheque, Ottawa: 65-2696.

Fig. 6. Making a sledge at Pelly Bay. Driftwood was rare so wooden sledges were not common. Runners were made from frozen fish wrapped in sealskin with caribou antler pieces tied as crossbars with sealskin lines. A sludge of pulverized moss and water was then put on the underside of the runner in a thick coat, frozen, coated with ice, and rubbed with wet polar bear fur to produce a hard, resistant coat of ice that allowed the sledge to run smoothly (Balikci 1970:48–49). Photograph by Douglas Wilkinson, Aug. 1963.

U. i Oslo, Etnografisk Mus: left, 15,550; bottom right, 15,562; top right, Natl. Mus. of Canada, Ottawa: IV-C-1731.

Fig. 7. Household utensils. left, Soapstone cooking kettle with holes at the top for suspension over a lamp. bottom right, Soapstone lamp, used to heat the cooking pot, placed on pieces of wood set into the surface of the snow platform inside the house. A piece of sealskin might be put under the lamp to absorb oil seepage. Oil is burned in a wick of moss or other material. top right, Lamp used for illumination inside the snowhouse. Such lamps were usually smaller than those for cooking. Length 52.5 cm, rest same scale. Collected by J. Bernard, Adelaide Peninsula, N.W.T., before 1921. left and bottom right collected by Roald Amundsen on King William I., N.W.T., 1903–1905.

horn indicators; two kinds of breathing-hole searchers for examining the orientation of the hole; and the ice scoop (fig. 9) (for a detailed description of this kit see VandeVelde 1958; Rasmussen 1931:151–161). The hunters spread in a fan formation, each man holding a dog on leash whose fine sense of smell could locate the seal's breathing hole under the snow cover. After the elaborate preparation of the breathing holes the watch began and lasted usually for several hours.

The usually very successful seal hunts at the open breathing holes began near the end of May when the ice was free of snow cover. All able-bodied Eskimos participated—men, women, and older children (Rasmussen 1931:160). Those who lacked harpoons were armed with sticks, and they simply pushed the seal back into the water until it came up again at a hole watched by a harpooner. Two seal-hunting techniques for individual hunters were also practiced during the spring. While stalking the seal, the hunter lying on the wet ice imitated the movements and sounds of the dozing seal who lay near the breathing hole and managed to crawl close enough for the kill (Rasmussen 1931:160). The second technique took place in the twilight of the arctic night. The seal spends the night in the sea water, under the ice, and has the peculiar habit of coming up early in the morning through the same breathing hole from

which he previously descended. The hunter first located this specific hole from a distance and then set up a watch above it for the rest of the night; then he harpooned the surfacing seal when it rose to breathe on the following morning.

Two localized sealing methods were also practiced. At Queen Maud Gulf a group of hunters stalked the large bearded seal cautiously, then at a distance of 100 yards or less they all jumped and screamed wildly and rushed at the seal, which was generally so stupefied and terrified by the noise that it could not move but remained paralyzed on the ice until harpooned (Balikci 1959–1960). The second technique was employed at Thom Bay where sea currents formed cracks in the ice used by the seals as natural breathing points. The hunter built an igloo over such a crack, covered it with snow, and chiseled out an artificial breathing hole, which somehow fascinated and attracted the seal to a position under the waiting harpooner (Rasmussen 1931:161).

Caribou hunting took place mostly in summer and fall when the migrating herds were heading south (Rasmussen 1931:169–178). Techniques for hunting the caribou (fig. 10) were essentially the same as those in other Central Eskimo areas (see "Caribou Eskimo," this volume).

Fishing was conducted in all seasons but rarely in midwinter (Rasmussen 1931:184). In early August schools of arctic char swimming upstream were caught at stone weirs that blocked the shallow rivers. The fish were speared in the central basin of the weir with the three-pronged leister and immediately strung on a line (figs. 11–12). No coordination of efforts took place in the central basin; every fisherman hurried to maximize his catch. Another method was employed in the fall: holes were cut through the thin river ice, the arctic char attracted with decoys and speared with the leister. These two were the most rewarding fishing methods. Secondary techniques included throwing the fishing harpoon with a detachable point from prominent rocks, fishing

Natl. Mus. of Canada, Ottawa: IV-C-2789.

Fig. 8. Blubber pounder of musk-ox horn with flattened striking surface and finger depressions cut into the handle end. It is used in winter to break down the fat in frozen blubber for the oil burned in lamps. Length 17.0 cm; collected by L.T. Burwash at Pelly Bay, N.W.T., 1925–1926.

with a barbless iron hook fixed in a bone sinker, and leaving a gorge wrapped in caribou meat in the water during the night (Birket-Smith 1945:70–75).

Musk-oxen were occasionally stalked in the fall and winter by small groups of hunters with the help of dogs (Ross 1835:350; Rasmussen 1931:182). When in danger the herd forms a circle with the males at the periphery facing the enemy and protecting the females and the young behind. The Netsilik first shot arrows at a bull. The enraged animal left the circle and charged but was quickly kept at bay by the dogs. The hunters then attacked the isolated animal with heavy spears.

Seldom were polar bears hunted and then preferably in spring, at the end of hibernation (Rasmussen 1931:183; Amundsen 1908:41). A spear was used to drive the bear out of the den as it was kept at bay by the dogs, the hunters attacking first with arrows and then with barbless harpoons and spears.

Other animals were of secondary importance. Foxes, wolverines, hares, and marmots were occasionally trapped and snared (Rasmussen 1931:187). Ptarmigan were shot with the blunt arrow point, the wild fowl were caught barehanded or stoned during the moulting period, and sea gulls were snared.

Gathering involved some berry picking in late August and the collecting of sea gull eggs in early June.

Among Netsilik bands the material culture of the Utkuhikhalingmiut around 1900 resembled most closely that of the Caribou Eskimos, the similarities reflecting a common inland adaptation (Rasmussen 1931:489 ff.).

Fig. 10. Rocks built up "like men" used to help channel the caribou into confined areas where they were hunted with bow and arrow. They "were erected in a row on top of a ridge leading to a lake. At the end of the line of cairns and near the lake the archers lay in ambush, concealed behind low piles of stones. The beaters, using wolf cries, drove the caribou down the line of cairns toward the concealed archers, who then attacked the caribou with a barrage of arrows" (Balikci 1970:41). Photograph by Richard Harrington, Spence Bay, 1951.

The hook-spear made of horn is an important instrument used at the stone weir. In early autumn an original and complex fishing technique was employed: a conical basin cut in the river ice and covered by a snow hut attracted the salmon trout caught with a leister (Rasmussen 1931:485). There is evidence that musk-ox hunting might have been an important yet sporadic activity

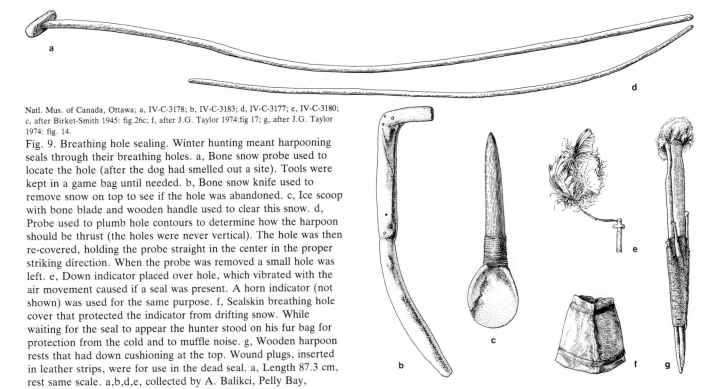

Fig. 9. Breathing hole sealing. Winter hunting meant harpooning seals through their breathing holes. a, Bone snow probe used to locate the hole (after the dog had smelled out a site). Tools were kept in a game bag until needed. b, Bone snow knife used to remove snow on top to see if the hole was abandoned. c, Ice scoop with bone blade and wooden handle used to clear this snow. d, Probe used to plumb hole contours to determine how the harpoon should be thrust (the holes were never vertical). The hole was then re-covered, holding the probe straight in the center in the proper striking direction. When the probe was removed a small hole was left. e, Down indicator placed over hole, which vibrated with the air movement caused if a seal was present. A horn indicator (not shown) was used for the same purpose. f, Sealskin breathing hole cover that protected the indicator from drifting snow. While waiting for the seal to appear the hunter stood on his fur bag for protection from the cold and to muffle noise. g, Wooden harpoon rests that had down cushioning at the top. Wound plugs, inserted in leather strips, were for use in the dead seal. a, Length 87.3 cm, rest same scale. a,b,d,e, collected by A. Balikci, Pelly Bay, N.W.T., 1959.

Fig. 11. Summer fishing at a stone weir in Pelly Bay area. top left, Repairing a fish weir. Such repair work was done by the first men to arrive at the site. Several extended families (about 20–30 individuals) might meet at such a summer camp. top right, Spearing fish using leisters. The men hold the line for stringing the fish in their mouths. The line was made of a sharp bear bone needle about 1 foot long on a sealskin thong (Balikci 1970:33–34). bottom left, Dragging the catch to shore. bottom right, Woman and child eating raw fish, probably Arctic char. The woman's hair is made up in hair sticks of wood, wound spirally with strips of light caribou skin and dark material (Birket-Smith 1945:47). Photographs by Douglas Wilkinson, Aug. 1963.

among the Utkuhikhalingmiut, with the herds being driven into lakes and speared like caribou. This inland adaptation of the group, with arctic char fishing and caribou hunting as the main subsistence base, developed during the nineteenth century following their migration to the Back River area. Prior to this movement the basic material culture and the round of subsistence activities of the Utkuhikhalingmiut band resembled closely that of the Netsilik with both groups sharing the same seal hunting complex in winter.

Considering the lack of quantitative data it is impos-

sible to assess the relative importance of the three main game species as food sources: fish, caribou, and seal. However, fish probably constituted the major part of the Utkuhikhalingmiut diet; fish were relatively easy to catch in large amounts, and there is no record of a "bad fishing year" (Balikci 1980).

Social and Economic Organization

The nuclear family was the smallest collaborative unit based upon the complementarity in the division of labor

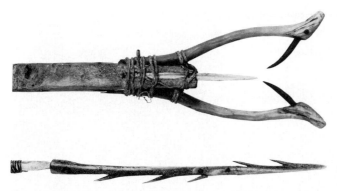

Fig. 12. Fishing. top, Leister with musk-ox horn prongs, iron side barbs, and a bone center spike, used to catch Arctic char either in weirs or from the ice. bottom, Harpoon with barbed head, antler foreshaft, and wood shaft, used to catch Arctic char in the summer. Fish are also caught with hooks. Length of head 34.0 cm; top, same scale. Both collected by Roald Amundsen on King William I., N.W.T., 1903–1905.

Fig. 14. Dogs jumping a crack in the ice during the spring break-up in May-June. The dogs are hitched in a center traced hitch. Photograph by Richard Harrington, Queen Maud Gulf, 1951.

between husband and wife. While the husband was the provider of food and maker of tools, the wife cooked, sewed and looked after the clothing, and reared the children. Although even young couples had their separate igloos adjoining their relatives' dwellings in a cluster of domes, almost never was the nuclear family an autonomous economic unit. The Netsilik had extended families usually comprising an elderly father with his married sons and their descendants (Balikci 1964:29). This unit followed a developmental cycle of its own; in time, after the death of the elderly father an alignment of brothers emerged that in turn was split into new extended families. Affinal ties could be exploited: a man with his brother-in-law or two unrelated men who had married two sisters could constitute the core of an "extended family," and a cousin or an uncle could join and remain part of the family. Generally the father-son and the brother-brother relationships were critically im-

Fig. 13. Container. Light colored fish skins are sewed in vertical strips between dark skin inserts. It was probably used to store dry moss. Diameter about 32.0 cm. Collected by Roald Amundsen, King William I., N.W.T., 1903–1905.

portant. The extended family (*ilaγi·t naŋminiri·t*) tended to be a residential unit occupying a cluster of snow-houses or tents. An individual or a nuclear family could leave for a prolonged period yet was expected to return.

In summer and fall the extended family functioned as a discrete economic unit in relation to caribou hunting at the crossing places and stone weir fishing. Although occasionally several extended families could exploit the same or adjoining sites, the cached game belonged to each, and there were no precise meat-sharing rules transcending the kinship units. The eldest hunter in the extended family acted as headman (*ihumataaq*): he decided about the movements of the family, selected hunting sites, and advised the younger men on hunting matters and travel. No clear-cut orders were given; the headman only advised and always consulted with the other hunters (Steenhoven 1959:18).

In midwinter several extended families congregated at the sealing camps (Balikci 1964:30). These were the largest communities in the Netsilik area. There is evidence that prior to the migration of numerous Netsilik families to the Chesterfield area around 1900, the average winter settlement comprised about 100 individuals (Damas 1969b). This stands in sharp contrast to the summer groupings inland, which probably averaged about 15 to 20 individuals with somewhat larger concentrations around the stone weir. The people of sealing camps were considered to be part of the regional -*miut* group. Throughout this grouping there was extensive continuity of kin linkages with a possible predominance of male-oriented kin ties over female-oriented kin ties (Damas 1969a). The presence of both is clear demonstration of bilaterality. However, under no condition should this grouping be considered as a kinship unit in a corporate sense. It is rather a band, specifically named and associated with a general territory and particular hunting grounds. It is a loose agglomeration in the sense

top, Nationalmuseet, Copenhagen: 1891; Public Arch. of Canada, Ottawa: bottom left, PA 129026; bottom right, PA 114694.

Fig. 15. Games and amusements. top, Handball and football games were common forms of amusement. Men and women use a ball made of sealskin filled with caribou hair or grass (Rasmussen 1931:357). bottom left, Imitating an adult woman carrying a child, a girl from Spence Bay carries a puppy in her parka hood. bottom right, Woman from Spence Bay playing the cup and pin game. The object is to toss up the "cup" (a horn, bone, or as here a wooden plug with holes drilled in it) and catch it on the pointed wooden stick. The game sometimes accompanied a story in which the holes represented incidents and had to be speared in proper order (Rasmussen 1931:358; Birket-Smith 1945:117–118). Bottom left and right, Photographs by Richard Harrington, 1951.

that nuclear or extended families can leave the band for prolonged periods while neighboring kinship units may join it. Patrilateral trends are visible at several levels: preference for patrilocal residence, the father-son or brother-brother bond at the core of the extended family, and the prevalence of male-oriented linkages across extended families. However, in the absence of clear patrilineal descent principles it is impossible to define the Netsilik midwinter community as a patrilinear band.

No clearly defined headmanship existed in the Netsilik band (Steenhoven 1959:59). The elder hunters con-

Natl. Mus. of Canada, Ottawa: IV-C-3272.

Fig. 16. Pulling game used for trials of strength. Two slightly rounded pieces of wood are joined by a strip of leather. Length 12.5 cm. Collected by A. Balikci at Pelly Bay, N.W.T., 1960.

Nationalmuseet, Copenhagen: top, 2903; bottom, 3029.

Fig. 17. Cutting figures—men, women, caribou—from firm snow as part of an archery game used to sharpen a bowman's skill (Rasmussen 1931:357). top, Man from Pelly Bay uses a block of snow with peat as center. bottom, Male figures with arrows. Photographs by Knud Rasmussen, Fifth Thule Expedition, 1921–1924.

sulted informally on community matters with the opinion of the most experienced and prestigious elder carrying greatest weight, although he functioned essentially as first among equals. The band was integrated rather by an efficient and rigid system of seal-meat-sharing partnerships (VandeVelde 1958). The seal was cut into 14 main parts, each bearing a particular name. A hunter had an equal number of sharing partners, named after a part of the seal. Sharing partners used to call each other after the corresponding seal portion. This system of dyadic partnerships, transcending kinship alignments, integrated the community as a network of reciprocal relationships and insured meat distribution throughout the band together with camp peace (Damas 1972). In midwinter the band constituted both a food production and food distribution unit (Balikci 1964:36). The extended family remained the basic commensal unit through all seasons with men and women eating in close proximity in two separate commensal circles. The nuclear family together or an individual could have a snack anytime after informally getting "permission" from the eldest female in the extended family who was in charge of food distribution within the group. In sum, the economic functions of the various social units changed with the seasons. In summer and fall the extended family acted as both a production and distribution unit, while in midwinter it was superseded in these functions by the band as an integrated network of extended families.

Rasmussen (1931:482) mentions specifically that the Utkuhikhalingmiut lacked the system of meal-sharing partnerships. For the period of Rasmussen's journey this group practiced intensive breathing-hole sealing, and shares were distributed just as among the Netsilingmiut. The upriver Hanningayurmiut and Uvaliarlit did not descend to the sea, and consequently the seal-meat-sharing pattern did not exist among them (David Damas, personal communication 1969).

Marriage

The Netsilik practiced female infanticide to a very high degree. The decision was made usually by the father immediately after birth. It was strictly a family affair and seemed related to the providing capacity of the father. Female infants were killed because women were not considered so important as the hunters for the survival of the group (Balikci 1967). In rejecting this ecological explanation, Freeman (1971) has considered Netsilik female infanticide as a repeated manifestation of male dominance. The result of this widespread practice was a remarkable imbalance in the sex ratio for the Netsilik: 150 males and 109 females counted by Rasmussen (1931:141) in 1923. This put a particular strain on society as far as the availability of marriageable women was concerned. In order to secure wives for their male children, mothers betrothed them to girls from their own kinship circle. First cousins were preferred, cross or parallel. This was in disharmony with kin terminology, since sibling terms were extended to cousins of the opposite sex, girls calling male cousins 'brother' and boys calling female cousins 'sister' (Balikci 1963). The practice of arranged cousin marriage must have worked imperfectly because there are many historic cases of wife stealing with or without the murder of the husband (Steenhoven 1959). Strangely enough, the scarcity of women did not prevent the establishment of polygynous unions. Rasmussen's (1931:85–90) 1923 census indicates 3 polygynous alignments out of a total of 61 marriages. Polyandrous arrangements were rare and highly unstable. The distrust of strangers was given as a reason for the preferred cousin marriage pattern. A cousin spouse was a trusted mate who remained near her parents after marriage and continued to provide them with services. A second factor might have been the imbalance of sexes making enforcement of kin exogamic practices unworkable (Damas 1975).

Spouse exchange (*kipuktu*) was a widespread practice; it could be initiated directly by the husbands or indirectly by the wives. It was a consequence of a strong friendship bond between two men, an expression of sexual desire for a particular person, or a practical arrangement involving the borrowing of a partner's wife for a specific trip. Spouse-exchange partners were often song fellows on the occasion of drum dances, the relationship acquiring thus a semiritual form. While some spouse-exchange partnerships were of short duration, others endured for life; still others, eroded by jealousy, ended in bitterness and hatred (Balikci 1959–1960).

Other dyadic partnerships were of lesser importance: avoidance partnerships expressing spontaneous feelings of shyness unconnected with kinship norms, formal bonds between two individuals with identical names leading to gift exchanges, and joking relationships spontaneously developing between nonkinsmen.

Social Control

There is substantial case material on conflict and aggressive behavior (Steenhoven 1959). Apparently a trivial matter with personality factors providing a suitable setting could provoke a fist fight. Competition for women was a more serious reason for conflict that could lead to murder. There is no evidence for actual murder being followed by blood revenge although the intentions of it have been frequently expressed. Highly successful hunters seem to have been the object of gossip and strong feelings of jealousy. Hostile sentiments could always lead to [an] individual seeking magical means. While the threat of this form of retaliation constituted a relative check on overt aggressiveness, it also promoted considerable suspiciousness (Rasmussen 1931:202).

Mockery and derision were enlisted as controls for deviance, yet if pushed too far they might anger the concerned individual and provoke his retaliation (Ras-

mussen 1931:18). Additional conflict resolution techniques were public fist fights, song duels, and approved execution, which was a very rare practice reserved for those regarded as being particularly evil sorcerers and for insane individuals. Simple withdrawal remained the most common strategy for conflict resolution or, more precisely, for conflict avoidance.

The rate of suicide was very high among the Netsilik (Balikci 1960). The immediate reasons determining suicides were disaster affecting a near relative (usually an offspring), personal misfortune such as illness, marital dissatisfaction, and in a few cases old age (Rasmussen 1931:138).

Religion

The Netsilik believed in a variety of supernatural beings: personal souls, the source of manly strength; name souls, considered as guardian spirits; and human ghosts, which were feared as becoming very dangerous if not appeased by the appropriate taboos (Rasmussen 1931:214ff.). Animals also had souls; and for the freshly killed seal, caribou, and bear special observances applied. Individually owned amulets sheltered special spirits who helped the hunter on the chase, strengthened a person's qualities, or protected him against evil ghosts. Further, there were the shaman's own protective spirits of which there was a great diversity: ghosts, various animals, elements of nature such as the sun or moon, and a number of monsters and bizarre beings. Other supernaturals inhabited the open country, preferring generally mountain sites. Although mostly they were humanlike in size, their characteristics varied greatly. Some monsters were bloodthirsty, dangerous to humans, and intensely feared by the Netsilik especially during the dark winter months (Rasmussen 1931:239–257).

Above all these lesser spirits were three major deities. Nuliayuk, a goddess living in the depth of the sea, was considered the mother of both sea and land animals; Nârssuk or Sila, the giant baby, was the weather god, master of the wind, rain, and snow; Tatqiq, the moon spirit, was a deity generally well disposed toward mankind (Rasmussen 1931:224–238). With the exception of Tatqiq, the name souls, and the amulet spirits, practically all other supernatural beings were inimical to mankind, and the Netsilik thus lived in perpetual fear of sudden attacks by malevolent spirits.

The Netsilik knew a number of disconnected creation myths that point to the following underlying assumptions. First, creation was conceived as a process of increased differentiation from the original chaotic condition. Second, human existence initially was dull and tasteless; following the appearance of suffering and pleasure it acquired meaning. Third, human wickedness seemed to be the source of all evil. Fourth, the creation of the visible world, the supernatural world, and the *425*

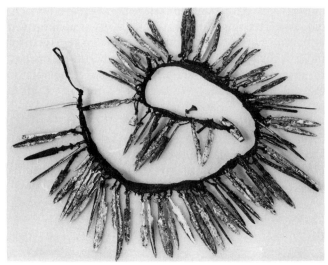

U. i Oslo, Etnografisk Mus.: 16,159.

Fig. 18. Shaman's belt. Although similar to the amulets worn by the rest of the community, the shaman's belt is differentiated by the objects hung from it. The band is caribou or sealskin; attached to it are miniature carved antler implements which protected the shaman. The belt and a fringed breast ornament are the shaman's only special apparel (Blodgett 1979:155–156). Length 92.0 cm. Collected by Roald Amundsen on King William I., N.W.T., 1903–1905.

Nationalmuseet, Copenhagen: 1642.

Fig. 19. Niaqúnuaq (Niagunguaq) from King William I. wearing a brow band made of the white belly skin of a caribou with 3 loops of beads on his forehead, indicating his status as a shaman. Photograph by Knud Rasmussen, Fifth Thule Expedition, 1921–1924.

human moral order took place simultaneously, and in myth the three are considered as a whole.

Three afterworlds provided shelter for the dead. The energetic hunters and the tattooed women lived in eternal bliss in villages located high in the sky or very deep under the tundra. The dead there live in a land of plenty where everything is happiness and joy. The lazy hunters remain just below the crust of the earth; they are perpetually hungry and apathetic, and their only food is the butterfly (Rasmussen 1931:315–319).

The Netsilik knew and rigidly observed a very large number of taboos concerning hunting activities and various game animals as well as the critical phases of a person's life cycle (birth and death) and certain physiological functions such as menstruation (Rasmussen 1931:258–266). The complex taboo system had the following underlying functions: first, it kept the distinction between land and sea animals and thus confirmed symbolically the separation of the world into two halves, land and sea; second, it reduced the level of anxiety generated by uncertainties implied in hunting and childbirth; third, since breaking of taboos was considered as the source of evil, it provided society with an understandable reason for misfortunes; and fourth, considering that many taboos were related to animal souls and locality sacredness, they strengthened religious beliefs by making the spiritual world omnipresent.

The Netsilik knew three distinct forms of "shamanism" (Rasmussen 1931:234–319). The active form involved a trance, the use of the shaman's secret vocabulary, and a very lively relation with protective spirits.

426

The passive technique (*qilaniq*) was considered less efficient and did not necessitate much training by the practitioner. Involving head lifting with a thong and questioning a helping spirit, it was mostly used for divinatory purposes. The last method was related exclusively to curing and consisted in the lesser shaman's visual capability to see the evil spirit in the body of the patient and force him to leave its abode. Of a different nature was *ilisiniq* or evil magic, which was a mechanical activity accompanied by a malevolent mental wish that could be performed by anyone.

In addition to performing the functions usually associated with Eskimo shamans (see "Copper Eskimo," this vol.), the shamans were the people who brought the world together. Environment, spirits, the afterworld, social life—all these elements were fused together by the shaman into one meaningful whole. In this role as integrator, in a stream of symbolic effusions, the shaman gave meaning to a multiplicity of situations that would have remained inexplicable to society without his intervention (Balikci 1963a).

Prehistory

In reference to prehistoric antecedents Mathiassen (1927, 1:87–89, 326–327, 2:162–163) emphasizes the separate identity of Thule culture considered as distinct from modern Central Eskimo patterns. An analysis of Thule and protohistoric Netsilik artifacts from Boothia Peninsula and Somerset Island indicates that Thule forms have been changed and adapted in this area to caribou hunting and fishing. It appears clearly that Netsilik implement culture is a logical development from the locally adapted Thule culture (VanStone 1962).

History and Culture Change

The process of culture change in the Netsilik area has followed a course similar to that in other regions of the Canadian North. There have been two acculturative phases: first, a period of slow culture change under the influence of the trading companies, the missionary churches, and the Royal Canadian Mounted Police; and second, a period of rapid transformations sponsored by the Canadian federal government.

The first trading contacts of the Netsilik took place at the end of the nineteenth century with the whaling fleets along northwest Hudson Bay. It was from the whalers that the Netsilik obtained their first steel tools and guns with an irregular supply of ammunition. In the 1920s several trading posts were established in and around the Netsilik area: Repulse Bay in 1920 by the Hudson's Bay Company, Perry River in 1926 and Gjoa Haven in 1927 by the Canalaskan Trading Company, Fort Ross shortly after and Spence Bay in 1949 (Usher 1971) by the Hudson's Bay Company. The Roman Catholic mission at Pelly Bay operated a small trading facility in the late 1930s. From these stores the Netsilik obtained four essential items: rifles, steel traps, canoes, and fishing nets. The general use of these four items profoundly transformed the subsistence activities and settlement pattern of the Netsilik within the framework of the fur-trading economy. With rifles seals were more efficiently hunted at the ice edge or along wide ice cracks, and this technique gradually brought breathing-hole sealing to an end. In summer seals were shot in open water from canoes—an entirely new seasonal activity. With rifles in hand the Netsilik could hunt caribou at any season and any place; the kayakers didn't need to wait for the migrating herds at the crossing places. Consequently both kayaks and bows and arrows went out of use. The use of nets made fishing easier. Stone weirs were also gradually abandoned, and the leister lost its traditional importance. Trapping foxes with steel traps was introduced as a new and all-important activity. Fox pelts were the principal commodity exchanged at the trading posts for the acquisition of the newly essential imported goods. The Netsilik rapidly changed from hunters to trappers, each running a long trapline from a central camp base.

There were some local variations to this basic pattern. Fur trapping was most intense around the Gjoa Haven and Spence Bay settlements. In 1961–1962, 1,901 white fox pelts were traded at Spence Bay, 1,691 at Gjoa Haven (including the Back River people), and only 238 at Pelly Bay. Following the missionary's directives to the Arviligyuarmiut to live off the land, this group adopted fox trapping as a very secondary activity clearly subordinated to rifle hunting (Balikci 1964). As for the Back River group, they continued to rely on their inexhaustible supplies of fish.

The intensive use of rifles in several areas of the District of Keewatin including the Netsilik region greatly reduced both the resident and migrating caribou herds. Decreased caribou availability determined changes in local clothing styles: imported cloth replaced caribou fur coats thus increasing the Netsiliks' dependence on the trading stores. As for the musk-oxen, they vanished altogether from the Netsilik area. No decreases in the availability of ringed seal and arctic char have been reported.

In the fur trading regions a new settlement pattern emerged—the permanent camp. These camps comprised not bands but extended families with adjoining collaterals. Generally families resided in the permanent camps all year with possible prolonged visits to the trading posts in summer and to fishing sites in fall. Men hunted and trapped alone or in very small groups with periodic visits to the trading posts, which increasingly acted as magnets for the scattered coastal camps.

The most profound changes took place in the field of economic organization. All game brought down with the rifle or collected with nets and steel traps was strictly individual property. The traditional meat-sharing practices cutting across kinship units disappeared and gave way to the individualistic rifle hunting–fur trapping pattern with the trader as integrator of the new exchange system.

Many Netsilik collectively converted to Christianity in the late 1930s and early 1940s. The competing efforts of Roman Catholic and Anglican missionaries resulted in all Back River people, half of the Gjoa Haven group, and the majority of the Spence Bay area population becoming Anglican and the rest joining the Catholic church. Apparently this conversion took place easily, with little or no opposition from shamans. The consequences from the point of view of traditional intellectual culture and religious beliefs and practices were most profound. The whole taboo system collapsed, shamanistic practices and minor rituals vanished, and beliefs in major deities and lesser spirits were rejected. Some regional differences might have occurred due to the speed of conversion. In 1963 Briggs (1970:3) was unable to find any informants among the Back River people who recalled shamanistic performances, while in 1960 in Pelly Bay elderly individuals were still interested in traditional religious beliefs (Balikci 1963a). Under missionary influence female infanticide, suicide, and polygyny were halted and vigorous efforts made to control

Natl. Film Board of Canada Phototheque, Ottawa: top left, 62-3253; right, 62-3257.
Fig. 20. Christmas celebration in large community igloos or kashims at Pelly Bay. top left, Playing a game of dexterity. In this traditional and competitive game a string is tied to each end of a piece of ivory that has small holes in it. The upper string is tied to a stick and stuck into the igloo wall, while the lower string is held by a hunter who twirls it so that the ivory piece spins rapidly. The men try to jab the twirling ivory with a small pick. The first man to do so wins and is given a prize. This game is played separately by men and women. right, Using a small bird bow and arrow, a man shoots prizes hung from the ceiling during the party. top left and right, Photographs by Douglas Wilkinson, Dec. 1961. bottom left, Feasting after the midnight mass. Father Vandevelde celebrated mass here, as the stone mission chapel was too small for the crowd. Four family-size igloos built in a circle were used as a base on which the 18-foot snow dome was raised. The inside area was 25–30 feet across, not counting the 4 individual igloos (Mary-Rousselière 1956:4–5). Photograph by Guy Mary-Rousselière, 1956.

premarital and extramarital sexuality. In contrast, cousin marriage continued to flourish among the eastern Netsilik. Missionary influence does not seem to have affected to any great extent the style of Netsilik interpersonal relations, their expression of sentiments, and their strategies of aggression management (Briggs 1970, 1972, 1978).

The Royal Canadian Mounted Police have had a detachment at Spence Bay since 1949. In the 1950s they patrolled the area providing administrative and medical services, registering vital statistics, and acting as game wardens. Considering that lawlessness is not a problem in this area their function in law enforcement has been a nominal one.

428   The presence of traders, missionaries, and RCMP constables transformed entirely the leadership pattern in the area. Although the *ihumataaq* retained much of his traditional authority in reference to domestic activities within his kinship circle, the trader manipulated the prestige structure of society by allowing or withdrawing credit to trappers and influenced economic activities in a variety of ways. The Netsilik became a single subordinate class of trappers entirely dependent on the trading store. The religious and social influence of the missionary was enormous. Not only did he introduce basic Christian beliefs and practices in the community, but also he imposed new behavioral norms following the western cultural model and advised individuals on a multiplicity of matters. The influence of the RCMP constables was much less important.

In the early 1960s the Canadian federal government initiated a period of massive cultural change by increasing the number of services. An area administrator was located at Spence Bay in 1962, and schools and nursing stations were established in Spence Bay, Gjoa Haven, and Pelly Bay. The permanent coastal camps were abandoned, and the whole Netsilik population concentrated in these three settlements. In 1958 the Hanningayurmiut of Garry Lake suffered a famine and the survivors were evacuated to the coastal settlements of western Hudson Bay. At the end of the 1960s the camp at Thom Bay relocated to Spence Bay, and shortly after all the Back River people resettled in Gjoa Haven. This completed the process of sedenterization among the Netsilik. Permanent low-cost housing was provided to all families, together with electricity and heating, water delivery, and garbage and sewage disposal facilities. Communications have been extended and improved by widening the radio-telephone network and building airstrips. Community clubs, associations, and councils have been established in all three settlements with local cooperatives performing increasingly important functions. With the locally elected executives of these agencies being composed of Eskimos it is possible to make guesses about the future forms of self-government among these communities.

The creation of towns provided new employment opportunities for the younger people with some knowledge of English. The relative importance of trapping decreased as did seal hunting. As the snowmobile replaced the sledge there was no need to keep large dog teams and no need to amass seal meat for dog food. Since the 1960s the caribou population in the area has been on the increase, although the caribou chase was facilitated by the snowmobile. Attempts at commercial fishing have also been made. In all three settlements production of handicrafts has become an important source of income. However, the new economy continues to be almost entirely dependent on government support. The Netsilik townsmen have become government wards.

Population

In the late nineteenth century, when whaling fleets and traders in Chesterfield Inlet and Repulse Bay were attracting numerous Netsilik families, occasioning important migratory movements, Boas (1888:450) assembled evidence that suggests a Netsilik population numbering between 450 and 500, excluding the Back River groups. Yet in 1923 Rasmussen's survey indicates a total of 259 individuals for the same groups (1931:84) plus at least 156 Netsilik who had moved to the southern coastal areas (1930:84–88). It is clear that over one-third of the Netsilik had emigrated from their traditional country. This occasioned obvious reductions in band size and winter settlements (Damas 1969b). For the same period Rasmussen (1931:473) estimated the Back River population at 164.

In the late twentieth century welfare measures and extended medical services drastically reduced the rate of child mortality (Villiers 1968:83) while a very high birth rate continued to be maintained. As a result the population jumped from about 550 in 1954 to 720 in 1967. In 1979 Gjoa Haven comprised 493 people, Pelly Bay 281, while Spence Bay's population was 470 with half that number consisting of South Baffin Islanders relocated by the Hudson's Bay Company in the 1930s together with a few Arctic Bay people (Northwest Territories. Government 1981).

Synonymy

The term Netsilik under a variety of spellings has been used by different authors to designate alternately Lake Netsilik on Boothia Isthmus, the geographic area around this lake, the Eskimo band whose summer hunting grounds were located there (referred to in the recent literature as the Netsilik proper, a usage followed here) and by extension all the bands between Committee Bay and Victoria Strait (Rasmussen 1925 and later all the members of the Fifth Thule Expedition). Further, the members of these Netsilik bands designate the Netsilik proper simply as *natsilik*, the source of the name. As for the term Netsilingmiut (*natsiliŋmiut* 'people of the ringed seal'), it is generally used by distant groups such as the Aivilingmiut and Iglulingmiut (Iglulik) or the Copper Eskimos (Jenness 1922:40) in reference to the group of Netsilik bands as a whole. In the literature the term Netsilingmiut is applied indiscriminately to the Netsilik proper (Birket-Smith 1945:16) or to all Netsilik groups collectively (Rasmussen 1931:84).

The terms Netsilik and Netsilingmiut have been spelled differently by various early explorers. Ross (1835:273) writes Neitchillee, M'Clintock (1859:229) Něitchĭllěe, C. F. Hall (1879:274) Neitchille, Gilder (1881:85) Netchillik, Schwatka (1884) Neitschilluk, Boas (1888) Netchilirmiut, and Amundsen (1908:292) Netchilli. The standard spelling Netsilingmiut seems to have been established first by Jenness (1922:49). As for the term Netsilik Eskimo, together with the abbreviated form Netsilik, it was used first by the members of the Fifth Thule Expedition (Rasmussen 1925:536). Other early spellings are in Hodge (1907–1910, 2:58).

Subgroups

In Rasmussen (1931:3, 8, 85–92) the Arviligyuarmiut are given as Arviligjuarmiut 'people of Pelly Bay'; the Arviqtuurmiut as Arvertormiut 'people of Bellot Strait'; the Ilivilirmiut as Ilivilermiut 'people of the mainland (Adelaide Peninsula)'; the Killirmiut as Kitlermiut 'people of the edge (farthest out to the sea toward the west)'; the Kuungmiut as Kûngmiut 'people of the river (Murchison River)'; the Qiqiqtarmiut as Qeqertarmiut 'people of the island (King William's Land)'; and the Utkuhikhalingmiut usually as Utkuhikjalingmiut.

Sources

There are two standard reference books on the Netsilik. The first was written by the famous Danish explorer and ethnographer Knud Rasmussen (1931), who, following the Fifth Thule Expedition of 1921–1924, provided rich descriptive material covering most aspects of culture with special emphasis on myth and religion. The second (Balikci 1970) is a descriptive summary of the literature on the Netsilik embodying some new data on the eastern Netsilik. Both books deal with the traditional aspects of Netsilik culture as it existed at the beginning of the twentieth century.

For the history of explorations, see Boas (1888) and Birket-Smith (1945:10–15). The extensive literature on the search for the Northwest Passage contains relatively little information on the Netsilik with the notable exception of Amundsen (1908). The process of ecological adaptation is described by Balikci (1968) and Freeman (1971). Band organization is well analyzed by Damas (1969a, 1969b), as are partnerships and nonkinship associations (Damas 1972, 1972a). Legal concepts and their application have been studied by Steenhoven (1959), and string games in a wider culture-historical context by Mary-Rousselière (1969). The process of acculturation among the eastern Netsilik has been described by Balikci (1964, 1978), Treude (1973), and Villiers (1968). Briggs's (1970, 1972, 1978) contributions are very important for the understanding of the emotional side of social life.

Three museums own extensive ethnographic collections from the Netsilik area: the Danish Nationalmuseum, Copenhagen; Universitetet i Oslo Etnografisk Museum, Norway; and the National Museum of Canada, Ottawa.

A distinct contribution to Netsilik ethnography was the production of a film series directed by Balikci (1966, 1975) that attempts a description of the annual migration cycle prior to the introduction of firearms in the area. In 1970 the National Film Board of Canada produced an hour-long film entitled *Esquimaux* on the same Netsilik families in the new town environment. A 17-minute version entitled *The Netsilik Eskimo Today* is also distributed by the National Film Board.

Iglulik

GUY MARY-ROUSSELIÈRE

Language, Territory, and Environment

The term Iglulik (ĭg'lōōlĭk) has been used since the Fifth Thule Expedition to designate, besides the Iglulingmiut proper, the Aivilingmiut and the Tununirmiut (including the subgroup Tununirusirmiut). According to Mathiassen (1928:1), "these groups . . . [are] so closely related that they must be regarded as forming one Eskimo tribe with in all essentials a uniform culture."

It is generally agreed that the present-day Iglulik are the descendants of those who brought the Thule culture into the area around the twelfth century A.D. They belong to the Inuit-Inupiaq (or Eastern Eskimo) linguistic group* and, like other Canadian Eskimos, call themselves *inuit* (singular *inuk*). Although there are minor internal differences, their language is sufficiently homogeneous to distinguish them, as a whole, from the neighboring groups.

They were separated linguistically and culturally from the Netsilingmiut group of Netsilik to the west; the Qairnirmiut and the Hauniqtuurmiut groups of Caribou Eskimo and the Sallirmiut on Southampton Island to the south; and the Akudnirmiut and Oqomiut groups of Baffinland Eskimo to the east.

The territory formerly inhabited by the Iglulik Eskimos extended approximately from the north of Baffin Island to Cape Fullerton in the south. It was delimited by Committee Bay and Prince Regent Inlet in the west and Lancaster Sound and Baffin Bay in the north then southwest to Foxe Basin (fig. 1). In addition, the Tununirmiut would at times make prolonged journeys to Somerset, Devon, and Cornwalles Islands.

The ringed seal, the bearded seal, and the Greenland whale were found throughout this entire area. In sum-

mer the narwhal came primarily to Eclipse Sound, Admiralty Inlet, and Lyon Inlet, and the white whale mostly to Igloolik and Repulse Bay. Igloolik was the chief region of the walrus, which could also be found in Repulse Bay and at the entrance to Wager Bay. Polar bear and caribou were common in most places, while muskoxen could be encountered only to the west of Rae Isthmus, in the Wager Bay area, and on Devon Island.

Waterfowl, particularly Brant and snow geese and king eiders, could be numerous in season. Arctic char ascended all large rivers and large streams.

Culture

Subsistence

The quest for game dominated the entire existence of the Iglulik Eskimo. The method of hunting seals through breathing holes (figs. 2–3) was identical with that of other Central Eskimo groups while hunting the animal as it slept on the spring ice was more widely practiced than farther west (for descriptions of breathing hole and surface sealing see "Copper Eskimo" and "Netsilik", this vol.).

Pursuits especially important to the Iglulik Eskimo were hunting walrus through thin ice (fig. 4) or on the floe edge, as well as hunting seals and walrus in open water from kayaks and the walrus as it slept on drift ice. At times, in order to avoid some of the danger inherent in hunting walrus in open water, several kayaks were tied together (Rae 1850:174). Groups of kayak hunters also pursued the Greenland whale (Parry 1824:509). Special harpoons and harpoon heads were used in walrus and narwhal hunting (Mathiassen 1928:47–53), and other types were used for whale hunting.

Polar bears were usually brought to bay by dogs and then attacked by lance, harpoon, or a knife attached to a long handle. A bear trap of stone is known in Paquet Bay. Caribou were hunted with bow and arrow primarily in the summer and autumn months, either by approaching the animal using various stratagems or by lying in wait behind a rock screen. The most common hunting method was by kayak, pursuing the caribou when it swam across a lake. Often beaters would drive the animals toward the hunter or toward the water

---

*The phonemes of Iglulik Eskimo are: (voiceless stops) *p, t, k, q*; (voiced fricatives) *v, y, γ, γ̇*; (voiceless fricatives) *s* and perhaps *ł*; (nasals) *m, n, ŋ*; (lateral) *l*; (short vowels) *i, a, u*; (long vowels) *i·, a·, u·*. Before nasals *γ̇* is [ŋ].

In the practical orthography generally in use the Iglulik phonemes are written: p, t, k, q; v, j, g, r; s, l; m, n, ng; l; i, a, u; ii, aa, uu.

Information on Iglulik Eskimo phonology and the transcription of words is from Guy Mary-Rousselière, Webster and Zibell (1976:276), and Anthony C. Woodbury (communication to editors 1982).

The Eskimo names of groups used as English designations are in the practical orthography, but with y for j. The sequence dn has been left as in the sources; though this cannot be phonemically correct its interpretation was unknown to the editors.

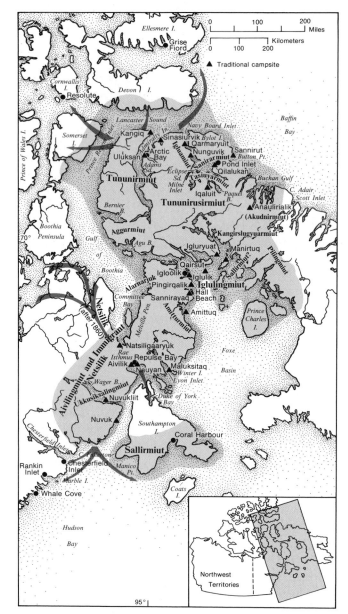

top, Natl. Film Board of Canada Phototheque, Ottawa: 63321; bottom, Public Arch. of Canada, Ottawa: PA129874.

Fig. 2. Seal hunting. top, Idlout searching for sleeping seal around Bylot I. Photograph by Douglas Wilkinson, Oct. 1952. bottom, Hunter pulling captured spotted seal from the water. At right is a small umiak for retrieving seals shot from the floe edge in open water. Photograph by Richard Harrington, 1952–1953.

Fig. 1. Territory of Iglulik groups and subgroups and the Sallirmiut in the late 19th century. For a discussion of the Sallirmiut see "Central Eskimo: Introduction," this vol. Unlabeled arrows indicate hunting and trading excursions.

through alignments of rock piles. In winter, caribou were sometimes captured in snow traps (Rae 1850:134). As for the musk-ox, it was hunted with the help of dogs, and in the final kill the bow and arrow or a lance was used.

Several kinds of traps were made of stone or ice to catch foxes and wolves: tower traps, box traps, or deadfalls. The wolf was taken by a special wolf-killer of baleen or enticed by a sharp blade covered with frozen blood.

In bird hunting, the bird-dart was used with the harpoon-thrower (fig. 6), particularly for eiders and geese, which were also caught with a snare. In moulting season geese were sometimes trapped in rock enclosures. Gulls were caught with bone hooks or by hand from inside a snowhouse. Ptarmigans were killed with bow and arrow, rocks, or a whip. Finally, at Pond Inlet murres were caught by means of a circular net with a handle. Eggs of all kinds were highly sought after.

Fishing techniques (fig. 7) resembled closely those of other Central Eskimo (see "Netsilik Eskimo," this vol.).

• ANNUAL CYCLE   A general pattern of yearly movements and utilization of game can be discerned throughout the Iglulik Eskimo area. A number of people, particularly the younger hunters and their wives, spent much of the summer and autumn inland hunting caribou, while the older men hunted marine animals. Both elements congregated in strand villages during the sewing period at the end of autumn, and in midwinter all Iglulik Eskimos moved to the sea ice where they could

MARY-ROUSSELIERE

Fig. 3. Ivory carving representing a seal hunting scene. right to left, A man harpoons a seal through a breathing hole; after the seal is harpooned it is pulled up through the hole and then butchered. The woman, far left, is scraping the skin. Length 34.0 cm; made at Repulse Bay, N.W.T., 1962.

exploit breathing-hole sealing and hunt at the floe edge. During the spring the large winter sealing villages dispersed for the period of hunting *uˑttuq* 'seal basking on the ice'. The spring was also the time for visiting, and sometimes prolonged journeys were undertaken during that season.

There were regional variations in the annual cycle within the Iglulik area. Beginning in the north, Button Point on Bylot Island was the most important winter and spring campsite. Here the Tununirmiut hunted seals at the breathing hole and along the floe edge where they also exploited narwhal and Greenland whale when they arrived sometime in June. As the ice receded into Eclipse Sound this group moved westward hunting *uˑttuq* while in the spring some elements would cross Lancaster Sound for polar bear or musk-oxen on north Devon Island. When the inland caribou hunters and the sea mammal hunters met again in the fall they would move into stone huts that would be their dwellings during much of the winter season.

The Tununirusirmiut of the Admiralty Inlet region centered their winter habitation at Adams Sound for breathing-hole sealing and a little later hunted at the floe edge to the north. The spring camps were sometimes used as points of departure for bear hunting in Lancaster Sound and at places as distant as Devon and Somerset islands. Other favorite locales included an open-water area where seals could be secured throughout the winter and caribou and fishing places in the southern parts of the Tununirusirmiut country.

The major winter villages of the Iglulingmiut proper were situated near open water where walrus could be hunted through thin ice or in the water itself at the same season that breathing-hole sealing was practiced. The normal pattern of surface sealing in the spring and the inland-coastal split of personnel into summer groups was followed around Iglulik.

Like the other groups, the Aivilingmiut alternated between hunting marine mammals on the ice and in open water with terrestrial hunting and fishing, but more importance seems to have been given to caribou hunting. At the end of summer in the area of Rae Isthmus, the caribou hunt was supplemented by fishing for arctic char and hunting musk oxen. The major centers of habitation were Repulse Bay and on Lyon Inlet as well as Wager Bay, a region especially rich in walrus, caribou, and musk-oxen. (An account of the traditional seasonal cycles of the various Iglulik Eskimo groups is also given in Mathiassen 1928:23–36.)

Transportation

The sledge was used most of the year, pulled by dogs harnessed in fan formation with traces of different lengths. It was formed of two runners made of whalebone, wood, or when these materials were lacking, frozen skins joined together with cross-pieces of wood, bone, or antler. Runners were shod with whalebone or a casing of wet vegetable mold that was left to freeze and then iced. When a sledge was not available, skins, baleen, or even a rounded block of ice could be used instead (Lyon 1824:201, 324).

The dogs, trained very young by the children, were driven with the help of various commands and a long whip. Late in spring their paws were protected with sealskin boots. In summer dogs carried a part of the camp equipment on their backs.

The sealskin kayak (*qayaq*) was formerly used everywhere. Several kayaks were lashed together to transport men or baggage. Sometimes several skin floats tied together or a bundle of *Cassiope tetragona* enveloped in tent skins was used as a raft.

The skin umiak (*umiaq*) seems to have disappeared by 1820. However, it is possible that it was still in use at Pond Inlet at the beginning of the twentieth century or even later (Mary-Rousselière 1954).

Structures

The snowhouse with an ice window was the usual winter dwelling (fig. 8), especially for the Aivilingmiut. Both among the Iglulingmiut and the Tununirmiut the snowhouse was usually lined with sealskins (Lyon 1824:394). It could shelter several families and was often used to form a complex in which domes were joined together by one or more porches made of snow.

In spring and autumn the Iglulik Eskimo used the *qaẏmaq*, or incomplete snowhouse roofed with skins. This name was also given to the ice hut sometimes used in the autumn, as well as to the hut made of whalebones, stones, and turf and roofed over with skins. This last

Public Arch. of Canada, Ottawa: top left, PA 129875; top right, PA 129871; bottom, PA 129869.
Fig. 4. Hunting walrus on thin ice, as practiced at Igloolik. Walrus do not usually keep a breathing hole like the seals, but where the sea has frozen between the floes, they break through the thin ice in order to breathe, but not always at the same place. This kind of hunt was very dangerous as the wounded walrus sometimes broke through the ice under the hunter. top left, Apparently the walrus was harpooned as it came up to breathe and it submerged but is held by the harpoon line. While some men pull on the line to retrieve it, one stands at the left with a gun and another one with a lance, ready for the kill when the animal reappears. bottom, The walrus has been killed and the dogs are pulling it over the ice. top right, The walrus is being cut up. Photographs by Richard Harrington, 1952–1953.

structure was a simplified version of the "domed hut" (Lyon 1824:235) described by Parry (1824:545). According to local tradition, these huts, with a membrane or intestine-covered window located at the top, were still inhabited in the mid-nineteenth centry. At Pond Inlet, huts made of solid materials, as well as snowhouses, were inhabited until the 1960s.

The ridge-type tent served as the summer lodging. This tent was usually made of seal skin, less frequently of caribou skin or of thinned walrus skin. The front part was of dehaired and transparent skin.

Cooking was done over a soapstone oil lamp in a cooking pot of the same material suspended above. In summer cooking was often done outside over a fire kindled from bones doused in oil. Fires were started by striking pyrite with flint or by a wooden fire drill driven by a cord or bow. Part of the meat was eaten raw or frozen and often in an advanced state of decay (Mathiassen 1928:203–208).

Clothing and Adornment

Both men and women usually dressed in caribou skins. They wore hooded double frocks; men, double breeches and the women, single. The masculine dress called for a long flap at the back and sometimes a shorter one in front. A Pond Inlet variant was the flapless frock with a slit in front similar to the one used in South Baffin,

Fig. 5. Pulling polar bear meat across the ice to the boat, using the skin as a sled. This kill occurred during a walrus hunting expedition in northern Foxe Basin, by a group from the camp of Alarniq (Alarnerk), south of Igloolik. Photograph by Guy Mary-Rousselière, 1956.

perhaps as an imitation of White men's coats. The woman's dress had two long narrow flaps. Underneath the woman's enormous hood was a pouch for carrying her baby (fig. 9). Wide armholes enabled the woman to bring her infant in front for nursing. Stockings and boots of caribou and sealskin shoes completed the man's dress. The woman's stockings and boots were very long, with an appendage on the side in the form of a pouch.

The underclothing alone was worn in the summer, sometimes covered with a sealskin garment, along with boots of dehaired sealskin. Garments and stockings of duck skin were sometimes worn (Lyon 1824:314).

Tattoos commonly decorated women's faces and also various parts of the body (Mathiassen 1928:159–202).

Technology

The principal raw materials used to make weapons and various utensils were: ivory, antler, bone, driftwood, soapstone, and slate. The primary tools included the adz, the bow-drill (fig. 10), the whittling knife, and the graver. Fired pottery was unknown, but the children made small lamps of clay, which they dried in the sun, and the adults sometimes cemented together fragments of limestone to make lamps.

Lyon (1824:237) also reports basketry.

Fat or flesh was removed from skins with the woman's knife, or ulu. Skins were then dried. Different sorts of bone (fig. 12) and stone scrapers were used to prepare the skins, which were also softened by chewing. Urine tanning was also known in the 1820s. The Iglulik Eskimos used bearded sealskin mainly to make ropes (fig. 13) and soles. Sewing was done with bone needles and a skin thimble. The seams of summer boots and kayaks had to be made watertight (Mathiassen 1928:109–114).

Art

Artistic talent was expressed in particular in manufacture of skin garments, which were often decorated with bands of different colors.

Rare objects of ivory or stone—needle cases, lamp trimmers, combs, or buttons—were sometimes embellished with engraved designs utilizing simple motifs like the dot-and-circle (fig. 14). Very few cases of figurative representation have been found. Some Thule culture decorative motifs survived in women's tattooing.

Social Organization

• KINSHIP The Iglulik Eskimo kinship system has two different terms for parallel cousins of the same sex, one for cross-cousins of the same sex, and four pairs of different terms for consanguineal uncles and aunts and their nephews or nieces. The terms are extended three generations, both ascending and descending. There is a term for the parents of a son-in-law or daughter-in-law.

Various behavior patterns accompany certain dyadic relationships. Between spouses there is affection, which is sometimes openly expressed, together with the subordination of the wife, although she may also exert a strong influence on her husband (Parry 1824:528). The relationships between parents and children, in particular between those of the same sex, are marked by affection and super-subordination. The parents give an almost unrestricted freedom to their very young children. Later the offspring will obey their parents and will continue to do so after maturity.

Between siblings, there was subordination of the

Royal Scottish Mus., Edinburgh: left, UC160; right, UC 147.
Fig. 6. Bird hunting. left, Dart used primarily for eider ducks has a shaft of 2 pieces of wood lashed together with baleen, 3 barbed ivory points at the center, and 2 barbed points at the distal end. The butt is tipped with an ivory piece that fits into the hook of the throwing board. right, The shaft of the dart was laid in the groove of the board and thrown from it for increased leverage. Length 42.0 cm, left same scale. Both collected by E. Parry, Melville Peninsula, N.W.T., 1821–1823.

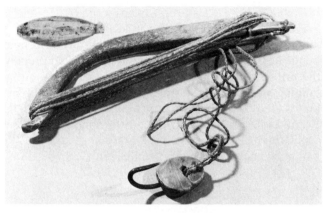

top, Smithsonian, Dept. of Anthr.: 10,400; bottom, Amer. Mus. of Nat. Hist., New York: 60/6626.

Fig. 7. Fishing gear. Arctic char are caught in open water and from the ice. When fishing through a hole in the ice a line with a lure (top, ivory with inset eyes) is used to attract the fish, which are then speared. The spear is sometimes used in conjunction with a hook and line or the fish may simply be hooked. bottom, Bone reel with braided sinew line with a metal hook set into an ivory lure. Width of reel 25.0 cm; collected by George Comer, Aivilik, N.W.T., 1910. top, Width 7.5 cm; collected by C.F. Hall, Igloolik, N.W.T., 1871.

younger, and, following puberty, reserve between siblings of different sexes. This reserve characterized, in particular, the relationship between brother-in-law and sister-in-law, who, formerly, could neither speak to each other nor name each other.

Adoption was a frequent occurrence, in particular the adoption by grandparents of grandchildren. Those adopted (*tiɣuaq*) very young were treated as natural children. Adoption also created special ties between the adopting parents and the natural parents.

For a child carrying the name of a deceased relative (the two were *atiɣiˑk*), one used the same term of relationship regarding him as would be used for his namesake. Two persons having the same eponym (but not necessarily all the namesakes) were *avvaɣiˑk*. A special familiarity existed between them.

Among other dyadic relationships, the following can be cited: partners in wife exchanges, joking partners, and friends. The *illuɣiˑk* (sg. *illuq*) consisted of two mutually chosen men who, at each encounter, would meet in the *qaɣɣiq* 'kashim' and exchange wives. It was not rare that the competition between them became bitter. Those who usually exchanged a certain piece of food would designate each other by the name of this piece.

The personal kindred of each individual included consanguines and some affines. The Eskimo ideal was to have a network, as extensive as possible, of kinship and fictive kinship relationships.

• MARRIAGE The incest taboo was nearly universally respected. Ideally this prohibition included first and second cousins..Nevertheless, examples have shown that marriages among such relatives also took place (Lyon 1824:353).

Most often the future bride and groom were engaged when very young, generally with the boy's parents offering a gift to the girl's parents. At maturity the young man performed a few months or a year in service with his father-in-law. Sometimes a wide age difference existed between the spouses; either the woman or the man could be the older.

Polygyny was formerly common, especially at Igloolik were the hazards of hunting were greatest, causing a lower proportion of men than women (Mathiassen 1928:20). Polyandry was rare as were situations of men having more than two wives.

Divorce was rather frequent, especially at the beginning of married life, but the arrival of children tended to stabilize marriage. Remarriage was the rule.

• NUCLEAR FAMILY The customary Central Eskimo division of labor existed between husband and wife (see "Netsilik Eskimo," this vol.).

The woman would give birth alone in a separate shelter called *iɣnivik*, and she would cut the umbilical cord herself with a piece of flint. The baby was given a name immediately, usually that of a recently deceased relative of either sex. After being cleansed with a bird skin, which would become its amulet, the baby was placed in the pouch of its mother's garment. The woman would then settle in another igloo or tent (*kiniɣvik*), where she would spend a variable length of time during which she was considered impure and dangerous. She had to observe numerous taboos that would determine the future of the baby. During its first two years, the baby spent most of its time in the pouch and was pampered by everyone. Infant mortality was very high. In 1822 two adults were counted for every child (Parry 1824:492).

For the most part, children's games imitated adult activities. A very young boy would have a small sledge, to which he harnessed puppies. As soon as he was old enough, about 11, his father would take him on hunting trips. A little girl would play at imitating her mother, and she was given the responsibility of a baby quite early, carrying a younger sibling in the pouch. She helped with the housework by bringing in the ice, hammering blubber for the lamp, and chewing seal skin to soften it. A girl was tattooed as soon as she reached puberty.

top, Mystic Seaport Mus., Conn.: Comer Coll. 63.1767.94; bottom, Dept. of Energy, Mines, and Resources, Geological Survey of Canada, Ottawa: 2904.

Fig. 8. Winter snowhouses, composed of blocks of snow cut with a snow knife. top, Building the snow vault; when completed it will be covered with loose snow and an entranceway built. Photograph by George Comer, 1897–1905. center, Winter village at Repulse Bay. The square light patch in the center on one of the houses is an ice window. Photographed by moonlight, at night, by Guy Mary-Rousselière, 1952. bottom, Inside a house at Cape Fullerton. Women and children sit on a platform covered with furs. In the corner is the cooking area with oil cooking lamps over which kettles are suspended. Photograph by Albert Peter Low, 1903.

MARY-ROUSSELIÈRE

IGLULIK

MARY-ROUSSELIÈRE

Fig. 9. Women's clothing. top, Women from Cape Fullerton on board the *Era*. Wearing bead-decorated parka is Niviarsannaq (nicknamed Shoofly by the whalers), wife of Angutimmarik, one of Therkel Mathiassen's main informants, and herself recognized as a wise woman and an expert seamstress. The parkas are of caribou skin, worn with the hair inside; the white ones are new, the dark ones older. The large armpit toggles are for the cord that supports the baby on the back. Photograph by Albert Peter Low, 1903–1904. bottom, Shoofly's parka. This caribou skin inner garment is elaborately beaded and decorated. The center front panels are red cloth with beadwork including the name Shoofly. Beadwork, including fringes is red, white, blue, and yellow; there are also dyed red bands of skin, small incisors, and metal danglers. The back view with the hood up shows the characteristic baby pouch. The back view with the hood down gives an indication of the large size of the hood. A beadwork scene of a man shooting a caribou decorates the hood, which also has strips of red cloth. Width at shoulders 72.0 cm; collected by George Comer, 1906.

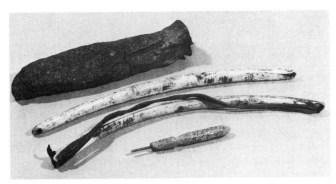

Fig. 10. Drill kit. Leather bag containing a man's tools including 2 bows (one strung with leather thong) and bone drill bit with metal point. The mouthpiece for the bow drill is missing but was a small block of wood, bone or antler, with a socket for the drill or a vertebra with the natural hollows serving as sockets. The mouthpiece is held with the teeth and the bow is wrapped around the drill and worked with one hand. Length of bag 26.0 cm; collected by George Comer on Southampton I., N.W.T., 1899.

Fig. 11. Knife, double-edged steel blade, secured with a triangular piece of metal and rivets to a wooden handle. It was used to skin and butcher game and occasionally as a snow knife. Length 32.5 cm; collected by Therkel Mathiassen at Igloolik, N.W.T., 1922.

Fig. 12. Bone scrapers for removing water from wet hides. top, Plain handle; bottom, finger notches cut in handle. Length of bottom 27.0 cm, top same scale; both collected by George Comer:top, Aivilik, N.W.T., 1899; bottom, Foxe Channel, N.W.T., 1910.

The Eskimos knew many indoor games. Among the most important were string figures (*ayaẏa·q*), cup-and-ball (*ayaɣaq*), and knucklebones (*inukkat*).

• EXTENDED FAMILY After his marriage or period of service with his in-laws a husband often lived with his wife in his parents' house. The father's authority and his concern with keeping his sons nearby to help in the hunt led, in effect, to predominant virilocality. As a

Fig. 13. Men from Southampton Island cutting thong from bearded seal skin. Photograph by Fred Bruemmer, Sept. 1967.

Fig. 14. Adornment. left, Ivory comb used to style the hair and remove lice; right, ivory hair ornaments decorated with dots. Length of right 7.0 cm; left, same scale. Both collected by George Comer on Southampton I., N.W.T., 1902.

result, the extended family generally formed the unit of cohabitation and cooperation. Distribution of food and skins was coordinated at this level. Meals of boiled meat were generally eaten in a group, with the men eating together first, then the women.

The father coordinated the group activities. Even in his old age, when leadership had passed on to his oldest son, he continued to be consulted. When an old man was no longer useful, it was not unusual for him to commit suicide. This was done most often by hanging and sometimes with the help of the old man's close relatives.

When death occurred, numerous taboos were observed. The corpse, bound up in bedding skins, was taken outside through an opening made in the igloo and carried some distance, the containing cord was cut, and then the corpse was covered with either rocks or snow depending on the time of year. Some personal effects of the decreased were placed nearby. Before death a person could bequeath his property. The remainder of the deceased's possessions went to the eldest son, or, in the case of a woman, to the eldest daughter.

Leadership

The core of the camp or village that formed in autumn generally consisted of one or several extended families.

The camp usually had a leader or *isumataq*. A large village might have several men so designated. He was generally a mature and experienced man, who was a good hunter and the head of a large family. The functions of the *isumataq* and the shaman were often combined. Except in the case of outstanding personalities, the *isumataq* was rather the first among equals, and only after consulting the other heads of families did he proceed to coordinate the activities, divide tasks, and sometimes distribute the game.

Ability in hunting conferred a definite prestige. Not only did it permit the support of a large family, but also it allowed for aid to be given to the less fortunate attracting a following. The poor hunter and the orphan were at the bottom of the social ladder.

The inhabitants of the village constantly visited one another, and since visiting usually elicited an offer of food, it helped in distributing provisions.

Ceremonies and Games

Village life gave rise to intense social activity. It was at the time of these great gatherings, especially when the provisions were abundant, that the major festivities took place.

The song and dance feast in the large *qaɣɣiq* was most common. This often occurred when a stranger came to visit, especially if this person had an *illuq* in the camp. Each *illuq* in turn would sing his personal song, with the support of the women's chorus, accompanying himself on the drum while dancing. They then engaged in friendly competitions of waist wrestling and boxing, each one alternately hitting his adversary on the shoulder or temple. Other adults would also compete and sing.

During the course of the *tivayuq* ceremony they proceeded to exchange wives; two masked individuals presided over the choice of partners.

440   The Iglulik Eskimos knew many outdoor games in

Fig. 15. A tug-of-war at Igloolik. Some of the women wear the more traditional parka with the long tail and child-carrying *amaut*. Others wear the evenly hemmed parka that first appeared in the whaling centers in the late 19th century. A few younger women wear more recent style winter parkas. Photograph by Fred Bruemmer, April 1966.

which boys and girls participated. They played ball divided in two teams, and, especially in the evening, they played a game involving imitating the wolf. Adults often participated in these games, which sometimes took on pronounced sexual overtones. They also played hide-and-seek, founder, and bow and arrow shooting. As for indoor games, there was the suspended *nuɣluktaq* into which several people tried to thrust a stick; exercises done on a skin robe stretched across the igloo; and blind man's buff. The younger children played many other games (Mathiassen 1928:218–228).

Feasts of boiled meat or of frozen caribou, to which the whole camp was invited, were also organized.

Conflict and Social Control

A village was often divided by opposing factions. Conflicts could arise from jealousy, avarice, unauthorized adultery, or the suspicion of witchcraft. Disputes were sometimes resolved by a song contest, where each one strove to ridicule the adversary.

Mockery was also a method of control used by the community against delinquents. This sometimes had the effect of forcing the asocial individuals to flee: the *qivittuq* was, as in Greenland, the misanthrope who lived far away from others.

When a man was feared because of his crimes or suspected misdeeds, the community could decide to eliminate him, with one man or a group executing the sentence. The Tununirmiut had the reputation of having little respect for human life. A murder generally led to a vendetta that ended when one of the parties went into exile (Gilder 1881:248). Cases of bow and arrow combats between two groups are known.

Religion

Eskimo traditions were related during the long winter evenings in the form of legendary narratives. It is mostly from these that one can extract a body of beliefs, however amorphous it may have been.

The notion of a soul was fundamental. All that exists has a soul or can have one. Man has a double soul: *inu·siq*, the breath of life, and *taŷniq*, the soul proper. One's name, *atiq*, is also a kind of soul, generally inherited from an ancestor. For some, each part of the body has its own soul. The soul of an animal that was killed takes over a new body, hence the necessity not to offend it. It is not essentially different from the human soul; the *aŷnakkayuktuq* legend shows a human soul reincarnated in a series of animal forms, and finally in the form of a man. Sickness comes from the loss of one of the souls or of part of the soul, which may have been stolen. The soul, once liberated from the body, generally stays near for a time. When offended it can turn against the living.

The world always existed, but daylight came from the cry of the raven: *qau! qau!* 'light'.

Formerly the Eskimo deities were mere humans. The moon-man (*tatqiq*), having had incestuous relations with his sister the sun (*siqiniq*), pursued her across the sky. Each one was armed with a torch, but the moon's burned out. The moon spirit is well disposed toward human beings and gives them fertility.

uiniŷumayuituq 'the one who did not want a husband' was married by her father to a dog, by whom she had two kinds of offspring, the Indians and the Whites. Fleeing her second husband, the petrel, she was thrown into the water by her father, who cut off her fingers when she grasped his boat. Her phalanges turned into various marine animals whose movements she now directs from her residence at the bottom of the sea. Her name is *aviliayuk* or *nuliayuk*, but she is often called *takanna·luk* 'the one from below'.

Much less important are *pakimna*, mistress of the caribou, and *sila*, the air. Thunder and lightning are sisters, and many of the stars are of human or animal origin.

Numerous supernatural beings populate the world and sometimes make themselves visible. They are dwellers of the sea, of the mountains, of the ground, of the sea shore. The *inuŷayait* are ghosts of the dead, and the *tuuŋ̇ŷait* auxiliary spirits.

The main dwelling place of the dead is situated in the earth (*alli·t* 'those from below') and is composed of four levels in which the lowest one is identified as the abode of *takanna·luk*. The other three constitute a sort of purgatory. The sky makes up the dwelling place of suicides, of those who died a violent death, and of the women who died in childbirth. These are the *ulluŷmiut* 'inhabitants of the daytime'. Some people, generally powerful shamans, are thought to have come back to life after their death.

Innumerable taboos accompanied each life situation, particularly birth and death. *Takanna·luk* was most offended when a woman concealed her menstrual period or a miscarriage. Everything that dealt with hunting was strictly regulated. In particular, an incompatibility existed between terrestrial game and marine game.

Amulets of all sorts brought aid and protection, and magic formulas uttered in certain circumstances were very effective.

The cause of a sickness or a stroke of fate could be discovered through *qilaniq* 'head-lifting' (fig. 16).

ilisiniq was a means of exercising maleficent influence on an enemy. A mischievous spirit or tupilak could be sent out after this enemy. One could also procure the services of an evil shaman who would try to steal the soul of the victim and set his spirits against it.

• SHAMANISM The *aŋakkuq* or shaman was usually the necessary intermediary between the community and the supernatural forces. In order to become an *aŋakkuq*, one had to be initiated by another shaman for several days to obtain instruction ('illumination'). Then, seeking solitude, the novice must become able to see his own body as a skeleton.

The *aŋakkuq* wore a special belt. His principal func-

Mystic Seaport Mus., Conn.: Comer Coll. 66.339.82.

Fig. 16. Demonstrating method for diagnosing illness or identifying a wrong that needs to be corrected so that the evil effect disappears. The head is lifted, a spirit called, and when it arrives the head becomes so heavy it can no longer be lifted. The performer then puts a question concerning the cause of illness or evil to the spirit who has been called and tries to lift the head. As long as he can lift the head without difficulty the answer is negative. An affirmative answer is given when the head cannot be lifted (Boas 1901–1907:135,512). Photograph by George Comer, at Cape Fullerton, N.W.T., April 1905.

tions consisted in healing, seeing into the future, influencing the weather, locating game and securing its return, searching for stolen souls, and fighting against malevolent spirits. These functions were exercised, in particular, during different seances, in which adults participated, whose essential aim was to discover the cause of misfortune.

In the most common seance (*sakavuq*), the *aŋakkuq* summoned his spirits and questioned them. Afterward, the assistants confessed the taboos infringed upon. The shaman could also, with the help of his spirits, go underground and visit *takanna·luk* to try to make her yield, or, after his doubled up body had been tied, take flight (*ilimaγtuγtuq*) toward the land of the *ulluγmiut* and the moon. Another kind of magic flight (*ikiaγqivuq*) would take him to faraway places.

Mythology

In addition to origin myths the folklore contains a large number of narratives, such as the odyssey of *kiviuq* and the story of the girl *navaγanna*, which are known with only a few variants from Alaska to Greenland. Here one finds epic tales, fantastic stories where humans and animals changed their forms and married each other, animal fables, or narratives of historic origin like those dealing with the *tunit* people and the Indians. In general these tales reflect the values most highly prized by the Eskimo—courage, generosity, resourcefulness, hospitality, and moderation.

External Relations

The Tununirmiut, Iglulingmiut, and Aivilingmiut had frequent intercourse with one another. But formerly the Tununirmiut seem to have been at least as frequently in contact with the Akudnirmiut, as witnessed by their costume and their language. At times some of them resided at Akudniq, from where they communicated with Foxe Basin by way of Anaulirialik (Lyon

left, Mystic Seaport Mus., Conn.: Comer Coll. 63.1767.161; right, Amer. Mus. of Nat. Hist., New York: 60/4440.

Fig. 17. Qingailisaq, a shaman. left, Wearing the coat he had made following a vision during a caribou hunting trip. The coat was made to duplicate one worn by a caribou woman (one of the caribou he slew turned into a woman giving birth to a boy). The open hands on the front were meant to ward off evil spirits. The figure of a child appears above the hands (Boas 1901–1907: 509). Photograph by George Comer, probably 1902. right, Qingailisaq's costume. Brown and white caribou fur are sewn into an elaborate mosaic pattern. The top has no hood but is worn with the hat. Most shamans did not wear a special costume but wore ordinary fur coats with special belts. Length of top 98.0 cm; collected by George Comer, 1902.

442

1824). Contacts with the Oqomiut were rarer and sometimes took place via Akudniq (M'Clintock 1859:151). The best known instance is that of the people who, before 1850, left southeast Baffin and Qillaq (Qidlaq) for Pond Inlet, some of whom emigrated later to North Greenland (Mary-Rousselière 1980:39, 43, 69). Boas (1888) mentions four visits by Cumberland Eskimos to Foxe Basin between 1750 and 1835. There has been little contact in either direction since then. The old Sallirmiut were known, but they were considered to be barbarians, and no one maintained relations with them. The Aivilingmiut had a low opinion of the Netsilik whom they feared. Relations between them were strained.

Before the arrival of the whalers, contacts with the Qairnirmiut and the Hauniqtuurmiut were quite rare. Nevertheless, the metal utensils and meat trays found by Parry in 1822 show that commercial relations must have existed (Parry 1824:503; Lyon 1824:346). Before White contact, the Tununirmiut were probably unaware of the existence of their Polar Eskimo neighbors (Mary-Rousselière 1980:39, 43, 69).

History

The lengthy intercourse with the Parry expedition in the 1820s gave the Aivilingmiut and the Iglulingmiut access to an abundance of metal and wooden objects.

The Tununirmiut had their first contacts with Scottish whalers in 1819 or 1820 (Lyon 1824:294). About that time, three ships ran aground in the area (Parry 1824:437; M'Clintock 1859:138–139, 147–148), furnishing them with an abundant supply of wood and iron. Later exchanges took place at the time of the whalers' annual visit, and the Eskimos obtained guns. However, these transient contacts did not profoundly change their way of life.

The situation was different with the Aivilingmiut when the whalers began to winter on Marble Island and at Repulse Bay in the 1860s. The American whalers not only employed the Eskimos during the summers but also lived in symbiosis with them during the winters. In exchange for replenishing the stores of fresh meat and other services, the natives "received little pay beyond their food, which consisted chiefly of the scraps left from the meals" (Low 1906:28). However, as early as 1864 the Nuvuk Eskimos had whaleboats from this source.

Repulse Bay constituted thenceforth a strong pole of attraction for the Iglulingmiut and the Netsilik. Families from Igloolik visited Repulse Bay and Marble Island, while others were going to Pond Inlet to replenish their supply of guns and ammunition. Little by little tea and tobacco (fig. 18) became necessities. For the Netsilik who practiced female infanticide, the possibility of finding wives in Aivilik was an additional incentive to emigrate. The movement was to continue until they reached

Chesterfield, where they eventually found themselves in the majority.

Trapping foxes and hunting musk-oxen took on growing importance. The gun facilitated hunting along the floe edge and favored individualism in the hunt. The introduction of the whaleboat was of great socioeconomic importance and modified the distribution of groups. An increased food supply was then available, and the number of dogs could be increased.

Interbreeding of Whites with Eskimos, especially with the Aivilingmiut, modified the population biologically. Venereal disease and alcohol introduced by the whalers contributed to the Eskimos' decline (Mathiassen 1928:21).

Traditional celebrations gradually gave way to Scottish dances, and the shaman began to lose his prestige. Murders, facilitated for the Tununirmiut by firearms, continued until the arrival of the Royal Canadian Mounted Police.

The period 1920–1960 has been referred to by some as that of the "big three": the Royal Canadian Mounted Police, the Hudson's Bay Company, and the missions. It was mostly from 1920 onward that Euro-Canadian penetration in Iglulik Eskimo territory was accentuated when the Hudson's Bay Company established posts at Repulse Bay and Pond Inlet. In 1922 the RCMP established itself at Pond Inlet from where it regularly visited Igloolik and Arctic Bay. From 1922 to 1967 the Eastern Arctic Patrol annually offered the Baffin Islanders the services of its medical team.

Anglican prayer books had arrived at Pond Inlet as early as 1910, but in particular in 1919. The following year an Eskimo introduced the new religion in the Iglulik area (Mathiassen 1928:235–236). In the south, the Catholic mission founded at Chesterfield in 1912 extended its influence as far north as Igloolik. In 1929 the two denominations began to open missions in the country.

This period is characterized by the development of trapping, but hunting remained at the base of the economy. The trading post was frequented by the neighboring Eskimos. The products they bought from the post were primarily those that facilitated their hunting existence—guns, ammunitions, tools, boats. Food

Natl. Mus. of Canada, Ottawa: IV-C-84.
Fig. 18. Pipe. Wooden stem is bound with sinew, and the soapstone bowl is rimmed with brass (probably a rifle shell case). Both men and women smoked, sometimes mixing the pure tobacco from the trading post with twigs or cotton-grass. Length 6.2 cm; collected by George Comer at Repulse Bay, N.W.T., 1907–1909.

products they used were often limited to tea, flour, molasses, or sugar.

The snowhouse along with the tent remained the usual dwelling, but the earth hut, which had disappeared in Igloolik and at Repulse Bay, experienced a revival in popularity. A few wooden cabins appeared at Pond Inlet.

Christmas and Easter attracted the men of the population to the post, but rarely women and children. No Euro-Canadian institutions encouraged the permanent settlement of the Eskimos.

Lay dispensers belonging to one or another organization took care of basic medical needs and visited the sick. Infant mortality began to decrease, but various epidemics reduced the population severely. After 1950, those infected with tuberculosis were sent to sanatoriums in the south, which was their first prolonged contact with White culture. The distribution of family allowances began in 1947 and gave widows a certain amount of independence.

Work on the Distant Early Warning line, starting in 1955, caused an influx of foreigners to the Iglulik area. The Foxe Main dump became an important pole of attraction, and a small permanent village grew nearby at Hall Beach.

The Netsilik continued to move into the area, and although they made up the majority in the south, they were more and more culturally assimilated by the Aivilingmiut. The opening of the Rankin Inlet mine in 1955 set in motion another southward migration. On Southampton Island, Oqomiut penetration converted the Aivilingmiut, who had moved there after the disappearance of the old Sallirmiut, into a minority. In the north a few Oqomiut families had been settled by the Hudson's Bay Company in 1936. After 1953 several Tununirmiut families emigrated to Resolute and Grise Fiord.

The Hudson's Bay Company manager assumed authority on the regional level, while in the camps the situation was not profoundly modified, since they retained the same composition and authority structure.

Christian faith was naturally tinged with syncretism, especially in the beginning. Some missionaries discouraged not only shamanistic practices but also the use of traditional names and songs. In 1948 religious hysteria broke out in Admiralty Inlet. The last avowed shaman died in 1964, but vestiges of old beliefs still lived on. Polygamy no longer existed; wife exchanges (at least as openly practiced) and divorce gradually disappeared; murders came to an end; and suicides became rarer than earlier.

In the 1950s the Canadian federal government intensified its activity in the Arctic. The administration first helped the mission schools to function more or less regularly. From 1955 a number of children of the area began to frequent the Chesterfield Catholic boarding school. In 1959 day schools were opened at Pond Inlet, Arctic Bay, and Iglulik. This development marked the beginning of the centralization process, which was to be completed almost everywhere by 1970. Hostels were built to house the children, but the parents reconciled themselves with difficulty to the separation. Gradually the camps disappeared as the natives moved to the main settlements. The government deliberately encouraged this movement, starting in 1966, by having low-rent housing constructed in these centers.

At the same time, nursing stations were built, where planes brought in medical teams several times a year and facilitated emergency evacuations. The concentration of population and the care of trained nurses contributed to the rapid decrease in mortality. In contrast, dental caries have become more frequent.

The number of Eskimos who depend primarily on hunting and trapping is diminishing. The introduction of the snowmobile in 1963 marked a revolution that rivaled that of the gun. Despite its many inconveniences it facilitated traveling great distances in a minimum of time, and it greatly diminished the need for meat, since the number of dogs decreased considerably.

The Hudson's Bay Company stores offer a wide choice of products, and the Eskimos now purchase much of their food, including a considerable quantity of soft drinks and sweets, and almost all their clothing.

Adult education centers have been created in several villages, while adolescents sometimes continue their studies outside in various schools.

Most of the adults, many of whom have learned trades in the south, hold permanent or temporary jobs. Since 1971 many from Pond Inlet and Arctic Bay have gone to work in the High Arctic oil fields. At Nanisivik, near Arctic Bay, a lead and zinc mine employed some Eskimos from the nearby village as well as from distant places.

Rapid urbanization resulted in the disappearance of the camp leader. The "settlement manager" sent by the government and the various associations whose directors are elected replaced the traditional leadership. The major association is the Community Council, which received increased responsibility when the settlements reached "hamlet" status.

Cooperatives were founded first at Igloolik in 1962, and since then in other centers. They have facilitated the carving and handicraft trade, and in 1977 each had a store that competed with that of the Hudson's Bay Company.

Generally the family structures remain strong (table 1), although the head of the extended family has lost some of his authority. Eskimo has remained the language spoken in the home, even by most teenagers, and people are showing an increasing pride in their cultural heritage. Frequent communications with the south and between settlements have brought about an increased

Table 1. Number of Unmarried Children per Iglulik Eskimo family

	Pond Inlet	Arctic Bay	Igloolik	Repulse Bay
1822				1.38 (0.75[a])
1898				1.75 (1.40[a])
1922	1.68	2.40	1.10	1.21
1951				2.52
1954			2.75	
1955	2.55	2.42		
1969				3.20
1970	3.49	3.08		
1973			4.16	

[a] Number of children per two adults. The number of children per family is higher because of the numerous cases of polygyny: 12 at Iglulik in 1822 (for 155 Eskimos); 7 at Repulse Bay in 1898 (for 102 Eskimos).

awareness of political problems and especially of land claims. However, with many of the young having lived outside the area and with television being available since 1974, people are increasingly influenced by Euro-Canadian social trends. The prosperity that has touched many Eskimos has brought on problems, including alcoholism and drug addiction. Suicides of young men, almost unheard of in the past, have become frequent. These facts, in the 1970s, gave rise to a back-to-the-land movement at Igloolik and Pond Inlet.

Population

In 1822–1823 the total population met by Parry (1824:492) at Winter Island and Igloolik numbered 219 Eskimos. Parry indicated Tununiq, Tununirusiq, Akulik, Pilik, and Nuvuk to be inhabited localities and also mentioned the northern Sallirmiut. In addition, his map showed "many Eskimaux" at several places along the west coast of Melville Peninsula. From these indications as well as local resources, and other data on the Tununirmiut† the following estimate can be made for the period of Parry's visit: Aivilingmiut, 130; Iglulingmiut, 210; Tununirmiut, 130; Tununirusirmiut, 50; total, 520. Most likely, 400 can be considered as the minimum and 600 the maximum for the 1820s.

Later information was generally incomplete and sometimes doubtful. However, the figures given for the Aivilingmiut and for Pond Inlet can probably be trusted (see table 2). But, contrary to the information given by

†The Pond Inlet population seems to have been reduced periodically by emigrations probably due in part to blood feuds. At least three are known: the most important in the 18th century seems to have involved about 50 persons (Mary-Rousselière 1954); the Qitdlarssuaq migration to Greenland took place around 1860; one reported by Gilder (1881) occurred about 1878.

Low, it is certain that, from about 1894 to 1910, the Admiralty Inlet area had no permanent inhabitants: the original Tununirusirmiut had disappeared.

Despite some additions from the Netsilik and Oqomiut, the present population of Pond Inlet, Arctic Bay, and Igloolik can be considered as descended from the aboriginal one. On the other hand, at Repulse Bay the Netsilik, though strongly assimilated by the Aivilingmiut, represent close to 60 percent of the population. In their former territory those of Aivilingmiut origin are now a minority and have been largely fused with the rest of the population through marriage.

In spite of programs promoting birth control, a demographic explosion is taking place due both to the reduction in infant mortality as well as perhaps to the decrease in breast feeding. About half the population is under 15 years of age.

Synonymy

The names of the three major groups constituting the Iglulik Eskimos were "more geographical than ethnographical" (Mathiassen 1928:21). Mathiassen based his 1922 census on genealogical and cultural data, rather than on residency (Netsilik immigrants were omitted). But subsequently these names have taken on a more ethnographic meaning.

The Tununirmiut (*tununiᵧmiut*) were first and foremost the inhabitants of Tununiq, in Milne Inlet; but in a broader sense this term designated all the inhabitants of the Pond Inlet region. These latter sometimes made a distinction among the Tasiuyarmiut (southern part of Eclipse Sound), the Sanirarmiut (southeast coast), and the Igluamiut (Navy Board Inlet). The present Tununirusirmiut (from Tununirusiq, in Adams Sound) are generally considered as a branch of the Tununirmiut, the old population of the area having disappeared at the end of the nineteenth century.

The name Iglulingmiut (*iᵧluliŋmiut*) comes from the old village of Igloolik (*iᵧlulik*), on the same island but distinct from the present settlement of Igloolik. Its meaning has been broadened to include all the inhabitants of northern Foxe Basin, who are sometimes called *itiviŋmiut* by the Pond Inlet people. They themselves distinguished among the Amitturmiut (southwest coast); the Kangirlugyuarmiut (Steensby Inlet); the Pilingmiut (east coast), also called Ualinarmiut in folklore; and the Sallirmiut of Rowley Island (not to be confused with the homonymous groups now and formerly on Southampton Island).

The Aivilingmiut, also called Nauyarmiut, were the inhabitants of Aivilik in Repulse Bay and its surrounding area. Boas (1901–1907:6) reports that an Eskimo tribe, the Nuvugmiut, which lived to the south of Wager

Table 2. Population, 1822–1981

Date	Pond Inlet	Admiralty Inlet	Igloolik	Repulse Bay	Total	Source
1822	130[a]	50[a]	155+ (210[a])	64+ (130[a])	520[a]	Parry 1824
1898				102		Boas 1901–1907
1904	144	40[a]	60[a]	138	328 (450[a])	Low 1906
1906			125[a]	271[b]		Sellers 1907
1906–1907	160		200 (150[c])			Bernier 1910
1910–1911		18				Bernier 1911
1922	171	22	146	165[d]	504	Mathiassen 1928
1930	70?	100?	100?	155?	425?	census 1930
1939	181 (154[e])	100	223[f] (245[a])			RCMP, Pond Inlet
1941	175	156	349			census
1944–1945	170[g]		238[h]			C.M.*
1950	203					Danielo 1955
1955	249 (288[i])	160				RCMP, Pond Inlet
1963	269	183	485			Bisset 1967
1967	343	199	680	151	1,373	RCMP, Pond Inlet; Crowe 1970
1970	389	240				RCMP, Pond Inlet
1972	408	264	867[j]	234	1,793	Gov. N.W.T.
1974	459	295	852[k]	246	1,851	Gov. N.W.T.
1981	616	387	1,025[l]	367	2,395	C.M.*

*Catholic Mission records, Pond Inlet, Igloolik, Repulse Bay.
[a] Estimate.
[b] Probably includes Aivilingmiut and Eskimos from Hudson Strait and other places (see Low 1906:138).
[c] Calculated from the number of male adults whose names were given to Bernier (1910:41).
[d] Netsilik inhabitants not included.
[e] Buchan Gulf (Anaulirialik) Eskimos not included.
[f] Agu Bay Eskimos not included.
[g] Heavy mortality due to epidemic.
[h] Hudson's Bay Company store was closed from 1943 to 1948.
[i] Including Tununirmiut families on Ellesmere and Cornwallis islands.
[j] Of which 275 reside at Hall Beach.
[k] Of which 293 reside at Hall Beach.
[l] Including 310 at Hall Beach.

Inlet, was wiped out by the Aivilingmiut before 1800, who were thus able to expand to the south of Nuvuk.

Sources

In their journals Parry (1824) and Lyon (1824) give a detailed description of the lives of the Iglulik Eskimos at the time of their first contact with the Whites. No other Arctic expedition narratives rival theirs in richness of ethnographic information.

Rae (1850) and Gilder (1881) both related some interesting details about the Aivilingmiut. In spite of his five years with the Eskimos, the notes left by C. F. Hall (1879) furnish only a few scattered bits of information. As for the Tununirmiut in the nineteenth century, a few brief pieces of information are found in M'Clintock (1859).

The particulars given to Boas by Comer (1921) and Mutch (1906), as well as those found in Low (1906), Bernier (1909, 1911), and Tremblay (1921) are instructive but sometimes require confirmation.

It is mainly in Rasmussen (1929, 1930) and Mathiassen (1928) that the essential ethnographic data are found. Unfortunately a good part of the material used by Rasmussen came from the Netsilik folklore. On the other hand, perhaps Mathiassen had a tendency to accentuate the differences that existed between the Thule and the Iglulik Eskimo cultures.

Since then a few anthropologists have studied several aspects of the Iglulik Eskimo culture: J.S. Matthiasson (1967) and Rousseau (1970) at Pond Inlet, Damas in Iglulik (1963) and Repulse Bay, Honda and Fujiki (1963) in Iglulik. Finally, Crowe (1970) has published a study on Iglulik human geography.

The most important source for this chapter is Mary-Rousselière's residence among Iglulik Eskimos at Pond Inlet, Igloolik, and Repulse Bay since 1944. His chief informants have been M. Ataguttaaluk (b. 1875, d. 1948), Qidlaq (b. 1880, d. 1960), H. Kappianaq (b. 1881, d. 1963), Quliktalik (Alrak) (b. 1888, d. 1963), Inuguk (b. 1893, d. 1975), W. Ukumaaluk (b. 1896, d. 1956), J.M. Anannguaq (b. 1892, d. 1973), L. Uutaq (b. 1893, d. 1967), Atuat (b. 1890, d. 1976), J. Qumangaapik (b. 1905, d. 1981), D. Arnatsiaq (b. 1909), S. Atagutsiaq (b. 1915, d. 1982), and Qanguq (b. 1916).

Caribou Eskimo

EUGENE Y. ARIMA

Language and Territory

The several similar but independent Inuit bands on the west side of Hudson Bay from Chesterfield Inlet to the tree line are known as Caribou Eskimos. They speak varieties of Inuit-Inupiaq differing slightly from those of their neighbors.*

These southernmost of Central Eskimos have lived below the Arctic Circle at roughly 61–65° north latitude and 90–102° west longitude since at least the late nineteenth century. Their area was about 300 miles square, extending east to west from Hudson Bay to the Dubawnt River and north to south from Chesterfield Inlet and the Thelon River to the first trees (fig. 1).

Four main groups of Caribou Eskimos—the Qairnirmiut, Hauniqtuurmiut, Harvaqtuurmiut, and Paallirmiut—were recognized by the Danish Fifth Thule Expedition of 1921–1924 (Birket-Smith 1929, 1:59–62; Rasmussen 1930:9). Later Gabus (1944a:26, 126) added a fifth, the Ahiarmiut to the southwest on the upper Maguse and Kazan rivers. The Qairnirmiut extended from the sea coast between Chesterfield Inlet to Rankin Inlet to their main region around Baker Lake. Some also lived as far inland as Beverly Lake. The Hauniqtuurmiut, much reduced in the twentieth century, lived near the coast south of the Qairnirmiut about the Wilson and Ferguson rivers. West of them were the Harvaqtuurmiut along the lower Kazan River below Yathkyed Lake and its tributary, the Kunwak River, extending inland to Beverly Lake and the lower Dubawnt River. The Paallirmiut to the south of the Hauniqtuurmiut and Harvaqtuurmiut were the most populous group with Birket-Smith distinguishing a coast-visiting subgroup on the lower Maguse River and an interior one around Yathkyed Lake extending west to Dubawnt Lake. Since about 1960 the Caribou Eskimos have become concentrated in several large settlements under Canadian government encouragement and subsidy. In 1982 most of the Qairnirmiut and Harvaqtuurmiut lived at Baker Lake (Qamanittuaq), most Paallirmiut and Ahiarmiut at Eskimo Point (Arviat); and the Hauniqtuurmiut remnants have been absorbed into the other groups at Whale Cove (Tikiraaryuaq) and Rankin Inlet (Kangiqliniq). Chesterfield Inlet (Igluligaaryuk) is a secondary center for Qairnirmiut, and Padlei, until it closed, was the Ahiarmiut center. In the early 1980s there were about 3,000 Caribou Eskimo (table 1).

The several main groups of Caribou Eskimos may be equated with the maximal bands distinguished for other Central Eskimos on the basis of their former scale of about 50 to 300 persons, group autonomy though without formal political organization, cooperation and sharing, and perhaps most of all the consciousness of group identity marked by behavioral or artifactual distinctions as in speech style or dress, territorial location, and group name.

External Relations

Intertribal relations were particularly close with the Aivilingmiut when they and the northernmost Caribou Eskimos associated with the nineteenth-century commercial whalers. Contact with Whites began in the eighteenth century with the founding of Churchill, and until the whaling period the Caribou Eskimos were middlemen in trade, passing European goods to the Iglulik, Netsilik, and Copper Eskimos. A well-known summer trading center was at Akiliniq on the northwest side of Beverly Lake, whose driftwood had long attracted Inuit from afar (Birket-Smith 1929, 1:161–163; Jenness 1922:48; Stefánsson 1914:4–7). A few enterprising Caribou Eskimos carried the trade themselves to the Back River and even Coronation Gulf. On the other hand, many of the Utkuhikhalingmiut and Hanningayurmiut (groups of Netsilik Eskimos) of the Back River shifted southward to the Thelon. Relations with the Chipewyan and Dogrib to the south and west were largely inimical although trade occurred (Birket-Smith 1929, 1:36, 164–165; Graham 1969:172–174, 214; Hearne 1958:217–218; Rasmussen 1930:15, 102–104).

*The phonemes of Caribou Eskimo are: (voiceless stops) p, t, k, q; (voiced fricatives) v, y, γ, γ̇; (voiceless fricatives) h ([h] and [s] vary dialectally); (nasals) m, n, ŋ; (laterals) l and perhaps ł; (short vowels) i, a, u; (long vowels) i·, a·, u·. Before nasals γ̇ is [ŋ].

In the practical orthography commonly in use these phonemes are written: p, t, k, q; v, j, g, r; h; m, n, ng; l; i, a, u; ii, aa, uu. Group names, place-names, and others used as English designations are in the practical orthography, but with y instead of j. Since these are based on a dialect with h for s, forms like Hila are used where Iglulik, for example, has Sila.

Information on Caribou Eskimo phonology and the transcription of words is from Eugene Y. Arima, S.T. Mallon, Anthony C. Woodbury, and Webster and Zibell (1976:276–277).

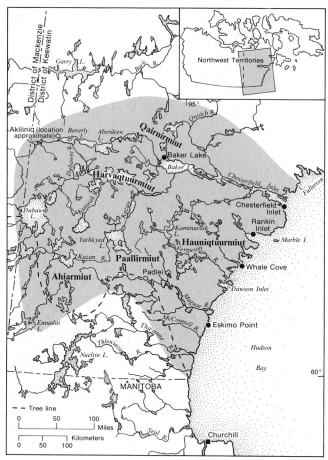

Fig. 1. Distribution of Caribou Eskimos in the mid-19th to mid-20th century.

Culture

Subsistence and Technology

Caribou Eskimo culture is best known as it was earlier in the century when Birket-Smith (1929, 1), Gabus (1944a), and Rasmussen (1930) pictured it as predominantly inland with a one-sided focus on the Barren Ground caribou. Musk-oxen were also important, particularly over the second half of the nineteenth century (Burch 1977:143–146). Technology may be conveniently described in the context of the annual round. The caribou provided not only food but also the raw materials for many artifacts in the skins used for clothing, bedding, tent and kayak covers, containers, and rawhide line; sinew for thread and braided lines; and antler and bone for hard implements like snow beaters, moss spades, scrapers, tool handles, gorges, bola weights, arrowheads, arrow straighteners, ice chisel blades, hooks, needles, and snow knives.

Each spring the majority of the caribou migrate from four winter ranges in the forests toward two main calving regions, one by Kaminuriak Lake near the center of the Caribou Eskimo area and the other about Beverly Lake to the northwest (Kelsall 1968:177–180; Parker 1972:24–28). The pregnant cows reach the Caribou Eskimos first, usually during May when the spring thaw forces the Eskimos' dwelling to be changed from snowhouse to a transitional qaɣmaq (snow walls roofed with skins), then to the conical tent, usually of seven or eight poles supporting a cover of a dozen caribou skins, hair side out. Since the ice on the lakes and rivers stays into June, the first caribou to arrive were shot. Formerly they were driven between long converging lines of stone cairns capped with dark upturned turf or stakes hung with waving scares (pieces of wood or skin, clothing, or bird wings) to the hunters who were concealed in shallow shooting pits (Birket-Smith 1929, 1:84, 110; Rasmussen 1930:40) since the native D-bows, though sinew-backed, and even the trade muzzle-loaders had but short range. In June there is a lull when the cows are calving on elevated rocky terrain while the others are still on their way. The bulls may come by the end of June, some joining the cows who have formed large postcalving aggregations continuing slowly in the lines of migration. Between mid-July and mid-August, after erratic local movements, the caribou move to near the tree line in a mid-summer migration. Thousands or even tens of thousands of caribou can concentrate against water barriers posed by the major lake and river system and funnel into crossing places at lake narrows or slow river sections where the Caribou Eskimos waited to lance (fig. 3) the swimming herds from their kayaks (cf. Arima 1975:147–153). Such hunting was very productive, and surplus meat was preserved by sun-drying in thin slices laid on flat rock or gravel.

Fish formed a major food source, particularly when shifts in caribou migratory pattern or population fluctuations left the Caribou Eskimos short. Especially productive was the interception of arctic char on their spawning runs by stone weirs built across shallow streams and their capture with leister or bag trap (Birket-Smith 1929, 1:119–120). Other summer fishing techniques included hooks and cast from shore, baited gorges set in shallows, and harpooning from banks, all displaced around the mid-twentieth century by imported gill nets and rod-cast spinning lures, which can take lake trout

Table 1. Population by Settlements, 1979

	Population	Percent Iniut
Eskimo Point	980	99.9%
Whale Cove	203	92.0
Rankin Inlet	956	72.3
Chesterfield Inlet	281	90.7
Baker Lake	1,017	86.4
Totals	3,437	87.06%

SOURCE: Devine and Wood 1981:46, 54, 66, 126, 145.

NOTE: These figures do not distinguish tribal affiliations and thus include immigrant Netsilik and Iglulik Eskimo.

448

Fig. 2. Skin preparation. When a caribou is skinned, the hide is dried and stored until ready to be used. To prepare the hide for use in clothing the woman usually sleeps on it for a night so that her body heat works on the fibers. It is then cleaned with a bone scraper (left); the fibers stretched and crushed with the stone scraper (center); the hide moistened and put away for a day; and finally scraped to the desired thickness with the scraper (right) with a metal blade and bone handle. The scrapers are held with the palm up and work is away from the body (Birket-Smith 1929:240–247). Length of left, 14.8 cm, rest same scale; all collected by D.B. Marsh, Eskimo Point area, N.W.T., before 1938.

in abundance from the rivers. Excess fish were preserved by splitting and drying or by caching in sand down against the permafrost (Arima 1966–1969). The plentiful summer period also provided ducks, geese, ptarmigans, gulls, and their eggs. Formerly a double-pointed dart without side prongs was used for waterfowl from the kayak. Also used for birds were the bolas, sling, ptarmigan bow, gull gorge, and sinew line noose (Birket-Smith 1929, 1:114–116). Ground squirrels and hares were snared as well. Plants had minor value as food, the practical and relished raw consumption of much of the meat and fish ensuring a sufficiency of vitamins. Several kinds of berries and a root were eaten, but the main plant food was the crop contents of the caribou and ptarmigan stomachs.

Frequent moves were made in summer by many families to reach different game. The Caribou Eskimos were strong walkers, carrying substantial back loads of implements, bedding, and the tent with tumplines over brow and chest. Dogs, of which there were only a couple in each family before the trapping economy, carried pack bags and dragged tent poles. Kayaks, with two to several lashed together by cross poles for stability, could transport passengers and baggage not only in short ferryings but also for long distances on calm waters (Arima 1975:156–158).

The summer hunts by the fast narrow kayaks at the crossing places were of key importance since they furnished not only a great quantity of food from the increasingly fat caribou but also skins for clothing with the right fur, not too long and loose but dense, following the molt, which took place about June for bulls and July for calving cows. Also, in August the skins healed from the numerous breathing holes made in the back by the warble fly larvae that exit to pupate in June. Clothing required the most skins, with six to eight needed for an adult outfit.

There were different degrees of organization in caribou lancing (Arima 1975:150–151). When the caribou were dispersed in small fly-harassed bands in July, one or two kayakers might wait by the shore while another frightened the animals with a white skin taken to be a wolf so that they fled into the water. Most organized was the driving of a herd by women and children into a crossing where several kayakers waited until the caribou were more than halfway across, then intercepted and herded them up current if there was one to tire them. A couple of the hunters lanced while the rest kept the animals from escaping. Migrating caribou usually needed no urging to take to water and, when in great numbers, were quite fearless, but when a herd was about to cross people kept quiet for precaution. For directing caribou to a preferred crossing spot, a single row of cairns or stakes was commonly used. Even a solitary cairn hung with a noisily flapping scapula could keep caribou from a spot where the current was too strong for kayak hunting. The caribou were usually lanced around the lower back to pierce the diaghragm, aorta, or vital organs. Slain caribou were towed ashore, up to five at a time, for skinning and butchering by the women, or if they had floated downstream, they might be brought back in pieces stowed inside or on top of the kayaks.

Caches of caribou and fish from the summer and fall maintained the groups gathered at the crossing places into winter (Birket-Smith 1929, 1:71; Gilder 1881:43–46; Hanbury 1904:70–71). Snow begins to accumulate in late September, and by late October there is usually enough in drifts to build snowhouses. Two or more families often built multiunit houses. Besides the usual antechambers of windbreak, passage tunnel, and storerooms, there was a special conical cooking chamber open at the high top to let out smoke and heat because most Caribou Eskimos boiled meat over open fires of tundra vegetation rather than the blubber lamp.

Fig. 3. Caribou lance. An iron point is secured with metal rivets to an antler foreshaft, which is in turn attached to the wooden shaft. The shaft tapers toward the foreshaft and is curved downward to aid in thrusting the weapon; it is used when hunting caribou from a kayak. Length 170.5 cm; collected by Christian Leden at Churchill, Man., 1913.

Fig. 4. Woman from Eskimo Point carrying a load of "moss," i.e., dwarf birch, willow, heather, etc., commonly used for fuel. The inland-oriented Caribou Eskimo used open fires instead of oil lamps for cooking (Birket-Smith 1929:87–89). Photograph by Donald B. Marsh, 1930s or 1940s.

Fig. 5. Spade made from a single piece of caribou antler, used to dig moss for fuel. Length 33.4 cm; collected by Knud Rasmussen at Baker Lake, N.W.T., 1922.

Preferred fuel plants (Arima 1966–1969) were bilberry, Labrador tea, dwarf birch, and cassiope, the last two resinous enough to burn even when damp. Willow, though abundant, did not burn well. Women gathered great bundles of fuel (figs. 4–5), some being set aside in the fall for winter. After snow came, the fuel had to be dug up and beaten with little spades shaped from the broad brow tine of the caribou's antlers. But fuel could not always be gathered in winter so that often only frozen food was eaten for days. Water did not have to be melted since winter camps were situated near lakes where a waterhole could be kept open. For illumination caribou fat, marrow, or fish oil was burned in a small saucerlike soapstone lamp or simply a flat stone with a depression. Although temperature in the snowhouses attained only 24–26°F through body heat (Hanbury 1904:77), the only serious difficulty from the lack of the blubber lamp was that stockings and inner parkas damp from perspiration and raw skins for clothing could be dried only by placement against the body overnight (Birket-Smith 1929, 1:245; Rasmussen 1930:45).

For magico-religious reasons, new clothing for winter was not made until snowhouses were built (Hanbury 1904:65). The arduous mechanical skin dressing, in which men assisted, involved scraping off flesh and connective tissue, breaking the fiber with a sandstone scraper, and thinning with an iron-edged scraper for a white, soft result. The clothing (figs. 6–9) was superlatively tailored, particularly among the Qairnirmiut, with decorative inserts of white belly fur, striped edges, and tassels. Special festive dress for women included a pair of

Fig. 6. Men's summer clothing. The parka has side slits for movement and the lower edge is fringed to prevent lifting by the wind. Men also wear skin trousers, boots, and mittens. left, Men at Baker Lake. Man on the far right wears a small bag, perhaps for ammunition. The old man on far left has his sun goggles raised on his forehead. Photograph by J.B. Tyrrell, 1893. right, Man from Padlei wearing goggles with a beaded band. Photograph by Richard Harrington, 1949–1950.

long tapered sticks to which the hair was bound at the sides with spiraling strips of light and dark fur or colored beaded cloth. Women also wore a brow band of shiny telescope brass (fig. 10) flanked by bead strands, short bead strands at the ears, and beadwork panels on the inner parka, plus facial tattooing. Some men wore beaded parkas, headbands, and ear tassels, but none had the tattoos.

Although most caribou winter in the forest, small bands remain on the tundra as in the vicinity of the lower Kazan River (Rasmussen 1930:27) or the coast between Rankin Inlet and Eskimo Point (Parker 1972:24, 45–46). They can be effectively hunted with rifles. Formerly with the bow and arrow caribou were extremely difficult to get in winter since they fled at the creaking of snow underfoot, and close approach was possible only in storms (Birket-Smith 1929, 1:107). Pitfalls were cut into the snow, covered with thin slabs and baited with urine; these were effective only if the caribou were numerous (Arima 1966–1969; Hanbury 1904:114–115). Fishing was a more certain pursuit in winter. While the ice remained thin enough, the fish were lured to the chiseled-out hole by a decoy jigged on a line and speared with the leister. With thick ice, a barbless iron hook set in a combined sinker and lure of bone or ivory was used. Despite fishing possibilities, after the caches from the summer and fall were exhausted, food shortage often occurred, sometimes becoming starvation.

In winter with caribou scarce and skittish, the large nonmigratory musk-ox was a vital complementary resource. It figured in the nineteenth-century shift from a diversified sea and land economy to a focus on these two prime land animals (Burch 1977:143–146). Musk-ox was mainly important as food, but its horn was utilized for soup ladles (fig. 13), ice scoops, bows, and leister prongs while the skin provided bedding and tenting. Musk-ox skin was valuable in the fur trade from 1820 until hunting prohibition in 1917, particularly when buffalo robes ran out in the south (Tener 1965:102). Before decimation in the late nineteenth century, the musk-ox extended across the Caribou Eskimo area nearly to the Hudson Bay coast (Ferguson 1938:136; Hearne 1958:87). Like polar and grizzly bears, musk-ox were formerly killed with bow and arrow or a heavy lance while held at bay by dogs. Bears were relished but apparently little hunted.

A major winter activity in the twentieth century was

Amer. Mus. of Nat. Hist., New York: top, 60/4320; bottom, 60/2684.
Fig. 7. Men's parkas. top, Outer parka of caribou skin with fringed border. bottom, Inner parka with caribou fur on the inside and fringed border. In warmer weather it would be worn without the accompanying outer garment, so was sometimes ornamented with beadwork. This example has simple decorative trim of skin strips. Back length 137.0 cm; collected by George Comer in Qairnirmiut territory, 1899. top, Same scale, collected by Comer in Qairnirmiut territory, 1902.

top left, Public Arch. of Canada, Ottawa: PA 112079; top right, Royal Canadian Mounted Police Mus., Regina, Sask.; bottom right, Hudson's Bay Company Lib., Winnipeg, Man.

Fig. 8. Women's garments have wide shoulders to allow the mother to bring the infant around front to nurse without having to take it out of the parka (Birket-Smith 1929:213–215). top left, Girls from Padlei. The one on left is wearing a beaded inner parka, the one on right an outer winter parka. The long hood of the parka is usually worn by girls only after their first menses (Birket-Smith 1929:223). Photograph by Richard Harrington, Feb. 1950. top right, Highly decorated inner parka, the front decorated with a square piece of cloth with bead pendants. Shoulders and cuffs are also decorated with beaded cloth, while the beaded work at the neck is from the fringe of the hood. Browbands hammered out of discarded pieces of metal became popular in the 19th century (Birket-Smith 1929:229). Photograph by Geraldine Moodie, 1906. bottom left, Eskimo woman with brass browband decorated with cloth and long strands of colored beads, part of which are tucked behind her ear. The waistband buttons, possibly of wood, are visible. She smokes a stone pipe with stem of willow bound with sinew. Photograph by Donald B. Marsh, 1938. bottom right, Third wife of Kakoot, a resident of the Ennadai Lake area. She wears brass browband, beaded hair sticks, decorated inner parka, and woolen shawl that replaced the outer parka in summer (Birket-Smith 1929:219). Photograph by Thierry Mallet, 1926.

452

Fig. 9. Young woman's parka. This caribou fur outer parka was worn over an inner parka with fur side toward the body. A girl's parka has a close-fitting hood and truncated tails. The parka develops as the girl does, the hood becoming fuller and the tails longer. The leather loops attached to the back lower hem allow it to be turned under and fastened; although reported as a sign that the wearer was in her menstrual period, it was probably a matter of fashion among young women (Driscoll 1980). Width at shoulders 61.0 cm; collected at Eskimo Point, N.W.T., 1938.

trapping, and the white foxes caught were eaten. In spring the numerous ptarmigans arriving before the caribou migration were often of critical importance by alleviating famine. They were shot with a small bow or sometimes simply stoned.

Seals were not hunted through breathing holes in winter except by a few Qairnirmiut at Chesterfield Inlet in the twentieth century because, according to Birket-Smith (1929, 1:126–127), the coast to the south was too shallow. In the spring, about a quarter of the Caribou

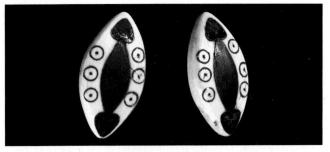

Fig. 11. Ornaments. Inlaid and engraved ivory ornaments have a metal eye on the back through which a leather belt was run. The strap was used to support a child carried in the parka. In the Central Arctic this strap was passed through a double or single loop at the parka neck opening and the ornament at each end of the belt pushed under the loops (Driscoll 1983). Length 7.5 cm; collected by E.W. Hawkes at Chesterfield Inlet, N.W.T., 1914.

Eskimos traveled to the coast before the end of May to shoot seals basking on the ice (Birket-Smith 1929, 1:36, 125). A thrusting harpoon about 40 feet long (Rae 1850:191) may have been used before. Seals, and walrus, were taken also at the floe edge. In July when the coastal ice broke up, sea mammals were pursued with watercraft, formerly a wider version of the kayak; by the 1920s, whaleboats and factory-made canoes were employed. Although sea mammal meat was generally disdained (Arima 1966–1969; Gabus 1944:30, 44), it did sustain people at the coast.

The Hauniqtuurmiut and a few Qairnirmiut burned sea mammal oil in semilunar soapstone lamps into the 1920s (Birket-Smith 1929, 1:91; Rasmussen 1930:11), although the Paallirmiut with more abundant plant fuel apparently used all blubber as dog feed (Gabus 1944:80). The dogs undoubtedly benefited from a period of rich sea mammal diet. From the strong skin of the bearded

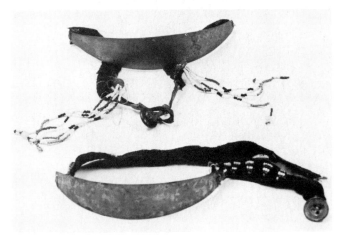

Fig. 10. Brow bands. The brass ornament, hammered out of old telescopes, is worn across a woman's forehead. Cloth strips decorated with beads are wrapped around the head and a leather loop with button closure secures the band. Width 2.9 cm; collected by Douglas Leechman at Chesterfield Inlet, N.W.T., 1934.

Fig. 12. Mittens. There is no difference in style between men's and women's mittens. These have fur on the inside of the hand with a decorative fur border at the bottom. Length 24.0 cm; collected by George Comer, in Qairnirmiut territory, 1899.

Fig. 13. Drinking vessels. top, Musk-ox horn ladle used with soup. It is dipped into the cooking pot and passed around those being served, who each sip from a corner. bottom, Skin cup with a wooden handle that is dipped into a water pail. A bird bone was used to suck water in the spring when lips are split in the dry air (Birket-Smith 1929:148). Height 8.0 cm, top same scale. Both collected by George Comer, in Qairnirmiut territory, 1899.

seal dog traces and boot soles were made; both products were traded to inland groups. Walrus ivory was used for artifacts such as snow knives, fish hooks, and needles in the past. Sea mammals had an important place in the exploitative system even in the twentieth century when their hunting had diminished. Still, each August the Caribou Eskimos returned inland for their great crossing-place hunts of the preferred caribou.

Social Organization

Caribou Eskimo social organization is comparatively poorly documented in the literature. The major named groups—Qairnirmiut, Hauniqtuurmiut, Harvaqtuurmiut, Paallirmiut, Ahiarmiut—lacked formalized leadership and hierarchical organization. They apparently did not aggregate regularly and totally, although the maximal gatherings of 100 to 300 individuals at trade centers prior to the concentration in permanent settlements (for example, Gabus 1944a:28; Lofthouse 1922:109, 111) may have included most of a group. There was considerable intermarriage among the three northern groups, and for the Qairnirmiut and Harvaqtuurmiut as recorded in Rasmussen's (1930:11–13, 22–23) listing of 1921–1922 almost one-quarter of 42 existing marriages were exogamous, mainly between

the two groups, while only one involved non–Caribou Eskimo (Arima 1966–1969). A few decades earlier during the whaling period, heightened interaction between the Qairnirmiut and the Iglulik and Netsilik Eskimos produced more "intertribal" marriages, on the order of 10 percent. Degree of exogamy has not been ascertained for the Hauniqtuurmiut, but it was high due to their being absorbed into the other Caribou Eskimo groups when they decreased greatly in numbers. The Paallirmiut and Ahiarmiut similarly intermarried with other groups.

Local groups or encampments regularly numbered about 50 individuals at most, and typically on the order of 10 to 25, while a few numbered still less, often consisting of isolated nuclear families, either conjugal or stem nuclear with extra unmated adult members. In the 1921–1923 period 25 local groups were recorded for the Caribou Eskimos exclusive of the Ahiarmiut, some in winter and some in spring (Birket-Smith 1929, 1:74; Rasmussen 1930:11–13, 22–23, 37–38), for an average camp size of 17.3 individuals if the population without Ahiarmiut was 432 (Birket-Smith 1929, 1:66). Fluctuations in groups over seasons and years are not documented well, but it was noted that aggregation was most pronounced in late summer at the caribou crossing places for the communal hunts and these concentrations tended to persist well into, if not through, the winter, because of the resultant cached food surplus (Birket-Smith 1929, 1:71; Gilder 1881:43–46; Hanbury 1904:70–71). Local group size likely diminished over the winter since fam-

Fig. 14. Ayaranee, son of Arloo, using a bow drill. The mouthpiece was often made of caribou vertebra or wood. The bow is made out of wood with a string of seal thong (Birket-Smith 1929:239). Photograph by Donald B. Marsh, near Eskimo Point, 1936–1937.

ilies might move off at any time to try other hunting and fishing localities. In summer, settlement became more scattered in the interior with small hunting groups of varying size predominant, but on the coast the lesser portion of the population that moved there would concentrate at a few places with good sea mammal hunting and trade opportunities; for example, the 108 Paallirmiut at the coast in the summer of 1923 were in four camps of 7 to 44 individuals. As for group composition, reconstruction through genealogical data of the Qairnirmiut and Harvaqtuurmiut camps of the 1921–1922 winter indicates that two of the 13 groups were each constituted by a nuclear family, four by an extended family with living primary kin links, and seven by a pair to several families, nuclear and extended, of which half had close cousin or avuncular linkages (Arima 1966–1969). In the 10 extended families out of a total of 18 family units, there were 10 parent-son links, six parent-daughter, five brother-brother, three brother-sister, and one brother-sister, indicating bilaterality in such family ties but with a definite emphasis on male bonds, at least for the Qairnirmiut and Harvaqtuurmiut. The ideal form was apparently a patrilocal extended family living in a large common or multiple-unit snowhouse, large tent, or smaller neighboring tents (Birket-Smith 1929, 1:83; Damas 1971:68; Gabus 1944a:53, 67–72; Steenhoven 1968:13). The family had a leader or *ihumataq* 'one who takes thought' in its eldest male unless he was mediocre. In a multifamily camp, an outstanding family head was often also a voluntarily followed group *ihumataq* (Birket-Smith 1929, 1:258–59; Steenhoven 1962:65).

Caribou Eskimo society was principally organized about kinship (fig. 15). Relationships were only slightly set by the partnerships based on seal or other game sharing, joking, same name, or singing and dancing, which ties were prominent among Copper and Netsilik Eskimos (Damas 1969b:127–129, 1969a:48–50, 1971:57–62). Spouse exchanges established some quasi-kin relationships and might be considered periodic marriages. Kinship terminology may be given in tentative charts based on Birket-Smith's (1929, 1:296) mainly Paallirmiut list and Qairnirmiut and Harvaqtuurmiut data (Arima 1966–1969). At variance from the so-called Eskimo type system (for example, Murdock 1949:227) are the two terms for same-sex cousins and bifurcate collateral terms for uncles, aunts, nephews, and nieces. Cospouse terms exist since polygyny was frequent; for example, in 1922–1923 almost one-fifth of the married men had two wives, very often sisters (Birket-Smith 1929, 1:67–68). Three wives were exceptional. Levirate and sororate were practiced as well. Female ego's terms for sister's children accord with sororate and sororal polygyny, as does that for mother's sister. Polyandry was sporadic and short-lived (Gabus 1944a:82).

Betrothals were commonly arranged in infancy (Birket-Smith 1929, 1:293; Gabus 1944a:97), as the boy's parents sought to ensure a wife for him in view of the shortage of girls due to female infanticide. Among the adults, however, women outnumbered men due to higher male mortality through hunting accidents, particularly freezing in storms. Marriage usually occurred without ceremony when the girl reached puberty and began cohabitation. Young couples could reside with either parental family as was practical (Birket-Smith 1929, 1:294; Steenhoven 1962:42) or, less commonly, separately, but there was a definite tendency to patrilocality. About one-tenth of the marriages among the Qairnirmiut and Harvaqtuurmiut in 1921–1922 involved cousins (Arima 1966–1969). Very rarely uncle-niece or aunt-nephew unions might occur. Since it was not impeded by formalized obstacles, divorce was not uncommon initially, but children tended to cement marriage. For the childless, adoption was common.

Murder entailed vengeance by close kin, but this involvement of the kinship system was rarely manifested among the Caribou Eskimos, at least in the twentieth century, because of the limited occurrence of killings and a reliance upon external police action (Birket-Smith 1929, 1:265; Steenhoven 1962:68–70). Witchcraft was closely related to murder since it was usually meant to kill, but it seems to have been comparatively infrequent (Rasmussen 1930:50).

Economic interaction was governed principally by residential association, which in turn was strongly influenced by kinship and exploitative task requirements. The land and its resources were held to be for all and not to be claimed by individuals or communities, although each group had a vaguely demarcated home area (Birket-Smith 1929, 1:261; Steenhoven 1962:57). All hunting returns were common local group property to an extent through well-developed sharing in the camp. Implements and clothing belonged to the individual who made or used them, and at death most such personal possessions were placed on the grave (Birket-Smith 1929, 1:263, 302–306; Gabus 1944a:134; Steenhoven 1962:46).

Knowledge and Beliefs

As may be expected, the economically all-important caribou was prominent in Caribou Eskimo thought. "If the conversation of the Eskimos does not turn upon new winter clothing, it is usually about the hunt and the contents of the meat caches" (Birket-Smith 1929, 1:95); all three subjects involve the caribou, of course. This focus on the caribou involved an extensive specially associated vocabulary whose specificity astonished Rasmussen (1930:139–144). There were, for example, at least 20 designations for the animal distinguishing maturation, sex, fatness, coat, and other features (Arima 1966–1969). In supernatural belief, as described primarily by Rasmussen (1930:48–65), the caribou, along with other land creatures including man, had a female

455

a

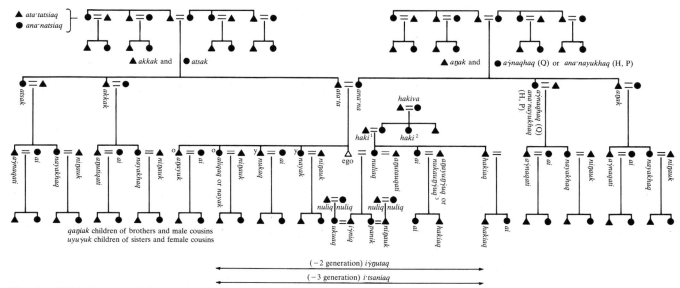

(+3 generation) ▲ *amauk* and ● *niŋiuq*

▲ *ata·tatsiaq*
● *ana·natsiaq*

▲ *akkak* and ● *atsak*

▲ *aŋak* and ● *aẏnaqhaq* (Q) or *ana·nayukhaq* (H, P)

qaŋiak children of brothers and male cousins
uyu·ẏuk children of sisters and female cousins

(−2 generation) *iẏŋutaq*
(−3 generation) *i·tsaniaq*

[1] Terms for wife's father's consanguineal relatives are the same as for those of the wife's mother.
[2] Terms for wife's mother's sibling's children are the same as for wife's sibling's children.
[3] *aŋayuŋẏuq* 'wife's older sister's husband'; *nukauŋẏuq* 'wife's younger sister's husband'.

b

(+3 generation) ▲ *amauk* and ● *niŋiuq*

▲ *ata·tatsiaq*
● *ana·natsiaq*

▲ *akkak* and ● *atsak*

▲ *aŋak* and ● *aẏnaqhaq* (Q) *ana·nayukhaq* (H, P)

anŋaq children of brothers or male cousins
▲ *iẏniqhaq*
● *panikhaq* } children of sisters or female cousins

(−2 generation) *iẏŋutaq*
(−3 generation) *i·tsaniaq*

[1] Terms for husband's father's consanguineal relatives are the same as for those of the husband's mother.
[2] Terms for husband's mother's sibling's children are the same as for husband's sibling's children.
[3] *aŋayuŋẏuq* 'husband's older brother's wife'; *nukauŋẏuq* 'husband's younger brother's wife'.

Q-Qairnirmiut
H-Harvaqtuurmiut
P-Paallirmiut
o-older than ego
y-younger than ego

c

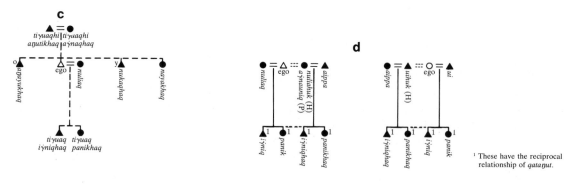

tiẏuaqhi | *tiẏuaqhi*
aŋutikhaq | *aẏnaqhaq*

tiẏuaq | *tiẏuaq*
iẏniqhaq | *panikhaq*

d

[1] These have the reciprocal relationship of *qataŋut*.

456

ARIMA

supernatural guardian of all life referred to as Pingna (*piŋna* 'the one up there'), who received souls at death, then let them be reincarnated. Otherwise, the animals belonged to the earth and lived independently without supernatural interference. To avoid alienating the fastidious caribou, various taboos were observed, mainly segregating land and sea products.

Numerous rules of conduct pertained to other aspects of life as well, especially the crises of birth and death. Protective amulets were worn, especially by children (Rasmussen 1930:79). Hila (*hila* 'air, atmosphere') represented all that one feared in the atmosphere: cold, dark, gales, and blizzards. Disasters brought about by Hila could be averted by magic words or the agency of shamans.

Shamanism

One became a shaman (*aŋatkuq*), usually under the guidance of an established practitioner through exposure and fasting to gain the pitying attention of Pingna and Hila, through "death" by drowning or shooting, or by simple external choice by helping spirits whether ghosts or animals (Gabus 1944a:193; Rasmussen 1930:52–58). With the aid of his spirits, the shaman primarily cured the sick and foresaw conditions such as those on a route of travel. Scepticism of shamanistic powers was not uncommon; however, in times of continued blizzards, famine, and sickness, the afflicted would come to congregate about the leading shamans who then elicited public confessions of taboo transgressions to appease the spirits and cured ailments through supernatural aid or prescribed specific taboos for them (Gabus 1944a:138, 142, 164).

Mythology

In mythology, most of the narratives recorded for other Central Eskimos were present among the Caribou Eskimos; however, their major accounts of the hero Kiviuq, the orphan Kaugyagyuk, the origin of Indians and Whites, and the origin of sun and moon were less full than the versions of the neighboring Iglulik and Netsilik Eskimos (see Rasmussen 1929:63–67, 77–81, 88–90, 287–290, 1931:232–236, 365–382, 418–420). Notably absent was the tradition of the origin of the sea mammals from Nuliayuk. Full versions existed of the fox wife, the owl who married a goose, Ilimarahugyuk who ate his children, the wolf mother Uivarahugiyaq, the woman who adopted a worm, girls who marry a falcon and a whale, the girl who became stone, the origin of fog, and the two men who abandoned each other on an island, as well as lesser accounts about the first times,

animals who acted like humans, the origin of flies, sky phenomena, dwarfs, giants, Indians, and other strange beings (Arima 1966–1969).

Recreation

The Caribou Eskimos were very fond of singing and when food was abundant, especially in autumn and winter when caches are full from the main caribou hunts, they held feasts followed by song fests which usually included drum dancing (Birket-Smith 1929, 1:268–271; Gabus 1944a:162–166; Gilder 1881:43; Rasmussen 1930:66–78). With the camp crowded into a special huge dance snowhouse or the largest tent, the men danced in turn with a big tambourine drum, nearly always singing a personal song. The poetic songs commonly alluded to hunting, travel, or the inabilities of the performer. There were also derisory satirical songs in which men with differences attacked each other, venting ill feeling and obtaining settlement by public opinion.

Alleviating monotony were a number of simple but enthusiastically played games: cup and pin, *nuɣluktaq* or the sticking of a suspended pierced bone piece, spin the soup ladle, and an elementary bone game. Caribou Eskimos could be great gamblers, particularly at festive gatherings (Birket-Smith 1929, 1:277; Rasmussen 1930:14). Athletic contests included trials of arm strength, wrestling, gymnastics on suspended lines, football, and "keep away" ball tossing. Toys included dolls, model artifacts, juggling pebbles, sling, dart, bow, crossbow, bull-roarer, and buzz disk on a thong. Particularly developed and engrossing were string figures (fig. 16).

Prehistory

In the highly conjectural ethnological interpretations of Eskimo development, the hypothesis of an inland origin in the New World became dominant (Rink 1875:70–71, 1885, 1887, 1887–1891, 1890; Murdoch 1888; Boas 1888a:39; Hatt 1969:101–109, 1916:248–249; Steensby 1917; Birket-Smith 1929, 2, 1930, 1951, 1952, 1959). Most elaborate was Steensby's (1917:153–156, 165–171) study holding that Eskimo culture had uniquely arctic-adapted traits like ice-hunting techniques in the central regions and was oldest there as an adaptation of Paleo-Eskimo migrants from the interior to the coast. Spreading, this culture was improved in Alaska through the stimulus of Pacific cultures into a "Neo-Eskimo" stage including the whaling umiak and baleen seal net absent in the central regions and the sea hunting kayak developed from the central riverine form. To this scheme Birket-Smith (1929, 2:128–130, 222, 230) added a Proto-

Fig. 15. Kinship terminology. Consanguineal and affinal terms for a, male ego, b, female ego; c, adoptive terms; d, spouse-exchange terms.

Eskimo stage for the original interior adaptation, having found suitable surviving representatives in the mainly inland Caribou Eskimos whose relatively sparse technological inventory he interpreted as primitive and ancient. He also added a latest "Eschato-Eskimo" stage for the neighboring Copper, Netsilik, and Iglulik Eskimos who were more coastal but had substantial land-oriented traits taken to indicate a recent advance from the interior to replace the archeological Thule culture, equated with Neo-Eskimo. The Caribou Eskimos were thus given great importance as the sole survivors of the original stage of Eskimo development.

But to Mathiassen (1930:605–606), the archeologist of the Fifth Thule Expedition, Caribou Eskimo artifacts did not appear ancient, nearly all forms being known from the Thule culture. He explained (1927, 2:200) the spare technology by the simple loss of sea-adapted traits and suggested that "a group of Eskimos, when from the west they got to the coast regions between Coronation Gulf and Boothia, were enticed into the country by the great herds of caribou. . . ." Excavations at two places on the Caribou Eskimo coast yielded remains related to the Thule culture (Birket-Smith 1929, 2:5–7; Mathiassen 1927, 1:108–113). Harp (1962:74), after surveying the middle and lower Thelon River in 1958, concluded that "the Caribou Eskimos derived from bands of Thule people who gradually turned for increased sustenance to the rich and proven food resources of the Barren Grounds herds"; he saw their culture as "a resurgence of the inland aspects of the age-old and almost universal dual [sea- and land-oriented] economy of the Eskimos" (1961:68). Finally, Burch (1979, 1978a) has offered a complicated but tenuous argument for the origin of the Caribou Eskimos from an overland migration of Copper Eskimos in the 1690s at the climax of the "Little Ice Age." These conjectures as to Caribou Eskimo culture history may give way to sounder interpretations supported by archeological evidence.

History

Historical records begin with Thomas Button (Fox 1635:120), who sailed up and down the west Hudson Bay coast in 1612–1613, and Jens Munk (1897, 2:28–29), who wintered at Churchill in 1619–1620 without meeting people although he noted heaps of chips from

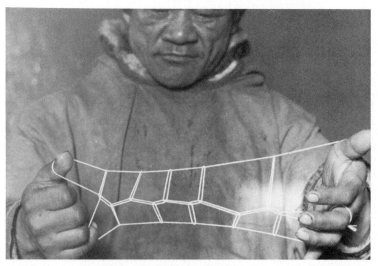

top left, Natl. Film Board of Canada Photothèque, Ottawa: 59920; bottom left, Public Arch. of Canada, Ottawa: PA 114713.
Fig. 16. Amusements and play. top left, Woman playing with her grandson using a buzz or whirling toy (Culin 1907:751). Photograph by Jean Roy, Chesterfield Inlet, 1950–1951. bottom left, Man from Padlei making a string figure of the sort used to illustrate stories. Photograph by Richard Harrington, 1949–1950. bottom right, Kokshok and his wife, playing inside the igloo. He has slipped her braids over his head. Photograph by Donald B. Marsh, just north of Eskimo Point, 1930s or 1940s.

ARIMA

timber cutting and remains of square dwellings. In 1689 the Hudson's Bay Company made an abortive attempt to establish a post at what became Churchill. Regular contact with European civilization developed only with the founding of Prince of Wales's Fort there by James Knight (1932) in 1717. Athapaskan Indians, specifically Chipewyans, were encouraged to come into Churchill from the northwest. Since guns were not entrusted to the Inuit until about 1770, the flintlock-equipped Indians drove them northward from Churchill (Glover 1969:xlvii; Graham 1969:174, 226, 236; Robson 1752:64). To pursue the Inuit trade, a small sloop sailed north along the coast in summer from Churchill to about Marble Island, ice permitting, from the 1720s, at first irregularly but virtually annually by midcentury (Hearne 1958:lxi, 217–218).

Caribou Eskimo subsistence pattern at the time is only sketchily recorded, but apparently they lived primarily on the coast in summer and inland in winter along lakes and rivers using caches of food and vegetation for fuel, and angling through ice (Graham 1969:229; Hearne 1958:103–105). They are recorded as far inland on the Thelon River as the woods above Beverly Lake where they cut timber (Hearne 1958:179). In the interior south of the Thelon the Chipewyans were following the caribou well into the tundra in summer (Burch 1978a:13–17). Inuit-Indian relations were variable with both hostilities and trade occurring. The Hudson's Bay Company encouraged peace, but the Chipewyans reported several of them being slain in 1720 and 1725, while in 1755 they killed 16 of 18 Inuit at Eskimo Point just after the sloop had traded there (Hudson's Bay Company 1718–1721, 1724–1725, 1756). In 1764 the Company secured a lasting peace at Eskimo Point between the Chipewyans and Caribou Eskimos at least (Hudson's Bay Company 1764–1765).

In the 1780s the Chipewyan summer excursions into the tundra were curtailed by the 1781 smallpox epidemic, which reportedly killed nine-tenths of those trading into Churchill (Hearne 1958:115) and by the opening of posts in the Athabasca country, which drew the Chipewyans to the southwest (Glover 1969:lli). From 1790 the summer trading voyages to the Caribou Eskimos were discontinued, and they were encouraged to trade directly into Churchill. They arrived, usually in small parties of men, from early spring by kayak, or by sled in which case they would build kayaks from timber at Churchill since they returned north before late summer to hunt caribou. During 1795–1813, some were hired by the post to hunt seals and white whales for oil, but the industry failed when the Inuit no longer wanted to linger after trading (Glover 1969:lv–vi). Glover (1969:li–lii) suggests that guns especially and also fishhooks and nets acquired in trade made year-round inland existence possible about this time. Firearms also facilitated sea mammal hunting. Frequent ammunition shortage, however, limited the effectiveness of guns until later in the nineteenth century. Rae (1850:189) noted on his coastal travels of 1846–1847 that up to Rankin Inlet the Inuit had guns but wanted powder and ball, while around Chesterfield Inlet even guns were scarce.

In the nineteenth century the Caribou Eskimos expanded southward in the interior from about the 1820s, and although Chipewyans in reduced numbers continued to summer on the tundra, they remained at peace with the Inuit who became the dominant population of even the southern Barren Grounds by the 1860s (Smith and Burch 1979:76–77). The Hudson Bay commercial whaling of 1860–1915 (W.G. Ross 1975) involving symbiotic White-Inuit relations marked a new stage of acculturation. The trade center shifted to the whaling area between Marble Island and Cape Fullerton. In 1882 the Hudson's Bay Company resumed its summer coastal trading voyages. The supply of firearms and ammunition improved greatly; moreover, the American whalers brought in modern repeating rifles developed in New England to replace the muzzle-loaders, which were still traded into the 1880s. As a result the ability to live on caribou must have been much increased, particularly for the difficult winter hunting period. A whaler, Robert Ferguson (1938:27–28) describes the Qairnirmiut in 1878 as hunting mostly caribou, and in the same year the explorer William Gilder (1881:41–46) visited a winter camp by a lake about 40 miles inland from Rankin Inlet where the people were living in large unheated snowhouses, burning oil only for light. Cooking was done over fires of vegetation, but most meat and fish was eaten frozen raw. In March several Qairnirmiut sleds arrived at Marble Island just at the best time for harpooning walrus at the floe edge, then returned to the mainland by the end of April, no doubt for the spring caribou migration (Ferguson 1938:107, 111, 137). Reports of large coastal camps of up to 150 persons in summer at Dawson and Rankin inlets (Lofthouse 1922:109–112; Rae 1850:22) suggest that a good part of the population lived again by the sea until the main caribou hunts of August and September. Open sea hunting continued, with Lofthouse observing in 1892 that "they often venture far out to sea, even out of sight of land sometimes, and shoot or spear fish, seals, and even whales from their kayaks." But the Caribou Eskimo had become primarily caribou and musk-ox hunters with the majority always inland. Their camps were found far to the interior, not only in the northwest about Beverly Lake but also toward Dubawnt Lake in the west and Ennadai Lake in the south (Hanbury 1904:41; J.B. Tyrrell 1898:65, 126–129; Tyrell 1897:105–107, 112).

In 1898 the Qairnirmiut population was reported as 146, and the Hauniqtuurmiut as 178 in 1902 (Boas 1901–1907:7, 377–378).

U. of Toronto, Thomas Fisher Rare Book Lib.: J.B. Tyrrell Coll. 1894.958.
Fig. 17. Man portaging a kayak on the Kazan River, above Yathkyed Lake. Photo retouched to show kayak shape. Photograph by J.B. Tyrrell, Aug. 1894.

In the twentieth century whaling declined but trade continued and intensified in the second and third decades as several posts opened in the Caribou Eskimo area (Birket-Smith 1929, 1:23; Vallee 1962:23–24). Missionaries and police quickly followed. Foxes were the basis of the trade, musk-ox having been hunted out by 1900 except in the extreme northwest of the area. When musk-ox hunting was banned in 1917 there was a coincidental severe decrease in caribou for several years, and hundreds starved to death (Burch 1977:146). Although times of plenty returned, scarcity recurred with frequency as the caribou population fluctuated and generally declined. For trapping purposes, the dog population was trebled (Vallee 1962:39) and was maintained to a large extent on caribou.

Population may have fluctuated considerably. In the early 1920s estimated total population was 500 at most (see table 2). Gabus (1944:28) in 1938–1939 estimated 300 Paallirmiut and 107 Ahiarmiut, and Steenhoven (1962:3) in 1955 listed 430 Paallirmiut and 50 Ahiarmiut with an estimate of total Caribou Eskimo population as possibly less than 1,000. Widespread famine came around 1950 when caribou decreased drastically due to overhunting (Kelsall 1968:200–236) or an extreme periodic population fluctuation (Parker 1972:22–23, 88). Some people died.

In the late 1950s the Canadian government encouraged the Caribou Eskimo to move into several concentrated settlements, mostly on the coast: Eskimo Point, Whale Cove, Rankin Inlet, Chesterfield Inlet, and, to the interior, Baker Lake (see table 1). Many of the Utkuhikhalingmiut of the Back River (Netsilik Eskimo) also were relocated to these centers, especially Baker Lake, and in addition a significant Aivilingmiut (Iglulik Eskimo) component was present in the coastal settlements, especially since the 1950s when workers were imported to the Rankin Inlet nickel mine. This concentration into permanent towns centered on White establishments was completed in the 1960s, and existence became heavily subsidized. Government prefabricated houses replaced snowhouses and tents; fur clothing disappeared; hunting and trapping were overshadowed by wage labor, handicrafts (figs. 18–19), and welfare; most food became store bought; alcohol consumption rose; dog teams decreased then virtually vanished with the coming of snowmobiles; and the children received White schooling, learning English instead of Eskimo. Change has been most rapid and obvious in material culture but is great in the social and mental realms as well. When hunters carve soapstone instead of pursuing the animals while their White-educated sons are largely jobless and aimless, Caribou Eskimo life has been thoroughly transformed and not for the better (Tagoona 1973).

By the late 1960s only the aged knew the old traditions and songs well. Youth was interested in White mass culture, media, and music. A real generation gap has developed, diluting the traditional closeness of the family (Anoee 1979). There is general recognition that the government education program initiated in 1959 has been a particularly potent acculturative agent. School attendance has been high, partly since the belief was fostered that nonattendance would stop family allowance benefits (Tagoona 1977:53–54); however, many parents who complied with Canadian compulsory education requirements actually would have preferred to teach their children their own way of life. The standard elementary curriculum has been inculcated at the expense of Caribou Eskimo learning in living skills (Mumgark 1978:108–110). In view of the inadequacy and irrelevance of much of the school curriculum, parents have often asked for more time to be given to Inuit studies but to little avail (Piryuaq 1978:123). Television, which arrived in the mid-1970s with satellite transmission, is seen to be another powerful acculturative force, and attempts are being made to inject native programming to counteract the strong White influence in the home itself but again to very limited effect as of the early 1980s. Radio broadcasting in the Eskimo language has fared better due to the simpler nature of the medium

Table 2. Band Population, 1922–1923

| | Adults | | Children | | |
	Male	Female	Male	Female	Totals
Quairnirmiut	25	30	24	11	90
Hauniqtuurmiut	13	18	13	10	54
Harvaqtuurmiut	17	21	23	15	76
Paallirmiut	47	59	59	47	212
Ahiarmiut[a]					35
					467

Source: Birket-Smith 1929, 1:66–68.
[a] Unnamed but indirectly reported. A few families at Angikuni Lake were not counted.

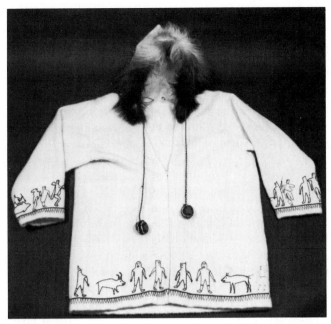

Fig. 18. Duffle coat. Cut in contemporary style, this cream-colored parka has a zipper front, hood trimmed with wolverine fur, and multi-colored drawstring. The cuffs and bottom border are embroidered with traditional scenes, such as sealing and caribou hunting. Length 127.0 cm; made by Oonark, Baker Lake, N.W.T., 1959.

and local stations operated in Eskimo Point and Baker Lake from the mid-1970s. Also the Caribou Eskimo have their share of popular native performers in the modern folk- and country-based Eskimo music, a few with records that are played on home stereos. But despite such technological trappings, by no means should it be assumed that the Caribou Eskimo have suddenly become merely another ethnic subculture to the Canadian-American mainstream.

From the 1960s the development of Inuit political organization was actively promoted by the Canadian government, which needed formally defined bodies to negotiate for land and other native rights. Caribou Eskimo fell into the area covered by Inuit Tapirisat of Canada and partly by their location nearer the White south came to be more conscious of the contention involved and to supply much leadership. They have been in the forefront of the Nunavut or "Our Land" movement begun in 1974 for Inuit self-determination in their own territory (Suluk 1981:30–37). They are prominent in the Inummarilirijikkut or Inuit Cultural Institute established in 1974 in Eskimo Point.

The basic problem confronting the Caribou Eskimo in the 1980s was the ever-increasing White encroachment on their land. Besides the overall state claim to territory, main White interest lies in the mineral riches of the land. The first mine, for nickel, operated at Rankin Inlet in the late 1950s and introduced mass labor to the Caribou Eskimo and other Inuit imported for the

Fig. 19. Earthenware pot. Four low relief creatures surround the vessel, which is glazed in browns and blues on green ground. Cups, bowls, plates, and clay figures are also made as part of contemporary craft projects. Height 31.2 cm; collected at Rankin Inlet, N.W.T., 1972.

purpose who found it futile (Mumgark 1978:111). Mining exploration increased in the 1960s and 1970s, intensifying greatly in the Baker Lake region when rich uranium deposits were discovered in early 1978 on the upper Thelon River. This intense uranium exploration by aircraft so disturbed the caribou that the Baker Lake Inuit and Inuit Tapirisat took six mining companies and the Canadian government to court in 1979 seeking an injunction against further mining exploration. But in this, the first case in Canada to discuss Inuit aboriginal rights, the judge ruled that although about 30,000 square miles of the District of Keewatin were subject to the rights of the Baker Lake Inuit, such were not property rights, since these had been handed over to the Hudson's Bay Company by King Charles II in 1670 (Inuit Tapirisat of Canada 1980:3). Caribou Eskimo land use had been defined by government-sponsored studies shortly before (Hoffmann 1976; Welland 1976). Another major front of White encroachment is that of ever-increasing game regulations. Of special concern as the 1980s began was proposed close regulation for the caribou, which reportedly were declining again from overhunting made easy by snowmobile use (Mumgark 1982, 1982a; Kallutjak 1982:9–15; Snowden 1982). Such White-imposed restrictions on hunting and fishing strike at the heart of Caribou Eskimo culture, which, however altered by acculturation, retains its caribou-focused identity. The old hunters quietly warn that Inuit should never accept such foreign interference in their lives (Anonymous 1980).

Synonymy

The Caribou Eskimo are a group of independent bands that have no native name for the cultural grouping as a whole. The descriptive designation Caribou Eskimos was first applied by the Danish Fifth Thule Expedition of 1921–1924 (Birket-Smith 1929, 1:9; Rasmussen 1930). Gabus (1944:126) translated this as Esquimaux-caribous. The term Agutit (Boas 1888a:42) may represent a tribal designation used by Iglulingmiut. Whalers applied the misnomer Kinipetu (Boas 1887:42, 1901–1907:6), Kinnepatoo (Ferguson 1938; Gilder 1881:41; Klutschak 1881:419), particularly to the Qairnirmiut but also to the tribe as a whole. The word has been explained as from *kinippatut* 'they are wet' or *kinipatu·t* 'see how wet they are', a woman's exclamation about her clothing (Birket-Smith 1929, 1:60; Rasmussen 1930:11).

Subgroups

The name of the Qairnirmiut (*qaiɣniɣmiut* 'people of the smooth bedrock') refers to the land behind Rankin Inlet. Other spellings are Qaernermiut (Birket-Smith 1929; Rasmussen 1930), Kaernermiout (Michea 1949:168), Kiaknukmiut (Boas 1901–1907:6), and Kiackenneck. The Aligattalingmiun (Jenness 1922:48) or Aligatalingmiut (Birket-Smith 1929, 1:62) are the Qairnirmiut west of Baker Lake.

The name of the Hauniqtuurmiut (*hauniqtu·ɣmiut*) means 'people of the place with bones' (referring to Wilson River). Variant spellings are Hauneqtôrmiut (Birket-Smith 1929; Rasmussen 1930), Sauniktumiut (Boas 1901–1907:6), and Aonarktormiut (Gabus 1944:126).

Harvaqtuurmiut is *haɣvaqtu·ɣmiut* 'people of the whirlpools' (a reference to Kazan River), also spelled Harvaqtôrmiut (Birket-Smith 1929; Rasmussen 1930), Harvaktormiut (Gabus 1944:126), and Savvanormiout (Michea 1949:168).

The name of the Paallirmiut, *pa·lliɣmiut* 'people of the dried willow branches' (referring to Maguse River), is also spelled Pâdlermiut (Rasmussen 1930:5–6), Padlermiut (Gabus 1944:126; Steenhoven 1962:3), Padlimiut (Boas 1901–1907:6), and Pâdlimiut (Birket-Smith 1929, 1:54–60). A group called Kuungmiut (*ku·ŋmiut* 'people of the river'), also Kûngmiut (Birket-Smith 1929,

1:62) and Kôungmiut (Boas 1901–1907:6), are Paallirmiut at the outlet of Yathkyed Lake. A group of Netsilik and other more distant Eskimo groups have the same name. The Paallirmiut near Maguse Lake are the Tahiuharmiut (Birket-Smith 1929, 1:62).

The name of the Ahiarmiut (Steenhoven 1962), also Ahearmiut (Gabus 1944:126), is *ahiaɣmiut* 'out-of-the-way dwellers'. The same name is also applied to a subgroup of Qairnirmiut north of Baker Lake.

Sources

The literature on Caribou Eskimos is still limited. Earlier references like those of Ellis (1748), Graham (1969), Hearne (1958), Rae (1850), Gilder (1881), Ferguson (1938), Lofthouse (1922), J.B. Tyrrell (1898), Tyrrell (1897), and Boas (1901–1907) furnish valuable details but lack comprehensiveness. Hanbury (1904) provides a more extended account. Full descriptions are supplied only since the 1920s, notably by Birket-Smith (1929), Rasmussen (1930), and Gabus (1944), all attending mainly to the Paallirmiut. Supplementing their basic ethnography are Steenhoven's (1962) study focused on law among the Paallirmiut and Ahiarmiut and government-sponsored community studies of Eskimo Point, Rankin Inlet, and Baker Lake made by Van Stone and Oswalt (1959), Dailey and Dailey (1961), and Vallee (1962). Less technical accounts are provided by Gabus (1943, 1944), Harper (1964), Leden (1927), Michea (1949), and Mowat (1952, 1959), although with the last it is difficult to separate fact from fiction. Ethnographic knowledge is relatively good for technology and mythology but less satisfactory for other aspects. Continuing ethnological study, including fieldwork by Thomas Correll, Ernest S. Burch, Jr., and Anthony Welland should expand coverage. Since Birket-Smith (1929) the question of Caribou Eskimo origins has drawn considerable attention, from Meyer (1976), Clark (1977), and Burch (1979, 1978a). Some of the most vital material on Caribou Eskimo has appeared by their authorship since the late 1970s in Inuit Tapirisat periodicals: *Arjungnagimmat* (formerly *Ajurnarmat*) and *Inuit Today*.

Baffinland Eskimo

WILLIAM B. KEMP

The Baffinland ('băfĭn‚lănd) Eskimo occupy the southern two-thirds of Baffin Island. Although Boas (1888:410) also included under this label the Iglulik people of northern Baffin Island and Igloolik, their distinct history and kinship patterns justify separating them even though no sharp linguistic or social boundary divides these northern groups from the Baffinland Eskimo (Damas 1963:39–62; Brody 1976:153–156; Wenzel 1981:77). According to Mathiassen (1928:22–23), some social connections did exist between the two populations, but the Iglulik considered the Clyde River Eskimo to be strangers.

The population of the Foxe Basin coast is unknown except for Boas's (1888:444) reference to the Pilingmiut there; they probably belonged to the Iglulik population (see the synonymy in "Iglulik," this vol.).

The Baffinland Eskimo are a coastal people who utilize selected parts of the interior and effectively exploit a wide range of marine, land, and freshwater resources. The cultural adaptations of the twentieth century have roots that extend far back, for Baffinland was first occupied by the Pre-Dorset people, who settled the north shore of Hudson Strait around 2200 B.C. The Dorset occupation followed and enlarged the known area of settlement between 500 B.C. and A.D. 1400 (M.S. Maxwell, personal communication 1982). About A.D. 1200, Thule culture, directly ancestral to the Eskimo culture of today, expanded into the region. Neither archeological data nor the historical record can substantiate a continuous occupation of territories within Baffinland over the last 4,000 years; however, a mapping of prehistoric and historic patterns of settlement and land use shows that much of the territory was persistently used over long periods of time (Boas 1888:pl. III; Freeman 1976, 2:117–122, 3:107–127).

In 1980 the Baffinland Eskimos lived in the six centralized communities of Clyde River (population 443), Broughton Island (378), Pangnirtung (839), Frobisher Bay (2,333), Lake Harbour (252), and Cape Dorset (784). There were also five small, all-Native hunting villages ranging in size from 12 to 30 people. An active use of the land and close kinship ties still characterize these smaller settlements, but even in the larger centers, harvesting is important, kinship controls many of the face-to-face interactions, and the Eskimo language continues to be spoken by adults and children.*

Environment

The environment of the Baffinland Eskimo comprises marine, land, and freshwater ecosystems. The northeastern sector of Baffin Island is mountainous, as are the southwestern coasts of Cumberland Sound and Frobisher Bay (Dunbar and Greenaway 1956:92–142). The central interior of the island is a low plain that contains the large freshwater bodies of Nettilling and Amadjuak lakes. Elsewhere rolling hills, plateaus, massive rock outcrops, structural valleys, lakes, and rivers combine to form complex patterns. Throughout, travel is difficult, and overland access to distant areas only occurs in the late winter and the spring (Boas 1888:574–575). In the south there is a short summer night and winter days of about five hours' duration, while the north has continual summer daylight and winter darkness. All regions are subject to sudden storms and strong winds. Heavy seas, blowing snow, and the packing or moving apart of loose sea ice can occur quickly, making the environment of the Baffinland Eskimo hazardous and difficult to predict.

The coastal zone of Baffinland is the most important living and harvesting area for the Eskimo. The marine environment has five phases: the open water of summer, the formation of new ice in the fall, the large expanse of land-fast ice bordered by the floe edge in winter, the deteriorating ice of spring, and the moving pack ice of early summer. In some years, the ice may not break up; in others, it may disappear early in the season. The coastal zone has fjords, deep embayments, protected harbors, rock and wave-cut cliffs, and exposed headlands. In places, groups of islands extend

*The variety of Inuit-Inupiaq spoken by the Baffinland Eskimo, called Southeast Baffin Eskimo, can be written with the same phonemes as Iglulik (see the orthographic footnote in "Iglulik," this vol.). Words and other elements appearing in italics are in a phonemic system broadly valid for northern Canada. In the group names and the mythological name Sedna the spellings of Boas (1888) have been retained.

the total territory utilized for settlement and harvesting and influence the formation of sea ice. A notable feature of the Baffin Island coastal zone is the extreme tides, some of the highest in the world, that influence all but the Davis Strait coast. Foxe Peninsula and Cumberland Sound have a tidal range of 25 feet, and the south coast, 38 feet (Canadian Hydrographic Service 1968). Along the entire coastline, currents and countercurrents are severe.

Territory

Boas (1888:421–442) subdivided the Baffinland Eskimo (as here defined) into seven regional populations that he referred to as tribes. The population of a particular territory was organized into nuclear and extended family units that were coupled with other family units to form a village. Within a particular geographic area, villages were linked together by kinship and the mutual use of hunting territory, to form larger territorial and social groupings now most often referred to as bands (Damas 1969b:126; Wenzel 1981:32). Territorial stability was important to the process of band development since it encouraged the strengthening of kinship alliances and fostered the creation of a very specific store of information that was best shared within a well-defined social network and between the generations that maintained this network over time (Kemp 1974:74–76).

A band occupying a particular area was given a general name by outsiders that described its geographical location in reference to the position of the outside group (Boas 1888:424–425; Brody 1976:153–154). Individuals or families were identified geographically by use of the suffix complex -miut 'the people of' appended to the name of the particular place and socially by use of the suffix complex -kut 'members of the family of' added to the name of a person. The location and characteristics of places within the geographical and social territory of the band were given by a dense network of place-names. Each band exploited the resources of its region; other groups were not excluded from it, but since the traditional hunting territory was more familiar to the resident population, and since kinship linkages within this territory were better defined, the tendency was to maintain loose boundary distinctions (L.F. Brooke 1974; Kemp 1974).

Foxe Peninsula and South Coast Settlements

The large territory stretching east from Foxe Peninsula to the shores of Frobisher Bay has been used throughout historical times (Kemp 1966–1970; Kemp in Freeman 1976, 3:107–116). Boas (1888:421–423) distinguished four separate groups here; the Sikosuilarmiut on the southern shore of Foxe Peninsula, the Akuliarmiut to

the west and east of Big Island, the Qaumauangmiut near the Middle Savage Islands, and the Nugumiut of Frobisher Bay. Boas knew that each of these designations covered several smaller territorial units. Although he was not able to state exact village sites, the general locations he gave were quite accurate, with the exception of the northern coast of Foxe Peninsula. Figure 1 gives a more precise map of settlements and hunting territory (Boas 1888:pl. III; Kemp 1966–1970; Kemp in Freeman 1976, 1:125–150, 3:107–128).

Settlement patterns and land use as reconstructed for about 1850 to 1950 show major settlements to the east and west of Cape Dorchester on Foxe Peninsula, from west of King Charles Cape east to Chorkbak Inlet, on the coast and coastal islands from Amadjuak to Markham Bay, from Crooks Inlet to the eastern shoreline of North Bay, from Balcom Inlet east past the Middle Savage Islands to Pritzler Harbour, in Countess of Warwick Sound in Frobisher Bay, and in Cyrus Field and Cornelius Grinnell bays located on the Davis Strait coast of Hall Peninsula. There is very little data on the patterns of settlement and land use prior to the mid-1800s, but there is no evidence against the long-term existence of these regional groupings.

All the groups had some contact with trading vessels, but the Middle Savage Islands and Big Island areas were the most important meeting places. Descriptions of contact and of the trade that ensued are summarized by W.G. Ross (1975) who in turn refers to published accounts of activity (Chappel 1817:69; McKeevor 1819:32; Lyon 1824:38; Parry 1824:15). Trade was sporadic from 1810 to 1860, when it became more regular (W.G. Ross 1975:25, 61). Some seasonal settlements were an artifact of this contact, but the trade did not create or greatly distort the areas shown on figure 1 (Kemp 1966–1970). In the 1890s a permanent whaling station operated for several years on Spicer Island, and beginning in 1911, the Hudson's Bay Company established trading posts in the area: 1911, Lake Harbour; 1913, Cape Dorset; 1914, Frobisher Bay (Kemp in Freeman 1976, 1:125, 128, 133). In the late 1800s, the whaling ship *Active* played a part in relocating people from Hudson Strait to the Hudson Bay area. People from Hudson Strait wintered in the Ottawa Islands, and in 1898 at least 100 Eskimos were transported to Southampton Island, some of whom stayed permanently (W.G. Ross 1975:133–134).

Before the trading post era, there was contact among all these territorial groups and between the Frobisher Bay and Cumberland Sound residents (Boas 1888:425, 429, pl. III). In 1912 the missionary A.L. Fleming visited the Hudson Strait coast and noted 82 Eskimos in that area who had resided in Frobisher Bay the previous year (W.G. Ross 1975:114). An important meeting place for the south coast in the 1800s was the Amadjuak and Nettilling lake regions, into which each group had travel

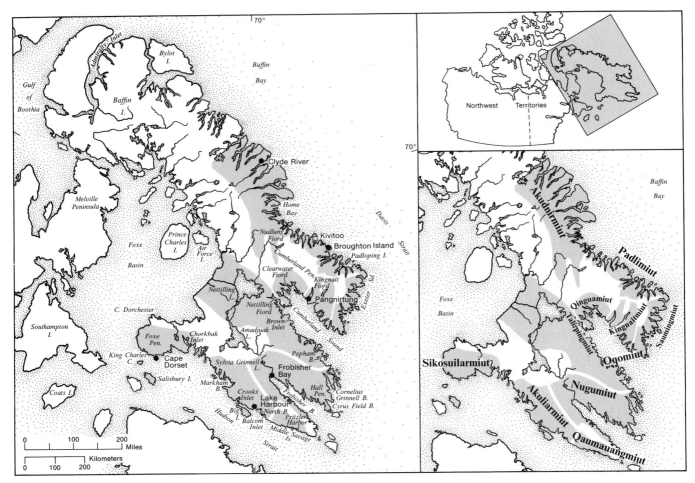

Fig. 1. Late 19th-century tribal territory (after Boas 1888).

routes to exploit late summer caribou (Boas 1888:421–423). Most of the south shore and Frobisher Bay population exploited the Amadjuak area, while the people of Cape Dorchester on Foxe Peninsula penetrated farther northeast into Nettilling Lake. After the advent of fox trapping, larger settlements split into smaller trapping units, but there was no great distortion in territorial boundaries. A mapping of territory after 1920 shows a large network of traplines across the entire area of south and east Baffin Island (Kemp in Freeman 1976, 3:107, 108, 117, 119, 121, 125). Contacts between southern Baffin Island and northern Quebec took place but without regularity (Boas 1888:462–463). A whaling station opened on Spicer Island in the 1880s attracted northern Quebec people (W.G. Ross 1975:63).

Cumberland Sound and Davis Strait

The Eskimos of the Cumberland Sound and Davis Strait region were reported by Boas (1888:424, 440–442) to be divided into the general groupings Akudnirmiut 'people of the center' and Oqomiut 'people of the lee side'. The Iglulik Eskimo of the northern part of Baffin Island were the Aggomiut 'people of the weather side'.

These names referred not to specific delimited areas but to relative location, and they were applied somewhat differently by people from different parts of the island. Boas applied the name Akudnirmiut to the people of the Home Bay region and north of it and, following northern usage, applied Oqomiut to those from Exeter Sound to Cumberland Sound. Between these two groupings, from Padloping Island north, in summer, as far as Nudlung Fiord, were the settlements of the Padlimiut, whom Boas regarded as an intermediate group of doubtful classification but perhaps best taken as a subdivision of the Akudnirmiut. The Oqomiut were described as formerly divided into four "subtribes" in four major settlement areas. On the southwest coast of Cumberland Sound Talirpingmiut settlements were spread from Popham Bay north to Brown Inlet; the head of the sound was utilized from Nettilling Fiord on the west side to Clearwater and Shark Fiord on the east side by the Qinguamiut; the east shore was inhabited from Pangnirtung Fiord south to the main settlement area in Kingnait Fiord by the Kingnaitmiut; and farther south were the Saumingmiut coastal settlements along the southwestern margin of the Cumberland Peninsula. Except for the transitional Padlimiut, no specific names

465

Bibliotheek van de Rijksuniversiteit, Ghent, Belgium.

Fig. 2. An Eskimo man brought from Baffinland to England by Martin Frobisher. He wears a parka with long flap down the back and holds bow and arrow and double-bladed paddle. A kayak is in the background as is a European sailing ship. Wash drawing by Lucas de Heere, probably after a lost original by John White; although dated 1576, this is almost surely the same man as fig. 3.

of subgroups were given by Boas for the Akudnirmiut, who did not have the same recurring associations with specific places that characterized the Oqomiut groups.

Whaling activity along Davis Strait began in the mid-1700s, and by 1850 all the Cumberland Sound and Davis Strait population was in contact with whalers. On Davis Strait, there were important trading areas on the north shore of Home Bay and at Kivitoo, but there were no permanent whaling stations. Boas (1888:425–426) noted that the boundaries of the Cumberland Sound "subtribes" were no longer distinct (as of 1880), attributing this to the presence of permanent whaling stations there after 1850, with a consolidation of groups due to the decline in population from disease—from 1,600 in 1841 to 300 in 1857 (Boas 1888:425). The Hudson's Bay Company entered Cumberland Sound in 1921 and established a post at Clyde River in 1923 and at Broughton Island in 1960 (Kemp in Freeman 1976, 1:137, 142, 146).

In both regions, there was frequent contact among the groups, although the difficult passage across the highland limited relations between the people at the head of Cumberland Sound and the Davis Strait groups. There was frequent contact, however, between the peo-

ple of Kingnait Fiord and those living around Padloping Island. The groups on the southwestern shores of Cumberland Sound moved west onto the highland for caribou hunting and sometimes encountered groups from the Frobisher Bay region. The Cumberland Sound people also frequented the interior of Baffinland, utilizing Nettilling Lake for caribou and seal hunting. Prior to 1850 there was often a small winter village established on the north shore of the lake (Boas 1888:433). Boas (1888:432) reported that there was some possible contact with the Foxe Basin people from Nettilling Lake, but these meetings were not frequent. The relations between groups living along Davis Strait were somewhat different. They moved their villages more frequently, and thus the size and seasonal location of settlements varied from year to year. In this region, contact was facilitated or hindered by the pattern of fjords and mountain valleys. Because of their location, these groups did not frequent the Nettilling Lake area (Boas 1888:440–441. The present settlement and hunting area of Clyde River was said by Boas (1888:442) to be infrequently used by the Home Bay people. After the trading post was established in 1923, several family units totaling about 30 people from Cumberland Sound took up residence in the Clyde River area (George Wenzel, personal communication 1982).

Culture

Economy

The Baffinland Eskimo regularly harvest 20 species of marine and land mammals, fish, and birds (Kemp 1971). Of these, all but the wolf is important for food. The ecological patterns of these species cover broad expanses of territory, and their exploitation is facilitated by the hunters' understanding of species behavior (Kemp 1981).

The seasonal cycle was first described by Boas (1888:471–516) for the Cumberland Sound Eskimo; at the time of his observations certain activities had already been influenced by the introduction of firearms and imported material goods. A hunting adaptation that was dependent on a continuing access to trade goods began to develop between 1850 and 1900. This dependency increased with the growth of a trapping economy, and by 1920 the pattern of seasonal activity was heavily influenced by winter fox trapping, which peaked in the late 1920s and has fluctuated since that time (Usher 1970–1971, 1:87). The availability of ammunition was a limiting factor; assumptions about indiscriminate killing of game because of the rifle fail to recognize the economic problems that severely restricted the supply of ammunition (Duffy 1981; Kemp 1982).

The seasonal economic cycle is characterized by win-

 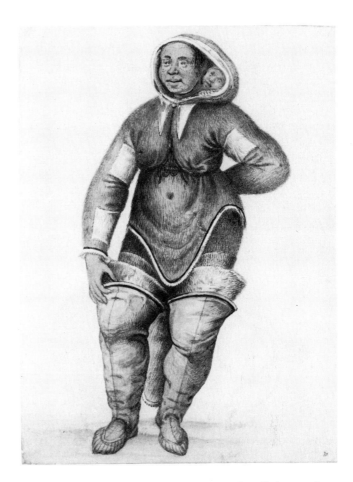

The British Mus., Dept. of Prints and Drawings, London: left, PS131736; right, 40470.

Fig. 3. Eskimo man, woman, and child brought from Baffinland to England by the Martin Frobisher Expedition, 1577. They died soon after they reached England. The adults wear sealskin parkas. The man's parka has a long flap down the back, a feature that disappeared from men's clothes in the 19th century. He leans on a hunting bow. The woman's costume includes the parka with apron flap, long flap down the back, enlarged hood for carrying the infant, and boots. Watercolors by John White, 1577.

ter breathing-hole and floe-edge hunting; spring hunting for basking seals, and for seals, beluga whales, and walrus at the floe edge; early summer fishing; late summer caribou hunting inland or in coastal locations; early fall fishing at stone weirs; late fall walrus and whale hunting; and a return to breathing-hole and floe-edge hunting as freeze-up progresses. Marine resources are critical to the Baffinland Eskimo, and the ringed seal has been the single most important resource (Boas 1888:471; Kemp 1971:112; Wenzel 1981:59). Walrus, narwhal, beluga whale, and polar bear are the other important species of marine mammals; their importance varies within the Baffinland region. Breathing-hole seal hunting was the main source of winter food. The floe edge was used to hunt walrus, and in the late winter along the south coast beluga whales were harvested from kayaks at the floe edge (Boas 1888:498–550; C.F. Hall 1865:459). Prior to the use of rifles, the most productive hunting was for the basking seal in the spring; Boas (1888:485) noted that a good hunter could kill up to 15 seals in a single day. After the increased availability of rifles and ammunition, midwinter floe-edge hunting and summer boat hunting gradually became

more productive parts of the seasonal cycle. The important hunts for beluga, narwhal, and walrus took place during the fall migration. In that season whales feed close to land, and walrus haul out onto the shore to rest, later feeding under the new sea ice that forms near shore. Narrow straits and peninsulas were favorite whale hunting spots, and at times kayaks were used to drive

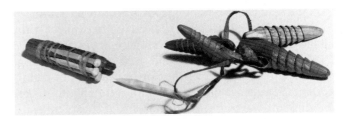

Merseyside County Mus., Liverpool: 1956.26.512.

Fig. 4. Seal plugs. left, Ivory pins, carried in a wood (as here) or leather case; for plugging the wounds in a seal to stop the flow of blood. right, wooden screw-type plugs, less frequently used than the pins. The ivory needle could be used for sewing wounds. Once the seal's wounds were plugged it could be dragged more easily. Length of case 7.0cm, rest same scale; all collected by Julian Bilby, Lake Harbour, Baffin I., 1909–1914.

Fig. 6. The division of a whale at Pangnirtung. Writing in the Eskimo syllabary has been cut into the skin. Photograph by George Anderson, 1946.

top, Boas 1964:fig. 48; bottom, Amer. Mus. of Nat. Hist., New York: 60/3143.
Fig. 5. Floats and drag, which are tied to the harpoon line and tire the animal. The boat follows and the kill is then made with a lance. top, Floats and drag; bottom, drag made of a wooden frame with a leather covering and lines. Diameter of drag 39.0cm; collected at Cumberland Sound, Baffin I., 1900.

In addition to the harvest of large land and sea mammals, fishing and the capture of small game provided both quantity and diversity. Fall fishing for arctic char at stone weirs was a major source of food. In winter ice-fishing, lures are used to attract the fish, which are then speared. The Eskimos know the exact location of spawning beds and could position themselves at the proper places for productive fishing. Ducks, geese, and other sea birds in molt were hunted by kayak. Eggs, in particular eider duck eggs, were an important source of food in early summer except in the Davis Strait area. Boas (1888:510–513) describes many ingenious Baffinland Eskimo ways of hunting birds on land and water (figs. 7–8). In summer various roots and other parts of plants were collected, and throughout the year clams and mussels were important in the southern part of the region.

the whales into smaller bays where they could be easily killed (Boas 1888:501).

Caribou hunting was the only major activity that took hunters inland (Freeman 1976, 1:207). Caribou hunting for food and winter clothing began in mid- to late August for most Baffinland groups. Before 1930, the hunts were often carried out adjacent to Nettilling, Amadjuak, and Sylvia Grinnell lakes. Crossing places at rivers and at the narrows of lakes were considered to be the best areas (Boas 1888:501–502). Hunting on the Cumberland Peninsula and along Davis Strait was confined to narrow mountain valleys that served to connect with inland caribou areas. Drives were also undertaken, but except in the Padloping Island area, caribou hunting was not productive along the northern shores of Cumberland Peninsula. Only those who were able to make the difficult walking trip inland left the coast. Informants speaking of the inland caribou hunt state that anyone could go who wanted to, and that if one village was leaving to venture inland, men from another would often join them (Kemp 1966–1970). Once inland, as many caribou as possible were taken before the first snows came. If more were killed than could be transported out, they were cached and retrieved in the winter.

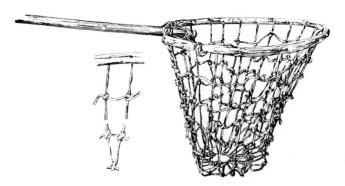

Amer. Mus. of Nat. Hist., New York:60/3137.
Fig. 7. Bird net. Leather netting attached to wood hoop frame with wood handle, used to catch dovekies during nesting season. Diameter of hoop 20.0cm; collected by James Mutch at Cumberland Sound, Baffin I., 1900.

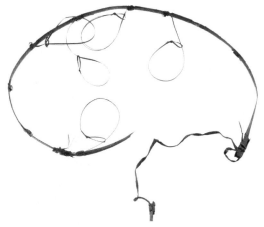

Smithsonian, Dept. of Anthr.: 153,908.
Fig. 8. Whalebone snare: a line of nooses set along the edge of a lake to catch waterfowl. It was placed across the water in shallow lakes to catch diving and swimming birds, which were then drawn to shore with the line. Length 140.0cm excluding ties; collected by Franz Boas, Hudson Strait, 1882-1884.

Technology

Boas (1888:471–562) provides an excellent description of the material culture and technology of the Baffinland Eskimo. The inventory of material goods, including hunting equipment, clothing, and housing, was closely integrated with the seasonal cycle. All the artifacts used within this region were similar in style and function to other areas in the Arctic, and there are still a great many artifacts in common use that differ little from those described by Boas (Kemp 1966–1970). Skillful selection and use of materials, careful workmanship, and consistent style characterized the artifacts of the Baffinland Eskimo.

Hunting implements included the breathing-hole harpoon with a long thin metal shaft (a major item of early trading) and small detachable metal head. Large marine mammals were hunted with a harpoon having a heavy wooden handle, ivory foreshaft, and a detachable head, usually of caribou antler, with a large triangular metal point. The head was tethered to a skin float. The bow and arrow was important for land hunting, with the single-curve bows manufactured from driftwood or antler and reinforced with sealskin rope (Boas 1888).

Transportation

The kayak was the chief means of marine transport although the large skin umiaks or women's boats were also used to move family groups. The kayak frames were made from driftwood and covered with the skin of large ringed seals. Suits of seal intestines were used when hunting from kayaks, these having dog fur sewed to the sleeves to reduce noise (Kemp 1966–1970). The style of the kayak seems to have differed from place to place within Baffinland (Boas 1888:487). In winter, dog traction and sleds of varying size were used. Both the number of dogs and the size of the sled increased with trapping, and the style of sled changed when wood became available from the whalers.

In the early twentieth century, dog traction was based upon the possession of two to six dogs per person in the Hudson Strait and Cumberland Sound region and from 6 to 12 along Davis Strait (Boas 1888:583). Informants from the Lake Harbour area reported that throughout much of the twentieth century they had only one or two dogs and that a team could only be formed by sharing among several families (Kemp 1966–1970). Boas (1888) attributes the difference in the number of dogs to problems of disease rather than food supply. Dog traction was the dominant means of winter transport until the mid-1960s when it was replaced by the motorized snowmobile.

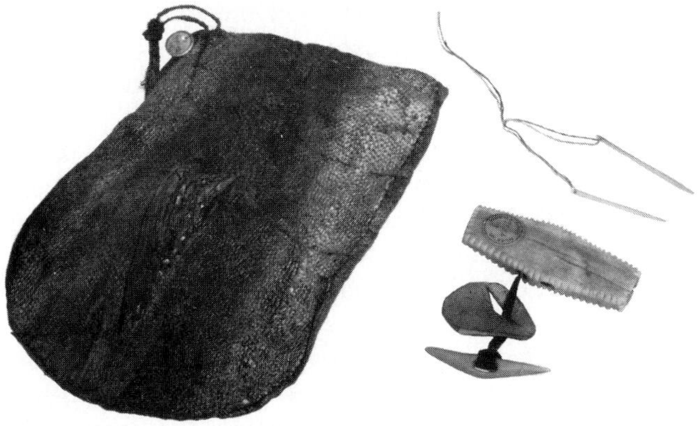

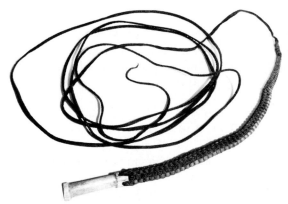

Merseyside County Mus., Liverpool: left, 1956.26.453; right, 1956.26.517.
Fig. 9. Sewing equipment. left, Fishskin bag used by a woman to keep thread and tools; right, ivory needlecase and needles. Length of case 7.4cm, left same scale. Both collected by Julian W. Bilby, Lake Harbour, Baffin I., 1909-1914.

Merseyside County Mus., Liverpool: 1956.26.456.
Fig. 10. Dog whip. The ivory handle is attached to the braided upper portion, which is made of strips of whale skin. The whip is used on sled dogs to encourage them to start moving, to discipline them, and at the side of the team when changing direction. Length 180.0 cm. Collected by Julian Bilby, Lake Harbour, Baffin I., 1909–1914.

Smithsonian, Dept. of Anthr.: 29,978.

Fig. 11. Goggles. Used to protect the eyes they are made of a single piece of wood carved with a visor and narrow eye slits. The leather head strap is split and tied together at the center back to prevent the 2 pieces from spreading too far apart. Length 14.5 cm; collected by W.A. Mintzer, Cumberland Sound, Baffin I., 1876.

Clothing

Clothing was made from caribou in winter and a combination of seal and caribou in summer. Pants of polar bear skin were worn to the top of the ankles, falling over sealskin boots in summer and caribou skin boots with sealskin soles in winter. Women's clothing had a large pouch for the child and a long tail in back and a shorter one in front (fig. 12). Davis Strait groups had a more rounded parka hood.

Structures

The type of dwelling used varied according to season and activity. Snowhouses were the primary winter dwelling of all the Baffinland groups. Some groups also reconditioned earlier Thule stone houses, covering the roofs with skin, arctic heather, and then another layer of skin (Boas 1888:448–449). Around 1930 this type of dwelling was made with a wooden frame and became the main winter house in most areas. Summer tents varied in size according to use and distance to be transported (fig. 14). The front tent skins were scraped extremely thin, or even split, allowing light to filter through, while the rear of the tent was covered with skins retaining hair for protection from the rain (Kemp 1966–1970).

Social Organization

The cultural life of the Baffinland Eskimo is based upon a well-defined system of social relationships that involves kinship positions and behavior (Graburn 1964; Kemp 1974; Wenzel 1981). The organization of the nuclear and extended family, the formation and segmentation of larger social groups, the sharing of food, the exchange of material resources, the flow of information, the expression of leadership, the education of children, and the regulation of activity in accordance with stages of the life cycle—all are controlled through kinship. The system of kinship that prevails throughout Baffinland is relatively homogeneous, although some variations in terms or in the preference for the use of particular terms exist. Kinship terms, not names, are the accepted forms of address between individuals, although nicknames or unique terms are often used between two individuals. It is kinship that directly regulates interpersonal behavior, and for the Baffinland Eskimo, this involves dyadic relationships in which the primary elements of behavior involve respect, obedience, and affection (Graburn 1964; Kemp 1966–1970; Wenzel 1981:83–86).

The Baffinland system of kinship is bilateral, and there is a standard set of terms that identify genealogical positions in relationship to the speaker. A speaker can provide the appropriate term for each position, but there is a significant distinction between the ideal term and the term actually used (Graburn 1964:21–24; Kemp 1974a:60–61). The associations that define an individual within a network of kin involve the biological ties of family and the acquired ties of marriage. In addition to these well-defined linkages, another set of associations can be established between individuals through processes such as name giving, name sharing, adoption, midwifery, and spouse exchange. These processes provide important alternatives for creating bonds between individuals. Name giving creates actual kinship positions, and in earlier times spouse exchange also did (Kemp 1974:57–58; Wenzel 1981:131). Fictive kinship provided alternatives for creating interpersonal alliances both within and outside consanguineal and affinal bonds. All the associations formed by real and fictive relationships were affected by age, order of birth, general circumstances of life history, and specific stage of the life cycle (Kemp 1974).

Naming

Interpersonal relationships for the Baffinland Eskimo cannot be understood apart from the meaning of the name and the process of naming (Kemp 1974). An individual can only be named after a deceased person, and the terminology used between individuals is based upon the fictive relationship designated by the name and not by the consanguineal or affinal bond. However, the symbolic role of this process is strong only for those who have a particular resemblance or association with the deceased. Each individual may have several names, with each one suggesting a separate set of kinship designations. Names are given by older people, and the parents are informed (Kemp 1966–1970). When kinship terminology is established by the name, the behavior is also a function of the fictive as opposed to the actual kin relationship. Names are not sex-specific, so that a child who had been given the name of a deceased person of the opposite sex would also be designated by a kin-

470

Fig. 12. Women's clothing. top left, Napachee making a beadwork belt. She wears a parka with a deep hood for carrying a baby. Photograph by Rosemary Gilliat, 1960. top right, Women from Cape Dorset. The women wear the traditional design parka with back and front flaps and a deep hood. The parka of the woman on the right is made of caribou fur, contrasting with the others made from duffle, a heavy woolen material originally imported by the Hudson's Bay Company. Photograph by R.A. Thierry, date not recorded. bottom, Women wearing parkas with short flaps in front, decorative beading, and (at right) metal spoon bowls. Photograph by Archibald Lang Fleming, 1913-1915.

ship term for the opposite sex. Thus, not only may a father refer to his son as if he were his mother, but also he would behave toward his son as he would toward his mother. The child might be dressed in girl's clothing,

the hair would be grown, and any behavior reminiscent of his deceased namesake would be noted and positively reinforced. As the child grew older, the expectations associated with the real kinship position would begin

471

Fig. 13. Man's summer garments. Sealskin jacket and trousers showing European influence in design and materials—the jacket is lined in plaid cloth and has front button closure. The trousers are lined with baby sealskin fur. Length of jacket 109.0 cm; collected by Julian Bilby, Lake Harbour, Baffin I., 1909-1914.

Fig. 14. Summer tent dwellings. top, Lake Harbour canvas tents, which replaced the traditional skin ones. Photograph by Max Sauer, 1933. bottom, Spotted seal skin tent on Baffin I. held secure by large boulders around its outer rim. Photograph by James Dewey Soper, Aug. 1924.

to emerge, but the symbolic reference of the name continues. When two people have the same name, they recognize an association between them, but it is not formally expressed in expected behavior.

Leadership

It is impossible to separate the traditional economic system of the Baffinland Eskimo from the social system (Wenzel 1981). Independence pervades most phases of social and economic interaction, and it follows that leadership was weakly developed outside the family or household. A particular individual was usually considered to be "the thinker," but this position was as much an expression of respect as it was a designation of leadership (Boas 1888; Kemp 1966–1970; Wenzel 1981). With the development of the trapping economy the fur traders often selected an individual within a family group to be the "camp boss." Outside the sphere of trading activity this position had little social or economic rel-

evance (Phillips 1967:79–80; Kemp in Freeman 1976). Economic decision making was generally left to each individual; but, for the most part, choices converge making joint effort a matter of course. As a result, economic responsibility beyond the family was a sum of the particular obligations between individuals, and allegiance to the group as a separate economic entity does not exist (Kemp 1966–1970). Both men and women play a role in economic decision making, with the woman frequently stating a preference for particular foods, and the activity to secure that food being directed by men. The primary expression of economic life is sharing. Networks of sharing and cooperation are within the nuclear family and extended family, and, to a much lesser extent, within the village or band. While hunting, the harvest will be divided among the hunters, with the person making the kill getting special parts of the more important species. All meat is equally divided as is the skin of the bearded seal (Boas 1888:582). Meat is shared within the village through group meals in summer (Boas

1888:577) or by a more formal division and eating of fresh kills in winter (Kemp 1966–1970). Since about 1965 networks of sharing have been somewhat displaced in the larger settlements by the introduction of a non-trapping money economy. There are no formal arrangements for sharing of money or technology, but there are pressures that force some equalization to take place (Kemp 1966–1970). The first spread of new technology such as snowmobiles was dependent on sharing—an employed person, for example, would buy a machine and then give his older vehicle to relatives still on the land.

Life Cycle

Age and sex underlay physical and mental levels of achievement, and together with kinship they helped determine the expected behavior of an individual within a network of roles (Kemp 1974). Children are involved in both physical and mental games, and their independent action is encouraged. Their role learning begins with play, which becomes useful work at about the age of 10 (Kemp 1974:74–84). The transition from play to work might involve the first killing of an animal for boys or the sewing of garments for girls, when the special event was marked by giving gifts to the child's midwife. Once work began and children matured, they became extremely important to the productivity of the system, carrying out many of the physically difficult tasks. Movement out of this stage usually involved marriage.

Marriage is usually based on an arrangement made between families, but older males may choose a woman. There is no clear pattern of residence after marriage.

Amer. Mus. of Nat. Hist., New York: 60-3358.
Fig. 16. Cup-and-pin game. Stylized bear carved of bone is attached by leather thong to wooden pin. Points are assigned to the various holes. Length 12.0 cm; collected by James Mutch at Cumberland Sound, Baffin I., 1900.

Occasionally polygamy occurs, but monogamous unions are the rule (Boas 1888:579).

The final stages of the life cycle are the mature family providers, followed by old age. Both men and women may be active in naming, telling of tales, and generally providing supervision and guidance to family activity. Older men may develop some power of leadership and be referred to as "the one who thinks or knows everything." As pointed out by Boas (1888:581), this form of leadership is mainly limited to decisions about hunting and seasonal shifts of the village.

The Spiritual World

The world of the spirit permeated every element of Baffinland Eskimo life, affecting both social and ecological relationships. Throughout the area there was a close similarity of beliefs and practices in this sphere. The supernatural world was made up of spirits whose powers were defined by the stories told about them. An individual's relationship with the spiritual world was expressed through the use of amulets and through the observation of taboos; direct intervention was through the shaman (Boas 1888; C.F. Hall 1865; Fleming 1932; Bilby 1923). A *tuᐧrŋaq* or guardian spirit controlled every object as its invisible *inua* 'its person, its owner' (Boas 1888:591). Men could acquire the *inua* of an object as a protector, but only the shaman could control the malevolent powers. Although every object contained its *inua*, some were more powerful than others. Bilby (1923:209) enumerated 50 central spirits, the most powerful of which was Sedna. She created all living things, was the protector of the Eskimo (Boas 1888:583–588; C.F. Hall 1865:524), and was the central figure for most of the ceremonies.

The shaman was responsible for organizing the feasts and celebrations. Important feasts were associated with

Smithsonian, NAA: Honigmann Coll.
Fig. 15. A keep-away game played by young women and older children at Apex, Frobisher Bay. Such games, which were played especially at the end of winter, served both as a means of social integration and as an outlet for aggression (Honigmann and Honigmann 1965:123). Photograph by John J. Honigmann, March-Aug. 1963.

the hunting of fall caribou, the coming of full winter darkness, and the emergence of basking seals on the spring ice (Boas 1888; Bilby 1923). All feasts were accompanied by individual song duels and by the activities of the shaman who must drive away the evil spirits that visit the land. The shaman was often expert in the use of trances and magic. At feast time, the population was divided by season of birth. Gifts were given and mates were exchanged (Boas 1888:602–606).

Sickness was treated by the shaman. If the person was gravely ill, a separate dwelling was built and the sick person remained alone. Death in a house meant that everything in it was to be destroyed. A series of taboos accompanied death, and grave goods were placed with the body. Graves could be visited a year after death and when relatives are traveling in the area (Boas 1888:612–614).

History

The history of contact between the Baffinland Eskimo and the outside world began in the sixteenth century when Martin Frobisher took several Eskimos to England (figs. 2–3).

Whalers first entered the waters of Davis Strait in the mid-1700s (Lubbock 1937). Whaling activity intensified and then began to decline around 1870 (W.G. Ross 1975:40). By 1910, fur trapping had replaced whaling as the primary economic force in Baffinland. Whaling initiated the shift from independence to dependency and was responsible for the introduction of disease (Boas 1888:425; W.G. Ross 1975:119, 124). The strength of the fur trade after 1900 led to outside control over the economic and material life of the Baffinland Eskimo (Phillips 1967:71–82).

In the early 1900s, Anglican missionaries entered the region, with the first baptisms taking place in 1905 (Fleming 1932:110). Missionaries introduced a syllabic system of writing, which remained the primary source of written communications in the 1980s. The missions were responsible for occasional schooling, and they were active in the development of early medical services. The missionaries were followed by the police, who entered the area as the main representatives of government and continued in this role until the late 1950s (Jenness 1964). The trader, missionary, and police dominated social and economic control over Eskimo life until the 1960s.

After 1930 there was a decline in the trapping economy and from this date until the late 1950s many Eskimo groups were unable to maintain a viable economy. Ammunition and material goods were often in short supply. There were untreated epidemics and chronic poor health (Duffy 1981). A shift from this situation began in the early 1950s when a network of radar stations was established across the northern part of the

Robert and Frances Flaherty Study Center at the School of Theology, Claremont, Calif.
Fig. 17. Inside the church at Lake Harbour where Bishop Archibald Lang Fleming was minister. Photograph by Robert Flaherty, 1911.

territory and serviced from Frobisher Bay. This brought about a different form of contact between the Baffinland Eskimos and outsiders and led to the rapid development of Frobisher Bay.

In 1955 the Canadian government brought bureaucracy to the north (Jenness 1964). Village centralization was initiated, and health, education, and social services were taken over by government departments (Phillips 1967:169–172). In 1967, a rental housing program further encouraged families to move into settlements; and slowly, attachments were made to the available services, amenities, and occasional wage labor. Communications improved, with the first radio around 1955, full telephone service in the mid-1970s, and television in most communities by 1980. Communities are served by scheduled airlines, and some medical services are available in each locale.

Hunters continue to exploit the land for food resources, and problems arise because of the equipment and food costs associated with hunting. Problems with the conservation of resources also appear because the hunting is concentrated around the communities. Nevertheless, many families continue to rely on hunting for their primary supply of food, especially during the spring and summer when they establish hunting camps. This need for both money and hunting has created a dual economy.

The main problem to be resolved in the 1980s involved the attempt of the Baffinland Eskimo to gain

Natl. Film Board of Canada Photothèque, Ottawa: 65-4895.
Fig. 18. Man from Frobisher Bay dressed in sealskin parka and wearing a wind mask. Photograph by Ted Grant, May 1965.

effective control over their lives. Land claims are an essential part of this process and the basic principles of these claims have been formally set out. There is an active interest in dealing with proposed developments of oil and gas exploration and transport by ice-breaking tankers that will carry liquefied natural gas. A common denominator of Inuit life has been, and continues to be, a deep and stable attachment to the land. Stability does not mean that significant change in the use and meaning of the land has taken place, but that the land and its resources have never been abandoned as a central force in the Inuit perceptions of their life and livelihood. In 1980 Canada was in the middle of constitutional debate over aboriginal rights, and there were attempts on the part of Baffinland Eskimos to join in a larger circumpolar solidarity in order to strengthen their ability to cope with the outside world and with the social, economic, and political evolution within their territory.

Synonymy

The Baffinland Eskimo referred to themselves in the 1980s as the Nunatsiaqmiut 'people of the beautiful land'.

The local group names collected by Boas (1888) are given in the text.

Sources

In 1883–1884, Franz Boas (1888) carried out field studies among the Baffinland Eskimo of Cumberland Sound and Davis Strait. Before this, Charles Francis Hall (1865) lived and traveled with the Eskimo of Frobisher Bay in the years 1860–1862. After Boas, no ethnographic studies were carried out until the 1960s; however, an interesting body of information was being accumulated in whaling logbooks, journals of the Hudson's Bay Company, mission records, patrol reports of the Royal Canadian Mounted Police, and the records of government agencies. This vast archival literature is being utilized by researchers such as W.G. Ross (1975) in his work on whaling. In 1960 the Canadian government began a program of community studies and evaluative research on the economic potential of the region that supported studies of Frobisher Bay (Yatsushiro 1963), Lake Harbour (Graburn 1963; Higgins 1967), and Cumberland Sound (Anders 1967). Dissertations have been written on Clyde River (Stevenson 1972; Wenzel 1980), and Pangnirtung (Mayes 1978). A major research program was undertaken in 1974 on historical and current land use for all the Baffinland communities (Freeman 1976, 1–3). Important long-term ethnographic studies have been conducted in Lake Harbour (Kemp 1966–1971). Work on socialization was carried out in Cumberland Sound by McElroy (1971). Hantzsch (1977) details travel in Baffinland from 1909 to 1911.

Inuit of Quebec

BERNARD SALADIN D'ANGLURE*

The inhabitants of the south shore of Hudson Strait and the east coast of Hudson Bay share many cultural characteristics, in language, social organization, technology, beliefs, and mythology. As with many other Eskimo groups, there is no traditional collective term for them other than the generic *inuit* 'human beings' or *inutuinnait* 'true human beings'. However, their cultural distinctness has been reinforced by the political and economic history of this region, as is indicated by their modern use of the name *inuit kupaimiut,* an adaptation to Inuit phonology of the expression *inuit* Quebec-*miut* 'people of Quebec'.

The first definite mention of the names of their local bands is in a 1773 manuscript by the Moravian missionary Jens Haven (Haven 1773). Using information from two Inuits originally from Ungava Bay, he enumerated 10 local bands, moving north and west from Nachvak: (1) Killinek (modern *killiniq*†), whose territory around the present Port Burwell is still known under this name; (2) *kangiva,* coinciding with Port-Nouveau-Québec (*kangirsualujjuaq*) on the east coast of Ungava Bay; (3) Tessiugak (*tasiujaq*), living along and at the mouth of the Rivière aux Feuilles, where there is now a village of the same name; (4) Aukpaluk (*aupaluk*), living in the region of Hopes Advance Bay where a small village still is called this; (5) *ungava,* which the modern Inuit describe as the region at the mouth of and somewhat north of the Rivière Arnaud (Payne), now exploited by the Payne Inuit (*kangirsuk*); (6) Tuak (*tuvaq),* who no doubt lived around Diana Bay, which is now called by the related term *tuvaaluk* 'big *tuvaq* (sea ice)', where Koartac village is situated; (7) Aiviktok (*aivirtuuq*), probably occupying the Point Frontenac region still called by this name that is the center of a very rich hunting zone exploited by the Inuit of Wakeham (Maricourt, Kangiqsujuaq, *kangirsujuaq*) (8) Novangok (*nuvunnguq*), certainly located in the sec-

tion of Cape Wolstenholme now known as *nuvuk* 'the cape' (-*nnguq* 'those who assemble at'), where the presence of an Inuit group is attested from the beginning of the seventeenth century (Asher 1860); (9) Iglurarsome (*illuajuk*), who seem to be the Inuit of southwest Baffin called *illuajummiut* 'occupants of little igloos' by those of the south shore of Hudson Strait who call themselves *illualummiut* 'occupants of big igloos' (Saladin d'Anglure 1968); Pitseolak and Eber (1975) and Graburn (1972) confirm these terms, which recall the Igdlumiut (*illumiut* 'occupants of igloos') mentioned by Boas (1888) as the southeast Baffin Inuit name for those of northern Labrador; (10) Ittibime (*itivi*), which includes all the Inuit of the east coast of Hudson Bay; *itivi* 'the other side' is used reciprocally by the Inuit of Ungava Bay and those of the east coast of Hudson Bay to designate each other's territories. The farther one gets from Ungava Bay, the region of the informants, the less precise are the names on this list.

Ungava, one of the terms recorded by Haven, was much used during the nineteenth century because it became official on maps for the bay, was adopted to label the region served by the Hudson's Bay Company post at Fort-Chimo, and finally was extended to cover the federal district created in 1895 in the northeast Labrador peninsula. Although at first it was only a relative geographical term used by the Moravians in Labrador for the unknown regions in the northwest, and then labeled the territory of a precise local band, Ungava gradually acquired, especially in English, a very extended regional meaning that was not supplanted even after the adoption in French of the term Nouveau-Québec for the same territory, which was incorporated into the province of Quebec in 1912.

L.M. Turner (1888) introduced into the scientific literature four other Inuit terms to designate the principal regional bands that he had observed or heard of during his stay in Ungava from 1882 to 1884. Suhinimyut (*siqinirmiut* 'occupants of the sunny side') designates the Inuit of the Atlantic coast of Labrador and of the shores of Ungava Bay west to Baie aux Feuilles; Tahagmiut (*tarramiut* 'occupants of the shady side') designates the Inuit of the west coast of Ungava Bay, southern Hudson Strait, and the northern part of the east coast of Hudson Bay, that is, the coast between Hopes Advance Bay and Cape Smith; Itivimiut (*itivimiut* 'oc-

---

*Translated from French by William C. Sturtevant.

†The Quebec Inuit words appearing in italics in this chapter, and some nonitalicized place-names and personal names, are in the orthography supplied by the author, which is based on the practical orthography in use locally. This orthography has generally the values of the Greenlandic orthography introduced in 1972 (see "Greenland Eskimo: Introduction," this vol.), including *g* for /ɣ/, *r* for /ɣ̇/, and *j* for /y/. The orthography is virtually phonemic in principle, though there are some inconsistencies in the writing of consonant clusters.

476

cupants of the other side of the country') designates the Inuit of the east coast of Hudson Bay from Cape Smith to the entrance of James Bay. He also recognized the Kikiktagmyut (*qikirmiut* 'occupants of the islands') along the coast of the Itivimiut as a distinct regional band. Neither the *qikirmiut* nor *nunamiut* 'occupants of the interior' are here considered one of the large regional bands. Although the distinctions among regional bands that L.M. Turner (1894) reported seem approximately correct, the terms that he proposed as their labels have the meanings he gave only for a speaker situated at Fort-Chimo. His ethnographic descriptions are the only ones based on scientific observation in this region, except for the well-documented reports of the Hudson's Bay Company managers for 1830 and 1834 (Finlayson and Erlandson in Davies 1963) and for 1849 (J. McLean 1932), and Hawkes's (1916) monograph, which is much less precise and based mainly on information from the Labrador coast. Adopting the European usage of Labrador for the whole peninsula known as the Quebec-Labrador peninsula, Hawkes grouped together as Labrador Eskimos all the Inuit occupying that region, unjustifiably obscuring the important differences among them.

The many labels reported or used for the Inuit hide a complex system of denomination of space and its occupants. At the first and best-defined level are occupied sites, particularly winter camps, with names designating their inhabitants. The second level consists of geographical terms, sometimes in semantic opposition, designating groups that utilize a network of camps and are in close relationship with each other. *ungava* 'toward the sea' with its inhabitants the *ungavamiut* is contrasted to *kangiva* 'toward the land' with its inhabitants the *kangivamiut*, as *aggu* 'exposed to the wind' contrasts with *urqu* 'protected from the wind', each of these last being associated with a local band. These terms refer to parts of the Ungava Bay coast and the south shore of Hudson Strait. In the same region *salluit* 'the thin ones' designates the coast between Capes Weggs and Wolstenholme, serving to label as *sallumiut* the inhabitants of Sugluk Inlet and Deception Bay. *saniraq* 'the side' is the territory of the band just to the south of *nuvuk* 'the cape', including Cape Wolstenholme and extending to Kovik Bay.

Other regions are defined less by a coastal section than by the basin of a large river that serves as a route for the seasonal migrations of a local band, for example the band of *kuugaaluk* 'the river', the *kuugaalummiut*. The generic name of an island or archipelago often designates the inhabitants: the *pujjunarmiut* are the inhabitants of *pujjunaq* (Mansel Island); the *arvilimmiut* of *arviliit* (Ottawa Islands); the *qumiutarmiut* of *qumiutait* (Sleeper Islands); the *qikirtamiut* of *qikirtait* 'the islands' (Belcher Islands).

On the third level are the regional bands, Siqinirmiut, Tarramiut, and Itivimiut. Each of these includes several local bands whose members intermarry and share linguistic and cultural characteristics.

Language

Dorais (1971–1972, 1) has indicated that there are two modern dialects, each subdivided into regional forms of speech. The first corresponds to the area of the Itivimiut, the second to that of the Tarramiut and Siqinirmiut together, the eastern boundary passing south of Port Burwell on the Labrador coast, where a new dialect begins. The main dialect boundary runs a little south of Cape Smith while the southwestern and southern limit is marked by the beginning of Subarctic Indian occupation. It is difficult to evaluate the influence that European establishments must have exercised on the linguistic evolution of the Inuit bands.

Territory

The zones occupied and exploited by the three regional bands comprise an immense region in the northern part of the Quebec-Labrador peninsula, including almost all the coasts, most of the adjacent islands, and a large part of the interior (fig. 1). This occupation was effectively limited by Indian use of the entire wooded part of the peninsula, particularly in Ungava Bay, where in 1811 Kohlmeister and Kmoch (1814) discovered traces of Indians on the Koksoak and George river banks and noticed the fright these produced in the Inuit who were with them, and at the tree line at the eastern juncture of James and Hudson bays where true Indian raids are attested since the end of the seventeenth century. The East Cree of this region, according to contemporary reports, massacred without hesitation Inuit families they encountered, taking only infant captives and scalps (Francis 1979). These scalps were even traded south, if J. McLean's (1932:268) 1849 comment is correct: "I have seen Esquimaux scalps, even among the timid, *têtes des boules* of Temiscamingue." No doubt these conflicts influenced the respective territorial extensions of these two groups both before and after the first commercial posts were established in the region.

The Islands

The ancient, regular occupation of the large islands and archipelagos off the east coast of Hudson Bay and the south shore of Hudson Strait is attested by archeological evidence, by the testimony of early voyagers, and by modern Inuit informants drawing on oral tradition.

Several hundred Inuit there hunted large marine mammals, polar bears, and the birds that abound on some of the islands. At the end of the nineteenth century

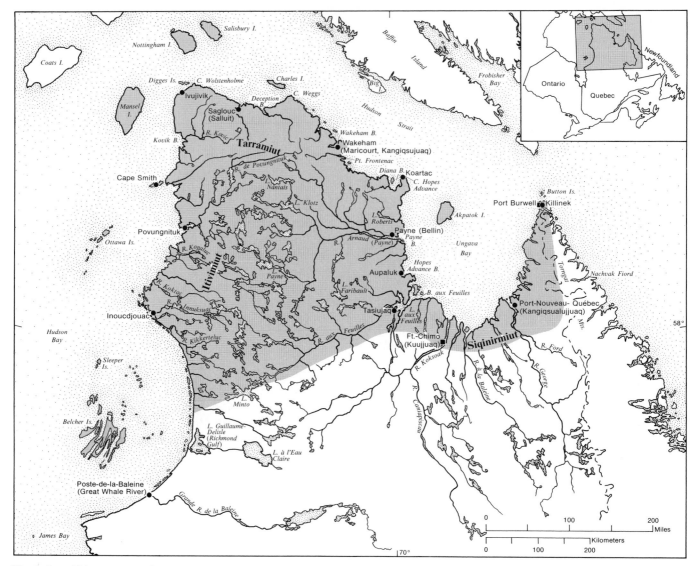

Fig. 1. Late 19th-century territory.

an important group of islanders still lived permanently in the Belcher Islands, and other, smaller groups occupied more temporarily the other islands—Sleeper, Ottawa, Mansel, Nottingham, Akpatok, and Button. These islands were valued refuge zones when violent conflicts broke out on the mainland, between Inuit and Indians or between Inuit groups (Saladin d'Anglure 1978).

The islands were also valuable for the episodic exploitation of specific resources less easily accessible on the mainland, such as polar bears (Akpatok and Ottawa islands) and walruses (Sleeper, Nottingham, and Akpatok islands).

Button and Nottingham islands, at the ends of Hudson Strait, served according to the Inuit as stopover points for people crossing the strait. The term *tujjaat* that designates both of them exactly expresses this use as a stopping place. Crossings were frequent via Nottingham Island, where walrus hunters from the mainland and from Baffin Island met (Boas 1888; Elton 1942;

Arima 1963; Pitseolak and Eber 1975); it was much riskier, although still possible, to cross the entrance of the strait (J. McLean 1932).

Oral tradition includes many stories and beliefs about the islands. The population of the Sleeper Islands disappeared after a murderous quarrel and a general poisoning from eating bad game. A single survivor was taken in by the Belcher Islands Inuit. It is also said that the brother and sister who are the origin of the sun and moon lived on the Ottawa Islands and that many of their descendents still live in the region around Inoucdjouac (Port Harrison, Inukjuak, *inujjuaq*). There are also dramatic stories of cannibalism occurring several times on Akpatok Island.

The Interior

Inuit exploitation and occupation of the interior of the Quebec-Labrador peninsula has been regularly mentioned since Low (1906) alluded to some hundred Inuit

478

living there. In 1912 Flaherty (1924) found numerous remains of camps and caribou hunters' blinds. Speck (1936) investigated the presence of Inuit bands in the interior southeast of Ungava Bay, and in 1948 J. Rousseau (1948) discovered archeological sites proving an ancient human occupation on the shores of Lac Payne. Many questions remain regarding the antiquity, the importance, and the regularity of this occupation, but several Inuit living in the 1970s said that they had grown up in these regions and descended from genuine inhabitants of the interior. Balikci (1964b) cautiously avoids this question, choosing instead a postcontact adaptation tied to the acquisition of guns. Saladin d'Anglure (1969) and Vézinet (1980) support the hypothesis of a traditional occupation of the interior.

In contrast to the District of Keewatin and Alaska, where important groups still live in the interior, the last inland groups of Arctic Quebec were integrated into coastal groups by 1930. They seem never to have been very numerous. The existence of rich lichen pasturages for caribou and the presence of large lakes and rivers filled with fish would explain both the attraction of the interior country for the coastal Inuit, who regularly went there to procure caribou skins and sinews necessary for their winter clothing, and the permanent occupation by a few small local bands. Rivers and lakes on the route of the autumn caribou migrations afforded in some spots excellent hideouts for hunters who profited from the slow crossings by the herds to provision themselves with meat and skins, the skins being at that season the most suitable for clothing. In the peninsula more than a dozen caribou crossing places are known; they were exploited jointly by the interior and coastal bands.

The resources of lakes and rivers of the interior plateau, seasonally exploited by the coastal groups, were sufficient for permanent occupation by some groups of families. This occupation, often precarious, sometimes was the result of ostracism from coastal groups. For other families, life in the interior could be the result either of a family tradition, which had developed an attachment to their native country and the mode of life associated with it, or of the choice of an alternative to their previous insular or coastal life. *angutinnguaq,* the famous song-duel singer who lived for the last part of his life in the Wakeham Bay region and then at Fort-Chimo, was one of these former inland dwellers whom circumstances had constrained to live on the coast. He composed a song in which he evoked his nostalgia for the interior and his inability to rid himself of it and be happy on the coast (Saladin d'Anglure et al. 1973).

Nantais, Klotz, and Payne lakes and the Povungnituk, Kogaluc, and aux Feuilles rivers were the principal sites of inland Inuit occupation. In the summer, coastal hunters from Hudson Strait, Ungava Bay, and Hudson Bay came to the same places. The trips from the coast were made in sleds, leaving in the spring and returning in the autumn, going up the rivers in kayaks or umiaks, and finally often on foot.

The Coast

Most Inuit bands, about 50 of them, occupied the coastal zone. Each included two to five families occupying the shore itself, the small coastal islands that were easily accessible in all seasons, the lower courses and mouths of the large rivers, and also all the fish-filled lakes near the coast.

In this region also the inhabitants met and conducted economic and matrimonial exchanges with people from the interior and the islands. The islanders who needed caribou skins and clothing exchanged their powerful dogs and their ivory. The inlanders, lacking ivory for their weapons and utensils and bearded sealskins for their boot soles, exchanged their bales of summer and autumn caribou skins. Still remembered on the east coast of Hudson Bay is one of the last of these transactions, about 1930, when an islander offered his ivory-shod sled and its harness to an interior hunter in exchange for a bale of skins and a complete suit of caribou clothing (Balikci 1964; Saladin d'Anglure 1956–1971; Trudel 1969).

Despite the relatively restricted area of Inuit habitats compared to the entire territory of modern Arctic Quebec with its forests and continually migrating caribou in the southern part, the Inuit made only episodic incursions into the southern margins and interior due to their fear of the Indians. Only the Belcher Archipelago and some islands closer to the coast offered both security and sufficient resources to allow permanent habitation. The Rivière aux Feuilles and Lac Minto were the southern limit of territory that could be permanently exploited with a supportable risk from the Indians. The Koksoak, Baleine and George rivers at the bottom of Ungava Bay were ascended by the Inuit in large umiaks in search of wood and caribou, but at considerable risk (Kohlmeister and Kmoch 1814). An intermediate region between the northern limit of the thin boreal forest and the southern shore of Hudson Strait was safer than the coast or interior, yet contained many caribou; most of the permanent and seasonal interior occupation was here. The coast in this intermediate region had fewer large marine mammals (compared to their abundance in Hudson Strait) and in general less diverse food resources. This is one reason for the greater seasonal alternation between coastal and interior habitats here; another is the larger number of river courses and navigable lakes that traverse this flat region and allow the use of kayaks on the Kikkerteluc, Koktak, Kogaluc, and Povungnituk rivers or umiaks on the Rivière Arnaud. Some families left the coast in April and did not return from the interior until the end of September.

The northern region includes the highest density of

coastal Inuit. They hunted the bowhead whale, walrus, beluga, and bearded seal in coastal locations that have very great tidal amplitudes and thus afford supplementary food resources in all seasons (algae and shellfish). The less abundant caribou were hunted on foot in the interior high plateaus in August and September, particularly for their skins. A few families, however, spent 6 or 12 months of the year in the interior near Lac Nantais. Wood was rare despite the presence of driftwood in some areas, and some families undertook long voyages toward the south in order to procure it. The islands were regularly exploited, but only a few families lived there permanently for long periods (Mansel, Nottingham, Salisbury, Akpatok, Button islands) while maintaining strong relations with the coast.

Demography

Various sources (for example, Haven 1773) allow the reconstruction of the distribution of the Inuit population in Arctic Quebec during the first half of the nineteenth century (table 1, with more precise totals by region than by habitat zone). There are numerous indications (Saladin d'Anglure 1956–1971) that starvation and famines accompanied by infanticide and even cannibalism were not rare. Despite a very flexible social organization and developed types of cooperation, violent conflicts followed by murders, battles, and feuds occurred regularly. Epizootic diseases and epidemics periodically decimated dogs and humans; infant mortality was high as was that of adults with frequent death in childbirth for women and from hunting accidents for men; and conception was widely spaced due to prolonged nursing (from two to four years). This population had achieved only a fragile demographic equilibrium.

Under these conditions simple reproduction was highly valued since there was a real problem in replacing generations. This is far from the concept of hunter-gatherer societies as characterized by abundance (Sahlins 1972).

Prehistory

Archeological research, episodic beginning in the 1940s and intensive in the 1970s (W.E. Taylor 1964a; Plumet 1977), has shown that Arctic Quebec was first occupied by successive migrations (probably from the northwest) between 2500 and 1000 B.C. Sites occupied by these Pre-Dorset people have been identified at Ivujivik, on Mansel Island, and at Poste-de-la-Baleine (Great Whale River). Sites dating between 800 B.C. and A.D. 1350 are numerous all along the coast from Poste-de-la-Baleine to Cape Chidley, on the main islands, and even in the interior on Payne and Roberts lakes (Vézinet 1980). The Dorset culture of these sites developed out of that

Table 1. Population, Early 19th Century

Region	Islands	Coast	Interior	Total
Northern	100	750	50	900
Central	50	450	100	600
Southern	150	300	70	520
Total	300	1,500	220	2,020

of their predecessors. In the fourteenth century the Dorset population of the region was supplanted by new immigrants, the Thule people, who also came from the northwest via southern Baffin Island. Very mobile thanks to their dog sleds, they rapidly invaded the coastal and island regions and also left traces of their passage at Payne and Roberts lakes (Vézinet 1980). More Thule sites than others are now known.

Traditional Culture

Beginning in the sixteenth century European ships searching for a Northwest Passage to China and Japan came in contact with the Inuit of the Atlantic coast of Labrador and perhaps also of the south shore of Hudson Strait. Despite the importance of these occasional contacts and the unsuccessful attempts to establish trading posts in the southern part of the region, the "Aboriginal Period" (Damas 1968a) lasted until the mid-nineteenth century. During this period the Inuit exploited all the habitation zones; most of the camps were on the coast or the nearby islands, with a few small groups living in the interior or on the offshore islands. The only permanent European establishments were, in the nearby Subarctic, the Hudson's Bay Company trading post established in 1837 at Great Whale River (now Poste-de-la-Baleine), and, on the Labrador coast, the Moravian Brethren's post founded in 1830 at Hebron.

The presence of these posts at Lac Guillaume-Delisle (Richmond Gulf), 1750-1756, Little Whale River, intermittently 1749-1820, and Fort-Chimo, 1830-1842, resulted in a southern displacement of the Inuit population (toward Poste-de-la-Baleine and the Koksoak and George river mouths). The choice of the mid-nineteenth century for the end of the aboriginal period remains somewhat arbitrary until all the ancient commercial and maritime archives can be systematically searched, but it is justified by the important changes occurring after 1850 (cf. Balikci 1964b). The following ethnographic reconstruction for this period is based on oral tradition and the available documents.

Technology and Domestic Equipment

In Arctic Qubec, *piuliniagaq* 'practical goods' (artifacts and raw materials to make them) are distinguished from *niqiksaq* 'alimentary goods' (edibles). Each primary domestic unit had to supply itself with raw materials and make its own tools, weapons, and equipment. These regularly included a fire-making kit of flint, iron pyrite, and dried moss; several scrapers and men's knives; a bow drill kit, and some adzes; cooking equipment with large oil lamps suitable for women (and some small lamps for traveling men) and a set of pots of various sizes including some small individual pots for tabooed women, all of steatite obtained at quarries rather evenly scattered over the peninsula. Little is known of these rarely studied quarries (Saladin d'Anglure 1978a); two of them, on the south shore of Hudson Strait, include very interesting petroglyphs (Saladin d'Anglure 1963).

Driftwood was another important material, for making tool handles and plates edged with whalebone. Ivory, bone, and horn, with schist, were used to make men's and women's utensils. Women also had cups and pails made from old kayak covers; semilunar knives; various kinds of stone, bone, or wood scrapers and skin softeners; bone or ivory needles; thimbles and finger guards; various birdskin or membrane containers; bladders and small-animal skins for keeping their oil lamp wicks; sewing thread; and menstrual napkins. Sewing thread, to be usable, had to be fresh and from caribou or beluga sinew. Lacking this, substitutes were known such as seagull esophagus dried and cut into thin strips in the Belcher Islands or guillemot (*Uria lomvia*) wing tendons used on the Digges Islands (Saladin d'Anglure 1956–1971).

Marine mammal skins were in much demand, especially of the bearded seal used for boot soles, straps, lines, and tent and boat covers. Ringed seal skins were much used for summer garments, boot tops, food containers, and small cords. But the most valuable skins were taken from caribou in midsummer for ceremonial clothing and at the end of summer for winter clothing. Skins with contrasting ventral white and dorsal brown were sought for their fine esthetic effects. Numerous substitutes were also known and used, especially, on the islands, skins of polar bears, dogs, eider ducks, guillemots, or even fish (Saladin d'Anglure 1956–1971). In the interior, the lack of marine mammal skins was made up for by greater use of caribou, dog, and fox skins.

Structures

In winter the dwelling was the snow igloo (*igluvigaq*), with porch, entryway, and often an annex for storing skins and food (fig. 2). Ordinarily it housed two families. In the northern region where large stores of walrus

Fig. 2. Dwellings at Little Whale River, 1874. top, Winter snowhouse. Man to left is cutting blocks of snow for the entranceway. Man on right is tending to the sled. A skin is on a semi-circular stretcher frame leaning against the igloo to the right. bottom, Two skin summer tents. Photographs by James L. Cotter.

and beluga oil could be accumulated during the summer and autumn, the oil lamps and the igloos were much larger. Other coastal groups had to use smaller lamps and houses. The interior people even had to do without heating, using caribou tallow for lighting and cooking over a twig fire in an ice porch.

The semisubterranean house (*qarmaq*) built of stones and turf with a skin roof (sometimes insulated with brush or turf) has been used since ancient times as attested by Inuit tradition, numerous well-preserved remains in various locations, and place-names such as *qarmait*, *qarmaaliut*, and *qarmatalik*. It was still used in the early twentieth century at Killinek, on the edge of the sparse forest at the foot of Ungava Bay, and on some archipelagoes such as the Ottawa Islands.

In the summer two types of tent were ordinarily used. The conical Indian-type tent (*nuirtaq*) with a central smoke hole and pole framework was used in the Belcher Islands (covered with undehaired ringed seal skins) and by the permanent or seasonal interior dwellers (covered with dehaired caribou skins). Small and with thin skins, this tent was suited to summer movements. The apse tent was larger and commoner, made of 10 to 15 bearded seal skins supported by a dozen wood poles. The sides were of translucent membranes, such as the fatty layer cut off in thinning a hide, serving as a window; the rest of the tent was not dehaired. These large tents occurred especially on the northern coasts. Coastal people elsewhere, lacking bearded seals, could use ringed seal or beluga skins. In cases of real necessity, one could even use salmon skins (Saladin d'Anglure 1956–1971).

Kashims (*qaggiq* sg.), used for recreational or ceremonial gatherings, are known from the southern shore of Hudson Strait (Stupart 1887) and from Ungava Bay, where in winter a large snow dome served for games, sports, and dances. In summer a huge skin tent sometimes covered a structure of backed benches of stone; there is such a kashim on *Airaqtuuq* Island near Cap Hopes Advance (Saladin d'Anglure 1956–1971; Plumet 1981). Large collective feasts were regularly held in these structures, as well as boxing and other athletic competitions, song meetings, games, dances, and shamanistic seances.

Clothing and Adornment

The same clothing style seems to have characterized all the Inuit of Arctic Quebec and to have differentiated them from southern Baffinland, where, for example, women's winter parkas had a pointed hood, tails pointed at the front corners, and decorative pieces at the throat to resemble walrus tusks, while on the mainland hoods and tails were rounded and no such decorations were used (figs. 3–4).

Differences from Labrador clothing were less striking and are more difficult to evaluate (due to the lack of data). Some distinctions in clothing existed among the regional bands, such as minor differences in cut, shape, or decoration. Thus, for example, thigh boots of dehaired sealskin were only used on the east coast of Hudson Bay (Saladin d'Anglure 1956–1971; Hawkes 1916). The white edging of women's winter parkas was narrow among the Tarramiut and broad among the more southern Inuit.

Some variations were due to differences in availability of materials, because of varying natural environments or individual performances. Only the families of good hunters had a wide variety of clothing that they replaced each year; they were set apart in the winter by their clothing of shorthaired caribou skins richly decorated with white fur inserts and in the summer by clothing of ringed seal skins for rainy days. Poor families unable to get autumn caribou skins wore their garments for more than a year or had to use sealskins instead for their parkas.

Finally, on the offshore islands genuine alternative solutions to the clothing problem were applied, such as the systematic use of eider duck skins reinforced or filled out with bits of sealskin or dogskin for parkas (fig. 5) and stockings. In the Belcher Islands this custom persisted into the 1960s. On the Mansel and Ottawa

Smithsonian, Dept. of Anthr.: 90,237.

Fig. 3. Woman's parka. This caribou skin outer garment is ornamented with trade goods including seed beads, pewter spoons, and lead drops in several shapes (probably fishing line sinkers). Each lead piece cost about 1½¢, and L.M. Turner (1894:211) estimated the trim on this parka to have cost about $4.00. Length 158.0 cm; collected by Lucien Turner at Ungava Bay, Que., 1882–1884.

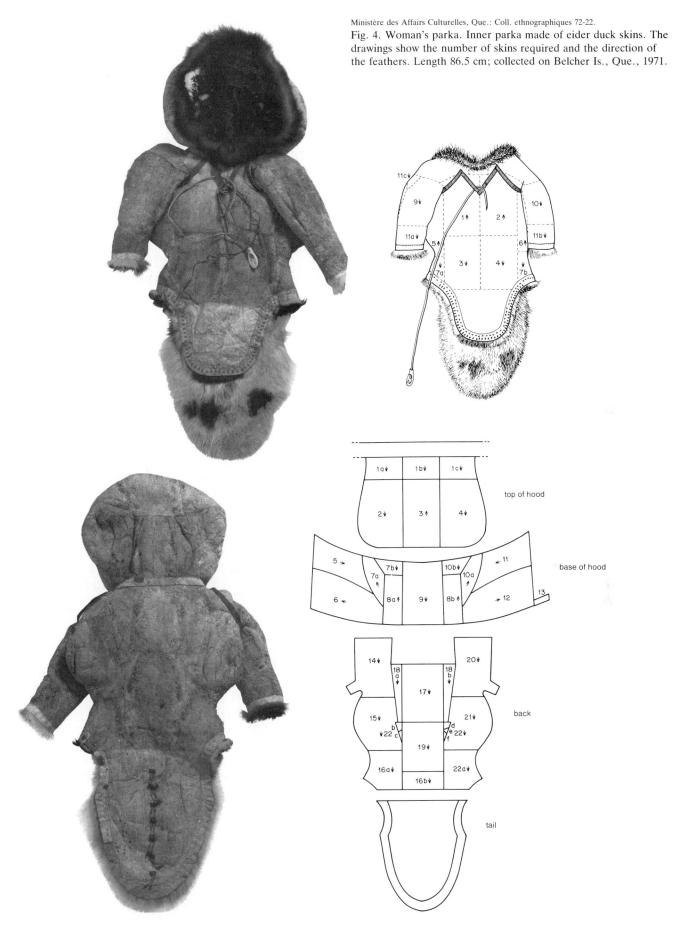

Ministère des Affairs Culturelles, Que.: Coll. ethnographiques 72-22.

Fig. 4. Woman's parka. Inner parka made of eider duck skins. The drawings show the number of skins required and the direction of the feathers. Length 86.5 cm; collected on Belcher Is., Que., 1971.

top of hood

base of hood

back

tail

Ministère des Affairs Culturelles, Quebec: Coll. ethnographiques 72-20.
Fig. 5. Man's feathered outer parka made of eider duck skins. Children's clothes were also made of eider skins. Length 78.0 cm; collected on Belcher Is., Que., 1971.

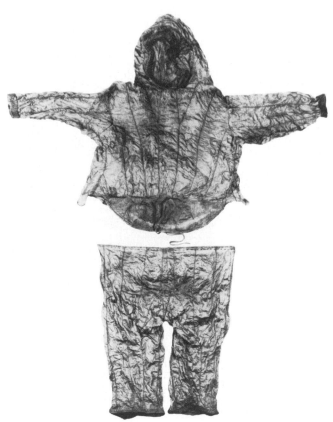

Natl. Mus. of Canada, Ottawa: top, IV-B-294; bottom, IV-B-295.
Fig. 6. Man's waterproof parka and trousers made of vertical strips of seal gut, worn over fur clothing when kayaking. Length of top about 78.7 cm, bottom same scale; both collected by E.W. Hawkes at Cape Wolstenholme, Que., 1914.

islands polar bear skins were used for men's pants and winter boots, and occasionally fish skins for children's and adolescents' parkas (Saladin d'Anglure 1956–1971).

Age and sex were also differentiating factors in clothing, in its form, decoration, and materials. The decoration on the uppers of ringed sealskin winter boots were vertical for men, horizontal for women. Fox and hare skins were almost completely reserved for women and children, hats and pants of birdskins for old people and young children, fawnskins and unborn caribou skins for the newborn and infants.

Tattooing, formerly universal for women's faces, arms, and breasts after puberty had almost disappeared in the Fort-Chimo area by the end of the nineteenth century (L.M. Turner 1894) but could still be seen on two elderly women at Saglouc (Salluit) in the 1960s (Saladin d'Anglure 1956–1971). Men were only rarely tattooed, on the nose or shoulder when they had killed a White man or a bowhead whale (Saladin d'Anglure 1956–1971; Pitseolak and Eber 1975). Tattooing was done with a needle, sinew thread, and an oil-soot mixture.

Little is known of traditional personal ornaments, except that a variety of talismans and amulets of wood, ivory, or animal parts were sewn onto parkas (fig. 8), and women wore necklaces of teeth and small ivory beads (before these were replaced by imported beads) and decorated their summer parkas with ivory pendants (fig. 9) (replaced by tin and beads).

Men wore their hair long, hanging to the shoulders and sometimes with a forehead band. Women also wore their hair long, but braided, rolled, and knotted in two small chignons in front of the ears, in which they often carried sewing equipment (Saladin d'Anglure 1956–1971).

Transport

In Arctic Quebec perhaps more than elsewhere the Inuit developed and maintained their transportation system, one of the most original and efficient there has ever been. The peninsular form of their large territory, the importance of the interior waterways and the coastal island network, and the nearness of standing trees no doubt combined to allow the continuing use of the umiak for collective movements into the 1920s (Flaherty 1924, 1979 for the east coast of Hudson Bay; Arima 1963 and Saladin d'Anglure 1956-1971 for Hudson Strait; Vézinet 1982 for Ungava Bay), of the kayak for individual hunting into the 1960s (Arima 1964; Freeman 1964; Saladin d'Anglure 1956–1971), and of the dog sled even into the 1980s.

The combined use of umiak, kayaks, and dogs allowed bands of 20 to 30 people to move in summer along the coasts and the large water-courses with weapons and baggage. Haven (1773) mentions 10 umiaks for 200 people at Aufaluk (Aupaluk?) and J.G. Taylor (1974a) the same ratio in Labrador. They could travel several hundred miles under sail or oars to exploit the elongated zones of their territory, along the coasts or

484

Smithsonian, Dept. of Anthr.: 90,191.
Fig. 7. Leather shoes with corrugated sole worn over waterproof boots to prevent slipping on ice. The textured surface is created by looping the leather strip sewn into the sole. Length 25.5 cm; collected by Lucien Turner, Ungava Bay, Que., 1882–1884.

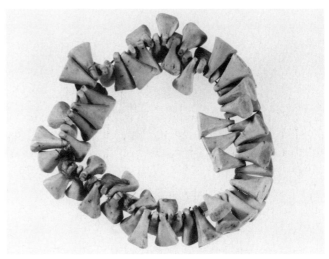

Smithsonian, Dept. of Anthr.: 90,234.
Fig. 9. Conical ivory pieces with a hole at the end for stringing. They were used as fringed borders and breast bands to decorate the parkas of men and women before trade goods became available. Length of each about 2.5 cm; collected by Lucien Turner at Ungava Bay, Que., 1882–1884.

up the rivers, or to search outside their territory for rare materials such as wood for construction, steatite, or walrus ivory (Arima 1963). At the entrance to Wakeham Bay Low (1901) met an umiak with masts rowed by two women and steered by a man; it contained three other women, some children, a dog team and sled, tents, and baggage and was escorted by eight men and youths in kayaks. In Ungava Bay Low encountered another umiak accompanied by seven kayaks, some 30 people, the dogs towing the umiak, going to their caribou hunting territory some 50 miles up the Rivière Arnaud (Low 1901). Dogs pulled an umiak like a sled, when the current was strong. "Two men stayed in the umiak, one in the bow and the other at the stern rudder. . . . They used a long line and the man driving the dogs had to run most of the time . . . those following on the river bank also had to run . . . in order to keep up with the boat" (Vézinet 1980).

Mus. of the Amer. Indian, Heye Foundation, New York: 12/7532.
Fig. 8. Charms. Carved ivory charms said by the owner to avert the evil consequences of the cannibalism his band was forced to resort to for survival (J.G.E. Smith 1980:45). Length of largest 4.5 cm; collected Akpatok I., Ungava Bay, N.W.T., 1895.

With a kayak and two to four dogs a family of four, an adult couple and two children, could travel along the interior lakes and rivers for one to three months in the summer and early autumn hunting caribou and fishing for lake trout. The dogs carried bags of provisions and utensils, and even sometimes an infant, and dragged the tent poles. On her back the woman carried perhaps a child and a bundle of skins for the tent or for bedding. The man in the kayak transported everything that would fit inside or on top. The old people, the sick, and some children and adolescents had been left on the coast (Low 1906). When a hunting region was reached, the man went on foot in search of game, carrying only a caribou skin, his weapons, and some dried food. The skin served as protection if he had to sleep out, and as a boat if he had to cross a watercourse—stuffing it with brush, tying the edges together, and using it as a float while paddling with a caribou scapula (Saladin d'Anglure 1979).

The families of the same band often left the coast together, dispersing as they entered the interior in order to increase their chances of encountering game. They sometimes met again at the *talu* (stone wall built as a bow hunter's blind) or at the *nallu* (collective blind where caribou swimming across lakes or rivers were hunted with kayak and lance) (Low 1899a; L.M. Turner 1894; Balikci 1964b; Saladin d'Anglure 1979; Saladin d'Anglure and Vézinet 1977). Some families went back down to the coast on foot and in the kayak as they had come, while others took apart their kayak and ingeniously converted it into a sled so they could stay in the interior until the snow allowed them to use the dog team to return to the coast more quickly (Saladin d'Anglure 1978).

Smithsonian, Dept. of Anthr.: 90,183.
Fig. 10. Goggles. Wooden eye shade has narrow eye slits, blackened front surface, and projecting knobs at the side over which the split ends of the leather head strap are slipped. Width 13.5 cm; collected by Lucien Turner at Ungava Bay, Que., 1882–1884.

Prov. Arch. of B.C., Victoria: 16396.
Fig. 11. Group of Eskimos in a large umiak at Wakeham Bay. Photograph by Albert Peter Low, 1903–1904.

In the spring the combined use of a dog team and kayak permitted them to move along the floe ice to hunt marine mammals both on the ice as well as in the open water. The boat was attached on top of the sled, to protect the equipment in case the ice broke. Sometimes the hunter used an old kayak cover filled with snow in the same fashion (Balikci 1960b).

There were many variants within these transport systems. For example, there were two kayak types. A large kayak for hunting and travel at sea, 20–25 feet long and covered with bearded sealskin, was used mainly by northern coastal people, and a small kayak 12–18 feet long was particularly adapted to portages across the isthmuses and to travel among the coastal archipelagoes and to the interior rivers and lakes (Freeman 1964; Saladin d'Anglure, Dorais, and Malgrange Saladin d'Anglure 1969; Vézinet 1980). The small kayak was more lightly covered, with ringed sealskins on the coast and in the islands or caribou skins in the interior, and was the kayak of the Belcher Islands people, inland people, and the coastal people who went into the interior during the summer (fig. 12).

There were also transformations from one system to another in addition to the kayak-sled method. A celebrated story of a migration lost on the ice in the early twentieth century on the east coast of Hudson Bay (Saladin d'Anglure 1978a; Myers 1977) illustrates the transforming of sleds into an umiak when the ice thawed, and then the retransforming of the umiak into sleds at freeze-up. The Inuit everywhere also knew the catamaran technique, tying two kayaks to solid cross-pieces when they had to transport heavy loads by water over short distances (Saladin d'Anglure 1956–1971; Freeman 1964). In the Belcher Islands during the first half

486

of the twentieth century there appeared a form of kayak with two hatches, parallleled only in south Alaska and the Aleutians, which seems to have been a recent adoption (Freeman 1964; Guemple 1967). A small triangular sail was sometimes installed in the kayak bow in the Belcher Islands and on the east coast of Hudson Bay (Burwash 1927; Freeman 1964).

Despite this ingenuity that allowed the islanders to reach the continent and the Tarramiut of Hudson Strait to cross to Baffin Island at the west entrance of the strait or to hunt walruses and polar bears on Akpatok Island, the Inuit were above all great walkers—the women carrying infants and the men carrying game, or dragging loads, game, or sleds. They did not know how to swim, and drowning was common. Kayaks often capsized during the harpooning of large mammals, and umiak shipwrecks were feared (Saladin d'Anglure 1956–1971; Graburn 1969).

Ownership

Since traditionally in Inuit territory there was no true ownership of land or hunting territories, permanent habitation structures were less used than in many other regions. On the other hand, there were use-rights resulting from prolonged occupation or from the construction and upkeep of fixed structures: walls for hunters' blinds, cairns for caribou drives, stone weirs, traps, food caches, and graves. And despite the great mobility of the band, several generations could succeed each other in the same region. One always knew one's place of birth, and a particular tie attached one to that place.

Tools of production belonged to their regular user, who was often the maker. An umiak owner was especially prestigious, because several related families depended on him for their summer mobility; such a grouping constituted a local band. Each umiak served about

20–30 people (fig. 11) (Stupart 1887; J.G. Taylor 1975; Vézinet 1982) who cooperated in the re-covering, maintenance, portage, and propulsion of this means of collective transport.

Subsistence

Production from hunting, fishing, and collecting was largely an individual activity, practiced by women (mainly collecting), by men (mainly hunting), or by both (fishing). Certain places in Arctic Quebec provided supplementary foods accessible all year round. They offered nearby bands an appreciated dietary complement and an assurance against famine. These included the guillemot rookeries, such as those of Cape Wolstenholme and the Digges Islands (Ascher 1860), and some zones free of winter ice where shellfish were abundant: mussels in the Inoucdjouac region, sea urchins and sea cucumbers in the Belchers. At Wakeham and Saglouc the 30-or-more-foot tidal amplitude allowed the Tarramiut during spring-tides to collect important quantities of mussels and edible algaes (*Fucus, Alaria, Laminaria*); in winter they dug holes in the floe ice at low tide in order to make such collections in cavities in the ice emptied by the ebb. Because of these possibilities, families from less favored regions in several known cases took refuge there (Saladin d'Anglure 1970).

In the summer on several islands the Inuit collected seagull and eider eggs (L.M. Turner 1894). On Akpatok Island men lowered themselves with leather cords over high cliffs in order to collect guillemot eggs (Saladin d'Anglure 1956–1971; Vézinet 1982). Plants were also collected, such as *Oxytropis* roots in the spring, willow buds and mountain sorrel in the summer, and numerous berries such as blackberries, bearberries, and black crowberries in the autumn.

Individual fishing was done by women with hand lines, through holes in lake ice for trout and char or crevices in the floe ice for cod. Men more often used a gig with a lure or a small harpoon. In the interior of the country they used set lines baited with caribou meat to fish the large, gray lake trout that they prepared by smoking (Saladin d'Anglure 1979; Balikci 1964).

Men hunted aquatic birds with a dart with a spear thrower (Hawkes 1916) and sometimes, as in the Belchers, threw bolas at flights of geese and ducks (Saladin d'Anglure 1956–1971; Balikci 1964), but the principal weapon for small and medium-sized game, ptarmigan, hares, migratory birds on the ground, and caribou was the bow with different kinds of arrows adapted to the different sizes and types of animal. Some women were trained for hunting from their infancy, when they had received the name and identity of a great hunter or when their father had no sons (Saladin d'Anglure 1970, 1970a). Stone or ice traps were used to capture foxes, and snares of caribou sinew or whalebone strips were used for birds. The ringed seal was pursued by men in kayaks in the summer, harpooned, and then killed with the lance. In winter it was hunted at breathing holes where the tides are weaker (the east coast of Hudson Bay), or at the edge of crevasses or in open water in the south shore of Hudson Strait (Low 1906; Balikci 1964; Saladin d'Anglure 1956–1971). In spring a special harpoon was used on the east coast of Hudson Bay for hunting seals warming themselves on the ice (Balikci 1964). Larger game such as bearded seal and polar bear was sometimes hunted alone, although this was dangerous. A bearded seal was harpooned after a long pursuit and dispatched with a lance. A polar bear was attacked with a lance or a knife after it was immobilized by the dogs.

Although individual production provided a significant part of daily needs, it was insufficient to fulfill the needs for new clothing each autumn, and to provide the stocks of meat and oil to feed families and dog teams and to fill the oil lamps during the winter. The organization of simple to complex forms of cooperation was encouraged by the gregarious habits of some game species at definite stages in their migratory cycles or the periodic abundance of species of a size that made individual hunting too difficult.

The Arctic anadromous char, descending from fresh water to the sea at the beginning of each summer and returning at the end, were concentrated in late June near the outlets of lakes where they had spent the winter, and in late August at the mouths of rivers up which they passed. The return upstream took place regularly for only a few days, occasioning spectacular collective fishing at stone weirs built in the river bed. Each band had weirs in one or two rivers from which they filled large stone caches wth fish, the temperature being sufficiently low at this time of year to allow long preservation. Women and children participated in this collective activity, waiting for the fish to arrive, catching some of them by hand, killing and cleaning them, and caching them. This was an important occasion for building up stored food supplies for the frequently difficult transitional period at the beginning of winter. This form of fishing was especially common and extensive among the people of the coasts and the islands, but there were several other hunting and fishing practices utilizing comparable forms of traps. On the south shore of Hudson Strait, with its large tides, the Inuit dammed up the char in summer in natural pools on the shore and harpooned them at low tide. In the Povungnituk territory and everywhere that geese nested hunters took advantage of their inability to fly during moult and drove large numbers into stone enclosures that were then closed so that they could be killed at will (Saladin d'Anglure 1956–1971).

There were two types of large collective hunts for caribou in the interior: with bow and arrow from wall

487

Fig. 12. Johnny Pov making a kayak at Povungnituk. top left, Johnny Pov (on right) planing the bottom lath. top right, In a large tent set up by Pov for the occasion, women take the scraped, softened sealskins and suspend them from a horizontal pole, then sew the skins together with sinew. Agnes Akinisie, Johnny Pov's wife (wearing a hair net) is to the right. center left, The sewn skins are placed on the kayak frame and are then (center right) lashed together across the top of the kayak. bottom left, Occasional softening of the damp skin by chewing may be needed. After lashing the kayak will be carried back into the tent where the women sew the top skins to the laced part. bottom right, Placing the wooden cockpit frame into the kayak. After it is completed it will be placed in a rack to dry. Photographs by Frederica Knight, summer 1959.

SALADIN D'ANGLURE

blinds toward the end of summer, and from kayaks at caribou crossings in autumn. *Nau Kilupaq* (Saladin d'Anglure and Vézinet 1977) has provided a remarkable drawing showing bow hunting in the Rivière Kovic area a the end of the nineteenth century. Depicted is a herd of 26 male caribou driven by some 30 Inuit (men running and women and children waving pieces of hide or cloth and shouting) toward a wall where nine hidden archers wait to shoot them (see also Balikci 1964; Vézinet 1980, 1982). More is known about hunting at caribou crossings (L.M. Turner 1894; Low 1899a; Saladin d'Anglure and Vézinet 1977; Vézinet 1980, 1982). One or several bands conducted these hunts at each crossing. There were lookouts at high places, rows of cairns with flags to frighten off any caribou attempting to escape from the gully leading to the crossing, hunters in kayaks waiting in ambush, and finally women and children hidden on the other shore ready to kill any wounded animals that approached them. When a herd began to swim in the crossing, hunters in kayaks tried to kill them by spearing their loins.

It required, ideally, some 60 autumn caribou skins (of females or young ones) to renew the wardrobe of a band of 30 people.

The collective hunt determined by the size of the game animals relates essentially to large marine mammals: walrus, belugas, and bowhead whales. Their yield, much greater than from other forms of hunting, no doubt explains the greater density of the Tarramiut population (J.G. Taylor 1975). Jens Haven is apparently the only early written source that gives some details about bowhead whale hunting by the Inuit on the south shore of Hudson Strait. According to him (in J.G. Taylor 1975), Aiviktok in Wakeham Bay territory was the most important place in all Labrador for hunting whales. Whaling was also done at Tuvak but to a lesser degree. Payne (1887:75) wrote that at Wakeham the Eskimos, when living there in larger numbers, did "not hesitate to surround one of these huge monsters in their kayaks" and sometimes succeeded in killing one with the aid of their harpoons and floats. Modern inhabitants of the region preserve this tradition (Arima 1963; Saladin d'Anglure 1967), and it is confirmed by the numerous whalebones scattered along the coast and the isles, by the many place-names based on *arviq* 'bowhead whale' and by the existence of marine traps for bowhead whales like that adjoining Ukiivik Island, which is a small bay almost closed at low tide, of which the entrance was blocked so that whales trapped inside could be safely harpooned (Saladin d'Anglure 1956–1971). Old Tarramiut still know some tales of hunting whales or whale calves. They confirm that whales were hunted from kayaks not umiaks (see also Arima 1963) and that calves and sleeping whales were easier to approach. The first harpooner threw his *igimaq* (articulated harpoon) with attached floats and *niutaq* (tambourine-shaped skin drag);

then the others joined in to chase the animal until it died under repeated blows from the *anguvigaq* (articulated lances) (Arima 1963; Saladin d'Anglure 1967a; Graburn 1969).

Walruses were hunted throughout the year. Ordinarily only a simple form of cooperation was required: three or four hunters could take a walrus that was surprised on floating ice in the spring or in open water in the summer, or when it surfaced to breathe by breaking through new ice in winter. But large collective hunts were organized when herds of walrus rested on the rocky beaches of the small islands during their seasonal migrations. In the Wakeham Bay region, well-known for its abundant walruses, toward mid-October large herds returning from the western entrance of Hudson Strait stopped on Ugliik, Uglialuk, and Uglijuaq islands. Hunters went ashore without allowing themselves to be seen, trying to surprise the resting walrus, and attempting to harpoon one before it could regain deep water. Walruses could also be surrounded in kayaks and forced toward the shore to be harpooned in shallow water. This was dangerous because an animal wounded in the water can turn against his assailant in a kayak and smash the frail boat. Herds of walrus coming from the Atlantic in the spring stopped on the Button Islands; in the autumn they returned. They stopped on Akpatok Island, which they left in July to go northwest to Nottingham Island whence they returned during the autumn. They were found in the islands and archipelagos in eastern Hudson Bay, especially the Sleeper and Belcher Islands. But despite the migrations, many walrus wintered over in these different places (Freeman 1964; Saladin d'Anglure 1967; Graburn 1969; Vézinet 1982). Walrus hunters had available a quality and quantity of products much superior to those of seal or caribou hunters—valuable ivory, large quantities of meat and fat—which gave them better dog teams, greater mobility, and relatively comfortable living conditions.

The third large marine mammal hunted collectively was the beluga whale, herds of which appeared at the ice edge after spring ended (fig. 13). Sometimes they were captured in great numbers in openings in the ice in this season and in the autumn during freeze-up. Like the walrus, the beluga followed seasonal migratory routes from the Atlantic into Hudson Bay, although some individuals wintered over in the bay as well as at many places along the route. But, in contrast to the walrus, the beluga stayed in shallow water, preferring river estuaries, small bays, and the proximity of the shore. The Inuit made use of these habits, trapping entire herds inside bays that turned into lakes at low tide, where remarkable hunts then took place. In addition, hunters in kayaks forced bowhead whales into coastal shallows where they were more easily harpooned, killed, and butchered at low tide.

Beluga were abundant along all the Arctic Quebec   *489*

coasts, from Ungava Bay to James Bay. This animal, like the walrus, furnished important supplies of meat and fat and provided the precious *maktaq* (edible skin) and sinews for sewing (Low 1906; Balikci 1963; Saladin d'Anglure 1967).

• DISTRIBUTION OF PRODUCTS   The distribution of the products of hunting, fishing, and collecting does not seem to have involved rules so elaborate as those among Central Eskimo groups, particularly for the ringed seal (Damas 1972a). A few rules and practices have been described by elderly Inuit, particularly among the Tarramiut (Saladin d'Anglure 1956-1971, 1967; Vézinet 1979).

Three levels in allocation practices can be distinguished: taking account, for the first level, of the degree of participation in production; for the second, of the needs of domestic groups and the ties that united them; and for the third, more ritualized, of the "first-fruits" nature of the product. The sharing-out determined by participation in production was especially effectuated when there had been cooperation; then one of the hunters, the "acquirer" of the game, customarily had particular privileges. The acquirer was recognized as the man who organized the cooperation, or who owned the collectively used means of production (umiak, fish weir, game blind), or who discovered the game (polar bear or stranded marine mammal), or who was the first to harpoon the animal or who killed it. The acquirer's privileges ordinarily were to control the distribution, along with having the first choice and often also a special part, primarily rare utilitarian parts such as ivory, baleen, or hide (Saladin d'Anglure 1967; Graburn 1969).

Once this part was subtracted the rest of the game was divided among the hunters present, following the order or degree of their participation in the capture. If the game had been killed immediately adjacent to a camp, all the domestic units there were considered participants, and each delegated one of their members to make the division. During collective caribou hunts the division of meat and sinew was quantitatively equal but that of skins qualitatively favored the ones first served.

The second level of division could apply to shares obtained from the first division, or to the products of individual or domestic production. Much less formal, it took account of relations of solidarity that existed between the owner of a part or all of a game animal and his relatives, neighbors, and friends. Circumstances played an important role in this division, which operated maximally in times of scarcity, but was not necessary in periods of abundance, and disappeared during times of famine when domestic units were more concerned with survival than with sharing (Payne 1889; Saladin d'Anglure 1967; Graburn 1969).

The third level applied to first fruits. All coresidents shared the first game of the season that was large or numerous enough to be collectively divided. But the true first fruits were the first game of each species killed by an adolescent boy or girl. In such a case the killer

Public Arch. of Canada, Ottawa: left, PA 129887; right, C8160.

Fig. 13. Harpoons used for hunting sea mammals. left, Adami of Port Harrison examines his harpoon and line while sitting on a snow platform inside the snowhouse. He wears a parka of canvas, serge pants, and sealskin boots. Photograph by Richard Harrington, winter 1947–1948. right, Man with harpoon next to 2 freshly killed belugas, with line and inflated float still attached. Photograph by George Simpson McTavish, at Little Whale River, Que., 1865.

had to divide the meat, skin, and other products of the animal among all the old people of the camp beginning with his or her midwife who received the part and the symbolic status of the acquirer. She presided over the division and praised her *angusiaq* 'the man she had made'. If it was a bird, it was torn apart, each participant trying to pull off the largest piece (Saladin d'Anglure 1967; Graburn 1969).

These various forms of division could be deferred—as could consumption—when an important part of production was stored. A product that was not divided at the moment of its production because it was abundant could become rare and then be divided when its owner brought it back to the camp from a cache. Similarly, the absence of a relative or the midwife might require that person's share to be saved.

For primary materials such as ivory, baleen, and skins, transactions sometimes involved exchanges or loans, when someone making a tool, garment, tent, or means of transport needed additional material.

• CONSUMPTION The indispensable materials were skins (for housing and bedding, boats and sled equipment, clothing, cooking and food preservation) and meat and fat (for human and dog food, heating, lighting, and cooking)—all derived from wild game, of which from 3 to 15 species were available, depending both on what habitat was chosen and what mobility the means of transport afforded (Saladin d'Anglure 1967a). A well-off Tarramiut family of three adults and two children, possessing a tent, a kayak, a dog team, and an umiak annually used about 15 bearded seal skins, 25 ringed seal skins, and 40 caribou skins (the last only for clothing and bedding). In other regions or for poorer families the bearded seal or caribou skins could be replaced by ringed seal skins in the ratio of two for one. These requirements had to be met by maintaining the necessary mobility that alone guaranteed the family relative autonomy in permanent and repeated efforts to maintain its equipment and preserve the unity of the domestic group.

The food required was subject to the same constraints. The dogs, indispensable for hunting and for winter movements, were in direct competition with humans for meat; an adult dog consumed about 400 kilograms of meat and fat per year (Saladin d'Anglure 1970a). A true symbiosis thus existed between dogs and humans, in relation to the game that they both ate, as is shown by the extreme measures to which they had recourse in times of shortage and famine. On such occasions both dogs and humans ate hides, famished humans fed on dogs, and, the ultimate recourse, humans ate each other. Famine cannibalism was not rare in Arctic Quebec when circumstances overrode human planning. Usually it was not due to the absence of supplies, which were scattered in all hunting locations, but to the loss of the mobility that allowed supplies to be

exploited (L.M. Turner 1888, 1894; Payne 1889; Lowe 1906; Saladin d'Anglure 1967; Graburn 1969; Vézinet 1980, 1982).

These Inuit were essentially carnivorous. Plants, algae, roots, and berries played a minimal, although no doubt indispensable, part in their diet, and even so some of their vegetable consumption came from animals, since they ate the small intestines of most game and the stomach contents of caribou. They ate meat and fat at each meal. Regularly—every two or three weeks for the Inuit of the south coast of the Hudson Strait—they liked to feast on fish or seafood for several days. In summer the variety of resources was larger because numerous migratory species were present and the vegetation cover was available, but they know how to maintain dietary variety from game alone, eating almost all parts of each animal. They were particularly fond of liver, giblets, tripe, cartilage, and brain (Saladin d'Anglure 1967, 1970; Malgrange-Saladin and Saladin d'Anglure 1973).

Food preparation, rudimentary as it may seem, was nevertheless subtle and required detailed knowledge in order to prepare meat properly depending on the part of the animal, the age and sex of the game and the circumstances of its killing, the season, whether consumption was to be immediate or deferred, the preservation technique, and incidentally, the tastes of the consumer. The meat of any game species could be aged (slightly, fully, or to the point of decomposition), slightly or fully boiled, uncooked, frozen, dried, or smoked. Drying served in the summer for filleted Arctic char; loins and ribs of ringed seals, belugas, and caribou; the entrails of ringed seals and braided small intestines of ringed and bearded seals; and pieces of skin and cut up flippers of belugas. Wet preservation, in skin or beluga stomach containers, served for beluga skin and fat, cuts of walrus meat and fat, and the oil of various sea mammals. In the autumn it sufficed to place sections of game or whole game animals under piles of stones, where later freezing preserved them through the winter.

Cooking was done on the coast in steatite pots over an oil lamp flame, or in the summer over a fire of driftwood or of fat mixed with old bones. The interior people cooked in the winter in an ice entryway over a brushwood fire and during summer movements could cook caribou meat superficially on a flat stone covered with damp lichen. Drinks were broth, fresh blood, and water. A family ate together every day, more because of cooperation in the preparation or division of food than because of collective meals. In contrast, when a camp received game that was unusually large (bearded seal, walrus, beluga, bowhead whale) or was rare for the season or due to shortage, it was consumed collectively and festively. Women ate collectively the heart and the flesh of the dorsal vertebrae of bearded seals and the flesh of beluga caudal vertebrae, while the men ate the lumbar vertebrae of bearded seals. In summer, *491* commensality was sometimes organized on the scale of the whole band, when an entire seal might be boiled. Hospitality was the general rule and a visitor was always called to share the meal of his hosts (Saladin d'Anglure 1967, 1970, 1979; L.M. Turner 1894; Low 1906; Graburn 1969).

Division of Labor

Division of labor was organized on the domestic level according to sex, age, and parental status; on the band level, additional criteria were competence, knowledge, and the ability to direct and maintain the cohesion of the group.

Sexual division assigned to women the care of infants, their carrying, and their feeding. They also prepared, cut and sewed skins to make clothing, bedding, tents, and boat coverings (fig. 14). They did small-scale hunting and fishing near the camp and collected plants, berries, algae, seafood, and eggs. They maintained and used oil lamps, prepared and cooked food (fig. 15), provided combustibles and water, and assisted men on their departure for and return from the hunt and during family traveling. Men were responsible for hunting and transportation, conducting the umiak, using the kayak, caring for the dog team, and preparing dog harnesses and traces. They made the domestic utensils, including those of the women, as well as their own weapons and tools. They built the igloo, set up the tent, and prepared and repaired the gear required for hunting, fishing, and trapping.

© Three Lions, Inc., New York.

Fig. 14. Lucy of Povungnituk stretching a sealskin on a frame normally used as a drying rack over an oil lamp. Photograph by Richard Harrington, 1959.

492

Division of labor by age assigned young people subordinate roles aiding adults of the same sex. From the age of six or seven, a daughter helped her mother in her various tasks, and at about age eight a boy began to accompany his father and make his first catches. Until they married young men and young women obeyed the adults in order to learn their future tasks. Their midwife (or a substitute) regularly supervised their progress, encouraging or criticizing them. She also praised their performances, and was rewarded on each occasion, at first by the family and then by the child or adolescent.

Technical specialization developed when a particular talent distinguished an individual's performances from others', but this could never be more than an occasional specialization, derived sometimes from a particular family experience that yielded a specialized knowledge of a region, of a type of game, or of a technique. In a band there was also the best bow, kayak, vessel, or knife maker, the best and most rapid sewer, the best hunter of caribou or walrus. But the subsistence economy, quite fragile in periods of shortage, required great versatility of everyone.

Ideally, a couple always hoped to have at least one son and one daughter to help them and tried in various ways, such as adoption and guardianship, to ameliorate the accidents of demography and the sex ratio. However, when a family lacked a son or a daughter, it could decide to train a daughter in masculine tasks or a son in feminine tasks, and this independently of the relations of homonymy, which often required dressing an infant according to the different sex of its namesake and initiating it into the tasks of the opposite sex. Formerly transvestites were often taken as spouses because of their double set of economic skills. Most productive activities required the collaboration of two people; a man needed the help of a younger man or a woman; a woman was aided by a younger woman or rarely a child.

At the band level, the division of tasks also followed lines of parental authority, but individual competence also played an important role, particularly for hunting and travel. The general rule was cooperation by each domestic unit in the manufacture of tents and kayak covers, balanced by reciprocity or in the case of the umiak cover, the right of collective use. The owner of an umiak had a certain recognized status of authority, especially if he was a good hunter and if he knew how to share his surplus production and play a generous host. He could only use this status sparingly if he wished to preserve the cooperation and participation of other families in the collective activities of the band.

Social Organization and Kinship

The traditional kinship system of the Inuit of Arctic Quebec was evidently quite similar to those of the Cen-

Fig. 15. Cooking. left, Woman in a snowhouse heating a kettle of water over a traditional seal-oil lamp supported by wooden sticks. Photograph by Bud Glunz, Jan. 1946. right, Deep frying bannock in seal oil over a primus stove in a snowhouse passageway, the walls protected from the heat with wood from packing cases. Photograph by Richard Harrington, Inoucdjouac, winter 1947–1948.

tral Eskimo, although it has not been studied on a comparable scale (Damas 1968a). However, regional monographs provide data on the kinship system of the east coast of Hudson Bay (Honigmann 1962; Willmott 1961; Guemple 1966) and of the south coast of Hudson Strait (Graburn 1964; Saladin d'Anglure 1967). The terminology reported is the same type as that reported for the Igloolik region (Damas 1963) in the terms for parents, uncles, aunts, nephews, and nieces but differs in the cousin terminology in that first cousins are distinguished but cross and parallel cousins are not differentiated. Separate terms are applied to uncle's wife (*arnaajuk*) and aunt's husband (*angutiarjuk*) and to spouse's nephews and nieces (*irniajuk* and *paniarjuk*).

The affinal terminology is also comparable, except that no term such as *nuliq* (used at Igloolik) designates the parents of one's child's spouse. There are some regional phonetic variants of the suffixes used in kinship terms, such as *-arjuk* 'little' among the Tarramiut, *-arruk* among the Itivimiut, and *-a'uk* in the Belcher Islands and at Poste-de-la-Baleine.

Kinship was readily recognized up to the sixth degree (*ilagalak* 'distant relative') in the four grandparental lines, but only kin of the first degree (*namminiq* 'near relatives') had important reciprocal rights and duties. Kinship was the usual channel of transmission for the personal name and the associated identity and provided the framework for solidarity in feuds.

Adoption was general, as among most Inuit groups.

It took various forms such as the temporary use of boarders as young helpers, the raising of orphans, or the adoption of children at birth. The terminology for adoptive relatives was the same as that for kin, with the addition (in reference) of the suffix *-taq* (*-saq* at Igloolik) (Guemple 1972b, 1979; Saladin d'Anglure 1967).

Marriage usually followed infant betrothals arranged by the families; often two families promised a brother and a sister in exchange for a sister and brother. In first marriages the authority of elders always overrode the wishes of the potential spouses; nevertheless, it was proper for the young woman to resist when the time came for her to leave her natal family (L.M. Turner 1894; Saladin d'Anglure 1967a). Marital residence was normally virilocal after a variable period of residence by the man with the family of his future in-laws. But when a couple had only daughters they could require a son-in-law and his family to live with them. Polygyny was general, practiced by good hunters able to support a large family. In some instances, such as that of a nineteenth-century Tarramiut, a man could have four simultaneous wives without being affluent (Saladin d'Anglure 1956–1971). Permanent or temporary spouse exchanges were very common, as were separations and remarriages; stepparents and stepchildren, and the children of remarried spouses, used the appropriate kin terms with the added suffix *-saq* (Saladin d'Anglure 1967).

493

Both consanguinal and affinal relationships were almost always concealed by the use of kinship terms of address and reference derived from the identity received with each personal name. This very complicated practice (Guemple 1965; Saladin d'Anglure 1970) was skillfully maintained by the elders who directed the choice of names and associated behavior, followed the interpretation of dreams, signs, and portents that they had no hesitancy in expressing. The transmission of names in order to replace deceased relatives or departed camp members with newborn children took place independently of sex and resulted in numerous transvestite practices in infancy and adolescence.

The midwife (*sanaji* 'she who makes') occupied an essential place in the kinship system, as the cultural mother responsible for the role and for settling the sex of the infant (it was believed that male babies could transform themselves into girls at birth, and sometimes the reverse) and for presiding over all the important rites of passage accompanying the first performances of the child, receiving important presents on such occasions. Terms derived from or resembling kinship terms accompanied the relations between the midwife and the children she delivered, and between children delivered by the same midwife; thus *uitsiaq* 'husband-in-law' and *nuliatsiaq* 'wife-in-law' were used reciprocally by a boy and girl with the same midwife (Saladin d'Anglure 1967, 1970a; Guemple 1969).

Adoption, infant betrothal, name transmission, spouse exchange, relations of economic sharing and exchange, and relations of co-production, commensality, and co-residence influenced one another. In fact these were the recognized social methods for ensuring the persistence of economic life and the reproduction of social groups.

The local bands of 20 to 30 people moved in summer to their series of seasonal hunting camps. Sometimes close relatives within a band decided to separate during the summer in order to maximize their catch and diversify the yield from the co-residents of the small hunting camps (Saladin d'Anglure 1967a; for the Ingloolik region, Damas 1963). Several bands might join together in winter to exploit a site where game, rarer during this season, was always accessible, or in order to participate in much-liked collective activities such as ballgames on the ice, boxing matches, archery contests, games involving gymnastics and physical strength (fig. 16), song and dance duels, and shamanistic performances. For such occasions large ceremonial igloos were built; these were still used on the south shore of Hudson Strait in the early twentieth century.

Authority structures were flexible and rarely involved coercion. Authority followed major recognized social principles such as seniority, which gave ancestral generations power over their descendants, elder over younger siblings, and husbands over wives. But important decisions involving movement, the hunt, and the choice between camps were collectively discussed and the advice of the best hunter was often followed.

An *angajuqqaq* was a leader who was a great hunter and also had a kinship status that gave him control over several brothers and brothers-in-law, sons or sons-in-law, and had shamanistic powers or the support of a shaman among his close relatives. He owned an umiak and had several wives. He had to reaffirm his competence continually with his performance and to reinforce the cohesion of his group by the sharing of his takes. The abuse of power resulted in ostracism or collective execution. The executioner then had to take in the wives and children of the victim (L.M. Turner 1894; Payne 1889; Saladin d'Anglure 1967). Leaders liked to confront each other, to establish a relationship known as *illuriik*, in which they were dueling adversaries and exchange partners. Women could also compete with each other in duels of throat-singing, and some were so sought after that men did not hesitate to kill in order to appropriate them. (Nungak and Arima 1969; Saladin d'Anglure 1978b). Murders and feuds involved confrontations that occasionally took on the appearance of pitched battles; they also led to population displacements with effects that are still felt.

Cosmogony, the Supernatural, and Transformations

A general sketch of mythology can be constructed from the scattered fragments recorded by Turner, Low, and Hawkes after missionary activities had already shattered the system, adding some remarkably well preserved versions orally transmitted among the Tarramiut

Bernard Saladin d'Anglure, Quebec.

Fig. 16. Nuqaqtatuq demonstrating exercises on a suspended bar, a traditional game of strength. Anyone who succeeded in doing 80 of these pullups was considered very strong; some managed to do only 3, others 10. The equipment, made of a snow beater and a seal thong, was fastened above the ice pane by running the strap through the snow wall and pinning it with a transverse piece of wood. Drawing by Davidialuk Alasuaq at Povungnituk, 1968.

494

or illustrated in the contemporary art of the Inuit of Povungnituk.

In primordial times a flood covered the earth; then the waters receded (Hawkes 1916). The first man was created from nothing and after a long voyage found a companion; from this couple the Inuit descended (L.M. Turner 1894). A few species of animals must have already existed because, as in the mythologies of neighboring regions, there is no story of their creation. These were the polar bear, the fox, the weasel, and the lemming, all endowed with important powers and playing a major role in shamanism. Others were created by the transformation of humans into gulls (some women walking along the shore were lost when their husbands went ahead by kayak; in order to rejoin them they metamorphosed themselves), and into crows, hawks, hares, wolves, etc. (L.M. Turner 1894; Nungak and Arima 1969; Saladin d'Anglure 1978). In these ancient times animals and humans were very similar, speaking the same language, and having the same customs except for a few distinctive details: the polar bears loved fat, and the wolves were fond of caribou tongue. They could all easily metamorphose, taking off their animal skins or putting them back on again. Marriages were not rare between them, although they were very unstable as in the case of the Eskimo who successively lost his fox wife, and then his goose wife (in the Wakeham region), or the eagle and the bowhead whale who lost their Inuit fiancées. In this period of instability, humans who did not succeed in procreating sometimes adopted animals, such as the woman who adopted a caterpillar and fed it with her own blood (Nungak and Arima 1969; Saladin d'Anglure 1978).

As among other Inuit, the sky was conceived of as a rigid dome resting on a flat earth with abrupt edges like those of the sea (L.M. Turner 1894). Two sisters transformed into celestial spirits poured rain out of their pails and caused the lightning and thunder (Hawkes 1916;

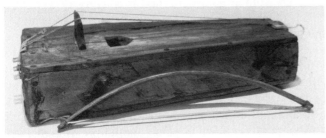

Natl. Mus. of Canada, Ottawa: IV-B-648.

Fig. 17. Fiddle. Trapezoidal wooden box with wooden bridge, bone pegs, and 3 twisted sinew strings, and a bow with a willow root string rather than the more common whalebone strip. It is held across the lap when played. The fiddle was not a native instrument but its exact derivation is unclear; Arima and Einarsson (1976) suggest the model was a Norse stringed instrument used by Orkneymen in the Hudson's Bay Company in the late 17th or early 18th centuries. Length 40.7 cm; collected by A. Balikci, at Povungnituk, Que., 1958.

Saladin d'Anglure 1956–1971). Winds were also personified: north winds were controlled by a giant male spirit resembling the *silaap inua* of neighboring groups; south winds were under the influence of a female spirit (L.M. Turner 1894), as was also the case with Baffinland Eskimo and Iglulik. The stars, the sun, and the moon were former humans who had become celestial spirits. The brother and sister who had an incestuous relationship after throwing their unworthy mother into the sea, attached to a beluga, lived on the Ottawa Islands according to the tradition of groups on the east coast of Hudson Bay, and the mother and beluga are still occasionally seen; to them were attributed descendants still living at Inoucdjouac (Saladin d'Anglure 1978a, 1956–1971). Other spirits in forms intermediate between animals and humans included mermaids (*iqalu nappaa*) who lived in rich regions at the bottom of the sea and regurgitated wealth, and the flying heads with human heads and bird feet who taught throat-singing to the Inuit (fig. 18) (Nungak and Arima 1969; Saladin d'Anglure 1978a, 1978b).

Sizes were no more stable than were the boundaries between kinds of beings. Thus dwarfs and children could change scale when they confronted a larger adversary. *Kaujjajuk*, a small mistreated orphan, was giantized by the Moon-man so he could take vengeance on his oppressors; similarly, a baby became a giant in order to punish the murderers of his parents (L.M. Turner 1894; Nungak and Arima 1969; Saladin d'Anglure 1978a, 1980b). These scale differences accounted for the order of the world: there was a superhuman set including giants (*inukpaq*), spirits, masters of elements, and giant animals like the giant bear (*nanurluk*); and a subhuman counterpart with dwarfs (*inugagudliq*), small animal species, and children. Finally there were ordinary humans (*inuk* sg.). Beings of the same scale had equivalents in other scales, and all went well when each was confined to his own scale. But problems resulted when beings of different scales accidentally came into contact. Dwarfs took the Inuit for giants and foxes for polar bears. "One day an Inuit visiting his traps tried to grasp a fox caught in a trap, but found his catch contested by a dwarf who claimed it was a bear that he had seen first and followed to the spot . . . Overpowered by the dwarf's strength, the Inuit's life was saved only by the intervention of his dogs" (Nungak and Arima 1969; Saladin d'Anglure 1980b). Inversely, giants took the Inuit for dwarfs and polar bears for foxes (Saladin d'Anglure 1978a, 1980a, 1980b). Just as with dwarfs and infants whose power could vastly increase when seriously menaced by humans, that of humans could be increased by a trick when threatened by a giant or amplified by the stupidity of giants.

The reality of the mythical times from which humanity gradually emerged is still present, although invisible and inaccessible to ordinary people except for those,

495

Bernard Saladin d'Anglure, Quebec.

Fig. 18. While an Eskimo was sleeping outside on the tundra, he dreamed that a *tunnituarruk* stole his boots and that he had to continue his journey in the snow with bare feet. The *tunnituarruk* are flying heads without bodies. They have bird's feet, breasts on their cheeks, sexual organs on their chin, and female tattoos on their face. They fly using their hair as wings. These beings are well known mythological creatures in the Povungnituk region. Throat-singing is their ordinary language. Drawing by Davidialuk Alasuaq at Povungnituk, 1971.

especially shamans (*angakkuq*, sg.), who by trials have succeeded in breaking human limits. Isolation, frustration, or physical or moral trials gave certain humans the extraordinary power to see and to manipulate mythic reality. Myths were always invoked to explain what was extraordinary, strange, and tragic. The production of game and the reproduction of life, essential but precarious, continually involved the mythic space-time in which both the species hunted and the deceased ancestors had to be pleased. In circular space-time both the past and the future were ahead as well as behind, as were both captured and potential game animals, and, from an adult's point of view, both infants and ancestors. Nothing was stable or absolute in daily life; as in the myths everything was in process and transformation: distinctions between humans and animals, distinctions of scale, distinctions between dead and alive, and even the distinction between man and woman. Myths relate many transformations from one sex to the other, and the Inuit still think that many fetuses are transformed into females if labor is overlong, or that a female fetus sometimes changes into a male (Saladin d'Anglure 1970, 1977, 1978a, 1978b, 1980, 1980a, 1980b).

Prescriptions and Prohibitions

To maintain the cosmic order and assure the reproduction of life the Inuit imposed a complex system of prescriptions and prohibitions, especially in the two broad domains particularly related to this reproduction: in hunting and relations with game animals, and in procreation and relations with children. These two domains were very explicitly fused in the semantics of the Inuit of Arctic Quebec. This is illustrated on the linguistic level by the term *naukkati* which means 'penis' on the east coast of Hudson Bay and 'harpoon' on the south shore of Hudson Strait; and on the level of beliefs and

social rules by the symbolism of the kayak, the bow being called *usuujaq* 'resembling a penis' and ownership being required in order for a man to marry. It was said of a hunter who married before acquiring a kayak, 'he mistakes his wife for a kayak' (Saladin d'Anglure 1978a, 1978b, 1956–1971). Procreation resulted in many rules and prohibitions, especially for the future mother but also for the father. Movements, activity, and obligingness were recommended for a pregnant woman so that the fetus would have a quick and easy birth and would become a quick and efficient hunter, or if female would be a skilled seamstress and have many sons. Both parents should attend to the knots of their laces and belts so that the umbilical cord would not strangle the baby. When building an igloo the future father should shape the last block of snow for the dome in a special way so his wife would have an easy birth. In the domain of hunting and game, precise rules governed a man's activities and circumscribed a woman's. Love of the game, respect for its specific personality and tastes, care with weapons in order to kill it gently (as gently as a pleasant tickling), and systematic sharing with the old and the poor, all assured a good life for future sons, numerous offspring for daughters, and many catches for all the hunters of the family and the band. A hunter had always to wipe his hands on his clothing to please the game, while a woman had to wash herself carefully to avoid frightening it, especially during her menstrual periods or after giving birth. Woman's vaginal blood, nonproductive, was in basic opposition to the blood of slain game, the daily food of everyone. This symbolic division of functions and activities along sexual lines was extended to the universe. Thus the earth mother, which according to some gave birth to the first humans and some animals and which produces plants and fruits and feeds many animals, was feminine. When a daughter was wanted, the tent was erected far from shore and facing inland. The sea, domain of the hunter and the large marine mammals, was masculine, prohibited to tabooed women who even had to stay away from the beach during their periods. When a son was wanted, the tent was erected as close as possible to the tide line to cause him to choose a hunter's life (Saladin d'Anglure 1956–1971, 1980, 1980a, 1980b). Accomplishment as a hunter came with his first killing of large game. For the first seal he had to untie the midwife's belt and slide his hand into her trousers, touching her crotch; she fell down, imitating a killed game animal. A woman's accomplishment came with her first menstruation, which was announced so that everyone would know she had become an adult. She was redressed with a special parka and tattooed to please the Sun-woman, to have a fortunate afterlife, and to distinguish her from men when she was old and postmenopausal. She should previously have learned the secrets of tailoring, of cooking and preserving meat, of lighting and the care of the lamp—

of which the soot and tarry oil served to inscribe the social and cosmic order indelibly on her face and limbs.

All kinds of compromises, trickery, and subtleties were allowed with the child's social sex before these great transitions in life. The multiple identities connected with homonymy were played on, children were often cross-dressed up to the moment they became adults, and then too use was made of the double reality of myth and daily life. Dreams and their interpretation were widely used to escape from the everyday and to get messages from another level of reality, from spirits, and from the dead. But in case of difficulties, sickness, and problems with production or reproduction, the ultimate recourse was always the shaman. First were tried private rituals, divination, and appeals for help from eponyms or the tutelary animals whose names were borne and often a bit of whose bodies were carried as talismans (L.M. Turner 1894; Hawkes 1916; Saladin d'Anglure 1956–1971); inherited incantations were recited, or profane talents and gifts were called on, to stop bleeding, conduct minor surgery, or resolve difficult births. But only the shaman had the ability to operate on the invisible world, to conduct dialogues with forces, spirits, and the dead.

Shamanism

Shamanism was a complex of beliefs, experiences, and practices that was the keystone of an immense biophysical structure erected by the Inuit. Here recur all the elements of myths and their reality, of the system of prescription and prohibition, and of rituals with their dialectic and their symbolic efficacy. The future shaman usually drew his ability to see the invisible, in mythic space-time, from much moral or physical suffering. Thus *Alariaq*, one of the last Hudson Strait shamans, was forcibly separated from his mother after losing his father, and cried for a whole week before feeling himself enlightened with a secret vision. He also had to withdraw, hiding far inland or in a cave in order to enter into contact with the Earth Mother, the vital forces of extrahuman beings (*tuurngaq*, sg.). He then had to learn and practice both the metaphorical language of myths and shamans, and the art of demonstrating his power. This came to him gradually, as he acquired new spirit-helpers.

Shamanism was an especially masculine art and power. *Pilurtuut*, last shaman of the Wakeham and Ungava region, wanted to transmit his name to one of his descendants; so an expecting daughter-in-law asked him to give his name to her child when it was born. It was a daughter; the frustrated shaman cried "I just simply don't want to menstruate," and, it is said, the child grew up to adolescence and died, during the 1930s, without ever menstruating (Saladin d'Anglure 1970). Menstrual blood is in opposition to game, and also to

shamanistic power, the super-reproducer of the social and cosmic order. However, there were women who attained shamanism. *Qasinga* of Saglouc was one of them, and she succeeded in many cures and difficult births. She had a river as a spirit-helper, which flowed as a torrent from her mouth when she shamanized. Once she was called to the bedside of a great hunter who lost consciousness and died. The hunter's soul left for the afterworld, but on his way he encountered a river that inexorably barred his way; he had to turn around and came back to life. It was *Qasinga*, with her spirit-helper, who had brought him back.

Spirit-helpers could be of many kinds; *Itiikuluk* of Port Burwell had a fly as spirit-helper; *Alariaq*, a walrus; others had an Indian. The collaboration was often caused by some particular circumstance. Only great shamans had the power of going to upper or lower otherworlds, or of having themselves pierced by a harpoon, in full view, and emerging unharmed. But besides such spectacular performances, the worth of a shaman's power depended on his ability to cure and foresee, especially the movements of game. L.M. Turner (1894) mentions that a famous shaman of the east coast of Hudson Bay was invoked as far away as Ungava Bay because of his shamanic power; to do this a miniature effigy of him was carried. Some shamans, despite their powers, were not good hunters so that they were largely materially dependent on the group they joined. A great shaman was recognized by a large territory, and one of average power by a band. *Juugalaq* of Wakeham Bay, a great hunter and the leader of a band, was associated with his younger brother, the shaman *Auvvik* (Saladin d'Anglure 1967). Some shamans unhesitatingly abused their power, breaking up and rematching couples, causing conflicts and band fissions (L.M. Turner 1894). In fact, the limits of their powers were set by group recognition. In cases of abuse a shaman could be killed or ostracized.

Shamanism, in brief, functioned to synthesize the junction of the masculine and feminine domains, the natural and human worlds, and the present with the otherworld of the dead and the spirits.

Annual Cycle

The spring and autumn equinoxes marked the boundaries of the two great periods of activity in the Inuit annual cycle. One period included the seasons named with the root *uki-*: *ukiaksaq* 'pre-autumn', *ukiaq* 'autumn', *ukiuq* 'winter'. The other was named with the root *upi-*: *upirngasaq* 'spring', *upirngalaaq* 'beginning of summer', *upingaaq* 'summer' (among the Tarramiut; the Itivimiut used *aujaq* for 'summer').

The first period was dominated by winter darkness and the departure of migratory species to their winter ranges—interior lakes for anadromous fish, southern regions for caribou and many birds, Atlantic waters or near several Hudson Bay and Ungava Bay islands for walrus. At this time these species were the object of intensive hunting, often collective and dangerous.

The second period was marked by increasing light, culminating in the *udlutusiit* 'the long days' of the summer solstice. The migratory species returned and most mammals successively gave birth, followed by bird brooding and the descent of anadromous fish to the sea.

The cycle of the Inuit of Wakeham Bay is representative for the Tarramiut area (Saladin d'Anglure 1967). For them, bow hunting of caribou began in August in order to procure short-haired skins for richly decorated fancy garments and for meat and sinew. Large hunts to supply long-haired skins for making winter garments took place in September, when the herds gathered to swim across lakes and rivers migrating south. At this time important meat caches were made, and the women had to hurry to scrape, soften, cut, and sew the fresh skins to complete new garments before walrus hunting began, due to stringent prescriptions regulating contact between terrestrial and marine products. Between mid-October and mid-November, for several days herds of wolves were hunted on the islands where they interrupted their return migration from Hudson Bay. Ample provisions of meat, fat, and ivory were needed for winter. After this the groups returned to their winter camps. Here they sometimes harpooned some walrus that broke through the new ice to breathe, but especially they hunted the ringed seal in ice holes, crevices, or at the ice edge. In the middle of winter hunting diminished and many prohibitions restricted the use of animal products. People largely lived off stocks from meat caches. When these were plentiful and transport conditions were favorable, large collective festivities were organized in ceremonial igloos (Payne 1889; L.M. Turner 1894). Under contrary conditions famines were not rare; then people tried to collect sea food and algae under the shore ice (Payne 1887, 1889).

In March with the birth of ringed seals winter taboos ceased and a period of active seal hunting began. With dogs, the small birth shelters and breathing holes were sought out, or seals whose curiosity was aroused ambushed at the floe edge. This was also an auspicious time for movement between camps and between territories. Winter reserves had long been exhausted and the territory had to be searched for old caches or small game (Payne 1889).

Abundance often returned with the end of April when the caribou returned northward for the birthing in May. The long days allowed extended trips across the lake ice to hunt caribou or fish. In June began the period of the most intensive hunting and collecting: hunting seals sunning themselves on floes, walrus hunting, hunting the belugas that arrived in herds and sometimes even bowhead whales, hunting migratory birds, and egg collecting. The fresh bearded seal skins were used to re-

cover boats and to make skin tents to replace the old tents covering the snow shelters of which the roofs had collapsed in April (Payne 1889; Low 1906). The presence of the coastal floe allowed the establishment of camps for intensive gathering of roots, eggs, and mollusks. Then came the large-scale fishing of Arctic char that had gathered near lake outlets before descending to the sea.

The floe broke up at the beginning of July, and the camps fell back onto the shore for intensive beluga hunting in small bays. Then the umiaks were launched to begin a long trip to take the band to the head of a large bay where the strongest adults left on foot for the interior to hunt caribou, while the elderly, the women with small children, and the rest of the band fished at river mouths or hunted small game (Low 1901; Saladin d'Anglure 1967).

Only the best hunters, well equipped with means of transport (umiak and many dogs) and able to accumulate large supplies of meat and fat for their teams, could perform this cycle over its maximum area, that is, exploit concurrently the resources of the coast, islands, and interior. Others tried within their means to approach it and often undertook shorter routes or even stayed permanently on the coast.

In neighboring areas there were variants of this cycle. Thus the Inuit of the region between Cape Wolstenholme and Rivière Kovic did not have to go very far into the interior to hunt caribou, since they were abundant near the coast at some times (Graburn 1969; Saladin d'Anglure and Vézinet 1977; Vézinet 1980). Similarly in the region of Diana Bay and the mouth of Rivière Arnaud large herds of caribou formerly approached the coast (Vézinet 1980, 1982).

More northerly bands exploiting the lowlands and the basins of the Povungnituk, Kogaluc, Koktak, Innuksuac, Arnaud, and aux Feuilles rivers often spent four to six months in the interior and the rest of the time on the coast. Some families left by sled in the spring to spend the summer and autumn hunting and fishing in the interior; others left on foot in July, the men backpacking or using their kayaks. These bands usually returned only after freeze-up and the first snowfalls (Saladin d'Anglure 1956–1971).

The system was flexible (a concept of Inuit social organization developed by Willmott 1960). Thus some families could spend several years on the islands, then go to live in the interior or on the coast, and vice versa, either to have access to different resources or because of interfamily or interethnic conflicts. Moreover, as J.G. Taylor (1975) has shown, in the eighteenth century the Inuit of Aupaluk and no doubt also Baie aux Feuilles spent the winter inland when the autumn caribou hunt had been very successful. Probably in similar fashion the capture of a bowhead whale on the south shore of Hudson Strait would have affected the annual cycle of a band, either providing them with better means of transport or giving them greater subsistence security on the spot.

History

Contact to First Settlements, 1610–1750

From the late sixteenth century the coastal waters of Arctic Quebec were traversed by ships flying the British, Danish, or French flags, in search of a Northwest Passage to China. Martin Frobisher, John Davis, George Weymouth, Henry Hudson, Thomas Button, Robert Bylot, Jens Munk, Luke Foxe, and Thomas James were only the best-known navigators who passed along the coasts and sometimes came ashore. Hudson disembarked on Digges Island in 1610 where he met an Inuit group. This first attested contact of Europeans with Inuit in the region was very ambiguous; beginning with euphoria and an exchange of gifts, it ended with a murderous assault (Asher 1860; Graburn 1969). Munk also met some Inuit, on the south shore of Hudson Strait, illustrated by an engraving published in the account of his expedition (Munk 1897; Oswald 1979). But after a half-century of fruitless searching in this part of the Arctic, exploration shifted west and north. The attempts by Foxe and James in 1631 were the last searches for the Northwest Passage along the Quebec-Labrador coast.

The founding of the British Hudson's Bay Company in 1667 resulted in new maritime activities along these coasts, particularly commercial ones but also military until the Treaty of Utrecht in 1713 established exclusive rights for the Hudson's Bay Company, denying the claims of its French competitors. Bacqueville de la Potherie (1722) provides a well illustrated account of Pierre Le Moyne d'Iberville's 1697 campaign in Hudson Bay, describing especially a confrontation between British and French ships near the north shore of Hudson Strait and French-Inuit commercial transactions near Cape Wolstenholme, even claiming that a commercial treaty was then established since the Inuit agreed to smoke the peace calumet offered by the French.

Until the mid-eighteenth century, no attempt at settlement was made in the territory occupied by the Inuit of Arctic Quebec, although in Subarctic Indian territory permanent trading posts flourished (the availability of wood in the southern zones facilitated the founding of European establishments). But despite the absence of trading posts the Inuit must have obtained wood and metal through indirect trade from southern Labrador, James Bay, or Baffin Island. Moreover, many wrecks of commercial and naval vessels near the coasts certainly provided nearby Inuit camps with precious supplies of European imports, as seems to be attested by

the discovery, at the end of the nineteenth century, of very old, completely rusted cannons among the Inuit of Stupart Bay (Stupart 1887; Payne 1889).

Only in 1750 did the Hudson's Bay Company build its first post on the southern edge of Inuit territory, Fort Richmond in Lac Guillaume-Delisle on the east coast of Hudson Bay, to develop the fur trade with the Inuit and exploit the minerals believed to be present. This was a complete failure in terms of mining as well as furs (yielding only £ 100 during six years' operation, Cooke and Holland 1978), and in relations with the Inuit, which became tense when a storekeeper and two Inuits were killed (Hudson's Bay Company Archives, Winnipeg). In addition the Inuit were harassed by Albany and Moose River Indians (West Main Crees) avid for scalps and slaves (some 20 such raids between 1707 and 1794 are mentioned in the Hudson's Bay Company accounts, according to Francis 1979). Thus in 1756 the Hudson's Bay Company transferred the post to Little Whale River where for some years it had organized summer beluga hunts. Three years later this store had to be closed and withdrawn to a region with a more numerous and accessible clientele, which turned out to be Poste-de-la-Baleine in Montagnais-Naskapi Indian territory. The new post operated there intermittently until 1855 when it became permanent.

Culture Change, 1750–1903

The century and a half following 1750 was characterized by slow settlement on the margins of Inuit territory: missionary establishments on the Labrador coast, trading posts on the edge of James Bay or the head of Ungava Bay, whaling stations on the north shore of Hudson Strait, all resulting only in episodic contacts either because of the seasonality of Inuit visits or because the establishments were temporarily or permanently closed.

These contacts did cause population displacements with permanent effects—from Ungava Bay to the Labrador coast, from the south shore of Hudson Strait to Baffin Island, from the northern peninsula to more southern settlements, and from Ungava Bay to the east coast of Hudson Bay.

The publication in London of a volume by two Moravians (Kohlmeister and Kmoch 1814), recounting their 1811 travels to the Inuit of Ungava Bay and describing that region as very suitable for a permanent establishment, caused the Hudson's Bay Company, jealous of its monopoly, to send overland expeditions in 1819–1820, 1827, and 1830 from its James Bay posts to the mouth of the Rivière Koksoak. The absorption in 1821 of the rival North West Company of Montreal left it a clear field in the south and allowed much more energy to be devoted to exploiting its Arctic territories. Hence Fort-Chimo was built in 1830 on the Rivière Koksoak to extract marketable resources collected both by Naskapi Indians and by Inuit, and to thwart Moravian Mission expansionary impulses in the region.

Three other locations in Ungava Bay were soon endowed with commercial posts, seasonal (Tasiujaq in 1833 and *Ungunniavik* in 1838) or permanent (Port-Nouveau-Québec in 1838). But great difficulties in communication and provisioning caused these outposts to be closed in 1842. Since the post at Poste-de-la-Baleine had itself been closed in 1822, there no longer remained any active European establishment near Inuit territory. These were certainly very difficult times for the Inuit who for 10 years had to undertake long voyages to the Labrador coast (or, after 1860, to the whaling stations on the north shore of Hudson Strait) in order to obtain metal blades, needles, and containers, a few rare firearms with ammunition, beads, and tobacco in exchange for their furs. However, activities among the Inuit were attempted by the Fort-George post, where from 1837 on an Inuit from the west coast of Hudson Bay worked as an interpreter. In 1839 he was sent among the Inuit of Lac Guillaume-Delisle to urge them to trade at Fort-George. Beginning then more or less regular commercial relations were undertaken with this group, who learned to mix peacefully with the Indians.

The situation in Arctic Quebec began to improve in 1851 with the reopening of Little Whale River, Poste-de-la-Baleine in 1852, then Fort-Chimo in 1866. The introduction of steamships overcame many of the navigational difficulties of sailing ships. Just when the Hudson's Bay Company finally consolidated its presence at both extremes of the peninsula, it had to abandon its rights there in 1867 in favor of the new Canadian confederation, which took over coastal exploration, geological and mineral surveying, and the control of access.

The increasing number of American whaling ships in Hudson Bay, as well as U.S. and Scandinavian claims to Arctic islands together with their development of scientific research in the Arctic, caused concern in Great Britain and its new Dominion. Canada decided to send its own maritime expeditions into the Arctic with scientific and administrative personnel, police (beginning in 1903), and photographic equipment, in order to investigate opportunities and resources and to assert Canadian sovereignty. Soon after the return of expeditions organized for the first International Polar Year, 1882–1883, the first Canadian expedition to Hudson Bay stationed teams of ice observers on the south shore of Hudson Strait to study the navigability of these important maritime channels. Four stations were built, at Killinek, *Aniuvajjuaq* (in the Wakeham area, also known as Stupart Bay), at *Saaqqajaaq* on the Digges Islands, and on Nottingham Island. During their two years of operation these stations were the sites of numerous exchanges with the Inuit and observations on the Tarramiut, whose customs were much more traditional than those of the southern Inuit, who were in more regular contact with the posts at Fort-Chimo and Little Whale River (Stupart 1887; Payne 1889; Gordon 1887).

From this period come the first series of photographs of Hudson Strait Inuit (Bell 1885), important for their quality and precision of details (especially those taken at Stupart Bay). In 1872–1873, G.S. McTavish had completed a set of photographs of Inuit gathered at the Little Whale River post (fig. 13) (Saladin d'Anglure 1982). R. Bell and A.P. Low of the Geological Survey of Canada continued the work of these pioneers, also providing detailed descriptions of their travels. After these important contacts with Euro-Canadians the Inuit of the south shore of Hudson Strait became regular customers of the Hudson's Bay Company stores, organizing annual expeditions to them. Constantly increasing desires for imported tea, tobacco, tools, cloth, firearms, metal, and lumber caused the emigration of many Tarramiut families toward the nearest trading posts. The southern regions, traditionally the least populous, became places for seasonal gatherings from distant camps to exchange hides, and for permanent settlement by some families employed by the stores.

The establishment in 1859 of an Anglican missionary at Little Whale River further accentuated these processes. The effects of the contacts and the attractions of Euro-Canadian products and ideas entailed profound changes in the lives and settlement patterns of the Inuit of Arctic Quebec. During the second half of the nineteenth century Inuit means of production were transformed, due to the general use of metal, the increased availability of wood (standing or imported), the development of means of transport (umiak, kayak, dog sled), and the increasing adoption of firearms. Conflicts seem to have increased, both because of competition over the trade with Whites, and because of the use of new, much more deadly weapons (Saladin d'Anglure 1978a).

Inuit-White relations during this period also saw some dramatic episodes such as the massacre of shipwrecked crews (Pitseolak and Eber 1975), especially that of the Hudson's Bay Company supply ship *Kitty* wrecked in Hudson Strait in 1859 (Cooke and Holland 1978). The perpetrators of this massacre, when met at *Aniuvajjuaq* in 1884 and 1885, were distinguished by a nasal tattoo, a sign of great exploits, and for this reason were prohibited from trading at Hudson's Bay Company posts. This detail is significant: in precisely this area the murderers' descendants in 1910 welcomed with open arms the competing company, Révillon Frères. Other massacres of shipwrecked men are reported by oral tradition in the region between Cape Smith and Cape Wolstenholme and in the Belcher Islands (Saladin d'Anglure 1978b).

The Inuit annual cycle of activities was quickly changed by the Euro-Canadian installations: long trips along the coasts to southern trading posts gradually replaced

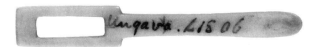

Smithsonian, Dept. of Anthr.: 90,317.

Fig. 19. Snuff paddle. Small ivory spoon used to bring snuff from bag to the nostril. Snuff was used by men and women; tobacco was also smoked and chewed. Length 6.7 cm; collected by Lucien Turner at Ungava Bay, Que., 1882–1884.

hunting and fishing trips among the islands, coast, and interior; moreover, the need to trap foxes to acquire imported goods involved a new exploitation of the interior, and the necessity of dog food for trapping and trading trips caused a recrudescence of walrus and beluga hunting (Balikci 1964, 1964b; Graburn 1969). There seems to have been some specialization by families, some going to the store, others to the interior for caribou hunting, still others to the islands for walrus hunting. Only the most capable hunters attained maximum mobility, as was also true under traditional conditions (Saladin d'Anglure 1967a).

One of the most striking effects of the early trading posts on the edge of the thin boreal forest was that the inhabitants of the southern and intermediate zones, traditionally less advantaged with regard to large game, suddenly found themselves favored by the proximity of commercial establishments and by the ease of access to standing timber because of the normalization of relations with the Indians. These Inuit tried to become commercial intermediaries for more northern Inuit or to offer various kinds of services to the Whites at the trading posts.

Beyond the small post settlements traditional social structures, habits of daily life, beliefs and rituals, the transmission of knowledge, and demography persisted for a long time, even though the first effects of the techno-economic changes were quickly felt and, with the arrival of Euro-Canadian settlers, new diseases appeared (especially infectuous ones) and sometimes were epidemic. The remarkable photographs taken by A.P. Low in 1897 and 1899 among the Wakeham and Fort-Chimo Inuit show the former with few exceptions still completely dressed in caribou skins, while the latter already used only cotton cloth (at least in summer). This distinction increased during the first half of the twentieth century; the Fort-Chimo Inuit said in the 1980s that those of Wakeham speak and live as their own grandparents did.

Commercial Competition and Missionization, 1903–1960s

Until the twentieth century the Inuit situation in Ungava (the name given the federal district created in 1895) corresponded in many ways to the description given by L.M. Turner (1887, 1894) after his stay at Fort-Chimo in 1882–1884. There he met Inuit families from different parts of the peninsula and learned more about those who lived permanently near the post. Some salmon and Arctic char fisheries and beluga hunting camps operated by Inuits were organized by the Hudson's Bay Company near Fort-Chimo and Poste-de-la-Baleine. For the Company these provided profits and also significant fresh food, and for the Inuit, appreciated employment. Moreover, several Inuit families in these regions soon established such close links with White traders as to result in mixed-blood descendants, the origin of a more acculturated class of Inuit whose influence is considerable.

There was a marked distinction between the Inuit living near the trading posts and those of northern camps who supplied nearly all the furs purchased by the Company; the latter had to make such long trips to deliver their skins that they often preferred to exchange them at low prices with intermediate groups. With the development of commercial competition this situation resulted in a bitter struggle between rival companies for the products of trapping.

In 1903 the French fur company Révillon Frères arrived in the north. It first opened two stores, one at Fort-George and the other at Fort-Chimo. With new products such as repeating rifles, canvas tents, and wooden dories, and sales techniques, the new company had some quick successes in these places. But as long as the traders had to wait in these villages for trappers to come from more game-filled regions, they had to bargain constantly for their clients' favors. It was necessary to go meet them on their own grounds; in 1905 Révillon Frères set up a new post at Baie aux Feuilles, on the route taken each year by trappers from Hudson Strait. The Hudson's Bay Company, seeing the risk of losing an important proportion of its customers, in 1906 opened a trading post at the same place (Brochu 1970).

In 1909 Révillon Frères opened a post at Port Harrison (now Inoucdjouac) on the other Inuit trading route. The same year with much secrecy the Hudson's Bay Company attempted a great coup by setting up a post at Cape Wolstenholme at the most distant point from its two earlier posts, in the hope of reversing the flow of furs by attracting northward and northwestward the trappers who customarily went south and southeast; but due to a failure in organization no one knew that the post had been opened and no one came there until the following year (Hudson's Bay Company Archives, Winnipeg). This allowed time for Révillon Frères to counter by opening their own post on the south shore of Hudson Strait, at Wakeham in 1910. This was a more strategic location, in the best marine mammal hunting territory with a dense population of Inuits. Four years later the Hudson's Bay Company also opened a post at Wakeham but never succeeded in seriously competing with Révillon Frères there.

World War I temporarily interrupted this pursuit of

customers and creation of new trading posts. Provisioning became more difficult, and local positions had be be consolidated.

In 1920 the Hudson's Bay Company opened a post at Inoucdjouac alongside its rival's; in 1921 the two companies built neighboring stores at Payne (Bellin) and Povungnituk. The same year Révillon Frères opened up beside the Hudson's Bay Company at Poste-de-la-Baleine, while the latter began a new post at Lac Guillaume-Delisle where Révillon Frères joined it in 1922. Again in 1922 Révillon Frères opened a post at Diana Bay near present Koartac; this was the last post formed. Fur prices reached record heights, the average price of a white fox skin being around $39 between 1924 and 1928. Several independent traders even tried to infiltrate the dense network of the two fur trade giants, at Saglouc in 1924, at Diana Bay in 1927, and at Lac Guillaume-Delisle in 1930 (after the two great companies left). The Hudson's Bay Company immediately reacted, installing a post in 1925 at Deception Bay a little east of Saglouc and the same year reopening its post at Port-Nouveau-Québec, which reinforced its position in Ungava Bay. In 1926 there was a shift in the history of the fur trade with the Inuit, when the Hudson's Bay Company gained majority control of the shares of the American affiliate of Révillon Frères. With this beginning of financial absorption there was a corresponding beginning, at least on paper, of administrative collaboration and then integration (Bernard 1977). In the territory itself it was much more difficult to change habits and attitudes since the competition had resulted in deep socioeconomic cleavages.

There were families in clientage with Révillon Frères or the Hudson's Bay Company, and some had been drawn into alliance with the post manager by subtle economic and kinship ties, changing location with him when he was reassigned. Poor trappers sometimes tried to get credit by shifting their allegiance, but they risked acquiring bad ratings in the confidential files kept by each post manager. With high prices good trappers gained considerable incomes during good years in the fox population cycle, and the importation of metal traps, improved rifles, tailored clothing, and even decked boats barely met their demands.

In a few years the traditional technology of the old hunting methods was supplanted by the imported technology of the trappers; the beautiful scenes illustrated in *Nanook of the North* (Flaherty 1922), filmed at Inoucdjouac, were relegated to memory. The skin umiaks and clothing shown were in their last years. Indeed wooden boats with sails and later motors completely replaced traditional collective vessels; caribou skin garments were more and more difficult to obtain as the animals became rarer due, apparently, to the general use of repeating rifles (Low 1906; Balikci 1964; Vézinet 1980; Trudel 1979).

The 1926 takeover evidently resulted in agreements on opening and closing trading posts and also on fixing prices. In practice the two companies closed their stores at Lac Guillaume-Delisle in 1927 and the Hudson's Bay Company opened a new store at Cape Smith; in 1929 Révillon Frères closed its post at Fort-Chimo while the Hudson's Bay Company shifted its Deception Bay store at Saglouc in order to counter S. Ford, its independent competitor who was very active along with his associate H. Hall who in 1927 opened a store at Diana Bay to compete with the Révillon Frères store. In 1927 ice observation stations were established at Nottingham Island, Wakeham, and Killinek equipped with the first airplanes in the region. Several families were employed by the ice observers and aviators, following them when stations were moved or emigrating to Coral Harbour on Southampton Island, as did the Inuit of Killinek and Wakeham, who took advantage of passing government ships.

The station remained at Nottingham, becoming a permanent metereological station, and the one at Wakeham was transferred for the same purpose to Cape-Hopes-Advance. These stations equipped for telegraph transmissions reinforced the Euro-Canadian presence in the Inuit region and provided employment and services for several families. With the telegraph era commercial competition also became sharper.

Despite agreements at the highest level, bitter competition in the villages persisted among the Hudson's Bay Company, Révillon Frères, and the independent traders. The economic situation changed profoundly with the crisis of the 1930s. The average price of a white fox fur fell to $17. Then in 1936 Révillon Frères was absorbed by the Hudson's Bay Company and the French departed. For many Inuit families this change was wrenching, and in the 1980s people still spoke of the distress that followed the departure.

Some Révillon managers among those most involved with the Inuit population reacted by creating their own Ungava Trading Company, taking with them many of the best trappers with their families and Peterhead boats. They spent the winter at Burgoyne Bay at the eastern tip of the Wakeham region, but the venture had no future and the company was dissolved within a year. Economic conditions continued to deteriorate, the average price for white fox skins falling to $12 and for ringed seal skins to $2. A new company, the Baffin Trading Company, appeared and tried to fill the gap left by the departure of Révillon Frères, opening posts at Inoucdjouac, Diana Bay, and Lac Guillaume-Delisle in 1939, and at Saglouc in 1941. The venture lasted 10 years. Meanwhile the Hudson's Bay Company reacted to the economic crisis, the war, and the disappearance of its principal competitor by closing several posts at Killinek, Baie aux Feuilles, Lac Guillaume-Delisle, and Wakeham.

After the opulent 1920s there was a return to an economy oriented mainly toward subsistence, but some technological changes were irreversible (the use of bows and arrows and umiaks was not revived) and traditional technology came out of the era much impoverished while the imported technology suffered from marked shortages. There were attempts to find substitutes: lacking tea, local plants were infused to make *tiirluk* 'tea substitute'; lacking cloth, flour sacks were used to make children's clothes. Without local stores interest in trapping was replaced by an emphasis on hunting. The period of false archaism lasted 20 years.

Although economic factors seem to have dominated Inuit life during the period described, because of the intensive development throughout their territory of commerce centered on the fur trade and the establishment of a very dense network of stores (one store per 100 inhabitants), another fundamental aspect of Inuit social life not only suffered from the Euro-Canadian invasion but also was the subject of direct attacks—traditional shamanism and the accompanying rituals and belief system. The crisis of the 1930s, as also the one of the 1980s, seems to have intensified religious manifestations responding to changes in Inuit society especially influenced by the Euro-Canadian model.

Beginning at the end of the eighteenth century Moravian missionaries were in contact with Ungava Inuit who came to trade furs at their coastal Labrador stores. However, it was not until 1860 that missionization began within Arctic Quebec itself, at first at Little Whale River among northern Inuit who went to trade there. From 1900 on, an Anglican missionary lived permanently at Fort-Chimo and another at Poste-de-la-Baleine. Among the Inuit settled near these two posts were trained the first Native catechists, who were sent into other regions with Bibles translated into Inuit and written in syllabics (a sort of stenography invented by a Wesleyan missionary).

Henceforth the authority of Inuit shamans was menaced by the missionaries, who openly attempted to deprive them of all their powers, defining these as expressions of Satan, just as they adopted old Inuit terms for spirit-helpers and the active forces of nature as translations for the evil forces and devil of the Christians. It was an unequal struggle, and despite some shamans' attempts to integrate Christian elements with their shamanism (such as *Piluqtuuti,* who took a biblical lion as his spirit-helper), one after another they submitted to White rule and were baptized. Thus *Arnaitualuk* gathered together his campmates in the Belcher Islands on the day he decided to dismiss forever his four spirit-helpers in order to turn Christian (Saladin d'Anglure 1956–1971).

The rules of Christian morality, especially those regarding marriage and monogamy, were rather strongly resisted as is testified by a song composed by Angu-

tinnguaraaluk about the first missionary at Fort-Chimo, whom he wanted to throw into the river (Saladin d'Anglure et al. 1973). But in the years after 1930 no shaman dared to proclaim himself as such in Arctic Quebec. Most Inuit were baptized, although most of them had received only minimal instruction from catechists who interpreted the Bible very loosely. These catechists, often chosen for their strong personalities, somewhat resembled new shamans with authority from the Whites.

During the 1910s and 1920s syncretistic religious movements arose in several camps and sometimes spread. About 1920 at Payne some Inuit began to announce the end of the world; they killed all their dogs in order to follow biblical prescriptions. Jesus being about to arrive, everyone gathered to pray while awaiting him. Unmistakable signs were apparent a little earlier in the neighboring Wakeham area: a down-covered newborn baby began to talk and then died. On the east coast of Hudson Bay another movement originated in a dream, and the catechist *Qirturaaluk* decided to go to Jerusalem by dogsled in the spring. In 1931 at Baie aux Feuilles the catechist *Mala*'s wife died and was resuscitated; the Bible was studied to interpret this, and it was decided that the apostles had taken Inuit form and, following the example of the people of Israel, everyone should wear distinctive symbols on their clothing, such as moons, suns, and Jacob's ladders (fig. 20). Flags were taken up to await the arrival of visitors who were welcomed with singing and clockwise processions around the tents then into the ceremonial tent and around the stove where everyone partook of the blood of Christ, in the form of tea. The Royal Canadian Mounted Police (RCMP), summoned from Port Burwell by the alarmed White traders, managed to stop the movement by threatening to imprison the instigators (Saladin d'Anglure 1956–1971; RCMP 1933).

In 1941 on the Belcher Islands in midwinter two hunters became convinced that God the Father and his son Jesus had taken their shapes; they were readily recognized as such by their campmates, except for a few unbelievers such as the catechist *Kikturiaq* who saw in them only the work of the Devil. At a turbulent meeting the same accusation was turned against *Kikturiaq,* who was struck with a harpoon, along with a young girl who supported him, and then beaten to death. A little later when "Jesus" left to hunt seals on the floe ice, women and children were encouraged to go naked over the ice to meet him, as the Bible foretells for the end of the world. Two women and three children froze to death. When the RCMP finally intervened nine dead were counted; those mainly responsible were jailed and then exiled to the mainland.

Some time later on *Milliit* Island, between Inoucdjouac and Povungnituk, a woman began to prophesy to the Inuit who flocked from all sides to listen. She had the gift of clairvoyance and revealed each person's *503*

Fig. 20. Participants in the syncretic religious movement at Baie aux Feuilles. Photograph by Lawrence J. Burpee, 1931.

hidden faults. She announted Jesus's return for a fine June day during ice breakup. She had a large ceremonial igloo built for praying and dancing, invited single people to marry, and rematched already constituted couples (Saladin d'Anglure 1956–1971, 1978a). Similar phenomena, called *mumiksimaniq* 'turning over' by the Inuit, occurred in nearly all the villages, especially between 1936 and 1950 but occasionally also in more remote times. These movements were almost always accompanied by food, clothing, or sexual taboos based on the Bible and on ancient Inuit traditions; they are only truly understandable in terms of shamanism and traditional beliefs about identity, reincarnation, and possession.

At the same time as some Inuit renounced polygamy under missionary pressures, others in districts farther from the missions turned to it with renewed emphasis, taking advantage of new regulations conferring responsibility on a Hudson's Bay Company outpost. Such was the case, for example, with *Uumajualuk* in the Belcher Islands and *Qalingu* on Mansel Island, who had three and four wives at the same time. Some antagonisms and jealousies were exacerbated during commercial competition. Sorcery accusations were common, and summary executions were not rare. In regions far from RCMP stations (Port Burwell from 1920 to 1934) or during periods when these police were absent from the territory (1938–1943) it was an attempt to provide justice, sometimes, according to the Inuit, with the encouragement of the local Whites (Saladin d'Anglure 1956–1971, 1978a).

The departure of a large number of the employees of closed trading posts had some unexpected results such as the appearance of "incubus" spirits (*uirsaq*, sg.) in their forms who came to possess the inconsolable Inuit mistresses they had abandoned. At Wakeham the Inuit catechist had to debaptize officially one of these "possessed" and give her a new Christian name in order to free her of her incubus, who 30 years later repossessed her and killed several of her successive husbands (Saladin d'Anglure 1956–1971).

In this socioeconomic and religious situation the Roman Catholic order of the Oblates of Mary Immaculate, which had successfully operated west of Hudson Bay, decided to deploy missionaries among the Inuit of Arctic Quebec, whom it considered to be abandoned and living as pagans. The first mission was created in 1936 at Wakeham, then another in 1938 at Ivujivik with two missionaries in each. In 1946 a Catholic mission was added at Poste-de-la-Baleine, where an Anglican mission had been since 1890. In 1947 missions were established at Saglouc, Diana Bay, and Lac Guillaume-Delisle; then in 1948 another mission, adjacent to the Anglican mission at Fort-Chimo. During 10 years several newly born and dying people were baptized, and only a few dozen Inuits were convinced to rejoin the Catholic faith, while a few people left the church.

The Anglican–Roman Catholic competition extended to the hospitals, whither for some years sick Inuits were evacuated by the annual visit of the hospital ship *C.D. Howe.* This persisted in the 1960s, even though the last new Catholic mission was situated at Povungnituk in 1955. The Anglicans tried to meet the situation by building missions at Saglouc in 1955, at Povungnituk in 1958, at Wakeham in 1963, and at Payne in 1965. But already under the new ecumenism sanctioned by Rome and due to the limited spiritual results achieved by its eight missions, the Oblate order decided to close them gradually except the one at Wakeham where there was the only small community of Catholic Inuits. Some Inuit Anglican missionaries were gradually trained and took charge of the new Anglican missions to respond to the needs of the local population and the lack of Euro-Canadian missionaries.

While the commercial companies contested for furs and the missionary institutions for souls, the federal and provincial governments mutually refused judicial and social responsibility over the Inuit of Arctic Quebec. The Ungava District was assigned to the Province of Quebec in 1912. When 10 years later the federal Eastern Arctic Patrol began annual inspection tours of police and health in the Eastern Arctic, they included the Inuit of Ungava, some of whom were on coastal islands turned over by the federal government. The only government unit in the north that took on any actual responsibilities for the Inuit was an RCMP detachment stationed after 1920 at Port Burwell. Social services and indigent aid during this time were left to the good will of the few Euro-Canadian residents (traders, missionaries, and meteorological station employees) or to passing ships whose crews too often exchanged gifts for women's sexual favors (Saladin d'Anglure 1956–1971).

The federal Department of Indian Affairs distributed aid—an individual average of $5.00—through police or trader intermediaries (Jenness 1964). An effort was made from 1930 on to provide aid at $10.00 per inhabitant, payable by the trading posts in clothing and food to needy families. Each year the federal government sent the bill to the Province of Quebec for reimbursement; but beginning in 1933 the province refused to pay, claiming that the Inuit should be assimilated with the Indians and thus removed from federal jurisdiction (Jenness 1964). In 1939 the Supreme Court of Canada ruled in favor of the province.

The combined effects of the Depression, the store closings, and World War II precipitated many Inuit families into a very critical situation; numerous cases of death from starvation were reported. Caribou had almost disappeared, making it difficult to prepare winter clothing, and marine game resources had suffered greatly from the systematic use of guns and resulting frequent losses of wounded animals.

The end of World War II and the inauguration of a national system of family allowances (in which the Inuit were included from 1948) signaled a marked increase in Inuit family income, although it was tempered by a renewed drop in fur prices in 1949 (Jenness 1964). Dur-

Natl. Film Board of Canada Phototheque, Ottawa: 95734.
Fig. 21. George River Eskimos cleaning char inside the freezing plant. Photograph by Rosemary Gilliat, Aug. 1960.

ing 1948–1951 the average annual individual income for the Arctic Quebec Inuit was about $90, including $30 from family allowances, $25 from trapping, $20 from government aid, and $15 from local employment. During this period the first federal schools and infirmaries were opened in what became the two principal regional administrative centers, Inoucdjouac and Fort-Chimo. These settlements quickly became over-populated, as the administrative and social services there attracted needy families and those whose supporters required hospitalization in the south, especially in the anti-tuberculosis program (Jenness 1964; Crowe 1974; Lachance 1979; Simard 1982). This was the beginning of a gradual abandonment of the seasonal camps and of a slow but irreversible sedentarization, which increased the need for schooling for the children. Efforts were made at Inoucdjouac to encourage good hunters and their families to return to living in game camps; the RCMP even organized the emigration of a dozen families from Inoucdjouac to the uninhabited game-rich islands of the Arctic archipelago. But these measures were rapidly counterbalanced by the increase in population caused by improved social and medical aid.

Elsewhere developments related to military defense during World War II and the Cold War that followed it, such as the construction of landing strips, military bases, and related services, attracted populations from nearby areas suffering from a scarcity of game and the drop in trapping revenues. Thus at Fort-Chimo the original village was supplanted by a new one that developed around the American army camp (before the troops withdrew in 1949), with immigrants from Baie aux

Feuilles, Port-Nouveau-Quebec, and Payne. At Poste-de-la-Baleine in 1955 a new military base attracted families from Lac Guillaume-Delisle, the Belcher Islands, and the east coast of Hudson Bay (Honigmann 1962; Balikci 1961). A measles epidemic in 1952 literally decimated the Inuit population of Ungava Bay, causing over 80 deaths.

During the twentieth century the Inuit population of Quebec grew rapidly, as is shown by the relatively accurate census figures available from 1931 on (table 2). The annual increase of about one percent between 1931 and 1951 was due to better medical care. The annual increase of about 2.6 percent in 1951–1969—implying a doubling of the population in less than 30 years—was a result of a decrease in infant mortality thanks to improved health services and nutrition, coupled with a reduction in general mortality because of air evacuation of serious medical cases to southern hospitals, and direct aid that suppressed famines. Infant feeding by formula shortened maternal lactation periods, decreasing the times between births.

State intervention was greatly extended in the decade following 1960. This year can be taken as marking the end of a way of life centered on hunting, fishing, and the fur trade, the end of snowhouses for permanent winter occupation, the end of summers spent in traditional hunting camps, and also the end of missionary predominance in schooling and health care.

Synonymy

There are no traditional names for the Inuit of Quebec in their own language or that of their Montagnais neighbors that distinguish them from other Eskimos. The general designations and attested regional group names are discussed at the beginning of this chapter, and the general names for the Eskimo are discussed in the synonymy in "Introduction," this volume.

Sources

The earliest and most important sources on the traditional life of the Inuit of Arctic Quebec are still largely unpublished, as has been demonstrated by research on the archives of the Moravians (J.G. Taylor 1974a, 1975), the Hudson's Bay Company (Francis 1979; Elton 1942; Trudel 1979), and the whalers (W.G. Ross 1975). Research on early iconography (engravings, drawings, photographs) relating to the Inuit also shows large gaps in knowledge (Saladin d'Anglure 1982). Between 1965 and 1971 B. Saladin d'Anglure and L.J. Dorais of Laval University undertook the systematic collection of syllabic texts, original Inuit drawings, and tape recordings, relating to the past of all of Arctic Quebec (Saladin d'Anglure 1976).

As for published sources, first must be mentioned the reports and journals of early navigators: Pricket in Asher (1860), Munk (1624), Bacqueville de la Potherie (1722), Chappell (1817), Lyon (1824), and the work of Kohlmeister and Kmoch (1814) that first described the east coast of Ungava Bay with precision and from an understanding of the Inuit language. Next there are the reports of Hudson's Bay Company post managers (E. Erlandson and N. Finlayson in Davies 1963); and the interesting 1849 description of the Fort-Chimo region

Table 2. Census Totals for Inuit of Quebec

Location	1931	1941	1951	1961	1969
Port Burwell	107	64[a]	21[a]	33	148
Port-Nouveau-Québec	86	108[a]	129	144	186
Fort-Chimo			287	297	523
Tasiujaq	288	257		82	59
Payne	116	357	306	107	178
Koartac	105			72	84
Wakeham	122	68	73	109	183
Saglouc	120	145	162	246	287
Ivujivik	79	148	103	95	114
Nottingham Island		24			
Qikirtajuaq	60	125	127		
Povungnituk	150	181	171	429	586
Inoucdjouac	225	402	473	378	448
Tasiujaq	60[a]	55	49		
Poste-de-la-Baleine	140[a]	160	141	387	508
Qikirtait	150[a]	150[a]	170[a]	180	207
Fort-George	40[a]	1	32	30	50
	1,848	2,221	2,244	2,689	3,561

[a] Estimates.

Inuit by J. McLean (1932). The occupants of the four permanent ice stations in the southern part of Hudson Strait left detailed observations (Stupart 1887; Payne 1887, 1889). Then came works by the geologists Bell (1885) and Low (1899, 1899a, 1901, 1903). Low (1906) includes a fine description of the life of Inuit bands around Cape Wolstenholme at the end of the nineteenth century.

The naturalist L.M. Turner (1887, 1894) conducted the first ethnographic research among the Inuit of the Fort-Chimo region. Hawkes (1916) issued a study that mainly concerns the Inuit of the Labrador coast, containing little data about Ungava. Peck (1925) translated Inuit texts and compiled an Inuit-English dictionary. Only after World War II was serious research undertaken among the Quebec Inuit. Schneider (1966) published an Eskimo-French dictionary of the speech of Ungava, unmatched elsewhere in the Canadian Arctic, a French-Eskimo dictionary (1970), a grammar (1967), and a dictionary of infixes (1968). An enlarged and corrected Inuit-English version of the first dictionary was compiled by Laval University (1985).

Beginning in 1949 several anthropologists and their graduate students conducted research in the area. There are studies of acculturation in the Belcher Islands (Desgoffe 1955), at Poste-de-la-Baleine (Honigmann 1951; Balikci 1961), and at Inoucdjouac (Willmott 1961). Research was carried out on technology and traditional economy: on the Belcher Islands kayak (Freeman 1964; Guemple 1967), at Ivujivik (Arima 1964), at Povungnituk (Balikci 1960b), on the Ivujivik umiak (Arima 1963), on the Povungnituk sled (Arima 1967), and on the material culture of the inland Inuit (Saladin d'Anglure 1969).

Several community studies deal with kinship and social organization and include information on traditional life: Willmott (1961) on Inoucdjouac; Graburn (1960, 1964) on Saglouc; Honigmann (1962) on Poste-de-la-Baleine; Balikci (1964) on Povungnituk; Saladin d'Anglure (1967) on Wakeham; Dorais (1983) on Koartac. Jean Malaurie and Jacques Rousseau (1964) edited a collective work that surveyed the human occupation of the Quebec-Labrador peninsula and contained articles on the Inuit area. Also separately cited are articles by W.E. Taylor, Neatby, J.K. Fraser, and Damas in a book edited by C.S. Beals (1968).

Probably the most interesting studies are those on knowledge, myths, art, and music (Nungak and Arima 1969, translated into French by Saladin d'Anglure; Graburn 1972; Saladin d'Anglure 1978a), many catalogues of Inuit engravings and sculpture illustrating historical, ethnographic, and mythological themes (Fédération des Coopératives du Nouveau Québec), the recording of throat-singing or gasping songs, mostly from Arctic Quebec (Groupe de recherche en sémiologie musicale, University of Montreal) by Nattiez et al. (1978), and the ethnomusicological work by Montpetit and Veillet (1977), on musical symbolism by Saladin d'Anglure (1978). There are works on games by Savoie (1970) and Beaudry (1978).

Anthropological efforts at renewing and synthesizing knowledge of Arctic Quebec Inuit culture and ethnohistory include an important study on prehistoric archeology at Ungava Bay (Vézinet 1982) and on the Inuit of the interior of the peninsula (Vézinet 1980). Original Inuit manuscripts have been published in syllabics by the Association Inuksiutiit (Saladin d'Anglure 1981 and Saladin d'Anglure and Vézinet 1977), as has the first historical novel written by an Inuit woman of Wakeham (Mitiarjuk 1983). The Centre d'Études Nordiques of Laval University has devoted particular efforts to research and scientific publication on Arctic Quebec; the Centre for Northern Studies and Research renewed McGill University's pioneering tradition of Inuit research (J. Fried 1955), and the Department of Indian Affairs and Northern Development, Ottawa, since 1950 has published numerous original works on the Inuit of Arctic Quebec. The research service of the Makkivik Corporation, Montreal, is compiling exhaustive inventories of land and local resource uses in the region. Inuit researchers increasingly investigate toponymy, genealogies, technology, and oral tradition, which will fill the deficit in knowledge on this region as compared to other Arctic areas. Since 1977 the journal *Études/Inuit/Studies* has assisted this development, as has the series *Inuksiutiit Allaniagait* of books in syllabics. The parallel efforts of the Kativik Educational Commission in syllabic publication and of the Service du Patrimoine Autochtone, Ministère des Affaires Culturelles, Quebec, complete these efforts. The former Commission Scolaire du Nouveau-Québec beginning in 1972 entrusted the Inuit with preparing educational manuals in syllabics, English, and French (Sivuak 1972, 1973; Alasuaq 1973).

The best bibliographic tool is certainly the *Inuit du Nouveau-Québec Bibliographie* published by the Ministère des Affaires Culturelles du Québec (Pageau 1975).

Historical Ethnography of the Labrador Coast

J. GARTH TAYLOR

The Inuit of the Labrador coast speak an Inuit-Inupiaq (Eastern Eskimo) dialect that has been referred to as "Labrador Inuttut" (L.R. Smith 1978:116).* They are cultural and racial descendants of the prehistoric Eskimo population who possessed what archeologists refer to as the eastern Thule culture. Archeological research suggests that the Thule/Inuit culture may have arrived in Labrador from eastern Baffin Island between A.D. 1300 and 1450 (Fitzhugh 1977a:38). At that time, northern Labrador may have been occupied by people of the older Dorset culture, which appears to have been rapidly displaced by the Thule Eskimos through replacement or absorption (Fitzhugh 1977a:32). By about 1500 the Thule people began to migrate southward from their initial settlements on the northern Labrador coast.

Territory and Environment

During the late eighteenth century, which is the earliest period for which there is detailed documentation on land use and occupancy, Inuit settlements were reported at widespread locations along the entire Atlantic coast, from the Button Islands down to Cape Charles (fig. 1) (J.G. Taylor 1977:50). Although the most permanent settlements have been usually located near the salt water, the Inuit of Labrador have also made seasonal use of the adjacent hinterland in their quest for caribou, fish, and, in more recent times, fur-bearing animals. The maximum limits of inland penetration appear to have occurred in the Nain-Okak region, where

caribou hunters sometimes crossed beyond the height of land to reach the wooded banks of the George River (J.G. Taylor 1969:163).

At various times during the historic period, Inuit from the coast of Labrador have traveled through the Strait of Belle Isle and along the north shore of the Gulf of Saint Lawrence. However, the precise nature and extent of Inuit occupation inside the Gulf of Saint Lawrence is still being debated (Martijn 1980b; J.G. Taylor 1980). It seems likely that ultimate clarification of this question, which is confused by the fact that the term "esquimaux" was formerly used for both Indians and Inuit in this area, will depend heavily on archeological research.

The most extreme proponent of the view that there was once a permanent and extensive occupation of Inuit within the Gulf of Saint Lawrence was Frank Speck (1931:568). He argued that the entire southeastern corner of the Labrador peninsula, including the heavily wooded interior of the Saguenay region, was occupied by Inuit during the seventeenth century. This claim has been effectively refuted (J.A. Burgesse 1949), and the so-called "Esquimaux of the Saguenay" have been identified as Micmac refugees who emigrated to the Saguenay region after 1646 (Mailhot, Simard, and Vincent 1980:61).

More conventional opinion has held that the Inuit once occupied the Gulf of Saint Lawrence as far west as Mingan (Hawkes 1916:4; Jenness 1965:10; Packard 1891:245). Much of the evidence for this claim has been questioned by Martijn (1980a:122), who suggests that Inuit may have reached the Mingan region during the period 1640–1690, but that these were probably temporary visitors who were on winter hunting excursions from a permanent base in the Bradore Bay–Saint Paul River area to the east. Even greater caution has been suggested by J.G. Taylor (1979:274), who feels that the old argument for a historic Inuit occupation in the Gulf of Saint Lawrence should be held in abeyance until new evidence can be produced.

Although the Inuit of Labrador have occupied more southerly latitudes than any other Eskimoan population, the cooling influence of the Labrador Current has given them a relatively harsh climate. On the northern coast, which is dominated by high mountain ranges and fringed by narrow coastal fjords, the landscape contains

---

*The phonemes of the form of Eskimo spoken in Labrador are: (voiceless stops) p, t, k, q; (voiced fricatives) v, y, γ, γ̇; (voiceless fricative) s; (nasals) m, n, ŋ; (laterals) l, ł; (short vowels) i, a, u; (long vowels) i·, a·, u·. The phonetic realization of certain phonemes and phoneme sequences varies dialectally, with some losses of contrast.

The current practical orthography, based on the more evolved subdialects, has the following letters corresponding to these phonemes: p, t, k, q and k; v, j, g, g; s; m, n, ng; l, ł; i, a, u; ii, aa, uu.

Information on Labrador Eskimo phonology and the transcriptions of words was obtained from Webster and Zibell (1976:278), Peacock (1974), F.W. Peacock (communication to editors 1973), Lawrence R. Smith (communication to editors 1974), Robert Underhill (communication to editors 1972), and Anthony C. Woodbury (communication to editors 1982). The editors are responsible for selecting from among these sources, and some inconsistencies may be the result.

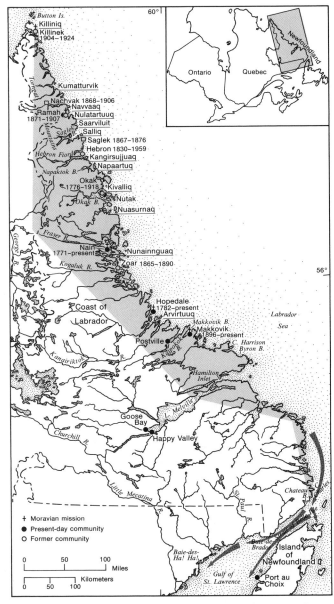

Fig. 1. Territory in the late 18th century. Arrows show excursions into the Strait of Belle Isle in earlier historic times. Eskimo place-names, written in the current practical orthography, are underlined.

most of the common forms of Arctic vegetation. There are no trees north of Napaktok Bay, where some of the more sheltered areas are dotted with small patches of black spruce and tamarack. Trees increase in size and quantity toward the south and, in the Nain-Okak region of the central coast, substantial stands of forest are found in the deep river valleys and on many of the numerous islands that shelter the wide bays in that section. Inland from the coast, the high, rolling plateau is still treeless in the Nain area; while in the south, from Hamilton Inlet to the Strait of Belle Isle, a dense cover of boreal forest reaches almost to the coast.

The Labrador Sea has provided the Inuit with an unusually rich selection of sea mammals, which in for-

mer times included the Greenland whale (*Balaena mysticetus*). Other species of sea mammal that have been important to the Inuit include the harp seal, ringed seal, bearded seal, harbor seal, walrus, and beluga. In winter most of the sea mammals migrated south or retreated to open water, beyond the outer edge (*sina*) of a stable band of fast ice that forms in the shelter of fjords and islands. The most important land animal in the Inuit economy was the migratory Barren Ground caribou.

External Relations

The Inuit who formerly lived on the northern coast of Labrador had trade relations and some kinship connections with the Inuit of northern Quebec. In addition, there have been occasional migrations both to and from Ungava Bay within the historic period. Travel between the Labrador coast and northern Quebec frequently entailed lengthy boat journeys, although sled routes through passes in the Torngat mountains were sometimes utilized in the winter months.

The Inuit of the central and southern coast have lived in relatively close proximity to their Algonquian neighbors, the Montagnais-Naskapi, who spent most of their time in the wooded Labrador interior. Traditional relations between Inuit and Indians in this area have usually been described as hostile, with open warfare a common feature in early historic times (Gosling 1910:165; Hawkes 1916:5). However, most arguments for warfare are based on misleading or false evidence (J.G. Taylor 1979a). Early relations may have been characterized more by avoidance than hostility, with limited trade and social interaction becoming more common after the advent of European settlement.

History

Contact until 1700

It is not yet known exactly when Labrador Inuit first made contact with Europeans. The fishermen and whalers who came in increasing numbers to exploit the rich waters around Newfoundland and southern Labrador after 1500 left little record of their encounters with native people. However, from the reports of explorers such as Jacques Cartier and Jean-François de La Rocque de Roberval, it would appear that Inuit were not present in southern Labrador during the early sixteenth century (Gosling 1910:161). The records of Basque whalers, who monopolized the Straits of Belle Isle from the early 1540s to the mid-1580s, have not yet yielded any positive proof of contact with Inuit, although they may possibly have been indicated in one reference to a skirmish between "savages" and codfishers or whalers in 1574 (Barkham 1980:54).

509

Evidence of European contact with the Labrador Inuit is contained in two handbills printed in Augsburg and Nuremberg in 1567 (fig. 2). In spite of some incredible details in the text and the European-looking hair and facial features in the drawing, the depiction of appearance is mostly correct.

Throughout the seventeenth century it appears that Inuit were frequenting both sides of the Strait of Belle Isle on a fairly regular basis. However, the scattered reports of this period do not specify whether these people resided permanently on the south coast, or whether they were "northerners" who simply came to obtain European wares and returned home again during the winter. Such reports do make it clear, however, that relations between the Inuit and European fishermen were generally hostile (Champlain 1922–1936, 5:168–169). Most of the skirmishes occurred in southern Labrador, where Inuit often stole boats and iron objects from the shore installations of European fishermen.

In spite of the violence that characterized most early White-Inuit encounters in southern Labrador, there are some accounts of peaceful trade contacts toward the end of the seventeenth century. For example, when the explorers Médard Chouart des Groseilliers and Pierre Esprit Radisson were sailing from New France to Hudson Bay in 1683 they purchased sealskins from some Inuit they encountered in the Nain-Okak region (Radisson 1896:8). Similarly Louis Jolliet, who explored the Labrador coast as far north as the Nain area, purchased seals and animal oil from several of the Inuit with whom he met. They seem to have been well supplied by this time with many articles of European manufacture, including wooden boats with sails and grapnels, barrels, sea chests, screws and nails, knives, cloth and various items of European clothing (Jolliet 1694:197, 201). Some of the European goods were of Spanish origin, but Jolliet did not know whether they had been obtained by trade or plunder. He was of the opinion that the Inuit did not yet have regular trade contacts, but that they only traded with fishing ships in Newfoundland when the opportunity arose (Jolliet 1694:193, 196).

French Colonial Period, 1700–1763

The early eighteenth century saw an expansion of French activity in southeastern Labrador, with rapid development of sedentary seal and cod fisheries (Trudel 1978:103). The seal fishery was conducted by Canadian grantees who were supplied by Quebec merchants and kept their posts open throughout the year; the cod fishery was pursued by ships that arrived from France each June and returned in September. Although hostilities remained common for several decades, both the sealers and cod fishermen engaged in sporadic trade with groups of Inuit who made summer excursions into the Strait of Belle Isle and to northern Newfoundland, where they

British Lib., Dept. of Printed Books, London.
Fig. 2. Eskimo woman and child kidnapped by French sailors in "Nova Terra" (probably Labrador) in 1566, in a handbill printed in Nuremberg to advertise their exhibition in Europe. This (and a near-duplicate printed in Augsburg) is the earliest European depiction of Eskimos done from life. The clothing and tattoo patterns appear to be accurate, except that the boots were misunderstood (Sturtevant 1980:47). Handcolored woodcut, printed in 1567.

ventured as far south as Port au Choix (Brouague 1719:67).

Evidence suggests that most of the Inuit who frequented the posts and fishing harbors of southern Labrador during this period were temporary visitors who returned each fall to their winter homes in the north. For example, Augustin le Gardeur de Courtemanche, a Canadian grantee who held the title Commander of Labrador, specified in his report on the "Eskimo coast" that the Inuit reside in Kesesakiou, which then referred to Hamilton Inlet (Courtemanche 1705:213). The same report suggests that some Inuit had wintered a few years earlier in Baie d'Haha, near Grand Mecatina, indicating that temporary winter residence may have occurred west of the Strait of Belle Isle from time to time. However, there are no further reports of Inuit wintering in the Strait of Belle Isle or on the Quebec North Shore until 1716, when François Martel de Brouague granted "permission" to a group of traveling Inuit to winter 15 leagues from his post at Baye de Phélypeaux (Brouague 1717:165).

The seasonal nature of Inuit presence in southern Labrador is also suggested in the records of Dutch whalers, who were trading with Inuit of Labrador during the early eighteenth century (Zorgdrager 1728:83). By 1733, when such contacts were an established tradition, whalers who wanted to take advantage of the Labrador trade were instructed to complete their Greenland voyage before crossing over to Labrador. Then, if the Inuit were available, the whalers could go ashore and trade with them. If the Inuit had not yet arrived, the captains were to wait for them "because experience has taught that the natives always return from the north to the south at a certain time" (Kupp and Hart 1976:13).

Trade relations became even more regular after 1743, when Louis Fornel explored Hamilton Inlet and left two men to establish a trading post at North West River. By this time the Inuit had developed a trade jargon for communicating with French fishermen. One of the most commonly heard phrases was "troquo balena," from French *troquons* 'let's trade' and *baleine* 'whale, baleen' (Fornel 1743:209). By mid-century it was believed that most of the baleen was brought from the north coast by Inuit middlemen, who sold it in Hamilton Inlet where they spent the winter (Jefferys 1768:147). Although rudimentary communication was now possible the French remained cautious; it was said that they always traded with a guard of several armed men, and as soon as trading was finished they sent the Inuit away.

British Colonial Period, 1763–1949

Relations between Europeans and Inuit were temporarily disrupted in 1763, when Labrador became a British possession and the French were no longer allowed on the coast. The British and Americans who attempted to take over the lucrative baleen trade had difficulties in the beginning, and open hostilities once again became commonplace (J.G. Taylor 1974a:7). In an effort to end this renewed conflict the governor of Newfoundland attempted, with the assistance of some Moravian missionaries from Greenland, to negotiate a "truce" with the Inuit in 1765 (J.G. Taylor 1972:135).

Although this early attempt to establish peaceful relations did not spell an immediate end to misunderstanding and bloodshed, it helped pave the way for the expansion of European settlement that soon followed. During the final decades of the eighteenth century several British trading companies opened fishing and furring posts in the area south of Hopedale. Such posts supplied Inuit visitors, whose regular homes lay to the north, with European food and trade goods in exchange for their baleen, blubber, and occasional labor. Some of the employees of these early British posts married Inuit women, giving rise to a permanent and ethnically

Institut für Völkerkunde, Göttingen, Federal Republic of Germany.

Fig. 3. Mikak and her son Tutauk, who were taken to England after being captured in a skirmish with a British naval vessel near Cape Charles in southern Labrador in 1767. Tutauk has frequently been mistaken for Karpik, a much older boy who was taken to England at the same time and who died there of smallpox. Mikak and her son were returned to Labrador and were living in the Nain area when the Moravians established their first mission in 1771. The woman has tattoo lines on her chin, cheeks, and brow, wears long beaded hair ornaments, and holds a medal she received in England. Oil painting by John Russell, 1768-1769.

distinct population referred to as Settlers. The Settlers, who identified more strongly with their European than Inuit ancestors, increased rapidly and expanded steadily northward during the nineteenth century.

The first Europeans to settle north of Hamilton Inlet were missionaries of the Unitas Fratrum or United Brethren, commonly known as Moravians. After an unsuccessful attempt to found a mission in 1752 near present-day Makkovik the Moravians returned to Labrador and opened stations at Nain in 1771, Okak in 1776, and Hopedale in 1782. The mission continued to expand its operations throughout the nineteenth century, with new settlements at Hebron in 1830, Zoar in 1865, Ramah in 1871, and Makkovik in 1895. In 1904 the Moravians opened a station at Killinek, near Cape Chidley.

Although the main concern of the early Moravians was the spreading of Christianity, they were involved in many aspects of Inuit life other than religion. To the Inuit, who had come to depend on a wide variety of European goods, an extremely important feature of the

511

Lord John Ulick Knatchbull Brabourne, Ashford, England.

Fig. 4. Attuiock (left) and Caubvick (right), who were taken to London in 1772 by Capt. George Cartwright. The Inuit used cloth and beads supplied by Cartwright to make these garments, which are trimmed with fur and cut in a traditional manner. Attuiock holds a lance of the type used to kill large sea mammals. Pastel drawings by Nathaniel Dance, 1773.

mission station was the Moravian-operated trading store. By maintaining regular trade with the Inuit, the Moravians hoped to make their mission as self-sufficient as possible while at the same time reducing one of the prime motives for Inuit journeys to European traders in southern Labrador.

The relative isolation of the Moravian mission stations and their growing Inuit congregations ended in the 1860s, when Newfoundland cod fishermen started frequenting the northern coast of Labrador in greater numbers than ever before. One writer, who visited Labrador twice in the late nineteenth century, estimated that approximately 30,000 fishermen in 1,000 to 1,200 vessels arrived on the Labrador coast between late June and early October (Packard 1891:240). These "floater" fishermen frequently traded with the Inuit at their summer fishing camps away from the mission, and in this manner the Inuit acquired novel trade goods, alcoholic beverages, and increased quantities of European food. The fishermen also introduced new diseases, which, combined with dietary change, contributed to a decline in the Inuit population.

The last vestiges of Moravian trade monopoly ended in 1926 when, after several years of financial difficulty, the mission transferred all its trading operations to the

Hudson's Bay Company. Although the Company had been operating on the coast of Labrador since the mid-nineteenth century, most of its earlier trade had been with Settlers and Indians. Direct competition with the Moravians had increased when the Company opened northern posts at Saglek (Lamson Fort) and Nachvak in 1867 and 1868. However, it was not until the Moravians gave up their trade operations in 1926 that the Company achieved significant control over the Inuit economy (Kleivan 1966:129).

Shortly after the Hudson's Bay Company had begun to exploit its new trade monopoly, the Newfoundland government also started to take over functions that had been formerly handled by the Moravians. In 1934 the Commission of Government for Newfoundland established a rural police force, which posted "Rangers" in several Labrador communities. The main function of the Rangers, who found very little crime to contend with, became the "scribbling task" of issuing government relief through the Depression (Jenness 1965:63).

The government did not take a more active role in directing the economic affairs of the Inuit until July 1942, when the Hudson's Bay Company, plagued by rising expenses and trade deficits, closed all its establishments in northern Labrador. These were taken over by the Newfoundland Department of Natural Resources, which put all responsibility for trade in the hands of its newly organized North Labrador Trading Operations. At the same time the Newfoundland government railroad started to operate a regular supply vessel on the Labrador coast in order to carry on the work formerly performed by Hudson's Bay ships.

In spite of increased government involvement in some aspects of Inuit life, the Moravian mission was still dominant in the fields of education and health care when Newfoundland-Labrador joined Canada in 1949. The Moravians had operated schools since the eighteenth century, and most of the Inuit of Labrador could read and write in their own language, using an orthography based on Roman letters, which was developed by the early missionaries. During the early twentieth century the mission opened boarding schools at Makkovik and Nain. At Makkovik, where Settlers outnumbered Inuit, instruction was given in English whereas at Nain the Inuit children continued to be taught in Inupiaq (Jenness 1965:64).

The Moravians also continued to provide the Inuit with medical assistance, as they had already been doing since the mission began. The first hospital in northern Labrador, founded at Okak in 1903, was built and operated by a Moravian medical missionary, Dr. S.K. Hutton. After this hospital was closed in 1908, when Hutton returned to England because of ill health, Inuit health care reverted largely to missionaries whose efforts were hampered by their limited medical training. They were assisted in this task by occasional visits from

512

the Grenfell Mission of the International Grenfell Association, which had in 1905 opened a large hospital at Saint Anthony in northern Newfoundland, and by government doctors who traveled on the summer mail boat (Jenness 1965:48).

Population

The distribution of Inuit population in the winter of 1772–1773 has been reconstructed from various archival sources, including surveys made by the Moravian missionary, Jens Haven, and by Lt. Roger Curtis of the Royal Navy (J.G. Taylor 1974a:15). These sources suggest a total population of 1,460 (table 1).

At the time of this estimate, there is no mention of any significant year-round Inuit occupation of the coast south of Arvertok, although there had been two households in Hamilton Inlet just eight years earlier (J.G. Taylor 1972:143). The Hamilton Inlet area may have been temporarily abandoned at this time, or its population may have been included in the relatively large estimate (270) for Arvertok. Within a few years, Inuit were once again wintering at Hamilton Inlet and other locations as far to the south as Chateau Bay (J.G. Taylor 1977:51). Many of these migrants to the south later returned to their places of origin on the central and northern coast; others were eliminated through disease or absorbed through intermarriage with an expanding Settler population.

In spite of such losses, the Inuit population seems to have remained fairly constant for almost a century. In 1861 a Moravian missionary reported that there were about 1,500 Inuit dwelling along the coast (Reichel 1861:276). Of this number, 1,163 belonged to the Moravian mission. One of the most noticeable changes in the distribution of population was the relative decline of numbers on the north coast. It was said that there were about 200 heathen living to the north of Hebron, an area that held almost twice that number in the eighteenth century. This depopulation, which was already obvious in 1840, resulted from emigration to Hebron and other Moravian stations to the south, as well as to Ungava, where the Hudson's Bay Company had established a trading post at Fort Chimo in 1830 (Kleivan 1966:149).

The population appears to have declined during the late nineteenth century, largely as a result of a series of epidemic illnesses (Kleivan 1966:95). Population statistics for 1905 (Stewart 1939:74) suggest that there were 1,004 Inuit in northern Labrador, distributed at Hopedale (123), Nain (233), Okak (329), Hebron (166), Ramah (75), and Killinek (78). In addition to these, Hawkes (1916:22) reported 35 Inuit living in Hamilton Inlet, and 5 "scattered survivors" farther south.

The population decline continued into the early twentieth century. One of the greatest demographic disasters at this time was the "Spanish influenza" of 1918–1919, in which more than one-third of the entire Inuit population within the Moravian mission area died within three months (Kleivan 1966:181). As a direct result of this epidemic, the old mission station of Okak was completely shut down. After the Moravians also closed Killinek in 1924, there were only a few Inuit families still living in the northern Torngat region. In the 1930s these families moved down to Hebron, which then became the most northerly outpost of permanent settlement on the coast.

Culture

Structures

Inuit of the Labrador coast formerly lived in semipermanent winter dwellings for up to six months of the year, beginning around the middle of October. The Labrador winter house (iɣluqsuaq) was a semi-subterranean structure with walls of sod or stone, a sod-covered roof supported on rafters of whale bones or timber, and a long covered entrance passage. The floor of the house was paved with flat stones while the raised sleeping platform, extending along back and side walls, was covered with split or adzed logs. One or two skylights, made up of translucent seal intestines, were set into the front half of the roof over the entrance tunnel (fig. 5).

During the early historic period winter houses increased in size from small, rounded single family huts to large, rectangular multi-family dwellings (Bird 1945:179). This development may have culminated in the late eighteenth century, when the average winter house was occupied by about 20 persons (J.G. Taylor

Table 1. Population, 1772–1773

Eskimo place-name	Location	Population
Arvirtuuq	Hopedale area	270
Nunainnguaq	Nain Bay	250
Nuasornak	Okak Bay (south portion)	140
Kivalliq	Okak Bay (north portion)	160
Napaartug	Napaktok Bay	140
Kangirsujjuaq	Hebron Fiord	120
Salliq	Saglek Bay and Fiord	100
Saarviliut	Bears Gut	40
Nulatartuuq	Ramah Bay	30
Navvaaq	Nachvak Bay and Fiord	80
Kumatturvik	Komaktorvik Fiord	30
Killiniq	Killinek Island	100
Total		1,460

Fig. 5. Dwellings at Hopedale. left, Sod-covered winter houses with household equipment on the roof. The rectangular inset in the roof in center is a window. The darker figures wear clothing of sealskin; the lighter clothing is European in materials and sometimes in form. right, Summer tent made of skins. The woman seated on the sled wears wool clothing while the standing couple wear sealskin parkas. A seal hook and paddle are on the deck of the kayak. Photographs by William Pierce, Sr., summer 1864.

1974a:71). During the nineteenth century, the size of winter dwellings diminished, and by the 1870s single-family houses were common at the southern stations, especially Nain and Hopedale, where an expanding Settler population was beginning to influence many aspects of Inuit culture (Kleivan 1966:36).

The appearance of the winter dwelling was already changing by the early nineteenth century, when the long, low entrance tunnel was gradually replaced by a much shorter and higher porch. As the century progressed, Inuit of the central and southern coast started using logs and planks from mission sawmills in their house construction. This was accompanied by the adoption of wood stoves, since traditional blubber lamps were inadequate for the poorly insulated plank houses (fig. 6) (Kleivan 1966:37).

The snowhouse (*iɣluviɣaq*) was used mainly as a temporary winter shelter. Simple snowhouses, consisting of a single dome, were used for overnight hunting trips, while a cluster of several domes joined by a common entrance tunnel could be used by families planning to camp at a good hunting location for a longer period of time (J.G. Taylor 1974a:75). A large type of snowhouse known as the *qaɣɣiq* was sometimes constructed for the purpose of communal feasting and recreation.

The tent (*tupiq*) was used during the period from late April until the middle of October. A typical tent had a framework of poles, one of which served as a ridge between the conical-shaped rear and the triangular entrance (Hill et al. 1765:Sep. 12). In addition to this ridgepole type, conical tents have also been reported (Hawkes 1916:63). Tents were usually covered with sealskins, although caribou hides were sometimes used

by those hunting caribou in the interior (J.G. Taylor 1969:152).

Transportation

The large open skin boat known as the umiak was used extensively to transport families and goods during the summer and to hunt whales during late autumn. When traveling from one place to another women rowed the umiaks with long wooden oars, hoisting a square sail on the single mast when winds were favorable. Men took over the umiaks during the whaling season, but they used single-bladed paddles instead of the large bulky oars. A steersman kept the boat on course by means of a wooden rudder (J.G. Taylor 1979b:294).

The umiaks used on the Labrador coast were blunt at bow and stern, with the same boxlike shape that was characteristic of this vessel elsewhere in the eastern arctic. They were covered with skins of the bearded seal; about seven were required for an umiak in excess of 30 feet (J.G. Taylor 1974a:38). In the late eighteenth century the umiaks carried an average load of about 20 people, often with tents, baggage, and dogs.

By the time Moravian missionaries arrived in Labardor wooden boats, which the Inuit had obtained on seasonal voyages to European settlements in the south, were already more common than umiaks. The transition to European boats was almost completed during the late nineteenth century, when commercial cod fishing was growing in importance. Between 1861 and 1876 the number of wooden boats between Nain and Hebron increased from 117 to 237, while the number of umiaks decreased from 14 to 4 (Kleivan 1966:46). By 1920 there

514

Moravian Church: Königsfeld, Federal Republic of Germany.
Fig. 6. Wooden model representing a house style typical of the late 19th century with an entry porch rather than the earlier long tunnel passage. A section of the rear roof is cut away for viewing the interior and the whole roof is removable to show the interior space and furnishings. There is a sleeping platform along the back wall; 2 roof supports in the middle; a table, drying rack, and wood stove (J.G. Taylor 1982). Length of base 28.3 cm; from Okak, Labrador, Newf.

was still one umiak in use at Killinek (Butler 1963:142). At that time fishing boats with outboard motors were already getting popular farther south.

The kayak was normally used at the coast for hunting sea mammals and birds between late April and the middle of December, but it was also used for spearing caribou at inland lakes during late summer (J.G. Taylor 1969:158). Labrador kayaks were relatively wide, flat-bottomed craft, similar in general shape and style to those of northern Quebec and southern Baffin Island. The size of kayaks was described by one observer (R. Curtis 1774:385) as "upwards of twenty feet by two." These dimensions apply remarkably well to a kayak obtained at Hopedale in 1851 (Nationalmuseet, Copenhagen, Pb 1), which has an overall length of 19 feet, 4 inches and a width (measured behind the cockpit) of exactly two feet. Kayaks started to decline in numbers and importance in the late nineteenth century, and, except for a few survivals on the north coast, had gone out of use by the 1930s (Kleivan 1966:47).

During the winter, transportation was provided by substantial wooden sledges that had solid crossbars and runners with whalebone shoes. Dog teams, harnessed to the sledge in fan-shaped formation, were relatively large; the average size of teams mentioned in sources of the late eighteenth century was 15.6 animals (J.G. Taylor 1974a:38). By the middle of the nineteenth century the Inuit had adopted skis of European type (Nationalmuseet, Copenhagen, Pc 3) and snowshoes of the Montagnais-Naskapi swallowtail variety (Nationalmuseet, Copenhagen, Pc 4). However, there is no evidence that either skis or snowshoes were used when the Moravian missionaries first arrived.

Clothing

Clothing styles, which were generally similar to those of south Baffin Island, had already changed considerably by the time from which the oldest extant museum specimens derive. For example, an eyewitness account from the late seventeenth century makes it clear that men's coats, like those of women, had a long flap or tail on the back (Jolliet 1694:188). This style, once common in Baffin Island as well, may have gone out of fashion in the early eighteenth century; by 1743 only the women had flaps on their coats (Fornel 1743:227). Men's coats were by this time cut straight across, as can be seen on pictorial references dating from the late eighteenth century and museum specimens from the mid-nineteenth century (Nationalmuseet, Copenhagen, Pd 2a).

The appearance of women's clothing also changed during early historic times. Documentary sources from the seventeenth and eighteenth centuries indicate that women wore hip boots of sealskin that widened toward the top (Jolliet 1694:195; Fornel 1743:227). According to early Moravian observers, these boots were big enough that they could "thrust" a child into them (fig. 7) (J.G. Taylor 1972:139). This old type of woman's boot seems to have been completely forgotten by the beginning of the twentieth century, leading Hawkes (1916:41) to comment that "there does not appear to be any particular difference between the boots of men and women in Labrador, such as obtains in other sections."

In addition to their everyday clothing, made from the hair-covered hides of seal, caribou, dog, and bear, the Inuit of Labrador had various types of specialized waterproof clothing made of depilated sealskin. One such item was a buoyant "combination suit," which covered the entire body except the face and was worn for flensing whales in relatively deep water (J.G. Taylor 1979b:297). Other waterproof sealskin clothing used in whale flensing were special mittens and wading pants that came up to the chest. Kayak hunters often wore a jacket of split seal intestines sewn in vertical strips and 515

Fig. 7. Labrador woman's clothing of the 18th century. The rather contrived effort to conceal the face with snow goggles and by pinning the hood in a non-Eskimo manner suggest that the artist was forced to use a non-Native model. However, the hooded parka is authentic and the depiction of the large boot may be the only detailed painting of this traditional article of clothing so often described in written sources of the 17th and 18th centuries. Oil painting by Angelica Kauffman, 1770s.

fastened around the cockpit of the kayak with a drawstring (Nationalmuseet, Copenhagen, Pd 1).

Subsistence

• TECHNOLOGY Two different harpoon types are mentioned in early sources. The winter or ice-hunting harpoon (*una·q*) had a fixed foreshaft (Nationalmuseet, Copenhagen, Pb 2d). The summer or kayak harpoon

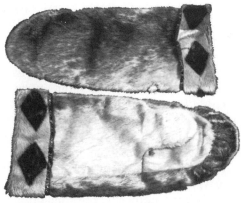

Fig. 8. Man's sealskin mittens with appliqué work in fur and cloth trim on cuffs. Length 36.0 cm; collected by E.W. Hawkes at

516 Hamilton Inlet, Labrador, Newf., 1914.

Fig. 9. Bag made of loonskin and decorated with beads and yarn. Length 17.5 cm excluding tassels; collected by E.W. Hawkes at Hamilton Inlet, Labrador, Newf., 1914.

(*naulaq*) had a moveable foreshaft (*iɣimaq*) and was used for hunting seals, walrus, and beluga in open water. It was commonly employed with a blown sealskin as float (*avataq*) and a drag anchor (*niutaq*), which consisted of sealskin stretched on a round wooden frame of about 10 inches diameter (Nationalmuseet, Copenhagen, Pb 1c). After a sea mammal was secured with this equipment, it was killed with a lance (*aŋuviɣaq*), which had a foreshaft of walrus ivory (Nationalmuseet, Copenhagen, Pb 1e). The kayak equipment also included a three-pronged bird spear and throwing board (Nationalmuseet, Copenhagen, Pb 1f, Pb 1d).

Inuit whalers in Labrador used specialized equipment for both hunting and flensing the Greenland right whale. The heavy whaling harpoon, which could only be used from umiaks, was similar to specimens collected in Baffin Island around 1900 (Boas 1901–1907:23). The head was attached by lines to two or three sealskin floats and a large drag anchor with a wide baleen frame and a diameter of about 22 inches (J.G. Taylor 1979b:296). A special flensing knife had a small bladder attached to the end of a wooden handle; this kept the knife afloat if it slipped out of the user's hand.

The bow, which was used for stalking land animals, was made of wood with an adjustable backing of sinew (Cartwright 1792, 1:238). During the main caribou hunt of late summer, animals were chased by kayakers and killed with lances. Both the bow and caribou lance were replaced by firearms at an early date, which may explain why they are not represented in many museum collections.

Both hooks and spears were used for fishing. The hooks, used for cod and arctic char, operated on the same lines as a jigger, catching fish in the side or belly (J.G. Taylor 1974a:36). The spear, used for salmon and char, was the familiar three-pronged *kakivak*. The spear was used at stone weirs (*saputit*) in summer and through

Natl. Mus. of Canada, Ottawa: IV-B-176.
Fig. 10. Man's roll-up tobacco pouch of sealskin decorated with seed beads. Width 16.5 cm; collected by Frank G. Speck at Aillik Bay, Labrador, Newf., 1914.

holes in the ice in winter (Kohlmeister and Kmoch 1814:29).

Although the Inuit of Labrador made use of small dip nets for catching capelin (J.G. Taylor 1974a:37) there seems to be considerable disagreement with regard to their use of larger gill nets for salmon and char. Hawkes (1916:3) thinks it probable that nets may have been used in aboriginal times, while Gosling (1910:29) argues that the Inuit did not use nets for catching salmon until after the arrival of the Moravians. Documentary sources tend to support Gosling's view insofar as they suggest that the Inuit did not have their own nets when the missionaries first arrived but that by the middle of the 1780s they were obtaining some nets from traders (Cartwright 1792, 3:167) as well as making some of their own (J.G. Taylor 1974a:37).

• ANNUAL CYCLE   The seasonal subsistence cycle for the period between 1771 and 1784, immediately prior to the acquisition of firearms, has been reconstructed from early Moravian diaries (J.G. Taylor 1974a:51–58). At that time, the Inuit usually settled into their winter houses around the middle of October. These were usually located at the mouths of fjords or on some of the more sheltered of the seaward islands.

The main subsistence pursuits of autumn, which lasted until the freezing of coastal waters in mid-December, were seal hunting and whaling. The harp seal, a major resource in all areas, was harpooned from kayaks during its autumn migration to the south. The Greenland whale, which was hunted with a fair degree of success in the Hopedale area, Okak Bay (north portion), Hebron Fiord, Saglek, and Nachvak, was pursued by crews of men in umiaks (J.G. Taylor 1974a:32–34). Both seal and whale meat were stored in stone caches for winter consumption.

After freeze-up, whaling ceased and seals were hunted at breathing holes in the new ice. Although the seals taken in this manner included some migratory harps that had been caught inshore by the sudden ice formation, these were captured less frequently than the nonmigratory bearded and ringed seals. Men and boys often left the winter camps for periods of several days, seeking areas that had just frozen over. Sealing on new

ice was extremely productive, and for the first few weeks after freeze-up it was still possible to store seals for later use.

Around the middle of January sealing at breathing holes became much less productive as the ice thickened and was covered with deep snow. Most sealing was restricted to the vicinity of strong currents and to the ice edge, where the process of breaking and refreezing sometimes resulted in patches of new ice. When weather was favorable, basking seals (uˑttuq, sg.) were hunted by the crawling method. Walrus were important in a few of the northern areas, such as Okak Bay and Nachvak Bay, where they appeared in the open water of the ice edge in February and March.

When sea mammals were scarce or difficult to catch other food sources were exploited. During January and February it was possible to secure various types of sea birds such as dovekies, eider ducks, guillemots, and puffins. In March and April people could fish through the ice for rock cod or arctic char. The former were caught in the sea; the latter in freshwater lakes and ponds. During hard winters it was often necessary to revert to caches of whale, seal, caribou, and fish in order to avert famine. Some people left their winter houses during the late winter months and built snowhouses close to better hunting and fishing localities.

As the sun grew stronger toward the end of April, both winter houses and snowhouses were abandoned in favor of tents. During the months of May and June most people moved out to islands, where they hunted seals, beluga, and eider ducks and gathered ducks' eggs. Most sealing at this time was carried out from kayaks in the ever-increasing patches of open water. Food was often so plentiful that caches could be made for the following winter.

As the fast ice broke up and drifted out to sea around the middle of June, the people who were scattered among the outer islands returned to summer gathering places in the bays. Seals and beluga, which also re-entered the bays at this time, continued to be the chief prey, although arctic char, salmon, cod, sea fowl, black bears, polar bears, and the occasional stray caribou were all supplementary food sources.

In early August many families went to hunt caribou in the interior in order to get skins for winter clothing. Those who were unable to stand the rigors of inland travel remained behind at the coast, where they continued to hunt sea mammals and catch fish. Salmon and char were stored in stone caches for the winter consumption of all, including the caribou hunters, and in return the people who remained at the coast were given furs for winter clothing by those who went inland. Most of the people who went to the interior for caribou returned to the coast during the first weeks of October.

The annual cycle as just described had started to change in significant ways by the beginning of the nineteenth century. One of the most profound changes was the decline of whaling, which had already occurred at Arvertok by around 1780 (J.G. Taylor 1974a:34). Although whales were hunted for several more decades at the more northerly whaling locations, returns diminished rapidly after 1800 and the last kill on record was made in 1823 (Taylor and Taylor 1977:59). Reasons for the abandonment of whaling have yet to be carefully analyzed but some of the factors that may have contributed are a decline in the number of whales, the dropping price of baleen, and changes in Inuit society and culture (J.G. Taylor 1977:52).

Another important change in the subsistence cycle was the introduction of inland caribou hunting during the late winter and early spring. The development of the winter-spring hunt, which increased in popularity during the early 1800s, was probably related to the acquisition of firearms. Guns were more effective than the traditional bow and arrow for hunting caribou on the frozen plateau and thus made feasible an alternative to coastal hunting during a relatively sparse period of winter (Taylor and Taylor 1977:76).

While the new winter caribou hunt was growing in importance, the traditional hunt of late summer was starting to disappear among mission Inuit. This development may have been initiated by missionaries' efforts to get the Inuit to spend their summer at the coast, where they could catch fish to help see them through the winter (Taylor and Taylor 1977:76). Among the Inuit of the central coast, the final demise of the summer hunt occurred in the late nineteenth century, when commercial fishing became an important source of earned income (J.G. Taylor 1979c:80). On the north coast, where prime caribou hides were still required for clothing and bedding, the late summer hunt persisted into the twentieth century.

One of the most significant changes to occur in the subsistence cycle during the early twentieth century was the intensification of fur trapping under the Hudson's Bay Company monopoly, from 1926 to 1942 (Kleivan 1966:129). As a result of the emphasis that the Company placed on trapping, men had to leave the mission villages for long periods during the winter, traveling farther inland than at any time within memory. The food requirements of trappers and their dog teams were probably a major factor in the decline of caribou populations at this time.

Social Organization

Little is known about traditional social organization until the arrival of the Moravians in 1771. At that time, one of the most striking features of family structure was the very high incidence of polygyny. In a census of the Nain area in 1776–1777, in which 36 marriages were represented, there were 13 cases of polygyny, seven of

Denver Art Mus.: left, 1951.227; right, 1936.207.

Fig. 11. Masks worn by Labrador Inuit in the *nalujuk* ritual, which was held on Epiphany (Jan. 6). The ritual, in which masked performers went from house to house, appears to have included a mixture of traditional Inuit and European elements (Speck 1935; Richling 1980). left, Fur mask said to represent a bat; right, sealskin mask of a human face. Height of bottom 21.5 cm, top same scale. Both collected by Frank G. Speck, Nain, Labrador, Newf., probably 1934.

which involved two wives and six of which involved three wives (J.G. Taylor 1974a:68).

The high incidence of polygyny in this particular sample was in part supported by the population structure, since there were more females than males. However, the high incidence of wife-stealing (J.G. Taylor 1974a:91) and the fact that girls were often taken for wives when only 10 years old (J.G. Taylor 1974a:69) both suggest that the demand for extra wives was even greater than could be supplied by the existing sex ratio imbalance. It appears that the possession of extra wives was a definite goal and that early contact Inuit society in this area should be described as truly "polygynous" (J.G. Taylor 1970:253). The co-wives in such unions were often close relatives, such as sisters or mother and daughter.

The average size of families listed in the Nain census of 1776–1777 was five persons (J.G. Taylor 1974a:67). Fewer than one-third of those represented could be classified as nuclear families. In addition to numerous "joint families," with more than two spouses, there were several "stem families," which included a variety of other members, such as widowed sisters and mothers, as well as unmarried children.

The household unit was usually larger than the individual nuclear, stem, or joint family. In a sample of 14 winter households, which averaged about 20 people, the majority of component family groups were closely related (J.G. Taylor 1974a:73). Although snowhouses and tents contained fewer people than the large winter houses, they were usually situated in a compact cluster with one or two others. Clusters of two or three snowhouses often shared a common entrance tunnel.

The most common kin ties within winter households were those between fathers and their married sons and

Niels W. Jannasch, Halifax, N.S.

Fig. 12. Harvesting turnips at the Moravian mission at Hebron. The women are dressed in traditional parkas but wear cloth skirts instead of trousers. Hebron, founded in 1830 and closed in 1959, became the northernmost Moravian mission after Killinek was closed in 1924.

between pairs of brothers (J.G. Taylor 1974a:75). Although the sample of 14 households included eight such virilocal ties, it also included six ties of an uxorilocal nature. The fact that virilocal kin ties were numerically preponderant in spite of the fact that females outnumbered males in the population structure suggests there may have been a preference for virilocality in the household unit.

Although settlements were sometimes composed of single household units, multi-household settlements were also very common. The average size of seasonal settlements in winter, spring, and late summer was 36.3, 26.7, and 38.2 respectively (J.G. Taylor 1974a:17, 18, 19). In larger settlements, the heads of component households were frequently siblings, and kin connections within such communities included both uxorilocal and virilocal ties.

The largest unit that normally came together in face-to-face contact was the local group of settlements that were recognized by a common territorial name. This group regularly gathered together in early summer, just prior to the annual caribou hunt. Similar gatherings could occur at other seasons, especially when there was an unusually productive whale or walrus hunt, or when a dead whale was discovered. When people of different settlements gathered, the people engaged in feasting and various competitive activities, such as boxing, football, and archery contests.

The average population of the 12 local groups listed in table 1 was 121.7 persons. As with smaller social units, the local group contained both virilocal and uxorilocal kin ties. In addition, there were marriages within the local group as well as to people in other territories (J.G. Taylor 1974a:79). Both in size and in composition, the local group of the Inuit of Labrador resembles a social unit that has also been identified among Inuit of the central arctic, where it has been referred to as a "band" (Damas 1969b:123).

Leadership appears to have been well developed at the family and household levels (J.G. Taylor 1974a:84). Above this level, temporary advisors were sometimes

Natl. Mus. of Canada, Ottawa; a, IV-B-205; b, IV-B-166; c, IV-B-168; d, IV-B-211; e, IV-B-191; f, IV-B-209; g, IV-B-178.

Fig. 13. Basketry. Coiled grass basketry, a native craft, was encouraged and marketed by the Moravian Mission. Basketry continued as a saleable craft in the 1980s. Decoration sometimes uses berry or commercial dyes, wool, embroidery thread, raffia, or carved lid handles. The variety of shapes includes a, basketry plaque; b, bowl with black and red yarn design; c, high-sided bowl; d, elliptical; e, bowl with braided handle; f, elliptical covered basket; g, flared sides from circular base, the orginal lid missing. Height of g 14.4 cm, rest to same scale. a, f, g collected by E.W. Hawkes at Cape Chidley, d at Okak; e at Hamilton Inlet, all in 1914. b–c collected by Frank G. Speck, 1914.

© Natl. Geographic Soc., Washington.

Fig. 14. Women from Hopedale making sealskin clothing for members of the Donald B. MacMillian Expedition of the National Geographic Society. The woman on the left uses an ulu. Photograph by Jacob Gayer, July 1925.

appointed to supervise economic activities involving several households, while a degree of political and religious influence was enjoyed by any man who was recognized as either a secular leader (aŋayuqqaˑq) or shaman (aŋakkuq). Serious disputes within the larger multi-household settlements or at the place group level were usually handled by informal "council meetings," which were attended by most of the men from the groups that were involved.

Some of the earliest social changes to occur in the early Moravian period were the decline of polygyny and native leadership, both resulting from direct or indirect missionary influence. The missionaries were also responsible for creating formal mechanisms of social control, in order to regulate both religious and secular activities in rapidly growing mission villages. Since the nineteenth century, missionaries appointed Inuit men and women as chapel servants, which they called kivγat, to help maintain order in both the church and the community (Hutton 1912:334). After 1901 they also introduced village councils, which included both appointed kivγat and men who were elected by the congregation (Kleivan 1966:78).

Religion

Religious beliefs and practices of the pre-Christian Inuit of Labrador have received relatively little attention in the literature. According to unpublished Nain diaries from the early 1770s, one of the most important figures in the belief system was the male spirit called Torngarsoak. He was said to have lived in the water and was propitiated whenever the people wanted seals or whales. His wife was an old woman called Superguk-soak, who lived in the interior and presided over land animals. In addition to these two figures, the Nain diaries also mention a woman named Nerchevik, who was said to "preside over the seals," and who obviously corresponds to the "sea goddess" known throughout the North American Arctic by various names.

There is abundant evidence of the importance of shamanism in the Labrador area (J.G. Taylor 1974a:85). Shamans were called upon to cure the sick, to increase hunting success, and to predict and control the weather. They usually demanded a heavy payment for curing, although the other functions were performed as a public service. Both male and female shamans invoked the aid of their *tuuɣŋaq* (guardian spirit) during performances which involved varying techniques, although most were carried out in darkness and included some singing and drumming. Many shamans claimed the ability to injure and kill their enemies by means of sorcery (J.G. Taylor 1974a:93).

The traditional religion of the Inuit of Labrador was modified at a very early date by persistent efforts of the Moravian missionaries. Following the first baptism at Nain in 1775, when one of the Inuit men named Keminguse became known as Peter, the missionaries continued to seek new converts among those who frequented the mission stations. Their progress remained slow until just after 1800, when a growing religious movement spread from Hopedale to Nain and Okak (Taylor and Taylor 1977:61). This movement, referred to in mission diaries as "the great awakening," prompted a rapid growth in population at the Moravian stations. Although the majority of Labrador Inuit became nominal Moravians in the early nineteenth century, there were still non-Christian Inuit on the north coast until 1935, when the last converts were baptized at Hebron.

Synonymy

The Eskimos of the Atlantic coast of Labrador refer to themselves simply as Labrador Inuit or as Labradormiut. Although there does not appear to be a more traditional name that applies exclusively to this group, they have been described as belonging to a "subdivision" called Siqinirmiut 'southerners', which also includes those people of Ungava Bay who live as far west as Rivière aux Feuilles (L.M. Turner 1894:176). This appears as Suhinimiut in Hodge (1907–1910, 2:647). However, it should be noted that, prior to the arrival of Europeans in the Ungava region, the Inuit of the Atlantic coast had relatively little contact with those of Rivière aux Feuilles from whom they were separated by wide uninhabited and sparsely populated areas on the south and east coasts of Ungava Bay (J.G. Taylor 1975:274). Also, the designation Siqinirmiut was collected at Fort-Chimo and does not appear to be generally known on the Atlantic coast.

J.G. Taylor (1974a:11–19) discusses the local names in the 1773 reports of Jens Haven and Roger Curtis and other sources.

Sources

In spite of the voluminous literature dealing in some way or other with the culture and history of the Inuit of Labrador, there exists no comprehensive historical enthography for this important group. The ethnographic description of Hawkes (1916) is of limited value because it includes observations on the entire Labrador-Ungava peninsula, and it is often impossible to know which ones pertain specifically to the Labrador coast. Moreover, the culture of the Inuit had already been greatly modified by a long period of contact prior to Hawkes's visit in the summer of 1914, and his coverage of earlier time periods rests heavily on secondary sources. A reconstruction of traditional ethnography based on primary source materials undertaken by the National Museum of Man, Ottawa, has produced works on a number of specialized topics, such as social structure (J.G. Taylor 1970), cultural ecology (J.G. Taylor 1974a), demography (J.G. Taylor 1975), traditional land use (J.G. Taylor 1977), changing subsistence patterns (Taylor and Taylor 1977), hunting technology (J.G. Taylor 1979b), and Indian-Inuit relations (J.G. Taylor 1979a). Kleivan (1966) has published a very useful study of cultural contact prior to 1955, and Jenness (1965) has described the administration of Inuit by various contact agents, from missionaries to government officials. Two collections of essays dealing with the Inuit occupation of north-central Labrador (Brice-Bennett 1977) and southern Labrador (Martijn and Clermont 1980) contain much interesting material. Gosling (1910) includes a very brief chapter on "The Eskimos" in his otherwise substantial history of Labrador. A good source of further readings is contained in the impressive bibliography compiled by the Finnish geographer V. Tanner (1944).

Most of the primary sources from the early historic period (until 1700) are vague and of limited ethnographic significance. The situation improves considerably during the French colonial period, with the reports of explorers and grantees such as Jolliet, Fornel, and Courtemanche. Some of these early French materials are reprinted with English translation in the twelve-volume publication entitled *In the Matter of the Boundary between the Dominion of Canada and the Colony of Newfoundland in the Labrador Peninsula* (Great Britain. Privy Council. Judicial Committee 1927).

For the early British colonial period there are interesting observations by Cartwright (1792), who recorded his dealings with the Inuit in a journal spanning 15 years of activity at Cape Charles and Sandwich Bay. However, by far the most valuable sources for Inuit history and ethnography since 1771 are contained in the diaries, letters, and other records of the Moravian missionaries in Labrador. These invaluable and extensive manuscripts, kept mostly in German, are housed in three major depositories: the Archiv der Brueder Unitaet in Herrnhut, East Germany, the Moravian Archives (British Province) in London, England, and the Moravian Archives (American Province) in Bethlehem, Pennsylvania. Since 1790 the Moravians have printed a serial publication known as the *Periodical Accounts relating to the Mission of the Church of the United Brethren, established among the Heathen*, which includes brief communications from Moravian missions around the world, including those in Labrador. The Labrador reports included in these *Periodical Accounts* consist mainly of very brief excerpts from station diaries that have been translated, sometimes inaccurately, from German into English. They give an interesting overview of developments throughout a long period of time but do not provide the serious scholar with a substitute for the original manuscript sources from which they are extracted.

Two of the earliest ethnographic collections of Inuit material culture from the Atlantic coast were made by the Moravian missionary F. Kruth in 1851–1853 and the German meteorologist K.R. Koch in 1882–1883. The Kruth collection is housed in Nationalmuseet, Copenhagen, and the Koch collection is in the Sammlungen des Instituts für Völkerkunde der Universität Göttingen, Federal Republic of Germany. Interesting materials that cover later times are in the König collection in the Museum für Völkerkunde, Berlin; the Hawkes collection in the National Museum of Man, Ottawa; the Sornborger and Daniels collections in the Peabody Museum of Archaeology and Ethnology, Cambridge, Massachusetts; the Woodward collection in the Pitt Rivers Museum, Oxford, England; and the Ward and Bryant collections in the Smithsonian Institution, Washington.

Greenland Eskimo: Introduction

HELGE KLEIVAN

The development of traditional Greenlandic culture and its differentiation into local and regional varieties depended to a large extent on the local ecological conditions, including very distinct climatic conditions, some of which changed significantly over time. The persistence of identity as Greenlandic Eskimos and the emergence of a sense of national unity, especially after the institution of home rule in 1979, were much influenced by the special circumstances of Norwegian-Danish colonial rule.

The Maritime Focus of Greenlandic Economy

The inhabited part of Greenland, and most particularly the long west coast, exhibits very considerable regional differences in physiography, climate, and biological resources. Each locality is marked by specific cultural manifestations that reflect these regional differences. Throughout human history in Greenland the main focus of economic activities has been a maritime one; however, inland caribou hunting has been, and continues to be, an important summer activity in some localities, particularly the Sukkertoppen, Holsteinsborg, and Egedesminde districts on the west coast. According to Birket-Smith (1924) geographical reasons probably account for the somewhat more inland economic emphasis of the Egedesminde district. On the whole, habitation and economic emphasis in Greenland contrast sharply with those of Canada and much of Alaska in the lack of any general strong orientation to inland hunting. In addition to the minor role played by caribou hunting in the traditional economy, there are two other exceptions to the predominantly maritime orientation of Greenland, neither of which have been Eskimo adaptations. Some of the Norse farms, both in the Ameralik Fjord area and on the southern part of the west coast, were located so far inland that they had to be devoted almost entirely to cattle raising. However, seal and walrus hunting as well as fishing were also important in the economy of the Norsemen ("History of Norse Greenland," this vol.). The second instance is the occurrence of sheep farming in the twentieth century (figs. 2–3). Although this occupation depends on the land for pastures, the herders maintain their economic viability through combining sheep husbandry with utilization of maritime resources.

The culture history of Greenland exhibits the extremes and nearly the whole range of Eskimo ecological adaptations; Greenland includes greater environmental variation than either the Alaska or the Canadian Arctic. In the Subarctic zone of the southern west coast, seal hunting was practiced from kayaks all year round. In the Arctic zone, on the west coast north of Holsteinsborg and in the Ammassalik district of East Greenland, various ice-hunting techniques, the use of dog sledges, and seal hunting from kayaks were all practiced according to the season. Among the Polar Eskimos of the Thule district, cultural adaption to a truly High Arctic zone was perfected: all the ice-hunting techniques known in the Eskimo culture area were utilized in a region where the sea is ice-covered for 9 to 10 months of the year and where there is a period of four months when hunting is rendered impossible because of darkness.

South Greenland exhibits a high degree of cultural specialization based on adaptation to year-round open water. Neither the techniques nor the technology necessary for ice hunting and transportation on the frozen sea can be of use. At the other extreme, for the High Arctic conditions of the Polar Eskimo, adaptation to hunting on the largely ice-covered sea had become so highly specialized that the kayak and other implements used during the short summer season had gone totally out of use by the time of initial European contact. These features were revived by newcomers from Baffin Island in the 1860s (Gilberg 1974–1975; Petersen 1962).

Human Habitation in the Greenland Environment

During the history of human occupation of Greenland, the widely varying cultural configuration of the Paleo-Eskimo and Neo-Eskimo phases, the medieval Norse culture, and the present-day Greenlandic and European adaptations have all been articulated with the physical environment in different ways. A condition that may have met the energy requirements and influenced the settlement pattern or the system of transportation in one cultural system could be irrelevant or even highly inhibiting to the optimal functioning of another system. Thus, for example, Melville Bay with its great glaciers

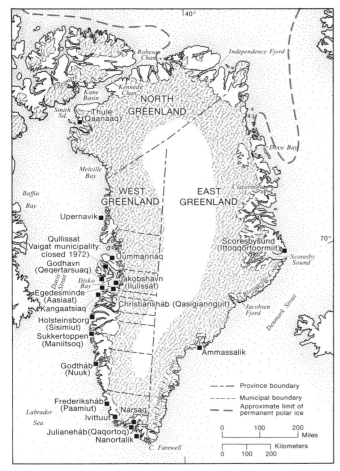

Fig. 1. Greenland provinces and municipalities.

and its unbroken ice cover during much of the year is quite inaccessible even for modern vessels and seems to constitute a barrier to human habitation and movements. But this area must have been perceived quite differently by the hunters of the Neo-Eskimo Thule culture phase who moved southward over Melville Bay to populate the west coast in the twelfth and thirteenth centuries. For them the wide expanse of sea ice was an excellent transport route, since they had dog-drawn sledges. The region was also well suited for occupation by Neo-Eskimos with their truly Arctic adaptation: several archeological sites have been discovered along the coasts of Melville Bay ("Neo-Eskimo Prehistory of Greenland," this vol.). But farther back in time, the system of winter transportation of the Dorset Paleo-Eskimos was less adequate for coping with comparable challenges, being limited to their small man-drawn sledges (W.E. Taylor 1965).

Contemporary attempts by Danes in Greenland to apply modern technology and adaptations that were developed in temperate regions may be compared with the traditional Eskimo adaptations on the southernmost part of the west coast. In this region in spring and summer the East Greenland Current carries great masses of drift ice around Cape Farewell toward the northwest. Julianehåb Bay and the coastal waters of the Nanortalik district can be packed with ice for days and even weeks at a time so that all shipping and coastal fishing activities come to a standstill. In the late summer and in early autumn when the quantities of drift ice diminish or disappear entirely, coastal fishing is comparatively successful in this region. Because of this periodic difficulty with drift ice in summer, the Danish government has been reluctant to invest in larger fish processing plants on this part of the coast. This reluctance to support the fishing industry in the area engenders much consternation among both the fishermen and local politicians.

A year in which wind or currents keep the ice away from coastal waters is called a "good year." Before the introduction of commercial fishing—an activity that was encouraged by the warming of the climate and the shifting ranges of the Atlantic cod (H. Kleivan 1964)—hunting migrating hooded seals was the most important activity both socially and economically for the people of this part of Greenland. Women and children in umiaks and kayaks moved out to the islands offshore to hunt and to socialize with neighbors and kin. Years with extraordinary quantities of drift ice could, of course, reduce mobility at sea, but these were still "good years." According to the hunters, hooded seals stayed no longer in such years. Years with little or no drift ice were called "poor years" by most people as this circumstance shortened the hunting period and reduced the catch of hooded seals.

European adaptations in Greenland are faced with very considerable problems, even when they do not extend beyond the margins of the area characterized by year-round open water. This fact has had far-reaching consequences for the people of Greenland in the twentieth century. For development planning and investments, the country is divided into two main areas: the hunting districts, which correspond to the Arctic and High Arctic zones, and the fishing districts, which correspond to the Subarctic open-water zones of the central and southern part of the west coast. Modernization has meant directed concentration of the growing population in the open-water regions, particularly in the four largest urban centers of that area. The west coast has always been populous, but traditionally the population has been dispersed into a great number of small settlements, many of which were depopulated during the 1950s and 1960s.

The importance of natural conditions in the hunting districts helps account for the retention of a considerable part of the material manifestations of Eskimo culture as functionally meaningful in the life of the people in those regions. However, the population of these marginal areas has also been drawn into the orbit of the market economy and is subject to related changes in social life and technology.

Nationalmuseet, Copenhagen: left, 11218; right, 81301.

Fig. 2. The sheep raising village of Igaliku built near the Norse settlement of Garðar. left, Gardens and grazing cattle in the foreground, ruins of Garðar to the right. Photograph by K. Stephensen, 1912. right, Harvesting grass to be used as fodder for cattle or sheep, with a house built of stones from the Norse ruin at right. Photograph by Poul Nørlund, 1926.

The Emergence of a Common Greenlandic Identity

Before Europeans arrived, the people widely dispersed along the fringes of Greenland were conscious of their common heritage, and similarly with their fellows in Canada, identified themselves as Inuit (West Greenlandic *inuit*). This Eskimo identity has been important in encounters with Europeans in Greenland (H. Kleivan 1969–1970; Kleivan 1969–1970) and with Indians and Europeans in Canada, but in communication with Inuit from other geographical areas, local identity was the important referent guiding attitudes and relationships.

Greenland at the dawn of the colonial era in the eighteenth century encompassed a multitude of local groups, each significantly distinct in culture. Local identity was expressed by the use of the place-name with the suffix complex -*miut* 'inhabitants of' (sg. -*miu*). The degree of social distinctness of such groups (Jenness 1922; Burch 1974) depended on their distance apart. Neighboring groups included affines and other kin to whom one could relate when visiting or in encounters at the margins of exploited areas. This was the case along much of the west coast, but such relative continuity did not exist everywhere. In the early historic period there were no contacts between the Polar Eskimo and the people of the Upernavik district on the northern west coast. There was probably also little between West and East Greenlanders until East Greenlanders began to visit and settle on the southern part of the west coast ("East Greenland Before 1950," this vol.).

In Greenland the presence and activities of the colonial power contributed decisively to the emergence of a new identity. This process, which commenced shortly after the arrival of the Norwegian priest Hans Egede in 1721, in the twentieth century provided the foundation for nation building among the Greenlanders. The emerging identity came to be expressed in the self-designation *Kalaaleq* (pl. *Kalaallit*), which according to early sources (P.H. Egede 1750; Kleinschmidt 1871; Cranz 1770) became common usage among people on the colonized west coast by the 1760s. The European presence in Greenland in the eighteenth and nineteenth centuries was not precisely an acculturative force, since here more than in any other part of the Eskimo world a hybrid culture developed early. It was a culture that clearly included many European features yet remained Greenlandic to such an extent that it served as the origins for the emerging national culture of Greenland. This new colonial culture grew to fill the vacuum left by intensive missionary work that had obliterated tradi-

Fig. 3. Shearing sheep at Igaliku. Photograph by Hans Berg, June 1969.

524

tional Eskimo intellectual culture or, for a time at least, had driven it underground.

The monopoly situation established by colonial rule in Greenland was less detrimental to the people under conditions of isolation than would have been more open policies. Within this closed system, several institutional arrangements were established to implement ideas current in Copenhagen, the center of colonial decision making.

Among the situational changes during the colonial period in Greenland, scarcely any were more important for cultural change than the establishment of a teacher's college at Godthåb in 1845 for training Greenlandic catechists. This institution contributed profoundly to the formation and dissemination of a homogeneous colonial intellectual culture. The main duties of these catechists were to teach pupils in the elementary schools and to serve the church. The textbooks used in the college were written in Greenlandic, covering not only the religious subjects that dominated the curriculum but also disciplines such as world history, zoology, and geography.

The catechists worked both in the colonial centers and in a great number of small settlements along the west coast. This area comprised colonial Greenland until East Greenland was opened for colonial control and missionary activities at the end of the nineteenth century and before the Thule area was incorporated at the beginning of the twentieth.

Although the teachings of the catechists emphasized Christianity, they also contributed to the spread of a common fund of elementary knowledge based on European educational ideas, but adapted to Greenlandic conditions. The great majority of Greenlanders acquired literacy during the eighteenth and early nineteenth centuries (Rink 1857). When the Greenlandic periodical *Atuagagdliutit* was established in 1861, it soon became favorite reading along the coast and undoubtedly enhanced the development of a sense of unity among Greenlanders ("Greenlandic Written Literature," this vol.).

Operating in an enormous geographical area with a high degree of variation in aboriginal culture, the joint educational and church system fostered a homogenization of social and cultural conditions. Despite dialect differences, this process was also facilitated through the dissemination and rapid acceptance of the unified system of orthography introduced by Kleinschmidt (1871).

Changes in the material aspects of life took place much more slowly, since Danish policy during most of the colonial period aimed at continuation of a hunting economy for the majority of Greenlanders. Except for the early introduction of firearms, much of the traditional hunting technology and many of the techniques of exploitation as well as means of transportation were maintained well into the twentieth century.

As colonial rule expanded throughout the eighteenth century to include the whole Greenland west coast, complex ethnic processes resulted in a population increasingly mixed with Europeans. Only the population mixture emanating from marriages between indigenous women and Danish or Norwegian men employed in the colonial service resulted in social processes of historic significance. First and foremost these marriages gave rise to a social differentiation that has not had many parallels in the colonial history of other parts of the Eskimo world. Sons of such marriages were encouraged to get training that could qualify them for jobs in the colonial service. This gave rise to what popularly is called "the great Greenlandic families," whose male members held positions as catechists, trade managers, interpreters, craftsmen and foremen throughout colonial history (H.E. Rasmussen 1983). These families, although bearers of an identity as Greenlanders and speakers of the Greenlandic Eskimo language, manifested a culture strongly marked by European features. They played a most significant role in the dissemination of the new culture that emerged in the early colonial period as the product of the encounter of European and Greenlandic Eskimo culture.

During the long process of colonialization and the accompanying social and cultural changes, Greenland emerged as one country, *Kalaallit Nunaat* 'the land of the Greenlanders'. Although communication between Copenhagen and Greenland was carried out in Danish throughout the entire colonial period, the central west coast dialect of Eskimo emerged as the administrative language in all inhabited parts of the island and, indeed, became the chief language of the country. When the Ammassalik Eskimos and the Polar Eskimos were drawn into the orbit of Danish rule, most of the colonial employees, priests, and catechists, as well as the servants of the Royal Greenland Trade Department who worked in those regions, were West Greenlanders. Thus, both European and hybrid colonial cultural influences were introduced in these formerly isolated areas mainly through West Greenlandic contact agents.

The changes that occurred on the west coast as early as the eighteenth century as a cumulative result of the activities of the colonial power were repeated, but in a somewhat attenuated form, in the first half of the twentieth century among East Greenlanders and Polar Eskimos. Although these groups retain their distinctive local identities and many local traditional cultural elements, individuals from those regions, acknowledging present-day realities, recognize that they form part of the people of Greenland in contrast to Danes or other foreigners (Petersen 1977a; Søby 1979).

Much of what happened in Greenland colonial history has contributed and given momentum to what deserves designation as a nation building process. Traumatic experiences during the intensive modernization

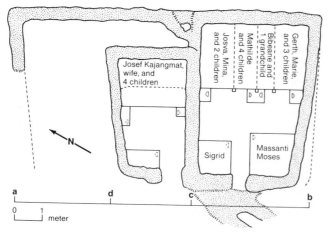

after Petersen 1974–1975:171–183.

Fig. 4. Plan of a longhouse at Sarpaq, Ammassalik District, with traces of former residences. In 1905 the entire house a–b was occupied as a "common house." b–c, House of the Aqipe family, an extended family; c–d, house of a nuclear family. The longhouse, the most common form of dwelling in East and West Greenland at the beginning of Danish colonization in 1721, remained predominant until the second half of the 19th century in West Greenland and until 1920–1940 in East Greenland. Several extended families sometimes lived together in a "common house." In this arrangement there was no mutual economy or single head of the house; the individual families were equal. Though the walls of the house were shared, the space and furnishings occupied by the extended family were not common property; however, food was sometimes distributed to all housemates. After one winter in a "common house" the residents made new arrangements for the next winter season.

period since 1950 furthered the political mobilization that finally led to the home rule system for Greenland, established May 1, 1979. But the immediately precipitating factors, however clear-cut, should not obscure the long-term historical forces that also gave impetus to political mobilization.

No observer of developments in Greenland would deny the possibility that home rule may eventually be transformed into full national independence. Such a development would depend on the emergence of a self-sustaining Greenlandic economy. If this should happen, there is little reason to believe that political separation would entail severance of all of the deeply rooted social ties between Danes and Greenlanders. On the contrary, these ties could actually be drawn tighter under such circumstances.

Greenland is the only major area within the Eskimo world that may face the possibility of future political independence. While Greenland can be regarded as the most isolated part of the Eskimo area, both in terms of its removal from other Eskimo groups, as well as in its distance from the administering nation, this very isolation may well provide the conditions for the emergence of an independent country.

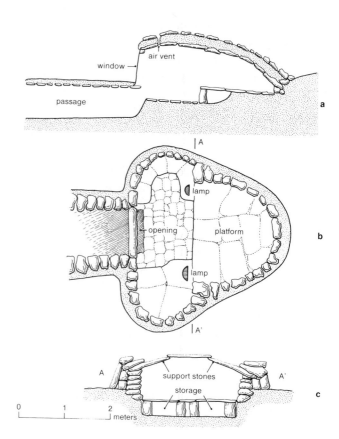

after Steensby 1910:311–321.

Fig. 5. Polar Eskimo winter house located east of the settlement of Uummannaq. a, Longitudinal section. The roof is constructed of inner and outer layers of stone, the cavity between being filled with earth and sod. c, Cross-section through A–A'. The heavy roof is held up by a cantilever system of 7 support stones that project into the interior to support the center roof stones and are anchored into the walls with counterbalance stones. b, Ground plan. The passage, about 3 meters long and 60–75 centimeters high, opens into the living area, about 3.9 meters wide, through a small rectangular entrance. A translucent window of gut-skin with a peephole in the center is located above the entrance. The main platform, about 2.1 meters wide at the front edge, is covered with skins of caribou or bear over a layer of dry grass and is used for sleeping and lounging. The interior walls and roof are lined with sealskin with the fur side turned toward the wall. The 2 side platforms are used for storage and support the oil lamps used for heating and lighting the room. Drying boards and cooking pots are suspended above them. The winter house is usually occupied by no more than 2 families.

History of Research in Greenland

Discussion of sources is included in each of the chapters of this section of the volume. Here are mentioned only a few of the most prominent figures and their chief or representative works.

Pioneering archeological investigations of the prehistory of Greenland were the excavations in the 1920s and 1930s by Mathiassen (1929, 1933, 1936) working in both East and West Greenland, by Larsen (1934, 1938) in East Greenland and the north coast of the island, and by Holtved (1944) for the Polar Eskimo. All continued their work into the second half of the century when they were joined by Meldgaard (1952, 1965) and Knuth (1952, 1968a). While the manpower that has been committed to Greenland archeology has been small, the results are significant. The Paleo-Eskimo cultures of Sarqaq and Independence I and II, as well as the Neo-Eskimo culture, Inugsuk, have all been delineated in Greenland and their roles in Eskimo prehistory extend well beyond the Greenland area ("Prehistory: Summary," this vol.).

The history of Greenland began with Icelandic sagas, and concern with the Norse colony and its disappearance has produced a virtual mountain of literature. Archeological work (Vebæk 1943, 1958) has supplemented the study of documentary material and the analysis of Eskimo legends in Norse research in Greenland.

The history of colonial Greenland is well served beginning in the eighteenth century with the writings of missionary Hans Egede (1745) and his sons Niels (1939, 1939a) and Poul (1939), continued with the work of Fabricius (1962) and Rink (1877). Gad's (1967–1976) monumental three-volume history of Greenland presents a comprehensive coverage of all periods of documented Greenlandic history.

Holm's (1888) ethnography of East Greenlanders belongs to the very dawn of ethnological fieldwork in the Arctic, being contemporary with Boas's (1888) research on Baffin Island. It was followed in the same region by Thalbitzer (1914–1941), while the Egedesminde monograph of Birket-Smith (1924) based on 1918 fieldwork was for many years the only balanced ethnography for West Greenland. For the Thule district, Holtved (1951) extended his investigations into Eskimo oral tradition and language. The interest in Eskimo folklore has been a dominant one in Greenland ethnology with Rasmussen's Polar Eskimo monograph (1908) and East Greenland material (1921–1925), and the work of Rink (1875) on the west coast being only representative of a large body of literature. Work on oral traditions includes Sandgren (1967) and Sonne (1982).

Linguistics has been also a major concern in Greenlandic studies for a long time beginning with the translations of religious works by eighteenth-century missionaries, continuing with the very important work of Kleinschmidt (1871), Petersen (1969–1971), Bergsland (1955), and Rischel (1974).

Study of cultural change and of Greenlandic identity has been carried out by H. Kleivan (1969–1970), Kleivan (1969–1970, 1974–1975), Jensen (1969–1970), and Brøsted and Gulløv (1978). Gulløv (1979) gives a critical account of home rule.

While much of the anthropological and historical writing on Greenland has been published in Danish, a great deal of the work of Scandinavians has been either written in English or translated into that language. Meanwhile, there has been a burgeoning of work on Greenlandic Eskimos written in French. Notable is Malaurie (1952) for the Thule region, but the bulk of French material focuses on East Greenlanders, for example by Victor (1938, 1972), Robert-Lamblin (1971), and Gessain (1969). The work of these anthropologists together with the early publications of Holm and Thalbitzer and that of Nooter (1972–1973) and Petersen (1965, 1974–1975) make the East Greenlanders the best-documented of Greenlandic groups with coverage rivaling that of any other Eskimo group.

The impressive volume of literature on the Eskimo of Greenland covers linguistics, archeology, physical anthropology, and the ethnological categories of material culture, oral tradition, religion, economy, and settlement patterns. Research approaches have included excavations, conventional ethnographical fieldwork, and ethnohistory.

In contrast to the concern with social organization that in the 1960s had become central to research in Alaska and the Canadian Arctic, that interest has lagged in Greenland. The very early disruption of traditional social organization in most of the subcontinent left little for the conventional social anthropologist to examine. Also, most work by Scandinavian ethnologists until after the end of World War II was in the continental European tradition; only after drastic social change was virtually complete did anthropologists trained to focus on social institutions appear. Søby's (1977–1978) work on Thule region kinship is one example of analysis of the social organization of Greenland Eskimos.

Paleo-Eskimo Cultures of Greenland

WILLIAM W. FITZHUGH

After an auspicious beginning (Solberg 1907), Paleo-Eskimo studies lagged considerably behind Neo-Eskimo archeology, for which projects have been completed in nearly every major part of Greenland. This situation is a result of geographical and historical conditions that have governed the development of this field, chief among them being the general absence of organic remains, the physically unobtrusive nature of Paleo-Eskimo sites, and the common occurrence of Paleo-Eskimo chipped stone implements in association with Neo-Eskimo artifacts. In addition, this field has been heavily influenced by Danish scholarly tradition.

Given the poor state of knowledge and the large distances between archeologically known regions, the following review of published information emphasizes regional chronology and phase descriptions and makes only passing reference to socioeconomic characteristics and internal and external relationships. Greenland Paleo-Eskimo archeology has been concerned largely with regional adaptations and interpretations in which migration and climate change have figured prominently as explanatory mechanisms. In large part this tendency has been reinforced by Greenland's geographic situation as a landmass occupied by a peripheral population whose segments have been separated by great distances and physical barriers. Another important factor has been the presence of a single point of contact with a High Arctic region of Canada, which must have acted to some degree as a "cultural filter" for population movements and cultural influences. In addition, Greenland's regional environments vary widely in ecological complexity and productivity, ranging from Peary Land's High Arctic deserts and permanently frozen coasts to the "Scandinavian" subarctic regions around Julianehåb with meadowlands and ice-free seas. For these reasons Greenland has long been viewed as an important area for studying historical, biological, and cultural relationships between man and his environment under relatively controlled, definable, but harsh physical conditions. These concerns are implicit in most of the Greenland archeological literature (Meldgaard 1977).

North Greenland

Peary Land

The administrative unit called North Greenland comprises the area from Melville Bay, south of Thule, east to Danmark Fjord. Although the history of Paleo-Eskimo archeology in North Greenland began in the more ecologically productive western portion of the province, it is in Peary Land that information on early cultures is most complete. Much of this area is a dry arctic desert, unglaciated and snow-free throughout the year. In the twentieth century its coast has been blocked by ice year-round, but the find of a Thule culture umiak at Kolnæs attests to earlier periods when navigation was possible (Knuth 1952). Nevertheless, occupation of Peary Land would have demanded a terrestrial adaption, similar to that of the Caribou Eskimos, rather than the sea hunting life known from most other areas of the Arctic.

Peary Land fauna include musk-ox, Arctic fox, Arctic hare, and ringed seal. Caribou have not been available in the twentieth century, and their remains are almost unknown in archeological sites in this region. Arctic char and trout are present in the lakes and streams. Birds include ptarmigan, brant goose, king eider, glaucous gull, ivory gull, oldsquaw, and kittiwake. Most of these animals have limited seasonal availability and even when present are not abundant.

Conditions for settlement in Peary Land, which was not occupied in the historic period, are among the most severe ever encountered by humans. In addition to impoverished and seasonal food supplies, four and one-half months of darkness make winter hunting difficult. Fuel is limited to driftwood and tiny woody plants such as dwarf willow (*Salix arctica*). Driftwood is deposited along the shore in summer during warm climatic periods when open ice leads permit it to be blown ashore. Further constraints exist in the availability of construction materials: rock, driftwood, bones, horn, and hide. Under conditions such as these, where biological production and the forces of physical attrition are delicately balanced, a small human population might live frugally for only a short period before their consumption outstripped the regenerative capacities of land and sea. In this case extinction or emigration followed by a subsequent fallow period is necessary before new colonization can occur. Periodic natural resource fluctuations make such adaptations even more precarious.

Paleo-environmental studies reveal general patterns of climatic and environmental change in North Greenland. Malaurie et al. (1972) have reported on vegetation and geomorphic history from the Thule region; Dansgaard et al. (1969, 1971) studied atmospheric and climatic history from ice-core borings; and Washburn (1965) studied postglacial geomorphology in northeastern Greenland. The most complete record comes from the climatically sensitive area of Peary Land (Knuth 1967; Fredskild 1969, 1972; Weidick 1972). These studies reveal that Peary Land responded late to global Hypsithermal warming but has been physically accessible to man for the past 5,000 years. Favorable conditions (partly ice-free fjords in summer) existed 2500–1600 B.C., 1000–600 B.C., and, perhaps, A.D. 1000–1300. These periods correspond closely to the settlement periods of Peary Land's various Eskimo cultures.

• INDEPENDENCE I CULTURE   Despite these rigors it is here that traces of one of Greenland's oldest and best-known cultures, Independence I, are found (Thostrup 1917; Knuth 1952, 1954, 1958, 1967, 1966–1967, 1977–1978, 1981, 1982). Independence I is one of the best-dated archeological complexes in the Arctic. Twenty-five radiocarbon determinations have been made, about half of which have been run on Arctic willow samples. Being locally grown, willow is more likely to give accurate dates than driftwood (which may have taken years to drift across the Arctic Ocean and in addition, may have been collected by people from older beach deposits), or marine animal bones, for which isotopic fractionation results in erroneously early dates (McGhee and Tuck 1976). Based on willow, the uncorrected radiocarbon age of Independence I is 4000–3650 B.P. (Knuth 1981:fig. 8), that is, 2050–1700 B.C. Considering statistical error, the actual occupation might have been as brief as two centuries.

The present geographic distribution of Independence I culture ranges from the Thule District to Cape Holbæk, Danmark Fjord. Additional evidence suggests cultures related to Independence I range from Port Refuge in northwestern Devon Island (McGhee 1979) and Labrador (Tuck 1975; Fitzhugh 1976a; Cox 1978) in Canada, to Clavering Island and perhaps Scoresbysund in East Greenland (fig. 1). In keeping with its environs Independence I has been described as a conservative culture with a low population density, a limited inventory of tool types, distinct dwelling structures, and a settlement and subsistence system directed at interior lake and coastal fishing and musk-ox hunting (Knuth 1967).

Independence I collections, numbering nearly 2,000 artifacts from 271 structures (Knuth 1981:110), include both stone and bone implements (fig. 2) (Knuth 1967:32a). Hunting weapons include wooden lances tipped with stemmed endblades for musk-ox hunting. Small stemmed endblades are relatively abundant, suggesting that the bow and arrow was used for bird and land game. The recovery of side prongs indicates use of multi-pronged darts or spears for hunting fish and birds. Burins were the dominant wood and bone carving tool, and these implements are found in larger numbers than any tool class except microblades. Burin spalls may have served as small engraving and cutting tools. Con-

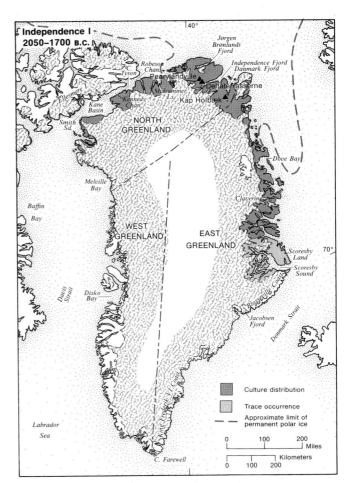

Fig. 1. Distribution of Independence I culture in Greenland.

cave side scrapers were used for shaft manufacture. Animal butchering was accomplished by broad-bladed stemmed or lanceolate knives and microblades, while heavy duty cutting of hide, flesh, and bone was by stone-bladed adzes and bone chisels. Hides were worked with large triangular convex end scrapers often having strongly flared ears or spurs. Tailored clothing was sewed with thin round-eyed needles made from goose or small mammal limb bones with the aid of bone bodkins. Needles were stored in tubular bone cases. No art or evidence of religious beliefs has been found.

Several features of this assemblage are of special note. In contrast with later Greenland Paleo-Eskimos there is no evidence of stone blubber lamps, bone lanceheads, or harpoons. Presence of harpoons is suggested, however, by chipped endblades and finds of barbed, male-socketed harpoons in West Greenland Sarqaq (Saqqaq)*

*In the *Handbook* Greenlandic place-names, including site names, are given in the reformed Greenlandic orthography introduced in 1972, but names of cultures, phases, or periods derived from place-names written in the earlier orthography are retained. Hence the Sarqaq culture is named after the site at Saqqaq (earlier spelled Sarqaq), the Old Nûgdlît culture after the Old Nuulliit site (earlier Gammel or Old Nûgdlît), and the Inugsuk period after the Inussuk site (earlier Inugsuk).

culture sites (Meldgaard 1977:29) and in Canadian Independence I sites (McGhee 1979:pl. 4g). In addition, Independence I assemblages have higher percentages of microblades, burins, and burin spalls than Independence II and West Greenland Sarqaq. Other distinctive features of the technology include roughness of form; relative massiveness of tools compared with other Arctic Small Tool tradition assemblages; pronounced tendency for multiple lateral notches; lack of facial grinding; and, frequently, fine edge serration.

Several types of structures have been identified at Independence I sites (Knuth 1967, 1981). The simplest are small areas of flagstone pavement, which are probably the floors of temporary shelters, summer tents, or windbreaks. Also common are rectangular stone slab boxes, about 40–60 centimeters on a side, made by setting four large slabs into the ground. These structures, called hearth boxes, contain boiling stones, charcoal, and remains of burned bones. Although found as isolated features, they are generally located in the center of dwelling floors, or "mid-passages," framed by parallel rows of slab rocks oriented perpendicular to the former shoreline along which such houses are situated (fig. 3). The hearth passages are often subdivided by transverse slabs and may contain flagstone pavements. Some are surrounded by a low gravel wall or a ring of stones defining the outer edge of the house (fig. 4). Absence of features and a relative lack of artifacts outside the margins of the mid-passage suggests that the lateral areas of these dwellings were floored with skins, which may also have formed roofs over which snow must have been mounded for insulation in winter. In such structures, Independence I people are thought to have survived the long, dark winter in a kind of semihibernation, or torpor, attempting to conserve meager supplies of meat and fuel stored in caches near their houses (Knuth 1967).

Independence sites in North Greenland generally are found on raised beaches near former river mouths and headlands, along musk-ox migration routes through the interior lowlands, and at fishing and hunting locations near interior lakes. Sites range from transient hunting or traveling camps with minimal remains to settlements, such as Pearylandville, whose 20 ruins may have been repeatedly occupied for short periods over many seasons. Reoccupation and modification of structures at a particular location make it difficult to determine site population levels, seasonality, or function. However, a general settlement pattern has been suggested for the Midsummer Lakes–Jørgen Brønlunds Fjord area with dispersed coastal occupations during the ice-free summer for sea hunting and driftwood collection; occupation of riverside camps in the fall and spring; and more long-term settlement at larger, more densely populated base camps at lakes during the dark winter months (Knuth 1967:60–61, 1981:94). Most sites contain bones of summer animal migrants, like geese and ptarmigan, and musk-ox calves; and specifically winter animals have been found. Nevertheless, it is thought that Independence I people stayed in Peary Land throughout the year and that the bias toward summer fauna results from winter residents eating cached summer-caught food.

Settlement maps have not been published for most Independence I sites in Peary Land. However, Independence I sites on Devon Island are composed of groups of ruins containing as few as 5 and as many as 22 houses, arranged in a loose linear pattern along fossil shorelines with 10–20 meters separating individual houses (McGhee 1976:16, 1979:12).

The Independence I people hunted all animals that presently inhabit Peary Land with the addition of the barnacle goose, which in the twentieth century does not summer north of Dove Bay, 600 miles to the southeast. Middens contain abundant remains of musk-ox, fox, Arctic hare, trout, goose, and, rarely, seal; caribou bones are not found, although imported caribou antler is used

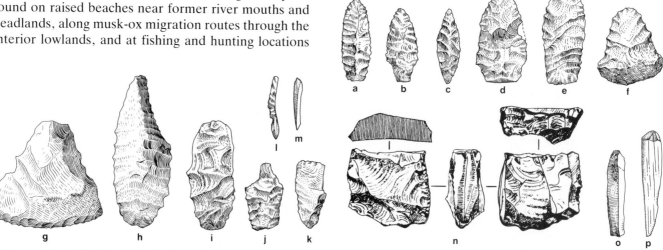

a–f, i–m, o–p, Knuth 1967:pl. 3; g–h, after Knuth 1954:fig. 103; n, Knuth 1954:fig. 104.

Fig. 2. Independence I implements. a–d, stemmed endblades; e, biface; f, end scraper; g, celt; h, concave side scraper; i–k, burins; l–m, burin spalls; n, microblade core; o, microblade; p, bone flint flaker point. Length of a 4.0 cm; rest same scale except n.

Fig. 3. Independence I mid-passage hearth at Pearylandville, Ruin 1. Photographed by Eigil Knuth, 1968.

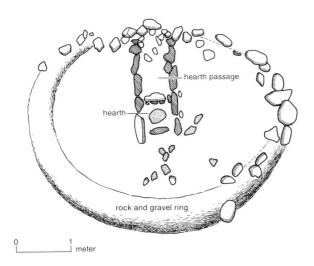

Knuth 1952:fig. 12.
Fig. 4. Plan of Independence I elliptical tent ring with mid-passage structure, House 11, Deltaterrasserne, site K, Jørgen Brønlunds Fjord. The passage is formed by a single line of thick slabs.

for tool making. A single dog bone has been recovered (Knuth 1967:32a). The economy was oriented primarily toward land hunting with relatively little use of marine resources.

The presence of the barnacle goose and large quantities of driftwood embedded in beach levels of this period indicate more ice-free conditions in Peary Land than is present in the twentieth century. Based on the age of the driftwood recovered from cultural and geological contexts, these conditions were fulfilled 2650–1550 B.C. (Knuth 1967:63). Further evidence of climatic warming 2000–1600 B.C. comes from pollen data (Fredskild 1969:581). Amelioration beginning about 2500 B.C.

probably enabled Independence I people to travel across the Canadian High Arctic to Greenland with their land hunting economy, tent houses, and open fires; and animals and driftwood may have been unusually plentiful and perhaps easier to hunt than today (McGhee 1972a). The absence of earlier cultures in Peary Land suggests that these pioneers arrived with a fully developed Independence I culture. They found driftwood and game, and utilized the area, perhaps sporadically, for 500 years shifting between the fjord mouths and inland lakes, conserving their precious resources until, probably, resource depletion and climatic deterioration brought the occupation to an end.

• INDEPENDENCE II CULTURE Several centuries later people returned to live in Peary Land with a culture known as Independence II. Dates for this occupation come from 13 determinations ranging between 1340 ± 130 and 420 ± 75 B.C. (Knuth 1981:fig. 9). Among these are four willow determinations and three musk-ox bone dates that place the settlement range at 1250–450 B.C. Several driftwood dates form the early part of this series, perhaps a result of people mining older beaches for fuel. The concentration of driftwood dates between 1450 and 750 B.C. suggests that relatively warmer, more ice-free conditions preceded and partially overlapped with the early Independence II period in Peary Land.

In Greenland, Independence II culture has approximately the same distribution as its predecessor, extending from Thule to Sophus Mullers Næs and possibly south to the Blosseville coast (fig. 5). In Canada, sites related to Independence II are found in eastern Ellesmere Island (Schledermann 1978; Knuth 1981) and at Port Refuge (McGhee 1976). Knuth (1968:70) has noted resemblances between Independence II bone tools and ones from the 22–23 meter terrace sites at Igloolik dated by Meldgaard (1962) to the late Pre-Dorset period about 1000 B.C. Groswater Dorset assemblages in Labrador, dating 800–200 B.C., and other "late Pre-Dorset" or transitional assemblages from the Eastern Arctic also exhibit similarities to Independence II.

Reconstruction of Independence II technology is facilitated by better organic preservation but parallels Independence I in overall poverty of tool classes and number of finds. Major changes in hunting weaponry include the replacement of the bow and arrow by a "clovenhoof" open-socketed lancehead equipped with a single lateral ovate sideblade (fig. 6). Widespread in the Eastern Arctic, this weapon was probably used for hunting musk-ox in North Greenland. Small self-pointed harpoon heads with bifurcate bases fitted with short foreshafts were used for hunting seals. Stone tool making was done with bone flakers. Bone and antler tool manufacture was conducted with a partly ground burin-knife. Butchering was accomplished by stone-bladed adzes, side-notched ovate knives, and microblades that were thinner and more slender than Independence I speci-

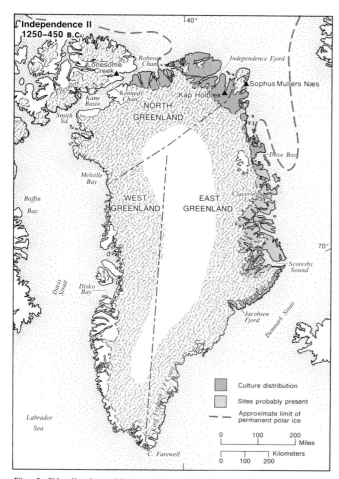

Independence II
1250–450 B.C.

Culture distribution
Sites probably present
Approximate limit of permanent polar ice

0   100   200
                    Miles
0   100   200
              Kilometers

Fig. 5. Distribution of Independence II culture in Greenland.

mens. Hide processing was facilitated by convex and eared end scrapers. Sewing needles were flat and had gouged oblong holes. Pendants and pins were produced.

Compared with Independence I this technology is notable for its absence of small endblades, presence of harpoons and bone lanceheads, reduction of burin use and diminution of overall tool size, absence of multiple notching and heavy serration on the lateral margins of tools, selection of chalcedony rather than flint for chipped stone tools, and increase in personal decorative and magico-religious objects. There are also significant differences in the frequencies of various tool types.

Independence II faunal evidence reflects a change toward greater use of maritime resources (Knuth 1967:35). Walrus remains have come from the Lonesome Creek site in Ellesmere Island, while most of the North Greenland sites contain some seal bones. Muskox, hare, and trout are also found, with ptarmigan, goose, duck, and gull being less common. Caribou continues to be absent, and fox remains are rare, although stone fox traps are found. Seal hunting sites used during the winter months are found on the coast for the first time, but the predominant winter settlement pattern remains an interior one, as before. Overall, the Inde-

pendence II settlement pattern is similar to its predecessor's but has a greater emphasis on summer seal hunting.

Independence II house forms are also closely related to structures of the previous period. Flagstone pavements without perimeter walls are found with hearths exhibiting concentrations of charcoal and boiling stones, but without standing hearth boxes. Presumably, these are the floors of summer tents. The most diagnostic Independence II form is a developed form of the Independence I "mid-passage hearth," or axial hearth structure (fig. 7). This resembles the earlier form but is longer and thinner, often converging slightly toward the end of the structure facing the sea. The hearth is formed by isolating a section of this new structure between thin vertical transverse slabs. "Wing pavements" are sometimes added. As in Independence I, these hearth passages constructions occur both as isolated features and as central features in structures whose perimeters are defined by a ring of gravel or boulders.

Several trends are noted in comparing Independence I and II settlement patterns. These include reduction in the variability of structure types, and elaboration and standardization of the hearth and its passage construction. In addition, at the site level, Independence II settlements are smaller and more dispersed. While more than 157 Independence I dwelling ruins have been found, only 31 Independence II ruins are known (Knuth 1967:52). Considering the longer dating span of Independence II, 800 years or more, it is possible to view Independence II sites as intermittent or sporadic occupations by a few families living in Peary Land for short periods of time, perhaps only seasonally. Knuth has suggested that the dispersed nature of the settlement results from the need to more efficiently utilize the available territory for seal hunting and driftwood collecting.

As with Independence I, the Independence II occupation in Peary Land lasted only a few centuries. Its disappearance is attributed to deteriorating climatic conditions beginning around 1000 B.C. that become severe about 150 B.C. (Fredskild 1973:190). The second half of this period was the coldest of the Holocene. Sea ice may have completely blocked the fjords and coasts of Peary Land and much of the remainder of North Greenland, for few driftwood samples date from this period. Vegetation after 150 B.C. became desertlike, its arid conditions caused by lack of moisture from the ice-covered sea. After the departure of Independence II people about 400 B.C. Peary Land remained unoccupied for almost 2,000 years.

Western North Greenland

The western portion of North Greenland is less well known archeologically than Peary Land. Environmen-

532

tally, this area is transitional between Peary Land and more temperate West Greenland. Land and marine resources, available in greater numbers than farther east, include caribou, musk-ox, seals, walrus, whales, and a variety of fish and sea birds. More favorable conditions are reflected in the occupation of portions of this region by the Polar Eskimos, who in the nineteenth century were the most northerly people on earth, and by a number of large archeological sites dating to the Neo-Eskimo period (Holtved 1944). Paleo-environmental information from Inglefield Land and nearby Ellesmere Island (Hattersly-Smith 1963; Tedrow 1970) is not so detailed as that for Peary Land. This region has been of continuing interest to archeologists because it is the only entrance point for populations or cultural influences passing between Canada and Greenland.

Nevertheless, little information is available on Paleo-Eskimo archeology in this region. Independence I sites are known from Robeson Channel in Hall Land, where, at Cape Tyson, Lauge Koch discovered the first Dorset culture implements and structures reported for this region (Mathiassen 1929:191–216; Knuth 1977–1978:17). Late Dorset artifacts have also been found in many of the Neo-Eskimo sites—Inuarfissuaq, Thule, Ruin Island, and others (Holtved 1944). Among the finds were harpoons, leisters, spatulas, knife handles, numerous stone and some meteoric iron tools, and many decorated objects, including some magnificent sculptural art (fig. 8). Among the finer objects are an ivory male figure wearing a coat with a high collar (Holtved 1944:

pl. 40:20; Meldgaard 1960b:pl. 21); an ivory female figurine wearing a topknot headdress (a "Thule" coiffure worn by Greenland women in the twentieth century) executed in Dorset carving style (Meldgaard 1960: pl. 24); and an antler multiple-face carving in which some faces appear to have European features (Meldgaard 1977:fig. 3).

Research at Old Nuulliit (Gammel Nûgdlît) adds considerably to this picture (Knuth 1977–1978). Dorset structures have been mapped from the seven-meter beaches, but they contained few implements. Primary attention has been given to 20 older house ruins belonging to an Independence I–related culture in several site groups at the 9–11 meter elevations (fig. 9).

Artifact collections (fig. 10) from these ruins include most classes found in Independence I in Peary Land. Important exceptions are the presence of small bipointed endblades, small burins, large chipped adzes without polished bits, and a miniature class of microblades accompanied by the typical larger tool forms of Independence I. In addition, there is an uncharacteristic abundance of tools and debitage, tool miniaturization, delicate workmanship, and lack of pronounced lateral notching—characteristics that are more commonly associated with early Sarqaq assemblages. In these respects the Old Nuulliit materials are typologically in-

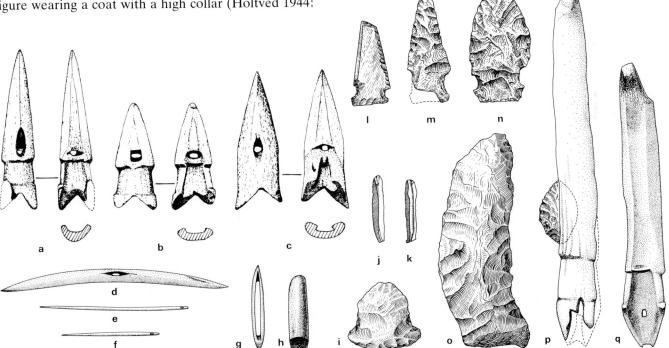

a–c, Knuth 1968:fig. 2; d–h, q, after Knuth 1968:2; i,o, after Knuth 1952:fig. 10; j–n,p, Knuth 1967:3.

Fig. 6. Independence II implements from Peary Land. a–b, harpoon heads with type A open socket; c, harpoon head with type B incised socket; d, bone gull hook or coarse needle; e–f, bone needles; g, bone bucklelike implement; h, bone flint-flaker point; i, flint end scraper; j–k, microblades; l, idealized burinlike tool; m–n, side-notched knives; o, asymmetric knife; p–q, "cloven-hoof" form of lance with sideblade. Length of a about 8.4 cm; rest same scale.

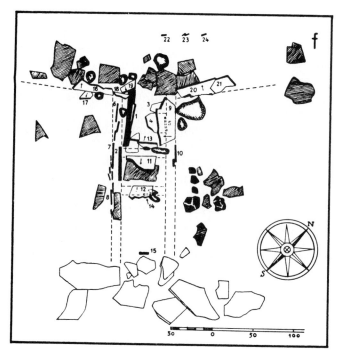

Knuth 1966–1967:203–204, pl. III f.

Fig. 7. Interior arrangement of an isolated Independence II hearth passage (Ruin a, Group II) at Cape Holbæk, Peary Land. The passage is formed by doubled sets of thin vertical slabs with the hearth set in the middle compartment between inclined slabs. Wing pavements are found at the rear of the dwelling. The outer wall of this particular structure was not marked, but it consists of a low ring of gravel or rocks.

termediate between Independence I and Sarqaq and seem closer to Alaska Denbigh than to other known eastern representatives of the Arctic Small Tool tradition (Knuth 1977–1978:40). This relationship is supported by three radiocarbon determinations: 3900 B.C. from Ruin C–3; 2970 B.C. from Ruin F–6; and 2110 B.C. from Ruin A–2 (Knuth 1981:93). However, because these dates are based on sea mammal products (polar bear, whale, and walrus tusk, respectively), materials prone to producing early dates, the excavator's preference for an occupation of about 3000–2200 B.C. might be revised to about 2500–2000 B.C. The presence of round, elliptical, or subsquare dwellings; absence of hearth boxes and passage features; and the early typological relationships of the artifact assemblage support the idea that the Old Nuulliit remains are among the oldest in the Eastern Arctic, predating both Independence I, Sarqaq, and Canadian Pre-Dorset as presently known. For this reason the designation Old Nûgdlît culture rather than Independence I has been assigned.

Finally, in a number of reports on North Greenland, Knuth (1967, 1977–1978) has discussed the matter of the "Shelter Ruins." These small, oval, multitiered stone structures rarely contained diagnostic artifacts and have been thought to be of Paleo-Eskimo origin. Research has determined that these structures date to the four-

534

teenth century A.D. and were used by Neo-Eskimo Thule culture (Knuth 1981). Similar structures occur in Thule context in Canada. In Labrador a variety of structures related to shelter ruins were used by Thule and historic Inuit people through the nineteenth century (S.A. Kaplan 1983).

West Greenland

The paleo-environment of the West Coast is better known than other areas of Greenland, and studies on this subject frequently have been integrated with archeological investigations. Projects have been conducted in palynology (Iversen 1934, 1952–1953; Fredskild 1967, 1967a, 1973); lichenometry (Beschel 1961); geomorphology and glaciology (Brink 1975; Weidick 1968, 1972); and ice-core studies (Hammer et al. 1978; Dansgaard 1980). Deglaciation of coastal zones occurred between 8000 and 4000 B.C., with earliest vegetation dating to 6700 B.C. Pollen spectra show an herb tundra period (6700–4900 B.C.) followed by a willow-grass zone (4900–2500 B.C.) in which climate and vegetation resembled those of the twentieth century. Optimal conditions began by 2500 B.C., when birch immigrated, and thereafter the climate grew warmer and drier than today, peaking at 1600 B.C. After this, cooler and moister conditions prevailed. During A.D. 100–1000, the climate was cool and dry with birch and willow dominating pollen assemblages. Following A.D. 1000 the influence of Norse weed introduction, grazing, and fuel gathering overrides climatic effects in the pollen assemblages. This summary is generally supported by glaciological data that indicate minor glacial advances at 6,000, 4,500, 2,500, 1,500,

Nationalmuseet, Copenhagen: left, L3.12031; right, L3.730.

Fig. 8. Dorset culture ivory sculptures. left, Front and back view of figure of a woman with topknot hairstyle. right, Carving of a man wearing high collar, a part of Dorset dress. left, Height 8.1 cm; Thule district; right, same scale, excavated in a house ruin, Inuarfissuaq, Thule district, 1935–1937.

Knuth 1977–1978:fig. 6.

Fig. 9. Old Nûgdlît culture tent dwelling (ruin C-3) with central hearth between stones a and b. Located on the north coast of Wolstenholme Fjord, Thule District.

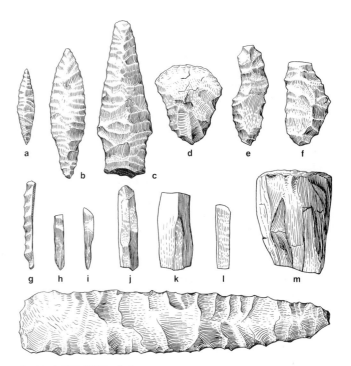

after Knuth 1977–1978:figs. 8–9.

Fig. 10. Old Nûgdlît culture implements. a–b, stemmed endblades; c, stemmed biface; d, end scraper; e, concave side scraper; f, burin; g–i, burin spalls; j–l, microblades; m, microblade core; n, celt. Length of n 27.5 cm; dimensions of a–m not known but all to same scale.

and 500 years ago. Studies of local glaciers show later advances at A.D. 1650, 1880, and in the 1960s. Even more precise data is available from ice-core analyses. The Millcent core (Hammer et al. 1978) contains evidence of both seasonal and yearly temperature variations that can be used to correlate with historical events, oral traditions, and prehistoric archeological evidence (for example, Petersen and Rix 1982).

The West Greenland environment is more favorable and faunally diverse and has greater opportunities for human settlement than does North Greenland because the sea is ice-free many months of the year. Its land game includes caribou, fox, and hare. Musk-ox, wolf, and lemmings are not known to have ever existed there. Sea mammals present in parts of the West Coast include harp, harbor, ringed, hooded, and bearded seals, both small and large whales, polar bear, and, in the northern and southern reaches of the coast, walrus. Land and sea birds are abundant, as are fish, including trout, char, halibut, cod, and many others. While resources are generally abundant, the absence of Eskimo occupation of the West Coast at the time of Norse settlement suggests that seasonal shortages of critical resources, such as seals or caribou, may occur occasionally in different

regions. Variation in the sea-ice distribution could be responsible for local faunal fluctuations that would make occupation by human hunters in these areas difficult or impossible under certain climatic conditions (Vibe 1967, 1970; S.A. Kaplan 1976).

Archeological studies of the Paleo-Eskimo period there began with Solberg's (1907) study of the West Greenland "stone age." However, Mathiassen (1929), famed for his excavation and publication of Neo-Eskimo sites, claimed that these chipped stone remains were not produced by an earlier culture but were a special variant of Neo-Eskimo culture. It was not until Mosegaard's 1948 collection from the Saqqaq (Sarqaq) site arrived in Copenhagen (Meldgaard 1952) and Knuth's early work in Peary Land that a Paleo-Eskimo occupation of West Greenland was recognized. Two distinct Paleo-Eskimo cultures are now known: Sarqaq and Dorset.

• SARQAQ CULTURE   Sarqaq culture is best known from the site of Sermermiut, located at the entrance of Jakobshavn Isfjord. Excavations conducted at this site (Larsen and Meldgaard 1958; Mathiassen 1958) resulted in stratigraphic separation of three components: Sarqaq, Dorset, and Neo-Eskimo. The original dating of Sarqaq there produced an age of 800 B.C. (Mathiassen 1958:22), but a date of 1410 ± 120 B.C. (Fredskild 1967a) conforms better with Sarqaq dates from Disko, Gothåb, Holsteinsborg, and elsewhere. As now established, the

Sarqaq period in West Greenland lasted about 2250–950 B.C. (Fredskild 1973:158; Tauber 1962; Meldgaard 1977:28; Petersen and Rix 1982:86; Gulløv 1982a). Its occupation began at the end of the warm Hypsithermal period and persisted during a period of increasingly colder climates. The Sarqaq distribution (fig. 11) extends from Upernavik in the north to Julianehåb on the west coast, and on the east coast north to the Blosseville region between Ammassalik and Scoresbysund (Meldgaard 1977; Andersen 1981).

Sarqaq collections consist largely of stone tools since these sites do not often contain preserved organic remains (fig. 12). The basic hunting weapon was the bow and arrow tipped with slender triangular stemmed and bipointed endblades with finely serrated edges whose faces range from unground to partially ground forms. Lances may have been either of the thrusting or detachable variety with large tanged endblades and transverse edge sideblades. The lack of harpoon endblades suggests that self-tipped harpoons may have been used. As in Independence I the basic manufacturing tool was the spalled burin, which has an angled tip and is bifacially ground at its distal end. Burin spalls are frequently reworked for small cutting and engraving purposes. Shaft

production employed tanged and lanceolate, concave side scrapers; cutting was done with large asymmetric and symmetric knife blades with pointed or rounded tips, and with smaller triangular transverse blades. Partly ground adz blades functioned as butchering, meat processing, and heavy wood or bone working tools. Hide processing employed triangular end scrapers. Small crescentic-shaped tools and chipped and ground slender stone rods served as bodkins or points. Food was cooked in skin bags with boiling stones and in open fires, and round dish-shaped soapstone lamps provided heat and light. In addition, an unusual form of harpoon was used. Unlike later Paleo-Eskimo harpoons, the Sarqaq form had a pointed proximal end with a line hole near the base and a strongly barbed tip (Meldgaard 1977:29). Lacking a foreshaft or toggling capability, this implement would have been relatively inefficient in capturing marine mammals, particularly in ice edge or breathing hole situations.

Sarqaq technology has a number of distinguishing features. Ninety-five percent of the stone tools are made from a slatelike stone called *ammaaq*. Chert and chalcedony tools are present only in small amounts. Implements are frequently unifacial and sometimes have pronounced longitudinal curvature. Workmanship is delicate, with minute edge serration being a relatively common feature in the projectile point classes. Partial grinding of the tool faces is found on bodkins, small endblades, burins, and bifaces. Also significant for comparison with other early Paleo-Eskimo assemblages is the high frequency (about 50%) of distally ground burins and burin spalls, the presence of delicate stemmed and triangular endblades, and low frequency of microblades (2–3%). Statistically, Sarqaq assemblages are dominated by burins and small endblades. This description presents Disko Bay Sarqaq culture at around 1350 B.C. as known from published sources. Undoubtedly, it will be expanded when information from Sarqaq collections from other places and periods becomes available.

Sarqaq culture sites are found in both outer and inner fjord locations. Although research on Sarqaq and Dorset culture in West Greenland has not been extensive, Sarqaq sites are frequently found on islands and passes near headlands and at the mouths of fjords where seals are plentiful. Such sites sometimes contain linear cobblestone pavements, perpendicular to the shore, with central hearths containing scorched boiling stones. Faunal remains have not been found in these sites, but it appears that they were occupied during the winter and spring. Sites are also found along the inner reaches and at the heads of the fjords at good fishing and caribou hunting locations. One such site, Itinnera (Itivnera) (Meldgaard 1961, 1977:30), dated to 1150 B.C., contained four circular dwelling areas with central slab hearth boxes and a well-preserved faunal collection dominated by caribou, with a small amount of seal and birds. Sarqaq

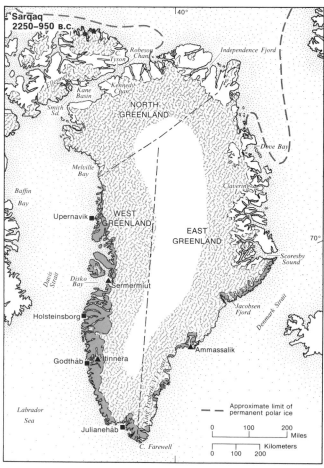

Fig. 11. Distribution of Sarqaq culture in Greenland.

people probably went there in the fall to hunt caribou (cf. Nelleman 1969–1970; Berglund, Grønnow, and Meldgaard 1983). Analysis shows that the Itinnera caribou were smaller in stature than modern animals, like East Greenland caribou, perhaps a result of poor nutrition experienced during the colder and moister conditions that prevailed during late Sarqaq times (Fredskild 1973:220; U. Møhl 1972; Hammer et al. 1978).

• DORSET CULTURE Two phases of Dorset culture are known in West Greenland (Meldgaard 1977). The earliest and most extensive occupation is known primarily from the middle levels at Sermermiut and dates to 550 B.C.-A.D. 150. Early Dorset culture is found throughout West and most of East Greenland, from Upernavik to Ammassalik (fig. 13) (Larsen and Meldgaard 1958; Mathiassen 1958; Fredskild 1967). Sites of a late Dorset culture that was established in the Thule District have not yet been found in West Greenland, but their existence has been signaled by a late Dorset harpoon head from Rittenbank (Larsen and Meldgaard 1958:71) in Disko Bay, and by a wooden figurine from Upernavik (Meldgaard 1977:33).

Early Dorset people in West Greenland employed a technology that differed significantly from their Sarqaq predecessors. In contrast to Sarqaq but in keeping with early Dorset traditions elsewhere, side-notching was a common attribute of their endblades, and the bow and arrow was not used. The scarcity of small triangular points suitable for harpoons—common in Canadian Dorset—indicates that their harpoon heads were "self-tipped" and lacked stone points, like Independence II harpoons. Knives employed a variety of notched endblades, and lances were fitted with lateral chert insets. End scrapers are made in triangular and "eared" forms. Slender burinlike tools with pointed tips, triangular sec-

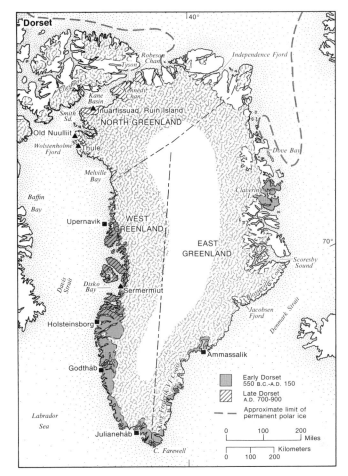

Fig. 13. Distribution of Dorset cultures in Greenland.

tions, and ground lateral edges diverge strongly from Canadian Dorset types, revealing closer ties to Independence II. However, microblades—which are rare in Sarqaq—are the most common find in Dorset assemblages, where they probably served as small knife blades. Small soapstone lamps were used for heat and light, and chipped and ground *ammaaq* celts were set into

a–q, Smithsonian, Dept. of Anthr.: Archeo. Coll.; Nationalmuseet, Copenhagen: r, L7.501; s, L13.520.

Fig. 12. Sarqaq implements. a, concave side scraper; b–d, stemmed endblades; e–f, slate points; g–h, microblades; i, chipped stone drill; j, polished stone awl; k–l, polished burinlike tools; m–q, endblades; r, ivory harpoon head; s, soapstone lamp. Length of p 7.5 cm, rest same scale.

adzes for heavy-duty cutting and chopping. Whereas *ammaaq* was the primary stone material in the Sarqaq tool kit, Dorset peoples chose a variety of colorful fine-grained, glassy flints and chalcedony (fig. 14).

This assemblage is easily distinguished from the North Greenland ones described above. Its isolation from contemporary Canadian Dorset is also evident, and it is different from Sarqaq in many respects, although Sarqaq relationships exist. West Greenland Dorset therefore probably did not develop from Sarqaq alone. Influence from an undiscovered transitional stage similar to Independence II and transitional Pre-Dorset and Dorset cultures in Canada must have occurred.

Little is known about Dorset settlement patterns, house forms, or economy. Mathiassen (1958) suggested West Greenland Dorset may have had a more maritime focus than Sarqaq. During the early part of the Dorset period in Greenland the climate seems to have been cool and moist, as during the late Sarqaq period (Fredskild 1973:234). It is likely that the Dorset expansion into West Greenland brought with it an improved capability for winter ice edge and breathing hole hunting. A similar change had occurred at this time in the central Canadian Arctic.

East Greenland

Very little Paleo-Eskimo archeology has been done in East Greenland, making it one of the least known areas of the Arctic. This region is much colder than the west coast because of the presence of the East Greenland Current and its ice pack for which the minimum permanent extension is off Scoresby Land. Caribou, the dominant land animal (extinct after A.D. 1900), occurred as a stunted form due to the severity of the environment. At various periods and places caribou may have been locally extinct in East Greenland. Marine mammals, birds, and fish are also present though not in the numbers available on the west coast. Geological and botanical conditions have been summarized by Washburn (1965), Weidick (1972), and Fredskild (1973).

Knowledge of Paleo-Eskimo cultures from East Greenland comes from artifacts found in Neo-Eskimo sites, surface collections, and brief survey reports. No project has yet explored the great potential of this region specifically for Paleo-Eskimo research. Dorset implements have been found in Clavering under conditions that raised questions about the possibility of contact between Thule and Dorset groups (Bandi and Meldgaard 1952). Independence I and II have also been found in this region, and Independence II and Sarqaq have been reported from the Blosseville region (Andersen 1981). At Ammassalik both Sarqaq and Dorset materials are found in Neo-Eskimo sites (Mathiassen 1933), again raising the possibility of Dorset-Thule contacts (Meldgaard 1960b).

Summary

The prehistory of Greenland offers a unique opportunity to study cultural development in a marginal northern environment. With a gateway in the High Arctic accessible only to those cultures adapted to its harshest extremes, Greenland has the potential of being a population trap far removed from the origin place of Es-

Fig. 14. Early Dorset implements. a, harpoon head; b–c, chalcedony points; d, chalcedony knife; e, chipped and ground slate point; f–g, notched knives; h, side blade; i, chipped and ground burinlike tool; j, chert lance point; k, chert knife; l–o, end scrapers; p, chalcedony scraper; q, chalcedony core; r–s, small chisels; t–u, chert microblades; v, slate celt; w, polished slate knife; x, polished slate lance point. Length of x 13.9 cm, rest same scale.

kimo societies 1,500 miles to the west in the Bering Sea region. At least twice Eskimo peoples moved into the Eastern Arctic, and each time these population waves reached northwestern Greenland after a short period traveling along a High Arctic corridor north of the Canadian mainland. Once arriving in Greenland Paleo-Eskimo cultures maintained sufficient contact with northern Canadian cultures, both receiving and donating new cultural forms, that their respective cultural developments remained on parallel courses. Closest connections were in the Thule District where Independence I and II peoples shared similar, contiguous, geographic regions with Canadian groups. Paleo-Eskimo cultures of West Greenland, with more extensive open-water hunting conditions, demonstrate more divergent courses from their Canadian counterparts.

Figure 15 summarizes the cultural data on Greenland prehistory. Such a presentation suffers from a number of problems arising when one attempts to interpret, date, and correlate events across disciplinary boundaries. Most apparent is the lack of archeological data on Paleo-Eskimo cultures. More than half the habitable area of the island is completely unknown, including most of the eastern and southwestern coasts. Two culture periods are identified in Disko Bay comprising a small part of a probable 3,000-year Paleo-Eskimo sequence. Only in Peary Land is knowledge complete enough that gaps in the sequence may with some confidence be taken to indicate absence of settlement rather than lack of data. Therefore, a synthesis of Greenland's early settlement has little to build upon.

The proposal by Steensby (1917) that the ethnographic Eskimos and their recent ancestors were members of a maritime-adapted Neo-Eskimo tradition that, in turn, had developed from an earlier land-based stone age Paleo-Eskimo culture has had a continuing effect on subsequent ideas of Eskimo origins. Elaborating a theory expressed by Boas (1888a:39, 1902:525–526), Steensby postulated that the original inhabitants of the North American Arctic and Greenland—the Paleo-Eskimos—had developed from Indian caribou-hunting cultures occupying the forest-tundra boundary west of

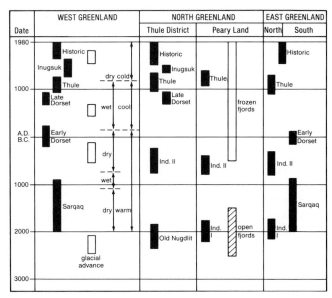

Fig. 15. Paleo-Eskimo culture and environmental history in Greenland, 3000 B.C. to present.

Hudson Bay. Successfully adjusting to life in the Barren Grounds by specializing in caribou and musk-ox like their purported descendants, the Caribou Eskimos, the Paleo-Eskimos soon spread to the arctic coast and from there west to Alaska and east to Greenland. The Greenland movement was thought to have occurred in two streams, one following a High Arctic route known as The Musk-Ox Way into North Greenland and the other a southern track into West Greenland, where a more diversified coastal economy emerged. Despite the absence of evidence of Paleo-Eskimo origins in northern Canada some archeologists have suggested that Pre-Thule (Paleo-Eskimo) Arctic peoples may have been Indians (McGhee 1978), and most employ Steensby's Neo-Eskimo and Paleo-Eskimo terminology to classify prehistoric Arctic cultures. Steensby's recognition of environmental factors distinguishing North and West Greenland cultural adaptations also remains important in interpretations of Greenland's culture history.

Neo-Eskimo Prehistory of Greenland

RICHARD H. JORDAN

Between A.D. 1000 and 1100 the 3,000-year period of Paleo-Eskimo occupation in Greenland was disrupted by two quite different cultural immigrations. The Norse established colonies in the Julianehåb (Qaqortoq) and Godthåb (Nuuk) Districts under the leadership of Eric the Red in A.D. 985. Even though the existing written sources state that the Norse discovered remains of earlier Eskimo occupations, there is no concrete evidence that southwestern Greenland was inhabited during the initial period of Norse colonization (G. Jones 1964: 60). Some time between A.D. 1050 and 1100, new Eskimo populations also arrived in the Thule District in the far northwestern portion of the island. These people, first termed the Thule culture by Mathiassen (1927), possessed a cultural inventory that apparently gave them a competitive advantage over the Late Dorset people in Canada and Greenland. In addition to the smaller sea mammals previously hunted by Paleo-Eskimos, the Thule people engaged in open-water hunting of large whales, thus greatly expanding their resource base. Rapid mobility was facilitated in the summer by kayak and umiak, and in winter by sleds pulled by dogs. Knowledge of the bow and arrow was a great aid in hunting caribou and presumably in sporadic warfare. Finally, the Neo-Eskimo had a flexible social organization that readily fragmented into small colonizing groups during expansionary periods. Not only did these factors result in the replacement of the previous Paleo-Eskimo inhabitants, but also they may have eventually contributed to the Norse demise.

Origin of the Neo-Eskimos in Greenland

The Thule culture developed out of Birnirk culture in North Alaska (Ford 1959; Stanford 1976) and the Punuk culture of the Bering Strait region (Collins 1937) and spread rapidly east to Canada and Greenland during a period of climatic amelioration. This warming period probably allowed the free migration of bowhead whales through Parry Channel in the Canadian Archipelago. These new environmental conditions were exploited by the Thule culture people, who shifted their hunting strategies from spring ice-lead whale hunting to open-water whale hunting in Canada (McGhee 1969–1970). The earliest sites in Canada are thus found in the

High Arctic Archipelago region along the former whale migration corridors, rather than in Central or Low Arctic regions. Population expansion seems to have been very rapid as indicated by the homogeneous nature of tool kits and artifact forms from Alaska to Greenland. However, the clearest evidence for this early Thule population spread is based on the High Arctic distribution of Sicco harpoons (W.E. Taylor 1963a) and other forms that exhibit ornamental multiple spurs and gouged slots for the insertion of chipped stone sideblades. These early Thule harpoons, found at Nuulliit (Nûgdlît) (see "Paleo-Eskimo Cultures of Greenland," footnote *, this vol.) and Ruin Island in the Thule District and indicate that northwestern Greenland was colonized by the Neo-Eskimos before Central and Low Arctic Canada.

North Greenland—Thule District

Most investigators agree that the earliest Neo-Eskimos initially colonized northwestern Greenland, although it is not known whether the first crossing was made from Ellesmere Island across the wider, but more southerly expanses of Kane Basin and Smith Sound, or farther to the north across the narrower Kennedy and Robeson channels. Archeological surveys undertaken in the Lake Hazen and Lady Franklin Bay regions of northern Ellesmere unearthed no evidence for the earliest Thule migrations. Rather, this region seems to have been utilized as a seasonal hunting area by later prehistoric Eskimos who were already well established in Greenland (Maxwell 1960:88). On the western shores of Kane Basin, Schledermann (1978, 1980) has excavated a number of sites that show very close affinities to the Nuulliit and Ruin Island sites in the Thule District. This may indicate that the first colonization of Greenland took place across Kane Basin and Smith Sound.

Most knowledge concerning the culture history of northwestern Greenland is a result of excavations undertaken by Holtved (1944, 1954), who divides the Neo-Eskimo continuum into five cultural periods: Thule, dominant in the twelfth and thirteenth centuries; Early Transitional; Inugsuk, early fourteenth to sixteenth centuries; Late Transitional; and Recent or Historic period. The Thule period finds from Inuarfissuaq site (Inuarfigssuaq) were thought to represent the earliest

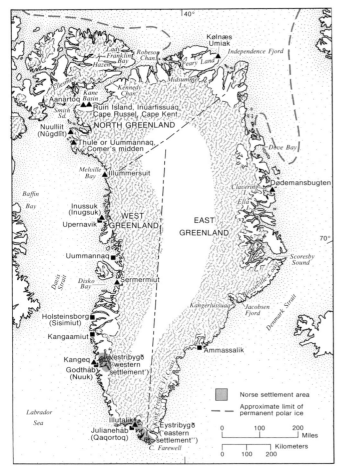

Fig. 1. Neo-Eskimo sites and locations of Norse settlements.

Neo-Eskimo immigrants into Greenland. This was succeeded by the Nuulliit and Ruin Island sites, which Holtved thought resulted from a second wave of migration from Alaska and Canada. This was followed by a transitional phase that culminated with the Inugsuk period, mainly defined by the presence of Norse artifacts. The last two periods involved the absence of Norse material, gradual loss of contact with the west coast of Greenland, and the introduction of European goods in the contact period.

Although Holtved's characterization of the cultural sequence in the Thule District adequately outlines the general historical trends, Jordan's (1979) seriation of harpoon forms suggests that an initial occupation of Greenland followed by in situ development and ultimate isolation from Canadian Eskimo and West Greenland influence is a more accurate assessment of the sequence. The relative site chronology from oldest to youngest seems to be the following: Nuulliit, Ruin Island, Inuarfissuaq, and the Thule or Uummannaq (Ūmánaq) site. Comer's Midden, so prominent in early accounts of Neo-Eskimo culture history, covers the entire time span from the early Thule, Inugsuk, and Historic periods, but is predominantly composed of In-

ugsuk period materials. All these sites except Nuulliit contain Norse material, which was probably obtained indirectly from Eskimo groups in northern West Greenland, though long-distance Norse trading voyages to the Thule District cannot be entirely ruled out (McGhee 1982a).

An accurate assessment of absolute chronology is still not entirely possible, even though a number of radiocarbon dates have been published (Tauber 1973). Four radiocarbon dates from Nuulliit on wood and walrus ivory fall between A.D. 910 ± 100 and 940 ± 100. Those from Ruin Island on walrus ivory and driftwood date A.D. 800 ± 100 to 830 ± 100, and A.D. 1020 ± 100 to 1070 ± 100 respectively (Tauber 1973:105–106). All but the eleventh-century dates may be too early since culturally related sites just across Kane Basin on Ellesmere Island have been dated to this general time period. Schledermann (1980) and Schledermann and Mc-Cullough (1980) have published a series of consistent radiocarbon dates that indicate that initial colonization of Ellesmere Island and Greenland by Thule people took place not much earlier than A.D. 1050 to 1100. Though continuous occupation undoubtedly persisted until the present, the sites excavated by Holtved (1944) are early in the sequence, only dating as late as the fifteenth century.

The relationship between the Late Dorset and early Thule populations is not completely understood. While Late Dorset material has been recovered from Neo-Eskimo midden deposits and houses at Inuarfissuaq and Ruin Island, there have been no isolated Dorset settlements excavated in northwest Greenland though they most certainly exist. The presence of Dorset materials in a Thule context does not necessarily mean direct contact between these two different Eskimo cultures. Dorset materials here probably result from finds inadvertently incorporated in the sods of Thule houses and middens on sites formerly occupied by Dorset peoples. In any case, the limited geographic distribution of Late Dorset materials, clearly related to Canadian Late Dorset, is confined to the Thule District and northern Disko Bay (Qeqertarsuup Tunua) (Larsen and Meldgaard 1958:71) and argues for a relatively short period of occupation. This Dorset colonization may have preceded the Thule by a few centuries. If so, it may be that some Late Dorset groups were forced out of the Canadian High Arctic by the Thule immigrants only to be overrun by them in Greenland. Dorset movement southward along the West Greenland coast might have been prevented by the Norse, who hunted as far north as Disko Bay.

While this interpretation remains speculative, there does seem to be a complete break in the cultural sequence in the Thule District with very little evidence for initial transmission of traits between these two cultures. Yet the Nuulliit site has produced a number of *541* technological items probably derived from the Canadian Dorsets. These include bone or ivory sled shoes, snow knives, and inferentially the domed snowhouse, the use of soapstone for cooking pots and lamps and, with less certainty, the intensive use of meteoritic iron for endblades and knives (fig. 2a). The presence of these traits in early Thule sites in Canada where the Dorsets were first encountered suggests that Thule groups in Greenland had already been influenced by the Late Dorset people. Evidence for later Dorset-Thule contact is present at the Thule site, which most likely dates to the fourteenth and fifteenth centuries (Holtved 1944; Jordan 1979). Here, flat open socket harpoon forms appear to be direct copies from the Dorset (fig. 2c–e). The origin of this new influence is not known, but it may have come from northeast Greenland where there is possible evidence for blending of relict Dorset and Thule cultures (Bandi and Meldgaard 1952).

Resources and Cultural Adaptations

The initial colonization of Greenland required no major alterations in cultural adaptations since the Thule District is essentially an extension of Arctic conditions stretching across the polar regions from Alaska through Canada. Despite its northerly geographic location between 76° and 81° north latitude, the Thule District is rich in faunal resources that can be exploited with open-water and ice-hunting techniques. As in many other Arctic areas, the ringed seal formed the backbone of

the economy and was probably hunted in all seasons. Bearded and harp seals were important during the summer. Bowhead whales also migrate into the area during late June or early July and were intensively hunted by the earliest Neo-Eskimos. The polar bear and walrus were particularly important in the Thule District. The most important land mammal was the caribou, which was hunted at the heads of fjords at least during the early cultural periods. While the musk-ox is not found in the Thule District, it was apparently hunted in northern Ellesmere Island by prehistoric groups from Greenland (Maxwell 1960). Other important resources include migratory bird populations, especially eiders, murres, and dovekies, which nest in great profusion on rocky islands and steep cliffs. Locally available fish resources include Arctic char and the Atlantic salmon. Thus the Thule District contains an abundant and diverse fauna that could be exploited by Arctic-adapted hunters throughout the year. Moreover, in the twentieth century it is a region much richer in resources than the Canadian High Arctic through which the Neo-Eskimos spread.

Neo-Eskimo sites from northwestern Greenland exhibit a pattern common throughout the Eastern Arctic. Winter settlements were scattered throughout the Thule District at good sea mammal hunting locations at the mouths of fjords, headlands, and outer islands. They range in size from three house ruins at Cape Russel to 60 at Nuulliit, though at the latter site all the houses may not have been inhabited simultaneously. These

Nationalmuseet, Copenhagen: a, L3.773; b, L3.787; c, L3.2158; d, L3.1252; e, L3.12901; f, L3.151; g, L3.8253; h, L3.575; i, L3.269; j, L3.2714; k, L3.2395; l, L3.1671; m, L3.1267; n, L3.1250.

Fig. 2. Neo-Eskimo artifacts from the Thule District. a, Knife with iron blade and whalebone handle; b, side prong from a bird dart, walrus ivory; c–d, harpoon heads, antler (a–d from Inuarfissuaq, Inglefield Land); e, harpoon head, walrus ivory from Nuulliit; f, toy oil lamp of soapstone from Cape Kent, Inglefield Land; g, figure of a whale(?), walrus ivory from Thule or Uummannaq; h, fishing lure, walrus ivory from Inuarfissuaq; i, arrowhead of caribou antler from Cape Kent; j, fragment of a wooden bow from Aanartoq, Inglefield Land; k, scraper of walrus ivory from Ruin Island off Inuarfissuaq; l, mounting for dog traces, whalebone; m, needlecase of walrus ivory; n, fragment of a sledge runner of whalebone (l–n from Inuarfissuaq). Length of a, 13.3 cm, b–i same scale; length of j, 21.5 cm, k–n same scale.

542

have been interpreted as nuclear family dwellings and were constructed of rock and sod, framed with whale ribs and driftwood (fig. 3). A sunken entrance tunnel projected from the front of the house, and a raised sleeping platform was constructed in the rear of the house interior. Floors and entrances were generally paved with flat stones. Some houses also exhibit multiple rooms or entrance tunnels, indicating that more than one nuclear family may have inhabited some of them. The earliest ruins also have a separate kitchen area built into the front of the house.

The material culture of the early Neo-Eskimo primarily reflects the subsistence and domestic pursuits of hunting, fishing, butchering, cooking, hide preparation, and tool manufacturing and repair (fig. 2). Equipment associated with sea mammal hunting during different seasons includes harpoons with a wide variety of bone, antler, or ivory heads, sealskin floats, ice picks, wound plugs, towing handles, and throwing boards for bladder darts. Birds were taken with side-barbed darts, blunt arrows, bolas, or gull hooks. Fish were caught either with hooks or with fish decoys and leisters. Terrestrial mammals were hunted with arrows tipped with bone

points. Composite bows were constructed of wood, baleen, and sinew. All large game was dispatched and butchered with a variety of lances and knives. Sled runners and shoes, trace buckles, and whip shanks provide evidence for dog-drawn sleds. Kayak and umiak boat fragments have been unearthed in early period sites. Tools for house construction consist of bone snow knives, bone mattocks for cutting sod, and bone and ivory adzes. Tools associated with women's activities include the ulu, bone scrapers, needles, needlecases, hide thimbles, and thimble holders. Cooking was done with oval or rectangular soapstone pots and semilunar and oval lamps. Items of clothing, such as gutskin jackets, birdskin jackets and trousers, sealskin boots, and bearskin mittens have been recovered from the Nuulliit site. Decorative or ornamental objects include combs; beads of soapstone, amber, and antler; and ivory pendants in the form of chains or human figures. Evidence for adult games includes the *ajagaq* (the Eskimo ring and pin game) and carved gambling pieces or amulets in the form of whales, seals, bears, dogs, foxes, and birds. Children's toys were represented by small replicas of harpoons, lances, bows, arrows, sled runners, umiaks, kayaks, ulus, snow knives, cooking pots, and lamps. With the exception of the bow and arrow, kayak, and leister, all the above items of material culture continued to be used by the Neo-Eskimo in the Thule District until the historic period. (For a detailed discussion of formal, functional, and geographic variations in Greenland Eskimo material culture, see Birket-Smith 1924; Holm 1914; Holtved 1962, 1967; Kroeber 1900; Porsild 1915; Steensby 1910; Thalbitzer 1914–1941; VanStone 1972.)

West Greenland and the Inugsuk Culture

The culture history of West Greenland is of particular interest because it is along this vast coast that native North Americans first encountered Europeans. However, there still exists a good deal of debate concerning the nature of Eskimo-Norse interaction, the degree of Norse influence on the Eskimo, if any, and the role the Eskimos played in the collapse of the Norse settlements between A.D. 1350 and 1450–1500 (Gad 1971–1982, 1; Holtved 1944; Ingstad 1966a; G. Jones 1964; Jordan 1979; Krogh and Albrethsen 1967; McGovern 1979, 1980, 1981; McGovern and Jordan 1982; Mathiassen 1931).

Archeological evidence for some form of Norse-Eskimo contact is certainly plentiful as most Eskimo sites along the west coast have produced Norse material. Mathiassen, the principal investigator of these sites, has published results that cover the entire West Greenland coast: the Upernavik District (1931a), Disko Bay region (1934, 1958), the Kangaamiut (Kangâmiut) area (1931), 543

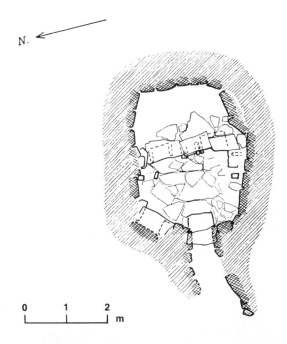

N.

0   1   2
|___|___| m

Holtved 1944:18–24.
Fig. 3. Plan of winter house 4, Cape Kent, Thule District. The dimensions of the room are 2.5 by 3.5 meters; a 1.5-meter-long sunken entrance projects from the front of the house. The floor was paved with stone; the lower portion of the walls were stone, the upper portion and roof probably whalebone or driftwood covered with sod. The platform at the back of the house, about 25 centimeters higher than the floors, had 2 built-in storage recesses at the ends of the front edge. Two sets of vertical stone slabs in front of the platform probably served to support soapstone lamps, while an additional storage recess was just to the left of the entrance tunnel.

and Julianehåb District (Mathiassen and Holtved 1936). Even though these publications shed light on Eskimo culture history and Norse-Eskimo contact, they provide no definitive understanding of Eskimo-Norse interaction. Mathiassen, however, never wavered from his conviction that Eskimo culture was greatly influenced by the Norse and that the Norse settlements were ultimately overrun by the Eskimos.

Data from excavations of Eskimo houses and middens at Inussuk (Inugsuk), an island located in the Upernavik District, first led Mathiassen (1931a:275) to define the Inugsuk culture as "a special Greenland culture . . . closely related to the Thule culture and a further development of it." Of all tool types recovered from Inussuk, 89 percent are also found in the Thule culture. Mathiassen (1931a:300) adds that "the Inugsuk culture must be looked upon as a later phase of the Thule culture influenced by mediaeval Norse culture" and that the early inhabitants of Inussuk "lived contemporaneously with the Norsemen in South Greenland . . . from the beginning of the thirteenth to the fifteenth century" (1931a:294).

The dating of Inugsuk period sites is obviously vital in evaluating Eskimo-Norse interaction. Only four radiocarbon dates from two Neo-Eskimo sites are available, and none of them provides the critical chronological information. Dates from the Inugsuk layers of the Sermermiut midden in Disko Bay are A.D. 1010±120 and 1240±120 (Mathiassen 1958). Based on the nature of the artifact assemblage and the harpoon forms, both these dates appear to be too early. A mid- to late fourteenth-century occupation of this site is more likely (Jordan 1979). The second site, Kangeq, lies on the outer coast just north of Godthåbsfjord and about 50 kilometers east of the Norsemen's Western Settlement (Vestribygð). The two radiocarbon determinations from this site are A.D. 1330±70 and 1460±60, which date the Eskimo occupation either to the time of the Western Settlement collapse around A.D. 1350 or to a century or more later (Gulløv 1982b). Whether there are earlier Inugsuk occupations in the vicinity of the Norse Western Settlement is unknown. Thus, it is still uncertain whether the Eskimo and Norse occupations of the Godthåb District were contemporaneous, which may have led to direct competition, or whether the Eskimos were able to move into this region because it was no longer occupied by the Norse.

It is almost certain, however, that Neo-Eskimo groups occupied more northerly regions of West Greenland at an earlier time. Norse artifacts in Eskimo sites with harpoon forms that are older in the Thule District than in West Greenland indicate that Eskimo expansion across Melville Bay probably occurred about A.D. 1200 and spread at least as far south as Disko Bay. This interpretation is supported by excavations at Illummersuit (Igdlummerssuit), a late Thule/early Inugsuk period

winter village on Tuttulissuaq (Tugtuligssuaq) Peninsula, a small ice-free region on the southern shores of Melville Bay (Jacobsen et al. 1980). If this tentative dating is correct it means that Eskimos and Norsemen probably contacted each other about A.D. 1200 in the Disko Bay region, since Norse sagas suggest this area was part of their northern hunting grounds, called the Norðrseta. Given the poor chronological placement of most West Greenland Inugsuk sites, it is not yet possible to decide whether Norse artifacts in Eskimo middens result from trading or raiding or whether they were obtained from Norse sites after abandonment.

Items that have been recovered at Inussuk and other West Greenland sites, upon which Mathiassen based his argument, fall into two categories—Norse-manufactured items and presumed copies of Norse material. The first category includes checker pieces and chessmen, soapstone spindle whorls, wooden spoon cases, fragments of Christian church bells, wooden fragments with Norse designs, sandstone whetstones, and iron and copper fragments (fig. 4). With the exception of iron, and possibly copper, used for endblades and knives, none of these items can be considered integral to Eskimo economy or technology.

Items that may have been Norse-inspired, according to Mathiassen (1931a), include ornamental bodkins and spoons, baleen saws and daggers, coopered tubs, knives with iron insets, and carved wooden dolls that faithfully

Nationalmuseet, Copenhagen: a, L4.885; b. L15.626; c, L3.610; d, L4.4077.
Fig. 4. Inugsuk period artifacts from West Greenland and the Thule District. a, Stave of a wooden barrel from Inussuk, Upernavik district; b, spindle whorl with runes, soapstone, Norse from Illutalik, Julianehåb District; c, chessman of turned whalebone, Norse from Inuarfissuaq, Inglefield Land; d, top, a whalebone disk mounted on a wooden stem, Norse from Inussuk. Length of a, 14.2 cm; rest same scale.

reproduce Norse clothing styles. The last certainly indicates direct contact and careful observation of the Norse (Gulløv 1982b). However, it is equally likely that the other items were independently invented or possibly introduced through direct or indirect contact with the Late Dorset people (Jordan 1979).

Although the Inugsuk culture reveals strong continuities with earlier sites in the Thule District, there are certain cultural ecological adjustments to Low Arctic environments and subtle changes in artifact form through time, which begin to differentiate West Greenland from Thule District cultures. For example, subsistence techniques underwent modification along the West Greenland coast. Seal ice-hunting techniques eventually disappeared south of the Holsteinsborg (Sisimiut) region with a concomitant improvement and elaboration of kayak-hunting techniques. Ringed seal hunting declined with an intensification of harp, hooded, and common seal hunting. Polar bear hunting declined as these animals become increasingly scarce south of Disko Bay. Cod and halibut fishing increased in importance, as did the procurement of a wider variety of bird species (Degerbøl et al. in Mathiassen 1931:134–139; Degerbøl 1936:131–133). Similarly, dog traction also disappeared south of Holsteinsborg, which is also another obvious adjustment to more southerly conditions.

Settlement patterns and house forms remain virtually unchanged until the historic period. The Eskimos continued to reside in clustered, nuclear family sod houses at good sea mammal hunting locations. Ideational systems, as reflected in art forms, show no major changes with the exception of the discontinuance of certain incised geometric motifs and an increased emphasis on the sexual organs of wooden dolls during the Inugsuk and Historic periods. Religious practices, on the other hand, do alter somewhat in Greenland at least by the mid-fifteenth century (Mathiassen and Holtved 1936:103–113; Meldgaard 1953; Rosing 1979). Interment in caves and rock crevices and the subsequent natural mummification supplemented the general practice of constructing stone cairns over the deceased. Rosing (1979) has described a particularly dramatic and extraordinarily well-preserved series of female mummies from the Uummannaq District, which were placed under a rock overhang and retained their clothing perfectly intact. The seal and caribou skins that covered the deceased have been radiocarbon dated to A.D. 1460 ± 50. While the origins of this practice remain unknown, it is in no way influenced by either pagan or Christian Norse practices.

Even though the Norsemen inhabited West Greenland's southern coast for nearly five centuries, Eskimo culture remained essentially unaffected. Despite the twin challenges of possible conflict with Norsemen and the need for new cultural ecological adjustments to Low Arctic environments, the Eskimos eventually occupied the entire West Greenland coast from Melville Bay to Cape Farewell, while the Norse culture ultimately collapsed sometime during the fifteenth century.

East Greenland

The coastal environment in East Greenland is not nearly so hospitable as in West Greenland. There are long stretches of coast with steep terrain that make settlement difficult. Nor is there nearly the number of continuous fjords and island skerries, which make for good hunting grounds and calmer waters. But most important, the climate and environment are dominated by the East Greenland Current with its frigid waters and permanent pack ice. Consequently the climate is much harsher than along the southwestern coast, which is influenced by the Irminger Current, a mixture of East Greenland and much warmer Gulf Stream waters.

These environmental conditions, which are radically different from those of West Greenland, have undoubtedly contributed to the linguistic and cultural divergence so evident between modern East and West Greenland populations. Relatively mild climatic conditions may have promoted one or more population expansions and periods of increased communication both across North Greenland and around Cape Farewell. Alternatively, colder climates and poorer hunting conditions may have contributed to population contraction and isolation. These factors all suggest a long and complex culture history in East Greenland.

Because of the lack of modern archeological investigations, a coherent cultural historical framework is not yet possible. At least five conflicting outlines of East Greenland prehistory and cultural development have been presented. The first, proposed by Mathiassen (1933, 1936a), states that the Inugsuk culture rounded Cape Farewell in the second half of the fourteenth century and gradually occupied the East Greenland coast as far north as Scoresby Sound. Larsen (1934) agrees with this general formulation but extends the Inugsuk culture even farther north to the Clavering Island region by the early sixteenth century. At some unspecified later time, these people encountered Thule groups who spread across North Greenland and formed the distinctive East Greenland "Mixed Culture." Bandi and Meldgaard (1952) assert that the Thule expansion across North Greenland occurred much earlier, during the thirteenth century, and met Late Dorset populations in northeast Greenland, forming a Paleo- and Neo-Eskimo "Blended Culture." Laughlin and Jørgensen (1956) suggest that there have been two historically discreet Neo-Eskimo populations in East Greenland. Their studies, based on East Greenland skeletons from the northeastern and southeastern coasts, indicate that there were two morphologically distinct populations that never combined.

This would indicate separate population expansions from the north and from the south with little, if any, contact between them. And finally, Gulløv (1982) suggests a single population movement into East Greenland from the north, which ultimately rounded Cape Farewell from the east during the early eighteenth century. These East Greenlanders eventually replaced the former West Greenland populations along the southwestern coasts. Thus, there is very little consensus among archeologists and physical anthropologists concerning the prehistory of the East Greenland Eskimos. The following outline should be considered provisional.

The earliest possible evidence for population expansion across North Greenland comes from a single radiocarbon date of A.D. 1180 ± 100 on dwarf willow from a presumed Thule stone tent ring near Midsummer Lake (Knuth 1967). The distinctive Thule-2 harpoon forms, presumably dating from the twelfth to fourteenth century, have also been recovered from a stone tent ring in North Greenland and from a grave on Ella Island in Northeast Greenland (Glob 1935; Knuth 1967). Dramatic evidence of this northern population movement, perhaps as late as the fifteenth century, comes from the discovery of a complete umiak or large open skin boat (Knuth 1951) in an area of permanently frozen seas (fig. 5). Small Thule and Inugsuk groups may have occasionally traversed the forbidding stretches of Peary Land both on foot and by boat any time between the twelfth and fifteenth centuries. These groups may have originated in northern Ellesmere Island or the northwestern portion of Greenland.

Bandi and Meldgaard (1952) have suggested that these Thule groups encountered Late Dorset people and that technological acculturation occurred. Their evidence is based on the excavation of a single house complex at Dødemansbugt on Clavering Island in which Dorset chipped stone material was found in direct association with Thule slate implements. Organic remains were rare and unfortunately contained no harpoon heads. Although their interpretation may be open to question, there still remains the distinct possibility that the association of these chipped and ground stone implements indicate that the relations between these two Eskimo groups were more peaceful in Northeast Greenland than elsewhere in the Eastern Arctic. Moreover, possible Dorset influence may also be detected in modern Ammassalik bone and ivory carvings. These are either miniature anthropomorphic and zoomorphic inlays on utilitarian tools, or the bizarre tupilaks (Greenlandic *tupilak*, pl. *tupilaat*), starvation figures composed of human and animal features sculptured in the round (Meldgaard 1960b).

During the sixteenth and seventeenth centuries nearly the entire East Greenland coast was populated by Inugsuk groups. Relatively small, circular semisubterranean houses clustered in small settlements are found

Nationalmuseet, Copenhagen.

Fig. 5. The Kølnæs umiak. The bottom framework, about 9.6 meters long, is viewed from the northwest. The eastern side is in place as found, while the western side, found collapsed on top of the bottom, has here been removed (Knuth 1951). Excavated in 1949, eastern Peary Land.

at good sea mammal hunting locations along nearly the entire length of East Greenland. Excavations of these settlements have been conducted from King Frederik VI Coast in the extreme south to Clavering Island in the far northeast—a distance of approximately 2,000 kilometers (Degerbøl 1936; Glob 1935; D.M. Johnson 1933; Larsen 1934, 1938; Mathiassen 1933, 1934a, 1936a; Richter 1934). Ringed seals formed the most important subsistence resource, though the high percentage of whale bone artifacts and quantities of baleen found in some middens indicate that large whales were still actively pursued. The house forms, the small clustered winter settlements, and the associated harpoons and other items of material culture are nearly identical to the Inugsuk culture found in West Greenland and the Thule District. Small quantities of Norse artifacts, found in these houses and middens, include a few fragments of iron and bell metal. Again the presence of Norse artifacts associated with Eskimo remains is another line of continuity with the Inugsuk culture.

Unfortunately there is not a single radiocarbon date from any of these East Greenland sites so that it remains virtually impossible to judge whether these East Greenland cultures originated in West Greenland and spread north (Mathiassen 1933, 1936a), or whether they originated in North Greenland and spread south (Gulløv 1982). It is also possible that there were two population expansions from the north and south that contacted each other in Northeast Greenland (Larsen 1934) or remained isolated from each other (Laughlin and Jørgensen 1956). It is not yet possible to decide which of these outlines of population expansion and cultural interaction is correct.

Protohistoric and Historic Periods

Since about 1600, Eskimo culture in Greenland has been altered by changes in both the physical and social environment. A severe period of climatic deterioration caused a drastic reduction in the population size and geographic distribution in East Greenland and a breakdown of communication between the Thule District and West Greenland. In addition, contact with European whalers along the West Greenland coast in the seventeenth century and with missionaries in the early eighteenth century (Bobé 1952; Gad 1971–1982, 1; Gulløv and Kapel 1979) brought about marked social and economic changes.

Events in the Thule District culminated in the complete isolation of the Polar Eskimo, the present inhabitants. Ellesmere Island and most of North Greenland were both abandoned, and communication ceased across Melville Bay. There were also changes in subsistence pursuits, technology, and house form. The distinctive pear-shaped stone house was adopted sometime after the 1500s (Holtved 1944). Surprisingly, use of the bow and arrow, leister, and kayak all disappeared; caribou hunting and open-water sealing were discontinued until these items and hunting practices were reintroduced in the 1860s by a small group of Eskimos from Baffin Island (Gilberg 1974–1975).

In West Greenland, the nucleated settlement pattern of numerous small houses was abandoned in the late seventeenth or early eighteenth century in favor of a more dispersed communal or longhouse pattern (Gulløv 1982; Petersen 1973, 1974–1975). Whale hunting may have diminished in importance, dog traction was abandoned south of Holsteinsborg, while open-water kayak techniques were refined, and the harp and common seals replaced the ringed seal in importance though the latter species remained dominant north of Disko Bay (Møhl 1979). The communal house pattern also appeared on the east coast of Greenland about A.D. 1700.

It was along this coast that the Neo-Eskimo fared the worst. East Greenland became nearly depopulated during the nineteenth century as a result of a severely deteriorating climate, which restricted sea mammal hunting and contributed to the collapse of caribou populations (Vibe 1967). The only settlement to survive this period was Ammassalik, whose inhabitants had become as isolated as their distant relatives in the Thule District.

Rather grim archeological evidence of this process comes from the Kangerlussuaq region where Larsen (1938) found several examples of communal houses that were partitioned to conserve heat as populations declined. One sod house from Jacobsen Fjord had been reduced twice until the final product was little more than a tiny hovel at the end of the entrance tunnel. In another house in the same fjord, a skeleton was found at the rear of the house. The man had evidently died on the sleeping platform and had not received the benefit of any form of burial (Larsen 1938:27–31, figs. 14–17). Cultural and biological responses to these conditions may have included blood feuds, competition over scarce resources, increased witchcraft, population shifts, and starvation. Yet, in the face of these disastrous conditions, or perhaps because of them, artistic styles and the elaboration and decoration of material objects flourished, as the Eskimos increasingly sought supernatural solutions to counteract their deteriorating subsistence resource base.

Summary of Neo-Eskimo History

The present Greenland Eskimos are the descendants of Thule culture people who initially colonized the Thule District during the late eleventh or early twelfth century. Primarily adapted to hunting sea mammals, including large baleen whales, they entered Greenland after having spread across the Canadian Archipelago during the period of climatic warming. For a century or two their culture was virtually identical to the early Thule in Alaska and Canada.

Some time during the late twelfth and early thirteenth centuries, they expanded south across Melville Bay to the west coast. Here they encountered the Norsemen whose cultural remains are found in nearly all Neo-Eskimo sites. This new phase has been termed Inugsuk, but the degree of Norse influence on Eskimo culture as well as the nature of Eskimo-Norse interaction remain uncertain. By the late fifteenth century, the Inugsuk culture occupied the entire West Greenland coast as far south as Cape Farewell. During the late seventeenth or early eighteenth century Eskimo social organization and residential patterns changed fundamentally as families began residing in communal houses, both in East and West Greenland.

Thule groups also expanded across the formidable expanses of North Greenland perhaps as early as the twelfth century. Along the northeast Greenland coast they may have merged with Late Dorset culture, indicating that relations were a good deal more congenial than in the Thule District, where the Dorset people had apparently been overrun. Population expansion and occupation of nearly the entire East Greenland coast occurred during the sixteenth to seventeenth centuries. Although these groups are initially closely related to the Inugsuk culture of West Greenland and the Thule District, the lack of absolute dates on any of these sites renders any exact outline of population movement and cultural interaction speculative.

The last few centuries reversed this expansionary pattern. Northernmost Greenland and Ellesmere Island were abandoned, and communication ceased between the Polar Eskimo and the West Greenlanders. The East Greenland coasts were depopulated very rapidly during the nineteenth century, leaving a single struggling settlement at Ammassalik. The arrival of the Norwegian missionary, Hans Egede, in 1721 marks the beginning of the modern period with the recolonization of Greenland by Scandinavians who have increasingly transformed Eskimo culture.

History of Norse Greenland

INGE KLEIVAN*

Shortly before the year 1000 southwest Greenland, which at that time was unpopulated, was settled from Iceland. This Norse population had disappeared by the time European expeditions and whalers came to Greenland in the sixteenth and seventeenth centuries, and the hope of finding some Norsemen alive and leading them back to Christianity was one of the most important motivations for the Danish-Norwegian colonization of West Greenland in 1721.

The Norse Culture

The Norse settlement in Greenland was the final phase of the Scandinavian expansion that had started before the Viking period. According to the Icelandic sagas, *Eiríks Saga Rauða* ('The Saga of Eric the Red') and *Grænlendinga Saga* ('The Greenlanders' Saga'), Eric the Red (*Eiríkr Rauði*), who was born in Norway but emigrated to Iceland, was exiled, and sailed out looking for a country rumors of which had circulated in Iceland. This is supposed to have taken place in 982. The sagas were not written down until the beginning of the thirteenth century and the details may not be reliable. Eric investigated the country he found and in order to make it sound attractive, he gave it an appealing name: Greenland (Krogh 1967:141–143). Indeed, the green fjords of southwest Greenland, where no domestic animals had ever pastured, must have been attractive to farmers from Iceland. It is related that 15 years before the Christian faith became law in Iceland, which would make it about 985, Eric sailed from Iceland with 25 heavily loaded ships, of which only 14 ever reached Greenland (Krogh 1967:143). In the following years many settlers arrived who took up residence in two large fjord complexes: Eystribygð 'eastern settlement' in the Julianehåb (Qaqortoq) area and Vestribygð 'western settlement' in the Godthåb (Nuuk) area. The Europeans who settled in Greenland after the Norse settlements had been given up for a long time wrongly believed that the eastern settlement was to be found on the east coast (Gad 1971–1982, 2:90, 400–401).

Most of the farms and all the churches were situated near the coast, but a few farms can be characterized as inland farms (Vebæk 1943). Topographical and archeological research has discovered the ruins of about 250 farms in the Eastern Settlement and 80 in the Western Settlement (Krogh 1982:65).That is more than is recorded in the written sources, but all the farms were hardly in use at the same time and probably some small high-lying farms were populated only in the summer. The written sources mention 12 churches, a monastery, and a nunnery, each with a church, in the Eastern Settlement, and four churches in the Western Settlement. However, ruins of 17 churches have been found in the eastern settlement and three in the western settlement (Krogh 1982a).

It has proved difficult to identify the churches and other place-names mentioned in the sources. One locality is quite sure: a bishop's grave found in Igaliku, which therefore must be identical with Garðar where the cathedral was situated (Nørlund and Roussell 1930) (see "Greenland Eskimo: Introduction," fig. 2, this vol.). Some other place-names may be identified from this point of departure (E.L. Andersen 1982).

Dwellings, stalls, and storerooms were built of peat and stones; some living rooms were lined with wood. Most of the churches were built of wood protected by walls of peat and stones, but some were real stone churches (fig. 1). The history of the construction of the farms in Greenland can not yet be described in detail since most of the excavated farms are from the later period of the Norse settlement. The first farms may have been longhouses, which consisted of a common room for all activities. Most of the later farms consisted of a number of detached buildings, but in one type of farm complex all the buildings were built attached with the cow shed in the middle. The peat walls of a detached cow shed had to be up to five meters high in order to protect the animals from the winter cold (Jansen 1972:80–99; Krogh 1982:73–95). Sheep and goats wandered around freely most of the year; pigs were rarely kept. Only a few bones of horses have been found. This must be seen in connection with the fact that most of the excavated animal bones are remnants of food, and the church had forbidden eating horses because of their cultic role in the old religion. The domesticated animals also included dogs (Degerbøl in Vebæk 1943:114; Hatting 1982).

Hay for winter fodder was gathered in the fjords and harvested on the home-fields, which were protected by

*Translated from Danish by Charles Jones and I. Kleivan.

Nationalmuseet, Copenhagen: 29870.

Fig. 1. The well-preserved Norse church at Hvalsey (Qaqortukulooq), probably built about 1300 and of the type built in Norway after 1250. The walls are of stone, and the roof was probably made of driftwood covered with turf. Photograph by Poul Nørlund, 1932.

dikes near each farm where animals were not allowed to graze. In some cases irrigation systems were constructed to bring water to the fields from lakes and rivers (Meldgaard 1965:40–41, 80–81; Krogh 1982:96–101).

In *Konungs Skuggsjá* ('The King's Mirror') written in Norway in the middle of the thirteenth century it was told that the farmers in Greenland raised cattle and sheep in large numbers and made butter and cheese in great quantities (Krogh 1967:52). Although grain cultivation was attempted, probably grain could only rarely ripen in this climate. On big farms in the Eastern Settlement millstones have been found, which may have been used for grain grown in Greenland (Krogh 1982:103–105).

The settlers were not only farmers but also to a great extent hunters and fishermen. Most of the animal bones found in archeological excavations of the middens do not come from domesticated animals but from various kinds of game, especially seals (Degerbøl 1936a; Møhl 1982).

The Norse settlers made trips to the northern part of the west coast in search of coveted animal products. Among their most important export commodities were tusks of walrus and narwhal and hides from seals, walruses, caribou, arctic foxes, and polar bears. They imported luxury foods such as grain and salt and other consumer goods such as iron and timber; they were also able to extract bog ore and make their own iron (Nielsen 1936).

The early Norsemen of Greenland traveled west to North America, which according to *Eiríks Saga Rauða* was discovered by Eric's son Leif the Lucky (*Leifr inn Heppni Eiríksson*), but according to *Grœnlendinga Saga* by Bjarni Herjólfsson. A Norse settlement from about 1000 has been excavated at L'Anse aux Meadows, Newfoundland (A.S. Ingstad 1977). The locality is probably situated in the Vínland of the sagas, whereas Markland is part of Labrador and Helluland is Baffin Island.

Objects of Norse origin have also been found in the Thule area in northwest Greenland (Holtved 1944:298–302, 1945) and in Arctic Canada, especially on the east coast of Ellesmere Island (Schledermann 1980, 1982). The question of whether the Norsemen themselves were ever that far north has not been answered with certainty.

Christianity was quickly accepted in Greenland, and the first church in the New World was built about the year 1000 at Brattahlíð (Qassiarsuk) where Eric had settled. By excavating the church and the churchyard, which both probably fell into disuse in the eleventh century, the remains of 144 persons have been found. The skeletons show that these Norsemen were tall people with an average height for women of 160 centimeters and for men of 173 centimeters (Krogh 1967:42). In 1126 Greenland received its first bishop, and a cathedral was built at Garðar (Nørlund and Roussell 1930).

As in Iceland, there was probably no real head of the state, but the chiefs on the big farms were powerful by virtue of the many men they employed, and as in Iceland the Norse society in Greenland was probably divided into two classes: freemen and bondsmen. Every summer people gathered to decide legal disputes; these meetings were also the occasions for various kinds of social activities. First the Althing probably met at Brattahlíð, later at Garðar. In 1261, a Norwegian delegation returned to King Hákon from a visit in Greenland to report that the Norse had agreed to pay taxes to the Norwegian Crown (Gad 1964, 1971–1982, 1:120–121), but this contact seems to have been of little importance at the time. For posterity, it had serious consequences because Norway including Greenland from the fourteenth century was united with Denmark, and Greenland remained part of Denmark when the union between Denmark and Norway was dissolved in 1814 (Gad 1979).

Sources illustrating the general historical development of both settlements are lacking. Only short runic inscriptions written in Greenland in West Norse or Latin on wood and stone have been found (fig. 2). The use of runic letters is closely related to the tradition in western Norway where runic letters were in use even in the fourteenth and fifteenth centuries (Stoklund 1982).

Archeological excavations of the cemetery at Herjólfsnes (Ikigaat) where the soil has been especially suitable for preserving textiles, have brought to light a unique collection of everyday clothes from the Middle Ages, made in Greenland of wool from Greenlandic sheep, but of European cut (Nørlund 1924). Besides woollen clothes the Norsemen used skin clothes. Many

Fig. 2. Rune stone, found in one of 3 cairns on Kingittorsuaq I.
northwest of Upernavik, the northernmost Norse monument
discovered in Greenland (72° 55′ north latitude). The inscription
says that Erlingr Sighvatsson, Bjarni þórðarson, and Eindriði
Oddsson (?) raised the cairns on the Saturday before Rogation
Day, but the year and hence the date are unknown. The style of
the runes indicates a date of about 1300 (Gad 1971–1982, 1:137;
G. Jones 1964:49; Thalbitzer 1904:25; Gordon and Taylor
1957:186–187, 260). Length 10.0 cm; acquired in 1824.

woollen liripipe hoods were found of a type that was
very popular in Europe especially in the fourteenth century. One cap, a so-called Burgundy cap, is considered
an important indication that the Norse may have had
contact with Europe at the end of the fifteenth century
(fig. 3).

There was no regular navigation from Europe at this
time. In 1378 the last bishop active in Greenland died
(Det Kongelige Nordiske Oldskrift-Selskab 1838–1845,
3:32). One of the last pieces of reliable information from
the Norse settlements deals with a wedding in the eastern settlement that took place on September 16, 1408,
in Hvalsey (Qaqortukulooq) church (fig. 1). Icelanders
who witnessed this wedding confirmed it after their return to Iceland in a document dated May 15, 1414 (Det
Kongelige Nordiske Oldskrift-Selskab 1838–1845, 3:152–
154). Later news of the settlements in Greenland is
uncertain.

A Papal brief from 1448 states that 30 years previously the Norse had been attacked by hostile barbari-

Fig. 3. Norse headgear. left, "Burgundy cap" of wool in a style
that was in fashion in France about 1450; right, hood. Both
excavated at the Herjólfsnes churchyard, Ikigaat, West Greenland,
1926.

ans, who destroyed churches and captured people as
slaves (Det Kongelige Nordiske Oldskrift-Selskab 1838–
1845, 3:165–176). The last important Papal brief about
Greenland is dated October 23, 1492. It deals with the
appointment of a new bishop at Garðar but states that
no ship had arrived at Greenland for 80 years and that
many of its inhabitants had denied Christianity, of which
the only remembrance is an old altar-cloth that is shown
in public once a year (Bobé 1936:3–4). There is no
evidence that the new bishop ever reached Greenland.
Accounts from Icelanders in the sixteenth century reflect speculations about the fate of the Norsemen rather
than facts (Det Kongelige Nordiske Oldskrift-Selskab
1838–1845, 3:505, 514–515), for the Icelanders did not
actually meet with Norse in Greenland.

Possible Evidence of Eskimo-Norse Contact

Norse Sources

Besides *Eiríks Saga Rauða* and *Grænlendinga Saga* there
are other Icelandic sagas dealing with the early history
of the settlers in Greenland: *Fóstbrœðra Saga, Eyr-
byggja Saga, Grænlendinga þáttr,* and *Flóamanna Saga.*
The sagas were written down 200–300 years after the
events they relate, and most of the stories are considered fictional. *Flóamanna Saga* tells that a Norseman
on the east coast met two troll women, cut off the hand
of one of them and stole their meat (Bárðarson 1932:43).
This is supposed to have happened soon after 1000, but
the story was probably not written down until about
1300. If it is based on facts the women may have been
Eskimos, but the Eskimos are not otherwise mentioned
in these sagas.

The earliest Icelandic source that mentions the Eskimos is Ari þorgilsson's *Íslendingabók,* dealing with
the history of Iceland from 870 to 1120, and written
between 1122 and 1132. It states that the first Norsemen
in Greenland found signs of people: human dwellings,
fragments of skin boats, and stone tools, both in the
east and the west (that is, the Eastern and the Western
Settlements), from which it appeared that they had belonged to the same people who inhabited Vínland,
the Skraelings (*Skrælingar*) (Holtsmark 1952:22). These
may have been remains of the Dorset Eskimos.

Approximately at the same time as the Norse settled
in southwest Greenland, a new migration of Eskimos
of the Thule culture from Canada to northwest Greenland began. The first testimony of Norse contact with
Eskimos is to be found in *Historia Norvegiæ,* which
may have been written in the end of the twelfth century.
The Eskimos are presented almost as a mythical people
with whom contact was hostile: "On the other side of
Greenland, toward the North, hunters have found some
little people whom they call Skraellings; their situation
is that when they are hurt by weapons their sores be- *551*

come white without bleeding, but when they are mortally wounded their blood will hardly stop running. They have no iron at all; they use missiles made of walrus tusks and sharp stones for knives" (Jansen 1972:35).

In the Icelandic annals that give brief details on navigation to Greenland and conditions there, the Eskimos are mentioned only once. It is stated that in 1379 they attacked the Norsemen, killed 18 men, and captured two boys and made them bondsmen (Det Kongelige Nordiske Oldskrift-Selskab 1838–1845,3:32).

An important account is due to the Norwegian cleric Ívarr Bárðarson (1930:29) who worked in Greenland in the middle of the fourteenth century; the manuscript based on his reports is, however, only preserved in copies from about 1500. It contains, in addition to information on various places in Greenland, a short description of a rescue expedition from the Eastern Settlement led by him to the Western Settlement in order to drive out the Eskimos. However, they saw neither Christians nor heathens. It is a valuable source with regard to Norse topography, but the expedition can hardly have investigated all the farms. Carbon-14 dating made in connection with archeological excavations of the farms of Niaquussat and Nipaatsoq in the Western Settlement shows that the habitation stopped at A.D. 1390 ± 50 years and 1410 ± 50 years. Carbon-14 dating from the Eskimo settlement Kangeq in the coastal area has given the result 1330 ± 70 years (radiocarbon dates noncalibrated) (Gulløv 1982b:232–234). These figures indicate that at any rate some farms may have existed for a longer time in the Western Settlement than is usually supposed and that both peoples may have lived in this area at the same time.

Finally there are two late sources that may be based on contact with the Eskimos. Both contain many fictional elements that mention meetings between "trolls" and Icelanders in Greenland (Det Kongelige Nordiske Oldskrift-Selskab 1838–1845, 3:436–441, 468–470).

Eskimo Legends

Eskimo oral traditions about the Norse are few, and most of the material was not recorded until the middle of the nineteenth century. The legends published by Rink (1875:308–321) are somewhat rewritten and the variants are worked together by Krogh (1967:127–137). Most of the original texts were first published in full in Greenlandic-Danish editions (*Kaladlit okalluktualliait—Grønlandske Folkesagn I–IV* 1859–1863; the three most important of these texts are published by Knuth 1968a:48–85 in somewhat modernized language including a translation in English).

One legend gives a short glimpse of a peaceful relationship between Norsemen and Eskimos; it is told that the place-name Pisissarfik 'the archery place' in Godthåbsfjord derives from an archery competition that took place between a Norseman and an Eskimo. The Norseman lost and was according to the rules set by himself hurled from the top of the mountain into the sea, but the two peoples continued to be friends.

The main theme of the legends about the Norse is why and how the Eskimos exterminated the Norse. Two explanations are given of how hostilities arose between the two people. According to one legend that has been recorded in several variants in the eighteenth, nineteenth, and twentieth centuries, a Norseman challenged an Eskimo to try to hit him with his bird dart. The Eskimo hit the Norseman and killed him, but the Norse did nothing about it. As far as this, the story offers a parallel to the first one. Later on, it is told, an Eskimo on his own initiative killed a Norseman, and the Norse took revenge by attacking an Eskimo settlement, killing all its inhabitants except two brothers, who fled out on the ice. The Norse chieftain, Uunngortoq, chased them and killed the younger brother; but the elder one, Qasape, escaped.

According to another legend it was Navaranaaq, an Eskimo servant girl in a Norse settlement, who caused conflict between the Eskimos and the Norse (fig. 4). The Norse decided to strike first and massacred a camp with Eskimo women and children while their men were out hunting. In both cases an Eskimo is made responsible for the origin of the enmity between the two people, but the merciless attack by the Norse is meant to justify the counterattack by the Eskimos that exterminated the Norse.

The sequels of both these introductory sections are variants of the same story. The Eskimos approached the Norse settlement in a boat that a shaman had made to look like ice in order not to arouse Norse suspicions. They surprised the Norse and set fire to their house. The Norse chief escaped but was chased and killed by an Eskimo who was particularly anxious to take revenge because a near relative of his had been killed and he had in addition seen the body being maltreated by the Norse.

According to another tradition recorded in the eighteenth century, but only once (N. Egede 1939:268), three pirate ships once came and looted a Norse settlement. The following year a whole fleet turned up and after the attack some of the survivors went south, and the Eskimos promised to help those who remained if they were ever attacked again. But when the pirates came again the following year, the Eskimos fled, at the same time bringing five Norse women and some children to safety. When they later returned to see what had happened, they found everything burned and destroyed. The Eskimos then married the five Norse women.

These legends many contain some historical truth, but there exists no way of having the details of the stories confirmed. Indications of localities are definitely

Nationalmuseet, Copenhagen: top, 12101; bottom, 12102.

Fig. 4. Two of 12 woodcuts by the Greenlander Aron of Kangeq (b. 1822, d. 1869) illustrating Eskimo legends of conflict with the Norse, first published in Godthåb (Rink 1860). top, Norsemen killing Eskimo women and children in camp, an attack that, according to a traditional motif, was brought on by false stories started by Navaranaaq, an Eskimo woman. bottom, Eskimos retaliating, burning the Norse house at Ameralik and killing all the escaping inhabitants except Uunngortoq, the Norse chief (Knuth 1960:19, 1968a:74–84).

unreliable, as variants locate the same event at different places. The story telling how the Eskimos by using the strategem of a boat disguised as ice surprised the Norse and set fire to their house was probably first associated with the Eastern Settlement. It was later on also located in the Western Settlement by Eskimos traveling along the west coast from south to north.

Some of the motifs in the Eskimo legends about the Norse are also known outside West Greenland. A striking example is the legend of Navaranaaq, which is also told by Polar Eskimos and East Greenlanders and by many Canadian Eskimos (Holtved 1943). In these cases the role of the Norse is played by Indians, Tunnit (Dorset Eskimos), or even more mythical people. This indicates that the legend was brought by immigrants from Canada to West Greenland where it was transferred to the Norse.

Even among the Polar Eskimos and the East Greenlanders legends have been recorded that are supposed to deal with Norsemen (Holtved 1951, 1:113; Rosing 1958:438), but probably they do not represent memo-

ries of the presence of Norsemen in these remote areas; the stories may have come from West Greenland or they may deal with Europeans from a later period.

Norse Traits Among the Eskimos

Several attempts have been made to show that the Norse and the Eskimos had contact with each other and that the Eskimos learned various practices from the Norse, but the evidence is meager. It has been suggested, for example, that the Eskimos got the idea for their longhouses from the large houses of the Norse (Thalbitzer 1914–1941:363), but the origin of the longhouse can be explained otherwise (Petersen 1974–1975:175–179).

Eskimo wooden vessels made by cooperage have also been explained as a result of Norse influence (Mathiassen 1931a:295–296), but according to archeological research, this technique seems to have been known during the Dorset period (Meldgaard 1965:95).

Very few Eskimo objects have been found in Norse ruins, but a great number of Norse articles have been found in Eskimo ruins. This has been interpreted partly as evidence of trade between the two people (Ingstad 1959:502–505), and partly to support a hypothesis that a number of Norse moved in with Eskimos and brought their things with them (Persson 1969:627). But the most likely explanation of the presence of a large number of Norse objects in Eskimo ruins is that the Eskimos looted the Norse settlements (Mathiassen and Holtved 1936:84–85). This does not have to have taken place during a state of hostilities; the objects could have been removed after the disappearance of the Norse.

Among the concepts that the Greenland Eskimos once were supposed to have learned from the Norse, some have turned out to be almost worldwide, such as the practice of not using the regular entrance when removing a dead person from a dwelling (Nansen 1891:244).

Other elements that the Greenland Eskimos supposedly learned from the Norse have turned out to be known to other Eskimos as well. In the case of the myth of the swan maiden (bird wife) (Nansen 1891:251), it has been demonstrated that the West Greenlandic variant is so similar to other Eskimo variants in North America there can be no doubt that it reached Greenland from this source and not through contact with the Norse (Kleivan 1962:35).

It is also claimed that the Greenland Eskimos learned the chain dance from the Norse (Thalbitzer and Thuren 1911:97), but such dances are also known by the western Eskimos (Johnston 1975:5,7), and the Greenland Eskimos could also have learned them through later contact with Europeans. A Dutch whaler wrote of the Greenland Eskimos in 1720 that "they are able to imitate all the skills and games of our people, when they have seen them but once" (Haan 1914:69).

Of the words that have been mentioned as possible

Norse loanwords in the Greenlandic language, most have been rejected. The few remaining are doubtful.

The similarity between Greenlandic and Scandinavian words can be coincidental. For instance, old lists of Greenlandic words include the word pannien, which has been compared with Norse *barn* 'child' (Egede 1925:36). But the Greenlandic word is in fact an inflected form of the widespread Eskimo word *panik* 'daughter'. Some loanwords thought to have been of Norse origin may be derived from early contact with Europeans after the disappearance of the Norse. For example, the Greenlandic word for 'sheep', *sava*, was mentioned in the nineteenth and twentieth centuries as a Norse loanword (Kleinschmidt 1871:316), but it entered Greenlandic in the first half of the eighteenth-century when the colonists brought sheep to Greenland (Kleivan 1978).

It is still claimed that *niisa* 'porpoise', *kuanneq* 'angelica', and *kalaaleq* 'Greenland Eskimo' are loans from the Norse (Bergsland quoted in Ingstad 1959:504–505). However, all these words are known in Labrador: the first and the third with the same definition, and the second meaning edible algae (Erdmann 1864:146, 205, 112). If the theory that these are loanwords from the Norse is accepted, then their presence among the Labrador Eskimos may be explained by contact with the Moravian missionaries there, who were heavily influenced by the linguistic work of the missionaries in West Greenland.

Racial Mixture

In support of a theory that interbreeding took place between Norse and Eskimos in Greenland, reference has been made to Hans Egede's impression of the inhabitants of a certain locality in southwest Greenland in 1723. He described them as "rather beautiful and white" (Egede 1925:96). Several similar observations exist, but these impressions of a European element in the Greenland Eskimo population may easily be explained as a result of contact with Europeans in the centuries after the disappearance of the Norse. Neither skeletons from Norse graves nor those from Eskimo graves have proved any interbreeding (Fisher-Møller 1942:61–63; B.J. Jørgensen 1953:85).

One researcher has used serological investigations to conclude that there is a possibility that interbreeding did take place between the Norse and the Eskimos in the Julianehåb area, where the old Eastern Settlement was situated (Persson 1969:627). This is however very doubtful; the difference between the population in this area and in other parts of West Greenland may be explained as a local variation; besides this area received many immigrants from southeast Greenland in the eighteenth and nineteenth centuries (B.J. Jørgensen 1975:151).

Eskimo Depictions of the Norse

Archeological excavations of Eskimo ruins at different sites in Greenland have produced wooden dolls carved like Eskimo dolls without arms or any hint of facial features, but with their clothing carved to resemble Norse clothing (fig. 5) (Mathiassen 1931a:287–290). These Eskimo carvings are regarded as evidence that the Norse and the Eskimos really were in contact in Greenland. Even in Arctic Canada similar dolls have been found in Ellesmere Island (Schledermann 1980) and in Baffin Island (Sabo and Sabo 1978). A comparative survey of all these carvings is made by Gulløv (1982b).

Explanations of the Norse Disappearance

There are three ways to explain what happened to the Norse: they died in Greenland, they emigrated, or they mixed with the Eskimos and were integrated into the Eskimo population. The Norse in Greenland lived in a marginal area and were therefore especially vulnerable to changes in their environment, and that is why most of the following theories propounded to explain how the Norse disappeared are related to ecological conditions.

The most accepted explanation is that their animal husbandry was made difficult by poor grazing conditions due to the climate's becoming colder and drier. The climate was relatively warm when the Norse settled in Greenland, but from about 1200 a colder period set in. The excessive grazing and cutting of brush, which the slowly growing flora could not keep up with, led to erosion; and the flora in some places could have been reduced by severe attacks of caterpillars.

Another aspect of the explanation due to economic failure is that the Norse could not manage when supplies from Europe failed. The lack of shipbuilding materials in Greenland made contact between the Norse and Eu-

Nationalmuseet, Copenhagen: L4.3225.
Fig. 5. Wooden doll, carved in the Eskimo manner (without arms or facial features) but differing in that its dress seems to be non-Native, probably Norse. Height 5.3 cm; excavated by Therkel Mathiassen at Inussuk, Upernavik District, 1929.

rope dependent on the Europeans and in the long run led to isolation. The question of why contact with Europe was broken is not clarified. It could be either because the Scandinavian countries were unable to keep up contact, or because preconditions for maintaining it did not exist in Greenland. This explanation, that the Norse could not survive without supplies from Europe, was formerly prominent, but archeological excavations of Norse ruins have shown that the Norse were prepared for self-sufficiency.

Subsistence based on hunting and fishing alone could have been insufficient. If the Norse went over to complete dependence on hunting and fishing, a deterioration of ecological conditions could have been disastrous as it has proved to be to various groups of Eskimos in Greenland through the ages.

The settlements could have been ravaged by epidemics as in Norway and other European countries. There is no proof of this.

Perhaps the Norse population could no longer propagate themselves. This theory, that the last Norse in Greenland were diseased and deformed, was formerly important but has been disproved by later investigations of the skeletal material on which it originally was based.

Strife within the Norse community might have weakened the population. It is not known to what extent this factor may have contributed to the extinction of the Greenland settlements.

Pirates may have attacked the Norse. The theories of strife and pirates are analogies based on conditions in Iceland. In addition, reference is made to the Eskimo legend of pirate attacks and the Papal brief of 1448; but some students think that the attackers mentioned in the brief may have been Eskimos.

Did the Eskimos kill the Norse? Norse sources mention few incidents of hostilities besides the expedition to drive the Eskimos out of the western settlement, where, however, no Eskimos were seen. Eskimo legends say the Eskimos exterminated the Norse. The supporters of this theory imagine that the inhabitants of solitary farms were gradually killed by Eskimos, and that the Norse population had already been weakened by other factors. It is further presumed that it would have been difficult for two peoples that were so different to accept each other.

If the second way of explaining Norse disappearance, emigration, is correct, this may have been because conditions in Greenland were unacceptable due to one or more of the above-mentioned factors. Norse could have emigrated to North America, or returned to Iceland or Norway, or more or less voluntarily accompanied pirates to the British Isles. One can imagine a gradual emigration, especially of young people, but there are no sources to support this hypothesis.

The third explanation is that the Norse mixed with the Eskimos and were integrated into the Eskimo population. A single Eskimo tradition indicates the possibility of interbreeding, but anthropometric investigations have brought forth no proof of this. The opponents of this theory have claimed that the racial and religious prejudices of the Norse would have prevented such interbreeding. But if they found themselves in a situation where it was a question of life or death, one can assume that they would have been more positively inclined to join the Eskimos.

None of the many different theories that have been propounded to explain why and how the Norse disappeared from Greenland has advanced sufficient evidence for the solution of this puzzle. Most probably there were several different factors operating.

The place where Eric the Red settled, Brattahlíð, which is the richest grazing area in all Greenland, was populated again in 1924 by a Greenlandic farmer. Much of the area where the Norse population once lived in the eastern settlement was in the 1980s being utilized by Greenlandic sheep raisers.

The mystery of the fate of the Norse has absorbed not only many European researchers but also the descendants of the Eskimos, who all know of the legends dealing with the Norse, which are published in Greenlandic in various editions of oral traditions (K. Lynge 1938–1939:124–139) and schoolbooks. The legends describing contact between these two people, ending in the ruin of the Norse, have also been a source of inspiration for several Greenlandic writers and artists (Aron in Knuth 1968a; Kristiansen 1954; Villadsen 1965; F. Nielsen 1970; Rosing 1973).

Sources

How the Norsemen lived and disappeared, and what their relations with the Eskimos were, have been the object of much interest (G. Jones 1964; Ingstad 1966a, 1966b; Gad 1971–1982; Krogh 1982). The sources of the history of Norse Greenland are ecological, archeological, and topographical investigations, European written sources, and Eskimo oral traditions. Surveys of archeological sources are found in Roussell (1941) and Jansen (1972), and maps with all recorded Norse ruins are published by Krogh (1982:247–261). Most of the early written sources on the Norse in Greenland are published in *Grønlands historiske Mindesmærker I-III* (Det Kongelige Nordiske Oldskrift-Selskab 1838–1845). Surveys of research of these sources and references to various editions are found in *Kultur-historisk leksikon for nordis middelalder I-XXII* 1956–1978 and in Jansen (1972). A survey of Eskimo oral traditions about the Norse is given by Kleivan (1982). A survey of research on many aspects of the way of life of the Norse including contributions by natural scientists is published in the journal *Grønland* (5–9) 1982.

History of Colonial Greenland

FINN GAD*

The history of Greenland is based on both archeological finds and written sources: up to the year 1000 exclusively on archeology; during the Norse period from 1000 to 1400 on both written sources and archeology; from 1400 to 1700 again essentially on archeology; and since 1700 to a growing degree on written sources, rarely published. The history of the Polar Eskimos and the East Greenlanders up to 1900 is based almost exclusively on archeological material.

1400–1721

During the Inugsuk culture period, Eskimos slowly migrated south, occupying the coastal areas of West Greenland; they passed Cape Farewell and migrated farther up the east coast during the fifteenth century (see "Neo-Eskimo Prehistory of Greenland," this vol.). The Norse population was gone. Occasional contact between Eskimos and Europeans seems to have taken place when Basque seafarers landed; in pursuit of large whales they sailed, according to tradition, north into Davis Strait.

In the centuries of great discoveries, the idea of reaching China and India through the Northwest Passage kept knowledge of Greenland alive in Europe. Maps by the Danish cartographer Claudius Clavus Swart and descriptions from the 1420s showed the king of Denmark-Norway to have possession of the westernmost land known to Europe at the time; Clavus also had some knowledge of the Eskimos. On this basis, Portugal urged the king of Denmark-Norway to seek the western passage to India.

The leitmotif of Danish-Norwegian-Icelandic actions during the following centuries was the obligation of the king of Denmark-Norway toward the Norse population that perhaps still survived in Greenland. After the Reformation of 1536 in these countries, it was considered the duty of the king to have "the true gospel" preached to the Norse Greenlanders. At the same time, European whaling moved westward and northward and was concentrated around the Svalbard archipelago. The Basques were defeated in the competition with the Dutch and English, who continued to compete aggressively with each other. For this reason and because of the still prevalent idea of a Northwest Passage, Martin Frobisher in 1576–1578 and John Davis in 1585–1587 went to Greenland, Frobisher being considered the European rediscoverer of Greenland. Reports of these two expeditions (Frobisher 1578; Davis 1589) contain the first substantial descriptions of Eskimos. Davis took down 40 Eskimo words, but they are difficult to interpret on the basis of his record.

By the terms of the agreement of 1261, the king of Denmark-Norway exercised sovereignty over the North Atlantic. This brought about negotiations between England and Denmark-Norway that resulted in England's dropping its interest in Greenlandic waters. Despite several attempts, it was not until 1605 that the Danish-Norwegian government succeeded in carrying out expeditions to the west coast of Greenland; these departed for three consecutive years. The Frobisher, Davis, and Danish-Norwegian expeditions all abducted Eskimos. These detestable practices did lead to better European knowledge of the Eskimos.

Denmark-Norway then began modest whaling in the North Atlantic, both as an exercise of sovereignty and in order to share in the profits. As the whales gradually moved south and west, the Dutch came to dominate in this competition. In 1614 a number of Dutch shipowners founded the Noordse Compagnie in Amsterdam, investing considerable capital in whaling; from this developed the Dutch sea ventures for whaling and trading on the west coast of Greenland.

Some Dutch merchants who had been excluded from the Noordse Compagnie emigrated to Denmark-Norway, especially after the English Navigation Act of 1651. This immigration promoted Danish-Norwegian shipping and whaling. Several whaling companies were set up in Bergen and Copenhagen at various times during the seventeenth century. Special Greenland companies were founded in Copenhagen; one of these, established in 1652, acquired a monopoly on this shipping for 30 years. It had ships out for three successive years without results. War between Denmark-Norway and Sweden prevented further activity.

In the 1654 expedition, four Greenlanders from the Godthåb area were abducted, including one man who died en route from Norway to Denmark. Portraits of all four were painted in Norway. The three survivors

556   * Translated from Danish by Charles Jones.

lived for some time at a castle in Schleswig, where the learned proto-ethnographer and traveler Adam Olearius (1656:163–171) studied their appearance and way of life and wrote about them. The doctor who accompanied them, who had learned some Eskimo, facilitated the recording of 114 Eskimo words, all written comprehensibly; later the total recorded reached about 300.

During the seventeenth century, Icelandic scholars who spoke and wrote about the Norse population of Greenland mentioned that they and the island itself belonged to Norway according to the agreement of 1261. Several Icelanders drew maps of Greenland, mistakenly putting Eystribygð on the east coast. All this stimulated the interest of the Danish-Norwegian Crown in resuming contacts with Greenland. But no private interests reacted until in 1671 a Bergen merchant attempted whaling and trade with Greenland. From 1673 to 1676 he had ships out; although he considered installing a station on the west coast of Greenland, he was forced to give up the entire project.

When the 1652 monopoly expired, the Icelandic historian Þormóðr Torfæus proposed in 1683 that contact be reestablished with Greenland and that Icelanders be settled there. This led to no actual policy, but along with the various reports from different countries and occasional foreign navigations of Davis Strait, it had a certain influence. In 1697 trading privileges were issued to Greenland companies in Bergen and Copenhagen. For several years, only one Copenhagen merchant engaged in the Greenland trade; later Bergen shipowners also began to take part.

The relatively constant traffic by ships from the Netherlands, Hamburg, and Denmark-Norway to West Greenland, interrupted by European wars, led Arngrimr Þorkilsson Vídalín, born in Iceland, to write a long proposal urging the colonization of the west coast of Greenland. This was extremely detailed, describing European knowledge at the time about this part of the world and the opportunities available there. At least indirectly, it formed the basis for later colonization.

Contemporary knowledge of the coastal population was due partly to the many abductions and partly to the relatively numerous reports from ships that had landed along the coast during the seventeenth century. Certain cultural traits can thus be dated. The kayak, with its equipment, seems to have been fully developed in its Greenlandic version by 1600, as was the watertight kayak coat. The winged harpoon was in use before 1650. At the same time the "jump coat," used when whaling, seems to have been in common use.

It was obvious that the people of the west coast of Greenland were not descendants of the Norse settlers, but hope was still alive that those people would be found. The idea of preaching "the true gospel" to the Norse inhabitants was the motive force behind Hans Egede's mission and colonization plans. It is probable that while studying in Copenhagen in 1704–1705 he heard of Vídalín's proposals, which had brought about realistic discussions of a Greenland trade. Likewise he must have known of the whaling that developed from Bergen immediately after 1700. In April 1708 shipowners in Bergen had applied for whaling privileges, and in October of the same year Hans Egede conceived the idea of a Greenland mission.

Egede, born on January 31, 1686, and married in 1707 to Giertrud Rasch (b. 1673, d. 1735), got into difficult conflicts as a 22-year-old priest on Lofoten, which strengthened his desire to go to Greenland. Although his father-in-law Niels Rasch, who had been to West Greenland as a ship's officer, told him that only "savages" lived there, Egede clung to his idea, trusting more in the written and printed word than in eyewitness accounts. In 1710 and 1711 he applied for the establishment of a mission, but consideration of his applications was hampered by the Great Northern War (1700–1720/21). Egede left his post and moved to Bergen but met with scant sympathy for his plans. In 1719 he submitted his final proposal, for establishing a company that by means of whaling and trade with the population of Greenland would create the economic basis for the founding and operation of a combined mission and trading post on the west coast of Greenland. The government wanted the trading company to be established before granting permission to the mission. In 1721 it was established, with great difficulty: merchants in Bergen were not very willing to invest, and Egede himself was one of the two largest contributors. The government granted the newly established Bergen company certain privileges, but not the desired monopoly on Greenland trade. It would have been undiplomatic to offend the Dutch at this time.

The Dutch activity on the west coast of Greenland had increased since 1713. A considerable number of whales was taken, and trade with the Eskimos of the west coast was quite profitable. This trade was carried on as barter: the Dutch skippers brought loads of shirts, stockings, gloves, brass articles, knives, sword blades, various tools, tin items, fishhooks, glass beads, faience, specially made women's knives (ulus), small wooden chests, and finally also coarse woollen cloth. They refrained from selling firearms, gunpowder, and bullets, out of consideration for their own personal safety.

Relations between the Eskimos and the Dutch were not always the best. Recalling abductions, the Greenlanders were on their guard against the foreigners. Nevertheless, they could not refrain from meetings at the market that took place every year when Dutch ships put in at Sydbay, the island of Tullukune, or Ukivik, a few nautical miles northwest of the present Holsteinsborg. Often coming from considerable distances in umiaks and kayaks, the Greenlanders brought blubber and hides. The trade seems to have been rather one-sided. *557*

Except for the beads, knives, fishhooks, sword blades, ulus, and some of the tools, the Greenlanders apparently had little need for the merchandise offered; their wants were evidently quickly satisfied. But the Dutch had such a great appetite for hides and blubber that they forced their merchandise on the Greenlanders. There is evidence that the Greenlanders hung all kinds of trade goods from their rafters as decorations. Dutch trade had a certain influence on the Greenlandic cultural pattern, but not so much by attracting them to the market in the best hunting season. There was usually extensive traveling north and south along the ice-free coasts from April/May to around August/September. Not everyone went to the market every year, either. The influence on the Eskimos' culture took place through the consumer goods bartered to them. Needs were created that could be satisfied only by outside supplies. Side effects of this contact with foreigners were sexual promiscuity and some use of strong drink. It is probable that tuberculosis got its foothold in Greenland through this contact.

1721–1782

In comparison with the Dutch influence, that of the little Norwegian colony established on July 3, 1721, on a skerry off the mouth of Godthåbfjord was insignificant, but it worried the Greenlanders, who were accustomed to foreigners coming in the spring and leaving in the summer. The new foreigners built houses and appeared to intend to stay.

Hans Egede had trouble making contact with the population of the surrounding area. The few words of Greenlandic he knew were useful but hardly sufficient for his purpose, which was to bring the gospel, in the Lutheran doctrine, to the Greenlanders. He spent the first months getting his building constructed, and the first years learning the language. His immediate attempts to trade with Greenlanders were unsuccessful, just as the projected whaling was a total fiasco.

In trading, competition from the Dutch was immediately noticed; it remained serious until 1777. Due to scarcity of capital and weak support from the state, the Bergen company had to give up in 1727, with huge losses. During the following years, the trade center was moved from Bergen to Copenhagen, where it remained.

Thereafter, Danish-Norwegian trade with Greenland was carried on by various enterprises: from 1728 to 1733/34 for the Crown, and from 1733/34 to 1749 by a Copenhagen merchant, who transferred it to the Royal Chartered General Trading Company, which went into liquidation in 1774. From 1774–1776 to 1950 the Royal Greenland Trade Department (*Den Kongelige Grønlanske Handel*) had a monopoly on trade in Greenland. The government of Denmark-Norway was hesitant

to grant a monopoly on this trade for reasons of foreign policy, but the Bergen company obtained the monopoly in 1723. From then on it was transferred from one trading company to another. It derived from the assertion of the sovereignty of the king of Denmark-Norway over the total extent of Greenland, known or unknown, according to the agreement of 1261. This same sovereignty forced the state step by step into an ever deeper involvement in the affairs of Greenland, which was also motivated by a sense of responsibility for the population of the island. Greenlanders were subjects to whom the king of Denmark-Norway had obligations.

State subsidies were necessary. Not until 1794 did the trade become profitable, partly because of the Dutch competition and partly due to the relatively large expenses involved in establishing, operating, and supplying a growing number of trading posts and in running the mission. The mission was the main objective, but the number of missionaries was not increased in proportion to the growing number of trading posts; the number of trading employees, on the other hand, was of course increased. If only for that reason, trade became predominant over missions in Greenland.

In 1728 the first colony was moved to its present location and called Godthåb 'Good Hope'. At about the same time an attempt was made to establish a whaling station farther north, but this project had to be abandoned, as the government in 1730 was prepared to dissolve the entire venture. When Egede pointed out the Crown's commitments to the Greenlanders who had already been baptized, the king, a deeply religious man, changed his mind in 1731. "The holy work" was able to continue, and the necessary expansion was begun. In 1734 Christianshåb was founded, in 1741 Jakobshavn, and in 1742 Frederikshåb. Concurrently with the slowly declining Dutch competition, the coverage of the coast was improved after 1750 by the founding of more trading stations: Claushavn in 1752, Fiskenæsset in 1754, Sukkertoppen and Ritenbenk in 1755 (both moved in 1781), Holsteinsborg in 1756–1764, Uummannaq (Ũmánaq) in 1758–1761, Egedesminde in 1759–1761, Upernavik in 1771, Godhavn in 1773, and Julianehåb in 1774–1776. After 1774 several whaling stations were established in Disko Bay. By 1782 all the West Greenland colonies had been established as well as many intermediate trading posts and whaling stations.

Finally the desire that Hans Egede had expressed in 1725 was fulfilled: the west coast was covered by trading posts so that the monopoly could dominate it. After previous notices during the course of the century, the final decree was issued on March 18, 1776, closing the coast to foreign ships except in emergencies. Explicit reservations were made for future installations.

Every colony had a merchant, later called a colonial manager. At certain places he was the only trader, but at larger settlements he had one or more assistants. In

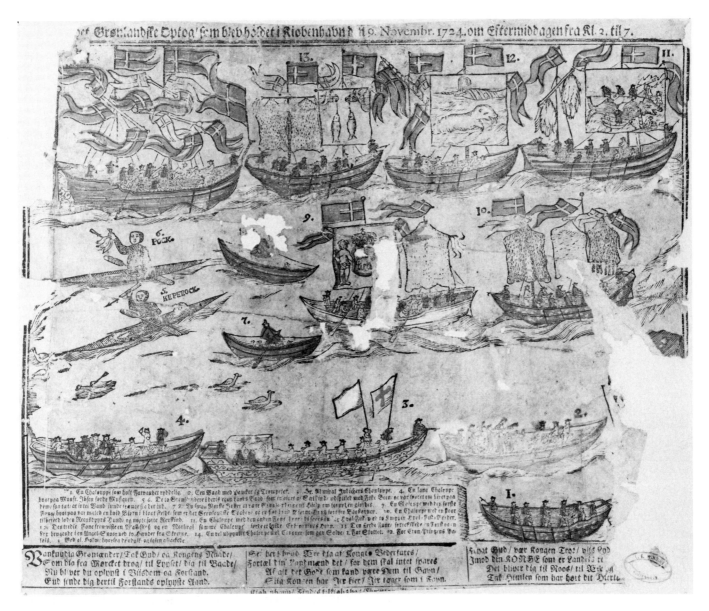

Fig. 1. The West Greenlanders Poq and Qiperoq in their kayaks at left, in a regatta at Copenhagen on Nov. 9, 1724, in celebration of the Greenland trade. The procession included an admiral's barge and 6 ships displaying bearskins and other Greenland products. At the royal palace a special song was sung: "Here we come Almighty Monarch/From Greenland's ice and cold to Denmark/Greenland lays the table of the Queen/Our regional tribute for her is foreseen/When only good trade/Can be made" (Dam-Mikkelsen and Lundbæk 1980). Contemporary hand-colored woodblock print.

addition the merchant supervised all practical work, for which each colony had hired craftsmen and "sailors," the latter functioning as simple laborers. Carpenters, coopers, and smiths were represented. The number of personnel could vary, but as a rule each large settlement had one merchant, one assistant, one cooper or carpenter, sometimes one smith, and four to eight "sailors." Among the "sailors" there was sometimes a man with skill in a craft, in which case a trained craftsman was not employed. Throughout the eighteenth century, by far the greatest number of those employed in trade in Greenland were "stationed" there. Because of the scarcity of capital, it was necessary to practice thrift, including imposing limits on stationed personnel.

The trading practice introduced at the very beginning was preserved right up to 1803–1804: in the spring and autumn the traders traveled in their respective districts, carrying "trading chests" with goods for barter. The quantity of Greenlandic products offered on certain occasions could not always be paid for by the supply of goods available for barter, in which case the difference was credited to the Eskimo in an account, or else a certain number of beads, fishhooks, sewing needles, or similar miscellany was added to round out the value.

Det Kongelige Bibliotek, Copenhagen: Egede 1741.

Fig. 2. West Greenlandic customs as depicted by the missionary Hans Egede: dances and a drum match (left) and football and handball games (right).

Occasionally Greenlanders came to the trading post to trade. It was impossible for the Greenlanders to check on whatever might have been credited to them. The barter itself helped to stabilize prices, so that the Greenlanders could react forcefully if prices were changed.

Smithsonian, Natl. Philatelic Coll.

Fig. 3. Stamp issued in April 1976 with a surtax for the Greenland Athletic Union. It features a drawing illustrating Greenlandic armwrestling, after a woodcut published by Hans Egede (1741).

Their products were in demand, and each district apparently delivered each year more or less the same quantity of skins, blubber, and whalebone.

Time and again it was impressed on the trading company employees that they must not buy so much from the Greenlanders that the latter did not have enough left for their daily needs, but this policy was often not followed. After 1750 bad hunting years occurred more and more often, resulting in famines. This called for active social welfare. Not dictated by any elevated philosophy, this policy was due to an obligation to protect the Eskimos, pure necessity, and the positive humanism of the mission.

When the Eskimos' produce was imported to Denmark, it was sold at auction. The income, together with the state subsidy, was meant to cover the salaries and other expenses of operating the trading company and the mission, the maintenance of buildings and equipment in Greenland and Copenhagen, supplies, shipping, and the growing quantity of goods bartered in exchange. These goods were mostly produced in Denmark; they were essentially the same as those brought by the Dutch.

During the course of the eighteenth century the variety of trade goods increased somewhat. Around 1740

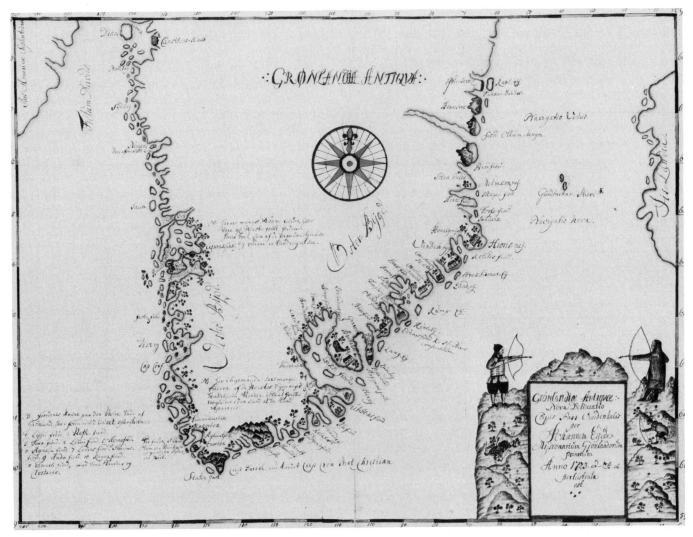

Fig. 4. *Grönlandia Antiqua*, manuscript map of Greenland north to Disko Bay, by Hans Egede, 1737, the west coast based in part on his explorations in 1723–1724 (for transcription of names see Bobé 1944:331).

the Dutch—to meet the Danish competition—began to sell the Greenlanders arms, gunpowder, and lead for making bullets. The Danish trading company tried in vain to prevent this; instead the inferior Dutch arms were bought up and replaced by better Danish ones. By the time the Dutch competition ceased, arms, gunpowder, and lead had become necessities for Greenlandic hunters. These consumer goods thus had an enormous influence on the Eskimo culture and increased dependence on outside supplies.

Beginning about 1755 tobacco came into ever greater use among the Greenlanders, serving as part or full payment for small services rendered, and in exchange for individual game birds, caribou and seal meat, fish, and the like used as fresh food supplies by those stationed in Greenland. Tobacco became a necessary commodity, even considered by some as the most important one.

All the commodities were as a rule sent to Greenland in small sailing ships, one to each colonial district. Shipping was expensive because the cost per unit was so great. This was one reason for the deficit of the operation. Income depended exclusively on what the Greenland hunter could produce, so that the trading company was interested in the maintenance of production capacity. Hunting as an occupation had to be supported. The trading company had a deliberate policy of attempting to keep the Greenlanders to "their national occupations," so that it was little inclined to take them into its employment. It sought by all means to preserve the dispersal of settlement, an essential precondition for hunting. This factor caused a certain conflict between the trading company and the mission.

Hans Egede's mission project—first intended for the Norse population, but when they could not be found, transferred to the Greenlanders—was based on the Lutheran evangelical religion; this was maintained during the following centuries. The implementation of this principle depended on the individual's becoming conscious of his faith by personal choice. The individual had to be able to read in order to assimilate doctrine and read the Bible. The language—the West Greenlandic Eskimo dialects—had therefore to be studied and learned and a writing system created, which gave Egede and his successors a great deal of difficulty. Translating texts into Greenlandic and composing hymns took time. Egede got linguistic assistance from his sons and the young Greenlanders he took into his house. Quite early he established a practice that was followed in later decades: on frequent trips he sought out contact with Greenlanders of the area, attempting to instruct them about Christianity. As soon as the Greenlandic boys taught by him were able, he sent them out on similar trips.

The problem soon came to a head, since all instruction demands a certain residential stability of those being instructed. The Greenlandic hunting cycle made instruction difficult, so that the missionaries desired a more permanent settlement. Their trips also met with many troubles, such as the changeable weather and difficulties in obtaining transportation. The training of catechists took time, and few Greenlanders wished to follow this un-Eskimo vocation; besides, catechists were paid badly and had to live for the most part from their own hunting or depend on their relatives. Often they were persons who were not able to hunt because of some physical handicap. At first an attempt was made to train boys from the orphanage in Copenhagen to be catechists in Greenland. Some good catechists were produced in this manner, but during the course of the century interest in the vocation declined so that no catechists were sent out. With much difficulty, the mission attempted to increase the number of Greenlandic catechists trained by the various missionaries.

The number of colonies grew, but the state subsidy was not increased proportionately; this, too, impeded the progress of the mission since more missionaries could not be employed. It was therefore even more amazing that the mission became important to the West Greenlandic population as quickly as it did. Among the most important reasons for this success were probably the authority radiated by Hans Egede; the close contact that his sons, Poul and Niels Egede, had with the Greenlanders they lived among; and especially the devoted work of Giertrud Rasch, particularly during the frightful smallpox epidemic of 1733–1734. Probably also significant was the collapse of the authority of the traditional angakok (Greenlandic *angakkoq,* pl. *angakkut*), which seems to have been taking place when the first colony was founded. Angakoks continued to exist and to arise, especially in outlying districts, but their influence quickly faded. A number of revivals throughout the decades promoted the spread of Christianity. By 1782 the majority of the population of West Greenland

had been baptized. In 1775, the first church building in modern Greenland was consecrated in Holsteinsborg, built with funds raised by the local Greenlanders.

In 1733 the German Moravians were allowed to establish a mission in Greenland. It was intended that they should assist Hans Egede, but this Lutheran priest did not fit into the pattern of their creed, so they established their mission in the immediate vicinity of Godthåb. This gave rise to an unbecoming competition between the two missions. For many years the Moravians worked in vain, but in 1739 a revival occurred among the Greenlanders visiting them. From then on their mission grew, essentially because the Moravians demanded less knowledge than the Royal Mission as a prerequisite for baptism (fig. 5). Many Greenlanders, especially from the south, settled at their mission station. Economically things began well, but eventually the residential concentration depleted the local hunting resources. It also created strife between the Greenlanders of the colony district and those of the Moravian parish. Partly due to this overpopulation, the Moravians set up two stations farther south; both enjoyed tolerable economic conditions.

In other fields also, the Moravians influenced their supporters among the Greenlanders. They taught them useful crafts, although not to a professional degree. The Moravian procedures for housekeeping and daily life fit well into the Greenlandic culture, and their decorative, well-kept stations were imitated. In the south they raised sheep. The Moravians' economy was entirely outside the province of the Royal Mission and the trading company, as they received support from congregations in Germany and the Netherlands.

The fact that the Moravian missionaries were laymen

New York Public Lib., Rare Books and Manuscripts Div.: Moravian Church 1762:pl. 6.
Fig. 5. Moravian minister (A) at Neu Herrnhut (Norliit), Greenland, baptizing 3 men (B) and 2 women (C) before a congregation of Greenlanders. Engraving first published in 1757 (for the original drawing, see Müller 1926:opp. 48).

influenced their teachings. Their exposition of the Bible was easy to grasp, and their demands for the understanding of dogma were simple. On the other hand, they emphasized the individual's consciousness of faith, which in daily life should manifest itself in obedient humility; this brought a previously unknown degree of authority and submission into the life of West Greenland.

The priests of the Royal Mission had a university education. It was not always knowledgeable, qualified, and especially active missionaries that were stationed in Greenland during the course of the century, although there were several outstanding persons among them. Nor were all the Danish catechists equally proficient and stable. Some of the better ones quit and went to work for the trading company, for better wages. The progress of the mission rested on the personality and linguistic abilities of the individual missionary and catechist. Some missionaries developed a great deal of proficiency in Greenlandic, while others had to manage with an interpreter. Most of the Danish catechists became quite skilled in the language, partly because they stayed in Greenland and partly because they married Greenlandic women. On the other hand, the catechists born in Greenland often had a poor knowledge of Danish, so that the language problem persisted. Few of the trading personnel learned more Greenlandic than was absolutely necessary.

At settlements that had a missionary or a catechist, both adults and children received instruction. The instruction of the Moravians was quite lenient. That imparted by the Royal Mission included only reading and writing, and, for adults, catechism exercises; other subjects were of no interest to the mission. Schools for children, organized as boarding schools, seem to have been established as early as the 1730s. In addition, each missionary trained the Greenlandic catechists he thought he needed (see also "West Greenland Before 1950," this vol.).

The instruction, services, and devotions, as well as the opportunity to buy coveted commodities at the trading post, attracted Greenlanders. The possibility of getting immediate help in difficult times was also attractive. Greenlanders moved into the colony settlements, which were almost all located where harbor and construction conditions were best and where fresh water was available, without taking hunting resources into account. This migration therefore had unfortunate social and economic consequences.

Among those who moved into the colonial settlement were many widows and orphans, so that a large part of the colony population was dependent on the trading company and the mission. The colony administration was thus forced to resort to measures of social welfare, distributing provisions and sometimes encouraging individual craftwork. In Eskimo society, physically handicapped persons and those without providers had led a miserable existence; the Christian view of man and humane attitudes made social welfare necessary and natural, but this contributed to the concentration at settlements.

In the course of the eighteenth century, marriages between European men and Greenlandic women became common. The children of these marriages, as well as the many illegitimate children, eventually became a problem—especially the boys and the poor. Legally they were considered Greenlanders, following mercantilistic colonial principles. But in only a few cases were they raised as Greenlanders, with, for instance, an Eskimo diet. Very few could earn their living as hunters so that they were unproductive from a Greenlandic point of view. Gradually an entire population group was composed of the so-called half-breeds; in the following centuries they formed the nucleus of the population of West Greenland. Not until after 1782 was the future of such children attended to. Before then, some had been employed by the mission and the trading company, although the latter was in principle opposed to this practice.

Greenlandic manpower was attractive because it was cheap. In Denmark-Norway the wages of even a priest consisted to a great extent of payment in kind or the proceeds of the priest's own crops. In principle, Greenlanders were to be kept to hunting and must not therefore be "spoiled" by "un-national food." The Greenlandic standard of living was considerably lower than that of Europeans stationed in Greenland, so that the wages in money of a Greenlander could also be kept lower. Payment in money was considered in any case only a supplement, to more or less cover needs not provided for by payment in kind. Greenlanders' needs were judged to be small, and they had to get their own payment in kind by hunting and fishing. Thus the concept of "Greenland wages," considerably lower than the wages of Europeans stationed in Greenland, was introduced. Once in practice, it became traditional and difficult to eradicate, especially since it aided economizing efforts.

For the trading company, the economy was the paramount problem. In addition to practicing thrift, it was necessary to create a source of income. From the very beginning, Europeans stationed in Greenland had supplemented their provisions by hunting and fishing, from which the surplus such as fox skins, could be sold to the trader at the ordinary price. This developed into a practice that was actually illegal: Europeans hired Greenlanders to hunt for them and gave them some of the payment they received. This practice was forbidden and attempts were made to stop it, but it was nevertheless the basis of, for example, the enormous development of seal hunting with nets at Uummannaq. When Europeans sold monopoly products to skippers, or the skippers bought products for their own advantage, this constituted "underhand trade," against which the administration was continually on guard.

This private enterprise was to a certain extent channeled by the trading company taking over production in Greenland. In the case of seal hunting with nets, for example, the train oil was at first rendered in Copenhagen, but in the late eighteenth century the first extraction began to take place in Greenland. Nevertheless, the problem was to produce as much blubber as possible in Greenland; the Greenland hunters did not produce enough, so the trading company attempted several times to establish whaling in Greenland, but as it was only willing to invest a small amount of capital, the results were likewise small. However, whaling out of Holsteinsborg in collaboration with Greenlanders remained quite constant.

Attempts were made to engage in fishing, but with no prospects of establishing fishing as a stable occupation. The exploitation of mineral deposits was considered but resulted only in local coal mining at Uummannaq and Godhavn, primitively organized.

When the Royal Greenland Trade Department was established in 1774–1776, it was the intention of the government to initiate large-scale whaling off Greenland and around Svalbard. A large fleet of whaling ships was purchased and built. With renewed investment and a large subsidy, this project was carried out, but it was quickly abandoned due to the expense of operations. Whaling was declining all over the world. In 1777 the Netherlands and Hamburg suffered great losses through shipwrecks on the east coast and southwest coast of Greenland. Dutch whaling was reduced and ceased completely during the Napoleonic Wars; that of Hamburg was reduced. Greenlandic whaling remained, but in a different form. The government sold most of the whaling ships. It suspected that the whalers stationed in Greenland were not operating correctly, so it sent two inspectors out to investigate the situation and also the entire operation of the trading company. Whaling was now to be carried on, as previously at Holsteinsborg, in collaboration between Greenlanders and Europeans, and from coastal stations.

Eight whaling stations were established. But neither Holsteinsborg nor the new stations were favorably located for whaling. The Greenlanders who moved to these stations were essentially occupied in whaling and the concomitant production of whale meat and blubber and in general were forced to abandon their traditional sealing. Therefore, they had to be paid with European supplies and supported during bad whaling periods. There was a scarcity of sealskins, as it was dificult to procure them from elsewhere; this gave rise to a growing use of European clothing at these stations.

All in all, during the period from 1721 to 1782, the society of West Greenland became quite dependent on contact with Europe. The organization of this contact was in its period of growth quite chaotic and dissimilar from place to place. It had to be made more orderly.

1782–1900

The basis of the new organization was created by the activities of the two stationed inspectors in 1780 and 1781. One of them especially, Johan Friedrich Schwabe, had a decisive influence; he formulated the so-called Instruction of April 19, 1782, which formed the basis for the entire administrative work, as well as part of the cultural work, of the following hundred years. At the same time, West Greenland was administratively divided into two inspectorates, with inspectors' headquarters at Godthåb and Godhavn; Schwabe was at Godhavn.

The main objective of the Instruction of 1782 was to formulate a set of regulations to protect the Greenlanders. Rules were set up for mixed marriages. Both legitimate and illegitimate children were as far as possible to be raised to be "competent Greenlanders," with the boys as hunters; if this was impossible, they should become either useful craftsmen or workers for the trading company or the mission. The employees of the Trade Department were instructed to see to it that no hunter sold produce needed by him or his family during the winter. Alcoholic beverages were not to be sold to Greenlanders, except to those employed in whaling, where they were considered a necessity. Proficient hunters were never to be enticed away from their occupation, while incompetent ones were to be set to an occupation that they could master.

Attention was paid to the semifraudulent practices of which the employees of the trading company were occasionally guilty. Verified weights and measures were made compulsory, and a set of regulations was prescribed for buying and selling. All regulations had punishment provisions, but these applied only to Europeans; no punishment was stipulated for Greenlanders.

Social welfare in the form of the distribution of provisions during periods of famine was regulated. Credit granted to Greenlanders was subject to proper accounting. The trader was instructed to take care that the population did not concentrate too much in his district.

The Instruction laid down certain conservation regulations for eider ducks. Down collecting had developed into ruthless exploitation, and the down trade outside the monopoly had greatly increased. Much had gone to English whalers, who in growing numbers were moving into Disko Bay and surrounding waters.

To make prices uniform along the entire coast, an annual schedule was introduced for commodities sold and products purchased, published in Greenlandic as well as Danish, so that Greenlanders themselves could check that it was being observed.

Among the commodities were those previously available, but for a long time they were divided by the schedule into a group sold to all, another group sold only to Europeans, and a third group that could be ordered only through the Royal Greenland Trade Department—the so-called commission goods. This division was not intended to function as discrimination against the Greenlanders; on the contrary, it was to prevent tempting the Greenlanders to buy commodities that were considered destructive of their way of life. Nevertheless, the use of certain forbidden goods crept into the Greenlanders' culture. During the 1790s stimulants such as tea and especially coffee were used in small quantities as bonuses for hunters. Both of these, like tobacco previously, became much coveted by the Greenlanders, as was also the case with certain provisions such as beans, flour, and bread, in spite of the Danish principles.

Imported supplies also entered through the wages that were paid partly in kind to the Greenlandic employees of the Trade Department and the mission, as well as in whaling and as social welfare in periods of famine. Such times of hardship occurred periodically, differing from place to place, into the twentieth century. Around 1782 they were particularly common and regular at the whaling stations. To counter them in the northern inspectorate, Schwabe set up the world's first relief fund, based on the earnings of the local occupations. A certain percentage of the Greenlanders' share in the whaling proceeds, as well as fines for violating the Instruction of 1782, were put into savings. The fund provided relief in kind to all in times of need, help to widows and others without providers, as well as occupational help. It was a bit difficult to set up a corresponding fund in the southern inspectorate, where only Holsteinsborg had actual whaling, but the fund was finally established; however, it was never so important there as in the north, where incomes were large when the whaling was good. The relief fund of the northern inspectorate was partially used to pay the first resident doctor in Greenland.

Medical assistance had previously been only occasional. The whaling ships had to have a barber-surgeon on board, and when whaling began to be carried on from stations, the barber went on shore although required to function at the same time as a whaling assistant. This situation was untenable in the long run, and at everyone's request a surgeon was stationed at Godhavn to provide necessary medical assistance to all. The Royal Greenland Trade Department could not afford to pay a permanent doctor in each inspectorate, let alone set up the most rudimentary hospital, or in general organize an up-to-date health service. So it was assistants and catechists who performed bloodletting and other medical services; and they as well as the surgeon at Godhavn carried out smallpox vaccination.

Prompted by the smallpox epidemics, which ever since 1733/34 had ravaged one or another locality, as well as by the last violent epidemic of 1800, in which entire districts were laid waste, a systematic program of vaccination was initiated in 1804, with successful results.

Although the financial means of the Royal Greenland Trade were still limited, by the late 1790s they were at least somewhat more substantial than previously. By rationalizing all its activities, working profits were created. To a certain extent this was also due to the good prices for Greenlandic products that prevailed during the unrest in Europe and to the neutrality that Denmark-Norway attempted to practice.

The good times ceased abruptly. The Trade Department suffered losses in several shipwrecks, and English whaling was to a growing extent a threatening competitor. English ships called at Greenland ports, disturbing the protectionist policy of the Danish monopoly, which could not and did not want to prevent Greenlanders from going on board. The Greenlanders neglected their jobs and hunting and often sold their animal hides, clothes, kayaks, and hunting gear for gin. The English bought down and other products and also collected them themselves, in violation of the monopoly regulations. All kinds of excesses followed in the footsteps of the crews. After some clashes, however, a working arrangement was reached.

The mission was far too weak to counterbalance this influence; it had not benefited from the good times. Due to economy measures during an acute Danish-Norwegian financial crisis around 1790, the state subsidy was lowered considerably. The Royal Mission had to cut down its operations, but the Moravians did not. The number of missionaries in the Danish mission was cut in half, without employing more catechists to replace them. The two inspectors understood that not only the progress of the trading company but also social and cultural development depended on the instruction and moral support given to the Greenlanders. If the mission could not manage economically to a sufficient extent, the trading company itself would have to take steps; it considered improving the wages and education of the catechists by establishing a catechist training college at its own expense. This plan advanced so far that instruction was about to begin, when the entire development was abruptly interrupted.

Military events in Europe forced Denmark-Norway over into Napoleon's camp from 1807 to 1814. For West Greenland this meant that communications and supplies were made difficult, which threatened the relationship with the mother countries. All development plans were immediately shelved in 1807. Without going into details of events and the situation in West Greenland in the war years, it must be emphasized that West Greenland managed from year to year, partly with the help of the English. Personnel was reduced as some people sailed home voluntarily. Greenlandic products could not be bought up, except to pay for foreign supplies. Commodities for barter were lacking, and the products, which could not be sent to Denmark, would lose their value if they were stored indefinitely. Gunpowder and bullets came into short supply, to the detriment of hunting in Greenland. Traditional Eskimo techniques supported the Greenlanders for some time except in whaling, which was almost entirely abandoned. Greenlanders employed in whaling, as well as the many who could not hunt, suffered hardship. Everything that depended on outside supplies for maintenance and operations, such as buildings and ships, fell into disrepair.

Parallel with the Napoleonic wars, a separate war was waged between Sweden and Denmark-Norway from 1813 to 1814, when it was brought to an end by the Treaty of Kiel. The Danish Crown relinquished Norway to Sweden, but without the dependencies of the Norwegian Crown: Greenland, Iceland, and the Faroese Islands. This provision formed the basis for the continuation of Greenland within the kingdom of Denmark.

The situation after 1815 was determined by the economic resources of Denmark. During the first decade, the entire economy of Europe was rather poor. Denmark was, if possible, even more hard pressed than other countries, especially due to the bankruptcy of the state in 1813. Not until around 1830 did prospects get brighter.

English whaling off Greenland continued for a few decades after 1815 but diminished greatly. As an offshoot of whaling, a few expeditions were carried out. One of these was that of John Ross to Baffin Bay in 1818. At Cape York, Ross encountered Polar Eskimos and made contact with them for a short time with the help of the West Greenlander Hans Zakæus (figs. 6–7). This group was not again visited until the end of the century. In 1806 William Scoresby, Sr., was near Scores-bysund; William Scoresby, Jr., explored it from 1819 to 1822. In 1823 Capt. D.C. Clavering and Edward Sabine followed in their wake and on Clavering Island contacted the last living inhabitants of the East Greenland coast north of 71° north latitude; this too was but an episode. Nevertheless, the nineteenth-century rediscovery and survey of the entire land area of Greenland had begun; it continued into the next century, until the entire geography of Greenland was known, in general or in detail.

In the 1760s the surveying of the mineral deposits of the west coast and a modest exploitation of some of them was gradually begun, but conditions, knowledge, methods, and means were poor. From 1807 to 1813 the geologist Karl Ludwig Giesecke was in West Greenland. He traveled along the coast and described several mineral deposits, including the cryolite at Ivittut that the Greenlanders had pointed out during the general mineral collection that took place from the 1780s on.

Scott Polar Research Inst., U. of Cambridge, England.

Fig. 6. Hans Zakæus (John Sakeouse, John Sackhouse, John Sackheouse, Jack Saccheous), a West Greenlander from Jakobshavn (Ilulissat) or Upernavik, who went to Scotland in 1816 aboard the Greenland whaler *Thomas & Ann*. At Leith, according to the legend on this engraving, he demonstrated his skill with lance and kayak, winning a race with a 6-oared whaleboat and performing the kayak roll. He could sign his name (facsimile at bottom), learned English, and said he attended school in Greenland. Engraving after an unknown original painting by Amelia Anderson, 1816.

Cryolite was first exploited after 1859, by a Danish consortium. When it became known that this mineral could be used to make aluminum, production increased, with a Danish and a Canadian company as buyers. The exploitation was based on a concession from the Danish state, which received an ever greater share of the profits, first in the form of a royalty and later as a partner. This income was transferred directly to the Greenland account and thus benefited Greenlandic society. By virtue of the regulations of the Instruction, stipulating that Greenlanders must not be taken from hunting, they were spared becoming miners. Until 1953 the cryolite mine was a closed area, even for Greenlanders.

Economic activity in the remainder of West Greenland was slowly reconstructed under hard-pressed conditions. In 1804 credit notes had been introduced for use in trading with Greenlanders. They had been a success, but the war years made them useless. After 1815 their use was resumed; they again facilitated trad-

Fig. 7. Capt. John Ross and Lt. William Edward Parry exchanging knives for narwhal tusks with Polar Eskimo. Behind them are the West Greenlander Hans Zakæus, in beaver hat, and 2 Polar Eskimos looking in a mirror. Zakæus was enlisted in Scotland by Ross as interpreter. The expedition ships are *Alexander* and *Isabella*. Lithograph after an unknown original drawing by Zakæus, Aug. 1818.

ing and slowly promoted a transition to a greater degree of a money economy. To facilitate purchases and sales and to supply the districts more efficiently, several small trading posts were established under the leadership of managers, mostly of Danish descent. Many of these married Greenlandic women.

By 1789 the population of West Greenland was estimated at 5,122. By 1905 it had doubled, but this growth was not continuous; a number of years passed with a stagnation or even a reduction of the population. From 1825 to 1840 the population increase is estimated to have been 23 percent, and in the following 15-year period approximately the same. Although these figures must be accepted with all due caution, they do indicate relatively favorable living conditions and survival opportunities for the population. Health conditions were apparently improved. Housing became somewhat more healthy when window glass and interior walls of wood were installed in the earth huts.

By the end of this period the reconstruction had been

completed, to the extent that everything was in the same modest shape as previously. The Royal Greenland Trade Department had been reorganized; better and cheaper commodities had appeared in the shops; and the prices the Greenlanders received for their products were raised a bit. The small trading posts increased trade, which again became profitable, although only modestly so.

An introduction of free trade was therefore considered. As early as 1788 the possibility of free trade had been discussed by a commission, which rejected it out of consideration for the Greenlanders. In addition, if this free trade should turn out to be unprofitable, it would be abandoned, so that the state would again have to take over operations, in a much worse situation than before. The state was in any case responsible for the expenses of the mission. And the social arrangements that had been implemented, such as the price policy, could not be enforced.

From 1820 to 1840 the desire to liberalize West Greenland grew stronger, leading to a free-trade experiment south of Sukkertoppen. In 1835 a commission was appointed to examine operations in Greenland in their entirety. At the same time, the free-trade experiment degenerated into just what the commission of 1788 had feared. A majority of the 1835 commission again rejected liberalization but did recommend that government policy should aim at liberalization. More-over, the entire operation should pay for itself: any profits should not revert to the state but be plowed back into Greenland as investments for the progress of Greenlandic society.

According to this new principle, Greenlandic manpower was to be used to a greater degree, so that Greenlanders must be trained for service in the trading company, for useful crafts, or for mission work. This training necessarily took place in Denmark at public expense, that is, at the expense of the Royal Greenland Trading Company. The first priest born in Greenland had already been ordained in 1815.

The commission had indicated that improved schooling was a prerequisite for training opportunities. Such an improvement in turn required better teacher training in Greenland. As a consequence, two training colleges for catechists were established in1845. Neither of them attracted many students, so that one was discontinued in 1875, after which all higher education was concentrated in Godthåb. The men working there thus became the cultural leaders, and the Greenlandic tradition and the West Greenlandic language became dominant.

Health services were improved by stationing one doctor in each inspectorate. Two modest hospitals were erected after 1850. Midwives were trained; by 1855 a total of eight were active in West Greenland.

In 1848 the natural scientist H.J. Rink traveled in

Nationalmuseet, Copenhagen: Graah 1832:pl.7.

Fig. 8. Winter quarters of the Danish explorer Lt. Wilhelm A. Graah and his West Greenland women umiak rowers and man kayaker, at Nukarbik, East Greenland. The women cook over oil lamps while the man drums and dances. Graah's 1829–1830 expedition was one of the earliest European contacts with this area (Oswalt 1979:139–144). Engraving by I. Holm after a drawing by H.G.F. Holm based on a lost sketch by Graah.

568

North Greenland and later in the south. His observations of the movements of glaciers were fundamental to glaciology as a science (Rink 1857). The Lutheran creed by now reigned supreme, all paganism was eradicated, and almost everyone could read and write, but proficiency in arithmetic was poor. In this sense the situation was more or less satisfactory, but Rink deplored the fact that the mission had eliminated the original Eskimo social institutions and traditions. But the Trade Department was also partly responsible for this.

According to the liberal Danish constitution of 1849, the newly established parliament was to look into a number of affairs. A commission was appointed for Greenland in 1851, which was to take a position on the monopoly. Although a liberal current permeated the work of parliament, this commission recommended the continuation of the monopoly as hitherto. Rink returned from his work on the commission and was appointed inspector of South Greenland.

The condition of society must at that time have given Rink an impression of stagnation. Everything existed at a very low level; poverty, shabbiness, and apparent hopelessness dominated the picture. The amount of products purchased declined. The population was no longer increasing. Rink was of the opinion that West Greenlanders had lost their self-respect. Along with the former Moravian Samuel Kleinschmidt (a teacher and linguist) and two other leading Danish officials in Godthåb, he thought the self-respect of the Greenlanders could be reestablished if they were able to discuss and administer their own social affairs. For this purpose Rink began in 1861 the publication of the first newspaper in Greenland, *Atuagagdliutit*. In addition, in accordance with the establishment of the free constitution and municipal self-government in Denmark, they thought that corresponding municipal self-government should be established in Greenland, at first only limited, but with a potential for development in collaboration with the officials stationed in each district.

This idea was implemented in the establishment of the so-called *forstanderskaber* in 1862 in the south and 1863 in the north. The independent male providers of each settlement elected a *forstander* (local chief). These met annually by districts in district councils under the chairmanship of the district missionary and with the colony chief trader as accountant. The council was to administer the colony treasury, the funds of which were derived from a 25 percent (later 20 percent) tax on all products purchased in the district, paid by the Royal Greenland Trade Department. This income was divided, with three-fourths going to the colony treasury and one-fourth to the so-called common treasury of the inspectorate. Funds from the common treasury were used to support measures in the entire inspectorate, while those of the colony treasuries were used for poor relief, occupation help, and house-building support. Any

Det Kongelige Bibliotek, Copenhagen: A.5934.

Fig. 9. Celebration of the king's birthday at Dyvelskløerne near Godthåb. Participants include Danish employees of the Royal Greenland Trade Department, and well-to-do Greenlandic hunters. Food and drink were served, and there was a shooting match, with the bird on a pole serving as target. Godthåb fjord is in left background. Hand-colored woodblock print, evidently sold in West Greenland, done about 1862 by a Greenlandic artist, probably Aron of Kangeq but perhaps Jens Kreutzmann (I. Kleivan, communication to editors 1983; Oldendow 1957:227).

surplus was to be refunded the producers in proportion to the value of the products purchased in each district during the year in question.

These municipal councils functioned more or less as intended, but they could not change the economic and occupational development. Conditions remained pressing. Between 1860 and 1870 the population declined, as did also the number of sealskins purchased from each inhabitant. From 1870 on per capita production was in general in great decline. Whaling in the north was stagnant. The European demand for Greenlandic products fell, as did prices.

The relationship between population and production gradually became noticeably dislocated: the population rose again, but per capita production continued to fall. Imports of food products rose, disturbing the balance of trade and the nutrition of the population. Alternative occupations had to be found in addition to the traditional ones, but there was not much to choose from; fishing seemed to be the only available economic opportunity.

Ever since the 1770s there had been repeated attempts to introduce efficient fishing. Some years it was profitable, but for long periods these efforts were quite in vain. At the end of the nineteenth century, the economy of West Greenland had still not been straightened out, and at the same time, there was political stagnation in Denmark.

However, the curtain had already risen on a new era. In the United States, Secretary of State William H.

Seward had raised the question of the military vulnerability of the North American continent. Alaska, Greenland, and the West Indies were brought into the strategic picture. Alaska was purchased, but negotiations with Denmark on the purchase of the Virgin Islands did not take place until 1916. Denmark flatly refused to sell Greenland, although during the course of several centuries it had liquidated its Oriental and African colonial possessions. Greenland was not considered a colony in the same sense.

The geographic and other scientific problems of Greenland were investigated by several expeditions from Europe and the United States. Fridtjof Nansen from Norway was the first to cross the ice cap, in 1888. In Denmark the Commission for the Geological and Geographic Survey of Greenland had been set up in 1878 (later called the Commission for Scientific Investigations in Greenland), and the scientific journal *Meddelelser om Grønland* 'Reports on Greenland' began publication in the same year.

Two expeditions were especially important. The "Umiak Expedition," led by the Danish naval officers Gustav Holm and V. Garde, traveling from the south along the east coast, in 1883–1885 reached the area around the present Ammassalik, making contact with the East Greenland Eskimos. Mostly due to the political stagnation in Denmark, a mission and trading station were not established at Ammassalik until 1894. It is claimed that Danish colonization saved this group of Eskimos from ruin. In 1901 its population was 436; in 1905, 501. Both the trading company and the mission applied the same methods and organization as in West Greenland, and several West Greenlanders participated in the operation.

The second expedition included Robert E. Peary's repeated sojourns at Cape York between 1891 and 1909 (fig. 10), which led to contact with the Polar Eskimos. In 1910, when Peary had left the Cape York area for good, Knud Rasmussen established the station at Thule, which he directed until his death in 1933. It was taken over by the state in 1936.

1900–1950

Rasmussen had taken part in the Danish Literary Expedition of 1902–1904, which reestablished contact across Melville Bay. The participants in this expedition criticized in Denmark the entire administration of Greenland. In the Godthåb district council, semipolitical action was taken. The Danish legislature began to be directly interested in the problems of Greenland. This led to the Greenland Church and School Act of 1905, by which the mission was disbanded. For quite some time there had been no unbaptized persons in West Greenland, and the mission had quickly gained ground

in the east. The church in Greenland was enabled to be organized as a part of the Danish established church. Not until 1910 was Thule missionized, with a priest born in Greenland as the missionary. The Moravians had in 1900 handed over their stations to the Royal Mission and the Royal Greenland Trade Department and left the island.

There had been so many catechists trained in West Greenland that they could be stationed at most settlements and thus carry out actual schooling; but the smallest stations had to be content with a literate hunter or other self-employed person who would take it upon himself to teach as a "reader," usually in his own house. Several churches, chapels, and school chapels were erected. In 1907 a large training college was built at Godthåb, the first really imposing edifice in Greenland.

The criticism that had been raised in Denmark led to the appointment in 1906 of a commission, the work of which resulted in the Administration Law of 1908, which above all dissolved the institution of the directorates. Each district was divided into communes (Danish *kommuner*), local semi–self-administering units, with elected councils to administer the municipal treasuries. Criticism was gradually acknowledged politically. In each inspectorate or province in West Greenland, an indirectly elected provincial council (Danish *landsråd*), was set up to administer the funds of the common treasury. The funds of the various treasuries derived from a 20 percent tax paid by the Royal Greenland Trade on income from the sales of monopoly products purchased in each commune. Sixty-six percent of this amount went to the municipal treasury, 22.5 percent to the provincial treasury, and 11.5 percent to the newly established Common Fund for Greenland. In addition a tax of 2 percent was imposed on wages; this tax was distributed to the various treasuries in the same proportion. An interest of 4 percent a year was paid on treasury funds, without their being invested in anything.

A certain organization of the administration of justice was introduced. Previously, traditional principles had been applied to Greenlanders, while the Danish Law of 1683 with amendments had applied to others stationed in Greenland, so that a nonstatutory distinction was made between persons under Greenlandic law and persons under Danish law. This was not discrimination, but a protection of the Greenlandic population against unfair laws. The Instruction of 1782 with amendments was still valid.

The 1908 law distinguished sharply between trade and administration, which quickly led to confusion, because the distinction was made only at the highest levels, in Denmark, not in Greenland itself. In 1912 these areas of law were combined again.

At the same time a serious attempt was made to find new occupational opportunities for Greenlanders. In 1906 a native Greenlandic priest began to carry on ef-

Fig. 10. Arctic explorers depended heavily on Eskimo means of transport, Eskimo clothing, and often Eskimo guides, hunters, and other aid. left, Eivind Astrüp in Eskimo clothing at Navy Cliff, Independence Bay, Greenland, during Robert E. Peary's North Pole Expedition (Peary 1898,1:348–352). Photograph by Peary, July 4, 1892. right, The MacMillan Arctic Expedition, based at Etah, on the face of a glacier. Photograph by Donald B. MacMillan, 1925.

ficient sheep raising in the southernmost part of West Greenland. This had actually been attempted since the 1770s; wool, also processed into yarn in Greenland, had been sold. But sheep raising had never had any real significance, nor had cattle raising, which since 1782 had been carried on privately at Igaliku in Julianehåb fjord. However, after 1906 sheep raising grew to be a productive but risky occupation in the southernmost part of Greenland.

At the same time, it seemed that cod fishing would turn out to be a disappointment. But after the Tjalfe Expedition of 1908–1909, which demonstrated abundant quantities of cod, this industry grew, until by 1923 it was the dominant occupation of southwest Greenland.

The First World War had relatively little effect on Greenland. In conjunction with the Danish sale of the Virgin Islands to the United States in 1916, the Danish government inquired as to the position of the United States government on the extension to all of Greenland of the monopoly and the prohibition of imports, in accordance with the Regulation of 1776 and the Treaty of Kiel of 1814. The United States government had no objections to this, and Denmark then obtained statements from a number of other countries. In 1921 the entire island was placed under the monopoly. The Nor-

wegian government made an unexpected protest, but after difficult negotiations the Treaty of East Greenland was concluded in 1924. Norwegian hunters obtained certain rights, but Denmark and Norway retained their separate views on sovereignty over the uninhabited parts of East Greenland. In 1925, 83 East Greenlanders moved from Ammassalik, which was becoming overpopulated, to Scoresbysund, where an apparently viable society of hunters developed.

At that time Norwegian hunting was relatively recent, but it developed under the auspices of the Treaty of East Greenland, although never playing any important role in Norwegian economy. Due to certain differences of opinion, and under the influence of activist circles in Norway, Norwegian hunters occupied certain parts of the east coast of Greenland in 1930. The case was brought before the International Court of Justice at The Hague, which on April 5, 1933, disallowed this occupation on the basis of Danish sovereignty over all of Greenland according to the Treaty of Kiel. The Treaty of East Greenland of 1924 continued to be valid; it was prolonged in 1944 until further negotiations and renewed with amendments in 1947 until 1967, when a new 10-year agreement was concluded.

By the two-hundredth anniversary of Hans Egede's landing in Greenland, interest in Greenland was quite lively in Denmark, including political circles. Prior to the revision of the Administration Law of 1908, a commission was appointed in 1920 in which Greenlanders participated for the first time. It submitted its report in 1923, and a new Administration Law was passed on April 18, 1925.

Once again it had been deemed advisable to continue the monopoly, but the new law reorganized the administration and the trade department placing them under the common direction of the Greenland administration, which from 1936 on was itself under the prime minister's department. Otherwise no changes were made in the central administration, which ever since the 1880s had experts attached as advisors. The principle was established that the economy of Greenland should be self-financing, so that until 1950 Greenland was excluded from the ordinary Danish finance laws and budgets, with the exception of old-age pensions, which were covered by Danish social budgets.

The changes introduced in 1925 applied to conditions in Greenland itself. West Greenland continued to be divided into two provinces, each with a chief administrative officer (Danish *landsfoged*) with seats in Godthåb and Godhavn. Each province was divided into districts (*syssel*) roughly corresponding to the colony districts. These in turn were divided into communes, each with its council. The communal councils were elected by all men over 22. The district councils (*sysselråd*) consisted of the communal chairmen of the district and the representatives of the provincial council (*landsråd*), plus an equal number of officials stationed in Greenland. They were headed by the "sheriff" (*sysselmand*), who was also a kind of chief of police in the district and the chairman of the district court. The district council elected one or two representatives to the provincial council. Each of these councils administered its own treasury, the funds of which were derived in the same manner as under the law of 1908, calculated by communes and apportioned thus: 50 percent to the communal treasury, 25 percent to the district treasury, 15 percent to the provincial treasury, and 10 percent to the Common Fund.

The tasks of the various councils were more or less the same as previously. The communal councils were now empowered to submit ordinances to the district council for approval. In the future all bills directly concerning Greenland were to be submitted to the provincial councils for their comments before passage or rejection in the Danish parliament. The opinions of the provincial councils could also be obtained in other cases. The provincial councils were empowered to raise and discuss on their own initiative issues of general interest in Greenland. They assembled at first every other year, then every year. Throughout the years various essential issues were discussed, and criticism was voiced. The communal councils met as it suited them; the district

councils only once a year. The jurisdiction of the communal councils was somewhat narrowed, as several fields were transferred to the district councils: through committees they supervised schools, cemeteries, health services, and whatever else was considered reasonable.

The Administration Law of 1925 established compulsory school attendance from the age of 7 to 14. More promising pupils could continue two years at a secondary school, of which there were three for boys and one for girls. Finally, young men could continue in a two-year course at a "high school." Some of these left with a final examination, while others went on to a two-year course for catechists and teachers. All the higher levels were free boarding schools. Instruction in Danish was increased at all levels at the request of the Greenlanders.

The health services were organized with a doctor in almost every district. Hospitals were to be built to gradually supplement the few existing ones. Training was organized for midwives and nurses. The main task of the health services was the eradication of tuberculosis, which caused 36 percent of mortalities among Greenlanders until 1925. All the doctors as well as some of the nurses were Danes stationed in Greenland; all the mid-wives were Greenlanders. Doctors' consultations, hospitalization, and medicine were free for all.

All institutions could recommend Greenlanders for higher education in Denmark, which likewise took place at public expense. An ever-growing number of Greenlanders benefited from this, although the number recommended each year was not very large.

The administration of justice was reorganized. The "sheriff" was the judge and at the same time the public prosecutor in cases against "persons under Greenlandic law." The court was assisted by from two to four assessors, lay judges like the "sheriff." The chief administrative officer of the province, a trained jurist, acted as examining magistrate in cases concerning "persons under Danish law."

This statutory distinction between the two kinds of inhabitants of Greenland also entailed differences in rights, for instance, the right to order alcoholic beverages. When persons under Greenlandic law were in Denmark, they possessed the full rights of Danish citizens, but were exempted from compulsory military service. Thus in principle Greenlanders were considered Danish citizens; distinctions that applied in Greenland were dictated by the continued desire to protect Greenlanders under the monopoly against untraditional measures from the Danish society and against the influence of presumably harmful consumer goods. There had been and still were very few court cases in Greenland. Danes still hesitated to introduce a criminal code with provisions for punishment; on a traditional basis a kind of common law slowly developed. Prison sentences were almost never meted out.

Fig. 11. Health center in Sukkertoppen, Greenland. Children's tubercular hospital is in the distance; hospital and doctor's residence are on the hill. A Greenlandic sod and stone house with entrance passage is in the foreground. Photograph by Maynard Owen Williams, 1925.

On the basis of the Administration Law of 1925, cod fishing was systematized. From 1923 on, split and beheaded cod was purchased by weight. Eventually, salt fish for export was produced from this cod at every fishing harbor. Self-employed Greenlanders were forced to adjust from hunting to fishing, which essentially was carried on as a one-man job in small boats. This adjustment involved a more rapid transition to a money economy, as the fishermen were to an ever-growing extent forced to purchase their necessities, including food, with income derived from fishing.

For 1925–1926 the budget was just under 2.9 million Danish crowns, with a deficit of under 65,000 crowns. For 1939–1940, the budget was just under 5.3 million crowns, with a deficit of over one million crowns. The principle that the economy of Greenland should be self-financing entailed that the development of new occupations, including attempts at fox raising, depended on the capital derived from profits from the sales of Greenlandic products. There was never any real capital formation, and the monopoly prevented private investment. Therefore fishing progressed slowly, as did also secondary industries connected with fishing. The primitive methods limited fishing to sheltered waters. Cod shoals on the banks in Davis Strait were left to the Portuguese, the French, and the Faroese. From 1936 on the Faroese acquired certain shore facilities. In 1937 Færingehavn south of Godthåb was internationalized. Greenlanders repeatedly expressed their concern over this development and wanted the protection of the monopoly against outside competition. In spite of all this, cod fishing became the dominant occupation in the south. Sealing in the north had gradually been pressed back to a few of the northernmost districts and the east coast. Thule had its own special kind of economy.

Around 1939 the situation was felt to be stagnant. A thorough discussion of conditions in Greenland was contemplated, but the Second World War interrupted all reform plans. When Denmark was occupied by German troops on April 9, 1940, it was up to Greenland to survive as Danish territory but on its own economy. This succeeded, essentially because of the cryolite, but also because the United States helped to establish sales outlets for Greenland products in the West.

Modern technology had come to Greenland on a modest scale from 1925 to 1940. Especially important was the radio, which made for closer communication with the outside world, particularly Denmark. Motor boats chugged along the coasts and in the fjords. The number of kayaks and umiaks was continually falling. However, sled transportation still played an important role in the north at that time. Steamships and later ocean liners crossed the Atlantic and made for safer and surer communications to the east coast and Thule. Small motorized schooners were used for domestic voyages. In the 1930s the first airplanes appeared over Greenland, direct harbingers of a new era and a completely new situation for Greenland.

The Second World War confirmed the strategic predictions of William H. Seward. The German threat to Allied shipping on the East Coast, the supply lines of the lend-lease program across the Atlantic, and the rapid development of aviation all gave Greenland a central position in defense policy. These factors, along with the Allied Powers' need for Greenlandic cryolite, led to the conclusion of the so-called Kauffman treaty between the United States and the free ambassador of Denmark in Washington, Henrik Kauffman. This treaty dealt with the defense of Greenland, but in reality assured the defense of the United States and its domination of the air space over the north Atlantic. The United States was granted the right to establish air bases on the ice-free coasts of Greenland. The chief administrative officers of the provinces of Greenland had, according to the Administration Law of 1925, the right to represent the Danish government in emergencies and to act according to their own discretion. They recognized the Kauffman treaty.

This development immediately led to American activity in certain fjords in Greenland, and closer relations between the United States and Greenland. The United States set up a consulate at Godthåb; a Canadian consulate followed. Commitments deriving from the agreements of 1916 and from Danish sovereignty over Greenland were observed. Nothing was changed by the direct participation of the United States in the war. Greenland made a considerable contribution to its own defense through the Northeast Greenland sled patrol.

The Danish administration in Greenland attempted to maintain the principles of the 1925 law and to continue internal development according to previous di-

573

rections, but in spite of this, contacts with Canada and the United States brought about a general change in the Greenlandic mentality. Different, although not always better, commodities were available, and more advanced needs were created among Greenlanders. It was shown that Greenland could manage by itself in an emergency as long as the cryolite held out and that this society could administer itself if no special development was to take place.

Greenlanders felt that administration policy toward Greenland after the war could not return completely to the provisions of the 1925 law. However, many, both in Greenland and in Denmark, felt in 1945–1946 that the wartime changes were destined to oblivion. This produced violent criticism in the following years, concentrated in a demand for a thorough investigation of all the problems of the island. Critics wanted the 225–year-old monopoly to be abandoned in favor of a liberalization, but the monopoly of the Royal Greenland Trade Department prevented its own dissolution. The war had shown that Greenland could not exist in a military vacuum. Nor could it continue to be an economic vacuum. This criticism was gradually acknowledged politically.

1950–1972

As agreed with the Greenland provincial councils, a comprehensive commission was appointed in 1949, with many Greenlanders participating. Its report, submitted in 1950, prompted the passage of eight laws that deliberately set the stage for the integration that followed in the Danish Constitution of 1953. The laws dealt with:

(1) administration. One provincial council was established for the whole of Greenland, elected directly with equal voting rights for all persons over 21 (later 20). The communes were combined into a few large ones, each having a local council directly elected by all voters resident in the commune.

(2) the public treasuries, the funds of which were henceforth to derive from sales taxes.

(3) the church.

(4) schools. These were divorced from the church and put under local direction. A new school system was set up, which was to lead to a more gentle transition to higher education in Denmark. This in turn was to be made more efficient and more comprehensive.

(5) health services, which were reorganized with hospitals and intensified nurses' training.

(6) The Royal Greenland Trade Department, which was changed into a temporary organization for the purchase and processing of Greenlandic products, the supply and distribution of commodities throughout Greenland, and transatlantic and domestic navigation. It was to work to make itself eventually unnecessary. A trade

conditions equalization fund set up later to equalize price fluctuations had an anti-liberalizing effect and was abolished.

(7) business. This law abolished the monopoly and opened Greenland to private enterprise, including cooperatives.

(8) an occupational loan fund.

A ninth law dealing with the administration of justice was passed in 1951. A provincial court was established in Godthåb and several local district courts were instituted. A police authority was set up in each court district, and lay bailiffs were to supervise law and order locally. After thorough and radical preparation, the Criminal Code of 1954 was passed, based partly on Greenlandic tradition and partly on modern principles of resocialization. Persons could be held in custody in an "open prison" at Godthåb. In all laws the distinction between population groups according to place of birth in or outside of Greenland was tacitly abolished.

Modernization was able to begin in all fields, but all plans were undone almost at once by a rapid rise in population. A drastic fall took place in infant and total mortality, due to the effective control of tuberculosis. A tuberculosis sanatorium was located at Godthåb; several hundred patients were sent to sanatoria in Denmark, and modern chemotherapy was used. The population born in Greenland rose from 22,148 in 1948 to 30,378 in 1960 and to 38,914 in 1969: a total increase of over 75 percent. Modernization likewise brought about a drastic increase in the population born outside of Greenland, from over 900 in 1948 to 2,762 in 1960 and 7,417 in 1969: an increase of over 700 percent. A number of Danes took their families to Greenland and settled there for some time as merchants, master craftsmen, and the like; office workers and officials stationed in Greenland usually took their families along.

The relatively large investment in all fields demanded thorough planning and the administration of large grants from the Danish state. Capital could not be derived from production in Greenland alone. The investment and operations expenses of the state rose from 41 million Danish crowns in 1951 to 567 million crowns in 1969, and can be estimated at 700 million crowns the following year. Taking inflation into account, state expenses in Greenland increased 400 percent between 1950 and 1970. Modernization entailed the concentration of construction and installation activities under one authority, the Greenland Technical Organization, with local representatives in each municipality.

The population explosion increased the demands on priorities; attention was concentrated on settlements located on open water, which brought about a concentration of the population at these settlements. This concentration seems to have taken place too quickly, so that people had a feeling of alienation, resulting in political dissatisfaction and the lack of social balance.

Greenlanders' passive acceptance of conditions was replaced by the insecurity of a society in development. Crime and the consumption of alcohol rose.

The rise in population made extraordinary demands on the school system. An acute shortage of teachers could be compensated for only by the stationing of Danish teachers in Greenland. The training of Greenlandic teachers was insufficient, although the training college was reorganized more than once. Although the Danish teachers seldom had a mastery of Greenlandic, the language policy of the past was maintained in principle; however, instruction in Danish was intensified due to the teacher situation, and partly also at the request of Greenlanders themselves. Although the transition to higher education was made easier, the number of Greenlanders educated to be qualified for the assumption of executive positions was insufficient.

The Criminal Code of 1954 was to be followed up by scientific investigations of its effects. An interdisciplinary social research committee appointed in 1955 had the opportunity to accomplish only modest results. Nevertheless, it was instrumental in the appointment of a political-administrative committee in 1960 to discuss again the problems involved. The report of this committee, submitted in 1964, resulted in a more stringent program for the future.

Fishing developed with an increasing number of motor boats, for which any person resident in Greenland could get a favorable loan. Small processing installations were built, both by private investment and with public funds. The cod changed its habitat, however, and it was feared that lower sea temperatures were coming. Cod fishermen were forced to go farther out into Davis Strait, which led to larger trawlers being built by the state. This meant an open competition with foreign fishermen on the banks. Among fish products, shrimp were considered the salvation of the Greenlandic fishing industry; salmon products also helped. Sealing and whaling declined drastically between 1923 and 1960, but thereafter sealing showed some progress.

On shore the new installations provided jobs for many women and men. Many others found jobs in the service occupations brought in by modernization. A proportionately small number of Greenlanders was employed in construction and installation, due to their lack of training and technical experience. Technical training was therefore organized at Godthåb, as well as navigation training. A number of Greenlanders started shops or kiosks; many of the shops prospered from the sale of special commodities. The shops of the Royal Greenland Trade Department were continually obstructed in competition by their obligation to import a balanced list of supplies, to which the private shops were not subject. Some of the shops of the department were taken over by cooperatives. The selection of retail commodities available exploded in the same manner as the population. Sealing, hunting, and fishing, as well as some reindeer and sheep raising could not sufficiently supply the Greenlanders with their daily necessities. They therefore became dependent on a rising import of foodstuffs. In general, the average standard of living was raised.

The increase in the standard of living of Greenlanders was coupled with better housing facilities. Standardized housing construction increased the number of dwellings, including apartment buildings, involving facilities of an urban nature, such as electricity, running water, sanitary installations, sewers, roads, garbage collection, and central heating. Hydroelectric power was undependable, and usually too far away, so that all power was based on oil motors, with a rise in oil and gasoline imports as a consequence.

In order to find new sources of income for Greenlanders, the work of the Greenland Geological Survey, begun in 1928, was intensified. Both Danish and foreign expeditions made a scientific contribution. Lead deposits were discovered by Lauge Koch at Mesters Bay in 1948, but their exploitation turned out to be unprofitable. Later mineral discoveries on the west coast were planned for exploitation. Prospecting and exploitation take place within a general framework, so that the state supervises these ventures and gets a share of the profit, for the benefit of Greenlandic society. Essentially foreign capital is involved in prospecting.

Planning for the near future and the tempo of modernization began to take on the unmistakable appearance of remote control. Greenlandic local assemblies often had to negotiate on local interests in consultations in Copenhagen. The Constitution of 1953 gave Greenland (and also the Faeroe Islands) two representatives in the Danish parliament. From 1960 to 1964, and again from 1971 to 1973, one of the Greenlandic representatives was also the minister for Greenland in the government. In 1964 a committee of Danish and Greenlandic politicians and some nonparliamentary experts was set up to keep watch on developments and to negotiate on various activities and priorities.

The 1941 treaty on the defense of Greenland had to be terminated, according to its own provisions. After negotiations with the United States, and in consideration of the establishment of the North Atlantic Treaty Organization, this treaty was resurrected in a somewhat altered form in 1951. The technical development of defense had changed, and the United States wanted to build the Distant Early Warning radar line. The lines of international antagonism had changed. Some of the air bases in Greenland became superfluous. The base at Søndre Strømfjord was converted to civil aviation and became the main port of entry and exit for passengers to and from Greenland, who are transported farther with helicopters and coastal ships. Under the new defense treaty, Dundas Base was built in 1951 near old Thule, entailing the moving of Thule to Qarnaq, or New Thule, actually a better hunting center than the old settlement. Strategically and with respect to traffic, Greenland occupies a less central position than during and immediately after the Second World War.

Sources

General surveys of the history of Greenland written in English are few. Bobé (1928–1929) and Ostermann (1928–1929) have contributed brief essays, while Bobé (1952) has published in English a biography of Hans Egede. Gad (1967–1976) is a detailed account in Dan-ish, with full documentation of the manuscript and printed sources, nearly all of which are in Danish. An English edition (Gad 1971–1982) is less thoroughly documented, but contains a short survey of the sources in volumes 2–3. The manuscript sources, in Danish or Greenlandic, are mostly preserved in official Danish archives. Official documents, such as orders and laws, and statistics referring to recent times are published in Danish and Greenlandic in several series issued by the Ministry for Greenland Affairs, Copenhagen. From the same source appear the official reports of various institutions and the long series of minutes of the different provincial councils, all in Danish or Greenlandic.

Polar Eskimo

ROLF GILBERG*

Territory and Environment

The Polar Eskimo, who speak an Inuit-Inupiaq (Eastern Eskimo) dialect (Holtved 1952), are the northernmost human population in the world. Their territory (called Avanersuup Kommunia, formerly Thule District) is on the west coast of North Greenland from 75° to 79°30′ north latitude and from 58° to 74° west longitude (fig. 1). It is separated from West Greenland to the south by the uninhabited shores of Melville Bay, and from the rest of North Greenland by the Humboldt Glacier. Bounded by the Greenland ice cap to the east, and by Kane Basin, Smith Sound, Baffin Bay, and Melville Bay to the west, the land of the Polar Eskimos can thus be regarded as an island in an ocean of ice. Within this vast region, the area used for settlement is relatively small.

The climate here is arctic, with long, cold winters and short, cool summers. January and February are the coldest months, with an average temperature of −30°C (−22°F). In July and August, the average temperature is about +5°C (+41°F). Because the water in this climate tends to freeze, there is little evaporation, and the precipitation is quite low. Winter storms disperse most of the little snow that falls, so that dogsledding on land may be difficult in windy places.

By the middle of October the fjord ice is strong enough to sled on safely. From December to June the sea is covered by ice. In June most of the snow on land disappears, and small pools of water collect on the sea ice; but dogsledding continues until storms in July break up the ice and bring open water. The ice foot is shore ice frozen to the bottom and separated from the sea ice by a crack made by the tide. When the sea ice has gone, the ice foot persists for some time, often serving as a sled road along the shore when the sea ice is absent or unusable.

On the basis of ice conditions the Polar Eskimo year might be divided into a nine-month sledding season (October to June) and a three-month kayak season (July to September). On the basis of the presence or absence of the sun, the year could be divided into four seasons: a four-month period of darkness from late October until late February when the Polar Eskimos can travel by moonlight; a two-month season with day and night, with the dark period getting shorter and shorter until it disappears in late April; a four-month season during which the sun shines continuously, late April to late August: and a two-month season with day and night, with the day getting shorter and shorter until it disappears completely in late October (Freuchen and Salomonsen 1960; Gilberg 1976a; Rasmussen 1921a). The Polar Eskimos themselves divide the year into five periods each having a specific name, *ukiaq* (mid-September to late November), *kaperlaq* (late November to mid-February), *qaammaaq* (mid-February to mid-April), *upernaaq* (mid-April to the end of June), and *aasaq* (July to mid-September).†

History

The first known written mention of the neighborhood of Smith Sound was made by William Baffin, who in 1616 reached Hakluyt Island. About 200 years passed before Whites came in contact with Polar Eskimos with the arrival of John Ross in August, 1818 (Rasmussen 1921:1–3). Polar Eskimos told Ross through the West Greenlandic interpreter Hans Zakæus that they considered themselves the only people in the world and that at first they had looked upon Whites as gods from the sky (Ross 1819).

The discovery and rough mapping of the northern waters led European whalers to penetrate farther north in Baffin Bay. They began to visit the Polar Eskimo at Cape York in early July to exchange wood and iron products for fox and polar bear skins. From 1849 to 1861 expeditions led by James Saunders, Edward A. Inglefield, Elisha Kent Kane, and Isaac Israel Hayes searching for the lost expedition of John Franklin visited the Polar Eskimo but influenced their culture very little (Laursen 1972).

Culture About 1850

During the first half of the nineteenth century the climate of North Greenland was relatively cold, dry, and

---

*Translated from Danish by the author and Charles Jones.

†No phonemic analysis for the dialect of the Polar Eskimos is known to the editors. Polar Eskimo words are given in the transcription provided by Gilberg.

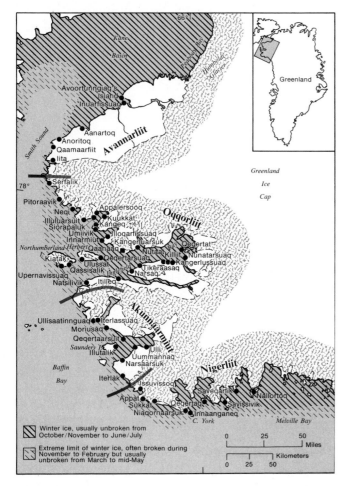

Fig. 1. Polar Eskimo territory in the early 20th century. During parts of the year hunting grounds extended north and west to Washington Land, Greenland, and Ellesmere I., Canada. Ice conditions after Vibe (1950).

stable. This period must have been a difficult one for people living north of Melville Bay, since the ringed seals left their fjords and migrated south to the central part of West Greenland, also causing a decline in the polar bear population (Vibe 1967:52).

The Polar Eskimo constituted a small, isolated, self-supporting society, numbering perhaps about 200 people. Living exclusively from hunting, they were settled along the coast in small, scattered groups of one to three families, totally dependent on the seasonal variations of their environment. Each year they had to struggle through two critical periods in which only a few exploitative possibilities were open to them, given their technology. During spring and fall they were forced to store meat supplies for summer and winter consumption.

Since the kayak was then unknown to the Polar Eskimo, small groups spent the summer isolated in skin-tent camps below mountains where birds could be hunted. When ice had covered the fjords and the sea, they could leave their bird rookeries by sled to begin accumulating

winter supplies, before the darkness slowed down all outdoor activities. Winter was spent in stone houses, which were a modified form of the winter house of the Thule culture whalers. Winter supplies were usually rather small due to the short time available for accumulating them, so that toward the end of the period of darkness famines were common.

Immigration of Canadian Eskimos in the 1860s

Around 1856 a small party of Eskimos, primarily or wholly Iglulik (Petersen 1962), migrated from Baffin Island to live among the Polar Eskimos, where they arrived in 1861. This immigration had an extremely important influence on the culture of the Polar Eskimo, as the Canadians introduced the following features (Rasmussen 1908:32):

(1) Many myths and songs, which indicates that much of the mythology recorded from the Polar Eskimo actually originated with the immigrants of the 1860s (Holtved 1967:178; Hauser 1975).

(2) The building of snowhouses with long low passages and entrances from below. Lacking these features, the Polar Eskimo snowhouses had been colder.

(3) The production and use of the three-pronged fishing spear for Arctic char.

(4) The production of the kayak and the technique of hunting with it. The Polar Eskimos explained that they had lost the ability to build kayaks when a disease exterminated all the old people, and the people who survived were too young to have learned this craft (Rasmussen 1908).

(5) The production of bows and arrows, and the use of them in hunting ptramigan and caribou. In spite of the small area that was free of permanent ice, large numbers of caribou roamed the district in the 1860s (Vibe 1967:168), yet the Polar Eskimo had considered the caribou and the ptarmigan to be unclean animals, unfit for human consumption. This opinion changed after 1865.

On the other hand, the Canadian immigrants adopted the Polar Eskimo sled type, as they found it better adapted to driving on sea ice, mainly because of the upstanders and the fan-shaped dog hitch with traces of equal length.

The new technology influenced the settlement pattern of the Polar Eskimo. The kayak allowed more flexibility in the summer: people were no longer bound to the bird mountains but could spread over the entire coast and better explore all available subsistence possibilities. There was also no longer any need for storing supplies for the summer, so that all efforts could be concentrated on accumulating sufficient supplies for the annual late winter crisis. The population did not increase, as mortality was still great; diseases brought by whalers had an especially bad effect on Polar Eskimo

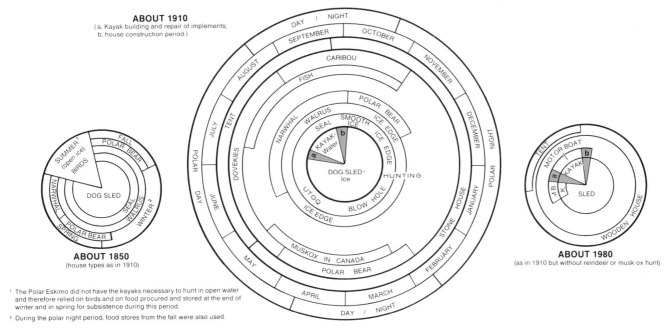

¹ The Polar Eskimo did not have the kayaks necessary to hunt in open water and therefore relied on birds and on food procured and stored at the end of winter and in spring for subsistence during this period.

² During the polar night period, food stores from the fall were also used.

Fig. 2. Seasonal cycle for about 1850, 1910, and 1980.

viability (for more details see Gilberg 1974–1975; Mary-Rousselière 1980; Petersen 1962; Rasmussen 1908:23–36; Uvdloriaq 1976).

Interbreeding and Migration

Nineteenth-century whalers may have borrowed a Polar Eskimo woman occasionally, but this does not seem to have left a serious imprint on the population of Thule District. The Canadian immigrants of the 1860s added nine females and seven males to the population. After contact with West Greenland was reestablished in 1904, some West Greenlandic women, mostly from Upernavik District, married Polar Eskimo hunters. From 1900 to 1959, 17 females were imported; in the 1960s, 13 women from West Greenland married into the Polar Eskimo population (fig. 3). The total of non-Polar Eskimos of both sexes added to the Polar Eskimo gene pool was 32 persons between 1900 and 1959, and 28 persons between 1960 and 1969 (Gilberg 1976).

Culture About 1900

Settlement Pattern

Ordinarily a man and his family spent only one or two winters at the same winter settlement. If a family decided to spend more than one winter in the same stone house, they retained the right to use it until they moved, whereupon this right reverted to the first family that moved in. The summer was spent in a skin tent at a summer settlement close to the place where the family had decided to spend the next winter, so that winter supplies of meat, accumulated during the summer and fall, would not be too far away.

This movement was due to the need to exploit various game animals. Settlements were usually located 50–100 kilometers apart and had good communication during the ice season; but they were rather isolated during the summer, when the ice was gone and the only means of transportation was the kayak, as the Polar Eskimo had no umiaks.

Generally a family would stay two or three years within one of the four subdistricts into which the Polar Eskimo divide their territory. Some settlements were inhabited year after year, although not always by the same individuals; others were inhabited only now and then, by small groups. Settlement sites had to have access to fresh water, either from lakes or from glacial ice floating in the fjords; there should be good sledding conditions to and from the sea ice or the ice cap; hunting conditions should be favorable; there should be plenty of flat stones and turf for house building; and there should be some shelter against bad weather, such as storms and heavy snowfall (Holtved 1944; Thomsen 1912).

Structures

In May the family moved into its skin tent, where it lived until September, when the nights became too cold. The summer camp might be moved, depending on the animals hunted. The tent was as a rule a one-family dwelling (fig. 4).

One nuclear family inhabited a stone house from September to May, perhaps accompanied by some parents

579

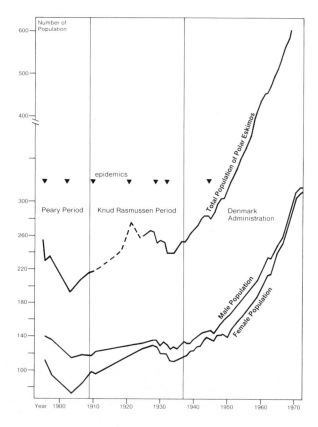

after Gilberg 1976:figs. 8, 10.
Fig. 3. Growth in the Polar Eskimo population, 1893–1973.

and Pitoraavik in February–March. For more on house types, see Holtved (1967:13–33), Steensby (1910:311–329), Ekblaw (1927–1928:161–173), and Rasmussen (1921:19–27).

Transportation

The sled, the most important Polar Eskimo means of transportation, was used up to 10 months of the year (fig. 6). Two parallel solid runners of oak or pine wood formed the foundation for a platform of boards, bound to the runners with skin straps, spaced so that an extra board could be laid between each, unbound. In the 1920s–1930s the loose boards were lashed to the fixed cross boards; after World War II a longitudinal board was nailed below all the loose and fixed cross boards. In this way the sled was at the same time flexible and stable; one runner could move separately from the other, which was advantageous when driving in rough ice. Along the entire length of the bottom edge of the runners were fastened sled shoes cut from tusks or, since 1900, made of strap-iron. In very cold weather water warmed in the mouth was spat on the edges of the runners to eliminate friction; this measure is especially useful in loose powdery frost and snow, which act almost like sand on the iron shoeing. Two upstanders with a couple of intercrossing straps were lashed to the runners at the back; these were used to keep the sled on course. Along the outside of the runners was placed a heavy side-thong, to which was attached the zigzag lashing across the sled load.

The Polar Eskimo kept their dogs tied up at all times. This made life in the settlements safer, especially for children, and no time was lost in gathering the dogs together when they were to be used. The risk that the dogs might eat straps and other skin products was reduced by removing the sharp points of their carnassial teeth. Dog boots, sewn from square pieces of skin, were sometimes used to protect their paws from sharp crystals on the sea ice in the spring.

The kayak introduced by Canadian immigrants in the 1860s was the fairly broad, heavy Baffin Island type, about five meters long with a triangular manhole. There was no kayak stool for the harpoon line, which instead was coiled up and fixed to a square wooden frame covered with skin on one side. This was thrown out together with the float when harpooning and functioned as a

or siblings of the spouses. It was heated by a blubber lamp that burned continuously, tended by the wife. Ventilation in a stone house was good. Warm air was kept inside by the pressure of the cold air in the depressed entrance passage. The temperature of the stone floor was around the freezing point, so that frozen meat and ice for drinking water were kept there; the air on and above the sleeping platform varied from 15°C (59°F) to 25°C (77°F), so that no clothing was needed. If the air in the house became too stale, a wad of dry grass was removed from the air hole in the roof, called the nose of the house, and fresh air was admitted from the entrance passage.

The snowhouse, built of spiralling blocks of snow, was for the Polar Eskimo only a temporary dwelling used while traveling and when hunting walrus at Neqi

top left and center right, © Natl. Geographic Soc., Washington; top right and bottom, Rolf Gilberg, Copenhagen; center left, Arktisk Institut, Charlottenlund, Denmark.
Fig. 4. Habitations. top left, Snowhouses, made of blocks of snow arranged in spirals, used during hunting trips. Children in front are playing at capturing a walrus. Photograph by Donald B. MacMillan, Pitoraavik, 1925. top right, Maassannguaq talks to his mother through a gutskin window in their winter house at Nallortoq (Cape Melville). Photograph by Aage Gilberg, March 1939. center right, Permanent winter sod house with entrance passage, Uummannaq. Additional sod slabs on the right and left were cut each fall to rebuild the walls and roof. Photograph by R.J.S. Tickle, before 1946. center left, Pualorsuaq, his wife Qiajuk, and child in front of their summer skin tent with wooden door. Photograph by Erik Holtved, Thule, 1937. bottom, Uummannaq in 1939. Largest building is the hospital, the next Peter Freuchen's store, with Knud Rasmussen's house adjacent. Photograph by Aage Gilberg.

GILBERG

POLAR ESKIMO

Rolf Gilberg, Copenhagen.
Fig. 5. Interiors of houses. top, Eqilana cooking in her winter house at Uummannaq. The wooden walls are covered with newspaper, to give additional warmth and light. A drying frame hangs from the ceiling on which boots and the cooking pot are hung. bottom, One-room wooden house built at Qaanaaq in 1953. Aminnguaq, wife of Iggianguaq Odaq, removes ashes from the coal stove. Photographs by Aage Gilberg. top, April, 1939; bottom, June 1963.

drag anchor. The kayak was often transported on a sled for hunting at the ice edge. After 1910, features of the West Greenlandic kayak type came gradually to the Polar Eskimo so that by the 1930s the construction of the Polar Eskimo kayak generally corresponded to that of West Greenland, with some modifications due to the materials available.

More on transportation is available (Ekblaw 1927–1928:15–21; K. Hansen 1969–1970; Herbert 1981; Holtved 1967:61–82; Steensby 1910:352–362).

Subsistence

The Polar Eskimo supported themselves exclusively by hunting (fig. 7). The variety of animal species in their area was not great, but in general there was enough of each species to feed the population. During famines any game present was hunted. The most common marine animals hunted were the bearded and ringed seal (all year), the walrus (all year), the narwhal (summer), the white whale (summer), and fish (summer and fall). On land, caribou (fall), fox (all year), hare (all year), polar bear (spring and fall), and musk-oxen (spring, in Canada) were hunted. A number of birds, such as the thick-billed murre (Brünnich's guillemot), dovekie (little auk) (fig. 8), sea gull, eider, and ptarmigan, were caught from spring to fall (Ekblaw 1927–1928:1–15; Holtved 1967:83–122; Macmillan 1918; Malaurie 1974; Rasmussen 1921:12–27; Vibe 1950).

Unlike the West Greenland Eskimo, among the Polar Eskimo males flensed most of the animals killed, before turning over the skins to the women for scraping and drying. Like other Eskimo, they had an established system for sharing the catch. In general, only hunters who had participated in the hunt and in the flensing of a large animal would get a true hunting share. However, if others happened to be present, they sometimes received small portions of meat as a present. Sometimes when a young man had made his first catch, the meat was distributed to everybody at the settlement, especially to the older people. A hunter was proud to have enough meat to give to others either directly or at a large gathering (Holtved 1967).

Until groceries such as coffee, tea, and biscuits could be bought at the store, the Polar Eskimo lived exclusively on animal food, which in 1980 still accounted for the greater part of their diet. Meat was eaten boiled, dried, frozen, or fermented. Certain meats were also eaten raw. Principal among these were blubber and the livers of seal and caribou eaten right after the kill and the tasty hide of narwhal and white whale (Greenlandic *mattak*). This hide is said to be important in preventing scurvy since it contains quantities of vitamin C when eaten raw (A. Gilbert 1948). The chief sources of meat were seals, walruses, narwhals, white whales, and dovekies. Bear and fox livers were not eaten: it was said that they "made one's skin peel off" (Ekblaw 1921, 1927–1928:185–193; Holtved 1967:142–144; Freuchen 1961:95–114). This is probably a reference to the results of hypervitaminosis A.

Clothing and Adornment

The men wore skin boots reaching to the knees, with soles of bearded seal skin and the upper parts usually of waterproof depilated sealskin. Stockings were usually made of hare or dog skin with the fur turned inward.

Fig. 6. Sled made primarily of bone with some ivory and wood. Pieces are attached with walrus skin thongs and occasionally sinew. As wood became available from European sources the composition but not the form of the sled changed. Length of runners 142.0 cm; collected by John Ross, Melville Bay area, Aug. 14, 1818. (See King 1983 for documentation and construction details.)

Between the boot sole and the stocking, an insole of dry grass was placed to insulate against the cold and absorb humidity and sweat. The men's trousers were made of polar bear skin with the fur side out. They were worn in all seasons, as were the boots. The thighs between the boots and the trousers were covered by fox tails in cold weather. Above the trousers, a soft, light inner coat made of dovekie or thick-billed murre skins was worn directly against the skin with the feather side in. Over this inner coat or shirt the men usually wore a coat made from three sealskins, with the hair side out. During the cold winter, however, a coat made of eight fox skins was worn. While traveling, and on hunting trips, sealskin mittens were worn. In the spring, when the sunlight is reflected sharply by snow and haze, it was necessary to use snow goggles carved from wood or antler to avoid snow blindness.

Women's boots were long, covering the thigh; the bootlegs were of white, depilated sealskin, dried in freezing weather to obtain the desired stiffness. The women also wore stockings of hare or caribou skin, edged at the top with a strip of polar bear skin. Their stiff footwear gave the women a somewhat tottering gait. The upper parts of the stockings were used as pockets, for storing small items such as a pipe and tobacco, or for warming the hands. The short female trousers were sewed from 23 pieces of blue and white fox skin. Under the trousers, very short underpants of haired sealskin were worn. Over the bird-skin inner coat, the women usually wore a coat made from two sealskins, but in cold weather they wore a coat made of seven fox skins, one of which was always white. If a woman carried a baby, she wore an outer coat (Green-landic *amaat*) made of sealskins or nine fox skins. This coat had an especially big head opening and a sacklike back in which the naked baby lay against its mother's skin. A loose hood of sealskin was worn with the *amaat* (fig. 9).

Children usually wore the same kind of clothing as adults of the same sex (fig. 10).

For more on clothing, see Ekblaw (1927–1928:173–185), Steensby (1910:333–346), Rasmussen (1921:17–19), Freuchen (1961:25–30), Holtved (1967:36–60), and Kroeber (1900:290–297).

Some of the female Canadian immigrants had their faces tattooed, but before they arrived this custom was unknown among the Polar Eskimo (Holtved 1967:57).

Hygiene varied a great deal among the Polar Eskimo. As it was rather difficult to produce fresh water in large quantities, body washing, performed with dovekie skins, was kept to a minimum. Hands and face were often washed with snow (A. Gilberg 1948).

Social Organization

Polar Eskimo society was loosely organized. It was based on the nuclear family, which was also the economic unit. Often a nuclear family settled among other relatives, making a kind of extended family unit that sometimes constituted the entire settlement. As there were no chiefs, society was governed by public opinion, under the influence of the shaman or a great hunter: these were often one and the same person. They could never command, but only suggest. They were respected by all, but only in critical situations did they become leaders of the people. Disagreements that could not be settled

584

Fig. 7. Hunting and hunting equipment. top left, 2 kayaks on the ice near Qaanaaq. Equipment visible includes a sealskin float, paddle, harpoon, and harpoon line. top right, Making a sealskin float. One ringed sealskin is removed whole, made airtight, and then inflated. The hair is removed using a sharp knife or an ulu. Once dehaired the skin is turned inside out, laced again to make it airtight, inflated, most of the blubber cut off, and hung to dry. The skin is then turned right side out, laced, and inflated for final drying (Holtved 1967:130–132). center left, Narwhal hunt in Whale Sound (Herbert I. in background). After kayakers harpooned the narwhal (marked by 2 floats in center distance), hunters in the motorboats approached for the final kill. top left and center left, Photographs by Rolf Gilberg, July 1963. bottom left, Qaqqutsiaq and Maassannguaq wearing kayak half-jackets of dehaired sealskin in the southwestern Greenland pattern. Qaqqutsiaq also wears kayak sleeves to protect his anorak sleeves from water dripping off the paddle (Holtved 1967:83). center right, Shooting screen of white linen mounted on a small sled, a West Greenlandic technique used for hunting seals and walrus on the ice, near Herbert I. bottom right, Skinning a walrus caught off Northumberland I. Harpoons with razor-sharp blades or powerful rifles are needed to penetrate walrus hide. During flensing the stomach contents were usually checked for half-digested bivalves, which were immediately eaten as a great delicacy (Holtved 1967:93–94). top right and bottom left, Photographs by Erik Holtved, 1936. center right and bottom right, Photographs by Fred Bruemmer, summer 1971.

otherwise were often resolved by one of the parties leaving the village voluntarily, but murder was not unknown. As the total Polar Eskimo population was only around 200–250 persons, everyone knew everyone else; there was considerable visiting and constant traveling around their territory. Only clothing, implements, and utensils were personal property; hunting grounds, food, and dwellings were owned in common with the right of use. Hospitality was a matter of course.

Men and women had more or less equal status. The men hunted, and the women performed domestic duties.

Around 1900 an average family had about four children (Gilberg 1976). Factors regulating family size were infanticide, high infant mortality, and the long nursing period (Freuchen 1961).

Life Cycle

When a woman was about to give birth, she left the family dwelling and moved to a private tent for herself in the summer, or to a private snowhouse in the winter. The period of confinement was usually remarkably short; if labor seemed to take a long time, the woman's husband would often place himself behind her with his arms around her and help to press the baby out. The umbilical cord was severed with a stone and tied with sinew.

Fig. 8. Hunting and preparing dovekies (*Alle alle*). In earlier times dovekies were used for clothing as well as food (Holtved 1967:112–113). left, Inuutersuaq Ulloriaq catching birds with a net near Siorapaluk. Photograph by Fred Bruemmer, May 1971. right, Preparing the birds. About 8 breasts were needed to feed one individual. Photograph by Maynard Owen Williams, on board the expedition ship *Bowdoin*, near Etah, 1925.

585

left, Nationalmuseet, Copenhagen:L211; center, Rolf Gilberg, Copenhagen; right, Smithsonian, Dept. of Anthr.: 176,631.

Fig. 9. Women's clothing. left, Arnarúniak (standing) and Inalliak wearing long boots and coats of skin. Arnaruniak also wears a separate hood and mittens. Photograph by Thomas N. Krabbe, at Thule, summer 1909. center, Women at Thule each with a young child in the pouch of the sealskin outer coat. Photograph by Aage Gilberg, 1939. right, Woman's necklace made of leather with ivory pendant attachments. Other ornaments were uncommon. Length 21.5 cm; collected by Henry Bryant, Qaanaaq, Inglefield Gulf, 1894.

On the day of giving birth, the mother was required to wash herself all over and forbidden to eat boiled meat, and entrails and eggs were taboo for a period. On the next day she sewed new clothing for herself, and threw her old clothes away. Her husband was also subject to taboos. Under the influence of the mission, these taboos gradually disappeared.

A Polar Eskimo mother nursed her infant for a couple of years, sometimes longer. Often she also gave her baby meat she had first chewed. There seems to have been a tendency toward three-year intervals between pregnancies, but after the 1940s this no longer prevailed and many siblings were born only a year apart. Since 1954 more than half of the Polar Eskimos have been born at the hospital in Qaanaaq.

During periods of famine, strangulation of both boys and girls younger than 3 or 4 years occurred, in order to save them from slow starvation due to lack of milk from the mother (or a substitute nurse) or from lack of food when the father died (Gilberg 1976).

On childbirth see Mylius-Erichsen and Moltke (1906:324, 459), Rasmussen (1908:65–68, 119–122), Malaurie (1975), Malaurie, Tabah, and Sutter (1952), J.D. Peary (1893:87), Freuchen (1961:106), Bessels (1875:111, 1884), F.A. Cook (1894), Gilberg (1971), and A. Gilberg et al. (1978).

For the Polar Eskimo, the name had its own soul, with a certain amount of vitality and character; the name was one's identity. The connection between the name-soul and identity was so intimate that new names seldom developed. Men and women did not use the same names, as they did in other parts of Greenland. When a person had died, his name was taboo and was never mentioned until it was given to a newborn. Any other Eskimo having the same name had to assume another of his names until a baby received the name; if he did not do this, it was believed that the name would lose its power. Children were thus often named after the last person who had died in the vicinity, or especially after their grandparents (Rasmussen 1908:116). In spite of the influence of Christianity, in 1980 the Polar Eskimos still followed this naming custom. In the 1960s the Polar Eskimos were given surnames by the Danish Ministry of Ecclesiastical Affairs.

A mother carried her infant on her back for the first two or three years. Small boys were said to be spoiled by their mothers because their childhood was so short; at the age of 12, they began going hunting with their fathers. They learned by imitation the use of hunting equipment and where and how to find game animals, and soon began to contribute actively to the support of their families. Girls were taught by their mothers how to maintain the home and to prepare skins, so that they would be desirable as wives when they grew up (Hovey 1918; Søby 1977–1978).

The family was the economic unit, in which husband and wife depended on each other, and each contributed important traditional skills. In premission times, small children were often betrothed by their parents; these arrangements were almost always respected when the children were old enough to marry. If a marriage was not arranged by the parents of both parties, only the consent of the girl's parents was required; but the boy's parents could put pressure on him if they disapproved of the marriage.

In the early twentieth century, Polar Eskimo girls

586

Smithsonian, Dept. of Anthr.: 209,180.

Fig. 10. Boy's clothing. Once a child was old enough to walk, garments similar to those of adults were worn. The murre-skin inner parka here was worn with the feathers against the skin (it was turned inside out for storage) with an outer parka, probably of foxskin. The trousers are polar bear fur and have a drawstring top. Stockings and boots completed the outfit. Length of trousers 54.0 cm; collected by Robert E. Peary, Smith Sound, 1896.

often married between the ages of 12 and 16, due to the excess of males in the population. Before marrying, a young man had to prove for several years that he was a good hunter and could support a household, so that most men did not marry until their mid-twenties (Freuchen 1961:55–95; A. Gilberg et al. 1978; Peary 1910:60; Rasmussen 1908:54–68). There seems to have been no Polar Eskimo wedding ceremony in premission times (Peary 1898, 1:496).

When Polar Eskimos married, this did not always mean that they would establish a household of their own, or even that they were able to support themselves. Usually they joined the household of a parent, generally the boy's; during this time, their production belonged to the entire household. The young couple still had a lot to learn about domestic chores and hunting. Gradually they became independent (Freuchen 1961:70–95).

As a rule, a settlement consisted of one to four often extended families, such as a father and his sons and their families, or a group of siblings and their families. As long as the father was in his prime, his sons would follow his choice of a settlement, but when they became independent they might not stay with him each year. When parents grew old, they would follow one of their sons in his choice of a settlement, since they were now dependent on his hunting prowess (Ekblaw 1927–1928:156–160; Holtved 1944:10–14).

A childless couple was pitied because they could not look forward to having anyone to take care of them in their old age. They could compensate for this by taking foster children or adopting children, usually from relatives. Sometimes two childless couples tried to have children by exchanging mates for a period. It also happened that a couple without children separated, or that the husband returned his wife to her parents and took another (Gilberg 1976).

The Polar Eskimo were monogamous. Polyandry seems never to have occurred among them, and only five incidents of polygyny are known: these lasted no more than a few years, as the missionary dissuaded the Eskimos from the practice (Gilberg 1976). There were no rules of preferred marriage, but marriages among relatives seem to have been avoided at least up to fourth cousins. This changed after World War II; up to 1970, 36 cases of cousin marriages had been recorded (Gilberg 1976).

Due to the virtual economic necessity for marriage, life was not pleasant for widows, widowers, and single persons. A man without a wife could not keep up his own household, unless he happened to have an adult daughter; he could move in with another couple, where he could get his clothing repaired, but he would in turn have to contribute his entire catch to this household. Steensby (1910:367) reported that many Polar Eskimos had several mates in succession; this situation may have prevailed until the 1940s, when the decline in mortality increased average longevity, and since then normally Polar Eskimos keep their spouses for life.

Old people would try to make themselves useful by taking care of grandchildren, doing small repairs of clothing or equipment, or collecting birds and fish. Peary (1907:383) noticed that Polar Eskimos seldom lived longer than 60 years. After that time social conditions improved, so that by the 1960s several reached 70 and over.

As the evil of a deceased person was believed to remain in the corpse, no one wanted to touch it, and only the closest relatives in the nuclear family participated in its disposal. It was sewn fully dressed into a skin, placed on the ground facing the rising sun, and covered with stones. For five days no activity was permitted in the settlement; all its residents were subject to various taboos during this period. The personal equipment of the deceased was buried with him (Kroeber 1900:310–323; Rasmussen 1921–1925, 3:29–27).

Fig. 11. Games and amusements. top left, Rock throw. top and bottom right, Pulling game. Each man grasps his part of a double handle, made of 2 pieces of wood lashed with sealskin thong, and tries to pull his opponent forward and raise him off the ground (Holtved 1967:155–156). top left and top and bottom right, Photographs by Robert E. Peary, Smith Sound, 1891–1897. bottom left, Bull-roarer, made of ivory with sinew cord through central holes, used as a toy. Length of ivory piece 7.5 cm; collected by Henry Bryant, Cape York, 1892.

Fig. 12. Women at work. left, Palloq preparing a bearded seal intestine for use for window panes in the winter house. The intestine is cleaned, blown up, dried in the wind, and then slit open lengthwise and rolled up for later use (Holtved 1967:135). Photograph by Erik Holtved, Inuarfissuaq, summer 1936. center, Smith Sound woman braiding sinew for a bowstring. Photograph by Robert E. Peary, 1891–1897. right, Oline and Mequ at Uummannaq collecting freshwater ice from the inland ice caps used for drinking water. Photograph by Aage Gilberg, summer 1938.

Fig. 13. Needlecase of ivory. Steel or ivory needles were fitted into the sealskin strips that could be drawn into the case; attached are thimble, carved ornaments, and a small ivory tube with wooden plug for additional needles. Length 36.0 cm; collected by Robert E. Peary, Smith Sound, 1891–1892.

Spouse Exchange

In premission times, it was common for the Polar Eskimos to exchange spouses, for religious or practical reasons or for amusement (Mylius-Erichsen and Moltke 1906:405). In order to influence nature, propitiate angry evil spirits, bring good weather, or make game animals appear, the shaman could command the entire settlement to exchange spouses; he would make up the couples. If the first combinations did not help, he would try others (Freuchen 1961:64). Or, before setting off on a long hunting trip, a hunter whose wife was pregnant, had a small baby, or for any other reason could not or did not want to accompany him, could ask a neighbor staying at home to exchange wives, if the wife of the neighbor was disposed to travel with him. Exchanges of spouses could last for a night, a week, or even years. The new combination was always treated like a real marriage by the rest of the community; the exchange was a private matter. If it resulted in children, these were not treated differently from other children of the same mother.

The mission did not condone exchanges of spouses, so that the practice disappeared.

Religion

Polar Eskimo religion centered on shamanism. They believed in the presence of certain mystical powers in nature that were easily offended and could become dangerous and malevolent.

The Polar Eskimo shaman, called *angakkoq* as among other Eskimos, knew how to fight the powers controlling life and death, not through prayer but by command. Thus the supernatural became the tool of the shaman. Old and young persons of both sexes could become shamans, but only if they were born with the necessary supernatural faculty.

Each person had an immortal soul, a body spirit, and a name spirit. The soul was outside the body, following it around like a shadow; when the soul left the body, the person became ill. Only a great shaman could see the soul; to cure a person who was ill, he would find the soul and bring it back. Otherwise the person would die. After death the soul went to meet ancestors either in the sky or in the sea.

As protection against an unforeseen fate, the Polar Eskimos used amulets, formulas, and taboos. Most men who lived a hazardous life had amulets sewn into their clothing; women wore them less since they spent most of their time at the settlement, which was distant from danger. Children had sewn into their clothing pieces of animals, the characteristics of which were believed to be transferred to the child. One had to be careful in using a formula, as it would lose its power if misused. Taboos were common in connection with critical situations. If they were broken, famine, bad weather, a dearth of game animals, or death would threaten not only the offender but also the entire group.

Polar Eskimo myths are published by Rasmussen (1908:159–358, 1921–1925, 3:45–162), Kroeber (1899), and Holtved (1951). For other aspects of religion, see Rasmussen (1908:126–157, 1921–1925, 3:1–44) and Kroeber (1900:303–326). For music see Hauser (1975, 1983) and Leden (1952).

Culture Change

To reach the North Pole during his expeditions of 1891–1909, Robert E. Peary needed Polar Eskimos for their experience in arctic travel. Because he could not use people still using bows and arrows, he paid for their services to him as hunters, guides, and drivers with rifles, ammunition, wood for sleds, steel knives (fig. 15), and Primus stoves. He paid women with steel sew-

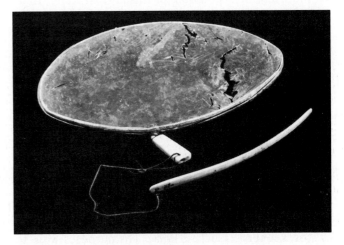

Fig. 14. Drum of seal intestine (now damaged) stretched over an elliptical frame with bone or ivory handle. The dancer beat it with the attached walrus rib. Width 36.0 cm; collected on the Crocker Land Expedition, Smith Sound, 1913–1917.

top, Smithsonian, Dept. of Anthr.: 176,632; bottom, Field Mus., Chicago: 13,869.

Fig. 15. Tools. European implements were obtained by the natives; when the handles broke the metal blade was reset in bone or ivory. top, Knife, metal blade with maker's mark, riveted to ivory handle with leather thong tied through holes at end. bottom, Saw blade riveted to ivory handle. top, Length 11.5 cm; collected by Henry Bryant, Qaanaaq, Inglefield Gulf, 1894. bottom, Same scale; collected by Robert E. Peary, Smith Sound, 1891–1892.

ing needles for making clothes for his expeditions. He also introduced tea, coffee, tobacco, sugar, and biscuits.

During this period, the Polar Eskimos expended a great deal of time and energy to help Peary reach the North Pole. At the outset of each expedition, he would visit the entire district to gather the most skillful hunters and the best dogs to work for him, often taking them out of the region. Thus the best manpower was removed from the economic system. It was to these selected hunters and their families that Peary introduced the new technology (Astrup 1898; Hensen 1912; Peary 1898, 1907, 1910; Steensby 1909).

During the nineteenth century there was no contact between the Polar Eskimo population and the Eskimo of West Greenland, except for the West Greenlander Hans Hendrik (b. 1834, d. 1889) who was an interpreter for the scientific expeditions of Elisha Kent Kane, Isaac Israel Hayes, Charles Francis Hall, and George Strong Nares (Laursen 1972). He lived among the Polar Eskimo from 1853 to 1872 and married one of them (Rink 1878; Mylius-Erichsen and Moltke 1906). In 1904 the Danish Literary Greenland Expedition reestablished contact with West Greenland across Melville Bay; since then, some Polar Eskimos have visited Upernavik District by sled every winter. Initially they came to buy European commodities. Later, after a trading post store had been established at Thule in 1910 they came to find wives.

Knud Rasmussen founded his trading post, Kap York Stationen Thule (Thule Station), in 1910 at Uummannaq (Ūmánaq) on North Star Bay with Peter Freuchen as storekeeper (Freuchen 1935). His purposes were to incorporate North Greenland into the Danish colony of Greenland, to make Thule Station a geographical and economic base for scientific expeditions to study Eskimo culture everywhere, to sell Polar Eskimo products, and to provide the Polar Eskimo with European merchandise.

The Polar Eskimo had previously been totally independent, producing themselves all their food, clothing, and equipment. But especially after Peary had bought all the old Polar Eskimo weapons and equipment for museums in the United States (VanStone 1972), they became dependent on imported merchandise. To be sure it became easier to obtain game with guns, but these were worthless without ammunition. Other drawbacks followed contact with Whites, such as diseases, which often became epidemics.

Improved technology (better rifles, larger sleds, steel fox traps, and the like), in conjunction with an increased number of marine animals (Vibe 1967) due to climatic changes, led to a more stable economic growth. That happened in the period after 1910 when the shop was built, at first slowly then more markedly after 1920; the climatic change reached its maximum around 1930.

Lutheran Christianity was introduced in 1909 by the Danish Mission Society and the Greenland Church Cause (G. Olsen 1910). In 1912 the first Polar Eskimo adults were baptized; in 1934 the last adult was baptized. For a good many years the priest and the shaman existed side by side in this society.

During the Knud Rasmussen period as little as possible was done to change the culture of the Polar Eskimo, except in the field of religion, so that they could still feel that they were free and independent. To strengthen this feeling, in 1927 Rasmussen established a hunters' council consisting of six members: three ex officio (the colony manager, the doctor, and the priest, always Whites or West Greenlanders) and three hunters, chosen each year by the six members of the council, one from each of the north, south, and central parts of the district. The hunters' council passed its first law, the Thule Law, in 1929. The entire population recognized the decisions of this council, which concerned issues such as inheritance and alimony, health regulations, game conservation, the settling of disagreements, and punishments and fines. The council had at its disposal a small amount of money deriving from taxes on tobacco and other commodities. Around 1930 the Thule district administrative center at Uummannaq was expanded by the addition of several buildings, including a church, a school, a larger shop, and a hospital (Sand 1935, 1938; Gilberg 1977).

Knud Rasmussen introduced a number of changes that slowly modified Polar Eskimo culture. Channeling all import and export through his trading post, he provided a continuous flow of European merchandise in exchange for fox and seal skins. He created political interest through the hunters' council. He established a health service, which markedly decreased deaths in epidemics and resulted in a continuously increasing population. During his period all the Polar Eskimos were converted to Christianity, and a school system was organized. He selected his European co-workers with great care, so that the Polar Eskimos got a rather good impression of Whites. Many new ideas were spread among the Polar Eskimo, who were still carrying on their traditional way of life, thus facilitating their integration in the greater community of Greenland.

Knud Rasmussen died in 1933, and in 1937 Denmark took over the administration of the district, which became a part of the Danish colony of Greenland. Mission activity and property were transferred to the Danish State Church. Rasmussen seems to have been successful in facilitating the integration of traditional Polar Eskimo with the rest of Greenland.

After the Greenland Provincial Council was founded in 1950, the Polar Eskimos elected a representative to its seat at Nuuk (Godthåb). In 1952, election rules for members of the hunters' council were changed so that three hunters were elected by universal suffrage for four years in a row. The hunters' council functioned and the Thule Law was valid until January 1, 1963, when the West Greenland municipal system of 1950 was extended to include Thule District. In 1953, all Polar Eskimos became Danish citizens, and the whole of Greenland became an integrated part of Denmark under the supervision of the Ministry for Greenland (Trap 1970). When Greenland Home Rule was introduced in May 1979, the Polar Eskimos elected one member to the National Council (Greenland Assembly).

After World War II, Polar Eskimo society received two sets of parallel and simultaneous outside influences: from the presence of Thule Air Base, and from political decisions made in Denmark.

The Korean War and the Cold War in Europe were factors that resulted in the construction of Thule Air Base by the United States in 1951–1955. During the late 1950s it was staffed by 6,000 troops but with the advent of satellites it lost some of its strategic significance and was in the 1980s inhabited by approximately 1,500 American soldiers and 1,500 civilian Danish service personnel.

Very few Polar Eskimos were ever employed on the base. Although there was almost no Eskimo fraternization with the American troops, the presence of the base greatly influenced conditions in the district. Oil pollution from supply ships and noise from jet planes made hunting impossible in the vicinity of Uummannaq. In addition, it was tempting for some of the Eskimos to collect refuse meat, wood, and other materials on the base garbage dump, rather than to devote themselves to hunting.

When the Polar Eskimos themselves realized where this development was leading, the hunters' council, strongly influenced by Danish authorities, decided in 1953 to move the 27 families living at Uummannaq north to Inglefield Gulf at Qaanaaq where a new, one-room, 20-square-meter wooden house was built for each family in compensation for the one they had previously lived in. The new Thule town was designed in Copenhagen and paid for partly by the United States.

In spite of the transference of the Thule town farther north, the Thule Air Base still has a great influence on Polar Eskimo society. Especially, the air field has increased communication with West Greenland and Denmark, and each year some young Polar Eskimos travel south for education. There they meet new cultures with other values, and they bring home new ideas (Gilberg 1977).

The closer association with Denmark meant an increase in the technological innovations, but new technology does not necessarily mean progress. New technology opens new possibilities, but at the same time often forces new restrictions on the already known possibilities.

Thus the introduction of the motorboat meant better summer communication and less work for the kayak hunter. He was now able to reach the hunting grounds more easily, and to go farther than before. The same boat can carry several hunters together with their hunting equipment, including the kayak. On the hunting ground the motorboat serves as a base where the tired hunter can get food and heat. He becomes economically dependent upon society for borrowing money and for service facilities. The motorboat can only be used for a short part of the year, and it requires a harbor. Only a few places in the district are suitable for motorboat anchorage. This fact has influenced the settlement pattern, limiting settlement to only a few places, but the game still lives on the usual hunting grounds. In 1966 Polar Eskimos owned 18 motorboats, all of which were shorter than 25 feet. The kayak was still in use (Gilberg 1971).

In the 1930s and 1940s the winter habitation, the stone house, had been replaced by a turf wall house (fig. 4, center right), and later a wooden house covered totally with turf walls. At first only the skillful and well-to-do hunters built new-style houses; later the entire community did so. The more wood used in building the house, the more difficult it became to move with a sled in the yearly migration cycle. The more successful hunters began to acquire wood houses at several settlements, where relatives borrowed them in their absence. With sealskin increasingly becoming the main export cash commodity, the skin tent was replaced by a canvas tent. The dwelling was heated by a blubber lamp of iron or a Primus stove (Holtved 1967).

By the 1960s no Polar Eskimos lived in stone houses or turf wall houses; they all lived in wooden houses. The hygiene and arrangement of the Eskimo house varies. Some like it extremely clean and orderly while others pay less attention to these considerations, but generally personal hygiene is of a high standard.

In spring and summer many Polar Eskimos still leave their wooden houses to live in tents at the hunting grounds. In camping during trips the tent is erected on top of the sled, which then serves as a sleeping platform. Heating and cooking is provided by the Primus stove. Many hunters have replaced the skin sled straps and dog harness with ones of nylon, which are not tempting for dogs to eat.

In the 1970s the Polar Eskimos began to use plastic shoeing below the wooden sled runner instead of iron, as it provides a much smoother drive. Some hunters prefer to keep the iron between the plastic and the wood, as the plastic wears off faster than iron. The local council has limited the use of snowmobiles to the main road between settlements, and they prefer that snowmobiles not be used at all, as they scare away game and cause accidents.

Often the kayak is painted white for camouflage and in order to make the sealskin last longer. Some hunters save the sealskin for trade purposes and use canvas for the kayak instead, waterproofing it with white paint. The traditional fur costume has been replaced with a European one, although when sledding most Polar Eskimos in the 1970s dressed in fur (Gilberg 1971). Since the mid-1970s cotton has replaced the grass in the boots.

The yearly migration from winter settlement to summer settlement and to new winter settlement ceased during the 1960s because of the expensive and non-moveable wooden house. The previously migrating hunter has become a permanent resident; but the game is still found at the old hunting grounds. As the hunter no longer follows the game as in the traditional system, the journey to the hunting ground becomes longer in time as well as in distance. Often he leaves his wife and children in the permanent wooden house in the village, where the family can buy food in the store should the meat scaffold be empty before the hunter returns. The food available in stores means that the annual late-winter hunger periods have disappeared.

The permanent settlement and larger houses have allowed the Eskimos to collect more belongings in their houses, as they are no longer limited in their possessions by what can be loaded on a sled. Previously scattered in small groups along the coast for better exploration of the hunting grounds, the Polar Eskimo now cluster around the five settlements having stores.

This concentration of the population in five main settlements has not created isolated clusters. Most Polar Eskimos still live as hunters, and in spite of the permanent settlements they maintain their geographical mobility, having constant contact with the rest of the society all year round. In this way the Polar Eskimo population still is a homogenous ethnic unit.

The size of the Polar Eskimo population in the nineteenth century and the beginning of the twentieth seems to have reminded stable at around 200–250. The cultural environment became more stable in the 1910s and 1920s. After the Peary expeditions stopped, the hunters could stay at home to provide for their own families. The whalers, who often brought diseases with them to Thule, by 1915 ceased to visit the district.

About 1930 the Polar Eskimo got their own hospital with a permanent doctor and a bigger shop. Simultaneously the number of harp seal, fox, and dovekies increased in the area due to a change of climate (Christian Vibe, personal communication 1971). This caused the fluctuation in population size to cease during the 1930s, when it began a regular increase of 1 to 1.5% a year. After the construction of the New Thule town in 1953 with a new hospital, larger store, and boarding school, with consequent changes, the size of the Polar Eskimo population increased markedly; thus in the 1950s there was an annual increase of 3 percent, and in the 1960s, 4 percent. During this period of fine hunting conditions, with selective pressure decreased to a minimum, the Polar Eskimo population doubled in 20 years. Due to family planning, the population increase in the 1970s was smaller, 2 percent yearly (see table 1). The population of the Thule area in 1982 was 770.

The inspector living in Qaanaaq was the jural representative, policeman, and chief of the Royal Greenland Trade Department in Thule. Until Home Rule, he was also secretary of the local council. The local council has eight members: three elected from the town of Qaanaaq, one from Qeqertarsuaq, one from Qeqertat, one from Moriusaq, and one from Savigsivik. The mayor is usually a Polar Eskimo, as also are most of the members. At the election of April 4, 1979, 71 percent of the 424 entitled to vote did so. For several years the mayor was a woman. Reports of the meetings at the local council have from the 1970s been published in the local newspaper, *HAINANG*, in both Greenlandic and Danish.

During the 1930s there was a rapid shift to a monetary system. The first to make use of it—mostly successful hunters investing in motorboats and wood for house construction and the like—had an initial advantage over those who continued to measure their values in "foxes" and who disliked cash as a medium of exchange. As the Polar Eskimo gradually got accustomed to the new system, their society developed an incipient class struc-

Table 1. Population, 1973 and 1981

Age	Males 1973	Males 1981	Females 1973	Females 1981	Total 1973	Total 1981
0–14	137	127	139	115	276	242
15–64	165	211	166	217	331	428
65 +	19	21	11	21	30	42
Totals	321	359	316	353	637	712

NOTE: 1981 figures include some West Greenlanders.

ture mainly based on money. This emphasis replaced traditional social structure with equal rights and duties for all, based only on hunting ability without accumulated capital in the form of meat or other valuables (Holtved 1950:289).

Presently the only alternative to the hunter's life for the Polar Eskimo man who wants to stay in the district is employment in the administration: possibly as a salesman in the store, a worker for the Greenland Technological Organization, or as a servant for an institution such as the hospital or school; or he can hire out himself and his dogs for "taxi-driving" for the officials of the administration. Some prefer this to the hunting life, and many young people are attracted by a job with a fixed salary. Thus a rudimentary social stratification is emerging, and the hunter is no longer the only active contributor to the maintenance of the society. However, the administration is not capable of absorbing all those who do not wish to become hunters. Quite a few young people try their luck in the south, either in West Greenland or in Denmark, but most of them come back because they feel awkward in these places as they lack experience in a foreign culture and are wary of being regarded as naive.

The 1960s and 1970s were times of rapid change for the Polar Eskimos. Especially the young and the old feel that they live between two cultures, and it is not uncommon that these people drink heavily to escape the dilemma. In contrast to the rest of Greenland, the Polar Eskimos have restricted the sale of alcohol.

Considering the changes that have occurred in the ecosystem since the mid-nineteenth century it appears that the Polar Eskimo who formerly lived in isolation and who were self-supporting from the resources in their area, by increasingly adopting outside influences, slowly have grown dependent on supplies from the south in order to maintain themselves. Modification of their technology allows a more effective tapping of their resources or in some cases the development of new ones.

In spite of ecological changes and acculturation problems, the Polar Eskimo population was in the 1970s still functioning as a homogeneous group, with all members of the society known to one another and speaking the same Eskimo dialect. The Polar Eskimo neither consider themselves Danes nor part of the West Greenland society; they think of themselves as a particular element in the Greenlandic population, accordingly, as a distinct ethnic group (Gilberg 1980, 1982).

Synonymy

The most widely accepted term, Polar Eskimos (Danish *polareskimoer*), was first applied by members of the Danish Literary Greenland Expedition who visited them in 1903–1904 (Mylius-Erichsen and Moltke 1906; Ras-

mussen 1908). Variants of this are Polar-Eskimo (Gilberg 1983), Polar Inuit (Hauser 1979), and Polar, with Inuit/Eskimo understood (National Geographic Society 1983).

At first contact they were labeled Arctic Highlanders (Ross 1819). Subsequently they were referred to by the name of Etah (Ita), their principal settlement (Hayes 1860:197), and derivatives: Itaner (Bessels 1879:351), Itanese (Bessels 1884:863), Ita-Eskimos (Boas 1885:102), Ĩtă'mi (Stein 1902:198), and Ita (Hodge 1907–1910, 1:625). Later, descriptive names include Smith Sound Eskimo (Kroeber 1900), Kap York Eskimoer and Kap Yorker (Meddelelser om Den Grønlandske Kirkesaq 1909–1940), Highland Eskimos (Whitney 1910), Polargrønlænder (Thomsen 1912), Thulegrønlænder (Freuchen 1954), Thule-eskimoer (Vibe 1956), and the Wild Gentlemen, cited by K. Hansen (1969–1970) with no source given. Boas (1888) included them in his Central Eskimo.

The Polar Eskimo self-designation is inuhuit 'great and beautiful human beings', the cognate of West Greenlandic *inusuit* 'large people'. They do not refer to themselves as *inuit*. In West Greenlandic they are called *Avanersuarmiut* 'those who live farthest north'.

When Knud Rasmussen established his trading post at Uummannaq he named it Kap York Stationen Thule, from the term for the northernmost inhabited land in Classical geography. The entire area gradually became known as Thule District. The local council for this District has officially named it Avanersuup Kommunia 'the northernmost commune'. When the administrative center was moved to Qaanaaq (Qânâq) in 1953, the new settlement was officially known as Thule, and often called New Thule. The name of the earlier Thule at Uummannaq was changed to Dundas after the English name for Thule Mountain. The Eskimos continued to use the names Uummannaq and Qaanaaq.

Sources

The first information about the Polar Eskimos was obtained in August 1818 by Ross (1819) through a West Greenland interpreter, Hans Zakæus. Ross met only 18 men, no women or children.

Although many expeditions visited the Polar Eskimos during the nineteenth century, little information on ethnography was published. The best is from the Hall expedition in the 1870s (Bessels 1875, 1884). Even Peary, who spent a great deal of his life among the Polar Eskimos, does not provide extensive ethnographic information.

The first good ethnographic information on the culture of the Polar Eskimos was given by the Danish Literary Greenland Expedition (Mylius-Erichsen and

Moltke 1906; Rasmussen 1908), which brought the Polar Eskimo into contact with West Greenland again in 1903–1904.

In spite of only a short summer visit in 1909 Steensby (1910) gives a comprehensive account of the Polar Eskimo society of that period. Freuchen (1935, 1961) lived among the Polar Eskimos from 1910 to 1920 and married a Polar Eskimo. Although some readers consider the writing of Freuchen questionable, most of his details, even in his novels, provide correct ethnographic data.

The best information about the Polar Eskimo is found in the material from Knud Rasmussen, who visited them in 1903–1904, 1906–1908, 1909, 1910–1914, 1916–1918, 1920, 1921, 1926, 1927, 1928, 1929, and 1930. As he could speak their dialect well, his material is especially valuable.

Holtved (1967) is another very good source. He visited the Polar Eskimo in 1935–1937 and 1946–1947.

Ekblaw (1921, 1927–1928) lived among the Polar Eskimos as a member of the Crockerland Expedition, 1913–1917; his contributions focus on the human geography of the Polar Eskimo.

A good source from the 1970s, Herbert (1981), discusses the accommodations of the traditional hunting culture to the twentieth-century situation. The newspaper *HAINANG*, published since 1957, provides detailed information.

A Polar Eskimo bibliography containing references up to 1975 is found in Gilberg (1976:57–87).

Jørgen Roos, a Dane, made three documentaries on the Polar Eskimo in the 1960s. Some parts of the Jette Bang film *Inuit* from 1938 also concern the Polar Eskimo. The photographer Ivars Silis took a series of color slides in 1971. Other photographs are in Herbert (1981).

Polar Eskimo material culture specimens are found in the following museums: American Museum of Natural History, New York; Australian Museum, Sydney; Department of Ethnography, Nationalmuseet, Copenhagen; Field Museum of Natural History, Chicago; State Hermitage Museum, Leningrad; Museum of the American Indian, Heye Foundation, New York; Museum of Mankind, London; National Museum of Natural History, Smithsonian Institution, Washington; Grønlands Landsmuseet, Godthåb. The Polar Eskimos themselves have founded a Polar Eskimo museum.

West Greenland Before 1950

INGE KLEIVAN*

Territory

The West Greenlanders live along the west coast of Greenland, up to Melville Bay, which is uninhabited (fig. 1). North of Melville Bay are the Polar Eskimos. The area of the West Greenlanders extends to the south as far as the Cape Farewell area. The East Greenlanders, who live in two separate areas on the east coast, are separated from the West Greenlanders by large stretches of coast that are difficult to traverse.

In this chapter "west coast" refers to the area of the West Greenlanders; the northern part of the "west coast" means, then, the area south of Melville Bay including Holsteinsborg.

Even within the area inhabited by West Greenlanders, geographical conditions have formed barriers between various regions, making contact among their inhabitants difficult. Groups were identified on the basis of the locality where they lived, the group term being formed by the addition of the suffix-complex -*miut* 'inhabitants of' to the place-names. In addition, designations such as North and South Greenlanders were used. At the time of the Danish-Norwegian colonization in 1721, the West Greenlanders did not regard themselves as a unit, but they have been unified by centuries of colonial administration.

Language

The language spoken in West Greenland belongs to the Inuit-Inupiaq (Eastern Eskimo) group. It consists of several dialects, the speakers of which have no difficulty understanding one another. The standard Greenlandic written language is based on the vernacular of the central west coast, where the first missionaries settled.†

Environment

The west coast of Greenland is indented by a number of very long, narrow fjords. Off the coast are innumerable islands. The interior is covered by an ice sheet. Only in the valleys of southwest Greenland is any forestlike vegetation to be found; most of the wood used by the Greenlanders was driftwood.

The ecological conditions on the west coast south of Holsteinsborg are subarctic as distinct from the arctic conditions of the northern part of the coast. Some important cultural differences between north and south correspond to this contrast in ecology.

During the time that Greenland has been inhabited, climatic fluctuations have affected the animal population and thus the economic opportunities of the Greenlanders. An especially important change was the reduction of the seal population in the mild periods of the first half of the twentieth century, while the cod supply increased (Mattox 1973).

The West Greenlander subsistence was primarily based on marine mammals, although almost all available food sources were exploited. The most important species of seal in Greenland is the ringed seal, which is a permanent resident all along the coast where it can keep its breathing holes open through one to two meters of ice. Next in importance is the harp seal. Other seals, present in lesser quantities, are the spotted seal or harbor seal, the bearded seal, and the hooded seal. The walrus was also available.

Toothed whales present are the common porpoise, the white whale or beluga, the narwhal, the pilot whale, and others. One of the baleen whales found is the minke whale. In the eighteenth century the big Greenland whale was of great importance.

---

*Translated from Danish by Charles Jones.

†West Greenlandic words cited in the *Handbook* are in the standard phonemic orthography introduced in 1972 (Grønlands Landsråds-Forhandlinger. Efterårssamling 1972:210–228; Grønland. Landsrådsvedtægt 1973). The phonemes are as follows: (stops) *p, t, k, q*; (voiceless fricatives) *f, s*; (voiced fricatives) *v, g* ([γ]), *r* ([ɣ̇]); (nasals) *m, n, ng* ([ŋ]); (voiced continuants) *l, j* ([y]); (short vowels) *a, i/e, u/o*; (long vowels and diphthong) *aa, ii/ee, uu/oo, ai*. As a concession to the earlier orthography, *e(e)* and *o(o)* are retained before the uvulars *q* and *r*, where they are in complementary distribution with *i(i)* and

u(u). Geminate consonants are written with double letters, with geminate *ng* rendered *nng*; *gg, rr*, and *ll* are voiceless. The orthography provides for the /š/ used by a minority of speakers to be written *S* but omits this distinction from the standard spellings.

In the earlier orthography *q* was written κ (*q* in some sources after about 1936) and long vowels and geminate consonants were indicated by accents: v̂ = long vowel (e.g. â for modern *aa*); v̌ = following consonant geminate (án for *ann*); v̄ = long vowel followed by geminate consonant (ān for *aann*). Many consonant clusters were written in which the first member was no longer pronounced and there were other special conventions (Schultz-Lorentzen 1945:7–13).

The polar bear occurs both on land and in the sea, especially on drift ice off the coast of South Greenland.

Of the land mammals, the caribou is the most important, but Arctic foxes and Arctic hares are also hunted and trapped.

Bird hunting centers around sea birds, especially black guillemots, thick-billed murres, dovekies, common and king eiders, ducks, and gulls. Ptarmigans are occasionally hunted.

Capelin, Greenland cod, Atlantic cod, shorthorn sculpin, Atlantic halibut, greenland halibut, lumpfish, haddock, and Greenland shark are taken in Greenland waters. Arctic char is taken from the rivers (Fabricius 1929; Vibe 1967; Salmonsen 1981).

External Relations

People from the southern parts of west and east Greenland met in the southernmost part of Greenland to hunt the hooded seal as well as for other activities (Graah 1932:80). Toward the end of the eighteenth century and the beginning of the nineteenth century, people from southern East Greenland began to settle on the west coast, and by the close of the nineteenth century, southeast Greenland was totally depopulated (see table 1). Other West Greenlanders who for a longer period of time had been familiar with various aspects of European culture used to look at the rather isolated southernmost population in Greenland as backward people (Kleivan and Kleivan 1961–1962).

There was no regular contact between the West Greenlanders and the Polar Eskimos in the eighteenth and nineteenth centuries, but the former realized there were people living in the north. Contact was first really established when the Danish Literary Expedition crossed Melville Bay by sled in 1903. Since then, West Greenlanders and Polar Eskimos have paid each other occasional visits. This contact has resulted in some marriages, and the two groups have also borrowed from each other culturally. The West Greenlanders admire the hunting prowess of the Polar Eskimos and have in certain cases imitated their hunting gear (Hansen 1969–1970:103–107).

History

Beginning in the sixteenth century the West Greenlanders came into occasional contact with European exploring expeditions and whalers (Gad 1967–1976, 3:13–61). Many Greenlanders made long journeys to places where they expected whalers to land, in order to barter with them. They traded skins, blubber, and baleen for fishhooks, knives, metal pots, glass beads, and European clothes. This trading contact did not result in any radical change in the social organization or ideology of

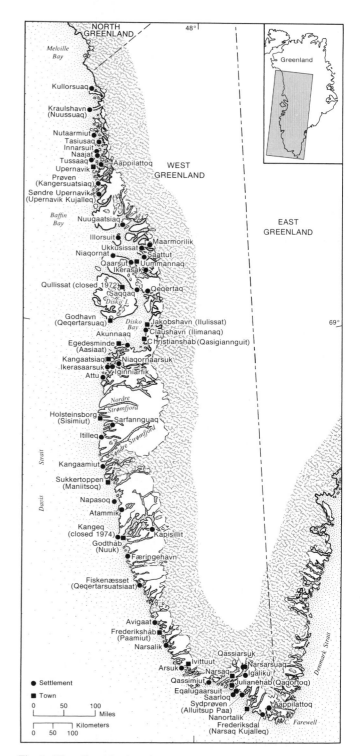

Fig. 1. West Greenland settlement area.

the Greenlanders, and it changed their technology only to a limited extent.

On the other hand the Danish-Norwegian colonization, begun in 1721, and the accompanying permanent settlement of Europeans in West Greenland resulted in the long run in decisive changes in many fields. During the eighteenth century missions and trading posts were established all along the west coast (Gad 1971–1982).

596

Table 1. Censuses of Greenlanders in West Greenland, 1789–1950

Date	Population
1789	5,122
1805	5,888
1820	6,282
1840	7,877
1860	9,648
1870	9,586
1880	9,720
1890	10,254
1900	11,118
1910	12,489
1920	13,441
1930	15,529
1940	17,472
1950	20,730

NOTE: Figures before the mid-19th century are slightly erroneous, since the remaining non-Christian populations of the outlying areas were not totally included.

SOURCES: 1789 and 1820, Rink 1877:227; 1805, Gad 1971–1982, 3:88; 1840, Grønlands Styrelse 1942–1944:418; 1860–1950, Udvalget for Samfundsforskning i Grønland 1963:34.

Trade

After European colonization began in 1721, trade between Greenland and Denmark-Norway was conducted successively by different companies, but in 1774 the Royal Greenland Trading Company was granted a monopoly. This was an economic measure, but it gradually resulted in the implementation of a policy of protection that attempted to avoid exposing the Greenlanders to uncontrolled contact with foreigners and possible demoralizing influences or exploitation (Sveistrup 1949). This monopoly and isolationist policy was not abandoned until the 1950s, when the period of modernization began.

The Royal Greenland Trading Company functioned primarily as a purchaser of native produce. It was not a factor in production except for involvement on a small scale in whaling (Gad 1971–1982, 2:385–395, 3:43–62, 203–243) and seal netting.

Among the most coveted European commodities were firearms. At first mainly used in caribou hunting, firearms soon were also applied to sealing on ice, and finally, around the middle of the nineteenth century (Rink 1877:115), to hunting from kayaks.

Missions

The Danish-Norwegian missionaries represented orthodox Protestantism, while the German missionaries, who from 1733 to 1900 operated at various localities in South Greenland, were Moravians. Among the missions and trading company, there were differences of opinion with regard to dealing with the Greenlanders; this somewhat complicated the impact of Christianity and of Europeans in general on the Greenlanders (Ostermann 1928–1929, 3; Israel 1969; Gad 1971–1982, 2).

By 1800 the majority of the West Greenlandic population had been baptized. In outlying districts adult baptisms took place as late as 1861 in the Upernavik area, and 1901 in Frederiksdal, where the last immigrants from southeast Greenland were baptized. Many traditional ideas continued in force alongside Christian concepts (Rink 1868; Rasmussen 1979; F. Lynge 1981).

However, much of the traditional nonmaterial culture of Greenland disappeared rather quickly. Thus, the missionaries in many cases reproached the Greenlanders for their drum dances, and in general gave them a feeling of guilt about aspects of their life that the Europeans connected with heathenness. Church festivals became the occasions when people met to celebrate. Christmas was especially celebrated as a great feast. European dancing became a popular form of amusement, except in the Moravian congregations, where dancing was considered sinful. Birthdays developed into social events of great importance.

The missionaries built up a school system with Greenlandic as the language of instruction, and they gradually trained Greenlandic catechists for education and religious duties. Church and school were closely linked until the beginning of the period of modernization.

Protest Movements

In the early period of contact some incidents of violence took place, mostly between Greenlanders and explorers or whalers. The Greenlanders had to accept the permanent presence at various settlements of missionaries and trade managers; the colonial history of Greenland is not, however, free of examples of protest actions by Greenlanders against European interference in their lives.

Thus, at certain places the number of shamans increased during the first period of colonization (Glahn 1921:78). There are also examples of prophetic movements among the converts. In the Sukkertoppen area in the 1780s the prophet Habakuk and his wife Maria Magdalene were the nucleus of a movement that established its own congregation and its own rituals. The local clergyman and the local trade manager feared that this movement was the first stage of a rebellion. However, the prophet was gradually deserted by his disciples, under the influence of Frederik Berthelsen, a Greenlandic catechist who was ordained in 1815 as the first Greenlandic priest (Söderberg 1974; Gad 1967–1976, 3:378–396).

In 1854 another noteworthy movement emerged from the Moravian congregation at Frederiksdal, as a reaction against the missionaries at a time when the Eskimos were plagued with hunger and disease.

In 1862 the first seeds of political autonomy were sown by the establishment of the so-called *forstander-skaber*, municipal councils, a Danish initiative. (For the colonial history of Greenland and the general history of contact with Europeans, see "History of Colonial Greenland," this vol.)

Culture

The following survey of the culture of West Greenland is based mainly on descriptions written in the eighteenth century. These contain much precise information on material culture, but their treatment of the nonmaterial aspects of culture, especially social organization, is inadequate on a number of points. Although certain regional differences existed, the nature of the source material makes it reasonable to treat the entire west coast as a unit.

Annual Cycle

The culture encountered by Europeans on their first meetings with West Greenlanders was a continuation of the Inugsuk culture, known from archeological excavations, which in turn had its roots in the Thule culture.

This was a hunting culture in which the resources were subject to seasonal fluctuations. These resources also differed in various localities, so that the subsistence of the Greenlanders was based on high mobility. The winter was spent in a permanent house, but in the spring, summer, and autumn, families lived in tents at scattered hunting camps.

Within the extensive area of West Greenland there were rather large regional differences in ecological adaptation (Birket-Smith 1928a:141–150). In the southernmost area, the great hunting season was from May to August, when families moved out to the outermost coastal islands to hunt hooded seals, which came with the drift ice. This sealing was so important that capelin fishing in the fjords in June was often left to women, children, and old men (Kleivan and Kleivan 1961–1962). Later in the summer, Arctic char in the rivers was exploited. During the rest of the year sealing was carried on from kayaks in open water, and to a lesser extent on the ice in the inner parts of the fjords. The caribou population of southernmost Greenland became extinct during the first period of colonization (Vibe 1967:163–166).

Off the outer coast of the central area there was usually open water all year. Harp seals were especially important here; they were hunted from kayaks. Capelin fishing began in June, and in July and August families sailed their umiaks and kayaks into the fjords to hunt caribou and to fish for Arctic char.

In the northern part of West Greenland, seals were hunted on the ice and at the ice edge in winter and spring, and from kayaks in the summer. Capelin and Arctic char were fished. Caribou were, as farther south, hunted both in summer and winter, but here they were not so important.

Social Organization

The most important social unit was the nuclear family. However, this unit was very seldom independent; most of the time it constituted part of an extended family, the members of which lived together and cooperated in production and consumption. An extended family consisted of several generations of closely related nuclear families, or several brothers with their wives and children; various unmarried relatives could also be included. For descriptions of the West Greenland population by age see figure 2.

The kinship system was bilateral (Birket-Smith 1927:99–100), but unfortunately no detailed investigations have been made of the correspondence between genealogical terms and behavior patterns. Generally speaking, relationships of super- and subordination were based on age and sex. Kinship was also important in social relations with people in distant localities.

Even relationships between nonrelated persons living at the same settlement were characterized by cooperation in production and consumption.

Finally, there were dyadic relationships that had mainly social objectives and were only to a lesser extent economically conditioned. During the first period of colonization inhabitants of different dwelling sites, for instance before about 1800, would meet regularly for song duels as an expression of a joking relationship. Relationships between persons with the same name were important, and later those between persons with the same birthday (after the missionaries started to record the dates of births).

The attitude in the traditional society toward strange Greenlanders was characterized by caution, and a lone hunter was not always safe when he met strangers.

Settlement Pattern

A winter settlement could consist of only one house, but there were usually several. Throughout the colonial period there was a trend toward greater concentration of the population. At first, missionaries urged the Greenlanders to live at the missions, in order that they could more easily instruct and control them. Some Greenlanders, too, were attracted by opportunities for trade and for getting help in times of scarcity, and probably also by the more intense social activity that developed at the missions. However, because it was better for the trading company that the Greenlanders lived

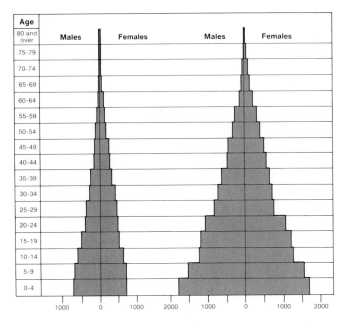

Age
80 and over				
75-79				
70-74				
65-69				
60-64				
55-59				
50-54				
45-49				
40-44				
35-39				
30-34				
25-29				
20-24				
15-19				
10-14				
5-9				
0-4				

Fig. 2. Population in West Greenland. left, 1855: total 9,644 (not including 248 Danes; 49 males and 95 females omitted from pyramid because of inadequate recording of age) (Rink 1857, 2:380). right, 1951: total 22,095 (including 1,105 Danes; 41 males and 55 females omitted from pyramid because of inadequate recording of age) (Denmark. Statistiske Department 1954:312).

close to good hunting grounds, it urged the Greenlanders to disperse. When the trading posts and missions were established, hunting conditions were not taken into much account, so that a large portion of the population continued to live in many small settlements.

In the twentieth century the authorities no longer actively supported a policy of dispersal, and the number of inhabited places fell from 181 in 1901 to 155 in 1949 (Udvalget for Samfundsforskning i Grønland 1963:22). As much of the population in this period shifted their main occupation to commercial fishing, it was no longer expedient to maintain a large number of settlements. Summer dispersal also declined gradually: more and more, people lived in their winter houses all year.

The composition of the population of a winter settlement, as well as that of an individual house, could vary somewhat from year to year. Although exact data are lacking, all indications are that kinship relations played an essential role in this composition. Two to eight families (Saabye 1942:60; Egede 1925:365) lived together in a winter house. These seem in general to have comprised extended families.

All the inhabitants of a winter settlement had the right to share common hunting grounds. This also applied to summer hunting camps, but in this case regular return to the same place seems to have granted a kind of priority to camp there and to exploit the resources (Petersen 1963).

It was necessary to be familiar with an area in order to exploit its resources effectively. Another reason for limiting movement was to be near relatives, who would feel obliged to help in case of need.

Families living in the same house during the winter could separate and use different summer hunting and fishing grounds. The people who lived together in the same tent and traveled by the same umiak (*umiaq*), the big skin boat, usually included more than one nuclear family but were usually related by kinship. There had to be a sufficient number both of active hunters and of women to row the umiak (Israel 1969:17–18).

The summer camps were sometimes smaller than the winter settlements, but they could also be considerably larger when families from various winter settlements stayed temporarily at the same summer camp to exploit the same abundant resource (Thorhallesen 1914:97).

When Greenlanders in an umiak and its accompanying kayaks approached an already inhabited summer camp where they too would like to camp, they slowly neared land and then stopped and lay still and silent some distance away. If those who were already there did not desire their presence, they indicated this by doing nothing, and the newcomers would go on, as if nothing had happened. But if the people on land wanted the newcomers to make camp with them, they called out to them and recommended the locality most heartily (Dalager 1915:11).

Native Trade

A limited amount of barter took place, in raw materials or finished products, both locally and between people living on different parts of the coast and having access to different resources. In the eighteenth century, for instance, there were some families living in Godthåbfjord, where there were especially good supplies of soapstone, who quarried this stone and made lamps and pots, which they took with them along the coast, trading them for baleen for fish lines and other products (Dalager 1915:15).

Structures

When colonization began in the eighteenth century, the Greenlanders lived in large rectangular houses with walls of stone and peat and sunken entrances several meters long. The roof was flat, made of driftwood, and covered with peat. Small windows in front were made of gutskin—seal intestines that were sewed together. The inside walls were covered with hides. Along the front wall, narrow platforms of peat and stone could be built for the use of the young men of the house and visitors, while the back wall was taken up by a wide platform in which each nuclear family had its permanent section. In front of each section there was a little projection for a soapstone lamp (Egede 1925:362–365).

The big longhouses were gradually abandoned in the nineteenth century and replaced by smaller houses (Birket-Smith 1924:148–153; Petersen 1974–1975) for which imported wood was used, first for platforms, ceilings, floors, and inner walls and later for the outer walls, and to make European-type roofs. The entrance was replaced by a porch at floor level, closed by a wooden door. Gradually, as houses were built with purchased materials, they began to represent a greater economic value, and they were lived in by the same family year after year. Intestine windows were replaced by glass, but as late as the 1920s some intestine windows were still in use (fig. 3) (Ostermann in Saabye 1942:111). A

few houses with flat roofs and walls of stone and peat, but lined with wood inside, were still in use in some outlying areas when the period of modernization began in the 1950s (Kleivan and Kleivan 1961–1962).

Houses were warmed by blubber lamps of soapstone, which also served for cooking food and for lighting (fig. 4). A moss wick was placed along one side of the lamp. Fires were started with fire drills (Egede 1925:372). During the nineteenth century many houses changed to heating with ovens, but blubber lamps were still kept for lighting. The introduction of ovens increased the need for fuel, so that women had to make longer and longer trips from the settlement to find brush (fig. 5).

top right, Nationalmuseet, Copenhagen: 1.45; bottom left, © Natl. Geographic Soc., Washington: 32819; bottom right, © Arktisk Institut, Charlottenlund, Denmark: 5851.

Fig. 3. Habitations. top left, Settlement at Kraulshavn (Nuussuaq), with rectangular sod houses and skin tents. Almost all households used tents as summer quarters. Photograph by Frederica de Laguna, Aug. 1929. top right, Wooden house at Egedesminde with sod walls (Birket-Smith 1924:151). The loft was used as a storage room; the rafters extending out from the house served as storage racks for kayaks and other household items. Photograph by Kaj Birket-Smith, 1918. bottom left, House at Holsteinsborg constructed mostly of sod, with glass window. In foreground skin is drying, stretched and pinned with bones. Photograph by Maynard Owen Williams, 1925. bottom right, Winter house of stone and earth with gutskin window (to right of entrance) Uummannatsiaq, Uummannaq District. Photograph by H.P. Steensby, about 1910.

600

INNUIT KAFFISOTON   ERKIKSANATOME   TIPEITSORTUT

Nationalmuseet, Copenhagen: 11462.

Fig. 4. Coffee drinking inside a communal winter house. Each area with a soapstone lamp probably represents the space of a different nuclear family. Watercolor by Israil Nicodemus Gormansen, a Greenlander of the Sukkertoppen district, April 1840.

To remedy this situation, some people began to cut peat for fuel (Rink 1877:91–93). Kerosene lamps were introduced in almost all houses during World War II; thereafter blubber lamps were used only occasionally, for example, in hunting cabins (Kleivan and Kleivan 1961–1962).

There is no evidence that the Greenlanders ever used snowhouses as permanent dwellings, but there are traditions that at some places snowhouses were built for temporary use on hunting trips during the winter (Birket-Smith 1924:148).

At their hunting grounds Greenlanders lived in tents with driftwood frames and coverings of sealskin weighted down with stones (Birket-Smith 1924:154–160). A tent frame consisted of a door frame on which long tent poles were leaned. A curtain of intestines sewed together covered the entrance. Tents with two layers of skins were quite warm and could be occupied from early spring to late autumn.

Canvas ridge tents gradually replaced those of skins. They were easier to transport but afforded less protection against the cold and rainy weather. Therefore, Greenlanders began to construct hunting cabins, especially for use in the cold season. The last skin tents were abandoned in the 1950s (Kleivan 1955).

There are no observations or traditions, either from the time of first contact or from the following period, indicating that the West Greenlanders had a special

building serving as a festival house or a men's house. However, the word *qassi*, corresponding to Yupik *qazjiq* 'kashim', appears often as a place-name, and in certain cases traditions indicate that these places may have been the sites of festival houses (Thalbitzer 1914–1941:670–674). A dictionary of Greenlandic from 1804 defines *qassi* as, among other meanings, a little house without windows "where both sexes used one another indis-

© Natl. Geographic Soc., Washington: 33438–A.

Fig. 5. Women carrying loads of brush for firewood, using tumplines. Photograph by Maynard Owen Williams, Holsteinsborg, 1925.

601

criminately, the married men particularly in exchanging wives" (Fabricius 1804:158).

Transportation

The means of transportation consisted of skin boats, and on the northern part of the coast of dogsleds. There were two kinds of skin boats: the large, open umiak, and the one-man kayak. All three means of transportation were also used for hunting.

The dog sled has two runners that curve up forward and are connected by a number of crossbars. It is about 2 to 2.5 meters long, with 75–100 centimeters between the runners. In back there are two uprights with which the driver can maneuver the sled in difficult terrain. The dogsled is tied together with skin straps, which makes it very elastic and resistant to bumps and blows. Formerly dogsleds had bone shoeing; this was replaced by iron. About seven dogs were harnessed to a sled, with towlines all of equal length, approximately three meters, attached to a front strap on the first crossbar (Birket-Smith 1924:242–252; E. Rosing 1975). The dogs are steered with the whip and verbal commands (Jensen 1961:53–55). The dogsled is used for transportation to hunting or fishing grounds on the ice and in hunting caribou. It can carry up to 100 kilograms, which the dogs can pull up to 75 kilometers a day, under favorable conditions. The number of dogsleds in West Greenland has greatly increased. In 1880 there were 287; in 1910, 728; in 1950, 1,301 (Grønlands Styrelse 1942–1944:565; Denmark. Statistiske Departement 1954:320).

The umiak was 8 to 12 meters long and consisted of a laced wooden frame covered with depilated, waterproof sealskins sewed together. When used for travel, it was always rowed by women, while an old man was often in charge of the steering oar (fig. 6). But when it was used for whaling, it was paddled by men using special paddles and standing up in the boat facing in the direction of travel. The umiak could also be equipped with a sail made of intestines sewed together, later replaced by a cloth sail (Birket-Smith 1924:252–260). It was a relatively light craft that could be carried over portages and pulled up on land and ice, but it was also easily torn by ice (the gashes were patched with blubber until the boat could be repaired). The umiak had a loading capacity of around 1,500 to 2,000 kilograms, but due to its flat bottom it was not seaworthy in rough weather. In 1880 there were 251 umiaks in West Greenland and in 1900, 339. Thereafter the number decreased quickly in southern Greenland due to the transition to commercial fishing and the introduction of wooden boats, but less quickly in northern Greenland. The last umiak in West Greenland was from the Egedesminde area; it was last used in 1966 for a trip to the caribou district in the interior and then given to the museum Kalaallit Nunaata Katersugaasivia in Godthåb.

© Natl. Geographic Soc., Washington: 33026–A.

Fig. 6. Skin umiak at Sukkertoppen. The women rowers wear decorative bead collars. A man steers with a stern oar. Photograph by Maynard Owen Williams, 1925.

A kayak is about five meters long and 60 centimeters wide, built as a light wooden frame covered with waterproof, depilated sealskin (fig. 7) (Birket-Smith 1924:260–271; P.S. Jensen 1975). To keep water from entering through the opening where he sits, the kayaker wears a special coat of depilated skin, laced tightly around the wooden ring at the mouth of the opening as well as around his wrists and face. Kayak equipment also includes a pair of kayak gloves of depilated skin that are also laced tightly (Birket-Smith 1924:181–188), and scrapers (fig. 8).

The keel fin or kayak rudder was invented by a hunter from Jakobshavn around 1867 (Steensby 1912:148). It is a short piece of wooden board or bone fastened to the keel of the kayak near the stern, which acts like a centerboard to keep the vessel from drifting with the wind. It proved useful in connection with the use of firearms and kayak shooting screens but was primarily adopted in northern Greenland.

The practice was for every man to have his own kayak, and for most of the colonial period even wage earners employed by the trading company and the mission commonly hunted and fished in order to supplement their wages. The number of kayaks declined in the 1920s, especially in the central areas around Sukkertoppen and Godthåb. The decreasing use of kayaks is related to the development of fishing, which in many areas was more profitable than sealing, and to the fact that more and more Greenlanders were able to assure themselves of a steady income through paid employment (H. Kleivan 1964).

In the twentieth century wooden rowboats began to replace kayaks and umiaks as means of transportation, and especially as fishing boats. Until around 1930 they were almost all built privately in Greenland, but then they began to be imported in greater numbers from Denmark (Grønlands Styrelse 1942–1944:569).

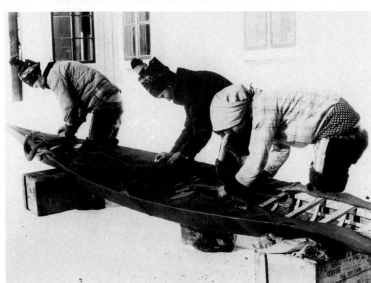

© Natl. Geographic Soc., Washington: top left, 33120–A; top right, 33861–A; © Arktisk Institut, Charlottenlund, Denmark: bottom left, 3711; bottom right, 3418.

Fig. 7. Kayaks. top, Man from Søndre Upernavik (Upernavik Kujalleq) demonstrating tipping and righting his craft (top left) and balancing after a complete roll (top right). Photographs by Maynard Owen Williams, 1925. bottom left, Building the wooden frame for a kayak at Søndre Upernavik. Photograph by Jette Bang, June 1939. bottom right, Sewing the skin covering on the frame at Godhavn (Qeqertarsuaq). An ulu lies on top of the cover. Photograph by Morten Porsild, 1924.

About 1940 a Greenlandic fisherman at Godthåb built a boat as a wooden frame covered with canvas. This model could carry more than similar wooden boats, and for the next couple of decades this rather cheap but fragile boat was quite popular for coastal and fjord fishing. A special light model was built for easy portage when caribou hunting, and another model for use with an outboard motor (Kapel 1973).

The first motorboats for fishing were bought by Greenlanders in 1924. In the southernmost and northernmost areas of the west coast, motorboats are also used in sealing. Seals are never harpooned from a motorboat but always shot. Sometimes a kayak is brought along on the motorboat, partly to be used in sealing, and partly for getting help if the motorboat should de-velop engine trouble or become icebound (Kleivan and Kleivan 1961–1962).

Subsistence

• SEALING   In sealing from kayaks a large number of specialized weapons are used (Birket-Smith 1924:283–320; Holtved 1962:27–66; P.S. Jensen 1975). Each has a definite place on the deck. The harpoon consists of a wooden shaft with a bone foreshaft in which is placed a detachable bone or antler head with an iron point. Harpoons with shafts terminated with an ivory knob are about 280 centimeters long, while those shafts ending in a couple of flat bone wings measure about 190 centimeters. The harpoon is thrown with a throwing-

603

Smithsonian, Dept. of Anthr.: top, 130,473; bottom, 130,468.

Fig. 8. Kayak scrapers used to remove ice from the deck. top, Older style scraper; bottom, later style with leather thong at handle ending with a bone knob. top, Length 22.0 cm; bottom same scale. Both collected by T. Holm. top, From a grave in Upernavik; bottom, from Godthåb, 1884–1886.

board. To the harpoon head is attached an 11–14 meter harpoon line that lies rolled up in front of the hunter, on the so-called kayak stand. The other end of the line is attached to an inflated sealskin float (fig. 9). When the hunter is within 18 meters of the seal he throws the harpoon and immediately puts the throwing-board between his teeth, in order to be ready to throw the sealing float out when the line is almost paid out. The seal dives, and the hunter takes his big lance and paddles after it.

Like the kayak harpoon, the big lance consists of a long wooden shaft and a bone foreshaft strapped together so the shaft can break off when the lance is shoved into an animal. But while the harpoon has a detachable head, the lance head is fastened to the foreshaft. The lance head has no barbs, so it can easily be pulled out of the wound and shoved in again, after the foreshaft is again put in place. The seal is finally dispatched with the sealer's small lance or with his hunting knife.

For small seals, the bladder dart could be used. The bladder dart was thrown with the same throwing-board as used for the bird dart.

The bird dart consisted of a wooden shaft with a blunt bone head; around the middle of the shaft were placed three or four lateral prongs with their heads directed forward and with barbs on their inner sides, to provide as wide an area of contact with the birds as possible.

The bladder dart and the bird dart went into disuse in the northern part of the West Greenland area around the beginning of the twentieth century but were in common use for a few decades longer in the southern part. The other kayak weapons were still in use in the 1960s, most often in combination with a rifle (fig. 10) (Kleivan and Kleivan 1961–1962).

To prevent water damage, the rifle at first was kept inside the kayak, which was not very practical. In the 1860s a hunter at Uummannaq constructed a special bag of depilated skin in which the rifle could lie on the front deck (Steensby 1912:147); this was imitated all along the coast.

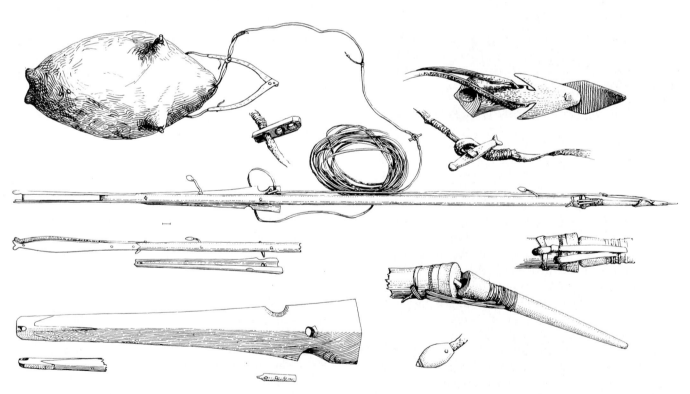

Smithsonian, NAA (drawing from Mason 1902:1.5).

Fig. 9. Sealing harpoon, throwing-board, and float used in open water. This type of harpoon is known as the "feathered" type because the bone projections at the base resemble feathers and are used to increase the weight and guide the flight. Length of shaft 207.0 cm; collected by N.P. Scudder at Holsteinsborg, 1879.

During the same period, the kayak shooting screen came into use in northwest Greenland (Steensby 1912:150). The idea was adopted from the shooting screen for ice hunting; both reduced the contrast between the hunter and his environment. The screen is a white cotton cloth stiffened with sticks and fastened across the front deck of the kayak, giving the impression that the kayak is a piece of floating ice (Hansen 1971:185–186).

Often several hunters set off together in the morning, but when they were out in the open sea, they spread out, keeping in sight so that they could assist each other if necessary.

In southern Greenland collective sealing sometimes occurred: as soon as a seal was sighted, several hunters began to shout and to throw their bladder darts at it, forcing it to dive quickly. It soon had to surface again in order to breathe, when it was then easy prey (Holtved 1962:106).

In some places kayaks could close off sounds at narrow places where in certain seasons seals passed in herds. The kayak hunters, having occupied the outlets, threw their bird darts and bladder darts to frighten the seals toward shore where they would be taken with the kayak weapons, as well as being stoned by women and children on land (Dalager 1915:12–13).

When experience showed that seals came close to land at certain places, sealers would lie in hiding behind a low stone wall and harpoon or shoot the passing seals (Birket-Smith 1924:321–322).

When a Greenlander hunted seals from the ice edge, he would carry his kayak so he could take it into the water to dispatch and retrieve the animal (Hansen 1971:157–162).

Nets for sealing (Hansen 1971:45–47, 142–143) seem to have been introduced by Europeans (Holtved 1962:107). They were placed across fjords and sounds with floats.

The best season for sealing at breathing holes (Hansen 1971:148–150) was in January, before the ice was covered with too much snow. The hunter either stood by a breathing hole or sat on a one-legged stool, with

Fig. 10. Seal hunting by Tobias Nielsen of Illorsuit, Uummannaq District. top, Shooting seals with a shotgun from behind a screen on the bow of the kayak. The wounded seal is then harpooned and if necessary dispatched with a rifle. center, Seal under water in left foreground, attached to harpoon line float on far side of kayak; floating harpoon has simple bone knob at proximal end, and throwing-board engaged with pin at balance point of shaft whence the harpoon is propelled. Two guns are in the gun sleeve on kayak deck. Hunter inflating towing-strap float wears a waist band, normal for hunting with guns in calm waters, rather than the full waterproof jacket; his mittens are on the harpoon-line stand. bottom, Towing the seal, with towing-strap float at rear, head toward front, both attached to kayak with a quick-release system. The rolled-up shooting screen is on the foredeck. Photographs by Kenneth Iain Taylor, 1959.

his feet resting on a small three-legged footstool, waiting for the seal to appear. When the seal rose it would be harpooned with a special ice harpoon, which differed from the kayak harpoon in that its foreshaft was not detachable. The shaft terminated in an ice chisel of tooth or bone, used to chop the breathing hole large enough for the seal to be hauled up. When the Greenlanders acquired iron from Europe, the ice chisel became a separate tool (Birket-Smith 1924:324–325; Hansen 1971:176), and instead of the ice harpoon, it gradually became common to use for breathing-hole sealing the kayak harpoon without its inflated sealing float.

When the weather had been very calm and cold and the ice had frozen a special form of breathing-hole sealing could be carried on. The hunter listened carefully in order to locate the breathing hole, and approached that spot for harpooning, his steps silenced by hairy skin fastened to the soles of his boots (Hansen 1971:144–145).

A special ice hunting method, "peep" hunting, was carried on by two men. One of them lay down on a low wooden bench or a skin on the ice in order to see into the water. The other stood up beside him, ready to strike with a very long harpoon, about 7.5 meters, which was already projecting through a smaller hole nearby. The prone man watched the movements of the seal under the ice and attempted to attract it with whistling sounds. When the seal was in the right position, he signaled to the harpooner (Hansen 1971:151–153).

Breathing-hole, smooth-ice, and "peep" hunting were gradually discontinued but were still practiced occasionally in the beginning of the twentieth century (Hansen 1971:144, 148, 151).

In the spring when seals were lying on the ice sunning themselves, a hunter stalked them with his harpoon, which might be fastened to a very small sled, the runners of which were shod with skin (Hansen 1971:152–154).

After the introduction of firearms it was no longer necessary to approach so closely to a seal. The hunter hides behind a shooting screen of white cotton cloth, stretched across a small sled that he pushes in front of himself, firing his gun through an opening in the screen (Hansen 1971:155–156, 185–186). This shooting screen was probably invented by a Danish trade manager in Egedesminde at the close of the eighteenth century (Gad 1971–1982, 3:167).

Ice-net sealing, like net sealing in open water, seems to have been unknown to or at least very little used by Greenlanders before it was introduced by Europeans in the eighteenth century. It is carried out especially in the early winter, when the ice is rather thin (Hansen 1971:146–148).

• WHALING Small whales, especially the white whale, were hunted from kayaks in the same way as seals (Hansen 1971:40–44, 138–141).

Larger whales were hunted from umiaks (Birket-Smith 1924:335–339). If the whale hit a boat and threw the men into the water, they could stay afloat for some time in their air-filled, waterproof combination suits. To keep the umiak from capsizing, several inflated floats were placed along the gunwales. Special harpoons with floats were used, as well as lances. When Greenlanders hunted whales, they preferred to use two or three umiaks, with 10 to 12 men in each (fig. 11). There is no information on how the crews of whaling umiaks were recruited.

Towing a whale to land could be just as difficult as killing the animal, and more whales were killed than could be towed home. But killed or wounded whales often later drifted to land.

In the eighteenth century the Royal Greenland Trading Company employed Greenlanders to participate in hunting large whales, but a rapid decline in the whale population soon set in, and the trading company stopped whaling. An attempt at whaling with a trading company ship was begun in 1924 but discontinued again in 1959. A Greenlander from Egedesminde began in 1949 to hunt small whales, especially minke whales, from a motorboat with a harpoon gun. This successful form of whaling was later adopted by others.

Off the north coast of West Greenland a herd of narwhals or white whales is sometimes trapped in a gap surrounded by large areas of compact ice.

• POLAR-BEAR HUNTING The polar bear, which appears only occasionally, is an especially coveted game animal. Bears are attacked with any weapon available, on land as well as at sea (Birket-Smith 1924:349–350; Hansen 1971:63–66). In northern Greenland, sled dogs assist in preventing the bear from escaping.

The polar bear has from ancient times been surrounded by a special aura. Not only is bear skin quite warm, but also since the time of first contact with Europeans it has commanded a very good price as a trading commodity.

• CARIBOU HUNTING Caribou hunting (Nellemann 1969–1970) was carried out with bow and arrow during trips to the interior in both summer and winter, but especially in late summer when the skins were best for making clothes. With umiaks and kayaks the Greenlanders sailed up the fjords and then continued on foot. Sometimes the boats were carried for some distance for crossing lakes and rivers in order to penetrate deeper into the interior.

The bow, which went out of use in the late eighteenth century, was usually made of driftwood, reinforced with plaited cords of sinew. The barbed or barbless arrowheads were of caribou antler; a blade was sometimes inserted. A quiver-bowcase of depilated waterproof sealskin was carried by a forehead strap (Holtved 1962:69–73; Birket-Smith 1924:339–347).

Eighteenth-century accounts describe women and children driving the caribou toward where the men lay hiding (fig. 11). The Greenlanders also used a row of

Fig. 11. Depictions of subsistence activities of West Greenlanders. left, A caribou hunt. Women drive the game toward concealed men with bows and arrows. Poles topped with turf complete the surround. right, Hunting right whales from umiaks. A sealskin float is attached to the whale in the foreground. Engravings by Johanne Fosie based on lost sketches by Hans or Poul Egede, 1721–1736.

poles topped with lumps of turf, resembling humans. Many remains of ancient stone cairns used for driving caribou can still be seen. Sometimes the caribou were driven into lakes, where men in kayaks killed them. Some fences were so arranged that the caribou dispatched themselves by falling off a cliff.

On the northern half of the west coast, dogsleds were used for caribou hunting in the winter. When a track was found, the hunters could also continue on foot or skis (the latter having been introduced by Europeans at the beginning of the colonial period).

The introduction of the rifle much increased the efficiency of a lone hunter. The technological and organizational change in caribou hunting that took place at the end of the eighteenth century, when drives seem to have been completely replaced by individual hunting, is probably also connected with a distinct decline in the caribou population at this time, due to climatic change and perhaps also the excessive exploitation of the population since the introduction of the rifle.

• FOX TRAPPING Greenlanders made little use of fox skin themselves but European demand led to the in-tensification of fox trapping for the fur trade. The most common method used a rectangular stone room with a flat stone placed vertically as a trap door (Holtved 1962:97–101; Hansen 1971:78–82, 167–169, 181–183).

• BIRD HUNTING Sea birds were hunted with the bird dart thrown at prey on the surface of the water, or at birds in flight (Holtved 1962:73–82). Occasional organized bird hunts were led by an especially skilled hunter who decided the morning departure time of hunters who attempted to surprise the birds or to exhaust them (Holtved 1962:78–80, 127–129; Hansen 1971:72–74). Sea birds were sometimes an important part of the diet, but land birds were never much hunted, except for ptarmigans, which were especially trapped in snares (Holtved 1962:73–75; Hansen 1971:83–84).

• FISHING The most important fish was the fat little capelin, which was easy to preserve by drying. In the early summer large numbers came in to the coast and were scooped up in nets made of plaited sinew thread (Glahn 1921:233–235; Holtved 1962:94–95).

A common method of catching Arctic char was to dam a bay or a river with a stone weir low enough to

Fig. 12. Hunting knife with metal blade made from a file and bone handle. The wooden sheath protects the kayak skin from the blade. Length 27.5 cm; collected by T. Holm at Godthåb, 1884–1886.

let water flow at high tide, but high enough to isolate the area at low tide. Then men, women, and children, caught the fish with leisters, hook spears, hooks on lines, scooping nets, bird darts, and with bare hands (Holtved 1962:95–96).

Shorthorn sculpin and Greenland cod were caught with jigs, either from kayaks or through holes in the ice. These fish constituted an emergency food reserve resorted to when no other supplies were available. Large fish such as Atlantic cod and Atlantic halibut were caught from kayaks in deep water at various banks or through the ice in the winter. Other fish caught were redfish, deepwater redfish, Greenland halibut, and sharks. Shark meat was usually eaten only by the dogs; shark livers might serve as lamp fuel and could be sold to the trading company as well. Fishing lines were thongs and sinew threads, but mostly baleen strips tied together, which were gradually replaced by European materials (Birket-Smith 1924:363–370). Lumpfish were taken with leisters from the shore in calm weather, when they could be seen from the rocks (Holtved 1962:93).

In the eighteenth and nineteenth centuries there were some attempts by officials and private Europeans to build up a fishing industry, but not until the beginning of the twentieth century was this venture successful (Mattox 1973). Fishing stations were established under the leadership of Danish instructors who were hired to teach the Greenlanders the use of long lines and other equipment. Long lines are also put under the ice for Greenland halibut, at times several kilometers from land, so that the fishermen must drive out in their dog sleds to inspect them.

In the market economy, the most important primary product of fishing was cod. Opportunities for selling cod began in earnest in 1911; in the following year fish houses were built at many places for salting cod. The first experiments with cod nets were conducted by a Greenlander around 1900; in 1912 the sale of cod nets was started (Grønlands Styrelse 1942–1944:592–593). In addition to long lines, pound nets began to be used for cod fishing around 1951, but a number of Greenlanders continued to jig from rowboats and kayaks, which yielded only limited catches. Mostly smaller motorboats were used at this time, so that fishing was still carried on in the inner coastal waters.

• NEW OCCUPATIONS Among the new occupational opportunities that the government attempted to create in the beginning of the twentieth century, fishing was significant for the greatest number of people. At certain localities in southern Greenland sheep raising also was initiated; attempts at fox raising, begun in 1914, and mink raising, begun in 1938, did not produce very positive results. Reindeer breeding started at Godthåbfjord in 1952.

Since the end of the eighteenth century coal has been mined on a small scale at various places on the coast from Disko Island to Svartenhuk. The coal mine at Qullissat, established in 1924, employed a number of Greenlanders until it was closed in 1972.

From the first century of colonization, the missions and the Royal Greenland Trading Company also employed a number of Greenlanders, especially the sons of European fathers and Greenlandic mothers who often had not been reared so that they could manage exclusively as hunters. Some women were employed as housemaids by Danish families.

• GATHERING Food gathering (Birket-Smith 1924:371–372) played no great part in the traditional economy of West Greenland, but added variety to the diet and was resorted to when hunting and fishing failed.

The eggs of sea birds were gathered both by men on hunting trips and by an entire family when the occasion arose. Mussels were also gathered at low tide, mostly by women; it was also generally women and children who gathered plant products (Hertz 1968). In hard times, berries and plant roots constituted a food reserve all winter, if the snow was not too deep (Glahn 1921:191). Seaweed was another reserve. Fresh plants and berries were eaten during the summer, and some were kept in sealskin bags with blubber to be used in wintertime.

• COOKING AND FOOD STORAGE Meat and fish were usually boiled, either in soapstone pots suspended over the blubber lamp inside the house or outside over a fire in the summer. On hunting trips, where heavy pots were not taken along, meat was sometimes roasted in thin slices on a flat stone, which served as a frying pan.

At the beginning of contact with Europeans, metal pots were introduced to replace the heavy soapstone ones, as were china and metal cutlery.

Seal, whale, and caribou meat was stored raw and frozen, or cut into small pieces and dried. Stored walrus and bearded seal meat was eaten more or less tainted as were fish such as Arctic char and cod. Capelin were dried whole in large quantities and stored in large bags of sealskin. Blubber was also stored in bags made of a whole stripped-off sealskin or in an inflated stomach, where it gradually turned into oil. Vegetable foods were preserved raw with blubber in such bags. Seal blood was poured into a stomach or intestines, where it coagulated; like most other food, it was eaten with blubber (Birket-Smith 1924:380–381, 389).

Europeans brought new methods of preservation to Greenland, especially smoking, which was used for Arctic char.

Storerooms were built of stone, often using a natural crack in a cliff as the back and side walls. Other storerooms were situated farther off, near hunting grounds. This distance functioned as a rationing mechanism, so that stores were not exhausted too quickly (Kleivan and Kleivan 1961–1962).

Death from starvation occurred only under extraordinary conditions. There are, nevertheless, several documented cases of starvation in the history of Greenland (Rink 1877:159, 265–267). The presence of Europeans generally functioned as a safety net, as they distributed rations in periods of famine.

• EUROPEAN FOOD AND STIMULANTS   During the first century of colonization, government officials were quite restrictive about the sale of European supplies to Greenlanders, in order not to make them dependent on imported foodstuffs. In the middle of the nineteenth century the restrictions were abandoned, but the supply of European foodstuffs available for purchase was nevertheless quite limited, consisting mostly of beans, peas, barley groats, rye, flour, biscuits, sugar, and dried fruit. The subsistence of the Greenlanders was still based on hunting and fishing. Not until the twentieth century, in connection with an increased access to cash income and the greater variety of food products available in shops, did the consumption of imported food begin to play a greater role. Hunting and fishing products continued, nevertheless, to be greatly appreciated.

Tobacco and later coffee quickly became coveted commodities. At times, a relatively large amount of the cash income of Greenlanders was spent on them (Sveistrup and Dalgaard 1945:378–384).

It was forbidden to sell alcohol to Greenlanders, although alcohol was sometimes served as a reward for work. Various rationing systems were then employed, until in 1954 the sale of alcohol was freed from all restrictions. By that time it had become common for Greenlanders to brew their own beer (Nellemann 1974–1975).

• COMMUNITY OF CONSUMPTION   West Greenlandic hunting society was characterized by various commensal units. There were several rules for the distribution of animals killed in hunting. When several men participated in killing the same animal, the one whose weapon hit the animal first was considered the actual killer but he only received a minor part, the rest being distributed to the other participants (Dalager 1915:18–19; Holtved 1962:106–107). The distribution system also applied to men in kayaks who met a hunter at sea after he had killed an animal alone (Kleivan and Kleivan 1961–1962); thus, it was a system of distribution comprising active hunters. There were different rules for different animal species. Small seals were usually not divided. There were local variations in the distribution rules for large seals, small whales, caribou, and polar bears (Birket-Smith 1924:279–281). In the Cape Farewell area the rule applied was that the person who first saw a polar bear was regarded as the one who had secured it, receiving the skin, the head, and some of the meat (Kleivan and Kleivan 1961–1962).

A large whale was free for all to flense as much of as they wished, regardless of whether they had participated in killing it, or even been out hunting at all (Glahn 1921:128–131).

At some localities capelin, which existed in large quantities, were carried by the women and children up onto rocks to dry, with the family that carried the most receiving the most, regardless of the performances of their men in scooping them out of the water (Glahn 1921:234). This system, and that of whale flensing, was to the advantage of larger families.

The first animal killed by a boy and the first kill of the season of certain animals such as the hooded seal and the walrus were ritually distributed to all the inhabitants of the settlement, a practice designed to assure successful hunting in the future. Even infants were considered as social persons for the purposes of such distribution (Birket-Smith 1924: 280–282; Kleivan and Kleivan 1961–1962).

When a seal was pulled up on land to be flensed, a small strip of belly skin with blubber on it was cut into small pieces for distribution to the children (Kleivan and Kleivan 1961–1962).

A very important form of distribution was the so-called meat gifts, given by a hunter to the inhabitants of his settlement. Hunters were expected to give away some of their kill, but this does not seem to have been an obligation in the same way as was the distribution to other hunters of parts of animals killed. Certain pieces of meat were given to certain age-sex categories of persons. Thus in earlier times each woman of the settlement would be given a rib (P.H. Egede 1939:73), each unweaned child a piece of the flipper, and a piece of blubber would be allotted to each lamp (Glahn 1921:169). The burden of supporting unproductive members of the society was accommodated through the meat-gift system.

The men participated in common meals, a very important form of communal consumption (Glahn 1921:170; Kleivan and Kleivan 1961–1962). There were also common meals to which people who lived in the same house each contributed. The men ate at one end of the house, and the women and children at the other, on the floor and on the platform, respectively (Glahn 1921:170–171).

As settlements grew it became more difficult to maintain a meat-gift system that could apply to everyone at the settlement, and it became more common to restrict meat gifts to relatives and close neighbors. As a money economy gained importance at the same time that a differentiation of occupations took place, seal meat became rare in many places, and was sold by successful hunters. This development began in some places while sealing was still generally carried out from kayaks but became more pronounced with the introduction of motorboats, as the economic obligations taken on by their owners considerably increased their need for cash. For the same reason, motorboat owners were unwilling to distribute parts of their kill to kayak hunters they met while returning home (H. Kleivan 1964:69–70).   *609*

Fig. 13. Sealskin bag used to carry fire-making tools. It is decorated with a skin-mosaic, the individual pieces sewed on with a patterned running stitch, a decorative technique also used on clothing. Width 29.5 cm; collected by C.F. Hall at Holsteinsborg, 1860.

Tools

For working in bone, wood, and soapstone, an adz, bow drill, and knife were used.

European metal blades for women's knives quickly became a common trading commodity, to which the woman's husband or a relative attached a handle. Various bone and stone scrapers were used. All these tools (Birket-Smith 1924:81–100) were in use at the beginning of the period of rapid culture change (Kleivan and Kleivan 1961–1962).

Skin Preparation

Skins were prepared in various ways (Birket-Smith 1924:100–109) depending on the animal and the use the skin was to be put to.

When sealskins were scraped clean of most of the blubber, they were stretched and dried. To remove the remaining blubber they were then washed in urine (replaced by European detergents), dried again, and then rubbed and scraped to make them soft. To depilate sealskin, it was soaked in urine after the first scraping. Seal intestines to be used for gutskin were soaked in salt water and then inflated.

Thongs were especially made of the hide of young walruses and bearded seals. Seals destined for this purpose were flensed in a special way: circular cuts were made and the middle parts of the skin were removed. When the hair was removed, the pieces of skin were cut up into long spirals.

For sewing, the sinews of various animals were used. Sinews from the back of a caribou provided especially long and thin thread, while sinews from small whales yielded strong thread especially used to sew boat skins.

A hunter had to have well-sewn skin clothing in order to survive, and it was equally necessary to keep his clothes dry. They were dried on wooden frames hung over the lamp, in later times over the oven.

Clothing

Most clothing was of sealskin, but caribou, dog, and bird skins were also used. Warmest were caribou skins, mostly used for winter coats. Clothing (Birket-Smith 1924:167–208) consisted of two layers: the outer coat and trousers had the hair outward, while the inner coat and trousers had it inward. Indoors, both men and women wore only their inner trousers.

At the beginning of contact with Europeans, men's coats were cut so they almost reached the knee (fig. 14); some had a little flap in front and in back. The coat and hood were sewn together. Men's trousers were quite short; their boots were of dipilated skin. Mittens were often equipped with two thumbs so that they could be turned around when the palms got wet (fig. 15). There were special suits of depilated skin and gutskin for use at sea (fig. 16).

To protect the eyes against the harsh light reflected from the sea and snow, especially in the spring, snow goggles or eyeshades were used.

Women's coats had considerably larger flaps than the men's. They were also broader at the shoulders, and had bigger hoods, although in general women went bareheaded. Women's coats used for carrying children were of a special cut, with the back and hood enlarged to make a place for the child (fig. 17). A belt fastened to a button in front kept the child from sliding down. Women's trousers reached below the knee. Their boots and stockings were relatively short, meeting the trousers. Seams, especially on women's clothes, might have insets of a different color, such as depilated white skin.

During the period of colonization, both men's and women's coats became shorter; the men's coats lost their flaps entirely, while those of the women's coats became narrower. The men's trousers became longer, and the women's shorter; boot lengths were altered correspondingly.

Trade with Europeans led Greenlanders both to purchase European clothing and to sew European fabrics in Greenlandic styles, such as anoraks and trousers. Colored glass beads were sewed to collars and cuffs on the women's coats.

Not for some time after the beginning of the twentieth century did it become common for Greenlanders to dress like Europeans; this occurred with the transition to a money economy and a greater degree of contact with Denmark. But the use of Greenlandic clothing had not died out by the 1950s. Particularly on the northern

Fig. 14. Portraits of West Greenlanders. left, The earliest known painting of Greenlandic Eskimos. Ihiob, Cabelou, Gunnelle, and Sigjo (left to right), captured in the Godthåb area by David Dannel on his 1654 voyage. Both women have chin tattooing and one of them wears a coat with high hood, wide shoulders, and flap in front and back. The man holds a bladder dart and a sinew-backed bow and arrow. Unknown artist, painted in Bergen, Norway, 1654. center, Maria, daughter of Epeyub, who visited Denmark with the missionary Sylow in 1746. She wears a long coat, hair in topknot, and ear ornament; her hands and chin are tattooed. She holds a small harpoon used for fishing (Birket-Smith 1924:361). Painting by Mathias Blumenthal, 1753, after a lost 1747 original by him. right, Poq (left), aged 22, and Qiperoq, aged 34, on a visit to Denmark where this portrait was commissioned by the Bergen Grønlandske Compagnie as a gift for King Frederik IV. They wear fur coats that were considerably longer than 20th-century styles. Poq holds bow and arrow and Qiperoq holds a bird dart and throwing-board. Painting by Bernhard Grodtschilling in Copenhagen, 1724.

part of the west coast hunters in the 1980s still wore skin clothing to a great extent; and a number of Greenlanders still wore skin boots and stockings in the winter, while European footwear was considered more suitable in the summer.

Greenlandic clothing was still worn at celebrations in the 1980s. For men this usually meant only a white cotton anorak. The women's costume has combined Greenlandic and European materials and styles. The space between the top of the long skin stockings and that of the short skin boots is thus decorated with lace and embroidered fabric, while the boots themselves and the skin trousers are richly decorated with colored skin embroidery. The anorak is of colorful silk or cotton without a hood. The bead collar with geometrical designs almost reaches the elbows (Kaalund 1979:125). This is an expensive costume, which confers prestige and at the same time stresses the ethnic identity of its owner.

Adornment

At the beginning of the period of contact with Europeans, men's hair was combed down on all sides and cut straight all the way around; the women wore their hair in a high topknot tied halfway up with a strip of skin, soon replaced by a silk ribbon (Cranz 1770:184).

At the beginning of the twentieth century, young girls in the cities began to adopt European hairstyles. Even as late as the 1950s one could still see an old woman or two with the topknot (Kleivan and Kleivan 1961–1962).

Girls were tattooed on the face and sometimes also on the hands, arms, and legs, by sewing lines under the skin with a bone needle and a sooty thread. Not all women were tattooed; it was more common for women in the south than those in the north (Glahn 1771:193). Tattooing was rather quickly abandoned. It did not conform to the European idea of feminine beauty, and it was soon also considered inappropriate for Christians.

Art

Tools, weapons, household equipment, and clothes could be artistically fashioned; beautifully elaborated hunting equipment undoubtedly had a magical function (H. Lynge 1970:242–244). In the middle of the nineteenth century, some Greenlanders illustrated Greenlandic oral traditions and various other publications printed at the newly established press in Godthåb (Oldendow 1959). Aron

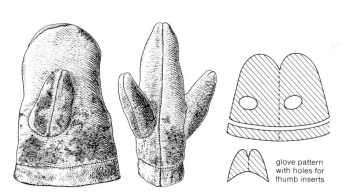

Smithsonian, Dept. of Anthr.: 37,546.

Fig. 15. Sealskin mittens with 2 thumbs. Length 8.5 cm; collected by N.P. Scudder at Holsteinsborg, 1879.

glove pattern with holes for thumb inserts

of Kaneq in particular became especially renowned for his woodcuts ("History of Norse Greenland," fig. 4, this vol.) (Knuth 1968a) and watercolors (Meldgaard 1982). At the beginning of the twentieth century, Jakob Danielsen painted watercolors depicting details of the hunting culture of northwest Greenland (Rosendahl 1967).

Division of Labor

Husband and wife cooperated quite closely. Cooperation was often also necessary between several men, women, or both in various kinds of hunting and work.

There was no consistent specialization of labor, except that based on sex and age. Men and women had different kinds of expertise (Dalager 1915:4–5). Both sexes needed technical skill in some situations and physical strength and endurance in others. All the men hunted and fished, unless prevented by illness or age. The women also fished a bit and gathered, but their contribution to the overall household food production was relatively small.

When women went along on caribou-hunting or whaling expeditions, their expertise as seamstresses was useful in making repairs. In caribou hunting they participated as beaters, and after the kill carried the game; in whaling they might function in towing the whales home.

When a hunter returned in his kayak with game, his wife took care of its further preparation. She flensed and cut up the animals, prepared the skins for various

612

uses, and sewed them. The men did the woodworking necessary for the house, while the women built walls of stone and peat (Saabye 1942:59). All utensils of wood, bone, stone, and iron were made by men. The women cooked, provided water and fuel, tended the blubber lamp, and took care of the children.

Life Cycle

• CHILDHOOD A baby was named immediately after birth, often after a recently deceased relative or other person. Such a name created a bond between the child and the relatives of the deceased. Later in life the child could also receive another name, often emphasizing some personal characteristic (Dalager 1915:1–2). Long after the introduction of Christian baptism, Greenlanders continued to give their children, along with a Christian name, a Greenlandic name (Bertelsen 1918).

Until a child could walk steadily, he was carried around in a special women's coat sewn for the purpose, on the back of its mother or some other woman, with whom the child thus acquired a feeling of close and secure contact. Later the child would be much left to older siblings and playmates.

Children were not punished physically and seldom verbally (Saabye 1942:64), but sometimes they were teased as an element in the process of socialization.

Nationalmuseet, Copenhagen: 115.

Fig. 16. A man from Attu wearing sealskin trousers, boots, and a waterproof skin jacket. The jacket could be tied around the face and wrists and fixed firmly around the rim of the kayak opening to keep the kayaker dry. Photograph by Kaj Birket-Smith, Egedesminde District, 1918.

KLEIVAN

Fig. 17. Women's clothing. left, Women and children at Egedesminde in front of a sealskin tent. They wear sealskin coats with hoods large enough to carry infants, trousers, and long boots. Their hair is in a characteristic topknot. Photograph by Arnold Heim, June 1909. right, Woman at Holsteinsborg stretching a boot on a square iron blade set into a flat piece of wood (Birket-Smith 1924:210). Photograph by Maynard Owen Williams, 1925.

Childless persons were eager to adopt children to help them in their work and take care of them when they grew old. Sometimes the adoptive parents paid a small amount to an unmarried mother for her child (P.H. Egede 1939:46).

Even parents who had their own children often also had adopted children. It was not uncommon for an adoptive child to do the hardest work, such as fetching water, and to have the poorest clothing. But from the moment a boy began to hunt, he was almost always well treated. A conflict could arise if one of an adopted child's biological parents were still alive and wanted him back at a time when his help was needed. An adult adopted as a child could then decide to continue to live with his adoptive parents and help them in their old age (Dalager 1915:25–26).

Children played games imitating adult activities, but a real knowledge of hunting techniques, for example, was first acquired when they accompanied experienced hunters on a hunt. Boys had a small kayak built for them at the age of six or seven.

Future hunters were also able to get theoretical insight into the many special situations that could arise by listening to hunters tell of their experiences. Indeed, the main topic of men's conversation was the hunt.

When a boy made his first kill, for instance a lumpfish, the occasion was commemorated with a celebration in which as many persons as possible tasted the meat (Kleivan 1955). But the most important rite of passage was held in connection with the first seal killed by a boy. The men of the community were invited to a meal, and the meat was also distributed to everyone in the settlement.

The status achieved by a boy by killing his first seal was also taken as a sign that he was sexually mature. An account from the middle of the eighteenth century describes such a boy being taken to a young girl to feel her sexual organs (Dalager 1915:4).

The celebration of the first kill took place in the homes of hunters at the beginning of the period of most rapid acculturation, but for most Greenlandic children the most important rites of passage since then were the beginning of school and confirmation (Kleivan and Kleivan 1961–1962).

• MARRIAGE A man usually married when he was able to support a wife; marriage between persons of approximately the same age seems to have been the norm. Adoptive siblings were not considered eligible for marriage to each other.

A marriage was accomplished by a man taking a woman by force. The girl was expected to resist, even if she was interested in marrying him.

There were no consistent rules for where a newly wedded couple should live, but the most common practice by far seems to have been that they lived with the husband's parents, that is, in an area where he was familiar with hunting conditions. If the wife's parents needed a hunter in the house, the couple might settle with them instead (Dalager 1915:23–24).

Usually a man had only one wife. In the mid-eighteenth century, it was estimated that less than one Greenlander out of 30 had two wives, and only a very few had three or four (Dalager 1915:6). One reason for polygyny could be the fact that the first wife had borne no children. But it could also happen that a man was so productive a hunter that the first wife thought it too difficult to take care of all his game and urged him to take a second wife. The relationship between co-wives was not always harmonious; it was often marred by jealousy.

One case of polyandry is reported from the early period of colonization. This was, however, quite unusual: the wife and both the husbands were all shamans (N. Egede 1939:129).

Either husband or wife could take the initiative in divorcing, but seldom did a couple with children divorce. In such a case, the children stayed with the mother (Dalager 1915:6). With the introduction of Christianity, polygamy and divorce were forbidden. Divorce was not legalized until the passage of a marriage law in 1955.

• OLD AGE Old people were respected for their experience, and they were in general treated lovingly by their families. If a widow had grown sons, she still occupied the dominant position in the family; but if she was taken into another family as a widow, her status was inferior. Such widows received food on an equal basis with the others but were last in line when skins were distributed for clothes (Dalager 1915:25). Skins could be scarce, especially after they could be converted into European commodities.

Examples of mercy killing of old people are known (N. Egede 1939:157), but this seems to have been rare. It was the responsibility of a family to take care of its old people.

The trading company and the mission helped the needy to a limited extent. In 1926 an old-age pension was introduced for all persons over the age of 55 in West Greenland; this regular supplement of cash income was in many cases important for the entire family, but the amount was so small that it was not expected to be the total subsistence of the pensioner. In 1932 the first old people's home was established. Before the period of modernization, such institutions were significant for only a tiny part of the aged population.

• ILLNESS AND DEATH The West Greenlanders practiced some medicine (Birket-Smith 1924:423-427): thus abscesses were cut and bandaged with blubber and moss; but in many cases they placed more faith in seances held by the shaman (Dalager 1915:28–30; Glahn 1921:76).

In the eighteenth century the first physicians were stationed in Greenland (Gad 1971–1982, 2:365) but during the period of colonization the health services were far from adequate to the needs of the highly dispersed population.

The contact with Europeans brought new diseases to Greenland, resulting in epidemics with a high mortality rate, such as smallpox and various children's diseases. The most serious illness during the late colonization period was tuberculosis, with the second most important cause of death being accidents, especially kayak drownings (Bertelsen 1935–1943, 1:28–71).

When it became obvious that a sick person was about to die, he was dressed in his finest clothes. The deceased was carried by his closest relatives some distance away from the houses of the settlement, and a stone coffin was built around him covered by piled-up stones. His personal property was placed in or by the grave. Those who had touched the dead person were subject to taboos. Women, but not men, showed that they had lost their spouse by neglecting their appearance; when the survivors met someone for the first time after the death of a relative, both sides burst into tears and laments (Dalager 1915:34–37, 41).

The introduction of Christianity led to burials in consecrated cemeteries, and to European-style coffins in graves dug into the earth. With the disappearance of taboos in relation to death, funerals were transformed from strictly personal events for the nearest relatives to social events involving the whole community.

Political Organization

Before the Danish-Norwegian colonization, the small, more or less isolated communities had no central authority. Nor was there any basis for a stratified society with leaders and priests; but a kind of limited leadership did exist. The words of skillful hunters carried more weight than those of others; they might take initiatives, but it was not considered good manners to dominate others.

The "great hunter," who brought much game home to his settlement and was generous in distributing it, had high prestige. Only a few men ever attained the status of "great hunter," and that only for the period when they were able to combine the vigor of manhood with experience in the many factors contributing to successful hunting. But former "great hunters" and their exploits continued to command respect.

All hunters engaged in fishing at the times of the year when it was especially productive. But men who began to fish only, as their hunting opportunities and expertise declined, were not esteemed. This attitude changed with the growth of the fishing industry.

The religious experts, the shamans, had to be active hunters also; society was not disposed to support them, and they received only limited gifts for their efforts. While the skills of good hunters were appreciated far into the twentieth century (Kleivan and Kleivan 1961–1962), the shamans lost their influence and positions quite rapidly in the eighteenth century (Dalager 1915: 30–31).

• LAW Articles regularly used by the individual, such as clothes, utensils, weapons, kayaks, and amulets, were personal property, and most often followed the owner to the grave on death. When the head of a family died, his oldest adult son inherited large objects of common use, such as the tent and umiak. If he had no adult son, they were inherited by his brother, but if the brother already had a tent and an umiak, they went to some other relative or friend. The one who inherited these objects was obliged to support the widow and minor children of the deceased.

Some property rights were clearly connected with use. If, for example, a man stopped using a fox trap that he had built, another man could begin using it and had the right to keep all the foxes he caught in it (Dalager 1915:18–23).

In the traditional society it was considered a just and useful act to kill a murderer, including anyone suspected of having taken the lives of others by sorcery. In the case of ordinary murderers, the family of the victim was obliged to seek revenge even after many years had passed (Dalager 1915:49). In the case of witches, it was often a shaman who designated the witch, and many might take part in killing him or her.

There was no formal institution for solving conflicts between individuals or groups, but the song duels provided an opportunity for submitting cases to a larger forum and releasing the tension.

A colonial common law slowly evolved, applying only to Greenlanders. This state of affairs was finally changed in 1954, when a modern criminal code for all inhabitants of Greenland was introduced (Goldschmidt 1963).

• SOCIAL CONTROL Song duels were an important means of social control. The two competitors, accompanying themselves on a drum, took turn singing songs in which they each insulted the other and praised themselves; this behavior would have been unthinkable in any other social context. No formal winner was recognized, the contest being decided by expressions of approbation and displeasure from the spectators.

Opponents belonged to different winter settlements: they could be individuals in conflict, or even whole settlements, the representatives of which took turns singing (Glahn 1921:61). Song duels could also take place between complete strangers who met at a hunting ground. Song duels had the communicative effect of demonstrating that a peaceful joking relationship had now been established between the opponents. They thus principally served to prevent violence and achieve a relaxation of tensions. Song duels were held in a festive atmosphere, often in connection with games and entertainment, such as various trials of strength in which

aggressions left over from the satirical songs could be let out. Many missionaries, although not all, strongly disapproved of the song duel as an institution over which they had no control. It died out in most localities by the end of the eighteenth century (Kleivan 1971).

Harmony was essential to the small Greenlandic communities, and development of hostile situations and direct confrontations were avoided as much as possible. People who disliked each other simply withdrew; in some cases one of the parties would prefer to move elsewhere. If one man involuntarily harmed another, for instance by spoiling his hunting, the offender would reproach himself, while the injured party would attempt to make light of the situation, perhaps by laughing (Saabye 1942:42). This pattern of behavior, along with a system of child rearing in which scolding was avoided, could lead to violent reaction when someone was directly reproached (Glahn 1921:62).

One reaction when face was lost was to go into the wilderness and try to live as a *qivittoq*. Some examples are known of these hermits having been able to survive alone for several years (Birket-Smith 1924:450; Saabye 1942:59, 110); they were exceptions but this contributed to keeping alive the idea that people who disappeared without their corpses ever having been found had in many cases gone off and become *qivittoq*s.

These *qivittoq*s were assumed to have come into the possession of various supernatural powers allowing them to survive in isolation, and they were regarded with fear. The fact that they become *qivittoq*s served as revenge against their relatives or others who had offended them; the very threat of going off into the interior was quite effective (Glahn 1921:60–61). Stories of *qivittoq*s are still very popular (Kleivan and Kleivan 1961–1962).

Oral Literature

Story-telling was a popular form of entertainment. Some stories confirm social ideals, and many contain origin motifs (Rink 1875:206). Many Greenlandic narratives are exciting stories of conflicts, while humorous themes are predominant in others. Most stories contain supernatural elements.

Some of the motifs present in West Greenlandic stories are also known to other Eskimos (Holtved 1943; Kleivan 1962, 1971); some are even present in other language areas.

Missionaries and trade managers translated European literature into Greenlandic, primarily religious works. A printing press was set up in Godthåb in 1857 (Oldendow 1959). Several collections of oral traditions have been published in Greenlandic and a Greenlandic literature has gradually developed (see "Greenlandic Written Literature," this vol.).

Music

The only musical instrument known to the West Greenlanders was the drum, consisting of a frame about 40 centimenters in diameter covered with tissue, preferably from the stomach of a bearded seal (Glahn 1771:272). The back of the frame, held with a handle, was beaten with a drumstick (Birket-Smith 1924:404–405). The drum was played at the seances of shamans, during song duels, and accompanying purely entertainment songs (Glahn 1921:81–89). The drummer also sang and danced at the same time.

The drum seems to have disappeared in most places around 1800. Only at a few very isolated localities, such as in the Uummannaq area, was the drum tradition preserved almost up to the period of modernization.

The Greenlandic song tradition was also preserved only in exceptional circumstances; European singing was popularized through church hymns.

Games

Many children's games reflected the adult world. In summer girls played house outdoors, marking with stones the outline of a house and the platform inside. They used little pots and lamps of soapstone and wooden dolls. Likewise, boys had little replicas of hunting gear, which they used against baby birds or animal figures made out of snow; they also trained their accuracy by throwing stones (Kleivan and Kleivan 1961–1962; Hansen 1979).

Some games that adults played were competitions in occupational skills, such as paddling and accuracy and distance competitions with hunting gear.

Pulling hooked fingers and arms, and a kind of boxing existed; even when losing, it was not considered good manners to show anger. Handball and football were also popular. Another sport, apparently only for men, consisted in swinging around in various positions on one or two stretched sealskin thongs (Egede 1925:382–384; Birket-Smith 1924:395–396).

Among sedentary games were the art of making string figures (Hansen 1974–1975) and the ring-and-pin game, played with a bone with holes and an attached pin or thin bone (Birket-Smith 1924:399–401; Sandgren 1978).

Contact with Europeans brought new games and sports to the Greenlanders. In 1933 the first sports club was formed in Godthåb, called *Aqissiaq*, after a legendary Greenlandic figure. By this time, soccer was played according to European rules, but the old Greenlandic form of football was also still played on special occasions.

Cosmology

In the eighteenth century the West Greenlanders thought the sky rested on a high, pointed mountain or a pillar, and that it rotated with the sun, moon, and stars (P.H. Egede 1939:43, 51). There are few myths explaining the origin of the world in its present form.

The West Greenlanders had variants of the common Eskimo myth of the origin of the sun and moon. In the earliest one recorded, written down in 1735, the story takes place at Disko Bay. By marking her lover with soot in the dark, a woman discovered that he was her brother. She lit a torch and ran off, followed by her brother; she became the sun and he the moon (P.H. Egede 1939:16–17).

The origin of death is variously explained, each myth in its own way attempting to preach that it is preferable for people to die, because if they were to live forever, it would be under conditions making life not worth living (P.H. Egede 1939:27, 45, 57–58).

The Greenlanders imagined various giant mythical animals, some being merely larger versions of ordinary animals, while others did not correspond to any known animal (fig. 18). One of the fearful ones was a huge creature with 6 or 10 legs, whose meat would grow back on its bones three times after it had been eaten (Rink 1866–1871,2:190; Birket-Smith 1924:221). It has been guessed that the origin of this myth may have been mammoth bones found by the Eskimos in Alaska, but it also represents the eternal dream of abundant and inexhaustable food resources.

The Greenlandic world was populated by various humanlike mythical beings. Many of these were said to dwell in the interior (Rink 1866–1871,2:189–190; Birket-Smith 1924:221–225).

• AFTERLIFE Every person was supposed to have a

Nationalmuseet, Copenhagen: L18.189.

Fig. 18. Ivory sculpture of a man riding a mythical creature. The leather thong originally went from the man's hands around the creature's throat. Height 11.0 cm; made by Ole Kreutzmann, Kangaamiut, 1930.

soul, which after death lived in one of the two lands of the dead: one in the sky, resembling the interior; or one in the lower world, resembling the coast. Conditions resembled those on earth, but with certain positive features emphasized in accordance with the values of Greenlandic society. It was best to be in the lower world, where there were many marine animals and perpetual sunshine.

Those who went into the sky lived in tents at the foot of a snow-covered mountain; there were plenty of caribou, birds, and Arctic char. Women who died in childbirth, whalers, and those who died at sea were destined to go to the lower world; it was primarily their way of dying not their moral behavior in life which decided where they were to go. All others would go to the sky (Egede 1925:397). According to other information, relatives and friends of a dying person could assure that he would go to the lower world by putting him on the floor. This movement started off his trip to the land of the dead in the right direction (P.H. Egede 1939:86). It took three days, or five days according to others (P.H. Egede 1939:53, 86), for the soul to get to the land of the dead. Especially during this period, the survivors were obliged to observe various taboos.

• THE CONCEPT OF INUA Animals, things, and concepts had a so-called *inua*. This word is a form of *inuk* 'human being' and means literally 'its person'. The concept of *inua* can be illustrated by an example: a Greenlander got sleepy and said that the *inua* of sleep had come to him. When asked what it looked like, he answered: "Much like a person, but he is nothing but sleep. He is always asleep and owns all sleep, which he pours out over people" (Glahn 1921:179).

• RELATIONSHIP TO ANIMALS The West Greenlanders imagined that animals were happy and sad, angry and grateful, in the same way as people. If, for instance, Greenlanders killed too many seals at a certain place, a group of seals in human form could come in an umiak of ice, the so-called *umiarissat*, to take revenge (Vebæk 1969–1970).

The dominant fear was not, however, that people might kill so many animals that they would risk vengeance from them, but that they could not kill enough. It was therefore of vital importance to maintain a positive and stable relationship between people and animals. The West Greenlanders attempted to ensure this by surrounding their relations to game animals with magical precautions (Søby 1969–1970). Some rituals dealt with the short-term situation, but most of them attempted to assure good hunting in the long run. The conduct of those who stayed at home was thought to influence the success of the hunt. On the one hand, they should act in the same way as they would like a game animal to do, and on the other hand, they should do nothing that could frighten the game away. The mother of one who had first sighted a bear should attempt to keep it from fleeing by turning her trousers down to her knees, so that her movements, and thereby those of the bear, would be impeded (S. Rink 1896:97). While the men were out whaling, the women who stayed at home should keep quiet inside with all the lamps out (Dalager 1915:56).

When a man was out hunting he could in various ways imitate an advantageous hunting situation, and this would have a magical effect. If he had looked in vain for hooded seals on the field ice, he might lay his harpoon throwing-board across the kayak stand, in imitation of a seal crawled up on the ice. It was believed that soon hooded seals would then appear (Rasmussen 1921–1925,3:334).

When the hunt was over, the hunter was supposed to ask the animal for forgiveness for having killed it. This he did by honoring it, for example with suitable death ceremonies. If this were done satisfactorily, the hunter would have good luck in the future, as the positive feelings of the dead animal would be transferred to potential future game.

The idea that it took several days for an animal's soul to leave its body was manifested especially in connection with the polar bear, an object of special attention. The head of a polar bear was put on the lamp stand inside the house, turned in the direction it had come from and decorated with small gifts such as knives, glass beads, and boot soles (S. Rink 1896:99). Three days (H. Lynge 1955:156) or five days (Rasmussen 1921–1925,3:339) after the bear had been killed its cranium was sunk into the sea.

The first kill made by a boy was the object of special attention. The seal's bones were collected at one place; sometimes they were taken out to sea and sunk at the place where the seal had been killed. The animal was thus returned to its proper element, to assure the boy's sealing success in the future (Dalager 1915:4).

The idea prevalent especially among the Canadian Eskimos that it was necessary to keep land and sea animals separate, as well as activities pertaining to them, was not predominant in Greenland, but local examples are known of similar taboo rules. Thus, people in Frederikshåb district said that one must not sew soles into a caribou hunter's boots with sinew thread from the narwhal or white whale, for the caribou would then hear the sound of a sea animal and be frightened (Rasmussen 1921–1925,3:334).

• LIFE CRISES The two social situations that were especially surrounded by magical precautions were birth and death. By carrying out certain rites of passage, a correct transition was ensured without danger to anyone. Failure to do this could bring illness and death. Violation of the taboos in connection with life crises often also had consequences for the relationship with game animals. For example, if a whale had been harpooned but could not be towed to land, this could be due to the fact that one of the rowers was wearing a coat that had been worn at a burial or had just had a miscarriage (P.H. Egede 1939:92–93).

A mother would give her newborn a ritual meal of water and fish (Egede 1925:374), thus initiating him as a member of society. A women in confinement would have to keep various taboos to ensure the life of the child, and in order not to harm others. No one was allowed to drink from her water pail or get light from her lamp (Egede 1925:396).

After a birth the mother had to observe the prescribed rules, such as abstaining from certain foods and certain kinds of work; and those surrounding her had to take precautions to avoid too close contact with her and her things. A pregnant woman who miscarried was also obliged to observe certain rules in order to avoid unfortunate consequences, but there was always the risk of a woman keeping a miscarriage secret to avoid having to observe these rules. A continuous period of bad weather and poor hunting with no other immediate explanation would often lead to suspicions of a secret miscarriage, and that the concealed fetus (*anngiaq*) was flying around near the mother. It was then the duty of the shaman to catch the fetus and make it harmless (Glahn 1921:99–100).

At a death precautions were taken to ensure that the deceased was not impeded in reaching one of the lands of the dead, and particuarly that the survivors managed the situation safely. To keep the deceased from returning to his dwelling, his corpse was taken out through the window of a house, or under the tent skins. Then the house of the deceased was virtually purified with fire and everyone who had touched the deceased had to wash himself. The nearest survivors had to avoid looking out over the sea, and they were required to cover their heads (Egede 1925:375–376).

The name of the deceased was not mentioned until it was again given to a newborn. This name taboo could mean that Greenlanders living nearby with the same name would for a time have to change to another name (Dalager 1915:1).

Special magical precautions were prescribed in the case of murder. The murderer ate some of the heart and liver of his victim to protect himself from revenge. Through this act the murderer would participate in the identity of the victim, so that the soul of the victim could not take revenge on him. When a witch was killed, similar precautions were taken, and the corpse would be carved up and strewn about (Egede 1925:256; Dalager 1915:49).

• MAGICAL AIDS The violation of taboos was thought to bring harm not only to the guilty party but also the entire society, mostly in the form of poor hunting due to bad weather. Everyone was thus obliged to observe these rules.

Among the much-used methods of bringing about

desired conditions were amulets (Birket-Smith 1924:446–448; H. Lynge 1955:56–77), often worn on a strap around the neck, and also attached to hunting gear.

Magical formulas were also private property (Birket-Smith 1924:445–446); they were used in deepest secrecy to promote either positive ends, such as good hunting, or negative ones, such as causing dissension between spouses or frightening away the game animals of another (Glahn 1921:67–68).

In certain cases when Greenlanders climbed a bird-cliff (F. Lynge 1981:83) or by boat passed places considered to be dangerous, they might throw some small objects on the cliff or into the sea, presumably for the *inua* of the locality, but information on this subject is vague (Birket-Smith 1924:444).

Shamans

In addition to the magical aids accessible to all, there were also persons with special abilities and greater knowledge (Glahn 1921:64–67), to whom one could resort when in need of help. These were primarily shamans, *angakkut* (sg. *angakkoq*). Both men and women could be shamans, but the overwhelming majority were men.

In addition to the knowledge and technical skill that a prospective shaman could acquire by being an attentive spectator at the seances of experienced shamans as well as through direct instruction by them, it was of decisive importance that he himself came into contact with supernatural powers. The novice accomplished this by going out alone into the wilderness, where his especially receptive frame of mind could be made even more receptive by continuously, and for a long time, rubbing a little stone in circular movements against a larger one. It is related that when the supernatural would reveal itself, sometimes in the form of a bear, the apprentice would lose consciousness; after three days he would awaken as a shaman (Egede 1925:393).

The shaman had acquired a spirit-helper, a *toornaq*; later he would acquire more. Various things and beings could serve as spirit-helpers. When the shaman held a seance, his spirit-helpers served as entertaining and frightening elements in the performance, as well as oracles. This latter role seems to have been especially reserved for a spirit-helper called *toornaarsuk* 'little spirit-helper'. Early sources contain obscure information as to the nature of this being, its appearance, and the extent of its power (Holtved 1963).

During a seance the shaman went into a trance, and a mysterious atmosphere was created by the use of darkness, the drum, and strange sounds, and by the shaman's use of archaic words and circumlocutions (P.H. Egede 1939:14, 41).

A seance would usually be held to explain why something had gone wrong: bad weather, poor hunting, illness, or death. It was the duty of the shaman to find

618

out who had violated a taboo and to get the guilty person or persons to confess in public. The revelation of taboo violations had a neutralizing effect, so that society could continue functioning under ordinary conditions.

The shaman could also arrange a wife-exchanging ceremony designed to avert hardship: for instance, to keep a sick person from dying or to end a famine (Egede 1925:217; Glahn 1921:66).

The most important function of the shaman was to act as an intermediary between people and the higher powers: the Sea Woman and the Moon Man. According to the myth this could be done during a seance, when the shaman's soul would leave his body, accompanied by one of his spirit-helpers. The fingerless Sea Woman was thought to live on the bottom of the sea. She had all the animals of the sea under her command, and could hold them back if she were offended. There were great difficulties involved in reaching the Sea Woman (Egede 1925:398). Like a tabooed woman who was not allowed to work or wash she would sit on the platform with her back to the room (Sonne 1975), and filth would be hanging in her hair because people had violated the taboo regulations. The shaman would appease her by cleansing her, with the result that the sea animals would swim to their accustomed haunts (P.H. Egede 1939:36–37). There is no evidence that the ritual was actually carried out in West Greenland.

The Moon Man also had some influence on hunting conditions. Sometimes the shaman would visit the Moon Man to procure seals. The Moon Man also punished violations of taboos. If a woman did not observe the prescribed regulations, the Moon Man punished the community with stormy weather and rain for several days (P.H. Egede 1939:28). Occasionally the Moon Man rode in his sled down to earth, where he got his food in the sea and had sexual intercourse with a woman. Sometimes he would even take a woman back with him. The Moon Man lived in a little house where the platform was covered with bearskin. Here the souls of the dead rested on their way to the land of the dead in the sky. In one end of the house, the Sun had a little room.

The third mythical figure living in the heavens was the Intestine Robber, who attempted to get her visitors to laugh. If she succeeded, she would cut their intestines out (P.H. Egede 1939:62).

There was another power that could interfere in the lives of humans and punish them in case of taboo violations. This was *Sila*, which as a common noun means 'the air, the weather, the world, the universe' and also 'consciousness'. *Sila* would get angry, for example, blowing up a big storm, if someone went visiting the same day that the shaman had performed a seance (P.H. Egede 1939:70). *Sila* does not seem to have been anthropomorphized as were the Sea Woman and the Moon Man.

Illness was thought to be due to a number of causes, such as the temporary absence of the soul, the violation of a taboo by the sick person or a close relative, or a foreign object entering the body by magic. It was the task of the shaman to make a diagnosis, during a seance. Just as was the case in finding the reason for poor hunting, the very fact of holding a seance and exposing the reason for illness seems to have had a beneficial effect, and it relieved psychic tension. In serious cases several shamans might be called in to hold a joint seance (Dalager 1915:28–29). The shaman could bring the soul back by blowing on the sick person (P.H. Egede 1939:38) and he could suck foreign objects out of the patient's body (Egede 1925:205). When a shaman served as a doctor, he could demand a reward (Egede 1925:395).

Some of a shaman's activities consisted in prophesying the near future. There was also another category of persons who were thought to have special prophetic abilities. These were usually old women, and their favorite method was to tie a strap around the head of a medium, often a sick person, and lift it with a stick (N. Egede 1939:165). The answers to the questions she would mumble would depend on whether the head felt heavy or light. One who practiced this art was caled *qilalik* (see "Netsilik," this vol.).

An ambivalent attitude toward shamans was prevalent. On the one hand they were respected, because their skills were to the benefit of others; but they were also feared, precisely because they had control over supernatural powers. In some cases the suspicion would arise that a shaman was using his skills to harm others by practicing witchcraft (P.H. Egede 1939:95, 106).

Witches attempted in secret to destroy the fundamental values of life for others. They were thought capable of causing death, illness, sterility, and poor hunting (Dalager 1915:33). Witches, who in many cases were old women, might remove something owned by the prospective victim, recite magic formulas over it, and place it in a grave, or place an object over which they had mumbled a magic formula on the victim's property, so that he would have an accident when he used it.

They could also make a so-called tupilak, an animal of bad omen, created by magic from various components and brought to life by a magical formula. The idea was to let it imitate a game animal so that the person one wanted to harm would harpoon it and die (Petersen 1964).

The belief in witches, like the belief in the consequences of taboo violations, gave an explanation for many events. It was also the basis for a kind of moral control: people attempted to behave well in order not to expose themselves to the dangers of witchcraft. Furthermore, accusations of witchcraft could create a scapegoat in difficult situations.

Within the period dealt with here there have been 619

great regional differences in the degree of acculturation. Generally speaking, contact with European culture has been more intensive for Greenlanders in the larger settlements than in the smaller ones, and on the central part of the coast more than in the northernmost and southernmost areas.

Synonymy‡

According to Poul Egede, writing during the early contact period in the eighteenth century, the West Greenlanders referred to themselves by the common Inuit-Inupiaq Eskimo term *inuit* 'human being' (sg. *inuk*), but they also used *kalaallit* (sg. *kalaaleq*), which they explained as the name they had been called by the earlier Norse settlers (P.H. Egede 1750:48, 68; Thalbitzer 1904:36). In the early twentieth century *inuit* was still in use in the sense of 'Greenlanders' and *kalaallit* was said to be a self-designation used only in southern Greenland (Thalbitzer 1904:26, 36; Schultz-Lorentzen 1927:66, 110), but since then *kalaallit* has come to be used as the general word for 'Greenlanders' in standard Greenlandic. Greenland, earlier *inuit nunaat* 'the land of the people', is now officially *Kalaallit Nunaat* 'the land of the Greenlanders'. The term *inuit* has come to be used in Greenland as a general name for 'Eskimos', stressing their common heritage (see the footnote in "The Pan-Eskimo Movement," this vol.).

Several interpretations of the name *kalaallit* have been proposed, the best known being the derivation from Old Norse *skrælingr* (Kleinschmidt 1871:164; Thalbitzer 1904:36; synonymy in "Introduction," this vol.). Another theory holds that *kalaallit* was an eighteenth-century borrowing from Danish *Kareler*, which appears in its Latin form (*Careli*) on a depiction of Greenland on a map of 1427 and on later maps (Thalbitzer 1904:31–32, 37; Petersen 1961). The local traditions recorded by Poul Egede regarding *kalaallit* and the fact that *Careli* is the Latin name of another northern people, the Karelians of Finland, cast doubt on this explanation.

Sources

Sources from the sixteenth, seventeenth, and the beginning of the eighteenth centuries are reports of explorers and whalers, and information from Greenlanders who had been kidnapped to Europe (Hakluyt 1965; Lyschander 1608; Olearius 1656; Poincy 1658; Haan 1914). These sources are of limited value due to defective communication with Greenlanders, and because observations in Greenland were only made during short visits in the summer.

After the Danish-Norwegian colonization of Green-

land was begun in 1721, it became possible to get deeper insight into the lives of Greenlanders. The first missionary to Greenland, Hans Egede, wrote a monograph and this, as well as his diary (1925) and those of his sons (Poul H. Egede 1939; Niels Egede 1939), contains much valuable information on the Greenlanders. Among other diaries from the eighteenth century, that of Glahn (1921) is especially worthy of mention. Glahn also wrote a critical review (1771) of a large work on Greenland published by Cranz (1765), the historian of the Moravian mission.

Of writings from the eighteenth century that concentrate on special subjects, Dalager (1915), who describes social life and Fabricius (Holtved 1962), dealing with hunting equipment and technique, are very important. There are also a number of descriptions of individual districts, such as the one by Thorhallesen (1914).

Descriptions of the Greenland society and diaries from the nineteenth century include Bluhme (1865) and Nansen (1891). Distinguished for his research on Greenland is H. Rink, who both describes and analyzes social and religious aspects of the culture of West Greenland and its changes in the colonial period (1857, 1868, 1877, 1966–1967).

Collections of oral traditions and oral literature have been made, for example, by Rink (1875), Thalbitzer (1904), Rasmussen (1921–1925), and H. Lynge (1955). Two collections of taboos each of them including about 500 examples recorded on the west coast in the first part of the twentieth century have been published (Rasmussen 1979; F. Lynge 1981). A survey of traditional and modern Greenlandic art has been made by Kaalund (1979).

Unprinted source material dealing with conditions in Greenland in the eighteenth and nineteenth centuries has been used especially by Ostermann (1928–1929), Sveistrup and Dalgaard (1945), Israel (1969), and Gad (1967–1976, 1971–1982). Social and medical problems are dealt with by Bertelsen (1935–1943). Works concerning especially the traditional material culture have been written by Steensby (1912), Porsild (1915), and Birket-Smith (1924, 1928a). The kayak and its implements have been described by P.S. Jensen (1975). Birket-Smith's monograph on the Egedesminde area (1924) is the most comprehensive ethnological work on West Greenland and contains many references to older literary sources.

Detailed instructions in hunting methods were written by Greenlandic hunters, first published in Greenlandic (Lindow 1922, 1923) and later translated into Danish (Hansen 1971). In Greenlandic, Sandgren (1972) has given a detailed description of equipment used in connection with traditional hunting methods and E. Rosing (1975) has described the sled. The Greenlandic newspaper *Atuagagdliutit*, which has been published at Godthåb since 1861, contains many valuable contri-

‡This synonymy was written by Inge Kleivan and Ives Goddard.

butions in which Greenlanders themselves have told about their lives.

In 1921, on the bicentennial of the beginning of colonization, a large work was published in Danish with detailed surveys of conditions at the various localities (Amdrup et al. 1921). A general description of Greenland was published shortly after in English (Vahl et al. 1928–1929). A good deal of information on conditions in Greenland before modernization is also to be found in various reports published by Danish official organs (Grønlands Styrelse 1942–1944).

The Nationalmuseum in Copenhagen has an archive based on questionnaires answered in the 1940s and 1950s, mostly dealing with material culture. This museum also has a large ethnographical collection from West Greenland. Museums containing smaller collections from West Greenland are Universitetets etnografiske museum in Oslo, Norway, and Kalaallit Nunaata Katersugaasivia in Godthåb, West Greenland. Photographic archives are possessed by Nationalmuseet, Arktisk Institut, and Det kongelige Bibliotek, all in Copenhagen, and Kalaallit Nunaata Katersugaasivia in Godthåb.

East Greenland Before 1950

ROBERT PETERSEN*

During the twentieth century East Greenland has been populated in two regions: Ammassalik, centered around 65°40′ north latitude, and the large Scoresbysund fjord (Scoresby Sound) at about 70° north latitude (fig. 1). The settlement at Scoresbysund dates only from 1925, when migration began from Ammassalik; a few immigrants from West Greenland also settled there. However, there were also two other East Greenland groups in historic times, about whom very little is known. The Northeast Greenlanders, north of Scoresbysund, as far as is known were contacted by Europeans only once, by Capt. D.C. Clavering in 1823, after which they died out (Clavering 1830:21–24). The Southeast Greenlanders lived northeast of Cape Farewell up to 64° north latitude, until they emigrated to the Cape Farewell region of West Greenland shortly before 1900.

Language

Modern East Greenlandic is mutually intelligible with West Greenlandic, but differs from it both phonologically and lexically, and in some slight grammatical details. Some characteristic deviations of the East Greenlandic dialect from West Greenlandic are a widespread shift of u to i, the lack of long voiceless fricatives, the general fricativization of intervocalic consonants, the nasalization of velar and uvular fricatives, and the rather extensive ellipsis of intervocalic voiced fricatives. The grammatical and stylistic differences are less, but a number of expressive suffixes that permit a variety of nuances difficult to explain make East Greenlandic seem comparatively archaic, whereas the phonological differences can be interpreted as indicating that East Greenlandic is more advanced.†

Research on Greenlandic dialects shows that the situation—and hence the culture history—was rather more complex than had been supposed. Nothing is known directly about the speech of the Northeast Greenlan-

ders. But similarities in phonology between the Ammassalik dialect and the Upernavik dialect in West Greenland are such that Upernavik can be considered basically East Greenlandic, although with adaptation of West Greenlandic vocabulary. This implies direct contacts between Upernavik and East Greenland, probably by migration from Northeast Greenland, which must have occurred around the northern part of the island (since contacts across the central ice cap are impossible) and this after the end of the great Thule migration into West Greenland but before the Polar Eskimo settled their present area. Archeological confirmation is required: the relevant regions have not been investigated by archeologists since the recognition of Paleo-Eskimo cultures in Greenland, yet more than 200 sites are known in the Northeast Greenland area even though some suitable regions have not been adequately surveyed. Probably the Northeast Greenland population before 1823 was larger than has been supposed.

There is evidence on the old Southeast Greenland dialect, which shows that it was almost identical to Ammassalik speech. The great lexical similarity between these two regions rules out the idea that taboos on the names of the dead were the principal cause of lexical innovation in East Greenlandic, for the area of similar speech is too large for such taboos to have accounted for the innovations. The modern speech of southern West Greenland, from Cape Farewell to Julianehåb, is now believed to have undergone heavy influence from Southeast Greenland beginning about 1650, and the dialect around Cape Farewell was influenced even more strongly by the migration of Southeast Greenlanders between 1830 and 1900. Archeological confirmation is also required for these conclusions about cultural influences and migration that are based on lexical and phonological evidence.

Environment

Ammassalik District

Ammassalik District is a bedrock area with irregular terrain and jagged mountains. The rim of ice-free coast is only about 100 kilometers wide at the widest. There

---

*Translated from Danish by Charles Jones.

†The orthography used for East Greenlandic is the official one adopted in 1980, with all spellings by Robert Petersen. The principles and phonetic values are the same as for the phonemic orthography for West Greenlandic introduced in 1972 (see the orthographic footnote in "West Greenland Before 1950," this vol.).

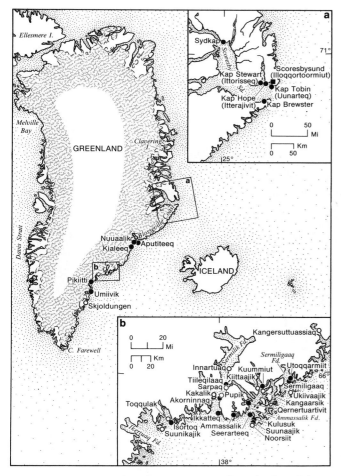

Fig. 1. East Greenland settlement areas: a, Scoresby Sound; b, Ammassalik.

There is quite a bit of precipitation, a good deal of which falls as snow. In winter the snow is often soft and deep, especially in hollows and valleys. In 1938 the precipitation at Ammassalik town was 765 mm (Anonymous 1942–1945,1:395). From 1931 to 1938 the average annual temperature was $-0.5°$ C, averaging $-7.6°$ C in February and $+7.9°$ C in July (Anonymous 1942–1945,1:393).

Ammassalik District is poor in land game since large amounts of snow alternating with winter rains create unfavorable conditions for herbivorous animals. The caribou that formerly were present have disappeared, and there are no hares in the area. There is a small number of arctic foxes (*Alopex lagopus*). On the other hand, the area is often visited by polar bears drifting with the storis; sometimes females hibernate here during the winter and give birth to their young around January 1.

Only a few species of birds breed in Ammassalik District, but in the fall the area is host to large flocks of dovekies (*Alle alle*), thick-billed murres (*Uria lomvia*), and common eiders (*Somateria mollissima*) on their way south. In the spring large flights of geese pass through on their way north (Vibe 1970).

The ringed seal (*Phoca hispida*) is the most numerous marine animal in Ammassalik District. The hooded seal (*Cystophora cristata*) and the bearded seal (*Erignatus barbatus*) are quite common, whereas the walrus (*Odobenus rosmarus*) and the harbor seal (*Phoca vitulina*) are rare. Narwhals (*Monodon monoceros*) and belugas (*Delphinapterus leucas*) enter the fjords occasionally (Vibe 1970).

The flora of the archipelago is quite sparse, but in the fjords sheltered fertile spots occur with many small flowers. In the fjord valleys are willow scrub, dwarf birch, and herb fields; the mountains have alpine vegetation.

Scoresbysund District

Scoresbysund District is situated in a basalt area with flat beaches, regular coastlines, and plateaus. The widest ice-free area in Greenland is located in the vicinity of Scoresby Sound with its relatively dry climate. The storis drifting off Scoresby Sound can extend far out to sea. The amount of ice that reaches Cape Farewell around New Year passes Scoresbysund as early as October. Although the winter ice can be quite thick in Scoresby Sound, the strong current generally creates openings at the mouth of the fjord. From 1926 to 1930, the average annual precipitation at Scoresbysund was close to 300 millimeters (Anonymous 1942–1945, 1:396). From 1931 to 1938, the average annual temperature was $-7.0°$ C, the average for February being $-16.4°$ C and that for July $+5.6°$ C (ibid.:393). Some of the summer precipitation falls at the coast as fog (Bøcher 1970). Also in

are long stretches of considerably narrower land area, and at many places the ice cap itself forms the coastline. Off the coast there are islands of various sizes: irregular, jagged, and indented. The nucleus of Ammassalik District, the area around the four fjords, lies in the shelter of the curved coast. South and north of the four fjords, the ice-free coast is quite narrow and divided by the ice cap into small isolated areas. North of 68° north latitude is the inaccessible Blosseville Coast, isolating Ammassalik District from Scoresbysund District.

Off the coast the cold East Greenland Current flows from the north, bringing a huge mass of drift ice, the storis. The ice passes so close to the coast that settlements can be located only where there is shelter. In the summer, however, the storis can drift so far out that one can sail even to relatively isolated places; but this travel is always undependable, and a change of wind can block the coast again in a short time.

Between the islands, ice forms in the winter, but it is unsafe at many places because the strong current running from the fjords and between the islands erodes the ice from below and forms holes. Thaws and offshore winds are also common in the winter and can destroy the winter ice.

the Scoresbysund area, and even farther north, caribou (*Rangifer tarandus eogroenlandicus*) were formerly to be found, but by 1900 they had totally disappeared from East Greenland (Vibe 1967:153). There are musk-oxen (*Ovibos moschatus*) in the area. Other land animals include the hare (*Lepus arcticus*), the ermine (*Mustella erminea*), and the arctic fox (*Alopex lagopus*). In the early twentieth century wolves (*Canis lupus*) were killed. The polar bear breeds in the area.

Large flocks of dovekies breed here, and there are bird cliffs with thick-billed murres and black-legged kittiwakes (*Rissa tridactyla*). Bird species breeding in the interior are the common loon (*Gavia immer*), the red-throated loon (*Gavia stellata*), the old squaw (*Clangula hyemalis*), the king eider (*Somateria spectabilis*), the barnacle goose (*Branta leucopsis*), and the pink-footed goose (*Anser brachyrhynchus*). Ptarmigans (*Lagopus mutus*) are also to be found.

Among marine animals, the ringed seal is abundant. Bearded seals, walruses, and harp seals are present only in small numbers, and the hooded seal is likewise a rare visitor. On the other hand, narwhals often enter Scoresbysund fjord (Vibe 1970).

Arctic vegetation is rich in species, especially on the coastal mountains, which are shrouded in fog during the summer. Farther up the fjord the climate is warmer and drier, with a subarctic flora including tall willow scrub and steppelike grass (Bøcher 1970).

Settlement Pattern

The Ammassalik population is primarily grouped around four fjords: Ikertuaq, Sermilik, Ammassalik, and Sermiligaaq. The last three of these are connected by straits through which their inhabitants maintain contact with one another. The area around these four fjords is constantly inhabited. North and south of them are stretches of coast that are partly uninhabited; people from the four fjords sometimes live in these outlying areas for some time before finally returning to the fjords. Before 1950 people sometimes lived at Kangersuttuassiaq, Nuuaalik, Kialeeq, and Aputiteeq north of Ammassalik. South of Ikertuaq, people sometimes lived at Pikiitti and Umiivik, at 64° and 65° north latitude, respectively. Skjoldungen, at 63° north latitude, was inhabited from 1938 to 1963.

The limited contact between the Ammassalik group and West Greenland, mostly maintained with the Southeast Greenlanders as intermediaries, ended when the latter emigrated to West Greenland. This contact took place when the Southeast Greenlanders traded at the southernmost West Greenlandic trading centers or met West Greenlanders at Aluk, slightly northeast of Cape Farewell. These contacts were undoubtedly the occasions of a good deal of merriment, as is the case

Fig. 2. Wooden maps. left, Representation of the coast between Kangersuttuassiaq and Sieralik; center, islands off the coastline shown on the map at left; right, representation of the peninsula between Kangersuttuassiaq and Sermiligaaq. Carved by Kunit from Umiivik. Length of left 14.2 cm; rest same scale. All collected by Gustav Holm, 1884–1885.

at similar meetings in West Greenland. All that is known with certainty is that trading took place, in which the East Greenlanders exchanged many items for European goods (Graah 1832:80). Some Ammassalik Eskimos may have also participated in the contacts at Aluk; it is known that some of them came to West Greenland to trade (Mikkelsen 1934:41).

During the time of the initial Danish colonization of Ammassalik District and immediately thereafter, there were no permanent settlements, that is, places where people regularly spent the winter. After one or more winters a new settlement was chosen. This movement must be considered an attempt to distribute as equally as possible the exploitation of the seal population of the area and at the same time as a search for a place where the seal population could support long-term hunting.

Thus Akorninnaq, Ikkatteq, and Tiileqilaaq on Sermilik fjord were inhabited for many years. Pupik, Kakalik, Sarpaq, and Innartuaq on the same fjord were often inhabited, although for short periods each time. On Ammassalik fjord, Suunaajik and Qernertuartivit were inhabited for a rather long time; and Noorsiit, Kangaarsik, Seerarteeq, and Kiittaajik were often inhabited. On Sermiligaaq fjord, Ukiivaajik and

Utoqqarmiit were often inhabited; and on Ikertuaq fjord, Toqqulak, Suunikajik, Iitsalik, and Isortoq.

People usually moved along the same fjord. With all the frequent moving, different families lived together at different times, so that people living on the same fjord considered each other as potential co-villagers.

Gradually permanent settlements were founded, first around missions. The town of Ammassalik was founded at Tasiilaq in 1894, Kap Dan at Kulusuk in 1909, and Kummiit in 1916. Until about 1920 the population of these three localities was mainly determined by the number of persons preparing for baptism. After two years of preparation the candidates were baptized and, as a rule, returned to their former settlement group.

In general, the average population of inhabited settlements was 20 to 30. But on the four fjords, settlements could be found with even less population, sometimes under 10 persons. When people spent the winter isolated from the four fjords, they often lived in settlements of up to 60 people; the tendency to dispersal was less at isolated settlements than in the central area. As a rule, people returned to the four fjords after just one winter spent away.

Scattered throughout Ammassalik District one can find abandoned house walls of stone and peat. During the time when people moved frequently, such walls were often repaired, lengthened, or shortened, according to the number of prospective inhabitants, and used again. But the East Greenlanders claim that settlement locations were mainly chosen according to hunting conditions. In any case, people could also move to a location with no standing house walls, or even to an island without drinking water, as ice could always be melted for this purpose.

In 1884, when the Ammassalik Eskimo were contacted for the first time, they were living in longhouses, which they continued to do until the 1920s. Generally each settlement had but one longhouse, with all inhabitants living in one room. The sleeping bench, which extended the entire length of the back of the house, was partitioned by stretched sealskins fastened to a number of poles. Each partition was inhabited by a complete or incomplete nuclear family. Nuclear families belonging to the same extended family had their partitions grouped together; several extended families could live in the same longhouse. Longhouses were inhabited from August or September to April or May.

During the summer, the various families of a longhouse lived separately, in tents at various hunting camps where they could fish, hunt seals, and so forth. Nevertheless, people were less isolated during the summer than in the winter. For one thing, the entire population of the district gathered at Qinngeq, at the head of Ammassalik fjord, to fish *ammassak* (capelin, *Mallotus villosus*). The hooded seal *(Cystophora cristata)* was hunted at the mouths of the fjords, when some hunting camps

were located on a group of islands close to each other, at Kulusuk in Ammassalik fjord and Ammaat-Ikkatteq in Sermilik fjord (Holm and Petersen 1921:623).

Ammassalik District

While longhouses were still in use, Ammassalik District was characterized by great mobility. From 1900 to 1925, people moved around so much that each settlement was inhabited about one out of every three years. Some of this moving about was doubtless due to the general search for new hunting grounds. At the same time it also kept different families from living together very long, and thus was probably a means of preventing latent conflicts from developing. A change of settlement-mates was likewise a change of housemates, as each settlement normally had but one longhouse.

The East Greenlanders themselves, however, state that the search for better hunting was the decisive factor in moving, and there are indeed many indications that hunting conditions played an important role in mobility. In the hunting districts of West Greenland, the degree of dispersal of the population is inversely proportional to the number of animals taken, and this number can vary from 10 to 20 percent each year. Unfortunately, comparable statistics are not available for East Greenland. But since 1920, trading in skins has reached such proportions that the number traded seems reliable as an indicator of variations in the numbers of animals taken. Just as in West Greenland, dispersal increased in East Greenland when hunting declined; but people who spent the winter isolated always joined others the next year regardless of hunting trends.

In cases where the dispersal and concentration of the population could be expressed as variations in the number of settlements, it was generally the number of small settlements in the central area that varied. But the degree of dispersal could also be expressed by the movement of people from larger inhabited settlements to smaller ones, as well as by a group spending the winter in an otherwise uninhabited area and then returning.

Without postulating any causality, there is nevertheless some connection between mobility and housing conditions. The decrease over the years in the average number of residents in a house in Ammassalik District is shown in the following figures: in 1894, 29.5 persons; 1900, 24.2; 1904, 21.8; 1915, 21.5; 1920, 22.1; 1925, 19.4; 1930, 14.0; 1935, 10.4; 1940, 8.9; 1945, 7.1. These data indicate the rapid dissolution of longhouses after about 1925 (Statistisk Protokol, Ministeriet for Grønland).

After 1930 the founding of new settlements increasingly declined. At about this time, it became common to wall the interior of houses with wood. It thus took more time and more work to build a house, and it was more difficult to transport the materials to a new lo-

625

Arktisk Institut, Charlottenlund, Denmark.
Fig. 3. Ammassalik as seen from the southwest. Photograph by Thomas Mathiesen, 1932.

cation. The wood used had to be purchased, and as there was no tradition of several families cooperating for purchases, it became more common to build houses for one family. Young hunters especially moved into their own houses (Høygaard 1938:86). Likewise, the introduction of the rifle had brought about changes in hunting life. Hunting tradition became less important, and so did the elder hunters, who were the bearers of this tradition. This gave young people more independence. It must be assumed that some families were forced to give up living in longhouses because they finally had no one to live with. Around 1940 there were no more longhouses, and each dwelling housed but one family, although often consisting of three generations.

About 1935 approximately 20 percent of the population moved to a new settlement each year, but after 1945 this figure dropped to around 10 percent. By 1950 Ammassalik District had only a few settlements with one family. The founding of new settlements was declining.

Scoresbysund District

In Scoresbysund District the same geographical mobility has not prevailed as in Ammassalik District. Since 1925, when the vicinity was settled, there has been an attempt to disperse the population voluntarily. Several settlements were founded along the huge fjord complex and at its mouth. As early as 1925, besides the town of Scoresbysund (*Ittoqqortoormiit* 'people with the big houses'), a number of smaller settlements were established in the area: Kap Stewart (*Ittorittermiit* 'people at the good peat place'), Kap Hope (*Ittaajuit* 'the small houses'), and Kap Tobin (*Uunarteq* 'the hot spring'). Later Sydkap (*Kangersuttuaq* 'the big fjord'), Kap Brewster (*Kangikajik* 'little cape'), and *Ukaleqarteq* 'hare land' were established.

Since the Scoresbysund Eskimos had the same family organization as the Ammassalik group, as well as the same hunting principles, it might seem strange that they did not have the same kind of geographic mobility. In good hunting years, concentration tendencies were often reinforced. People who moved from Ammassalik District to the areas around Scoresbysund saw game animals in a quantity to which they were not accustomed (Abelsen 1935–1936:123). This was thus a time of improved hunting for these immigrants. Although no hunting statistics were kept, figures from sales of hunting products give the direct impression of improved conditions. Even though a latent greater need for money could have increased the sales of hunting products in proportion to actual hunting results, common observations leave no doubt that in the Scoresbysund area the hunting of small seals, walruses, polar bears, and

626

narwhals was better than in Ammassalik District. Thus the basis of subsistence was better, resulting in the reinforcement of concentration tendencies.

In addition, the population of Scoresbysund District was a small, isolated group. The need for a greater sense of community seems to be reinforced in such a group, as is indicated by the strong tendency in Ammassalik District for families to rejoin others after a winter in isolation. It is also noteworthy that the Ammassalik Eskimos did not reside for long periods in isolation. Short periods of habitation were possible in this district because stone and peat houses could be easily erected at a new locality. With the introduction of wood in housing construction, residences became more stable, and people began to concentrate in somewhat larger permanent settlements. In Scoresbysund District, people lived in wooden houses right from the beginning, so that habitation was less flexible than in Ammassalik District. Although hunting in Scoresbysund District could also be subject to slack periods, these were by no means so extreme as those known from Ammassalik District. The slack periods could result in temporary want, but even then there was an attempt to respect hunting restrictions (Boassen 1939:4).

Due to the lack of large seals in the area, after a few years it became difficult to procure enough skin for the umiaks brought from Ammassalik District, so that these craft soon disappeared from the Scoresbysund area (Abelsen 1935–1936:129), decreasing considerably the capacity of the population to move.

House stoves here used local coal deposits as fuel. But Kap Stewart was far from the coal fields, and this settlement was poorly situated with respect to the spring ice edge, making for poorer spring hunting. In 1933 the population of Kap Stewart moved to Kap Hope (Abelsen 1935–1936:123).

Culture

Since most of the population of Scoresbysund originates from Ammassalik District, much of the material culture is common to both areas. On the other hand, immigration to Scoresbysund has taken place so recently that some implements originally present in Ammassalik had disappeared by the time of moving. The material culture described here is that of Ammassalik District, with an indication of deviations to be found at Scoresbysund.

Structures

Longhouses were built with walls consisting of peat with stones in between, or stones with peat in between, depending on the relative availability of these materials in the immediate vicinity of the house. The ground plan of a longhouse was trapezoidal, the front side being a

Photothèque, Musée de l'Homme, Paris: left, E 13245; right, C 43–1351–92.
Fig. 4. Traditional winter houses of stones and sod. The walls are partially subterranean and the roof flat. left, 8 houses in a village. right, Interior of a house. Woman seated on a wooden platform, beside an oil lamp, heating a pot suspended from the drying rack. Photographs by Robert Gessain, Ammassalik District, 1934–1935.

Nationalmuseet, Copenhagen: L 154a.

Fig. 5. Summer tent dwellings at Ammassalik each occupied by a single family. Photograph by Thomas N. Krabbe, Sept. 1908.

bit shorter than the back. A long entrance was attached to the front side at an angle; it was depressed and functioned as a cold trap.

The longhouse had but one room. The sleeping bench extended the entire length of the back wall. Along the front wall ran a narrow window bench, interrupted only by the entrance (Thalbitzer 1914–1941:35). A line of poles at the front edge of the sleeping bench divided it into various nuclear-family partitions; these poles also supported the roof beam, which ran the entire length of the house. From this beam a number of rafters ran to both the front and the back walls; these rafters in their turn supported a framework of wood, which supported the roof. The lowest layer of the roof consisted of peat flakes. These were covered by peat litter, which in turn was covered by outer tent sheets. Around 1930 the tent sheets were replaced by roofing felt, which lasted longer since tent sheets tended to rot quickly on house roofs. But the roofing felt was fragile; it often tore, with leaky roofs as the result (Høygaard 1938:85).

The window panes were gut casings slit in one place with hot metal; the burnt edge prevented the casings from splitting. Casing windows were translucent but not transparent. After 1930 glass panes began to appear (Mikkelsen 1934:71).

When wood became available, it was first used as a surface for the sleeping bench, then as the floor in front of the bench, and gradually extended to the walls and to the floor under the bench. Finally wood was used for the roof (Mikkelsen 1934:71). This replacement process had little effect on the ground-plan of longhouses, although the houses often became shorter. The entrance was no longer depressed; it was shortened and furnished with doors. Several houses appeared at the individual settlements.

The East Greenland tent was reminiscent of that used in West Greenland. Timbers supported the two sheets, the hairy inner sheet and the hairless outer sheet.

Transportation

Originally Ammassalik District had a rather massive, small dog sled with the runners curved upward in the front and with wide vertical upstanders. It is said that formerly only three or four dogs were harnessed to a sled.

After 1930, possibly even somewhat later, a new type of dog sled appeared in Ammassalik District, larger than the previous type. The new sled is two to three meters long and approximately 65 centimeters wide. It runs on a pair of skis, from which it is raised about 20 centimeters by a number of supports. Under the narrow vertical props is a brake, consisting of a serrated piece of curved metal held in place by a strong rubber band; it can be tramped down in the snow. This is at present the only type of dog sled to be found in Ammassalik District; it can carry a heavier load than the previous type, and its ski runners are well adapted to the soft snow found in the valleys. The dogs are harnessed in the form of a fan, but since they are given traces of various lengths they can easily run in tandem, two side by side.

In Scoresbysund District, the West Greenland dog sled has been adopted.

As in the rest of Greenland, the umiak has been used in East Greenland as a means of transportation during the summer and autumn (fig. 6). Skins of the hooded seal and the bearded seal were used in its manufacture. Not every household had its own umiak. During the winter the umiak was placed on a rack outside the house and used for storing food and household articles that were not destined for immediate consumption (Thalbitzer 1914–1941:42–44).

The umiak was used for a long time; the last one disappeared from Ammassalik about 1970. Wooden boats were introduced late (table 1).

The East Greenland kayak is much like the one used in West Greenland, differing in that it has a flat *masik*, a Y-shaped cross strap, and divided cross straps on the deck (Thalbitzer 1914–1941:45).

After the disappearance of the longhouse, it was impossible to repair the kayak skin in the winter because a kayak could not be brought into a small house. Outdoor repairs were impossible at that season, because the wet skin patches quickly froze stiff. Therefore, after 1930 shorter winter kayaks were built for use in addition to summer kayaks of normal length.

Equipment and Tools

Hunting equipment used in the kayak once included the winged harpoon, now used rarely, but the knob

left, Nationalmuseet, Copenhagen: Graah 1832:pl.1; right, Photothèque, Musée de l'Homme, Paris: D.43.1385.92.

Fig. 6. Umiaks. left, Umiak with mast, rowed (as usual) by women, as seen by Wilhelm A. Graah in 1829–1830. Engraving by Bagge after lost original drawing by H.G.F. Holm, 1832. right, Umiak in foreground and kayaks with shooting screens in background. Photograph by Robert Gessain, Ammassalik, 1935.

harpoon is still in use. The foreshaft is locked to the harpoon shaft by two tight straps and a pivot on the foreshaft that corresponds to a depression at the front of the harpoon shaft. The harpoon head has two spurs but no barb. At the end of the line a double harpoon float could be attached, consisting of two curved seal-skin floats sewed together with two connecting flippers. Today the float is made out of uncurved black skin. The large lance is constructed basically like the harpoon, but with its blade on the foreshaft. The throwing stick is the same type as that used in West Greenland but is often richly decorated with riveted bone figures of animals or people. In general, the wooden articles of the Ammassalik Eskimo are richly decorated with riveted pieces of bone representing geometric figures, animals, or persons, attached in various patterns.

Kayak equipment also includes a hunting knife, beautifully elaborated wound plugs, and towing equipment (Thalbitzer 1914–1941:46–48). Around 1950 the rifle began to be used in the kayak; it gradually replaced the lance.

Unlike kayak hunting tools, the former ice-hunting tools have fallen into disuse, as have the practices connected with this type of hunting. A special harpoon was used for breathing-hole hunting, and a different one for peephole hunting; the latter was long, with a so-called hinge harpoon nailed to the foreshaft with a swiveling axis (Thalbitzer 1914–1941:50). All these ice-hunting harpoons fell out of use at a rather early period, due to the use of the rifle in ice hunting. The peephole harpoon was last used in 1959 as a kind of curiosity.

Seal nets were introduced from West Greenland for

Table 1. Hunting Equipment

	1895	1905	1915	1925	1935	1944	1950	1958	1959
Dog sleds									
Ammassalik	21	65	80	99	70	68	82		
Scoresbysund	0	0	0	10	26	39	39		
Umiaks									
Ammassalik	12	35	32	34	32	24	28		
Scoresbysund	0	0	0	2	1	0	0		
Wooden boats									
Ammassalik	0	0	0	1	2	5	8		
Scoresbysund				0	0	0	2		
Kayaks									
Ammassalik	[a]	[a]	136	135	162	189	161		
Scoresbysund				15	21	27	27		
Seal nets									
Ammassalik	[a]	[a]	32	28	59	81	77	146	[a]
Scoresbysund				0	0	17	35	[a]	15

SOURCES: Denmark. Statistiske oplysninger 3:562, 565, 570; Sammendrag af grønlandske fangstlister 1960.
[a] No data.

Fig. 7. Fishing decoy with soapstone sinker and leather line. Fish were not caught with hooks, but speared with a leister. Length of sinker 9.5 cm; collected at Ammassalik before 1926.

sealing from ice, but they have never been used so widely in the East as in the West, perhaps because the danger of losing the net in ice drift is too great.

For fishing, which has not been carried on very much in known times, the shorthorn sculpin jig has been used, as well as a scoop net for capelin fishing and a two-pronged "salmon harpoon," a type of spear with two small toggle harpoons at the prongs for fishing char (*Salvelinus alpinus*). Of these, the salmon harpoon has fallen into disuse, since nets are now used in char fishing (Thalbitzer 1914–1941:53 ff.).

Men formerly used stone tools to carve wood and

bonelike materials. The bow drill was a special characteristic of East Greenland culture as well as of other cultures related to the Thule culture. Besides its primary function, it was also used to split bone items. Through indirect contact with West Greenland, iron articles were introduced and shaped to make cutting tools and similar items. When stores were established at Ammassalik, tools could be purchased, which influenced tool culture a great deal.

Women's traditional household articles were but little different from those of West Greenland. The ulu, the women's knife, had its blade and handle connected by two bones. Wooden dishes and water containers were more richly decorated (fig. 8), and some water containers had built-in straws. These containers were made with staves (Thalbitzer 1914–1941:38 ff.).

Clothing

For clothing, sealskins, with as well as without hair, and gut casings were used. Polar bear skin was used for hunting clothes and for edging. Fur coats, especially the women's, were shorter than in West Greenland. The women's *kamik*s, or top boots, were also quite short, leaving a bare area around the middle of the thigh. The use of hide strips for attaching soles resulted in elevated seams. Indoors both the men and the women wore very short trousers, *naassit* (Thalbitzer 1914–1941:29–34).

Subsistence

The meat of all the species of seals, as well as whale meat and polar bear meat, is eaten, as are also a number

Fig. 8. Decorated containers. left, Wooden water bucket decorated with ivory carvings of whale, seals, and fish. center, Bentwood cup with ivory figures of people, seals, belugas, bears, and birds attached to the sides. The handle is sinew. right, Wood tool box, richly ornamented with ivory. left, Height 6.8 cm; rest same scale. All collected at Ammassalik: left, by Gustav Holm, 1884–1885; center, before 1925; right, before 1929.

of sea birds, such as murre, eider, kittiwake, and grouse. Fish that were and are eaten are shorthorn sculpin *(Myxocephalus scorpius)*, Greenland cod *(Gadus ogac)*, and char. All these foods can be eaten boiled or dried, and even raw-frozen, but never fresh and raw. In the winter, the Greenland shark *(Somniosus microcephalus)* can be eaten after a complicated boiling process.

In the summer, seal meat is often dried and put into blubber sacks. Also a number of vegetables gathered in the late summer are put into blubber sacks: crowberries *(Empetrum nigrum)*, roseroot *(Sedum rosea)*, and angelica *(Angelica)*, as well as the leaves of fireweed *(Epilobium)* and lousewort *(Pedicularis)*.

To preserve dried winter stores, rock caves were used and carefully sealed. Such storage caves were often at least a couple of kilometers from the house, so that the supplies would not be exhausted too quickly. Rations were brought out according to need or desire; whatever was not to be eaten immediately was put into the *mingiisivik*, a little room outside the house, or under the umiak. Frozen whole seal carcasses lay on the ground around the house, because the dogs were always tied.

Religion

In the original cosmology of East Greenland there was the earth, the land of the dead under the sea, and another land of the dead in the sky. While the two lands of the dead seem to have been immaterial, this world was material, but possessing a supernatural element that was the cause of everything that took place on the earth. This supernatural element gave life, and some of it continued to give life after death.

That a person is an independent being with a will, an intellect, and powers of perception, is connected with the fact that he has a soul, *tarneq*. This soul, identical with the person in question, becomes at death a free soul, which after a period of purification takes up residence in one of the lands of the dead. A person has also special qualities and special knowledge connected with his name, which he shares with others who have the same name, or *ateq*. This name soul remains on earth after death and takes up residence in a newborn child who has been given the same name. This child inherits with his name some qualities of former bearers of the name. In addition, a person is warm, breathes, and performs actions that can be considered as organic processes. At death a person loses these vital processes, which during life are started and maintained by a kind of a soul, *inuuseq*. There is no information as to what happens to this soul after death.

The various parts of a human being move and have strength, so they must also have a soul. Thus "member souls" are mentioned. It is not certain what relationship exists among these various souls, or whether they are

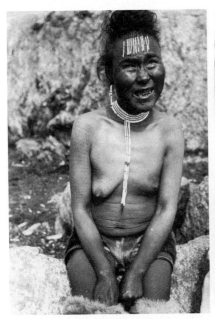

Arktisk Institut, Charlottenlund, Denmark.

Fig. 9. Women and children's clothing and adornment. left, Mannaate in indoor dress: outer breeches, boots, bead necklace and ear ornaments, and decorative beads attached to hair over her forehead. She is liberally tattooed on her arms and right breast. Such tattooing was done at age 13–15 (Thalbitzer 1914–1941:608). center, Eekeettsuk (left) and Igimarajik, wives of the shaman Ajukutooq, wearing their hair in the customary topknot of adult women. Ajukutooq's youngest son Ningaawa wears an amulet harness; usually these had a case in front and back to protect both sides of the body against spirit intrusion (Thalbitzer 1914–1941:625). right, Woman wearing an anorak with fur inside and the back full enough to carry a small child. Her topknot is decorated with a beaded hairband. (The English term anorak is a borrowing through Danish of Greenlandic *annoraaq*, a jacket of this sort, with or without a hood, in historic times of cloth and worn as a windbreaker.) Photographs by William Thalbitzer, Ammassalik, 1906.

only various manifestations of the same soul. There is apparently a paradoxical relationship between these soul concepts, but since a dogmatic formulation is lacking one can only confuse the issue by attributing to them more significance than the East Greenlanders themselves did.

Thus, according to these old concepts, a human being consisted of a material body and a supernatural soul, or souls. It is claimed that the moon brought souls to children about to be born, but no one seemed to know the origin place of these souls.

It is obvious that ordinary logic cannot be directly applied to these basic religious concepts. Nevertheless, a certain relationship was expected to exist between matter and the soul. If the balance was disturbed, for example by soul theft, in which a soul was removed from its body, resulting in too little soul in the mixture, the person would sicken and die unless the soul was returned. Too much soul, caused by the intrusion or the contamination of magically infected matter, made the person mentally disturbed, and in extreme cases could also cause death (Petersen 1966–1967:272). Therefore one had to be careful in the phases of life in which the soul was more loosely connected to the body than usual: at birth, death, or the transition from one phase of life to another, for example, at the onset of menstruation. Any act that could disturb the transition of the soul from one phase to another was taboo. By abstaining from a number of acts and by concluding purification through magical formulas, people tried to prevent a liberated soul from possessing an object or other persons (Rasmussen 1921–1925, 1:35–45).

By knowing secret rules and formulas, one could learn to manipulate the supernatural presence in human beings and objects. The objective of such magic was to disturb soul balance by contamination or imitation, in order to bring bad luck. In magic there was often no direct con-nection between the act and the intended result, but in *tupilak* magic, an animal composed of various animals was magically brought to life; this animal, in the shape of one of the component animals, was then to attack the intended victim. In sorcery in general, including *tupilak* magic, the intended victim might have greater magical power than the one practicing the magic. In this case, the victim would suspect mischief and send the magic charm back to its creator, who could then avoid bad luck only by making a public confession to neutralize the magic.

Such designs against people could be detected by shamans. The East Greenland shamans could have different numbers of auxiliary spirits and thus occupy different degrees. The lowest degrees could explain the causes of illness and other secrets, the next ones could cure them. Others could visit the moon, and the greatest shamans could visit the Sea Woman (fig. 13) and *Asiaq*.

The shaman often performed in a trance, either in a tent with his audience outside or in a house with the lights out. With his arms tied behind his back, sitting on a skin on the floor, he could contact the spirits with his drum. If the shaman's soul went on a trip during the seance, one of his auxiliary spirits occupied his body until the return of his own soul.

It is not known how many shamans there were in East Greenland. If by a shaman is meant someone who in a public performance has documented a previous initiation, consisting in being eaten up by a bear spirit and then coming to life again, then there were not very many shamans. Shamanism does not seem to have been inherited in East Greenland.

One did not have to be a shaman to seek help in the spirit world. Methods similar to those used in sorcery were used in positive magic, for example, love magic and magic to resist the sorcery of others (C. Rosing 1946:49 ff.). Magic formulas, to be sung or spoken in order to change the weather, get good hunting results, cure illness, or purify an unclean person, could be used by anyone who knew them, but not too often. They were kept secret from those who did not know them but could be purchased (Rasmussen 1921–1925, 1:48–55).

Although there was no real worship, there were several divinities in the mythology of East Greenland. One could send a shaman to them in difficult times. These approaches followed determined formulas, giving the impression of passive spirits who had to grant a request only if the shaman carried out the ritual correctly. Only the Moon Man seemed to have an independent will.

Immap ukuua, the mother of the sea, was the guardian of the marine game animals, watching over the observation of the taboo rules. If gross violations of taboo were committed, she could keep animals for herself so that a shaman would have to try to get them back. In East Greenland the Eskimo myth connecting the Sea

Smithsonian. Dept. of Anthr.: 168,939.
Fig. 10. Wooden shade decorated with ivory strips and with ivory beads on strap, used to protect the eyes against snow blindness. Wooden goggles were also used for the same purpose. Width 14.2 cm; collected at Ammassalik before 1893.

Natl. Mus. of Canada, Ottawa: left, IV–A–341; center, IV–A–373; right, IV–A–342.
Fig. 11. Wooden dolls, which characteristically have no feet or arms. Female dolls are recognizable by the hair topknot and the emphasized breasts. They served as children's toys and perhaps as amulets. left, Height 8.0 cm; rest same scale. Left and right collected by C. Ryder, 1892; center collected 1925, all from Ammassalik.

Woman with the girl who married the dog was lacking, but otherwise she is the same deity as found in the West (Rasmussen 1921–1925, 1:95ff.). The Sea Woman who kept the game animals for herself was in certain West Greenland myths connected with bad weather. Only in East Greenland was there a divinity called *Asiaq* 'the far traveler', who could withhold game animals by sharp cold and unfavorable winds. She too could be visited by a shaman, who could procure a change of weather and thus animals.

According to East Greenland myths, the Moon Man had become a kind of divinity by committing incest with his sister, the Sun. He too had some kind of supervision over the observation of taboo prohibitions, especially those of the death taboo (Thalbitzer 1957:243, 275). Taboo violations turned into filth on the moon, which a shaman had to clean up, whereby the filth turned into narwhals, bears, foxes, and birds (Rasmussen 1921–1925, 1:82). Through the tide, the Moon Man was also connected to the sea, to certain whales, and to the formation of marine animals. He seems likewise to have played a role in the formation of human beings, fetching souls for children about to be born (Holm 1888:131). While Sea Woman must be considered a kind of underworld divinity, the position of the Moon Man is not clear. His insistence on the observation of taboo prescriptions as well as his connection with the marine animals leaves the impression that the boundary between his area and that of Sea Woman was diffuse.

Nalaarsik, the man on Vega, is also mentioned as a

person who became angry about the violation of taboos, but there is no additional information on this spirit.

Other divinities seem not to have existed in East Greenland. But in nonliving things, in flowers, in small animals, and even in concepts, there was a kind of soul, *inua*. This is a power with consciousness but seemingly without a will; nevertheless, it was dangerous to insult or ignore it. One had to show attention to the *inua* of the locality at certain places such as dangerous glaciers, graves, and trout streams. One had to offer a sacrifice to the *inua* of the locality in order to succeed in one's undertaking. This approaches worship (cf. Holtved 1968:132).

In other ways one was expected to pay attention to the presence of the supernatural. In critical situations, especially in case of death, one had to avoid disturbing the presence of the supernatural by abstaining from certain actions. For three days the soul of the deceased remained in the vicinity, and then it took a year for it to reach one of the lands of the dead. For three days the survivors had to stay inside, wear their clothes in a certain manner, and refrain from working. Then a male survivor could be purified by magic words; and then following certain prescriptions, he was to go hunting. When he had taken game, he was allowed to resume normal pursuits. A female survivor, on the other hand, still had to observe a number of prescriptions in her work, in her association with others, in her relation to the hunt, and in her diet, which was very strict. When a year had passed, she was to be purified by magic words. The name of the deceased was not to be men-

Nationalmuseet, Copenhagen: L 118a.
Fig. 12. Ukuttiaq and his wife using a fire drill. Two people are needed, one to turn the hard wooden drill, while the other presses it into the cavity of the hearth, which has been greased with blubber. In less than a minute smoke and sparks were obtained (Thalbitzer 1914–1941:531). Photograph by Johan Petersen, Ammassalik, 1900.

Fig. 13. Drawings of shamans by the East Greenlander Kaarale Andreassen. left, A shaman, bound up, performing during a seance. right, Shaman on a spirit flight visiting the supernatural Sea Woman. Drawings done in 1920 on the basis of Ammassalik traditions of customs then obsolete (Ostermann 1938:94–129).

tioned until it was passed on to a child (Rasmussen 1921–1925, 1:12, 42).

There are a few creation myths. One concerns a man who came from the sky and made the earth pregnant; their descendants filled the world. There was an earthquake, and the earth cracked. Some of the people fell into the cracks and became *innertivit* 'fire spirits', who lived under the shore. The remainder continued to reproduce and filled the earth again. Then there came a great flood that submerged the earth; only a few people managed to seek refuge on the top of a mountain near Ammassalik; from these the East Greenlanders are descended (Rasmussen 1921–1925, 1:71 ff.). In these myths, no fundamental difference is emphasized between the world of the creation and the world of the East Greenlanders. It was not even clear whether, for example, the moon originated in mythological times. But *Asiaq* was said to have wandered from the very beginning of time, trying to find a husband.

In 1894, F.C.P. Rüttel, who previously worked in West Greenland, came as the first missionary to East Greenland. In 1904 he was replaced by Christian Rosing, born in Greenland, whose work was continued first by his sons and later by other Greenlandic clergymen.

Christianity was quick to find adherents in the vicinity of Ammassalik town. Here neophytes were given instructions in the basic principles of Christianity before being baptized. The newly Christian families returned to their homes, so that for many years the mission stations were principally inhabited by catechumens preparing for baptism. In 1916 a new mission station was founded under the leadership of an East Greenlandic catechist, Kaarali Andreassen (Holm and Petersen 1921:647). The last adult baptism commemorated the two hundredth anniversary of the landing of the mis-

sionary Hans Egede in West Greenland (Mikkelsen 1934:84).

The East Greenland mission had deliberately avoided concentrating the population around the mission stations. Various practices such as polygamy, blood vengeance, and magic were combatted in the name of Christianity. The East Greenlandic missionaries managed to avoid creating antagonism among the shamans; some of the most reputable of these, such as Mitsivarniannga and Maratsi, were among the first converts to Christianity. Although missionaries did not oppose the song tradition of the East Greenlanders, and old songs are still sung in East Greenland, people have stopped composing new songs, which may be linked to the demise of the satirical song.

All people who moved to Scoresbysund were Christians.

Songs and Tales

Many of the East Greenland tales were variants of themes found elsewhere in the Eskimo area; they contained a mixture of old myths and epic tales, old as well as self-experienced, and expressed the attitude of the East Greenlanders to their environment.

Oral entertainment had many forms. Certain definite routines were performed, *uaajeerneq* and *tivaneq*, in which a certain situation was performed in disguise. While the routines were determined, the performance was left to the imagination of the performer.

There were a number of genres of East Greenlandic song, ranging from nature poetry to judicial settlements. In the 1980s many songs were still known and sung.

The satirical song, a part of Eskimo song tradition,

was sung a great deal in East Greenland when individuals felt offended. Although the reaction of the audience, which was a kind of judgment, probably depended more on the performance than on sober justice, nevertheless the satirical song can be considered a judicial presentation, the main function of which was to prevent an offense from developing into open conflict. The "documents in the case" were presented to an audience consisting of supporters of both parties; if the main objective was to make them public and pacify a threatening conflict, then the satirical song was a kind of juridical act. The two parties in a song duel were not allowed to make use of other means; if one of them felt that his life was threatened, he could save himself by challenging his opponent in song (fig. 14). One had to treat his opponent in a song duel as a beloved guest; a song duel was a celebration that everyone attended in his finest clothes.

Arktisk Institut, Charlottenlund, Denmark.

Fig. 14. Drumming. Drums were made of a wood hoop covered with skin, preferably from the stomach of a polar bear, bearded seal, crested seal, or shark. The drumstick was struck against the hoop, not the skin head (Thalbitzer 1914–1941:640–641). top, Drum dance challenge in Ammassalik. bottom left, Man from Ammassalik drumming and singing to his 2 wives and daughter. Photographs by William Thalbitzer, 1906. bottom right, Man "masked" (face distorted) for the drum dance. Photograph by Jette Bang, late 1930s.

• OWNERSHIP   In the longhouse food was shared without compensation even with those who were not close relatives, so that one could get the impression of collective property. This impression is reinforced by the fact that anyone could share in a large animal that had been killed by simply arriving in time for the event of distribution.

But on closer examination it turns out that there was a difference between distribution to persons who were able to reciprocate and distribution to those who had no reasonable opportunity for doing so. People who had similar opportunities for giving gave each other both produce and work without demanding compensation, while those without support were often expected to perform work or have something to give in order to receive. One of the reasons for this "potential reciprocity" among the various households could be that people were usually satisfied with a "debt of gratitude" and that a strict observance of balanced reciprocity could easily disturb the necessary hunting ability. Balanced reciprocity existed among members of various settlements as a kind of barter.

In principle, property was private. Stores of skins and food, tents, and the like, which were used by entire families, were owned by the households. Animals taken by a man were incorporated into the property of his household. In principle, an animal was always taken by one person, even if others had helped. In the case of a large animal, the "hunter" could not just dispose of the whole animal; those who had helped him had the right to certain parts of the animal. Only if the man was all alone, also on his way home, could he dispose of the entire animal. But he did not have to share small seals with others.

The man considered to have "taken" an animal was the one who put the first bullet or harpoon into it, regardless of who had killed it. Animals that were shared were narwhals, belugas, walruses, and polar bears, and, in certain cases, hooded seals and bearded seals. The one entitled to a part of an animal in East Greenland cut out the part himself. In net hunting or fishing, the owner of the net was considered to be the one who had "taken" the animal or animals.

In the longhouse there was a widespread sharing of food with housemates, even among those who were not relatives. This sharing could take the form of measured portions, raw or cooked, or of common meals. But in each case the division was made by the head of a family offering others items from the food stores of his household. If the head of a family did not want to offer anything to others, in spite of the possible dissatisfaction of his housemates, there was no question that only the head of a family could dispose of the property of the household.

Skins, blubber, and other hunting produce, as well as other property, were not subject to such common distribution.

Families or persons without providers could procure skins, bubber, and the like, which were not usually shared, by working for hunting families, rowing, sewing, flensing and the like; or by fishing or gathering plants and selling their produce in exchange for what they needed.

Finding an ownerless object, such as driftwood, conferred ownership on the finder, if he marked his find by dragging it over the highwater mark. If a seal was taken that another had lost after having harpooned it, it belonged to the new taker, who returned the harpoon to its owner.

The right of disposal was not identical with the right of use. For example, a man might have the use of his brother's food stores, being able to eat from them without asking permission, without having the right to share them with others, or to sell them. These rights belonged only to the brother and his wife. In families of three generations, it was often the oldest member who had the right of disposal of the family's common property. But personal items such as clothes, hunting equipment, and household items were private in the sense that only the one who used them had the right of disposal. The right of disposal included the right of transfer by gift, loan, or sale. One weakness in the study of these principles of ownership is that normally no sanctions were applied, either when an expected gift was not forthcoming or even in the case of direct violation of the principles, for instance, theft. It is thus probable that theft was eventually "legalized" by the first owner giving up his claim as useless.

Exploitation of the common hunting area takes place at alternating localities, some of which are utilized seasonally, others more irregularly. The entire area in which East Greenlanders hunt can be considered common property. The use of any locality is totally, and without formalities, assigned to any household that, under certain conditions, desires to utilize it. Afterward the locality reverts to common ownership. A seasonally determined cessation of exploitation is not considered as abandonment by a household of its prior claim to the exploitation of a locality; this claim is considered abandoned if the household in several seasons goes to other hunting grounds. Such a prior claim to exploitation can be inherited within the household, so long as the opportunities afforded by the locality are exploited. A prior claim to exploitation includes no private territorial right; rather it is connected to fixed points within the hunting ground, so that there are no set territorial boundaries, but rather prior claims to tent rings and the like (Petersen 1963:280).

• SOCIAL UNITS   The society is organized into households, which are economic, residential, and organiza-

636

Nationalmuseet, Copenhagen: left, L5304; center, L19.161; right, L5305.

Fig. 15. Masks from Ammassalik. left, Wooden mask representing a woman; the grooves probably indicate tattoo lines. center, Wooden dance mask; right, skin mask, possibly used for curing as amulets were sewn under the edges for protection (Kaalund 1979:54). left, Height 37.0 cm, rest same scale; left and right collected by Johan Petersen, 1910; center, collected by Christian Kruuse, 1901–1902.

tional units consisting of an extended family with complete or incomplete nuclear families. The kinship system is bilateral with emphasis on virilocality, which is not, however, absolute. Marriage hardly constitutes an alliance; it is entered into with very little ceremony. Within a household a couple can live with their sons and daughters and the nuclear families of these. The normal extended family in one household consists of three generations. If there are four, the oldest generation usually resides with their youngest son (and his children and grandchildren), his older brothers having established separate households as soon as they became grandparents. The occupants of a household live together, migrate together, and have a common economy and a recognized head. Labor is distributed according to sex and age.

A settlement consisting of several households is quite loosely connected; it can easily be joined and as easily dissolved. Only with important tasks does real common activity take place in which people help each other in expectation of reciprocity. The settlement is loosely cemented by common norms, a common language, possible ties of friendship or kinship, and especially by the reciprocal sharing of food.

No head of a family is subordinate to any other head of a family. In this sense the society is egalitarian. But by various abilities and various degrees of support from their families, some achieve more prominent status than others, being, for example, the one to whom others turn.

History

Education

In 1904 a little school was founded in Ammassalik, in which the priest taught children preparing for baptism. Since then schools have been established around Ammassalik District, which by 1950 had nine schools (Mikkelsen 1950:259). As far as possible, children in Greenland were taught in their own locality. By 1950 most adult East Greenlanders could read and write; some of them had learned to read from their friends. By 1950 there was an evening school for adults.

From the very establishment of Scoresbysund in 1925, schools or school chapels were founded.

The school system in both areas was under the church. This is partly due to the tradition in Greenland whereby the school system developed from the desire of the Protestants that their adherents should be able to read the Bible and other religious works. In addition, the school system and the church shared their personnel.

Administration

Administratively, East Greenland was separated from West Greenland, with contact between them taking place

637

through Denmark. Special rules applied to East Greenland, and the colonial manager was directly subject to the Greenland Administration in Copenhagen.

In the 1940s colonial councils were set up for Ammassalik and Scoresbysund Districts, with Danish and Greenlandic members. These councils had the authority to pass local ordinances and to prosecute their violation. They were led by an inspector for East Greenland, who for several years was Ejnar Mikkelsen, an East Greenland pioneer.

At first the health services were administered by the colonial manager and the priest. In 1932 a nurse was appointed in Ammassalik, but not until 1945 did the district have its own doctor (Mikkelsen 1950:260). Scoresbysund District got its first doctor even later.

For many years, the sale of sealskins was the only source of income for the Ammassalik Eskimos; later Greenland shark fishing was added. At first the Eskimos could only purchase tools, guns, and ammunition at the shop at Ammassalik; but after 1905 textiles, sugar, flour, and the like could also be purchased. In 1916 these restrictions were abolished, and the only limitations were those imposed by the stock of the shop. At first the colonial manager was instructed to buy skins only when he deemed that domestic consumption would not suffer (Mikkelsen and Sveistrup 1944:97).

In Scoresbysund local coal deposits were used for heating houses, so that seal blubber as well as sealskins could be sold.

Population

The decline in the population of the Ammassalik area from 1884 to 1894 is often attributed to blood feuds and famine, but this interpretation cannot explain how the population could rise to 411 in the course of only six years (table 2). A better explanation is that the population of the Ammassalik area had begun to take advantage of the vacuum created by the emigration of the Southeast Greenlanders to West Greenland, by utilizing the new hunting grounds and thus maintaining the trade contacts with West Greenland. The emigration of the Southeast Greenlanders to West Greenland must be seen in connection with the unfavorable ice conditions at the end of the nineteenth century (Vibe 1967:202). Some of the seal population had gone to West Greenland.

After the founding of a colony at Ammassalik, this trade in the southern area lost its importance, and the population returned to Ammassalik District; by 1899 they had all returned to the area around the four fjords. Individual families had by then moved from Sermilik fjord to West Greenland. Thus a direct decline in the population had not occurred, but there was a stagnation. An expected annual increase of 2½ to 3 percent, encountered in areas without extensive health services,

Table 2. Population of East Greenland

	Ammassalik District	Scoresbysund District
1884	413	
1894	247	
1900	411	
1905	501	
1910	565	
1915	602	
1920	663	
1925	659	89
1930	771	115
1935	855	161
1940	935	211
1945	1,105	251
1950	1,207	261

SOURCES: Holm 1888:200; Ministeriet for Grønland, Statistisk Protokol; Beretninger vedrørende Grønland 1946, 1947; Report on Greenland 1951:2

was not forthcoming. This increase would have amounted to about 150 persons between 1884 and 1899.

Thereafter the population of Ammassalik District continued to grow. The population in 1899, 403 persons, was doubled in the whole of East Greenland by 1927, that is, after the foundation of Scoresbysund with a small contribution of population from West Greenland. These figures are interesting in that almost no exchange of population took place with other areas, due to the isolation of East Greenland. Except for very few officials and their families from Denmark and West Greenland, neither immigration or emigration occurred.

Excluding Scoresbysund, the 1899 population of Ammassalik District was doubled by 1932. This figure was again doubled by 1952, including a considerable number of immigrants. For many years, the population of Ammassalik town consisted especially of converts preparing for baptism. In 1895 its population was 11; by 1921 it had varied between 60 and 111, and by 1945 between 74 and 130.

The 1925 population of Scoresbysund District was doubled by 1936; immigrants from Ammassalik had arrived in 1927 and 1935. Further immigrants arrived later; by 1950 the original population had almost quadrupled (Robert-Lamblin 1968:105 ff.). Scoresbysund District did not have a variation in the population of the individual localities. The 1945 population was 251, of which 91 lived in Scoresbysund town.

Economy

Danish economic policy in East Greenland, as in many parts of Greenland up to 1950, was based on seal hunting as the chief occupation. Radical changes were avoided. But changes in the material culture, due to new supplies and the presence of a centralized administration, had a stabilizing influence on settlement in Ammassalik District. No sudden changes occurred, but the smallest settlements died out gradually.

The sales of seal skins grew in Ammassalik from 54 skins in 1894–1895 to approximately 5,000 skins around 1930; between 1930 and 1950 sales varied from slightly under 5,000 skins to around 6,000 skins annually. In 1930–1931, 11 polar bear skins and 22 fox skins were sold. In the same year, 22 barrels of blubber, 534 sealskins, 77 polar bear skins, and 61 fox skins were sold in Scoresbysund (Mikkelsen 1934:150). These are figures of sales only, not of the number of animals taken.

The 1950s

By 1950 East Greenland consisted of two inhabited areas with almost no small settlements; settlement was more permanent than ever before; housing was smaller and more mobile. Due to the introduction of the rifle, many hunting techniques had fallen into disuse and others had evolved. The society was in many ways still self-sufficient: the means of communication and transportation were manufactured domestically, and in Ammassalik District houses were built by the inhabitants. Many tents were still made of skins, hunting clothing was likewise made of skins, and food was procured locally, as was fuel for the heating and illumination of houses.

Shamans and other distinguished individuals had disappeared, but the society, cemented not by leaders but by the reciprocity of free hunters, was still functioning.

Education, health services, and housing were to be improved. Around 1950 new arrangements appeared on the scene that exercised a radical influence on conditions, creating both benefits and problems.

Synonymy

The East Greenlanders are called in West Greenlandic *tunumiut* or *tunuamiut* 'inhabitants of the back side'. The two main subgroups are the *ammassalimmiut* 'the Ammassalik Eskimo' and the *ittoqqortoormeermiit* 'the Scoresbysund Eskimo' (formerly known as Scoresbysund*imiut*). The Southeast Greenlanders were the *timmiarmiit*.

Sources

Useful summaries of the natural conditions, history, administration, and culture of the various districts of Greenland were compiled by Trap (1970a), including sections by Vibe (1970) on zoogeography and by Bøcher (1970) on botany. Vibe (1967) has also described the effects of climatic fluctuations on animal abundance; Paine (1971a) is relevant here also. Boassen (1939) is a brief note claiming that Scoresbysund hunters respected hunting regulations.

An outline of the history of Greenland, 1500–1945, is by Gad (1946). Mikkelsen (1934, 1950, 1950a, 1965) has published several works on the history of East Greenland, focusing on more recent times. A brief summary of the old Eskimo religion is by Holtved (1968). Petersen (1964) has described the tupilak stories and their religious significance, has surveyed the relation between burial forms and the death cult (1966–1967), and compared East and West Greenlandic dialects (1975).

Robbe (1981) has written on personal names and Robert-Lamblin (1981) on sex roles, both at Ammassalik. Rasmussen (1921–1925, 1) collected East Greenlandic myths and legends. C. Rosing (1946) presents the reflections of the second missionary to the Ammassalik district on the paganism of the East Greenlanders but also gives much valuable ethnographic data. P. Rosing (1930–1931) describes the hunting, social, and cultural life of the people about Ammassalik in the 1920s. Holm and Petersen (1921) is a handbook on the geographical and cultural situation of Ammassalik 200 years after Danish colonization of Greenland began. Høygaard (1938) is a preliminary report on hygienic conditions in Ammassalik District. Borchersen (1963) is a description by an administrative officer of the introduction of industrial fishing to Ammassalik. Gessain (1967, 1969) has produced a monograph on modernization at Ammassalik and a paper on the modern early importance of the kayak there (1968).

Robert-Lamblin (1968) has studied the Scoresbysund community. Petersen (1972) is a study of the relationship between hunting and ownership in an East Greenland hunting community, while Petersen (1978) treats hunting and urbanization and Nooter (1972–1973) discusses similar topics. Enel (1981) has published on modern market craftwork. Statistical information is found in the yearly editions of *Beretninger vedrørende Grønland*.

639

Greenlandic Written Literature

ROBERT PETERSEN*

Literature written in Greenlandic is distinguished from compositions that were intended for oral presentation and kept alive in tales and songs. Not all oral literature is anonymous: some remains associated with the names of specific authors, as in the case of some East Greenlandic songs.

Hardly any Greenlandic written literature has been translated into any other language. In addition, publication opportunities for Greenlandic literary works have been limited, so that a large part of the production of several writers is still only in private possession. Poetry is sometimes first published long after the death of the authors.

From the arrival of the Egede family in Greenland in 1721 into the middle of the nineteenth century, a number of missionaries dominated the literary life of the island. As an orthodox Lutheran, Hans Egede considered it important for Greenlanders to be able to read "the correct doctrine"; as quickly as possible, he and his assistants attempted to invent an orthography and get books printed. The first printed literature of Greenlandic Eskimo origin was written down by Hans Egede, when two converted Greenlanders paid homage to the Danish crown prince on his birthday in 1729. Considering the lack of social stratification in Greenland, this poem was surprisingly servile (Egede 1741:119 ff.). From the hands of the missionaries came, naturally, translations of the Bible in 1744, the Articles of Faith in 1742, and Martin Luther's Catechism in 1757. A number of hymns, especially ancient ones, were adapted to Greenlandic. The latest Greenlandic hymnbook still contains works by Hans Egede (b. 1686, d. 1758) and his son Poul Egede (b. 1708, d. 1789). Their relative Niels Brønlund Bloch (b. 1720, d. 1792), also a missionary, and born in northern Norway, published the first Greenlandic hymnbook in 1761. Another missionary, Otto Fabricius (b. 1744, d. 1822), published several works, including a Greenlandic grammar in 1802, which was a revision of Poul Egede's 1760 *Grammatica grønlandica*, and a Greenlandic dictionary, revised from Poul Egede's pioneer work of 1750. Fabricius also published several translations of the Bible and a new hymnbook in 1801.

Knud Kjer (b. 1802, d. 1865) came to Greenland as a newlywed missionary in 1823; he lost his wife before a year had passed. He remarried and worked in Greenland until 1831, adapting a number of Danish songs and hymns to Greenlandic and composing many hymns himself. At the time, the ancient Greenlandic songs had already been partially forgotten. Kjer thought it unfortunate that they were replaced only by religious hymns and adapted a number of secular songs to Greenlandic, including some drinking songs. There is a cheerful tone in his composition, and his own misfortunes cannot be detected in his hymns. Through his compositions, Kjer attempted to inform the Greenlanders of his time about trends in European literature. Thus he adapted *Den tapre Landssoldat*, which takes place in the Danish-Prussian war of 1848–1850. In other works he transferred themes to Greenlandic conditions, such as in his adaptation of Carl Maria von Weber's *Der Freischütz*, where the hunters' chorus is converted into Greenlandic caribou hunting. In a more original mode, he took inspiration from the Danish "golden-age romanticism" by treating a theme from Greenlandic oral tradition in the form of love tragedy in verse in *Ingik*. After his return to Denmark, Kjer also published a hymnbook called *Kikiaktok* 'The Crucified One'.

Rasmus Berthelsen (b. 1827, d. 1901) was the first Greenlander who took up this tradition of composing hymns. For many years until his death, he was a teacher at the teachers' college in Godthåb (established in 1845). In 1858 he published hymns for church festivals, and in 1859 even more hymns. Their quality is inconsistent, but one of them, *Gûterput qutsingnermio* 'Our God in the Highest', is today probably the most popular hymn in Greenlandic. In 1861 Berthelsen became the first editor of the Greenlandic-language periodical *Atuagagdliutit* 'Readings'; he also wrote a number of articles for it.

Johannes Ungâralak (b. 1840, d. 1886), a hunter with little schooling, wrote a number of articles on the life around Salliit, just north of Cape Farewell, where he lived. They were full of spelling mistakes, but at the same time so lively and detailed that they must still be considered as pearls of Greenlandic literature. He evoked for posterity the drama of daily life in a small settlement.

Carl Julius Spindler (b. 1838, d. 1918) is another

 *Translated from Danish by Charles Jones.

European writer who deserves mention. He spent the period from 1863 to 1888 as a Moravian missionary at various mission stations in Greenland; even when he had left Greenland, he wrote several hymns in Greenlandic, totaling over 1,000 verses. Spindler also wrote various songs about the daily life of Greenlanders. In his 1879 collection *Eríniugkat nûtigdlit 105* '105 Songs with Music' he identified himself as a Greenlander. In 1891 he published his first epic poem in Greenlandic, *Qajarnaq*, dealing with the first Greenlander baptized by the Moravian missionaries, in 1739.

Henrik Lund (b. 1875, d. 1948) grew up in the area around Cape Farewell. For his first post as a catechist he traveled with his wife to Ammassalik in East Greenland, where a mission station had been founded three years previously. He had often seen East Greenlanders in his childhood. Although Lund remained in East Greenland from 1898 to 1909, no poems of his from that time have ever been published, and the still vital East Greenlandic song tradition seems to have exercised no influence on him. After his return to West Greenland in 1910, Lund became the head catechist of Sydprøven. In 1918 he moved to Narsaq, where he worked until his death. In 1936 he was ordained a priest; shortly before his death he was decorated with the order Ingenio et Arti for his writing.

Lund's writing extends from descriptions of nature to songs of social criticism. He described the progress of south Greenlandic nature through the seasons. His contemporaries populated nature with spirits; Lund denied the existence of these but wrote of the "life of nature" as experienced by the poet. One of his descriptions of nature deals with a fjord suitable for sheep raising. In a way it is a very prosaic song, but at the same time perhaps one of the best lyrical productions in Greenlandic; the poet, carried on the wings of song, saw opportunities for "the man of the future." Several of Lund's poems dealt with the occupations of south Greenland, fishing and seal hunting. As a schoolteacher he could raise his finger to remind people of the severe winter, which they so often had a tendency to forget in the joys of summer.

A few of his poems were descriptions of characters, such as Matînarssuaq, who according to the tales once returned home from a storm by the use of a magic song; and Paaliiterajik, whose violin bow once caught on a bent nail, so that he thought an angel had taken hold of it. This was obviously a parody of legends of chivalry, in which an angel could prevent the evil knight from killing innocent people by holding back his sword. *Nunarput utorqarssuangoravit*, written by Lund in 1912, has been described by Thalbitzer (1948, 2:244), a Danish professor of Eskimo languages, as "the national anthem of Greenland." Actually, this poem was a polemic article. The previous year Lund had been elected to the South Greenland Provincial Council.

Earlier poets had played on the sense of sight; Lund played just as much on the sense of hearing:

The small bushes rustle
in the spring-clothed valley,
where masses of snow have retreated
and the stream of life rushes.
　Light from above
　hits this place.
I can hear the voice of eternity.

Lund wrote romantically about spring, but gloomily about autumn, for example:

Soon we shall see the earth
Under a blanket of snow,
Clothed in mourning
And weeping in the wind,
After having said goodbye
To all the little birds.

Lund also expressed his thoughts about society:

Since the world does not stand still
He who does not try to keep up with it
He will be weakened.

Josva Kleist (b. 1879, d. 1937) is still little known as a poet; many of his works have not been published. The strict rules of prosody were technically difficult for him, but his poems of social criticism contain a depth that has caused them to be often quoted.

Jonathan Petersen (b. 1881, d. 1965) as a composer and a poet has been of great importance for Greenlandic song culture. In his youth he experienced the lay revival movement, which led to the formation of organizations resembling the YMCA and YWCA; many of his poems have a Christian theme. His hymns are quite varied. He had an almost confidential relationship with God, as can be seen, for instance, in *Nipaitdlisimatitdlunga* 'While I Sit in Silence', the theme of which is taken from the calling of Samuel in the Old Testament. He was also a patriotic poet, considering Greenland as a kind of absraction of the area where he spent his childhood. Although his songs are often rather heavy, one can be surprised by the lightness of those about spring. He often composed the music for his own songs as well as for those of other writers. Nevertheless, Petersen is remembered in Greenland as a linguist. Although he was not a pioneer, no one equaled his familiarity with the details of the language situation in Greenland. Petersen's novel *Inûnerup sarfâne* 'At the Stream of Life', described the issues debated in the 1920s and the social patterns of the 1930s. Since its publication was delayed until 1957, this book must be considered mainly as a historical contribution.

The first work of fiction from the hand of a Greenlander, *Singnagtugaq* 'The Dream', was written by Mathias Storch (b. 1883, d. 1957), a clergyman. The main character in this novel, like Storch himself, was born in a little settlement in the north of West Greenland 641 and studied at the teachers' college in Godthåb; Storch's contemporaries in Godthåb considered it a roman à clef. With stern wit Storch described a number of unfortunate situations: the hardships of a foster child, the barrier between Danes and Greenlanders, a farcical meeting of the elected council. As a common denominator he points out the low state of popular enlightenment.

Peter Gundel (b. 1895, d. 1931), a fisherman at Jakobshavn, wrote a number of short stories that were published in *Avangnâmioq*, a monthly for northern West Greenland. These were character descriptions based on subjects from old Greenland of which *Atâtaga akiniúpara* 'I have revenged my father' was the most significant. After a long wait a young man meets his father's murderer. He has felt the obligation to avenge his father as a heavy burden and expects to have peace of mind when the revenge has been carried out. But when this is finally done, he cannot find the peace he hoped for. Gundel seems to have wanted to write about life in Greenland in the old days; his stories were only a way of attempting to enlighten Greenlanders about their past. Yet he also took an eager part in discussing the issues of the day; he wrote about child rearing and education, for example, a rather uncommon activity for a fisherman. He could read Danish, and one of his short stories seems to have been inspired by Giuseppe Verdi's opera *Il Trovatore*.

Augo Lynge (b. 1899, d. 1959), a teacher, edited *Tarqigssût* 'The Lamp Trimmer', a periodical that served as a forum for social debates of the 1930s. He was active in politics and in various organizations, being elected first a member of the Greenland Provincial Council and then the first representative of South Greenland to the Danish parliament, where he served until he perished in a shipwreck. He wrote many of his thoughts in verse, for young people. His short novel *Ukiut 300-ngornerat* 'The 300th Anniversary' is an attempt, starting at the three hundredth anniversary of Hans Egede's landing on Greenland, to describe his own concepts of the future development of society in Greenland. This is the strong point of the book, and it is not nullified by a greatly oversimplified crime story.

Pâvia Petersen (b. 1904, d. 1943) had tuberculosis at an early age, which frustrated his need for activity, but adversity made him a patriotic writer. Probably inspired by the great Danish writer Nikolai F.S. Grundtvig, he emphasized the "soul of the nation," expressed in the cultural and linguistic unity of Greenlanders, and also directed attention to the cultural relationship between Greenlanders and the other Eskimo groups. Like his father, Jonathan Petersen, he also wrote some of the music for his own songs. It was especially in describing the nature of Greenland that he created important works. Like other Greenlandic writers, he wrote enthusiastically of the self-realization of spring and of summer travels in "the great school of nature"; but in contrast to most of the others, he also described the joys of autumn. In his play *Ikíngutigît* 'The Friends' and in a short story *Aussaq ukiordlo asangningnerdlo* 'Summer, Winter, and Love', he turned against superficial modernism, which imitated the external symbols of new conditions without realizing the obligations entailed by them. His novel *Niuvertorutsip pania* 'The Trading Post Manager's Daughter', posthumously published in 1944, featured as the title character the daughter of Danish-Greenlandic parents, who is just about to leave Greenland to go to school in Denmark when her mother dies. She must remain to keep house for her father. Although she is disappointed at having to forgo her education, in her new role she becomes the central personality of the settlement. This was a good description of Greenland around the turn of the century, in which the social immaturity of the Greenlanders results from the lack of relevant education.

Frederik Nielsen (b. 1905), from a village on Godthåbfjord, began to write songs at an early age. His early works are of varying quality, but there are some pearls among them, including his adaptation of the patriotic poem *Fänrik Ståls Sägner* 'The Tales of Ensign Stal' by the Finn J.L. Runeberg. This poem was adapted while studying in Denmark to be a teacher, probably under the influence of the national consciousness that was prevalent in the Danish-German border area. He was also influenced by Grundtvig. His 1934 novel *Tûmarse* told the story of an enterprising hunter who founds a hunting settlement. The seriousness of hunting life becomes evident in Tûmarse's heroic attempt to save a drowning kayak hunter without being able to see who it is; later he discovers that it is his own son. During a famine, Tûmarse himself dies trying to get help. In the face of the harsh conditions of life, the local catechist provides a humorous relief; for many years he has conducted religious services every Sunday, but upon retirement he goes hunting immediately to avoid the priest's speech of thanks; his principled wife refuses to flense his take.

In 1943, Nielsen published a collection of poetry, *Qilak, nuna, imaq* 'Sky, Earth, Sea', which was enlarged in 1962; it contains a miscellany ranging from stories and tales to descriptions of characters and patriotic songs. The shadow of the Second World War was evident in his sigh for peace on earth. Later he published *Arnajaraq*, the theme of which was taken from *Snow White and the Seven Dwarfs*, but the dwarfs were described as mythical Greenlandic dwarfs, which brings life and vitality to this story. As a teacher, Nielsen traveled extensively giving various lectures; a selection appeared in 1965 under the title *Oqalugiautit sarqúmîssatdlo avdlat* 'Lectures and Other Publications'. After several years' work he published in 1970 *Ilivse tássa nunagssarse* 'This Land Shall Be Yours', a family saga of the Eskimos who came from Canada and settled in Greenland. Stylistically this book has several weaknesses, but its strength lies in an imposing narrative ability, where Greenlandic legends are woven into the fabric of the story. In 1957 Nielsen became the first head of Radio Greenland.

Hans Lynge (b. 1906) at an early age came into contact with circles involved in amateur theater production in Godthåb; while attending the teachers' college there, he participated actively in performances. When he later went to Julianehåb as a catechist, he wanted to stage plays; he translated some Danish works and soon began to write plays himself, most of which take place in precolonial Greenland. Not all these plays have been published. His novel *Erssíngitsup piumassâ* 'The Demand of the Invisible', which was published in mimeographed form in 1938 and first printed in 1967, is probably the most significant character description Greenlandic literature has yet seen. It begins with a happy family, but when the children grow up they discover that the man they thought was their father is actually his murderer. According to the ancient norms, they must kill him in revenge. This drama brings the family to a crisis, in which the mother commits suicide and the youngest brother goes away to live alone, suffering qualms of conscience and material poverty. His girlfriend finds him one day, and they live together for a long time without having any intimate contact with each other. Not until the girl becomes seriously ill does the young man begin to see a connection. His senses can now observe nature, and by seeing how a watercourse cuts and flays the earth to form the difficult transition to the rich and lovely summer, he understands that his own adversities have been the path to the insight he now has into the secrets of nature. In alliance with nature he becomes a shaman and cures his girlfriend. They return to their settlement and find his brother in a state of mental confusion, also due to the dissolution of the family; the shaman helps him, too. H. Lynge penetrated into a character and reached such general insights that just by describing the course of nature he could tell about his character. At the same time he gave such a personal quality to the transformation that the young man had to undergo to win wisdom that this novel also deals with the coming of age of a new artist, a new writer, and his insight into the parallellism between the course of nature and that of human life.

Lynge's other works include *Inugpait*, which he published in 1955 after having collected legends and tales from the time around the beginning of the colonization in Upernavik District. He is also a painter and sculptor and was associated with the founding of the organization Greenlandic People's Art.

Kristen Poulsen (b. 1910, d. 1951) was also a catechist, living at many different places in Greenland and writing poems at each one. Not many of them have been published. Poulsen wrote serious poems on the Greenlandic identity that he thought should unite all Greenlanders. He often adapted tales in a bold style and had a very lively ability to express himself in verse. He could also write about serious problems in a humorous vein, with considerable effect. While working as a catechist around Cape Farewell, Poulsen met a former East Greenlandic shaman, Aattaaritaa; using him as a model, Poulsen wrote the novel *Angákoq Papik* 'Papik the Shaman', which was published posthumously. It contains much information about life in Southeast Greenland in the nineteenth century; but this master of verse wrote rather stereotyped prose.

Villads Villadsen (b. 1916), also a catechist, has taught especially in East Greenland and northern West Greenland. He has written several poems to be sung, often with a moral. In 1958 he published a novel, *Jense,* describing a confrontation between Danes and Greenlanders at Ammassalik. There are many successful passages in this book, but it is weakened by a tendency to philosophize. In 1965 Villadsen published *Nalussûnerup târnerane* 'In the Darkness of Heathenism', the first Greenlandic book written entirely in verse. The first section concerns the last meeting between the Eskimos and Norsemen, describing a regular battle. The other sections deal with murder stories from East Greenland before the population was converted to Christianity. With an impressive stylistic assurance he describes characters, their feelings and their quests; also his descriptions of nature reveal a surprisingly varied expressiveness. In one section he tells about the East Greenlanders who went to West Greenland to become Christians. Finally they could see Nunattuk, where they expected to meet the first West Greenlanders. The adversities of the journey are described indirectly, through the old woman, Saaqivaat, "whose tuft of hair resembled a bent finger" and whose face "reminded one of the tangle of sled tracks on melting ice," when she saw again the region that recalled so many memories. She became straighter, a sparkle came into her eye, and her speech revealed strength. Thus Villadsen describes the indomitability that allowed these people to survive. He wrote just as incisively when he described murderous thoughts or the foaming sea, or when he expressed a reflection: "Such power has envy, when it is allowed to grow. Still today it attacks innocent people, but in another shape."

Otto Sandgreen (b. 1914) comes from Disko Island, but as a clergyman he has lived in the outlying districts of Greenland. He is a writer of a different sort from other Greenlandic writers. One of his first books, *Nuánersorâse Avangnâta* 'You are the Joys of North Greenland', contains a number of descriptions of dog-sled trips over seldom-trafficked paths; the author's assured style contributes to its strength. Later he published a number of works from East Greenland, including a collection of myths: *Ernerminik akiniússissoq* 643

'The Man Who Avenged His Son' in 1964, and in 1967 descriptions of the last shamans in East Greenland, *Isse issimik kigutdlo kigúmik I-II* 'An Eye for an Eye and a Tooth for a Tooth I-II', dealing with a family from Sermilik that included several shamans. For these books Sandgreen received the Greenland literary prize. In 1972 he published *Piniartorssuaq* 'The Great Hunter', describing the knowledge and techniques of a "great hunter." In 1973 appeared his account of Georg Qúpersimân, a former shaman from East Greenland.

H.C. Petersen (b. 1925) had to interrupt his education because of illness but resumed it later. After several years as a teacher and educational consultant he became the principal of the folk high school at Holsteinsborg. His novel *Náparsímavik pissariaqarpoq* 'The Hospital is a Necessity' has a strength derived from personal experience. The main character, in the hospital for a long time, realizes the economic, psychological, and social blows to which he and his friends are continually subjected. Hope and disappointment alternate, but the book concludes with his recovery.

Otto Rosing (b. 1896, d. 1965) left West Greenland at the age of eight, when his father became a missionary in East Greenland. He spent the rest of his childhood in Ammassalik, where he often accompanied his father on church trips. He became a minister himself, working from 1932 to 1940 in Ammassalik but spending the rest of his career mostly in the northern part of West Greenland. First he wrote biographies of personalities in the history of Greenland: for example, Carl Julius Spindler; the linguist Samuel Kleinschmidt; and Hans Hendrik, who in the nineteenth century took part in various polar expeditions. In 1955 Rosing published *Taseralik,* a novel dealing with a locality of the same name on Nordre Strømfjord in West Greenland, where in the old days people from north and south met. In spite of a great deal of romanticizing, this is not a bad book; before writing it, the author conducted comprehensive period-historical studies. It is distinguished by a richness of detail and an accurate description of situations. Rosing's second historical novel, *Gulúnguaq,* published in 1967, describes (on the basis of Hans Egede Saabye's notes) a witchhunt in Disko Bay in the eighteenth century. This novel is less assured than *Taseralik,* and there seems to be a tendency to mix elements of the East and West Greenlandic cultures. In 1968 Rosing's descriptions of his official trips were published under the title *Tikipok* 'He Came'; the trips are related in short, easily read stories.

Among later poets can be mentioned Amos Amondsen (b. 1923), who has several songs in *Erinarssûtit,* published in 1967 by Knud Petersen. His patriotic songs especially are distinguished by stylistic strength.

Five poets—Isak Lund (b. 1889, d. 1973), Abel Kristiansen (b. 1900, d. 1975), Amandus Petrussen (b. 1927), Moses Olsen (b. 1940), and Kristian Olsen (b. 1942)—are presented in the poetry collection *Puilassoq pikialârtoq* 'The Welling Spring'. Of the five, three have been in the service of the church, and all have been teachers. Moses Olsen was a member of the Danish parliament from 1971 to 1973. These poems range over various subjects, from dedications to memories of childhood and from stories to philosophical thoughts. All the poets write about their surroundings. A surprising little gem in the midst of all the metrical formalism is *Qiúngôrtup ivngerutâ* 'The Song of One Freezing' by Petrussen, who in the form of an old Eskimo song, with genuine *parallellismus membrorum* 'thought rhyme', complains about the poor insulation of modern houses. The two Olsens differ from the other three in not making as much use of singable texts and in having less of a tendency to naturalism.

Ole Brandt (b. 1918, d. 1981), also a teacher, had two short works in *Agdlagarsiat* 'The Letter', published in 1970 under the editorship of Jens Poulsen and containing the works of several previously unknown authors. Among these, Brandt is prominent with a poem about the quick-witted bachelor Anada and a story of a young "great hunter," Qanersso, who died at a very early age after saving his settlement from the threat of famine. This subject is a traditional one from the area around Nordre Strømfjord. Brandt's 1971 novel *Qôqa* comes from the same area and deals with a "great hunter" who stops a blood feud. This book, based on a considerable amount of ethnohistorical study, contains an immense amount of information on life in West Greenland 250 years ago. It was followed by other novels in what became a family saga, *Tugdluartoq,* with vivid stories that contributed to the search for cultural identity in Greenland. In 1980 Ole Brandt received a cultural prize for his works.

During the 1970s the contemporary community and its problems have provided motifs for new books, especially by young authors. Jørgen Berglund (b. 1947), under the pseudonym of Hans Hendrik, wrote *Nutaraq* 'Immature', about a young Greenlander during his education in Denmark and after his return to Greenland, where he found that he had created a distancing between himself and his townmates. Hans Anthon Lynge (b. 1945) published *Seqajuk* 'Hopeless Person', telling about young people, their common situation, and their problems as a group that was forming a community faction—one of the few Greenlandic books translated into other languages. In 1979–1980 Lynge was editor of a cultural periodical *Alikutagssiaq* and a frequently published author. Identity problems played an important role in a work by Inoraq Olsen (b. 1939), *Taimane silarssuaq angmarmat* 'When the World Opened Itself' set among young Greenlanders being educated in Denmark, where cultural alienation is becoming more and more obvious. A similar problem is seriously described in the novel *Bussimi naapinneq* 'Encounter in a Bus', by Mâliâraq Vebæk (b. 1918), about the nightmarish situation of an uneducated Greenlander woman in Denmark, with difficult adaptation problems and a tragic end. It is a strong story, but weakened by being written as a dream.

Greenlandic literature has developed from the song to a stage of creative activity where the naturalistic novel has played a great role. But new tendencies indicate that this literature is beginning to be influenced by outside currents. In the early 1960s it seemed to be stagnant, as no new names appeared; but a feeling of powerlessness has been replaced by one of optimism. There seems to be more material than there is any possibility of publishing.

Naturally, literature demanding oral performance has played a certain role. Interaction between a reciter and his audience was a precondition for the oral tradition. The first Greenlandic literary activities were hymn composition, beginning with Rasmus Berthelsen, and the writing down of myths and contemporary tales, which was especially made possible by the foundation in 1861 of *Atuagagdliutit,* a periodical containing a large number of Greenlandic myths. Hymn composition was partially replaced by the composition of singable poems, in which descriptions of nature, patriotic feelings, and social criticism found expression. The first patriotic songs published after 1900 were abstractions of the authors' native areas, but they developed a love of Greenland in which the "spirit of the people," expressed in the community of language and culture, was formed and in which the history of the people gradually became a synonym for Greenlandic identity.

Thus interest was awakened in the prehistory of the Eskimos, and kinship with other groups of Eskimos came to play a role in emphasizing the special characteristics of the Greenlanders in the kingdom of Denmark. This was done with no desire of returning to "the good old days," nor did it lead to any militant attitude, although the role of Danes in the recent political and practical life of Greenland has been criticized, especially by younger writers.

Theater as a form of expression played a role especially in the 1920s and 1930s; it is perhaps not so strange that this took place in a relatively early period in the development of Greenlandic literature. The prehistory of Greenland has been the most common subject for theater; still lacking is drama dealing with contemporary society and its problems, except for radio plays on contemporary themes, which are often presented by Radio Greenland. Not all these radio works are known to the general public.

In contrast, novels and short stories have dealt with both the past and the present, and even to a certain extent with the future.

There is a variegated collection of literature translated into Greenlandic, including some of the classics of world literature. These translations can play a part in shaping the literature of the future, but as more and more Greenlanders can read Danish, a great deal of this influence can take place through Danish literature and translations into Danish.

Especially in the field of poetry, a definite outside influence seems to have caught on; the younger poets are more and more ignoring the strict rules of prosody and avoiding singable texts.

Sources

Greenlandic myths and legends translated into Danish were published by Rasmussen (1921–1925) in three volumes, one on East Greenlandic, one on southern West Greenlandic and one on northern West Greenlandic and Polar Eskimo. Thalbitzer (1948) provides a brief history of written Greenlandic literature from 1721 until about 1945, which contains many details even though it is not entirely reliable. Rosing (1963) published legends and narratives collected in the Ammassalik district from early times to about 1900; some of these stories were written down by East Greenlanders while others were collected by Rosing. Berthelsen (1957) briefly describes and evaluates novels and songs written in Greenlandic. Three periodicals are relevant. *Atuagagdliutit,* established in 1861, published translations, narratives, news, essays, and debates, all in Greenlandic. *Grønlandsposten,* established in 1942, was published at first in Danish. These two were unified in 1953 into a single periodical, *Atuagagdliutit/Grønlandsposten.* Between 1913 and 1957 the periodical *Avangnâmioq* published, in Greenlandic, materials such as those in *Atuagagdliutit* but especially those of northern West Greenlandic interest.

Alaska Eskimo Modernization

NORMAN A. CHANCE

The archeology, ethnography, and culture history of the Alaska Eskimo is reasonably well understood. The many scholarly studies available demonstrate how Alaska Eskimo technology was designed to meet the conditions of the far northern environment and how the nonmaterial elements of Eskimo culture—particularly the social structure and belief system—became equally well adapted to solving traditional problems of human life in the Arctic. Knowledge of this cultural patterning has been helped by the fact that for many years Eskimos lived in a world of relative stability where, given the techniques they had developed, they could adjust to their northern setting indefinitely. The changes that did occur in their technology and social life did little to disrupt this stability, and each new generation could predict with a fair degree of accuracy the course its future would follow. Furthermore, when these predictions were not realized, religious or other cultural mechanisms were used to explain this failure.

The more explicit history of Eskimo-White contact is also well documented. The arrival of Russian fur traders among the Aleuts in the late 1700s and American commercial whalers in north Alaska in the middle to late 1800s began a process of change that dramatically transformed the traditional world of the Eskimo. The introduction of rifles, iron and steel implements, drugs and medicines, and other items of western manufacture resolved many of the insecurities associated with an aboriginal subsistence economy. This, in turn, stimulated changes in other spheres of Native life. Although use of the rifle made hunting easier, it reduced somewhat the need for sharing and cooperation among kin groups, lessened the prestige of the traditional hunter, and brought into question the validity of Native religion by raising doubts about the importance of certain rituals and taboos connected with hunting. This questioning of religion affected the traditional means of social control in that the threat of supernatural punishment for deviation from approved Eskimo practices lost much of its force.

White whalers and fur traders were followed by missionaries, school teachers, nurses, doctors, construction workers, and government and military personnel, all of whom contributed to the Eskimos' growing awareness of western society and technology. However, for many years the changes brought about by this knowledge were relatively slow, resulting in gradual modifications of their traditional culture. This was largely due to the fact that the newcomers had to adapt much of their way of life to that of the Eskimo. In the early contact period, the adjustment problems were often as much the concern of the Whites as of the Eskimos.

After World War II, the situation underwent an almost complete reversal. Steadily increasing contacts with Whites led many Eskimos to adopt numerous material and social traits of western society. By the 1950s they were purchasing large quantities of western goods and services; building multi-room houses; wearing suits, dresses, and other forms of western-style clothing; participating in more modern dances, games (fig. 2), and religious and secular holiday activities. At the same time, interest in traditional activities such as hunting and fishing, games and dances, skin sewing, and skilled crafts had lessened and in some instances disappeared. Although this pattern still varies among individuals and groups at different times and places, it is quite clear that the modern Eskimo have tended to identify themselves more and more with western cultural patterns, discarding in the process much of their ethnic heritage. As Lantis (1957:126) wrote in the 1950s: "Eskimos are trying just as hard today to adapt as they did 500 or 900 years ago; the difficulty is that they are adapting not to the Arctic but to the Temperate Zone way of living. The new people with their new standards have nearly overwhelmed the Eskimos, not in numbers but in wishes and wants." Other studies also discuss the acculturative trend among Alaska Eskimos at this time (Chance 1966; Gubser 1965; Hughes 1960; Oswalt 1963; Spencer 1959; VanStone 1962a). For a comparative analysis, see Hughes (1965).

This brief introduction suggests that the process of modernization is largely an external and uncontrollable force in which the acquiring of industrial technology and accompanying western cultural patterns lead to the eventual destruction of the Eskimo way of life. By implication, the task of anthropologists and other scholars concerned with the modernizing process of Native peoples is to study their response and mode of adaptation to these events. Indeed, many studies of the "modern" Eskimo and other minority peoples focus on the importance of changing values, attitudes, techniques, and cultural practices, as well as internal social and psycho-

© Natl. Geographic Soc., Washington: 130694–T.
Fig. 1. Women of Mekoryuk, Nunivak I., in the schoolhouse making baskets for local use and for export. Photograph by Amos Burg, Sept. 1941.

logical attributes that constrain the individual or group from becoming more modernized. Unfortunately, this approach to the study of modernization not only tends to disregard historical relationships of economic and political power vis-a-vis other more technologically developed societies but also has little or nothing to say for the future. A concept that telescopes a long historical past into the phrase "traditional" and poses the future as a never-ending present has a rather limited potential as a form of scientific inquiry.

To understand the process of modernization of the Alaska Eskimo—as opposed to their culture history—it is necessary to take fully into account the historical relations *between* Native and Euro-American populations, including the economic and political factors promoting such contact, and only then analyze the ways in which Eskimos have tried to adapt to these conditions. To disregard the first area of inquiry is to lose sight of the long history of economic exploitation of the Eskimo, a factor that must be thoroughly understood if one is to comprehend their present status and future attempt at cultural survival.

History

Modernization never occurs in a social vacuum. With the industrialization of the United States, many White Americans have been able to increase their opportunities and choices. In contrast, Eskimos, Indians, and many other minorities find themselves limited not only by geographical and social isolation, lack of educational and occupational skills, racism, and economic exploitation but also by social behavior and cultural beliefs of their own that are less than effective as applied to life in a rapidly changing industrialized society. What are these interlocking historical constraints that limited Alaska Eskimo modernization and how have these constraints affected their present economic, social, and political development?

Exploitation and misery stemmed from early Eskimo-

Fig. 2. Eskimo ball games. left, North Alaska Coast girls at Point Barrow playing baseball. Photograph by Ted Spiegal, spring 1964. right, Southwest Alaska Eskimos at summer fishing camp on Nelson I. concentrating on Lappball. Photograph by James H. Barker, 1977.

White contact. Russian fur traders, who conscripted Pacific Eskimo to work for them, almost exterminated the sea otters. During Russian rule in Alaska, 1799–1867, American whalers also left their mark in northern coastal villages among Eskimos reduced by European diseases and alcohol-induced disorders.

More formal expression of American colonialist thinking came with Congress's passing of the first Organic Act of 1884, following the U.S. purchase of Alaska from the Russians in 1867. This act, in addition to establishing a government in Sitka, directed the secretary of the interior to provide proper education for all Alaska children, irrespective of race. The policy implemented by the U.S. commissioner of education and summed up in his report of 1898 was "to provide such education as to prepare the natives to take up the industries and modes of life established in the States by our white population, and by all means not try to continue the tribal life after the manner of the Indians in the western states and territories" (U.S. Bureau of Education 1898:xlix).

As with any colonial power, America's view of the Alaska Eskimo (and Indian) population was based on a set of moral assumptions, beliefs, and myths that together provided the rationale to maintain the tradition. The most predominant racial myths of the colonial period were associated with conservative forms of Christianity and "social Darwinism." Viewing the Eskimos as uncivilized heathens, Protestant, fundamentalist, Russian Orthodox, and other incoming missionaries actively worked to convert the Native population to the "superior ways" of the western world. Along with their particular form of religious teaching, they attempted to limit the use of the Native language, change cultural practices, destroy the Eskimo religion, instill guilt over existing sexual mores and other "barbarous customs," and promote new forms of behavior and thought more acceptable to their own world.

Not having to deal with problems of hostile warfare or issues of land ownership, which characterized colonization of the American West, the missionaries, supported by the mandate of the Organic Act of 1884 and the few resident government officials and traders, set out to assimilate the Eskimo as quickly as possible. Dr. Sheldon Jackson, the first Alaska superintendent for education (and ex–general secretary of the Presbyterian missions) began the slow task of establishing schools for the Natives. Through the efforts of missionaries, teachers, and other Whites, Christian conversion slowly took hold.

Becoming Christianized, the Eskimos still found themselves relegated to an inferior status through the commonly accepted myth of social Darwinism. Simply stated, this theory explained the dominance of Whites in technological, social, and cultural spheres as a result of their natural superiority. That is, human beings in-

648

Fig. 3. Entertaining with an electric guitar at Newtok in the Southwest Alaska Eskimo area. Photograph by Alex Harris, July 1977.

variably arrange themselves according to their innate abilities. Since Whites are obviously more "advanced" than Eskimos, this difference must represent a unilinear law of nature.

Additional support for this moral belief was derived from the assumption that mental abilities were superior to physical abilities. Since the Eskimo appeared to place greater emphasis on the development of physical prowess and endurance in hunting than in mental development, further evidence of their inferior status was provided, a myth still occasionally expressed in the form of compliments about "these technologically oriented people" and "their particular fitness for technical occupations" (B.F. Sater 1970:4).

Failure of the Eskimo and other Native Americans to assimilate quickly into the social and economic mainstream was often explained by reference to these assumptions of natural inferiority characteristic of the colonial period. To speed up this process, Congress enacted in 1887 the Dawes Severalty Act designed to encourage the Native to engage in farming, "thus civilizing him and ridding our nation of the burden and blight of the Indian problem." Although farming was not possible in arctic Alaska, domesticated reindeer herding (a so-called second stage of unilinear social evolution) was introduced in 1890 as an alternative in the hope that this economic activity could provide an improved livelihood for Eskimos whose original subsistence base was rapidly declining due to the excessive killing of whales, walrus, and seal. Although a significant effort, the long-term result was failure (Lantis 1950a).

Similar failures of the federal government to bring about rapid assimilation did not deter it from continuing to promote its assimilationist policies. Typical of such efforts was the following guideline laid down by the commissioner of Indian affairs in 1889, which influenced federal relations with Eskimos and Indians for many years: "Indians must be absorbed into our national life, not as Indians but as American citizens. The Indian must be 'individualized' and treated as an individual by the Government. *The Indian must conform to the White man's ways, peaceably if they will, forceably if they must.*" The Indian must be prepared for the new order through a system of compulsory education, and *the traditional society of Indian groups must be broken up* (U.S. Federal Field Committee for Development Planning in Alaska 1968:432). During the next few years schools became more prevalent in accessible coastal villages all the way to Point Barrow.

By the beginning of the twentieth century, the gold rush and the extension of the homestead laws to include Alaska brought more White miners, prospectors, and similar migrants to the north. However, no provision was made to designate or protect Native landholdings in either coastal or interior Alaska. In villages and towns inhabited by both Eskimos and Whites, increasing complaints concerning "uncivilized" Natives handicapping the progress of White school children soon brought an end to the original policy of integrated schools. By 1905 the federal government assumed responsibility for schooling of all Native children in Alaska. Not surprisingly, these schools were of inferior quality in regard to either improving traditional skills or preparing the Eskimo to qualify for more advanced vocational or professional training.

As the United States became more industrialized, greater attention was given to exploiting Alaska's rich natural resources. Eskimos' involvement in this development depended largely on their geographical proximity to the economic source of employment. Industries seeking baleen, ivory, and other sea mammal products at the turn of the century not infrequently employed Eskimos living in northern coastal villages. The commercial salmon fishing industry in the Bristol Bay area hired Eskimos from southwestern Alaska. Rising fur prices in the early 1900s also provided Eskimos with a new source of cash income that lasted until the Depression that began in 1929. However, at no time could Eskimos be assured of a secure economic base other than that derived from their traditional subsistence hunting and fishing. Rogers (1969:22) described the economic constraints placed on the Eskimo:

During the colonial period the native was treated as part of the environment in which the exploitation was undertaken. If they could be turned to a use in serving the purpose of getting the resource out as easily and cheaply as possible, they might be enslaved (as with the Aleut) or re-

top, © Natl. Geographic Soc., Washington.

Fig. 4. Transportation. top, Mail delivery by airplane, received by kayakers from Mekoryuk, Nunivak I. Photograph by Amos Burg, Sept. 1941. bottom, Cyril Merculief driving motor boat. The village of St. George, Pribilof Islands, is in the background. Photograph by Andy Klamser, June 1979.

cruited. . .as a local work force in the harvest and processing of marine resources. If not, they were ruthlessly pushed aside while their traditional resources were exploited to the point of extinction by seasonally imported work forces (as was the case with the coastal Eskimo). The impact was on the whole destructive to traditional ways and to the native people themselves, and their economic participation was marginal at best. Whether they participated or not, their very survival required adaptation of their traditional ways to the new conditions imposed by the altered environment.

World War II and its aftermath brought profound changes to Alaska. With the influx of military personnel and their dependents, service industry employees, and postwar settlers, for the first time Alaska's non-Native population assumed numerical dominance. Alaska's strategic location in the rapidly expanding Cold War brought about a fundamental shift in the economic base from natural resource exploitation to military preparedness. Construction of facilities for defense, transportation, education, and health and expansion of related services and trade greatly increased job opportunities for all Alaskans including Eskimos.

However, as in the past, these boom periods were invariably followed by reduced government expenditures with attendant rise in unemployment. The Eskimos who moved from their small villages to new construction centers, being the last hired and first fired, suffered particularly during the "bust" segment of the cycle. They did receive far better health care than previously, and educational opportunities continued to expand. Increased jobs, educational experience, and geographical mobility assisted significantly in expanding the Eskimos' knowledge of White Alaska and the outside world.

Alaska statehood in 1959 stimulated a new consciousness in and about the Native population. The new government took steps to incorporate Eskimo (and Indian) schools into the state system. High school training became somewhat more easily available following increased funding and construction of facilities. University scholarships were accessible to the few who could qualify. A temporary return to the old termination policy by the Bureau of Indian Affairs in the 1950s had relatively little impact on the Alaska Eskimo, who had no reservation land to terminate.

Economic Development

In the early 1960s, when the defense economy had begun to level off and its employment and income-producing capacity declined, the federal and state governments again increased their efforts to improve the economic and social conditions of Alaska Eskimos, Aleuts, and Indians. Expansion of manpower training, area economic development programs, health-care facilities, and community-action projects were only some of the innovative efforts undertaken at that time. Nevertheless, initial results were not encouraging.

In their detailed report, the U.S. Federal Field Committee for Development Planning in Alaska (1968:3) concluded that: "A great contrast exists today between the high income, moderate standard of living, and existence of reasonable opportunity of most Alaskans and the appallingly low income and standard of living, and the virtual absence of opportunity for most Eskimos, Indians, and Aleuts of Alaska." Of even greater long-range significance was their statement concerning the impact of economic development on the Eskimo and other northern minorities: "The economic position of Alaska Natives, and of the communities in which they live, is steadily falling further behind statewide averages" (ibid.:528).

What factors account for this condition?

650   The 1960 U.S. census report placed the number of

Alaska Natives at approximately 53,000, of which 52 percent were Eskimo and 14 percent Aleut. Over 70 percent of this population lived in 178 villages or rural towns that were predominantly native in composition. Half of these were communities of 155 people or less. Although there was some migration to more urban centers, 80 percent of these villages grew in size between 1950 and 1967 and over half grew more rapidly than the rate of net annual increase. The expectation by some that Eskimo villages would decline and disappear in the 1960s did not materialize. Clearly, the large majority of Eskimos continued to live in village communities far removed from areas of rapid economic growth (fig. 5).

It would be incorrect to assume that those Eskimos who migrated from isolated areas, particularly the southwest and northwest, to the growth centers of interior and south-central Alaska could expect greatly improved economic and social conditions. On the contrary, an economic study by Rogers (1969:26) drawing on statistics from the 1960 census concluded that "the relative well-being of the native people in all of these regions does not vary significantly."

Just how appalling the economic situation was for both rural and urban Eskimos and other natives in the mid-1960s was described by an analyst for the Federal Field Committee:

> Among Alaska Natives generally, more persons are unemployed or are seasonally employed than have permanent jobs. More than half of the work force is jobless most of the year; for them, food gathering activities provide basic subsistence. Only one-fourth of the work force has continuing employment. . . . 50 to 60 percent are jobless in March and September. . . . At these times only half of those employed have permanent jobs. In the summers, when no

U. of Alaska, Arctic Environmental Information and Data Center, Anchorage.
Fig. 5. Nuiqsut, an old North Alaska Coast Eskimo village site in the Colville River delta, as resettled with frame houses after village corporations were instituted. Photograph by J.C. LaBelle, Aug. 1974.

Fig. 6. A retired St. Lawrence Island Eskimo boat captain, who had led many successful whale hunts, near barrels of stove oil that has replaced sea mammal oil for heating and lighting. Photograph by Charles C. Hughes, 1955.

Indian Arts and Crafts Board, Washington: W–65.99.7.
Fig. 7. *Sea Birds*, a woodcut printed in black. Size 12.3 by 13.0 cm. Made by James Okpealuk, Eskimo, 1965.

estimates are compiled, joblessness among Natives across the state may drop to 20 or 25 percent.

In urban areas, Natives work at a variety of permanent and temporary jobs. Some few are self-employed, but the larger number are employees. While some are carpenters, electricians, and equipment operators, more are unskilled workers or construction laborers. . . . In urban areas, Native unemployment appears to be higher than among non-Natives. Lacking education and marketable skills, the villager is not usually equipped to compete in the job market.

Year-round jobs in most villages are few. Typically the opportunities are limited to positions such as school maintenance man, postmaster, airline station agent, village store manager, and possibly school cook or teacher aide. In these places, other adults gain income through the sale of furs, fish, or arts and crafts; find seasonal employment away from the villages as firefighters, cannery workers, or construction laborers; depend upon welfare payments, make their National Guard income stretch mightily; or, as is usually the case, (1) provide for the bulk of their food supply by fishing, hunting, trapping, and other activities of food gathering; and (2) rely upon a combination of means to obtain the cash needed for fuel, some food staples, and for tools and supplies necessary to the harvest of fish and wildlife (Arnold 1968:12–13).

Other research studies undertaken at the same time (Sessions 1967; U.S. Public Health Service. Division of Indian Health 1966) come to the similar conclusion that poverty implied for urban and rural Eskimos in the 1960 census continued through the decade while income levels for White Alaskans grew steadily (Sullivan 1969).

During the late 1960s and early 1970s governmental concern over this widening economic gap was reflected in numerous research studies and reports. Anticipating significant economic development from power projects, oil and gas exploration, timber, and other natural resources, the U.S. Department of the Interior (1967:25–

26) foresaw that future employment opportunities would enable Natives "to make the transition from their present subsistence existence to a more self-supporting one with adequate income and employment." Instead of stressing "assimilation," emphasis was placed on "equal opportunity," "equal standards of living," and "equal participation in Alaskan growth and development."

Implicit in most of these statements was the judgment that equal opportunity was the crucial ingredient to Eskimo (and Indian) development. What has since become clear is that such policies usually meant that *if* the Eskimos have equal qualifications, they should have the same opportunity for advancement. Unfortunately, this view almost totally disregarded the earlier history of disadvantageous relationships between Eskimos and White Alaskans (cf. Chance 1970).

This concept of equality carried another hidden assumption as well. It subtly eroded the principle of compensation for past injustices by questioning the "unequal" allocation of funds to Eskimo and other Native groups that were economically deprived. In response, critics of government policies began promoting the principle that given the past history of economic and social exploitation, a very strong case could be made for preferential rather than equal treatment of Eskimos in job opportunities and social and cultural development programs. Where past events provided Eskimos with less than equal qualifications, they deserved a better than equal opportunity.

Finally, the concept of equal opportunity raised the issue of the Eskimos' right to develop their distinct culture as well as participate in the economic life of Alaska. Although full access into the dominant Alaska society was not an option available to most Eskimos, *651*

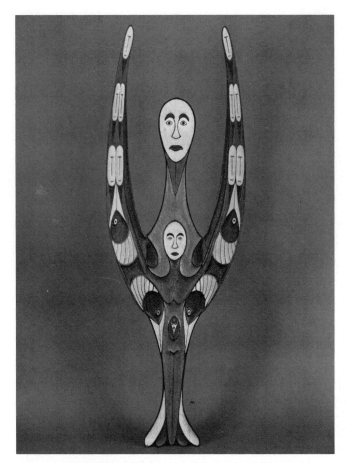

Indian Arts and Crafts Board, Washington: B–75.5.2.

Fig. 8. *Loon Mother*, polychromed red cedar sculpture. Height 218.5 cm. Made by John Hoover, an Aleut, 1974.

if it were, the implication was still that the industrial-urban sector of American society had all the advantages and these should be shared with the Eskimo. This subtle form of White paternalism was not infrequently a hidden feature of "full participation" policy, a paternalism that continued to devalue the present and future contributions of Eskimo culture to the rest of American society. In so doing, negative stereotyping and Eskimo feelings of self-disparagement were further encouraged.

This attitude was clearly reflected in a letter written by an Eskimo from the northwestern part of Alaska to his state legislator expressing deep concern over the economic future of the people of his village:

> Again spring is here with us, and work or jobs are pretty dim in our area. Last year, all the men were without work all summer long. My total earnings for 1967 were less than $300. and that worries a man with a family of eight. We hate to get welfare but it is our only solution. It is tough without work and hunting only does not meet our needs. Sometimes we have bad luck even tho we hunt. We have to worry what are next meal will be.
>
> But I really thank BIA office in Nome for giving us help when help is most needed. Even tho we hate to ask for help, our children give us courage to write and ask for help. . . .

> There's over 25 men in our village and not even one has work prospects. Only three men have steady jobs in our village—that's the store manager, postmaster, and BIA janitor, plus one BIA cook. We need help to get work. I know labor market is scarce. But we should get training for older men without high school education (Arnold 1969:18).

The problems posed by this Eskimo were characteristic of many older men in small rural villages.

Possible solutions were viewed as closely tied to the potential contained in exploiting Alaska's natural resources. As the magnitude of Alaska's oil and gas resources became known to the nation, projections of future economic growth appeared highly encouraging, but not in terms of Eskimo participation. According to the U.S. Federal Field Committee for Development Planning in Alaska (1968:521): "The leading growth industry—oil and gas—is one of the most capital intensive and technology intensive of all commodity-producing industries and employs almost no unskilled or semi-skilled labor." Although Alaska's economic growth would create new jobs at minimum entry levels, the report went on to state that these new positions "may well be more than offset by the disappearance of unskilled and semi-skilled jobs in declining industries or trades, and resulting from automation, modernization, and upgrading of work in general. Under these circumstances, programs to place additional Natives in minimum-entry jobs may succeed only to the extent they *redistribute* unemployment rather than alleviate it" (ibid.:521). The results of this study made it very clear that the geographical mobility of the Eskimo to new growth centers was not sufficient to insure their active involvement in Alaska's economic development. To fit the occupational needs of a rapidly modernizing state, the Eskimo and other Native groups had to have at least the equivalent of a high school education.

Indian Arts and Crafts Board, Washington: W–65.56.

Fig. 9. *Wood-skin Houses, King Island*, an etching printed in black. Size 25.2 by 35.5 cm; made by Bernard T. Katexac, the first Eskimo to be given a Bureau of Indian Affairs art scholarship, used at the University of Alaska (Ray 1967b: 88–89), 1965.

acceptable in the general sense when referring to the preschool, primary, elementary, secondary and adult education needs of our people. . . (Anonymous 1970).

From 1884 on, governmental efforts to provide the Eskimo with good education had failed. Participation in Alaska's economic future appeared minimal at best. Political organization seemed the best way to bring about changes that had been promised but had never materialized.

Political Consciousness

The one most dramatic event that set in motion the political development of Eskimos and other Natives was the achieving of Alaska statehood in 1959. The Statehood Act specified that the state should select approximately 104 million acres within 25 years. Since Congress had never determined conclusively the status of Native land rights, this act posed a severe threat of land expropriation, countering the Organic Act of 1884, which stipulated that Natives would not be disturbed in the use or occupancy of their land and that the determination of their title would be reserved to Congress.

In October 1966 eight regional Native associations that had formed to protect land rights combined to establish the Alaska Federation of Natives (AFN) (see Lantis 1973). By April 1967 the AFN had submitted title claims to 370 million of Alaska's 375 million acres. Almost equally momentous was the announcement in 1968 of the major Prudhoe Bay petroleum discoveries and the North Slope oil rush and the 900-million-dollar sale of land leases by the state to oil corporations that followed in September 1969 (Rogers 1970:5).

In response to these events the federal government halted disposal of Alaska public lands that were subject to Native claims until the U.S. Congress defined what the rights were and the process of settlement. For the first time in Alaska, Eskimos, Aleuts, and Indians found themselves in a position of real political strength. Equally important, a new generation of Native leaders, well educated and aggressive, began to assume positions of responsibility in Native-based and controlled organizations.

Nevertheless, the problems they faced were immense. Competing regional interest groups, separate languages, and historical distrust among Eskimos, Indians, and Aleuts threatened internal communication and decision making within the AFN. Contacts among native villages and towns, regional associations, and the AFN had to be increased and strengthened. Aiding in this communication was the Native newspaper *Tundra Times,* whose increased circulation enabled each village in the state to receive copies. The most serious problem was the lack of political understanding of much of the Native population.

Sensitive to the needs of its varied constituency, the AFN leaders established a position on land claims that contained the following elements: (1) enough land to sustain a subsistence economy for those Native Americans who choose to retain their traditional lifeways, (2) adequate compensation for lands taken in the past, (3) a just monetary settlement for extinguishment of Indian title to the remaining land, including a perpetual royalty interest in the mineral resources of that land, and (4) native control over the money and the land they receive (Wolf 1969:7). After several years of negotiation, the Alaska Native Claims Settlement Act was passed and signed into law on December 18, 1971. In addition to settling the dispute over who owned Alaska land,

right, *Tundra Times,* Anchorage, Alaska.
Fig. 13. left, William L. Hensley from Kotzebue Sound, President of the NANA Regional Corp., dancing at the dedication ceremony of the NANA oil rig. Photograph by Lael Morgan, Aug. 1980. right, Howard Rock (b. 1911, d. 1976), from the North Alaska Coast area, editor of the influential newspaper *Tundra Times* from its first issue, Oct. 1, 1962, through the issue for April 21, 1976. Photograph by Sue Gamache.

this act gave the Eskimos, Indians, and Aleuts 962.5 million dollars and 44 million acres, at which time the natives relinquished all claims to the remaining acreage of Alaska. The problems of implementing this act are tasks that continue to face Eskimo and other Native leadership.

In a blunt statement to White Alaskans, the vice-president of the AFN summarized the history and potential of the Alaska Native:

> For the most part you have easily gotten used to the Alaska Native, because he has needed your help and your assistance, and a fairly large, complex "industry" has emerged based on his needs. The relationship between one who gives and one who receives when it has been institutionalized is very easy to accept, to adjust to and forget. As long as the arrangement is accepted or tolerated, there is nothing that is disconcerting in this relationship. But what happens as the Alaska Native assumes his rightful place as an equal partner in the economic, political and other power structures of this state? What happens when instead of coming in and asking for help, he comes in by right and asserts his right to share equally in the opportunities and benefits of economic and social development? (Borbridge 1970:202).

The economic and social potential contained in the Alaska Native Claims Settlement Act can assist greatly in upgrading the quality of life of the Native population. But the villages still contain many Eskimos, Aleuts, and Indians whose cash income is minimal and whose educational opportunities are insufficient to ensure jobs for those wishing to migrate to more economically viable towns and cities. Although subsistence hunting and fishing are still available, few younger people have the interest or skills to engage in such activity. Disparagement of more traditional Eskimo, Aleut, and Indian ways by Native youth continues to broaden the generational gap with its resulting community conflict and dislocation. Some young people resolve the problem by moving from their small isolated villages to larger towns and cities. Here, problems of alienation, social control, insecurity, and economic discrimination manifest themselves in delinquency and emotional disorders. It is hardly surprising that mental illness is the key health problem among Alaska Natives in this period of westernization (Wilson 1969).

Resentment growing out of tensions found in villages, towns, and cities is still largely focused inward in keeping with traditional Eskimo (and Indian) cultural patterning. It is not likely to remain that way in the future as the Alaska Natives come to have a clearer understanding of the exploitation to which they have been historically exposed. Only by revising White assumptions about economic, social, and political development will the Eskimo, Indian, and Aleut be able to participate fully in the process of building modern Alaska.

656

The Land Claims Era in Alaska

ERNEST S. BURCH, JR.

The land claims era was formally inaugurated on December 18, 1971, with the passage of the Alaska Native Claims Settlement Act (ANCSA). Land ownership and use were major issues leading to ANCSA's passage, and they have been major issues ever since. But they have not been the only ones. Education, employment, and political involvement have remained on the agenda of active Native concerns. But, in contrast to the general Native subordination that characterized the early part of the modernization period, the land claims era has been distinguished by a striking re-assertion of Native control over Native affairs, a resurgence of pride in being Native, and an increasingly aggressive involvement by Natives in the general economic, political, and social life of the state. ANCSA thus marked a major turning point in the social history of Alaska's Native peoples.

With the sole (and major) exception of the Pribilof Aleuts (D.K. Jones 1980), the federal government did not interfere in the life of Native people in Alaska nearly so much as it had historically in the continental United States (Jenness 1962; Lantis 1966; Rogers 1968, 1971). There were few reservations, and most of those that did exist were established with the reasonably voluntary agreement of the Natives involved and were situated on their traditional homelands. Natives in most areas felt free to live wherever they wished and to hunt and fish both wherever and whenever they desired. Except in the vicinity of a few major towns and cities, there was relatively little conflict over land between Natives and non-Natives.

The Alaska Statehood Act, which was passed on July 7, 1958, changed all this. According to the act, the state disclaimed any right to land and property held by Alaska Natives or held in trust for them by the United States. However, the act also granted the State the right to select more than 104 million acres (out of a total of over 362 million acres) from the public domain that were "vacant, unappropriated or unreserved" at the time of their selection. The state proceeded to select much of the best land in the state, including a great deal that the Natives considered to be theirs. As oil and mineral exploration expanded during the 1960s, many individuals, mining and oil companies, and various agencies of both the state and federal governments joined the fray, each claiming some right to large sections of

real estate. By 1975 some 20 percent more Alaska land had been claimed than actually existed (Brewer 1975:264).

Disputes over land ownership were not the only issues facing the Natives in the early 1960s. Another was Project Chariot, a plan by the Atomic Energy Commission to create a harbor on the northwest Alaska coast through a series of nuclear explosions. A similar issue was the Rampart Dam Project, whereby the U.S. Army Corps of Engineers would have dammed the Yukon River and flooded an immense area in the center of the state. The final major source of controversy was the sudden enforcement in 1961 of the Migratory Waterfowl Treaty with Canada and Mexico. All these schemes were developed without prior consultation with or notice to the people involved, most of whom happened to be Natives.

With initial funding and guidance from a number of non-Natives who were equally distressed by these examples of governmental high-handedness, the Natives began to organize to defend their interests (Lantis 1973). During the 1960s the original local Native organizations grew into regional organizations. In October 1966 eight of the regional organizations banded together to form the Alaska Federation of Natives (AFN) (Ervin 1976; Rogers 1968a). The AFN subsequently carried out most of the lobbying and formal negotiations leading to the passage of ANCSA (M.C. Berry 1975; Hanrahan and Gruenstein 1977; G. Martin 1975).

Alaska Native Claims Settlement Act of 1971

ANCSA provided that 44 million acres of land be made available for selection by Alaska Natives, and that $962.5 million in cash be granted to the Natives over an 11-year period (Arnold et al. 1978). In return, the Natives agreed to the extinguishment of all claims of aboriginal right. Both the land and the cash were to be conveyed to the people through 13 regional corporations and more than 200 village corporations, all of which were created by the act itself.

ANCSA encompassed the entire territory of Alaska, and nearly all the Native groups living within it. It did not contain specific provisions dealing directly with education, local or regional government, or health and welfare services. However, it did set forth a number of

657

requirements concerning land distribution, the most important of which were those concerning easements (American Indian Policy Review Commission 1976:30–31; N. Harvey 1978) and the so-called National Interest Lands (*Alaska Geographic* 1981; *Tundra Times* 1981).

Native Regions

ANCSA divided Alaska into 12 Native regions each of which constitutes the domain from which one regional corporation could select land and from which it would recruit its shareholders (fig. 1).

Eight of the 12 regions are occupied primarily by Aleut or Eskimo-speaking people (table 1). Some Inupiaq Eskimo speakers also live in the primarily Athapaskan Indian Doyon Region, in the villages of Beaver, Evansville, Allakaket, and Hughes (Burch 1979a:138ff.). Other people of Eskimo and Aleut descent residing outside Alaska are affiliated with the "thirteenth Region," which has no geographic base or land entitlement.

The boundaries of the Native regions created under ANCSA were drawn to make them conform reasonably closely with areas represented by regional associations during the negotiations leading to the act's passage. The legislatively mandated districts thus conform to spontaneously created units developed over at least a 10-year period. The units, in turn, reflected a social history that was relatively unified for some decades before that. The fit with still earlier ethnic domains is much looser, although, within the Eskimo-Aleut area, the Arctic Slope, NANA, Aleut, Koniag, and Chugach Regions do reflect broad cultural and linguistic groupings of considerable antiquity.

Native Corporations

The land and most of the cash provided under ANCSA were to be granted to or administered by the regional corporations, the village corporations, and a small special category of corporations involving Natives living in urban areas (Arnold et al. 1978:163 ff.). Within the Eskimo-Aleut area, three villages—Gambell and Savoonga, on Saint Lawrence Island, and Elim, all within the Bering Straits Region—opted to gain title to previously existing reservation lands rather than participate in the ANCSA benefits (Morgan 1975). Mergers of regional and village corporations have been undertaken in the NANA and Koniag Regions.

The regional corporations were given four primary responsibilities. First, they were to receive all cash payments made under the act and to invest or distribute the money to the village corporations and individuals. Second, they were to become owners of the surface estate of some of the land, and owners of the subsurface estate of all the land selected under ANCSA. Third, they were to supervise the creation of the village corporations and generally to aid the village corporations in making land selections and in operating businesses or other ventures. Finally, they were to operate one or more businesses themselves, for a profit. The situation of the regional corporations in the Aleut and Eskimo part of Alaska as of 1980 is summarized in table 2.

The village corporations were created as smaller versions of the regional corporations. Like them, they were to receive cash and land and to make further disbursements and conveyances to individuals. In contrast to the regional corporations, they could organize for either profit or nonprofit purposes.

The Native regions differ considerably from one an-

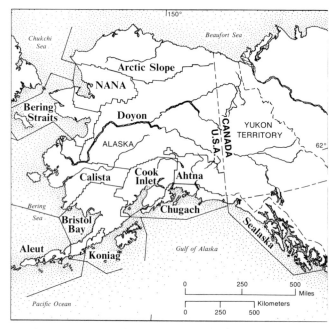

Fig. 1. Native regions created by the Alaska Native Claims Settlement Act of 1971.

Table 1. Aleut and Eskimo Regions Created by ANCSA

Region	Major Language Groups (Krauss 1980)	Area in Acres
Aleut	Aleut	7.1 million
Arctic Slope	Inupiaq	54.1 million
Bering Straits	Inupiaq, Central Yupik, Siberian Yupik	14.8 million
Bristol Bay	Central Yupik, some Pacific Yupik (and some Tanaina Athapaskan)	26.0 million
Calista	Central Yupik (with some Tanaina Athapaskan)	35.8 million
Chugach	Pacific Yupik	9.1 million
NANA	Inupiaq	23.1 million
Koniag	Pacific Yupik	4.6 million

other in their geographic extent and in the size of their Native population. They also differ in their apparent potential for resource development. All these factors were taken into consideration by the framers of ANCSA, who allocated land and cash entitlements among the corporations in different proportions in an effort to spread the benefits of the settlement as evenly as possible among all the individuals and groups involved. The same objective led to provision (7i), which stated that 70 percent of "all revenues received by each regional corporation from the timber resources and subsurface estate patented to it" shall be divided annually among all of the regional corporations "according to the number of Natives enrolled in each." This provision resulted in more than a decade of litigation and negotiation, ending in a complex agreement signed by the regional corporations on June 29, 1982.

The regional and village corporations entered into a remarkable variety of business enterprises (Alaska Native Foundation 1977; *Anchorage Daily News* 1981:30–37; *Northland News* 1981:15 ff.). Oil field services, mining operations, hotels, shipping companies, reindeer herds, and stock and bond portfolios are just a few of the ways they have invested their money. Their success has been equally varied. For example, Bering Straits Regional Corporation nearly folded in the late 1970s, while neighboring NANA Regional Corporation has made a modest but steady profit for several years.

Enrollment

ANCSA specified that an "Alaska Native" was any U.S. citizen who is at least one-fourth degree of Alaska Indian, Eskimo, or Aleut blood, or who, in the absence of hard evidence on the matter, was generally regarded as "Native" by individuals for whom the relevant data were available. In order to be eligible for ANCSA ben-

efits, however, a Native also had to be living on December 18, 1971, the date that the legislation was passed. People who did not meet both criteria, or who did but who failed to enroll with the secretary of the interior, were not entitled to benefits.

Natives were to enroll by village and by region. As soon as their registration had been approved by the secretary of the interior, they automatically became shareholders in the relevant village and regional corporations. Their stock cannot be bought or sold until January 1, 1992. (The courts have determined that it can be inherited, however.) At that point the old stock will be canceled, and new stock, which will not be subject to any special transfer restrictions, will be issued.

Land Selection

Land ownership was the most fundamental issue in the land claims movement. It was also the one matter supposedly settled by ANCSA. But 10 years after ANCSA's passage a very large number of land issues remained unresolved. Ownership patents had been granted for less than 8 percent of the land included in the settlement. Another 41 percent had reached the "interim conveyance" stage, at which point Native corporations had control of the land, but final ownership had not been transferred (*Northland News* 1981:14). The remaining 51 percent still had to be dealt with.

The Cash Settlement

ANCSA provided that nearly one billion dollars be paid to Alaska Natives in compensation for land lost. Most of the money was to go to the regional and village corporations to be invested by them for the benefit of their shareholders. Ten percent was to be paid by the corporations directly to individuals, of whom there were

Table 2. Aleut and Eskimo Regional Corporations, 1980

Corporation	Land Entitlement (Acres)	Cash Entitlement (In Millions)	Number of Shareholders	Number of Villages	Total Assets (Millions)	Net Worth (In Millions)
The Aleut Corporation	1.25 million subsurface, 52,000 surface	$ 40.1	3,249	14	$19.0	$13.7
Arctic Slope Regional Corporation	4.6 million	46.5	3,738	8	81.3	24.3
Bering Straits Native Corporation	2.9 million	79.5	6,333	20	32.1	4.6
Bristol Bay Native Corporation	2.2 million surface, 2.9 million subsurface	67.0	5,400	29	55.5	43.1
Calista Corporation	5.9 million	165.0	13,308	56	98.3	57.8
Chugach Natives, Inc.	1 million	24.0	1,912	5	14.1	8.8
Koniag, Inc.	1 million	41.3	3,344	9	32.4	15.5
NANA Regional Corporation	2.3 million	59.9	4,828	11	66.8	44.0

SOURCES: *Anchorage Daily News* 1981:32; *Alaska Native News* 1982:11.

nearly 77,000 by the time enrollment was completed (Arnold et al. 1978:151–152, 209 ff.; *Northland News* 1981:14).

The cash provisions of ANCSA proved nearly as difficult to implement as other aspects of the act (Burch 1979c:19–21), but the payments were all distributed by November 1981. Individual shares ranged from about $300 to $5,000, the precise amount depending on a formula that took various factors, such as the amount of land entitlement, into account. People who received more land tended to get less money, and vice versa, although other factors also entered into the calculation. The balance of the money went to the Native corporations, where it served as the major source of capital.

Effects of the Act

No single legislative act could have dealt satisfactorily with the huge number and variety of problems related in one way or another to land claims in Alaska, and ANCSA seems to have created as many difficulties as it solved (*Alaska Native News* 1982; Lazarus and West 1976; Morgan 1977). Nevertheless, it did establish a framework within which interested parties could assert specific claims in a structured manner. Equally important, Congress demonstrated a willingness to postpone certain important deadlines set forth in ANCSA when events proved them beyond reasonable chance of attainment. Congress also has been flexible enough to amend the act in areas where developments showed the original version to be flawed. ANCSA is thus not just a piece of legislation, but a dynamic phenomenon involving several acts of Congress, a seemingly endless series of negotiations, contractual agreements, and court settlements, and a broad array of economic enterprises, political campaigns, and cultural programs.

1991 will be a threshold year for Alaska Natives because it will be the last in which their shares in regional and village corporations are not transferable. After that the stock becomes just like that of any other corporation, subject to sale and to the vagaries of the marketplace. The possibility exists that non-Natives will buy out at least the profitable Native corporations, leaving the Natives with only the unprofitable ones, and perhaps with nothing at all. By that time there also will be an entire generation of Natives—those born after December 18, 1971—who do not hold shares in a Native corporation.

Native leaders are acutely aware of the problem and have taken steps to deal with it (Hensley 1981). They are concentrating on two main areas—development of new Native leadership, and creation of a heightened sense of cultural awareness and ethnic identity. Their assumption is that only if being Native becomes a quality exceeding material gain in importance will Alaska Natives long survive the stock crisis of 1991.

U.S. Dept. of Interior, Indian Arts and Crafts Board, Washington: W–73.29.3. Fig. 2. *Land Claims Dance*, teak sculpture on mahogany base. Height 40.6 cm. Made by Richard Seeganna, King I., Alaska, 1973.

Other Issues

ANCSA, and the general Native rights movement that helped produce it, have permeated every aspect of Native life in Alaska. Other changes that might have come about independently have come to be related to it in one way or another.

Subsistence

Subsistence was the single most emotional issue in the state of Alaska in the early 1980s. The subsistence issue is not a single problem but several different ones unified only in that they all deal in some way with hunting and fishing (*Anchorage Daily News* 1981:39–44; *Tundra Times* 1978, 1981). One subsistence issue is whether to develop Alaska lands in preference to leaving them in their still reasonably pristine state. A second, and the most emotional one, concerns who is to be permitted to hunt and fish in a state whose population has grown too large for everyone to do it, particularly if the fish and game populations should decline.

A third subsistence issue concerns who should control hunting and fishing in the first place: the federal government, the state government, or regionally based "user" groups.

Education

In 1973 the state-operated school system was in the process of taking over a large number of Bureau of Indian Affairs schools from the federal government.

Subsequently the state system was replaced by 21 Regional Educational Attendance Area school districts (REAAs), each of which operates under a locally elected board (Darnell 1979; Getches 1976, 1977). In areas where the local population is Native, this transfer effectively placed education under Native control. Of the 21 REAAs, six had largely Eskimo or Aleut populations. A separate school system, operated by the North Slope Borough, is also under largely Eskimo control. Each of these school systems had a number of difficulties getting started.

Village Life

Village studies have not been carried out, or at least not been published, during the land claims era. However, a number of analyses sponsored by the Department of the Interior Bureau of Land Management in anticipation of outer continental shelf oil lease sales present comprehensive and useful information on village life. Fienup-Riordan (1982) has written on the Central Yupik area, Ellanna (1980) on the Bering Strait–northern Bering Sea area, Davis (1979b) on Kodiak Island, and Worl Associates (1978) on most of the Arctic Slope. Other useful sources on village Alaska include the *Anchorage Daily News* (1965, 1981), Kruse, Kleinfeld, and Travis (1982), and Morgan (1974, 1974a).

Physically, most villages were transformed between 1960 and 1980. A series of housing programs sponsored by the federal and state governments, and in many areas by Native regional corporations, replaced virtually all the old houses with new, much larger dwellings of more or less standardized construction. Imposing, locally controlled schools, kindergarten through grade 12, replaced the small Bureau of Indian Affairs schools that ended with eighth grade. The old village stores were supplanted by virtual supermarkets. Electricity, telephone service, and television were made available in every village; only the very largest towns had any of these services in 1960. Transportation changed to plane, snowmobile, and all-terrain-vehicle instead of dog team and boat.

The extent to which Eskimo and Aleut villages changed culturally and socially during the same period is less clear. There seems to be considerable variation in this respect, not only between one Native region and another but also among the several villages found within each region. The one really significant and pervasive change has been the extent to which Natives have taken over control of their own affairs at the regional and village levels (McBeath and Morehouse 1980).

661

Contemporary Canadian Inuit

FRANK G. VALLEE, DEREK G. SMITH, AND JOSEPH D. COOPER

This chapter describes changes in the personal and social situations of the Inuit during the period since 1960 (emphasizing events and trends of the 1970s) in the Canadian Arctic within the Northwest Territories.

Modernization, Invasion, and Incorporation

Modernization is a general term for the process of cultural and socioeconomic changes that accompany industrialization. Canada is proceeding rapidly toward advanced industrialization, and the effects are felt even in its remotest hinterlands. Groups that were previously autonomous or that had only tenuous external connections have come to be a part of the surrounding society, thereby losing much of their autonomy. Some writers refer to the Inuit as being drawn into ever-widening continental orbits; some depict them as being caught in the embrace of the dominant society; some favor the imagery of eating, referring to Inuit individuals and groups as being swallowed by the all-absorbing mass society. These are metaphors for invasion and incorporation; among the results are conflict, succession, accommodation, and incorporation. The spread of the Canadian economy, culture, and polity is an invasion that began only in the nineteenth century in most parts of the Arctic, one outcome of which is the on-going incorporation of Inuit into the society called Canada. Invasion is "an ecological process involving the movement of one type of population or land [and resource] use into an area already occupied by or subject to a different type of population or land use" (Theodorson and Theodorson 1969:215).

External forces and people have expanded into Arctic regions for reasons originating outside the Arctic; the Inuit did not decide to set up military installations, oil rigs, hospitals, pipelines, and the like. But because they did not invite it does not mean that the Inuit have resisted this expansion. Where resistance has occurred it has not been to modernization as such, but to the excesses of technological change, such as the disruption of ecosystems by oil exploration; or to societal changes, such as the disruption of interpersonal relations by bureaucratic decisions to move people for educational, health, or other purposes; or to planning without due regard to native rights and opinions (Usher 1970–1971,

3:73). Few of the manifestations of resentment can be construed as signs of a counter-modernization movement. Evidence from the many studies of the contemporary scene point to a continuing Inuit effort to adapt in a positive way to the sweeping changes in their environment (for example, Honigmann and Honigmann 1970; J.S. Matthiasson 1977; Paine 1977; Rowley 1972).

Incorporation is not the same as assimilation. The latter term implies that a category of people is absorbed as individuals into another society through their links into personal networks through marriage, work, religion, politics; the category is in a sense digested. But where a category of people maintains some cultural and social distinctiveness but at the same time is part of a larger collectivity whose governance they are under, they may be regarded as incorporated, but not digested. A people may be incorporated without achieving either equality of condition or opportunity or, indeed, without identifying with the larger collectivity to any significant extent. The evidence is that the Inuit are resolved not only to persist but also to develop as a distinctive collectivity, a kind of nationality group within Canada.

Population Characteristics and Trends

The Inuit provide a classic example of the demographic transition that accompanies modernization among preindustrial peoples: from a slow-growing or zero-growth population in which a high birth rate is canceled out by a high death rate, to one in which a sharp decline in the death rate results in a population explosion. Freeman (1971a) documents this transition for the East Arctic and provides a provocative discussion of its consequences.

The population of the Northwest Territories has increased rapidly since 1951 due to both high rates of natural increase among Inuit and Indians and vastly increased immigration of Euro-Canadians. While the number of Inuit has risen in that period, they declined as a proportion of the total population (table 1).

Table 2 summarizes some of the main Inuit population characteristics for the 1960s and 1970s. The rate of natural increase is very high, almost four times the national rate in 1969; birth and death rates are much above the national average. While death rates decreased

Table 1. Population of the Northwest Territories, 1951–1980

Year	Total	Indian and Inuit		Inuit		Others	
1951	16,004	10,860	67.8%	6,500	40.6%	5,144	32.2%
1961	22,998	13,233	57.5	8,070	35.0	9,765	42.5
1971	34,810	18,580	53.4	11,400	32.7	16,230	46.6
1980	46,069	23,922	51.9	15,727	33.6	22,141[a]	48.1

[a] Includes an estimated 4,500 Métis, people of mixed native and European origin.
SOURCES: Canada. Census Division 1973: Bull. 1.3–2, table 4–32; Canada. Bureau of Statistics. Census Division 1963: Bull. 1.3–2, table 82–26; Canada. Bureau of Statistics, Census Division 1951, 2: table 5–56; Northwest Territories. Government 1983:25; unpublished 1981 Canadian census.

(Freeman 1971a:219), infant mortality rates were still very high when compared to other Canadian groups. Again, compared with Canadian rates, the average age of death among Inuit is markedly lower. The Inuit population had high birth and mortality rates and low life expectancy. The high ratio of children to adults means that a relatively small number of adults must support a relatively large number of dependents (table 3). Given high rates of unemployment and underemployment and widespead poverty, the situation is extremely grave. The 1971 census shows the Inuit population as becoming increasingly younger, probably due to high birth rates and decreasing rates of infant mortality. The Euro-Canadian population is also becoming younger, but in this case apparently due to continuing immigration of younger married people with young families.

Regionally there is much variation. For example, Inuit outnumber non-Native people six to one in the Baffin and Keewatin regions, which contain over 67 percent of the total number of Inuit in the Northwest Territories. In the Mackenzie Delta region they comprise only 30 percent of the population (D.G. Smith 1967:10). The western Northwest Territories has had a much larger proportion of Euro-Canadians since the late fur trade period (the 1930s), followed by mining, defense, and oil development activities.

Inuit have the highest rate of natural increase in Canada, but unlike many groups whose origin is outside Canada they do not gain members from immigration. In earlier periods the Canadian Inuit population was augmented by immigrants from Alaska. However, during the 1960s and 1970s this movement was of little numerical significance. Regarding the emigration of Canadian Inuit there is no information available.

The Census of Canada provides some information that permits an estimate of the numbers of Inuit residing outside their historic homelands in Northern Labrador, Arctic Quebec, and Northwest Territorial regions beyond the tree line. In 1971 about 8 percent of the Canadian Inuit population was enumerated in locations other than these homelands whereas in 1961 less than 5 percent of the Inuit population was so enumerated (De Vries and Vallee 1975). Because the Inuit are not treated as a separate category at the census subdivision level and because cross-tabulation of characteristics is not provided for them in the published census reports, very little is known about Inuit residing outside their regions of origin in terms of age, sex, education, and length of residence.

Urbanization and Sedentarization

Studies of modernization among preindustrial people report trends toward larger population groupings associated with a more settled, or sedentary, way of life, particularly for hunters and gatherers. For the Canadian Arctic many authors have noted the important on-going migration into settlements and the taking up of permanent residence in urban settings (for summary statements, see Hughes 1965:15). Of course, the change from migratory to contemporary settlement living was not an abrupt one. Traditional migration cycles were altered with the advent of trapping and the setting up of trading posts (Graburn 1969:124ff.), so that by the

Table 2. Natural Increase and Selected Birth and Death Rates (per 1,000 population) By Ethnic Category, 1969 and 1979

| | Northwest Territories | | | | All Groups[c] | | All Canada[c] | |
| | Inuit | | Non-Native | | | | | |
	1969[a]	1979[b]	1969[a]	1979[c]	1969	1979	1969	1979
Live Births	44.9	30.9	28.0	25.3	38.0	27.0	17.6	15.5
Illegitimate Births	14.5	—	12.0	—	18.5	—	9.2	9.2
Stillbirths	12.6	6.2	15.3	5.3	14.0	5.8	10.0	7.7
Prenatal Deaths	43.0	22.8	43.3	10.7	22.7	19.1	12.4	11.8
Neonatal Deaths	30.7	18.8	15.4	11.4	20.9	12.9	13.5	7.2
Infant Deaths	90.5	37.5	20.5	17.9	31.2	29.7	5.4	10.9
Crude Death Rate	10.1	5.6	4.1	4.2	6.8	5.0	7.3	7.1
Natural Increase	39.2	26.0	23.8	21.4	31.2	22.1	10.3	15.5

SOURCES: [a] Canada. Department of National Health and Welfare. Northern Health Service 1970–1979.
[b] Canada. Department of Naitonal Health and Welfare. Medical Services Branch 1980.
[c] Canada. Statistics Canada 1980: table 1.

Table 3. Northwest Territories Population by Age Groups

Age Grouping	Census Year	All Groups	Indian and Inuit	All Others
0–14	1951	67%	77%	23%
	1961	58	66	34
	1971	53	61	39
20+	1951	33	57	43
	1961	42	49	51
	1971	47	46	54

SOURCES: Canada. Census Division 1973, 1:Bull. 1.4–3, table 5; Canada. Bureau of Statistics. Census Division 1963, 1:Bull. 1.3–2, table 82; Canada. Bureau of Statistics. Census Division 1951, 2:table 5.

mid-1920s the transhumance associated with the earlier hunting phase was abandoned over much of the Arctic. What replaced it was a pattern of more restricted movement of families from campsite to campsite to fish, hunt, and trap. The families were oriented to trading posts, but most of them did not become rooted in these posts as permanent residents. The more restricted movement began after World War II and was fostered by official policies and programs. As it became increasingly difficult to obtain a livelihood from full-time exploitation of wildlife, many Inuit were impelled to go to a settlement, although many would alternate between settlement and camp living (Graburn 1969:219). The establishment of educational, health, recreational, and other services in settlements also attracted the Inuit.

Although settlement living was becoming quite common in the 1950s, the majority of Inuit did not reside permanently in places with more than 200 inhabitants. In fact, most settlements had fewer than 150 people. The 1960s saw a substantial rise in the number of Inuit living in settlements on a permanent basis, and settlements have increased sharply in size, most of them at least doubling their populations between 1961 and 1971, and some of them having had five- to eight-fold increases in that decade. Population concentration has been a product of several factors: the collapse of the fur trade; federal government policies to introduce effective administration of educational, health, and welfare programs; subsidized housing; mechanization of hunting practices; and the gradual acquisition of urban preferences by Native people. In 1961, in the region under review, there were eight places with more than 200 inhabitants and five with more than 500; in 1981 there were 24 places with more than 200 inhabitants and 13 of these had more than 500. By 1981 more than 70 percent of the Inuit population in the Northwest Territories lived in communities with more than 500 inhabitants. Many of the studies carried out since the 1960s pay special attention to this phenomenon of urbanization and sedentarization, calling attention to the economic, cultural, social, and psychological implica-

tions (see Honigmann and Honigmann 1965, 1970; Honigmann 1975; Hughes 1965; J. Ferguson 1971).

Technological Adaptations

The most visible and measurable examples of Inuit adaptation to modern conditions are those pertaining to material culture. For example, during the 1960s, items of clothing and housing designed and manufactured outside the Arctic supplanted traditional Inuit items. There are scores of general stores in the Arctic, stocking a range of items comparable to that found in villages and small towns in other parts of Canada.

For earlier periods the ramifying effects on Inuit economy and social organization of technological innovations such as the rifle and steel traps have been described (Balikci 1960a:142; Vallee 1967a:35). While these previous technological innovations improved the traditional hunting skills of the Inuit, a new means of transportation to and from the hunt site has introduced as many problems as it has solved. The snowmobile had an important impact both on hunting and on the hunter in the development of a new set of social and economic problems.

Since the 1960s snowmobiles increasingly replaced dog sleds (Graburn 1969:163; Freeman 1974–1975:149; Usher 1972). Snowmobiles are faster than dogsleds, can carry larger loads of fur and meat, and do not have to be "fed" when they are not in use. The disadvantages are both directly and indirectly related to the new technology. The decline in the use of sled dogs has also brought with it a decline in the hunt for sea animals, and an increase in the potential for emergencies on a hunt—for instance, a snowmobile cannot be eaten or

Natl. Film Board of Canada Phototheque. Ottawa: 20461.
Fig. 1. Caribou Eskimo igloo interior. Man ("Pork") at right works on a snow knife while his wife Hattie sews caribou skin moccasins and his grandson Ikkat listens to phonograph. Photograph by George Hunter, Baker Lake, March 1946.

find its own way home. The increasing use of snow-mobiles has also brought about a marked increase in the outlay costs of the hunt in terms of the high purchase and maintenance costs of the vehicle, which is prone to breakdowns in rough Arctic terrain, coupled with the high cost of oil and gasoline in the Arctic. These factors have kept the snowmobile from gaining total acceptance among the Inuit, and the dog sled has persisted as a secondary means of transportation in the Arctic.

Not only did modern technology transform the traditional cultural patterns of those Inuit who continue to hunt and trap, but also it had a profound impact upon those who chose to live in the larger settlements. Technological innovations especially affected communication, long distance transportation, and housing. Motor-propelled boats and air travel linked the many scattered communities and settlements throughout the year, thus ensuring the flow of people, materials, and information from the south to the north on an almost regular basis. Planned communities using newly developed permafrost building techniques assured that more people received better shelter, water supply, and sewerage. Since many of these projects have become Inuit initiated as well as directed, the general policy has been to offer such housing at reasonable cost to the purchaser (Canada. Minister of Supply and Services 1978:85).

The development of orbital satellite communication (for example, the Anik satellite system) offers the potential for a greater social, political, and cultural revitalization. This may involve simple voice communication, or point to point transmission of video information, in uses ranging from popular entertainment and education to the holding of conferences by widely separated groups. An Inuit-owned and operated broadcasting corporation has been formed to provide television programs that are more than 90 percent in the Inupiaq language and strongly oriented toward the issues confronting the Inuit people (see Anonymous 1982; Graburn 1982). This and several other innovations appear to hold much promise for an improved awareness of the cultural experience of the Inuit as well as providing a means of achieving social and political unity among the scattered communities of the Arctic.

Pluralism and Stratification

One outcome of Euro-Canadian invasion has been the development and crystallization of social stratification. Dunning (1959), Hughes (1965:26), Vallee (1967a:123–125), Graburn (1969:228–229), and others have referred to an emerging castelike structure. A complex association of cultural, ethnic, and stratification dimensions does allocate Euro-Canadians to a superordinate position and Natives to a subordinate one. In a castelike situation these two sections would be integrated by a consensus on values. Here they are integrated by reg-

ulation and control of the Native sector by Euro-Canadians, particularly in economic and political spheres (D.G. Smith 1975:132). Also, northern society is not a single system of stratified ranks with Euro-Canadians at the upper end and Native people at the bottom. Rather, it consists of two complementary, partly parallel systems of stratification, one composed of Euro-Canadians, and the other of Native people. The two systems derive from different historical sources and reflect different cultural ideas of worth, esteem, prestige, and power.

Stratification among Euro-Canadians is strongly influenced by the ranking model provided by the government agencies for which most of them work, particularly in the Eastern and High Arctic where there are few Euro-Canadians who are not linked in some way to the public service.

Mailhot (1968:4–5) and Ervin (1968:12–14) suggest that there is no clear pattern of stratification in the Native sector. Vallee (1967a) and D.G. Smith (1975:21–28), on the other hand, distinguish three major categories: Kabloonamiut ('people of the White man'), who have a definite orientation to a settlement way of life; "people of the land," who have a definite commitment to traditional lifeways; and an intermediate category who follow a regime partly (in many ways poorly) adapted to both settlement and traditional lifeways. Graburn (1969:228) is probably correct in saying that these intra-Inuit class distinctions are only temporary and may not constitute long-term divisions, or, as D.G. Smith (1975:29) has said, at best they may be "incipient class structures."

In the 1970s a "new middle class" emerged among the Inuit, composed of a small number of young men and women who had more formal education than the Inuit average and were drawn into the expanding clerical and managerial sectors. Many of them were recruited into local and regional political and governmental positions previously occupied by Euro-Canadians. Some were active in the promotion of Inuit goals within the Northwest Territories as well as on the national scene. Some have emerged as entrepreneurs in small businesses.

Northern Native people, along with Native people throughout Canada, are becoming incorporated into the nation's lower class. This process has not been completed, but Fainberg (1965) and Slobodin (1966) see northern Native people as becoming "proletarianized." Graburn (1969:220), while not using this terminology, is in essential agreement, as is Brody (1975:229).

Employment

Employment data for the 1960s (Krolewski 1973:31–32) show that only 45 percent of Inuit aged 15 to 65 were active in the labor force compared to 74 percent

665

left, Natl. Film Board of Canada Phototheque, Ottawa: 20466.

Fig. 2. The fur trade, an important economic factor before the 1960s. left, Caribou Eskimos dealing with trader A. "Sandy" Lunan (on right) at a Hudson's Bay Company store, Baker Lake. Each stick represented a "skin" or 50 cents in trade. Photograph by George Hunter, March 1946. right, Iglulik Eskimo from Arctic Bay baling white fox skins. Photograph by Eric Mitchell, manager of Hudson's Bay post in Arctic Bay, 1955.

of Euro-Canadians. In 1961, 57 percent of Inuit workers were listed as fishermen, trappers, and hunters. The number of hunters and trappers decreased markedly in the 1960s, accompanying the trend to urbanization and sedentarization. Unemployment and underemployment were widespread. Many general labor jobs were seasonal, only sporadically available, and of brief duration.

Most casual workers rely on seasonal (usually summer) employment for the cash necessary to engage effectively in more traditional activities, such as trapping, during the winter. Income from wage employment is modest, for even the permanently employed in the 1960s had an average annual income per worker of $4,000, or about $950 per capita. The corresponding income for the casually employed, the majority of Native workers, was $1,500, or $195 per capita (cf. D.G. Smith 1975:91). There is extensive reliance on social assistance payments.

The history of employment in the North has been one of "boom and bust," with periods in which much employment was available (such as the building of the Distant Early Warning radar line, the building of Inuvik, intensive oil and gas exploration) followed by times in which employment opportunities were markedly reduced. This pattern, along with marked seasonality of employment, was accompanied by very unstable and unreliable occupational training and retraining programs aimed at incorporating Native people more extensively into the full range of occupations. These programs have met with only modest success. Most Native

workers are still involved in menial and unstable occupations other than those for which they had been trained. In addition, some Native people have been trained for as many as a half dozen jobs and are employed in none of them, or they have been employed in one or two of them only briefly.

The Cooperative movement has enjoyed considerable success in Inuit communities, facilitating access to store goods, home appliances, and transportation equipment such as canoes, outboard motors, snowmobiles, and even motorcycles. In the production aspect of the coops, furs play a large role, but Inuit art has become an internationally recognized symbol for Canada itself. Inuit play a very prominent role in directing their coops, which were often government supported in their early phases.

The occupational aspirations of younger Native people correlate very closely with those of their Euro-Canadian counterparts. Their occupational preferences span the full occupational spectrum, with considerable emphasis on skilled and semiprofessional occupations (D.G. Smith 1971, 1974). There is an influx of younger Inuit into the skilled, clerical, and managerial sectors, but their numbers are small. It was among people whose occupational aspirations were not fulfilled that social problems were most prominent (Clairmont 1963). In many ways, Native people have become attitudinally, but not structurally, incorporated into the Canadian social system, and this is particularly visible in the occupational sphere.

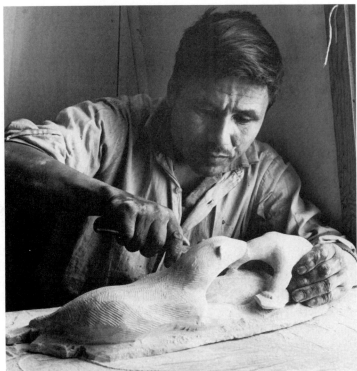

Fig. 3. Commercial stone sculpture became an important product of the Eskimo cooperatives in the 1960s. left, Iglulik artist Katak of Repulse Bay filing a soapstone animal figurine. Photograph by Villy Svarre, Aug. 1961. right, Pacôme Qulaut, an Iglulik sculptor. Photograph by Fred Bruemmer, April 1966.

Commercial Arts*

In 1950 the 9,000 Inuit of the Northwest Territories were dependent hunters and trappers who relied on imported guns, ammunition, some clothing, basic foods, tea, and tobacco. There was practically no wage employment and the price of fox furs was very low. Over 50 percent of the monetary income came from forms of relief. Since then the manufacture of commercial arts has contributed considerable income and has provided employment in the increasingly monetized economy.

In 1948 James Houston, a Canadian artist visiting the North, discovered some small toys and souvenirs and was employed by the Canadian Handicrafts Guild, with the support of the federal government, to return north in 1949–1953 as a crafts officer to encourage the production of these crafts to supplement Inuit income, which then averaged $25 per month per family. Traveling to many settlements in northern Quebec and the Northwest Territories, he successfully encouraged this cottage industry, and the Hudson's Bay Company stores bought the items with funds supplied at first by the federal government.

The commercialization of the arts—some ivory but largely soapstone carvings (fig. 3)—grew rapidly, yielding a total of $2,000 in 1950 and over $20,000 per year in the mid-1950s. The products were bought by Hudson's Bay Company store managers (who at first often favored good trappers) and sold through the Bay stores and the Canadian Handicrafts guild outlets. Within two years, they were also being exported to the United States and England. Local Whites, DEW-line personnel, and visiting ships' crews also began to buy directly from the Inuit in the North. In the 1950s there was a great expansion in the dollar volume as well as the size of the sculptures. Prices were still low (Inuit rewards were 25¢ to $2.50 an hour), providing about $25.00 per month on the average to over 1,000 families in the Eastern and Central Arctic.

In the late 1950s the market became overstocked, and certain types of carvings did not sell; northern stores occasionally stopped buying, forcing many families back on welfare. Government administrators, on the other hand, saw the commercial arts as a way of getting people off welfare and, when the market collapsed, started buying through their northern offices. This led to further government involvement as wholesalers. Eventually the Crown Corporation Canadian Arctic Producers (CAPRO) was set up in Ottawa to market the arts. Further government involvement followed the inception of commercial printmaking at Cape Dorset and a

*This section on arts is by Nelson H.H. Graburn.

few other settlements. These high-price items were marketed directly through CAPRO, and the Eskimo Arts Council was formed to oversee the quality of the products.

Throughout the 1960s, producers' cooperatives were founded in many settlements. Most of these purchased sculptures (and a few prints, fig. 4) and competed with the Hudson's Bay Company pushing up artists' income and retail prices. These coops later branched out into crafts workshops, retail stores, and oil distributorships, and by the late 1960s two federations of cooperatives were set up (one in Quebec and one in the Northwest Territories), owned and controlled by the local coops. These institutions became more subsidized by the government as the volume of business rose, and indirect subsidies went to high-level promotional efforts, films, tours, and exhibitions, such as *Sculpture Inuit* in 1971 and *The Inuit Print* in 1976. Other subsidies paid local crafts officers and for new crafts ventures, such as dolls, ookpiks, batik, jewelry, textiles, pottery, and clothing manufacture.

By the 1970s, the arts income of Cape Dorset's 600 Inuit exceeded one million dollars per year, and the total Inuit arts income was five to seven million dollars per year. The average artist in communities such as Cape Dorset, Lake Harbour, Rankin Inlet, and Baker Lake made $1,000–3,000 per year, and some artists made $35,000–50,000 per year. Late in the 1970s, there emerged problems due to overpricing and lowered demand. In many areas other forms of employment provided substitute income, but the cooperatives, which had become the largest employers in the North, were in trouble, and their expenses often exceeded their income and subsidies, requiring more government intervention. Should other employment increase, greater division of labor would leave fewer artists who would in turn emerge as self-conscious creators, as has already happened in Alaska. On Canadian Inuit commercial arts see Graburn (1971, 1978, 1978a), Martijn (1964), and Treude (1972).

The Polity

Since about 1960 the process of bringing the Inuit under Canadian governance has been nearly completed. Modes of political organization that are of long standing outside the Canadian Arctic have been introduced to the Inuit: people are defined as citizens belonging to political units of varying degrees of inclusiveness—settlements, hamlets, towns, provinces, or territories, and the Canadian state. A person's interests are represented in legislative bodies at each of these levels, the bodies consisting of elected, and, in some cases, appointed members. The elected members are officially defined as representing constituencies rather than particular groupings within them, such as kinship or ethnic groups.

In the Arctic, the rules of eligibility to vote and stand for office in these political units do not differ from those obtaining elsewhere in Canada.

The Inuit are linked into the polity at the federal, territorial, and local community levels. Until 1962, only the southern and western parts of the Northwest Territories were represented at the federal level in the Mackenzie River riding; the northern and eastern parts, containing the bulk of the Inuit population, were without elected representation. In 1962 the Mackenzie River riding was replaced by the Northwest Territories riding, which included the entire territorial population. Then in 1975 this constituency was divided into two: the Western Arctic and Nunatsiak. Since that date the Northwest Territories sends two federal members to Ottawa where they sit with 280 members from across the country in the House of Commons.

At the territorial level, significant political changes occurred in the decade from 1965 to 1975 in the government of the Northwest Territories (Harvey 1975). This territorial government is superficially similar to provincial governments in Canada, but it lacks many of the powers vested in provinces. The federal government retains control over nonrenewable natural resources and health. Under a commissioner appointed by the federal government, the Territories government legislates in education, local government, housing, and public works; it controls most renewable resources.

Territorial legislation is enacted by the Northwest Territories Legislative Council (since 1975 referred to as the N.W.T. Assembly). Until 1974, when the Northwest Territories Act was amended by the government of Canada, this Council was composed of 10 elected members plus four members appointed by the federal government. The amendment abolished membership by appointment, replaced the Commissioner as presiding officer with an elected Speaker, and increased the number of elected members to 15, this number being increased to 22 in 1979 (Northwest Territories. Government 1983:38–40). Ten are elected from constituencies above the tree line, in the Arctic part of the Northwest Territories.

The need for representative and responsible government for the Territories, and for the Arctic parts in particular, was the subject of a Commission of Inquiry into the Future of Government in the Northwest Territories, commonly known as the Carrothers Commission after its Chairman, A.W.R. Carrothers. Most of the recommendations of this Commission (Carrothers 1966, 1:140–214) have been implemented. Further progress was recommended in the *Report on Constitutional Development in the Northwest Territories,* commonly known as the Drury Report (Drury 1980). Issues of political development in the Territories are discussed by several authors in Keith and Wright (1978:252–335).

Before 1965 the Mackenzie Delta was the only part

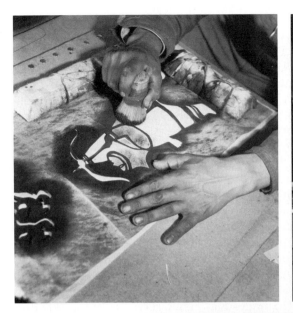

Natl. Film Board of Canada Phototheque, Ottawa: top left 95810, top right 68–6209, center left 95819; center right and bottom, *Native Press*, Yellowknife, N.W.T.

Fig. 4. Inuit commercial prints. top left, Iyola, in the art center at Cape Dorset, stippling paint through a sealskin stencil to produce a print of *The Archer* by the artist Niviaksiak ("Coastal Northern Labrador After 1950," fig. 3, this vol.). Photograph by Rosemary Gilliat, Aug. 1960. top right, Caribou Eskimo artist Oonark of Baker Lake at work. Photograph by John Reeves, March 1968. center left, Baffinland Eskimo Luktak cutting a design by Kenojuak onto a stone block at the Cape Dorset art center. Photograph by Rosemary Gilliat, Aug. 1960. center right, Ningosiak (Baffinland Eskimo) pulling print from a stone block. Photograph by Tessa Macintosh at Cape Dorset, 1976. bottom, Copper Eskimo Cooperative at Holman Island where a small artisan group makes silkscreened greeting cards, tablecloths, placemats, and Inuit dolls and hand puppets. Photographed in 1977.

669

of the Arctic that had an elected representative on the Northwest Territories Council. In 1965, the territorial franchise was extended over the Arctic regions, and three new Arctic constituencies were created. By 1970 there were five territorial constituences in the Arctic and six in the remainder of the Northwest Territories; by 1980 there were 10 in the Arctic and 12 in the remainder.

Local government takes different forms in the region. The considerable increase in the size of settlements during the 1960s was accompanied by a growing need for local administration and control. There was a tendency in the late 1950s and early 1960s to vest control and administration in government-appointed officials with, in some cases, advisory councils with no legislative or executive powers (for example, Vallee 1967a:214ff.). During the late 1960s the Northwest Territories government mounted a campaign to incorporate settlements as local legislative bodies, with varying degrees of authority ranging from settlement councils with quite limited power, to village and town councils whose powers are comparable to those of the same kinds of bodies elsewhere in Canada (Harvey 1975:11). Between these extremes are hamlet councils. In 1962 there was only one incorporated village in the region, no hamlets, and three settlement councils; by 1980 there were two incorporated towns (Inuvik and Frobisher Bay), 23 hamlets, and only eight unincorporated settlements (Northwest Territories. Government 1983:85–212).

Legislation may endow people with citizen status, but the people concerned may be indifferent or hostile to that status, or may be prevented from exercising the rights associated with it. Accounts of statutory rights and obligations tell nothing about the significance of political incorporation for the Inuit, nor do they provide answers to questions about the Inuits' commitment to and participation in the polity. Published studies of Arctic committees analyze patron-client and brokerage roles and relationships in the Eastern Arctic (Paine 1971) and illuminate decision-making processes and the distribution of power in local settings. But the political culture of the Inuit population with regard to the Northwest Territories and levels is essentially unknown.

Indicators of Inuit participation in federal and territorial politics can be drawn from the Reports of the Chief Electoral Officer for Canada for five territorial and five federal elections between 1965 and 1980 (Vallee 1981). Despite the great numerical superiority of the Inuit in the Arctic parts of the Northwest Territories, not one had run for federal office before 1979, when Peter Ittinuar won the federal seat of Nunatsiaq, defeating two other candidates of Inuit origin. Between 1965 and 1972, 15 of the 21 candidates for election to the Northwest Territories Legislative Council were Euro-Canadian, one was Indian, and five were of Inuit ancestry (in whole or in part). In the territorial election

of 1975, the first held after the number of constituencies was increased, there was a sharp rise in Inuit participation. The eight Arctic constituencies were contested by nine Euro-Canadians and 14 Inuit. Of the successful candidates, three were Euro-Canadian and five Inuit. In the 1979 territorial election, in which 10 Arctic constituencies were contested by 28 candidates, five of these were Euro-Canadian and the remainder of Inuit origins. Seven Inuit were elected.

Until the 1975 election, the occupations of territorial candidates bore out the oft-noted role of local Euro-Canadians as influential persons mediating between the Inuit and the society at large (Vallee 1971:83). The largest category among non-Inuit candidates consisted of owners or managers of community enterprises, like stores and small charter airlines. In the 1975 election the occupational base was broadened with the addition of several hunters and trappers and Inuit employees in the skilled trades and public services. But in the 1979 election four of the Inuit candidates were listed in the business category, and 10 as clerical-managerial employees of local authorities or Inuit associations. There was a shift away from Euro-Canadians acting as mediators between the Inuit and the larger society (Vallee 1981:16).

Voter turnout in Arctic communities for both federal and territorial elections is close to national and provincial averages in Canada, and Inuit participation in the voting process is slightly higher than it is for Euro-Canadians, although the differences are not significant. No clear-cut correlation was found in the data between voting turnout and variables such as length of time exposed to Canadian political modes or cultural group affiliations within the Inuit category (Vallee 1981:23).

Thus, during the 1960s and 1970s the Inuit participated notably as voters and supporters, and later as leaders, in various government bodies. These councils and official representatives connected with them came to mediate relations between individual Inuit and the larger society.

One important trend has been toward the political enfranchisement of the entire population of the Northwest Territories. There has also been a growing recognition that the Arctic region, with its substantial Inuit majority, has a special status in the polity. Pressure for recognition of this special status comes primarily from nongovernmental organizations, without precedent in traditional Inuit society. Trappers' councils and local cooperatives (Vallee 1964) began to assume an importance beyond their narrowly defined terms of reference during the 1960s. But it was during the 1970s that the organizational capacity of the Inuit assumed national dimensions.

The Committee for Original Peoples Entitlement (COPE) was established in 1970 as a body representing the interests of all Inuit and other Native people, especially in the Western Arctic. Early in its history the organization found itself under heavy pressure to concentrate its efforts on negotiating a land claim settlement in the Western Arctic where resource development and exploration were very active. The pressure from resource development and exploration was not so heavy in the Central and Eastern Arctic, with the result that the concentration on land claims issues as such did not peak there until the late 1970s (Crowe 1979:31–39). By 1978 COPE had reached an agreement in principle with the federal government over land claims for the Western Arctic, but negotiations were interrupted by a change in the federal government and, although they were resumed, a final agreement had not been reached by 1983.

Many of the functions of COPE other than those pertaining to land claims were taken over by the Inuit Tapirisat of Canada (ITC), which was founded in 1971, and which represents the interests of more than 25,000 Inuit in Canada in the Northwest Territories, Quebec, and Labrador. Its constituent parts are Inuit regional organizations as well as a number of special purpose corporations and committees such as the Inuit Broadcasting Corporation (IBC), the Inuit Development Corporation (IDC), the Inuit Cultural Institute (ICI), and the Inuit Committee on National Issues (ICNI). As with COPE, which became a regional affiliate of ITC, the concerns of the Inuit Tapirisat are with the rights and welfare of people, not as members of political constituencies, but as Inuit (fig. 5).

In 1977 and again in 1979 this organization presented its Nunavut proposal, advocating the division of the Northwest Territories into two separate parts, one of which would be called Nunavut 'our land'. In a plebiscite on the issue of this division held in April 1982 no less than 85 percent of the voters in the Eastern Arctic voted in favor. The predominantly Euro-Canadian population in the portion of the Northwest Territories below the tree line voted against division (Anonymous 1982a). Western Inuit have opposed the Nunavut proposal as incompatible with their view of political development and resolution of land claims.

The Nunavut proposal is not simply one dealing with the rearrangement of boundaries. It also has a direct bearing on land claims as well as on the guaranteeing of Inuit rights in the new Canadian constitution (Anonymous 1982b). The Nunavut proposal resembles other proposals put forth by native groups in Canada in their quest for collective rights as "nationality" rather than "ethnic" groups; Nunavut and many others share the following aims:

> Collective recognition as distinct peoples, including the protection of traditional cultures and lifestyles, and aboriginal rights.
> Political rights to self-governing institutions of various kinds within the Canadian state.
> Economic rights to lands, resources and their benefits as a base for self-sufficiency and development of native communities and families, including protection of existing economic resources (Jull 1980:10).

The communication networks and common fronts established by these organizations foster the development of a pan-Inuit identity and solidarity. This process was extended beyond Canada's boundaries with the approval of a charter establishing the Inuit Circumpolar Conference, which brings together Inuit from Alaska, Canada, and Greenland (Anonymous 1980a; "The Pan-Eskimo Movement," this vol.).

Education

Of the many externally initiated changes during the 1960s none had a stronger impact than the dramatic

left and right, Dept. of Ind. Affairs and Northern Development, Hull, Que.
Fig. 5. Political involvement. left, Inuit Tapirisat of Canada (ITC) land claims committee meeting with Netsiliks from Spence Bay. Photograph by John Evans, Aug. 5, 1975. right, Miriam Ekkootna and Peter Arseevaryoo, Caribou Eskimos from Baker Lake, casting ballots for the name of the eastern territory to be created from the Northwest Territories. Photograph by B.A. Deer, 1962.

671

spread of a modern educational system into every part of the Canadian Arctic. The federal government mounted a massive campaign to provide universal formal education for Inuit residents. As part of the growing autonomy of the Northwest Territories government, responsibility for the administration of formal education was shifted to it in 1969.

Before 1947 what little formal education existed was provided by the missions, in a very sporadic way at a few federal government day schools and in a more regular, sustained way at a few residential schools (Jenness 1964:123ff.). The residential schools were often miles from the students' homes, with negative consequences for family life and cultural continuity. Precise figures are lacking, but it is doubtful that more than 20 percent of the Inuit population had received even a few years of formal schooling before 1950. Between 1947 and 1959, the federal government built 24 elementary schools in Arctic settlements in the Northwest Territories, and between 1960 and 1970, 18 more. In 1960 there were 1,425 Inuit children enrolled in schools; by 1975 that figure had more than tripled to 4,951 (Northwest Territories. Commissioner 1975:56). For the year 1955–1956 only 17 percent of school-age Inuit were enrolled in school. For 1960–1961 the percentage was 56 percent, and for 1970–1971, 83 percent (Simpson et al. 1968:3ff.; Northwest Territories. Commissioner 1970:104–105).

Considering the recency of universal, full-time education to grade 8 in local schools in the Arctic, it is hardly surprising that the Inuit profile of school attendance diverges from the national one, despite the sharp increase in enrollments during the 1960s. The average age of Inuit pupils is significantly higher than for non-Inuit pupils at the same grade levels in Canadian schools. Also very few Inuit students remain in school past grade six. Only 68 Inuit were enrolled in grades 10 to 12 in the Northwest Territories for the 1970–1971 school year. An additional 40 were following high school courses outside the Territories that year, but the total number remaining in the school track that leads to the possibility of pursuing higher education is very low (Northwest Territories. Government 1971:120–125). Unfortunately the published reports after 1971 do not present data on grade distribution by ethnic origin. Some of those that abandon the academic track take trades training in programs to which the Northwest Territories government gives strong support; others go directly into employment, usually on a part-time basis; still others go trapping or hunting; and some simply remain outside both the school and labor force. Since attending high school means moving to a town in the north or even southern Canada, many drop out rather than leave their home settlements. Psychological research during the 1960s suggested that whatever difficulties Inuit children might have in school are not due to intellectual ability.

On conventional tests of intellectual development Inuit children have proved virtually equivalent to Euro-Canadian children. Berry (1972:231–232) concludes that "Eskimo differ very little from southern norms on tests involving perceptual skills or those abilities tapped by 'performance scales' of conventional intelligence tests." Other researchers agree (Preston 1964; Vernon 1966; MacArthur 1967, 1969) that, on the whole, Inuit are intellectually well equipped in cognitive skills to deal with the educational system, despite its Euro-Canadian biases.

Attempts to explain the tendency to leave school before completion of even junior high school stress the effects of culture (for example, Hobart and Brant 1966). At Inuvik in the Mackenzie Delta the abandonment of schooling was explained by the lack of congruence in cultural values between the native familial environment and the school environment (Honigmann and Honigmann 1970:188ff.).

D.G. Smith (1975) argues that structural aspects of the plural social system, such as the faulty integration of native and outsider segments, should be given at least equal consideration in any attempt to explain school performance. The results of large-scale surveys in the Mackenzie Delta in the late 1960s and early 1970s led to the conclusion that there are no pronounced differences in occupational prestige evaluation and preference among young persons of Inuit, Indian, Métis, and non-Native origin. However, there is a divergence in aspirations, the non-Native aspiring much more to professional occupations than do Native children. This suggests that a complex set of cultural and structural factors place narrow limits upon what native children expect to happen to them in the work world. These limitations on their aspirations and expectations result not only from their own perceptions of reality but also from those of influential Euro-Canadians, such as teachers (D.G. Smith 1974:20).

Mass education is widely regarded as the key component in plans to incorporate hitherto isolated peoples into the surrounding society. Policy and programs tend to favor either the universalist or the milieu approach (Vallee 1967a:151). Proponents of the universalist approach argue for educational content and methods similar to those prevailing in the country as a whole, assuming that the pupils should be equipped to make their way in the broader society. Where local language and custom differ sharply from the dominant national ones, they may be ignored or discouraged. Where the family or community is perceived as unfavorable to the child's educational progress, the authorities are advised to send the child to another location for schooling. In contrast, the proponents of the milieu approach argue that the main thrust of the educational system should be to ensure that Inuit children do not devalue and turn away from the Inuit way of life. They assume that the ma-

672

jority of children will remain in the Arctic and probably in their region of origin. In this view teachers should be familiar with the Inuit language and culture. The removal of children from their communities for schooling in distant places is abhorred.

After the period of missionary responsibility for education, characterized by a locally oriented program that stressed basic literacy and religion, the federal government's massive campaign was informed by universalism. The educational programs during the early 1960s stressed cultural replacement rather than cultural continuity (Hobart and Brant 1966:48, 65). An only slightly modified version of the Province of Alberta school curriculum gave the program a definite non-Arctic orientation. The use of the Inupiaq language in school precincts was either discouraged or forbidden. Teachers and administrators were recruited on the basis of professional criteria. They were not discouraged from acquiring some degree of competence in the Inuit language and some knowledge of Inuit culture, but these achievements were not specially rewarded. The policy of residential schooling, requiring separation of pupils from their home communities, received strong official support.

In the late 1960s the authorities undertook a campaign to redress the universalist imbalance, injecting a number of milieu elements into it by mounting a program to recruit and train Inuit youths as teachers and teaching assistants; providing more intensive training and orientation for White teachers in Inuit language and cross-cultural education; developing a hostel system to serve pupils-in-residence closer to their home communities; increasing substantially the Inuit content of the curriculum; and providing for more participation by Inuit in decision-making about schooling in their communities (Northwest Territories. Government 1969; Mouat 1970; Simpson et al. 1968; A. Stevenson 1973). This movement toward more Inuit content and decision-making in education was strengthened in the late 1970s and early 1980s as a result of pressures from Inuit organizations; an important aim of the Nunavut proposal is to achieve control in the field of education.

Health

Discussions of the consequences of modernization for Inuit individuals usually focus on costs calculated on the basis of indicators of ill-health and personal disorganization.

The Inuit population shows high rates of mortality and morbidity, particularly in infancy and among the elderly, although there is considerable variation in these rates between communities (Hildes 1960, 1966:499; Lederman, Wallace, and Hildes 1962). Major causes of mortality and morbidity are infectious diseases and injury by accident and violence. No diseases specific to Arctic regions are known (Hildes 1966:500), but rates and patterns of disease and death are distinctive, due both to environmental features and to changing sociocultural features (Willis 1962:1–29, 253; Hildes 1966:499). Especially important among the latter are: change from traditional to store foods (Schaefer and Steckle 1980); widespread poverty in a population thoroughly connected with a cash economy; movement from small dispersed settlements to larger settlements, in many of which sewerage and garbage disposal and the availability of safe drinking water are problems; widespread abuse of alcohol; malnutrition; and overcrowded housing. These conditions are a major cause of high rates of infectious disease among the Inuit, particularly pulmonary diseases such as tuberculosis, pneumonia, and bronchitis, as well as viral, bacterial, protozoal, and parasitic enteric diseases. These diseases have often been endemic, and many such as tuberculosis have occurred in local epidemics, often leaving residual effects such as high incidences of corneal scarring, chronic otitis media, encephalitis, and meningitis (Hildes 1966:500; Schaefer 1959, 1959a; Reed and Hildes 1959; Schaefer and Steckle 1980:10). Other results are visual and hearing defects among the younger people, and elevated rates of mental retardation. All these medical problems contribute to lower school and occupational success.

The efforts of medical health teams, with better community cooperation, improved health conditions during the 1970s. Yet many of the rates still considerably exceeded the national average. Nearly 40 percent of the Inuit death rate is still attributable to accidents with respiratory, circulatory, and neoplasmic diseases representing the next three major causes, totaling approximately 35 percent (Canada. Department of National Health and Welfare 1970–1979). While many types of diseases that have beset the Inuit have come under greater control—the incidence of tuberculosis was by the 1980s at its lowest rate in the history of the Northwest Territories (90/1,000,000)—other diseases, such as measles, shigellosis, and salmonellosis, increased substantially during the late 1970s. Gonorrhea emerged as a serious medical problem during the 1970s, with a rate of 3,563/100,000 in 1979 as compared to 209/100,000 for Canada as a whole, while syphilis and other sexually transmitted diseases remained much below the national rate.

The variety and range of mental disorders among Inuit are similar to those for southern Canada, but the lack of reliable epidemiological data makes it difficult to identify the prevalence of each type. Boag (1966, 1967, 1972), Vallee (1966a, 1968), and Foulks (1972) note the frequency of reports over the years concerning hysteria and conversion hysteria. Several reports imply a reduction of the incidence of these classic Inuit hysterias with increasing culture contact, accompanied by

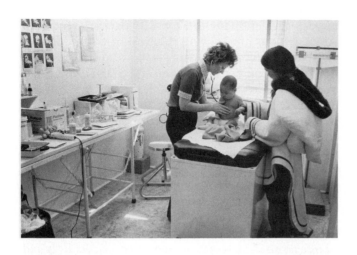

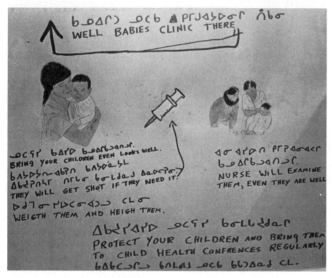

WELL BABIES CLINIC THERE

BRING YOUR CHILDREN EVEN LOOKS WELL.

THEY WILL GET SHOT IF THEY NEED IT!

WEIGTH THEM AND HEIGH THEM.

NURSE WILL EXAMINE THEM, EVEN THEY ARE WELL

PROTECT YOUR CHILDREN AND BRING THEM TO CHILD HEALTH CONFRENCES REGULARLY

top, *Native Press*, Yellowknife, N.W.T.; bottom, Natl. Film Board of Canada Phototheque, Ottawa: 68–5901.
Fig. 6. Health care services. top, Government nursing station at Cape Dorset. Baffinland Eskimo mother wearing parka of traditional design with short front flap, long back flap, and deep hood for carrying infant. Photograph by Tessa Macintosh, 1976. bottom, Sign at Netsilik clinic in Spence Bay in Eskimo, written in syllabics, and English. Photograph by John Reeves, March 1968.

a rising incidence of psychosomatic disorders (Boag 1967). It appears that a raised incidence of manic depressive, extreme passive-depressive, and self- and other-directed aggression symptoms, and an increase in the use and abuse of alcoholic intoxicants, all tend to accompany extensive culture contact and social change. In general, contact and social change appear to have intensified and exacerbated mental disorder patterns already in existence since aboriginal times (Clairmont 1963; S. Parker 1964; Chance 1965; Vallee 1968). Psychodynamically and socially "deviant" manifestations seem to be more prevalent among those who aspire to positions and statuses dominated by Euro-Canadians but have not found legitimate means of achieving them. As Vallee (1968:566–568) notes, these phenomena are related to: cultural discontinuity (abrupt and disjunctive

separation at the communal level from traditional ways); social incongruence at the individual level between aspirations and means of achieving them; anxiety-producing separations such as those attendant upon extensive hospitalization or periods in residential schools in isolation from family, home, community connections, and Inuit customs; and personal and communal crises such as death, threatened starvation, and disease.

During the 1970s various programs were implemented by the government health services of the Northwest Territories to overcome many of these problems. However, there was only one resident psychiatrist in the Northwest Territories as of 1979 (see Canada. Department of National Health and Welfare. Medical Services Branch 1980:57). As a result much of the work was undertaken by mental health coordinators working through existing social service programs and visiting psychiatric consultants. The main emphasis was to establish a local support network with the treatment of patients in their own locales reserving evacuation to the south for exceptional cases. While it is still too early to assess the impact of this service, it appears that the slight decline of psychiatric problems is attributable to these programs (Canada. Department of National Health and Welfare. Medical Services Branch 1980:5).

A third level of costs experienced by the Inuit, and one directly linked to health and psychiatric problems, has been the rise in social deviance, much of it linked to the use of alcohol (Finkler 1982a:3). There was about a 30 percent increase in alcohol-related offenses from the 1960s to the early 1980s (Finkler 1982; RCMP 1961–1979). During the early 1970s the number of Inuit incarcerated in Northwest Territories correctional institutions increased by 70 percent, and the number of violent crimes committed by 13 percent, with assault representing the largest category of all violent crimes reported (an average of 93% of the total). In other categories of arrest, 50 percent of the total charges laid in the Territories against Inuit have related to the operation of motor vehicles while intoxicated, with the remainder otherwise related to alcohol use (see RCMP 1961–1979; Finkler 1982, 1982a).

In order to control problems of alcohol-related behavior a number of programs and policies were undertaken by all levels of government agencies and local communities. The courts and law enforcement officials used legal sanctions in only the most severe and persistent cases of alcohol abuse and attempted to direct both potential and actual offenders into treatment programs. Local social services tried to supervise chronic alcohol abuse and provide greater support for developing adequate housing, health, employment, and educational opportunities. Between 1975 and 1980 at least 14 of 33 Inuit communities held plebiscites on alcohol control, and all 14 approved either total prohibition or strict community control on either consumption or

674

distribution (Northwest Territories. Government 1983:82–215 for community data; Northwest Territories. Government 1981a; Canada. Department of National Health and Welfare. Medical Services Branch 1980:58; Finkler 1982:9–10).

Sources

For the period of the 1960s and early 1970s there are many accounts by anthropologists and other social scientists of changes in the Inuit way of life in the Canadian Arctic. Many of these are based on studies of single communities or districts, but a growing number are primarily comparative, attempting to generalize about types of community or situation for large regions such as the Eastern Arctic (for example Brody 1975; Paine 1971); or for the Canadian Arctic as a whole (for example, Honigmann 1975; Jenness 1964; Vallee 1971); or for the Canadian Arctic in circumpolar perspective (for example, Hughes 1965; Jenness 1968). To this cross-national dimension Jenness (1964, 1968) adds a sound historical one.

Every region of the Canadian Arctic has been covered to some extent in the literature for the period. The coverage has been most thorough for the Mackenzie Delta, where a multidisciplinary research program launched in 1967 had produced 10 monographs by 1975. This program and the great bulk of social science research in the Canadian Arctic is government-sponsored, most of it through the Department of Indian Affairs and Northern Development (until 1965 known as the Department of Northern Affairs and National Resources). The Northern Research Division of that Department coordinates these research and publication activities, which are summarized in an annotated bibliography (Canada. Northern Research Division 1975). Many of the authors cited in this chapter have done their studies and published under the aegis of this Department, although in most cases they have also published these research findings in scholarly journals and books, an indication of the generally good quality of their research.

Social and economic impact studies in connection with projected fuel extraction, pipeline, and communications developments represent another research thrust (for references, see Castonguay and Lanari 1976). These studies, sponsored by private corporations as well as government, are uneven in quality insofar as analysis is concerned although they do contain interesting factual materials.

A document of considerable political and social significance is the Report of the Berger Inquiry into Pipeline Development (Berger 1977), which solicited and paid attention to the opinions about northern development in many communities in the Northwest Territories.

During the 1970s there were established several publication series that deal exclusively with matters pertaining to the Inuit. The source most used in this chapter is the bilingual (English and Inuit) bimonthly *Igalaaq*.

675

The Grise Fiord Project

MILTON M.R. FREEMAN

In the Canadian North, Inuit communities such as on Southampton Island, in northwest Hudson Bay, retain distinct factions having separate dialects and modes of living nearly 40 years after being brought together. Though some cultural exchange has undoubtedly occurred, presumably very real forces exist within the societies to prevent amalgamation, homogenization, or indeed any large-scale exchange that would obscure distinct collective identities. The same is true elsewhere in the Canadian North, for example, at Great Whale River, Spence Bay, Resolute Bay, and Grise Fiord, where immigrant groups maintain distinct subcultural differences many years after establishing proximate residence.

The causes and consequences of these population shifts among Inuit groups are not well documented for the most part. Some of these movements, for example, of North Alaska Inupiaqs into the Mackenzie Delta region or of people from the Delta to Banks Island, appear to have been economically motivated (Usher 1970–1971:23ff.). The heroic journey of the last Canadian Inuit immigrants to Greenland has also been recorded (Rasmussen 1908:23–36) and analyzed (Petersen 1962), as have population shifts occasioned by the advent of nineteenth-century commercial whaling into northwest Hudson Bay (Robinson 1973). However, all these early migrations appear to have resulted from initiatives taken by the Inuit themselves; since then, some relocations have been taking place as a result of initiatives, if not pressures, emanating from the locally influential representatives of Euro-Canadian society whose goals and values are quite dissimilar to those of the Inuit. The politics of two such relocation schemes have been analyzed: one, involving transfer of Baffin Island Inuit to Devon Island, Somerset Island, and the Boothia Peninsula (Jenness 1964:59–64; see also Mowat 1966:10–11) and the other involving the movement of northern Labrador Inuit to more southerly coastal locations (Jenness 1965:79–85; see also Ben-Dor 1966).

In the decade of the 1960s, there were numerous examples in the Canadian North of relocations, as in the Labrador instance, for reasons of "administrative expedience." The high cost of maintaining small and somewhat remote communities and the presumed manifold benefits (for example, better educational facilities, occupational opportunities, and exposure to a more progressive milieu) of relocation in larger population centers resulted in the disappearance of many small settlements. Examples might be the Cape Hope Islanders in James Bay, removed to Great Whale River, Quebec, in 1960; Reindeer Station residents to Inuvik and Tuktoyaktuk in 1968; and Padloping Islanders moved to Broughton Island in 1969.

Schemes such as these, where the total population is relocated, are of great cultural and social significance to the migrants; nevertheless, they allow in large part the maintenance of premigration social relationships, providing, of course, that a significant portion of the original population continues to coreside in the new location. The Grise Fiord situation, like other colonization schemes involving small numbers of migrants, is significantly different because of the attenuated social universe that had to readjust to the demands of a novel situation.

This essay outlines certain of the events surrounding the establishment of a colonizing settlement at Grise Fiord on the southern coast of Ellesmere Island; the events described cover the years 1953–1973.

History

In September 1953, four families arrived at Craig Harbour, in southeast Ellesmere Island, as the first colonists of an experimental relocation project destined both to exploit the rich game resources of uninhabited regions of the Canadian High Arctic and to reduce pressure on game in the relatively heavily settled Low Arctic areas. The immigrants came principally from the Port Harrison district on the east coast of Hudson Bay (Inuit of Quebec); however, to assist these immigrants from the low latitudes in their adjustment to life in the High Arctic, they were accompanied by one Iglulik family from north Baffin Island (Pond Inlet). Since that time, the growth of a locally resident population in the region has been due to natural increase and further immigration (see table 1) (Freeman 1969:table 1); by 1973, the resident population numbered 111.

In 1962 a federal day school was opened in the community, and a teacher and a mechanic have been resident since that date. In 1969 a second teacher was added to the school, and an administrator and nurse became additional residents in 1971.

Table 1. Population

Year	Families	Individuals
1954	7	36
1955	9	43
1956–1957	9	46
1957–1958	9	43
1958–1959	12	58
1959–1960	14	58
1960–1961	16	81
1961–1962	15	70
1962–1963	15	73
1963–1964	17	85
1964–1965	17	82
1965–1966	18	86
1966–1967	17	91
1967–1968	17	89
1968–1969	16	88
1969–1970	15	90
1970–1971	15	96

SOURCE: RCMP records in Riewe 1971.

The economy at Grise Fiord was based almost exclusively on hunting and trapping until the 1960s. A construction program that started in 1961 enabled men to obtain periodic, short-term wage employment; but only since 1966, when the cooperative contracted to service the community, has the opportunity for year-round wage employment been available for some men. Changes occurring since then have principally resulted in an increase in average family income, decrease in fox trapping, and changed consumption patterns in the direction of more imported high-cost capital goods. Hunting activity barely changed in overall intensity throughout this period (table 2) (Bruemmer 1968).

Hunting Activities

The Grise Fiord area is, without doubt, a superior sealing location, for not only are ringed seal (*Phoca hispida*) abundant and very close to the settlement at all seasons (fig. 1), but also they are generally of a very large size. Winter hunting at the breathing holes (a technique referred to as *nippatuq*)* is extensively practiced from the beginning of November until the end of April when basking seals (*uuttuq*, sg.) haul out on the ice by breathing holes. In late spring also, the hunters from northern Baffin Island practice communal hunting at the large breathing holes on the now water-covered ice; this technique (*qulangissiyut*) utilizes harpoons only. No local hunters hunt seals at the floe edge because of the distance to open water, the darkness of winter, and the profitability of other techniques that can be practiced nearer to the settlement.

In the open-water months of August and September, harp seal (*Phoca groenlandica*) and white whales also come close to the settlements. Walrus, which are sometimes taken during the open-water season and on the floating ice-pans and among the opening leads in the ice in July too, can be obtained near open water during the winter months.

Polar bears are more especially hunted in the period immediately following the return of light (March through May), and long hunting journeys have been undertaken in search of this quarry (Bruemmer 1969).

Peary caribou are scarce, occurring in small herds in scattered localities, and are mainly hunted in November, which is the earliest that suitable snow cover allows winter travel inland from the coast. Since 1969 caribou hunting has been combined with musk-ox hunting.

Other species of wildlife contribute, in quantitative terms, quite small amounts to the local economy.

Cultural Difference and Social Distance Between the Immigrant Groups

Shortly after arriving on Ellesmere Island, the immigrant families moved to a campsite on Lindstrom Peninsula 50 miles to the west of Craig Harbour. A small trading store was constructed alongside the Royal Canadian Mounted Police detachment at Craig Harbour in the summer of 1954, and one family of Hudson Bay Inuit resided in a wooden house at this location until both the detachment and store moved to Grise Fiord in 1956. The other households constructed frame dwellings from canvas and scrap lumber (obtained from Craig Harbour), insulated with local plant material in the double walls and with imported buffalo and reindeer hides; seal-oil lamps provided heat. Although frame tents were known in the Port Harrison region of Hudson Bay, they were usually heated by driftwood-burning stoves; permanent winter dwellings (*qammat*) constructed by Baffin Island Inuit are unknown at Port Harrison. Due to the inadequacy in winter of a frame tent-cum-shack heated by seal-oil lamp and their lack of knowledge concerning *qammat* construction, Port Harrison immigrants continued to live in snowhouses for their first three winters on Lindstrom Peninsula. By the fourth winter, improvements to their wooden dwellings and the introduction of fuel-oil-burning stoves enabled all Port Harrison families to discontinue living in snowhouses at the permanent winter camp.

Knowledge of *qammat* construction was never attained by Port Harrison immigrants, nor was another

---

*The editors have no independent sources of information on the dialects spoken at Grise Fiord. The transcriptions of Eskimo words in this chapter are those of the author, with some editorial modifications based mostly on the transcriptions for central Canadian dialects in Schneider (1970), and the orthographic proposals of Gagné (1961) and later writers, but with *y* written for j.

677

Table 2. Hunting Returns

Year	Ringed Seal[a]	Bearded Seal	Harp Seal	Walrus	Beluga	Narwhal	Polar Bear	Wolf	Caribou	Arctic Fox	Arctic Hare[a]	Ptarmigan[a]
1954	302	50	6	3	1	6	27	[b]	15	365	[b]	[b]
1955	404	22	27	23	11	0	18	[b]	28	409	[b]	[b]
1956–1957	560	34	[b]	46	6	0	13	1	15	184	90	151
1957–1958	485	32	[b]	39	15	0	8	2	13	664	70	300
1958–1959	539	27	[b]	46	5	0	17	3	0	667	20	50
1959–1960	500	25	[b]	50	25	0	22	2	2	54	50	200
1960–1961	600	25	[b]	38	35	0	16	0	23	534	50	400
1961–1962	955	40	[b]	40	10	3	18	3	20	1,015	40	125
1962–1963	537	23	70	21	75	0	45	1	28	38	100	95
1963–1964	620	[b]	[b]	19	83	20	16	6	11	325	100	75
1964–1965	652	20	70	31	20	0	29	3	12	550	150	40
1965–1966	515	30	25	30	48	27	36	3	37	63	62	47
1966–1967	400	35	15	35	118	0	45	5	12	83	30	26
1967–1968	500	25	20	19	0	7	17	5	24	221	100	79
1968–1969	1,000	20	68	15	0	10	27	12	75	274	[b]	24
1969–1970	530	20	68	7	0	49	29	12	46	174	[b]	92
1970–1971	[b]	[b]	[b]	[b]	[b]	[b]	25	9	[b]	17	[b]	[b]

SOURCE: RCMP records in Riewe 1971.
[a] Estimates.
[b] Data not available.

adaptive feature of Baffin Island winter life, namely, lining snowhouses (*illuvigaq*, sg.) with caribou skins to improve the comfort and length of life of the dwelling. Since Baffin Island families did not live in skin-lined snowhouses on Lindstrom Peninsula, that information could only have been transmitted verbally. According to both Hudson Bay and Baffin Island informants, social relations between the immigrant groups were not good. The former group in particular speak of the unhelpful attitude of the Baffin Islanders: indifference, ridicule, and even hostility were not uncommon features of intergroup relations, rather than the cooperation hoped for, and perceived, by the authorities (Fryer 1954:142).

A further example of the lack of cooperation was in

Fig. 1. Hunting migrating ringed seals in the tidal cracks in front of the village, Grise Fiord. Photograph by Rick Riewe, June 1971.

regard to obtaining fresh water. The Hudson Bay immigrants came from a region where streams, rivers, and lakes provide drinking water all year round, but in the far north fresh water is obtained from ice in the sea. The recognition of suitable freshwater ice (*nilak*) requires skill, for many of the promising-looking pieces are indeed salty when melted even if seemingly fresh when tasted in situ.

The elder kinsman of the Hudson Bay group was designated camp leader by the RCMP; his widow and others believe the fatal heart attack he suffered within the first year resulted from this weight of responsibility. Following his death, his brother was assigned the leadership, but as he also lacked leadership qualities the camp increasingly failed to function as a social, political, or productive unit, though as need arose it did function as a single unit of distribution. In view of the small size of each of the two social and productive units, both groups continued to urge kinsmen in their former communities to follow them north.

In 1955 the two groups considered the possibility of splitting the camp into two separate camps, and a location two miles eastward was chosen by the Hudson Bay families as their campsite. However, no move took place until 1958 when both groups had about doubled the number of households through immigration and marriages. This physical separation of the two groups was maintained when, following the establishment of the federal day school at a location adjacent to the RCMP buildings, the Inuit moved their camps about five miles east to consolidate the newly established Grise Fiord settlement. In 1964, two years after moving to

Fig. 2. Akpaleeapik building an igloo. Such temporary structures were commonly used during hunting and trapping excursions especially from late Oct. through April. Photograph by Fred Bruemmer, April 1967.

Fig. 3. Dog team pulling a sled on Ellesmere I. Photograph by Fred Bruemmer, April 1967.

Grise Fiord, all the houses were moved into one row of dwellings east of the police and school buildings.

Technology

Among contemporary Inuit in the east Canadian Arctic, many items of technology are subject to substitution, especially if the substitution leads to evident increase in functionality or results in economy of time or effort. Typical Port Harrison sleds at Grise Fiord are shorter and narrower than Baffin Island sleds. Though Hudson Bay immigrants admit the narrow sled is more liable to overturn in rough ice conditions, especially during the dark period, the Baffin Island sled has not been widely adopted by them. However, following the first visit from Greenlanders in 1958, the shorter and much wider Polar Eskimo sled began being used by several of the more innovative Hudson Bay hunters.

Though there are other important innovative changes in sled technology made by the Hudson Bay hunters now living at Grise Fiord (Freeman 1969:775), in other ways both groups have held to former techniques, as for example the design of dog harnesses, the practice of rearing pups, and the use of either boiling or cool water to prepare sled runners prior to the application of the mud winter shoeing (see Freeman 1969:779–781 for further discussion).

Although women are often held to be more culturally conservative than men, even middle-aged women have discarded techniques of a lifetime practice and adopted new and presumably improved ways. The most marked of such innovative changes has been with respect to preparation of sealskin by Hudson Bay women (Freeman 1969:775). Hudson Bay families have also adopted the furred overboot (*maannguat*) worn by Baffin Island

people (fig. 4). This boot, which ties over the ankle and has a double fur sole, is worn over the winter sealskin boot (*niuyurriak*) or the sealskin boot with leggings of caribou, bear, sheep, or wolf skin (*kamippaq*, sg.).

Kinship and Ritual Relationship

Spouse selection is necessarily limited, more especially because marriage between Baffin Island and Hudson Bay Inuit remains very rare at Grise Fiord (see Freeman 1969:776). In view of this, and the degree of relatedness of people within the two groups, men have undertaken journeys to obtain spouses; in 1957 one of these expeditions resulted in a Pond Inlet man (son of a special constable at Alexandra Fiord) marrying a Port Harrison woman at Grise Fiord. In this exceptional case, residence after marriage was with the Hudson Bay group, in accord with the initial uxorilocality that appears to be usual in that area (Freeman 1967:162).

Although adoption, like marriage, is an acceptable and effective means of extending one's network of kin (an altogether desirable goal in Inuit society), adoptions occurring at Grise Fiord for the most part remain within, rather than between, each of the immigrant groups. The first case of adoption across group boundaries occurred in 1968 when a childless Port Harrison family adopted the child of a Baffin Island woman living at Grise Fiord.

Name sharing can be either planned, in which case the partners will refer to each other as *sauniq*, or accidental, whereupon they are *atikulugiit* (pl.) or *avvariit* (pl.). The exact nature of the *sauniq* relationship varies from group to group. For example, a Port Harrison family will choose an infant's *sauniq* only from among living persons, whereas at Pangnirtung the *sauniq* is always chosen from the recently deceased. This custom

679

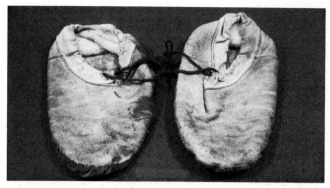

Natl. Mus. of Canada; Ottawa: IV–C–3571.
Fig. 4. Overboots, sheepskin with green braided wool ties laced through canvas cuff, worn over sealskin boots. They are of the Baffin Island type but were made by a Quebec Inuit woman from Inoucdjouac living at Grise Fiord. Length about 30.5 cm; collected by Milton M.R. Freeman, 1966.

has remained unchanged in both groups following immigration (see Guemple 1965 for discussion of the *sauniq* relationship).

At the birth of an infant, in addition to a competent adult serving as midwife, at least one other adult is usually present. Among Port Harrison Inuit such a person is the sponsor, or *sanariarruk*, of that child. This relationship, which is very important in Port Harrison society, has as a ritual component dressing the child immediately after birth and expressing the wish, for example, that it be a successful hunter, a skillful seamstress, a person of integrity and wisdom. The child is the sponsor's *angusiaq* (if a male child) or *annaliaq* (if female). These are terms of address as well as reference (Guemple 1969).

Among Baffin Island Inuit, by contrast, the nonmidwife adult is present primarily to provide physical support to the mother during labor; if this adult has any special role in relation to the neonate it is incidental and of no ritual importance. On Baffin Island the institution is less important than at, for example, Port Harrison: the adult who assisted the child's mother at its birth may call the child *angusiaq* or *annaliaq* according to sex, and the child uses the same term in addressing the adult. The term *sanariarruk* is not known to informants. No changes in terminology have occurred since Baffin Island and Port Harrison people came together at Grise Fiord; however, some Baffin Island adults at Grise Fiord now specifically request the role of sponsor prior to a child's birth, dress the neonate, and wish for its good fortune.

Customs

The belief is held on Baffin Island that a spirit force resides in an iceberg and imparts to it the strength to resist being cut into pieces. All Grise Fiord people now "kill" the spirit by shooting at the iceberg before attempting to cut blocks of ice for domestic use, even though this belief and practice were entirely unknown to Hudson Bay immigrants prior to their arrival in the far north.

An area of customary behavior that appears to be very resistant to change concerns food preferences. The acceptability of the meat of foxes or young gulls and dried whale meat by Port Harrison people and its rejection or low value in the eyes of the Pond Inlet people is matched by the latter's taste for summer-cached walrus meat *(igunaq)* and avowed preference for narwhal *mattak* (whale skin) over beluga *mattak*.

Language and Cognition

As the dialects spoken by the two immigrant groups are quite dissimilar, there were certain difficulties experienced during the early years of coresidence. Terms used in connection with hunting, travel conditions, and technology more especially were mutually unintelligible (table 3). The difficulty was in time overcome, not by developing a lingua franca, but by maintaining a high degree of dialect constancy together with a comprehension of the other's linguistic expression.

The former Hudson Bay Inuit refer to Baffin Island people at Grise Fiord as *maanimiut* 'the people living here' while continuing to call themselves *inuyyuamiut* 'the Port Harrison people'. Though cultural exchange has occurred since immigration, there exists no doubt in the minds of Grise Fiord people that they comprise two distinct social and cultural groups; and as the preceding examples illustrate, distinct behavioral, attitudinal, and linguistic differences serve to maintain the perceived differences.

Appraisal of the Relocation Scheme

How would one appraise a relocation program? In terms of how well the original objectives have been met, or

Table 3. Examples of Linguistic Variation

Pond Inlet Dialect	Port Harrison Dialect	English Meaning
naggutik	*tukkilik*	'winter crack in the sea ice' (useful for seal net site)
talligak	*takumigauk*	'white screen' (for hunting seals in spring)
anguvigaq	*ikilik*	'short lance with an attached barbed head'
isumaiguttuk	*qauyimailivuk*	'canine rabies'
iyyuq	*sirmiq*	'mud covering for sled runners in winter'
turruuk	*mirqutuuq*	'long-haired dog'
illuina	*qamut*	'sled runner'

680

FREEMAN

Fig. 5. The community of Grise Fiord with frame and prefabricated houses. Photograph by Fred Bruemmer, April 1967.

in terms of some objective measure of improvements in the physical and social well-being of the participants? Perhaps the degree of persistence of a new colony can itself be taken as some degree of success. This particular colonization scheme may be assessed according to these various criteria.

The stated goal of the scheme was to relocate families from the Hudson Bay region where population pressure on resources was apparently creating certain physical hardship in some areas and where the probability of an increasing dependence on welfare appeared great. In view of the colonial nature of the government service operating in the Canadian north at that time (see Jenness 1964:93–94), it seems likely that unstated decisions of a political nature also influenced the decision to establish population centers of Canadian citizens in the thinly populated regions of the far north.

Not unexpectedly, the Hudson Bay Inuit looked upon the transfer to far distant places with less enthusiasm than did the northern Baffin Island families who were to accompany them north. For one thing, they knew they would be cut off from effective contact with their kin far to the south and would be living in a world not only quite dissimilar to their own region but also totally unknown to any of their group. The Baffin Island families, on the other hand, not only were considerably closer to their kin and familiar regions immediately to the south but also had knowledge of the northerly regions through earlier hunting trips or through the periodic residence by some of their group at RCMP detachments or as members of police patrols into the region.

Thus, notwithstanding the accounts of superior hunting conditions sent back to kinsmen of the Hudson Bay families now residing in the Grise Fiord area, there occurred very little further immigration from Hudson Bay, though further immigration of Baffin Island families did occur through the years. (The last family arrived in 1966, and a single young woman immigrated in 1970) (see Freeman 1969: table 1).

To place into some further perspective the differential attractiveness of Grise Fiord as a settlement area to the two groups, it should be stressed that some pressure had to be exerted to "persuade" at least one of the original families to journey north from Hudson Bay (see Freeman 1971a:117–118, 1971b:43–44) and that subsequent efforts by members of both groups to leave Grise Fiord were officially opposed.

Postmigration Benefits

Viewed in the government's terms, there is no doubt that Grise Fiord residents enjoyed improved standards of health and physical well-being as a result of their move to that new location. Reports of the RCMP and the medical officers and administrative personnel visiting the community attest to the continuation of that situation. In objective terms there can be no doubt that hunting returns, more especially as they ensured the necessities of meat for human and dog food, and skins for clothing and other essential needs, were improved over both groups' former situations, with the Hudson Bay group experiencing the far greater improvement.

In subjective terms, both improvements incurred costs. The Hudson Bay group, having a longer period of dependency on store foods and coming from a very different part of the Arctic, regarded the resources of Grise Fiord as seriously lacking variety. The scarcity of Arctic char, ducks and geese, eggs, berries (several varieties), shellfish, caribou, and (for Baffin Islanders) the highly prized skin of the narwhal—all constituted missing items in the seasonal diet of the immigrants.

Both groups came to Grise Fiord from camps situated at a distance from the administrative-trading centers of their respective regions; therefore, following the move to Grise Fiord where a single settlement was constituted in 1962, they experienced certain amenities otherwise lacking in camp life. The proximity to a store (albeit of very limited capability to satisfy consumer demand), to medical aid, to communication facilities (radio, post office, periodic aircraft arrivals)—all represented increased security and access to amenities. There were certain additional benefits to be derived from the administrative presence, such as occasional film showings, dances, parties, the use of certain facilities, and additional visiting potential. The small number of households in the community allowed significant physical improvements to be made to each, utilizing surplus materials within the community.

Despite the benefits of small size, there are certain disadvantages too, more especially when the compactness encapsulates powerfully divisive forces. It should be apparent from the foregoing material that there remained in fact quite discrete social groupings within the

681

small confines of the settlement. Temporary alignments might cross these group lines, but sometimes disputes within a group caused further factionalism (see Freeman 1971b, 1971c).

Another serious problem of small size was the shortage of potential spouses for the young people approaching marriageable age. It should be remembered that very strong reservations exist toward marriage across group lines and that within each group the young unmarried people often share a degree of consanguinity that precludes marriage. This particular problem appears more acute for the Hudson Bay families, as the nearest potential spouses reside at Resolute Bay, which is also a small community, and moreover, one where intergroup marriages appear more acceptable (Bissett 1968: table 23). The Baffin Island families, on the other hand, can with greater facility reach the large population of potential spouses in northern Baffin Island and Igloolik (as well as those at Resolute Bay).

Prospects

Following the establishment of a one-classroom federal school at Grise Fiord in 1962 and the subsequent increased contact with visitors, the extreme isolation of this community has progressively decreased. Certain events illustrate some of the consequences of both the earlier remoteness and the later situation of more self-awareness on the part of the Inuit residents.

In 1966 the Canadian government placed the administration of Inuit housing into the hands of local committees; in Grise Fiord this was from the start a virtually all-Inuit committee. This event had signal importance for the community; indeed, it was the first time any transaction between the distant government administration and Grise Fiord Inuit was free from control or undue influence by authoritarian local non-Inuit. A growing awareness of not only the need to exert meaningful influence over local affairs but also the knowledge of how this was being achieved elsewhere (a direct result of the increased information flow into the community) resulted in other significant moves. Examples included formal complaints against the conduct of a local RCMP officer (twice in 1966), a successful petitioning of the Territorial government for a more enlightened program of musk-ox management in the region (in 1966), and an equally successful agitation to obtain a more equitable quota of polar bear (in 1967) once this important

Fig. 6. A community council meeting held in the school. Photograph by Fred Bruemmer, April 1967.

resource became subject to strict government control. In 1970 the community made a concerted and subsequently successful effort to obtain more satisfactory health-care facilities through a series of petitions to various levels of government.

Despite these and other exercises of a generally satisfactory nature, the Grise Fiord community has become very aware of its numerical and hence political weakness and has seen some of its achievements in gaining more local autonomy as being related to the role of Grise Fiord as a showplace community, a place to which important personages are taken for brief camera-toting visits. A series of position statements by nearly all the male heads of household in 1972 (Riewe 1973) attests to the increasing concern that in matters of the greatest import to the Inuit, namely the fundamental issue of control of the local game resources and the whole matter of perpetual safeguards over the integrity of the northern ecosystem, decisions are being taken that they have little power to influence.

The long-term viability of a small artificial community such as Grise Fiord has always been in doubt. The inevitable in- and out-movement of people to any northern community would, due to the increasing urbanization and sophisticated tastes of the overall population, make small remote communities appear increasingly less attractive places to move to. The motives and ideals that spawned such colonial projects in the past have been replaced in the Canadian Arctic by other imperatives (see, for example, Rohmer 1973).

Contemporary Inuit of Quebec

BERNARD SALADIN D'ANGLURE*

Beginning about 1960 the socioeconomic life of the Inuit of Arctic Quebec was transformed when services were taken over by the government, compulsory education was introduced, and sedentarization ensued. The Inuit were rapidly impelled toward a Canadian model for village municipal structures, and toward increasing dependence both on transfer payments (family allowances, pensions, and other aid) and on new mechanized means of individual transport capable of carrying hunters and trappers back to their former ranges. Each trapper or trapper's family soon owned a trapline, sometimes 100 kilometers long; the region was crisscrossed by these lines, ownership of which was usually passed on to relatives. It was necessary to cover great distances to reach the starting points of these lines, near the old winter camps (Balikci 1964; Audet 1974). There was a similar problem in marine mammal hunting, since the faunal resources of waters near the new villages rapidly diminished under hunting pressure. In addition some families were forced to leave their ancestral territory, where services were lacking, to settle in already organized communities in which they failed to become integrated. This was the case with the Inuit from Cape Smith who were forced to move to Povungnituk after the Hudson's Bay Company store at Cape Smith was closed and nearly a third of the group was medically evacuated to the south in 1955.

Thus, in the early 1960s there began an era of dependence on the welfare state, and of increased consumption of imported goods, sedentarization, and the mechanization of transport.

After the competition of the trading companies for furs and of the missionaries for souls, there arose a competition between the federal and provincial governments for the control of Arctic Quebec and its inhabitants. The radical change in Quebec's position regarding the Inuit could be seen as resulting from the advent in 1960 of provincial government by the Liberal party, one of whose slogans was *Maîtres chez nous* 'masters in our own house', just when federal agencies were massively intervening in Arctic Quebec. Jean Lesage, the prime minister of Quebec, had himself been minister of Indian affairs and northern development for the federal government in Ottawa, and his minister of

natural resources was the Quebec nationalist René Lévesque.

The Struggle over Economic Development and Political Hegemony

In the 1950s many investigations had been carried out in northern Quebec relating to the extraordinary development of mining and hydroelectric power that occurred in the heart of the peninsula. Several Quebec ministers were involved in these assessments of natural resources, especially minerals and hydroelectric power. It was proposed to extend the railroad from Schefferville to Ungava Bay, where there was a coastal outcrop of iron ore; a very detailed plan for a port and mining village at Hopes Advance Bay was prepared in 1955. The same year important teams measured the water supply of affluents of the Arnaud and aux Feuilles rivers in the interior of Inuit country. These teams wintered over and were resupplied by air. On the south shore of Hudson Strait between Cape Smith and Wakeham Bay prospectors discovered mineral beds, including an important asbestos deposit.

One of the first measures taken by the Lesage government was negotiating for the replacement of the Royal Canadian Mounted Police by the Sûreté du Québec at Poste-de-la-Baleine (Great Whale River) and Fort-Chimo (*Kuujjuaq*) in 1961. In the next two years Quebec provincial administrators were posted in these two villages. In 1963 the Direction Générale du Nouveau-Québec was created, with rather broad powers, and immediately sent agents to take places alongside the federal agents at Wakeham (Maricourt, Kangiqsujuaq), Povungnituk, and Inoucdjouac (Port Harrison, Inukjuak, *Inujjuaq*). Provincial social service benefits were offered to the Inuit at the same time as a teaching network with primary classes taught in Inupiaq. Three years later these services were installed in all the villages, paralleling those already established by the federal government, the Quebec health services supplanting the federal services in the district dependent on Fort-Chimo. At Tasiujaq, an abandoned locality on Baie aux Feuilles, the province built a school, store, and houses in response to the wishes of a group of families who had emigrated from there to Fort-Chimo. This was the only village without any Euro-Canadian antagonism.

*Translated from French by William C. Sturtevant.

683

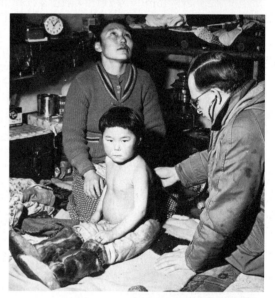

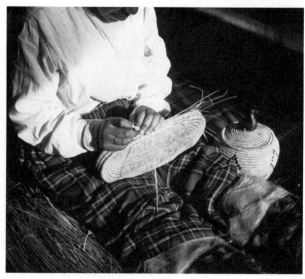

684

Rivalry between federal and provincial governments extended throughout Arctic Quebec, lasting about 10 years until the federal government decided in 1970 to propose to the Inuit the transfer of its responsibilities to the province of Quebec. Meanwhile the federal administrative center for Arctic Quebec had been moved from Ottawa to Quebec City, and French speakers were recruited as agents. At this time the budgets of the two governmental levels were estimated to include $10 million each devoted to the administration of the region. The competition seemed more and more useless and inefficient, especially since both were inspired by the same philosophy of "community development" with an imposing bureaucracy (Simard 1982). The influence of the state on Inuit life and territory had become invasive. A mixed federal-provincial commission, the Neville-Robitaille Commission, was sent into all the Inuit villages of northern Quebec to consult the population on the "transfer." The great majority of the Inuit reacted negatively; they mistrusted the Quebec government, the "little government" as they called it.

While the rival administrations opposed each other in the field, but acted in concert to fuse at a high level, two important Inuit movements developed in Arctic Quebec. One reacted against the waste of energy resulting from this opposition, and against the increasing dependence on the welfare state into which the Inuit had sunk; this was the cooperative movement that arose mainly from the first carvers' societies. The other reacted against the proposed fusion as simply one more understanding between Whites erected on the backs of the Inuit who would gain no power from it; this was the Northern Quebec Inuit Association, a political movement founded in 1971 that arose from the aspirations of a young Inuit elite, who were graduates of the first Anglophone schools at Inoucdjouac or Fort-Chimo, members of the old families settled around the first trading posts, mixed-bloods, or the early permanent employees of government agencies.

The first Quebec cooperative was founded in 1959 at Port-Nouveau-Québec (George River, Kangiqsualujjuaq) thanks to the activities of a federal development agent. Cooperatives started thereafter, under the federal community development program, joined the Fédération des Coopératives du Nouveau-Québec, which was created in 1967. The Povungnituk cooperative, begun in 1960, originated entirely differently, growing from a carvers' society (incorporated in 1958) that resulted from activities in 1955–1957 by P. Murdock, the former Hudson's Bay Company manager in the village. He convinced the local carvers to form a corporation, like those he had known in Newfoundland (Simard 1982). The Roman Catholic missionary A. Steinman took over his development work in 1957, and Murdock returned to work for the Inuit cooperative movement in 1966. Meanwhile the Povungnituk cooperative had been quite successful thanks to the community's enthusiasm and Steinmann's efforts. In 1962 it yielded the Inuit of the village a profit of about $112,000 out of a total income of about $222,000, making them the richest in the area (Vallee 1967; Simard 1982), with three-quarters of the village participating in the cooperative's activities. This success led other communities to emulate it, such as Ivujivik in 1967, Inoucdjouac in 1965, and Saglouc (Salluit) in 1967.

The average annual individual income at Povungnituk reached $493 in 1962, including $249 from the cooperative, $98 from government wages, $74 from the Hudson's Bay Company and private wages, $57 from allowances, and $15 from assistance (Vallee 1967; Simard 1982). State economic intervention had gradually limited the Hudson's Bay Company to managing (very profitable) general stores; the spectacular development of cooperatives then reduced government agencies to the second rank as sources of Inuit income.

The economic success of the Povungnituk cooperative put it ahead of all the other Inuit cooperatives in the Canadian Arctic, as was evident at the pan-Arctic conference on cooperation held in the village in 1966. The Fédération des Coopératives du Nouveau-Québec underwent no less spectacular development, for after only three years of activities its business amounted to $4 million (Simard 1982) and provided one-third of Inuit monetary income for the entire region. It was engaged not only in carving, engravings, and crafts but also in local food selling, hunting and fishing camps for tourists, commercial fishing, eiderdown collecting, general stores, restaurants, hotels, billiard halls, movie houses, heating-oil distribution, and construction (Simard 1982).

These numerous activities, and the enthusiasm and

Natl. Film Board of Canada Photothèque, Ottawa: top left, 64–4322; top right, 73–5093; center left, 64–4353; center right, Dept. of Indian Affairs and Northern Development, Hull, Que; bottom right, © Three Lions Inc., New York.

Fig. 1. Contemporary life. top left, Children learning to read English at the federal day school in Fort-Chimo. Photograph by Gar Lunney, May 1964. top right, Men at Koartac repairing a snowmobile. Photograph by Dunkin Bancroft, May 1973. center left, Residents of Fort-Chimo during a municipal council meeting. Photograph by Gar Lunney, May 1964. center right, Tubercular child at Inoucdjouac (Port Harrison), examined by T.J. Orford, government physician, preparing for evacuation in the spring to a southern sanatorium. Photograph by Bud Glunz, Jan. 1946. bottom left, Elizabeth Sirpaluq, Annie Mikpiaq, unidentified man, and Alacee Quingalik of Povungnituk playing a game using seal bones. Photograph by Fred Bruemmer, Sept. 1968. bottom right, Woman of Inoucdjouac stitching a coiled grass basket, a type made for export. Completed one at right has carved stone handle representing a bird. Photograph by Richard Harrington, March 1959.   685

economic strength of the Fédération, inevitably impinged on the political domain, particularly since its regional emphasis demolished the narrow community development policies applied by the two levels of government.

Hence when the Neville-Robitaille Commission failed in its consultations with the Inuit over "transfer," a group of delegates from the cooperatives proposed the creation of an Inuit regional government, during a visit to the Quebec minister of natural resources in February 1971. The cooperatives were already much involved with community life, even sometimes subsidizing village councils (as at Povungnituk), and took an interest in regional development involving the complementary diversity of resources and local efforts. The minister's reaction to the proposition was very favorable, and he promised to undertake a legal study of it. As soon as they heard of this, newspapers in the provincial capital ran headlines asserting that the Inuit had "chosen Quebec" (implying "not Canada"), and this interpretation—at the least a biased one—caused much commotion in northern Quebec where several Inuit opposed to political domination by Quebec decided to react. Their leader was Charlie Watt, a young mechanic, originally from Fort-Chimo, employed by the federal government. He obtained the support of the Department of Indian Affairs and Northern Development and of the office of the Secretary of State to found the Northern Quebec Inuit Association.

This association, openly opposed to the regional government project proposed by the cooperatives, claimed to speak for the Inuit of Arctic Quebec and took control of defending Inuit interests in all political negotiations with the different governments. A few months later, when Quebec Prime Minister Robert Bourrassa announced the impending opening of the hydroelectric development project for James Bay and northern Quebec and the creation of the Société de Développement de la Baie James with a mandate to negotiate expropriation of the Natives, the Northern Quebec Inuit Association was recognized as the sole Inuit representative at the negotiating table along with delegates of the Indians (Grand Council of the Cree) and the provincial and federal governments. Their decision was ratified as the James Bay and Northern Quebec Agreement of 1975. This was the end of the political dream of the Inuit cooperative movement, and the beginning of a new era in which Inuit power was structured bureaucratically.

When the Agreement was signed, after 15 years of directed "economic and social development," Inuit life in Arctic Quebec had been profoundly modified. Before, there had been 12 settlements (including Port Burwell and Belcher Islands, administratively part of the North West Territories) mostly consisting of a few buildings occupied or managed by outsiders from the south (missionaries, shopkeepers, policemen) but each

surrounded by a network of seasonal camps occupied by the majority of Inuit families. Now there were 14 large villages—those at Baie aux Feuilles, Hopes Advance Bay, and Akulivik built at traditional campsites—well established, with prefabricated houses, electricity, oil heating, drinking water supplies, garbage collection, telephone service by radio or satellite, schools, and hospital. Air links served each village several times per week; snowmobiles had replaced dog sleds (which had practically disappeared) and motorboats had replaced kayaks. English became the language of communication, and knowledge of French increased. Community freezers stored local meat and fish, while the consumption of imported goods and food reached alarming levels (considering their cost and frequent maladaption to local conditions).

Inuit Take Control

Antagonisms between different agencies representing interests of southern Canada lessened or even disappeared, and a new class of Inuit officials filled many administrative and technical positions. A generation of "modernized" educated Inuit rejected the traditional image of Inuit life represented by their parents or grandparents; avidly assimilating White culture, they adopted also its abuses and evils. Alcohol use was general and drug problems common, with all their criminal consequences. To maintain order, municipalities and village councils employed auxiliary police. In the 1970s many adolescents went south to complete their educational and technical training, and when they returned introduced new behavior and sometimes new beliefs to their villages. In this way Christian sects such as the Pentecostals and Jehovah's Witnesses gained followers and began proselytizing in the North, as did the Baha'i. At Ivujivik a syncretistic movement appeared. Inuit-operated community radio services began in several places, and a specialized communication corporation, Taqramiut Nipingat, participated in experiments in satellite transmissions in the Inuit language. Between 1960 and 1970 the population increased at the unprecedented annual rate of 3.5 percent, due to a marked decrease in infant mortality. Adoption also declined significantly. The population grew much more youthful; in 1969, 57 percent was less than 20 years old.

Little of traditional technology remained after the invasion of plastic and metal manufactured goods, although a few hunting and sewing implements and some skin garments could be found. Hunting and fishing kept their importance for food and the production of sealskins; trapping in good years provided significant supplemental income; but carving was the newest and most important source of Inuit income. However, there was a large disparity between wage-earning families and others: in 1968–1969 the average annual individual income in families with wages was $1,500, but only $350 in non-wage-earning families; the overall average was $700 (Simard 1970). With ideas and habits of life from southern Canada, separations and divorces reappeared (separations were common under traditional conditions). Marriage increasingly followed individual preferences. Contraception appeared in several forms, including sterilization. A degree of village endogamy was apparent, while rare instances of polygyny perhaps represent a return to an ancestral custom. Domestic units tend to be based on nuclear families. The Inuit lost an important element of their traditional social structure with the disappearance of the midwives who had functioned as cultural mothers until those whose births they attended reached adulthood.

The James Bay and Northern Quebec Agreement

The James Bay and Northern Quebec Agreement of 1975 marked a historic turning point for the Arctic Quebec Inuit, as did the dissent it aroused among the Inuit of the northwestern peninsula (about one-third of the adult population of northern Quebec). The old Euro-Canadian antagonisms were replaced by Inuit antagonisms—the confrontation of two philosophies, two views of society, two concepts of social relations, and also two modes of administration. The Inuit majority followed the Northern Quebec Inuit Association and accepted the extinguishment of the aboriginal rights to their territory in exchange for compensation, while the minority refused this extinguishment and formed the association named Inuit Tungavingat Nunami 'the Inuit who stand up on their land'. This minority consisted of the inhabitants of Povungnituk and Ivujivik, and some from Saglouc, who were the pioneers of the cooperative movement.

From the governments' point of view, the Agreement allowed federal withdrawal from administration, with considerable budgetary savings (Rouland 1978), while retaining certain responsibilities. The provincial government was the main beneficiary, gaining a green light for its development projects, much more concrete recognition of its rights in the area, and exclusive political responsibility over the region. The coming to power of a separatist government in Quebec in 1976, led by René Lévesque who in 1961 had been involved at the start of Quebec political interest in northern Quebec, made the Agreement seem to correspond with Quebec nationalism, and set aside the federal control that had dominated the situation in northern Quebec up to that time.

From the point of view of the Northern Quebec Inuit Association and the Inuit majority, the Agreement seemed to be a victory for the Inuit bureaucratic elite, especially those originally from Fort-Chimo. For the price of extinguishing their land rights, the Agreement gave them immediate administrative power on the local and regional levels, and cultural recognition with some special rights, in the domain of the traditional life of hunting, fishing, and trapping, as also in education and justice. They received monetary compensation totaling dozens of millions of dollars.

Community corporations organized in each village were given exclusive rights over one percent of the territory (land category 1) in which there could be no mineral extraction without both their permission and monetary compensation. In other parts of the territory (land category 2) the Inuit have exclusive rights to hunting, fishing, and trapping, and any mineral or other exploitation there must respect these rights. In the third and largest part of the territory the Inuit have the same rights as non-Inuit, and large government projects can be developed. The Agreement provides for an autonomous educational commission, assigning great power to village parents' committees and assuring Inuit cultural needs by requiring that teaching be conducted at least partially in Inupiaq. The administration of justice must be adapted both to the nature of the territory by becoming more mobile, and to Inuit cultural characteristics by modifications in the Quebec and Canadian codes and procedures. Development is to be controlled at the municipal level through regaining all the local responsibilities previously in the hands of federal or provincial agents, and at the regional level by the establishment of a regional government with jurisdiction, throughout the territory, over administration, transportation, communications, justice, health, social services, education, economic development, the environment, resources, and managing the appropriation of land. Monetary compensation is estimated at $60 million basic indemnity plus $30 million as indemnity on future development. The Makivik Corporation was entrusted with managing these funds and using them according to procedures well specified by the Agreement (Rouland 1978). Several hundred Inuit are employed under the terms of the Agreement, so that an Inuit bureaucratic administration replaced the earlier ones.

Unfamiliar with the technical and legal language of the Agreement, impressed by the enumeration of powers to be retrieved as well as by the amounts of money mentioned and the number of jobs provided, and gratified by the emphasis in the texts on Inuit cultural identity and its characteristic ways, an overwhelming majority of the Inuit agreed to ratify the Agreement, without (according to some subsequent testimony) understanding all its aspects (Rouland 1978; Simard 1982).

From the point of view of the dissident minority (the Inuit Tungavingat Nunami) who always wished to preserve a community mode of operation, refusing both incorporation and federal or provincial funds in order to keep their options open (they financed their three villages through a voluntary 5 percent tax on sales of the cooperatives or on payments for carvings), aboriginal territorial rights as part of the Inuit cultural heritage are not negotiable or extinguishable. Everything else except that principle was negotiable. As for the sums offered to the Inuit as reparations, the Inuit Tungavingat Nunami argument is that they are incomensurate with the rights ceded; the real value of the money would even drop rapidly with inflation. In reality, behind this stance lay the communal philosophy of the cooperative movement that was so successful in the 1960s, especially in the northwestern part of the peninsula. This movement had motivated and drawn in the generation of active, unschooled adults, by means of carving and participation in community organizations and had integrated some traditional values with the modern socioeconomic structure.

Thus there was an opposition between two regions, two models of society, two generations, and two categories of Inuit differently affected by contacts with Euro-Canadian agents. The strength of the dissidents' argument should not be underestimated, given that one of the results of the Agreement was to reduce to one percent the lands on which the Inuit kept exclusive rights—lands in category 1. The dissidents appeared as the defenders of Inuit tradition and hoped to cause negotiations to be reopened on the matter of aboriginal rights. Certainly as long as the Agreement excludes one-third of the Inuit population of northern Quebec it remains a weak formulation always suseptible to questioning.

The crisis of the 1980s will perhaps resolve the dilemma, somewhat ironically: the effects of the crisis have in fact destroyed some illusions of the Inuit bureaucratic elite that administers the Agreement; inflation has considerably reduced the amounts promised as compensation, and several economic development projects of the Makivik Corporation have received major setbacks; cooperation by Quebec and Ottawa government agencies is deficient, the Inuit having continually to request respect for the spirit if not the forms of the Agreement, especially for financial readjustments.

Cultural awareness has reappeared throughout the peninsula. While in the 1970s only economic development and Inuit power were emphasized, in the 1980s priority was given to the development of many cultural projects—investigation of Inuit place-and personal names, the creation of museums, preparation of works in Inuit on the language and traditional culture—all undertaken by the Inuit themselves. And in these activities the dissidents played a very active role.

In July 1982 a conference on cultural development was organized by the Quebec Ministry of Cultural Affairs; delegates from all Inuit villages of Arctic Quebec met at Povungnituk. There was unanimity on the need for a reevaluation of Inuit culture, in alimentation and the hunting economy as well as in education and the transmission of knowledge. From many villages came echoes of a return to traditional practices: to dog sleds because of the costs and problems of snowmobiles, to skin and fur clothing, to traditional foods, to the old camps, even a new interest in old beliefs and shamanism.

The Inuit corporations resulting from the James Bay and Northern Quebec Agreement are developing their activities: Air Inuit assures air transport between the villages; Kigiaq deals with construction; Sanak handles training; *Taqralik* magazine publishes information in English and in Eskimo syllabics; Tusaqvik prepares radio broadcasts in Inuit. Avataq completes its museum and cultural center and supports several research projects; the Inuit Elders meet to decide on cultural priorities; Taqramiut Nipingat explores future communication; Kativik Health Service published a trilingual manual for mothers; the Kativik Education Commission works on Inuit curricula; the Kativik government administers the territory; and the Makivik Corporation, under the presidency of Mary Simon, an Inuit from Fort-Chimo, manages its financial support program and its investments under its mandate. The Inuit Tungavingat Nunami dissidents do not take part in these corporations. Using the profits from their carvings, they hire lawyers to attack the treaties and agreements that have dispossessed them. Rejecting the Kativik Education Commission they have themselves assumed the task of educating their children. They maintain a small museum and have undertaken an Inuit encyclopedia and a dictionary of the Inuit language.

Coastal Northern Labrador After 1950

ANNE BRANTENBERG AND TERJE BRANTENBERG

The coastal area of Labrador north of Cape Harrison includes the communities Postville (223 inhabitants in 1981), Makkovik (307), Hopedale (425), and Nain (938). The Inuit inhabitants constitute a majority compared to the descendants of European and Canadian Settlers who emigrated to the area mainly after 1830. The Montagnais-Naskapi Indians of this region are treated in volume 6.

In 1949 Newfoundland and with it Labrador entered the Confederation of Canada. Government dominance succeeded the local authority of the Moravian Mission. The coast was opened up through better means of transportation and communication. A new educational system and economic development also served to integrate Northern Labrador into the wider society.

During the 1970s various new opportunities gave rise to several initiatives and organizations that have strengthened participation by local residents in local-level and Native politics. Some governmental services have been transferred, providing the basis for local and outside enterprises.

At the same time, the many changes in conditions of life have decreased social control and increased poverty, alcohol abuse, and criminality. The longlasting influence of mission and government accentuates the problems of adjustment. Northern Labrador is still a marginal area; the policies of the wider society are still based more on its own premises than on those of the area's resources and residents.

Economic and Cultural Situation under Provincial Government

Government Administration

In the 1940s the administration and economy of Northern Labrador was in great disarray and undergoing considerable change. The former monopoly of the Moravian Mission was declining. In 1926 economic difficulties had forced the Mission to transfer its trading operations to the Hudson's Bay Company. However, falling prices on local products caused the Company to cease most of its activities along the coast. In the absence of any other trading interests, the government of Newfoundland took over responsibility for trade and public serv-ices through the Department of Mines and Resources in Saint John's.

Newfoundland's confederation with Canada in 1949 had far-reaching consequences for Labrador and particularly the northern coast. Despite disagreements between the provincial and federal governments as to responsibility for the Indian and Inuit populations, the Newfoundland government maintained and enlarged its administrative services for the northern coast. In 1951 these services were transferred to the Department of Public Welfare, and the following year a separate Division of Northern Labrador Affairs (DNLA) was established. This was later renamed the Labrador Service Division (LSD) as part of the Department of Recreation and Rehabilitation.

The central organization of the Division in Saint John's and its local staff began to support the local communities through planning and administration of such activities as the operation of general stores, power plants, and refrigeration units, the installation of sewerage and water, housing projects, the operation of local fisheries, the processing and marketing of fish products, seal-skins, and furs, and assisting fishermen in obtaining boats and fishing gear. Until 1967 the responsibility for social welfare services rested with the local depot-manager; it was then transferred to the Welfare Office in Happy Valley.

The establishment of this separate provincial service for the northern coast was made possible through a series of negotiations and agreements between the provincial and federal governments after 1953, with the federal government providing most of the financing. (The Annual Reports of Northern Labrador Service Division, government of Newfoundland, give more details.) However, the federal government did not formally recognize its constitutional responsibility toward the province's Natives until the middle of the 1960s. Not until 1975 were negotiations opened for representatives from the Native populations of Northern Labrador.

The provincial government initiated its activities in the region as a relief or emergency operation. Hence, governmental commitment was, from the 1940s to the 1960s, primarily concerned with the infrastructure, and less money and effort were spent on economic development. This concentration on "holding operations" was primarily based on the assumption that there was hardly any economic future for Northern Labrador (Jenness 1965:80). The population's long-term interests were to be met in terms of relocation to urban centers in the south and opportunities for wage labor by industrial development in other parts of Newfoundland (Kennedy 1977:285).

The raison d'être of the province's special services to the Inuit (and Indians) in Northern Labrador was related to notions of welfare and integration: to assimilate the Natives into Newfoundland society and culture. The Division's Annual Report of 1953 stated that "Eskimos and Indians have not as yet developed to the stage where they can be expected to compete on an equal footing with Whites in earning a livelihood, and who, at least for some time to come, will need patient understanding and guidance in their adjustment to economic and cultural conditions into which they are increasingly being enmeshed and absorbed" (Government of Newfoundland and Labrador. Division of Northern Labrador Affairs 1953:82).

The provincial government was opposed to establishing any permanent special services for the nonstatus Indians and Inuit in the province. Public funding earmarked for the Native population of Northern Labrador was consequently diverted into services provided to each community (Nain, Hopedale, Makkovik, Postville, Davis Inlet, and North West River), but excluding those Inuit and Indians who had migrated to the urban centers like Happy Valley and Goose Bay. Thus, the government solved the problem of defining criteria for eligibility on an individual basis due to the high degree of ethnic intermarriage along the coast. People were not aware of the reasons for the public services, as these were presented and understood as government services, not as stemming specifically from their constitutional status as indigenous people.

Transportation and Communication

Prior to Confederation, Northern Labrador's main link with the outside was the government mail boat between Saint John's and Nain. Regular freight and passenger traffic was first started in 1954 by the Canadian National coastal boats, which long served as the main means for intercommunity and outside travel during the open-water period from June or July through October or November. Airplane transportation, introduced in the 1930s, became increasingly important to the Moravian Mission, the International Grenfell Association (which provided health services), and the government, since the only other means of transport in winter was by dog team. In fact, dog teams were regularly used to carry mail within and out of Northern Labrador as late as the early 1950s. In 1956 a regular air mail winter service started operating out of Goose Bay every second month.

Thus, the introduction of air mail accompanied by mail order catalogues, old-age pensions, and family allowances and other transfer payments provided new sources of income and a growing dependence on market goods. In 1963 a regular weekly air service was started connecting the northern communities to Goose Bay. This was extended to bi-weekly flights in 1971, and since then air strips have been built in most communities.

Since the 1940s radio telephone has been an essential link for the northern coast; two-way radio equipment was soon used by the Royal Canadian Mounted Police, the International Grenfell Association, and the government in each community. During the 1950s a regular telephone service was developed. Direct distance dialing was installed along the coast beginning in 1974, reaching Nain in 1979. The Moravian Mission operated a radio station in Nain from 1950 to 1957. However, whereas Hopedale had for several years been receiving Canadian Broadcasting Corporation network broadcasting, Nain received the same service only in 1975. In 1975 an FM station was started in Makkovik; a similar station was started in Nain in 1981. During the early 1970s videotape equipment and programs were introduced; they were in regular use by various associations and agencies in the 1980s. In 1975 Nain was the first community to receive Canadian television coverage through a Canadian communications satellite; other communities have received television since then.

Newspapers were not regularly available on the northern coast until the inception of the bilingual *Kinatuinamot Illengajuk* in 1972. The quarterlies *The Labrador Moravian* (printed in Makkovik since 1972) and *Them Days* (printed by the Labrador Heritage Society since 1975) focus on the Moravian congregations past and present and the social history of Settlers, respectively. In the 1970s several newspapers and newsletters were published mostly in Happy Valley.

Thus, there has been an opening up of Northern Labrador not only in terms of changing administration but also in terms of opportunities for travel and communication.

Settlement and Population

In the course of the 1950s the centers became more important for the local population. Lower prices on the sealskins and furs important in a camp/homestead adaptation, increasing dependence on market-produced goods (food and technology), and increased possibilities for more or less permanent jobs in the settlements as well as the introduction of compulsory schooling (in 1949) and the closing of boarding schools, improved services in health care (small hospitals in Makkovik, Hopedale, and Nain built after 1954) and administration (trade, social welfare)—these factors resulted in more households spending a longer time in the settlements and other households leaving their hunting and fishing camps and homesteads to settle permanently in the towns.

By 1951 most of Northern Labrador's population was concentrated into four Moravian settlements: Makkovik (100 inhabitants), Hopedale (200), Nain (310), and Hebron (208) and in three other settlements: Kaipokok Bay area (160 inhabitants), Nutak (202), and the Indian community Davis Inlet.

Due to the dispersed population and distances—a 260-mile coastline between Makkovik and Hebron—the government faced problems in providing to the northern communities services comparable to those of other Canadians. In addition, the Moravian Mission and the International Grenfell Association also felt concern for the health and living conditions of the Inuit. At the same time the potential for economic development farther south, especially lumber and uranium exploitation in the Makkovik-Postville area, was great. These factors lie behind the decision to close Nutak and Hebron, Labrador's two most northern communities. The difficulties in obtaining firewood at Hebron gave additional problems (Government of Newfoundland and Labrador, Division of Northern Labrador Affairs 1960:114; Jenness 1965; Kleivan 1966:40, Kennedy 1977:278, 1978:144).

The 200 inhabitants of Nutak and Okak Bay area were relocated in 1956, most of them to Nain. The nearly 300 inhabitants of Hebron were then moved in 1959, most of them to Makkovik.

These moves revealed the growing dependence on the remaining settlements' services and increasing competition and exploitation of resources. At the same time, some of Northern Labrador's prime hunting and fishing resources remain unharvested during much of the year. The situation also shows the disparity between what the government and other outside agencies thought the people wanted and needed and what the people themselves thought best. Relocation meant breaking up Inuit family units and moving to unknown, more or less alien milieus.

Many of those relocated to Makkovik later moved northward to rejoin kin and exploit the richer resource base there. Population figures illustrate this, as 140 Inuit lived in Makkovik in 1963, but only 76 remained in 1972.

Many Labrador Inuit became both suspicious of and averse to government programs after the relocation. Throughout the years afterward negative feelings were publicly expressed and initiatives taken to establish at least seasonal camps in the abandoned areas.

After this relocation, Nain became the northernmost and largest community in Northern Labrador. In 1961 Nain had 465 inhabitants, Hopedale 218, Makkovik 168, and Postville 84. In the same year some 660 Inuit and some 500 Settlers inhabited the region, but Nain was the only community with an Inuit majority, about 75 percent.

The existing relations between the two local groups, Inuit and Settlers, account for some uncertainty with regard to the exact ethnic composition at any time. Thus the 674 local residents of Nain in 1970 may be divided into 76 percent Inuit and 14 percent Settlers while the remaining 10 percent were children under 20 years of age from ethnically mixed marriages. However, the offspring of mixed parentage are redistributed on either side of the ethnic border, usually within one, or at the most, two generations.

In this process language performance is important both as a criterion of ethnic status and as the means by which such offspring are able to make ethnic commitment and affirm an identity. The relation between ethnic origin and self-identification is not always obvious. Ethnic identity depends on context and opportunities.

Clear-cut, objective criteria for ethnic group membership are lacking. Ethnic status does not imply differential rights to the natural resources since Inuit and Settlers have always occupied the same ecological niches. Both groups have adopted items from each other's culture. The Settlers, being a local minority, have to a great extent been bilingual. Public services, cash income, and modern technology are available to Inuit and Settlers alike.

The degree of similarity and shared culture are reflected in everyday life, especially among individuals in public places like the wharf, the store, and the community hall. The number of interethnic marriages is another indication (13 percent of the married couples in Nain in 1970).

However, there are differences. These are also reflected in everyday life, especially on the group level in mutual ethnic stereotypes. People continue to refer to themselves and others as Inuit or Eskimos and Settlers, Whites, or *Qallunaangayuk* (sg.). They ascribe particular cultural content and stereotypes to these categories, react and interpret the reactions to changing circumstances and new opportunities accordingly.

This could traditionally be expressed within the Moravian Mission, which allowed Settlers to define themselves as Whites, Inuit to remain Inuit, albeit Moravian defined. Now there are more opportunities to present oneself simply as a local resident or Labradorian.

Education and Language

After the Confederation, responsibility for education was transferred from the Moravian Mission to the Department of Education in Saint John's and the Labrador East Integrated School Board in Happy Valley. As the curriculum then changed its basically religious character in the Moravian school to that of a broad secular program, the aim of education shifted from enabling the

691

pupils primarily to participate in the economic, social, and religious activities of their own community to that of obtaining skills for Canadian society. Thus, education has been an instrument to achieve the governmental policy of integrating the Labrador Native population.

However, the school seemingly fails to inspire and educate pupils according to the expected level of knowledge and grade. In Nain in 1970–1971 only four of the 16 pupils over the age of 14 were in grade 8 where they all should have been according to the age-grade norm. High turnover among the teachers reinforces the problem of getting the pupils through the classes as intended. Even for those few with higher education, school has not meant out-migration and careers in the south. They had to go to North West River for high school and to Newfoundland for vocational schools and university. However, 23 of the 39 from Nain who left Labrador for education before 1971 returned with or without graduation. Growing demands for high schools in the local communities brought grade 9 to Nain in 1976 and up to grade 11 in 1979. On the other hand, the curriculum also lacks relevance for local careers and does not include local history and culture.

There are not many opportunities for reinvestment of school-acquired expertise in the local community. The majority of administrative and other skilled jobs are already filled with "outsiders": the Labrador Service Division staff from south Canada, the nurses from England, teachers from England, the United States, and south Canada, and many of the carpenters building houses during the summer from the island of Newfoundland. Most jobs available for local persons involve training on the job rather than formal education. In addition, most people still have a combined adaptation where wage work constitutes only one element.

Natl. Film Board of Canada Photothèque, Ottawa: 95717.

Fig. 1. Tents at a summer camp at Ikkudliayuk, coast of Labrador, Newf., a traditional Inuit fishing ground. Photograph by Rosemary Gilliat, Aug. 1960.

692

For this adaptation the curriculum is broadly speaking irrelevant. The compulsory school terms deprive the households of necessary help and hinder the needed training by participation. This holds especially true for the boys, whose help is needed and whose training takes place on sea and inland, in the camps and homesteads outside Nain. Girls' work and training are essentially connected with housework and child care in and around the home for most people in Nain the year round, at least during school terms. Thus pupils from hunting-fishing homes have problems in combining participation in school and home.

The problems are accentuated for Inuit pupils. The mission school was ethnically segregated and bilingual as each group was taught separately in its own language. In 1983 the school was monolingual and may be said to segment and accentuate the differentiation between the local groups by favoring the language and other cultural traits of one of them, namely the English-speaking Settlers.

The school is instrumental in the process of growing monolingualism among Settlers and growing acquisition of bicultural skills among the Inuit. The Labrador dialect of Inuit is predominantly a spoken language, except in a religious context and the bilingual newspaper. The consequences of the reduced use and competence in the Inuit language and growing "anglification," especially among schoolchildren, is therefore serious.

Many parties have worked for reintroducing Inuit in the schools. Conferences and workshops have been arranged to better the situation, the Faculty of Education at Memorial University of Newfoundland established a Division of Native and Northern Education, and the provincial and federal governments allocate money for Indian and Inuit education.

Language classes once a week started in Nain in 1973 for grades 4 through 9. In 1979 the Nain school had 18 English-speaking teachers and six Inuit-speaking teachers' aides. About 70 percent of the 266 pupils that year were Inuit. However, the content of the curriculum remains Canadian, and there are still few Natives as teachers and administrators. Requests for establishing an Inuit school board have been turned down.

Economic Development

The communities of Northern Labrador have always been highly dependent on the renewable land and sea resources for subsistence and market production. Inuit and Settlers still have close and daily contact with land and sea.

Harvesting of the highly varied natural resources is restricted not only by the seasonality of the various species but also by a short fishing season during the open-water period. Also, commercial production has been limited by the trading agencies' tendency to specialize in a few species. Thus, fluctuating market prices on fish, sealskins, or furs have resulted in recurring crises for the local population, who to a large extent rely on unemployment insurance benefits and social assistance in the off-season. Thus, subsistence still provides an important addition and necessity to most households in the form of caribou, seal, fish, and birds.

The local resource harvesting is characterized by a small-scale technology. The majority of fishermen operate their own motorboats (open 28-foot "trapboats") (fig. 2) in addition to speedboats and a limited number of longliners. Dogteams were supplanted by snowmobiles during the late 1960s and early 1970s. During the late 1960s the codfishery, formerly the main commercial fish resource along the coast, was virtually wiped out due to overfishing at Hamilton Banks by deep-sea trawlers.

The Northern Labrador Service Division had started a commercial fishery of pickled char in 1942, and in 1968 production of smoked char was started. The Division enlarged the operations by installing a smokery and fish plant with two blast freezers in Nain in 1970–1971 and another plant in Makkovik in 1973. Char fishing was supplemented in 1969 when the Division started to purchase salmon, until then a little-used resource in Northern Labrador. The char and salmon fishery developed considerably in the following years.

In 1973 commercial char fishing was restricted to Labrador fishermen. Salmon licenses were issued some years later. In the 1970s both salmon and char catches declined gradually. Char stocks have declined in size and numbers in most areas, and quotas on local char stocks were enforced in 1979. However, in the early 1980s the inshore codfishery has shown signs of recovery. In 1980 the government-operated commercial fishery secured

Fig. 2. Char fisherman and motorboats at Ugjuktok Fiord. Photograph by Fred Bruemmer, July 1968.

employment for 653 fishermen and 376 plant workers along the northern coast.

Since 1974 the Department of Fisheries has explored possibilities for diversifying the fishery to other commercial fish species, and fisheries for turbot and scallops are being developed. Shrimp beds were also being exploited. In 1978 three shrimp licenses were reserved for Labrador by the federal Department of Fisheries.

Opportunities for wage labor in the construction of the U.S. air base at Goose Bay during World War II caused some out-migration from Northern Labrador to Goose Bay and Happy Valley in southern Labrador. In the 1950s and 1960s construction of radar and weather stations also provided periods of wage labor. However, the majority of workers have returned to fishing and hunting when prices on fish and other products have been on the rise. Also, the depressed economy with a high rate of unemployment in Newfoundland and the closing down of the U.S. Air Force at Goose Bay in 1975 have restricted opportunities for out-migration.

Within Northern Labrador the government's gradual extension of its services and housing programs has provided a market for local wage labor that alongside transfer payments and unemployment insurance benefits has provided vital subsidies to the local economy. Development of the fishery and construction work during the 1970s enabled resettled and out-migrated Inuit and Settlers to return to Northern Labrador. However, the increased level of income has been offset by rising prices on food, gas, and stove oil and increasing dependence on cash-demanding technology.

The sealfishery and hunting have declined in importance since 1960. The environmentalists' campaigns to end the seal hunt have led to falling prices and have deprived households of an important traditional cash source to supplement their sometimes extremely low income. In a local economy like that of Nain 88 percent of the people earned less than $2,400 in 1970 from fishing and wage labor, with unemployment benefits not included. Low prices and the rising costs of harvesting seals and other game resources have made it more difficult for households to obtain a highly valued and nutritious food supply. Among the Inuit seal meat has a social value and is shared among hunters, relatives, and neighbors, thus serving as an expression of prestige and solidarity within the Inuit community. So restrictions on subsistence activities like sealhunting render households not only more dependent on store food but also more dependent on those who can afford to hunt more.

The caribou is another major subsistence resource in Northern Labrador. According to studies started in 1969 by the Provincial Wildlife Service the population has been on the increase and in 1980 was estimated at 225,000 animals. Caribou management has been a recurring issue in Northern Labrador due to hunting regulations imposed by the Newfoundland government. Hunting has been closed during the autumn when the skin and meat is prime, and quotas of one animal per family member have been imposed as well as regulations against hunting for others (the old or disabled). Thus, caribou regulations have contributed to conditions of real poverty in the northern communities where store supplies of food were scarce, expensive, and of poor quality. After receiving considerable pressure the government amended regulations in 1978 and opened hunting all year round with no bag limit. During 1979–1980 the kill for Northern Labrador was about 2,500 caribou. Negotiations with the Quebec government for shared management have met with difficulties as Quebec allows sports hunting of the northern herds, whereas the caribou have been reserved for subsistence hunting in Northern Labrador.

This economic development has, on the local level, been met somewhat differently by the Inuit and the Settlers as could be seen in Nain in the early 1970s. Different value orientations, especially the focal value of sharing among the Inuit compared to being self-sufficient among the Settlers, produce contrasting economic adaptations. An example is the different responses to the introduction of snowmobiles in Nain in 1964. Among the Inuit, the dependence of one household on another often results in the sharing of snowmobiles instead of individual acquisition. However, most Settlers have snowmobiles and this may be interpreted in terms of the Settler emphasis on corporateness and independence, thus making them more dependent on personally owned means of transportation.

Dogteams or snowmobiles are of great importance because both Inuit and Settlers still value subsistence as supplementing the often fluctuating income from fisheries, more or less temporary jobs, and social assistance. For the Inuit hunting, in addition to providing meat, also contributes to prestige-giving exchange-relations through the practice of meat sharing. This is partly why many Inuit sometimes prefer hunting to more cash-yielding activities like intensive fishing or odd jobs in the spring, summer, and fall.

Generally speaking, the Inuit have some problems in maintaining economic viability throughout the yearly cycle especially with regard to firewood and meat. This is due to the sharing practices that make their adaptation a compromise between satisfaction of the needs of one's family and the rules imposed by one's ethnic group. The Settlers' stress on self-sufficiency makes individual planning and saving easier. Thus piles of wood and stored meat are more common in Settler than in Inuit households.

There have been more Settlers than Inuit who worked at steady jobs. In Nain in 1970, the figures were 75 percent versus 25 percent. Settlers have been used as middlemen by White agencies, for example as interpreters, due to their bilingual skills and knowledge of local circumstances. Many Settlers have also more readily than most Inuit taken advantage of the new opportunities opened up by greater governmental commitments and by increased consumer spending. Thus there are small entrepreneurs who are employed in the sale of snowmobile parts, there are small general stores, a snackbar, and sale of home-baked bread and cookies.

The differences in value orientations and in economic preferences and strategies are also reflected in the two groups' respective relationships with trading agencies. Due to the economic cycle, during some periods of the year many Inuit accumulate debts in the store, and this situation has sometimes resulted in conflicts with White traders and depot-managers (Kleivan 1966:24). Settlers also make use of credit, but generally speaking to a lesser extent and with fewer disputes. They also often have other relations with the Whites—as neighbor, employee, or kin. Thus, the two local ethnic groups react differently to the changing economic situation in a community like Nain. This is also emphasized in their mutual stereotypes, which help maintain the ethnic border in spite of similar circumstances: as to resource basis, transfer payments, and other new sources of income.

Industrial Development

In spite of its geographical isolation from the rest of Canada, the natural resources of Labrador have attracted a variety of outside interests. The formerly vast cod stocks attracted a large fishing fleet from Canada and foreign countries during the early twentieth century. Forests, minerals, and rivers have provided for large-scale industrial development. Most of these infringements took place outside southern Labrador.

After the discovery of uranium deposits in the 1940s, large-scale mineral explorations were carried out throughout the 1950s and 1960s. Brinex, the exploration arm of Brinco (British Newfoundland Corporation created in 1953 as a syndicate of international corporations and capital) in 1975–1976 considered plans for uranium mining in Michelin Lake and Kitt's Pond in the Makkovik-Postville area. In mid-1977 Brinex postponed its application to proceed with mining and after considerable protest from the communities and organizations of Northern Labrador, the provincial government halted the project due to environmental uncertainties in 1980.

Exploration for petroleum started in 1966, and in 1971 drilling explorations in Saglek Bay started.

Large-scale proposals for year-round transportation of liquified gas from the Northwest Territories along the coast of Labrador to southern markets were shelved by the National Energy Board in 1982. Future market prices may well make such plans feasible and pose a gigantic threat to the renewable resource base of the Labrador Coast. This as well as plans of the provincial government for an all-year deepwater port (Port Labrador) and plans for extensions of the Trans-Labrador Highway to strengthen the urban centers of Goose Bay and Happy Valley have been opposed by the coastal fishing and hunting communities.

Governmental Policies and Native Response

Political and Economic Participation

With Confederation in 1949, Northern Labrador gradually became more involved with and dependent upon Canadian society. Since the 1960s this process has accelerated rapidly with drastic and far-reaching consequences for the Native population. The most significant events of this period have been an extension of various public services, changes in the province's administrative policies, the establishment of local government, and most important, the emergence of a regional ethnopolitical movement.

During the 1960s it became evident that the expectations for a growing labor market and opportunities for relocation south were not going to be fulfilled. If the population of Northern Labrador was to be integrated into Newfoundland society, this had to take place within the existing communities of the region. However, living conditions in the north were still far behind the national average. All communities lacked many of the most basic public facilities such as sewerage and water, problems that were exacerbated by a rapidly growing population. At the same time, the all-important regional administration was still led and run by a predominantly Newfoundland staff.

In 1969, to overcome the dilemma between the administration's integrative policy and its bureaucratic control over local affairs, the LSD (in cooperation with the Department of Municipal Affairs) held meetings in the communities advocating the establishment of community councils. Until then, local leadership in the Moravian communities had been vested in elected bodies of church elders. With the decline of Moravian influence, the authority of the elders was undermined as well. Also, the elders did not meet the formal requirements for incorporating the communities with the province in order to be eligible for various provincial and federal grants.

In some communities, like Nain, Settlers saw the council as a means for replacing the traditional influence of Inuit elders; in Makkovik the council has been dominated by Settlers (Kennedy 1981). Both groups, however, supported the councils from the outset as a means to provide funding for community development, to communicate with the government, and to achieve local control. From 1970 to 1978 community councils were established in each settlement, and councils have grad-

ually taken over many of the LSD's responsibilities in housing, water and sewerage, and planning. The development of local government was stimulated by the formation of the Combined Councils of Northern Labrador in 1972, which from the start received considerable support from the Extension Service of the Memorial University of Newfoundland, Saint John's. The Combined Councils was the first regional body where representatives from all the various communities could present their local problems and develop common political goals. Since 1978 this field has been extended by the formation of the Combined Councils of Labrador with members from all over Labrador.

During the same period there has been a marked increase in various government programs and services. Since 1974 welfare services have been provided by local welfare officers and social workers. The health service, still provided by the International Grenfell Association, has been extended by new clinics in several communities and by a health program for Native communities with elected health representatives from each community. In 1981 the nursing station at Nain received the first resident medical practitioner for the northern coast.

Of particular importance have been several government-sponsored programs for community development, the most noteworthy being the Extension Service of the Memorial University. Since 1972 this service has provided initiative and support for economic and political development in coastal Labrador by assisting community councils and other local and regional associations with training in communications skills; arranging seminars, workshops, and conferences; and carrying out studies on local problems like food availability. In 1979 the Service was complemented by the establishment of the Institute for Northern Studies at Goose Bay with the purpose of solving problems in human and resource development in Labrador.

Since the early 1970s, the body of elders and the local school board have been supplemented by local recreation or sports committees, fisheries committees, health committees, and craft councils (included in the Labrador Craft Producers Association, founded in 1977) with local craft stores or Handicraft Centres. Particularly noteworthy has been the formation of several local women's groups, who joined in the Labrador Women's Group in 1978. These groups have initiated several projects such as a day-care center for fish plant workers in Nain, the start of a Women's Centre and a counseling group for women. The group has also been active on other issues such as petitioning the government for a resident doctor and for improving the quality of food in the government-operated stores. In 1978 the Nain Radio Society was formed to obtain funding for and to operate a local radio station. The station, Canadian North Torngat Radio, went on the air for the first time in June 1981.

In 1976 the Labrador Resources Advisory Council was established to advise the provincial government on Labrador views on oil and gas matters. This was soon to include other resource issues like the inshore fisheries, community development, and uranium mining. However, since it was an umbrella organization of various Labrador interests, the Native associations withdrew due to disagreement on the Council's policy of accepting industrial development on a project-by-project basis before land claims were settled. The council was dissolved in 1982 due to lack of government funding.

The combined growth of local-level and Native politics in Northern Labrador has had important implications for the provincial government's administrative policies. The provincial government, strongly committed to free enterprise and minimal government intervention in the economy, had long seen the economic operations of the Labrador Service Division as a "necessary evil." During the 1970s the government had transferred some of its former services (like sales of oil and gas and construction) to private interests, thus providing a basis for local and outside enterprises. In 1978 a major revision in the government administration was signaled by the transference of LSD's fishing operations from the Department of Rural Agriculture and Northern Development to the Department of Fisheries. The same year the government invited proposals for the leasing of its fish plants, holding units, and collecting service in Northern Labrador. Both decisions were made without any previous notice or consultation with the local population and its organizations.

In Nain and other communities the government's decisions were met with protests. Many people, in spite of their previous criticism of governmental inefficiencies, felt that the local fisheries represented common interests and were not to be controlled by individual Labradorians or by outside private interests (Kinatuinmot Illengajuk 1978:no. 21–24). At the initiative of the Labrador Inuit Association (LIA), a Fishery Emergency Policy Committee was formed with fishermen and fishplant workers from all six of the northern communities as well as members of LIA and Labrador Resources Advisory Council. The Committee was to negotiate for a takeover of fish plants in Nain and Makkovik and shrimp licenses for Labrador through the establishment of a regional cooperative. Another proposal was submitted by a joint venture of a Nova Scotia fishery company and a group of Nain businessmen (Kinatuinamot Illengajuk 1980:no. 36–37). The committee's proposal was approved by the government; and with the support of LIA, the Extension Service of Memorial University, and cooperative consultants, the committee launched a cooperative educational program in all six communities. In December 1980 the Torngat Fish Producers Co-Operative Society Ltd. was formally incorporated, with a board of directors elected from each community in Northern Labrador. During 1981 fishing operations were run in joint-management with the Department of Fisheries, and in 1982 the cooperative achieved full control of the fishing industry in Northern Labrador.

In the 1980s the provincial government operated stores in Nain, Davis Inlet, Hopedale, Makkovik, and Postville, which were run by the LSD, since 1979 renamed the Labrador Development Division of the Department of Rural Development. Government services were still mainly provided by the federal and provincial Native people's agreements. In 1981 the agreement amounted to $38 million over a five-year period.

Ethnopolitical Organizations

During the 1960s and early 1970s the influence of the English language and culture was rapidly replacing the traditional Inuit language and values in Northern Labrador. Except for a growing concern among Moravian Inuit church elders and individual ministers as to the future of Inuit culture and identity, issues of Inuit (and Indian) politics were nonexistent. However, outside Labrador, Indians and Inuit were organizing national and regional associations to secure their indigenous rights.

In February 1972 the Native movement was introduced to Northern Labrador by representatives from the Northern Quebec Inuit Association (NQIA), who visited Nain by travelling on snowmobiles from Port-Nouveau-Québec (George River). The purpose was to inquire whether the Inuit of Labrador wanted to establish a regional association of the national Inuit association, Inuit Tapirisat of Canada (ITC). Receiving positive support from the Nain Inuit (but much anxiety among White government employees and Settlers), ITC officials visited the main Inuit communities during the summer, and an interim Labrador Inuit committee was subsequently elected in Nain. During September 1973 ITC leaders revisited the coast and elections were held for president and board members (3 from Nain, 2 from Makkovik, 2 from Hopedale, 1 from Happy Valley). In October 1973 the Labrador Inuit Association was established as an affiliate member of ITC. In later years the communities of Postville and Rigolet have also been represented on the LIA's board.

The foremost task of the LIA, in addition to strengthening Inuit culture, was to organize land claims on the basis of the unextinguished aboriginal rights of the Inuit population. Initially, this led to some difficulties, not only because people were unfamiliar with the concept of indigenous rights and what it would mean for themselves (Inuit as well as Settlers), but also due to the presence of another recently formed association, the Native Association of Newfoundland and Labrador (NANL), founded in 1973 in Newfoundland by persons of Micmac ancestry. NANL recruited both Inuit and Settlers, some of the Settlers also serving as board members. LIA was pursuing a more restricted policy of recruitment by requiring at least one-quarter Inuit ancestry for full membership. This was to secure Inuit control and to establish the LIA as a legitimate representative of Inuit interests with the provincial and federal governments. However, within the Inuit-Settler communities Settlers were concerned about being excluded from a land claims settlement. In Makkovik Settlers were joining NANL, while opposing the LIA.

In 1974 both associations applied to the federal government for funding of their land claims; LIA's application was turned down as NANL had Inuit on their board. However, LIA revised its policy toward the Settlers by opening full membership for all Native Settlers (defined as "a white man who settled in Labrador prior to 1940 and who has remained there since, and his children" [D.I.N.A. 1980]). The association also stated its obligation "to respect the rights of native settlers, to invite participation by native settlers in all the objectives of the Association and to share equally with them all benefits such as the Association might obtain for its members" (Kinatuinamot Illengajuk 1977:2).

Through meetings between the NANL and LIA in 1974 and 1975, LIA was established as the sole representative for Inuit and Settlers in Labrador. NANL later split into two associations, one for the Indians of the island of Newfoundland, the other—the Naskapi-Montagnais Innu Association—for the Labrador Indians.

In 1975 LIA obtained funding for its land use and occupancy study and legal research to present a comprehensive claim to the federal and provincial governments. In 1977 the association presented to both governments its "Statements of Claims to Certain Rights in the Land and Sea-Ice of Northern Labrador by the Inuit and Native Settler People" (D.I.N.A. 1980). This was the first land claim ever presented by any native group in the province. The claim covers land and sea-ice between Cape Chidley in the north and Lake Melville in the south.

In 1978 LIA's land use and occupancy study was finished (Brice-Bennett 1977). The study presents ample archeological and historical data on Inuit presence on the coast and a detailed documentation of past and present land use and resource harvesting. The study also describes the cultural significance of the land and its resources to the Inuit and Settler populations.

The federal government formally accepted LIA's claim in 1978. The provincial government, however, was initially against any recognition of Native rights in Newfoundland. This government was also refusing to include LIA in any land claims negotiations with the federal government. This was a crucial matter as the provincial government has jurisdiction over land and resources that would eventually be part of an agreement.

In October 1980 the Newfoundland government reversed its hard stance on the land claims issue and announced its willingness to enter into tripartite negotiations, provided the claims were acceptable to the federal government (Peckford 1980). Other conditions were that any claims settlement was to extinguish all native claims in the province and that self-government was not to be included on the agenda for negotiations (Kinatuinamot Illengajuk 1980).

Since 1975 LIA has received increasing support from both Inuit and Settlers and in the 1980s was firmly entrenched as the main political organization on the northern coast. One of its most significant achievements has been to provide a basis for extensive Inuit-Settler cooperation. In spite of LIA's primary focus on Inuit concerns, Settlers have from its establishment had important positions within the association (LIA's first president was of Settler background). In fact, LIA has not only buttressed Inuit identity but also generated, in spite of initial tensions and ambiguity, a strong feeling of shared interests and common identity among Settlers and Inuit as Native residents of Northern Labrador (in contrast to Newfoundland influence and presence). Thus, while most Inuit and Settlers live different and separate lives at the household level, LIA has generated a complementarity of ethnic group interests not previously existent in Inuit-Settler relations (Kleivan 1966; Brantenberg 1977; Paine 1977:249–264).

Dept. of Ind. Affairs and Northern Development, Hull, Que.
Fig. 3. Tagak Curley, President of Inuit Tapirisat of Canada (at right), interviewed by Elijah Menarik of the CBC Montreal Production Centre of the Northern Service, on Curley's participation in organizing the Labrador Inuit Association. The interview formed part of "Tarqravut/Our North," a 5-minute weekly news and information television program transmitted to northern Canada via satellite in both Eskimo and English versions. Photograph by Francis J. Menten, Nov. 1973.

697

This process has been facilitated not only by the association's policy toward Settlers but also by its multipurpose character. The variety of problems and growing needs confronting local people as well as their lack of political influence created a niche for LIA in establishing itself as a major intermediary between government agencies and the local communities. Thus LIA has provided initiative and funding for a variety of programs and services like summer student employment, emergency repair, the Nain newspaper (Kuinatuinmot Illengajuk), Labrador Friendship Centre in Goose Bay providing services to recently relocated Natives, and Labrador Legal Services providing for the first time legal assistance including Native court workers, to Labrador Natives. Through LIA Inuit have been involved with the Inuit Cultural Institute at Rankin Inlet, receiving training in collecting and preserving Inuit cultural traditions. This led to the establishment of an Inuit Cultural Office at Nain and in 1978 to the Labrador Inuit Cultural Centre, Torngarsuk, an affiliate of LIA with the purpose of preserving and strengthening Inuit culture, language, and education.

Some of the Centre's projects involve producing school textbooks in Inupiaq and developing Inuit literature. The Centre has also worked for introducing the common Inuit writing system, which was being used in the schools in the late 1980s alongside the Moravian system. Also, LIA has organized an Inuit housing nonprofit corporation in Labrador, an extension of the ITC's housing arm, providing assistance for improving substandard housing.

Another aspect of the LIA's intermediary role has been to act as an advocate on local and regional issues. Through a series of petitions the association has voiced local concerns on governmental policies on education, health, game laws, protection of the inshore fisheries, food supplies, and the management of government-operated stores and fisheries as well as industrial resource development. In some instances like the question of changing existing caribou hunting regulations LIA has been able to achieve some revisions in provincial policies. LIA's call for a moratorium on all offshore oil and gas exploration, however, has been ignored. The association has provided studies on the effects of uranium mining, housing, health care delivery, and the social, economic, and legal problems of hunting. LIA has also organized trips to Scotland and Ontario to study implications there of petroleum development and uranium mining.

Through LIA's affiliation with ITC, Labrador Inuit have been included in the field of Native politics on a national level. Since 1973 Labrador Inuit have regularly participated in ITC meetings outside Labrador. On the basis of the importance of marine resources for Inuit and Settlers, LIA appeared before the National Energy Board, opposing the proposal for tanker shipment of oil and gas through the Northwest Passage, Davis Strait, and the Labrador Sea. The association has also made representations to the Environmental Assessment and Review Process panel on the Beaufort Sea Hydrocarbons proposal to ask for an extension of the review process to include impacts of proposed tanker routes in the Labrador Sea south of 60° north latitude. LIA is one of the six regional Inuit associations represented on the Inuit Committee on National Issues, established by ITC in 1979 in connection with the constitutional debate in Canada. The association is also involved with the Inuit Circumpolar Conference, the first international Inuit organization with members from Alaska, Canada, and Greenland. LIA sent four representatives to ICC's first meetings in Alaska in 1977, where LIA's president was elected vice-chairman of ICC's interim committee. LIA has also participated in ICC's meetings in Greenland.

At the outset LIA was to a large extent dependent on support from ITC (and White resource personnel with previous experience from varied ITC work). However, through its many activities, administrative work, fieldwork, and community representation LIA has provided Inuit and Settlers of Northern Labrador with unique experiences. The association not only has become more independent of outside support but also has served to recruit personnel to positions in other fields of activity such as community councils and community health representatives. Thus, LIA has served to develop local control and political participation within Northern Labrador and to reduce the distance between local communities and southern politicians and administrators. LIA, with the Extension Service of Memorial University, the community councils, and other regional associations, has brought about a rapid decline in the formerly pervasive Moravian and provincial influence. Most important, LIA has provided Labrador Inuit with means for rediscovering their Inuit ancestry and reducing the former isolation from other Inuit and indigenous groups outside Labrador.

Gains and Losses

In spite of the gradual improvement in various public services provided to Northern Labrador, living conditions for the majority of Inuit and Settlers are still characterized by material need. As increasing contact with the outside has resulted in rising demands and expectations, most households find that incomes from fishing, seasonal wage labor, and transfer payments are rapidly falling behind the rising costs of living. Subsistence is still an economic necessity and an expression of Native identity. However, reduced cash returns from hunting and fishing contribute to a situation where the household economy is becoming more precarious and life more severe.

698

Since 1970 increasing contact with Canadian society enabled Inuit and Settlers to achieve more control in running their local affairs as well as to participate in political fields outside Labrador. This development, however, has been accompanied by a loss of social control and common values within the local communities. Thus, the small communities of Northern Labrador have experienced the emergence of a cluster of problems associated with modern urban life such as alcoholism, crime, marital conflicts, and violence.

These divergent developments are a dramatic and tragic expression of the dilemmas facing the population of Northern Labrador in its relationship to outside influence. On the one hand, the domination of the Moravian Mission and the provincial government (in spite of their highly different policies), served to alienate Inuit from their indigenous past. Traditional values and institutions have been suppressed and downgraded as "pagan" or "backward." Both Inuit and Settlers have faced outsiders who, for very different reasons, defined them as being either "too White" or "too Inuit."

On the other hand, Inuit and Settlers have been able to overcome some of this ambiguity and conflict in their relations between themselves and with the outside by establishing a positive self-identification. This identity underlines their common dependence on Northern Labrador and its resources as their shared homeland.

Since the 1940s, the Newfoundland government has provided "special services" for Indians and Inuit in Labrador. The intent of this policy was to integrate the Native populations within Newfoundland society and culture. To the Natives of Northern Labrador this policy has provided benefits as well as the shortsighted policies of centralization and relocation. In the 1980s Inuit and Settlers were still the recipients of "Native" funding. In spite of its Native designation, the underlying policy was that of economic, political, and cultural integration. Native language and cultural identity was a secondary theme as expressed in the educational system. Thus, the conflicts and ambiguities remain. However, these problems are now becoming explicit and argued by Inuit and Settlers themselves. To them Native culture and identity have become the primary issue and the base for further integration with Newfoundland and Canada in general.

Contemporary Greenlanders

HELGE KLEIVAN

This chapter does not survey all the situational changes in Greenland from the early 1950s through the late 1970s. Rather, it is a critical review (influenced by Bodley 1982 and Berreman 1981) of data relevant to understanding both the positive and the negative effects of the model of "economic development" implemented in Greenland. Particular attention is devoted to the responses of Greenlanders to the policy of societal transformation that was applied.

Colonial Underdevelopment

During World War II Greenland was separated for five years from the colonial power. It was then obvious both to Greenlanders and to the small number of Danes working in the country that many postwar changes were necessary.

The socioeconomic conditions of 1945 were those of underdevelopment: there was widespread poverty, inadequate and unhygienic housing, an alarming health situation (table 1), and deteriorating possibilities for maintaining production technology. In addition, indigenous institutions, like the meat-giving system and other mechanisms for mutual aid, had largely broken down in the centralized communities and were eroding in many of the outlying settlements, where the majority of people still lived in 1945.

This situation had developed over a very long period, despite the undeniable fact that Danish colonial rule had been marked by an unusually benevolent attitude. That the conditions were closely related to the monopoly trade system operating throughout the whole colonial era in Greenland was diagnosed and well understood as early as 1862 (Rink 1862).

The Progress of Political and Economic Reform, 1945–1965

In 1945, when Greenlanders expressed their wishes for the immediate future (for example, N. Rosing 1945:38–40), equality of salaries between Greenlanders and Danes was a typical theme. Another wish was to attain equal legal status for people of the two ethnic groups. The suggestion that education should be improved, particularly in the form of more and better instruction in the Danish language, was frequently heard. Under the prevailing circumstances learning the language of those that were wealthy and influential offered the surest hope for the future.

Generally the wish was for a greater degree of independence for Greenlanders. There was no indication of hostility toward Denmark and the Danes. On the contrary, the hope was to escape colonial status and to achieve a position of equality with the Danes.

The provincial councils united in a joint meeting in 1945, where many ideas for reform were discussed. Some of the proposals had an almost symbolic character, stressing the need for communication among Greenlanders, for example, the desire to expand the range of the small broadcasting station at Godthåb (Nuuk) and to acquire a ship to travel along the west coast. Another proposal was to develop a single provincial council for the whole country, but this was not accepted in Copenhagen, apparently because some of the top colonial administrators saw it as a possible instrument for advancing "separatist" tendencies among Greenlanders (Sørensen 1981:129).

In 1946 a delegation from the provincial councils went to Copenhagen to work together with Danish civil servants and politicians on a committee to consider the problems of the region. The committee's five-year plan for development of the country largely reflected the viewpoint of Danes who knew very little about the actual situation and the prevailing sentiments in the Greenlander population. The most significant recommendations were to begin investments to strengthen the economy and to improve health and education through building hospitals and schools. The general attitude revealed in the recommendations was a fear that development might proceed at too fast a pace for the unprepared population. For the same reason, the committee would not consider abolishing the trade monopoly and opening the country to influences from abroad. The Greenlandic members of the committee supported this conclusion (Rigsdagens Grønlandsudvalg 1946).

In time the general postwar anticolonial attitude resulted in a strong reaction in the Danish press against the recommendations of 1946 as they began to be implemented. The plan was thought to be an attempt to retain a colonial situation. The public debate was so heated that Danish politicians realized that they would

Table 1. Life Expectancy for Persons born in Greenland, 1946–1980

	1946–1951	*1961–1965*	*1971–1975*	*1976–1980*
Men	32.2	56.7	59.0	57.2
Women	37.5	63.2	65.4	66.6

SOURCE: Ministeriet for Grønland 1981.

have to respond to the pressure. Thus it was Danish public opinion that led to the social experiment in development planning for Greenland. This experiment was to change the lives and future of tens of thousands of people living almost 4,000 kilometers away from where the scheme was conceived and designed.

The Social Democratic government that took office in 1947 was determined to change Danish policy toward Greenland. In 1948 Prime Minister Hans Hedtoft proposed abolishing colonial status for Greenland and giving Greenlanders the right to vote in parliamentary elections. He visited Greenland, talked to many people along the west coast, and held a joint meeting with the members of the two provincial councils. His visit was a great success and the Greenlandic politicians listened enthusiastically to his presentation. Like the Danish Parliament, they endorsed his ideas for changes of vast dimensions.

The "Big Commission"

A Greenland Commission to study the situation and propose recommendations was appointed on November 29, 1948. It consisted of four Danish and four Greenlandic politicians. A fifth Greenlandic member, representing the Greenlandic Association of Housewives, took part in the deliberations of the "big Commission," as it was called. All the other people—more than 100—participating in the work came from the various ministries of the government administration. The speed and energy with which the work was conducted was remarkable. By February 1950 the commission had published six volumes, totaling 1,100 pages. These volumes addressed issues of the economy, demography, health, education, housing, and administrative reform. This plan is popularly referred to as G–50 in distinction to the later G–60 plan.

The 1950 Plan

Raising the standard of living was to be accomplished mainly by developing an economy based on industrial fishing. This then was the impetus for the introduction of wage labor on a large scale, distinct from the previous period when a very few Greenlanders had salaried incomes as employees of the trading company, churches,

© Natl. Geographic Soc., Washington: 126621–TR.

Fig. 1. Salting split codfish in Itilleq, Holsteinsborg District. Photograph by Andrew H. Brown, summer 1954.

and schools. Industrialization was to be developed in the colonies, which henceforth were called towns. As the majority of the population (55% in 1950) lived in the many small communities (here called settlements) G–50 called for the people of Greenland to be relocated. In practical terms the envisaged migration from settlement to town would be the free choice of individuals. It was explicitly stated that coercive measures would not be applied. The two means to be used to encourage people to move would be propagandizing and, perhaps most effective, a concentration of investments only in the places that were economically promising, in short, the towns (table 2).

The Chairman of the "big Commission" wrote after the presentation of G–50: "One should not forget that

Table 2. Investments in Greenland 1951–1980

	In Millions of Kroner				
	1951–1955	*1956–1960*	*1960*	*1970*	*1980*
Towns	124.5	162.2	41.3	288.7	542.7
Settlements	12.6	22.3	4.5	7.7	58.2
Total	137.1	184.5	45.8	296.4	600.9

NOTE: Municipal investments are not included for 1960. The table comprises all State investments and most municipal and home-rule investments. Private investments are partly included.
SOURCE: Ministeriet for Grønland 1968, 1981.

701

such a conscious and intended transformation of a so-ciety, which we are here referring to, means intervening in a most decisive way in the existence of each and every human being. From certain points of view, one might say that it is a social experiment on a large scale, but that urgently requires the utmost attention and care in implementation. And it must above all be avoided that the endeavor to develop the economic, cultural, and social conditions acquires a convulsive character" (Koch 1950:296).

Two of the political-administrative reforms resulting from G–50 were regarded as the most important by Greenlanders: (1) the abolition of the trade monopoly and the opening of the country to contacts with the outside world, and (2) the establishment of one *landsråd* (Provincial Council) with its seat in Godthåb. Although the council was primarily advisory the Danish parliament practically always followed its recommendations and proposals. Some Greenlandic politicians in the early 1970s interpreted this tendency as a confirmation that the proposals and comments of the council exhibited the submissiveness characteristic of colonial subjects.

The development plan of 1950 contained a strange inconsistency: modernity was to be introduced in a great variety of fields as quickly as possible, but without educating Greenlanders for skilled construction and other work. The rationale was that the Greenland labor force should be reserved for the increase of productivity within the developing economy of the country, such as fisheries and fishing industries in West Greenland, and hunting in the northern districts of Uummannaq and Upernavik in addition to the East Greenland and Thule areas where large-scale fisheries could not be developed for ecological reasons. At the outset the transformation of society was expected to last some 10 to 15 years but in the field of housing construction perhaps 2 years, because practically all Greenland dwellings (probably 4,000–5,000 houses) were deemed to have reached the condemned stage. The initial decision not to educate Greenlanders in construction work, as carpenters, electricians, painters, plumbers, and so on, appears all the stranger in light of the housing goal. It was not until well into the 1960s that it was fully realized that craftsmen in these fields would be needed indefinitely, and preparations for vocational training schools commenced in a number of West Greenland towns.

This particular feature of development planning had far-reaching consequences. It necessitated an extraordinary increase in the number of Danes who had to be brought to Greenland (fig. 2). This measure increased the feeling among the indigenous people of being placed in the humble position of lowest-level workers, and often as mere spectators, at a time when the fast-growing urban communities boomed with construction. Nothing contributed more than the labor policy to making many Greenlanders think that economic develop-

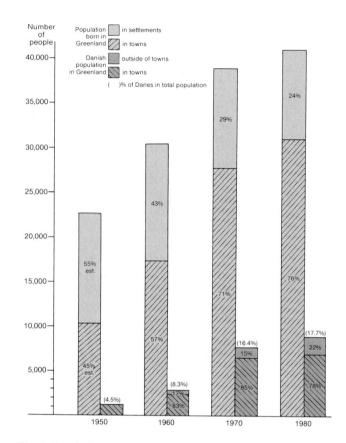

Fig. 2. Population growth in Greenland from 1950 to 1980.

ment contained a strong component of advantages for all the foreigners implementing the plans.

The Constitution of 1953

The formal abolition of colonial status took place on June 5, 1953, when an amended constitution was adopted through a national referendum in Denmark. This decision by the Danish people meant that Greenland was integrated as part of the Kingdom of Denmark and its people elected representatives to fill the two seats it obtained in the Parliament. The legislation regulating Greenlandic participation in parliamentary elections was not extended to include East Greenland and the Thule area until 1961.

To the people of Greenland what was significant was the assumption that the Constitution had finally given them equality with the Danes. They continued to insist on observance of the promise given them, but 12 years later expectations had not been met. A prominent member of the Provincial Council expressed his feelings during debate in the Council:

We who were born and grew up in the colonial period cannot deny that we had unquestioning faith in the Danes in Greenland. Indeed, they had much higher salaries than we had, and therefore we considered them to be happier than us, and they served as models for us. Under these circumstances no one should wonder that we thought that when our country was made part of Denmark and we had achieved the same duties and rights as Danish citizens, we would get the same high salaries as they did, and be as happy as they. But we were disappointed. After the changes in the Constitution that made Greenland part of Denmark, no changes occurred. Therefore, it was proposed that a committee be established that should work for normalization up here. The proposal was adopted, and G–60 was born out of this (Ministeriet for Grønland 1965:79).

The 1960 Plan

It became increasingly obvious during the 1950s that the minimal Greenlandic participation in implementation of the development schemes was a serious shortcoming. Feelings of frustration of Greenlandic politicians surfaced in the 1959 meeting of the Provincial Council, but the political criticism expressed was not directed toward anything like home rule. On the contrary, the demand was to "normalize" conditions, that is, to reduce the power of civil servants in the Ministry for Greenland and to give the Provincial Council an influence that corresponded more or less to that of a county council in Denmark. Normalization was a shorthand expression for full integration into the political-administrative system of Denmark. Furthermore, strong criticism was given about the lack of opportunities for employment given even educated Greenlanders. Finally complaints were expressed against the two large state institutions that controlled economic and technical development, The Royal Greenland Trade Department and the Greenland Technical Organization. It was suggested that private enterprise should be given better opportunities. The debate ended with the proposal that the Parliament should establish a committee to clarify the aims and objectives of development in Greenland.

The Greenland Committee of 1960, which ended its work in 1964, complied with some of the demands for "normalization." But the significance of G–60 (as it was popularly called) was a breathtaking increase in investments in Greenland (table 2).

In short, the recommendations of G–60 are self-contradictory. On the one hand, the aim is to normalize conditions and to increase Greenlandic participation. On the other hand, the recommendations, by greatly increasing the financial input, raised new demands for more Danish labor for the rest of the 1960s and far into the 1970s (Ministeriet for Grønland 1964). The increase in the total Danish labor force in Greenland gave new intensity to a vicious circle that was clearly discernible during the 1950s. More Danes meant more dwellings to be built to house Danes, and these houses according to the conventional wisdom would have to be built by still other Danes. In 1950 scarcely 300 habitations in Greenland were reserved for Danes employed by state institutions. In 1965 the figure had increased to about 1,400, and in 1970 the number of such habitations had passed 1,900. In addition there was housing for privately employed Danes (Ministeriet for Grønland 1971, 1973).

The lowest echelon Danish laborers had to accept quarters in barracks in some of the larger towns during their summer work period in Greenland. In contrast to the dwellings of the Danish middle-class employees, the workers' quarters were so small that the Danish labor unions protested, which resulted in some improvements. This stratification was a reminder to the Greenlanders that within the new order—in which they assumed that they would eventually achieve equality—equality was quite an elastic concept.

The level of cash income among Greenlanders did increase throughout the period of economic development and was some 2.5 times higher in real value in 1960 than in 1947. Nevertheless, the Danes in Greenland, who in 1960 made up 8 percent of the total population (fig. 2), accounted for almost 50 percent of total private incomes (Boserup 1963:10–13). A few years later, with intensification of the development process due to the recommendations from G–60, the same differences in income level were manifest. In 1967 the Danish 15 percent of the population accounted for 50 percent of incomes (H. Kleivan 1969:146).

Neither the 1950 plan nor the 1960 plan recommended large-scale migration from Greenland to Denmark. Greenlanders as well as Danish authorities had realized early in the twentieth century that only a fraction of the growing population with its expanding consumption of imported manufactured goods could continue as hunters of marine mammals. The assumption during the first decades of the twentieth century was that commercial fishing with a comparatively simple technology should be developed to solve the economic problems.

Although the population expanded rapidly after World War II, both the 1950 and the 1960 plans took for granted that the fisheries could form the backbone of the economy for the increasing population. The answer was to develop a capital-intensive and highly advanced fish processing industry in combination with a modern fishing fleet. In response to the dwindling cod resources in coastal waters, the 1960 commission decided that the fleet should be enlarged to include also larger, ocean-going longliners and trawlers, to compete with the advanced fishing fleet of European nations operating in Davis Strait and other waters around Greenland.

The tremendous growth of population was not a concern of the economists on the 1960 commission (Boserup 1963:480–481). Neither was the amount of capital being called for to invest in Greenland. Planners considered that Denmark was wealthy enough and populous enough to support the Greenland development.

Results of Political and Economic Development

Greenlanders in Denmark

Although the development plans did not actively stimulate permanent migration to Denmark, the possibility was not excluded that some Greenlanders would move to Denmark or would stay on there after their education was finished. There is no fully reliable record of the total number of Greenlanders resident in Denmark. In November 1971 figures from public registers and from lists of Greenlanders in Danish educational institutions gave a total of 3,299 persons, excluding individuals under the age of 14 (Barfod et al. 1974:36). An unofficial estimate by people working in a Greenlandic voluntary association in Copenhagen suggested a total between 5,000 and 6,000.

Some of these are Greenlandic women married to Danes, and a few are Greenlandic men married to Danish women. Others, after having been educated in Denmark, have stayed on, but well-informed people think the number in this category is very small. The prevailing pattern, by far, is for Greenlanders to return home after they have finished their education, or after a few years of work in Denmark. While the number of Greenlanders going to Denmark for vacation is considerable, the number of young people attending schools or courses will probably diminish since many vocational training centers and other educational opportunities opened in West Greenland during the 1970s and early 1980s.

Improvements in Health and Housing

Massive efforts in the health sector, such as building new hospitals, increasing medical services and personnel on all levels, and a general improvement of hygiene related to the improvements in housing, quickly caused a dramatic drop in infant mortality. Another important factor contributing to a population explosion in Greenland in the period before 1965 was the energetic and very successful struggle against tuberculosis in the 1950s and 1960s.

Tuberculosis was the cause of 36 percent of deaths in the period 1924–1933 (Beretninger vedr. Grønlands Styrelse, No.1, 1942). Around 1950, 7 percent of the Greenlandic population suffered from tuberculosis. But it was quickly brought under control during the 1960s.

Although the health situation improved remarkably between 1950 and 1980, mortality from all causes in 1982 was from 1.5 to 10 times higher than in corresponding age groups in Denmark. Infant mortality was about 40 percent in Greenland as against 8 percent in Denmark.

Changes in the size and levels of housing have, of course, been important factors in the general improvement of health. Living space in 1955 was about four square meters per person, as against 13 per person in 1976. In 1976 a majority of Greenlanders lived in dwellings with running water and central heating, amenities that were practically unknown in 1950. And between 1966 and 1980, the total usage of electricity in Greenland more than tripled.

left, © Natl. Geographic Soc., Washington; right, © Danish Ministry of Foreign Affairs.
Fig. 3. The town of Narsaq. left, The older part of the settlement, with the winter waterpipe leading to the factory, and Qaqqarsuaq mountain in the background. right, Sheep and lamb slaughterhouse, freezing plant, and canning factory. At lower right, outside the sheep enclosure, are the remains of a Norse house. Photographs by Mogens Lindhard, 1952–1953.

Development investments were overwhelmingly concentrated in the towns, although a majority of the Greenlanders lived in the settlements (table 3). The people who remained in the settlements, despite the many forms of indirect coercion that were used to get them to migrate to the towns, throughout the whole period of reforms and economic development waited for years for improvements in housing as well as in the production sector.

The differences between towns and peripheral settlements were still quite marked in 1983, with regard to housing, water supplies, and general hygienic conditions. A socio-medical researcher stated in the early 1980s that the differences in living conditions between towns and settlements, and between the various regions of Greenland, seem to be reflected also in differences in health and mortality. On the basis of official statistics, he calculated that age-corrected mortality rates are 1.25 times higher in settlements than in towns (Bjerregaard 1983). Furthermore, the rapidly increasing economic and social differentiation among contemporary Greenlanders—one of the most prominent social results of development policies—according to socio-medical specialists seems to be paralleled by differences both in health and in mortality between the different socioeconomic groups.

Among health and socio-medical problems, the high and increasing incidence of suicide is prominent (I. Lynge 1969, 1976a). Although there is no contemporary analysis of the phenomenon, suicide, as well as increased cases of violence and homicide, are clearly among the human costs of the transformation of society. In the same context are fast-rising mortality figures due to accidents, high consumption of alcohol, and venereal diseases manifesting a frequency 100 times higher than in Denmark.

Table 3. **Population Distribution according to Size of Town or Settlement, 1960–1981**

Population	Number of inhabited places			Percentage of total population		
	1960	1970	1981	1960	1970	1981
1– 99	84	82	61	9.7	5.0	3.6
100– 249	46	30	29	22.1	10.8	9.6
250– 499	10	12	10	9.4	8.8	7.6
500– 999	7	6	4	13.7	10.0	6.0
1,000–1,499	4	2	3	14.2	5.1	8.0
1,500–1,999	4	2	2	21.2	7.2	7.1
2,000–2,999	—	4	2	—	22.3	10.0
3,000–3,999	1	2	3	9.7	14.4	20.3
4,000 +	—	1	2	—	16.4	27.8
Total	156	141	116	100.0	100.0	100.0

NOTE: Not including 16 outpost facilities operated largely by Danes, totaling 3.6 percent of the population in Greenland.
SOURCE: Ministeriet for Grønland 1981.

The massive efforts to improve health and hygiene have resulted in a very steep rise in the average life expectancy figure (table 1). The slight decrease in the life expectancy of men, but not women, may be due to the greater vulnerability of men to death from suicide, accidents, and homicide.

"Normalization"

The concept of "normalization" did not emerge in the political vocabulary of Greenland until the late 1950s. It implies a definition of the current state of affairs as abnormal. The concept of normalization defined the political institutions of Greenland as inadequate and abnormal compared to the model of Danish society. Normalization was also used in the Greenland debate in a much wider sense to include nonpolitical phenomena such as the alleged need to give the Danish language priority as one of the keys to achieving normality.

For nearly 20 years, until the late 1960s, the development process was based on a wholesale and rather one-sided attempt to achieve equality by completely integrating Greenland into the political system of Denmark. In retrospect it is astonishing how long it was before "normalization" was replaced by demands for self-determination.

During this period it was suggested that Greenlanders begin paying taxes. The reasoning seemed to be that taxation as a duty of citizenship would strengthen the claim for equality. Everybody knew that average incomes among Greenlanders were sufficiently low so that very many people would avoid tax assessments. On the other hand, quite a few Danes, who earned considerable profits as owners of stores in the towns (H. Kleivan 1969) and as owners of firms involved in construction work, would constitute the heaviest taxpayers. The decision to introduce income taxes was adopted by the Provincial Council in 1970, but at a time when preoccupation with normalization had ended and other and more radical solutions to the political problems were proposed.

But before then, Greenlandic politicians suggested that the authorities should dismantle all regionally specific institutions as soon as possible. Field after field under the Ministry for Greenland was singled out for transfer to other ministries: the police were transferred to the Ministry of Justice and church affairs to the Ministry of Church Affairs, and it was planned to transfer educational matters to the Ministry of Education.

This normalization policy was pursued with the full support of the Provincial Council and often initiated by it. Even to outside observers it was quite obvious during most of the 1960s that a claim for more rather than less Greenlandic political control was rapidly emerging especially among younger educated Greenlanders.

Yet in the 1960s even the most modest suggestions

for self-determination were seen as unrealistic by established politicians in Greenland. The huge capital transfers from Denmark to finance the large development projects and the welfare reforms accompanying them seemed to paralyze political thinking in the Provincial Council.

The more or less vague political ideas of the 1940s and 1950s emanated from the small number of Greenlanders who had access to education and professional training, such as schoolteachers, priests, catechists, trade managers or assistants in the Royal Greenland Trade, and telegraph operators. Greenlanders from these professions were also the overwhelming majority in the provincial councils (Sørensen 1981).

Although the postwar development plans for Greenland were almost totally designed by Danes, the statements in favor of reforms voiced by prominent Greenlanders at the end of World War II were used to justify this expanding program of economic development. As Greenlandic society changed throughout the 1950s and 1960s, the articulation of indigenous hopes for more political influence came from a small but growing educated elite. The strength and style of these expressions changed. In the late 1940s the ideas were stated as humble and polite suggestions or in the form of questions. When young educated Greenlanders, strongly politicized and radical, entered the political arena at the end of the 1960s, suggestions and questions changed into strongly expressed demands for fundamental political changes. But it was not until 1971, when young radicals were elected to the Provincial Council, that there was a breakthrough into a new era in Greenland politics.

One of the issues that most strongly concerned the young radical politicians was the heavy concentration of the population in the towns with all the attendant human costs and its destruction of a way of life that, despite centuries of slow acculturative influences, had retained many indigenous features. The other central issue in their political argumentation was the strong Danification of the school system, an area in which their personal experiences gave them detailed knowledge. In their struggle against these processes, they came to represent a decentralist and humanitarian policy toward the people living in the settlements. In education they saw Danification as producing frustration among the young and alienation from their Greenlandic identity and values.

Fig. 4. Contemporary towns. top, Uummannaq, July 1973. A stone church is on the left with some older-style stone and sod houses on right surrounded by more modern structures. center, Holsteinsborg (Sisimiut), Sept.–Oct. 1969. bottom, Prøven (Kangersuatsiaq) in Upernavik District, July 1973. Boats, metal drums, and 2 fish-drying platforms border a structure in the foreground. Photographs by Mogens S. Koch.

706

The formal efforts at decolonization within the political sphere can be viewed as mainly cosmetic. In 1967 new legislation introduced a political reform, removing the Danish governor as ex-officio chairman of the Provincial Council. Thereafter the Council elected its own chairman, who was assisted by a new Council secretariat. The governor became merely a participant in the Council proceedings. This was a further step toward a functioning parliamentary democracy, although the real decision-making power remained with the parliament in Copenhagen. Greenlanders were reminded that they had an inalienable right to direct their own affairs. Yet in everyday reality the change was superficial, as social problems mounted, and the populace was increasingly impatient for the fulfillment of the promised equality.

Demography

In the early period of welfare reforms, from 1950 to 1960, not only was there a marked reduction of mortality, but also, for reasons not well described, a very strong increase in fertility. The number of children borne by mothers born in Greenland steadily increased culminating with 1,674 in 1964. A family planning campaign then resulted in a particularly marked drop in the birth figure, from 1,418 in 1968 to 999 in 1970, and a further drop to 665 in 1974 (fig. 5). This occurred simultaneously with an increase of 35 percent in the number of women within the age-group 15–50 in the period 1965–1975. The reduced fertility applies to the whole age group, but the decrease apparently started first, in the early 1960s, for women over 30 and last, in the later 1960s, for younger women.

The population pyramids for 1955 through 1980 (fig. 6) indicate the salient features of the changes in the demographic structure of contemporary Greenlanders. The base of the pyramid broadened from 1955 through 1965, whereas the pyramids for 1975 and 1980 clearly show the strong effect of the family planning campaign.

During the 1950s Greenland already had a particularly young population, 40.5 percent being under the age of 14. In 1960 this figure had risen to 44.3 percent, and in 1965, 47.5 percent. As more children reach school age, a considerable proportion of development investment is required to build new schools and hire more teachers. Most of the teachers were brought in from Denmark because of a lack of Greenlandic teachers, and new housing had to be built for them. During the same period many other Danish specialists in various fields were hired for work in Greenland, and they needed housing. This aggravated the problem of supplying decent housing for the many Greenlandic families having more children.

In addition the very intensive program carried out from before 1950 into the 1970s to concentrate the population, mainly in the towns singled out for the most intensive industrial development, increased the demand for housing for the migrants from the outlying settlements. This applied particularly to Pamiut, Godthåb, Maniitsok, and Sisimiut, towns in the subarctic "open water area" of the southern west coast, and to towns in the Disko Bay region, which was a secondary area of intensive industrialization because of the rich shrimp resources in these waters.

A consequence of the population explosion is the demand for job opportunities. Despite a large increase in investments, particularly after the recommendations of the G–60 plan began to be implemented in 1964–1965, the problem of unemployment was very serious.

Another result of the population explosion is the rising number of new families established throughout the 1970s and 1980s, which produces another demand on capital for housing. These young families, and a significant proportion of quite young, unmarried mothers,

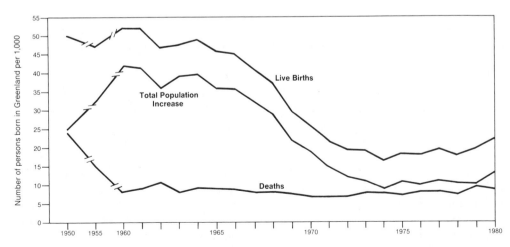

Fig. 5. Birth rate, death rate, and total population increase per 1,000 people born in Greenland for 1950–1980. Children of women born outside Greenland are not included.

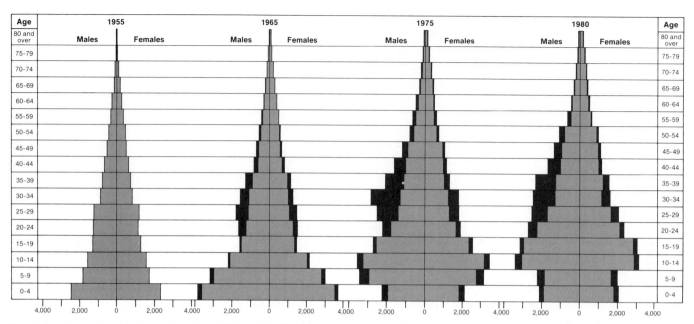

Fig. 6. Total population in Greenland from 1955 to 1980 (for whom adequate recordings of age were available). The population born outside Greenland is indicated in black. For 1955, 1,835 persons born outside Greenland were included in the total of 26,933, but a breakdown of their ages was not available.

contribute to an increase in the birth rate from the late 1970s up to about 1990. Births rose from 724 in 1975 to 906 in 1980. However, the future birth rate will not reach the high level of the 1960s, when the annual net increase in the indigenous population fluctuated around 4 percent. It was estimated that there would be a slow growth of the population to about 55,000 Greenlanders by 2000. The population was 41,459 in 1981.

Family Planning

Systematic family planning was introduced in the 1960s, mainly through the use of the intrauterine device. The health authorities applied a very direct and active approach to inform Greenlanders about contraception (Misfeldt 1977). By the end of 1970, 3,800 women, the great majority Greenlanders, had received the IUD (Ministeriet for Grønland 1973:10). But the family planning effort was not just another example of the many more or less coercive initiatives forced on the population. Certainly there was motivation for family planning, as more and more children survived and the number of young to be supported steadily increased. Furthermore the welfare state had stipulated a pension to be paid at the age of 60; this probably reduced the economic motivation to have many children, preferably sons, to provide support for the aged, which was a primary motive for childbearing in the traditional society. Field experiences in southern Greenland towns as well as peripheral settlements in 1961–1962 and the following years gave convincing evidence of motivational change. Statements in favor of family planning

were always most strongly voiced by the women, including unmarried as well as married mothers.

When family planning had just begun the Association of Greenlandic Women appealed to the authorities to disseminate information about it. Medical specialists were sent to Greenland in 1964 and 1968 to give information on family planning and instructions in the available techniques for birth control in a large number of communities. Although the introduction of the IUD led to a marked drop in the number of children borne by Greenlandic women after 1964, contraception education meetings were held along the West Greenland coast even into the middle 1970s. After Denmark adopted legalized abortion, the women's associations in Greenland raised a debate on the issue. The organized pressure by Greenlandic women through their associations no doubt played a significant role in the decision to legalize abortion in Greenland in 1974.

Changes in Family and Household

The household and family arrangements of traditional type underwent considerable modifications under the slow and modest economic changes during colonial times. A marked shift from extended family patterns to households based on the nuclear family occurred rather quickly after commercial fishing advanced in the years before World War II. Nevertheless, considerable differences remained between towns and settlements, with nuclear family households being more common in towns and the largest, townlike settlements.

The prevalence of nuclear family households does not

necessarily imply that traditional patterns of care for the aged have been entirely replaced by social welfare institutions. Providing fish and meat to aged parents who live separately appears to be more frequent than would be inferred from household censuses. Welfare payments to the old have been set at a rather low level on the assumption that old people receive considerable assistance in the form of food from their children, even when they live in separate houses. This principle apparently was too generally applied, as the facts of life differ from locality to locality. Old people had difficulties in making ends meet in the communities where gifts in the form of food were calculated as frequent (From et al. 1975).

Up to World War II young people still living in the household of their parents apparently were under stricter control by parental authority than has been observed in the postwar situation, when the young could more often spend their evenings with their friends without being called home. This alleged reduction in social control by the head of the household is probably related mainly to the fact that economic development provided easier access to money also for young people. Formerly economically dependent on their fathers, participation in commercial fishing and the increase in other job opportunities allowed them more independence.

Illegitimacy

Within a few years after economic development began, there was a rapid rise in the number of children borne by young unmarried mothers. Among the speculative explanations for this is one to the effect that a shift in women's clothing styles from sealskin trousers to European textiles led to increased sexual intercourse. This explanation has not been supported by a demonstrated correlation, district by district, between the periods of style change and of increased illegitimacy. Much more likely is a relationship to the lessening of parental authority directly generated by economic development. Probably also relevant is the remarkable increase during the postwar years in geographical mobility among both sexes of Greenlanders. More striking is the extraordinary surplus of males aged about 20 to 50 in the transient Danish population, compared to the balance in the Greenlandic sex ratio (fig. 6). The ethnicity of the fathers of illegitimate children has not been investigated, but appearances often suggest Danish ancestry.

In earlier times unmarried mothers were not very frequently recorded, and both they and their children were stigmatized. As the number of such births in the 1950s and 1960s increased everywhere, in some districts reaching 50 percent or more of the total number of births by Greenlandic mothers, the stigma correspondingly abated. The economic status of unmarried mothers and their children was considerably improved by the welfare practices implemented in Greenland as an integral part of development policy. The unmarried mother regularly receiving her small welfare check is not a liability to her kin and neighbors, and some may even envy her the regularity of her source of money. When the unmarried mother remained in her original social environment, the lack of a father in the household was often compensated for by the presence of a network of close kin and neighbors, grandparents playing a significant role in this respect. This was the case both when the unmarried mother lived under the same roof as her parents, and when they lived in separate households but with the geographic proximity typical of village life. Such compensation sometimes is reflected in adaptations of kinship terminology. Thus a child calls the mother's father *ataataq* 'father' rather than *aataq* 'grandfather'. This is another example of the oft-mentioned flexibility of Eskimo culture and social life in the face of considerable changes.

Illegitimate children encountered potential social problems most frequently in the social setting of the rapidly growing towns. In a rather protracted transitional period, especially during the 1950s and 1960s, a significant proportion of the population of the towns had immigrated from smaller settlements. This movement often meant an uprooting of the close network of kin and neighbors, in which the individual could seek comfort and consolation under more stable conditions.

Smithsonian, Dept. of Anthr.: 417,719.

Fig. 7. Eiderdown blanket with feather border. Size 105.0 by 144.0 cm; collected in West Greenland, 1956.

The extraordinary ease with which Eskimo children have been described as getting attached to others than their biological parents—apparently without psychologically harmful effects—presupposes the retention of social networks often lacking in the social setting of new townspeople.

Population Movements

People usually moved from small communities to larger villages of several hundred inhabitants, or directly to towns where few if any of the occupants were known to the newcomers. These movements, whether they involved a single family or resulted from a more direct form of coercion such as the closing down of a whole community through removing public services, often generated very grave problems of adaptation for the families that moved.

If the father of the family moving was an able fisherman or hunter, the economic viability of the kinsmen and neighbors left behind often was reduced. In a community of 50 to 60 individuals the loss of one contributing member of the group was a serious matter. After a few of the most economically active individuals were persuaded to move, coercion from the authorities was not required to get the rest to move.

The problems of adapting to new and unfamiliar circumstances in the towns, or in one of the few settlements singled out for development, were very considerable. Moving to a middle-size settlement was by no

Grafisk Værksted, Godthåb, Greenland.
Fig. 8. *Aningaaq Maliinalu* 'the Moon and the Sun'. Linoleum block print by the Greenlandic artist Anne-Lise Løvstrøm (b. 1960).

means easier than moving to a town. Inhabitants in a close-knit settlement often revealed an esprit de corps easily mobilized against any outsider, even against countrymen from the next community "with its strange customs." Outright mobbing has been reported in several such situations. People who themselves lived in overcrowded houses, and who saw newcomers being allocated one of the few newly built houses, could not be expected to know the details and technicalities of the official relocation programs.

With few exceptions, official documents on relocation begin with the assurance that population movement from countryside to town is a worldwide and inevitable phenomenon. In southern West Greenland such movements were already prevalent in the 1930s and 1940s. What is not stated is that such movements are related to social circumstances greatly influenced by political considerations. The fact that people move to town is taken as proof that nearly everyone would like to live in a town, not that sociopolitical policies are determinative. Documents on the relocation of population as a mechanism to further the policy of economic development are full of self-fulfilling prophecies.

Education

Educational reforms begun on the basis of the G-50 recommendations meant a definite break with the past. The church and the school were the only colonial institutions dominated by Greenlanders. They had developed as one entity throughout the whole colonial period but were now formally separated.

The church after the new development policy began in fact acquired an even more distinctly Greenlandic character. It has been the pioneer institution in realizing that Greenlandic needs can be adequately met by an alternative education to that given in Denmark (Kleivan 1979:130–131). This view contrasts to the strongly marked Danification of the new school system.

Although the catechists and most of the ministers continued to teach in the schools, the number of Greenlandic-speaking teachers soon became inadequate in the face of population growth during the 1950s and 1960s. It was necessary to bring an ever-increasing number of Danish teachers to Greenland. In addition, a number of Greenlanders without formal teacher training were engaged as instructors in the schools.

A dramatic imbalance was introduced between Greenlandic and Danish-speaking personnel within the new school system. In 1950 approximately 85 percent of the total teaching staff was Greenlandic-speaking, as against 63 percent in 1960, and only 29 percent in 1970 (Berthelsen 1973:12). It was not until the late 1970s that this situation was alleviated, and in 1980 the percentage of Greenlandic-speaking teachers had increased to 53 (Ministeriet for Grønland 1981:101).

Grafisk Værksted, Godthåb, Greenland.
Fig. 9. *Angákok* 'the shaman'. The shaman, viewed from above, is beating a drum surrounded by his spirit-helpers. Size 33.0 by 40.0 cm; silkscreen by the Greenlandic artist Jeremias Karlsen, 1975.

The Danish language was introduced in teaching in 1925, partly as a response to requests from a few prominent Greenlanders who saw Danish as an important instrument for social progress. Due to a lack of Danish-speaking teachers, the teaching of Danish acquired some significance only in the teachers' college and in the few existing secondary schools. The elementary schools were little affected by the 1925 decision.

There was a growing interest in learning Danish during the years preceding the development plans but as a secondary language, to assist social, cultural, and economic advancement. It was never questioned that Greenlandic was the appropriate principal language.

The old school system, with its culture-conserving features, through the sole use of Greenlandic as the language of instruction and in the limited reading materials available, could be perceived as adequate in a society with an economy based on hunting and small-scale fishing, largely isolated from outside influences through a rigid trade monopoly. But in a society facing changes in almost all aspects, such an immutable system with its limited perspectives could not continue.

The new school curriculum was expanded to include most of the disciplines of elementary schools in Den-

mark. But it took time to develop new educational materials adapted to some degree to the conditions of Greenlandic children.

Even before 1950 seven years of school education was compulsary, and this was maintained by the Education Act of 1950. To strengthen the teaching of Danish, the act set up a system by which Danish became the language of instruction for many children after the second grade, who then were taught Greenlandic only as a subject (except that religion was taught in Greenlandic). After a few years this system was criticized as discriminatory, favoring children from Danish-oriented families.

During the period of assimilationist policies many pupils were sent to Denmark for studies lasting from three months to two years. They often faced serious problems of reintegration on their return to Greenland.

In 1967 a new education act was passed (Kleivan 1969–1970: 251–262), closely modeled on the Danish Education Act. Seven years of compulsory schooling remained required, but possibilities were added for kindergarten classes and for extending education up to five years beyond the compulsory period. Literacy was often to be introduced first in Danish and only later in Greenlandic; soon objections were raised to this provision. Increasing ethnic consciousness in the 1970s led to attempts to strengthen the Greenlandic aspects of education, but implementation was delayed by the scarcity of Greenlanders qualified as teachers (Cram 1978).

In 1980 authority over education was transferred from Denmark to the Home Rule administration in Godthåb. The Greenlandic Parliament (*Landsting*) passed legislation giving prominence to Greenlandic as a medium of instruction as well as a topic of study. Compulsory schooling was extended to nine years, with the option of continuing for another 2 + 2 years (Ministeriet for Grønland 1982:97).

The great majority of Greenlandic teachers have always been educated at the teachers' college in Godthåb, established in 1845. A 1964 act on teachers' training established a system closely corresponding to that of Denmark, but including the subject of Greenlandic. One year of the total four-year training period was spent in Denmark (a provision dropped under Home Rule). As an emergency measure to increase quickly the number of Greenlandic-speaking teachers, a preliminary two-year program for teachers, with the Greenlandic language as the main discipline, was established in 1973; it was discontinued in 1978, after having educated 68 new teachers (Ministeriet for Grønland 1979:108).

The supply of new teachers to the school system has been somewhat eroded because some graduates of the teachers' college are hired for nonacademic jobs, such as in the Greenland church, the broadcasting system, the newspapers, and in public administration. Consequently there has been a delay in supplying the school system with an adequate number of fully trained Greenlandic-speaking teachers.

Several specialized training programs have been introduced in Greenland, for example, in journalism and preschool teaching. These programs, like the training of special health assistants, were especially designed for Greenland needs and are not copies of Danish models.

The seeds for the development of university-level studies were planted in the 1980s with the establishment of an Inuit Institute in Godthåb. In addition to conducting research the institute will give courses in Greenlandic culture and language that will correspond to courses in the same discipline at Copenhagen University. A program for training priests in Greenland started in 1983 in Godthåb. Only a small part of the this education will have to take place outside Greenland.

Under Home Rule the aim is that the highest possible level of education can be obtained within Greenland (Møller 1983:33). University studies generally and studies in very specialized fields will still have to be conducted in Denmark. Throughout the 1950s and 1960s many young Greenlanders were sent to Denmark for vocational training. In the late 1960s and early 1970s considerable investments were made to provide such training in institutions in Greenland. Significant results were achieved in this area by 1981, when the Home Rule administration also took over vocational training.

Godthåb, as a center for administration, as well as education, health services, and industries, has been haunted with housing problems and social problems ensuing from societal transformation and fast growth. So several of the new vocational training centers have been located in other towns along the west coast. Training programs were available in Greenland for, among others, motor operators, iron and metal work, building and construction, trade and office work, the merchant navy, social workers, pilots and mechanics for the Greenland airline, telecommunications workers, and health workers. Training for the fisheries, planned to be the backbone of Greenland's economy, is of course another important field. In addition to fishery training in Greenland, specialties such as fishing economy, fishery biology, and the development of new fishing methods, fish processing and its nutritional aspects, and the development of fishery-based consumer products, are being studied by young Greenlanders both in Denmark and in Norway.

There is also a training center for young people entering sheep farming.

Economy in 1983

Hunting and Fishing

Since the commencement of Home Rule, a more efficient attempt to develop courses in hunting is in evidence. There must be continued recruitment to hunting, which faces many problems in this era of development but still has considerable economic importance in addition to the great social and symbolic significance it has for all Greenlanders. However much the society has been transformed, a gift of seal meat is still a solemn medium for the expression and confirmation of social relations and respect.

That part of the hunting population would be recruited into the labor force of a multinational mining operation, as happened in the Uummannaq district in the 1970s, probably was not anticipated for the early stage of economic development. For some hunters temporary work in mining gave quick access to capital for improved hunting technology. For others it meant leaving hunting as a principal occupation (Dahl 1977; Dahl and Berg 1977; F. Hansen 1977; Hertz 1977; Dahl and Lyberth 1980). In 1976, 674 people over the age of 14 were occupied in sealing and hunting (table 4). For 1980 this figure is 700 to 800 persons, "for whom hunting is the only or, at least, the most important source of income. When the members of the families of these hunters are included, it can be estimated that this occupation forms the principal economic base for some 2,500 persons. Beyond this a considerable number of people are dependent on hunting as an essential supplement to their income from, for example, fishing or salaried employment" (Ministeriet for Grønland 1981:45).

The concepts of town and settlement imply that one is to be developed, and the other usually to be left without resources and therefore to become increasingly unattractive. The geographically much more comprehensive categories of "fishing districts" and "hunting districts" have a similar function. They designate, on the one hand, subarctic areas within which development of large-scale fishing is possible, and shall take place in centralized localities (towns) and, on the other hand, Arctic and High Arctic areas where development of large-scale fishing is precluded for obvious reasons.

Where fishing is not possible, planners realized that hunting would remain for quite some time essentially the only occupation. These hunting districts then were allocated a somewhat larger proportion of investments than were the settlements in the fishing districts.

Because of this difference in investment allocation, the migration from hunting districts to fishing districts was more modest, less dramatic, and less coercive in character, than was migration from peripheral settlements in the fishing districts to the nearest towns.

Why were the two segments of the Greenlandic population dealt with so differently in implementing the plans to make large-scale fishing the main component of the economy? In Greenlandic public opinion, hunting was very important in both economic and dietary terms and definitely also as an adaptation representing continuity with the past. On the other hand, most

Table 4. Occupational Status of Those Age 14 and Over, 1976

	Persons born in Greenland Number	Percent	Persons born outside Greenland Number	Percent
Occupations				
Fisheries	2,342	5.8	77	1.1
Sealing and hunting	674	1.6	6	0.1
Sheep breeding	111	0.3	12	0.2
Mining	34	0.1	6	0.1
Manufacturing	2,462	6.1	363	5.2
Construction	1,308	3.2	967	13.9
Public works	162	0.4	125	1.8
Trade and commerce	1,769	4.3	325	4.6
Transport	1,168	2.9	434	6.2
Public administration	895	2.2	527	7.5
Education, religion, cultural activities	1,052	2.6	655	9.4
Health and social institutions	1,717	4.2	422	6.1
Service trades	1,087	2.7	313	4.5
Not known	369	0.9	151	2.2
Total	15,150	37.3	4,383	62.9
Unemployed persons				
Children living at home	18,234	44.9	1,717	24.7
Students living elsewhere	407	1.0	10	0.1
Housewives	3,073	7.6	375	5.4
Retired	2,326	5.7	47	0.7
Total	24,040	59.2	2,149	30.9
Occupation not stated	1,406	3.5	432	6.2
Total	40,596	100.0	6,964	100.0

NOTE: Population in outpost facilities not included.
SOURCE: Census and count of dwellings in Greenland on Oct. 26, 1976; Ministeriet for Grønland 1981.

Greenlandic politicians of the Provincial Council endorsed the policy of population concentration in the towns, particularly the relocation of the population from the peripheral settlements of the fishing districts.

Public opinion in Denmark, to which development policy planners were more sensitive in the early phase of the process, maintained an attitude of deep respect and admiration for "the true hunters of the Arctic." Less frequent accounts of the more acculturated Greenlanders of the subarctic area, who increasingly depended on fishing, apparently had less appeal, although a few decades earlier the same people were described as the most skilled and courageous kayak men in the world. So the settlement dwellers of the southern and central part of the west coast could be squeezed into the towns under the rationale of giving them "a higher standard of living."

Greenland is still a country with a dual economy. Hunting and a little small-scale fishing is the most typical economic activity of the population in East and North Greenland, and small-scale fishing supplemented with some hunting prevails around the smaller settlements on the west coast. Although this production helps people obtain money necessary in their everyday life, this sector of the economy still has a considerable subsistence orientation. Self-employment, of course, is much more typical in the localities mentioned than is the case in the towns and the largest settlements, where the fishing harbors and the industrial fish processing plants are located.

But the strong drive toward industrialization and big-unit operation within the fisheries is conspicuously manifest in the rapid change of fishing technology. The number of boats in the fishing fleet was smaller in 1980 than in 1968 but each vessel was much larger.

A few figures will demonstrate the fast-growing importance of fishing in the economy of modern Greenland, and most particularly with regard to capital-intensive large-scale fishing. In the period 1950–1953 the average annual fish production was about 21,000 tons, and cod accounted for about 95 percent of the total catch. In 1980 the total Greenland catch was approximately 100,000 tons, and half of the income derived from shrimp fishing. The statistics give no indication as to the quantity of fish that derives from small-scale fishing, using rowing boats and small motorboats.

Incomes from hunting were 15.1 million kroner in 1980, 12.7 million from the sale of sealskins, and 2.4 million from the sale of reindeer products and whale meat. Some hunters and small-scale fishermen in addition obtain a moderate part of their money income from the sale of seal meat to Greenland wage laborers.

The export-oriented fishing industry of Greenland is very vulnerable for a number of reasons—fluctuations in world market prices, resource reduction due to temperature changes, and resource depletion due to intensive fishing.

Within the international regulation of fisheries and quotas, Greenland authorities see the sale of fishing licenses as a possible source of income, as long as their own fleet is not yet capable of utilizing the whole Greenland quota. The idea of selling licenses is the more tempting in the light of Greenland's decision to leave the European Economic Community (EEC) in the middle 1980s.

Sheep Raising

As a new adaptation sheep raising acquired economic importance in southern West Greenland from the beginning of the twentieth century. Long before, a small number of cows, goats, and sheep had been kept in the areas where the Norsemen had their pastures and farms in medieval times—in the three southernmost municipalities of the west coast, Narsaq, Qaqortoq, and Nanortalik. Sheep raising was stimulated by the colonial authorities as an attempt to improve economic viability for the population in the south. As a source of income sheep raising mostly has been combined with other economic activities, particularly fishing.

The recurring problem in Greenland sheep raising is the lack of sufficient pastures to produce enough winter fodder to keep the number of animals alive in the years where frost and thaw alternate so that ice covers the meager pastures. To avoid catastrophes killing most of the animals, a long-term plan for extending pastures, and for cultivating new areas to increase the number of farms, was initiated. As long as Greenland remains within the EEC, sheep raising is being supported from the EEC development fund.

Training in sheep raising lasts three years, one of which is spent on a sheep farm in Iceland. Like all other trades in Greenland, the sheep herders have a well-functioning organization to take care of their interests.

In 1980 there were about 80 families depending on this activity, and some 50 of them had it as their main occupation. Including all family members and assistants on the farms, approximately 350 people are dependent on this economic activity. The number of families has declined since 1970. By the end of 1981 the number of sheep was 23,600. In that year 15,200 animals were delivered to the Royal Greenland Trade Department slaughterhouse in Harsaq, a state-owned plant to be taken over by the Home Rule administration. In addition, 6,000 animals were sold by the farmers directly to consumers.

Minerals

Except for the almost depleted cryolite mine in West Greenland, the only mining activity in Greenland is the Greenex-operated lead and zinc mine in the Uummannaq area, where about 40 percent of the mineworkers were Greenlanders by the end of 1982. Exploration for oil and gas resources is planned in the Jameson Land area north of Scoresby Sound, East Greenland.

Home Rule Administration

The Emergence of Greenlandic Political Parties

Several attempts to form political organizations in Greenland in the 1960s failed. The Inuit party, designed as a party with particular ethnic appeal, veered one-sidedly to the interests of Greenland civil servants. The Sukaᴋ party, which was meant to be a social democratic party on Greenlandic terms to represent the interest of those dependent on wage labor, collapsed partly because it lacked an adequate local organizational structure (H. Kleivan 1969–1970).

The real beginnings of political organizations first as movements and later as regular parties were in the 1970s. The *Siumut* 'Forwards' movement began in 1971 and

was formalized as a political party in 1977. The most prominent founding members were Jonathan Motzfeldt, Lars Emil Johansen, and Moses Olsen. All three became members of the first Home Rule administration elected for the period 1979–1983, with Motzfeldt as the administration's first chairman, the prime minister.

In opposition to *Siumut,* whose program can be characterized as moderate socialist, the *Atassut* 'Connecting link' movement was established in 1977. Formalized as a political party in 1981, this party in Danish political terminology must be termed conservative-liberal, although its candidate in Parliament has "technical" cooperation with the Social Democratic Party of Denmark. Its most clearly expressed political objectives are to work for the maintenance of a close relationship with Denmark, for the family, and against conflict in society. Also in 1977 the group *Inuit Ataqatigiit* 'Human fellowship' was established. Later organized as a political party, its main objective is full independence for Greenland, and it takes a strong, Marxist anti-imperialist position, considerably to the left of *Siumut.*

The leaders of *Inuit Ataqatigiit* consider the new system of Home Rule, so definitely the result of the *Siumut* leaders' energetic struggle for self-determination, to be Danish colonialism under a new cloak. Finally, the *Sulissartut Partiat* 'The Workers' Party' was established by two leading members of the Greenlandic trade union (S.I.K.) shortly before the introduction of Home Rule. It took a position close to that of *Inuit Ataqatigiit,* got about 5 percent of the vote in the election to the Greenland provincial assembly on April 4, 1979, and was dissolved after three years.

The emergence of identity as Greenlanders (*Kalaaleq,* pl. *Kalaallit*) is a product of the unifying effect of colonial rule, but considerable regionalist attitudes have continued to exist. Until the formation of political movements, later transformed into political parties, candidates running for a seat in the Provincial Council, or (after 1953) for one of Greenland's two seats in the Danish Parliament, did so on a personal basis. They represented themselves as individuals, and the element of likes and dislikes was sometimes apparently more important than the electorate's knowledge of the candidates' specific political ideas.

The existence of political parties has changed political life in many respects. Although there are many ambiguities in the total arsenal of political argument as to what is in the best interest of the Greenlandic people, national rather than regionalist viewpoints are heard more often than was the case some few years ago. This tendency has evidently been stimulated by political confrontations with the outside world, such as the struggle with Denmark over ownership of mineral resources, and the struggle with the EEC over fishery resources in Greenland waters.

Another tendency, indicative of an increasingly differentiated and stratified society, is that political party alignment is beginning to reflect economic or class interests.

The Establishment of Home Rule

Popular discontent was expressed politically in 1971 when two men who later became prominent leaders of the *Siumut* party were elected to the Provincial Council and a third was elected to the Danish Parliament. In 1972 they convinced the Minister for Greenland, Knud Hertling (the first Greenlander to hold the position of minister in the Danish government) that it was time to set up a committee to study possibilities for giving the Provincial Council greater political influence on Greenland affairs.

After a formal request from the Provincial Council in autumn 1972, the Minister decided to establish a committee with only Greenlandic members. In February 1975 this committee suggested that a system of home rule should be developed as soon as possible, increasing gradually the influence of the Provincial Council. On October 9, 1975, the Minister for Greenland established a Commission on Home Rule in Greenland, consisting of seven Danish and seven Greenlandic representatives (five from the Provincial Council and the two Greenland members of Parliament). The federation of Greenland municipalities sent observers to the commission meetings. The work was concluded in June 1978, with a report containing proposals for a Home Rule Act and other legislation (Kommissionen om Hjemmestyre i Grønland 1978; Lovtidende A 1978:1879; Dahl 1983; Foighel 1980; Harhoff 1982).

A crucial concern in the negotiations in the Home Rule Commission was that of aboriginal rights. The *Siumut* representatives demanded full ownership of nonrenewable resources for "the resident population of Greenland," bringing the negotiations to a crisis. Finally the Danish prime minister interfered very bluntly, stating that it was totally unacceptable that any part of the national territory should not be under the full sovereignty of the kingdom of Denmark; if Greenland insisted on full ownership of the nonrenewable resources, it would have to leave the commonwealth. Knowing the existing complex relationships of dependency and the very great annual capital transfers from Denmark to Greenland, the prime minister was sure that he would prevail. The *Siumut* representatives agreed to a compromise, originally suggested by the *Atassut* representatives who maintained that there should be joint Danish-Greenlandic ownership. According to Section 8 (1) in the Greenland Home Rule Act of 29 November 1978, "the resident population of Greenland has fundamental rights to the natural resources of Greenland" (Lovtidende A 1978:1879). The concept of "fundamental rights" has never been legally defined, and according to spe-

cialists in that field, it has no legal merit, although it must be thought to have moral content. The *Siumut* politicians were deeply disappointed at this outcome of their energetic efforts. Nevertheless, they felt they had to accept the compromise in order to avoid a lengthy postponement of Home Rule. A joint Danish-Greenlandic Mineral Resources Administration was established, in which both parties have the right to veto proposals. *Siumut* leaders have indicated that they will ask for re-negotiation of the ownership of resources. The establishment of *Inuit Ataqatigiit* was precipitated by the compromise in the Home Rule Commission. They protested strongly and stated that the Danish refusal to recognize the inalienable rights of the people of Greenland made Home Rule nothing but a continuation of colonial rule.

The Commission emphasized that the home rule system should be introduced within "the framework of the unity of the Realm." According to the chairman of the Commission, the new system thus was not established "through a treaty based on international law, but exclusively on the basis of constitutional law through a Danish act by means of which the Danish Parliament delegates a certain, precisely defined, part of its competence to home rule" (Foighel 1980:6). Nevertheless, beyond the legal formalism, Home Rule is the application to the indigenous people in Greenland of the general principle of international law called self-determination (Sanders 1981:8–9). For that very reason indigenous peoples in other countries follow the development of Home Rule in Greenland with great interest. The negotiations in the Commission on Home Rule, and the Home Rule Act itself are a strong reminder that "self-determination" is not a clearly defined principle. Transfer of the right to self-determination through a home rule scheme can be designed with varying degrees of respect for the indigenous population. The arrangement for Greenland leaves ample room for the state authorities to safeguard state interests and control (Brøsted 1979).

Authority over foreign relations, defense policy, and the financial system remains with the government of Denmark. Greenlandic norms and ideas may have had little influence on the design of Home Rule, but it is highly significant that the Greenlandic language is defined as "the principal language." Since Danish has been the principal language of the administration and remains important in everyday communication with Danish authorities, the Act provides that "Danish must be thoroughly taught. Either language may be used for official purposes."

A schedule to the Home Rule Act lists the areas to be transferred to Greenlandic control, over the period 1979–1984. They include: local government; taxes; the established church and other religions; fishing, hunting, agriculture, and reindeer breeding; historic preserva-   *715* tion; country planning; regulation of business; social welfare; labor market affairs; education and cultural affairs, including vocational education; economic development; health services; rent regulation and housing; transportation; and protection of the environment (Foighel 1980:17–18).

Areas not listed but of particular importance to Greenland may be transferred to Home Rule in the future after a request from Greenland and with the agreement of the Danish authorities.

There is an interesting difference between the Faeroese and the Greenlandic home rule systems. In the Faeroe Islands home rule applies only to areas where the people of the islands can support the expenses. In Greenland, on the other hand, many areas that depend on heavy government subsidies have been or will be transferred to home rule.

It was agreed by all parties in the Commission for Home Rule that the new system should lead neither to savings nor to extra expenses for the government of Denmark. The subsidies are being transferred as a lump sum, so that the Home Rule authorities can apply their own priorities in allocating funds to the various areas. This is a great advance over the previous situation, where the detailed allocation priorities were made by Danish authorities.

When Home Rule was implemented on May 1, 1979, the government subsidies necessary for areas transferred at that time amounted to approximately 300 million Danish kroner. The capital transfers increased considerably in following years, as area after area was transferred to Home Rule.

The Home Rule Act provided for the replacement of the Provincial Council by a popularly elected provincial assembly (Danish *landsting*), which elects the provincial executive council (Danish *landsstyre*) to act on its behalf.

Elections to the assembly take place every four years. In the election to the first assembly in 1979, *Siumut* gained the majority of the seats, 13 out of 21, and *Atassut* formed the opposition with its 8 seats. In the second election in April 1983, the number of seats was increased by five. In the second assembly *Atassut* received 12 seats, *Siumut* 12, and *Inuit Ataqatigiit* 2.

Danes in Greenland

Between 1975 and 1978 the number of Danes in Greenland declined, probably because of uncertainty over changes in the conditions for Danes that might result from the introduction of home rule. Thereafter the figure rose again; by the end of 1981, 9,279 persons, or about 18 percent of the total population of 51,435 persons, were born outside Greenland. Almost all of these were Danes.

As more and more fields of responsibility have been transferred from Danish control to the administration in Godthåb, the recruitment of Danes has increased. By January 1, 1982, 3,108 persons, one-third of the total population of 9,719 in Godthåb, were Danes. One of the main objectives of Home Rule is that young Greenlanders be trained for the jobs in question.

Danes do vote in Greenland elections, bringing from Denmark the deep-rooted sense of the citizen's duty to vote. In Godthåb they rejected the possibility of dominating the municipal council. With the evolution of political parties in Greenland, Danes could vote within a Greenlander-controlled framework yet approximate the principal political alignments in Denmark. *Siumut* attracted social democrats and those who voted for the Peoples' Socialist Party in Denmark; *Atassut* corresponds to the interests of Danish liberals and conservatives; *Inuit Ataqatigiit* provides an alternative for Danes with more uncompromising attitudes on the left. There is therefore little reason for Danes in Greenland to develop their own political platform. The transient Danish population has little motivation for such an action, and the more permanent Danish inhabitants seem content that Greenlanders be the sole actors in a political arena where alternative viewpoints are expressed. However, it is possible that Danes employed at the military bases of Thule and Søndre Strømfjord (1,500 in 1983) may vote as an effective bloc. Previously enjoying a sort of extra-territoriality, with Home Rule they were given the vote and subjected to Greenlandic taxation, although in other ways they hardly participate in Greenlandic society.

Through more than 30 years of economic development conceived and implemented by foreign specialists far removed from the realities of Greenland life, the country has been made highly dependent on the world market. The one-sided concentration on large-scale fishing and advanced fish processing for the export market has implied underdevelopment of other sectors of the economy (Dahl 1982–1983). This dependency makes Greenland vulnerable to the effect of changes in the international economy, and to policies of foreign governments.

These problems are well illustrated by Greenland's relations with the EEC. When Denmark voted to join the EEC in 1972, Greenland voted against joining but was nevertheless included. The *Siumit, Inuit Ataqatigiit,* and *Sulissartut* parties campaigned to withdraw from the EEC, arguing that Greenland would lose control of its own resources, especially uranium and fish. *Atassut,* on the other hand, maintained that EEC membership promoted financial aid for the development of fishing and sheep farming. In 1982 a referendum resulted in a narrow majority favoring withdrawal from the EEC (Ministeriet for Grønland 1982:118, 285). The Danish government reluctantly concurred and began negotiations to arrange for the most favorable terms for exporting Greenland's fish products to the large Western European market. The EEC treaty has special provisions for Overseas Lands and Territories—former dependent areas of member states—and the Home Rule administration, with Danish support, requested such status.

During the period of intensive transformation of Greenlandic society, higher wages and various fringe benefits were offered to Danes to motivate them to work in Greenland. This has been particularly pronounced in fields demanding higher education, such as health, education, technology, and administration. In addition hundreds of construction workers come in the summer period.

Before the introduction of Home Rule, the assumption was that this system of salary discrimination would be abandoned as Greenlanders were trained to replace Danish personnel. This process has taken much longer than expected, and the system was still operating after the Home Rule administration was established.

This situation has been severely criticized by many Greenlanders. The fact that a number of Greenlandic civil servants have gained dispensation from the so-called birthplace criterion and receive the same salaries as Danes in comparable positions has been particularly repugnant and has damaged efforts to create solidarity among Greenlanders.

"Development on Greenlandic terms" is undercut if particular groups of Greenlanders can enjoy economic privileges that were originally introduced with the expressed purpose of attracting Danish specialists to the country. In 1982 Greenlandic journalists, already enjoying the same salary as their Danish colleagues working in Greenland, demanded an arrangement that would give them paid vacation trips, similar to the contracts under which a few Danish journalists work in the Greenland press and radio.

Home Rule executive Jonathan Motzfeldt stressed the need to eliminate colonial practices such as salary disparity (*Atuagagdliutit/Grønlandsposten*, No. 30, July 28, 1982). He admitted that there will be certain areas in which special arrangements will continue to be necessary, such as physicians for the health service and highly educated technicians, but "it is both politically and psychologically important to move toward a situation where all people in this country live under the same conditions, and that these conditions correspond to the economic capacity of the country."

Another obstacle to attaining social solidarity is the size of the bureaucracy, a legacy from the colonial period. The administrative staffs of Greenland's national and state institutions and of each of the 17 municipal districts are disproportionately large for a society of 50,000 people (Dahl 1982–1983).

East Greenland After 1950

ROBERT PETERSEN

The problems of modern East Greenland are not merely direct results of technical development. In Ammassalik District, there is discordance between the growth of population and technical development. Isolation is crucial in Scoresbysund District.

Population

Population statistics in Greenland divide the population into those born in Greenland and those born outside Greenland. This criterion generally but not precisely follows the ethnic boundary. The East Greenland population born in Greenland includes a number of West Greenlanders, although these are probably fewer than the East Greenlanders living outside East Greenland. The population has increased considerably, and the foreign element has more than doubled. The geographic distribution of the population has also shifted in the direction of greater concentration (table 1).

In Ammassalik District in 1955 there were 17 inhabited settlements; 59 percent of the total population lived at the three largest of these. In 1969 there were 14 inhabited settlements; the population of the same three largest had risen to 72 percent of the district total.

In Scoresbysund District the same tendency has prevailed. In 1955, 49 percent of the population of the district lived in its capital; by 1969 this figure had risen to 60 percent. During the entire period, only three settlements were inhabited in the district.

The composition of the population by age groups has also changed, partly due to the increased number of children and partly due to the fact that the number of unmarried persons 15 years of age and over has stagnated in Ammassalik District and declined in Scoresbysund District (table 1). Since as far as is known the average age at first marriage has not gone down, this lack of increase of unmarried persons must be interpreted as being due to the emigration of persons in this group.

A stagnation in the number of births has occurred in Ammassalik District; in 1960, 108 children were born, but in 1969 the figure was only 107. Scoresbysund District has registered a noticeable decline in the number of births: from 19 in 1960 to 3 in 1969. This decline should be seen as the result of a campaign for the use of intrauterine devices for contraception.

In spite of the plateau in the total number of births in Ammassalik District from 1960 to 1969, the number of illegitimate births rose in this period from 16 to 44. In Scoresbysund District, this figure fell from three to one in the same period. Although only the number of births has been registered, it can be assumed that the increase also indicates that the number of unwed mothers rose in Ammassalik District, and thus the number of family units without male providers.

The statistics show a steep increase in population, especially at the large settlements. The age distribution has shifted, partly through an increase in the number of children and partly due to some emigration among young persons seeking education or work elsewhere. Since the job supply is limited, the increase in the number of women who must support families in Ammassalik District is alarming.

Culture Change

Money Economy and Subsistence Economy

Assuming that the quantity of game animal resources is proportional to the area hunted, the concentration of population must demand the utilization of existing but previously unexploited niches, especially if the previous lack of exploitation was due to the fact than one could not convert products into a form that fit into the pattern of consumption. A money economy has entailed the possibility of converting from one kind of produce to another.

The rise of income from the sale of skins from 1955 to 1969 seems quite marked, but it was mostly due to more favorable prices; the rise in production was less. Some of the income rise is equalized by development of retail prices in Greenland. Prices are to a great extent uniform all over Greenland. With 1950 as the base of 100, the Greenland retail price index has risen thus: 1955, 142; 1960, 163; 1965, 204; 1967, 230 (*Grønland 1969–1970, 1971*).

Skin sales depend considerably on the number of animals taken, as illustrated in table 2. Although these figures do not cover the entire economy, they present a good part of it. It is clear that the population of Scoresbysund District derives considerably more, in terms

Table 1. Population

	1955 born in Greenland	1955 Total	1960 born in Greenland	1960 Total	1965 born in Greenland	1965 Total	1980 born in Greenland	1980 Total
Ammassalik District	1,459	1,546	1,826	1,981	2,166	2,356	2,413	2,694
Ammassalik town	310	372	502	612	650	780	954	1,114
Kuummiit	305	306	388	390	587	593	459	484
Kulusuk (Kap Dan)	225	230	257	258	387	398	382	390
under 15 years old				908		1,189		984
15+, unmarried				246		363		956
Scoresbysund District	315	398	379	490	406	510	421	496
Scoresbysund town	187	196	231	247	257	291	332	391
under 15 years old				199		247		164
15+, unmarried				80		52		200

SOURCES: Denmark. Statistisk tabelværk IX, 1969; Grønland 1969, 1970:78, 1971; Beretninger vedrørende Grønland 1961: 86, 1966:14; Ministeriet for Grønland 1980.

of both money and natural produce, from hunting than that of Ammassalik District, whose population is four times larger.

Shortly before 1960 cod fishing was intensified in Ammassalik District, expecially at Kuummiit and Kulusuk, where salt-fish storages were built. There has been no fish production in Scoresbysund District.

In aboriginal Eskimo culture, people themselves procured materials and fashioned them for their necessities. Although this custom was preserved in the first decades of colonization, people began to need money for small current expenses for tools and gear; likewise the transition to rifle hunting created a need for ammunition. This need for money could be satisfied by even a modest income. Gradually, as the consumption habits of the East Greenlanders began to change, new and larger investments became necessary.

Figures in table 3 indicate this development in the field of hunting. One must presume that the decline in the number of row boats in Ammassalik District is due to the increase in the number of motor boats. Although the motor boats used there are small, they cost considerably more than wooden row boats. Usually money must be borrowed to purchase a motor boat; this loan can be obtained under favorable conditions when an Eskimo has saved enough for the down payment. Motor boats are the most common objective of saving, although outboard motors are also becoming more ordinary.

A motor boat loan often entails a strict economy for its owner. He must often intensify his hunting and perhaps ignore others' expectations of shares in the take in order to meet his financial obligations. The money economy interferes in many ways in the traditional patterns of life.

Traditional Greenlandic hunting boats are noted for

Table 2. Money Economy

		Ammassalik Seals taken	Ammassalik Skins sold	Ammassalik Kroner income	Scoresbysund Seals taken	Scoresbysund Skins sold	Scoresbysund Kroner income
Seal hunting	1949–1950		4,863			914	
	1955–1956	7,949	7,503	89,500	4,853	4,404	81,400
	1960–1961	10,030	5,218		4,315	4,923	
	1965–1966	6,733	6,148				
	1967	8,696	7,818				
	1969			460,000			598,000
	1980			1,663,000			646,000
Cod Fishing	1955			3,400			
	1960			362,000			
	1965			281,000			
	1969			233,500			
	1980			3,146,000			

SOURCES: Beretninger vedrørende Grønland nr.6, 1957, 1961, 1966, 1969; Sammendrag af Grønlands fangstlister 1955, 1956, 1960, 1961, 1965, 1966, 1967; Ministeriet for Grønland 1981.

Table 3. Hunting Equipment

	Row boats	Motor boats	Ice nets
Ammassalik District			
1950	8	0	77
1958	97	4	146
1968	48	16	
Scoresbysund District			
1950	2	0	35
1958	3	0	158
1968		8	

SOURCES: Sammendrag af Grønlands fangstlister 1959, 1960; Grønland 1970, 1971; for motor boats, Robert-Lamblin 1968:115.

their silence. A motor boat makes noise, and if a seal suddenly appears in the vicinity, it can get scared and flee, to the detriment of possible kayak hunters in the same area. The kayak hunters consider motor boats detrimental to hunting; motor boats can therefore lead to conflict.

The extension of hunting grounds has been a successful attempt to alleviate the population problem in Ammassalik District, but other means of increasing income are also sought.

The ancient East Greenland tradition of carving wood and ivory has since the time of contact afforded the Eskimos a limited extra income, especially through the production of masks or grotesque figures called tupilak figures, or tupilaks (fig. 2). The Greenland Handicraft Association, a Danish enterprise, has organized the purchase of these figures. The Royal Greenland Trade Department also purchases some, and some are sold to

Natl. Mus. of Canada, Ottawa: IV–A–474.
Fig. 2. Tupilak, originally a magical creature (Petersen 1964), which has become a popular souvenir. This example is carved from a whale tooth. Length 13.0 cm; collected at Ammassalik before 1973.

tourists. This is in fact the only way in which tourism is made profitable for the inhabitants of East Greenland. The size of incomes from the sale of these figures is unknown, but especially at Kulusuk several persons have made this their main source of income, while others have thus got considerable supplemental income.

Wages and social payments must be mentioned as sources of income because of their relative size and because they involve the circulation of money.

In 1938–1939 Ammassalik District had five wage earners, whose combined earnings were 8,622 Danish kroner. During the same year Scoresbysund District had four wage earners, earning a total of 7,946 kroner (Denmark. Statistiske oplysninger VI:871). In the 1960s there were many more categories of wage earners, and it is more difficult to determine their exact number. Among the residents of Ammassalik District in 1965 who were born in Greenland, 262 persons were engaged in hunting or fishing, while 273 were wage earners of various types. In Scoresbysund District 39 persons were engaged in hunting and 65 were wage earners (Denmark. Statistisk tabelværk IX, 1969). These figures do not reveal how the various categories were distributed among the different households. Most paid jobs were in service occupations.

On the basis of calculations of the family incomes of workers, salaried employees, and public servants in Greenland, the total wage income of East Greenland in 1965 can be estimated at 7.8 million kroner for Ammassalik District and 1.1 million kroner for Scoresbysund District (Statistiske undersøgelser 28:44). During the same year social benefits totaling just under 700,000 kroner were paid out in Ammassalik District; in Scoresbysund District the sum was under 150,000 kroner. These figures do not include the operational expenses of social institutions (Grønlands landsråds forhandlinger 1966:517, 522). Such payments count as income for individuals.

Musée de l'Homme, Paris.
Fig. 1. Gaba using a throwing-board to launch a seal-hunting harpoon; the line is coiled on a stand and attached to a sealskin float on the kayak deck behind him. Photograph by Pierre Robbe, Ammassalik, about 1970.

Formerly several persons were "supported" by various hunting families. Too little is known about the extent of this help in kind to be able to describe its development or make any comparison.

Housing

Housing is the source of the greatest economic pressure. Until around 1950 most of the inhabitants of Ammassalik District lived in earth houses with interior walls of wood. Since then, this housing has been replaced by wooden houses built by Danish carpenters. In Scoresbysund District, the people have lived in wooden houses from the very foundation of the settlement in 1925.

Around 1950 a campaign involved the improvement of housing. By 1965 Ammassalik District had 317 houses, and Scoresbysund District 70; in both districts, more than half the total number had been built in the 10 years since 1955. Approximately two-thirds of the houses in both areas are owned by those who live in them. Slightly more than half the total dwellings in both areas were built with state loans (Denmark. Statistisk tabelværk IX, 1969).

The cheapest wooden houses cost about 30,000 Danish kroner: not very much, but quite a bit in an area that only a couple of generations ago managed without any money at all and that still produces all its own food. Mortgage payments and maintenance have become a heavy burden; the houses must therefore be utilized as much as possible, which means that even in the 1970s the owners themselves lived in them, as it is unusual to rent. This in turn means that people are limited in mobility by their houses to a greater extent than when they lived in earth houses with interior walls of wood. A wooden house cannot be moved around. That this situation was burdensome was revealed in the late 1950s, as desires to redisperse the population began to be made known. This was not the case in Scoresbysund District, probably due to the better economic situation there as well as fewer new houses.

Beginning in 1960, a number of houses were built at isolated places, where some households spent the winter and then returned to the four fjords. Hunting as well as health conditions have been good at these places. Almost all the active hunters in 1969 could consider trying these new hunting grounds to get their economy straightened out. In order to spend the winter in isolation, one has to take along whatever one may need during the winter; this involves a certain investment, for which one can borrow. Loan applications for this purpose must be made one or two years before the winter in question; the authorities are favorably disposed. Formerly, spending the winter in isolation was a spontaneous reaction to a bad hunting year. That loans must be applied for up to two years in advance indicates that spending the winter in isolation is now a response to long-term economic pressure. There are now six or seven places where people spend the winter each year; except for Pikiitti, the residents change each year.

Although this pioneer initiative in East Greenland is primarily the result of economic obligations, it can on a long view be considered an attempt to solve the overpopulation problem of Ammassalik District. Also, the former short winter periods spent in isolation were related to the population situation; this is shown by table 4, in which annual variations in the population and the area exploited are evened out into 10-year averages. Since the inhabited part of Ammassalik District consists of a long coastal belt, the area exploited is here expressed by the kilometer distance between the northernmost and southernmost settlements. In 1968 the area exploited was spread out over 875 kilometers of coast.

Clothing

Clothing was formerly made from sealskins from the stores of each household by the female members of the household. For the period from 1920 to 1930 it has been calculated that from 1,500 to 2,000 sealskins were used annually for clothing and tents; an estimated 6,000 to 7,000 seals were taken annually during the same period (P. Rosing 1930–1931:35; Mikkelsen and Sveistrup 1944:47,86). In the 1970s clothing was purchased, either as cloth or ready-made; almost only hunting clothes were made of sealskins. By purchasing clothes only the sewing is saved, since seal hunting and skin preparation are still carried out. But since skins are the most important source of income in East Greenland, it generally pays to sell all the skins and purchase clothing.

In 1930–1931, 14,440 Danish kroner were spent on dry goods in Ammassalik District; in 1960 the figure was 432,000 kroner. Corresponding figures for Scoresbysund District are 3,100 and 133,000 kroner (Statistiske oplysninger VI:838–840; Beretninger vedrørende Grønland nr. 6, 1962).

Table 4. Greatest Distance Between Ammassalik Settlements

	1906–1915	1916–1925	1926–1935	1936–1945	1946–1955	1956–1965
Kilometers	174.8	347.9	282.0	330.3	467.2	448.5
Population	569	667	780	961	1,289	2,013

In conjunction with the anti-tuberculosis campaign, several hunters, after sanatorium treatment, had to spend long periods of convalescence in dwellings erected for this purpose. Since many of these houses were built at larger settlements, this entailed a greater concentration of the population.

At the district centers hospitals, old people's homes, children's sanatoria, and kindergartens were built. In addition to performing their primary tasks, these also created new jobs.

Education was developed. Many new teachers arrived, and many of these were Danes. New schools were built, and in Ammassalik town a boarding house was built for children of the district attending Ammassalik school (fig. 3). The number of subjects taught grew, and the teaching of Danish was intensified.

The school situation in East Greenland is ambivalent. Except for kayak paddling and tool making and using, which can be included in orientation, instruction at school is not concerned with the training of a hunter; recruitment to this occupation will therefore be limited to children who do poorly in school.

School children who have stayed at the boarding house at Ammassalik have had difficulties adjusting to the working rhythm of their households when they returned home. After a year of school in Denmark, to which entire classes are sent, not one child wishes to become a hunter.

The increased efforts in the field of education are still not sufficient for East Greenlanders looking for work in West Greenland, where the level of education is even higher; if they are to be able to compete on an equal basis, the level of education in East Greenland must be raised. At the same time, the dispersal of the hunting population over a larger area can only entail a poorer education as the price of better hunting training. This well illustrates the dilemma of East Greenland.

Just as schooling given to children in Denmark indirectly reinforces the concentration of the population, seasonal work engaged in by young people in West Greenland also has a centripetal influence. Many young people from outlying areas of Greenland, including East Greenland, work in the fish factories of West Greenland during the summer; a considerable number of these are from small settlements where hunting is still the main source of income. When they return home they have difficulties readjusting to hunting life; at the same time they can find no other employment in their settlements, so that they often move to larger settlements, especially to the district centers. Among this category of young people there are many who would prefer to move to West Greenland, but many of these abandon such plans as they get married and settle down.

At the local centers various installations have created

Fig. 3. The elementary school at Ammassalik in 1969, which accommodated 227 pupils: 27 aged 6 in kindergarten, 190 aged 7–14, and 10 aged 15–17. Of the 13 teachers 3 were Greenlanders and 10 were Danes, only one of whom spoke Greenlandic fluently, and the school languages were Danish and West Greenlandic, rather than East Greenlandic. Photograph by Robert Petersen.

new jobs and thus new sources of income. Salt fish storages have been built in Kuummiit and Kulusuk. Several shops have been built in the two districts; and schools, hospitals, roads, harbors, and workshops are built at the larger settlements. The concentration of population is creating a need for itself.

Political Development

Shortly before 1950, local councils were set up in East Greenland: the District Councils, composed of a number of officials and elected members. This arrangement applied only to East Greenland. In the late 1950s it was decided to extend to East Greenland the system prevailing in the rest of Greenland. In 1961 a municipality system like that in West Greenland was established. There were no more ex officio members in the new municipal councils, which acquired elected chairmen and their own secretariats. From both Ammassalik and Scoresbysund constituencies, members were elected to the Greenland Provincial Council.

Municipal politics has been greatly concerned with modernization problems, especially the population problems, which are quite substantial. The Ammassalik municipal council supports both pioneer activity in the outlying areas and a labor exchange for jobs outside the municipality. "An illogical policy, but a realistic one," remarked one of the councilors.

In recent years various organizations have been politically active in order to support the ideas they advocate, especially the temperance organizations and the women's organizations, which have participated in elections, in alliance with similar groups in the rest of Greenland. East Greenland hunters' organizations, on the other hand, have shown surprisingly little interest in political activity, except for their membership in KNAPP (Greenland Federation of Fishermen's and Hunters' Organizations). This may be due to the fact that the local hunters' organizations in East Greenland have not yet established mutual cooperation within the districts; in addition, the hunters' attitudes have not yet been formulated in political contexts.

The isolation of Ammassalik District was broken when an airport was built at Kulusuk and an air service established in Søndre Strømfjord in West Greenland. In the summer, this service is weekly; in the winter, fortnightly. In addition, several ships land in Ammassalik District each summer.

The communication between Kulusuk and West Greenland has made the isolation of Scoresbysund District even more noticeable. Three or four ships visit this district each summer, and airplane service is likewise occasional. A trip from Scoresbysund to the rest of Greenland can easily cost several thousand Danish kroner. The first member of the Greenland Provincial Council from Scoresbysund was almost never at home, although the sessions lasted only six weeks a year.

Since even radio contact is poor, Scoresbysund District residents have the problem of being part of a larger entity from which they are isolated.

Conclusion

The transformation of East Greenland from a traditional hunting society to the present incipient differentiation of the social structure has taken place more rapidly than in West Greenland, undoubtedly because authorities have been able to use the situation in West Greenland as a model.

In many fields this development has occurred surprisingly easily, but some consequences have been neither desired nor foreseen. For instance, East Greenlanders have stopped composing songs; the song tradition has continued but with a constant repertoire. The song duel, a means of preventing disagreement from developing into open conflict, has fallen into disuse.

On the other hand, certain customs have been maintained although the conditions for their existence have been changed. In hunting with a motor boat, each participant hunts for himself, just as when a kayak is used. There is no sharing of the pool, as in the case when a motor boat is used in West Greenland, so that the boat owner risks bearing all the expenses but getting no share of the proceeds. Pool-sharing can be expected to come into use in East Greenland, too; but until this problem is solved it will be a source of conflict. The differentiation of society will also lead to a situation where the number of persons will grow who can share in the hunt without being able to reciprocate. New conflicts and new norms in this field must be expected.

If East Greenland is to continue as a hunting area, a solution must be found to the question of how more permanent settlement can be made compatible with greater hunting mobility. It will also in the long run be necessary for education to aim at improving the hunter's fortune. Improved education should not automatically lead to an abandonment of hunting; it should make it easier to alternate between hunting and other occupations.

How many persons can live in a hunting area depends not only on the quantity and accessibility of resources but also on the desired standard of living. At present it cannot be determined how many persons can earn their living from hunting in East Greenland, so it will still be necessary to attempt both to extend the hunting area and to create new jobs, if necessary outside of East Greenland. The solutions of these two problems will entail paradoxical situations, but unless they can be solved together, it will not be possible to create harmonious conditions in East Greenland.

The Pan-Eskimo Movement

ROBERT PETERSEN

Even before World War I Rasmussen (1912–1913, 2:48) intended to write a book on all the Inuit-Inupiaq groups after he had realized his plan to visit all their communities. About 10 years later he succeeded in crossing the North American Arctic along the coast from Greenland to Alaska and even paid a short visit to the Siberian Eskimos. His knowledge of the ethnic, cultural, and linguistic heritage of the Inuit-Inupiaq and Yupik played a decisive role in both the planning and the completion of the Fifth Thule Expedition. Rasmussen (1928) published in Greenlandic the first part of his description of the long trip among the Inuit groups, namely the experiences and results of the expedition's visit to the west coast of Hudson Bay, while the West Greenlandic participant in the expedition also published an account (J. Olsen 1927). Rasmussen, unfortunately, did not publish the second part of his narrative, although he intended to do so (Rasmussen 1928:5). But the two books in Greenlandic, and other descriptions in Danish and English, clearly revealed the close relationship among the different Inuit groups.

The Fifth Thule Expedition was the first step toward direct contacts between the Greenland Inuit and the other Inuit west of Davis Strait. But even before then knowledge of the other Inuit to the west was common in Greenland. The periodical *Atuagagdliutit,* published in Greenlandic since 1861, included several narratives from Northwest Passage expeditions and also described contacts between the Church of Greenland and the Labrador Mission.

In the 1950s, parallel to the growing interest of the Danish, Canadian, and United States governments in the study of different solutions to the problems of changing situations, the Greenlandic Provincial Council wanted to establish new and more formal contacts with the Canadian Inuit. A trip, planned by the Ministry of Greenland and sponsored by the Greenlandic Provincial Council, took place in August-September 1956, when a Greenlandic delegation visited Pangnirtung and Frobisher Bay. Two years later a Canadian Inuit delegation visited different places in West Greenland. The separation between the Canadian and Greenlandic Inuit began to diminish; these formal visits were the first steps in establishing new contacts.

Informal contacts between the Canadian Inuit and Alaskan Inupiaq were much easier. North Alaskans had visited the now displaced Chiglit on Herschel Island, and in the twentieth century Inuvialuit from the Mackenzie delta area met Inupiaqs from North Alaska and also sometimes Yupiks from southern Alaska and even Eskimos from Siberia (Nuligak 1972:36). At various traditional trading locations contacts between different Inuit-Inupiaq groups formed a chain from Alaska to the Canadian Arctic (Chance 1966:12 ff.).

Given such conditions, it is understandable that the contacts themselves gained in importance, and in the eastern part of the Inuit area they resulted in political and cultural projects. The different southerners also formulated similar interests for closer relations with the Eskimo.* Ideas about closer cultural exchange were put forward; among the different proposals was an idea for a shared orthography for the Inuit-Inupiaq language (Lefebvre 1957).

Only in the 1970s did the Eskimo really begin to establish voluntary organizations, which soon became both cultural and political channels for the articulation of their wishes.

In the 1970s new Eskimo orthographies were prepared. The Alaska Native Language Center, Fairbanks, prepared orthographies for the Yupik languages, while the orthography used for North Alaska Inupiaq was revised. In Greenland the 1851 orthography was revised in 1973. The Inuit Language Commission of Canada elaborated a parallel system, with both Latin alphabet and syllabic writing, and finalized its proposals in 1976. Even though there are differences due to dialectal diversity and to partly different traditions, the main principles were the same (Petersen 1980). The new systems facilitated widespread understanding of written materials, especially in the area from northern Alaska to Greenland.

The Inuit Circumpolar Conference

In May 1973 in France an international congress considered the problems and possibilities of oil and gas

---

*Especially within the context of the Pan-Eskimo movement the term Inuit has come to be preferred by many as a general designation replacing Eskimo in all its uses. However, this chapter conforms to the usage of the rest of the volume in using Eskimo as the general term and reserving Inuit to apply unambiguously to the Eskimo of Canada and Greenland. See "Introduction," this vol.—Editors.

activities in the Arctic (Malaurie 1975a). Participants were researchers and technicians from all phases of the oil and gas industry from various countries. Representatives of Canadian Inuit and northern Indian organizations took part, as well as some Inuit from the Greenlandic organizations in Denmark. A dialogue and exchange of experiences began. The Canadians James Wah-Shee, president of the Federation of Natives North of 60, and Joe Jacquot, representing the Métis and non-status Indians in northern Canada, continued on to Copenhagen to discuss the possibilities of an "Arctic peoples' conference" together with the Greenlandic associations in Denmark. The latter, with Angmalortoq Olsen from Peqatigiit Kalaallit and Arqaluk Lynge from Unge Grønlænderes Råd, took responsibility for planning the conference.

The conference itself, The Arctic Peoples' Conference, was held in the parliament building, Christiansborg, Denmark, in November 1973. The participants were the Saami (Lapp) organizations in Norway, Sweden, and Finland, the different Greenlandic organizations, and both Inuit and Indian organizations from the Northwest Territories and the Yukon Territory. The Alaska Federation of Natives was unable to take part because its negotiations on Alaskan land claims were reaching a crucial stage, and Greenlandic participation from political bodies was inadequate because a parliamentary election was called at this time so all the political bodies and politicians of Greenland were engaged in campaigns. The mass media paid only moderate attention to the conference. The conference itself was a great experience for the participants, as they realized that they could understand their different situations without profound explanations. Two resolutions were issued demanding recognition of Arctic populations as peoples, and claiming more direct influence upon development planning in Arctic areas (Boye 1974:68–70).

A working group was set up to examine the possibilities for continuation of this kind of cooperation, but other time-consuming activities of the persons involved besides the lack of the necessary financial support prevented further formal cooperation as a direct continuation of the Conference.

The next initiative came from Alaska, where the dynamic Mayor Eben Hopson of Barrow, Alaska, established contacts with other Eskimo groups and with a financing foundation in order to examine the possibility of Eskimo cooperation beyond the borders of the different countries that had gained sovereignty in the Eskimo area. Invitations were sent to different Canadian Inuit organizations and to the groups that had organized the Arctic Peoples' Conference. The attitude of this group was that Greenlandic participation in such cooperative Eskimo efforts ought not to be organized from Copenhagen, but in Greenland itself. This idea was of course accepted in Greenland, and the responsibility

for the Greenlandic part of the organization was divided between the Secretariat of the Greenland Provincial Council and the staff of Knud Rasmussen Folk-high-school, the active organizers in Greenland.

The first contact between the Greenlandic groups and the main organizing body in Barrow, Alaska, was established in October 1975 in Port Alberni, British Columbia, when Vice-Mayor Billy Neakok from Barrow met the Greenlandic delegates during the first conference of the World Council of Indigenous Peoples. While the Greenlandic and Canadian Inuit accepted the invitation to the Inuit Circumpolar Conference, no answer came from the Siberian Eskimo.

The prime mover in the preparation of the conference during the next two years was Mayor Eben Hopson, who located financial support for the preparatory work and the conference assembly and encouraged different groups to take responsibility. He engaged people both to organize the planning itself and to examine the financial possibilities.

In March 1976 the first preparatory meeting was held in Alaska, with participants from Alaska, Canada, and Greenland. Among other things discussed were questions of representation and objectives. The basis for the representation was decided: in Alaska, the regional Native corporations; in Canada, the Native associations; and in Greenland, the island-wide voluntary associations.

Transportation was one of the serious problems, because it might determine the size of the delegations. At this time there was no regular air route between Canada and Greenland, and transportation via Copenhagen would be too expensive. A charter plane from Søndre Strømfjord (Kangerlussuaq) to Barrow, Alaska, with intermediate landings in Frobisher Bay and Yellowknife brought the Greenlandic delegates and the Canadian participants (except the delegates from COPE, Committee for Original Peoples' Entitlement, from the Mackenzie Delta area).

On June 13–16, 1977, the Inuit Circumpolar assembly met to establish the Inuit Circumpolar Conference. Eighteen delegates from each region participated (54 in all), and more than 300 outside visitors came to Barrow. There were Eskimo observers, representatives of churches and governments, of the World Council of Indigenous Peoples, and also Saami representatives and different Eskimo artists. Correspondents from the mass media covered the conference.

Participants recognized in many ways their shared Eskimo origins and similarities in the minoritylike situations of the Eskimo peoples. However, regional differences in cultural heritage and community traditions were manifested, as were differences due to the history of influences from three different majority societies.

The main purposes of this assembly were to create the Inuit Circumpolar Conference (ICC), to discuss its objectives and charter, and in this way to create the first bodies for Eskimo cooperation in cultural, community, and environmental matters.

The Inuit Circumpolar Conference was established as a permanent body for Eskimo cooperation. Mayor Eben Hopson was elected president, but differences appeared when the draft charter was discussed. Some groups of delegates had obtained authority from their organizations to discuss and pass the charter, while other groups had no such authority and therefore wanted to take the draft charter home to discuss it within their organizations and even within their own communities. Working groups were set up to discuss and formulate a framework for exchanges in experiences, and an interim committee was given the task of discussing and formulating a draft charter (Anonymous 1977:14).

Preparation of the ICC Charter

The interim committee of the ICC had four members from each region. Charlie Edwardson, Jr., from Barrow, Alaska, was elected chairman. He called a meeting in September 1977 in Montreal. This meeting became dramatic: tensions due to a Quebec provincial bill about language policy made it difficult for the meeting hosts, the Northern Quebec Inuit Association, to call attention to itself in that period. Thus the meeting was moved to Ottawa. After the principles of the draft charter were discussed, the members from each of the three areas were asked to produce a proposal for such a charter before the next meeting of the interim committee.

In December 1977 the interim committee held its second meeting in Washington, D.C., when a Greenlandic proposal for a draft charter was read. For the next meeting were scheduled treatment of this proposal and of further expected proposals. But the 1978 meeting, to be held in Nain, Labrador, was not held, mainly for financial reasons.

In early 1979 Eben Hopson, finding the situation impossible, proposed to revitalize the three-member ICC executive resolutions committee as a cheaper method for completing the charter preparatory work. In February 1979 this committee met in New York to explore its possibilities and to discuss two proposals for a draft charter. The head of the planning staff, Charles R. White, was asked to unify the two proposals into one, which would be discussed in Greenland when Alaskan and Canadian representatives came to Godthåb (Nuuk) in connection with the celebration of the introduction of home rule in Greenland. But there were too many activities and too many events in Godthåb during those days, so instead, the Executive Resolutions Committee met in Inuvik, Northwest Territories, in July to deal with the unified draft charter proposal. The unification was carried out, but then COPE presented a new proposal for a charter lasting more than one year. Thus

after the Inuvik meeting there were still two proposals for a draft charter.

In autumn 1979 the establishment of home rule authorities in Greenland allowed them to consider new activities; the secretariat of the Greenland Provincial Council began to analyze the draft charter proposal and to compare it with the Home Rule act for Greenland. They found that the different versions might create some problems, partly because of different definitions of the same terms in the different areas. They made comparisons with the Nordic Council, which could serve as a model since it, too, was a charter for voluntary cooperation between people with a common heritage but living in three different countries. The Nordic Council is a forum for the exchange of ideas and the discussion of common objectives, without obligating the different governments to follow its decisions. The former chairman of the Greenland Home Rule Commission, Dr. Isi Foighel, was asked to prepare a proposal that might unite such a body with the Greenland home rule activities. This proposal was prepared in the beginning of 1980 and taken by the Greenlandic delegation to the conference planning meeting in Alaska in March 1980. It was passed with some amendments, and decisions were made to hold the next ICC meeting at Godthåb in the end of June and the beginning of July 1980. At a preparatory meeting at Godthåb in the days immediately before the meeting itself, the last amendments to the draft charter proposals, proposals for the ICC bylaws, and the conference program were finalized.

The Second ICC Assembly

The meetings were held at the Teacher Training School in Godthåb, where the staff remained after summer holidays had begun. An air route between Godthåb and Frobisher Bay in Canada was opened in the spring of 1980, which made the transportation much easier than before.

Mayor Eben Hopson, seriously ill, could not attend. He died during the conference, after learning that the charter had passed.

The main purpose of the meeting was to pass the ICC charter, which was effected unanimously (Anonymous 1980b:15ff., 1980c). It contained a definition of objectives and set up membership rules and different bodies to carry out ICC activities. It required ratification by the regional authorities, to bring about their participation in financing.

The ICC was organized with a president, six members of the executive committee, and a secretariat to coordinate and manage the assembly decisions. There are 54 delegates, 18 from each region (Greenland, Arctic Canada, and Alaska), who must live in the Eskimo homeland. In defining membership in Eskimo communities, the question of ancestry was omitted. "Circumpolar" is defined so as to include Eskimo communities in the Subarctic area, even south of the timberline.

Hans-Pavia Rosing from Greenland was elected president of the ICC (fig. 1), and in this connection the secretariat was opened in Godthåb. The meeting established several ICC working groups, one on cultural exchanges and educational questions, one on communications and transportation, another on village technology, another on the housing situation, and finally one on health and social conditions.

After the Second ICC Assembly

The progress of the ICC assembly in Godthåb was observed by representatives from the three countries, who studied the draft charter with interest and paid much attention to the charter as adopted. Their statements showed understanding of the demands of the body, especially the demand by the Eskimo living in the three countries to discuss matters of mutual interest without making them foreign affairs.

The ICC is a forum for the Eskimos from Alaska, Canada, and Greenland to exchange information about their conditions, experiences, and problems, through the different working groups. This time the organizers provided both the human and the financial resources needed to carry out the decisions of the conference. The working groups met several times following the Godthåb conference, recommending that the different organizations use common experiences and ideas in the solution of both common and regional problems.

The ICC has, beyond this, demonstrated moral support for the Eskimo and other Arctic people under stress. Of course such activities contribute to a better

Grønlands Landsmuseum, Godthåb.
Fig. 1. Hans-Pavia Rosing, president of the Second Inuit Circumpolar Conference, speaking at the conference in the Teacher Training School at Godthåb, Greenland. Photograph by Erik Holm, June–July 1980.

consciousness among the Eskimo of their own situation. An important example in this connection was information about indigenous whaling in Alaska (Anonymous 1980b); the ICC brought the Alaskan Eskimo Whaling Commission into contact with the Greenland home rule authorities, who then cooperated with the Danish delegation to the International Whaling Commission. Such information is important not only for international commissions of different kinds but also for the different Eskimo groups.

The ICC inherited the desire expressed by the Arctic Peoples' Conference that the Eskimo people participate on an equal basis in the planning of development projects in the Arctic. One of the main objectives discussed in the Barrow conference was common environmental policy. So it was obvious that the ICC should support the protests expressed by the Canadian Inuit organizations against the Arctic Pilot Project, which proposed icebreaker-tanker transport of oil or liquified natural gas from the Canadian Arctic archipelago via Lancaster Sound, and in some places rather close to the west coast of Greenland (Hess 1982:5). The fear of deleterious environmental impact played an important role, and the information provided led to official protests from both Greenlandic and Danish authorities.

The Possible Role of the ICC

In the steps that led to the establishment of the ICC the influences from three different majority societies are notable, even though many of the political attitudes in the United States, Canada, and Denmark are rather similar. But there are differences, and beyond this both the pace and the kind of influence from the historical contact between the Eskimo and the three majority societies created differences in experiences and ways of thinking. One of the observable differences was in the stress given to different aspects of democracy. In some regions it was especially representative democracy as a means for practical solution of community questions that was emphasized, while in other areas local and general participation in decision making seems to be the main point. These different attitudes may result in uneven influence upon matters of shared concern, and some means must be found to maintain the symbiotic character of the ICC. The results of the differences in basic political attitudes may be reinforced by differences in election rules and electoral periods that effect the terms and stability of representation by delegates to the ICC.

This point may become more important since the membership rules leave open the possibility for adding new members of the ICC; among others, the Siberian Eskimo may come under consideration at some future time. During the early years of the ICC, however, this must be regarded as a rather unlikely possibility.

Despite its youth, the ICC has already been important in working for better awareness of mutual identity and of many shared interests. It prepared the way for increased consciousness of mutual values, and for their possible importance even in the modern communities. But during the first years of its existence its success is more obvious among the groups who fought for its establishment; its final success must depend on the public understanding and utilization of its results by the rest of the Eskimo people. The formation of the ICC is the beginning of cooperation. Hans-Pavia Rosing asserted in April 1982 that the ultimate Eskimo unity would be an Eskimo nation, even though he could not predict when this might come into being (Hess 1982:5).

Contributors

This list gives the academic affiliations of authors at the time this volume went to press. The dates following the entries indicate when each manuscript was (1) first received in the General Editor's office; (2) accepted for the first time by the General Editor; (3) sent to the author for final approval after revisions and editorial work.

ACKERMAN, ROBERT E., Department of Anthropology, Washington State University, Pullman. Prehistory of the Asian Eskimo Zone: 4/7/74; 11/23/77; 3/9/83.

ANDERSON, DOUGLAS D., Department of Anthropology, Brown University, Providence, Rhode Island. Prehistory of North Alaska: 3/12/73; 12/26/73; 3/21/83.

ARIMA, EUGENE Y., Ottawa, Ontario. Caribou Eskimo: 1/8/73; 5/30/75; 12/20/82.

BALIKCI, ASEN, Department of Anthropology, University of Montreal, Quebec. Netsilik: 2/21/74; 3/26/75; 12/20/82.

BRANTENBERG, ANNE, Tromsø, Norway. Coastal Northern Labrador After 1950: 8/3/81; 5/20/83; 5/24/83.

BRANTENBERG, TERJE, Institutt for Samfunnsvitenskap, Universitetet i Tromsø, Norway. Coastal Northern Labrador After 1950: 8/3/81; 5/20/83; 5/24/83.

BURCH, ERNEST S., JR., Department of Anthropology, Smithsonian Institution, Washington, D.C. Kotzebue Sound Eskimo: 5/5/72; 2/6/73; 12/20/82. The Land Claims Era in Alaska: 7/29/82; 2/24/83; 5/20/83.

CHANCE, NORMAN A., Department of Anthropology, University of Connecticut, Storrs. Alaska Eskimo Modernization: 5/31/73; 12/5/73; 5/20/83.

CLARK, DONALD W., Archaeological Survey of Canada, National Museums of Canada, Ottawa, Ontario. Pacific Eskimo: Historical Ethnography: 5/8/72; 7/1/73; 11/24/82. Prehistory of the Pacific Eskimo Region: 5/5/72; 7/17/73; 2/7/83.

COLLINS, HENRY B. (emeritus), Department of Anthropology, Smithsonian Institution, Washington, D.C. History of Research Before 1945: 9/30/73; 1/24/75; 2/15/83.

COOPER, JOSEPH D., Ottawa, Ontario. Contemporary Canadian Inuit: 7/28/76; 5/2/83; 5/13/83.

DAMAS, DAVID, Department of Anthropology, McMaster University, Hamilton, Ontario. Central Eskimo: Introduction: 6/9/75; 3/23/82; 12/6/82. Copper Eskimo: 7/17/72; 12/26/72; 12/20/82. Introduction: 7/6/79; 2/8/83; 3/24/83.

DAVIS, NANCY YAW, Cultural Dynamics, Ltd., Anchorage, Alaska. Contemporary Pacific Eskimo: 3/10/75; 1/5/83; 12/7/82.

DUMOND, DON E., Department of Anthropology, University of Oregon, Eugene. Prehistory of the Bering Sea Region: 1/8/74; 1/18/74; 2/1/83. Prehistory: Summary: 9/21/79; 3/15/82; 2/4/83.

FITZHUGH, WILLIAM W., Department of Anthropology, Smithsonian Institution, Washington, D.C. Paleo-Eskimo Cultures of Greenland: 7/12/76; 6/5/78; 6/2/83.

FREEMAN, MILTON M.R., Department of Anthropology, University of Alberta, Edmonton. Arctic Ecosystems: 4/15/75; 12/27/76; 2/15/83. The Grise Fiord Project: 8/6/73; 2/5/75; 5/20/83.

GAD, FINN, Gentofte, Denmark. History of Colonial Greenland: 2/11/74; 2/18/75; 5/13/83.

GILBERG, ROLF, Etnografisk Samling, Nationalmuseet, Copenhagen, Denmark. Polar Eskimo: 1/25/74; 1/28/75; 5/9/83.

HALL, EDWIN S., JR., Department of Anthropology, State University of New York, Brockport. Interior North Alaska Eskimo: 5/4/72; 12/11/72; 11/26/82.

HARP, ELMER, JR. (emeritus), Department of Anthropology, Dartmouth College, Hanover, New Hampshire. History of Archeology After 1945: 2/17/76; 2/4/83; 3/23/83.

HUGHES, CHARLES C., Department of Family and Community Medicine and Department of Anthropology, University of Utah, Salt Lake City. Asiatic Eskimo: Introduction: 8/1/77; 12/27/82; 12/14/82. History of Ethnology After 1945: 1/13/83; 2/24/83; 3/22/83. Saint Lawrence Island Eskimo: 10/30/72; 6/4/73; 12/16/82. Siberian Eskimo: 1/24/77; 1/10/83; 12/17/82.

JORDAN, RICHARD H., Department of Anthropology, Bryn Mawr College, Pennsylvania. Neo-Eskimo Prehistory of Greenland: 8/3/76; 6/5/78; 5/10/83.

KEMP, WILLIAM B., Department of Geography, McGill University, Montreal, Quebec. Baffinland Eskimo: 8/3/81; 12/26/82; 1/14/83.

KLEIVAN, HELGE (deceased), Institut for Eskimologi, Københavns Universitet, Copenhagen, Denmark. Contemporary Greenlanders: 3/10/83; 5/16/83; 6/6/83. Greenland Eskimo: Introduction: 4/7/80; 4/14/82; 5/10/83.

KLEIVAN, INGE, Institut for Eskimologi, Københavns Universitet, Copenhagen, Denmark. History of Norse Greenland: 6/21/74; 12/29/76; 5/24/83. West Greenland Before 1950: 6/21/74; 5/13/82; 5/26/83.

LANTIS, MARGARET (emerita), Department of Anthropology, University of Kentucky, Lexington. Aleut: 2/25/74; 9/23/75; 11/24/82. Nunivak Eskimo: 4/5/76; 1/27/77; 11/22/82.

MARY-ROUSSELIÈRE, GUY, Roman Catholic Mission, Pond Inlet, Northwest Territories. Iglulik: 11/17/72; 3/25/75; 12/21/82.

MAXWELL, MOREAU S., Department of Anthropology, Michigan State University, East Lansing. Pre-Dorset and Dorset Prehistory of Canada: 6/21/73; 2/15/74; 11/23/82.

MCCARTNEY, ALLEN P., Department of Anthropology, University of Arkansas, Fayetteville. Prehistory of the Aleutian Region: 5/5/72; 7/14/77; 2/1/83.

MCGEE, ROBERT, Archaeological Survey of Canada, National Museums of Canada, Ottawa, Ontario. Thule Prehistory of Canada: 4/4/72; 7/6/73; 12/10/82.

MCSKIMMING, ROBERT J., Calgary, Alberta. Physical Environment: 4/11/78; 1/25/83; 2/23/83.

NEATBY, L.H., Saskatoon, Saskatchewan. Exploration and History of the Canadian Arctic: 8/23/74; 1/8/76; 11/23/82.

PETERSEN, ROBERT (West Greenlander), Inuit Institut, Godthåb, Greenland. East Greenland Before 1950: 1/24/74; 3/19/75; 5/6/83. East Greenland After 1950: 1/24/74; 3/19/75; 5/10/83. Greenlandic Written Literature: 1/24/74; 3/19/75; 5/6/83. The Pan-Eskimo Movement: 7/1/82; 7/20/82; 5/6/83.

RAY, DOROTHY JEAN, Port Townsend, Washington. Bering Strait Eskimo: 9/5/72; 4/25/73; 12/14/82.

SALADIN d'ANGLURE, BERNARD, Département d'anthropologie, Université Laval, Ste-Foy, Québec. Contemporary Inuit of Quebec: 4/7/75; 7/13/83; 7/15/83. Inuit of Quebec: 4/12/73; 7/13/83; 7/15/83.

SMITH, DEREK G., Department of Sociology/Anthropology, Carleton University, Ottawa, Ontario. Contemporary Canadian Inuit: 7/28/76; 5/2/83; 5/13/83. Mackenzie Delta Eskimo: 5/2/73; 3/10/75; 12/15/82.

SPENCER, ROBERT F., Department of Anthropology, University of Minnesota, Minneapolis. North Alaska Coast Eskimo: 8/16/72; 7/17/74; 11/23/82. North Alaska Eskimo: Introduction: 8/16/72; 8/20/73; 11/26/82.

STAGER, JOHN K., Department of Geography, University of British Columbia, Vancouver. Physical Environment: 4/11/78; 1/25/83; 2/23/83.

SZATHMARY, EMÖKE J.E., Department of Anthropology, McMaster University, Hamilton, Ontario. Human Biology of the Arctic: 2/23/82; 3/15/82; 2/23/83.

TAYLOR, J. GARTH, Canadian Ethnology Service, National Museums of Canada, Ottawa, Ontario. Historical Ethnography of the Labrador Coast: 1/30/72; 6/6/73; 12/21/82.

VALLEE, FRANK G., Department of Sociology/Anthropology, Carleton University, Ottawa, Ontario. Contemporary Canadian Inuit: 7/28/76; 5/2/83; 5/13/83.

VANSTONE, JAMES W., Department of Anthropology, Field Museum of Natural History, Chicago, Illinois. Exploration and Contact History of Western Alaska: 5/3/72; 12/15/72; 1/21/83. Mainland Southwest Alaska Eskimo: 5/3/72; 1/23/73; 11/22/82. Southwest Alaska Eskimo: Introduction: 5/17/74; 8/4/82; 11/23/82.

WOODBURY, ANTHONY C., Department of Linguistics, University of Texas, Austin. Eskimo and Aleut Languages: 8/30/82; 2/23/83; 2/24/83.

Bibliography

This list includes all references cited in the volume, arranged in alphabetical order according to the names of the authors as they appear in the citations in the text. Multiple works by the same author are arranged chronologically; second and subsequent titles by the same author in the same year are differentiated by letters added to the dates. Where more than one author with the same surname is cited, one has been arbitrarily selected for text citation by surname alone throughout the volume, while the others are always cited with added initials; the combination of surname with date in text citations should avoid confusion. Where a publication date is different from the series date (as in some annual reports and the like), the former is used. Dates, authors, and titles that do not appear on the original works are enclosed by brackets. For manuscripts, dates refer to time of composition. For publications reprinted or first published many years after original composition, a bracketed date after the title refers to the time of composition or the date of original publication.

Abelsen, Sejer
1935–1936 Scoresbysund nunasinerdlo [Scoresbysund and Its Settlement]. *Atuagagdliutit*: 105, 122-126, 129, 155-158, 163. Nûngme.

Abrahamson, G.
1963 Tuktoyaktuk—Cape Parry Area Economic Survey. Ottawa: Department of Northern Affairs and National Resources, Industrial Division, Projects Section.

Abrahamson, G., P.J. Gillespie, D.J. McIntosh, P.J. Usher, and H.A. Williamson
1964 The Copper Eskimos: An Area Economic Survey, 1963. Ottawa: Department of Northern Affairs and National Resources, Industrial Division.

Abrahamson, John D.
1968 Westward Alaska: The Native Economy and Its Resource Base. Report prepared for the Federal Field Committee for Development Planning in Alaska, Anchorage. Mimeo.

Ackerman, Robert E.
1961 Archeological Investigations into the Prehistory of St. Lawrence Island, Alaska. (Unpublished Ph.D. Dissertation in Anthropology, University of Pennsylvania, Philadelphia.)

_____
1962 Culture Contact in the Bering Sea: Birnirk-Punuk Period. Pp. 27-34 in Prehistoric Cultural Relations Between the Arctic and Temperate Zones of North America. John M. Campbell, ed. *Arctic Institute of North America Technical Paper* 11. Montreal.

_____
1964 Prehistory in the Kuskokwim-Bristol Bay Region, Southwestern Alaska. *Washington State University, Laboratory of Anthropology, Report of Investigations* 26. Pullman.

_____
1970 Archaeoethnology, Ethnoarchaeology, and the Problems of Past Cultural Patterning. Pp. 11-48 in Ethnohistory in Southwestern Alaska and the Southern Yukon. M. Lantis, ed. Lexington: University of Kentucky Press.

_____
1973 Post Pleistocene Cultural Adaptations on the Northern Northwest Coast. Pp. 1-20 in International Conference on the Prehistory and Paleoecology of Western Arctic and Subarctic. Scott Raymond and Peter Schledermann, eds. Calgary: University of Calgary, Archaeological Association.

_____
1976 The Eskimo People of Savoonga. Phoenix: Indian Tribal Series.

_____
1979 Southwestern Alaska Archeological Survey, 1978: Akhlun-Eek Mountains Region. (Preliminary Report to the National Geographic Society, Washington.) Pullman: Washington State University, Laboratory of Anthropology, Arctic Research Section.

_____
1979a Observations on Prehistory: Gulf of Alaska, Bering Sea and Asia During Late Pleistocene-Early Holocene Epochs. (Paper presented at 14th Pacific Science Congress, Khabarovsk, U.S.S.R.)

_____
1980 Southwestern Alaska Archeological Survey: Kagati Lake, Kisaralik-Kwethluk Rivers. (Final Research Report to the National Geographic Society, Washington.) Pullman: Washington State University, Laboratory of Anthropology, Arctic Research Section.

Ackerman, Robert E., T.D. Hamilton, and R. Stuckenrath
1979 Early Cultural Complexes on the Northern Northwest Coast. *Canadian Journal of Archaeology* 3:195-210.

Adam, Paul
1973 Future of Fisheries as a Basic Resource for Arctic Communities: With Accent on the Greenland Case. Pp. 519-531 in Le Peuple esquimau aujourd'hui et demain/The Eskimo People To-Day and To-Morrow. Jean Malaurie, ed. (Fourth International Congress of the Fondation Française d'Études Nordiques) Paris, The Hague: Mouton.

Adams, John W., and Alice B. Kasakoff
1976 Factors Underlying Endogamous Group Size. Pp. 149-173 in Vol. 2 of Regional Analysis. Carol A. Smith, ed. New York: Academic Press.

Ager, Lynn Price
1974 Storyknifing: An Alaskan Eskimo Girls' Game. *Journal of the Folklore Institute* 11(3):189-198.

Aigner, Jean S.
1966 Bone Tools and Decorative Motifs from Chaluka, Umnak Island. *Arctic Anthropology* 3(2):57-85.

_____
1970 The Unifacial, Core and Blade Site on Anangula Island, Aleutians. *Arctic Anthropology* 7(2):59-88.

_____
1974 Studies in the Early Prehistory of Nikolski Bay: 1937-1971. *Anthropological Papers of the University of Alaska* 16(1):9-25. Fairbanks.

_____
1976 Dating the Early Holocene Maritime Village of Anangula. *Anthropological Papers of the University of Alaska* 18(1):51-62. Fairbanks.

_____
1976a Early Holocene Evidence for the Aleut Maritime Adaptation. *Arctic Anthropology* 13(2):32-45.

_____
1978 Activity Zonation in a 4000 Year Old Aleut House, Chaluka Village, Umnak Island, Alaska. *Anthropological Papers of the University of Alaska* 19(1):11–25. Fairbanks.

_____
1978a The Lithic Remains from Anangula, an 8500 Year Old Aleut Coastal Village. *Universität Tübingen, Institut für Urgeschichte, Urgeschichtliche Materialhefte* 3. Tübingen, Germany.

Aigner, Jean S., and Douglas Veltre
1976 The Distribution and Pattern of Umqan Burial on Southwest Umnak Island. *Arctic Anthropology* 13(2):113-127.

Aigner, Jean S., Bruce Fullem, Douglas Veltre, and Mary Veltre
1976 Preliminary Reports on Remains from Sandy Beach Bay, a 4300-5600 B.P. Aleut Village. *Arctic Anthropology* 13(2):83-90.

Alaska Geographic
1981 Alaska National Interest Lands. *Alaska Geographic* 8(4).

731

Alaska Native Foundation
1977   Alaska Native Foundation: A Status Report. Anchorage: Alaska Native Foundation.

Alaska Native News
1982   ANCSA: From Tribalism to Tribal Corporations. *Alaska Native News* 1(1):9-12.

Alaska State Housing Authority
1971   Kotzebue, Alaska: Comprehensive Development Plan. Anchorage: Alaska State Housing Authority.

Alaska. Governor's Commission on Cross-cultural Education
1970   Time for Change in the Education of Alaska Natives: A Statement of Preliminary Findings and Recommendations Relating to the Education of Alaska Natives. Juneau.

Alasuaq, A.
1973   Guide de la couturière (Manuel scolaire en syllabique avec traduction anglaise et française). Povungnituk: Commission Scolaire du Nouveau-Québec.

Aldrich, Herbert L.
1889   Arctic Alaska and Siberia; or Eight Months with the Arctic Whaleman. Chicago: Rand, McNally.

Alekseev, Valeri P.
1964   The Craniology of the Asiatic Eskimo. *Arctic Anthropology* 2(2):120-125.

1979   On Eskimo Origins. *Current Anthropology* 20(1):158-161.

1979a   Anthropometry of Siberian Peoples. Pp. 57-90 in The First Americans: Origins, Affinities, and Adaptations. W.S. Laughlin and A.B. Harper, eds. New York: Gustav Fischer.

Alekseev, Valeri P., S.A. Arutiunov, and D.A. Sergeev
1972   Results of Historico-Ethnological and Anthropological Studies in the Eastern Chukchee Area. *Inter-Nord* 12:234-243. Paris.

Alexander, Herbert L.
1969   Prehistory of the Central Brooks Range: An Archaeological Analysis. (Unpublished Ph.D. Dissertation in Archaeology, University of Oregon, Eugene.)

1974   The Association of Aurignacoid Elements with Fluted Point Complexes in North America. Pp. 21-31 in International Conference on the Prehistory and Paleoecology of Western North American Arctic and Subarctic. Scott Raymond and Peter Schledermann, eds. Calgary: University of Calgary Archaeological Association.

Allen, Henry T.
1887   Report of an Expedition to the Copper, Tanana, and Koyukon Rivers, in the Territory of Alaska, in the Year 1885. Washington: U.S. Government Printing Office.

Allen, J.A.
1877   The Influence of Physical Conditions on the Genesis of Species. *Radical Review* 1:108-140. New Bedford, Mass.

Allen, P.W., and R.O. Weedfall
1966   Weather and Climate. Pp. 9-44 in Environment of the Cape Thompson Region, Alaska. Norman J. Wilimovsky and John N. Wolfe, eds. Washington: U.S. Atomic Energy Commission.

Allen, W.T.R., and B.S. Cudbird
1971   Freeze-up and Break-up Dates for Water Bodies in Canada. (*CLI-1-71*) Toronto: Canadian Meteorological Service.

Amdrup, Georg C., et al.
1921   Grønland i tohundredaaret for Hans Egedes Landing, I-II. [Greenland in the Two Hundred Years Before the Arrival of Hans Egede]. *Meddelelser om Grønland* 60-61. Copenhagen.

American Indian Policy Review Commission
1976   Special Joint Task Force Report on Alaska Native Issues. Washington: U.S. Government Printing Office.

Amsden, Charles W.
1977   A Quantitative Analysis of Nunamiut Eskimo Settlement Dynamics. (Unpublished Ph.D. Dissertation in Archaeology, University of New Mexico, Albuquerque.)

Amundsen, Roald E.G.
1908   Roald Amundsen's "The Northwest Passage." Being the Record of a Voyage of Exploration of the Ship "Gjöa", 1903-1907. 2 vols. New York: E.P. Dutton.

Anchorage Daily News
1965   The Village People. (Special series of articles on the condition of Alaska's Native peoples.) *Anchorage Daily News*.

1981   The Village People Revisited. (Special issue summarizing developments among the Native population during the first ten years of ANCSA.) *Anchorage Daily News*, December 5, 1981.

Anders, G., ed.
1967   Baffinland-East Coast: An Economic Survey. Ottawa: Department of Indian Affairs and Northern Development, Industrial Division.

Andersen, Erik L.
1982   De norrøne stednavne i Østerbygden. Tema: Nordboerne, I [The Norse Place-names in the Eastern Settlement. Theme: The Norse, I]. *Grønland* (5-7):163-176. Copenhagen.

Andersen, John
1981   Kaptajn Ejnar Mikkelsens Mindeekspedition 1980 Scoresbysund-Angmagssalik [The Captain Ejnar Mikkelsen's Commemorative Expedition—1980 Scoresbysund-Ammassalik]. (Manuscript in Andersen's possession.)

Anderson, Douglas D.
1962   Cape Krusenstern Ipiutak Economic and Settlement Patterns. (Unpublished M.A. Thesis in Anthropology, Brown University, Providence, R.I.)

1968   A Stone Age Campsite at the Gateway to America. *Scientific American* 218(6):24-33.

1970   Athapaskans in the Kobuk Arctic Woodlands, Alaska? *Canadian Archaeological Association Bulletin* 2:3-12. Ottawa.

1970a   Akmak: An Early Archeological Assemblage from Onion Portage, Northwest Alaska. *Acta Arctica* 16. Copenhagen.

1970b   Microblade Traditions in Northwestern Alaska. *Arctic Anthropology* 7(2):2-16.

1972   An Archaeological Survey of Noatak Drainage, Alaska. *Arctic Anthropology* 9(1):66-117.

1974-1975   Trade Networks Among the Selawik Eskimos, Northwestern Alaska, During the Late 19th and Early 20th Centuries. *Folk* 16-17:63-72. Copenhagen.

1978   Western Arctic and Sub-Arctic. Pp. 29-50 in Chronologies in New World Archeology. R.E. Taylor and C.W. Meighan, eds. New York: Academic Press.

1978a   Tulaagiaq: A Transitional Near Ipiutak-Ipiutak Period Archeological Site from Kotzebue Sound, Alaska. *Anthropological Papers of the University of Alaska* 19(1):45-57. Fairbanks.

1979   Archaeology and the Evidence for the Prehistoric Development of Eskimo Culture: An Assessment. *Arctic Anthropology* 16(1):16-26. Fairbanks.

1980   Continuity and Change in the Prehistoric Record from North Alaska. Pp. 233-251 in Alaska Native Culture and History. Y. Kotani and W.B. Workman, eds. *National Museum of Ethnology, Senri Ethnological Studies* 4. Osaka, Japan.

Anderson, Douglas D., and Wanni W. Anderson
1977   Selawik Inupiat (Eskimo) Archeological Settlement, Re-

sources and Subsistence Lifeways. Northwestern Alaska. Final Report. (Unpublished manuscript in Department of Anthropology, Brown University, Providence, R.I.)

Anderson, Douglas D., et al.
1977   Kuuvangmiit Subsistence: Traditional Eskimo Life in the Latter Twentieth Century. Washington: U.S. Department of the Interior, National Park Service.

————   1981   The Kotzebue Basin. *Alaska Geographic* 8(3).

Anderson, H. Dewey, and Walter C. Eells
1935   Alaska Natives: A Survey of Their Sociological and Educational Status. Stanford, Calif.: Stanford University Press.

Anderson, James E., and James A. Tuck
1974   Osteology of the Dorset People. *Man in the Northeast* 8:89-97.

Anderson, Patricia M.
1982   Reconstructing the Past: The Synthesis of Archaeological and Palynological Data, Northern and Northwestern Canada. (Unpublished Ph.D. Dissertation in Archaeology, Brown University, Providence, R.I.)

Anderson, Wanni W.
1974-1975   Song Duel of the Kobuk River Eskimo. *Folk* 16-17:73-81. Copenhagen.

Andrews, Clarence L.
1939   The Eskimo and His Reindeer in Alaska. Caldwell, Id.: Caxton Printers.

Andrews, J.T., Robert McGhee, and Lorna McKenzie-Pollock
1971   Comparison of Elevations of Archaeological Sites and Calculated Sea Levels in Arctic Canada. *Arctic* 24(3):210-228.

Anoee, Martina Pihujui
1979   Remembered Childhood. *Ajurnarmat* 1–7 (Education edition).

Anonymous
1850   Pokhod geodezista Mikhaila Gvozdeva v Beringov proliv, 1732 goda [Expedition of the Surveyor Mikhail Gvozdev to the Bering Strait in 1732]. *Sbornik Morskoĭ* 4:389-402.

————   1942-1945   Statistiske oplysninger om Grønland [Statistical Information on Greenland]. Copenhagen: Beretninger vedrørende Grønland.

————   1964   Lærebog i fangst for Syd- og Nordgrønland [Hunting and Fishing Textbook for South and North Greenland]. Copenhagen: Den Kongelige Grønlandske Handel.

————   1970   Policy Planning Statement of the Arctic Slope Region. (Manuscript, copy in Arctic Research Laboratory, Barrow, Alas.)

————   1977   The Conference Report; Inuit Circumpolar Conference, Barrow, Alaska, June 1977. Mimeo.

————   1978   Inside the Life and Culture of Kodiak. *Elwani Magazine*. Anchorage.

————   1980   Inuit and the Law. *Arjungnagimmat* (Summer):35-37. Eskimo Point, N.W.T.

————   1980a   Charter Approved, International Inuit Organization Established. *Igalaak* 2(10)August:1, 4. Ottawa.

————   1980b   Inuit Circumpolar Conference, Nuuk, Greenland, June 1980: Nuuk Conference Ratifies ICC Charter. *The Arctic Coastal Zone Management Newsletter* 29-30. Anchorage.

————   1980c   Kátuvfigtâp maligtarissagssai tamanit isumakatiginekarput/ Enighed om den nye organisations vedtægter. *Atuagagdliutit/ Grønlandsposten* 120-121(27):21.

————   1982   Inuit Broadcasting Corporation Replaces Inukshuk. *Igalaak* 4(4):5. Ottawa.

————   1982a   Yes Vote in Eastern Arctic. *Igalaaq* 4(7):1-3. Ottawa.

————   1982b   Rankin Conference Unites Nunavut on Land Claims, Constitution, Bill C-48. *Igalaaq* 4(3):1-2. Ottawa.

Arbess, Saul E.
1966   Social Change and the Eskimo Co-operative at George River, Quebec. (*NCRC 66-1*) Ottawa: Department of Northern Affairs and National Resources, Northern Co-ordination and Research Centre.

Arctic Environmental Information and Data Center
1976   Community Studies of the NANA Region: Ambler, Buckland, Deering, Kiana, Kivalina, Kobuk, Kotzebue, Noatak, Noorvik, Selawik, Shungnak. Anchorage: University of Alaska, Arctic Environmental Information and Data Center for the Alaska Department of Community and Regional Affairs.

Arima, Eugene Y.
1963   Report on an Eskimo Umiak Built at Ivujivik, P.Q. in the Summer of 1960. *Anthropological Series* 59, *National Museum of Canada Bulletin* 189. Ottawa.

————   1964   Notes on the Kayak and Its Equipment at Ivujivik, P.Q., *Anthropological Series* 62, *National Museum of Canada Bulletin* 196:221-261. Ottawa.

————   [1966-1969] [Ethnographic Notes from Approximately Six Months' Fieldwork Among Caribou Eskimos at Baker Lake, N.W.T.] (Manuscripts in Arima's possession.)

————   1967   Itivimiut Sled Construction. *Anthropological Series* 70, *National Museum of Canada Bulletin* 204:100-123. Ottawa.

————   1975   A Contextual Study of the Caribou Eskimo Kayak. *Canada. National Museum of Man. Mercury Series. Ethnology Service Paper* 25. Ottawa.

Arima, Eugene Y., and Magnús Einarsson
1976   Whence and When the "Eskimo Fiddle"? *Folk* 18:23-40. Copenhagen.

Armstrong, Sir Alexander
1857   A Personal Narrative of the Discovery of the Northwest Passage; With Numerous Incidents of Travel and Adventure During Nearly Five Years' Continuous Service in the Arctic Regions While in Search of the Expedition Under Sir John Franklin. London: Hurst and Blackett.

Armstrong, Terence
1966   The Administration of Northern Peoples: The USSR. Pp. 57-88 in The Arctic Frontier. Ronald St. J. Macdonald, ed. Toronto: University of Toronto Press.

Arnold, C.D.
1980   A Paleoeskimo Occupation on Southern Banks Island, N.W.T. *Arctic* 33(3):400-426.

Arnold, Robert D.
1968   Alaska Natives Today: An Overview. Pp. 1-36 in Alaska Natives and the Land, by Federal Field Committee for Development Planning in Alaska. Washington: U.S. Government Printing Office.

————   1969   Characteristics of the Economy of Village Alaska and Prospects for Change. (Paper presented at the 20th Alaska Science Conference, University of Alaska, College.)

————   1976   Alaska Native Land Claims. Anchorage: Alaska Native Foundation.

————, et al.
1978   Alaska Native Land Claims. Rev. ed. Anchorage: Alaska Native Foundation.

Arundale, Wendy H.
1976   The Archaeology of the Nanook Site: An Explanatory Approach. (Unpublished Ph.D. Dissertation in Archaeology, Michigan State University, East Lansing.)

1981   Radiocarbon Dating in Eastern Arctic Archaeology: A Flexible Approach. *American Antiquity* 46(2):244-271.

Arutiūnov, S.A.
1979   Problems of Comparative Studies in Arctic Maritime Cultures Based on Archeological Data. *Arctic Anthropology* 16(1):27-31.

Arutiūnov, S.A., and D.A. Sergeev
1962   Drevneéskimosskie mogil´niki na Chukotke [Paleo-Eskimo Cemeteries in Chukotka]. *Anadyr´. Chukotskiĭ Kraevedcheskiĭ Muzeĭ. Zapiski* 3:13-20.

1964   New Finds in the Old Bering Sea Cemetery at Uelen. Pp. 327-332 in The Archaeology and Geomorphology of Northern Asia: Selected Works. (*Anthropology of the North: Translations from Russian Sources* 5). Henry N. Michael, ed. Toronto: Published for the Arctic Institute of North America by University of Toronto Press.

1966   Raskopki drevnikh zakhoroneniĭ i zhilishch na Chukotke v 1965 godu [Excavations of Ancient Burials and Dwellings in Chukotka in 1965]. *Sovetskaiā Étnografiiā* 6:68–78.

1968   Two Millennia of Cultural Evolution of Bering Sea Hunters. *Arctic Anthropology* 5(1):72-75.

1969   Drevnie kul´tury aziatskikh éskimosov (Uélenskiĭ mogil´nik) [Ancient Cultures of the Asiatic Eskimos (Uélen Cemetery)]. Moscow: Akademiiā Nauk SSSR., Institut Étnografii Imeni N.N. Miklukho-Maklaiā.

1972   Ecological Interpretation of Ancient Harpoon Heads. *Inter-Nord* 12:305-311. Paris.

1975   Problemy étnichiskoĭ istorii Beringomoriā: Ékven mogil´nik [Problems in the Ethnic History of the Bering Sea: Ékven Cemetery]. Moscow: Akademiiā Nauk SSSR., Institut Étnografii Imeni N.N. Miklukho-Maklaiā.

Arutiūnov, S.A., I.I. Krupnik, and M.A. Chlenov
1982   Kitovaiā alleiā—drevnosti ostrovov proliva Seniāvina [Whalebone Boulevard—Antiquities of the Seniavin Strait Islands]. Moscow: Izdatel´stvo "Nauka".

Arutiūnov, S.A., M.G. Levin, and D.A. Sergeev
1964   Ancient Cemeteries of the Chukchi Peninsula. *Arctic Anthropology* 2(1):143-154.

Asher, Georg M., ed.
1860   Henry Hudson the Navigator: The Original Documents in Which His Career is Recorded, Collected, Partly Translated, and Annotated with an Introduction by G. Asher. London: The Hakluyt Society.

Astrup, Eivind
1898   With Peary Near the Pole. H.J. Bull, trans. London: C.A. Pearson. (Original: Blandt Nordpolens Naboer, H. Aschehoug, Kristiana, 1895.)

Atamian, Sarkis
1966   The Anaktuvuk Mask and Cultural Innovation. *Science* 151(3716):1337-1345.

Audet, Michel
1974   Le Réseau spatial des Qikirtajuarmiut et l'ouverture d'un nouveau village à Akulivik. (Unpublished M.A. Thesis in Anthropology, Université Laval, Quebec.)

Auger, F.
1974   Poids et plis cutanés chez les Esquimaux de Fort Chimo (Nouveau-Québec). *Anthropologica* n.s. 16(1):137-159.

Auger, F., P.L. Jamison, J. Balslev-Jørgensen, T. Lewin, J.F. De Peña, and J. Skrobak-Kaczynski
1980   Anthropometry of Cirumpolar Populations. Pp. 213-255 in The Human Biology of Circumpolar Populations. F.A. Milan, ed. Cambridge and London: Cambridge University Press.

Baba, Osamu
1943   The Aleuts in the Kuriles. *Japanese Journal of Ethnology* 8:1-22; 9:27-40.

Babb, James D. Jr., comp.
1972   Age and Sex Characteristics of Alaska's Population. *Alaska Review of Business and Economic Conditions* 9(1). College.

Back, Sir George
1836   Narrative of the Arctic Land Expedition to the Mouth of the Great Fish River, and Along the Shores of the Arctic Ocean in the Years 1833, 1834, and 1835. London: J. Murray. (Reprinted: Hurtig Reprint, Edmonton, Alta., 1970.)

Bacon, G.H.
1971   Archeological Survey and Excavation Near Murphy Lake in the Arctic Foothills. Pp. 208-271 in Final Report of the Archeological Survey and Excavation Along the Alyeska Pipeline Service Company Pipeline Route. John P.Cook, ed. (Manuscript in Department of Anthropology, University of Alaska, Fairbanks.)

Bacqueville de la Potherie, Claude C. LeRoy
1722   Histoire de l'Amérique septentrionale. 4 vols. Paris: Nyon.

Baer, John L.
[1855]   Language of the Indian Tribe on the Island of Chak-lock. Pp. 19-26 in [List of Tchuktchi Words Collected in Glasenap Harbor, Straits of Seniavine West Side of Behrings Straits] (Manuscript No. 338-C in National Anthropological Archives, Smithsonian Institution, Washington.)

Bailey, Alfred M.
1971   Field Work of a Museum Naturalist: Alaska—Southeast; Alaska—Far North, 1919-1922. (*Museum Pictorial* 22) Denver: Denver Museum of Natural History.

Bailey, George W.
1880   Report Upon Alaska and Its People: The Cruise of the *Richard Rush* in 1879. Pp. 2-27 in *U.S. Congress. Senate. 46th Cong. 2d sess. Senate Executive Document No.* 132. (Serial No. 1885) Washington.

Balikci, Asen
1959-1960   [Fieldnotes on the Netsilik Eskimo.] (Manuscript in Balikci's possession.)

1960   Suicidal Behavior Among the Netsilik Eskimos. (*NCRC* 60-2) Ottawa: Department of Northern Affairs and National Resources, Northern Coordination and Research Centre.

1960a   Some Acculturative Trends Among the Eastern Canadian Eskimos. *Anthropologica* n.s. 2(2):139-153. Ottawa.

1960b   A Note on the "Poor Kayak" of the Western Labrador Eskimo. *Man* 60 (January):9.

1961   Relations inter-ethniques à la Grande Rivière de la Baleine, baie d'Hudson, 1957. *Anthropological Series* 50, *National Museum of Canada Bulletin* 173. Ottawa.

1963   Le Régime matrimonial des Esquimaux Netsilik. *L'Homme* 3(3):89-101.

1963a   Shamanistic Behavior Among the Netsilik Eskimos. *Southwestern Journal of Anthropology* 19(4):380-396.

1964   Development of Basic Socioeconomic Units in Two Eskimo Communities. *Anthropological Series* 69, *National Museum of Canada Bulletin* 202. Ottawa.

1964a   Les Esquimaux de la péninsule du Labrador: Études ethnographiques. *Anthropological Series* 62, *National Museum of Canada Bulletin* 194:262-280. Ottawa.

1964b   The Eskimos of the Quebec-Labrador Peninsula: Ethnographic Contributions. Pp. 375-394 in Le Nouveau-Québec: Contribution à l'étude de l'occupation humaine. J. Malaurie and J. Rousseau, eds. Paris: Mouton.

734

1966 Ethnographic Filming and the Netsilik Eskimos. *ESI Quarterly Report* (Spring-Summer). (Reprinted: *Polar Record* 15(94):64-69, 1970.)

1967 Female Infanticide on the Arctic Coast. *Man* 2(4):615-625.

1968 The Netsilik Eskimos: Adaptive Processes. Pp. 78-82 in Man the Hunter. Richard B. Lee and Irvin DeVore, eds. Chicago: Aldine.

1970 The Netsilik Eskimo. Garden City, N.Y.: Natural History Press.

1975 Reconstructing Cultures on Film. Pp. 191-200 in Principles of Visual Anthropology. Paul Hockings, ed. The Hague: Mouton.

1978 The Netsilik Inuit Today. *Études/Inuit/Studies* 2(1):111-119.

1980 Charr Fishing Among the Arviligjuarmiut. Pp. 7-11 in Salmonid Fishes of the Genus Salvelinus. E. Balon, ed. The Hague: W. Junk Publishers.

Balikci, Asen, and Quentin Brown
1966 Ethnographic Filming and the Netsilik Eskimos. Newton, Mass.: Educational Services.

Bancroft, Hubert H.
1886 History of Alaska, 1730-1885. (*The Works of Hubert H. Bancroft* 33). San Francisco: The History Book Company. (Reprinted: Antiquarian Press, New York, 1959.)

1868a Native Races of the Pacific States of North America. Vol. 1: Wild Tribes. (*The Works of Hubert H. Bancroft* 1). San Francisco: The History Book Company.

Bandi, Hans-Georg
1958 Einige Gegenstände aus Alaska und British Kolumbien, gesammelt von Johann Wäber (John Weber), Bern/London, während der dritten Forschungsreise von James Cook 1776-1780. Pp. 214-220 in *Proceedings of the 32d International Congress of Americanists*. Copenhagen, 1956.

1968 Rapport préliminaire sur le "Projet de recherches archéologiques de l'Île St.-Laurent 1967" de l'Université de Berne (Suisse) et de l'Université d'Alaska. *Bulletin de la Société Suisse des Américanistes* 32:3-14. Geneva.

1969 Eskimo Prehistory. Ann E. Keep, trans. (*Studies of Northern Peoples* 2) College: University of Alaska Press. (Original: Urgeschichte der Eskimo, Gustav Fischer, Stuttgart, 1965).

1976 Arkheologiia ostrova sviatogo Lavrentiia Aliaska [The Archaeology of St. Lawrence Island, Alaska]. Pp. 485-491 in Beringiia v Kainozoe: Materialy vsesoiuznogo simpoziuma "Beringiiskaia Susha i ee Znachenie dlia razvitiia golarkticheskikh flor i faun v Kainozoe," Khabarovsk, 10-15 Maia 1973 [Beringia in the Cenozoic: Theses of the Reports of the All-Union Symposium "The Bering Land Bridge and Its Significance for the Development of Holarctic Floras and Fauunas in the Late Cenozoic," Khabarovsk, 10-15 May, 1973]. Vladivostok: Academy of Sciences of the USSR, Far Eastern Scientific Center.

Bandi, Hans-Georg, and Jørgen Meldgaard
1952 Archaeological Investigations on Clavering Ø, Northeast Greenland. *Meddelelser om Grønland* 126(4). Copenhagen.

Banfield, Alexander W.F.
1961 A Revision of the Reindeer and Caribou, Genus *Rangifer*. *Biological Series* 66, *National Museum of Canada Bulletin* 177. Ottawa.

1977 The Mammals of Canada. Rev. ed. Toronto: University of Toronto Press.

Bang, H.O., J. Dyerberg, and N. Hjørne
1976 Investigations of Blood Lipids and Food Composition of Greenlandic Eskimos. Pp. 141-145 in Circumpolar Health. R.J. Shephard and S. Itoh, eds. Toronto: University of Toronto Press.

Bank, Theodore P., II
1952 A Preliminary Account of the University of Michigan Aleutian Expeditions, 1950-1951. *The Asa Gray Bulletin* 1(3):211-218. Ann Arbor.

1952a Experiences of Scientific Exploration in the Aleutian Islands. *The Asa Gray Bulletin* 1(1):77-86. Ann Arbor.

1952b Botanical and Ethnobotanical Studies in the Aleutian Islands, I: Aleutian Vegetation and Aleut Culture. *Papers of the Michigan Academy of Science, Arts, and Letters* 37:13-30. Ann Arbor.

1953 Botanical and Ethnobotanical Studies in the Aleutian Islands, II: Health and Medical Lore of the Aleuts. *Papers of the Michigan Academy of Science, Arts, and Letters* 38:415-431. Ann Arbor.

1953a Cultural Succession in the Aleutians. *American Antiquity* 19(1):40-49.

1953b Ecology of Prehistoric Aleutian Village Sites. *Ecology* 34(2):246-264.

1953c Biological Succession in the Aleutians. *Pacific Science* 7(4):493-503.

1962 Ethnobotany of Northern Peoples and the Problem of Cultural Drift. Pp. 279-280 in Vol. 4 of *Proceedings of the Ninth Pacific Science Congress*. Bangkok, Thailand, November 18th-December 19th, 1957.

Baraga, Friedrich
1878-1880 A Dictionary of the Otchipwe Language Explained in English. New ed. 2 vols. Montreal: Beauchemin and Valois. (Reprinted: Ross and Haines, Minneapolis, 1973.)

Bárðarson, Ívarr
1930 Det gamle Grønlands beskrivelse [The Description of Ancient Greenland]. Finnur Jónsson, ed. Copenhagen: Levin and Munksgaard.

Barfod, Pie, et al.
1974 Grønlændere i Danmark, 1971-72 [Greenlanders in Denmark, 1971-1972] *Nyt fra Samfundsvidenskaberne* 34. Copenhagen.

Barkham, Selma de L.
1980 A Note on the Strait of Belle Isle During the Period of Basque Contact with Indians and Inuit. *Études/Inuit/Studies* 4(1-2)51-58.

Barnum, Francis P.
1901 Grammatical Fundamentals of the Innuit Language as Spoken by the Eskimo of the Western Coast of Alaska. Boston: Ginn.

Barrow, Sir John, ed.
1818 A Chronological History of Voyages into the Arctic Regions, Undertaken Chiefly for the Purpose of Discovering a Northeast, North-west, or Polar Passage Between the Atlantic and Pacific. London: J. Murray.

1846 Voyages of Discovery and Research within the Arctic Regions, from the Year 1818 to the Present Time... New York: Harper.

Barsukov, I., ed.
1886-1888 Tvoreniia Innokentiia Mitropolita Moskovskago [The Works of Innocent, Metropolitan of Moscow]. 3 vols. in 2. Moscow: Synodic.

Beaglehole, J.C., ed.
1967   The Voyage of the Resolution and Discovery 1776-1780.
          Cambridge, England: The University Press.

Beals, C.S.
1968   Science, History and Hudson Bay. 2 vols. Ottawa: Depart-
          ment of Energy, Mines and Resources.

Beaudry, Nicole
1978   Le Katajjaq: Un jeu inuit traditionnel. Études/Inuit/Studies
          2(1):35-53.

Beechey, Frederick W.
1831   Narrative of a Voyage to the Pacific and Beering's Strait to
          Co-operate with the Polar Expeditions Performed in His Maj-
          esty's Ship Blossom... in the Years 1825, 26, 27, 28... 2 vols.
          London: Colburn and Bentley.

_____
1832   Narrative of a Voyage to the Pacific and Beering's Strait, to
          Co-operate with the Polar Expeditions; Performed in His
          Majesty's Ship 'Blossom', Under the Command of Captain
          F.W. Beechey, in the Years 1825, 26, 27, 28. 2 vols. London:
          Colburn and Bentley.

Befu, Harumi
1964   Eskimo Systems of Kinship Terms—Their Diversity and Uni-
          formity. Arctic Anthropology 2(1):84-98.

_____
1970   An Ethnographic Sketch of Old Harbor, Kodiak: An Eskimo
          Village. Arctic Anthropology 6(2):29-42.

Befu, Harumi, and Chester S. Chard
1964   A Prehistoric Maritime Culture of the Okhotsk Sea. Amer-
          ican Antiquity 30(1):1-18.

Béland, Jean-Pierre
1978   Atikamekw Morphology and Lexicon. (Unpublished Ph.D.
          Dissertation in Linguistics, University of California, Berke-
          ley.)

Bell, Robert
1885   Observations sur la côte du Labrador le détroit et la baie
          d'Hudson. Rapport des Opérations à 1882-1883-1884. Ot-
          tawa: Ministère de l'Intérieur Commission Géologique et
          d'Histoire Naturelle et du Musée.

Bell, R. Raines, and Christine A. Heller
1978   Nutrition Studies: An Appraisal of the Modern North Alas-
          kan Eskimo Diet. Pp. 145-156 in Eskimos of Northwestern
          Alaska: A Biological Perspective. Paul L. Jamison, Stephen
          L. Zegura, and Frederick A. Milan, eds. Stroudsburg, Pa.:
          Dowden, Hutchinson and Ross.

Belov, Mikhail Ivanovich
1956   Arkticheskoe moreplavanie s drevneĭshikh vremen do sere-
          diny XIX veka [Arctic Voyages from the Earliest Times to
          the Middle of the Nineteenth Century]. Moscow: Moskoĭ
          Transport.

Ben-Dor, Shmuel
1966   Makkovik: Eskimos and Settlers in a Labrador Community:
          A Contrastive Study in Adaptation. (Newfoundland Social
          and Economic Studies 4) St. John's, Newf.: Memorial Uni-
          versity of Newfoundland, Institute of Social and Economic
          Research.

_____
1977   Inuit-Settler Relations in Makkovik, 1962. Pp. 306-325 in The
          White Arctic: Anthropological Essays on Tutelage and Eth-
          nicity. Robert Paine, ed. (Memorial University of Newfound-
          land, Institute of Social and Economic Research, Social and
          Economic Paper 7) Toronto: University of Toronto Press.

Benmouyal, Joseph
1978   Étude archéologique de sites eskimo aux Îles Belcher, T.N.O.
          Canada. National Museum of Man. Mercury Series. Archae-
          ological Survey Paper 76. Ottawa.

Bennett, Marsha E.
1979   Northern Gulf of Alaska: Petroleum Development Scena-
          rios; Sociocultural Impacts. (Alaska Outercontinental Shelf
          Socioeconomic Studies Program, Technical Report 36) An-
          chorage: U.S. Department of the Interior, Bureau of Land
          Management.

Bentham, Robert, and Diamond Jenness
1941   Eskimo Remains in S.E. Ellesmere Island. Proceedings and
          Transactions of the Royal Society of Canada, ser. 3, sect. 2,
          Vol. 35:41-55. Ottawa.

Bentzon, Agnete Weis, and Torben Agersnap
1973   Urbanization, Industrialization and Changes in the Family in
          Greenland During the Reform Period Since 1950. Pp. 21-28
          in Circumpolar Problems: Habitat, Economy, and Social Re-
          lations in the Arctic. Gösta Berg, ed. Oxford, England: Per-
          gamon Press.

Benveniste, E.
1953   The "Eskimo" Name. International Journal of American Lin-
          guistics 19(3):242-245.

Beregovaiā, Nina Aleksandrovna
1954   Arkheologicheskie nakhodki na ostrove Chetyrekhstol-
          bovom (Medvezh'i ostrova k severu ot ust'iā r. Kolymy)
          [Archeological Discoveries on Four Columns Island (The Bear
          Islands North of the Mouth of the Kolyma River)]. Sovetskaiā
          Arkheologiiā 20:288-312.

_____
1960   Arkheologicheskie nakhodki na ostrove Shalaurova [Arche-
          ological Discoveries on Shalaurova Island]. Akademiiā Nauk
          SSSR. Institut Arkheologii. Trudy Dal'nevostochonoĭ Arkhe-
          ologicheskoĭ Ekspediisii 1:183-195.

Beresford, William
1789   A Voyage Round the World: But More Particularly to the
          North-west Coast of America, Performed in 1785, 1786, 1787,
          and 1788, in the King George and Queen Charlotte... G.
          Dixon, ed. London: G. Goulding.

Berg, Hans
1973   Sheep Rearing in South Greenland: An Analysis of the Pres-
          ent-day Problems of Adaptation. Pp. 29-37 in Circumpolar
          Problems: Habitat, Economy, and Social Relations in the
          Arctic. Gösta Berg, ed. Oxford, England: Pergamon Press.

Berg, O., and J. Adler-Nissen
1976   Housing and Sickness in South Greenland: A Sociomedical
          Investigation. Pp. 627-635 in Circumpolar Health. R.J. Shep-
          hard and S. Itoh, eds. Toronto: University of Toronto Press.

Berger, Thomas R.
1977   Northern Frontier, Northern Homeland: The Report of the
          Mackenzie Valley Pipeline Inquiry. 2 vols. Toronto: James
          Lorimer in Association with Publishing Centre, Supply and
          Services, Canada.

Berglund, Jørn, Bjarne Grønnow, and Morten Meldgaard
1983   Aussivigssuit—the Large Summer Camps: Archaeological,
          Ethnographical, and Zooarchaeological Investigations at a
          West Greenland Caribou Hunting Summer Camp Site. Med-
          delelser om Grønland. In press.

Bergmann, C.
1845-1847 Über die Verhältnisse der Wärmeekonomie der Thiere zu
          ihrer Grösse. Goettinger Studien 1-3:595-708. Göttingen.

Bergsland, Knut
1951   Kleinschmidt Centennial IV: Aleut Demonstratives and the
          Aleut-Eskimo Relationship. International Journal of Amer-
          ican Linguistics 17(3):167-179.

_____
1955   A Grammatical Outline of the Eskimo Language of West
          Greenland. Oslo: University of Oslo. Mimeo. (Microfiche,
          from: Inter-Dokumentation, Zug, Switzerland).

_____
1956   Some Problems of Aleut Phonology. Pp. 38-53 in For Roman
          Jakobson: Essays on the Occasion of His Sixtieth Birthday,
          11 October 1956. Morris Halle, Horace G. Lunt, Hugh
          McLean, and Cornelius H. van Schooneveld, eds. The Hague:
          Mouton.

736

1958   Aleut and Proto-Eskimo. Pp. 624-631 in *Proceedings of the 32d International Congress of Americanists.* Copenhagen, 1956.

1959   Aleut Dialects of Atka and Attu. *Transactions of the American Philosophical Society* n.s. 49(3). Philadelphia.

1959a   The Eskimo-Uralic Hypothesis. *Journal de la Société Finno-Ougrienne* 61(2):1-29. Helsinki.

1964   Morphological Analysis and Syntactical Reconstruction in Eskimo-Aleut. Pp. 1009-1015 in *Proceedings of the 9th International Congress of Linguists.* The Hague: Mouton.

1966   [Review of] Ĭazyk sirenikskikh ėskimosov [The Language of the Sireniki Eskimos], by G.A. Menovshchikov. *Voprosy Ĭazykoznaniĭa* 4:140-148. Moscow.

1967.   The Eskimo Shibboleth *INUK/YUK*. Pp. 203-221 in Vol. 1 of To Honor Roman Jakobson: Essays on the Occasion of His Seventieth Birthday, 11 October 1966. The Hague: Mouton.

1968   Eskimo-Aleut Languages. Pp. 706-707 in Vol. 8 of Encyclopedia Britannica. 24 vols. Chicago: Encyclopedia Britannica Incorporated.

Bergsland, Knut, and Moses Dirks, comps.
1978   Introduction to Atkan Aleut Grammar and Lexicon. Anchorage: University of Alaska, National Bilingual Materials Development Center.

———, comps.
1978a   Eastern Aleut Grammar and Lexicon. Anchorage: University of Alaska, National Bilingual Materials Development Center.

Bergsland, Knut, and Hans Vogt
1962   On the Validity of Glottochronology. *Current Anthropology* 3(2):115-153.

Berkh, Vasiliĭ Nikolaevich
1823   Puteshestvīe uchenika morekhodstva Andreĭa Ustĭugova, i sluzhiteleĭ Rossīĭskoĭ Amerikanskoĭ kompanīi Fedora Kolmakova i Petra Korsanovskago v 1819 godu [Journey of the Apprentice Seaman Andreĭ Ustĭugov and of the Russian-American Company Employees Fĕdor Kolmakov and Pĕtr Korsanovskiĭ, in 1819]. *Sĕvernyĭ Arkhiv* Pt. 8(4):46-51. St. Petersburg.

1823a   Khronologicheskaĭa istorīĭa otkrytīĭa Aleutskikh ostrovov [The Chronological History of the Discovery of the Aleutian Islands]. St. Petersburg: N. Grecha. (Translation: U.S. Works Progress Administration, Seattle, 1938.)

1974   A Chronological History of the Discovery of the Aleutian Islands or the Exploits of Russian Merchants [1823]. Richard A. Pierce, ed; Dmitri Vrenov, trans. Kingston, Ont.: Limestone Press.

Bernard, Alain
1977   Dépendance et capitalisme marchand: Le cas des Inuit de la rive sud du détroit d'Hudson, 1930-1956. *Études/Inuit/Studies* 1(2):1-29.

Bernardi, Suzanne R.
1912   Whaling with Eskimos of Cape Prince of Wales. *The Courier Journal,* October 20:1-2. Louisville, Ky.

Bernier, Joseph E.
1909   Report on the Dominion Government Expedition to Arctic Islands and the Hudson Strait on Board the D.G.S. "Arctic", 1906-1907. Ottawa: Department of Marine and Fisheries.

1910   Report on the Dominion of Canada Government Expedition to the Arctic Islands and Hudson Strait on Board the D.G.S. "Arctic" [1908-1909]. Ottawa: Department of Marine and Fisheries.

1911   Report on the Dominion Government Expedition to the Northern Waters and Arctic Archipelago of the D.G.S. "Arctic" in 1910. Ottawa: Department of Marine and Fisheries.

Berreman, Gerald D.
1954   Effects of a Technological Change in an Aleutian Village. *Arctic* 7(2):102-107.

1955   Inquiry into Community Integration in an Aleutian Village. *American Anthropologist* 57(1):49-59.

1956   Drinking Patterns of the Aleuts. *Quarterly Journal of Studies on Alcohol* 17:503-514.

1964   Aleut Reference Group Alienation, Mobility and Acculturation. *American Anthropologist* 66(2):231-250.

1981   The Politics of Truth: Essays in Critical Anthropology. (*Sunderial Series in Humanistic Social Sciences 1*) New Delhi: South Asian Publishers.

Berry, J.W.
1972   Psychological Research in the North. Pp. 230-250 in Social Psychology: The Canadian Context. J.W. Berry and G.T.S. Wilde, eds. Toronto: McClelland and Stewart.

1976   Acculturative Stress in Northern Canada: Ecological, Cultural, and Psychological Factors. Pp. 490-497 in Circumpolar Health. R.J. Shephard and S. Itoh, eds. Toronto: University of Toronto Press.

Berry, Mary Clay
1975   The Alaska Pipeline: The Politics of Oil and Native Land Claims. Bloomington: Indiana University Press.

Bertelsen, Alfred
1918   Navnegivning i Grønland [Personal Names in Greenland]. *Meddelelser om Grønland* 56:221-287. Copenhagen.

1929   Sanitation and Health Conditions in Greenland. Pp. 363-386 in Vol. 3 of Greenland. M. Vahl et al., eds. Copenhagen: C.A. Reitzel, London: Humphrey Milford.

1935-1943   Grønlandsk medicinsk statistik og nosografi: Undersøgelser og erfaringer fra 30 aars grønlandsk lægevirksomhed, I-IV. [Medical Statistics and Nosography of Greenland: Investigations and Experiences Resulting from 30 Years of Medical Practice in Greenland]. *Meddelelser om Grønland* 117(1-4). Copenhagen.

Berthelsen, Christian
1957   Oqalugtualiautivut taigdliautivutdlo [Our Novels and Poems]. Godthåb: no publisher.

1960   De grønlandske kulturtraditioner i relation til nutidens oplysnings-arbeyde [Greenland Cultural Traditions in the Context of Modern Educational Practice]. Pp. 217-223 in *Grønland 1960.* Copenhagen.

1973   Development of the Educational System in Greenland 1950-1970. Copenhagen: Ministry of Education in Greenland.

Bertholf, E.P.
1899   Report of Lieutenant Bertholf, September 1, 1898. Pp. 103-114 in Report of the Cruise of the U.S. Revenue Cutter 'Bear' and the Overland Expedition for the Relief of the Whalers in the Arctic Ocean from November 27, 1897 to September 13, 1898. Washington: U.S. Government Printing Office.

1899a   Report of Second Lieut. E.P. Bertholf, R.C.S., Point Hope, Alaska, July 15, 1898. Pp. 18-27 in Report of the Cruise of the U.S. Revenue Cutter 'Bear' and the Overland Expedition for the Relief of the Whalers in the Arctic Ocean from Nov. 27, 1897, to Sept. 13, 1898. Washington: U.S. Government Printing Office.

Beschel, Roland E.

1961   Dating Rock Surfaces by Lichen Growth and Its Application to Glaciology and Physiography (Lichenometry). Pp. 1044-1062 in Vol. 2 of Geology of the Arctic, Proceedings. Gilbert O. Raasch, ed. 2 vols. Toronto: Toronto University Press.

1970   The Diversity of Tundra Vegetation. Pp. 85-92 in Productivity and Conservation in Northern Circumpolar Lands. W.A. Fuller and P.G. Kevan, eds. (*IUCN Publication n.s. 16[8]*) Morges, Switzerland: International Union for Conservation of Nature and Natural Resources.

Bessels, Emil

1875   Einige Worte über die Inuit (Eskimo) des Smith-Sundes, nebst Bemerkungen über Inuit Schädel. *Archiv für Anthropologie* 8:107-122.

1879   Die amerikanische Nordpol-Expedition. Leipzig, Germany: Engelmann.

1884   The Northernmost Inhabitants of the Earth: An Ethnographic Sketch. *American Naturalist* 18(9):861-882.

Bilby, Julian W.

1923   Among Unknown Eskimo: An Account of Twelve Years Intimate Relations with the Primitive Eskimo of Ice-bound Baffin Land, with a Description of Their Ways of Living, Hunting Customs and Beliefs. London: Seeley Service.

Binford, Lewis R.

1972   Demography; Nunamiut Hunters and the Malthusian Argument. (Unpublished manuscript in Binford's possession).

1978   Nunamiut Ethnoarchaeology. New York: Academic Press.

Binford, Lewis R., and W.J. Chasko, Jr.

1976   Nunamiut Demographic History: A Provocative Case. Pp. 63-143 in Demographic Anthropology: Quantitative Approaches. Ezra B.W. Zubrow, ed. Albuquerque: University of New Mexico Press.

Bird, Junius B.

1945   Archaeology of the Hopedale Area, Labrador. *Anthropological Papers of the American Museum of Natural History* 39(2):117-188. New York.

1972   The Physical Characteristics in Northern Canada. Pp. 1-24 in The North. William C. Wonders, ed. (*Studies in Canadian Geography*) Toronto: University of Toronto Press.

Birket-Smith, Kaj

1924   Ethnography of the Egedesminde District, with Aspects of the General Culture of West Greenland. *Meddelelser om Grønland* 66. Copenhagen.

1927   Det eskimoiske slægtskabssystem: En analysisk undersøgelse [The Eskimo Kinship System: An Analytical Investigation]. *Geografisk Tidsskrift* 30:96–111. Copenhagen.

1928   Five Hundred Eskimo Words: A Comparative Vocabulary from Greenland and Central Eskimo Dialects. *Report of the Fifth Thule Expedition 1921–24*. Vol. 3(3). Copenhagen.

1928a   The Greenlanders of the Present Day. Pp. 1–207 in Vol. 2 of Greenland. M. Vahl et al., eds. Copenhagen: Reitzel; London: Oxford University Press.

1929   The Caribou Eskimos; Material and Social Life and Their Cultural Position. *Report of the Fifth Thule Expedition 1921–24*. Vol. 5(1-2). Copenhagen.

1930   The Question of the Origin of Eskimo Culture: A Rejoinder. *American Anthropologist* 32(4):608-624.

738   1936   The Eskimos. W.E. Calvert, trans. London: Methuen.

1940   Anthropological Observations on the Central Eskimos. *Report of the Fifth Thule Expedition, 1921–24*. Vol. 3(2). Copenhagen.

1941   Early Collections from the Pacific Eskimo; Ethnographical Studies. *Nationalmuseets Skrifter Etnografisk Række* 1:121-163. Copenhagen.

1945   Ethnographical Collections from the Northwest Passage. *Report of the Fifth Thule Expedition, 1921–24*. Vol. 6(2). Copenhagen.

1951   Recent Achievements in Eskimo Research. *Journal of the Royal Anthropological Institute of Great Britain and Ireland* 77(2):145–157. London.

1952   Present Status of the Eskimo Problem. Pp. 8-18 in Vol. 3 of *Selected Papers of the 29th International Congress of Americanists*, Sol Tax, ed. Chicago: University of Chicago Press.

1953   The Chugach Eskimo. *Nationalmuseets Skrifter, Etnografisk Række* 6. Copenhagen.

1959   The Eskimos. W.E. Calvert, trans. Rev. ed. London: Methuen.

1959a   The Earliest Eskimo Portraits. *Folk* 1:5-14. Copenhagen.

Bissett, Don

1967   Northern Baffin Island: An Area Economic Survey. 2 vols. Ottawa: Department of Indian Affairs and Northern Development.

1968   Resolute: An Area Economic Survey. Ottawa: Department of Indian Affairs and Northern Development, Industrial Division.

Bjerregaard, Peter

1982   Samfundsmedicin i Grønland. [Public Health in Greenland]. Copenhagen. Mimeo.

Black, Lydia, ed. and trans.

1977   The Konyag (the Inhabitants of the Island of Kodiak) by Iosaf [Bolotov] (1794-1799) and by Gideon (1804-1807). *Arctic Anthropology* 14(2):79-108.

1979   Volcanism as a Factor in Human Ecology: The Aleutian Case. (Unpublished manuscript in Black's possession.)

1980   Early History. Pp. 82-105 in The Aleutians. L. Morgan, ed. *Alaska Geographic* 7(3).

1981   The Nature of Evil: Of Whales and Sea Otters. Pp. 109-153 in Indians, Animals, and the Fur Trade. Shephard Krech, III, ed. Athens: University of Georgia Press.

1982   [Review of] Kitovaîa alleîa—drevnosti ostrovov proliva Senîavina [Whalebone Boulevard—Antiquities of the Seniavin Strait Islands, by S.A. Arutîunov, I.I. Krupnik, and M.A. Chlenov, Moscow, 1982.] *Arctic* 35(4):563-565.

1982a   Aleut Art; Unangam Aguqaadangin: Unangan of the Aleutian Archipelago. Anchorage: Pribilof Islands Association.

1983   Some Problems in the Interpretation of Aleut Prehistory. *Arctic Anthropology* 20(1):49-78.

Black, Robert F.

1966   Late Pleistocene to Recent History of Bering Sea-Alaska Coast and Man. *Arctic Anthropology* 3(2):7-21.

1974   Late-Quaternary Sea Level Changes, Umnak Island, Aleutians: Their Effects on Ancient Aleuts and Their Causes. *Quaternary Research* 4(3):264-281.

1974a   Geology and Ancient Aleuts, Amchitka and Umnak Islands, Aleutians. *Arctic Anthropology* 11(2):126-140.

1975   Late-Quaternary Geomorphic Processes: Effects on the Ancient Aleuts of Umnak Island in the Aleutians. *Arctic* 28(3):159-169.

1976   Geology of Umnak Island, Eastern Aleutian Islands as Related to the Aleuts. *Arctic and Alpine Research* 8(1):7-35.

Black, Robert F., and William S. Laughlin
1964   Anangula: A Geologic Interpretation of the Oldest Archeologic Site in the Aleutians. *Science* 143(3612):1321-1322.

Blake, Weston, Jr.
1966   End Moraines and Deglaciation Chronology in Northern Canada with Special Reference to Southern Baffin Island. *Geological Survey of Canada, Department of Mines and Technical Surveys Paper* 66-26. Ottawa.

Bliss, K.J.
1979   International Whaling Commission Regulations and the Alaskan Eskimo. *Natural Resources Journal* 4:943-956.

Bliss, L.C.
1970   Primary Production Within Arctic Tundra Ecosystems. Pp. 77-85 in Productivity and Conservation in Northern Circumpolar Lands. W.A. Fuller and P.G. Kevan, eds. (*IUCN Publications n.s. 16(7)*) Morges, Switzerland: International Union for Conservation of Nature and Natural Resources.

Bliss, L.C., and Joan Kerik
1973   Primary Production of Plant Communities of the Truelove Lowland, Devon Island, Canada—Rock Outcrops. Pp. 27-36 in Primary Production and Production Processes, Tundra Biome. L.C. Bliss and F.E. Wielgolaski, eds. Edmonton: University of Alberta, Department of Botany.

Bliss, L.C., G.M. Courtin, D.L. Pattie, R.R. Riewe, D.W.A. Whitfield, and P. Widden
1973   Arctic Tundra Ecosystems. *Annual Review of Ecology and Systematics* 4:359-399.

Blodgett, Jean
1979   The Coming and Going of the Shaman, Eskimo Shamanism and Art. Winnipeg: The Winnipeg Art Gallery.

1979a   The Historic Period in Canadian Eskimo Art. *The Beaver* (Summer):17-27.

Bloom, Joseph D.
1972   Population Trends of Alaska Natives and the Need for Planning. *American Journal of Psychiatry* 128(8):998-1002.

1972a   Psychiatric Problems and Cultural Transitions in Alaska. *Arctic* 25(3):203-215.

1973   Migration and Psychopathology of Eskimo Women. *American Journal of Psychiatry* 130(4):446-449.

Bloom, Joseph D., and W.W. Richards
1976   Alaska Native Regional Corporations and Community Mental Health. Pp. 567-571 in Circumpolar Health. R.J. Shephard and S. Itoh, eds. Toronto: University of Toronto Press.

Bluhme, Hans E.
1865   Fra et ophold i Grønland 1863-64 [From a Sojourn in Greenland 1863-64]. Copenhagen: F. Wøldikes Forlagsexpedition.

Boag, Thomas J.
1966   Mental Health in the Arctic. *Proceedings of the Fourth World Congress of Psychiatry, Excerpta Medica International Congress Series* 150. Madrid.

1967   Psychological Problems in the North. (Paper read at the Annual Meeting of the Canadian Psychiatric Asociation, Quebec City.)

1972   Mental Health of Native Peoples of the Artic. Pp. 250-258 in Social Psychology: The Canadian Context. J.W. Berry and G.T.S. Wilde, eds. Toronto: McClelland and Stewart.

Boas, Franz
1885   The Eskimo of Baffin Land. *Transactions of the Anthropological Society of Washington* 3:95-102. Washington.

1888   The Central Eskimo. Pp. 399-669 in *6th Annual Report of the Bureau of American Ethnology for the Years 1884-1885*. Washington.

1888a   The Eskimo. *Proceedings and Transaction of the Royal Society of Canada for the Year 1887*. Vol. 5, sect. 2:35-39. Montreal.

1901   A.J. Stone's Measurements of Natives of the Northwest Territories. *Bulletin of the American Museum of Natural History* 14(6):53-68. New York.

1901-1907   The Eskimo of Baffin Land and Hudson Bay. *Bulletin of the American Museum of Natural History* 15. New York.

1902   Some Problems in North American Archaeology. *American Journal of Archaeology* 2d ser. Vol. 6:1-6. (Reprinted: Pp. 525-529 in Race, Language and Culture, by Franz Boas, Macmillan, New York, 1940.)

1964   The Central Eskimo [1888]. Lincoln: University of Nebraska Press.

Boassen, Egede
1939   Scoresbysundime umingmaqarpoq [Musk-ox Live About Scoresbysund]. *Avangnâmioq*: 4. Qeqertarsuaq.

Bobé, Louis
1928-1929   [A Short Survey of Greenland History.] *Greenland* 3. Copenhagen.

1936   Diplomatarium groenlandicum 1492-1818: Akstykker og breve til oplysning om Grønlands besejling, kolonisation, og missionering. [Diplomatarium groenlandicum 1492-1814: Acts and Letters Concerning the Sea Voyages, Colonization, and Missions of Greenland]. *Meddelelser om Grønland* 55(3). Copenhagen.

1944   Hans Egede, Grønlands Missionær og Kolonisator. *Meddelelser om Grønland* 129(1). Copenhagen.

1952   Hans Egede: Colonizer and Missionary of Greenland. Copenhagen: Rosenkilde and Bagger.

Bockstoce, John R.
1972   The Archeology of Cape Nome. (Manuscript at University Museum, University of Pennsylvania, Philadelphia.)

1977   Eskimos of Northwest Alaska in the Early Nineteenth Century: Based on the Beechey and Belcher Collections and Records Compiled During the Voyage of H.M.S. Blossom to Northwest Alaska in 1826 and 1827. *University of Oxford, Pitt Rivers Museum Monograph Series 1*.

1977a   Eskimo Whaling in Alaska. *Alaska Magazine* 43(9):4-6.

1977b   Steam Whaling in the Western Arctic. New Bedford, Mass.: Old Dartmouth Whaling Society.

1979   The Archaeology of Cape Nome, Alaska. *University of Pennsylvania, University Museum Monograph* 38. Philadelphia.

1980   Battle of the Bowheads. *Natural History* 89(5):52-61.

Bodley, John H.
1982   Victims of Progress. 2d ed. Menlo Park, Calif.: The Benjamin Cummings Publishing Company.

Bodmer, Walter F., and Luigi L. Cavalli-Sforza
1976 Genetics, Evolution, and Man. San Francisco: W.H. Freeman.

Bøcher, Tyge W.
1970 Plante- og dyreliv: Plantevækst [Plant and Animal Life: Vegetation]. Pp. 83-93 in J.P. Trap's Grønland (Danmark 14). Niels Nielsen, Peter Skautrup and Christian Vibe, eds. Copenhagen: G.E.C. Gads Forlag.

Bøcher, Tyge W., Kjeld Hulmen, and Knud Jakobsen
1968 The Flora of Greenland. T.T. Ellington and M.C. Lewis, trans. Copenhagen: P. Haase and Son.

Boessen, E.M.
1976 Involvement of Natives in Health Care. Pp. 584-588 in Circumpolar Health. R.J. Shephard and S. Itoh, eds. Toronto: University of Toronto Press.

Bogojavlensky, Sergei
1969 Imaangmiut Eskimo Careers: Skinboats in Bering Strait. (Unpublished Ph.D. Dissertation in Social Relations, Harvard University, Cambridge, Mass.)

Bogoras, Waldemar
1904-1909 The Chukchee. *Memoirs of the American Museum of Natural History* 11. New York. (Reprinted: AMS Press, New York, 1975.)

———
1913 The Eskimo of Siberia. (The Jesup North Pacific Expedition 8(3), Franz Boas, ed.) *Memoirs of the American Museum of Natural History* 12. New York. (Reprinted AMS Press, New York, 1975.)

———
1922 Chukchee. Pp. 631-903 in Pt. 2 of Handbook of American Indian Languages. Franz Boas, ed. *Bureau of American Ethnology Bulletin* 40. Washington.

———
1925 Early Migrations of the Eskimo Between Asia and America. Pp. 216-235 in Vol. 1 of *Proceedings of the 21st International Congress of Americanists*. Göteborg, 1924.

———
1929 Elements of the Culture of the Circumpolar Zone. *American Anthropologist* 31(4):579-601.

———
1975 The Eskimo of Siberia [1913]. New York: AMS Press.

Bogoraz, Vladimir Germanovich see Bogoras, Waldemar

Bonnichsen, Robson
1979 Pleistocene Bone Technology in the Beringian Refugium. *Canada. National Museum of Man. Mercury Series. Archaeological Survey Paper* 89. Ottawa.

Borbridge, John, Jr.
1970 Native Organization and Land Rights as Vehicles for Change. Pp. 195-206 in Change in Alaska: People, Petroleum, and Politics. G.W. Rogers, ed. College: University of Alaska Press.

Borchersen, J.
1963 Østergrønland efter krigen. [East Greenland After the War.] *Grønland* 6:201-214.

Borden, Charles E.
1975 Origins and Development of Early Northwest Coast Culture to About 3000 B.C. *Canada. National Museum of Man. Mercury Series. Archaeological Survey Paper* 45. Ottawa.

———
1979 Peopling and Early Cultures of the Pacific Northwest. *Science* 203(4384):963-971.

Bornemann, Claus
1956 Spiritus i Grønland [Alcohol in Greenland]. *Grønland* 3:99-12.

———
1973 Economic Development and the Specific Aspects of the Society in Greenland. Pp. 391-429 in Le Peuple esquimau aujourd'hui et demain/The Eskimo People To-Day and To-Morrow. Jean Malaurie, ed. (Fourth International Congress

of the Fondation Française d'Études Nordiques) Paris, The Hague: Mouton.

Boserup, Mogens
1963 Økonomisk politik i Grønland. [Economic Policy in Greenland]. Copenhagen: Grønlandsudvalget af 1960.

———
1973 The Economic Future of the Greenland Society as a Problem of Regional Policy. Pp. 461-476 in Le Peuple esquimau aujourd'hui et demain/The Eskimo People To-Day and To-Morrow. Jean Malaurie, ed. (Fourth International Congress of the Fondation Française d'Études Nordiques) Paris, The Hague: Mouton.

Bourquin, Theodor
1891 Grammatik der Eskimo-Sprache, wie sie an der Labradorküste gesprochen wird. London: Moravian Mission Agency.

Bowers, Peter M.
1982 The Lisburne Site: Analysis and Cultural History of a Multicomponent Lithic Workshop in the Iteriak Valley, Arctic Foothills, Northern Alaska. *Anthropological Papers of the University of Alaska* 20(1-2):79-112. Fairbanks.

Boye, Ellen
1974 Samarbeyde rundt om Nordpolen [Cooperation around the North Pole]. *Grønland* 3:65-70. Copenhagen.

Brack, D.M.
1962 Southampton Island Area Economic Survey; with Notes on Repulse Bay and Wager Bay. Ottawa: Department of Northern Affairs and National Resources, Industrial Division, Area and Community Planning Section.

Brantenberg, Anne
1977 The Marginal School and the Children of Nain. Pp. 344-358 in The White Arctic: Anthropological Essays on Tutelage and Ethnicity. Robert Paine, ed. (*Memorial University of Newfoundland, Institute of Social and Economic Research. Social and Economic Paper* 7) Toronto: University of Toronto Press.

Braund, S.R., and S.R. Behnke
1979 Lower Cook Inlet Sociocultural Systems Analysis. (*Alaska Outercontinental Shelf Socioeconomic Studies Program, Technical Report* 47) Anchorage: U.S. Department of the Interior, Bureau of Land Management.

Brevig, Tollef Larson
1944 Apaurak in Alaska: Social Pioneering Among the Eskimos. Joseph Walter Johnshoy, ed. and trans. Philadelphia: Dorrance.

Brewer, Max C.
1975 Land Commitments in Alaska. *Arctic* 28(4):263-274.

Brice-Bennett, Carol, ed.
1977 Our Footprints are Everywhere: Inuit Land Use and Occupancy in Labrador. Nain: Labrador Inuit Association.

Briggs, Jean L.
1970 Never in Anger: Portrait of an Eskimo Family. Cambridge, Mass.: Harvard University Press.

———
1972 Eskimo Women. (Unpublished manuscripts in Department of Sociology and Anthropology, Memorial University of Newfoundland, St. John's.)

———
1975 The Origins of Non-Violence: Aggression in Two Canadian Eskimo Groups. Pp.134-203 in Vol. 6 of The Psychoanalytic Study of Society. Warner Muensterberger and Aaron H. Esman, eds. New York: International Universities Press.

———
1978 The Origins of Non-violence: Inuit Management of Aggression. Pp. 54-93 in Learning Non-aggression, Ashley Montagu, ed. New York: Oxford University Press.

Brink, N.W. Ten
1975 Holocene History of the Greenland Ice Sheet Based on Radio-carbon-dated Moraines in West Greenland. *Meddelelser om Grønland* 201(4). Copenhagen.

740

Brochu, Michel
1970   Les Grandes phases de l'histoire économique du Nouveau-Québec indien et esquimau. *L'Action Nationale* 60(1):27-41.

Brody, Hugh
1975   The People's Land: Eskimos and Whites in the Eastern Arctic. New York: Penguin Books.

_____
1976   Inuit Land Use in North Baffin Island and Northern Foxe Basin. Pp. 153-171 in Vol. 1 of Report: Inuit Land Use and Occupancy Project. Milton M.R. Freeman, ed. 3 vols. Ottawa: Department of Indian and Northern Affairs.

_____
1978   Ecology, Politics and Change: The Case of the Eskimo. *Development and Change* 9:21-40.

Broensted, Henning
1973   Ruling in Greenland and Forms of Integration into Denmark: The Established Legal Components. Pp. 553-570 in Le Peuple esquimau aujourd'hui et demain/The Eskimo People To-Day and To-Morrow. Jean Malaurie, ed. (Fourth International Congress of the Fondation Française d'Études Nordiques) Paris, The Hague: Mouton.

Brøsted, Jens
1979   Beskåret hjemmestyre—et kritisk essay om den grønlandske hjemmestyreordning. [Reduced Home Rule—A Critical Essay on the Greenland Home Rule System.] Copenhagen: Rhodos radius.

Brooke, John M.
[1855] Vocabularies of Tchucktches on Tchuklook. P. 1 in [Vocabularies of Central Siberian Yupik and Chukchi, from Arakamchechen and Yttygran Islands, Strait of Seniavin.] (Copy by George Gibbs; manuscript No. 341 in National Anthropological Archives, Smithsonian Institution, Washington.)

Brooke, Lorraine F.
1974   Band Composition and Ethnography for the Markham Bay Region of Southern Baffin Island, 1930's. (Unpublished manuscript in Department of Anthropology, Sir George Williams University, Montreal.)

Brooks, Alfred H.
1953   Blazing Alaska's Trails. Burton L. Fryxell, ed. College: University of Alaska and Arctic Institute of North America. (Reprinted in 1973.)

Brouague, François Martel de
1717   Relation des Esquimaux de l'année 1717 à Labrador: Joint à la lettre de M. de Brouague de 1717. (Manuscript in Bibliothèque Nationale, Mss. Françaises, Nouvelles Acquisitions 9284:163-167, Paris.)

_____
1719   [Letter to the Conseil de Marine, France, Dated Labrador, Sept. 6, 1719] (Manuscript, C 11A-109, in Archives des Colonies, Archives Nationales, Paris.)

Brower, Charles D.
[1945] The Northernmost American: An Autobiography. (Unedited manuscript in the Stefánsson Collection, Dartmouth College Library, Hanover, N.H.)

_____
1950   Fifty Years Below Zero: A Lifetime of Adventure in the Far North. London: The Travel Book Club.

Brown, Archie, John Fennel, Michael Kaser, and W.T. Willetts, eds.
1982   The Cambridge Encyclopedia of Russia and the Soviet Union. Cambridge, England: Unversity Press.

Bruce, Miner W.
1894   Report of Miner W. Bruce, Teller Reindeer Station, Port Clarence, Alaska, June 30, 1893. Pp. 25-121 in *3d Report on Introduction of Domesticated Reindeer into Alaska.* Sheldon Jackson, comp. Washington: U.S. Government Printing Office.

Bruemmer, Fred
1968   Eskimos of Grise Fiord. *Canadian Geographical Journal* 77(2):64-71.

_____
1969   The Long Hunt. Toronto: Ryerson Press.

Bryan, Alan L.
1969   Early Man in America and the Late Pleistocene Chronology of Western Canada and Alaska. *Current Anthropology* 10(4):339-365.

Buckley, James D., and Eric H. Willis
1969   Isotopes' Radiocarbon Measurements VII. *Radiocarbon* 11(1):53-105.

_____
1970   Isotopes' Radiocarbon Measurements VIII. *Radiocarbon* 12(1):87-129.

Burch, Ernest S., Jr.
[1960-1961] [Fieldnotes from Kivalina, Alaska.] (Manuscript in Burch's possession.)

_____
1970   Marriage and Divorce Among the North Alaskan Eskimos. Pp. 152-181 in Divorce and After. Paul Bohannan, ed. Garden City, N.Y.: Doubleday.

_____
1970a   The Eskimo Trading Partnership in North Alaska: A Study in "Balanced Reciprocity." *Anthropological Papers of the University of Alaska* 15(1):49-80. College.

_____
1971   The Nonempirical Environment of the Arctic Alaskan Eskimos. *Southwestern Journal of Anthropology* 27(2):148-165.

_____
1972   The Caribou/Wild Reindeer as a Human Resource. *American Antiquity* 37(3):339-368.

_____
1974   Eskimo Warfare in Northwest Alaska. *Anthropological Papers of the University of Alaska* 16(2):1-14. Fairbanks.

_____
1975   Inter-regional Transportation in Traditional Northwest Alaska. *Anthropological Papers of the University of Alaska* 17(2):1-11. Fairbanks.

_____
1975a   Eskimo Kinsmen: Changing Family Relationships in Northwest Alaska. (*Monographs of the American Ethnological Society* 59) St. Paul, Minn.: West Publishing Company.

_____
1976   Overland Travel Routes in Northwest Alaska. *Anthropological Papers of the University of Alaska* 18(1):1-10. Fairbanks.

_____
1976a   The "Nunamiut" Concept and the Standardization of Error. Pp. 52-97 in Contributions to Anthropology: The Interior Peoples of Northern Alaska. Edwin S. Hall, Jr., ed. *Canada. National Museum of Man. Mercury Series. Archaeological Survey Paper* 49. Ottawa.

_____
1977   Muskox and Man in the Central Canadian Subarctic, 1689-1974. *Arctic* 30(3):135-154.

_____
1978   Traditional Eskimo Societies in Northwest Alaska. Pp. 253-304 in Alaska Native Culture and History. Y. Kotani and W. B. Workman, eds. *National Museum of Ethnology, Senri Ethnological Studies* 4. Osaka, Japan.

_____
1978a   Caribou Eskimo Origins: An Old Problem Reconsidered. *Arctic Anthropology* 15(1):1-35.

_____
1979   The Thule-Historic Eskimo Transition on the West Coast of Hudson Bay. Pp. 189-211 in Thule Eskimo Culture: An Anthropological Retrospective. Allen P. McCartney, ed. *Canada. National Museum of Man. Mercury Series. Archaeological Survey Paper* 88. Ottawa.

_____
1979a   Indians and Eskimos in North Alaska, 1816-1977: A Study in Changing Ethnic Relations. *Arctic Anthropology* 16(2):123-151.

_____
1979b   Ethnography of Northern North America: A Guide to Recent Research. *Arctic Anthropology* 16(1):62-146.

1979c   Native Claims in Alaska: An Overview. *Études/Inuit/Studies* 3(1):7-30.

1980   Traditional Eskimo Societies in Northwest Alaska. Pp. 253-304 in Alaska Native Culture and History. Y. Kotani and W. B. Workman, eds. *National Museum of Ethnology, Senri Ethnological Studies* 4. Osaka, Japan.

1981   The Traditional Eskimo Hunters of Point Hope, Alaska: 1800-1875. [Barrow]: North Slope Borough.

1981a   Studies of Native History as a Contribution to Alaska's Future. (Special lecture presented to the 32d Alaska Science Conference; manuscript in Burch's possession.)

Burch, Ernest S., Jr., and Thomas C. Correll
1972   Alliance and Conflict: Inter-regional Relations in North Alaska. Pp. 17-39 in Alliance in Eskimo Society. Lee Guemple, ed. *(Proceedings of the American Ethnological Society, 1971.* Suppl.) Seattle: University of Washington Press.

Burgess, Stephen M.
1974   The St. Lawrence Islanders of Northwest Cape: Patterns of Resource Utilization. (Unpublished Ph.D. Dissertation in Anthropology, University of Alaska, Fairbanks.)

Burgesse, J. Allan
1949   Esquimaux in the Saguenay. *Primitive Man* 22(1-2):23-32.

Burland, Cottie A.
1973   Eskimo Art. London: Hamlyn.

Burpee, Lawrence J., ed.
1927   An Historical Atlas of Canada. Toronto: Thomas Nelson and Sons.

Burwash, Lachlan T.
1927   The Eskimo, Their Country and Its Resources: Economic Survey of the East Coast of Hudson Bay and James Bay from Richmond Gulf to Rupert House, Including the Belcher and Other Adjacent Islands. Ottawa: Department of the Interior, North West Territories and Yukon Branch.

Bushnell, David I., Jr.
1928   Drawings by John Webber of Natives of the Northwest Coast of America, 1778. *Smithsonian Miscellaneous Collections* 80(10). Washington.

Butler, Kenneth C.
1963   Igloo Killinek. William Wheeler, illus. Toronto: Longmans.

Byard, Pamela J.
1980   Population, History, Demography, and Genetics of the St. Lawrence Island Eskimos. (Unpublished Ph.D. Dissertation, in Anthropology, University of Kansas, Lawrence.)

Campbell, John M.
1959   The Kayuk Complex of Arctic Alaska. *American Antiquity* 25(1):94-105.

1961   The Tuktu Complex of Anaktuvuk Pass. *Anthropological Papers of the Univesity of Alaska* 9(2):61-80. College.

1962   Anaktuvuk Prehistory: A Study in Environmental Adaptation. (Unpublished Ph.D. Dissertation in Anthropology, Yale University, New Haven, Conn.)

_____, ed.
1962a   Prehistoric Cultural Relations Between the Arctic and Temperate Zones of North America. *Arctic Institute of North America Technical Paper* 11. Montreal.

1962b   Cultural Succession at Anaktuvuk Pass, Arctic Alaska. Pp. 39-54 in Prehistoric Cultural Relations Between the Arctic and Temperate Zones of North America. John M. Campbell, ed. *Arctic Institute of North America Technical Paper* 11. Montreal.

1968   Territoriality Among Ancient Hunters: Interpretations from Ethnography and Nature. Pp. 1-21 in Anthropological Archeology in the Americas. Betty J. Meggers, ed. Washington: Anthropological Society of Washington.

1968a   The Kavik Site of Anaktuvuk Pass Central Brooks Range. *Anthropological Papers of the University of Alaska* 14(1):33-42. Fairbanks.

1970   Arctic. Pp. 239-244 in Current Research. Francis A. Riddell, ed. *American Antiquity* 35(2):239-277.

Canada. Bureau of Statistics. Census Division
1951   Census of Canada, 9th, 1951. Vol. II: Cross-classification of Characteristics. Ottawa: Dominion Bureau of Statistics (Statistics Canada).

1963   Census of Canada, 1961. Bulletin 1.3: Population. 2: Ethnic Groups by Age Groups. Ottawa: Queen's Printer.

Canada. Census Division
1973   1971 Census of Canada; Special Bulletin by the Census Division, Statistics Canada. Ottawa: Census Division.

Canada. Department of Mines and Resources
1944   Report of the Department for the Fiscal Year Ended March 31, 1944. Ottawa: King's Printer.

Canada. Department of National Health and Welfare. Medical Services Branch
1980   Report on Health Conditions in the Northwest Territories for 1979. Ottawa: Queen's Printer.

Canada. Department of National Health and Welfare. Northern Health Service
1970-1979   Reports on Health Conditions in the Northwest Territories. Ottawa: Queen's Printer.

Canada. Minister of Supply and Services
1978   Government. Pp. 61-129 in Canada Year Book, 1978-79. Ottwa: Statistics Canada.

Canada. Northern Research Division
1975   Abstracts of Publications of the Northern Research Division (North of 60) Ottawa: The Division.

Canada. Royal Northwest Mounted Police *see* RCMP = Royal Canadian Mounted Police

Canada. Statistics Canada
1974   1971 Census of Canada. Vol. I, Bull. 1.4-3: Ethnic Groups by Age Groups. Ottawa: Statistics Canada.

1976   Census of Canada. Vol. I, Population: Geographic Distributions. Ottawa: Queen's Printer.

1980   Vital Statistics. Ottawa: Statistics Canada.

Canada. Surveys and Mapping Branch
1971   The National Atlas of Canada. Ottawa: Department of Energy, Mines and Resources.

Canadian Hydrographic Service
1968   Pilot of Arctic Canada. Vol. 2. Ottawa: Department of Energy, Mines and Resources.

Cantwell, John C.
1887   A Narrative Account of the Exploration of the Kowak River, Alaska. Pp. 21-52 in Report of the Cruise of the Revenue Marine Steamer Corwin in the Arctic Ocean, in the Year 1885, by Capt. M.A. Healy U.S.R.M. Washington: U.S. Government Printing Office.

1889   A Narrative Account of the Exploration of the Kowak River, Alaska. Pp. 47-98 in Report of the Cruise of the Revenue Marine Steamer Corwin in the Arctic Ocean in the Year 1884, by Capt. M.A. Healy U.S.R.M. Washington: U.S. Government Printing Office.

Carlson, Roy L.
1979   The Early Period on the Coast of British Columbia. *Canadian Journal of Archaeology* 3:211-228.

Carrothers, A.W.R.
1966   Report of the Advisory Commission on the Development of Government in the Northwest Territories. Ottawa: Department of Indian Affairs and Northern Development.

Cartwright, Sir George
1792   A Journal of Transactions and Events, During a Residence of Nearly Sixteen Years on the Coast of Labrador: Containing Many Interesting Particulars, Both of the Country and Its Inhabitants Not Hitherto Known. 3 vols. Newark, England: Allin and Ridge.

Castonguay, R., and R. Lanari
1976   Bibliographie: Études d'impact socioéconomique relatives à des projets de pipeline et à certains projets de développement nordique. Ottawa: Department of Indian Affairs and Northern Development, Northern Research Division. Mimeo.

Chalmer, John W., W.J. Eccles, and H. Fullard, eds.
1966   Philip's Historical Atlas of Canada. London: George Philip and Son.

Champlain, Samuel de
1922-1936   The Works of Samuel de Champlain [1626]. Henry P. Biggar, ed. 6 vols. Toronto: The Champlain Society. (Reprinted: University of Toronto Press, Toronto, 1971.)

Chance, Norman A.
1960   Investigation of the Adjustment of the Eskimos at Barter Island, Alaska to Rapid Cultural Changes. Arctic 13(3):205.

1960a   Culture Change and Integration: An Eskimo Example. American Anthropologist 62(6):1028-1044.

1965   Acculturation, Self-identification, and Personality Adjustment. American Anthropologist 67(2):372-393.

1966   The Eskimos of North Alaska. New York: Holt, Rinehart, and Winston.

1970   Directed Change and Northern Peoples. Pp. 180-194 in Change in Alaska: People, Petroleum, and Politics. George W. Rogers, ed. College: University of Alaska Press.

[1970a]   [Study of Native Education in Alaska; Ethnographic Fieldnotes.] (Manuscripts in Chance's possession.)

1972   Premises, Policies and Practices: A Cross-cultural Study of Education in the Circumpolar North. Pp. 1-11 in Education in the North. Frank Darnell, ed. Fairbanks: no publisher.

1974   Modernization and Educational Reform in Native Alaska. Pp. 332-352 in Rethinking Modernization: Anthropological Perspectives. John J. Poggie and Robert N. Lynch, eds. Westport, Conn.: Greenwood Press.

Chappell, Edward
1817   Narrative of a Voyage to Hudson's Bay in His Majesty's Ship Rosamond Containing Some Account of the Northeastern Coast of America and the Tribes Inhabiting That Remote Region. London: Mawman.

Chard, Chester S.
1955   Eskimo Archaeology in Siberia. Southwestern Journal of Anthropology 11(2):150-177.

1955a   An Early Pottery Site in the Chukchi Peninsula. American Antiquity 20(3):283-284.

1957   The Southwestern Frontier of Eskimo Culture. American Antiquity 22(3):304-305.

1958   New World Migration Routes. Anthropological Papers of the University of Alaska 7(1):23-26. College.

1958a   An Outline of the Prehistory of Siberia. Pt. 1: The Pre-metal Periods. Southwestern Journal of Anthropology 14(1):1-33.

1959   The Western Roots of Eskimo Culture. Pp. 81-87 in Vol. 2 of Proceedings of the 33rd International Congress of Americanists. San José, Costa Rica, 1958.

1959a   Archaeological Work Near Magadan. Anthropological Papers of the University of Alaska 8(1):77-78. College.

1960   Additional Materials from Lake El'Gytkhyn, Chukchi Peninsula. Anthropological Papers of the University of Alaska 9(1):1-10. College.

1960a   Recent Archaeological Work in the Chukchi Peninsula. Anthropological Papers of the University of Alaska 8(2):119-130. College.

1961   Eskimo Remains from Shalaurova Island, Siberia. Anthropological Papers of the University of Alaska 10(1):73-76. College.

1961a   Northeast Asia. Asian Perspectives 4(1-2):7-16.

1962   Time Depth and Culture Process in Maritime Northeast Asia. Asian Perspectives 5(2):213-216.

1962a   Northeast Asia. Asian Perspectives 5(1):16-20.

1962b   New Developments in Siberian Archaeology. Asian Perspectives 5(1):118-126.

1963   The Old World Roots: Review and Speculations. Anthropological Papers of the University of Alaska 10(2):115-121. College.

1963a   Northeast Asia. Asian Perspectives 6(1-2):8-18.

1967   Northeast Asia: Bibliography (Annotated). Asian Perspectives 10:23-38.

1973   Northeast Asia. Asian Perspectives 14(1):1-28.

1974   Northeast Asia in Prehistory. Madison: University of Wisconsin Press.

Chernenko, M.B.
1957   Puteshestviia po Chukotskoi zemle i plavanie na Aliasku kazach'ego sotnika Ivana Kobeleva v 1779 i 1789-1791 gg. [The Travels in Chukchi Country and Voyages to Alaska of the Cossack Captain Ivan Kobelev in 1779 and 1789-1791]. Letopis' Severa 2:121-141. Moscow.

Chichlo, Boris
1981   Les Nevuqaghmiit ou la fin d'une ethnie. Études/Inuit/Studies 5(2):29-47.

Chitty, Dennis H.
1967   The Natural Selection of Self-regulatory Behaviour in Animal Populations. Pp. 51-78 in Vol. 2 of Proceedings of the Ecological Society of Australia. 2 vols. Canberra.

Chlenov, M.A.
1973   K Kharakteristike sotsial'noi organizatsii aziatskikh ėskimosov [Characteristics of the Social Organization of the Asiatic Eskimos]. IX Mezhdunarodnyi Kongress Antropologicheskikh i Ėtnograficheskikh Nauk: Doklady Sovetsnoi Delegatsii. Moscow.

Christensen, Niels O.
1968   Certain Socioeconomic Conditions in Greenland: A Brief Survey. Archives of Environmental Health 17:464-473.

Christy, Miller, ed.
1894   The Voyages of Captain Luke Fox of Hull and Captain Thomas James of Bristol in Search of a Northwest Passage, in 1631-1632. London: Hakluyt Society.

Clairmont, Donald H.
1962   Notes on the Drinking Behaviour of the Eskimos and Indians in the Aklavik Area. (NCRC-62-4) Ottawa: Department of

Northern Affairs and National Resources, Northern Co-ordination and Research Centre.

1963 Deviance Among Indians and Eskimos in Aklavik, N.W.T. (*NCRC-63-9*) Ottawa: Department of Northern Affairs and National Resources, Northern Coordination and Research Centre.

Clark, Annette McFadyen
1970 The Athabaskan-Eskimo Interface. *Bulletin of the Canadian Archaeological Association* 2:13-23. Ottawa.

1974 Koyukuk River Culture. *Canada. National Museum of Man. Ethnology Service Paper* 18. Ottawa.

Clark, Annette McFadyen, and Donald W. Clark
1976 Koyukuk Indian-Kobuk Eskimo Interaction. Pp. 193-220 in Contributions to Anthropology: The Interior Peoples of Northern Alaska. Edwin S. Hall, Jr., ed. *Canada. National Museum of Man. Mercury Series. Archaeological Survey Paper* 49. Ottawa.

Clark, Brenda L.
1977 The Development of Caribou Eskimo Culture. *Canada. National Museum of Man. Mercury Series. Archaeological Survey Paper* 59. Ottawa.

Clark, Donald W.
1964 Incised Figurine Tablets from Kodiak. *Arctic Anthropology* 2(1):118-134.

1966 Perspectives in the Prehistory of Kodiak Island, Alaska. *American Antiquity* 31(3):358-371.

1966a Two Late Prehistoric Pottery-bearing Sites on Kodiak Island, Alaska. *Arctic Anthropology* 3(2):157-184.

1968 Archaeological Survey on the Koyukuk River, Alaska. (Manuscript in National Museum of Man, Ottawa.)

1970 The Late Kachemak Tradition at Three Saints and Crag Point, Kodiak Island, Alaska. *Arctic Anthropology* 6(2):73-111.

1970a Petroglyphs on Afognak Island, Kodiak Group, Alaska. *Anthropological Papers of the University of Alaska* 15(1):13-17. College.

1972 Archeology of the Batza Tena Obsidian Source, West-Central Alaska. *Anthropological Papers of the University of Alaska* 15(2):1-21. College.

1974 Contributions to the Later Prehistory of Kodiak Island, Alaska. *Canada. National Museum of Man. Mercury Series. Archeological Survey Paper* 20. Ottawa.

1974a Koniag Prehistory. *Tübinger Monographien zur Urgeschichte* 1. Stuttgart, Germany.

1975 Technological Continuity and Change within a Persistent Maritime Adaptation: Kodiak Island, Alaska. Pp. 203-227 in Prehistoric Maritime Adaptations of the Circumpolar Zone. William Fitzhugh, ed. The Hague, Paris: Mouton.

1977 Hahanudan Lake: An Ipiutak-related Occupation of Western Interior Alaska. *Canada. National Museum of Man. Mercury Series. Archaeological Survey Paper* 71. Ottawa.

1979 Ocean Bay: An Early North Pacific Maritime Culture. *Canada. National Museum of Man. Mercury Series. Archaeological Survey Paper* 86. Ottawa.

1980 Relationships of North Pacific and American Arctic Centres of Slate Grinding. *Canadian Journal of Archaeology* 4:27-38.

Clark, Gerald H.
1977 Archaeology on the Alaska Peninsula: The Coast of Shelikof Strait, 1963-1965. *Anthropological Papers of the University of Oregon* 13. Eugene.

Clavering, D.C.
1830 Journal of a Voyage to Spitzbergen and the East Coast of Greenland in His Majesty's Ship Griper. *Edinburgh New Philosophical Journal* 9:1-30.

Cline, Michael S.
1975 Tannik School: The Impact of Education on the Eskimos of Anaktuvuk Pass. Anchorage: Alaska Methodist University Press.

Coats, Robert R.
1950 Volcanic Activity in the Aleutian Arc. *U.S. Geological Survey Bulletin* 974-B:35-49. Washington.

Coats, William
1852 The Geography of Hudson's Bay: Being the Remarks of Captain W. Coats in Many Voyages to that Locality Between the Years 1727 and 1751. (*Works Issued by the Hakluyt Society* 11) London: Printed for the Hakluyt Society.

Coccola, Raymond de, and Paul King
1956 Ayorama. New York: Oxford University Press.

Cohen, Ronald
1962 An Anthropological Survey of Communities in the Mackenzie–Slave Lake Region of Canada. (*NCRC-62-3*). Ottawa: Department of Northern Affairs and National Resources, Northern Co-ordination and Research Centre.

Colbert, M.J., G.V. Mann, and L.M. Hursh
1978 Nutrition Studies: Clinical Observations on Nutritional Health. Pp. 162-173 in Eskimos of Northwestern Alaska: A Biological Perspective. Paul L. Jamison, Stephen L. Zegura, and Frederick A. Milan, eds. Stroudsburg, Pa.: Dowden, Hutchinson and Ross.

Colby, W.B., and J.F. Cleall
1974 Cephalometric Analysis of the Craniofacial Region of the Northern Foxe Basin Eskimo. *American Journal of Physical Anthropology* 40(2):159-170.

Collier, John
1973 Alaskan Eskimo Education: A Film Analysis of Cultural Confrontation in the Schools. New York: Holt, Rinehart, and Winston.

Collins, Henry B., Jr.
1928 Check-stamped Pottery from Alaska. *Journal of the Washington Academy of Sciences* 18(9):254-256. Washington.

1930 Prehistoric Art of the Alaskan Eskimo. *Smithsonian Miscellaneous Collections* 81(14). Washington.

1931 Ancient Culture of St. Lawrence Island, Alaska. Pp. 135-144 in *Explorations and Field-work of the Smithsonian Institution in 1930*. Washington.

1932 Prehistoric Eskimo Culture on St. Lawrence Island. *Geographical Review* 22(1):107-119.

1934 Eskimo Archaeology and Somatology. *American Anthropologist* 36(2):309-313.

1935 Archeology of the Bering Sea Region. Pp. 453-468 in *Annual Report of the Smithsonian Institution for 1933*. Washington.

1937 Archeology of St. Lawrence Island, Alaska. *Smithsonian Miscellaneous Collections* 96(1). Washington.

1937a Culture Migrations and Contacts in the Bering Sea Region. *American Anthropologist* 39(3):375-384.

1937b Archeological Excavations at Bering Strait. Pp. 63-68 in *Explorations and Field-Work of the Smithsonian Institution in 1936*. Washington.

1939   On the Origin and Relationships of the Old Bering Sea Culture. Pp. 297-298 in *Proceedings of the 2d International Congress of Anthropological and Ethnological Sciences.* Copenhagen, 1938.

1940   Outline of Eskimo Prehistory. Pp. 533-592 in Essays in Historical Anthropology of North America, Published in Honor of John R. Swanton in Celebration of His Fortieth Year with the Smithsonian Institution. *Smithsonian Miscellaneous Collections* 100. Washington.

1941   Prehistoric Eskimo Harpoon Heads from Bering Strait. *Journal of the Washington Academy of Sciences* 31(7):318-324. Washington.

1943   Eskimo Archaeology and Its Bearing on the Problem of Man's Antiquity in America. *Proceedings of the American Philosophical Society* 86(2):220-235. Philadelphia.

1950   Excavations at Frobisher Bay, Baffin Island, N.W.T. *Annual Report of the National Museum of Canada for the Fiscal Year 1948-1949, Bulletin* 118:18-43. Ottawa.

1951   The Origin and the Antiquity of the Eskimo. Pp. 423-467 in *Annual Report of the Smithsonian Institution for 1950.* Washington.

1951a   Excavations at Thule Culture Sites Near Resolute Bay, Cornwallis Island, N.W.T. *Annual Report of the National Museum of Canada for the Fiscal Year 1949-1950, Bulletin* 123:49-63. Ottawa.

1952   Archaeological Excavations at Resolute, Cornwallis Island, Northwest Territories. *Annual Report of the National Museum of Canada for 1950-1951, Bulletin* 126:48-63. Ottawa.

1953   Radiocarbon Dating in the Arctic. *American Antiquity* 18(3):197-203.

1953a   Recent Developments in the Dorset Culture Area. *Memoirs of the Society for American Archaeology* 9(3):32-39. Salt Lake City.

1954   Arctic Area. *Instituto Panamericano de Geografía e Historia, Publicación 160, Programa de Historia de América* 2. Mexico City.

1954a   Comments on Morris Swadesh's Symposium 'Time Depths of American Linguistic Groupings.' *American Anthropologist* 56(3):364-372.

1954b   The Position of Ipiutak in Eskimo Culture—Reply. *American Antiquity* 20(1):79-84.

1955   Excavations of Thule and Dorset Culture Sites at Resolute, Cornwallis Island, N.W.T. *Annual Report of the National Museum of Canada for the Fiscal Year 1953-1954, Bulletin* 136:22-35. Ottawa.

1955a   Archaeological Research in the North American Arctic. *Arctic* 7(3-4):296-306.

1956   The T-1 Site at Native Point, Southampton Island, N.W.T. *Anthropological Papers of the University of Alaska* 4(2):63-89. College.

1956a   Archaeological Investigations on Southampton and Coats Islands, N.W.T. *Annual Report of the National Museum of Canada for 1954-55, Bulletin* 142:82-113. Ottawa.

1957   Archaeological Investigations on Southampton and Walrus Islands, N.W.T. *Annual Report of the National Museum of Canada, for 1955-1956, Bulletin* 147:22-61. Ottawa.

1957a   Archaeological Work in Arctic Canada. Pp. 509-528 in *Annual Report of the Smithsonian Institution for 1956.* Washington.

1958   Present Status of the Dorset Problem. Pp. 557-560 in *Proceedings of the 32d International Congress of Americanists.* Copenhagen, 1956.

1960   [Comments on] The Archeology of Bering Strait, by J.L. Giddings. *Current Anthropology* 1(2):131-136.

1961   Eskimo Cultures. Encyclopedia of World Art. Vol. 5: cols. 1-28. New York: McGraw Hill.

1962   Bering Strait to Greenland. Pp. 126-139 in Prehistoric Cultural Relations Between the Arctic and Temperate Zones of North America. John M. Campbell, ed. *Arctic Institute of North America Technical Paper* 11. Montreal.

1963-1964   Recent Trends and Developments in Arctic Archaeology. Pp. 373-377 in *Proceedings of the 6th International Congress of Anthropological and Ethnological Sciences.* Paris, 1960.

1964   The Arctic and Subarctic. Pp. 85-114 in Prehistoric Man in the New World. Jesse D. Jennings and Edward Norbeck, eds. Chicago: Published for William Marsh Rice University by the University of Chicago Press.

1969-1970   Prehistoric Cultural Relations Between Japan and the American Arctic: Eskimo and Pre-Eskimo. Pp. 358-359 in Vol. 3 of *Proceedings of the 8th International Congress of Anthropological and Ethnological Sciences.* 3 vols. Tokyo and Kyoto, 1968.

1971   Composite Masks: Chinese and Eskimo. *Anthropologica* n.s. 13(1-2):271-278. Ottawa.

Collins, Henry B., Jr., Austin H. Clark, and Egbert H. Walker
1945   The Aleutian Islands: Their People and Natural History. *Smithsonian Institution War Background Studies* 21. Washington.

Collins, Henry B., Frederica De Laguna, Edmund Carpenter, and Peter Stone
1973   The Far North: 2000 Years of American Eskimo and Indian Art. Washington: National Gallery of Art. (Reprinted: Indiana University Press, Bloomington, 1977.)

Collinson, Richard
1889   Journal of H.M.S. Enterprise, on the Expedition in Search of Sir John Franklin's Ships by Behring Strait, 1850-1855. T.B. Collinson, ed. London: Sampson, Low, Marston, and Rivington.

Comer, George
1910   A Geographical Description of Southampton Island and Notes Upon the Eskimo. *Bulletin of the American Geographical Society* 42:84-90.

1921   Notes on the Natives of the Northwestern Shores of Hudson Bay. *American Anthropologist* 23(2):243-244.

Commission on Social Research in Greenland
1961   Reports. 6 vols. Copenhagen.

Condon, Richard G.
1982   Seasonal Variation and Interpersonal Conflict in the Central Canadian Arctic. *Ethnology* 21(2):151-164.

Cook, Frank A.
1967   Fluvial Processes in the High Arctic. *Geographical Bulletin* 9(3):262-268.

Cook, Frederick A.
1894   Medical Observations Among the Esquimaux. *American Gynecological and Obstetrical Journal* 4:282-289.

Cook, James
1799   Cook's Voyages Round the World, for Making Discoveries Toward the North and South Poles. Manchester, England: Sowler and Russell.

Cook, James, and J. King
1784   A Voyage to the Pacific Ocean Undertaken, by the Command of His Majesty, for Making Discoveries in the Northern Hemisphere. Performed Under the Direction of Captains Cook, Clarke, and Gore, in His Majesty's Ships the Resolution and Discovery; in the Years 1776, 1777, 1778, 1779, and 1780. 3 vols. London: G. Nicol and T. Cadell.

Cook, John P.
1969   The Early Prehistory of Healy Lake, Alaska. (Unpublished Ph.D. Dissertation in Anthropology, University of Wisconsin, Madison.)

————, ed.
1977   Pipeline Archeology. Fairbanks: University of Alaska, Institute of Arctic Biology.

Cook, John P., E. James Dixon, Jr., and Charles E. Holmes
1972   Archaeological Report, Site 49 RAT 32, Amchitka Island, Alaska. (*USAEC Report HN-20-1045*) Las Vegas: Holmes and Narver.

Cooke, Alan
1973   The Eskimos and the Hudson's Bay Company. Pp. 209-223 in Le Peuple esquimau aujourd'hui et demain/The Eskimo People To-day and To-Morrow. Jean Malaurie, ed. (Fourth International Congress of the Fondation Française d'Études Nordiques) Paris, The Hague: Mouton.

Cooke, Alan, and Clive Holland
1978   The Exploration of Northern Canada, 500 to 1920: A Chronology. Toronto: Arctic History Press.

Coon, Carleton S., Stanley M. Garn, and Joseph B. Birdsell
1950   Races: A Study of the Problems of Race Formation in Man. Springfield, Ill.: Charles C. Thomas.

Cooper, P.F.
1967   The Mackenzie Delta—Technology. (*MDRP 2*) Ottawa: Department of Indian Affairs and Northern Development, Northern Co-ordination and Research Centre.

Corbin, James E.
1971   Aniganigurak (S-67): A Contact Period Nunamiut Eskimo Village in the Brooks Range. Pp. 272-296 in Final Report of the Archeological Survey and Excavation Along the Alyeska Pipeline Service Company Pipeline Route. John P. Cook, ed. (Manuscript in Department of Anthropology, University of Alaska, College.)

1976   Early Historic Nunamiut House Types: An Ethnographic Description with Archaeological Identification, Comparison and Validation. Pp. 135-176 in Contributions to Anthropology: The Interior Peoples of Northern Alaska. Edwin S. Hall, Jr., ed. *Canada. National Museum of Man. Mercury Series. Archaeological Survey Paper* 49. Ottawa.

Correll, Thomas C.
1972   Ungalaqlingmiut: A Study in Language and Society. (Unpublished Ph.D. Dissertation in Anthropology, University of Minnesota, Minneapolis.)

Courtemanche, Augustin le Gardeur de
1705   Descriptions de la coste des Esquimaux: Memoire du voiage qu'a fait le Sieur de Courtemanche à la coste des Esquimaux depuis Kegasca jusqu'au havre Saint Nicolas. (Manuscript in Bibliothèque Nationale, Mss. Françaises, Nouvelles Acquisitions 9275:211-213, Paris.)

Cox, D.W., N.E. Simpson, and R. Jantti
1978   Group-specific Component, Alpha$_1$-Antitrypsin and Esterase D in Canadian Eskimos. *Human Heredity* 28:341-350.

Cox, Steven L.
1978   Palaeo-Eskimo Occupations of the North Labrador Coast. *Arctic Anthropology* 15(2):96-118.

Coxe, William
1787   Account of the Russian Discoveries Between Asia and America, to Which Are Added the Conquest of Siberia and the History of the Transactions and Commerce Between Russia and China. 3d ed. London: T. Cadell.

1803   Account of the Russian Discoveries Between Asia and America to Which Are Added, the Conquest of Siberia and the History of the Transactions and Commerce Between Russia and China. 4th enl. ed. London: Cadell and Davies.

Cram, Jack
1978   Northern Teachers in Northern Schools: The Greenland Experience. *Polar Record* 19(120):209-216.

Cranz, David
1765   Historie von Grönland, enthaltend die Beschreibung des Landes und der Einwohner, und insbesondere die Geschichte der dortigen Mission der Evangelischen Brüder zu Neu-Herrnhut und Lichtenfels. Barby, Germany: H.D. Ebers.

1767   The History of Greenland: Containing a Description of the Country, and Its Inhabitants; and Particularly, a Relation of the Mission Carried on for Above These Thirty Years by the Unitas Fratrium, at New Herrnhuth and Lichtenfels, in That Country. 2 vols. London: Printed for the Brethren's Society for the Furtherance of the Gospel Among the Heathen and Sold by J. Dodsley.

1770   Historie von Grönland enthaltend die Beschreibung des Landes und der Einwohner insbesondere die Geschichte der dortigen Mission der Evangelischen Brüder zu Neu-Herrnhut und Lichtenfels. 3 vols. 2d ed. Barby and Leipzig, Germany: H.D. Ebers und Weidmann's Erben.

Creider, Chet
1981   Place of Articulation Assimilation and the Inuktitut Dialect Continuum. Pp. 91-100 in The Language of the Inuit: Historical, Phonological and Grammatical Issues. Louis-Jacques Dorais, ed. *Études/Inuit/Studies* 5. Suppl.

Crowe, Keith J.
1970   A Cultural Geography of Northern Foxe Basin, N.W.T. (*N.S.R.G. 69-2*) Ottawa: Department of Indian Affairs and Northern Development, Northern Science Research Group.

1974   A History of the Original Peoples of Northern Canada. Montreal: Arctic Institute of North America and McGill-Queen's University Press.

1979   A Summary of Northern Native Claims in Canada: The Process and Progress of Negotiations. *Études/Inuit/Studies* 3(1):31-39.

Culin, Stewart
1907   Games of the North American Indians. Pp. 3-809 in *24th Annual Report of the Bureau of American Ethnology for the Years 1902-1903*. Washington.

Cuoq, Jean-André
1886   Lexique de la langue algonquine. Montreal: J. Chapleau.

Curtis, Edward S.
1907-1930 The North American Indian: Being a Series of Volumes Picturing and Describing the Indians of the United States and Alaska. Frederick W. Hodge, ed. 20 vols. Norwood, Mass.: Plimpton Press. (Reprinted: Johnson Reprint, New York, 1970.)

Curtis, Roger
1774   Particulars of the Country of Labrador, Extracted from the Papers of Lieut. Roger Curtis, of His Majesty's Ship 'Otter', with a Plane Chart of the Coast. *Philological Transactions of the Royal Society of London* 64(2):372-387.

Cyriax, Richard J.
1939   Sir John Franklin's Last Arctic Expedition: A Chapter in the History of the Royal Navy. London: Methuen.

DRHA = Documents Relative to the History of Alaska
1936-1938   Alaska History Research Project, 1936-1938. (Manuscripts in the Library of Congress, Washington.)

Dahl, Jens
1977   Minearbejdere i Ūmánaq kommune [Mine Workers in the Uummannaq District]. Vedbæk, Denmark: Kragestedet.

1982-1983   Hjemmestyre med udviklings problemer: Kontakt 3 [Home Rule and Problems of Development]. Copenhagen: Mellemfolkeligt Samvirke.

1983   Det grønlandske hjemmestyre: En kommenteret bibliografi [Greenland Home Rule: An Annotated Bibliography]. Københavns Universitet Institut for Eskimologi 11. Copenhagen.

Dahl, Jens, and Hans Berg
1977   Minedrift i et fangersamfund [Mining in a Hunting Community]. Vedbæk, Denmark: Kragestedet.

Dahl, Jens, and Karl J. Lyberth
1980   Grønlandske migrantarbejdere i Marmorilik, 1973-1978. [Greenlandic Migrant Workers in Marmorilik, 1973-1978]. Københavns Universitet Copenhagen, Institut for Eskimologi 8, Copenhagen.

Dahlberg, A.A.
1980   Craniofacial Studies. Pp. 168-192 in The Human Biology of Circumpolar Populations. F.A. Milan, ed. Cambridge, England: Cambridge University Press.

Dahlberg, A.A., R. Cederquist, J. Mayhall, and D. Owen
1978   Eskimo Craniofacial Studies. Pp. 94-113 in Eskimos of Northwestern Alaska: A Biological Perspective. Paul L. Jamison, Stephen L. Zegura, and Frederick A. Milan, eds. Stroudsburg, Pa.: Dowden, Hutchinson and Ross.

Dailey, Robert C., and Lois A. Dailey
1961   The Eskimo of Rankin Inlet: A Preliminary Report. (NCRC-61-7) Ottawa: Department of Northern Affairs and National Resources, Northern Co-ordination and Research Centre.

Dalager, Lars
1915   Grønlandske relationer indeholdende Grønlændernes liv og levnet, deres skikke og vedtægter samt temperament og superstitioner tillige nogle korte reflectioner over missionen sammenskrevet ved Friderichshaabs colonie i Grønland anno 1752 af Lars Dalager Kjøbmand [Accounts from Greenland Containing the Lives and Living of the Greenlanders, Their Practice and Customs and Also Temperament and Superstitions Together with Some Brief Reflections on the Missions, Written at Frederikshåb Colony in Greenland in the Year 1752 by Lars Dalager, Merchant]. Det Grønlandske Selskabs Skrifter 2. Copenhagen.

Dall, William H.
1870   Alaska and Its Resources. Boston: Lee and Shepard.

1873   Notes on the Pre-historic Remains in the Aleutian Islands. Proceedings of the California Academy of Sciences 4:283-287. San Francisco.

1875   Alaskan Mummies. American Naturalist 9(8):433-440.

1877   On Succession in the Shell-heaps of the Aleutian Islands. Pp. 41-91 in Tribes of the Extreme Northwest. (Contributions to North American Ethnology 1) Washington: U.S. Government Printing Office.

1877a   Tribes of the Extreme Northwest. Pp. 1-106 in Vol. 1 of Contributions to North American Ethnology. John W. Powell, ed. 9 vols. Washington: U.S. Government Printing Office.

1880   On the Remains of Later Pre-historic Man Obtained from Caves in the Catherina Archipelago, Alaska Territory and Especially from the Caves of the Aleutian Islands. Smithsonian Contributions to Knowledge 22(318). Washington.

1881   On the So-called Chukchi and Namollo People of Eastern Siberia. American Naturalist 15(10):857-868.

1884   On Masks, Labrets, and Certain Aboriginal Customs. Pp. xxxi-xxxiv in 3d Annual Report of the Bureau of American Ethnology for the Years 1881-1882. Washington.

Damas, David
1960   A Reexamination of the Concept of "Eskimo Type" Social Organization with Respect to the Central Eskimo. (Unpublished M.A. Thesis in Anthropology, University of Chicago, Chicago.)

1962-1963   [Fieldnotes on the Copper Eskimo.] (Manuscript in Damas's possession.)

1963   Igluligmiut Kinship and Local Groupings: A Structural Approach. Anthropological Series 64, National Museum of Canada Bulletin 196. Ottawa.

1968   [Fieldnotes on the Aivilik and Netsilik Eskimo.] (Manuscript in Damas's possession.)

1968a   The Eskimo. Pp. 141-172 in Vol. 1 of Science, History and Hudson Bay. C.S. Beals, ed. 2 vols. Ottawa: Department of Energy, Mines and Resources.

1969   Survey of Eskimo Groupings. Appendix to Characteristics of Central Eskimo Band Structure. Pp. 135-138 in Contributions to Anthropology: Band Societies. Anthropological Series 84, National Museum of Canada Bulletin 228. Ottawa.

1969a   Environment, History, and Central Eskimo Society. Pp. 40-64 in Ecological Essays. David Damas, ed. Anthropological Series 86, National Museum of Canada Bulletin 230. Ottawa.

1969b   Characteristics of Central Eskimo Band Structure. Pp. 116-134 in Contributions to Anthropology: Band Societies. D. Damas, ed. Anthropological Series 84, National Museum of Canada Bulletin 228. Ottawa.

1969c   Contributions to Anthropology: Ecological Essays. Anthropological Series 86, National Museum of Canada Bulletin 230. Ottawa.

_____, ed.
1969d   Contributions to Anthropology: Band Societies: Proceedings of the Conference on Band Organization, Ottawa, August 30 to September 2, 1965. Anthropological Series 84, National Museum of Canada Bulletin 228. Ottawa.

1971   The Problem of the Eskimo Family. Pp. 54-78 in the Canadian Family: A Book of Readings. K. Ishwaran, ed. Toronto: Holt, Rinehart and Winston of Canada.

1972   The Structure of Central Eskimo Associations. Pp. 40-55 in Proceedings of the 1971 Annual Spring Meeting of the American Ethnological Society, Suppl. L. Guemple, ed. Seattle: University of Washington Press.

1972a   Central Eskimo Systems of Food Sharing. Ethnology 11(3):220-240.

1972b   The Copper Eskimo. Pp. 3-50 in Hunters and Gatherers Today. M.G. Bicchieri, ed. New York: Holt, Rinehart and Winston.

1975   Three Kinship Systems from the Central Arctic. Arctic Anthropology 12(1):10-30.

1975a   Demographic Aspects of Central Eskimo Marriage Practices. American Ethnologist 2(3):409-418.

Dam-Mikkelsen, Bente, and Torben Lundbæk, eds.
1980   Etnografiske genstande i det kongelige danske Kunstkammer 1650-1800/Ethnographic Objects in the Royal Danish Kunstkammer 1650-1800. *Nationalmuseets Skrifter, Etnografisk Række 17.* Copenhagen.

Danielo, Etienne
1955   The Story of a Medicine Man. *Eskimo* 36(June):3-6.

Dansgaard, W.
1980   Palaeo-climatic Studies on Ice Cores. Pp. 237-246 in Das Klima. H. Oeschger, B. Messerli, and M. Svilar, eds. Berlin, Heidelberg, New York: Springer.

Dansgaard, W., S.L. Johnson, H.B. Clausen, and C.C. Langway, Jr.
1971   Climatic Record Revealed by the Camp Century Ice Core. Pp. 37-56 in The Late Cenozoic Glacial Ages. Karl K. Turekian, ed. New Haven, Conn.: Yale University Press.

Dansgaard, W., S.L. Johnson, J. Møller, and C.C. Langway, Jr.
1969   One Thousand Centuries of Climatic Record from Camp Century on the Greenland Ice Sheet. *Science* 166(3903):377-381.

Darnell, Frank, ed.
1972   Education in the North: Selected Papers of the First International Conference on Cross-Cultural Education in the Circumpolar Nations and Related Articles. College: University of Alaska, Arctic Institute of North America and the Center for Northern Educational Research.

_____
1979   Education Among the Native Peoples of Alaska. *Polar Record* 19(122):431-446.

Davies, K.G., ed.
1963   Northern Quebec and Labrador Journal and Correspondence, 1819-35 (*Hudson's Bay Record Society Publication* 24) London: Hudson's Bay Record Society.

Davis, Craig W., Dana C. Linck, Kenneth M. Schoenberg, and Harvey M. Shields
1981   Slogging, Humping and Mucking Through the NPR-A: An Archeological Interlude. 5 vols. *University of Alaska, Anthropology and Historic Preservation Cooperative Park Studies Unit, Occasional Paper* 25. Fairbanks.

Davis, John
1589   The First Voyage of M. John Davis, Undertaken in June 1585 for the Discoverie of the Northwest Passage. Written by M. John Marchant. London: no publisher.

Davis, Nancy Yaw
1969   A Village View of Agencies. (Manuscript in Davis's possession, and at the University of Alaska, Anchorage.)

_____
1970   The Role of the Russian Orthodox Church in the Five Pacific Eskimo Villages as Revealed by the Earthquake. Pp. 125-146 in the Great Alaska Earthquake of 1964: Human Ecology. Washington: National Research Council, Division of Earth Sciences, Committee on the Alaska Earthquake.

_____
1971   The Effects of the 1964 Alaska Earthquake, Tsunami, and Resettlement of Two Koniag Eskimo Villages. (Unpublished Ph.D. Dissertation in Anthropology, University of Washington, Seattle.)

_____
1979   Kodiak Native Sociocultural Impacts. Western Gulf of Alaska: Petroleum Development Scenarios. *Alaska OCS Socioeconomic Studies Program, Bureau of Land Management, Technical Report* 41. (Available through National Technical Information Service, Springfield, Va. 22161.)

_____
1979a   Social Implications of ANCSA. Pp. 166-227 in Alaska Native Claims Settlement Act, 1971-1979: Commission Study 44. Anchorage: Federal State Land Use Planning Commission for Alaska.

_____
1979b   Western Gulf of Alaska Petroleum Development Scenarios, Kodiak Native Sociocultural Impacts. *Alaska OCS Socioeconomic Studies Program, Bureau of Land Management, Technical Report* 41. (Available through National Technical Information Service, Springfield, Va. 22161.)

Davis, Stanley D.
1980   Hidden Falls: A Multicomponent Site in the Alexander Archipelago of the Northwest Coast. (Paper read at the Annual Meeting of the Society for American Archaeology, Philadelphia.)

Davis, Wilbur A.
[1960]   Archaeological Investigations of Inland and Coastal Sites of the Katmai National Monument, Alaska: Report to the U.S. National Park Service. (*Archives of Archaeology* 4) Madison: University of Wisconsin Press.

Davydov, Gavrila Ivanovich
1810-1812   Dvukratnoe puteshestvīe v Ameriku morskikh ofitserov Khvostova i Davydova, pisannoe sim posliednim [A Double Voyage to America by the Naval Officers Khvostov and Davydov, Written by the Latter]. St. Petersburg: Morskaīa Tipografiīa.

_____
1977   Two Voyages to Russian America, 1802-1807. Richard A. Pierce, ed.; Colin Bearne, trans. (*Materials for the Study of Alaska History* 10) Kingston, Ont.: Limestone Press.

de Coccola, Raymond *see* Coccola, Raymond de

Degerbøl, Magnus
1936   The Former Eskimo Habitation in the Kangordlugssuak District, East Greenland. *Meddelelser om Grønland* 104(10). Copenhagen.

_____
1936a   Animal Remains from the West Settlement in Greenland with Special Reference to Livestock. *Meddelelser om Grønland* 88(3). Copenhagen.

Dekin, Albert A., Jr.
1969   Paleo-Climate and Prehistoric Cultural Interaction in the Eastern Arctic. (Paper presented at the 34th Annual Meeting of the Society for American Archaeology, Milwaukee.)

_____
1970   Paleo-climate and Paleo-ecology of the Eastern North American Arctic During Its Occupancy by Man [2500 B.C. to Date]. (Paper presented at the 3d Annual Meeting of the Canadian Archeological Association.)

_____
1975   Models of Pre-Dorset Culture: Towards an Explicit Methodology. (Unpublished Ph.D. Dissertation in Archaeology, Michigan State University, East Lansing.)

_____
1976   Elliptical Analysis: An Heuristic Technique for the Analysis of Artifact Clusters. Pp. 79-88 in Eastern Arctic Prehistory: Paleo-eskimo Problems. M. Maxwell, ed. *Memoirs of the Society for American Archeology* 31. Salt Lake City.

De Laguna, Frederica
1934   The Archaeology of Cook Inlet, Alaska. Philadelphia: Published for the University Museum by the University of Pennsylvania Press. (2d ed., Alaska Historical Society, Fairbanks, 1975.)

_____
1947   The Prehistory of Northern North America as Seen from the Yukon. *Memoirs of the Society for American Archaeology* 3. Salt Lake City.

_____
1952   Discussion of Kaj Birket-Smith's Present Status of the Eskimo Problem. Pp. 18-21 in Vol. 3 of *Selected Papers of the 29th International Congress of Americanists.* Sol Tax, ed. Chicago: University of Chicago Press.

_____
1956   Chugach Prehistory: The Archaeology of Prince William Sound, Alaska. *University of Washington Publications in Anthropology* 13. Seattle.

De Laguna, Frederica, Francis A. Riddell, Donald F. McGuin, Kenneth D. Lane, and J. Arthur Freed
1964   Archeology of the Yakutat Bay Area, Alaska. *Bureau of American Ethnology Bulletin* 192. Washington.

Denmark. Statistiske Departement
1954 ...Statistik Aarbog...Annuaire Statistique...Statens Statistiske Bureau, ed. Copenhagen.

Denniston, Glenda B.
1966 Cultural Change at Chaluka, Umnak Island: Stone Artifacts and Features. *Arctic Anthropology* 3(2):84-124.

———
1972 Ashishik Point: An Economic Analysis of a Prehistoric Aleutian Community. (Unpublished Ph.D. Dissertation in Anthropology, University of Wisconsin, Madison.)

———
1974 The Diet of the Ancient Inhabitants of Ashishik Point, an Aleut Community. *Arctic Anthropology* 11(Suppl.):143-152.

Derry, D.E.
1971 The Archeology and Anthropology of a Recent Eskimo Habitation at Prudhoe Bay, Alaska. Pp. 6-116 in Final Report of the Archeological Survey and Excavation Along the Alyeska Pipeline Service Company Pipeline Route. John P. Cook, ed. (Manuscript in Department of Anthropology, University of Alaska, College.)

Desgoffe, Claude
1955 Contact culturel: Le cas des Esquimaux des îles Belcher. *Anthropologica* 1:45-71. Ottawa.

Devine, Marina, and Deborough Wood *see* Northwest Territories. Government

Desautels, Roger J., Albert J. McCurdy, James D. Flynn, and Robert R. Ellis
1970 Archaeological Report, Amchitka Island, 1969-1970. (*USAEC Report TID-25481*) [Los Angeles]: Archaeological Research, Incorporated.

DeVries, John, and Frank G. Vallee, eds.
1975 Data-book on Language Characteristics of the Canadian Population. (Unpublished report prepared for the Development Committee of Research on Language, the Individual and Society, The Canadian Council, Ottawa.)

Dikov, Nikolaĭ Nikolaevich
1958 Predvaritel´nyĭ otchet o polevykh arkheologicheskikh issledovaniĭakh Chukotskogo kraevedcheskogo muzeĭa v 1957 godu [Preliminary Report on the Archeological Field Investigations of the Chukotka Regional Studies Museum in 1957]. *Anadyr´. Chukotskiĭ Kraevedcheskiĭ Muzeĭ. Zapiski* 1:45-57.

———
1958a Predvaritel´nyĭ otchet o rabote arkheologicheskoĭ ėkspeditsii Chukotskogo kraevedcheskogo muzeĭa 1956 godu [Preliminary Report on the Field Work of the Archeological Expedition of the Chukotka Regional Studies Museum in 1956]. *Anadyr´. Chukotskiĭ Kraevedcheskiĭ Muzeĭ. Zapiski* 1:32-44.

———
1959 Predvaritel´nye dannye o rabote arkheologicheskoĭ ėkspeditsii Chukotskogo kraevedcheskogo museĭa v 1958 godu [Preliminary Data on the Field Work of the Archeological Expedition of the Chukotka Regional Studies Museum in 1958]. *Magadan. Oblastnoĭ Kraevedcheskiĭ Muzeĭ. Zapiski* 2:89-93.

———
1960 Drevnĭaĭa kul´tura kontinental´noĭ Chukotki [The Early Culture of Continental Chukotka]. *Nauchnaĭa Konferentsiĭa po Istorii Sibiri, Sektsiĭa Arkheologii, Tezisy Dokladov i Soobshcheniĭ* 4:26-27.

———
1961 Pervye arkheologicheskie issledovaniĭa na ostrove Aĭon [First Archeological Investigations on Aĭon Island]. *Anadyr´. Chukotskiĭ Kraevedcheskiĭ Muzeĭ. Zapiski* 2:38-42.

———
1961a Pervaĭa arkheologicheskaĭa kollektsiĭa iz Vnutrikontinental´noĭ Chukotki [First Archeological Collection from the Interior of Chukotka.] *Anadyr´. Chukotskiĭ Kraevedcheskiĭ Muzeĭ. Zapiski* 2:3-10.

———
1961b O Raskopkakh Ust´-Bel´skogo mogil´nika po dannym 1958 goda [Excavations at the Ust´-Belaĭa Cemetery, According

to 1958 Data]. *Anadyr´. Chukotskiĭ Kraevedcheskiĭ Muzeĭ. Zapiski* 2:10-14. (Translation: *American Antiquity* 28(4):534-536, 1963.)

———
1961c Predvaritel´nye dannye ob arkheologicheskikh rabotakh na Chukotke v 1959 godu [Preliminary Data on Archeological Field Work in Chukotka in 1959]. *Anadyr´. Chukotskiĭ Kraevedcheskiĭ Muzeĭ. Zapiski* 2:21-35.

———
1963 Archaeological Materials from the Chukchi Peninsula. Chester S. Chard and James B. Griffen, eds. *American Antiquity* 28(4):529-536.

———
1965 Po Chukotke, k predkam ėskimosov [Across Chukotka, to the Forefathers of the Eskimos]. *Magadan. Oblastnoĭ Kraevedcheskie Muzeĭ. Zapiski* 5:53-59.

———
1965a The Stone Age of Kamchatka and the Chukchi Peninsula in the Light of New Archaeological Data. *Arctic Anthropology* 3(1):10-25.

———
1966 Drevnosti Seshana [Seshan Antiquities]. *Magadan. Oblastnoĭ Kraevedcheski Muzeĭ. Zapiski* 6:155-160.

———
1966a Chegitunskie drevneėskimosskie mogil´niki [Paleo-Eskimo Burials on the Chegitun]. *Magadan. Oblastnoĭ Kraevedcheskie Muzeĭ. Zapiski* 6:125-132.

———
1967 Arkheologicheskoe izuchenie Severo-Vostoka v sovetskoe vremĭa [Archeological Study of the Northeast in the Soviet Era]. *Magadan. Akademiĭa Nauk SSSR, Sibirskoe Otdelenie. Severo-Vostochnyĭ Kompleksnyĭ Nauchno-issledovatel´skiĭ Institut. Trudy* 31:46-62.

———
1967a Uėlenskiĭ mogil´nik po dannym raskopok v 1956, 1958, i 1963 godakh [Uėlen Cemetery According to the Excavations of 1956, 1958, and 1963]. *Istoriĭa i Kul´tura Narodov Severa Dal´nego Vostoka. Magadan. Akademiĭa Nauk SSSR, Sibirskoe Otdelenie. Severo-Vostochnyĭ Kompleksnyĭ Nauchno-issledovatel´skiĭ Institut. Trudy* 17:45-79.

———
1968 The Discovery of the Palaeolithic in Kamchatka and the Problem of the Initial Occupation of America. Roger Powers, trans. *Arctic Anthropology* 5(1):191-203.

———
1969-1970 Paleolithic Culture of Kamchatka. Pp. 350-352 in Vol. 3 of *Proceedings of the 8th International Congress of Anthropological and Ethnological Sciences*. Tokyo and Kyoto, 1968.

———
1971 Naskal´nye zagadki drevneĭ Chukotki (petroglify Pegtymelĭa) [Cliff-face Enigmas of Ancient Chukotka (The Pegtymel Petroglyphs)]. Moscow: Izdatel´stvo "Nauka."

———
1971a Drevnie kul´tury Kamchatki i Chukotki [Early Cultures of Kamchatka and Chukotka]. Avtoreferat Dissertatsiĭa na Soiskanie Uchenoĭ Stepeni Doktora Istoricheskikh Nauk. Ob´edinennyĭ Uchenyĭ Sovet po Istoriko-filologicheskim i Filosofskim Naukam. Sibirskoe Otdelenie, Akademiĭa Nauk SSSR. Novosibirsk.

———
1972 Les Pétroglyphes de Pegtymel' et leur appartenance ethnique. *Inter-Nord* 12:245-261. Paris.

———
1974 Chiniĭskiĭ mogil´nik (K istorii morskikh zveroboev Beringova proliva) [Chini Cemetery (On the History of the Seahunters of the Bering Strait)]. *Severo-Vostochnyĭ Kompleksnyĭ Nauchno-Issledovatel´skiĭ Institut. Trudy* 47. Novosibirsk: Izdatel´stvo "Nauka."

———
1977 Arkheologicheskie pamĭatniki Kamchatki, Chukotki i Verkhneĭ Kolymy (Aziĭa na styke s Amerikoĭ v drevnosti) [Archaeological Sites of Kamchatka, Chukotka and the Upper Kolyma (Asia Joining America in Ancient Times)]. Moscow: Izdatel´stvo "Nauka."

749

1979   Drevnie kul'tury severo-vostochnoĭ Azii: Aziĭa na styke s Amerikoĭ v drevnosti [Early Cultures of Northeast Asia (Asia Joining America in Ancient Times)]. Moscow: Izdatel'stvo "Nauka."

Dikova, T.M.
1965   New Data on the Characteristics of the Kanchalan Site. *Arctic Anthropology* 3(1):91-97.

Dixon, E. James, Jr.
1975   The Gallagher Flint Station, an Early Man Site on the North Slope, Arctic Alaska, and Its Role in Relation to the Bering Land Bridge. *Arctic Anthropology* 12(1):68-75.

1979   A Predictive Model for the Distribution of Archaeological Sites on the Bering Continental Shelf. (Unpublished Ph.D. Dissertation in Anthropology, Brown University, Providence, R.I.)

Dixon, R. Greg
1980   The Moose River Site, 1978. Pp. 32-48 in Archaeological Survey Projects, 1978. *Alaska State Division of Parks. Office of History and Archaeology. Miscellaneous Publications. History and Archaeology Series* 22. Anchorage.

Dixon, R. Greg, and William Johnson
1971   A Core and Blade Site on the Alaska Peninsula. (Unpublished manuscript in Don E. Dumond's possession.)

Dolgikh, Boris O.
1960   Rodovoĭ i plemennoĭ sostav narodov Sibiri v XVII veke [Clan and Tribal Structure of the Peoples of Siberia in the 17th Century]. Institut Ėtnografii im. N.N. Miklukho-Maklaĭa. *Trudy*, n.s. 55, Moscow.

1972   The Formation of the Modern Peoples of the Soviet North. Chester S. Chard, trans. and ed. *Arctic Anthropology* 9(1):17-26 (Original in *Sovetskaĭa Ėtnografiĭa* (3):3-15. 1967.)

Dorais, Louis-Jacques
1971-1972   La Structure du vocabulaire moderne de la langue esquimaude du Québec-Labrador. 2 vols. (Unpublished Ph.D. Dissertation, École Pratique des Hautes Études, sect. 4, Paris.)

1975   Kinngaqmiut uqausingit: The Inuit Language in Cape Dorset, N.W.T. Quebec: Université Laval, Association Inuksiutiit Katimajiit.

1975a   Iqalungmiut uqausingit: Southeast Baffin Inuit Language. Quebec: Université Laval, Association Inuksiutiit Katimajiit.

1975b   Inuit uqausingit: Manuel de langue inuit (Nouveau-Québec). Quebec: Université Laval, Association Inuksiutiit Katimajiit.

1976   Aivilingmiut uqausingit: The Aivilik Inuit Language. Quebec: Université Laval, Association Inuksiutiit Katimajiit.

1977   Les Dialectes inuit de l'arctique oriental canadien, une comparaison phonologique. *Études/Inuit/Studies* 1(2):47-56.

1978   Lexique analytique du vocabulaire inuit moderne au Québec-Labrador. (*Centre International de Recherche sur le Bilinguisme* A 14) Quebec: Les Presses de l'Université Laval.

1978a   Iglulingmiut uqausingit: The Inuit Language of Igloolik N.W.T. Quebec: Université Laval, Association Inuksiutiit Katimajiit.

1980   The Inuit Language in Southern Labrador from 1694-1785. *Canada. National Museum of Man. Mercury Series. Ethnology Service Paper* 66. Ottawa.

1980a   Les Inuit du Labrador méridional: Données linguistiques. *Études/Inuit/Studies* 4(1-2):167-174.

————, ed.
1981   The Language of the Inuit: Historical, Phonological and Grammatical Issue. *Études/Inuit/Studies* 5. Suppl.

1981a   Some Notes on the Language of East Greenland. Pp. 43-70 in The Language of the Inuit: Historical, Phonological, and Grammatical Issues. Louis-Jacques Dorais, ed. *Études/Inuit/Studies* 5. Suppl.

1983   Les Tuvaalummiut; histoire socio-économique de Quaqtaq: Québec arctique. Quebec: Ministère des Affaires Culturelles. In press.

Dorais, Louis-Jacques, and Ronald Lowe
1982   Recent Research on the Mackenzie Area Dialects. (Paper read at the 3d Inuit Studies Conference, London, Ont.)

Doty, William F.
1900   The Eskimo on St. Lawrence Island, Alaska. Pp. 186-223 in *9th Annual Report on Introduction of Domestic Reindeer into Alaska, 1899.* Sheldon Jackson, comp. Washington: U.S. Government Printing Office.

Douglas, Mary
1966   Population Control in Primitive Groups. *British Journal of Sociology* 77:263-273.

Draper, H.H,
1976   A Review of Recent Nutritional Research in the Arctic. Pp. 120-129 in Circumpolar Health. R.J. Shephard and S. Itoh, eds. Toronto: University of Toronto Press.

1980   Nutrition. Pp. 257-284 in The Human Biology of Circumpolar Populations. F.A. Milan, ed. Cambridge and London: Cambridge University Press.

Draper, H.H., and Catherine K.W. Wo
1978   Metabolic Parameters: Plasma Vitamin E and Cholesterol Levels in Alaskan Eskimos. Pp. 189-197 in Eskimos of Northwestern Alaska: A Biological Perspective. Paul L. Jamison, Stephen L. Zegura, and Frederick A. Milan, eds. Stroudsburg, Pa.: Dowden, Hutchinson and Ross.

Driscoll, Bernadette
1980   The Inuit Amautik: I Like My Hood to Be Full. Winnipeg, Man.: The Winnipeg Art Gallery.

1983   The Inuit Parka: A Preliminary Study. (Unpublished M.A. Thesis in Anthropology, Carleton University, Ottawa.)

Driver, Harold E.
1969   Indians of North America. 2d rev. ed. Chicago: University of Chicago Press.

Driver, Harold E., and William C. Massey
1957   Comparative Studies of North American Indians. *Transactions of the American Philosophical Society* n.s. 47(2). Philadelphia.

Drury, C.M.
1980   Constitutional Development in the Northwest Territories: Report of the Special Representative. Hull, P.Q.: Department of Supply and Services, Canada.

Duffy, R.Q.
1981   Inuit Population and Social Change on Southern Baffin Island: An Archival Review. Montreal: McGill University, Department of Geography.

Dumond, Don E.
1960-1975   [Notes from 10 Seasons of Fieldwork on the Alaska Peninsula.] (Manuscript in Dumond's possession.)

1964   A Note on the Prehistory of Southwestern Alaska. *Anthropological Papers of the University of Alaska* 12(1):33-45. College.

1965   On Eskaleutian Linguistics, Archaeology, and Prehistory. *American Anthropologist* 67(5):1231-1257.

1969   Prehistoric Cultural Contacts in Southwestern Alaska. *Science* 166(3909):1108-1115.

1969a   Toward a Prehistory of the Na-Dene, with a General Comment on Population Movements Among Nomadic Hunters. *American Anthropologist* 71(5):857-863.

1969b   The Prehistoric Pottery of Southwestern Alaska. *Anthropological Papers of the University of Alaska* 14(2):19-42. College.

1969-1970   Eskimos and Aleuts. Pp. 102-104 in Vol. 3 of *Proceedings of the 8th International Congress of Anthropological and Ethnological Sciences.* 3 vols. Tokyo and Kyoto, 1968.

1971   Early Racial and Cultural Identifications in Southwestern Alaska. *Science* 171(3966):88-90.

1971a   A Summary of Archaeology in the Katmai Region, Southwestern Alaska. *Anthropological Papers of the University of Oregon* 2. Eugene.

1972   The Alaska Peninsula in Alaskan Prehistory. Pp. 29-47 in For the Chief: Essays in Honor of Luther S. Cressman. Fred W. Voget and Robert L. Stephenson, eds. *Anthropological Papers of the University of Oregon* 4. Eugene

1972a   Prehistoric Population Growth and Subsistence Change in Eskimo Alaska. Pp. 311-328 in Population Growth: Anthropological Implications. Brian Spooner, ed. Cambridge, Mass.: MIT Press.

1973   Late Aboriginal Population of the Alaska Peninsula. (Paper read at the Annual Meeting of the American Anthropological Association, New Orleans, 1973.)

1974   Prehistoric Ethnic Boundaries on the Alaska Peninsula. *Anthropological Papers of the University of Alaska* 16(1):1-7. Fairbanks.

1974a   Remarks on the Prehistory of the North Pacific: To Lump or not to Lump. Pp. 47-55 in International Conference on the Prehistory and Paleoecology of Western North American Arctic and Subarctic. Scott Raymond and Peter Schledermann, eds. Calgary: University of Calgary Archaeological Association.

1977   Concluding Note: Subsistence and Seasonality. Pp. 101-110 in Archaeology on the Alaska Peninsula: The Coast of Shelikof Strait, 1963-1965. *Anthropological Papers of the University of Oregon* 13. Eugene.

1977a   The Eskimos and Aleuts. London: Thames and Hudson.

1979   Eskimo-Indian Relationships: A View from Prehistory. *Arctic Anthropology* 16(2):3-22.

1980   The Archeology of Alaska and the Peopling of America. *Science* 209(4460):984-991.

1981   Archaeology on the Alaska Peninsula: The Naknek Region, 1960-1975. *Anthropological Papers of the University of Oregon* 21. Eugene.

1983   Trends and Traditions in Alaskan Prehistory: The Place of Norton Culture. *Arctic Anthropology* 19(2):39-51.

Dumond, Don E., and Robert L. Mace
1968   An Archaeological Survey Along Knik Arm. *Anthropological Papers of the University of Alaska* 14(1):1-21. College.

Dumond, Don E., Leslie Conton, and Harvey M. Shields
1975   Eskimos and Aleuts on the Alaska Peninsula: A Reappraisal of Port Möller Affinities. *Arctic Anthropology* 12(1):49-67.

Dumond, Don E., Winfield Henn, and Robert Stuckenrath
1976   Archaeology and Prehistory on the Alaska Peninsula. *Anthropological Papers of the University of Alaska* 18(1):17-29. Fairbanks.

Dunbar, Maxwell J.
1968   Ecological Development in Polar Regions: A Study in Evolution. Englewood Cliffs, N.J.: Prentice Hall.

Dunbar, Moira, and Keith R. Greenaway
[1956]   Arctic Canada from the Air. Ottawa: Queen's Printer.

Duncan, Irma W., and Edward M. Scott
1972   Lactose Intolerance in Alaskan Indians and Eskimos. *The American Journal of Clinical Nutrition* 25(September):867-868.

Dunn, Ethel
1968   Educating the Small Peoples of the Soviet North: The Limits of Cultural Change. *Arctic Anthropology* 5(1):1-31.

Dunn, Stephen P., and Ethel Dunn
1963   The Transformation of Economy and Culture in the Soviet North. *Arctic Anthropology* 1(2):1-28.

Dunning, R.W.
1959   Ethnic Relations and the Marginal Man in Canada. *Human Organization* 18(3):117-122.

Eagan, C.J.
1963   Local Vascular Adaptations to Cold in Man. *Federation Proceedings* 22:947-951.

Efimov, Alekseĭ Vladimirovich
1948   Iz istorii russkikh ėkspediṫsiĭ na Tikhom okeane [The History of Russian Expeditions to the Pacific Ocean]. Moscow: Voennoe izdateĺstvo.

1950   Iz istorii velikikh russkikh geograficheskikh otkrytiĭ. [The History of the Great Russian Geographical Discoveries]. Moscow: Gos. izd-vo Geogr. dnt-pbl.

————, ed.
1964   Atlas geograficheskikh otkrytiĭ v Sibiri i v severo-zapadnoĭ Amerike XVII-XVIII vv. [Atlas of the Geographical Discoveries in Siberia and Northwestern America, 17th and 18th Centuries]. Moscow: Akademiǐa Nauk SSSR, Institut Ėtnografii.

Egede, Hans P.
1741   Det gamle Grønlands nye perlustration eller natural historie, og beskrivelse over det gamle Grønlands situation, luft, temperament og beskaffenhed [The New Perlustration or Natural History of Old Greenland, and Description of the Situation, Air, Temperament, and Character of Old Greenland]. Copenhagen: J.C. Groth.

1745   A Description of Greenland Shewing the Natural History, Situation, Boundaries, and Face of the Country... London: C. Hitch. (Reprinted: T. and J. Allman, London, 1818.)

1925   Relationer fra Grønland, 1721-36, og Det gamle Grønlands ny perlustration, 1741 [Relations from Greenland 1721-36, and New Perlustration of Old Greenland, 1741]. Louis Bobé, ed. *Meddelelser om Grønland* 54. Copenhagen.

Egede, Niels
1939   Beskrivelse over Grønland [1769] [Description of Greenland]. H. Ostermann, ed. *Meddelelser om Grønland* 120:232-269. Copenhagen.

1939a   Tredie Continuation af Relationerne Betreffende Den Grønlandske Missions Tilstand og Beskaffenhed [1744]. H. Ostermann, ed. *Meddelelser om Grønland* 120:123-232. Copenhagen.

Egede, Poul H.
1750   Dictionarium grönlandica-danico-latinum. Copenhagen: G.F. Kisel.

1760   Grammatica grönlandica-danico-latina. Copenhagen: G.F. Kisel.

1939   Continuation of relationerne betreffende den grønlandske missions tilstand og Beskaffenhed [1741]. [Continuation of the Relations Regarding the State and Condition of the Greenland Mission]. H. Ostermann, ed. *Meddelelser om Grønland* 120. Copenhagen.

Ekblaw, Walter E.
1921   The Ecological Relations of the Polar Eskimo. *Ecology* 2(2):132-144.

——— 1927-1928   The Material Response of the Polar Eskimo to Their Far Arctic Environment. *Annals of the Association of American Geographers* 17:147-198; 18:1-24.

Ellana, Linda J.
1980   Bering-Norton Petroleum Development Scenarios and Sociocultural Impacts Analysis. Vol 1. *Alaska OCS Socioeconomic Studies Program, Final Technical Report* 54. Fairbanks. (Available from NTIS, Springfield, Va.)

Elliott, Henry W.
1898   The Seal Islands of Alaska. Pp. 3-288 in Vol. 3 of Seal and Salmon Fisheries and General Resources of Alaska. 4 vols. Washington: U.S. Government Printing Office.

Ellis, Henry
1748   A Voyage to Hudson's Bay by the *Dobbs Galley* and *California* in the Years 1746 and 1747, for Discovering a North West Passage; with an Accurate Survey of the Coast, and a Short Natural History of the Country. Together with a Fair View of the Facts and Arguments from Which the Future Finding of Such a Passage is Rendered Probable. London: H. Whitridge. (Reprinted: S.R. Publishers, East Ardsley, U.K., 1967.)

Ellis, William *see* Rickman, John

Elton, Charles S.
1942   Voles, Mice and Lemmings: Problems in Population Dynamics. Oxford, England: Clarendon Press.

Enel, Catherine
1981   Signification sociale d'un artisanat touristique au Groenland oriental. *Études/Inuit/Studies* 5(2):125-142.

Erdmann, Friedrich, ed.
1864   Eskimoisches Wörterbuch gesammelt von den Missionaren in Labrador. Budissin, Germany: E.M. Monse.

Eriksson, A.W., W. Lehmann, and N.E. Simpson
1980   Genetic Studies on Circumpolar Populations. Pp. 81-168 in The Human Biology of Circumpolar Populations. F.A. Milan, ed. Cambridge and London: Cambridge University Press.

Ervin, Alexander M.
1969   New Northern Townsmen in Inuvik. (*MDRP-5*) Ottawa: Department of Indian Affairs and Northern Development, Northern Science Research Group.

——— 1976   The Emergence of Native Alaskan Political Capacity, 1959-1971. *The Musk Ox* 19:3-14.

——— 1981   Contrasts Between the Resolution of Native Land Claims in the United States and Canada Based on Observations of the Alaska Native Land Claims Movement. *Canadian Journal of Native Studies* 1(1):123-139.

Eyerdam, Walter J.
1936   Mammal Remains from an Aleut Stone Age Village. *Journal of Mammalogy* 17(1):61.

Fabricius, Otto
1788   Field-ræven (Canis lagopus). *Kongelike Danske Videnskabers Selskabs Skrivter* n.s. 3. Deel: 423-448. Copenhagen.

——— 1801   Forsøg til en Forbedret Grønlandsk Grammatica [Attempt at an Improved Greenlandic Grammar]. 2 vols. Copenhagen: C.F. Schubart.

——— 1804   Den grønlandske Ordbog, forbedret og forøget. [The Greenlandic Dictionary, Revised and Enlarged]. Copenhagen: C.F. Schubart.

——— 1929   Fauna groenlandica: Pattedyr og fugle [1780], [The Fauna of Greenland: Mammals and Birds]. G. Helms, ed. and trans. *Det Grønlandske Selskabs Skrifter* 6. Copenhagen.

——— 1962   Otto Fabricius' Ethnographical Works. Erik Holtved, ed. *Meddelelser om Grønland* 140(2). Copenhagen.

Fainberg, L.A.
1955   K voprosu o rodovom stroye u ėskimosov. *Sovietskaiă Ėtnografiiă* 1(2):82-89. (Translation: On the Question of the Eskimo Kinship System. Charles C. Hughes, trans. *Arctic Anthropology* 4(1):244-256, 1956.)

——— 1965   The Contemporary Situation of the Eskimos (1940-1960) and the Problem of Their Future in the Works of American and Canadian Ethnographers. *Soviet Anthropology and Archaeology* 4(1):27-45.

Faries, Richard, ed.
1938   A Dictionary of the Cree Language as Spoken by the Indians of the Provinces of Quebec, Ontario, Manitoba, Saskatchewan and Alberta. Toronto: The General Synod of the Church of England in Canada.

Farquharson, Don R.
1976   Inuit Land Use in the West-central Canadian Arctic. Pp. 33-61 in Vol. 1 of Inuit Land Use and Occupancy Report. Ottawa: Department of Indian and Northern Affairs.

Fassett, H.C.
1960   The Aleut Sea Otter Hunt in the Late Nineteenth Century. Robert F. Heizer, ed. *Anthropological Papers of the University of Alaska* 8(2):131-135. College.

Fay, Francis H.
1960   Carnivorous Walrus and Some Arctic Zoonoses. *Arctic* 13(2):111-122.

Fedorova, Svetlana Grigor'evna
1964   K voprosu o rannikh russkikh poseleniiakh na Aliaske [On the Question of Early Russian Settlements in Alaska]. *Letopis' Severa* 4:97-113. Moscow.

——— 1971   Russkoe naselenie Aliaski i Kalifornii [The Russian Population in Alaska and California]. Moscow: Nauka.

——— 1971a   Issledovatel Chukotki i Aliaski kazachii sotnik Ivan Kobelev [The Cossack Captain Ivan Kobelev, Explorer of Chukotka and Alaska]. *Letopis' Severa* 5:156-172. Moscow.

——— 1973   The Russian Population in Alaska and California: Late 18th Century–1867. (*Materials for the Study of Alaska History* 4) Kingston, Ont.: Limestone Press.

Feldman, Sheldon A., Arthur Rubenstein, C. Bruce Taylor, Kang-Jey Ho, and Lena Lewis
1978   Metabolic Parameters: Aspects of Cholesterol, Lipid and Carbohydrate Metabolism. Pp. 174-183 in Eskimos of Northwestern Alaska: A Biological Perspective. Paul L. Jamison, Stephen L. Zegura, and Frederick A. Milan, eds. Stroudsburg, Pa.: Dowden, Hutchinson and Ross.

Ferguson, J.D.
1961   The Human Ecology and Social Economic Change in the Community of Tuktoyaktuk, N.W.T. (*NCRC-61-2*). Ottawa: Department of Northern Affairs and National Resources, Northern Co-ordination and Research Centre.

Ferguson, Jack
1971   Eskimos in a Satellite Society. Pp. 15-28 in Minority Canadians. Vol. 1: Native Peoples. Jean Leonhard Elliot, ed. Scarborough, Ont.: Prentice-Hall of Canada.

Ferguson, Robert
1938   Arctic Harpooner: A Voyage on the Schooner Abbie Bradford, 1878-1879. Leslie D. Stair, ed. Philadelphia: University of Pennsylvania Press.

Ferrell, R.E., R. Chakraborty, H. Gershowitz, W.S. Laughlin, and W.J. Schull
1981   The St. Lawrence Island Eskimos: Genetic Variation and Genetic Distance. *American Journal of Physical Anthropology* 55(3):351-358.

Fetter, Sharon, and Anne D. Shinkwin
1978   An Analysis of Archaeological Materials from the Cathedral Mountain Area, North-central Alaska. *Anthropological Papers of the University of Alaska* 19(1):27-43. Fairbanks.

Fienup-Riordan, Ann
1982   Navarin Basin Sociocultural Systems Analysis. *Alaska OCS Socioeconomic Studies Program, Final Technical Report* 70. Anchorage. (Available from NTIS, Springfield, Va.)

Finkler, Harold
1982   Policy Issues in the Delivery of Correctional Services in the Northwest Territories. (Paper presented to the American Society of Criminology, Annual Meeting, November 4-6.)

1982a   Violence and the Administration of Criminal Justice in Northern Canada. (Paper presented to the Conference on Violence, University of Alaska Justice Center, Anchorage October 11-13.)

Finnie, Richard
1940   Lure of the North. Philadelphia: David McKay.

Fischer-Møller, Knud
1942   The Mediaeval Norse Settlements in Greenland: Anthropological Investigations. *Meddelelser om Grønland* 89(2). Copenhagen.

Fisher, John
1973   Bibliography for the Study of Eskimo Religion. *Anthropologica* n.s. 15(2):231-271. Ottawa.

Fisher, Raymond H.
1977   Bering's Voyages: Whither and Why. Seattle: University of Washington Press.

1981   The Voyage of Semen Dezhnev in 1648: Bering's Precursor. (*Hakluyt Society 2d ser. No.* 156) London: The Hakluyt Society.

Fitzhugh, William W.
1972   Environmental Archeology and Cultural Systems in Hamilton Inlet, Labrador: A Survey of the Central Labrador Coast from 3000 B.C. to the Present. *Smithsonian Contributions to Anthropology* 16. Washington.

1976   Environmental Factors in the Evolution of Dorset Culture: A Marginal Proposal for Hudson Bay. Pp. 139-149 in Eastern Arctic Prehistory: Paleoeskimo Problems. M.S. Maxwell, ed. *Memoirs of the Society for American Archeology* 31. Salt Lake City.

1976a   Paleoeskimo Occupations of the Labrador Coast. Pp. 103-118 in Eastern Arctic Prehistory: Paleoeskimo Problems. M.S. Maxwell, ed. *Memoirs of the Society for American Archaeology* 31. Salt Lake City.

1976b   Preliminary Culture History of Nain, Labrador: Smithsonian Fieldwork, 1975. *Journal of Field Archeology* 3(2):123-142.

1977   Population Movement and Culture Change on the Central Labrador Coast. *Annals of the New York Academy of Sciences* 288:481-497. New York.

1977a   Indian and Eskimo/Inuit Settlement History in Labrador: An Archaeological View. Pp. 1-42 in Our Footprints Are Everywhere. C. Brice-Bennett, ed. Nain: Labrador Inuit Association.

Fitzhugh, William W., and Susan A. Kaplan
1982   Inua: Spirit World of the Bering Sea Eskimo. Washington: Smithsonian Institution Press.

Fladmark, K.R.
1971   Early Microblade Industries of the Queen Charlotte Islands, British Columbia. (Paper presented at the 1970 Meeting of the Canadian Archeological Association, Calgary, Alta.)

Flaherty, Robert
1922   *Nanook of the North*, Film produced by Revillon Frères.

———   1924   My Eskimo Friends: Nanook of the North. New York: Doubleday, Page.

———   1979   Robert Flaherty, Photographer and Film-maker: The Inuit 1910-1922; an Exhibition Organized by the Vancouver Art Gallery. Catalogue.

Fleming, Archibald L.
1932   Perils of the Polar Pack: The Adventures of the Reverend E.W.T. Greenshield, KT.O.N. of Blacklead Island, Baffin Land. Toronto: Missionary Society of the Church of England in Canada.

Foighel, Isi
1980   Home Rule in Greenland. *Meddelelser om Grønland: Man and Society* 1. Copenhagen.

Foote, Don C.
[1959] The Economic Base and Seasonal Activities of Some Northwest Alaskan Villages: A Preliminary Study; Report for Bio-environmental Studies of Project Chariot, U.S. Atomic Energy Commission. (Manuscript in possession of the Arctic Institute of North America, Montreal.)

———   [1959–1962] [Fieldnotes from Point Hope, Noatak, and Kivalina.] (Manuscript in possession of the University of Alaska Archives, College.)

———   1964   American Whalemen in Northwestern Arctic Alaska. *Arctic Anthropology* 2(2):16-20.

———   1965   Exploration and Resource Utilization in Northwestern Arctic Alaska Before 1855. (Unpublished Ph.D. Dissertation in Geography, McGill University, Montreal.)

———   [1966] Human Geographical Studies in Northwest Arctic Alaska: The Upper Kobuk River Project. Final Report. (Mimeographed report in Ernest S. Burch's possession.)

———   1969   Human Ecological Studies at Igloolik, N.W.T. (International Biological Program Progress Report in Department of Geography, McGill University, Montreal).

———   1969-1970   An Eskimo Sea-mammal and Caribou Hunting Economy: Human Ecology in Terms of Energy. (Paper read at the *8th International Congress of Anthropological and Ethnological Sciences*. Tokyo and Kyoto, 1968.)

Foote, Don C., and Alan Cooke
[1960] The Eskimo Hunter at Noatak, Alaska. Report for Bio-Environmental Studies of Project Chariot, U.S. Atomic Energy Commission. Mimeo. (Copy in possession of the Arctic Institute of North America, Montreal.)

Foote, Don C., and H.A. Williamson
1966   A Human Geographical Study. Pp. 1041–1107 in Environment of the Cape Thompson Region, Alaska. N.J. Wilimovsky and J.N. Wolfe, eds. Oak Ridge, Tenn.: U.S. Atomic Energy Commission.

Foote, Don C., Victor Fischer, and George W. Rogers
1968   St. Paul Community Study: An Economic and Social Analysis of St. Paul, Pribilof Islands, Alaska. *University of Alaska, Institute of Social, Economic, and Government Research Report* 18. Fairbanks.

Ford, James A.
1959   Eskimo Prehistory in the Vicinity of Point Barrow, Alaska. *Anthropological Papers of the American Museum of Natural History* 47(1). New York.

753

Fornel, Louis
1743   Relation de la découverte qu'a fait le Sieur Louis Fornel en 1743 de la baie des Eskimaux nommée par les sauvages Kessessakiou. Pp. 204–229 in Vol. 2 of Inventaire des pièces sur la Côte de Labrador conservées aux Archives de la Province de Québec, 1940–42. Quebec: R. Paradis.

Forsius, Henrik
1980   Ophthalmology. Pp. 193–211 in The Human Biology of Circumpolar Populations. Frederick A. Milan, ed. Cambridge and London: Cambridge University Press.

Fortescue, Michael
1981   Endoactive-exoactive Markers in Eskimo-Aleut, Tungus and Japanese: An Investigation into Common Origins. Pp. 5-42 in The Language of the Inuit: Historical, Phonological and Grammatical Issues. Louis-Jacques Dorais, ed. Études/Inuit/Studies 5. Suppl.

1983   Affixal-inflectional Interaction in West Greenlandic in the Light of the Western Dialects of Inuktitut and the Thule-Copper Connection. (Manuscript in Institut for Eskimologi, University of Copenhagen, Copenhagen.) In press.

1983a   A Comparative Manual of Affixes for the Inuit Dialects of Greenland, Canada and Alaska. Meddelelser om Grønland, Man & Society 4. Copenhagen.

Fortuine, Robert, comp.
1968   The Health of the Eskimos: A Bibliography 1857-1967. Hanover, N.H.: Dartmouth College Libraries.

1975   Health Care and the Alaska Native: Some Historical Perspectives. Polar Notes 14:1-42.

Foulks, Edward F.
1972   The Arctic Hysterias of the North Alaskan Eskimo. (Anthropological Studies 10) Washington: American Anthropological Association.

Fox, Luke
1635   North-west Fox or, Fox from the North-west Passage: Beginning with King Arthur, Malga, Octhvr, the Two Zeni's of Iseland, Estotiland, and Dorgia. London: B. Alsop and Thos. Fawcet. (Reprinted: Johnson Reprint, New York, 1965.)

Francis, Daniel
1979   Les Relations entre Indiens et Inuit dans l'est de la baie d'Hudson, 1700-1840. Études/Inuit/Studies 3(2):73-83.

Franklin, Sir John
1823   Narrative of a Journey to the Shores of the Polar Sea, in the Years 1819, 1820, 1821, and 1822. London: J. Murray.

1828   Narrative of a Second Expedition to the Shores of the Polar Sea, in the Years 1825, 1826, 1827. London: John Murray. (Reprinted: Hurtig, Edmonton, Alta., 1971.)

Fredskild, Bent
1967   Postglacial Plant Succession and Climatic Changes in a West Greenland Bog. Review of Paleobotany and Palynology 4:113-127.

1967a   Palaeobotanical Investigations at Sermermiut, Jakobshavn, West Greenland. Meddelelser om Grønland 178(4). Copenhagen.

1969   A Postglacial Standard Pollendiagram from Peary Land, North Greenland. Pollen et Spores 11(3):573-583.

1972   Palynological Evidence for Holocene Climatic Changes in Greenland. Pp. 277-306 in Climatic Changes in Arctic Areas During the Last Ten Thousand Years. Y. Vasari, H. Hyvarinen, and S. Hicks, eds. Acta Universitatis Ouluensis, ser. A., Geologica 1. Oulu, Finland.

1973   Studies in the Vegetational History of Greenland: Palaeobotanical Investigations of Some Holocene Lake and Bog Deposits. Meddelelser om Grønland 198(4). Copenhagen.

Freeman, Milton M.R.
1964   Observations on the Kayak-complex, Belcher Islands, N.W.T. Anthropological Series 62, National Museum of Canada Bulletin 194:56-91. Ottawa.

1967   An Ecological Study of Mobility and Settlement Patterns Among the Belcher Island Eskimo. Arctic 20(3):154-175.

1969   Adaptive Innovation Among Recent Eskimo Immigrants in the Eastern Canadian Arctic. Polar Record 14(93):796-781.

1969-1970   Studies in Maritime Hunting, I: Ecologic and Technologic Restraints on Walrus Hunting, Southampton Island, N.W.T. Folk 11-12:155-171. Copenhagen.

1969-1972   Patrons, Leaders and Values in an Eskimo Settlement. Pp. 113-124 in Symposium on The Contemporary Cultural Situation of the Northern Forest Indians of North America and the Eskimo of North America and Greenland. Vol. 3 of Proceedings of the 38th International Congress of Americanists. Stuttgart-München, 1968. 4 vols. München, Germany: Klaus Renner.

1970   Not by Bread Alone: Anthropological Perspectives on Optimum Population. Pp. 139-149 in The Optimum Population for Britain. L.R. Taylor, ed. London and New York: Academic Press.

1971   A Social and Ecological Analysis of Systematic Female Infanticide Among the Netsilik Eskimo. American Anthropologist 73(5):1011-1018.

1971a   The Significance of Demographic Changes Occurring in the Canadian East Arctic. Anthropologica n.s. 13(1-2):215-236. Ottawa.

1971b   Tolerance and Rejection of Patron Roles in an Eskimo Settlement. Pp. 34-54 in Patron and Brokers in the East Arctic. Robert Paine, ed. (Newfoundland Social and Economic Papers 2) St. John's: Memorial University of Newfoundland, Institute of Social and Economic Research.

1971c   Patrons, Leaders and Values in an Eskimo Settlement. Pp. 113-124 in Vol. 3 of Proceedings of the 38th International Congress of Americanists. 4 vols. Stuttgart-München, 1968. München, Germany: Klaus Renner.

1974-1975   Studies in Maritime Hunting, II: An Analysis of Walrus Hunting and Utilisation: Southampton Island, N.W.T., 1970. Folk 16-17:147-158. Copenhagen.

1976   Report: Inuit Land Use and Occupancy Project. 3 vols. Ottawa: Department of Indian and Northern Affairs.

Freuchen, Peter
1935   Arctic Adventure: My Life in the Frozen North. New York: Farrar and Rinehart.

1954   Thule Distrikt. Pp. 316-334 in Dette er Island Færøerne og Grønland [This is Iceland, the Faroe Islands and Greenland]. Niels Th. Mortensen, ed. Odense, Denmark: Arnkrone.

1961   Book of the Eskimos. Dagmar Freuchen, ed. Cleveland: World Publishing Company.

1962   Peter Freuchens bog om eskimoerne. [Peter Freuchen's Book on the Eskimos]. Copenhagen: Gyldendal.

Freuchen, Peter, and Finn Salomonsen
1960   The Arctic Year. London: Jonathan Cape.

Frey, D.G., and J.B. Stahl
1958   Measurements of Primary Production on Southampton Island in the Canadian Arctic. Limnology and Oceanography 3(2):215-221.

Fried, Jacob, ed.
1955   A Survey of the Aboriginal Populations of Quebec and Lab-rador. (*Eastern Canadian Anthropological Series* 1) Mon-treal: McGill University.

Fried, Morton H.
1967   On the Concepts of "Tribe" and "Tribal Society." Pp. 3-20 in Essays on the Problem of Tribe. June Helm, ed. (*Pro-ceedings of the 1967 Annual Meeting of the American Eth-nological Society*) Seattle: University of Washington Press.

Friis, Herman R.
1967   The Pacific Basin: A History of Geographical Exploration. (*Special Publication* 38) New York: American Geographical Society.

Frobisher, Sir Martin
1578   A True Discourse of the Late Voyages of Discovery for Find-ing of a Passage to Cathaya and India by the North West. London: no publisher. (Reprinted: The Three Voyages of Martin Frobisher...Works Issued by the Hakluyt Society, 1st ser. Vol. 38, London, 1867.)

From, Anders et al.
1975   Sociale Problemer i Grønland: Levevilkår og sociale prob-lemer i Vestgrønland. [Social Problems in Greenland: Living Conditions and Social Problems in West Greenland]. *So-cialforsknings Instituttet Publikation* 64. Copenhagen.

Fryer, A.C.
1954   Eskimo Rehabilitation Program at Craig Harbour. *Royal Ca-nadian Mounted Police Quarterly* 20(2):139-142. Ottawa.

Gabus, Jean
1943   Touctou; chez les hommes qui-vivent-loin-du-sel. Neuchâtel, Switzerland: Editions Victor Attinger.

[1944]   Iglous: Vie des Esquimaux-caribou; Mission ethnographique suisse à la Baie d'Hudson, 1938-1939. Neuchâtel, Switzer-land: Editions Victor Attinger.

1944a   Vie et coutumes des Esquimaux caribous. Paris: Payot.

Gad, Finn
1946   Grønlands Historie. En oversigt fra ca. 1500 til 1945 [History of Greenland: A Summary from ca. 1500 to 1945]. *Grøn-landske Selskabs Skrifter* 14. Copenhagen.

1964   Grønlands tilslutning til Norgesvældet 1261 [Greenland's Af-filiation with the Kingdom of Norway in 1261]. *Grønland* 7:259-272. Copenhagen.

1967-1976   Grønlands Historie. 3 vols. Copenhagen: Nyt Nordisk For-lag.

1971-1982   The History of Greenland. 3 vols. Montreal: McGill-Queen's University; Copenhagen: Nyt Nordisk Forlag.

1979   La Grönlande, les Isles de Ferröe et l'Islande non comprises: A New Look at the Origins of the Addition to Article IV of the Treaty of Kiel of 1814. *Scandinavian Journal of History* 4(3):187-205.

Gagné, Raymond C.
1961   Tentative Standard Orthography for Canadian Eskimos. Ot-tawa: Department of Northern Affairs and Natural Re-sources, Welfare Division.

Gagnon, Paul
1959   Reports on Villages: Kivalina, Noatak, Noorvik. Juneau: Alaska Rural Development Board. (Copies in the library of the Arctic Institute of North America, Montreal.)

Gal, Robert
1982   Excavation of the Tunalik Site, Northwestern National Pe-troleum Reserve in Alaska. *Anthropological Papers of the University of Alaska* 20(1-2):61-78. Fairbanks.

Gambell, Vene C.
1898   Notes With Regard to the St. Lawrence Island Eskimo. Pp. 141-144 in *8th Report on Introduction of Domestic Reindeer into Alaska, 1898.* Sheldon Jackson, comp. Washington: U.S. Government Printing Office.

Gamo, Masao
1964   Structural Principles of Alaskan Eskimo Bands. *Japanese Journal of Ethnology* 28(2):1-32. (Japanese with English ab-stract.)

1980   The Band Structure and Acculturation Among the Eskimos of Nelson Island, Southwestern Alaska. Pp. 157-167 in Alaska Native Culture and History. Y. Kotani and W.B. Workman, eds. *National Museum of Ethnology, Senri Ethnological Stud-ies* 4. Osaka, Japan.

Geist, Otto W., and Froelich G. Rainey
1936   Archaeological Excavation at Kukulik, St. Lawrence Island, Alaska: Preliminary Report. (*University of Alaska Miscel-laneous Publication* 2) Washington: U.S. Government Print-ing Office.

Geoghegan, Richard H.
1944   The Aleut Language, the Elements of Aleut Grammar, with a Dictionary in Two Parts Containing Basic Vocabularies of Aleut and English. Washington: U.S. Department of the Interior.

Gerlach, S. Craig
1982   Small Site Archaeology in Northern Alaska: The Shoreline Bluff Survey. *Anthropological Papers of the University of Alaska* 20(1-2):15-49. Fairbanks.

Gessain, Robert
1967   Angmagssalik, trente ans après. *Objets et Mondes* 7(2). Paris.

1968   Le Kayak des Ammassalimiut: Evolution démographique. *Objets et Mondes* 8(4):247-264. Paris

1969   Ammassalik ou la civilisation obligatoire. Paris: Flammarion.

Gessain, Robert, and Joëlle Robert-Lamblin, eds.
1975   Tradition et changement au Groenland oriental: Dix années d'enquêtes du Centre de Recherches Anthropologiques—Musée de l'Homme. *Objets et Mondes* 15(2):117-285. Paris.

Gessain, Robert, Louis-Jacques Dorais, and Catherine Enel
1982   Vocabulaire du groenlandais de l'est. *Musée de l'Homme. Documents du Centre de Recherches Antropologiques* 5. Paris.

Getches, David H.
1976   A Primer on Laws Important to Alaska Native Education. Fairbanks: University of Alaska, Center for Northern Edu-cational Research.

1977   Law and Alaska Native Education. Fairbanks: University of Alaska, Center for Northern Educational Research.

Giddings, James L., Jr.
1949   Early Flint Horizons on the North Bering Sea Coast. *Journal of the Washington Academy of Sciences* 39(3):85-90. Wash-ington.

1951   The Denbigh Flint Complex. *American Antiquity* 16(3):193-203.

1952   Observations on the "Eskimo Type" of Kinship and Social Structure. *Anthropological Papers of the University of Alaska* 1(1):5-10. College.

1952a   The Arctic Woodland Culture of the Kobuk River. *University of Pennsylvania, University Museum Monograph* 8. Phila-delphia.

1956   Forest Eskimos: An Ethnographic Sketch of the Kobuk River People in the 1880's. *University of Pennsylvania, Museum Bulletin* 20(2):1-55. Philadelphia.

1956a   A Flint Site in Northernmost Manitoba. *American Antiquity* 21(3):255-268.

1957   Round Houses in the Western Arctic. *American Antiquity* 23(2):121-135.

1960   The Archeology of Bering Strait. *Current Anthropology* 1(2):121-138.

1960a   First Traces of Man in the Arctic. *Natural History* 69(9):10-19.

1961   Kobuk River People. *University of Alaska, Studies of Northern Peoples* 1. College.

1961a   Cultural Continuities of Eskimos. *American Antiquity* 27(2):155-173.

1962   Seven Discoveries of Bering Strait. *Proceedings of the American Philosophical Society* 106(2):89-93. Philadelphia.

1964   The Archeology of Cape Denbigh. Providence, R.I.: Brown University Press.

1965   A Long Record of Eskimos and Indians at the Forest Edge. Pp. 189-205 in Context and Meaning in Cultural Anthropology. Melford E. Spiro, ed. New York: Free Press.

1967   Ancient Men of the Arctic. New York: Knopf.

Giddings, James L., Jr., and Donald D. Anderson
1984   Beach Ridge Archeology of Cape Krusenstern National Monument (Order No. 024-005-00797-1). Washington: U.S. Government Printing Office.

Gilberg, Aage
1948   Eskimo Doctor. Karin Elliott, trans. New York: W.W. Norton. [Original: Verdens nordligste læge, Steen Hasselbalchs Forlag, Copenhagen, 1940.]

Gilberg, Aage, Lisbet Gilberg, Rolf Gilberg, and Mogens Holm
1978   Polar Eskimo Genealogy. *Meddelelser om Grønland* 203(4). Copenhagen.

Gilberg, Rolf
1971   Polareskimoerne, Thule distriktet, Nordgrønland: Økologiske betragtninger over deres bosætning og demografi. [The Polar Eskimo, Thule District, North Greenland: Ecological Comments on Their Settlement and Demography.] (Unpublished Ph.D. Dissertation in Anthropology, University of Copenhagen, Copenhagen.)

1974-1975   Changes in the Life of the Polar Eskimos Resulting from a Canadian Immigration into the Thule District, North Greenland in the 1860's. *Folk* 16-17:159-170. Copenhagen.

1976   The Polar Eskimo Population Thule District, North Greenland. *Meddelelser om Grønland* 203(3). Copenhagen.

1976a   Thule. *Arctic* 29(2):83-86.

1977   En arktisk handelsstation i "Ingenmandsland." [An Arctic Tradingpost in "No-Man's-Land"]. *Grønland* 25(9-10):247-254. Copenhagen.

1980   Polareskimoerne—en grønlandsk minoritet. [Polar Eskimos—a Greenland Minority]. *Vår Verden* 3(2):16-18. Trondheim, Norway.

1982   Sjælen er det, som gør dig til et menneske [The Soul is What Makes You a Human Being]. *Grønland* 30(1-2):47-59. Copenhagen.

1983   INUHUIT/Polar-Eskimo: A Greenland Minority. Pp. 65-73 in Arctic Culture: The Greenland Eskimo-Reader 3. Rolf Gillberg, ed. Copenhagen: National Museum.

Gilder, William H.
1881   Schwatka's Search: Sledging in the Arctic in Quest of the Franklin Records. New York: Charles Scribner's Sons. (Reprinted: Abercrombie and Fitch, New York, 1966).

Gill, Don
1973   Floristics of a Plant Succession Sequence in the Mackenzie Delta, Northwest Territories. *Polarforschung* 43(1-2):55-65.

Glahn, Henrik C.
1771   Anmærkninger over de tre første bøger af Hr. David Crantzes Historie om Grønland [Remarks on the First Three volumes of Mr. David Crantz's History of Greenland]. Copenhagen: Gerhard Giese Salikath.

1921   Missionær i Grønland: Henrik Christopher Glahns dagbøger for aarene 1763-64, 1766-67 og 1767-68 [The Diaries of the Greenland Missionary Henry Christopher Glahn for the Years 1763-64, 1766-67, and 1767-68]. H. Ostermann, ed. *Grønlandske Selskabs Skrifter* 4. Copenhagen.

Glarborg, Kirsten
1962   Child Rearing in West Greenland. Pp. 106-120 in Child and Education: Proceedings of the Fourteenth International Congress of Applied Psychology, Copenhagen, 1962.

Glennan, William S.
1972   A Descriptive Report of Lithic Specimen from Kagati Lake, Southwest Alaska. (Paper read at the International Conference on Prehistory and Paleoecology of the Western North American Arctic and Subarctic. Peter Schledermann, ed. University of Calgary, Calgary, Alta.)

Glob, Peter V.
1935   Eskimo Settlements in Kempe Fjord and King Oscar Fjord. *Meddelelser om Grønland* 102(2). Copenhagen.

Glover, Richard
1969   Introduction: Andrew Graham, the Royal Society Collections and His 'Observations.' Pp. xiii-lxxii in Andrew Graham's Observations on Hudson's Bay, 1767-1791, by Andrew Graham. *Publications of the Hudson's Bay Record Society* 27. London.

Glushankov, I.V.
1969   Aleutskaía ékspedítsiía Krenítsyna i Levashova. *Priroda* 12:84-92. (Translation: The Aleutian Expedition of Krenitsyn and Levashov. Mary Sadouski and R.A. Pierce, trans. *The Alaska Journal* 3(4):204-210.)

Golder, Frank A.
1903   Tales from Kodiak Island. *Journal of American Folk-lore* 16(60):16-31.

1907   A Kodiak Island Story: The White-faced Bear. *Journal of American Folk-Lore* 20(79):269-299.

1909   Eskimo and Aleut Stories from Alaska. *Journal of American Folk-Lore* 22(83):10-24.

1914   Russian Expansion on the Pacific 1641-1850: An Account of the Earliest and Later Expeditions Made Under the Russians Along the Pacific Coast of Asia and North America, Including Some Related Expeditions to the Arctic Regions. Cleveland: Arthur H. Clark.

1922-1925   Bering's Voyages: An Account of the Efforts of the Russians to Determine the Relation of Asia and America. 2 vols. *American Geographical Society Research Series* 1-2. New York.

Goldschmidt, Verner
1955-1956   The Greenland Criminal Code and Its Sociological Background. *Acta Sociologica* 1:217-264.

1963   New Trends in Studies on Greenland Social Life: Criminal Law in Changing Greenland. *Folk* 5:113-121. Copenhagen.

Gordon, Andrew R.
1887   Report of the Hudson's Bay Expedition of 1886 Under the Command of Lieut. A.R. Gordon, R.N. Ottawa: Department of Marine and Fisheries.

Gordon, Bryan H.C.
1970   Arctic Yukon Coast: Including a Description of the British Mountain Complex at Trout Lake. Pp. 67-86 in Early Man and Environments in Northwest North America. R.A. Smith and J.W. Smith, eds. Calgary: University of Calgary Archaeological Association.

1975   Of Men and Herds in Barrenland Prehistory. *Canada. National Museum of Man. Mercury Series. Archeological Survey Paper* 28. Ottawa.

1976   Migod—8000 Years of Barrenland Prehistory. *Canada. National Museum of Man. Mercury Series. Archeological Survey Paper* 56. Ottawa.

Gordon, E.V., and A.R. Taylor
1957   An Introduction to Old Norse. Oxford, England: Clarendon Press.

Gordon, George B.
1906   Notes on the Western Eskimo. *Transactions of the Department of Archaeology, Free Museum of Science and Art*, 2(1):69-101. Philadelphia.

1917   In the Alaskan Wilderness. Philadelphia: John C. Winston.

Gormly, Mary
1977   Early Culture Contact on the Northwest Coast, 1774-1795: Analysis of Spanish Source Material. *Northwest Anthropological Research Notes* 11(1): 1-80. Moscow, Idaho.

Gosch, Christian C.A.
1897   Munk's Expedition to Hudson Bay. In Vol. 2 of Danish Arctic Expedition, 1605-1620. London: Printed for the Hakluyt Society.

Gosling, W.G.
1910   Labrador: Its Discovery, Exploration and Development. New York: John Lane.

Gough, Barry M., ed.
1973   To the Pacific and Arctic with Beechey: The Journal of Lieutenant George Peard of H.M.S. 'Blossom.' Cambridge, England: Cambridge University Press.

Government of Newfoundland and Labrador. Division of Northern Labrador Affairs.
1952-1957   Annual Reports. St. John's: Government of Newfoundland and Labrador, Department of Public Welfare.

Graah, Wilhelm A.
1832   Undersøgelses-reise til østkysten af Grønland efter kongelig Befaling udført i Aarene 1828-31. [Voyage of Exploration to the East Coast of Greenland by Order of the King Carried out in the Years 1828-31]. Kaj Birket-Smith, ed. Copenhagen: Gyldendal-Nordisk Forlag.

Grabowski, Henning
1973   Das Arbeitskräftepotential der NANA-Region, Alaska. *Polarforschung* 43(1-2):75-78.

1974   Probleme städtischen Wachstums im arktischen Alaska. *Polarforschung* 44(2):165-176.

Graburn, Nelson H.H.
1960   The Social Organization of an Eskimo Community: Sugluk, P.Q. (Unpublished M.A. Thesis in Anthropology, McGill University, Montreal.)

1963   Lake Harbour, Baffin Island: An Introduction to the Social and Economic Problems of a Small Eskimo Community. (*NCRC-63-2*) Ottawa: Department of Northern Affairs and National Resources, Northern Co-ordination and Research Centre.

1964   Taqagmiut Eskimo Kinship Terminology. (*NCRC-64-1*) Ottawa: Department of Northern Affairs and National Resources, Northern Co-ordination and Research Centre.

1969   Eskimos without Igloos: Social and Economic Development in Sugluk. Boston: Little, Brown.

1971   Traditional Economic Institutions and the Acculturation of the Canadian Eskimos. Pp. 107-121 in Studies in Economic Anthropology. *American Anthropological Association Studies* 7. Washington.

1972   Eskimos of Northern Canada. 2 vols. New Haven, Conn.: Human Relations Area Files.

1976   Eskimo Art: The Eastern Canadian Arctic. Pp. 39-55 in Ethnic and Tourist Arts: Cultural Expressions from the Fourth World. Nelson H.H. Graburn, ed. Berkeley: University of California Press.

1978   Commercial Inuit Art: A Vehicle for the Economic Development of the Eskimos of Canada. *Inter-Nord* 15:131-142. Paris.

1978a   Inuit pivalliajut: The Cultural and Identity Consequences of the Commercialization of Canadian Inuit Art. Pp. 185-200 in Consequences of Economic Change in Circumpolar Regions. L. Müller-Wille, P.J. Pelto, L. Müller-Wille, and R. Darnell, eds. *University of Alberta, Boreal Institute for Northern Studies Occasional Paper* 4. Edmonton.

1979   Indian-Eskimo Relations. *Arctic Anthropology* 16(2):184-195.

1982   Television and the Canadian Inuit. *Études/Inuit/Studies* 6(1):7-17.

Graham, Andrew
1969   Andrew Graham's Observations on Hudson's Bay 1767-91. Glyndwr Williams, ed. *Publications of the Hudson's Bay Record Society* 27. London.

Grainger, E.H.
1962   Zooplankton of Foxe Basin in the Canadian Arctic. *Journal of the Fisheries Research Board of Canada* 19(3):377-400. Ottawa.

Grant, J.C. Boileau
1929   Anthropometry of the Cree and Saulteaux Indians in Northeastern Manitoba. *Anthropological Series* 13, *National Museum of Canada Bulletin* 59. Ottawa.

1930   Anthropometry of the Chipewyan and Cree Indians of the Neighborhood of Lake Athabaska. *Anthropological Series* 14, *National Museum of Canada Bulletin* 64. Ottawa.

Gray, Asa, and Merritt Fernald
1950   Gray's Manual of Botany: A Handbook of the Flowering Plants and Ferns of the Central and Northeastern United States and Adjacent Canada. 8th ed. New York, Cincinnati, Boston, Atlanta, Dallas, and San Francisco: American Book Company.

Grayson, Donald K.
1969   The Tigalda Site: An Eastern Aleutian Midden. (Unpublished M.A. Thesis in Anthropology, University of Oregon, Eugene.)

Great Britain. Parliament. House of Commons. Sessional Papers
1852-1853   Further Correspondence and Proceedings Connected with the Arctic Expedition: Continuation of Arctic Papers, Session 1852. Vol. 60(82). London.

1854-1855   Further Papers Relative to the Recent Arctic Expeditions in Search of Sir John Franklin. Vol. 35(1898). London.

Great Britain. Privy Council. Judicial Committee
1927   In the Matter of the Boundary Between the Dominion of Canada and the Colony of Newfoundland in the Labrador Peninsula. 12 vols. London: W. Glowes and Sons.

Greely, A.W.
1886   Three Years of Active Service: An Account of the Lady Franklin Bay Expedition of 1881-84 and the Attainment of

the Farthest North. 2 vols. New York: Charles Scribner's Sons.

Green, Paul
1959　　I am Eskimo, Aknik my Name. With Abbe Abbot. Juneau: Alaska-Northwest Publishing Company.

Grekov, Vadim Ivanovich
1960　　Ocherki iz istorii russkikh geograficheskikh issledovaniĭ v 1725-1765 gg. [Essays from the History of Russian Geographical Explorations, 1725-1765]. Moscow: Izdatel'stvo Akademii Nauk SSSR.

Grenfell, Sir Wilfred et al.
1922　　Labrador, the Country and the People. New York: Macmillan.

Griffin, James B.
1953　　A Preliminary Statement on the Pottery from Cape Denbigh, Alaska. Pp. 40-42 in Asia and North America: Trans-Pacific Contacts. M.W. Smith, ed. *Memoirs of the Society for American Archaeology* 9. Salt Lake City.

————
1960　　Some Prehistoric Connections Between Siberia and America. *Science* 131(3403):801-812.

————
1962　　A Discussion of Prehistoric Similarities and Connections Between the Arctic and Temperate Zones of North America. Pp. 154-163 in Prehistoric Cultural Relations Between the Arctic and Temperate Zones of North America. J.M. Campbell, ed. *Arctic Institute of North America Technical Paper* 11. Montreal.

————
1969-1970　Northeast Asian and Northwestern American Ceramics. Pp. 327-330 in Vol. 3 of *Proceedings of the 8th International Congress of Anthropological and Ethnological Sciences*. Tokyo and Kyoto, 1968.

Griffin, James B., and Roscoe H. Wilmeth, Jr.
1964　　The Ceramic Complexes at Iyatayet. Appendix I. Pp. 271-303 in The Archeology of Cape Denbigh, by J.L. Giddings. Providence, R.I.: Brown University Press.

Griffiths, Helen M.
1971　　Arctic Handknitted: One Hundred Percent Qiviut. *Handweaver and Craftsman* 22(2):6-8, 38.

Griggs, Robert F.
1934　　The Edge of the Forest in Alaska and the Reasons for Its Position. *Ecology* 15(2):80-96.

Grinnell, Joseph
1901　　Gold Hunting in Alaska. Elizabeth Grinnell, ed. Elgin, Ill.: David C. Cook.

Grønland. Landsrådsvedtægt
1973　　Landsrådsvedtægt om ændringen i den grønlandske retskrivning 14. maj 1973 [Provincial Council Ordinance on the Changes in the Greenlandic Orthography, 14 May, 1973]. Copenhagen: Ministeriet for Grønland.

Grønlands Landsråds Forhandlinger Efterårssamling
1972　　Beretning til Landsrådet fra Landsrådets Sprog- og retningsudvalg [Report to the Provincial Council from the Provincial Council Committee on Language and Orthography]. Godthåb.

Grønlands Styrelse
1942-1944　Beretninger vedrørende Grønlands Styrelse. [Reports Concerning Greenland's Government]. Copenhagen.

Gubser, Nicholas J.
1965　　The Nunamiut Eskimo: Hunters of Caribou. New Haven, Conn.: Yale University Press.

Guemple, D. Lee
1965　　Saunik: Name Sharing as a Factor Governing Eskimo Kinship Terms. *Ethnology* 4(3):323-335.

————
1966　　Kinship Reckoning Among the Belcher Island Eskimos. (Unpublished Ph.D. Dissertation in Anthropology, University of Chicago, Chicago.)

————
1967　　The Pacalik Kayak of the Belcher Islands. *Anthropological Series* 70, *National Museum of Canada Bulletin* 204:124-163. Ottawa.

————
1969　　The Eskimo Ritual Sponsor: A Problem in the Fusion of Semantic Domains. *Ethnology* 8(4):468-483.

————, ed.
1972　　Alliance in Eskimo Society. *Proceedings of the American Ethnological Society for 1971*. Suppl. Seattle: University of Washington Press.

————
1972a　　Eskimo Band Organization and the "D P Camp Hypothesis." *Arctic Anthropology* 9(2):80-112.

————
1972b　　Kinship and Alliance in Belcher Island Eskimo Society. Pp. 56-78 in Alliance in Eskimo Society. L. Guemple, ed. *Proceedings of the American Ethnological Society for 1971*. Suppl. Seattle: University of Washington Press.

————
1979　　Inuit Adoption. *Canada. National Museum of Man. Mercury Series. Ethnology Service Paper* 47. Ottawa.

Guggenheim, Paul
1945　　Anthropological Campaign on Amchitka. *Scientific Monthly* 61(July):21-32.

Gulløv, Hans Christian
1979　　Home Rule in Greenland. *Études/Inuit/Studies* 3(1):131-142.

————
1982　　Migration et diffusion: Le peuplement inuit de l'ouest du Groënland a l'époque post-médiévale. *Études/Inuit/Studies* 6(2):3-20.

————
1982a　　Nuup Kommuneani Qangarnitsanik Eqqaassutit—INUIT—kulturip nunaqarfii/Fortidsminder i Nuuk kommune Inuitkulturens bopladser. [Monuments of the Past in Godthåb (Nuuk) District. Settlements of the Eskimo Culture]. Copenhagen: Kalaallit Nunaata katersugaasiviata Nationalmuseumillu naqaitertitaat/Grønlands Landsmuseum og Nationalmuseet.

————
1982b　　Eskimoens syn på europaeren—de såkaldte nordbodukker og andre tvivlsomme udskæringer, Tema: Nordboerne, I. [The Eskimo's View of the European—the so-called Norse Dolls and other Disputed Carvings, Theme: The Norse, I]. *Grønland* 5-7:226-234. Copenhagen.

Gulløv, Hans C., and Hans Kapel
1979　　Haabetz Colonie 1721-1728: A Historical-archaeological Investigation of the Danish-Norwegian Colonization of Greenland. *National Museum of Denmark Ethnographical Series* 16. Copenhagen.

————
1979-1980　Legend, History, and Archaeology: A Study of the Art of Eskimo Narratives. *Folk* 21-22:347-380. Copenhagen.

Gunther, Erna
1972　　Indian Life on the Northwest Coast of North America as Seen by the Early Explorers and Fur Traders During the Last Decades of the Eighteenth Century. Chicago: University of Chicago Press.

Gurvich, I.S., and L.A. Fainberg
1964　　Reply to C.C. Hughes' "Under Four Flags: Recent Culture Change Among the Eskimo." *Current Anthropology* 6(1):59-60.

[Gvozdev, Mikhail]
1851　　Pervyĭ pokhod russkikh k Amerikie 1732 goda [The First Expedition of Russians to America in 1732]. *Zapiski Gidrograficheskago Departamenta* 9:78-107.

Gzowski, Peter
1975　　A Northern Tragedy: How Lawrence Thrasher, a 16-Year Old Eskimo Died Trying to Be a Man. *Maclean's Magazine* (January): 33-36.

Haan, Lourens F.
1914   Beskrivelse af Straat Davids tilligemed sammes indvaaneres sæder skikkelse og vaner som ogsaa deres fiskefangst og andere handlinger [1720] [Description of Davis Strait Together with the Habits, Appearance and Customs of the Inhabitants as Well as Their Fishing and Other Means of Livelihood]. Louis Bobé, ed. *Det Grønlandske Selskab Aarskrift* 63-68. Copenhagen.

Hadleigh-West, Frederick *see* West, Frederick Hadleigh

Hadley, Martha E.
1969   The Alaskan Diary of a Pioneer Quaker Missionary. Dora, Fla.: Loren S. Hadley.

Hakluyt, Richard
1907-1910   Principal Navigations, Voyages, etc. of the English Nation [1589]. 8 vols. New York: E.P. Dutton.

1935   The Original Writings and Correspondence of the Two Richard Hakluyts. (Works Issued by the Hakluyt Society 2d ser. Nos. 76-77) 2 vols. London: Cambridge University Press.

1965   The Principal Navigations, Voiages and Discoveries of the English Nation [1589]. 2 vols. Cambridge, England: Cambridge University Press.

Hale, Lynn Zeitlin
1979   The NANA Region Environment: A Summary of Available Information. Anchorage: Arctic Environmental Information and Data Center.

1979a   Bibliography and Index of Information on the NANA Region. Anchorage: Arctic Environmental Information and Data Center.

Hall, Charles F.
1865   Arctic Researches and Life Among the Esquimaux: Being the Narrative of an Expedition in Search of Sir John Franklin, in the Years 1860, 1861, and 1862. New York: Harper.

1879   Narrative of the Second Arctic Expedition Made by Charles F. Hall: His Voyage to Repulse Bay, Sledge Journeys to the Straits of Fury and Hecla and to King William's Land, and Residence Among the Eskimos During the Years 1864-69. J.E. Nourse, ed. Washington: U.S. Government Printing Office.

Hall, Edwin S., Jr.
1969   Speculations on the Late Prehistory of the Kutchin Athapaskans. *Ethnohistory* 16(4):317-333.

1970   The Late Prehistoric/Early Historic Eskimo of Interior Northern Alaska: An Ethnoarcheological Approach? *Anthropological Papers of the University of Alaska* 15(1):1-11. College.

1971   Excavations of Tukuto Lake: The Late Prehistoric of Early Historic Eskimos of Interior Northwest Alaska. (Manuscript in Hall's possession.)

1971a   Kangiguksuk: A Cultural Reconstruction of a Sixteenth Century Eskimo Site in Northern Alaska. *Arctic Anthropology* 8(1):1-101.

1973   Archaeological Investigations in the Noatok River Valley, Summer 1973. (Manuscript at SUNY-College, Brockport, N.Y.)

1974   Archaeological Investigations in the Noatak River Valley, Summer, 1973. Pp. 460-523 in The Environment of the Noatak River Basin, Alaska. Stephen B. Young, ed. *Contributions from the Center for Northern Studies* 1.

1975   The Eskimo Storyteller: Folktales from Noatak, Alaska. Knoxville: University of Tennessee Press.

1975a   An Archaeological Survey of Interior Northwest Alaska. *Anthropological Papers of the University of Alaska* 17(2):13-30. Fairbanks.

1976   A Preliminary Analysis of House Types at Tukuto Lake, Northern Alaska. Pp. 98-134 in Contributions to Anthropology: The Interior Peoples of Northern Alaska. Edwin S. Hall, ed. Canada. *National Museum of Man. Mercury Series. Archaeological Survey Paper* 49. Ottawa.

1978   Technological Change in Northern Alaska. Pp. 209-229 in Archaeological Essays in Honor of Irving B. Rouse. R.C. Dunnell and Edwin S. Hall, Jr., eds. The Hague: Mouton.

Hall, Edwin S., Jr., and Robert Gal, eds.
1982   Archaeological Investigations by the U.S. Geological Survey and the Bureau of Land Management in the National Petroleum Reserve in Alaska: Introduction. *Anthropological Papers of the University of Alaska* 20(1-2):1-2. Fairbanks.

Hamelin, Louis-Edmond
1968   Types of Canadian Ecumene. Pp. 20-30 in Readings in Canadian Geography. Rev. ed. R.M. Irving, ed. Toronto: Holt, Rinehart and Winston of Canada.

Hammer, C.U., H.B. Clausen, W. Dansgaard, N. Gundestrup, S.J. Johnson, and N. Reeh
1978   Dating of Greenland Ice Cores by Flow Models, Isotopes, Volcanic Debris and Continental Dust. *Journal of Glaciology* 20(82):3-26.

Hammerich, Louis L.
1951   Kleinschmidt Centennial VI: Can Eskimo be Related to Indo-European? *International Journal of American Linguistics* 17(4):217-223.

1953   The Dialect of Nunivak. Pp. 110-113 in *Proceedings of the 30th International Congress of Americanists*. Cambridge, 1952.

1954   The Russian Stratum in Alaskan Eskimo. *Word* 10(4):401-428 (Suppl. to *Slavic World* 3).

1958   The Western Eskimo Dialects. Pp. 632-639 in *Proceedings of the 32d International Congress of Americanists*. Copenhagen, 1956.

1960   Some Linguistic Problems in the Arctic. Pp. 83-89 in The Circumpolar Conference in Copenhagen. Helge Larsen, ed. *Acta Arctica* 12. Copenhagen.

1976   The Eskimo Language. Pp. 43-80 in Papers on Eskimo and Aleut Linguistics. Eric P. Hamp, ed. Chicago: Chicago Linguistic Society.

Hamp, Eric P., ed.
1976   Papers on Eskimo and Aleut Linguistics. Chicago: Chicago Linguistic Society.

Hanbury, David T.
1904   Sport and Travel in the Northland of Canada. New York: Macmillan.

Hanrahan, John, and Peter Gruenstein
1977   Lost Frontier: The Marketing of Alaska. New York: W.W. Norton.

Hansen, Finn
1977   Den økonomiske aktivitet i Umanaq. Bly- og Zincminens etablering og første driftsår [Economic Activity in Uummannaq: The Establishment and First Year of Operation of the Lead and Zinc Mine]. Vedbæk, Denmark: Kragestedet.

Hansen, J.P. Hart
1976   Criminal Homicide in Greenland. Pp. 548-558 in Circumpolar Health. R.J. Shephard and S. Itoh, eds. Toronto: University of Toronto Press.

Hansen, Keld
1969-1970   The People of the Far North. *Folk* 11-12:97-108. Copenhagen.

————, ed.
1971   Grønlandske fangere fortæller [Greenlandic Hunters Relate]. Copenhagen: Nordiske Landes Bogforlag.

1974-1975   String Figures from West Greenland. *Folk* 16-17:213-226. Copenhagen.

1979   Legetøj i Grønland [Toys in Greenland]. Copenhagen: Nationalmuseet.

Hanson, Wayne C.
1965   Seasonal Cycle of 137Cs in Some Alaskan Natives and Animals. *Health Physics* 11:1401-1406.

1965a   Radioactivity Measured in Alaskan Natives, 1962-1964. *Science* 147(3658):620-621.

1967   Cesium-137 in Alaskan Lichens, Caribou, and Eskimos. *Health Physics* 13:383-389.

1969   Anaktuvuk Pass Village Census. Richland, Wash.: Battelle Memorial Institute.

Hanson, Wayne C., D.G. Watson, and R.W. Perkins
1967   Concentration and Retention of Fallout Radionuclides in Alaskan Arctic Ecosystems. Pp. 233-245 in *Proceedings of an International Symposium on Radioecological Concentration Processes*. Stockholm, 1966.

Hantzsch, Bernard A.
1977   My Life Among the Eskimos: Baffinland Journeys in the Years 1909 to 1911. Leslie H. Neatby, ed. and trans. (*Mawdsley Memoir Series* 3) Saskatoon: University of Saskatchewan.

Haraldson, S.S.R.
1976   Evaluation of Alaskan Native Health Service: Alternative Approaches to Meeting Basic Health Needs. Pp. 559-564 in Circumpolar Health. R.J. Shephard and S. Itoh, eds. Toronto: University of Toronto Press.

Harding, Lee
1974   Mackenzie Delta: Home of Abounding Life. *Canadian Geographical Journal* 88(5):4-13.

Hare, F. Kenneth
1970   The Tundra Climate. Pp. 32-38 in The Tundra Environment. *Transactions of the Royal Society of Canada* 4th ser. Vol. 8. Toronto.

Hare, F. Kenneth, and John E. Hay
1974   The Climate of Canada and Alaska. Pp. 49-192 in Climates of North America. R.A. Bryson and F.K. Hare, eds. Amsterdam: Elsevier.

Hare, F. Kenneth and Morley K. Thomas
1974   Climate Canada. Toronto: Wiley Publishers of Canada.

Harhoff, Frederik
1982   Det grønlandske hjemmestyres grund og grænser [Greenlandic Home Rule—Basis and Limits]. *Ugeskrift for Retsvaesen*: 101-115. Copenhagen.

Harington, C.R.
1968   Denning Habits of the Polar Bear (*Ursus maritimus* Phipps). *Canadian Wildlife Service Report Series* 5. Ottawa.

Harp, Elmer, Jr.
1951   An Archaeological Survey in the Strait of Belle Isle Area. *American Antiquity* 16(3):203-220.

1953   New World Affinities of Cape Dorset Eskimo Culture. *Anthropological Papers of the University of Alaska* 1(2):37-54. College.

1958   Prehistory in the Dismal Lake Area, N.W.T., Canada. *Arctic* 11(4):219-249.

1959   The Moffatt Archaeological Collection from the Dubawnt Country, Canada. *American Antiquity* 24(4):412-422.

1961   The Archaeology of the Lower and Middle Thelon, Northwest Territories. *Arctic Institute of North America Technical Paper* 8. Montreal.

1962   The Culture History of the Central Barren Grounds. Pp. 69-75 in Prehistoric Cultural Relations Between the Arctic and Temperate Zones of North America. John M. Campbell, ed. *Arctic Institute of North America Technical Paper* 11. Montreal.

1964   The Cultural Affinities of the Newfoundland Dorset Eskimo. *Anthropological Series* 67, *National Museum of Canada Bulletin* 200. Ottawa.

1964a   Evidence of Boreal Archaic Culture in Southern Labrador and Newfoundland. *Anthropological Series* 61, *National Museum of Canada Bulletin* 193(1):184-261. Ottawa.

1969-1970   Late Dorset Eskimo Art from Newfoundland. *Folk* 11-12:109-124. Copenhagen.

1974-1975   A Late Dorset Copper Amulet from Southeastern Hudson Bay. *Folk* 16-17:33-44. Copenhagen.

1976   Dorset Settlement Patterns in Newfoundland and Southeastern Hudson Bay. Pp. 119-138 in Eastern Arctic Prehistory: Paleoeskimo Problems. M. Maxwell, ed. *Memoirs of the Society for American Archeology* 31. Salt Lake City.

Harp, Elmer, Jr., and David R. Hughes
1968   Five Prehistoric Burials from Port aux Choix, Newfoundland. *Polar Notes: Occasional Publication of the Stefánsson Collection* 8:1-47. Hanover, N.H.

Harper, Francis
1964   Caribou Eskimos of the Upper Kazan River, Keewatin. *University of Kansas. Museum of Natural History Miscellaneous Publications* 36. Lawrence.

Harper, Kenn
1974   Some Aspects of the Grammar of the Eskimo Dialects of Cumberland Peninsula and North Baffin Island. *Canada. National Museum of Man. Mercury Series. Ethnology Service Paper* 15. Ottawa.

1979   Suffixes of the Eskimo Dialects of Cumberland Peninsula and North Baffin Island. *Canada. National Museum of Man. Mercury Series. Ethnology Service Paper* 54. Ottawa.

Harrington, John J., ed.
1867   The Esquimaux.... Published at Port Clarence, R.A. and Plover Bay, E.S. San Francisco: Turnbull and Smith Printers.

Harrington, Richard
1952   The Face of the Arctic: A Cameraman's Story in Words and Pictures of Five Journeys into the Far North. New York: H. Schumann.

Harrison, Gordon S.
1972   The Alaska Native Claims Settlement Act and Federal Indian Policy. Pp. 38-48 in Alaska and Japan: Perspectives of Past and Present. Tsugo Arai, ed. Anchorage: Alaska Methodist University.

1972a   The Alaska Native Claims Settlement Act, 1971. *Arctic* 25(3):232-233.

Harvey, Nancy
1978   Easement Logjam Broken After Months of Waiting. *Tundra Times*, March 8:3, 12.

Harvey, Ross M.
1975   Government in Transition. Pp. 8-12 in Annual Report of the Northwest Territories. Yellowknife: Government of the Northwest Territories.

Hatt, Gudmund
1914   Arktiske Skinddragter i Eurasien og Amerika: En Etno-
        grafisk Studie. Copenhagen: J.H. Schultz. (Translation: *Arc-
        tic Anthropology* 5(2):3-132, 1969.)

1916   Moccasins and Their Relation to Arctic Footwear. *Memoirs
        of the American Anthropological Association* 3(3):151-250.
        Lancaster, Pa.

1916a   Kyst- og indlandskultur i det arktiske. [Coastal and Inland
        Culture in the Arctic]. *Geografisk Tidsskrift* 23:284-290. Co-
        penhagen.

1969   Arctic Skin Clothing in Eurasia and America: An Ethno-
        graphic Study. Kirsten Taylor, trans. *Arctic Anthropology*
        5(2):3-132. (Originally: Arktiske skinddragter i Eurasien og
        Amerika, J.H. Schultz, Copenhagen, 1914).

Hattersley-Smith, G.
1963   Climatic Inferences from Firn Studies in Northern Ellesmere
        Land. *Geografiska Annaler* 45(2-3):139-151.

Hatting, Tove
1982   Nordboernes husdyr. Tema: Nordboerne, I [Domestic Ani-
        mals of the Norsemen. Theme: The Norse, I]. *Grønland* (5-
        7): 252-257. Copenhagen.

Haurwitz, Bernard
1975   Long Waves in the Polar Atmosphere. Pp. 175-180 in Climate
        of the Arctic. Gunter Weller and Sue Ann Bowling, eds.
        Fairbanks: University of Alaska Geophysical Institute.

Hauser, Michael
1975   Structure of Form in Polar Eskimo Drumsongs. *Proceedings
        of the 23d International Folk Music Council.* Pt. 1: Introduc-
        tion and Form-type.

1979   Om trommesangstraditionen blandt Inuit, særling i Grønland
        [On the Drum Song Tradition Among Inuits, Especially in
        Greenland]. *Grønland* 27(8):217-250. Copenhagen.

[1983] Traditional Music and Music Traditions in Greenland: An
        Annotated Bibliography. *Meddelelser om Grønland.* In press.

Haven, J.
1773   A Brief Account of the Dwelling Places of the Eskimaux to
        the North of Nagvack to Hudsons Strait, Their Situation and
        Subsistence. London: Archives of the Moravian Church.

Hawkes, Ernest W.
1913   The "Inviting-in" Feast of the Alaskan Eskimo. *Canada.
        Department of Mines, Geological Survey Memoir* 45, *An-
        thropological Series* 3. Ottawa.

1914   The Dance Festivals of the Alaskan Eskimo. *University of
        Pennsylvania. Museum. Anthropological Publications* 6(2):5-
        41. Philadelphia.

1916   The Labrador Eskimo. *Canada. Department of Mines. Geo-
        logical Survey Memoir* 91, *Anthropological Series* 14. Ottawa.

Hawkins, James E.
1956   The Kotzebue, Noatak-Kobuk Region: A Preliminary Eco-
        nomic Study. Juneau: Alaska Rural Development Board.

Hay, John E.
1969   Aspects of the Heat and Moisture Balance of Canada. (Un-
        published Ph.D. Dissertation in Geography, University of
        London, London.)

Hayes, Isaac I.
1860   An Arctic Boat Journey in Autumn of 1854. Boston: Brown,
        Taggard and Chase.

Healy, Michael A.
1887   Report of the Cruise of the Steamer 'Corwin'. Pp. 5-20 in
        Report of the Cruise of the Revenue Marine Steamer 'Cor-
        win' in the Arctic Ocean, 1885. Washington: U.S. Govern-
        ment Printing Office.

1889   Report of the Cruise of the Revenue Marine Steamer 'Cor-
        win' in the Arctic Ocean in the Year 1884. Washington: U.S.
        Government Printing Office.

Hearne, Samuel
1958   A Journey from Prince of Wales's Fort in Hudson's Bay to
        the Northern Ocean in the Years 1769, 1770, 1771, and 1772
        [1795]. Richard Glover, ed. New ed. Toronto: Macmillan.

Heathcote, Gary M.
1981   On Alekseyev on Eskimo Origins. *Current Anthropology*
        22(5):582-594.

1982   Exploratory Craniometry on Western Arctic Skeletal Groups.
        (Unpublished Ph.D. Dissertation in Anthropology, Univer-
        sity of Toronto, Toronto.)

Heinrich, Albert C.
[1955] A Survey of Kinship Forms and Terminologies Found Among
        the Inupiaq-speaking Peoples of Alaska. (Unpublished man-
        uscript in the University of Alaska Archives, College.)

1955a   An Outline of the Kinship System of the Bering Straits Es-
        kimos. (Unpublished M.A. Thesis in Education, University
        of Alaska, College.)

1960   Structural Features of Northwestern Alaskan Eskimo Kin-
        ship. *Southwestern Journal of Anthropology* 16(1):110-126.

1963   Eskimo-type Kinship and Eskimo Kinship: An Evaluation
        and a Provisional Model for Presenting Data Pertaining to
        Inupiaq Kinship Systems. (Unpublished Ph.D. Dissertation
        in Anthropology, University of Washington, Seattle.)

1963a   Personal Names, Social Structure, and Functional Integra-
        tion. *Montana State University, Anthropology and Sociology
        Paper* 27. Missoula.

1972   Divorce as an Alliance Mechanism Among Eskimos. Pp. 79-
        88 in Alliance in Eskimo Society. D.L. Guemple, ed. (*Pro-
        ceedings of the Annual Meeting of the American Ethnological
        Society for 1971, Suppl.*) Seattle: University of Washington
        Press.

Heizer, Robert F.
1943   Aconite Poison Whaling in Asia and America: An Aleutian
        Transfer to the New World. *Anthropological Papers* 24, *Bu-
        reau of American Ethnology Bulletin* 133:415-468. Washing-
        ton.

1947   Petroglyphs from Southwestern Kodiak Island, Alaska. *Pro-
        ceedings of the American Philosophical Society* 91 (3):284-
        293. Philadelphia.

1949   Pottery from the Southern Eskimo Region. *Proceedings of
        the American Philosophical Society* 93(1):48-56. Philadelphia.

1952   Notes on Koniag Material Culture. *Anthropological Papers
        of the University of Alaska* 1(1):11-24. College.

1952a   Incised Slate Figurines from Kodiak Island, Alaska. *Amer-
        ican Antiquity* 17(3):266.

1956   Archaeology of the Uyak Site Kodiak Island, Alaska. *Uni-
        versity of California Anthropological Records* 17(1). Berke-
        ley.

Helm, June
1968   The Nature of Dogrib Socioterritorial Groups. Pp. 118-125
        in Man the Hunter. Richard B. Lee and Irven DeVore, eds.
        Chicago: Aldine.

Helm, June, and David Damas
1963   The Contact-traditional All-Native Community of the Ca-
        nadian North: The Upper Mackenzie "Bush" Athapaskans
        and the Iglugligmiut. *Anthropologica* n.s. 5(1):9-21. Ottawa.

761

Henn, Winfield
1978   Archaeology on the Alaska Peninsula: The Ugashik Drain-
        age, 1973-1975. *Anthropological Papers of the University of
        Oregon* 14. Eugene.

Henry, Victor
1879   Grammaire comparée de trois langues hyperboréennes:
        Grönlandais, Tchiglerk, Aléoute. Pp. 405-509 in Vol. 2 of
        Proceedings of the 3d International Congress of Americanists.
        Brussels.

Hensley, Willie
1981   Success and Failures Leading to 1991. *Tundra Times*, Oct. 7.

Henson, Matthew A.
1912   A Negro Explorer at the North Pole. New York: Frederick
        A. Stokes.

Herbert, Wally
1981   Hunters of the Polar North: The Eskimos. Time-Life Books:
        Peoples of the Wild. Amsterdam: Elsevier.

Hertz, Ole
1968   Plant Utilization in a West Greenland Hunting Community.
        Folk 10:37-44. Copenhagen.

_____
1977   En økologisk undersøgelse af minedriftens virkninger for fan-
        gerne i Uvkusigssat. [An Ecological Inquiry into the Effects
        of Mining on the Whalers in Ukkusissat]. Vedbæk, Denmark:
        Kragestedet.

Hess, Bill
1982   No Political Boundaries Can Divide Inuit People: Rosing.
        Tundra Times April 21:5.

Hewes, Gordon W.
1947   Aboriginal Use of Fishery Resources in Northwestern North
        America. (Unpublished Ph.D. Dissertation in Anthropology,
        University of California, Berkeley.)

Hibben, Frank C.
1943   Evidence of Early Man in Alaska. *American Antiquity* 8(3):254-
        259.

Hickey, Clifford G.
1969   The Kayak Site: An Analysis in the Spatial Aspect of Culture
        as an Aid to Archaeological Inference. (Unpublished M.A.
        Thesis in Anthropology, Brown University, Providence, R.I.)

_____
1976   An Economic View of Adaptation. Pp. 235-298 in Contri-
        butions to Anthropology: The Interior Peoples of Northern
        Alaska. Edwin S. Hall Jr., ed. *National Museum of Man.
        Mercury Series. Archaeological Survey Paper* 49. Ottawa.

_____
1979   The Historic Beringian Trade Network: Its Nature and Origins.
        Pp. 411-434 in Thule Eskimo Culture: An Anthropological
        Retrospective. Allen P. McCartney, ed. *Canada. National
        Museum of Man. Mercury Series. Archaeological Survey Pa-
        per* 88. Ottawa.

Higgins, G.M.
1967   South Coast-Baffinland: An Area Economic Survey. Ottawa:
        Department of Indian Affairs and Northern Development,
        Industrial Division.

Hildes, J.A.
1960   Health Problems in the Arctic. *Canadian Medical Association
        Journal* 83 (December):1255-1257.

_____
1966   The Circumpolar People—Health and Physiological Adap-
        tations. Pp. 497-508 in The Biology of Human Adaptability.
        Paul T. Baker and J.S. Weiner, eds. Oxford, England: Clar-
        endon Press.

Hill, J., J. Haven, C. Drachard, and A. Schloezer
1765   [Journal von der Recognitions Reise auf der Küste von Lab-
        rador der Vier Brüder John Hill, Jens Haven, Chr. Drachard
        und A. Schloezer von London aus bis wieder dahin im Jahr
        1765.] (Manuscript in Moravian Mission, London.)

Himmelheber, Hans
1938   Eskimokünstler: Teilergebnisse einer ethnographischen Ex-
        pedition in Alaska von Juni 1936 bis April 1937. Stuttgart:
        Strecker and Schröder.

_____
1951   Der gefrorene Pfad: Mythen, Märchen und Legenden der
        Eskimo. 3d ed. Eisenach, Germany: Erich Röth.

Hinz, John
1944   Grammar and Vocabulary of the Eskimo Language, as Spo-
        ken by the Kuskokwim and Southwest Coast Eskimos of
        Alaska. Bethlehem, Penn.: The Moravian Church. (Re-
        printed in 1955.)

Hippler, Arthur E.
1969   Barrow and Kotzebue: An Exploratory Comparison of Ac-
        culturation and Education in Two Large Northwestern Alaska
        Villages. Minneapolis: University of Minnesota, Training
        Center for Community Programs.

_____
1969a   The Big Villages in Northwest Alaska: A Dimension in the
        Acculturation of the Alaskan Eskimo. College: University of
        Alaska, Institute of Social, Economic and Government Re-
        search.

_____
1970   From Village to Town: An Intermediate Step in the Accul-
        turation of Alaska Eskimos. Minneapolis: University of Min-
        nesota, Training Center for Community Programs.

_____
1970a   Eskimo Acculturation: A Selected, Annotated Bibliography
        of Alaskan and Other Eskimo Acculturation Studies. Col-
        lege: University of Alaska, Institute of Social, Economic and
        Government Research.

_____
1974   The North Alaska Eskimos: A Culture and Personality Per-
        spective. *American Ethnologist* 1(3):449-469.

Hippler, Arthur E., and Stephen Conn
1973   Northern Eskimo Law Ways and Their Relationships to Con-
        temporary Problems of "Bush Justice:" Some Preliminary
        Observations on Structure and Function. *University of Alaska,
        Institute of Social, Economic and Government Research, Oc-
        casional Paper* 10. Fairbanks.

_____
1974   The Changing Legal Culture of the North Alaska Eskimo.
        Ethos 2(2):171-188.

Hirsch, David I.
1954   Glottochronology and Eskimo and Eskimo-Aleut Prehistory.
        American Anthropologist 56(5):825-838.

Hoare, W.H.B.
1927   Report of Investigations Affecting Eskimo and Wild Life,
        District of Mackenzie, 1924-1925-1926. Ottawa: Department
        of the Interior.

Hobart, Charles W.
1970   Some Consequences of Residential Schooling of Eskimos in
        the Canadian Arctic. *Arctic Anthropology* 6(2):123-135.

_____
1976   Socio-economic Correlates of Mortality and Morbidity Among
        Inuit Infants. Pp. 452-461 in Circumpolar Health. R.J. Shep-
        hard and S. Itoh, eds. Toronto: University of Toronto Press.

Hobart, Charles W., and C.S. Brant
1966   Eskimo Education, Danish and Canadian: A Comparison.
        Canadian Review of Sociology and Anthropology 3(2):47-66.

Hobfoll, Stevan E., Robert Morgan, and Raymond Lehrman
1980   The Development of a Training Centre in an Eskimo Village.
        Community Development Journal 15(2):146-148.

Hodge, Frederick W., ed.
1907-1910   Handbook of American Indians North of Mexico. 2 vols.
        Bureau of American Ethnology Bulletin 30. Washington.

Hoegh, Erling
1973   The Historical Development of Political Institutions in
        Greenland. Pp. 371-390 in Le Peuple esquimau aujourd'hui
        et demain/The Eskimo People To-Day and To-Morrow. Jean

Malaurie, ed. (Fourth International Congress of the Fondation Française d'Études Nordiques) Paris, The Hague: Mouton.

Höhn, E. Otto
1963   Roderick MacFarlane of Anderson River and Fort. *The Beaver* (Winter):22-29.

Høygaard, Arne
1938   De hygieniske Forhold i Angmagssalik, Østgrønland. [The Public Health Conditions in Ammassalik, East Greenland]. *Det Grønlandske Selskab Aarsskrift* 79-93. Copenhagen.

Hoffman, David
1976   Inuit Land Use on the Barren Grounds: Supplementary Notes and Analysis. Pp. 69-84 in Vol. 2 of Report: Inuit Land Use and Occupancy Project. 3 vols. Milton M.R. Freeman, ed. Ottawa: Department of Indian and Northern Affairs.

Hoffman, Walter J.
1897   The Graphic Art of the Eskimos: Based Upon the Collections in the National Museum. Pp. 739-968 in *Annual Report of the United States National Museum for 1895*. Washington.

Holm, Gustav F.
1888   Ethnologisk skizze af Angmagsalikerne [Ethnological Sketch of the Ammassalik People]. *Meddelelser om Grønland* 10(2):43-182. Copenhagen.

1914   Ethnological Sketch of the Angmagsalik Eskimo. *Meddelelser om Grønland* 39. Copenhagen.

————, coll. and trans.
1957   Østergrønlandske sagn og fortællinger [East Greenland Legends and Tales]. William Thalbitzer, ed. *Det Grønlandske Selskabs Skrifter* 21. Copenhagen.

Holm, Gustav F., and Johan Petersen
1921   Angmagssalik District. Pp. 560-661 in Vol. 2 of Grønland i Tohundredaaret for Hans Egedes Landing. G.C. Amdrup, Louis Bobé, Ad. S. Jensen, and H.P. Steensby, eds. *Meddelelser om Grønland* 61. Copenhagen.

Holmberg, Heinrich J.
1856   Ethnographische Skizzen über die Völker des russischen Amerika. *Acta Societatis Scientiarum Fennicae* 4:281-421. Helsinki.

Holmes, C.E.
1971   The Prehistory of the Upper Koyukuk River Region in North-central Alaska. Pp. 326-400 in Final Report of the Archeological Survey and Excavation Along the Alyeska Pipeline Service Company Pipeline Route. John P. Cook, ed. (Manuscript in the Department of Anthropology, University of Alaska, College.)

Holtsmark, Anne, ed.
1952   Ari þorgilsson hinn Fróði Íslendingabók: Nordisk filologi tekster og lærebøger til universitets-bruk. A. tekster 5. Oslo.

Holtved, Erik
1943   The Eskimo Legend of Navaranâq: An Analytical Study. *Acta Arctica* 1. Copenhagen.

1944   Archaeological Investigations in the Thule District, I-II. *Meddelelser om Grønland* 141(1-2). Copenhagen.

1945   Har Nordboerne været i Thule Distriktet [Were the Norsemen in Thule District]? *Nationalmuseets Arbejdsmark*: 79-84. Copenhagen.

1950   Thule Distriktet [The Thule District]. Pp. 269-290 in Vol. 2 of Grønlands Bogen [The Book of Greenland]. Kaj Birket-Smith, Ernest Mentze, and M. Friis Møller, eds. 2 vols. Copenhagen: J.H. Schultz Forlag.

1951   The Polar Eskimos, Language and Folklore: Pt. I: Texts; Pt. II: Myths and Tales. *Meddelelser om Grønland* 152(1-2). Copenhagen.

1952   Remarks on the Polar Eskimo Dialect. *International Journal of American Linguistics* 18(1):20-24.

1954   Archaeological Investigations in the Thule District, III: Nûgdlît and Comer's Midden. *Meddelelser om Grønland* 146(3). Copenhagen.

————, ed.
1962   Otto Fabricius' Ethnographical Works. *Meddelelser om Grønland* 140(2). Copenhagen.

1963   Tôrnârssuk, an Eskimo Deity. *Folk* 5:157-172. Copenhagen.

1967   Contributions to Polar Eskimo Ethnography. *Meddelelser om Grønland* 182(2). Copenhagen.

1968   Eskimoisk religion [Eskimo Religion]. In Illustreret religionshistorie. J.P. Asmussen and J. Laessøe, eds. 3 vols. Copenhagen: Gad.

Honda, Katsuichi, and Takane Fujiki
1963   Kanada Eskimo; Text by Katsuichi Honda, photos by Takane Fujiki. Tokyo: Asahi Shimbun-sha.

Honigmann, John J.
1951   An Episode in the Administration of the Great Whale River Eskimo. *Human Organization* 10(2):5-14.

1962   Social Networks in Great Whale River: Notes on an Eskimo, Montagnais-Naskapi, and Euro-Canadian Community. *Anthropological Series* 54, *National Museum of Canada Bulletin* 178. Ottawa.

1972   Housing for New Arctic Towns. Pp. 228-244 in Technology and Social Change. H. Russell Bernard and Pertti J. Pelto, eds. New York: Macmillan.

1975   Five Northern Towns. *Anthropological Papers of the University of Alaska* 17(1):1-68. Fairbanks.

Honigmann, John J., and Irma Honigmann
1965   Eskimo Townsmen. Ottawa: Saint Paul University, Canadian Research Centre for Anthropology.

1970   Arctic Townsmen: Ethnic Backgrounds and Modernization. Ottawa: Saint Paul University, Canadian Research Centre for Anthropology.

Hooper, Calvin L.
1881   Report of the Cruise of the U.S. Revenue Steamer Corwin in the Arctic Ocean, November 1, 1880. Washington: U.S. Government Printing Office.

1884   Report of the Cruise of the U.S. Revenue Steamer Thomas Corwin, in the Arctic Ocean, 1881. Washington: U.S. Government Printing Office.

Hooper, William H.
1853   Ten Months Among the Tents of the Tuski with Incidents of an Arctic Boat Expedition in Search of Sir John Franklin as Far as the Mackenzie River, and Cape Bathurst. London: John Murray.

Hopkins, David M.
1967   The Cenozoic History of Beringia: A Synthesis. Pp. 451-484 in The Bering Land Bridge. David M. Hopkins, ed. Stanford, Calif.: Stanford University Press.

1972   The Paleogeography and Climatic History of Beringia During Late Cenozoic Time. *Inter-Nord* 12(December):121-150. Paris.

1979   Landscape and Climate of Beringia During Late Pleistocene and Holocene Time. Pp. 15-41 in The First Americans: Origins, Affinities, and Adaptations. W.S. Laughlin and A.B. Harper, eds. New York: Gustav Fisher.

763

Hovey, Edmund O.
1918   Child-life Among the Smith Sound Eskimos. *American Museum Journal* 18(5):360-371.

Hrdlička, Aleš
1910   Contributions to the Anthropology of Central and Smith Sound Eskimos. *Anthropological Papers of the American Museum of Natural History* 5(2). New York.

————
1930   Anthropological Survey in Alaska. Pp. 19-347 in *46th Annual Report of the Bureau of American Ethnology for the Years 1928-1929.* Washington.

————
1941   Diseases of and Artifacts on Skulls and Bones from Kodiak Island. *Smithsonian Miscellaneous Collection* 101(4). Washington.

————
1941a   Artifacts on Human and Seal Skulls from Kodiak Island. *American Journal of Physical Anthropology* 28(4):411-421.

————
1943   Alaska Diary, 1926-1931. Lancaster, Pa.: Jacques Cattell.

————
1944   The Anthropology of Kodiak Island. Philadelphia: The Wistar Institute of Anatomy and Biology.

————
1945   The Aleutian and Commander Islands and Their Inhabitants. Philadelphia: The Wistar Institute of Anatomy and Biology.

Hudson's Bay Company
1718-1721   [Fort Churchill Post Journal.] (Manuscript B. 42/a/1 in Hudson's Bay Company Archives, Provincial Archives of Manitoba, Winnipeg, Canada.)

————
1724-1725   [Fort Churchill Post Journal.] (Manuscript B. 42/a/5 in Hudson's Bay Company Archives, Provincial Archives of Manitoba, Winnipeg, Canada.)

————
1756   [Fort Churchill Post Journal.] (Manuscript B.42/a/47 in Hudson's Bay Company Archives, Provincial Archives of Manitoba, Winnipeg, Canada.)

————
1764-1765   [Fort Churchill Post Journal.] (Manuscript B.42/a/62 in Hudson's Bay Company Archives, Provincial Archives of Manitoba, Winnipeg, Canada.)

Hughes, Charles C.
1958   An Eskimo Deviant from the "Eskimo" Type of Social Organization. *American Anthropologist* 60(6):1140-1147.

————
1960   An Eskimo Village in the Modern World. Ithaca, N.Y.: Cornell University Press.

————
1964   The Eskimos from The Peoples of Siberia. *Anthropological Papers of the Univeristy of Alaska* 12(1):1-13. College.

————
1965   Under Four Flags: Recent Culture Change Among the Eskimos. *Current Anthropology* 6(1):3-69.

————
1966   From Contest to Council: Social Change Among the St. Lawrence Island Eskimos. Pp. 255-263 in Political Anthropology. Marc J. Swartz, Victor W. Turner, and Arthur Tuden, eds. Chicago: Aldine.

————
1968   Structure, Field, and Process in Siberian Eskimo Political Behavior. Pp. 163-189 in Local-level Politics. Marc J. Swartz, ed. Chicago: Aldine.

————, ed.
1975   Eskimo Boyhood: An Autobiography in Psychosocial Perspective. Lexington: University Press of Kentucky.

————
1977   [Fieldnotes from Trip to St. Lawrence Island.] (Unpublished manuscript in Hughes's possession.)

Hughes, Charles C., and Jane M. Hughes
1954-1955   (Fieldnotes on Sociocultural Study of Gambell Village, St. Lawrence Island.) (Manuscript in C.C. Hughes' possession.)

Hughes, Jane Murphy
1960   An Epidemiological Study of Psychopathology in an Eskimo Village. (Unpublished Ph.D. Dissertation in Anthropology, Cornell University, Ithaca, N.Y.)

Hulley, Clarence C.
1970   Alaska: Past and Present. 3d ed. Portland, Oreg.: Binfords and Mort.

Hultén, Eric
1982   Flora of Alaska and Neighboring Territories: A Manual of the Vascular Plants. Stanford, Calif.: Stanford University Press.

Humphrey, Robert L.
1966   The Prehistory of the Utukok River Region, Arctic Alaska: Early Fluted Point Tradition with Old World Relationships. *Current Anthropology* 7(5):586-588.

Hunter, J.G.
1971   Fisheries Research Board Studies in Canada's Arctic. *Canadian Geographical Journal* 82(3):100-107.

Hurlich, M.G., and A.T. Steegmann, Jr.
1979   Hand Immersion in Cold Water at 5°C in Sub-Arctic Algonkian Indian Males from Two Villages: A European Admixture Effect? *Human Biology* 51(3):255-278.

Hurt, Wesley R., Jr.
1950   Artifacts from Shemya, Aleutian Islands. *American Antiquity* 16(1):68-69.

Hutton, Samuel K.
1912   Among the Eskimos of Labrador: A Record of Five Years' Close Intercourse with the Eskimo Tribes of Labrador. London: Seeley, Service.

————
1929   An Eskimo Village. London: Society for Promoting Christian Knowledge; New York: Macmillan.

Hylander, William L.
1977   The Adaptive Significance of Eskimo Craniofacial Morphology. Pp. 129-169 in Oro-Facial Growth and Development. A.A. Dahlberg and T.M. Grober, eds. The Hague: Mouton.

Iglauer, Edith
1966   The New People: The Eskimo's Journey into Our Time. New York: Doubleday.

Ingstad, Anne Stine
1977   The Discovery of a Norse Settlement in America: Excavations at L'Anse aux Meadows, Newfoundland, 1961-1968. Oslo: Universitets-forlaget.

Ingstad, Helge M.
1954   Nunamiut: Among Alaska's Inland Eskimos. F.H. Lyon, trans. London: Allen and Unwin.

————
1959   Landet under leidarstjernen: En ferd til Grønlands norrøne bygder [Land Under the North Star: A Journey to the Norse Settlements of Greenland]. Oslo: Gyldendal.

————
1966   Westward to Vinland: The Discovery of pre-Columbian Norse House-sites in North America. Erik J. Friis, trans. Toronto: Macmillan of Canada.

————
1966a   Land Under Pole Star: A Voyage to the Norse Settlements of Greenland and the Saga of the People that Vanished. Naomi Walford, trans. New York: St. Martin's Press.

————
1966b   Vejen til Vinland [The Way to Vinland]. Copenhagen: Fremad. (Translation: Westward to Vinland, St. Martin's Press, New York, 1969).

Inuit Tapirisat of Canada
1980   ITC News. April 1980:3-4. Ottawa.

Iokhel´son, Vladimir Il´ich
1919   Aleutskiĭ iazyk v osvi͡eshchenii grammatiki Veniaminova. [The Aleut Language in the Light of Veniaminov's Grammar].

Bulletin of the Imperial Academy of Sciences 13:133-154, 287-315. St. Petersburg.

1925 Archaeological Investigations in the Aleutian Islands. *Carnegie Institution of Washington Publication* 367. Washington.

1933 History, Ethnology and Anthropology of the Aleut. *Carnegie Institution of Washington Publication* 432. Washington.

Irving, Lawrence
1953 The Naming of Birds by Nunamiut Eskimo. *Arctic* 6(1):35-43.

1958 On the Naming of Birds by Eskimos. *Anthropological Papers of the University of Alaska* 6(2):61-77. College.

1960 Birds of Anaktuvuk Pass, Kobuk and Old Crow: A Study in Arctic Adaptation. *United States National Museum Bulletin* 217. Washington.

Irving, Lawrence, and Simon Paneak
1954 Biological Reconnaissance Along the Ahlasuruk River East of Howard Pass, Brooks Range, Alaska, with Notes on the Avifauna. *Journal of the Washington Academy of Sciences* 44(7):201-211. Washington.

Irving, William N.
1951 Archaeology in the Brooks Range of Alaska. *American Antiquity* 17(1):52.

1953 Evidence of Early Tundra Cultures in Northern Alaska. *Anthropological Papers of the University of Alaska* 1(2):55-85. College.

1955 Burins from Central Alaska. *American Antiquity* 20(4):380-383.

1957 An Archeological Survey of the Susitna Valley. *Anthropological Papers of the University of Alaska* 6(1):37-52. College.

1962 1961 Field Work in the Western Brooks Range, Alaska: Preliminary Report. *Arctic Anthropology* 1(1):76-83.

1962a A Provisional Comparison of Some Alaskan and Asian Stone Industries. Pp. 55-68 in Prehistoric Cultural Relations Between the Arctic and Temperate Zones of North America. J.M. Campbell, ed. *Arctic Institute of North America Technical Paper* 11. Montreal.

1964 Punyik Point and the Arctic Small Tool Tradition. (Unpublished Ph.D. Dissertation in Anthropology, University of Wisconsin, Madison.)

1968 Prehistory of Hudson Bay: The Barren Grounds. Pp. 26-54 in Science, History and Hudson Bay. C.S. Beals, ed. Ottawa: Department of Energy, Mines and Resources.

1969-1970 The Arctic Small Tool Tradition. Pp. 340-342 in Vol. 3 of *Proceedings of the 8th International Congress of Anthropological and Ethnological Sciences.* 3 vols. Tokyo and Kyoto, 1968.

Irving, William N., and C.R. Harington
1973 Upper Pleistocene Radiocarbon-dated Artifacts from the Northern Yukon. *Science* 179(4071):335-340.

Isham, James
1949 James Isham's Observations on Hudson's Bay, 1743 and Notes and Observations on a Book Entitled: A Voyage to Hudsons Bay in the Dobbs Galley, 1749. E.E. Rich, ed. Toronto: The Champlain Society.

Israel, Heinz
1969 Kulturwandel grönländischer Eskimo im 18. Jahrhundert: Wandlungen in Gesellschaft und Wirtschaft unter dem Einfluss der Herrnhuter Brüdermission. *Abhandlungen und Berichte des Staatlichen Museums für Völkerkunde Dresden* 29.

Itoh, Shinji
1980 Physiology of Circumpolar People. Pp. 285-303 in The Human Biology of Circumpolar Populations. F.A. Milan, ed. Cambridge and London: Cambridge University Press.

Ivanov, S.V.
1930 Aleut Hunting Headgear and Its Ornamentation. Pp. 477-504 in *Proceedings of the 23d International Congress of Americanists.* New York, 1928.

Iversen, Johanes
1934 Moorgeologische Untersuchungen auf Grönland. *Meddelelser fra Dansk Geologisk Forening* 8(4):341-358. Copenhagen.

1952-1953 Origin of the Flora of Western Greenland in the Light of Pollen Analysis. *Oikos* 4(2):85-103. Copenhagen.

JR = Thwaites, Reuben G., ed.
1896-1901 The Jesuit Relations and Allied Documents: Travel and Explorations of the Jesuit Missionaries in New France, 1610-1791. The Original French, Latin, and Italian Texts, with English Translations and Notes. 73 vols. Cleveland: Burrows Brothers. (Reprinted: Pageant, New York, 1959.)

Jackson, Sheldon
1895 Report on Introduction of Domestic Reindeer into Alaska. *53d Congress, 3d sess., Sen. Executive Document* No. 92 (Serial No. 3280). Washington: U.S. Government Printing Office.

1897 Report on Introduction of Domesticated Reindeer into Alaska, 1896. Washington: U.S. Government Printing Office.

1904 Fourteenth Annual Report on the Introduction of Domesticated Reindeer into Alaska. Washington: U.S. Government Printing Office.

Jacobi, A.
1937 Carl Heinrich Mercks ethnographische Beobachtungen über die Völker des Beringmeers, 1789-91. *Baessler-Archiv* 20(3-4):114-137. Berlin.

Jacobsen, Johan Adrian
1884 Capitain Jacobsen's Reise an der Nordwestküste Amerikas, 1881-1883, zum Zwecke ethnologischer Sammlungen und Erkundigungen, nebst Beschreibung persönlicher Erlebnisse, für den deutschen Leserkreis. A. Woldt, ed. Leipzig, Germany: M. Spohr.

1977 Alaskan Voyage, 1881-1883: An Expedition to the Northwest Coast of America. Erna Gunther, trans. Chicago: University of Chicago Press.

Jacobsen, N. Kingo, Chr. Bay, B. Fredskild, B. Grønnow, B. Holm Jacobsen, M. Meldgaard, N. Gylling Mortensen, and N. Thingvad
1980 Report of Activities at Tugtuligssuaq, Melville Bugt, 1978-79. *Geografisk Tidsskrift* 80:29-44. Copenhagen.

Jacobson, Steven A.
1977 A Grammatical Sketch of Siberian Yupik Eskimo, as Spoken on St. Lawrence Island, Alaska. Fairbanks: University of Alaska, Native Language Center.

1979 Report on Nunivak Dialect and Orthography Problems. (Manuscript in Alaska Native Language Center, University of Alaska, Fairbanks.)

1980 Report on Norton Sound Yup'ik. (Manuscript in Alaska Native Language Center, University of Alaska, Fairbanks.)

1983 [Central Alaskan Yupik Dictionary, with Postbase Dictionary, Inflectional Tables, English to Yupik Index, Dialect Survey, and Linguistic Introduction.] Fairbanks: University of Alaska, Native Language Center. In press.

[1984] [St. Lawrence Island Central Siberian Yupik Dictionary.] Fairbanks: University of Alaska, Native Language Center. In press.

James, James A.

1942 The First Scientific Exploration of Russian America and the Purchase of Alaska. *Northwestern University Studies in the Social Sciences* 4. Evanston, Ill.

Jamison, Paul L.

1978 Anthropometric Variation. Pp. 40-78 in Eskimos of Northwestern Alaska. A Biological Perspective. Paul L. Jamison, Stephen L. Zegura, and Frederick A. Milan, eds. Stroudsburg, Pa.: Dowden, Hutchinson and Ross.

Jamison, Paul L., and Stephen L. Zegura

1974 A Univariate and Multivariate Examination of Measurement Error in Anthropometry. *American Journal of Physical Anthropology* 40(2):197-203.

Jansen, Henrik M.

1972 A Critical Account of the Written and Archaeological Sources' Evidence Concerning the Norse Settlements in Greenland. *Meddelelser om Grønland* 182(4). Copenhagen.

Jarvis, D.H.

1899 Report of First Lieutenant D.H. Jarvis. Pp. 28-114 in Report of the Cruise of the U.S. Revenue Cutter 'Bear' and the Overland Expedition for the Relief of the Whalers in the Arctic Ocean from November 27, 1897 to September 13, 1898. Washington: U.S. Government Printing Office.

Jayewardene, C.H.S.

1975 Violence Among the Eskimos. *Canadian Journal of Criminology and Corrections* 17(4):307-314.

Jefferys, Thomas

1768 The Great Probability of a Northwest Passage... Containing the Account of a Discovery of Part of the Coast and Inland Country of Labrador, Made in 1753. London: Printed for the Author.

Jenness, Diamond

1921 The Cultural Transformation of the Copper Eskimo. *Geographical Review* 11(4):541-550.

1922 The Life of the Copper Eskimos. *Report of the Canadian Arctic Expedition, 1913-18*. Vol. 12(A). Ottawa.

1923 The Copper Eskimos: Physical Characteristics of the Copper Eskimos. *Report of the Canadian Arctic Expedition 1913-18*. Vol. 12(B). Ottawa.

1923a Origin of the Copper Eskimos and Their Copper Culture. *Geographical Review* 13(4):540-551. New York.

1923b The Copper Eskimos: Osteology of the Western and Copper Eskimos. (Including a Special Report Upon the Dentition, by S.G. Ritchie and J. Stanley Bagnall.) *Report of the Canadian Arctic Expedition 1913-18*. Vol. 12(G). Ottawa.

1924 Eskimo String Figures. *Report of the Canadian Arctic Expedition 1913-18*. Vol. 13(B). Ottawa.

1924a Myths and Traditions from Northern Alaska, the Mackenzie Delta, and Coronation Gulf. *Report of the Canadian Arctic Expedition 1913-18*. Vol. 13(A). Ottawa.

1925 A New Eskimo Culture in Hudson Bay. *Geographical Review* 15(3):428-437. New York.

1927 Notes on the Phonology of the Eskimo Dialect of Cape Prince of Wales, Alaska. *International Journal of American Linguistics* 4(2-4):168-180.

1928 Comparative Vocabulary of the Western Eskimo Dialects. *Report of the Canadian Arctic Expedition 1913-18*. Vol. 15(A). Ottawa.

1928a The People of the Twilight. New York: Macmillan.

1928b Eskimo Language and Technology. In Comparative Vocabulary of the Western Eskimo Dialects. *Report of the Canadian Arctic Expedition 1913-18*. Vol. 15(A). Ottawa.

1928c Archaeological Investigations in Bering Strait, 1926. *Annual Report of the National Museum of Canada for the Fiscal Year 1926, Bulletin* 50:71-80. Ottawa.

1933 The Problem of the Eskimo. Pp. 373-396 in The American Aborigines: Their Origin and Antiquity. D. Jenness, ed. Toronto: University of Toronto Press.

1940 Prehistoric Culture Waves from Asia to America. *Journal of the Washington Academy of Sciences* 30(1):1-15. Washington.

1941 An Archaeological Collection from the Belcher Islands in Hudson Bay. *Annals of the Carnegie Museum* 28(11):189-206. Pittsburgh, Pa.

1944 Grammatical Notes on Some Western Eskimo Dialects. *Report of the Canadian Arctic Expedition, 1913-18*. Vol. 15(B). Ottawa.

1946 Material Culture of the Copper Eskimos. *Report of the Canadian Arctic Expedition 1913-18*. Vol. 16. Ottawa.

1952 Stray Notes on the Eskimo of Arctic Alaska. *Anthropological Papers of the University of Alaska* 1(2):5-13. College.

1952a Discussion of Helge Larsen's The Ipiutak Culture: Its Origin and Relationships. Pp. 30-34 in Vol. 3 of *Selected Papers of the 29th International Congress of Americanists*. Sol Tax, ed. Chicago: University of Chicago Press.

1957 Dawn in Arctic Alaska. Minneapolis: University of Minnesota Press.

1962 Eskimo Administration, I: Alaska. *Arctic Institute of North America Technical Paper* 10. Montreal.

1964 Eskimo Administration, II: Canada. *Arctic Institute of North America Technical Paper* 14. Montreal. (Reprinted in 1972.)

1965 Eskimo Administration, III: Labrador. *Arctic Institute of North America Technical Paper* 16. Montreal.

1967 Eskimo Administration, IV: Greenland. *Arctic Institute of North America Technical Paper* 19. Montreal.

1968 Eskimo Administration, V: Analysis and Reflections. *Arctic Institute of North America Technical Paper* 21. Montreal.

Jensen, Bent

1961 Folkways of Greenland Dogkeeping. *Folk* 3:43-66. Copenhagen.

1969-1970 Development Policy and Greenland Man: Field Studies, Impressions and Points of View. *Folk* 11-12:287-307. Copenhagen.

1973 Human Reciprocity: An Arctic Exemplification. *American Journal of Orthopsychiatry* 43(3):447-458.

Jensen, P. Scavenius

1975 Den grønlandske kajak og dens redskaber [The Greenland Kayak and Its Equipment]. Copenhagen: Nyt Nordisk Forlag Arnold Busck.

Jochelson, Waldemar *see* Iokhel´son, Vladimir Il´ich

Jørgensen, Jørgen B.

1953 The Eskimo Skeleton: Contributions to the Physical Anthropology of the Aboriginal Greenlanders. *Meddelelser om Grønland* 146(2). Copenhagen.

1975 Befolkningen [The Population]. Pp. 149-151 in Julianehåb 1775-1975. Mimeo.

Johnson, Albert W., Leslie A. Viereck, Ross E. Johnson, and Herbert Melchior
1966 Vegetation and Flora. Pp. 277-354 in Environment of the Cape Thompson Region, Alaska. Norman J. Wilimovsky and John N. Wolfe, eds. Washington: U.S. Atomic Energy Commission.

Johnson, D. McI.
1933 Observations on the Eskimo Remains on the East Coast of Greenland Between 72° and 75° North Latitude. *Meddelelser om Grønland* 92(6). Copenhagen.

Johnson, Philip L.
1969 Arctic Plants, Ecosystems and Strategies. *Arctic* 22(3):341-355.

Johnson, Philip R., and Charles W. Hartman
1969 Environmental Atlas of Alaska. College: University of Alaska, Institute of Environmental Engineering and Institute of Water Resources.

Johnson, William D.
1962 An Exploratory Study of Ethnic Relations at Great Whale River. (*NCRC-62-7*) Ottawa: Department of Northern Affairs and National Resources, Northern Co-ordination and Research Centre.

Johnston, Thomas F.
1974 Eight North Alaskan Eskimo Dance-songs. *Tennessee Folklore Society Bulletin* 40(4):123-136.

1975 Alaskan Eskimo Dance in Cultural Context. *Dance Research Journal* 7(2):1-11.

1976 Eskimo Music by Region: A Comparative Circumpolar Study. *Canada. National Museum of Man. Mercury Series. Ethnology Service Paper* 32. Ottawa.

1976a The Eskimo Songs of Northwestern Alaska. *Arctic* 29(1):7-19.

1976b The Social Background of Eskimo Music in Northwest Alaska. *Journal of American Folklore* 89(354):438-448.

1977 Differential Cultural Persistence in Inuit Musical Behavior, and Its Geographic Distribution. *Études/Inuit/Studies* 1(2):57-72.

1978 Alaskan Eskimo Musical Revitalization. *Proceedings of the 42d International Congress of Americanists* 5: 247-254. Paris, 1976.

Jolliet, Louis
1694 Journal de Louis Jolliet allant à la descouverte de Labrador (Manuscript in Archives du Service Hydrographique, Paris; Printed: *Rapport de l'Archiviste de la Province de Québec pour 1943-44.*)

Jones, Dorothy C.
1970 Changes in Population Structure in the Aleutian Islands. *University of Alaska, Institute of Social, Economic, and Government Research, Research Note* A-2. Fairbanks.

Jones, Dorothy K.
1980 A Century of Servitude: Pribilof Aleuts Under U.S. Rule. Lanham, Md.: University Press of America.

Jones, Dorothy M.
1969 A Study of Social and Economic Problems in Unalaska: An Aleut Village. (Unpublished Ph.D. Dissertation in Anthropology, University of California, Berkeley.)

1972 Contemporary Aleut Material Culture. Pp. 7-19 in Modern Alaska Native Material Culture. Wendell H. Oswalt, ed. Fairbanks: University of Alaska Museum.

1973 Patterns of Village Growth and Decline in the Aleutians. *University of Alaska, Institute of Social, Economic, and Government Research, Occasional Paper* 11. Fairbanks.

1973a Race Relations in an Alaska Native Village. *Anthropologica* n.s. 15(2):167-190. Ottawa.

1976 Aleuts in Transition: A Comparison of Two Villages. Seattle: University of Washington Press.

Jones, Gwyn
1964 The Norse Atlantic Saga: Being the Norse Voyages of Discovery and Settlement to Iceland, Greenland, and America. New York: Oxford University Press.

Jones, Richard S.
1972 Alaska Native Claims Settlement Act of 1971 (Public Law 92-203): History and Analysis. Washington: Library of Congress, Congressional Research Service.

Jónsson, Finnur, ed.
1932 Flóamannasaga. Published by Samfund til udgivelse af gammel nordisk litteratur. Copenhagen: H. Jørgensen.

Joppien, Rüdiger
1978 John Webber's South Sea Drawings for the Admiralty: A Newly Discovered Catalogue Among the Papers of Sir Joseph Banks. *The British Library Journal* 4(1):49-77. London.

Jordan, Richard H.
1977 Inuit Occupation of the Central Labrador Coast Since 1600 A.D. Pp. 43-48 in our Footprints Are Everywhere. C. Brice-Bennett, ed. Nain: Labrador Inuit Association.

1978 Archaeological Investigations of the Hamilton Inlet Labrador Eskimo: Social and Economic Responses to European Contact. *Arctic Anthropology* 15(2):175-185.

1979 Inugsuk Revisited: An Alternative View of Neo-Eskimo Chronology and Culture Change in Greenland. Pp. 149-170 in Thule Eskimo Culture: An Anthropological Retrospective. Allen P. McCartney, ed. *Canada. National Museum of Man. Mercury Series. Archeological Survey Paper* 88. Ottawa.

Jull, Peter
1980 Canada's Native People and the Constitution. *Igalaaq* 3(1) November. Ottawa.

Kaalund, Bodil
1979 Grønlands kunst: Skulptur, brugskunst, maleri [The Art of Greenland: Sculpture, Crafts, Painting]. Copenhagen: Politiken. (Translation by Kenneth Tindall, University of California Press, Berkeley, 1983.)

Kachadoorian, Reuben
1966 Geographic Setting. Pp. 45-56 in Environment of the Cape Thompson Region, Alaska. Norman J. Wilimovsky and John N. Wolfe, eds. Washington: U.S. Atomic Energy Commission.

Kakarak, John A., and William Oquilluk
1964 The Eagle Wolf Dance. (Manuscript in the authors' possession.)

Kallutjak, Leo
1982 Leo Kallutjak. About Wildlife Management. *Inuktitut* 50(May):9-15. Ottawa.

Kapel, Hans
1973 Sejldugsjollen fra Kangeq [The Canvas Dinghy from Kangeq]. *Grønland* 3:81-90. Copenhagen.

Kaplan, Lawrence D.
1981 Phonological Issues in North Alaskan Inupiaq. *Alaska Native Language Center Research Paper* 6. Fairbanks.

1981a On Yupik-Inupiaq Correspondences for ï: A Case of Inupiaq Innovation. Pp. 81-90 in The Language of the Inuit. Louis-Jacques Dorais, ed. *Études/Inuit/Studies* 5. Suppl.

1982   Diomede Inupiaq and the Legendary Fourth Vowel. (Paper read at the 3d Inuit Studies Conference, London, Ont.)

1982a   [Alaskan Inupiaq Dialect Notes.] (Manuscript in Alaska Native Language Center, Fairbanks.)

Kaplan, Susan A.
1976   An Inquiry into Environmental and Cultural Change in Greenland. (Unpublished M.A. Thesis in Anthropology, Bryn Mawr College, Bryn Mawr, Penn.)

1980   Neo-Eskimo Occupations of the North Labrador Coast. *Arctic* 33(3):646-658.

1983   Economic and Social Change in Labrador Neo-Eskimo Culture. (Unpublished Ph.D. Dissertation in Anthropology, Bryn Mawr College, Bryn Mawr, Penn.)

Kari, James M., comp.
1977   Dena'ina Noun Dictionary. Fairbanks: University of Alaska, Native Language Center.

Kari, James M., and Mildred Buck
1975   Ahtna Noun Dictionary. Fairbanks: University of Alaska, Native Language Center for Northern Educational Research.

Kashevarov, A.F.
1879   Zhurnal vedennyĭ pri baĭdarnoĭ ėkspedit͡sii, naznachennyĭ dli͡a opisi si͡evernago berega Ameriki, 1838 goda...Vsesoyuznoe geograficheskoe obshchestvo [Journal Kept During a Canoe Expedition, Designed as a Description of the Northern Coast of America, in 1838...]. *Zapiski po obshcheĭ Geografii* 8:275-361.

Kay, H.K.
1979   General Development Plan—Cambridge Bay, N.W.T.: Current and Recent Research and Studies Relating to Northern Social Concerns. Vol. 3(1). Toronto: Underwood and McLelland.

Keim, Charles J.
1969   Aghvook, White Eskimo: Otto Geist and Alaskan Archaeology. College: University of Alaska Press.

Keith, Robert F., and Janet B. Wright, eds.
1978   Northern Transitions, II: Second National Workshop on People, Resources and the Environment (North of 60°). Ottawa: Canadian Arctic Resources Committee.

Keithahn, Edward L.
1963   Eskimo Adventure: Another Journey into the Primitive. Seattle: Superior Publishing Company.

Kelsall, John P.
1957   Continued Barren-ground Caribou Studies. *Canada. Wildlife Service. Wildlife Management Bulletin* 1(12). Ottawa.

1968   The Migratory Barren-ground Caribou of Canada. (*Canada. Wildlife Service Monograph* 3) Ottawa: Queen's Printer.

Kemp, Kenneth L.
1981   Differential Development of Village Size Social Units. (Unpublished Ph.D. Dissertation in Anthropology, University of New Mexico, Albuquerque.)

Kemp, William B.
[1966-1970]   [Unpublished Fieldnotes, Fieldwork on South Baffin Island, 1966-1970.] (Manuscript in Kemp's possession.)

1966-1971   [Ethnographic Fieldnotes from Lake Harbor.] (Unpublished manuscript in Kemp's possession.)

1971   The Flow of Energy in a Hunting Society. *Scientific American* 225(3):105-115.

1974   Final Report to the National Museum of Canada—Field Work on South Baffin Island 1966-1970. Ottawa: National Museum of Man, Ethnology Division.

1981   Inuit Land Use and Ecological Knowledge: A Report on the First Phase of a Research Project Carried Out Among the Inuit of Northern Quebec. Montreal: Makivik Research Department.

1982   Historical Development of Current Patterns of Inuit Culture and the Implication with Respect to Future Development. (Unpublished report in Kemp's possession.)

Kenai Peninsula Borough School District
1980-1981   Alexandrovsk: English Bay in Its Traditional Way. 2 vols. Homer, Alas.: Alexandrovsk Magazine.

1981-1982   Fireweed Cillqaq: Life and Times in Port Graham. 2 vols. Written by Port Graham High School Students. Soldotna, Alas.

Kennedy, John
1977   Northern Labrador: An Ethnohistorical Acount. Pp. 264-306 in The White Arctic: Anthropological Essays on Tutelage and Ethnicity. Robert Paine, ed. (*Newfoundland Social and Economic Paper* 7) St. Johns: Memorial University of Newfoundland, Institute of Social and Economic Research.

1981   Holding the Line. Ethnic Boundaries in a Northern Labrador Community. (*Newfoundland Social and Economic Studies* 27) St. Johns: Memorial University of Newfoundland, Institute of Social and Economic Research.

Kerfoot, Denis, and J. Ross Mackay
1972   Geomorphological Process Studies, Gary Island, N.W.T. Pp. 115-129 in Mackenzie Delta Area Monograph. Denis Kerfoot, ed. St. Catherines, Ont.: Brock University, Department of Geography.

Khromchenko, Vasiliĭ Stepanovich
1824   Otryvki iz zhurnala plavanii͡a g. Khromchenki, v 1822 godu. [Excerpts from the Journal of the 1822 Voyage of Mr. Khromchenko]. *Si͡evernyĭ Arkhiv* 10:254-276, 303-314; 11:38-64, 119-131, 177-186, 235-248, 297-312.

1973   V.S. Khromchenko's Coastal Explorations in Southwestern Alaska, 1822. James W. VanStone, ed. *Fieldiana: Anthropology* 64. Chicago.

King, Jonathan C.H.
1981   Artificial Curiosities from the Northwest Coast of America: Native American Artifacts in the British Museum Collected on the Third Voyage of Captain James Cook and Acquired Through Sir Joseph Banks. London: British Museum Publications.

[1983]   A Preliminary Description of a Polar Eskimo Sledge Collected by Sir John Ross. *Inter-Nord*. In press.

Kipling, Rudyard
1895   The Second Jungle Book. New York: Century Company.

Kir'i͡ak, M.A.
1979   Pervye mezoliticheskie i neoliticheskie stoi͡anki zapadnoĭ chukotki (oz. Tytyl' v verkhov'i͡akh M. Ani͡ui͡a) [The Earliest Mesolithic and Neolithic Sites of Western Chukotka (Lake Tytyl' on the Upper Reaches of the Lesser Anyui River)]. Pp. 39-52 in *Severno Vostochno-Aziatskai͡a Kompleksnai͡a Arkheoḽogicheskai͡a Ėkspedit͡sia, SVKNII DVNTs AN SSSR*. Magadan.

Kitto, Franklin H.
1930   The Northwest Territories. Ottawa: Department of the Interior.

Kjellström, Rolf
1974-1975   Senilicide and Invalidicide Among the Eskimos. *Folk* 16-17:117-124. Copenhagen.

Kleinfeld, Judith
1972   Alaska's Urban Boarding Home Program: Interpersonal Relationships Between Indians and Secondary Students and Their

Boarding Home Parents. (*ISEGR Report 32*) Fairbanks: University of Alaska.

1972a Effective Teachers of Indian and Eskimo High School Students. (*ISEGR Report 34*) Fairbanks: University of Alaska.

Kleinschmidt, Samuel P.
1851 Grammatik der grönländischen Sprache, mit theilweisem Einschluss des Labradordialekts. Berlin: G. Reimer. (Reprinted: Georg Olms Verlag Buchhandlung, Hildesheim, Germany, 1968.)

1871 Den grønlandske Ordbog. [The Greenlandic Dictionary]. H.F. Jørgensen, ed. Copenhagen: L. Klein.

Kleivan, Helge
1964 Acculturation, Ecology and Human Choice: Case Studies from Labrador and South Greenland. *Folk* 6(1):63-74. Copenhagen.

1966 The Eskimos of Northeast Labrador: A History of Eskimo-White Relations, 1771-1955. *Norsk Polarinstitutt Skrifter* 139. Oslo.

1969 Dominans og kontrol i moderniseringen af Grønland [Dominance and Control in the Modernization of Greenland]. Pp. 141-165 in Grønland i fokus. Jan Hjarnø, ed. Copenhagen: Nationalmuseet.

1969-1970 Culture and Ethnic Identify: On Modernization and Ethnicity in Greenland. *Folk* 11-12:209-234. Copenhagen.

Kleivan, Helge, and Inge Kleivan
1961-1962 [Fieldnotes on the Ethnography of West Greenlanders.] (Unpublished manuscript in the possession of the Kleivans.)

Kleivan, Inge
1955 [Fieldnotes on the Ethnography of West Greenlanders.] (Unpublished manuscript in I. Kleivan's possession.)

1962 The Swan Maiden Myth Among the Eskimo. *Acta Arctica* 13. Copenhagen.

1969-1970 Language and Ethnic Identity: Language Policy and Debate in Greenland. *Folk* 11-12:235-284. Copenhagen.

1971 Song Duels in West Greenland—Joking Relationship and Avoidance. *Folk* 13:9-36. Copenhagen.

1974-1975 Examples of Greenlandic Humour with Regard to Culture Contacts and Interethnic Relationships. *Folk* 16-17:189-212. Copenhagen.

1978 "Lamb of God"—"Seal of God"? Some Semantic Problems in Translating the Animal Names of the New Testament into Greenlandic. Pp. 339-345 in Papers from the Fourth Scandinavian Conference of Linguistics. Kirsten Gregersen et al., eds. Odense, Denmark: University Press.

1979 Language and the Church in Greenland. Pp. 123-144 in Eskimo Languages, Their Present-day Conditions: Majority Language Influence on Eskimo Minority Languages. Bjarne Basse and Kirsten Jensen, eds. Aarhus, Denmark: Arkona.

1982 Grønlandske sagn om nordboerne; Tema: Nordboerne, II [Greenlandic Traditions Concerning the Norsemen; Theme: The Norse, II]. *Grønland* 8-9:314-329. Copenhagen. In press.

Klutschak, H.W.
1881 Als Eskimo unter den Eskimo: Eine Schilderung der Erlebnisse der Schwatka'schen Franklin Aufsuchungsexpedition in den Jahren 1878-80. Vienna: A. Hartleben.

Knight, James
1932 The Founding of Churchill, Being the Journal of Captain James Knight, Governor-in-Chief in Hudson Bay, from the 14th of July to the 13th of September, 1717. J.F. Kenney, ed. Toronto: J.M. Dent and Sons.

Knuth, Eigil
1951 Et Umiak-fund i Pearyland. [An Umiak Find in Pearyland]. *Nationalmuseets Arbejdsmark*: 77-87. Copenhagen.

1952 An Outline of the Archaeology of Peary Land. *Arctic* 5(1)17-33.

1954 The Paleo-Eskimo Culture of Northeast Greenland Elucidated by Three New Sites. *American Antiquity* 19(4):367-381.

1958 Archaeology of the Farthest North. Pp. 561-573 in *Proceedings of the 32d International Congress of Americanists*. Copenhagen, 1956.

1960 Aron of Kangeq, 1822-1869: The Seal Hunter Who Became Father of the Greenland Art of Painting. Copenhagen: The Danish National Museum.

1966-1967 The Ruins of Musk-ox Way. *Folk* 8-9:191-219. Copenhagen.

1967 Archaeology of the Musk-ox Way. *École Pratique des Hautes Études. Contributions du Centre d'Études Arctiques et Finno Scandinaves* 5. Paris.

1968 The Independence II Bone Artifacts and the Dorset-evidence in North Greenland. *Folk* 10:61-80.

1968a Âlut Kangermio—Aron fra Kangek—Aron of Kangeq, 1822-1869. K'avdlunâtsiánik Agdlagtok Âlut Kangermio: Nordboer og Skrælinger—The Norsemen and the Skraelings. Clive Bayliss, trans. Godthåb: Det Grønlandske Forlag.

1977-1978 The "Old Nûgdlît Culture" Site at Nûgdlît Peninsula, Thule District, and the "Mesoeskimo" Site Below It. *Folk* 19-20:15-47. Copenhagen.

1981 Greenland News From Between 81° and 83° North. *Folk* 23:91-111. Copenhagen.

1982 Jordens nordligste ruinpladser [The Northernmost Ruins in the World]. *Forskning i Grønland* 1:17-26. Copenhagen.

Koch, H.C.
1950 Grønlandskommissionen og dens forslag [The Greenland Commission and its Proposal]. *Grønlandsbogen* 2:291-320. Copenhagen.

Koertvelyessy, T.
1972 Relationships Between the Frontal Sinus and Climatic Conditions: A Skeletal Approach to Cold Adaptation. *American Journal of Physical Anthropology* 37(2):161-172.

Kohlmeister, B., and G. Kmoch
1814 Journal of a Voyage from Okkak on the Coast of Labrador to Ungava Bay, Westward of Cape Chudleigh. London: W.M. McDowall.

Kommissionen om Hjemmestyre i Grønland
1978 Hjemmestyre i Grønland, I-IV [Home Rule in Greenland, I-IV]. *Betænkning* 837. Copenhagen.

Det Kongelige Nordiske Oldskrift-Selskab
1838-1845 Grønlands historiske Mindesmærker [Greenland's Historical Monuments]. Finn Magnusen and Carl Christian Ragn, eds. 3 vols. Copenhagen: Trykt i det Brünnichske Bogtrykkeri.

Kotani, Yoshinobu
1980 Paleoecology of the Alaska Peninsula as Seen from the Hot Springs Site, Port Möller. Pp. 113-121 in Alaska Native Culture and History. Y. Kotani and W.B. Workman, eds. *National Museum of Ethnology, Senri Ethnological Studies* 4. Osaka, Japan.

Kotzebue, Otto von
1821 A Voyage of Discovery into the South Sea and Beering's Straits for the Purpose of Exploring a North-East Passage,

Undertaken in the Years 1815-1818. 3 vols. London: Longman, Hurst, Rees, Orme, and Brown.

1967　A Voyage of Discovery into the South Sea and Bering's Straits [1821]. (*Bibliotheca Australiana* 17-19) Amsterdam: N. Israel; New York: Da Capo Press.

Kowta, Makoto
1963　Old Togiak in Prehistory. (Unpublished Ph.D. Dissertation in Anthropology, University of California, Los Angeles.)

Krader, Lawrence
1952　Neolithic Find in the Chukchi Peninsula. *American Antiquity* 17(3):261-262.

Krauss, Michael E., ed. and trans.
1963-1970　Eyak Texts. College: University of Alaska and Massachusetts Institute of Technology. Mimeo.

1973　Eskimo-Aleut. Pp. 796-902 in *Linguistics in North America. Current Trends in Linguistics.* Thomas A. Sebeok, ed. Vol. 10. The Hague, Paris: Mouton. (Reprinted: Plenum Press, New York, 1976.)

1973a　The Alaska Native Language Center Report for 1973. Fairbanks: University of Alaska.

1975　Native Peoples and Languages of Alaska. Map. Fairbanks: University of Alaska, Native Language Center.

1975a　St. Lawrence Island Eskimo Phonology and Orthography. *Linguistics* 152(May):39-72.

1979　Na-Dene and Eskimo Aleut. Pp. 803-901 in The Languages of Native America: Historical and Comparative Assessment. Lyle Campbell and Marianne Mithun, eds. Austin: University of Texas Press.

1980　Alaska Native Languages: Past, Present and Future. *Alaska Native Language Center Research Paper* 4. Fairbanks.

1982　Siberian Yupik Prosodic Systems and the Yupik Continuum (with Inupiaq Connections). (Paper read at the 3d Inuit Studies Conference, London, Ont.)

Kristiansen, Uvdloriánguaq
1954　Nunagssarsiaq [The Country That Was Discovered]. "kalâtdline qaumarsautigssîniaqatigit". *Naqitertitat* 14. Godthåb.

Kroeber, Alfred L.
1899　Tales of the Smith Sound Eskimo. *Journal of American Folk-Lore* 12(46):166-182.

1900　The Eskimo of Smith Sound. *Bulletin of the American Museum of Natural History* 12(21): 265-327. New York.

1939　Cultural and Natural Areas of Native North America. *University of California Publications in American Archaeology and Ethnology* 38:1-242. Berkeley. (Reprinted in 1963.)

Krogh, Knud J.
1967　Viking Greenland, with a Supplement of Saga Texts. Helen Fogh and Gwyn Jones, trans. Copenhagen: The National Museum. (Original: Erik den Rødes Grønland. Sagatekster ved Hans Bekker-Nielsen, Nationalmuseet Gyldendal, Copenhagen, 1967.)

1982　Grønland: Erik den Rødes Grønland [Eric the Red's Greenland]. 2d rev. ed. Copenhagen: Nationalmuseet.

1982a　Bygdernes Kirker. Tema: Nordboerne, II. [Churches of the (Norse) Settlements. Theme: The Norse, II]. *Grønland* 8-9:263-274. Copenhagen.

Krogh, Knud J., and Svend E. Albrethsen
1967　Vikingernes Grønland. Copenhagen: Nationalmuseet. [Transl.: Norse Greenland, by Jean Olsen, 1971.]

Krolewski, A., comp.
1973　Northwest Territories Statistical Abstract. Ottawa: Department of Indian Affairs and Northern Development, Policy and Planning Branch.

Krupnik, I.I., and M.A. Chlenov
1979　Dinamika étnolingvisticheskoĭ situafsii u aziatskikh éskimosov (Konets XIX v.—1970-e gg.). [Dynamics of the Ethnolinguistic Situation Among the Asiatic Eskimos, Late 19th Century to the 1970s]. *Sovetskaĭa Étnografiĭa* 2:19-29.

Kruse, John A.
1982　Subsistence and the North Slope Inupiat: The Effects of Energy Development. (*Man in the Arctic Program, Monograph* 4) Anchorage: University of Alaska, Institute of Social and Economic Research.

Kruse, John A., Judith Kleinfeld, and Robert Travis
1981　Energy Development and the North Slope Inupiat: Quantitative Analysis of Social and Economic Change. (*Man in the Arctic Program, Monograph* 1) Anchorage: University of Alaska, Institute of Social and Economic Research.

1982　Energy Development on Alaska's North Slope: Effects on the Inupiat Population. *Human Organization* 41(2):97-106.

Kuno, Y.
1956　Human Perspiration. Springfield, Ill.: Charles C. Thomas.

Kunz, Michael L.
1982　The Mesa Site: An Early Holocene Hunting Stand in the Iteriak Valley, Northern Alaska. *Anthropological Papers of the University of Alaska* 20(1-2):113-122. Fairbanks.

Kupfer, George, and Charles W. Hobart
1978　Impact of Oil Exporation Work on an Inuit Community. *Arctic Anthropology* 15(1):58-67.

Kupp, Jan, and Simon Hart
1976　The Dutch in the Strait of Davis and Labrador During the 17th and 18th Centuries. *Man in the Northeast* 11 (Spring):3-20.

Lachance, Denis
1979　Les Inuit du Québec. Pp. 289-303 in Perspectives anthropologiques. Montreal: Éditions du Renouveau Pédagogique.

LaFortune, Bellarmine
[1929-1942] History of the Mission of King Island. (Manuscript, at Gonzaga University, Spokane, Wash.; copy in St. Joseph's Church, Nome, Alaska.)

Lange, Philip
1977　Some Qualities of Inuit Social Interaction. Pp. 108-128 in The White Arctic: Anthropological Essays on Tutelage and Ethnicity. Robert Paine, ed. (*Memorial University of Newfoundland. Institute of Social and Economic Research. Social and Economic Paper* 7) Toronto: University of Toronto Press.

Langsdorff, Georg H. von
1813-1814　Voyages and Travels in Various Parts of the World During the Years 1803, 1804, 1805, 1806, and 1807. 2 vols. London: H. Colburn.

Lantis, Margaret
[1933-1934] [Atka Fieldnotes.] (Manuscript in Lantis's possession.)

1938　The Alaskan Whale Cult and Its Affinities. *American Anthropologist* 40(3):438-464.

1938a　The Mythology of Kodiak Island, Alaska. *Journal of American Folk-Lore* 51(200):123-172.

1946　The Social Culture of the Nunivak Eskimo. *Transactions of the American Philosophical Society* n.s. 35(3):153-323. Philadelphia.

1947　Alaskan Eskimo Ceremonialism. (*Monographs of the American Ethnological Society* 11). New York: J.J. Augustin.

770

1950   Mme. Eskimo Proves Herself an Artist. *Natural History* 59(2):68-71.

1950a   The Reindeer Industry in Alaska. *Arctic* 3(1):27-44.

1953   Nunivak Eskimo Personality as Revealed in the Mythology. *Anthropological Papers of the University of Alaska* 2(1):109-174. College.

1957   American Arctic Populations: Their Survival Problems. Pp. 119-130 in Arctic Biology. Henry P. Hansen, ed. (18th Annual Biology Colloquium) Corvallis: Oregon State College.

1959   Folk Medicine and Hygiene: Lower Kuskokwim and Nunivak-Nelson Island Areas. *Anthropological Papers of the University of Alaska* 8(1):1-75. College.

1960   Eskimo Childhood and Interpersonal Relationships: Nunivak Biographies and Genealogies. (*Monographs of the American Ethnological Society* 33) Seattle: University of Washington Press.

1966   The Administration of Northern Peoples: Canada and Alaska. Pp. 89-119 in The Arctic Frontier. R.St.J. MacDonald, ed. Toronto: University of Toronto Press.

1968   Environmental Stresses on Human Behavior. *Archives of Environmental Health* 17:578-585.

1970   The Aleut Social System, 1750 to 1810, from Early Historical Sources. Pp. 139-301 in Ethnohistory in Southwestern Alaska and the Southern Yukon. Margaret Lantis, ed. Lexington: University of Kentucky Press.

1972   Factionalism and Leadership: A Case Study of Nunivak Island. *Arctic Anthropology* 9(1):43-65.

1973   The Current Nativistic Movement in Alaska. Pp. 99-118 in Circumpolar Problems: Habitat, Economy and Social Relations in the Arctic. G. Berg, ed. New York: Pergamon Press.

Larsen, Dinah W.
1972   Notes on the Material Culture of the Eskimos of Northwestern Alaska. Pp. 35-42 in Modern Alaskan Native Material Culture. Wendell Oswalt, ed. College: University of Alaska Museum.

Larsen, Helge E.
1934   Dødemandsbugten: An Eskimo Settlement on Clavering Island. *Meddelelser om Grønland* 102(1). Copenhagen.

1938   Archaeological Investigations in Knud Rasmussens Land. *Meddelelser om Grønland* 119(8). Copenhagen.

1948   The Ipiutak Culture and Its Position within the Eskimo Culture. Pp. 419-421 in *Proceedings of the 28th International Congress of Americanists*. Paris, 1947.

1950   Archaeological Investigations in Southwestern Alaska. *American Antiquity* 15(3):177-186.

1951   De dansk-amerikanske Alaska—ekspeditioner 1949-1950. *Geografisk Tidsskrift* 51:63-93. Copenhagen.

1952   The Ipiutak Culture: Its Origin and Relationships. Pp. 22-34 in *Selected Papers of the 29th International Congress of Americanists*. Sol Tax, ed. Chicago: University of Chicago Press.

1953   Archaeological Investigations in Alaska Since 1939. *Polar Record* 6(45):593-607.

1954   The Position of Ipiutak in Eskimo Culture. *American Antiquity* 20(1):74-79.

1958   The Material Culture of the Nunamiut and Its Relation to Other Forms of Eskimo Culture in Northern Alaska. Pp. 574-582 in *Proceedings of the 32d International Congress of Americanists*. Copenhagen, 1956.

1961   Archaeology in the Arctic, 1935-1960. *American Antiquity* 27(1):7-15.

1962   The Trail Creek Caves on Seward Peninsula, Alaska. Pp.284-291 in *Proceedings of the 34th International Congress of Americanists*. Vienna, 1960.

1968   Trail Creek: Final Report on the Excavation of Two Caves on Seward Peninsula, Alaska. *Acta Arctica* 15. Copenhagen.

1969-1970 The Eskimo Culture and Its Relationship to Northern Eurasia. Pp.338-340 in Vol. 3 of *Proceedings of the 8th International Congress of Anthropological and Ethnological Sciences*. Tokyo and Kyoto, 1968.

1973   The Tareormiut and the Nunamiut of Northern Alaska: A Comparison Between Their Economy, Settlement Patterns, and Social Structure. Pp. 119-126 in Circumpolar Problems, Habitat, Economy, and Social Relations in the Arctic. Gösta Berg, ed. New York: Pergamon Press.

Larsen, Helge E., and Jørgen Meldgaard
1958   Paleo-Eskimo Cultures in Disko Bugt, West Greenland. *Meddelelser om Grønland* 161(2). Copenhagen.

Larsen, Helge E., and Froelich Rainey
1948   Ipiutak and the Arctic Whale Hunting Culture. *Anthropological Papers of the American Museum of Natural History* 42. New York.

Laughlin, William S.
1950   Genetic Analysis of Racial Traits (11): Blood Groups, Morphology and Population Size of the Eskimos. Pp. 165-174 in Cold Spring Harbor Symposia on Quantitative Biology 15. Cold Spring Harbor, N.Y.

1951   The Alaska Gateway Viewed from the Aleutian Islands. Pp. 98-126 in Papers on the Physical Anthropology of the American Indian. W.S. Laughlin, ed. New York: Viking Fund.

1951a   Notes on an Aleutian Core and Blade Industry. *American Antiquity* 17(1):52-55.

1952   Contemporary Problems in the Anthropology of Southern Alaska. Pp. 66-84 in Science in Alaska: Selected Papers of the National Academy of Sciences, National Research Council, Washington, November 9-11, 1950. Henry B. Collins, ed. (*Arctic Institute of North America Special Publication* 1). Montreal.

1952a   The Aleut-Eskimo Community. *Anthropological Papers of the University of Alaska* 1(1):25-46. College.

1957   Blood Groups of the Anaktuvuk Eskimos, Alaska. *Anthropological Papers of the University of Alaska* 6(1):5-15. College.

1958   Neo-Aleut and Paleo-Aleut Prehistory. Pp. 516-530 in *Proceedings of the 32d International Congress of Americanists*. Copenhagen, 1956.

1962   Bering Strait to Puget Sound: Dichotomy and Affinity Between Eskimo-Aleuts and American Indians. *Arctic Institute of North America Technical Paper* 11:113-125. Montreal.

1962a   Generic Problems and New Evidence in the Anthropology of the Eskimo-Aleut Stock. *Arctic Institute of North America Technical Paper* 11:100-112. Montreal.

771

1963   Eskimos and Aleuts: Their Origins and Evolution; Physiological and Cultural Adaptation to Facilitate the Evolutionary Success of Eskimo-Aleut Stock. *Science* 142(3593):633-645.

1963a   The Earliest Aleuts. *Anthropological Papers of the University of Alaska* 10(2):73-91.

1963b   Primitive Theory of Medicine: Empirical Knowledge. Pp. 116-140 in Man's Image in Medicine and Anthropology. Iago Galdston, ed. New York: International Universities Press.

1966   Aleutian Studies: Introduction. *Arctic Anthropology* 3(2):23-27.

1966a   Paleo-Aleut Crania from Port Möller, Alaska Peninsula. *Arctic Anthropology* 3(2):154.

1966b   Genetical and Anthropological Characteristics of Arctic Populations. Pp. 469-496 in The Biology of Human Adaptability. Paul T. Baker and J.S. Weiner, eds. London: Oxford University Press.

1967   Human Migration and Permanent Occupation in the Bering Sea Area. Pp. 409-450 in The Bering Land Bridge. David M. Hopkins, ed. Stanford, Calif.: Stanford University Press.

1968   Hunting: An Integrating Biobehavior System and Its Evolutionary Importance. Pp. 304-320 in Man the Hunter. Richard B. Lee and Irven DeVore, eds. Chicago: Aldine.

1974-1975   Holocene History of Nikolski Bay, Alaska, and Aleut Evolution. *Folk* 16-17:95-115.

1975   Aleuts: Ecosystem, Holocene History, and Siberian Origin. *Science* 189(4202):507-515.

1980   Aleuts: Survivors of the Bering Land Bridge. New York: Holt, Rinehart, and Winston.

Laughlin, William S., and Jean S. Aigner
1966   Preliminary Analysis of the Anangula Unifacial Core and Blade Industry. *Arctic Anthropology* 3(2):41-56.

1975   Aleut Adaptation and Evolution. Pp. 181-201 in Prehistoric Maritime Adaptations of the Circumpolar Zone. W. Fitzhugh, ed. The Hague, Paris: Mouton.

Laughlin, William S., and J.B. Jørgensen
1956   Isolate Variation in Greenlandic Eskimo Crania. *Acta Genetica et Statistica Medica* 6:3-12. Basel, Switzerland.

Laughlin, William S., and Gordon H. Marsh
1951   A New View of the History of the Aleutians. *Arctic* 4(2):75-88.

1954   The Lamellar Flake Manufacturing Site on Anangula Island in the Aleutians. *American Antiquity* 20(1):27-39.

1956   Trends in Aleutian Chipped Stone Artifacts. *Anthropological Papers of the University of Alaska* 5(1):5-21. College.

Laughlin, William S., and W.G. Reeder, eds.
1966   Studies in Aleutian-Kodiak Prehistory, Ecology and Anthropology. *Arctic Anthropology* 3(2):1-240.

Laughlin, William S., and William E. Taylor, Jr.
1960   A Cape Dorset Culture Site on the West Coast of Ungava Bay. *Anthropological Series* 48, *National Museum of Canada Bulletin* 167:1-28. Ottawa.

Laughlin, William S., and Susan I. Wolf
1979   Introduction. Pp. 1-11 in The First Americans: Origins, Affinities and Adaptations. William S. Laughlin and Albert B. Harper, eds. New York: Gustav Fischer.

Laursen, Dan
1972   The Place Names of North Greenland. *Meddelelser om Grønland* 180(2). Copenhagen.

Lawrence, Erma, and Jeff Leer, comps.
1977   Haida Dictionary. Fairbanks: University of Alaska, Native Language Center, and The Society for the Preservation of Haida Language and Literature.

Lazarus, Arthur, Jr., and W. Richard West, Jr.
1976   The Alaska Native Claims Settlement Act: A Flawed Victory. Pp. 132-165 in American Indians and the Law. Lawrence Rosen, ed. New Brunswick, N.J.: Transaction Books.

LeClerq, Chrétien
1910   New Relation of Gaspesia with the Customs and Religion of the Gaspesian Indians [1691]. W.F. Ganong, ed. and trans. Toronto: The Champlain Society.

Leden, Christian
1927   Über Kiwatins Eisfelder: Drei Jahre unter kanadischen Eskimos. Leipzig, Germany: F.A. Brockhaus.

1952   Über die Musik der Smith Sund Eskimos und ihre Verwandtschaft mit der Musik der amerikanischen Indianer. *Meddelelser om Grønland* 152(3). Copenhagen.

Lederman, J.M., A.C. Wallace, and J.A. Hildes
1962   Biological Aspects of Aging. Pp. 201-207 in *Proceedings of the 5th International Congress on Gerontology*. New York: Columbia University Press.

Lee, Molly
1981   Pacific Eskimo Spruce Root Baskets. *American Indian Art Magazine* 6(2):66-73.

1981a   Alaskan Eskimo Baleen Baskets. *Historic Nantucket* 29(1):19-24.

Lee, Thomas E.
1967   Fort Chimo and Payne Lake, Ungava, Archeology, 1965. *Université Laval. Centre d'Études Nordiques, Travaux Divers* 16. Quebec.

1969   Archaeological Findings, Gyrfalcon to Eider Islands, Ungava, 1968. *Université Laval, Centre d'Études Nordiques, Travaux Divers* 27. Quebec.

Leechman, Douglas
1943   Two New Cape Dorset Sites. *American Antiquity* 8(4):363-375.

Leer, Jeff
1977   [Yupik Stress Patterns]. (Manuscript in Alaska Native Language Center, University of Alaska, Fairbanks.)

1977a   Short Dictionary of Alaska Peninsula Sugcestun. Fairbanks: University of Alaska, Native Language Center.

1978   A Conversational Dictionary of Kodiak Alutiiq. Fairbanks: University of Alaska, Native Language Center.

1978a   Introduction for Linguists [to Conversational Alutiiq Dictionary, Kenai Peninsula Alutiiq]. (Manuscript in Alsaka Native Language Center, University of Alaska, Fairbanks.)

1978b   Conversational Alutiiq Dictionary. Anchorage: National Bilingual Materials Development Center.

Lefebvre, G-R.
1957   A Draft Orthography for the Canadian Eskimo: Towards a Future Unification with Greenlandic. (*NCRC-57-1*). Ottawa: Northern Coordination and Research Center.

Leffingwell, Ernest D.
1919   The Canning River Region Northern Alaska. *U.S. Geological Survey Professional Paper* 109. Washington.

Leighton, Alexander H., and Charles C. Hughes
1955   Notes on Eskimo Patterns of Suicide. *Southwestern Journal of Anthropology* 11(4):327-338.

Leighton, Alexander H., and Dorothea C. Leighton
1940   [Fieldnotes on Cultural Study of Gambell, St. Lawrence Island.] (Manuscript in C.C. Hughes and D.C. Leighton's possession.)

772

Le Jeune, Roger
1973   L'enterprise coopérative chez les Amérindiens du Nouveau-Québec. Pp. 337-348 in Le Peuple esquimau aujourd'hui et demain/The Eskimo People To-Day and To-Morrow. Jean Malaurie, ed. (Fourth International Congress of the Fondation Française d'Études Nordiques). Paris, The Hague: Mouton.

Lemoine, Georges, ed.
1911   Dictionnaire français-algonquin. Quebec: L'Action Sociale. [False Title Page: Chicoutimi, G. Delisle, Bureau du journal "Le Travailleur," 1909.]

Lent, Peter C.
1966   The Caribou of Northwestern Alaska. Pp. 481-518 in Environment of the Cape Thompson Region, Alaska. Norman J. Wilimovsky and John W. Wolfe, eds. Washington: U.S. Atomic Energy Commission.

Lethbridge, T.C.
1939   Archaeological Data from the Canadian Arctic. *Journal of the Royal Anthropological Institute of Great Britain and Ireland* 69(2):187-233. London.

Levin, Maksim Grigor´evich
1958   Anthropological Types of the Northeastern Paleoasiatics and Problems of Their Ethnogenesis. Pp. 607-613 in *Proceedings of the 32d International Congress of Americanists.* Copenhagen, 1956.

1958a   Ėtnicheskaĭa antropologiĭa i problemy ėtnogeneza narodov Dal'nego vostoka: Trudy severovostochnoĭ ėkspediĭsii II [Ethnic Anthropology and the Problems of the Ethnogenesis of the Peoples of the Far East: Investigations of the Northeastern Expedition, Pt. 2]. *Akademiĭa Nauk S.S.S.R., Institut Etnografii. Trudy* n.s. 36. Moscow.

1959   Ancient Eskimo Cemetery in Uellen (Chukotka). Pp. 65-71 in Vol. 2 of *Proceedings of the 33d International Congress of Americanists.* San José, Costa Rica, 1958.

1964   Fieldwork on the Chukchi Peninsula in 1957. Pp. 296-304 in The Archaeology and Geomorphology of Northern Asia: Selected Works. (*Anthropology of the North: Translations from Russian Sources* 5) Henry N. Michael, ed. Toronto: Published for the Arctic Institute of North America by University of Toronto Press.

1964a   An Early Eskimo Cemetery at Uelen: A Preliminary Report on the Excavations of 1958. Pp. 305-318 in The Archaeology and Geomorphology of Northern Asia: Selected Works. (*Anthropology of the North: Translations from Russian Sources* 5) Henry N. Michael, ed. Toronto: Published for the Arctic Institute of North America by University of Toronto Press.

Levin, Maksim Grigor´evich, and L.P. Potov, eds.
1956   Narody Sibiri [The Peoples of Siberia]. Moscow: Izdatel´stvo Akademii Nauk SSSR.

Levin, Maksim Grigor´evich, and D.A. Sergeev
1964   The Penetration of Iron into the Arctic: The First Find of an Iron Implement in a Site of the Old Bering Sea Culture. Pp. 319-326 in The Archaeology and Geomorphology of Northern Asia: Selected Works. (*Anthropology of the North: Translations from Russian Sources* 5) Henry N. Michael, ed. Toronto: Published for the Arctic Institute of North America by University of Toronto Press.

1970   Ancient Cemeteries in the Chukotsky Peninsula and Some Aspects of the Eskimo Problem. Pp. 289-294 in Vol. 10 of *Proceedings of the 7th International Congress of Anthropological and Ethnological Sciences.* Moscow 1964.

Lin, Peter C., comp.
1971   Alaska's Population and School Enrollments. *University of Alaska, Institute of Social, Economic, and Government Research. Review of Business and Economic Conditions* 8(5). College.

Lindow, Harald, ed.
1922   Piniarnermik ilitsersûtit. [Textbook for Hunters and Hunting]. Godthåb: sineríssap kujatdliup naqiteriviane naqigtigkat.

————, ed.
1923   Piniarnilerssârutit. Piniarniartunut Ilíniutigssat. [Guide/Textbook/Instructions for Hunting]. Qeqertarsuaq: avangnâta naqiteriviane naqitigkat.

Linnamae, Urve
1975   The Dorset Culture: A Comparative Study in Newfoundland and the Arctic. *Newfoundland Museum, Department of Tourism, Historic Resources Division, Technical Paper* 1. St. John's.

Linnamae, Urve, and B.L. Clark
1976   Archeology of Rankin Inlet, N.W.T. *The Musk-Ox* 19:37-73. Saskatoon.

Lippold, Lois K.
1966   Chaluka: The Economic Base. *Arctic Anthropology* 3(2):125-131.

Lipshiĭs, B.A.
1950   Ėtnograficheskie materialy po severo-zapadnoĭ Amerike v arkhive I.G. Voznesenskogo [Ethnographical Materials on Northwestern America from the Archives of I.V. Voznesenskiĭ]. *Vsesoĭuznoe Geograficheskoe Obshchestvo. Izvestiĭa* 82(4):415-420.

1955   O kollekĭsiĭakh Muzeĭa antropologii i ėtnografii, sobrannykh russkimi puteshestvennikami i issledovateliami na Alĭaske i v Kalifornii [The Collections of the Museum of Anthropology and Ethnography Gathered by the Russian Travelers and Explorers in Alaska and California]. *Akademiĭa Nauk SSSR. Muzeĭ Antropologii i Ėtnografii Sbornik* 16:358-369. Moscow.

Lisĭanskiĭ, ĬUriĭ Fedorovich
1814   A Voyage Round the World in the Years 1803, 4, 5, & 6: Performed by Order of His Imperial Majesty Alexander the First, Emperor of Russia, in the Ship Neva. London: Printed for J. Booth.

Lisiansky, Urey see Lisĭanskiĭ, ĬUriĭ Fedorovich

Litke, Fedor Petrovich
1835-1836   Voyage autour du monde, exécuté par order de Sa Majesté l'empereur Nicolas Ier, sur la corvette le Séniavine, dans les années 1826, 1827, 1828 et 1829, par Frédéric Lutké... Paris: Didot Frères.

Little, Ronald L., and Lynn A. Robbins
1982   Draft Final Ethnographic Baseline: St. Lawrence Island. Napa, Calif.: John Muir Institute; Anchorage: Alaska Outer Shelf Office, Socioeconomic Studies Program, Minerals Management Service.

Lloyd, Trevor
1973   The Development of the North American Arctic and the Future of the Eskimo Society. Pp. 51-62 in Le Peuple esquimau aujourd'hui et demain/The Eskimo People To-Day and To-Morrow. Jean Malaurie, ed. (Fourth International Congress of the Fondation Française d'Études Nordiques) Paris, The Hague: Mouton.

Lobdell, John E.
1980   Prehistoric Human Populations and Resource Utilization in Kachemak Bay, Gulf of Alaska. (Unpublished Ph.D. Dissertation in Anthropology, University of Tennessee, Knoxville.)

Lofthouse, Joseph
1922   A Thousand Miles from a Post Office; or, Twenty Years' Life and Travel in the Hudson's Bay Regions. London: Society for Promoting Christian Knowledge.

Long, Austin
1965   Smithsonian Institution Radiocarbon Measurements, II. *Radiocarbon* 7:245-256.

Lopatin, Ivan A.
1960   The Cult of the Dead Among the Natives of the Amur Basin. The Hague: Mouton.

Lot-Falck, Eveline
1957   Les Masques Eskimo et Aléoutes de la collection Pinart. *Journal de la Société des Américanistes* n.s. 46:5-43. Paris.

Love, Gordon
1976   The Biota of the Nikolski Strandflat. *Anthropological Papers of the University of Alaska* 18(1):43-49. Fairbanks.

Lovtidende A
1978   Lov No. 577 om Grønlands Hjemmestyre af 29. November 1978. [Law No. 577 of November 29, 1978 on Greenland Home Rule]. Copenhagen.

Low, Albert P.
1896   Report on Explorations in the Labrador Peninsula, Along the East Main, Koksoak, Hamilton, Manicuagan and Portions of Other Rivers in 1892-93-94-95. Pp. 5-386 in *Canada. Geological Survey. Annual Report for 1895.* Vol. 8, Rep. L. Ottawa.

1899   Report of an Exploration in the Hudson Strait Region. *Canada. Geological Survey. Summary Report for 1897, Annual Report* 10(A):84-92. Ottawa.

1899a   Report of Exploration on the East Coast of Hudson Bay. *Canada. Geological Survey. Summary Report for 1898, Annual Report* 11(A):124-133. Ottawa.

1901   Report of an Exploration of Part of the South Shore of Hudson Strait and Ungava Bay. *Canada. Geological Survey. Summary Report for 1899, Annual Report* Vol. 11(L):1-41. Ottawa.

1903   Report on an Exploration of the East Coast of Hudson Strait from Cape Wolstenholme to the South End of James Bay. *Canada. Geological Survey. Annual Report for 1900.* Vol. 13. Ottawa.

1906   Report on the Dominion Government Expedition to Hudson Bay and the Arctic Islands on Board the D.G.S. Neptune, 1903-1904. Ottawa: Government Printing Bureau.

Lowther, Gordon R.
1962   An Account of an Archaeological Site on Cape Sparbo, Devon Island. *Anthropological Series 57, National Museum of Canada Bulletin* 180:1-19. Ottawa.

Lubart, Joseph M.
1965   A Study of Basic Personality Traits of the Caribou Eskimos: A Preliminary Report. Pp. 301-332 in Developments in Psychoanalysis at Columbia University: Proceedings of the 20th Anniversary Conference. George S. Goldman and Daniel Shapiro, eds. New York: Hafner.

1969   Field Study of the Problems of Adaptation of Mackenzie Delta Eskimos to Social and Economic Change. *Psychiatry* 32(4):447-458.

1969a   Psychodynamic Problems of Adaptation—Mackenzie Delta Eskimos: A Preliminary Study (*NSRG-7*) Ottawa: Department of Indian Affairs and Northern Development, Northern Science Research Group.

Lubbock, Alfred B.
1937   The Arctic Whalers. Glasgow: Brown, Son and Ferguson.

Lucier, Charles V.
1954   Buckland Eskimo Myths. *Anthropological Papers of the University of Alaska* 2(2):215-233. College.

1958   Noatagmiut Eskimo Myths. *Anthropological Papers of the University of Alaska* 6(2):89-117. College.

Lucier, Charles V., James W. VanStone, and Della Keats
1971   Medical Practices and Human Anatomical Knowledge Among the Noatak Eskimos. *Ethnology* 10(3):251-264.

Lütke, Frédéric *see* Litke, Fedor Petrovich

Lundsgaarde, Henry P.
1962   The Comparative-generational Approach to the Analysis of Social Change: An Aleut-Eskimo Example. Mimeo.

Lunt, Horace G.
1958   Fundamentals of Russian: First Russian Course. New York: Norton.

Lutz, Bruce J.
1970   Variations in Checked Pottery from an Archeological Site Near Unalakleet, Alaska. *Anthropological Papers of the University of Alaska* 15(1):33-48. College.

1972   A Methodology for Determining Regional Intracultural Variation within Norton, an Alaskan Archaeological Culture. (Unpublished Ph.D. Dissertation in Anthropology, University of Pennsylvania, Philadelphia.)

1973   An Archaeological *Karigi* at the Site of UngaLaqLiq, Western Alaska. *Arctic Anthropology* 10(1):111-118.

Lynge, Finn
1981   Fugl og sæl—og menneskesjæl [Bird and Seal—and Human Soul]. Copenhagen: Nordiske Landes Bogforlag.

Lynge, Hans
1955   Inugpait eller fornemme mennesker, som Melville Bugtens eskimoer kalder sig selv: Upernavik Norddistrikts ældre historie [Inugpait, or People of Distinction, as the Melville Bay Eskimos Call Themselves: Early History of the Northern District of Upernavik]. *Meddelelser om Grønland* 90(2). Copenhagen.

1970   The Art and Poetry of Greenland. Pp. 241-255 in Greenland Past and Present. Knud Hertling, Erik Hesselbjerg, Svend Klilgaard, Ebbe Munck, and Olaf Petersen, eds. Copenhagen: Edvard Henriksen.

Lynge, Inge
1969   Omkostninger ved udviklingen: Samfund og politik i Grønland; Problemer og perspektiver [Costs of Development: Society and Politics in Greenland; Problems and Perspectives]. *Mentalhygiejne* 7-8:192-195. Copenhagen.

1976   Alcohol Problems in Western Greenland. Pp. 543-547 in Circumpolar Health. R.J. Shephard and S. Itoh, eds. Toronto: University of Toronto Press.

1976a   Behov for en våbenlov i Grønland. [The Need for a Gun Law in Greenland I-III.] *Atuagagdliutit/Grønlandsposten* 24:7. Godthåb.

Lynge, Kristoffer
1938-1939   Kalâtdlit oqalugtuait oqalualâvilo, I-III. [Myths and Legends of the Greenlanders]. Nûngme: Kujatâne landskassip naqitertitai. (Reprinted: Det grønlandske Forlag, Godthåb, 1957.)

Lyon, George F.
1824   The Private Journal of Captain G.F. Lyon of H.M.S. Hecla, During the Recent Voyage of Discovery under Captain Parry. London: John Murray.

1825   A Brief Narrative of an Unsuccessful Attempt to Reach Repulse Bay, Through Sir Thomas Rowe's "Welcome," in His Majesty's Ship Griper, in the Year MDCCCXXIV. London: J. Murray.

Lyschander, Claus C.
1608   Den grønlandske chronica... [The Greenlandic Chronicle]. Copenhagen: Trykt udi Hans Kongl. Majestets privil. Bogtrykkerie.

MacArthur, R.S.
1967   Sex Difference in Field Dependence for the Eskimo: Replication of Berry's Findings. *International Journal of Psychology* 2:139-140.

1969   Some Cognitive Abilities of Eskimo, White and Indian-Métis Pupils Aged 9-12 Years. *Canadian Journal of Behavioural Science* 1:50-59.

McBeath, Gerald A., and Thomas A. Morehouse
1980   The Dynamics of Alaska Native Self-Government. Lanham, Md.: University Press of America.

McCartney, Allen P.
1967   An Analysis of the Bone Industry from Amaknak Island, Alaska. (Unpublished M.A. Thesis in Anthropology, University of Wisconsin, Madison.)

1969   Prehistoric Aleut Influence at Port Möller, Alaska. *Anthropological Papers of the University of Alaska* 14(2):1-16. College.

1970   "Pottery" in the Aleutian Islands. *American Antiquity* 35(1):105-108.

1971   A Proposed Western Aleutian Phase in the Near Islands, Alaska. *Arctic Anthropology* 8(2):92-142.

1972   Dorset Artifacts from Northwestern Hudson Bay. *The Musk-ox:* 10. Saskatoon.

1974   Maritime Adaptations on the North Pacific Rim. *Arctic Anthropology* 11(Suppl.):153-162.

1974a   Prehistoric Cultural Integration Along the Alaska Peninsula. *Anthropological Papers of the University of Alaska* 16(1):59-84. Fairbanks.

1974b   1972 Archaeological Site Survey in the Aleutian Islands, Alaska. Pp. 113-126 in International Conference on the Prehistory and Paleoecology of Western North American Arctic and Subarctic. S. Raymond and P. Schledermann, eds. Calgary: University of Calgary, Department of Archaeology.

1975   Maritime Adaptations in Cold Archipelagoes: An Analysis of Environment and Culture in the Aleutian and Other Island Chains. Pp. 281-338 in Prehistoric Maritime Adaptations of the Circumpolar Zone. W. Fitzhugh, ed. The Hague, Paris: Mouton.

1977   Prehistoric Human Occupation of the Rat Islands. Pp. 59-113 in the Environment of Amchitka Island, Alaska. M.L. Merritt and R.G. Fuller, eds. (*TID-26712*) [Washington]: Energy Research and Development Administration, Technical Information Center.

1977a   Thule Eskimo Prehistory Along Northwestern Hudson Bay. *Canada. National Museum of Man. Mercury Series. Archaeological Survey Paper* 70. Ottawa.

_____, ed.
1979   Thule Eskimo Culture: An Anthropological Perspective. *Canada. National Museum of Man. Mercury Series. Archaeological Survey Paper* 88. Ottawa.

McCartney, Allen P., and Christy G. Turner, II
1966   Memorandum on the Anangula Core and Blade Complex. (Unpublished manuscript in McCartney's possession.)

1966a   Stratigraphy of the Anangula Unifacial Core and Blade Site. *Arctic Anthropology* 3(2):28-40.

M'Clintock, Sir Francis L.
1859   The Voyage of the 'Fox' in the Arctic Seas: A Narrative of the Discovery of the Fate of Sir John Franklin and His Companions. London: J. Murray.

McCoy, Donald R.
1956   The Special Indian Agency in Alaska, 1873-1874: Its Origins and Operation. *Pacific Historical Review* 25(4):355-367.

McCracken, Harold
1930   God's Frozen Children. Garden City, N.Y.: Doubleday, Doran and Company.

McElroy, Ann P.
1971   The Influence of Modernization on Female Eskimo Role Identification. (Paper presented at the 70th Meeting of the American Anthropological Association, New York City.)

MacFarlane, Roderick R.
1891   Notes on and List of Birds and Eggs Collected in Arctic America, 1861-1866. *Proceedings of the U.S. National Museum* 14:413-446. Washington.

1905   Notes on Mammals Collected and Observed in the Northern Mackenzie River District, Northwest Territories of Canada, with Remarks on Explorers and Explorations of the Far North. *Proceedings of the U.S. National Museum* 28:673-764. Washington.

McGhee, Robert
1968   Copper Eskimo Prehistory. (Unpublished Ph.D. Dissertation in Archeology, University of Calgary, Alberta.)

1969-1970 Speculations on Climatic Change and Thule Culture Development. *Folk* 11-12:173-184. Copenhagen.

1970   Excavations at Bloody Falls, N.W.T., Canada. *Arctic Anthropology* 6(2):53-72.

1971   An Archeological Survey of Western Victoria Island, N.W.T. *Anthropological Series* 87, *National Museum of Canada Bulletin* 232:157-191. Ottawa.

1971a   Excavation at Kittigazuit. *The Beaver* 302(2):34-39.

1972   Copper Eskimo Prehistory. *National Museums of Canada. Publications in Archaeology* 2. Ottawa.

1972a   Climatic Change and the Development of Canadian Arctic Cultural Traditions. Pp. 39-60 in Climatic Change in Arctic Areas During the Last Ten Thousand Years. Y. Vasari, H. Hyvärinen, and S. Hicks, eds. *Acta Universitatis Ouluensis, ser. A. Geologica* 1. Oulu, Finland.

1974   Beluga Hunters: An Archaeological Reconstruction of the Mackenzie Delta Kittegaryumiut. *University of Newfoundland. Institute of Social and Economic Resources. Social and Economics Studies* 13. St. John's.

1976   Paleoeskimo Occupations of Central and High Arctic Canada. Pp. 15-39 in Eastern Arctic Prehistory: Paleoeskimo Problems. Moreau S. Maxwell, ed. *Memoirs of the Society for American Archaeology* 31. Salt Lake City.

1976a   Parsimony Isn't Everything: An Alternative View of Eskaleutian Linguistics and Prehistory. *Canadian Archaeological Association Bulletin* 8:62-81.

1976b   The Burial at l'Anse Amour. (Report to the National Museums of Canada, Ottawa.)

1978   Canadian Arctic Prehistory. Toronto, New York: Van Nostrand, Reinhold.

1979   The Paleoeskimo Occupations of Port Refuge, High Arctic Canada. *Canada. National Museum of Man. Mercury Series. Archeological Survey Paper* 92. Ottawa.

1982   Norsemen and Eskimos in Arctic Canada. Pp. 38-52 in Vikings in the West. Eleanor Guralnick, ed. Chicago: Archaeological Institute of America.

1982a   Possible Norse-Eskimo Contacts in the Eastern Arctic. Pp. 31-40 in Early European Settlement and Exploitation in Atlantic Canada. G.M. Story, ed. St. John's: Memorial University of Newfoundland.

McGhee, Robert, and James A. Tuck, Jr.
1975   An Archaic Sequence from the Strait of Belle Isle, Labrador. *Canada. National Museum of Man. Mercury Series. Archeological Survey Paper* 34. Ottawa.

1976   Undating the Canadian Arctic. Pp. 6-14 in Eastern Arctic Prehistory: Paleoeskimo Problems. Moreau S. Maxwell, ed. *Memoirs of the Society for American Archaeology* 31. Salt Lake City.

McGovern, Thomas H.
1979   Thule-Norse Interaction in Southwest Greenland: A Speculative Model. Pp 171-188 in Thule Eskimo Culture: An Anthropological Retrospective. Allen P. McCartney, ed. *Canada. National Museum of Man. Mercury Series. Archaeological Survey Paper* 88. Ottawa.

1980   Cows, Harp Seals, and Churchbells: Adaptation and Extinction in Norse Greenland. *Human Ecology* 8(3):245-275.

1981   The Economics of Extinction in Norse Greenland. Pp. 404-434 in Climate and History. T.M.L. Wigley, M.J. Ingram, and G. Farmer, eds. London: Cambridge University Press.

McGovern, Thomas H., and Richard H. Jordan
1982   Settlement and Land Use in the Inner Fjords of Godthaab District, West Greenland. *Arctic Anthropology* 19(1):63-79.

Mackay, J. Ross
1964   Arctic Landforms. Pp. 60-62 in The Unbelievable Land. I.N. Smith, ed. Ottawa: Department of Northern Affairs and National Resources.

1972   Some Observations on the Growth of Pingos. Pp. 141-148 in Mackenzie Delta Area Monograph. Denis Kerfoot, ed. St. Catherines, Ont.: Brock University, Department of Geography.

Mackay, J. Ross, and D.K. Mackay
1972   Break-up and Ice Jamming on the Mackenzie River, Northwest Territories. Pp. 87-94 in Mackenzie Delta Area Monograph. Denis Kerfoot, ed. St. Catherines, Ont.: Brock University, Department of Geography.

McKeevor, Thomas
1819   A Voyage to Hudson's Bay During the Summer of 1812: Containing a Particular Account of the Icebergs and Other Phenomena Which Present Themselves in These Regions; Also, a Description of the Esquimeaux and North American Indians; Their Manners, Customs, Dress, Language, etc. London: Phillips.

Mackenzie, Sir Alexander
1801   Voyages from Montreal on the River St. Lawrence, Through the Continent of North America to the Frozen and Pacific Oceans in the Years 1789 and 1793 with a Preliminary Account of the Rise, Progress, and Present State of the Fur Trade of That Country. London: T. Cadell, Jr., and W. Davies, etc.

MacLaren, Ian A.
1958   The Biology of the Ringed Seal (*Phoca hispida* Schreber) in the Eastern Canadian Arctic. *Canada. Fisheries Research Board Bulletin* 118. Ottawa.

1961   Methods of Determining the Numbers and Availability of Ringed Seals in the Canadian Eastern Arctic. *Arctic* 14(3):162-175.

1962   Population Dynamics and Exploitation of Seals in the Eastern Canadian Arctic. Pp. 168-183 in The Exploitation of Natural Animal Populations: A Symposium of the British Ecological Society, Durham, 28-31 March 1960. E.D. Le Cren and M.W. Holdgate, eds. Oxford, England: Blackwell.

MacLean, Edna Ahgeak
1980   Abridged Iñupiaq and English Dictionary. Fairbanks: University of Alaska, Native Language Center.

1981   Siglit Inuvialuktun Dialect Paradigms. (Manuscript in Alaska Native Language Center, University of Alaska, Fairbanks.).

McLean, John
1932   John McLean's Notes of a Twenty-five Year's Service in the Hudson's Bay Territory [1849]. W.S. Wallace, ed. (*Publications of the Champlain Society* 19) Toronto: The Champlain Society.

McLenegan, Samuel B.
1887   Exploration of the Noätak River, Alaska. Pp. 53-80 in Report of the Cruise of the Revenue Marine Steamer 'Corwin' in the Arctic Ocean, 1885, by M.A. Healy. Washington: U.S. Government Printing Office.

1889   Exploration of the Kowak River, Alaska: Notes on the Natural History Resources, 1884. Pp. 99-108 in Report of the Cruise of the Revenue Marine Steamer 'Corwin' in the Arctic Ocean in the Year 1884, by M.A. Healy. Washington: U.S. Government Printing Office.

MacMillan, Donald B.
1918   Food Supply of the Smith Sound Eskimos. *American Museum Journal* 18(3):161-176.

MacNeish, Richard S.
1956   The Engigstciak Site on the Yukon Arctic Coast. *Anthropological Papers of the University of Alaska* 4(2):91-111. College.

1956a   Archaeological Reconnaissance of the Delta of the Mackenzie River and Yukon Coast. *National Museum of Canada Bulletin* 142:46-81. Ottawa.

1959   Men Out of Asia, as Seen from Northwest Yukon. *Anthropological Papers of the University of Alaska* 7(2):41-70. College.

1962   Recent Finds in the Yukon Territory of Canada. Pp. 20-26 in Prehistoric Cultural Relations Between the Arctic and Temperate Zones of North America. John M. Campbell, ed. *Arctic Institute of North America Technical Paper* 11. Montreal.

1964   Investigations in Southwest Yukon: Archaeological Excavations, Comparisons, and Speculations. *Papers of the Robert S. Peabody Foundation for Archaeology* 6(2). Andover, Mass.

MacPherson, A.H.
1965   The Origin of Diversity in Mammals of the Canadian Arctic Tundra. *Systematic Zoology* 14(3):153-173.

Mailhot, José
1968   Inuvik Community Structure—Summer 1965. (*MDRP-4*) Ottawa: Department of Indian Affairs and Northern Development, Northern Science Research Group.

1978   L'Etymologie de "Esquimau:" Revue et corrigée. *Études/Inuit/Studies* 2(2):59-69.

Mailhot, José, J.-P. Simard, and S. Vincent
1980   On est toujours l'Esquimau de quelqu'un. *Études/Inuit/Studies* 4(1-2):59-76.

Malaurie, Jean N.
1952   Problèmes économiques et humains au Groenland; Note sur Thulé. *Annales de Géographie* 61(326):291-297. Paris.

1956   The Last Kings of Thule: A Year Among the Polar Eskimos of Greenland. Gwendolen Freeman, trans. New York: Thomas Y. Crowell.

776

1973   Du Droit des minorités esquimaudes nord-américaines et de la population groenlandaise: Notions implicites au diagnostic de sous-développement. Pp. 27-49 in Le Peuple esquimau aujourd' hui et demain/The Eskimo People To-day and To-Morrow. Jean Malaurie, ed. (Fourth International Congress of the Fondation Française d'Études Nordiques) Paris, The Hague: Mouton.

————, ed.
1973a   Le Peuple esquimau aujourd'hui et demain. The Eskimo People To-day and To-morrow. Jean Malaurie, ed. (Fourth International Congress of the Fondation Française d'Études Nordiques) Paris, The Hague: Mouton.

1974   Les Esquimaux polaires (nord-ouest du Groenland): Extraits d'un "Atlas d'écologie animale et humaine: Les Esquimaux polaires." Inter-Nord 13-14(December):163-170. Paris.

1975   Les Derniers rois de Thulé: Avec les Esquimaux polaires, face à leur destin. 3d. ed. rev. Paris: Plon.

————, ed.
1975a   The Fifth International Congress on Arctic Oil and Gas: Problems and Possibilities. 2 vols. Paris: Mouton.

Malaurie, Jean N., and Jacques Rosseau, eds.
1964   Le Nouveau-Québec: Contribution à l'étude de l'occupation humaine. (Bibliothèque Arctique et Antarctique 2) Paris: Mouton.

Malaurie, Jean N., Léon Tabah, and Jean Sutter
1952   L'Isolat esquimau de Thulé (Groenland). Population 7(4):675-692.

Malaurie, Jean N., Y. Vasari, H. Hyvärinen, G. Delibrias, and J. Labeyrie
1972   Preliminary Remarks on Holocene Paleoclimates in the Regions of Thule and Inglefield Land, Above All Since the Beginning of Our Own Era. Pp. 105-136 in Climatic Changes in Arctic Areas, During the Last Ten Thousand Years. Y. Vasari, H. Hyvärinen, and S. Hicks, eds. Acta Universitatis Ouluensis, ser. A. Geologica 1. Oulu, Finland.

Malgrange-Saladin, Geneviève, and Bernard Saladin d'Anglure
1973   Une enquête alimentaire chez les Inuit de Maricourt-Wakeham (Kangiqsujuaq) Nouveau-Québec. (Unpublished report at the Anthropology Labroratory, Université Laval, Quebec.)

Mandelbaum, David G., ed.
1951   Selected Writings of Edward Sapir. Berkeley: University of California Press.

Manning, T.H.
1956   Narrative of a Second Defence Research Board Expedition to Banks Island with Notes on the Country and on the History. Arctic 9(1-2):3-77.

Mansfield, A.W.
1967   Seals of Arctic and Eastern Canada. 2d ed. Canada. Fisheries Research Board Bulletin 137. Ottawa.

Manville, Richard H., and Stanley P. Young
1965   Distribution of Alaskan Mammals. U.S. Fish and Wildlife Circular 211. Washington.

Markham, Sir Albert H., ed.
1880   The Voyages and Works of John Davis, the Navigator. London: Hakluyt Society.

Marsh, Donald B.
[1967]   A History of the Work of the Anglican Church in the Area Now Known as the Diocese of the Arctic. Toronto: no publisher.

Marsh, Gordon H.
1954   A Comparative Survey of Eskimo-Aleut Religion. Anthropological Papers of the University of Alaska 3(1):21-36. College.

1956   A Stone Lamp from Yukon Island, Alaska. Anthropological Papers of the University of Alaska 4(2):113-115. College.

Marsh, Gordon H., and William S. Laughlin
1956   Human Anatomical Knowledge Among the Aleutian Islanders. Southwestern Journal of Anthropology 12(1):38-78.

Marsh, Gordon H., and Morris Swadesh
1951   Kleinschmidt Centennial V: Eskimo Aleut Correspondences. International Journal of American Linguistics 17(4):209-216.

Martijn, Charles A.
1964   Canadian Eskimo Carving in Historical Perspective. Anthropos 59(3-4):545-596.

1980   The "Esquimaux" in the 17th and 18th Century Cartography of the Gulf of St. Lawrence: A Preliminary Discussion. Etudes/Inuit/Studies 4(1-2):77-104.

1980a   La Présence Inuit sur la côte-nord du golfe St-Laurent à l'époque historique. Études/Inuit/Studies 4(1-2):105-125.

1980b   The Inuit of Southern Quebec-Labrador: A Rejoinder to J. Garth Taylor. Études/Inuit/Studies 4(1-2):194-198.

Martijn, Charles A., and Norman Clermont, eds.
1980   Les Inuit du Québec-Labrador meridional/The Inuit of Southern Quebec-Labrador. Études/Inuit/Studies 4(1-2).

Martin, George C.
1913   The Recent Eruption of Katmai Volcano in Alaska: An Account of One of the Most Tremendous Volcanic Explosions Known in History. National Geographic Magazine 24(2):131-181.

Martin, Guy
1975   The Politics of Passage. Juneau: Alaska Department of Education.

Mary-Rousselière, Guy
1954   Issingut, the Starvation Camp. Eskimo 34 (December):9-13.

1956   Christmas Igloo. The Beaver (Winter):4-5.

1964   Paleo-Eskimo Remains in the Pelly Bay Region, N.W.T. Anthropological Series 61, National Museum of Canada Bulletin 193(1):162-183. Ottawa.

1969   Les Jeux de Ficelle des Arviligjuarmiut. Anthropological Series 88, National Museum of Canada Bulletin 233. Ottawa.

1976   The Paleoeskimo in Northern Baffinland. Pp. 40-57 in Eastern Arctic Prehistory: Paleoeskimo Problems. Moreau S. Maxwell, ed. Memoirs of the Society for American Archaeology 31. Salt Lake City.

1979   A Few Problems Elucidated...and New Questions Raised by Recent Dorset Finds in the North Baffin Island Region. Arctic 32(1):22-32.

1980   Qitdlarssuaq—l'histoire d'une migration polaire. Montreal: Les Presses de l'Université de Montréal.

Masnick, G.S., and S.H. Katz
1976   Trends in Fertility in a Northern Alaska Community. Pp. 259-268 in Circumpolar Health. R.J. Shephard and S. Itoh, eds. Toronto: University of Toronto Press.

Mason, J. Alden
1928   A Remarkable Stone Lamp from Alaska. University of Pennsylvania Museum Journal 19(2):170-194. Philadelphia.

1930   Excavations of Eskimo Thule Culture Sites at Point Barrow, Alaska. Pp. 383-394 in Proceedings of the 23d International Congress of Americanists. New York, 1928.

Mason, Otis T.
1891   The Ulu, or Woman's Knife, of the Eskimo. Pp. 411-416 in Annual Report of the United States National Museum for 1890. Washington.

1896   Influence of Environment Upon Human Industries or Arts. Pp. 639-665 in Pt. 1 of *Annual Report of the Smithsonian Institution for 1895*. 2 Pts. Washington.

1902   Aboriginal American Harpoons: A Study in Ethnic Distribution and Invention. Pp. 189-304 in *Report of the United States National Museum for 1900*. Washington.

1907   Environment. Pp. 427-430 in Vol. 1 of Handbook of American Indians North of Mexico. Frederick W. Hodge, ed. 2 vols. *Bureau of American Ethnology Bulletin* 30. Washington.

Masterson, James R., and Helen Brower
1948   Bering's Successors, 1745-1780: Contributions of Peter Simon Pallas to the History of Russian Exploration Toward Alaska. Seattle: University of Washington Press. (Reprinted from *Pacific Northwest Quarterly* 38(1-2), 1947.)

Mathiassen, Therkel
1927   Archaeology of the Central Eskimo. 2 vols. *Report of the Fifth Thule Expedition 1921-24*. Vol. 4(1-2). Copenhagen.

1928   Material Culture of the Iglulik Eskimos. *Report of the Fifth Thule Expedition, 1921-24*. Vol. 6(1). Copenhagen.

1929   Eskimo Relics from Washington Land and Hall Land. *Meddelelser om Grønland* 71(3). Copenhagen.

1930   The Question of the Origin of Eskimo Culture. *American Anthropologist* 32(4):591-607.

1930a   Archaeological Collections from the Western Eskimos. *Report of the Fifth Thule Expedition, 1921-24*. Vol. 10(1). Copenhagen.

1930b   Notes of Knud Rasmussen's Archaeological Collections from the Western Eskimo. Pp. 395-399 in *Proceedings of the 23d International Congress of Americanists*. New York, 1928.

1931   Ancient Eskimo Settlements in the Kangâmiut Area. *Meddelelser om Grønland* 91(1). Copenhagen.

1931a   Inugsuk, a Mediaeval Eskimo Settlement in Upernavik District, West Greenland. *Meddelelser om Grønland* 77(4):147-340. Copenhagen.

1931b   The Present Stage of Eskimo Archaeology. *Acta Archaeologica* 2(2):185-199. Copenhagen.

1933   Prehistory of the Angmagssalik Eskimos. *Meddelelser om Grønland* 92(4). Copenhagen.

1934   Contributions to the Archaeology of Disko Bay. *Meddelelser om Grønland* 93(2). Copenhagen.

1934a   Eskimo Finds from the Kanderdlugssuak Region. *Meddelelser om Grønland* 104(9). Copenhagen.

1935   Eskimo Migrations in Greenland. *Geographical Review* 25(3):408-422. New York.

1936   The Eskimo Archaeology of Julianehaab District. *Meddelelser om Grønland* 118(1). Copenhagen.

1936a   The Former Eskimo Settlements on Frederik VI's Coasts. *Meddelelser om Grønland* 109(2). Copenhagen.

1958   The Sermermiut Excavations, 1955. *Meddelelser om Grønland* 161(3). Copenhagen.

Mathiassen, Therkel, and Erik Holtved
1936   The Eskimo Archaeology of Julianehaab District, with a Brief Summary of the Prehistory of the Greenlanders. *Meddelelser om Grønland* 118(1). Copenhagen.

Matthiasson, John S.
1967   Eskimo Legal Acculturation: The Adjustment of Baffin Island Eskimos to Canadian Law. (Unpublished Ph.D. Dissertation in Anthropology, Cornell University, Ithaca, N.Y.)

1975   You Scratch My Back and I'll Scratch Yours: Continuities in Inuit Social Relationships. *Arctic Anthropology* 12(1):31-36.

1977   The Continuation and Transformation of Traditional Inuit Power Bases into the Modern Context. *University of Oklahoma Papers in Anthropology* 18(2). Norman.

Mattox, William G.
1973   Fishing in West Greenland, 1910-1966: The Development of a New Native Industry. *Meddelelser om Grønland* 197(1). Copenhagen.

Maxwell, James A.
1978   America's Fascinating Indian Heritage. Pleasantville, N.Y.: Reader's Digest Association.

Maxwell, Moreau S.
1960   An Archaeological Analysis of Eastern Grant Land, Ellesmere Island, Northwest Territories. *Anthropological Series* 49, *National Museum of Canada Bulletin* 170. Ottawa.

1960a   The Movement of Cultures in the Canadian High Arctic. *Anthropologica* n.s. 2(2):177-189. Ottawa.

1962   Pre-Dorset and Dorset Sites in the Vicinity of Lake Harbour, Baffin Island, N.W.T.: A Preliminary Report. *Anthropological Series* 57, *National Museum of Canada Bulletin* 180:20-55. Ottawa.

1967   The Origin and Development of Dorset Culture. (Paper presented at the 32d Annual Meeting of the Society for American Archaeology, Ann Arbor.)

1973   Archaeology of the Lake Harbor District, Baffin Island. *Canada. National Museum of Man. Mercury Series. Archaeological Survey Paper* 6. Ottawa.

1974-1975   An Early Dorset Harpoon Complex. *Folk* 16-17:125-132.

1976   Pre-Dorset and Dorset Artifacts: The View from Lake Harbor. Pp. 58-78 in Eastern Prehistory: Paleoeskimo Problems. Moreau S. Maxwell, ed. *Memoirs of the Society for American Archaeology* 31. Salt Lake City.

May, Alan G.
1951   Mummies from Alaska. *Natural History* 60(3):114-119.

Mayes, Robert G.
1978   The Creation of a Dependent People: The Inuit of Cumberland Sound, Northwest Territories. (Unpublished Ph.D. Dissertation in Social Geography, McGill University, Montreal.)

Mayhall, J.T.
1976   Inuit Culture Change and Oral Health: A Four-year Study. Pp. 414-420 in Circumpolar Health. R.J. Shephard and S. Itoh, eds. Toronto: University of Toronto Press.

Maynard, Washburn
1898   The Fur-Seal Fisheries. Pp. 289-309 in Vol. 3 of Seal and Salmon Fisheries and General Resources of Alaska. 4 vols. Washington: U.S. Government Printing Office.

Meany, Edmond S.
1906   Alaskan Mummies. *Washington Magazine* 1:459-468. Seattle.

Meares, John
1790   Voyages Made in the Years 1788 and 1789, from China to the North West Coast of America. To Which Are Prefixed an Introductory Narrative of a Voyage Performed in 1786 from Bengal in the Ship Nootka. Observations on the Probable Existence of a North West Passage, and Some Account of the Trade Between the North West Coast of America and China and the Latter Country and Great Britain. London: Printed at the Logographic Press.

Meehan, J.P.
1955   Body Heat Production and Surface Temperatures in Response to Cold Stimulus. *Journal of Applied Physiology* 7:537-541.

Meldgaard, Jørgen
1952   A Palaeo-Eskimo Culture in West Greenland. *American Antiquity* 17(3):222-230.

_____
1953   Fra en Grønlandsk Mumiehule [From a Greenland Mummy Cave]. *Nationalmuseets Arbejdsmark* 14-20, 106-107. Copenhagen.

_____
1960   Prehistoric Culture Sequences in the Eastern Arctic as Elucidated by Stratified Sites at Igloolik. Pp. 588-595 in Men and Cultures. Anthony F.C. Wallace, ed. *Selected Papers of the Fifth International Congress of Anthropological and Ethnological Sciences*, 1956. Philadelphia: University of Pennsylvania Press.

_____
1960a   Origin and Evolution of Eskimo Cultures in the Eastern Arctic. *Canadian Geographical Journal* 60(2):64-75.

_____
1960b   Eskimo Sculpture. Jytte Lynner and Peter Wait, trans. London: Methuen.

_____
1961   Sarqaq-folket ved Itivnera [The Sarqaq People, at Itinnera]. *Grønland* 9:15-23. Copenhagen.

_____
1962   On the Formative Period of the Dorset Culture. Pp. 92-95 in Prehistoric Cultural Relations Between the Arctic and Temperate Zones of North America. John M. Campbell, ed. *Arctic Institute of North America Technical Paper 11*. Montreal.

_____
1965   Nordboerne i Grønland: En vikingebygds historie [The Norsemen in Greenland: History of a Viking Settlement]. Copenhagen: Munksgaards Forlag.

_____
1977   The Prehistoric Cultures in Greenland: Discontinuities in a Marginal Area. Pp. 19-52 in Continuity and Discontinuity in the Inuit Culture of Greenland. Hans P. Kylstra, ed. Groningen, The Netherlands: University of Groningen Arctic Center.

_____
1982   Aron: En af de mærkværdigste billed-samlinger i Verden [Aron: One of the Most Remarkable Picture Collections in the World]. Copenhagen: Nationalmuseet.

Mendenhall, Walter C.
1902   A Reconnaissance from Fort Hamlin to Kotzebue Sound, Alaska by Way of Dall, Kanuti, Allen, and Kowak Rivers. *U.S. Geological Survey Professional Paper 10, ser. A, Economic Geology* 20. Washington.

Menovshchikov, Georgiĭ Alekseevich
1958   Ėskimosskie skazki [Eskimo Tales]. Magadan: Magadanskoe Knizhnoe Izdatel'stvo.

_____
1959   Ėskimosy; nauchno-populi͡arnyĭ istoriko-ėtnograficheskiĭ ocherk ob aziatskikh ėskimosakh [The Eskimos: A Popular Scientific Historical Ethnographic Outline of the Asiatic Eskimo]. Magadan: Magadanskoe Knizhnoe Izdatel'stvo.

_____
1962   O perezhitochnykh i͡avleni͡iakh rodovoĭ organisat͡sii u aziatskikh ėskimosov: Iz polevykh nabli͡udeniĭ [Surviving Elements of Clan Organization Among Asiatic Eskimos: From Field Investigations]. *Sovetskai͡a Ėtnografii͡a* 6:29-34.

_____
1962-1967   Grammatika i͡azyka aziatskikh ėskimosov. [Grammar of the Language of Asiatic Eskimos.] 2 vols. Leningrad: Izdatel'stvo "Nauka", Leningradskoe Otdelenie.

_____
1963   Paleoėskimosskie toponimy severo-vostochnoĭ Sibiri [Paleo-Eskimo Place-names in Northeastern Siberia]. *Voprosy I͡Azykoznanii͡a* 12(6):121-125.

_____
1964   I͡Azyk sirenikskikh ėskimosov: Fonetika, ocherk morfologii, teksty i slovar'. [The Language of the Sireniki Eskimos: Phonetics, Morphological Sketch, Texts, and Dictionary.] Moscow and Leningrad: Izdatel'stvo "Nauk."

_____
1974   Skazki i mify narodov Chukotki i Kamchatki: aziat. ėskimosy, chukchi, kereki, kori͡aki i itel'meny [Tales and Myths of the Peoples of the Chukotka Peninsula and Kamchatka: Asiatic Eskimo Chukchi, Kerek, Koryak and Kamchadal]. Moscow: Akademii͡a Nauk SSSR., Institut Vostokovedenii͡a.

_____
1975   I͡Azyk naukanskikh ėskimosov: foneticheskoe vvedenie, ocherk morfologii, teksty, slovar'. [The Language of the Naukan Eskimos: Introduction to Phonetics, Morphological Sketch, Texts, and Dictionary.] Leningrad: Izdatel'stvo "Nauka."

_____
1980   O Proiskhozhdenii ėtnonima 'Aleut' [On the Origin of the Ethnonym 'Aleut']. *Sovetskai͡a Ėtnografii͡a* 1:109-116.

_____
1980a   I͡Azyk ėskimosov Beringova proliva [The Language of the Bering Strait Eskimos]. Leningrad: "Nauka" Leningradskoe Otdelenie.

Menovshchikov, G.A., and N.B. Shnakenburg
1956   Ėskimosy [The Eskimo]. Pp. 934-949 in Narody Sibiri. M.G. Levin and L.P. Potov, eds. Moscow: Izdatel'stvo Adademii Nauk SSSR. (Translation: "The Eskimo" from The Peoples of Siberia. Charles C. Hughes, trans. *Anthropological Papers of the University of Alaska* 12(1):1-13, 1964.) College.

Merbs, Charles F.
1968   Burial Patterns in the Canadian Arctic. (Paper presented at the 33d Annual Meeting of the Society for American Archaeology, Santa Fe.)

_____
1968a   Human Burials of Silumiut, a Thule Culture Site North of Chesterfield Inlet, Northwest Territories. (Preliminary Report to the National Museum of Man, Ottawa.)

Merck, Carl H.
1980   Siberia and Northwestern America, 1788-1792: The Journal of Carl Heinrich Merck, Naturalist with the Russian Scientific Expedition Led by Captains Joseph Billings and Gavril Sarychev. Fritz Jaensch, trans.; Richard A. Pierce, ed. (*Materials for the Study of Alaska History* 17) Kingston, Ont.: Limestone Press.

Merritt, Melvin L., and R. Glen Fuller, eds.
1977   The Environment of Amchitka Island, Alaska. (*TID-26712*) [Washington]: Energy Research and Development Administration, Technical Information Center.

Mertie, J.B., Jr.
1938   The Nushagak District, Alaska. *U.S. Geological Survey Bulletin* 903. Washington.

Metayer, Maurice
1973   Unipkat, tradition esquimaude de Coppermine, Territoires-du-Nord-Ouest, Canada. 3 Pts. *Centre d'Études Nordiques, Collection Nordicana*, 40, 41, 42. Quebec.

Meyer, Carolyn
1977   Eskimos: Growing Up in a Changing Culture. New York: Atheneum.

Meyer, David
1976   Eskimos of West Hudson Bay, 1619-1820. *Na'pāo* 6(1-2):41-59. Saskatoon.

Meyers, Walter E.
1957   Eskimo Village. New York: Vantage Press.

Michael, Henry N.
1958   The Neolithic Age in Eastern Siberia. *Transactions of the American Philosophical Society* 48(2). Philadelphia.

Michea, Jean
1949   Terre stérile, six mois chez les Esquimaux caribou. Paris: Bould and Gay.

Mickey, Barbara Harris
1955 The Family Among the Western Eskimo. *Anthropological Papers of the University of Alaska* 4(1):13-22. College.

Miertsching, Johann A.
1967 Frozen Ships: The Arctic Diary of Johann Miertsching, 1850-1854. Leslie H. Neatby, trans. and ed. Toronto: Macmillan of Canada.

Mikkelsen, Ejnar
1934 De østgrønlandske Eskimoers Historie [The History of the East Greenland Eskimo]. Copenhagen: Gyldendal.

1950 Øst-grønland [East Greenland]. Pp. 251-268 in Vol. 2 of Grønlandsbogen. Kaj Birket-Smith, Ernest Mentze, and M. Friis Møller, eds. 2 vols. Copenhagen: J.H. Schultz-Forlag.

1950a Scoresbysund kolonien gjennem 25 år [The Scoresbysund Settlement Through 25 Years]. *Det grønlandske Selskabs Årsskrift*: 15-29. Copenhagen.

1965 Scoresbysund kolonien [The Scoresbysund Settlement]. *Grønland* 11:369-378, 12:409-428. Copenhagen.

Mikkelsen, Ejnar, and P.P. Sveistrup
1944 The East Greenlanders' Possibilities of Existence, Their Production and Consumption. *Meddelelser om Grønland* 134(2). Copenhagen.

Milan, Frederick A.
1964 The Acculturation of the Contemporary Eskimo of Wainwright, Alaska. *Anthropological Papers of the University of Alaska* 11(2):1-81. College.

1974-1975 Historical Demography of Alaska's Native Population. *Folk* 16-17:45-54. Copenhagen.

1979 The Human Biology of Circumpolar Populations. (*International Biological Programme* 21) Cambridge, England: Cambridge University Press.

Milan, Frederick A., J.P. Hannon, and E. Evonuk
1963 Temperature Regulation of Eskimos, Indians, and Caucasians in a Bath Calorimeter. *Journal of Applied Physiology* 18(2):378-382.

Milan, Leda Chase
1974 Ethnohistory of Disease and Medical Care Among the Aleut. *Anthropological Papers of the University of Alaska* 16(2):15-40. Fairbanks.

Mills, Elaine L., ed.
1981 The Papers of John Peabody Harrington in the Smithsonian Institution, 1907-1957. Vol. 1: A Guide to the Field Notes, Native American History, Language, and Culture of Alaska/Northwest Coast. Millwood, N.Y.: Krauss International Publications.

Ministeriet for Grønland
1964 Betænkning fra Grønlandsudvalget af 1960. [Deliberations of the Greenland Committee of 1960]. *Betænkning* 363. Copenhagen.

1965 Grønlands Landsråds forhandlinger 1965: Ekstraordinær samling maj 1965. [Greenland Provincial Council Debates: Extraordinary Session, May 1965]. *Beretninger vedrørende Grønland* 2A. Godthåb.

1968 From Outpost to Town: The Migration Policy in Greenland. *The Community of Greenland* 2. Copenhagen.

1970-1982 Grønland, 1968-81: Årsberetninger udarbejdet af Ministeriet for Grønland [Greenland, 1968-81: Annual Report Prepared by the Ministry for Greenland]. Copenhagen.

Mirsky, Jeannette
1970 To the Arctic! The Story of Northern Exploration from Earliest Times to the Present. Chicago: University of Chicago Press.

Misfeldt, Jens
1977 Familieplanlægning i grønlandske lægedistrikter [Family Planning in Greenland Medical Districts]. *Ugeskrift for Læger* 139:1501-1504. Copenhagen.

Mitlîanskaîa, Tamara Benîsianovna
1976 Khudozhniki Chukotki [Artists of Chukotka]. Moscow: Izdatel´stvo Izobrazitel´noe Iskusstvo.

Miyaoka, Osahito
1974 An Eskimo Tribe Near "Mount Saint Elias (Alaska)." *Arctic Anthropology* 11(1):73-80.

1976 Word-initial Differentiation in Western Eskimo. Pp. 202-210 in Papers on Eskimo and Aleut Linguistics. Eric P. Hamp, ed. Chicago: Chicago Linguistic Society.

1978 Esukimo no gengo to bunka. [The Language and Culture of the Eskimos.] Tokyo: Kobundo.

Mochanov, IÛriĭ A.
1969 Mnogosloĭnaîa stoîanka Bel´kachi I i periodizaîsiîa kamennogo veka IÂkutii [The Multilevel Bel´kachi I Site and the Periodization of the Stone Age in Yakutia]. Akademiîa Nauk SSSR. IÂkutskiĭ Filial Sibirskogo Otdeleniîa, Institut IÂzyka, Literatury i Istorii. Moscow: Izdatel´stvo "Nauka."

1969a The Bel´kachinsk Neolithic Culture on the Aldan. Roger Powers, trans. *Arctic Anthropology* 6(1):104-14.

1969b The Ymyiakhtakh Late Neolithic Culture. Roger Powers, trans. *Arctic Anthropology* 6(1):115-118.

1969c Drevneĭshie ètapy zaseleniîa severo-vostochnoĭ Azii i Alîaski: K voprosu o pervonachal´nykh migraîsiîakh cheloveka v Ameriku [The Earliest Stages of the Settlement of Northeastern Asia and Alaska: The Problem of the Initial Migrations of Man to America]. *Sovetskaîa Ètnografiîa* 1:79-86.

1969d The Early Neolithic of the Aldan. Roger Powers, trans. *Arctic Anthropology* 6(1):95-103.

1970 Arkheologicheskaîa razvedka po reke Amguni i Chuchagerskomy Ozera [Archeological Reconnaissance Along the Amgun River and Chuchagersk Lake]. Pp. 154-182 in Po Sledam Drevnikh Kul´tur. IÂkutsk: IÂkutsk Knizhnoe Izdatel´stvo.

1970a Dîuktaĭskaîa peshchera—novyĭ paleoliticheskiĭ pamîatnik severo-vostochnoĭ Azii (Rezul´taty Rabot 1967) [The Diuktai Cave—A New Paleolithic Site in Northeast Asia (Results of Work in 1967)]. Pp. 40-64 in Po Sledam Drevnikh Kul´tur. IÂkutsk: IÂkutskoe Knizhnoe Izdatel´stvo.

1972 Novye dannye o Beringomorskom puti zaseleniîa Ameriki (Stoîanki Maĭorych—pervyĭ verkhnepaleoliticheskiĭ pamîatnik v doline Kolymy) [New Data on the Bering Sea Route of the Settlement of America (The Maĭorych Site—First Upper Paleolithic Monument in the Kolyma Valley)]. *Sovetskaîa Ètnografiîa* 2:98-101.

1973 Early Migrations to America in the Light of a Study of the Diuktai Paleolithic Culture in Northeast Asia. (Paper presented to the 9th International Congress of Anthropological and Ethnological Sciences, Chicago).

1976 Paleolit Sibiri [The Paleolithic of Siberia.] Pp. 540-565 in Beringiîa v Kaĭnozoe: Materialy Vsesoîuznogo Simpoziuma "Beringiĭskaîa Susha i ee Znachenie dlîa razvitiîa golarkticheskikh flor i faun v Kaĭnozoe," Khabarovsk, 10-15 Maîa 1973 [Beringia in the Cenozoic: Theses of the Reports of the All-Union Symposium "The Bering Land Bridge and Its Role in the History of Holarctic Floras and Faunas in the Late Cenozoic," Khabarovsk, 10-15 May, 1973]. Vladivostok: Academia Nauk SSSR.

1977   Drevneĭshie ėtapi zaseleniĭa chelovekom severo-vostochnoĭ Azii. [The Earliest Stages of the Settlement of Northeast Asia by Man]. Novosibirsk: Nauka, SNB. Otdelenie.

1980   Early Migrations to America in the Light of a Study of the Dyuktai Paleolithic Culture in Northeast Asia. Pp. 119-133 in Early Native Americans. D.L. Browman, ed. The Hague: Mouton.

Mochanov, I͡Uri A., and S.A. Fedoseeva
1975   Absoli͡utnai͡a Khronologii͡a Golot͡senovykh kul′tur severo-vostochnoĭ Azii [Absolute Chronology of Holocene Cultures of Northeastern Asia] I͡Akutii͡a i ee Sosedi v Drevnosti, c.38-49. Institut I͡Azyka, Literatury i Istorii, Iakutskiĭ Filial Sibirskogo Otdelenii͡a, Akademii͡a Nauk SSSR. I͡Akutsk.

1976   Osnovyne ėtapy drevneĭ istorii severo-vostochnoĭ Azii [The Major Stages of the Early History of Northeastern Asia]. Pp. 515-539 in Beringii͡a v Kaĭnozoe [Beringia in the Cenozoic]. Vladivostok: Akademii͡a Nauk SSSR.

Møhl, Jeppe
1979   Description and Analysis of the Bone Material from Nugarsuk: An Eskimo Settlement Representative of the Thule Culture in West Greenland. Pp. 380-394 in Thule Eskimo Culture: An Anthropological Retrospective. Allen P. McCartney, ed. Canada. National Museum of Man. Mercury Series. Archaeological Survey Paper 88. Ottawa.

1982   Ressourceudnyttelse fra norrøne og eskimoiske affaldslag belyst gennem Knoglematerialet [Resource Utilization from Norse and Eskimo Refuse Layers Illustrated through the Bone Material]. Grønland 8-9: 286-295. Copenhagen.

Møhl, Ulrik
1972   Animal Bones from Itivnera, West Greenland: A Reindeer Hunting Site of the Sarqaq Culture. Meddelelser om Grønland 191(6). Copenhagen.

Møller, Aqigssiaq
1983   Hjemmestyrets uddannelsespolitik [The Home Rule Educational Policy]. Den Grønlandske Kirkesag 119:33-35. Copenhagen.

Moll, T.A., and P.T. Inėnlikėĭ
1957   Chukotsko-russkiĭ slovar′ [Chukchi-Russian Dictionary]. Leningrad: Gosudarstvennoe uchebno-pedagogicheskoe izdatel′stvo Ministerstva Prosveshchenii͡a RSFSR, Leningradskoe Otdelenie.

Momatink, Yva, and John Eastcott
1977   Still Eskimo, Still Free—The Inuit of Umingmaktok. National Geographic Magazine 152(5):624-647.

Montpetit, Carmen, and Céline Veillet
1977   Recherches en ethnomusicologie: Les katajjait chez les Inuit du Nouveau-Québec. Études/Inuit/Studies 1(1):154-164.

Moore, J.W.
1974   The Benthic Algae of Southern Baffin Island. 1: Epipelic Communities in Rivers. Journal of Phycology 10(1):50-57.

Moore, Riley D.
1923   Social Life of the Eskimo of St. Lawrence Island. American Anthropologist 25(3):339-375.

Moore, T.E.L.
1851   Narrative of the Proceedings of Commander T.E.L. Moore, of Her Majesty's Ship 'Plover', from September 1849 to September 1850. Great Britain. Parliament. House of Commons Sessional Papers 33(97):28-34. London.

Morgan, Lael
1974   And the Land Provides: Alaskan Natives in a Year of Transition. Garden City, N.Y.: Anchor Press.

1974a   The Villages Are Alive and Well, Thank You. Alaska 40(8):33-39.

1975   Going It Alone. Alaska 41(7):33-38, 76-78.

1977   Time to Review Alaska Land Claims Settlement. Alaska 43(5):9-11, 14, 76-78, 81-82.

Morison, Samuel E.
1971   The European Discovery of America: The Northern Voyages, A.D. 500-1600. New York: Oxford University Press.

Morlan, Richard E.
1978   Early Man in Northern Yukon Territory: Perspectives as of 1977. Pp. 78-95 in Early Man in America from a Circum-Pacific Perspective. Alan L. Bryan, ed. University of Alberta, Occasional Papers of the Department of Anthropology 1. Edmonton.

1980   Taphonomy and Archacology in the Upper Pleistocene of the Northern Yukon Territory: A Glimpse of the Peopling of the New World. Canada. National Museum of Man. Mercury Series. Archaeological Survey Paper 94. Ottawa.

Morrison, David
1981   A Preliminary Statement on Neo-Eskimo Occupations in Western Coronation Gulf, N.W.T. Arctic 34(3):261-269.

Morton, Arthur S.
1939   A History of the Canadian West to 1870-1871: Being a History of Rupert's Land (The Hudson's Bay Company's Territory) and of the North-west Territory (Including the Pacific Slope). London, New York: T. Nelson and Sons. (2d ed., University of Toronto Press, Toronto, 1973.)

Moser, Jefferson F.
1899   The Salmon and Salmon Fisheries of Alaska: Report of the Operations of the United States Fish Commission Steamer Albatross for the Year Ending June 30, 1898. Washington: U.S. Government Printing Office.

1902   Alaska Salmon Investigations in 1900 and 1901: Salmon Investigations of the Steamer Albatross in the Summer of 1900. Bulletin of the U.S. Fish Commission 21:177-248. Washington.

Mouat, W. Ivan
1970   Education in the Arctic District. The Musk-Ox 7:1-9. Saskatoon.

Mouratoff, G.J., and E.M. Scott
1973   Diabetes Mellitus in Eskimos After a Decade. Journal of the American Medical Association 226:1345-1346.

Mowat, Farley M.
1952   People of the Deer. Boston: Little, Brown.

1959   The Desperate People. Boston: Little, Brown.

1966   The Executioners. Maclean's 79(13):7-11, 24-26.

Müller, Gerhard F.
1758   Opisanie morskikh puteshestviĭ po Ledovitomu i po Vostochnomu moriu s Rossiĭskoĭ storony uchinennykh. [Description of Maritime Travels to the Icy and Eastern Seas made from the Russian Side]. Ezhemi͡esi͡achnyi͡a Sochineniĭa i Izvi͡estiĭa o Uchenykh Di͡elakh 1:99-120, 195-212, 291-325, 387-409; 2:9-32, 99-129, 195-232, 309-336, 394-424. St. Petersburg: Imp. Akademii͡a Nauk.

1761   Voyages from Asia to America: For Completing the Discoveries of the North West Coast of America. To Which is Prefixed a Summary of the Voyages Made by the Russians on the Frozen Sea, in Search of a North East Passage. Serving as an Explanation of a Map of the Russian Discoveries, Published by the Academy of Sciences at Petersburgh. Thomas Jefferys, trans. London: T. Jefferys.

Müller, Karl
1926   Der Weg des Matthäus Stach: Ein Lebensbild des ersten Grönland-Missionars der ersten Brüdergemeinde. Aus alten Briefen und Tagebuchblättern. Berlin: Im Furche Verlag.

Müller-Beck, Hansjürgen
1967   On Migrations of Hunters Across the Bering Land Bridge in the Upper Pleistocene. Pp. 375-408 in The Bering Land Bridge. David M. Hopkins, ed. Stanford, Calif.: Stanford University Press.

Muir, John
1917   The Cruise of the Corwin: Journal of the Arctic Expedition of 1881 in Search of De Long and the Jeanette. William Frederic Badé, ed. Boston and New York: Houghton Mifflin.

Mumgark, Andy
1978   Return to Kuuvik. *Ajurnarmat* (Autumn):107-115. Eskimo Point, N.W.T.

————
1982   Hunters of the Keewatin: Hunting the Caribou/Kivallirmi angunasutiit: tuktunik angunasuarniq. *Inuktitut* 50(May):36-37, 40-41. Ottawa.

————
1982a   Hunters of the Keewatin: Hunting Regulations/Kivallirmi angunasutiit. *Inuktitut* 50(May):32-34. Ottawa.

Munk, Jens
1624   Navigatio septentrionalis... Copenhagen: H.H. Waldkirch.

————
1897   The Expedition of Captain Jens Munk to Hudson's Bay in Search of a North-West Passage in 1619-20. Vol. 2 of Danish Arctic Expeditions 1605-1620. C.C.A. Gosch, ed. London: Hakluyt Society.

Munn, Henry T.
1919   Southampton Island. *Geographical Journal* 54:52-55. London.

Murdoch, John
1884   A Study of the Eskimo Bows in the U.S. National Museum. Pp. 307-316 in *Report of the United States National Museum.* Washington.

————
1885   Natural History. Pp. 89-200 in Report of the International Polar Expedition to Point Barrow Alaska. Pt. 4. Washington: U.S. Government Printing Office.

————
1888   Dr. Rink's "Eskimo-Tribes." *American Anthropologist* 1(2):125-133.

————
1888a   On the Siberian Origin of Some Customs of the Western Eskimos. *American Anthropologist* 1(4):325-336.

————
1892   Ethnological Results of the Point Barrow Expedition. Pp. 19-441 in *9th Annual Report of the Bureau of American Ethnology for the Years 1887-1888.* Washington.

Murdock, George P.
1949   Social Structure. New York: MacMillan.

Murdock, George P., and Timothy J. O'Leary
1975   Ethnographic Bibliography of North America. 4th ed. 5 vols. New Haven, Conn.: Human Relations Area Files Press.

Murie, Margaret E.
1977   Island Between. Fairbanks: University of Alaska Press.

Murie, Olaus J.
1959   Fauna of the Aleutian Islands and Alaska Peninsula. (*North American Fauna* 61) Washington: U.S. Fish and Wildlife Service.

Murphy, Jane M., and Charles C. Hughes
1965   The Use of Psychophysiological Symptoms as Indicators of Disorder Among Eskimos. Pp. 108-160 in Approaches to Cross-Cultural Psychiatry. Jane M. Murphy and Alexander H. Leighton, eds. Ithaca, N.Y.: Cornell University Press.

Mutch, James S.
1906   Whaling in Ponds Bay. Pp. 485-500 in Boas Anniversary Volume: Anthropological Papers Written in Honor of Franz Boas, Presented to Him on the 25th Anniversary of His Doctorate, 9th August 1906. New York: G.E. Stechert.

Myers, M., ed.
1977   Joe Talirunili, a Grace Beyond the Reach of Art. Montreal: La Fédération des Cooperatives du Nouveau-Québec.

Mylius-Erichsen, Ludwig, and Harold Moltke
1906   ...Grønland: Illustreret skildring af den Danske litterære Grønlandsexpeditions rejser i Melvillebugten og ophold blandt jordens nordligst boende mennesker Polareskimoerne, 1903-04. [Greenland: Illustrated Description of the Travels of the Danish Literary Greenland Expedition in Melville Bay and Their Stay Among the Northernmost-Dwelling People in the World, the Polar Eskimos 1903-04]. Copenhagen: Gyldendalske Bogenhandel, Nordisk Forlag.

Nagle, Christopher
1978   Indian Occupations of the Intermediate Period on the Central Labrador Coast: A Preliminary Synthesis. *Arctic Anthropology* 15(2):119-145.

Naish, Constance M., and Gillian L. Story
1976   English-Tlingit Dictionary: Nouns. Rev. ed. Sitka, Alaska: Sheldon Jackson College.

Nansen, Fridtjof
1891   Eskimåliv [Eskimo Life]. Stockholm: Hugo Gebers Förlag. (Translation by W. Archer, Longmanns, Green, London, 1893.)

Nash, Ronald J.
1969   The Arctic Small Tool Tradition in Manitoba. *University of Manitoba. Department of Anthropology Occasional Paper* 2. Winnipeg.

————
1972   Dorset Culture in Northeastern Manitoba, Canada. *Arctic Anthropology* 9(1):10-16.

————
1976   Cultural Systems and Culture Change in the Central Arctic. Pp. 150-155 in Eastern Arctic Prehistory: Paleoeskimo Problems. Moreau S. Maxwell, ed. *Memoirs of the Society for American Archaeology* 31. Salt Lake City.

National Geographic Society
1983   Peoples of the Arctic. *National Geographic Magazine* 163(2). Map. Washington.

Nattiez, J.J., C. Charron, N. Beaudry, and D. Harvey
1978   Inuit Games and Songs: Vocal Games and Songs of the Eskimos of Northeastern Canada. Recorded in Ungava Bay, Baffin Land and the Hudson Bay Area. [Sound recording] UNESCO Collection. Philips, The Netherlands. 1 disc. 33⅓ rpm. 12 in.

Naylor, Larry, and Lawrence A. Gooding
1978   Alaska Native Hire on the Trans-Alaska Oil Pipeline Project. *Alaska Review of Social and Economic Conditions* 15(1):1-19.

Neatby, Leslie H.
1968   History of Hudson Bay. Pp. 69-125 in Vol. 1 of Science, History and Hudson Bay. C.S. Beals, ed. 2 vols. Ottawa: Department of Energy, Mines and Resources.

————
1970   The Search for Franklin. New York: Walker.

Nei, M., and A.K. Roychoudhury
1982   Genetic Relationship and Evolution of Human Races. *Evolutionary Biology* 14:1-60.

Nellemann, George
1960   *Mitârneq*: A West Greenland Winter Ceremony. *Folk* 2:99-113. Copenhagen.

————
1961   Vinterfiskeriet på Jakobshavns Isfjord. [Winter Fishing in Jakobshavns Isfjord, West Greenland.] *Geografisk Tidsskrift* 60:39-53. Copenhagen.

————
1962   De stærke drikkes histoire i Grønland [The History of Alcohol in Greenland]. *Grønland:* 191-199.

————
1969-1970   Caribou Hunting in West Greenland. *Folk* 11-12:133-153. Copenhagen.

1974-1975   How to Teach a Nation to Drink—or the "Bender" as a Status Symbol. *Folk* 16-17:227-232. Copenhagen.

Nelson, Edward W.
1899   The Eskimo About Bering Strait. Pp. 3-518 in *18th Annual Report of the Bureau of American Ethnology for the Years 1896-1897*. Washington. (Improved reprint, Smithsonian Instn. Press, 1984, W. W. Fitzhugh intro.)

Nelson, Richard K.
1969   Hunters of the Northern Ice. Chicago: University of Chicago Press.

1980   Shadow of the Hunter: Stories of Eskimo Life. Chicago: University of Chicago Press.

Nelson, Willis H., and Frank Barnett
1955   A Burial Cave on Kanaga Island, Aleutian Islands. *American Antiquity* 20(4):387-392.

Neuman, Daniel S.
1914   Mary's Igloo Potlatch. *Nome Daily Nugget*, January 20.

Neuman, Elizabeth
1914   Nidl-Gah-Ruit. Pp. 16-19 in The Aurora: Nome High School Annual. Nome, Alas.

Nielsen, Frederik
1970   Ilivse tássa nunagssarse: inuit nunatâmingnut nunasiartorneránik oqalugtuaq [This Land Shall Be Yours: A Story of How the Inuit Settled in Their Country]. Godthåb: Det Grønlandske Forlag.

Nielsen, Niels
1936   Evidence of Iron Extraction at Sandnes, in Greenland's West Settlement. *Meddelelser om Grønland* 88(4). Copenhagen.

Noble, William C.
1971   Archaeological Surveys and Sequences in Central District of Mackenzie, N.W.T. *Arctic Anthropology* 8(1):102-135.

Nørlund, Poul
1924   Buried Norsemen at Herjolfsnes: An Archaeological and Historical Study. *Meddelelser om Grønland* 67(1). Copenhagen.

Nørlund, Poul, and Aage Roussell
1930   Norse Ruins at Gardar: The Episcopal Seal of Mediaeval Greenland. *Meddelelser om Grønland* 76(1). Copenhagen.

Nooter, Gert
1972-1973   Change in a Hunting Community of East Greenland. *Folk* 14-15:163-204. Copenhagen.

1976   Leadership and Headship: Changing Authority Patterns in an East Greenland Hunting Community. *Mededelingen van het Rijksmuseum voor Volkenkunde* 20. Leiden.

1980   Improvisation and Innovation: Social Consequences of Material Changes. Pp. 113-121 in From Field-Case to Show-Case: Research, Acquisition and Presentation in the Rijksmuseum voor Volkenkunde, Leiden. W.R. Van Gulik, H.S. van der Straaten, and G.D. van Wengen, eds. Amsterdam: J.C. Gieben.

Northland News
1981   [ANSCA, Its Implementation and Consequence: A Series of Special Articles.] *Northland News* December 1:13-22.

Northwest Territories. Commissioner
1970   Annual Report. Yellowknife: Northwest Territories, Department of Information.

1975   Annual Report. [Yellowknife]: Department of Information.

Northwest Territories. Government
1969   Annual Report of the Department of Education. Yellowknife, N.W.T.

1971   [Survey of Education.] (Unpublished report to Northwest Territories Legislative Council, Yellowknife, NWT.)

1981   NWT Data Book. Yellowknife: Outcrop.

1981a   Annual Report for 1980. Yellowknife, N.W.T.

1983   NWT Data Book, 1982-83. Yellowknife: Outcrop.

Norton, Frank R.B., and J. Eugene Haas
1970   The Native Villages. Pp. 357-399 in The Great Alaska Earthquake of 1964: Human Ecology. Washington: National Research Council, Division of Earth Sciences, Committee on the Alaska Earthquake.

Nowak, Michael
1970   A Preliminary Report on the Archeology of Nunivak Island, Alaska. *Anthropological Papers of the University of Alaska* 15(1):19-32. College.

[1974]   The Archeology of Nunivak Island, Alaska. (Final report to the National Science Foundation, Washington, Grant GS-3023). Mimeo.

1975   Subsistence Trends in a Modern Eskimo Community. *Arctic* 28(1):21-34.

1977   The Economics of Native Subsistence Activities in a Village of Southwestern Alaska. *Arctic* 30(4):225-233.

1978   U.S. Fish and Wildlife Service Archaeological Reconnaissance of Kodiak National Wildlife Refuge: June-August 1977. Mimeo.

1979   Ocher and Ocean Bay: Archaeological Investigations at KOD 224. (Manuscript in Nowak's possession.)

1982   The Norton Period on Nunivak Island: Internal Change and External Influence. *Arctic Anthropology* 19(2):75-91.

Nuligak
1966   I, Nuligak. Maurice Métayer, ed. and trans. Toronto: Peter Martin Associates. (Reprinted: Pocket Books, New York, 1972.)

Nungak, Zebedee, and Eugene Arima
1969   Unikkaatuat sanaugarngnik atyingualiit Puvirngniturngmit: Eskimo Stories from Povungnituk, Quebec. *Anthropological Series* 90, *National Museum of Canada Bulletin* 235. Ottawa.

O'Bryan, Deric
1953   Excavation of a Cape Dorset Eskimo House Site, Mill Island, West Hudson Strait. *Annual Report of the National Museum of Canada for 1951-52, Bulletin* 128:40-57. Ottawa.

Oeschger, H., T. Riesen, and J.C. Lerman
1970   Bern Radiocarbon Dates VIII. *Radiocarbon* 12(2):358-384.

Ohyi, Haruo
1975   The Okhotsk Culture, a Maritime Culture in the South Okhotsk Sea Region. Pp. 123-158 in Prehistoric Maritime Adaptations of the Circumpolar Zones. W. Fitzhugh, ed. The Hague, Paris: Mouton.

Oka, M., S. Sugihara, and M. Watanabe
1961   Alaska: Report of the Meiji University Alaska Research Group. Tokyo: Kokin Shoin.

Okada, Hiroaki
1980   Prehistory of the Alaska Peninsula as Seen from the Hot Springs Site, Port Möller. Pp. 103-112 in Alaska Native Culture and History. Y. Kotani and W.B. Workman, eds. *National Museum of Ethnology, Senri Ethnological Series* 4. Osaka, Japan.

Okada, Hiroaki, and Atsuko Okada
1974   Preliminary Report of the 1972 Excavations at Port Möller, Alaska. *Arctic Anthropology* 11(Suppl.):112-124.

Okada, Hiroaki, and Bin Yamaguchi
1975   Human Skeletal Remains Excavated at the Hot Springs Village Site, Port Möller, Alaska Peninsula, in 1972. *Bulletin of*

the *National Science Museum* (*Series D: Anthropology*)1:25-42. Tokyo.

Okada, Hiroaki, Atsuko Okada, Yoshinobu Kotani, and Keishi Hattori
1976   The Hot Springs Village Site (2): Preliminary Report of the 1974 Excavations at Port Möller, Alaska. Tokyo: Hachioji.

Okladnikov, Alekseĭ Pavlovich
1947   Drevnie kul´tury severo-vostoka Azii po Dannym arkheologicheskikh issledovaniĭ 1946 g. v Kolymskom krae [The Early Cultures of Northeastern Asia from Data of the Archeological Investigations of 1946 in the Kolyma Region]. Akademiīa Nauk *SSSR. Institut Istorii, Vestnik Drevneĭ Istorii* 1:176-182.

_____
1953   O pervonachal´nom zaselenii chelovekom vnutrenneĭ chasti Chukotskogo poluostrova [On the Original Settlement by Man of the Interior of the Chukchi Peninsula]. *Izvestiīa Vsesoīūznogo Geograficheskogo Obshchestva* 85(4):405-412.

_____
1958   Ancient Cultures and Cultural and Ethnic Relations on the Pacific Coast of North Asia. Pp. 545-556 in *Proceedings of the 32d International Congress of Americanists*. Copenhagen, 1956.

_____
1958a   Drevneĭshie kul´tury primor´īa v svete issledovaniĭ 1953-1956 gg [The Earliest Cultures of the Maritime Region in the Light of the 1953-1956 Investigations]. *Akademiīa Nauk SSSR. Otdelenie Istoricheskikh Nauk. Sbornik Stateĭ* 1958:5-80.

_____
1959   Ancient Population of Siberia and its Cultures. *Russian Translation Series of the Peabody Museum of Archaeology and Ethnology, Harvard University* 1(1). Cambridge, Mass.

_____
1959a   Ancient Cultures in the Continental Part of North-east Asia. Pp. 72-80 in Vol. 2 of *Proceedings of the 33d International Congress of Americanists*. San José, Costa Rica, 1958.

_____
1960   A Note on the Lake El´gytkhyn Finds. Chester S. Chard, trans. and ed. *American Antiquity* 26(1):97-98.

_____
1960a   Archaeology of the Soviet Arctic. Pp. 35-45 in The Circumpolar Conference in Copenhagen, 1958. Helge Larsen, ed. *Acta Artica* 12. Copenhagen.

_____
1965   The Soviet Far East in Antiquity: An Archaeological and Historical Study of the Maritime Region of the USSR. (*Anthropology of the North: Translations from Russian Sources* 6) Henry N. Michael, ed. Toronto: Published for the Arctic Institute of North America by University of Toronto Press.

_____
1970   Yakutia Before Its Incorporation into the Russian State. *Anthropology of the North: Translations from Russian Sources* 8) Henry N. Michael, ed. Montreal and London: McGill-Queen's University Press.

Okladnikov, Alekseĭ Pavlovich, and Nina A. Beregovaīa
1971   Drevnie poseleniīa Baranova mysa [Early Settlements of Cape Baranov]. Novosibirsk: Izdatel´stvo "Nauka," Sibirskoe Otdelenie.

Okladnikov, Alekseĭ Pavlovich, and I.A. Nekrasov
1959   New Traces of an Inland Neolithic Culture in the Chukotsk (Chukchi) Peninsula. Sophie D. Coe, trans., Chester S. Chard, ed. *American Antiquity* 25(2):247-256.

_____
1962   Ancient Settlements in the Main River Valley, Chukchi Peninsula. Morgan Usadel, trans. Chester S. Chard, ed. *American Antiquity* 27(4):546-556.

Okun´, Semen Benĭsionovich
1951   The Russian-American Company. Carl Ginsburg, trans. (*Russian Translation Project Series of the American Council of Learned Societies* 9) Cambridge, Mass.: Harvard University Press.

Oldendow, Knud
1957   Bogtrykkerkunsten i Grønland og mændene bag den: En boghistorisk oversigt [Typography in Greenland and the Men Behind It: A Bibliographic Survey.] Copenhagen: no publisher.

_____
1959   Printing in Greenland. Copenhagen: Munksgaard; Montreal: Davies Book Company.

Olearius, Adam
1656   Vermehrte newe Beschreibung der muscowitischen und persischen Reyse, etc. Schleswig, Germany: no publisher.

Olsen, Angmalortok
1978   Processes of the Dissolution of the Greenlandic Societies and Necessities and Possibilities in Rebuilding a New Greenlandic Society. Pp. 431-459 in Le Peuple esquimau aujourd'hui et demain/The Eskimo People To-Day and To-Morrow. Jean Malaurie, ed. (Fourth International Congress of the Fondation Française d'Études Nordiques) Paris, The Hague: Mouton.

Olsen, Gustav
1910   Beretning om missionen ved Kap York [Report Concerning the Mission at Cape York]. *Meddelelser fra den Grønlandske Kirkesag* 17. Copenhagen.

Olsen, Jacob
1927   Aikilinermiulerssârut [An Account of the Canadian Inuit]. Copenhagen: Nationalmuseet.

Olson, Dean F.
1969   Alaska Reindeer Herdsmen: A Study of Native Management in Transition. *University of Alaska, Institute of Social, Economic, and Government Research Report* 22. College.

Oquilluk, William A.
1973   People of Kauwerak: Legends of the Northern Eskimo. Anchorage: Alaska Methodist University Press.

Orlova, E.P.
1941   Aziatskie ėskimosy [The Asiatic Eskimos]. *Izvestiīa Vsesoīūznogo Geograficheskogo Obshchestva* 73(2):201-222.

Orth, Donald J.
1967   Dictionary of Alaska Place Names. *U.S. Geological Survey Professional Paper* 567. Washington.

Oschinsky, Lawrence
1960   Two Recently Discovered Human Mandibles from Cape Dorset Sites on Sugluk and Mansel Islands. *Anthropologica* n.s. 2(2):212-227. Ottawa.

_____
1962   Facial Flatness and Cheekbone Morphology in Arctic Mongoloids: A Case of Morphological Taxonomy. *Anthropologica* n.s. 4(2):349-377. Ottawa.

_____
1964   The Most Ancient Eskimos: The Eskimo Affinities of Dorset Culture Skeletal Remains. Ottawa: University of Ottawa, Canadian Research Centre for Anthropology.

Osgood, Cornelius
1937   The Ethnography of the Tanaina. *Yale University Publications in Anthropology* 16. New Haven, Conn.

Ostermann, Hother B.S., ed.
1921   Missionær i Grønland Henric Christopher Glahans Dagbøger for Aarene 1763-64, 1766-67 og 1767-68 [The Diaries for the Years 1763-64, 1766-67, and 1767-68 of H.C. Glahan, Missionary in Greenland]. *Det Grønlandske Selskabs Skrifter* 4, Copenhagen.

_____
1928-1929   The History of the Mission. Pp. 269-349 in Vol. 3 of Greenland. M. Vahl, G.C. Amdrup, L. Bobé, and Ad. S. Jensen, eds. 3 vols. Copenhagen: C.A. Reitzel; London: Oxford University.

_____
1938   Knud Rasmussen's Posthumous Notes on the Life and Doings of the East Greenlanders in Olden Times. *Meddelelser om Grønland* 109(1). Copenhagen.

_____, ed.
1939   Knud Rasmussen's Posthumous Notes on East Greenland Legends and Myths. _Meddelelser om Grønland_ 109(3). Copenhagen.

_____, ed.
1942   The Mackenzie Eskimos After Knud Rasmussen's Posthumous Notes. _Report of the Fifth Thule Expedition 1921-24._ Vol. 10(2):5-164. Copenhagen.

1952   The Alaskan Eskimos, as Described in the Posthumous Notes of Dr. Knud Rasmussen. _Report of the Fifth Thule Expedition, 1921-24._ Vol. 10(3). Copenhagen.

Oswalt, Wendell H.
1949   Dated Houses at Squirrel River, Alaska. _Tree Ring Bulletin_ 16(1):7-8.

1952   Pottery from Hooper Bay Village, Alaska. _American Antiquity_ 18(1):18-29.

1952a   The Archaeology of Hooper Bay Village, Alaska. _Anthropological Papers of the University of Alaska_ 1(1):47-91. College.

1955   Prehistoric Sea Mammal Hunters at Kaflia, Alaska. _Anthropological Papers of the University of Alaska_ 4(1):23-61. College.

1955a   Alaska Pottery: A Classification and Historical Reconstruction. _American Antiquity_ 21(1):32-43.

1957   A Western Eskimo Ethnobotany. _Anthropological Papers of the University of Alaska_ 6(1):16-36. College.

1960   Eskimos and Indians of Western Alaska 1860-1868: Extracts from the Diary of Father Illarion. _Anthropological Papers of the University of Alaska_ 8(2):101-118. College.

1962   Historical Populations in Western Alaska and Migration Theory. _Anthropological Papers of the University of Alaska_ 11(2):1-14. College.

1963   Napaskiak: An Alaskan Eskimo Community. Tucson: University of Arizona Press.

1963a   A Mission of Change in Alaska: Eskimos and Moravians on the Kuskokwim. San Marino, Calif.: The Huntington Library.

1964   Traditional Storyknife Tales of Yuk Girls. _Proceedings of the American Philosophical Society_ 108(4):310-336. Philadelphia.

1966   This Land Was Theirs: A Study of the North American Indian. New York: John Wiley. (2d ed. in 1973; 3d ed. in 1978.)

1967   Alaskan Eskimos. San Francisco: Chandler.

1972   The Eskimos (Yuk) of Western Alaska. Pp. 73-95 in Modern Alaskan Native Material Culture. Wendell H. Oswalt, ed. Fairbanks: University of Alaska Museum.

1978   The Kuskowagmiut: Riverine Eskimos. Pp. 103-143 in This Land Was Theirs: A Study of North American Indians. 3d ed. New York: Wiley.

1979   Eskimos and Explorers. San Francisco: Chandler and Sharp.

1980   Kolmakovskiy Redoubt: The Ethnoarcheology of a Russian Fort in Alaska. _University of California, Institute of Archaeology, Monumenta Archaeologica_ 8. Los Angeles.

Oswalt, Wendell H., and James W. VanStone
1967   The Ethnoarcheology of Crow Village, Alaska. _Bureau of American Ethnology Bulletin_ 199. Washington.

Pacifique
1939   Leçons grammaticales théoriques et pratiques de la langue micmaque. Sainte Anne de Restigouche, Que.: Bureau du Messager Micmac.

Packard, A.S.
1885   Notes on the Labrador Eskimo and Their Former Range Southward. _American Naturalist_ 19(5):471-481, (6):553-560.

1891   The Labrador Coast. New York: N.D.C. Hodges.

Pageau, Pierrette
1975   Inuit du Nouveau-Québec: Bibliographie. (_Dossier_ 13) Quebec: Ministère des Affaires Culturelles, Direction Générale du Patrimoine.

Paine, Robert, ed.
1971   Patrons and Brokers in the East Arctic. (_Memorial University of Newfoundland, Institute of Social and Economic Research. Social and Economic Paper_ 2) Toronto: University of Toronto Press.

1971a   Animals as Capital: Comparisons Among Northern Nomadic Herders and Hunters. _Anthropological Quarterly_ 44(3):157-172.

_____, ed.
1977   The White Arctic: Anthropological Essays on Tutelage and Ethnicity. (_Memorial University of Newfoundland, Institute of Social and Economic Research, Social and Economic Paper_ 7) Toronto: University of Toronto Press.

Pallas, Peter Simon
1781-1793   Neue nordische Beyträge zur physikalischen und geographischen Erd- und Völkerbeschreibung, Naturgeschichte, und Oekonomie. 7 vols. St. Petersburg: J.Z. Logan.

Parker, G.R.
1972   Biology of the Kaminuriak Population of Barren-ground Caribou. Pt. 1: Total Numbers, Mortality, Recruitment, and Seasonal Distribution. _Canadian Wildlife Service Report Series_ 20. Ottawa.

Parker, Seymour
1962   Eskimo Psychopathology in the Context of Eskimo Personality and Culture. _American Anthropologist_ 64(1):76-96.

1964   Ethnic Identity and Acculturation in Two Eskimo Villages. _American Anthropologist_ 66(2):325-340.

Parran, Thomas, et al.
1954   Alaska's Health: A Survey Report to the United States Department of the Interior. Pittsburgh: University of Pittsburgh, Graduate School of Public Health.

Parry, Sir William E.
1821   Journal of a Voyage for the Discovery of a North-west Passage from the Atlantic to the Pacific: Performed in the Years 1819-1820. London: John Murray.

1824   Journal of a Second Voyage for the Discovery of a Northwest Passage from the Atlantic to the Pacific: Performed in the Years 1821-22-23, in His Majesty's Ships Fury and Hecla. London: John Murray.

Payne, F.F.
1887   Flora and Fauna of Prince of Wales Sound, Hudson Straits. Pp. 70-83 in Report of the Hudson's Bay Expedition of 1886 Under the Command of Lieut. A.R. Gordon, R.N. Ottawa: Department of Marine and Fisheries.

1889   Eskimo of Hudson's Strait. _Proceedings of the Canadian Institute_ ser. 3, Vol. 6:213-230.

Peacock, F.W.
1974   Eskimo-English Dictionary. St. Johns: Memorial University of Newfoundland.

Peary, Josephine Diebitsch
1893   My Arctic Journal: A Year Among Ice-fields and Eskimos. New York: Contemporary Publishing Company.

Peary, Robert E.
1898   Northward Over the "Great Ice:" A Narrative of Life and Work Along the Shores and Upon the Interior Ice-cap of Northern Greenland in the Years 1886 and 1891-97. 2 vols. New York: Frederick A. Stokes.

1907   Nearest the Pole: A Narrative of the Polar Expedition of the Peary Arctic Club in the S.S. Roosevelt, 1905-1906. New York: Doubleday, Page and Company.

1910   The North Pole, Its Discovery in 1909 Under the Auspices of the Peary Arctic Club. New York: Frederick A. Stokes.

Peck, Edmund J.
1925   A Dictionary of the Eskimo Language. Hamilton, Ont.: Mission Fund.

Peckford, Brian
1980   Statement on the Question of Native Land Claims in the Province. St. John's, Newf. Mimeo.

Pelto, Pertti J., and Ludger Müller-Wille
1972   Snowmobiles: Technological Revolution in the Arctic. Pp. 166-199 in Technology and Social Change. H. Russell Bernard and Pertti J. Pelto, eds. New York: Macmillan.

Penrose, L.S.
1954   Distance, Size and Shape. Annals of Eugenics 18:337-343.

Perrot, Michel, and J. Robert-Lamblin
1975   Publications en langue française concernant la coté est du Groenland. Objets et Mondes 15:271-284.

Persson, Ib
1969   The Fate of the Icelandic Vikings in Greenland. Man 4(4):620-628.

Persson, Ib, and P. Tingsgard
1965   A Deviating Gc Type. Acta Genetica 15:51-56. Basel, Switzerland.

Peter, Katherine, comp.
1979   Gwich'in Junior Dictionary. Anchorage: University of Alaska, National Bilingual Materials Development Center.

Petersen, Robert
1961   Karelerne på Grønland; en genopfriskning af en gammel ordtydning [The Karelians in Greenland; A Revival of an Old Word Interpretation]. Grønland 12:462-468. Copenhagen.

1962   The Last Eskimo Migration into Greenland. Folk 4:95-110. Copenhagen.

1963   Family Ownership and Right of Disposition in Sukkertoppen District, West Greenland. Folk 5:269-281. Copenhagen.

1964   The Greenland Tupilak. Folk 6(2):73-88. Copenhagen.

1965   Some Regulating Factors in the Hunting Life of Greenlanders. Folk 7:107-124. Copenhagen.

1966-1967   Burial-Forms and Death Cult Among the Eskimos. Folk 8-9:259-280. Copenhagen.

1969-1970   On Phonological Length in the Eastern Eskimo Dialects. Folk 11-12:329-344. Copenhagen.

1972   Acquisition and Sharing of the Bag in East Greenland. Inter-Nord 12(December):282-286. Paris.

1973   On the Variations of Settlement Pattern and Hunting Conditions in Three Districts of Greenland. Pp. 153-161 in Circumpolar Problems: Habitat, Economy, and Social Relations in the Arctic. Gösta Berg, ed. New York: Pergamon Press.

1974-1975   Some Considerations Concerning the Greenland Longhouse. Folk 16-17:171-188. Copenhagen.

1975   The East Greenlandic Dialect in Comparison with West Greenlandic. Objets et Mondes 15(2):177-182.

[1977]   On the Variation and the Common Traits Among the Greenlandic Dialects. (Manuscript at Institut for Eskimologi, University of Copenhagen.)

1977a   On the West Greenlandic Cultural Imperialism in East Greenland. Pp. 187-195 in Cultural Imperialism and Cultural Identity: Proceedings of the 8th Conference of Nordic Ethnographers/Anthropologists. Carola Sandbacka, ed. Finnish Anthropological Society Paper 2. Helsinki.

1978   On Hunting and Urbanization in East Greenland. Pp. 75-81 in Vol. 5 of Proceedings of the 42d International Congress of Americanists. Paris, 1976.

1980   A New Writing System for the Canadian Inuit (Eskimo). International Journal of American Linguistics 46(2):136-144.

1982   [Letter to William C. Sturtevant, June 13, 1982.] (Manuscript in National Anthropological Archives, Smithsonian Institution, Washington.)

Petersen, Robert, and Lotte Rix
1982   Klimasvingninger og grønlændernes forhistorie [Climatic Variation and the Prehistory of Greenland]. Tidsskriftet Grønland 3:82-100.

Petitot, Émile
1876   Sur les Populations indigènes de l'Athabaskaw-MacKenzie. Bulletins de la Société d'Anthropologie de Paris ser. 2. Vol. 9(6):831-836. Paris.

1876a   Vocabulaire français-esquimau: Dialecte des Tchiglit des bouches du Mackenzie et de l'Anderson. (Bibliothèques de Linguistique et d'Ethnographie Américaines 3) Paris: E. Leroux.

1876b   Monographie des Esquimaux Tchiglit du MacKenzie et de l'Anderson. Paris: E. Leroux.

1879   De l'Origine asiatique des indiens de l'Amérique arctique. Les Missions Catholiques de Lyon 11 (543):529-532, (544):540-544, (545):550-553, (546):564-566, (547):576-578, (548):589-591, (549):600-604, (550):609-611.

1883   De la Formation du langage. Association Française pour l'Avancement des Sciences, 12e Session: 697-701. Rouen, France.

1886   Traditions indiennes du Canada Nord-Ouest. (Les Littératures populaires de toutes les nations 23) Paris: Maisonneuve Frères et Charles Leclerc.

1887   Les Grands Esquimaux. Paris: E. Plon, Nourrit.

1890   Origine asiatique des Esquimaux: Nouvelle étude ethnographique. Rouen, France: E. Cagniard.

1893   Exploration de la région du Grand Lac des Ours (fin des quinze ans sous le cercle polaire). Paris: Téqui.

1970   Les Amérindiens du nord-ouest Canadien au 19e siècle selon Émile Petitot. Vol. 1: Les Esquimaux Tchiglit. Donat Savoie, ed. (Mackenzie Delta Research Report 9) Ottawa: Department of Indian Affairs and Northern Development, Northern Science Research Group.

Petroff, Ivan see U.S. Census Office 1884

Petterson, John S., Lawrence A. Palinkas, and Bruce M. Harris
1982   North Aleutian Shelf: Non-OCS Forecast Analysis. 2 vols. (Alaska Outercontinetal Shelf Socioeconomic Studies Program, Technical Report 75) Anchorage: U.S. Department of the Interior, Minerals Management Service.

Pêwê, T.L.
[1983]   Alpine Permafrost in the Contiguous United States. Map.
          United States Geological Survey Circular. In press.

Phillips, R.A.J.
1967   Canada's North. Toronto: Macmillan of Canada.

Pilling, James C.
1887   Bibliography of the Eskimo Language. *Bureau of American
          Ethnology Bulletin* 1. Washington.

Pinart, Alphonse
1871   Diary of a Voyage from Unalaska to Kodiak. (Manuscript
          in Bancroft Library, University of California, Berkeley.)

———
1872   Catalogue des collections rapportées de l'Amérique Russe.
          Paris: J. Claye.

———
1873   Eskimaux et Koloches, idées religieuses et traditions des Kan-
          iagmioutes. *Revue d'Anthropologie* 2:673-680. Paris.

———
1875   La Caverne d'Aknañh, Île d'Ounga, (Archipel Shumagin,
          Alaska). Paris: E. Leroux.

Piryuaq, Barnabas
1978   Nomads No Longer. *Ajurnarmat* (Autumn):117-123. Eskimo
          Point, N.W.T.

Pitelka, Frank A.
1969   Ecological Studies on the Alaskan Arctic Slope. *Arctic*
          22(3):333-340.

Pitseolak, P., and D. Eber
1975   People from Our Side: A Life Story with Photographs by
          Peter Pitseolak and Oral Biography by Dorothy Eber. Ed-
          monton, Alta.: Hurtig.

Pjetturrson, Jorgen
1973   Bilingualism in Greenland and Its Resulting Problems. Pp.
          533-551 in Le Peuple esquimau aujourd'hui et demain/The
          Eskimo People To-Day and To-Morow. Jean Malaurie, ed.
          (Fourth International Congress of the Fondation Française
          d'Études Nordiques) Paris, The Hague: Mouton.

Plumet, Patrick
1969   Archéologie de l'Ungava: Le problème des maisons longues
          à deux hémicycles et séparations intérieures. *École Practique
          des Hautes Études. Contributions du Centre d'Études Arc-
          tiques et Finno-Scandinaves* 7. Paris.

———
1976   Archéologie du Nouveau Québec: Habitats paleo-esquimaux
          à Poste de la Baleine. *Université Laval. Centre d'Études Nor-
          diques, Paleo-Québec* 7. Quebec.

———
1977   Le Peuplement préhistorique du Nouveau-Québec. *Géogra-
          phie Physique et Quaternaire* 31(1-2):185-199.

———
1979   Thuléens et Dorsétiens dans l'Ungava (Nouveau-Québec).
          Pp. 110-121 in Thule Eskimo Culture: An Anthropological
          Retrospective. Allen P. McCartney, ed. *Canada. National
          Museum of Man. Mercury Series. Archaeological Survey Pa-
          per* 88. Ottawa.

———
1981   Les Structures de blocs dans l'Arctique québeçois. In Mega-
          liths to Medicine Whale: Boulder Structures in Archeology.
          Proceedings of the 11th Annual Chacmool Conference. Cal-
          gary: The Archeological Association of the University of Cal-
          gary.

———
1982   Les Maisons longues dorsetiennes de l'Ungava. *Géographie
          Physique et Quaternaire* 36(3):253-289.

Poincy, Louis de *see* Rochefort, Charles de

Porsild, Morton P.
1915   Studies on the Material Culture of the Eskimo in West Green-
          land. *Meddelelser om Grønland* 51(5). Copenhagen.

———
1918   On "Savssats": A Crowding of Arctic Animals at Holes in
          the Sea Ice. *Geographical Review* 6(3):215-228.

Porter, Lee
1979   Ecology of a Late Pleistocene (Wisconsin) Ungulate Com-
          munity Near Jack Wade, East-Central Alaska. (Unpublished
          M.S. Thesis in Geology, University of Washington, Seattle.)

Porter, Robert P. *see* U.S. Census Office 1893

Portlock, Nathaniel
1789   A Voyage Round the World: But More Particularly to the
          Northwest Coast of America...London: Printed for J. Stock-
          dale and G. Goulding.

Pospisil, Leopold
1964   Law and Societal Structure Among the Nunamiut Eskimo.
          Pp. 395-431 in Explorations in Cultural Anthropology: Essays
          in Honor of George Peter Murdock. Ward H. Goodenough,
          ed. New York: McGraw-Hill.

Pospisil, Leopold, and William S. Laughlin
1963   Kinship Terminology and Kindred Among the Nunamiut Es-
          kimo. *Ethnology* 2(2):180-189.

Powers, William R., ed.
1973   Paleolithic Man In Northeast Asia. *Arctic Anthropology* 10(2).

Powys, Llewelyn
1927   Henry Hudson. London: John Lane.

Preston, C.E.
1964   Psychological Testing with Northwest Coast Alaskan Eski-
          mos. *Genetic Psychology Monographs* 64(May):323-419.

Price, Larry W.
1972   The Periglacial Environment, Permafrost, and Man. Wash-
          ington: Association of Geographers.

Pruitt, William O., Jr.
1960   Animals in the Snow. *Scientific American* 202(1):60-68.

———
1965   The Ecology of Snow. *Canadian Society of Wildlife and Fish-
          ery Biologists, Occasional Paper* 1:1-8. Ottawa.

———
1970   Tundra Animals: What Is Their Future? *Transactions of the
          Royal Society of Canada* 4th ser., Vol. 8:373-385. Ottawa.

———
1978   Boreal Ecology. (*Institute of Biology, Studies in Biology* 91).
          London: Edward Arnold.

Putnins, P.
1970   The Climate of Greenland. Pp. 3-128 in Climates of the Polar
          Regions. S. Orvig, ed. (*World Survey of Climatology* 14) New
          York: Elsevier.

Quimby, George I., Jr.
1940   The Manitunik Eskimo Culture of East Hudson's Bay. *Amer-
          ican Antiquity* 6(2):148-165.

———
1945   Periods of Prehistoric Art in the Aleutian Islands. *American
          Antiquity* 11(2):76-79.

———
1946   Toggle Harpoon Heads from the Aleutian Islands. *Fieldiana:
          Anthropology* 36(2):15-23. Chicago.

———
1948   Prehistoric Art of the Aleutian Islands. *Fieldiana: Anthro-
          pology* 36(4):77-92. Chicago.

Quinn, David B.
1977   North America from Earliest Discovery to First Settlements:
          The Norse Voyages to 1612. New York: Harper and Row.

———, ed.
1979   New American World: A Documentary History of North
          America to 1612. Vol. 4: Newfoundland from Fishery to
          Colony; Northwest Passage Searches. New York: Arno Press.

RCMP = Royal Canadian Mounted Police
1875-Annual Reports. Ottawa: King's Printer.

Radisson, Pierre E.
1896   Relation du voiage du sieur Pierre Esprit Radisson, Esc.^er au
          nord de l'Amérique ès années 1682, et 1683. Pp. 2-52 in
          Report on Canadian Archives, 1895. Ottawa.

Rae, John

1850   Narrative of an Expedition to the Shores of the Arctic Sea in 1846 and 1847. London: T. and W. Boone.

1866   On the Esquimaux. *Transactions of the Ethnological Society of London* n.s. 4:138-153. London.

1963   Correspondence, 1844-1855. E.E. Rich, ed. Toronto: Hudson's Bay Record Society.

Rainey, Froelich G.

1941   Eskimo Prehistory: The Okvik Site on Punuk Islands. *Anthropological Papers of the American Museum of Natural History* 37(4):453-569. New York.

1941a   The Ipiutak Culture at Point Hope, Alaska. *American Anthropologist* 43(3):364-375.

1941b   Mystery People of the Arctic. *Natural History* 47(3):148-155.

1947   The Whale Hunters of Tigara. *Anthropological Papers of the American Museum of Natural History* 41(2). New York.

Rainey, Froelich G., and Elizabeth K. Ralph

1959   Radiocarbon Dating in the Arctic. *American Antiquity* 24(4):365-374.

Ralph, Elizabeth K., and Robert E. Ackerman

1961   University of Pennsylvania Radiocarbon Dates IV. *Radiocarbon* 3:4-14.

Ralph, Elizabeth K., H.N. Michael, and M.C. Han

1973   Radiocarbon Dates and Reality. *MASCA Newsletter* 9(1). Philadelphia: University Museum.

Rasmussen, Hans-Erik

1983   Social endogami og symbol-brug i Vestgrønland. [Social Endogamy and Symbol Use in West Greenland]. (Unpublished M.A. Thesis, Københavns Universitet, Institut for Eskimologi, Copenhagen.)

Rasmussen, Knud

1905   En Folkevandring [A Migration]. Pp. 42-54 in *Norske Geografiske Selskab Aarbok, 1904-1905*. Oslo.

1908   The People of the Polar North: A Record. G. Herring, ed. London: K. Paul, Trench, Trübner. (Original: Nye Mennesker, Gyldendal, Copenhagen, 1905.)

1912-1913   Silarssuarmiulerssárutit inuit Kavdlunâjúngitsut inûsiánik ugperissánigdlo univkât [A Description of the Original Peoples of the World]. 2 vols. Copenhagen: Rosenberg-ip nakiteriviane.

1921   Greenland by the Polar Sea: The Story of the Thule Expedition from Melville Bay to Cape Morris Jesup. Asta and Rowland Kenney, trans. London: William Heinemann. (Original: Grønland langs Polhavet, Gyldendalske Boghandel, Copenhagen, 1919).

1921a   Thule Distriktet [The Thule District]. *Meddelelser om Grønland* 60:517-567. Copenhagen.

1921b   Eskimo Folk-Tales. W. Worster, ed. and trans. London and Copenhagen: Gyldendal.

1921-1925   Myter og sagn fra Grønland [Myths and Legends from Greenland]. 3 vols. Copenhagen: Gyldendal, Nordisk Forlag.

1925   The Danish Ethnographic and Geographic Expedition to Arctic America: Preliminary Report of the Fifth Thule Expedition. *Geographical Review* 15(4):521-592. New York.

1927   Across Arctic America: Narrative of the Fifth Thule Expedition. New York: G.P. Putnam's Sons.

1928   Inuit nunáinik kaujatdlainialungnek I... [An Attempt to Walk Around the Inuit Lands]. Copenhagen: B. Lunos Bogtrykkeri.

1929   Intellectual Culture of the Iglulik Eskimos. *Report of the Fifth Thule Expedition 1921-24*. Vol. 7(1). Copenhagen.

1930   Intellectual Culture of the Hudson Bay Eskimos. *Report of the Fifth Thule Expedition 1921-24*. Vol. 7(1-3). Copenhagen.

1931   The Netsilik Eskimos: Social Life and Spiritual Culture. *Report of the Fifth Thule Expedition 1921-24*. Vol. 8(1-2). Copenhagen.

1932   Intellectual Culture of the Copper Eskimos. *Report of the Fifth Thule Expedition 1921-24*. Vol. 9. Copenhagen.

1932a   South East Greenland: The Sixth Thule Expedition, 1931, from Cape Farewell to Angmagssalik. *Geografisk Tidsskrift* 35(4):169-197. Copenhagen.

1932b   The Eagle's Gift: Alaska Eskimo Tales. Isobel Hutchinson, trans. Garden City, N.Y.: Doubleday, Doran.

1933   Explorations in Southeastern Greenland. Preliminary Report of the Sixth and Seventh Thule Expeditions. *Geographical Review* 23(3):385-393. New York.

1952   The Alaskan Eskimos, as Described in the Posthumous Notes of Knud Rasmussen. Hother Ostermann and E. Holtved, eds. W.E. Calvert, trans. *Report of the Fifth Thule Expedition, 1921-24*. Vol. 10(3). Copenhagen.

Rasmussen, Lars Toft

1979   500 leveregler, gamle ord og varsler fra Vestgrønland [500 Rules of Conduct, Old Sayings, and Omens from West Greenland]. Regitze M. Søby, ed. *Det Grønlandske Selskabs Skrifter* 23. Copenhagen.

1982   Inuits: Protecting Their Eskimo Heritage. *Christian Science Monitor*, April 13:12-13. Boston.

1983   Canada's Eskimos One Step Closer to Having a Homeland. *Christian Science Monitor*, January 5:7. Boston.

Rathburn, Robert R.

1981   The Russian Orthodox Church as a Native Institution Among the Koniag Eskimo of Kodiak Island, Alaska. *Arctic Anthropology* 18(1):12-22.

Rausch, Robert

1951   Notes on the Nunamiut Eskimo and Mammals of the Anaktuvuk Pass Region, Brooks Range, Alaska. *Arctic* 4(3):147-195.

Ray, Charles K., Joan Ryan, and Seymour Parker

1962   Alaskan Native Secondary School Dropouts: A Research Report. College: University of Alaska, Native Education Project.

Ray, Dorothy Jean

1961   Artists of the Tundra and the Sea. Seattle: University of Washington Press.

[1961-1968]   [Ethnographic Notes of Fieldwork Between Stebbins, Alaska and Kotzebue Sound.] (Manuscripts in Ray's possession.)

1964   Nineteenth Century Settlement and Subsistence Patterns in Bering Strait. *Arctic Anthropology* 2(2):61-94.

1964a   Kauwerak, Lost Village of Alaska. *The Beaver* 295(Autumn):4-13.

1965   Birch Bark Baskets of the Kobuk Eskimos. *Alaska Sportsman* 31(3):15-17.

788

1966   H.M.W. Edmonds' Report on the Eskimos of St. Michael and Vicinity. *Anthropological Papers of the University of Alaska* 13(2). College.

1967   Eskimo Masks: Art and Ceremony. Photographs by Alfred A. Blaker. Seattle: University of Washington Press.

1967a   Land Tenure and Polity of the Bering Strait Eskimos. *Journal of the West* 6(3):371-394.

1967b   Alaskan Eskimo Arts and Crafts. *The Beaver* 298(Autumn):80-91.

1969   Graphic Arts of the Alaskan Eskimo. *Native American Arts* 2:4-87. Washington.

1971   Eskimo Place-names in Bering Strait and Vicinity. *Names* 19(1):1-33.

1972   Eskimo Sculpture. Pp. 93-97 in American Indian Art, Form and Tradition: An Exhibition Organized by Walker Art Center, Indian Art Association, and the Minneapolis Institute of Art, 22 October-31 December, 1972. New York: Dutton.

1972a   The Bering Strait of Alaska, 1650-1900. (Manuscript in D.J. Ray's possession.)

1974   The Billiken...the Story of This Strange Creation That Has Become Identified with Alaska. *The Alaska Journal* 4(1):25-31.

1975   The Eskimo of Bering Strait, 1650-1898. Seattle: University of Washington Press.

1975a   Early Maritime Trade with the Eskimo of Bering Strait and the Introduction of Firearms. *Arctic Anthropology* 12(1):1-9.

1977   Eskimo Art: Tradition and Innovation in North Alaska. Seattle: University of Washington Press.

1980   Artists of the Tundra and the Sea. Rev. ed. Seattle: University of Washington Press.

1981   Aleut and Eskimo Art: Tradition and Innovation in South Alaska. Seattle: University of Washington Press.

1981a   Arts and Crafts in the Kotzebue Basin. *Alaska Geographic* 8(3):154-168.

1982   Reflections in Ivory. Pp. 255-267 in Inua: Spirit World of the Bering Sea Eskimo, by W.W. Fitzhugh and Susan A. Kaplan. Washington: Smithsonian Institution Press.

Ray, Patrick H.
1885   Ethnographic Sketch of the Natives of Point Barrow. Pp. 35-87 in Report of the International Polar Expedition to Point Barrow, Alaska in Response to the Resolution of the House of Representatives of December 11, 1884. Washington: U.S. Government Printing Office.

Reed, H., and J.A. Hildes
1959   Corneal Scarring in Canadian Eskimos. *Canadian Medical Association Journal* 81(September):364-366.

Reed, Irene, Osahito Miyaoka, Steven Jacobson, Paschal Afcan, and Michael Krauss
1977   Yup'ik Grammar. Fairbanks: University of Alaska, Native Language Center and Yup'ik Language Workshops.

Reeves, Brian O.K.
1971   On the Coalescence of the Laurentide and Cordilleran Ice Sheets in the Western Interior of North America with Particular Reference to the Southern Alberta Area. Pp. 205-228 in Aboriginal Man and Environments on the Plateau of Northwest America. Arnoud H. Stryd, ed. Calgary: The Students' Press.

Reger, Douglas R.
1977   An Eskimo Site Near Kenai, Alaska. *Anthropological Papers of the University of Alaska* 18(2):37-52. Fairbanks.

1981   A Model for Culture History in Upper Cook Inlet, Alaska. (Unpublished Ph.D. Dissertation in Anthropology, Washington State University, Pullman.)

Reichel, L.T.
1861   Report of the Visitation of the Mission in Labrador by Brother L.T. Reichel in the Summer of 1861. Pp. 263-277 in Periodical Accounts Relating to the Missions of the Church of the United Brethren Established Among the Heathen. Vol. 24. London: Society for the Furtherance of the Gospel.

Reinhard, K.R.
1976   Resource Exploitation and the Health of Western Arctic Man. Pp. 617-627 in Circumpolar Health. R.J. Shephard and S. Itoh, eds. Toronto: University of Toronto Press.

Renner, Louis L.
1979   Pioneer Missionary to the Bering Strait Eskimo: Bellarmine Lafortune, S.J. Dorothy Jean Ray, collaborator. Portland, Oreg.: Binford and Mort.

Rennie, D.W.
1963   Comparison of Nonacclimatized Americans and Alaskan Eskimos. *Federation Proceedings* 22:828-830.

Rennie, D.W., B.G. Covino, M.R. Blair, and K. Rodahl
1962   Physical Regulation of Temperature in Eskimos. *Journal of Applied Physiology* 17:326-332.

Rich, Edwin E.
1958-1959   The History of the Hudson's Bay Company, 1670-1870. 2 vols. (*Hudson's Bay Record Society Publications* 21 and 22) London: Hudson's Bay Record Society.

Richardson, Sir John
1851   Arctic Searching Expedition: A Journal of a Boat-voyage Through Rupert's Land and the Arctic Sea, in Search of the Discovery Ships Under the Command of Sir John Franklin. London: Longman, Brown, Green, and Longmans.

Riches, David
1966   Cash, Credit, and Gambling in a Modern Eskimo Economy: Speculations on Origins of Spheres of Economic Exchange. *Man* n.s. 10(1):21-33.

1974   The Netsilik Eskimo: A Special Case of Selective Female Infanticide. *Ethnology* 13(4):351-361.

1976   Alcohol Abuse and the Problem of Social Control in a Modern Eskimo Settlement. Pp. 65-80 in Knowledge and Behavior. Ladislav Holy, ed. *The Queen's University of Belfast, Papers in Social Anthropology* 1.

1977   An Inuit Co-operative: The Contradiction. Pp. 212-231 in The White Arctic: Anthropological Essays on Tutelage and Ethnicity. Robert Paine, ed. (*Memorial University of Newfoundland, Institute of Social and Economic Research, Social and Economic Paper* 7) Toronto: University of Toronto Press.

Richling, Barnett
1980   Images of the "Heathen" in Northern Labrador. *Études/Inuit/Studies* 4(1-2):233-242.

Richter, Søren
1934   A Contribution to the Archaeology of North-east Greenland. *Oslo Universitet Etnografiske Museum Skrifter* 5(3):65-213.

[Rickman, John]
1782   An Authentic Narrative of a Voyage Performed by Captain Cook and Captain Clarke in His Majesty's Ships Resolution and Discovery During the Years 1776, 1777, 1778, 1779, and 1780, in Search of a North-west Passage Between the Continents of Asia and America—by W. Ellis, assistant surgeon.

2 vols. London: Printed for G. Robinson, J. Sewell, and J. Debrett.

Riewe, Roderick R.
1971   I.B.P.—Devon Island. Progress Report: Mammalian Carnivore Study. Winnipeg: University of Manitoba.

———
1973   Preliminary Data on Mammalian Carnivores Including Man in the Jones Sound Region, N.W.T. Pp. 315-340 in Devon Island I.B.P. Project, High Arctic Ecosystem. L.C. Bliss, ed. Edmonton: University of Alberta Printing Services.

———
1977   The Utilization of Wildlife in the Jones Sound Region by the Grise Fiord Inuit. Pp. 623-644 in Truelove Lowland, Devon Island, Canada: A High Arctic Ecosystem. L.C. Bliss, ed. Edmonton: University of Alberta Press.

Riggs, Anna E.
1980   Finger Masks: Vivid Symbols of Eskimo Spirits. *Alaska Journal* 10(1):88-90.

Righter, Elizabeth, and Richard Jordan
1980   Report of a Comprehensive Archaeological Reconnaissance and National Register Eligibility Test at the Terror Lake Hydroelectric Project Site, Kodiak Island, Alaska. San Francisco: WAPORA, Inc. Berwyn, Penn., for International Engineering Company.

Rigsdagens Grønlandsudvalg
1946   Betænkning afgivet den 12. juni 1946 af Rigsdagens Grønlandsudvalg i Forening med en af de grønlandske Landsråd valgt Delegation af Repræsentanter for Grønlands Styrelse [Deliberation of 12 June 1946 by the Parliamentary Committee on Greeland in Conjunction with a Delegation of Representatives Chosen by the Greenland Provincial Council for Greenland Government.] Copenhagen.

Rink, Hinrich J.
1857   Grønland geographisk og statistisk beskrevet [Greenland: Geographically and Statistically Described]. 2 vols. Copenhagen: A.F. Høst.

———
1860   Kaladlit Assilialiait. Grønlandske træsnit [Greenlandic Woodcuts]. Godthåb: Inspektoratets bogtrykkeri, L. Møller og R. Berthelsen.

———
1862   Om Aarsagen til Grønlændernes og lignende, af Jagt levende, Nationers materielle Tilbagegang ved Berøringen med Europærene [The Reason for the Material Decline of the Greenlanders and Similar Peoples Living by Hunting After Contact with the Europeans]. *Dansk Maanedsskrift* 2:85-110. Copenhagen.

———
1866-1871   Eskimoiske eventyr og sagn [Eskimo Adventures and Tales]. 2 vols. Copenhagen: C.A. Reitzel.

———
1868   Om grønlændernes gamle tro og hvad der af samme er bevaret under Kristendommen. [Concerning the Greenlanders' Ancient Beliefs and What Has Been Preserved of Them Under Christianity]. Pp. 192-256 in *Aarbøger for Nordisk Oldkyndighed og Historie*. Copenhagen.

———
1875   Tales and Traditions of the Eskimo: With a Sketch of Their Habits, Religion, Language and Other Pecularities. Robert Brown, ed. Edinburgh and London: W. Blackwood and Sons. Copenhagen: C.A. Reitzel.

———
1877   Danish Greenland, Its People and Products. London: H.S. King.

———
1878   Memoirs of Hans Hendrik, the Arctic Traveller, Serving Under Kane, Hayes, Hall and Nares, 1853-1876. London: Trübner.

———
1885   The Eskimo Dialects as Serving to Determine the Relationship Between the Eskimo Tribes. *Journal of the Royal Anthropological Institute of Great Britain and Ireland* 15(2):239-245. London.

———
1887   The Migrations of the Eskimo Indicated by Their Progress in Completing the Kayak Implements. *Journal of the Royal Anthropological Institute of Great Britain and Ireland* 17(1):68-74. London.

———
1887-1891   The Eskimo Tribes: Their Distribution and Characteristics, Especially in Regard to Language. 2 vols. *Meddelelser om Grønland* 11. Copenhagen.

———
1890   On a Safe Conclusion Concerning the Origin of the Eskimo, Which Can Be Drawn from the Designation of Certain Objects in Their Language. *Journal of the Royal Anthropological Institute of Great Britain and Ireland* 19(4):452-458. London.

———
1914   The East Greenland Dialect According to the Annotations Made by the Danish East Coast Expedition to Kleinschmidt's Greenlandic Dictionary [1877]. Pp. 203-223 in The Ammassalik Eskimo. Pt. 1(4). *Meddelelser om Grønland* 39. Copenhagen.

———
1966-1967   The Reason Why Greenlanders and Similar People Living by Hunting, Decline Materially Through Contact with the Europeans [1862]. George Nellemann, ed. *Folk* 8-9:224-241. Copenhagen.

———
1975   Tales and Traditions of the Eskimo: With a Sketch of Their Habits, Religion, Language, and other Pecularities. New York: AMS Press.

Rink, Signe Moller, comp.
1896   Kahjakmænd: Fortællinger af grønlandske sælhundefangere [Kayakers: Stories Told by Greenlandic Seal Hunters]. Odense, Denmark: Milo'ske Boghandel.

Rischel, Jørgen
1974   Topics in West Greenlandic Phonology: Regularities Underlying the Phonetic Appearance of Wordforms in a Polysynthetic Language. Copenhagen: Akademisk Forlag.

———
1975   Asymmetric Vowel Harmony in Greenlandic Fringe Dialects. Pp. 1-48 in *9th Annual Report of the Institute of Phonetics, University of Copenhagen*. Copenhagen.

———
1978   [Greenlandic Eskimo Dialectology]. (Lecture delivered to the Berkeley Group in American Indian Linguistics, Berkeley, Calif., May 8, 1978.)

Ritter, John T.
1976   Gwich'in (Loucheux) Athapaskan Noun Dictionary: Fort McPherson Dialect. Whitehorse, N.W.T.: The Queen's Printer for the Yukon.

Robbe, Pierre
1981   Les Noms de personne chez les Ammassalimiut. *Études/Inuit/Studies* 5(1):45-82.

Robert-Lamblin, Joëlle
1968   Enquête sociologique au Scoresbysund (Côte orientale du Groënland—1968). *Journal de la Société des Américanistes de Paris* 57:101-125.

———
1970   Démographie et acculturation: Une nouvelle phase dans l'histoire des Ammassalimiut emigrés au Scoresbysund; l'introduction du controle des naissances. *Journal de la Société des Américanistes de Paris* 59:147-154.

———
1971   Les Ammassalimiut émigrés au Scoresbysund: Étude démographique et socio-économique de leur adaptation. *Bulletin et Mémoires de la Société d'Anthropologie de Paris* 12th ser. Vol. 8:5-131. Suppl.

———
1980   Le Kayak aléoute. *Objets et Mondes* 20(1):5-20.

———
1981   "Changement de sexe" de certains enfants d'Ammassalik: Une rééquilibrage du *sex ratio* familial? *Études/Inuit/Studies* 5(1):117-126.

790

Roberts, Arthur O.
1978   Tomorrow Is Growing Old: Stories of the Quakers in Alaska. Newberg, Oreg.: Barclay Press.

Roberts, Derek F.
1973   Climate and Human Variability. (*Addison-Wesley Module in Anthropology* 34). Reading, Pa.: Addison-Wesley Publishing.

Roberts, Helen H., and Diamond Jenness
1925   Eskimo Songs: Songs of the Copper Eskimos. *Reports of the Canadian Arctic Expedition 1913-18.* Vol. 14. Ottawa.

Robinson, Samuel I.
1973   The Influence of the American Whaling Industry on the Aivilingmiut, 1860-1919. (Unpublished M.A. Thesis in Anthropology, McMaster University, Hamilton, Ont.)

Robson, Joseph
1752   An Account of Six Years' Residence in Hudson's Bay from 1733 to 1736, and 1744 and 1747. London: Printed for J. Payne and J. Bouquet.

Roch, Ernst, ed.
1975   Arts of the Eskimo: Prints. Texts by Patrick Furneaux and Leo Rosshandler. Barre, Mass.: Barre Publishers.

Rochefort, Charles de
1658   Histoire naturelle et morale des Îles Antilles de l'Amérique enrichie de plusieurs belles figures des Raretez les plus considérables qui y sont d'écrites. Rotterdam: A. Leers.

Rogers, George W.
1968   Eskimo Administration in Alaska. *Arctic* 20(4):269-270.

1968a   Alaska's Native Population as an Emerging Political Force. *Inter-Nord* 10:148-150. Paris.

1969   The Cross-cultural Economic Situation in the North: The Alaska Case. (Paper presented at the Conference on Cross-cultural Education in the North, Montreal.)

————, ed.
1970   Change in Alaska: The 1960's and After. Pp. 3-14 in People, Petroleum, and Politics. 20th Alaska Science Conference, 1969, University of Alaska. College: University of Alaska Press.

1971   Goodbye, Great White Father-figure. *Anthropologica* 13(1-2):279-306. Ottawa.

1973   Native Pauperization and Social Segregation in Alaska. Pp. 91-110 in Le Peuple esquimau aujoud'hui et demain/The Eskimo People To-Day and To-Morrow. Jean Malaurie, ed. (Fourth International Congress of the Fondation Française d'Études Nordiques) Paris, The Hague: Mouton.

Rohmer, Richard H.
1973   The Arctic Imperative: An Overview of the Energy Crisis. Toronto: McClelland and Stewart.

Rosendahl, Philip
1967   Jakob Danielsen: En grønlandsk maler. [A Greenlandic Painter]. Copenhagen: Rhodos.

Rosing, Christian
1946   Østgrønlænderne: Tunuamiut Grønlands Sidste Hedninger [The East Greenlanders: The Tunuamiut, Greenland's Last Heathens]. Karl Rosing, trans. William Thalbitzer, ed. *Det grønlandske Selskabs Skrifter* 15. Copenhagen.

Rosing, Emil
1975   Qimusseq [The Sled]. Godthåb: Ministeriet for Grønland.

Rosing, Jens
1958   Nordbominder fra Angmagssalik [Norse Relics from Ammassalik] *Grønland* 11:438-439. Copenhagen.

1963   Sagn og saga fra Angmagssalik. [Legends and Sagas from Ammassalik]. Copenhagen: Rhodos.

1973   Ting og undere i Grønland [Things and Wonders in Greenland]. Copenhagen: Wormianum.

1979   Himlen er Lav [The Sky is Low]. Copenhagen: Wormianum.

Rosing, Nikolaj
1945   Udviklingen i vort Land, smaa Ændringer, der kunne foretages [The Development in Our Country, Small Changes That Can Be Accomplished]. *Grønlandsposten*, February 16:38-40. Godthåb.

Rosing, Peter
1930-1931 Angmagssalingmiut [The People of Ammassalik]. *Atuagagdliutit* 20-26, 33-42. Godthåb.

Ross, Sir John
1819   A Voyage of Discovery, Made Under the Orders of the Admiralty, in His Majesty's Ships Isabella and Alexander, for the Purpose of Exploring Baffin's Bay, and Inquiring into the Probability of a North-West Passage. London: J. Murray.

1835   Narrative of a Second Voyage in Search of a North-West Passage, and of a Residence in the Arctic Regions During the Years 1829, 1830, 1831, 1832, 1833. Philadelphia: E.L. Corey aud H. Hart.

Ross, Richard E.
1971   The Cultural Sequence at Chagvan Bay, Alaska: A Matrix Analysis. (Unpublished Ph.D. Dissertation in Anthropology, Washington State University, Pullman.)

Ross, W. Gillies
1971   Whaling and the Decline of Native Populations. *Arctic Anthropology* 14(2):1-8.

1975   Whaling and Eskimos: Hudson Bay 1860-1915. *Canada. National Museum of Man. Publications in Ethnology* 10. Ottawa.

1977   Commercial Whaling and Inuit in the Eastern Canadian Arctic. (Paper presented at the 10th Annual Meeting of the Canadian Archaeological Association, Ottawa.)

Rosse, Irving C.
1883   Medical and Anthropological Notes on Alaska. Pp. 5-53 in Cruise of the Revenue-Steamer 'Corwin' in Alaska and the N.W. Arctic Ocean in 1881. Washington: U.S. Government Printing Office.

Rouland, N.
1978   Les Inuit du Nouveau-Québec et la Convention de la Baie James. Quebec: Association Inuksiutiit Katimajiit and Centre d'Études Nordiques, Université Laval.

Rousell, Aage
1941   Farms and Churches in the Mediaeval Norse Settlements of Greenland. *Meddelelser om Grønland* 89(1). Copenhagen.

Rousseau, Jacques
1948   By Canoe Across the Ungava Peninsula via the Kogaluk and Payne Rivers. *Arctic* 1(2):133-135.

Rousseau, Jérôme
1970   L'Adoption chez les Esquimaux Tununermiut (Pond Inlet, T. du N.-O.) *Université Laval. Centre d'Études Nordiques. Travaux Divers* 28. Quebec.

Rowley, Graham W.
1940   The Dorset Culture of the Eastern Arctic. *American Anthropologist* 42(3):490-499.

1972   The Canadian Eskimo Today. *Polar Record* 16(101):201-205.

Rubel, Arthur J.
1961   Partnerships and Wife-Exchange Among the Eskimo and Aleut of Northern North America. *Anthropological Papers of the University of Alaska* 10(1):59-72. College.

Rubtsova, Ekaterina Semenovna
1954-   Materialy po iazyku i fol'kloru eskimosov: Chaplinskiĭ dialekt. Pt. 1. [Materials on the Language and Folklore of the

Eskimo: Chaplino Dialect]. Moscow-Leningrad: Izdatel´stvo Akademii Nauk SSSR, Institut IA͡zykoznaniia.

1971   Ėskimossko-russkiĭ slovar´. [Eskimo-Russian Dictionary]. Moscow: Izdatel´stvo "Sovetskai͡a Ėnt͡siklopedii͡a."

Rudenko, Sergeĭ Ivanovich
1947   Drevnie nakonechniki garpunov Aziatskikh ėskimosov [Early Harpoon Heads of the Asiatic Eskimos]. *Akademii͡a Nauk SSSR. Institut Ėtnografii. Trudy* n.s. 2:233-256. Moscow.

1961   The Ancient Culture of the Bering Sea and the Eskimo Problem. Paul Tolstoy, trans. (*Arctic Institute of North America, Anthropology of the North: Translations from Russian Sources* 1.) Toronto: University of Toronto Press.

Rundall, T.
1849   Narrative of Voyages Towards the North-West in Search of a Passage to Cathay and India, 1496 to 1631. London: Printed for the Hakluyt Society.

Russell, Frank
1898   Explorations in the Far North: Being the Report of an Expedition Under the Auspices of the University of Iowa During the Years 1892, 1893, and 1894. Iowa City: University of Iowa.

Russian-American Company
1818-1865   [Records; Communications Sent.] (Manuscripts in National Archives, Washington.)

Rutherford, A.A., J. Wittenberg, and Roscoe Wilmeth
1981   University of Saskatchewan Radiocarbon Dates IX. *Radiocarbon* 23(1):94-135.

Rychkov, I͡U. G., and V.A. Sheremet´eva
1980   The Genetics of Circumpolar Populations of Eurasia Related to the Problem of Human Adaptation. Pp. 37-80 in The Human Biology of Circumpolar Populations. F.A. Milan, ed. Cambridge and London: Cambridge University Press.

Saabye, Hans Egede
1942   Brudstykker af en dagbog holden i Grønland i aarene 1770-1778 [Extracts from a Diary Kept in Greenland in the Years 1770-1778]. H. Ostermann, ed. *Meddelelser om Grønland* 129(2). Copenhagen.

Saario, Doris J., and Brian Kessell
1966   Human Ecological Investigations at Kivalina. Pp. 969-1039 in Environment of the Cape Thompson Region, Alaska. N.J. Wilimovsky and J.N. Wolfe, eds. Oak Ridge, Tenn.: U.S. Atomic Energy Commission.

Sabo, George, and Debby Sabo
1978   A Possible Thule Carving of a Viking from Baffin Island, N.W.T. *Canadian Journal of Anthropology* 2:33-42.

Sahlins, Marshall
1972   Stone Age Economics. Chicago: Aldine-Atherton.

Sai͡apin, A.K., and N.N. Dikov
1958   Drevnie sledy kamennogo veka na Chukotke: nakhodki na beregu ozera Ėl´gygytgyn [Early Traces of the Stone Age in Chukotka: Finds on the Shore of Lake Ėl´gygytgyn]. *Anadyr´. Chukotskiĭ Kraevedcheskiĭ Muzeĭ. Zapiski* 1:17-31.

Saladin d'Anglure, Bernard
1956-1971   [Research Notes on the Inuit of Arctic Quebec.] (Unpublished Fieldnotes at the Department of Anthropology, Université Laval, Quebec.)

1963   Discovery of Petroglyphs Near Wakeham Bay. *The Arctic Circular* 15(1):6-13.

1967   L'Organisation sociale traditionelle des Esquimaux de Kangirsujuaak (Nouveau-Quebéc). *Université Laval. Centre d'Études Nordiques. Travaux Divers* 17. Quebec.

1967a   Mission chez les Esquimaux Tarramiut du Nouveau-Québec (Canada). *L'Homme* 7(4):92-100.

1968   Tape-recorded interviews with Papikaktuq at Salliut, Quebec. Deposited in Laboratoire d'Anthropologie, Université Laval, Quebec.

1969   Quelques aspects originaux de la culture matérielle des "Nunamiut", Esquimaux de l'intérieur du Nouveau-Québec. Ottawa: Musée National du Canada, Service Canadian d'Ethnologie Documents de Recherche, Pt. 2:36-55.

1970   Nom et parenté chez les Tarramiut du Nouveau-Québec (Canada). Pp. 1013-1039 in Échanges et Communications: Mélange offerts a C. Lévi-Strauss a l'occasion de son 60e anniversaire. Jean Pouillon and P. Maranda, eds. Paris: Mouton.

1970a   Sanaaq, récit esquimau composé par Mitiarjuk. Vol. 1. (Unpublished Ph.D. Dissertation in Anthropology, École Prâtique des Hautes Études, sect. 5, Paris.)

1976   Écrivains esquimaux en syllabique. Pp. 226-236 in Papers on Eskimo and Aleut Linguistics. E.P. Hamp, ed. Chicago: Chicago Linguistic Society.

1977   Iqallijug, ou les reminiscences d'une âme-nom Inuit. *Études/Inuit/Studies* 1(1):33-63.

1978   L'Homme (angut), le fils (irniq) et la lumière (qau); ou le cercle du pouvoir masculin chez les Inuit de l'Arctique central. *Anthropologica* n.s. 20(1-2):104-144. Ottawa.

1978a   La Parole changée en pierre: Vie et œuvre de Davidialuk Alasuaq, artiste Inuit du Québec arctique. *Canada. Ministère des Affaires Culturelles, Cahier du Patrimoine* 11. Quebec.

1978b   Entre cri et chant: Les Katajjait, un genre musical féminin. *Études/Inuit/Studies* 2(1):85-94.

1979   Tuktuit Mitsaanut (Inuit and Caribou). *Inuksiutiit Allaniagait* 2. Quebec: Laval University.

1980   Violences et enfantements inuit ou les nœuds de la vie dans le fil du temps. *Anthropologie et Sociétés* 4(2).

1980a   "Petit-Ventre" l'enfant-géant du cosmos inuit: Ethnographie de l'enfant et enfance de l'ethnographie dans l'Arctique central inuit. *L'Homme* 20(1):7-46.

1980b   Nanuq super-mâle. L'ours blanc dans l'espace imaginaire et le temps social des inuit de l'Arctique canadien. *Études Mongoles* 11:63-94. Paris.

1981   Unikkaatuat Ujaranguititait [Words Changed to Stone: The Life and Work of Davidialuk Alasuaq, Inuit Artist from Arctic Quebec] *Inuksiutiit Allaniagait* 3. Quebec: Laval University.

1982   Les Premières images photographiques des Inuit de l'Ungava (Québec-arctique) 1872-1900. (Unpublished mansucript at the Ministère des Affaires Culturelles, Direction du Patrimoine Autochtone, Quebec.)

Saladin d'Anglure, Bernard, and Monique Vézinet
1977   Chasses collectives au caribou dans le Québec arctique. *Études/Inuit/Studies* 1(2):97-110.

Saladin d'Anglure, Bernard, L.-J. Dorais, and Geneviève Malgrange-Saladin d'Anglure
1969   Enquête toponymique dans le Nouveau-Québec esquimau. (Unpublished report on file at the Commission de Géographie, Quebec.)

Saladin d'Anglure, Bernard, Jimmy Innaarulik, Mark Schneider, and Lucien Schneider
[1973] Musique inuit du Nouveau-Québec. (Unpublished report at the Ministère des Affaires Culturelles, Quebec.)

Salmonsen, Finn, ed.
1981   Grønlands fauna: Fisk, fugle, pattedyr [Greenland's Fauna: Fishes, Birds, Mammals]. Copenhagen: Gyldendal.

Sampath, H.M.
1976   Modernity, Social Structure, and Mental Health of Eskimos in the Canadian Eastern Arctic. Pp. 479-489 in Circumpolar Health. R.J. Shephard and S. Itoh, eds. Toronto: University of Toronto Press.

Sand, Rudolf
1935   Knud Rasmussens virke i og for Thule-Distriktet [The Work of Knud Rasmussen in and for the Thule District]. Pp. 381-392 in Vol. 3 of Mindendgave [Memorial Edition]. Peter Freuchen et al., eds. Copenhagen: Gyldendal.

————
1938   Nogle træk af Thules historie [A Few Passages from the History of Thule]. *Grønlandske Selskab Aarsskrift*: 43-59. Copenhagen.

Sanders, Douglas
1981   Some Central Themes in Relations Between Indigenous Peoples and Nation-States. Mimeo.

Sandgreen, Otto
1967   Isse issimik kiğutdlo kigúmik, I-II. [An Eye for an Eye and a Tooth for a Tooth, I-II]. Godthåb.

————
1972   Piniartorssuaq (piniutinik, sananeqarnerinik taigutáinigdlo) [The Great Hunter: Hunting Implements, How They Are Made and Drawings]. Godthåb: Det Grønlandske Forlag.

————
1978   Ajagarnek: Ring og pind spil [Ring and Pin Game]. Godthåb: Det Grønlandske Forlag.

Sapir, Edward
1916   Time Perspective in Aboriginal American Culture: A Study in Method. *Canada Department of Mines. Geological Survey Memoir 90, Anthropological Series* 13. Ottawa.

Sarychev, Gavriil Andreevich
1802   Puteshestvīe Flota Kapitana Sarycheva po sīevero-vostochnoĭ chasti Sibiri, Ledovitomu morīu i Vostochnomu okeanu, v prodolzhenie os´mi lĭet, pri Geograficheskoĭ i Astronomicheskoĭ morskoĭ Ekspedīt͡sii, byvsheĭ pod nachal´stvom Flota Kapitana Billingsa, s 1785 po 1793 god. [The Voyage of Captain of the Fleet Sarychev to the Northeastern Part of Siberia, the Icy Sea and the Eastern Ocean in the Course of Eight Years, with the Geographical and Astronomical Naval Expedition Formerly Under the Command of Captain of the Fleet Billings, 1785-1793]. St. Petersburg: Tip. Shnora.

————
1806-1807   Account of a Voyage of Discovery to the North-east of Siberia, the Frozen Ocean, and the North-east Sea. 2 vols. London: Printed for R. Phillips by J.G. Barnard.

————
1811   Puteshestvīe Flota Kapitana Sarycheva po sīevero-vostochnoĭ chasti Sibiri, Ledovitomu morīu i vostochnomu okeanu v prodolzhenie os´mi lĭet, pri Geograficheskoĭ i Astronomicheskoĭ morskoĭ Ekspedīt͡sii, byvsheĭ pod nachal´stvom Flota Kapitana Billingsa, s 1785 po 1793 god. [The Voyage of Captain of the Fleet Sarychev to the North-eastern Part of Siberia, the Icy Sea and the Eastern Ocean in the Course of Eight Years, with the Geographical and Astronomical Naval Expedition Formerly Under the Command of Captain of the Fleet Billings, 1785-1793]. 2d ed. St. Petersburg: Tip. Shnora.

Sater, Beverly F.
1970   Conference Report. Pp. 3-5 in A Report of the Conference on Arctic Research and Resource Development, May 8, 9, and 10, 1970. B.F. Sater, ed. Washington: Arctic Institute of North America.

Sater, John E., ed.
1969   The Arctic Basin. Rev. ed. Washington: The Arctic Institute of North America.

Sater, John E., A.G. Ronhovde, and L.C. VanAllen
1971   Arctic Environment and Resources. Washington: The Arctic Institute of North America.

Sauer, Martin
1802   An Account of a Geographical and Astronomical Expedition to the Northern Parts of Russia for Ascertaining the Degrees of Latitude and Longitude of the Mouth of the River Kovima, of the Whole Coast of the Tshutski, to East Cape, and of the Islands in the Eastern Ocean, Stretching to the American Coast. Performed...by Commodore Joseph Billings in the Years 1785 to 1794. London: T. Cadell, jun.

Savoie, Donat
1970   Two Eskimo Games at Port Nouveau-Quebec, P.Q. *The Musk-Ox* 7:70-74. Saskatoon.

Sawden, Feona, and Tupou L. Pulu
1979   Quangirllat Pici: Old Beliefs. Fairbanks: Alaska Native Language Center, National Bilingual Materials Development Center.

Schaefer, Otto
1959   Medical Observations and Problems in the Canadian Arctic, I. *Canadian Medical Association Journal* 81(August)248-253.

————
1959a   Medical Observations and Problems in the Canadian Arctic, II. *Canadian Medical Association Journal* 81(September):386-393.

————
1969   Carbohydrate Metabolism in Eskimos. *Archives of Environmental Health* 18:144-147.

————
1977   Are Eskimos More or Less Obese Than Other Canadians? A Comparison of Skinfold Thickness and Ponderal Index in Canadian Eskimos. *American Journal of Clinical Nutrition* 30:1623-1628.

Schaefer, Otto, and Jean Steckle
1980   Dietary Habits and Nutritional Base of Native Populations of the Northwest Territories. Yellowknife: Science Advisory Board of the Northwest Territories.

Schaefer, Otto, P.M. Crockford, and B. Romanowski
1972   Normalization Effect of Preceding Protein Meals on "Diabetic" Oral Glucose Tolerance in Eskimos. *Canadian Medical Association Journal* 107(October):733-738.

Schaefer, Otto, J.A. Hildes, P. Greidanus, and D. Leung
1976   Regional Sweating in Eskimos and Caucasians. Pp. 46-49 in Circumpolar Health. R.J. Shephard and S. Itoh, eds. Toronto: University of Toronto Press.

Schledermann, Peter
1971   The Thule Tradition in Northern Labrador. (Unpublished M.A. Thesis in Anthropology, Memorial University of Newfoundland, St. John's.)

————
1975   Thule Eskimo Prehistory of Cumberland Sound, Baffin Island, Canada. *Canada. National Museum of Man. Mercury Series. Archaeological Survey Paper* 38. Ottawa.

————
1978   Preliminary Results of Archaeological Investigations in the Bache Peninsula Region, Ellesmere Island, N.W.T. *Arctic* 31(4):459-474.

————
1980   Notes on Norse Finds from the East Coast of Ellesmere Island, N.W.T. *Arctic* 33(3):454-463.

————
1981   Eskimo and Viking Finds in the High Arctic. *National Geographic Magazine* 159(5):575-601.

————
1982   Nordbogenstande fra Arktisk Canada. Tema: Nordboerne, I [Norse Objects from Arctic Canada. Theme: The Norse, I]. *Grønland* (5-7):218-225. Copenhagen.

Schledermann, Peter, and Karen McCullough
1980   Western Elements in the Early Thule Culture of the Eastern High Arctic. *Arctic* 33(4):833-841.

793

Schneider, Lucien
1966   Dictionnaire alphabético-syllabique du langage esquimau de l'Ungava et contrées limitrophes. *Université Laval. Centre d'Études Nordiques. Travaux et Documents* 3. Quebec.

———
1967   Grammaire esquimaude du sous-dialecte de l'Ungava. Quebec: Ministère des Richesses Naturelles, Direction Générale du Nouveau-Québec.

———
1968   Dictionnaire des infixes des Esquimaux de l'Ungava. Quebec: Ministère des Richesses Naturelles, Direction Générale du Nouveau-Québec.

———
1970   Dictionnaire français-esquimau du parler de l'Ungava. *Université Laval. Centre d'Études Nordiques. Travaux et Documents* 5. Quebec.

Schrader, Frank C.
1904   A Reconnaissance in Northern Alaska, Across the Rocky Mountains, Along Koyukuk, John, Anaktuvuk, and Colville Rivers and the Arctic Coast to Cape Lisburne in 1901. *U.S. Geological Survey Professional Paper* 20. Washington.

Schrire, Carmel, and William L. Steiger
1974   A Matter of Life and Death: An Investigation into the Practice of Female Infanticide in the Arctic. *Man* 9(2):161-184.

Schultz-Lorentzen, Christian W.
1927   Dictionary of the West Greenland Eskimo Language. *Meddelelser om Grønland* 69. Copenhagen.

———
1945   A Grammar of the West Greenland Language. *Meddelelser om Grønland* 129(3). Copenhagen.

Schwalbe, Anna B.
1951   Dayspring on the Kuskokwim: The Story of Moravian Missions in Alaska. Bethlehem, Pa.: Moravian Press.

Schwatka, Frederick
1884   The Netschilluk Innuits. *Science* 4(98):543-545.

Schweger, Charles
1971   Paleoecology of the Onion Portage Region, North-western Alaska. (Manuscript at University of Alberta, Edmonton.)

Seeman, Berthold C.
1853   Narrative of the Voyage of H.M.S. Herald During the Years 1845-51, Under the Command of Captain Henry Kellett, Being a Circumnavigation of the Globe, and Three Cruizes to the Arctic Regions in Search of Sir John Franklin. 2 vols. London: Reeve.

Sekora, Palmer
1973   Aleutian Islands National Wildlife Refuge Wilderness Study Report. Mimeo.

Sellers, L.E.
1907   Patrol Report, Fullerton to Lyons Inlet, May 1, 1906. (*Sessional Paper* 28) Pp. 116-129 in *Canada. Report of the Royal North-west Mounted Police for 1906.* Ottawa.

Seltzer, Carl C.
1933   The Anthropometry of the Western and Copper Eskimos, Based on Data of Vilhjálmur Stefánsson. *Human Biology* 5(3):313-370.

Semenov, A.V.
1965   The Ancient Culture of the Koryak National District. *Arctic Anthropology* 3(1):107-115.

Sergeev, Dorian Alexeevich
1959   Pervye Drevneberingomorskie pogrebeniia na Chukotke [The First Old Bering Sea Burials on Chukotka]. *Akademiia Nauk SSSR. Institut Étnografii, Kratkie Soobshcheniia* 31:68-75.

———
1962   Perezhitki ott͡sovskogo roda u aziatskikh ėskimosov [Survivals of the Patrilineal Clan Among the Asiatic Eskimos]. *Sovetskaia Étnografiia* 6:35-42.

Sergeev, Dorian Alexeevich, and S.A. Arutiūnov
[1975]   The Asiatic Eskimos. (Unpublished manuscript in National Anthropological Archives, Smithsonian Institution, Washington.)

Sergeev, Mikhail Alekseevich
1955   Nekapitalisticheskiĭ put' razvitiia malykh narodov severa [The Non-capitalistic Path of Development of the Small Nationalities of the North]. *Akademiia Nauk SSSR. Institut Étnografii, Trudy* n.s. 27:1-569. Moscow-Leningrad.

Service, Elman R.
1962   Primitive Social Organization: An Evolutionary Perspective. New York: Random House.

Sessions, Frank Q.
1967   Fairbanks Community Survey: A Profile of Poverty. (*ISEG Report* 16) College: University of Alaska.

Sexé, Marcel
1923   Two Centuries of Fur-Trading, 1723-1923: Romance of the Révillon Family. Paris: Draeger Frères.

Shade, Charles I.
1949   Ethnological Notes on the Aleuts. (Unpublished B.A. Honor Thesis in Anthropology, Harvard University, Cambridge, Mass.)

Shapiro, Harry L.
1931   The Alaskan Eskimo: A Study of the Relationship Between the Eskimo and the Chipewyan Indians of Central Canada. *Anthropological Papers of the American Museum of Natural History* 31(6):347-384. New York.

Shapsnikoff, Anfesia T., and Raymond L. Hudson
1974   Aleut Basketry. *Anthropological Papers of the University of Alaska* 16(2):41-69. Fairbanks.

Shaw, Robert D.
1981   The Expansion and Survival of the Norton Tradition on the Yukon-Kuskokwim. (Paper read at the Annual Meeting of the Alaska Anthropological Association.)

Shea, Brian T.
1977   Eskimo Craniofacial Morphology, Cold Stress and the Maxillary Sinus. *American Journal of Physical Anthropology* 47(2):289-300.

Shelekhov, Grigoriĭ Ivanovich
1981   A Voyage to America, 1783-1786. Richard A. Pierce, ed.; Marina Ramsay, trans. (Transl. from the 1812 edition with indication of variations from 1787 and 1793 editions.) Kingston, Ont.: Limestone Press.

Shelikhov, Grigor see Shelekhov, Grigoriĭ Ivanovich

Shephard, Roy J.
1980   Work Physiology and Activity Patterns. Pp. 305-338 in The Human Biology of Circumpolar Populations. F.A. Milan, ed. Cambridge and London: Cambridge University Press.

Shephard, Roy J., and S. Itoh, eds.
1976   Circumpolar Health: Proceedings of the 3d International Symposium, Yellowknife, N.W.T. Toronto: University of Toronto Press.

Shephard, Roy J., and A. Rode
1976   On the Body Composition of the Eskimo. Pp. 91-96 in Circumpolar Health. R.J. Shephard and S. Itoh, eds. Toronto: University of Toronto Press.

Sherwood, Morgan B.
1965   Exploration of Alaska, 1865-1900. New Haven, Conn.: Yale University Press.

Shields, Harvey M.
1977   Salvage Archaeology in Katmai National Monument, 1974. (Anthropology and Historical Preservation Cooperative Park Studies Unit) *University of Alaska Occasional Paper* 2. Fairbanks.

Shinen, Marilene
1963   Notes on Marriage Customs of the St. Lawrence Island Eskimos. *Anthropologica* n.s. 5(2):199-208. Ottawa.

Shinkwin, Anne, and Mary Pete
1982 Alaskan Villagers' Views on Problem Drinking: "Those Who Forget." *Human Organization* 41(4):315-322.

Silook, Roger S.
1976 Seevookuk: Stories the Old People Told on St. Lawrence Island. Anchorage: Alaska Publishing Company.

Simard, Jean-Jacques
1970 *Le Nouveau Québec: Le petit peuple du peut-être dans la terre du futur.* (Unpublished Manuscript in the Department of Sociology, Université Laval, Quebec.)

⸺
1982 La Revolution congelée: Coopération et développement au Nouveau-Québec Inuit. (Unpublished Ph.D. Dissertation in Social Sciences. Université Laval, Quebec.)

Simpson, Alexander
1845 The Life and Travels of Thomas Simpson, the Arctic Discoverer. London: R. Bentley. (Reprinted: Baxter Publishing, Toronto, 1963.)

Simpson, D.W., and K. Bowles
1973 Integration of Eskimo Manpower into the Industrial Society: Difficulties—Programs—Attitudes. Pp. 348-367 in Le Peuple esquimau aujourd'hui et demain/The Eskimo People To-Day and To-Morrow. Jean Malaurie, ed. (Fourth International Congress of the Fondation Française d'Études Nordiques) Paris, The Hague: Mouton.

Simpson, D.W., et al.
1968 The Role and the Impact of the Education Program in the Process of Change in Canadian Eskimo Communities. Pp. 1-42 in Symposium on the Educational Process and Social Change in a Specialized Environmental Milieu. (*Occasional Publication* 4) Edmonton: University of Alberta, Boreal Institute.

Simpson, H.W., Mary C. Lobban, and Franz Halberg
1970 Arctic Chronobiology: Urinary Near-24 Rhythms in Subjects Living on a 21-Hour Routine in the Arctic. *Arctic Anthropology* 7(1):144-164.

Simpson, John
1875 Observations on the Western Eskimo and the Country They Inhabit, from Notes Taken During Two Years at Point Barrow. Pp. 233-275 in Royal Geographical Society, Arctic Geography and Ethnology. London.

Simpson, Thomas
1843 Narrative of the Discoveries on the North Coast of America; Effected by the Officers of The Hudson's Bay Company During the Years 1836-39. London: R. Bentley.

Sivuaq, Paulusi
1972 Ce qu'un chasseur doit savoir. Povunguituk, P.Q.: Commission Scolaire du Nouveau-Québec.

⸺
1973 Contes et légendes inuit. 2 vols. Povunguituk, P.Q.: Commission Scolaire du Nouveau-Québec.

Slobodin, Richard
1962 Band Organization of the Peel River Kutchin. *Anthropological Series* 55, *National Museum of Canada Bulletin* 179. Ottawa.

⸺
1966 Métis of the Mackenzie District. Ottawa: Saint Paul University, Canadian Research Centre for Anthropology.

Smith, Barbara S.
1980 Russian Orthodoxy in Alaska: A History Inventory, and Analysis of the Church Archives in Alaska with an Annotated Bibliography. [Juneau]: Alaska Historical Commission.

Smith, Derek G.
1967 The Mackenzie Delta: Domestic Economy of the Native Peoples. (*MDRP-3*) Ottawa: Department of Indian Affairs and Northern Development, Northern Co-ordination and Research Centre.

⸺
1971 The Implications of Pluralism for Social Change Programs in the Canadian Arctic. *Anthropologica* n.s. 13(1-2):193-214. Ottawa.

⸺
1974 Occupational Preferences of Northern Students. *Canada. Northern Science Research Group, Social Science Note* 5. Ottawa.

⸺
1975 Natives and Outsiders: Pluralism in the MacKenzie River Delta, Northwest Territories. (*MDRP-12*) Ottawa: Department of Indian Affairs and Northern Development, Northern Research Division.

Smith, G. Warren
1973 Arctic Pharmacognosia. *Arctic* 26(4):324-333.

Smith, James G.E., ed.
1979 Indian-Eskimo Relations: Studies in the Inter-Ethnic Relations of Small Societies. *Arctic Anthropology* 16(2).

⸺
1980 Arctic Art: Eskimo Ivory. New York: Museum of the American Indian.

Smith, James G.E., and Ernest S. Burch, Jr.
1979 Chipewyan and Inuit in the Central Canadian Subarctic, 1613-1977. *Arctic Anthropology* 16(2):76-101.

Smith, Lawrence R.
1975 Labrador Inuttut Surface Phonology. *International Journal of American Linguistics* 41(2):97-105.

⸺
1978 A Survey of the Derivational Postbases of Labrador Inuttut (Eskimo). *Canada. National Museum of Man. Mercury Series. Ethnology Service Paper* 45. Ottawa.

Smith, Lorne
1972 The Mechanical Dog Team: A Study of the Ski-dog in the Canadian Arctic. *Arctic Anthropology* 9(1):1-9.

Smith, Philip S.
1913 The Noatak-Kobuk Region, Alaska. *U.S. Geological Survey Bulletin* 536. Washington.

Smith, Philip S., and John B. Mertie
1930 Geology and Mineral Resources of Northwestern Alaska. *U.S. Geological Survey Bulletin* 815. Washington.

Smith, Thomas G.
1973 Censusing and Estimating the Size of Ringed Seal Populations. *Canada. Fisheries Research Board. Arctic Biological Station Technical Report* 427. Ste. Anne de Bellevue, Quebec.

⸺
1973a Management Research on the Eskimo's Ringed Seal. *Canadian Geographical Journal* 86(4):118-125.

⸺
1973b Population Dynamics of the Ringed Seal in the Canadian Eastern Arctic. *Canada. Fisheries Research Board Bulletin* 181. Ottawa.

⸺
1979-1980 How Inuit Trapper-Hunters Make Ends Meet. *Canadian Geographic* 99(3):56-61.

Smith, Valene L.
1966 Kotzebue: A Modern Alaskan Eskimo Community. (Unpublished Ph.D. Dissertation in Anthropology, University of Utah, Salt Lake City.)

Smolīak, A.V.
1957 Materialy k kharakteristike sotsialisticheskoĭ kul'tury i byta korennogo naseleniĭa Chukotskogo raĭona [Materials to Show the Nature of Socialist Culture and Mode of Life of the Indigenous Population of the Chukchi Region]. *Akademiīa Nauk SSSR. Institut Ėtnografii. Trudy. Sibirskiĭ Ėtnograficheskiĭ Sbornik* 11 n.s. 35:3-37. Vladivostok.

Snowden, Donald
1982 [Kaminuriak Herd Film/Video Project; Transcript of Tapes.] St. John's, Newf.: Donald Snowden Productions.

So, J.K.
1980 Human Biological Adaptation to Arctic and Subarctic Zones. *Annual Review of Anthropology* 9:63-82.

795

Søby, Regitze M.
1969-1970   The Eskimo Animal Cult. *Folk* 11-12:43-78. Copenhagen.

1977-1978   The Kinship Terminology in Thule. *Folk* 19-20:49-84. Copenhagen.

1979   Language and Identity in Thule. Pp. 145-154 in Eskimo Languages: Their Present Day Conditions; Majority Language Influences on Eskimo Minority Languages. Bjarne Basse and Kirsten Jensen, eds. Aarhus, Denmark: Arkona.

Söderberg, Bertil
1969   Jingle Rattles of Puffin Beaks. *Ethnos* (1-4):58-68.

Söderberg, Staffan
1974   Profetens roll i religionsmötet: Iakttagelser från religionsmötet Västgrönlands [The Role of the Prophet in the Encounter Between Religions. Observations from the Encounter Between Religions in West Greenland]. Lund, Denmark.

Sørensen, Axel Kjær
1981   Udkast til Grønlands historie i det 20. århundrede [Sketch of Greenland's History in the 20th Century]. Mimeo. Århus, Denmark: Historisk Institut.

Solberg, Ole
1907   Beiträge zur Vorgeschichte der Osteskimo: Steinerne Schneidegeräte und Waffenschärfen aus Grönland. *Videnskabs-selskabets Skrifter II, Hist.-Filos. Klasse* 2. Christiania.

Solecki, Ralph S.
1950   New Data on the Inland Eskimo of Northern Alaska. *Journal of the Washington Academy of Sciences* 40(5):137-157. Washington.

1950a   A Preliminary Report of an Archaeological Reconnaissance of the Kukpowruk and Kokolik Rivers in Northwest Alaska. *American Antiquity* 16(1):66-69.

1951   Archaeology and Ecology of the Arctic Slope of Alaska. Pp. 469-495 in *Annual Report of the Smithsonian Institution for 1950.* Washington.

1951a   Notes on Two Archaeological Discoveries in Northern Alaska, 1950. *American Antiquity* 17(1):55-57.

Solecki, Ralph S., and R.J. Hackman
1951   Additional Data on the Denbigh Flint Complex in Northern Alaska. *Journal of the Washington Academy of Sciences* 41(3):85-88. Washington.

Solecki, Ralph S., Bert Salwen, and J. Jacobson
1973   Archaeological Reconnaissances North of the Brooks Range in Northeastern Alaska. *University of Calgary, Department of Archaeology Occasional Paper* 1. Calgary.

Sonne, Birgitte
1975   Den besudlede kvinde: Havkvinden i ritual og myte. [The Defiled Woman: The Sea Woman in Ritual and Myth]. *Tidsskriftet Grønland* 104-117. Copenhagen.

1980   The Happy Family: Myths, Ritual and Society on Nunivak. Copenhagen: Københavns Universitet, Institut for Religionssociologi.

1982   The Ideology and Practice of Blood Feuds in East and West Greenland. *Études/Inuit/Studies* 6(2):21-50.

Spaulding, Albert C.
1953   The Current Stutus of Aleutian Archaeology. *Memoirs of the Society for American Archaeology* 9:29-31. Salt Lake City.

1962   Archaeological Investigations on Agattu, Aleutian Islands. *University of Michigan, Museum of Anthropology, Anthropological Paper* 18:3-74. Ann Arbor.

Spaulding, Philip T.
1955   An Ethnohistorical Study of Akutan: An Aleut Community. (Unpublished M.A. Thesis in Anthropology, University of Oregon, Eugene.)

Spearman, Grant
1979   Land Use Values Through Time in the Anaktuvuk Pass Area. *University of Alaska Occasional Paper* 22. Fairbanks.

Speck, Frank G.
1931   Montagnais-Naskapi Bands and Early Eskimo Distribution in the Labrador Peninsula. *American Anthropologist* 33(4):557-600.

1935   Labrador Eskimo Mask and Clown. *The General Magazine and Historical Chronicle* 37(2):159-172.

1936   Inland Eskimo Bands of Labrador. Pp. 313-330 in Essays in Anthropology in Honor of Alfred Louis Kroeber. Berkeley: University of California Press.

Spencer, Robert F.
1958   Eskimo Polyandry and Social Organization. Pp. 539-544 in *Proceedings of the 32d International Congress of Americanists.* Copenhagen, 1956.

1959   The North Alaskan Eskimo: A Study in Ecology and Society. *Bureau of American Ethnology Bulletin 171.* Washington. (Reprinted in 1969.)

1972   The Social Composition of the North Alaskan Whaling Crew. Pp. 110-120 in Alliance in Eskimo Society. Lee Guemple, ed. (*Proceedings of the American Ethnological Society for 1971. Suppl.*) Seattle: University of Washington Press.

1979   Play, Power, and Politics in Native North America. Pp. 67-76 in *Proceedings of the American Ethnological Society for 1977.* St. Paul, Minn.: West Publishing Company.

Spencer, Robert F., and Jesse D. Jennings
1965   The Native Americans. New York: Harper and Row. (2d ed. in 1977.)

Spuhler, James N.
1979   Genetic Distances, Trees, and Maps of North American Indians. Pp. 135-183 in The First Americans: Origins, Affinities and Adaptations. W.S. Laughlin and A.B. Harper, eds. New York: Gustav Fischer.

Stanford, Dennis J.
1970   Interim Summary: Point Barrow Research. (Manuscript at the University of New Mexico, Albuquerque.)

1976   The Walakpa Site, Alaska: Its Place in the Birnirk and Thule Cultures. *Smithsonian Contributions to Anthropology* 20. Washington.

Steegmann, A.T., Jr.
1972   Cold Response, Body Form, and Craniofacial Shape in Two Racial Groups in Hawaii. *American Journal of Physical Anthropology* 37(2):193-221.

1975   Human Adaptation to Cold. Pp. 130-166 in Physiological Anthropology. Albert Damon, ed. New York: Oxford University Press.

Steenhoven, Geert van den
1959   Legal Concepts Among the Netsilik Eskimos of Pelly Bay. *Canada. Department of Northern Affairs and National Resources. Northern Coordination and Research Centre Report* 3. Ottawa.

1959a   Song and Dance: Characteristic Life Expression of the Eskimo. *Eskimo* 50: 3-6. Churchill, Country Inhabitants, Catholic Missions.

1962   Leadership and Law Among the Eskimos of the Keewatin District, Northwest Territories. The Hague: Uitgeverij Excelsior.

1968   Ennadai Lake People 1955. *The Beaver* 298(Spring):12-18.

Steensby, Hans P.
1905   Om Eskimokulturens Oprindelse; En Etnografisk og An-
          thropogeografisk Studie [The Origin of Eskimo Culture: Eth-
          nographic and Anthropogeographic Study]. Copenhagen:
          Salmonsen.

1909   The Polar Eskimos and the Polar Expeditions. *Fortnightly
          Review* 92(November):891-902.

1910   Contributions to the Ethnology and Anthropogeography of
          the Polar Eskimos. *Meddelelser om Grønland* 34(7). Copen-
          hagen.

1912   Etnografiske og antropogeografiske rejsestudier i Nord-
          Grønland, 1909 [Ethnographic and Anthropogeographic Field
          Studies in North Greenland, 1909]. *Meddelelser om Grønland*
          50:133-173. Copenhagen.

1917   An Anthropogeographical Study of the Origin of the Eskimo
          Culture. *Meddelelser om Grønland* 53(2). Copenhagen.

Stefánsson, Vilhjálmur
1908   Notes on the Theory and Treatment of Diseases Among the
          Mackenzie River Eskimo. *Journal of American Folk-Lore*
          21(80):43-45.

1913   My Life with the Eskimo. New York: Macmillan.

1913a   The Distribution of Human and Animal Life in Western Arc-
          tic America. *Geographical Journal* 41(5):449-459.

1914   Prehistoric and Present Commerce Among the Arctic Coast
          Eskimo. *Canada. Geological Survey Museum Bulletin 6, An-
          thropological Series* 3. Ottawa.

1919   The Stefánsson-Anderson Arctic Expedition of the American
          Museum: Preliminary Ethnological Report. *Anthropological
          Papers of the American Museum of Natural History* 14(1).
          New York.

1921   The Friendly Arctic: The Story of Five Years in Polar Re-
          gions. New York: Macmillan.

1933   [Introduction to] The Anthropometry of the Western and
          Copper Eskimos, Based on Data of Vilhjalmur Stefánsson,
          by Carl C. Seltzer. *Human Biology* 5(3):313-370.

_____, ed.
1938   The Three Voyages of Martin Frobisher in Search of a Pas-
          sage to Cathay and India by the North-west, A.D. 1576-8.
          From the Original 1578 Text of George Best. London: Ar-
          gonaut Press.

1943   The Friendly Arctic: The Story of Five Years in Polar Re-
          gions. 2d ed. New York: Macmillan.

Stein, Robert
1902   Geographische Nomenklatur bei den Eskimos des Smith-
          Sundes. *Petermanns Geographische Mitteilungen* 48:195-201.
          Gotha, Germany.

Steinmann, André-Pierre
1977   La Petite barbe: J'ai vécu 40 ans dans le Grand Nord. Mon-
          treal: Editions de L'Homme.

Stejneger, Leonhard
1895   Aleut Baidarkas in Kamchatka. *Science* 2(29):62-63.

Stejneger, Leonard H.
1936   Georg Wilhelm Steller: The Pioneer of Alaskan Natural His-
          tory. Cambridge, Mass.: Harvard University Press.

Stephens, C.A., ed.
1900   At the School House Farthest West: A Tale of School-teach-
          ing in Alaska. *Youth's Companion* 74(16):197-198; (17):213-
          214; (18):225-226; (19):240-241.

Stephenson, R.O., and R.T. Ahgook
1975   The Eskimo Hunter's View of Wolf Ecology and Behavior.
          Pp. 286-291 in The Wild Canids: Their Systematics, Behav-
          ioral Ecology, and Evolution. Michael W. Fox, ed. New York:
          Van Nostrand, Reinhold.

Stern, Richard O.
1977   A Selected Annotated Bibliography of Sources on Reindeer
          Herding in Alaska. *University of Alaska, Institute of Arctic
          Biology, Occasional Publications on Northern Life* 2. Col-
          lege.

_____, et al.
1980   Eskimos, Reindeer and Land. *University of Alaska, Agri-
          cultural Experiment Station, School of Agriculture and Land
          Resources Management Bulletin* 59. College.

Stevenson, A.
1973   The Changing Canadian Eskimo. Pp. 181-196 in Le Peuple
          esquimau aujourd'hui et demain/The Eskimo People To-day
          and To-morrow. Jean Malaurie, ed. (Fourth International
          Congress of the Fondation Française d'Études Nordiques)
          Paris, The Hague: Mouton.

Stevenson, D.S.
1968   Problems of Eskimo Relocation for Industrial Employment:
          A Preliminary Study. (*NSRG 68-1*) Ottawa: Department of
          Indian Affairs and Northern Development, Northern Science
          Research Group.

Stevenson, David
1972   The Social Organization of the Clyde Inlet Eskimos. (Un-
          published Ph.D. Dissertation in Anthropology, University of
          British Columbia, Vancouver.)

Stewart, T.D.
1939   Anthropometric Observations on the Eskimos and Indians
          of Labrador. *Field Museum of Natural History Anthropolog-
          ical Series* 31(1). Chicago.

Stewart, T.D., and Marshall T. Newman
1951   An Historical Résumé of the Concept of Differences in In-
          dian Types. *American Anthropologist* 53(1):19-36.

Stoklund, Marie
1982   Nordboruner. Tema: Nordboerne, I. [Norse Runes. Theme:
          The Norse, I]. *Grønland* 5-7:197-206. Copenhagen.

Stoney, George M.
1900   Naval Explorations in Alaska: An Account of Two Naval
          Expeditions to Northern Alaska, with Official Maps of the
          Country Explored. Annapolis, Md.: U.S. Naval Institute.

Stratton, Lee, Project Coordinator
1981   Chugach Region Community Subsistence Profiles: A Re-
          source Book for the North Pacific Rim and the Native Com-
          munities of the Region. Mimeo.

Street, John M.
1969   An Evaluation of the Concept of Carrying Capacity. *Profes-
          sional Geographer* 21(2):104-107.

Stuckenrath, Robert, Jr., William R. Coe, and Elizabeth K. Ralph
1966   University of Pennsylvania Radiocarbon Dates IX. *Radio-
          carbon* 8:348-385.

Stupart, R.F.
1887   The Eskimo of Stupart Bay. *Proceedings of the Canadian
          Institute.* ser. 3. Vol 4:93-114. Toronto.

Sturtevant, William C.
1980   The First Inuit Depiction by Europeans. *Études/Inuit/Studies*
          4(1-2):47-49.

Sukernik, R.I., S.V. Lemza, T.M. Karaphet, and L.P. Osipova
1981   Reindeer Chukchi and Siberian Eskimos: Studies on Blood
          Groups, Serum Proteins, and Red Cell Enzymes with Regard
          to Genetic Heterogeneity. *American Journal of Physical An-
          thropology* 55(1):121-128.

Sullivan, James W.
1969   Personal Income Patterns in Alaska. *Alaska Review of Busi-
          ness and Economic Conditions* 6(1). College.

Suluk, Thomas
1981   [Interview in] The Nunavut Concept: A Proposal for Inuit Self-Determination. *Arjungnagimmat* (Winter):19-37.

Sveistrup, Poul P.
1949   Economic Principles of the Greenland Administration Before 1947. *Meddelelser om Grønland* 150(1). Copenhagen.

Sveistrup, Poul P., and Sune Dalgaard
1945   Det danske styre af Grønland, 1825-1850 [The Danish Administration of Greenland, 1825-1850]. *Meddelelser om Grønland* 145(1). Copenhagen.

Sverdrup, Otto N.
1904   New Land; Four Years in the Arctic Regions. Ethel H. Hearn, trans. 2 vols. London: Longmans and Green.

Swadesh, Morris
1946   South Greenlandic (Eskimo). Pp. 30-54 in Linguistic Structures of Native America, by Harry Hoijer et al. *Viking Fund Publications in Anthropology* 6. New York.

1951   Kleinschmidt Centennial, III: Unaaliq and Proto Eskimo. *International Journal of American Linguistics* 17(2):66-70.

1952   Unaaliq and Proto Eskimo, II: Phonemes and Morphophonemes. *International Journal of American Linguistics* 18(1):25-34.

1952a   Unaaliq and Proto Eskimo, III: Synchronic Notes. *International Journal of American Linguistics* 18(2):69-76.

1952b   Unaaliq and Proto Eskimo, IV: Diachronic Notes. *International Journal of American Linguistics* 18(3):166-171.

1952c   Unaaliq and Proto Eskimo, V: Comparative Vocabulary. *International Journal of American Linguistics* 18(4):241-256.

1962   Linguistic Relations Across Bering Strait. *American Anthropologist* 64(6):1262-1291.

1968   Eskimo-Aleut Languages. Pp. 706-707 in Vol. 8 of Encyclopaedia Britannica. 23 vols. Chicago, London, Toronto: Encyclopaedia Britannica, Inc.

Swinton, George
1972   Sculpture of the Eskimo. Greenwich, Conn.: New York Graphic Society.

Szathmary, Emöke J.E.
1979   Eskimo and Indian Contact: Examination of Craniometric, Anthropometric and Genetic Evidence. *Arctic Anthropology* 16(2):23-48.

1981   Genetic Markers in Siberian and Northern North American Populations. *Yearbook of Phyical Anthropology* 24:37-73. Washington.

Szathmary, Emöke J.E., and N. Holt
1983   Hyperglycemia in Dogrib Indians of the Northwest Territories, Canada: Association with Age and a Centripetal Distribution of Body Fat. *Human Biology*. In press.

Szathmary, Emöke J.E., and Nancy S. Ossenberg
1978   Are the Biological Differences Between North American Indians and Eskimos Truly Profound? *Current Anthropology* 19(4):673-701.

Taggart, Harold F., ed.
1954   Journal of William H. Ennis. *California Historical Society Quarterly* 33(1):1-11, (2):147-168.

1956   Journal of George Russell Adams. *California Historical Society Quarterly* 35(4):291-307.

Tagoona, Armand
1973   Tagoona Remembers. *Inuit Monthly* 2(6):22-23, 59-60.

1977   Education. *Inuit Today* 6(5):53-55.

Tanner, Väinö
1944   Outline of the Geography, Life, and Customs of Newfoundland-Labrador. *Acta Geographica* 8(1). Helsinki.

1947   Outlines of the Geography, Life and Customs of Newfoundland-Labrador (the Eastern Part of the Labrador Peninsula). Based Upon Observations Made During 'the Finland-Labrador Expedition' in 1939 and Upon Information Available in the Literature and Cartography. 2 vols. New York: Macmillan.

Tauber, Henrik
1962   Copenhagen Radiocarbon Dates V. *Radiocarbon* 4:27-34.

1973   Copenhagen Radiocarbon Dates X. *Radiocarbon* 15(1):86-112.

Taylor, J. Garth, ed.
1969   William Turner's Journeys to the Caribou Country with the Labrador Eskimos in 1780. *Ethnohistory* 16(2):141-164.

1970   Structure of Early Contact Labrador Eskimo Social Units. Pp. 251-255 in Vol. 2 of *Proceedings of the 38th International Congress of Americanists*. Stuttgart, München, 1968.

1972   Eskimo Answers to an Eighteenth Century Questionnaire. *Ethnohistory* 19(2):135-145.

1974   Netsilik Eskimo Material Culture: The Roald Amundsen Collection from King William Island. Oslo: Universitetsforlaget.

1974a   Labrador Eskimo Settlements of the Early Contact Period. *Canada. National Museum of Man. Publications in Ethnology* 9. Ottawa.

1975   Demography and Adaptations of Eighteenth Century Eskimo Groups in Northern Labrador and Ungava. Pp. 269-278 in Prehistoric Maritime Adaptations of the Circumpolar Zone. W.W. Fitzhugh, ed. The Hague: Mouton.

1977   Traditional Land Use and Occupancy by the Labrador Inuit. Pp. 49-58 in Our Footprints Are Everywhere. C. Brice-Bennett, ed. Nain: Labrador Inuit Association.

1978   Did the First Eskimos Speak Algonquian? Pp. 96-103 in *Papers of the Ninth Algonquian Conference*. William Cowan, ed. Ottawa: Carleton University.

1979   The Case of the Invisible Inuit: Reconciling Archaeology, History and Oral Tradition in the Gulf of St. Lawrence. Pp. 267-277 in Thule Eskimo Culture: An Archaeological Retrospective. Allen P. McCartney, ed. *Canada. National Museum of Man. Mercury Series. Archaeological Survey Paper* 88. Ottawa.

1979a   Indian-Inuit Relations in Eastern Labrador, 1600-1976. *Arctic Anthropology* 16(2):49-58.

1979b   Inuit Whaling Technology in Eastern Canada and Greenland. Pp. 292-300 in Thule Eskimo Culture: An Archaeological Retrospective. Allen P. McCartney, ed. *Canada. National Museum of Man. Mercury Series. Archaeological Survey Paper* 88. Ottawa.

1979c   L'Exploitation du caribou par les Inuit de la côte du Labrador (1694-1977). *Recherches Amérindiennes au Québec* 9(1-2):71-81.

1980   The Inuit of Southern Quebec-Labrador: Reviewing the Evidence. *Études/Inuit/Studies* 4(1-2):185-194.

1982   Labrador Crafts: Inuit House Models. *Them Days* 8(2): unpaged.

Taylor, J. Garth, and Helga R. Taylor
1977   Changing Land Use and Occupancy in the Okak Region: 1776-1830. Pp. 59-82 in Our Footprints are Everywhere. C. Brice-Bennett, ed. Nain: Labrador Inuit Association.

Taylor, Kenneth I.
1966   A Demographic Study of Karluk, Kodiak Island, Alaska, 1962-1964. *Arctic Anthropology* 3(2):211-240.

Taylor, William E., Jr.
1959   Review and Assessment of the Dorset Problem. *Anthropologica* 1(1-2):24-42. Ottawa.

——
1960   A Description of Sadlermiut Houses Excavated at Native Point, Southampton, Island, N.W.T. *Anthropological Series 45, National Museum of Canada Bulletin* 162:53-100. Ottawa.

——
1962   Pre-Dorset Occupations at Ivugivik in Northwestern Ungava. Pp. 80-91 in Prehistoric Cultural Relations Between the Arctic and Temperate Zones of North America. John M. Campbell, ed. *Arctic Institute of North America Technical Paper* 11. Montreal.

——
1963   Implications of a Pre-Dorset Lance Head from the Eastern Canadian Arctic. *Arctic* 16(2):129-134.

——
1963a   Hypotheses on the Origin of Canadian Thule Culture. *American Antiquity* 28(4):456-464.

——
1964   Interim Account of an Archaeological Survey in the Central Arctic, 1963. *Anthropological Papers of the University of Alaska* 12(1):46-55. College.

——
1964a   The Prehistory of the Quebec-Labrador Peninsula. Pp. 181-210 in Le Nouveau-Québec: Contribution à l'étude de l'occupation humaine. Jean Malaurie and Jacques Rousseau, eds. Paris: Mouton.

——
1965   The Fragments of Eskimo Prehistory. *The Beaver* 295 (Spring):4-17.

——
1966   An Archaeological Perspective on Eskimo Economy. *Antiquity* 40(158):114-120.

——
1967   Summary of Archaeological Field Work on Banks and Victoria Islands, Arctic Canada, 1965. *Arctic Anthropology* 4(1):221-243.

——
1968   The Arnapik and Tyara Sites: An Archaeological Study of Dorset Culture Origins. *Memoirs of the Society for American Archaeology* 22. Salt Lake City.

——
1972   Found Art—and Frozen. *Arts Canada* 162-163:32-47. Toronto.

——
1972a   An Archaeological Survey Between Cape Parry and Cambridge Bay, N.W.T., Canada in 1963. *Canada. National Museum of Man. Mercury Series. Archaeological Survey Paper* 1. Ottawa.

Taylor, William E., Jr., and George Swinton
1967   Prehistoric Dorset Art. *The Beaver* 298(Autumn):32-47.

Tedrow, J.C.F.
1970   Soil Investigations in Inglefield Land, Greenland. *Meddelelser om Grønland* 188(3). Copenhagen.

Tein, T.S.
1979   Arkheologicheskie issledovaniîa na O. Vrangelîa [Archeological Investigations on Wrangell Island]. Pp. 53-63 in Novye Arkheologicheskie Pamîatniki Severa Dal´nego Vostoka [New Archeological Monuments of the Northern Far East.] Magadan: Akademiîa Nauk SSSR.

Tener, J.S.
1965   Muskoxen in Canada: A Biological and Taxonomic Review. *Canadian Wildlife Service Monograph* 2. Ottawa.

Tester, F.J.
1976   Community Attitudes and Perception of Waste Management Problems at Resolute, Northwest Territories. Pp. 635-642 in Circumpolar Health. R.J. Shephard and S. Itoh, eds. Toronto: University of Toronto Press.

Thalbitzer, William
1904   A Phonetical Study of the Eskimo Language Based on Observations Made on a Journey in North Greenland 1900-1901. *Meddelelser om Grønland* 31. Copenhagen.

——
1911   Eskimo. Pp. 967-1096 in Vol. 1 of Handbook of American Indian Languages. Franz Boas, ed. 2 vols. *Bureau of American Ethnology Bulletin* 40. Washington.

——
1914   Ethnographical Collections from East Greenland (Angmagsalik and Nualik) Made by G. Holm, G. Amdrup and J. Petersen and Described by W. Thalbitzer. The Ammasalik Eskimo, 1(7). *Meddelelser om Grønland* 39:319-755. Copenhagen.

——
1914-1941 The Ammassalik Eskimo: Contributions to the Ethnology of the East Greenland Natives. *Meddelelser om Grønland* 39-40, 53. Copenhagen.

——
1916   Et Manuskript af Rasmus Rask om Aleuternes Sprog, sammenlignet med Grønlændernes [A Manuscript by Rasmus Rask on the Language of the Aleuts Compared with that of the Greenlanders]. *Kongelige Danske Videnskabernes Selskabs Oversigt* 3:211-249. Copenhagen.

——
1922   The Aleutian Language Compared with Greenlandic: A Manuscript by Rasmus Rask, Dating from 1820, Now in the Royal Library at Copenhagen. *International Journal of American Linguistics* 2(1-2):40-57.

——
1923   Language and Folklore: The Ammassalik Eskimo, Pt. 2(3). *Meddelelser om Grønland* 40(2):113-564. Copenhagen.

——
1948   Grønlandsk litteraturhistorie [History of Greenlandic Literature] Pp. 244 in Grønlandsbogen II. Kaj Birket-Smith, Ernst Mentze and M. Friis Møller, eds. Copenhagen: Schultz.

Thalbitzer, William, and Hjalmar Thuren
1911   Dans i Grønland: Festskrift til H.F. Feilberg [Dance in Greenland: Festschrift for H.F. Feilberg]. *Danske Studier* 77-97. Copenhagen.

Theodorson, George A., and Achilles G. Theodorson
1969   A Modern Dictionary of Sociology. New York: Crowell.

Thompson, Charles T.
1969   Patterns of Housekeeping in Two Eskimo Settlements. (*NSRG 69-1*) Ottawa: Department of Indian Affairs and Northern Development, Northern Science Research Group.

Thompson, Raymond M.
1948   Notes on the Archaeology of the Utukok River, Northwestern Alaska. *American Antiquity* 14(1):62-65.

Thomsen, Thomas
1912   Nogle meddelelser om Polargrønlænderne. [Some Notes on the Polar Eskimos]. *Det Grønlandske Selskab Årsskrift* 70-89. Copenhagen.

Thorhallesen, Egil
1914   Beskrivelse over missionerne i Grønlands søndre Distrikt hvilke han som Vice-provst visiterede i aarene 1774-1775 [1776] [Description of the Missions in the Southern District of Greenland, Which He Visited as Assistant Pastor in the Years 1774-75]. Louis Bobé, ed. *Det Grønlandske Selskabs Skrifter* 1. Copenhagen.

Thornton, Harrison R.
1931   Among the Eskimos of Wales, Alaska, 1890-93. Neda S. Thornton and William M. Thornton, Jr., eds. Baltimore: The Johns Hopkins Press.

799

Thorson, Robert M., David C. Plaskett, and E. James Dixon
1980   A Reported Early-Man Site Adjacent to Southern Alaska's Continental Shelf: A Geologic Solution to an Archeologic Enigma. *Quaternary Research* 13(2):259-273.

Thorsteinsson, R.
1958   Cornwallis and Little Cornwallis Islands, District of Franklin, Northwest Territories. *Geological Survey of Canada Memoir* 294. Ottawa.

Thostrup, Christian B.
1917   Ethnographic Description of the Eskimo Settlements and Stone Remains in North-east Greenland. *Meddelelser om Grønland* 44(4). Copenhagen.

Thrasher, Anthony Apakark
1976   Thrasher: Skid Row Eskimo. In collaboration with Gerard Deagle and Alan Mittrick. Toronto: Griffin House.

Tikhmenev, Pëtr Aleksandrovich
1861-1863   Istoricheskoe obozrēnīe obrazovanīīa Rossīĭsko-Amerikanskoĭ Kompanīi i dēĭstvīīa eīa do nastoīashchago vremeni [Historical Survey of the Formation of the Russian-American Company and of Its Activities to the Present Time]. 2 Pts. St. Petersburg: E. Veĭmar. (Translation by Dimitri Krenov, U.S. Works Progress Administration, Seattle, 1939-1940.)

1978   A History of the Russian-American Company. A.S. Connelly, trans., R.H. Pierce, ed. Seattle: University of Washington Press.

Townsend, Charles H.
1887   Notes on the Natural History and Ethnology of Northern Alaska. Pp. 81-102 in Report of the Cruise of the Revenue Marine Steamer 'Corwin' in the Arctic Ocean, 1885, by M.A. Healy. Washington: U.S. Government Printing Office.

Townsend, Joan B.
1970   The Pedro Bay Site, Iliamna Lake, Alaska. (Paper presented at 35th Annual Meeting of the Society for American Archaeology, Mexico City, April 30.)

1970a   The Archaeology of Pedro Bay Alaska. (Paper presented at the 35th Annual Meeting of the Society for American Archaeology, Mexico City, April 30.)

1979   Indian or Eskimo? Interaction and Identity in Southern Alaska. *Arctic Anthropology* 16(2):160-182.

Townsend, Joan B., and Sam-Joe Townsend
1961   Archaeological Investigations at Pedro Bay, Alaska. *Anthropological Papers of the University of Alaska* 10(1):25-58. College.

1964   Additional Artifacts from Iliamna Lake, Alaska. *Anthropological Papers of the University of Alaska* 12(1):14-16. College.

Trap, Jens P.
1970   Thule kommune. [Thule Municipality.] Pp. 600-613 in Vol. 14 of Grønland. N. Nielsen, P. Skautrup and Christian Vibe, eds. 5th ed. Copenhagen: G.E.C. Gads Forlag.

Trautman, Milton A.
1964   Isotopes, Inc. Radiocarbon Measurements IV. *Radiocarbon* 6:269-279.

Tremaine, Marie
1953-1975   Introduction. Pp. 5-9 in Vol. 1 of Arctic Bibliography. 16 vols. Washington: U.S. Government Printing Office.

Tremblay, Alfred
1921   Cruise of the Minnie Maud: Arctic Seas and Hudson Bay, 1910-11 and 1912-13. A.B. Reader, comp. and trans. Quebec: Arctic Exchange and Publishing.

Treude, Erhard
1972   Genossenschaften in der kanadischen Arktis. *Polarforschung* 42(2):138-150.

1973   Studien zur Siedlungs-und Wirtschaftsent wicklung in der östlichen kanadischen Zentralarktis. *Die Erde: Zeitschrift der Gesellschaft für Erdkunde* 104(3-4):247-276. Berlin.

Trollope, Henry
1854   Orders and Proceedings of Commander Henry Trollope, Her Majesty's Discovery Ship 'Rattlesnake.' Pp. 155-156 in Great Britain. Admiralty. Papers Relative to the Recent Arctic Expedition in Search of Sir John Franklin and the Crews of H.M.S. 'Erebus' and 'Terror'. Vol. 11. London: Eyre and Spottiswoode.

Trudel, François
1969   Histoires de vie—îles Belcher: Notes de terrain. (Unpublished report at the Université Laval, Quebec.)

1971   La Population de l'archipel des Belcher: Une culture insulaire? (Unpublished Ph.D. Dissertation in Anthropology, Université Laval, Quebec.)

1978   The Inuit of Southern Labrador and the Development of French Sedentary Fisheries (1700-1760). Pp. 99-122 in Papers from the Fourth Annual Congress, 1977. Richard J. Preston, ed. *Canada. National Museum of Man. Ethnology Service Paper* 40. Ottawa.

1979   L'Importance du caribou dans la subsistance et la traite chez les Inuit de la côte orientale de la baie d'Hudson (1839-1910). *Recherches Amérindiennes au Québec* 9(1-2):141-150.

Tuck, James A.
1975   Prehistory of Saglek Bay, Labrador: Archaic and Palaeo-Eskimo Occupations. *Canada. National Museum of Man. Mercury Series. Archaeological Survey Paper* 32. Ottawa.

1976   Paleo-eskimo Cultures of Northern Labrador. Pp. 89-102 in Eastern Arctic Prehistory: Paleo-eskimo Problems. Moreau S. Maxwell, ed. *Memoirs of the Society for American Archeology* 31. Salt Lake City.

Tundra Times
1978   Subsistence: Tradition and a Way of Life. *Tundra Times*, January 1978:3.

[1981]   Rural Guide to Alaska Lands Act. *Tundra Times*, Special Edition.

Turner, Christy G., II
1963   Two Carbon-14 Dates circa 8,000 BP and Associated Core and Flake Industry from the Aleutian Islands. (Unpublished paper presented at the 28th Annual Meeting of the Society for American Archaeology, Boulder, Colo.)

1970   Archaeological Reconnaissance of Amchitka Island, Alaska. *Arctic Anthropology* 7(2):118-128.

1972   Preliminary Report of Archaeological Survey and Test Excavations in the Eastern Aleutian Islands, Alaska. *Arctic Anthropology* 9(2):32-35.

1973   Report on 1973 Anthropological Fieldwork on Akun Island, Alaska. (Unpublished report, Department of Anthropology, Arizona State University, Tempe.)

1974   The Use of Prehistory for Direct Comparative Baselines in the Study of Aleut Microevolution and Adaptation. Pp. 205-215 in International Conference on the Prehistory and Paleoecology of Western North American Arctic and Subarctic. Scott Raymond and Peter Schledermann, eds. Calgary, Alta.: University of Calgary, Department of Archaeology.

1975   Evidence of Russian Contact in the Krenitzin Islands, Eastern Aleutians, Alaska. (Paper prepared for IBP Aleut Population and Ecosystem Analysis.)

1976 The Aleuts of Akun Island: A Study of the Peoples of One of the Islands of the Eastern Aleutians. *The Alaska Journal* 6(1):25-31.

Turner, Christy G., II, and Jacqueline A. Turner
1974 Progress Report on Evolutionary Anthropological Study of Akun Strait District, Eastern Aleutians, Alaska, 1970-1971. *Anthropological Papers of the University of Alaska* 16(1):27-57. Fairbanks.

Turner, Christy G., II, Jean S. Aigner, and Linda R. Richards
1974 Chaluka Stratigraphy, Umnak Island, Alaska. *Arctic Anthropology* 11(Suppl.):125-142.

Turner, Christy G., II, Linda R. Richards, and Jacqueline A. Turner
1976 The Relation of Aleut Population Size to Seasonality of Marine Fauna. (Paper read at the 41st International Congress of Americanists. Mexico City, 1974.)

Turner, Lucien M.
1882-1884 Language of the "Koksoagmyut" Eskimo at Fort Chimo, Ungava, Labrador Peninsula. 3 vols. (Manuscript No. 2505-a in National Anthropological Archives, Smithsonian Institution, Washington.)

———
1886 Contributions to the Natural History of Alaska...Washington: U.S. Government Printing Office.

———
1888 On the Indians and Eskimos of the Ungava District, Labrador. *Proceedings and Transactions of the Royal Society of Canada for the Year 1887.* Sect. 2, Vol. 5:99-119. Montreal.

———
1894 Ethnology of the Ungava District, Hudson Bay Territory. John Murdoch, ed. Pp. 159-350 in *11th Annual Report of the Bureau of American Ethnology for the Years 1889-1890.* Washington.

Tussing, Arlon R., and Robert D. Arnold
1973 Eskimo Population and Economy in Transition: Southwest Alaska. Pp. 123-169 in Le Peuple esquimau aujourd'hui et Demain/The Eskimo People To-Day and To-Morrow. Jean Malaurie, ed. (Fourth International Congress of the Fondation Française d'Études Nordiques) Paris, The Hague: Mouton.

Tussing, Arlon R., George W. Rogers, and Victor Fischer
1971 Alaska Pipeline Report: Alaska's Economy, Oil and Gas Industry Development, and the Economic Impact of Building and Operating the Trans-Alaska Pipeline. Seattle: University of Washington Press; Fairbanks: University of Alaska, Institute of Social, Economic and Government Research.

Tuten, Merry Allyn
1977 A Preliminary Study of Subsistence Activities on the Pacific Coast of the Proposed Aniakchak Caldera National Monument. *Cooperative Park Studies Unit Occasional Paper* 4. Fairbanks, Alas.

Tyrrell, James W.
1897 Across the Sub-arctic of Canada: A Journey of 3,200 Miles by Canoe and Snowshoe Through the Barren Lands. Toronto: W. Briggs.

Tyrrell, Joseph B.
1898 Report of the Doobaunt, Kazan and Ferguson Rivers and the Northwest Coast of Hudson Bay. *Canada. Annual Report of the Geological Survey* n.s. 9(F). Ottawa: S.E. Dawson.

———, ed.
1931 Documents Relating to the Early History of Hudson Bay. (*Publications of the Champlain Society* 18) Toronto: The Champlain Society.

Udvalget for Samfundsforskning i Grønland
1963 Befolkningssituationen i Vestgrønland: Bebyggelsespolitik og befolkningsudvikling. (*USG 7*) [The Population Situation in West Greenland: Construction Policy and Population Development]. Copenhagen.

Uhl, William R., and Carrie Uhl
1977 Tagiumsinaaqmiit: Ocean Beach Dwellers of the Cape Krusenstern Area: Subsistence Patterns (*Occasional Paper* 14). Fairbanks: University of Alaska, Anthropology and Historic Preservation. Cooperative Park Studies Unit.

———
1979 The Noatak National Preserve. Nuatakmiit: A Study of Subsistence Use of Renewable Resources in the Noatak River Valley. Fairbanks: University of Alaska, Anthropology and Historic Preservation, Cooperative Park Studies Unit.

Uhlenbeck, C.C.
1905 Uralische Anklänge in den Eskimosprachen. *Zeitschrift der deutschen morgenländischen Gesellschaft* 59:757-765. Leipzig, Germany.

U.S. Bureau of Education
1896-1905 Education in Alaska. Reports of the Commission of Education. Washington: U.S. Government Printing Office.

———
1898 Education in Alaska, 1896-1897, [by] Sheldon Jackson. Washington: U.S. Government Printing Office.

U.S. Bureau of Indian Affairs
1971 Report on Annual Land Operations. Juneau. Mimeo.

U.S. Bureau of Indian Affairs. Planning Support Group
[1977] Savoonga: Its History, Population and Economy. *BIA Planning Support Group Report* 242. Billings, Mont.

[1977a] Gambell: Its History, Population and Economy. *BIA Planning Support Group Report* 243. Billings, Mont.

———
1978 Alaska Natives Regional Profiles. Prepared for the Alaska Federation of Natives, Inc. *BIA Planning Support Group Report* 269. Billings, Mont.

U.S. Bureau of the Census
1915 Indian Population of the United States and Alaska, 1910. Washington: U.S. Government Printing Office.

———
1980 Census of Population, Vol. 1, Pt. 3: Alaska, PC80-1-B3, tables 15-22. Washington: U.S. Government Printing Office.

———
1982 General Population Characteristics, Pt. 3: Alaska, PC80-1-B3, table 55, Census of Population. Vol. 1. Washington: U.S. Government Printing Office.

U.S. Census Office
1884 Report on the Population, Industries, and Resources of Alaska. 10th Census: 1880. Washington: U.S. Government Printing Office.

———
1893 Report on Population and Resources of Alaska at the Eleventh Census: 1890. Washington: U.S. Government Printing Office.

U.S. Congress. Senate. Special Subcommittee on Indian Education
1969 Indian Education: A National Tragedy—a National Challenge. *Report of the Committee on Labor and Public Welfare. 91st Cong., 1st sess.* Washington: U.S. Government Printing Office.

U.S. Department of the Interior
1967 Alaska Natural Resources and the Ramparts Project. Washington: U.S. Government Printing Office.

U.S. Federal Field Committee for Development Planning in Alaska
1967 Villages in Alaska and Other Places Having a Native Population of 25 or More, Estimates 1967. Anchorage: no publisher.

———
1968 Alaska Natives and the Land. Washington: U.S. Government Printing Office.

———
1969 Estimates of Native Population in Villages, Towns, and Boroughs of Alaska, 1969. Compiled by Federal Field Committee for Planning in Alaska, with the Cooperation of a Division

of Planning and Research, Office of the Governor, State of Alaska. Anchorage.

1971   Alaska Community Inventory. Anchorage: U.S. Government Printing Office.

U.S. Department of the Treasury. Special Agents Division
1898   Seal and Salmon Fisheries and General Resources of Alaska. 4 vols. Washington: U.S. Government Printing Office.

U.S. Public Health Service. Division of Indian Health
1966   The Hooper Bay Community Health Study. Pt. 1. Anchorage: Alaska Native Health Area Office.

University of Alaska. Institute of Social, Economic and Government Research
1973   Age and Race by Sex Characteristics of Alaska's Village Population. *Alaska Review of Business and Economic Conditions* 10(2). Fairbanks.

Usher, Peter J.
1965   Economic Basis and Resource Use of the Coppermine-Holman Region, N.W.T. (*NCRC-65-2*) Ottawa: Department of Northern Affairs and National Resources, Northern Co-ordination and Research Centre.

1970-1971   The Bankslanders: Economy and Ecology of a Frontier Trapping Community. 3 vols. (*NSRG71-1*). Ottawa: Information Canada.

1971   Fur Trade Posts of the Northwest Territories, 1870-1970. (*NSRG 71-4*) Ottawa: Department of Indian Affairs and Northern Development, Northern Science Research Group.

1971a   The Canadian Western Arctic: A Century of Change. *Anthropologica* n.s. 13(1-2):169-183. Ottawa.

1972   The Use of Snowmobiles for Trapping on Banks Island. *Arctic* 25(3):171-181.

1976   Evaluating Country Food in the Northern Native Economy. *Arctic* 29(2):105-120.

Uvdloriaq, Inuterssuaq
1976   Qitdlarssuákúnik oqalualâq. Godthâb: Det Grønlandske Forlag.

Vahl, Martin, F.C. Amdrup, L. Bobé, and A.S. Jensen, eds.
1928-1929   Greenland. 3 vols. Copenhagen: C.A. Reitzel; London: H. Milford, Oxford University Press.

Valaam Monastery
1978   The Russian Orthodox Religious Mission in America, 1794-1837, [1894]. Richard A. Pierce, ed.; Colin Bearne, trans. Kingston, Ont.: Limestone Press.

Vallee, Frank G.
1962   Kabloona and Eskimo in the Central Keewatin. (*NCRC-62-2*) Ottawa: Department of Northern Affairs and National Resources, Northern Co-ordination and Research Centre.

1962a   Sociological Research in the Arctic. (*NCRC-62-8*) Ottawa: Department of Northern Affairs and National Resources, Northern Co-ordination and Research Centre.

1964   Notes on the Cooperative Movement and Community Organization in the Canadian Arctic. *Arctic Anthropology* 2(2):45-49.

1966   The Co-operative Movement in the North. Pp. 43-48 in People of Light and Dark. Maja van Steensel, ed. Ottawa: Department of Indian Affairs and Northern Development.

1966a   Eskimo Theories of Mental Illness in the Hudson Bay Region. *Anthropologica* n.s. 8(1):53-83. Ottawa.

1967   Povungnetuk and Its Cooperative: A Case Study in Community Change. (*NCRC-67-2*) Ottawa: Department of

Northern Affairs and National Resources, Northern Co-ordination and Research Centre.

1967a   Kabloona and Eskimo in the Central Keewatin. Ottawa: Saint Paul University, Canadian Research Centre for Anthropology.

1968   Stresses of Change and Mental Health Among the Canadian Eskimos. *Archives of Environmental Health* 17(October):565-570.

1971   Eskimos of Canada as a Minority Group. Pp. 75-88 in Minority Canadians, I: Native Peoples. Jean L. Elliott, ed. Scarborough, Ont.: Prentice-Hall of Canada.

1981   Inuit Participation in the Canadian Polity: Working Paper on Voting and Representation. (Unpublished manuscript in Social Science Data Archives, Carleton University, Ottawa.)

Vancouver, George
1798   A Voyage of Discovery to the North Pacific Ocean and Round the World in which the Coast of North-West America Has Been Carefully Examined and Accurately Surveyed in the Years 1790-1795. 3 vols. London: G.G. Robinson and J. Edwards.

VandeVelde, Frans
1958   Liste d'instruments Netsilik pour la chasse à l'agler. (Unpublished manuscript in Mission Catholique, Pelly Bay, N.W.T.)

Van Gulik, W.R., H.S. Van der Straaten, and G.D. Van Wengen
1980   From Field-Case to Show-Case: Research, Acquisition and Presentation in the Rijksmuseum voor Volkenkunde (National Museum of Ethnology), Leiden. Amsterdam: J.C. Gieben.

VanStone, James W.
1954   Pottery from Nunivak Island, Alaska. *Anthropological Papers of the University of Alaska* 2(2):181-193. College.

1955   Archaeological Excavations at Kotzebue, Alaska. *Anthropological Papers of the University of Alaska* 3(2):75-155. College.

1957   An Archaeological Reconnaissance of Nunivak Island, Alaska. *Anthropological Papers of the University of Alaska* 5(2):97-117. College.

1958   Commercial Whaling in the Arctic Ocean. *Pacific Northwest Quarterly* 49(1):1-10.

1959   Russian Exploration in Interior Alaska: An Extract from the Journal of Andrei Glazunov. *Pacific Northwest Quarterly* 50(2):37-47.

1960   An Early Nineteenth-century Artist in Alaska: Louis Choris and the First Kotzebue Expedition. *Pacific Northwest Quarterly* 51(4):145-158.

1960a   A Successful Combination of Subsistence and Wage Economies on the Village Level. *Economic Development and Cultural Change* 8(2):174-191.

1962   An Archaeological Collection from Somerset Island and the Boothia Peninsula, N.W.T. *Royal Ontario Museum, Art and Archaeology Division, Occasional Paper* 4. Toronto.

1962a   Point Hope: An Eskimo Village in Transition. Seattle: University of Washington Press.

1962b   Notes on Nineteenth Century Trade in the Kotzebue Sound Area, Alaska. *Arctic Anthropology* 1(1):126-128.

1963   A Carved Mammoth Tusk from Alaska. Pp. 69-73, 123-124 in *1962 Annual of Art and Archaeology Division, Royal Ontario Museum. University of Toronto.*

1964   Some Aspects of Religious Change Among Native Inhabitants in West Alaska and the Northwest Territories. *Arctic Anthropology* 2(2):21-24.

1967   Eskimos of the Nushagak River: An Ethnographic History. *University of Washington Publications in Anthropology* 15. Seattle.

1968   Tikchik Village: A Nineteenth Century Riverine Community in Southwestern Alaska. *Fieldiana: Anthropology* 56(3). Chicago.

1970   Ethnohistorical Research in Southwestern Alaska: A Methodological Perspective. Pp. 46-69 in Ethnohistory in Southwestern Alaska and the Southern Yukon: Method and Content. M. Lantis, ed. (*Studies in Anthropology* 7) Lexington: University of Kentucky Press.

1970a   Akulivikchuk: A Nineteenth Century Eskimo Village on the Nushagak River, Alaska. *Fieldiana: Anthropology* 60:3-123. Chicago.

1971   Historic Settlement Patterns in the Nushagak River Region, Alaska. *Fieldiana: Anthropology* 61. Chicago.

1972   The First Peary Collection of Polar Eskimo Material Culture. *Fieldiana: Anthropology* 63(2). Chicago.

————, ed.
1973   V.S. Khromchenko's Coastal Explorations in Southwestern Alaska, 1882. D.H. Kraus, trans. *Fieldiana: Anthropology* 64. Chicago.

1976   The Bruce Collection of Eskimo Material Culture from Port Clarence, Alaska. *Fieldiana: Anthropology* 67. Chicago.

————, ed.
1977   A.F. Kashevarov's Coastal Explorations in Northwest Alaska, 1838. David H. Kraus, trans. *Fieldiana: Anthropology* 69. Chicago.

1980   The Bruce Collection of Eskimo Material Culture from Kotzebue Sound, Alaska. *Fieldiana: Anthropology* n.s. 1. Chicago.

VanStone, James W., and Wendell H. Oswalt
1959   The Caribou Eskimos of Eskimo Point. (*NCRC-59-2*) Ottawa: Department of Northern Affairs and National Resources, Northern Coordination and Research Centre.

1960   Three Eskimo Communities. *Anthropological Papers of the University of Alaska* 9(1):17-56. College.

Vasil´ev, V.A., ĨU. B. Simchenko, and Z.P. Sokolova
1966   Problems of the Reconstruction of Daily Life Among the Small Peoples of the Far North. *Soviet Anthropology and Archeology* 5(2):11-21. (Translated from *Sovetskaĩã Ètnografiĩã* 3:9-22, 1966.)

Vasilevich, Glafira Makar´evna
1969   Èvenki; Ist.-ètnogr. ocherki (XVIII-nachalo XX v.) [Evenki; Historic-ethnographic Essays (from the 18th to the Beginning of the 20th Century)], Leningrad: Akademiĩã Nauk SSSR., Institut Ètnografii Im. N.N. Miklukho-Maklaĩã.

Vasil´evskii, R.S.
1964   Ancient Koryak Culture. Barbara P. Merbs, trans. Chester S. Chard, ed. *American Antiquity* 30(1):19-24.

1969   A Contribution to the History of the Ancient Culture of the Okhotsk Coast (Based on the Archaeological Materials from M.G. Levin's Collection from Zav'ialova Island). *Arctic Anthropology* 6(1):165-170.

1969a   The Origin of the Ancient Koryak Culture on the Northern Okhotsk Coast. *Arctic Anthropology* 6(1):150-164.

1969-1970   The Problem of the North Pacific Sea Hunters' Culture. Pp. 359-361 in Vol. 3 of *Proceedings of the 8th International Congress of Anthropological and Ethnographical Sciences*. 3 vols. Tokyo and Kyoto, 1968.

Vdovin, Inokentiĩ Stepanovich
1949   [Foreword to] Materialy po ĩãzyku aziatskikh èskimosov [Materials on the Language of the Asiatic Eskimos], by Waldemar Bogoras. Leningrad: Uchpedgiz.

1961   Èskimosskie Èlementy v kul´ture Chukcheĩ i Korĩãkov [Eskimo Elements in the Culture of the Chukchis and Koryaks]. *Adedemiĩã Nauk SSSR. Institut Ètnografii, Trudy* Vol. 64. *Sibirskiĩ Ètnograficheskiĩ Sbornik* 3:27-63. Vladivostok.

1973   Politique législative, économique, sociale et culturelle de l'URSS en faveur de développement des Esquimaux et des Tchouktches. Pp. 601-622 in Le Peuple esquimau aujourd'hui et demain/The Eskimo People To-Day and To-Morrow. Jean Malaurie, ed. (Fourth International Congress of the Fondation Française d'Études Nordiques) Paris, The Hague: Mouton.

Vebæk, Christen L.
1943   Inland Farms in the Norse East Settlement: Archaeological Investigations in Julianehaab District, Summer 1959. *Meddelelser om Grønland* 90(1). Copenhagen.

1958   Ten Years of Topographical and Archaeological Investigations in the Mediaeval Norse Settlements in Greenland. Pp. 732-743 in *Proceedings of the 32d International Congress of Americanists*. Copenhagen, 1956.

Vebæk, Mâliârak
1969-1970   Umiaríssat, a Boat of Ill Omen. *Folk* 11-12:79-81. Copenhagen.

Veltre, Douglas W.
1979   Korovinski: The Ethnohistorical Archaeology of an Aleut and Russian Settlement on Atka Island, Alaska. (Unpublished Ph.D. Dissertation in Anthropology, University of Connecticut, Storrs.)

Veniaminov, Ivan Evĩeevich Popov, comp.
1840   Zapiski ob ostrovakh Unalashkinskago otdĩela [Notes on the Islands of the Unalaska District]. 3 vols. in 2. St. Petersburg: Russian-American Company.

1846   Zamĩechaniĩã o koloshenskom i kad´ĩakskom ĩãzykakh i otchasti o prochikh rossiĩsko-amerikanskikh, s prisovokupleniem rossiĩsko-koloshenskago slovarĩã, soderzhashchago bolĩee 1000 slov, iz koikh na nĩekotoryĩã sdĩelany porĩãsneniĩã [Remarks on the Tlingit and Koniag Languages, and partly on Others of Russian America, with the Addition of a Russian-Tlingit Vocabulary Containing More than 1,000 Words, Some with Explanations.] St. Petersburg: Akademiĩã Nauk. (Typescript translation by R.H. Geoghegan in Alaska State Library, Juneau.)

1846a   Opyt grammatiki aleutsko-lis´evskago ĩãzyka [An Essay upon the Grammar of the Fox Dialect of the Aleut Language]. 2 Pts. St. Petersburg. Akademiĩã Nauk.

Vernon, P.E.
1966   Educational and Intellectual Development Among Canadian Indians and Eskimos. *Educational Review* 18:79-91, 186-195.

Vesilind, Priit J.
1983   Hunters of the Lost Spirit. *National Geographic Magazine* 163(2):151-197.

Vézinet, Monique
1975   Étude de la toponymie des Inuit des îles Belcher en tant que modalité de leur appropriation de l'espace. (Unpublished M.A. Thesis in Anthropology, Université Laval, Quebec.)

1979　　　L'Economie traditionnelle du caribou chez les Inuit du Québec arctique. *Recherches Amérindiennes au Québec* 9(1-2):83-92.

1980　　　Les Nunamiut, Inuit au Cœur des Terres. Quebec: Ministère des Affaires Culturelles.

1982　　　Occupation humaine de l'Ungava: Perspective ethno-historique et écologique (*Collection Paléo-Québec* 14). Montreal: Laboratoire d'Archéologie de l'Université du Québec à Montréal.

Vibe, Christian
1950　　　The Marine Mammals and the Marine Fauna in the Thule District (Northwest Greenland) with Observations on Ice Conditions in 1939-41. *Meddelelser om Grønland* 150(6). Copenhagen.

1956　　　Thule og Scoresbysund, Grønlands to nordligste fangst-distrikter [Thule and Scoresbysund, the Two Northernmost Hunting Areas in Greenland]. *Grønland* 4:414-427. Copenhagen.

1967　　　Arctic Animals in Relation to Climatic Fluctuations. *Meddelelser om Grønland* 170(5). Copenhagen.

1970　　　The Arctic Ecosystem Influenced by Fluctuations in Sunspots and Drift-ice Movements. Pp. 115-120 in Productivity and Conservation in Circumpolar Lands: Proceedings of the Conference, October 15-17, 1969. W.A. Fuller and P.G. Kenan, eds. *International Union for Conservation of Nature and Natural Resources Publications* n.s. 16. Morges, Switzerland.

1970a　　Dyreverdenen: Faunens historie og udforskning [Fauna: Faunal History and Exploration]. Pp. 93-105 in J.P. Trap's Grønland. N. Nielsen, P. Skautrup and Christian Vibe, eds. 5th ed. Copenhagen: G.E.C. Gads Forlag.

Victor, Paul E.
1938　　　Boréal: La joie dans la nuit. Paris: Grasser.

1972　　　Eskimos nomades des glaces. Paris: Hachette.

Villadsen, Villads
1965　　　Nalussûnerup târnerane. [In the Darkness of Heathenism]. Godthåb: Det Grønlandske Forlag.

Villiers, D.
1968　　　The Central Arctic, an Area Economic Survey. Ottawa: Department of Indian Affairs and Northern Development, Industrial Division.

Voblov, I.K.
1952　　　Ėskimosskie prazdniki [Eskimo Festivals]. *Akademiiā Nauk SSSR. Institut Ėtnografii. Trudy. Sibirskiĭ Ėtnograficheskiĭ Sbornik* 1 n.s. 18:320-334. (Translation: Eskimo Ceremonies, Charles C. Hughes, trans. *Anthropological Papers of the University of Alaska* 7(2):71-90, 1959.)

Voevodskiĭ, S.V.
[1858]　　[Vocabularies from Near Mount Saint Elias, Kodiak Island, Prince William Sound, Bristol Bay, and Unalaska.] (Manuscript, copies in National Anthropological Archives, Smithsonian Institution, Washington, and Bancroft Library, University of California at Berkeley.)

Vowinckel, E., and S. Orvig
1970　　　The Climate of the North Polar Basin. Pp. 129-252 in Climates of the Polar Regions. S. Orvig, ed. (*World Survey of Climatology* 14) New York: Elsevier.

Wanner, James A.
1977　　　Clinal Variation in Eskimo Craniofacial Morphology. (Unpublished Ph.D. Dissertation in Anthropology, University of Colorado, Boulder.)

Washburn, A.L.
1965　　　Geomorphic and Vegetational Studies in the Mesters Vig District, Northeast Greenland: General Introduction. *Meddelelser om Grønland* 166(1). Copenhagen.

Waxell, Sven L.
1952　　　The American Expedition. M.A Michael, ed. London: William Hodge.

Webster, D.H., and Wilfried Zibell
1970　　　Iñupiat Dictionary. Fairbanks: University of Alaska and Summer Institute of Linguistics.

1976　　　Report of Canadian Eskimo Language Survey, 1968. Pp. 272-327 in Papers on Eskimo and Aleut Linguistics. Eric P. Hamp, ed. Chicago: Chicago Linguistic Society.

Weick, E.R., G.T. Armstrong, D.C.E. Mathurin, and S.K. MacBain
1973　　　Economic Development of the Canadian North and Its Consequences for the Canadian Eskimo Society. Pp. 196-208 in Le Peuple esquimau aujourd'hui et demain/The Eskimo People To-day and To-Morrow. Jean Malaurie, ed. (Fourth International Congress of the Fondation Française d'Études Nordiques) Paris, The Hague: Mouton.

Weidick, Anker
1968　　　Observations on Some Holocene Glacier Fluctuations in West Greenland. *Greenland Geologiske Undersøgelse Bulletin* 73; *Meddelelser om Grønland* 165(6). Copenhagen.

1972　　　Notes on Holocene Glacial Events in Greenland. Pp. 177-204 in Climatic Changes in Arctic Areas During the Last Ten Thousand Years. Y. Vasari, H. Hyvärinen, and S. Hicks, eds. *Acta Universitatis Ouluensis, ser. A, Geologica* 1. Oulu, Finland.

Welland, Tony
1976　　　Inuit Land Use in Keewatin District and Southampton Island. Pp. 83-114 in Vol. 1 of Report: Inuit Land Use and Occupancy Project. Milton M.R. Freeman, comp. 3 vols. Ottawa: Department of Indian and Northern Affairs.

Weller, Gunter, and Sue Ann Bowling, eds.
1975　　　Climate of the Arctic. Fairbanks: University of Alaska, Geographical Institute.

Wells, James K.
1974　　　Ipani Eskimos: A Cycle of Life in Nature. Anchorage: Alaska Methodist University Press.

Wells, Roger, Jr., and John W. Kelly
1890　　　English-Eskimo and Eskimo-English Vocabularies, Preceded by Ethnographical Memoranda Concerning the Arctic Eskimos in Alaska and Siberia. *U.S. Bureau of Education, Circular of Information* 2. Washington.

Wenzel, George W.
1980　　　Social Organization as an Adaptive Referent in Inuit Cultural Ecology: The Case of the Clyde River and Aquiqtiuk. (Unpublished Ph.D. Dissertation in Social Geography, McGill University, Montreal.)

1981　　　Clyde Inuit Adaptation and Ecology: The Organization of Subsistence. *Canada. National Museum of Man. Mercury Series. Ethnology Service Paper* 77. Ottawa.

West, Frederick Hadleigh
1959　　　On the Distribution and Territories of the Western Kutchin Tribes. *Anthropological Papers of the University of Alaska* 7(2):113-116.

1966　　　Archaeology of Ogotoruk Creek. Pp. 927-967 in Environment of the Cape Thompson Region, Alaska. Norman Wilimovsky and John N. Wolfe, eds. Oak Ridge, Tenn.: U.S. Atomic Energy Commission, Division of Technical Information.

1967　　　The Donnelly Ridge Site and the Definition of an Early Core and Blade Complex in Central Alaska. *American Antiquity* 32(3):360-382.

1981   The Archaeology of Beringia. New York: Columbia University Press.

Weyer, Edward M., Jr.
1930   Archaeological Material from the Village Site at Hot Springs, Port Möller, Alaska. *Anthropological Papers of the American Museum of Natural History* 31(4):239-279. New York.

———
1931   An Aleutian Burial. *Anthropological Papers of the American Museum of Natural History* 31(3) New York.

———
1932   The Eskimos: Their Environment and Folkways. New Haven, Conn.: Yale University Press. (Reprinted: Archon Books, Hamden, Conn., 1962.)

Whalley, George
1960   Coppermine Martyrdom. *Queen's Quarterly*:591-610. Kingston, Ont.

Whitney, Harry
1910   Hunting with the Eskimos: The Unique Record of a Sportsman's Year Among the Northernmost Tribe—the Big Game Hunting, the Native Life, and the Battle for Existence Through the Long Arctic Night. New York: The Century Company.

Whitten, Norman E., Jr.
1964   Towards a Classification of West Alaskan Social Structure. *Anthropological Papers of the University of Alaska* 12(2):79-91. College.

Whymper, Frederick
1869   Travel and Adventure in the Territory of Alaska: Formerly Russian America—Now Ceded to the United States—and in Various Other Parts of the North Pacific. New York: Harper and Brothers.

Wiens, John A.
1966   On Group Selection and Wynne-Edwards' Hypothesis. *American Scientist* 54(3):273-287.

Wilcox, Ray E.
1959   Some Effects of Recent Volcanic Ash Falls with Especial Reference to Alaska. *U.S. Geological Survey Bulletin* 1028-N:409-476. Washington.

Wilimovsky, Norman J., and John N. Wolfe, eds.
1966   Environment of the Cape Thompson Region, Alaska. Oak Ridge, Tenn.: U.S. Atomic Energy Commission, Division of Technical Information.

Wilkinson, Douglas
1970   The Arctic Coast. Toronto: N.S.L. Natural Science of Canada.

Williamson, Robert G.
1973   Eskimo Value Persistence in Contemporary Acculturation. Pp. 265-288 in Le Peuple Esquimau Aujourd'hui et Demain [The Eskimo People To-Day and To-Morrow.] Jean Malaurie, ed. (Fourth International Congress of the Fondation Française d'Études Nordiques) Paris, The Hague:Mouton.

Willis, J.G.
1962   Disease and Death in Canada's North. (Conference on Medicine and Public Health in the Arctic and Antarctic, Document 20) Geneva: World Health Organization.

Wilmeth, Roscoe
1969   Canadian Archeological Radiocarbon Dates. *Anthropological Series* 87, *National Museum of Canada Bulletin* 232:68-127. Ottawa.

———
1978   Canadian Archaeological Radiocarbon Dates. Rev. ed. *Canada. National Museum of Man. Mercury Series. Archaeological Survey Paper* 77. Ottawa.

Willmott, William E.
1960   The Flexibility of Eskimo Social Organization. *Anthropologica* n.s. 2(1):48-59. Ottawa.

1961   The Eskimo Community at Port Harrison, P.Q. (*NCRC-61-1*) Ottawa: Department of Northern Affairs and National Resources, Northern Coordination and Research Centre.

Wilmsen, Edwin N.
1964   Flake Tools in the American Arctic: Some Speculations. *American Antiqutity* 29(3):338-344.

Wilson, Ian R.
1978   Archaeological Investigations at the Antigun Site, Central Brooks Range, Alaska. *Canada. National Museum of Man. Mercury Series. Archaeological Survey Paper* 78. Ottawa.

Wilson, Martha
1969   Health Status of the Alaska Native People. (Paper presented at the 20th Alaska Science Conference, University of Alaska, College.)

Wintemberg, W.J.
1939-1940 Eskimo Sites of the Dorset Culture in Newfoundland. *American Antiquity* 5(2):83-102, (4):309-333.

Wissler, Clark
1917   The American Indian: An Introduction to the Anthropology of the New World. New York: Douglas C. McMurtrie.

Wolf, Grace
1969   Native Politics: An Overview. (Paper presented at the 20th Alaska Science Conference, University of Alaska, College.)

Wolforth, John R.
1965   The Mackenzie Delta: Its Economic Base and Development: A Preliminary Study. (*MDRP 1*) Ottawa: Department of Indian Affairs and Northern Development, Northern Coordination and Research Centre.

Wolpoff, M.
1968   Climatic Influence on Skeletal Nasal Apperture. *American Journal of Physical Anthropology* 29(4):405-423.

Woodbury, Anthony C.
1978   [Linguistic Notes from 3 Months' Fieldwork in Chevak, Alaska.] (Manuscript in Woodbury's possession)

———
1981   Study of the Chevak Dialect of Central Yup'ik Eskimo. (Unpublished Ph.D. Dissertation in Linguistics, University of California, Berkeley.)

Woolfe, Henry D.
1893   The Seventh, or Arctic District. In Report on Population and Resources of Alaska at the Eleventh Census: 1890. Vol. 8. Washington: U.S. Government Printing Office.

Workman, Karen W.
1977   Chugachik Island: A Kachemak Tradition Site in Upper Kachemak Bay, Alaska. *Anthropological Papers of the University of Alaska* 18(2):1-22. Fairbanks.

Workman, Karen W., and John E. Lobdell
1981   The Seal Beach Site (*SEL 079*): A Multicomponent Hunting Station on Chugachik Island, Kachemak Bay, Alaska. (Paper delivered to the 8th Annual Meeting of the Alaska Anthropological Association, March 20-21, Anchorage.)

Workman, William B.
1966   Prehistory at Port Möller, Alaska Peninsula, in Light of Fieldwork in 1960. *Arctic Anthropology* 3(2):132-153.

———
1966a   Archaeological Reconnaissance on Chirikof Island, Kodiak Group: A Preliminary Report. *Arctic Anthropology* 3(2):185-192.

———
1969   Southwest Alaskan Cross-ties with the Bering Sea Region: A Discussion Based on the Data from Chirikof Island, Southwest Alaska. (Paper presented at the 34th Annual Meeting of the Society for American Archaeology, Milwaukee.)

———
1969a   Contributions to the Prehistory of Chirikov Island, Southwestern Alaska. (Unpublished M.A. Thesis in Anthropology, University of Wisconsin, Madison.)

805

1977   New Data on the Radiocarbon Chronology of the Kachemak Bay Sequence. *Anthropological Papers of the University of Alaska* 18(2):31-36. Fairbanks.

1978   Prehistory of the Aishihik-Kluane Area, Southwest Yukon Territory. *Canada. National Museum of Man. Mercury Series. Archaeological Survey Paper* 74. Ottawa.

1979   The Significance of Volcanism in the Prehistory of Subarctic Northwest North America. Pp. 339-371 in Volcanic Activity and Human Ecology. P.D. Sheets and D.K. Grayson, eds. New York: Academic Press.

1980   Continuity and Change in the Prehistoric Record from Southern Alaska. Pp. 49-101 in Alaska Native Culture and History. Y. Kotani and W.B. Workman, eds. *National Museum of Ethnology, Senri Ethnological Series* 4. Osaka, Japan.

1981   Beyond the Southern Frontier: The Norton Culture and the Western Kenai Peninsula. (Paper delivered to the 8th Annual Meeting of the Alaska Anthropological Association, March 20-21, Anchorage.)

Workman, William B., and John E. Lobdell
1979   The Yukon Island Bluff Site (*SEL 041*): A New Manifestation of Late Kachemak Bay Prehistory. (Paper presented to the 6th Annual Meeting of Alaska Anthropological Association, Fairbanks.)

Workman, William B., John E. Lobdell, and Karen W. Workman
1980   Recent Archaeological Work in Kachemak Bay, Gulf of Alaska. *Arctic* 33(3):385-399.

Worl Associates
1978   Beaufort Sea Region: Socioeconomic Baseline. *Alaska OCS Report* 11. (Available through the National Technical Information Service, Springfield, Va. 22161.)

Worl, Rosita
1980   The North Slope Inupiat Whaling Complex. Pp. 305-332 in Alaska Native Culture and History. Y. Kotani and W.B. Workman, eds. *National Museum of Ethnology, Senri Ethnological Studies* 4. Osaka, Japan.

Wrangell, Ferdinand Petrovich von
1839   Obitateli sîevero-zapadnykh beregov Ameriki [The Inhabitants of the Northwest Coasts of America]. *Syn Otechestva* 7:51-82. St. Petersburg.

1839a   Statistische und ethnographische Nachrichten über die russischen Besitzungen an der Nordwestküste von Amerika. K.E. von Baer, ed. St. Petersburg: Buchdruckerei der Kaiserlichen Akademie der Wissenschaften.

1970   The Inhabitants of the Northwest Coast of America [1839]. James W. VanStone, trans. *Arctic Anthropology* 6(2):5-20.

Wright, James V.
1972   The Shield Archaic. *Canada. National Museum of Man. Publications in Archaeology* 3. Ottawa.

1972a   The Aberdeen Site, Keewatin District, N.W.T. *Canada. National Museum of Man. Mercury Series. Archaeological Survey Paper* 2. Ottawa.

Wynne-Edwards, Vero C.
1962   Animal Dispersion in Relation to Social Behaviour. New York: Hafner.

Yarborough, Michael R.
1974   Analysis of Pottery from the Western Alaska Peninsula. *Anthropological Papers of the University of Alaska* 16(1):85-89. Fairbanks.

Yatsushiro, Toshio
1963   Frobisher Bay 1958 (*NCRC 63-6*). Ottawa: Department of Northern Affairs and National Resources, Northern Coordination and Research Centre.

Yesner, David R.
1980   Maritime Hunter-Gatherers: Ecology and Prehistory. *Current Anthropology* 21(6):727-735.

1981   Archeological Applications of Optimal Foraging Theory: Harvest Strategies of Aleut Hunter-Gatherers. Pp. 148-170 in Hunter-Gatherer Foraging Strategies. B. Winterhalder and E. Smith, eds. Chicago: University of Chicago Press.

Yesner, David R., and Jean S. Aigner
1976   Comparative Biomass Estimates and Prehistoric Cultural Ecology of the Southwest Umnak Region, Aleutian Islands. *Arctic Anthropology* 13(2):91-112.

Young, Steven B., and Edwin S. Hall, Jr.
1969   Contributions to the Ethnobotany of the St. Lawrence Island Eskimo. *Anthropological Papers of the University of Alaska* 14(2):43-53.

Zagoskin, Lavrentiĭ Alekseevich
1956   Puteshestviiâ i issledovaniiâ leĭtenanta Lavrentiiâ Zagoskina v Russkoĭ Amerike v 1842-1844 g.g. [The Travels and Explorations of Lt. Lavrentiĭ Zagoskin in Russian America, 1842-1844]. M.B. Chernenko, G.A. Agranat, and E.E. Blomkvist, eds. Moscow: Gosudarstvennoe Izdatel´stvo Geograficheskoĭ Literatury.

1967   Lieutenant Zagoskin's Travels in Russian America, 1842-1844: The First Ethnographic and Geographic Investigations on the Yukon and Kuskokwim Valleys of Alaska. Henry N. Michael, ed. (*Anthropology of the North: Translations from Russian Sources* 7) Toronto: Published for the Arctic Institute of North America by University of Toronto Press.

Zolotarevskaiâ, I.A., E.E. Blomkvist, and E.V. Zibert
1958   Ethnographical Material from the Americas in Russian Collections. Pp. 221-231 in *Proceedings of the 32d International Congress of Americanists*. Copenhagen, 1956.

Zorgdrager, C.G.
1728   Flourishing Rise of the Old and Present Greenland Fishery. Amsterdam: no publisher.

Index

Italic numbers indicate material in a figure caption; roman numbers, material in the text.

All variant names of groups are indexed, with the occurrences under synonymy discussing the equivalences. Variants of group names that differ from those cited only in their capitalization, hyphenation, or accentuation have generally been omitted; variants that differ only in the presence or absence of one (noninitial) letter or compound element have been collapsed into a single entry with that letter or element in parentheses.

The entry Eskimo and Indian words indexes, by language, all words appearing in the standard orthographies and some others.

825